The Annals of Loch Cé : A Chronicle of Irish Affairs from A.D. 1014 to A.D. 1590

Brian MacDermot, William Maunsell Hennessy

bibliolife
old books. new life.

THE

ANNALS OF LOCH CÉ.

A CHRONICLE OF IRISH AFFAIRS

FROM A.D. 1014 TO A.D. 1590.

EDITED, WITH A TRANSLATION,

BY

WILLIAM M. HENNESSY, M.R.I.A.

PUBLISHED BY THE AUTHORITY OF THE LORDS COMMISSIONERS OF HER MAJESTY'S
TREASURY, UNDER THE DIRECTION OF THE MASTER OF THE ROLLS.

VOL. I

LONDON:

LONGMAN & Co., AND TRÜBNER & Co, PATERNOSTER ROW ;
ALSO BY PARKER & Co., OXFORD;
MACMILLAN & Co, CAMBRIDGE,
A. & C. BLACK, EDINBURGH; AND A. THOM, DUBLIN.

1871.

CONTENTS.

PREFACE.

PREFACE.

THE history of the Irish manuscript which has fur-History of the MS. H. 1. 19, in the Library of Trinity College, Dublin. nished the greater portion of the text of these volumes, was long involved in considerable obscurity. Nor has this obscurity been yet entirely dissipated; for, although the MS. has formed the subject of investigation by three of the most competent Irish scholars and antiquaries of the present century—namely, the late Rev. Dr. Todd, Dr. O'Donovan, and Professor O'Curry—nothing very satisfactory has been ascertained regarding either its original materials, or its history from the time when it passed out of the hands of its owner and part compiler, Brian Mac Dermot of Carrick-MacDermot, county of Roscommon, who died in the year 1592, until the year 1766. In this latter year it seems to have been purchased in Dublin, at the sale of the books of Dr. John O'Fergus, by Dr. Thomas Leland, Fellow of Trinity College, Dublin, and author of a History of Ireland, who placed it in the MS. Library of that University, where it is now, No. 19 of class H., Tab. 1. There is no evidence to show how it became the property of Dr. O'Fergus, [1] who was a large collector of

---

[1] "The O'Ferguses were the hereditary physicians to the O'Malleys in *Iar-Umhall*, or West Umhallia, now comprising the barony of Murrisk, in Mayo, and all that district to the north-east of Croagh Patrick. The late distinguished Dr. John Fergus of Dublin, the correspondent of O'Conor of Belanagare, was of this family." O'Donovan's *Catal. of Irish MSS.* in Trin. Coll., Dublin.

Irish MSS.; but in the year 1734 it appears to have been in the possession of a well known Irish scholar, Mr. John Conry, or O'Mulconry, a member of a very learned and industrious family of Irish historiographers, the assistant of Dr. O'Brien in the compilation of his Irish Dictionary, and transcriber of many valuable manuscripts. This fact we learn from Bishop Nicolson's "Irish Historical Library,"[1] published in that year, in the 4th appendix to which (p. 243) the writer gives a list of "Annals and Chronicles" brought to him since the printing of the foregoing sheets (*i.e.* the body of his work) in which is included a MS. "communicated" to him by Mr. John Conry, corresponding to the original of these volumes. It seems also to have passed through the hands of Roger O'Flaherty, the author of "Ogygia," who died about the year 1717; at least the profuse marginal notes added by him throughout a portion of the volume would warrant this conclusion. But it is uncertain at what period O'Flaherty's connexion with the MS. began or ended.

The uncertainty attending the history of the MS. has led to so many changes in its title, that it would appear as if each successive possessor had given it a new name.

The name by which Dr. Nicolson indicates the MS. is "Annals of the Old Abbey of Inis-Macreen, an island in Lough-Kea." At the time of its purchase by Dr. Leland, in 1766, and down to the year 1836, it was known as a continuation of the Annals of Tighernach, and in fact lettered on the back "Tigernachi Continuator." In 1836, however, Dr. O'Donovan pronounced it to be, not the Annals of Inis-Macreen, but the same as the Book of the O'Duigenans of Kilronan, or Annals of Kilronan (a chronicle which the Four Masters had made use of when compiling their Annals), and always referred to it

The MS. noticed by Bishop Nicolson.

Known by various titles.

---

[1] Irish Historical Library; Dublin, 1724.

by that title. This opinion of Dr. O'Donovan, in which
Dr. Todd coincided, has been called in question by Pro-
fessor O'Curry, who has left a very full account of the
MS., and who considers that it should be called the
" Annals of Loch-Cé (or Lough-Key)," the name by which
the Chronicle is at present known.

It is due to the memory of these three eminent
scholars, that the result of their separate examinations of
the MS. should be published, in order that the reasons
which influenced them, in arriving at the several conclusions which they have expressed, may be appreciated

The following is Dr. O'Donovan's account, extracted
from his *Catalogue of the Irish MSS in the Library of*
Trinity College, Dublin (page 104, sq.), with some anno-
tations by the late Dr. Todd, which, for the sake of distinction, are enclosed within brackets :—

Dr. O'Do-
novan's ac-
count of H.
1. 19.

" This book is lettered on the back ' Tigernachi Continuator.' It is in quarto, and in its original state consisted
[principally] of vellum. It is now imperfect, both at the
beginning and end, and has chasms in different parts of it, to
supply which paper has been written on, but the principal part
is blank, and none of the chasms have [has] been completely
filled.

" The Annals of Tigernach, of which the book is said to be a
continuation, were compiled in the Monastery of Clonmacnoise,
of which Tigernach was abbot. He died 1088 ; but Augustine
Mac Raidin, a canon of the order of St. Augustine in the
Island of Saints in Lough Ree, continued the work from the
death of Tigernach down to 140[5], which was the year of his
own death.

" There must be a [gross] mistake in calling this *Tigernachi*
Continuator, because if it were only a continuation of Tigernach, it would not commence earlier than the year [1088 or]
1089, whereas the first article that presents itself is an account
of the battle of Clontarf, fought in the year 1014, *i.e.* 74 years
before the death of Tigernach. At the year 1088 no notice is
taken of the death of Tigernach (in H. 1. 18, fol. 163 b,
line 39), nor is there any notice given that the work is a continuation of any annals, but appears to be one entire piece, the
work of one person ; and I will make it appear in the course of
my observations, that it is no other than [an ancient copy of]

the book of the O'Duigenans of Kilronan, [of] which [the Four
Masters had a copy, which] began with the year 900, and
ended with 1563 ; (see Michael O'Clery's Testimonium to the
Annals of the Four Masters).

"Mr. O'Reilly, in his MS. notice of this [volume], was satis-
fied that it was not 'the Continuation of Tigernach,' but still
he was not prepared to state what it was.   His words are—
'I think this book cannot properly be called 'the Continuation of Tigernach,' though I am at present unprepared to say
what it should be called.   But of this I am certain, that it
differs materially from a copy of Tigernach, and a part of his
Continuator, now in my possession.'

"That this book was in the possession of the O'Duigenans
appears from several entries in the margin ; thus, at the top
of the page containing the years 1462–3, the following memorandum appears : 'Ꞇꞃꙇ ꝺuꙇꝇeóᵹꙁ ocuꞃ .u.xx. meꙁmꞃuꙇm
ꙁꞇꙁ ꙇꞃꙇn ꝉeꙁꞃuꞃ ꞃꙁ, per me David Duigenan ;' 'three leaves
and five score of vellum that are in this book, per me, D. D.'
And again, on the page which was originally left blank between
the years 1541 and 1542, the name ꝺꙁꞃꙇꝺe O'ꝺuꙇꞃᵹenꙁꙇn is
written inversely (sic).   On the same page the following entry
appears, which shows that it was in the possession of the family
of Mac Dermot.   'Hugh, the son of Brian, who was the son of
Rory Mac Dermot, died in Grangenamanagh on the 14th day
of March, 1648.   Mulroney, the son of Hugh Mac Dermot,
wrote this small scrap in 1654.'   On the same page the death
of Mac Dermot (Brian Oge), in 1636, is recorded, and his character described in glowing bardic terms ; [this was inserted long
after the original writing].   Again, on a leaf of paper inserted
between folios 1 and 2, is a memorandum from which it appears that this MS. was in Mac Dermot's country in the year
1698.

"'I am this day at Baile-an-chairn-Oillthrialla, the tenth
day of November, 1698.   John Mac Namee.'   This Baile-an-
chairn is now called [in English] Heapstown, (which is a
literal translation of its Irish name), and lies in Mac Dermot's
country.   [This place takes its name from a vast cairn of
stones which was piled to form the monument of Oilill, the
brother of Niall of the nine hostages, from whom the territory
of Tir-Oilella, now corruptly Tirerrill, a barony in the south-
east of the county of Sligo, has derived its name].

"The notices of the Mac Dermots of Moylurg [and of their
bards the O'Duigenans of Kilronan], and of their neighbouring
chiefs [and bards], are more numerous than those of any other
in Ireland throughout this chronicle ; and this is sufficient to
identify it with the district ; for in like manner, the Annals of

Ulster will be found to dwell more upon the history of the Maguires and their neighbours than upon any others.

"The Four Masters had the book of the O'Duigenans of Kilronan, in 1636 ; and at that time it commenced with the year 900, and ended with 1563 ; [and] it is' plain that this is not the copy of it they had, for it is stated in the testimonium that the Book of the O'Duigenans ended with the year 1563, whereas the present Chronicle ends with 1571. We learn also from the Stowe Catalogue (p. 76) that Charles O'Conor of Belanagare had a copy of the Book of Kilronan in his posses- sion in the year 1728 ; and by comparing an extract [there given] from the same book, A.D. 1464, with the same year in this Chronicle, it will be found they differ materially ; [and this is owing to a defect in this Chronicle at that year].[1]

"From the preceding evidences I draw the following con- clusions.

"[1st]. That the copy of the Book of Kilronan which the Four Masters used, was imperfect at the end (wanting from 1563 to 1571, and [perhaps] more).

"[2ndly]. That this present Chronicle is a copy of the book, made [2] before it was as defective as when it fell into the hands of the Four Masters.

"[3rdly]. That this copy had lost several pages at the begin- ning, and in the middle, which were afterwards attempted to be partially restored on vellum and paper [afterwards inserted].

"This volume in its present state contains 99 leaves of vellum, and 31 leaves of paper, which shows that it has not lost much vellum since David O'Duigenan found it to contain 'three leaves and five score of vellum.' The vellum part is in general closely written, but the paper part is mostly blank.

"There is a diversity of handwriting on the vellum, and even the small quantity that is written on the paper is not all in the one hand. The writing on the vellum is beautifully executed.

"In the beginning of the book the original writing has been

---

[1] "[O'Conor says] 'This extract is taken from the Book of Kilronan, which has the approbation of the Four Masters annexed to it, by me, Cathal O'Conor, 2 Aug., 1728.'" Note by O'Donovan.

[2] "It can be inferred from a mem- orandum [in the hand in which all the MS. was originally written], that [a part of] this copy was made for one of the Mac Dermots by a Philip Badly in the year 1580. Iṛ ım ṛ5ıtech ꝺo ḃaṛc Ḃhṛıaın mıc Ɗıaṛmaꝺa ao. ꝺo., 1580. Mıṛı Ṗılıp ḃaꝺt. "I am wearied of the bark (recte book) of Brian Mac Dermot, A.D. 1580. I, Philip Badley" [Badhlaie, Bailey]. Note by O'Donovan.

gone over with good black ink,[1] but towards the conclusion, and in some parts of the middle, the original writing appears in its virgin [pristine] beauty; but the ink is faded, though by no means so much so as to render the writing illegible.

"Owing to the book having been a long time without a cover, the first page is much soiled, worn, and nearly effaced. Its contents, however, have been copied on paper [now bound up with the book] on the 10th November, 1698, [by John Mac Namee] for the purpose, as [he] says, of preventing its being further *obscured.* The same has been copied upon one of the supplementary pages of the book, so that there are [now] three copies of the same page.

"It commences with the year 1014, and goes consecutively to 1138, where there is a chasm from thence to 1170. Here six leaves of blank paper were inserted, on which the deficiency might be supplied, but nothing has been written on them.

"After the year 1061 four leaves of paper were inserted by the bookbinder, though there does not appear any occasion for them, as there is no chasm, the year 1062 following in regular succession. On one of these, which is smaller than the rest, are written some verses which have no connexion with this MS., or with the family of Mac Dermot, from which it is clear that it found its way into this book by accident, and was in mistake bound up with it. The name [of] Francis Oge appears in it, who was in all probability Doctor Francis Sullivan, who collected the greater part of the MSS. we have hitherto described.

"At the head of the page containing the year 1170 is written 'ın naınm Oé an Cıonnrcna ro,' *i.e.* 'in the name of God this beginning;' which suggests that this part of the Chronicle was written by a different hand from Philip Badley. [And] a comparison of the writing will prove this to the caligraphist.

"From [after] the year 1170 the Chronicle goes on in consecutive annual [chronological] order to the year 1316, where another chasm occurs in the original vellum, in which 146 years more are lost, that is, up to the year 1462. With an intention of supplying this defect 22 leaves of blank paper were inserted, but no part of the chasm is filled up on the six first leaves. On the seventh leaf the death of Conor O'Doherty,

---

[1] "Mr. O'Reilly says, 'In the beginning of the book it is as black as if written only yesterday.' He did not observe that the original writing was restored by going over it with black [ink. To prove] that this is the case, however, requires no great skill in caligraphy.—*See* Mason's Catalogue, T. Coll. Dublin; class H. 16." Note added by Dr. O'Donovan.

chief of Ardmire, and lord of Inishowen, is [recorded] under the year 1413. [At] the years 1414, 1416, 1426, 1427, 1428, 1441, 1442, 1443, 1446, 1448, 1449, 1453, 1455, and 1460, very little is written on the paper except the dates.

"At the end of eight leaves more of the inserted paper, the same matter which is written on the seventh and succeeding leaves is again repeated, beginning with the year 1413, and leaving the same blanks as above described. At the end of eight leaves more the repetition of the former matter is concluded.

"From the year 1462 the Chronicle runs on regularly on vellum, and up to the year 1497. The writing is by different hands, and in different inks.

"There are vacant spaces left at the end of every year, evidently with a view of adding more matter.

"From the year 1497 to the end of the year 1542, which the writer marks as bissextile, the matter is very closely written on fifteen leaves of vellum. Here nearly two pages were left blank, which have been since filled up by an account of the deaths of George Oge Bingham in 1595, of Brian Oge, the son of Brian Mac Dermot, in 1636, of Randal, Earl of Antrim, in the same year, and of Hugh, the son of Brian Mac Dermot, in 1648.

"From the commencement of the year 1542 to the end of the volume, there is no chasm excepting that two or three pages [towards the very end] are almost illegible. The last page is altogether illegible, for which reason it cannot be said with certainty whether this chronicle had been carried lower down than the year 1571, which is the last date that appears.

"The Four Masters have *all*[1] the entries in this Chronicle,

---

[1] This is a most unaccountable mistake on the part of O'Donovan. See his edition of the Four Masters, Introduction, p. lxv., note b, where he refers to the MS. in the following words:—"There is a most curious and valuable manuscript volume of Irish annals, which was in the possession of the O'Duigenans, preserved in the Library of Trinity College, Dublin, H. I. 19; but it does not appear to be the one used by the Four Masters. It perfectly accords with all the passages quoted by Ware and Harris from the Annals of Lough Kee; and it may be safely conjectured that it is a compilation made by the O'Duigenans from the Annals of Lough Kee, Roscommon, and Kilronan. The editor has made copious additions to the work of the Four Masters from this manuscript, calculated to throw much light on historical facts but slightly touched upon by the Masters themselves." O'Donovan has also committed a grave error in stating, as he has in the foregoing note, that the present chronicle "perfectly accords with all the passages quoted by Ware and Harris from the Annals of Lough Kee." At least, it is certain that the original of the present volumes was not used by either of these writers.— Vid. *infra*, pp. xxxii.-xxxiv.

but some of them, especially those relating to Mac Dermot and his neighbours, they have not unfrequently abridged, leaving out some important references to names and situations of places, which are of great importance to the topographer. An editor of the second part of the Annals of the Four Masters should carefully compare their text with this Chronicle.

" J. O'DONOVAN,

"December 7, 1836."

Dr. Todd's description of H. 1. 19. Dr. Todd's account does not differ materially from that of Dr. O'Donovan, in conjunction with whom his investigation of the MS. would appear to have been conducted. His opinions were embodied in a paper read before the Royal Irish Academy on the 9th of January, 1837, an abstract of which has been published in the proceedings of that body.[1] Dr. Todd having kindly placed his original notes in my hand a short time before his lamented death, with authority to dispose of them as I might think fit, it appears to me that the most appropriate use to which I can put them, is to reproduce them here without curtailment.

"The Rev. James H. Todd, A.M., M.R.I.A., Fellow of Trinity College, mentioned the fact that an authentic, although imperfect, copy of the Annals of Kilronan, or Book of the O'Duigenans, had recently been discovered by Mr. John O'Donovan in the Library of Trinity College, Dublin.

" The volume is in quarto, and in its original state consisted entirely of vellum. It is now imperfect both at the beginning and at the end, and has also some chasms, which have been filled with paper leaves, inserted probably with an intention of supplying the deficiencies from some other copy; but this has not been done except in a very few cases, and the paper leaves are therefore almost entirely blank.

" Mr. Todd stated that the volume is lettered on the back *Tigernachi Continuator*, and that it was supposed to be the continuation of the Annals of Tigernach, composed by Augustin Mac Raidin (or Mac Raith), a canon of the Augustinian Monastery of All Saints in Lough Righ, in the river Shannon.

"But the continuation of Tigernach began with the year 1089,

---

[1] *Proceedings R. I. Academy*, vol. 1 p. 22.

and could not have extended beyond 1405, the year in which
Mac Raith died; whereas the present volume, notwithstanding
its imperfect state, begins with the year 1014, and ends with
the year 1571, one hundred and sixty-four years after the death
of the Continuator of Tigernach. Accordingly, this mistake was
detected and mentioned by Mr. O'Reilly, in the unpublished
catalogue of the Trinity College Irish MSS., drawn up by
him for Mr. Mason. (Here Dr. Todd quotes Mr. O'Reilly's
opinion, as given above in Dr. O'Donovan's notice, p. xii.)
The Library of Trinity College possesses a complete copy of the
Continuation of Tigernach, which enables us to determine this
question beyond doubt.

"Mr. Todd then proceeded to state the evidence for Mr.
O'Donovan's conjecture that this volume is no other than the
Annals of Kilronan, in the county Roscommon, compiled by
the O'Duigenans :—

"1. The book was in the possession of the O'Duigenans, as
appears by many entries contained in it; one of these, which
occurs on the upper margin of the page containing the year
1462, may be quoted as an example :—

"'Τρι ɔuilleóʒa ocuρ u.xxιᴄ. meampuim aᴄa iρın leaburρa
per me, David Duigenan.

"'Three leaves, and five score of vellum are in this book, by
me, David Duigenan.'

"And again, on a page which was originally left blank, between
the years 1541 and 1542, the name Ɔabıɔe O''Ɔuıbʒenaın is
written.

"2. Throughout the Chronicle notices of the Mac Dermots
of Moylurg, and of their family bards, the O'Duigenans of Kilronan, are more frequent than of any other clans or chieftains
of Ireland, a circumstance tending strongly to identify this
volume with the Annals of Kilronan, which we know contained
the local chronicles of the Mac Dermots' country. On the page
just alluded to, is an entry of which the following is a translation :—

"'Hugh, son of Brian, who was the son of Rory Mac Dermot, died in Grangenamanagh on the 14th day of March, 1648.
Mulrony, the son of Hugh Mac Dermot, wrote this short note
in 1654.'

"On the same page is recorded the death of the Mac Dermot
of 1636, who is styled Brian Oge, and his character drawn with
bardic eloquence.

"These and similar entries throughout the volume, made at
different dates, and several of them long after the original

writing of the Chronicle itself, prove that the volume was considered as a family record of the Mac Dermots, and the deaths or births of remarkable members of the family recorded from time to time in its blank leaves; such entries are often made even at the present day in the blank leaves of a family Bible or prayer-book.

"Between the first two parchment leaves of the volume, is a sheet of paper on which the contents of the first page, that had become almost illegible, were transcribed in the year 1698. To this the transcriber has affixed the following note[1] :—

"'I am this day at Baile-an-chairn-Oillthrialla, the 10th day of November, 1698.—John Conmidhe.'

"This entry proves that in 1698 this book was in the Mac Dermot's country; for *Baile-an-Chairn*, the town of the Cairn, now called *Heapstown*, which is a literal translation of its Irish name, is situated in the Mac Dermots' country. It derived its name from a large *cairn* erected as a monument to Oilill, the brother of Niall of the nine hostages, and the territory has hence been called Tir-Oilella, and corruptly Tirerrill, a barony in the south-east of the county Sligo.

"John Conmidhe, or (as the name is now written and pronounced) Mac Namee, was probably a travelling bard or scholar, who in a visit to the Mac Dermot's country, was able to read and transcribe the page which had become effaced in consequence of the book being kept without a cover. His name suggests no connexion with the family of Mac Dermot, or with the O'Duigenans of Kilronan.

"The Mac Namees were originally petty chiefs of Meath (*Cu Midhe*, 'dog of Meath'), and a branch of the family became afterwards hereditary bards of Tyrone—where they are still very numerous.

"Under the year 1061, and in the same beautiful hand in which the parchment and original part of the MS. was written, we find the following note :—

"'Iſ ım ẛᵹiᴄech ᴅo ḃaɼc ḃɼıan mıc Oıaɼmaᴅa Œ°.O°. 1580. Mıɼı Ṗılıp ḃaᴅlaıᵹ.

"'I am weary of the book of Brian Mac Dermot; A.D. 1580. I, Philip Badley.'

From this we may perhaps infer that Philip Badley was employed by one of the Mac Dermots to transcribe or compile this volume, from more ancient documents, and that he was engaged in this task in 1580.

---

[1] It was very common for Irish scribes to introduce their own names into their works, accompanied by panegyrics of their employers.

" 3. In confirmation of the foregoing evidence in support of Mr. O'Donovan's conjecture, it may be added that a comparison of this Chronicle with the Annals of the Four Masters, supplies strong proof of their having had a copy of it before them. They have abridged many of the passages relating to the Mac Dermots, as being of merely local interest; this we know was their uniform practice in regard to the other ancient chronicles from which they derived their materials, and as they tell us expressly that the Annals of the O'Duigenans of Kilronan were in their hands, these coincidences go far to prove the identity of that Chronicle with the volume now before us.

" It is fair, however, to mention that if the present volume be indeed the Annals of Kilronan, it is not exactly the same as the copy made use of by the Four Masters. They tell us that their copy commenced with the year 900, and ended with the year 1563, whereas the present copy begins with the year 1014, and ends with 1571, and appears to have formerly gone even later.

" These discrepancies, however, are not sufficient to overturn the evidence already adduced. For the copy of the Annals of Kilronan in the possession of the Four Masters may have been imperfect at the end; as this copy is both at the end and at the beginning. It may be added that this copy was evidently written by persons who were *compiling*, and not merely *transcribing*, for they throughout left blanks for subsequent entries, some of which have been inserted in their proper places. This circumstance appears to give to this volume the character of an original copy of the Chronicle, and might lead to the conclusion that the copy used by the Four Masters was a more modern and unfinished transcript.

" There is, however, a circumstance which would seem to indicate that the Annals of Kilronan, which were in the hands of those eminent antiquarians, was a document altogether different from the present Chronicle. It would seem that the copy which belonged to the Four Masters was in existence in 1728, and was then in the possession of Charles O'Conor of Belanagare, who extracted from it an entry relating to the last king of the O'Conor race, who died in the year 1464. This entry is published by Dr. O'Conor in his Cat. of the Stowe Library. It does not agree with the Dublin MS., where the death of O'Conor is simply mentioned under that date, without any of the particulars relative to his funeral, or the honors paid him by the neighbouring chieftains at his interment, which are given in the extract quoted by Mr. O'Conor.

"This at first sight would seem to be a difficulty fatal to
Mr. O'Donovan's opinion, that the Dublin MS. is a copy, and
apparently an original copy, of the Annals of Kilronan; but
we must not admit this conclusion hastily. For the passage
extracted by Mr. O'Conor, may have been a modern insertion
from the hand of some members of the O'Conor family, and
not an original or integral part of the Chronicle—such in-
sertions are common in this class of Irish MSS., and we have
already seen instances of them in the very volume before us.

"To this consideration Mr. Todd added his own doubts
whether the *Book of Kilronan,* from which the foregoing extract was taken, can properly be considered the same as *the
Annals of Kilronan,* or *Book of the O'Duigenans,* mentioned by
the Four Masters. The *Book of Kilronan,* which was in the
possession of Charles O'Conor in 1728, is described by him as
the Book of *the Church* of Kilronan, not as the family
Chronicle of the O'Duigenans; he tells us indeed that the
Four Masters had affixed to it their approbation, and this
perhaps has led to the idea that it was the same as the Annals
of Kilronan, which they undoubtedly used. But they have
expressly called these Annals *the Book of the O'Duigenans,* and
they tell us that they began with the year 900; a circumstance inconsistent with what we are told of the Book in
Charles O'Conor's possession, which must have begun much
earlier, since that eminent antiquary extracted from it "a
Chronicle of the Kings of Connacht from the arrival of St.
Patrick," which Chronicle is described by Dr. O'Conor in his
Catalogue of the Stowe Library, as beginning with the arrival
of St. Patrick, and ending with the year 1464. It is preserved in the Stowe Library, Press I., No. 3, fol. 23. A
transcript of it, if it could be obtained for the Academy from
his Grace the Duke of Buckingham, would be of great value
and importance.

"On the whole, then there can be no question that, whether
the Dublin MS. be, or be not, the Kilronan Annals which were
in the hands of the Four Masters, it is undoubtedly a Chronicle
of the Mac Dermots' country, composed by the O'Duigenans of
Kilronan. This is abundantly proved by the internal evidence of the volume, and will not be doubted by any person
who is competent to form an opinion on the subject. It has
been suggested that the intermediate part of the MS. belonged
to another chronicle, or was written at a different date from
the rest, because additional notes and passages are inserted
more frequently than in the preceding or following passages.
Mr. Todd stated that he was unable to concur in this opinion.
It is certainly true that this intermediate part of the volume

appeared to be written by perhaps four or five different hands, whereas the first part was all by the same scribe, and the last part, with the exception of some few entries, also by the writer of the first; but the hand of the first scribe may be traced also in the intermediate part, and a handwriting which occurs very frequently in the intermediate part, is found also in several places in the third. There cannot therefore be any great difference of date between these three portions of the volume. The intermediate part, containing at present twenty-four leaves of parchment, certainly bears marks of having once been separated from the rest; on its first and last pages occur the entries by David Duigenan, already quoted, who (if an opinion may be hazarded from his handwriting) appears to have lived in the beginning of the 17th century. The phenomena may be accounted for by supposing two or more scribes engaged simultaneously in the transcription of the work.

"The number of parchment leaves when they were counted by David Duigenan, was five score and three, which may mean either 103, or if the Irish method of counting, which allowed six score to the hundred was adopted, 123; the number of parchment leaves at present in the volume is 99.

"The principal chasms in the MS. are between the years 1138 and 1170, and between the years 1316 and 1462. In the former of these chasms several leaves of paper have been inserted which are entirely blank. The latter has also been filled up with paper, on which some very brief and scanty notices have been entered between the years 1413 and 1461. Two copies of this paper portion of the volume have been made, one of them of a date much more recent than the other. The older appears to have been written in the 16th century.

"Throughout the volume several marginal notes occur which are for the most part summaries of the text, both in Irish and English. Many of the English notes are, in Mr. Todd's opinion, in the handwriting of Roderick O'Flaherty, the celebrated author of Ogygia.

"Mr. Todd concluded by remarking that the discovery of this copy of the Book of the O'Duigenans of Kilronan will be of great importance if ever the liberality of Government, or the contributions of individuals, should place at our disposal funds for the publication of the Ancient Annalists of Ireland; the Annals of the Four Masters will of course be the first to be put to press, and it is of great importance to collect in the first instance the original documents made use of by those learned antiquaries in the compilation of their work. What these were they have themselves told us in their preface, a

translation of which has appeared in the Transactions of the
Academy, in a paper read before the Academy by Mr. Petrie.
By this recovery of the Annals of Kilronan, we are now in
possession of almost all these documents. The Book of Clon-
macnoise, or Annals of Tigernach, is published by Dr.
O'Conor, and a copy of it, well worthy of collation, is in the
Library of Trinity College. The Book of the Island of Saints,
in Lough Righ, is also in Trinity College. The Book of
Senait Mac Manus, or the Ulster Annals, is published by Dr.
O'Conor, and a very ancient copy is in Trinity College Library.
The Book of Mac Firbis, or the Book of Leacan, is in the
Library of the Academy, and is now completed by the copy
of Lord Roden's MS., just finished at the expense of the
Academy; and when we add to this list the Book of the
O'Duigenans of Kilronan, there remain not more than two
or three of the original Annalists, to which we have not now
easy access."

Professor O'Curry's description[1] is much more specific
and detailed than either of the foregoing. Written at a
period twenty-five years later, it naturally exhibits a
more intimate acquaintance with the contents and
history of the MS. than could have been acquired by
either Dr. Todd or O'Donovan, at the time of their investigation. It is as follows:—

Professor O'Curry's description of H 1. 19.

" And first, of the Annals which have been known for some
time under the name of the Annals of Kilronan, but which,
I think, it will presently be seen should be called the Annals
of *Inis Mac Nerinn* in *Loch Cé.*

" The only copy of these Annals known to exist at present is
that in the Library of Trinity College, Dublin, Class H 1. 19.
It is on vellum, of small folio size; the original writing in
various hands, but all of them fine and accurate Several
leaves having, however, been lost from the original volume in
various parts of it, the chasms are filled up, sometimes with
paper and sometimes with vellum, and some of the missing
annals restored, although in an inferior style of penmanship.
These restorations are principally in the handwriting of Brian
Mac Dermot. The chief defects in the body of the book are
observable from the year 1138 to 1170, where thirty-two years
are missing; and from the year 1316 to 1462, where 142
years are missing. The year 1468 is also omitted.

[1] *Lectures on the Manuscript Materials of Irish History,* Dublin, 1861,
p. 93, sq.

"The following notices will sufficiently show the names of the chief transcriber, of the owner, and the time of transcribing the volume.

"At the end of the year 1061 we find this notice :—'I am fatigued from Brian Mac Dermot's book; Anno Domini 1580. I am Philip Badley.'

"The Christian name of the scribe appears in several places from this to the end of the year 1588; but a memorandum at the end of the year 1515 is conclusive in identifying not only the chief transcriber, but the date of the original transcript, as well as the place in which, and the person for whom, the volume was transcribed or compiled :—

"'I rest from this work. May God grant to the man [that is, the owner] of this book, to return safely from Athlone ; that is Brian, the son of Ruaidhrigh Mac Dermot. I am Philip who wrote this, 1588, on the day of the festival of Saint Brendan in particular. And *Cluain Hi Bhraoin* is my place.'

"Of this Badley, if that be his real name, I have never been able to learn anything more than what he has written of himself in this volume. I may observe, however, that the name of Philip is not uncommon in the learned family of *O'Duibhghenainn* or Duigenan; and *Cluain I Bhraoin*, where Philip wrote this book, was at this time the residence of a branch of the *O'Duibhghenainn* or O'Duigenans, as will appear from the following entry in these Annals, in the handwriting of the owner of the book, Brian Mac Dermot, at the year 1581 :— 'Fercaogadh O'Duigenan, the son of Fergal, son of Philip, died at *Cluain I Bhraoin*.'

"We find, too, the name of *Dubhthach* [O'Duigenain] set down as a scribe in the book, at the end of the year 1224.

"The following memorandum at the end of the page at which the year 1462 commences (the book is not paged), gives us further reason still for supposing that the O'Duigenans had some connexion with this book. It runs thus :—'Three leaves and five scores of vellum that are contained in this book, per me, David Duigenan.' This memorandum is without date; and I may observe that, as the book contains at present but ninety-nine of the original leaves, four leaves must have been lost since this memorandum was written.

"I have not, however, quoted these memoranda merely in order to show by what particular scribe the Annals in question were written. A mistake has, it appears to me, been long current with regard to the identity of the MS., and I believe I am in a position to correct it.

"It is my opinion that the notices just referred to are suffi-

cient to show that these are not those Annals, or that 'Book
of the *O'Duibhghenainns* of Kilronan,' which was one of the
books mentioned by the Four Masters as having been used by
them in their compilation, and which extended from the year
900 to the year 1563. The present volume begins with the
year 1014, and in its original form ends (imperfectly) with the
year 1571; and we find that one of the O'Duigenan family
was a transcriber in the early part of it, and that it was transcribed at *Cluain I Bhraoin*. But it is, I think, more than
probable that the volume is but a transcript of the original
Book of the O'Duigenans of Kilronan, made, as far as it went,
for Brian Mac Dermot; and that to the text of this transcript
that noble chief himself, and other scribes, made several additions, carrying the annals down to the year 1590, or two
years before his death in 1592. Such is the opinion at which
I have arrived as to this manuscript.

"That the present volume was carried down to the year
1590, I am rather fortunately in a position to prove beyond
any doubt, having myself discovered a part of the continuation
in the British Museum in the year 1849. This part contains
sixteen consecutive years, and part of a dislocated year, extending from the latter part of 1568 to 1590, but still leaving
a chasm in the volume from 1561[1] to 1568. This continuation
is written partly on vellum and partly on paper, in various
hands, among which that of Brian Mac Dermot is still very
plainly distinguishable; and the following translation of an
entry, at the year 1581, with Brian's note on it, seems to complete the identification of the volume :—

" ' Calvagh (*Calbhach*), the son of Donnell, son of Teige
(*Tadhg*), son of Cathal O'Conor, the heir of Sligo and of Lower
Connacht, without dispute, died on Friday between the two
Easters [that is, between Easter Sunday and Low Sunday] in
this year.'

"To this article Brian Mac Dermot adds the following
note :—

" ' And the death of this only son of Donnell O'Conor and
Mòr Ni Ruairc is one of the most lamentable events of Erinn.
And there never came, of the descendants of Brian Luighnech
[O'Conor], a man of his years a greater loss than he, nor is it
likely that there will come. And this loss has pained the
hearts of all Connacht, and especially it has pained the scholars
and poets of the province of Connacht. And it has divided my

---

[1] This is obviously an error, as appears from the preceding paragraph,
in which O'Curry himself states that
the MS. H. 1. 19 ends with the year
1571. The chasm is from the year
1571 to 1577.—Ed.

own heart into two parts. Uch! Uch! how pitiable my condition after my comrade and companion, and the man most dear and truthful to me in the world!

"'I am Brian Mac Dermot who wrote this, upon Mac Dermot's Rock; and I am now like *Olioll Oluim* after his sons, when they were slain, together with *Art Aenfhir*, the son of Conn of the Hundred Battles, in the battle of *Magh Mucruimhé*, by *Mac Con*, the son of *Mac Niadh*, son of *Lughaidh*; or like *Deirdré* after the sons of *Uisneach* had been treacherously slain in *Eamhain Mhacha* [Emania], by *Conchobhar* the son of *Fachtna*, son of *Rossa Ruadh*, son of *Rudhraidhe*, [Conor Mac Nessa]; for I am melancholy, sorrowful, distressed, and dispirited, in grief and in woe. And it cannot be described or related how I feel after the departure of my companion from me, that is the Calvach. And it was on the last day of the month of March that he was interred in *Sligech* (Sligo).'

"Mac Dermot's Rock (*Carraig Mhic-Diarmada*), and the Rock of Loch Cé (*Carraig Locha Cé*), were the popular names of a castle built on an Island in Loch Cé, near Boyle, in the present county of Roscommon. This castle was the chief residence and stronghold of Mac Dermot, the native chief and prince of *Magh Luirg* (or Moylorg), an extensive territory in the same county of Roscommon.

"The above Brian Mac Dermot, the owner, restorer, and continuator of these Annals, was chief of Magh Luirg between the years 1585 and 1592, though in what year he succeeded his father, Rory (*Ruaidhri*), the son of Teige (*Tadhg*), I am not able to say.[1] The father was chief in 1540 and 1542.

"Of Brian Mac Dermot himself, we find in the Annals of the Four Masters—under the year 1585 (in which year all the native chiefs of Erinn were called by proclamation to a parliament in Dublin),—that *Tadhg*, the son of *Eoghan* Mac Dermot, attended this Parliament as deputy from Mac Dermot of Magh Luirg; that is Brian the son of *Ruaidhri*, son of *Tadhg*, son of *Ruaidhri Og*, which Brian was then a very old man. And at the year 1592, the same Annals record the death of this Brian Mac Dermot in the following words:—

"'Mac Dermot of Magh Luirg,—*Brian*, the son of *Ruaidhri*, son of *Tadhg* Mac Dermot, died in the month of November; and the death of this man was the more to be lamented, because there was no other like him of the *Clann-Maolruanaidh* [the tribe name of the Mac Dermots], to succeed him in the chieftainship.'

---

[1] Brian must have succeeded in the year 1568, under which date the death of his father, Ruaidhri, is recorded in the present chronicle. *See* vol II., p. 397.—Ed.

"It would appear, I think, that these cannot be the so-called Annals of Kilronan; but that they are those called the Annals of Loch Cé, quoted by Sir James Ware in his work on the Bishops of Erinn, is by no means certain.

"Dr. Nicolson (Protestant Bishop of Derry, and afterwards Archbishop of Cashel), in his valuable 'Irish Historical Library,' published in Dublin in 1724, p. 36, thus speaks of the Annals of Loch Cé, quoted by Sir James Ware:—

" 'The Annals of this monastery are frequently quoted by Sir James Ware; but all that he ever saw was a fragment of them (part in Latin and part in Irish), beginning at 1249, and ending at 1408. He supposes the author to have been a Canon-Regular of the said Abbey, and to have lived about the middle of the Fifteenth Century. His copy, perhaps, has had some farther loss since it fell into other hands; seeing all that can be now said of it is '*Pars Annalium Cœnobii S. Trin. de Loghkœa, incipiens ab An. 1249, et desinens An. 1381, ex Hibernico Idiomate in Anglicum versa.*'

"The same writer (Appendix No. 6, page 243) says:—

" 'The most valuable collection of Irish MSS. that I have met with, in any private hand, here in Dublin, next to that of the Lord Bishop of Clogher, was communicated to me by Mr. John Conry, who has great numbers of our Historico-Poetical Composures, and (being a perfect master of their language and prosodia) knows how to make the best use of them. Amongst these, there's—

" '1. An ancient copy of the *Annales Senatenses* (Annals of Ulster), written on vellum and in a fair character, but imperfect at the beginning and end; for it begins at the year 454, ten years later than the Duke of Chandois', and ends (about 50 years sooner) at 1492.

" '2. There is also in the same Letter and Parchment, and the same folio Volume, a copy of the Annals of the Old Abbey of *Inch-Maccreen*, an island in the Lake of *Loghkea*, very different from those of the Holy Trinity, an abbey (in the same Loch) of a much later foundation. This book commences at the year 1013, and ends with 1571.

" '3. He has likewise the original Annals of Donegal (or the Quatuor Magistri), signed by the proper hands of the Four Masters themselves, who are the compilers of that Chronicle,' etc., etc., etc.

"This, indeed, is a most valuable notice from the very candid Bishop Nicolson.

"The Annals of the Old Abbey of Inis Macreen, properly *Inis Mac Nerinn*, an island in *Loch Cé*, which he mentions, are beyond any doubt those which I have already identified as such. According to Conry's report to the bishop, these Annals commenced with the year 1013, and ended with 1571; but it is quite clear that the year 1013 is a mere mistake for 1014, with which the book commences in its present, and I am sure in its then condition. For it commences with an account of the battle of Clontarf; and as the original page is much defaced and the date totally illegible, and as the date of that great event is given by the Four Masters under the year 1013, it seems probable that, without looking to the copy of the whole annal, and the date mentioned below, Conry gave that year as the commencement of the book to the bishop. The last page of the year 1571, with which the volume (without the British Museum addition) ends, is also illegible, showing plainly that the book had been a long time lying without a cover, probably in the ruined residence of some departed member of the Mac Dermot family, before it passed into Conry's hands. Still, notwithstanding that Conry gave this book the name of the Annals of the Abbey of *Inis Mac Nerinn* of *Loch Cé*, it is quite clear from the circumstances under which they were written, that they were not the annals of that abbey, if any such annals ever existed.

"There is some mystery as to the way this volume passed from the hands of *John Conry*. It was, however, purchased at the sale of the books of Dr. John O'Fergus, in 1766, by Dr. Leland, the historian, along with the Annals of Ulster,—a transcript made for the doctor of the first volume of the Annals of the Four Masters,—and the imperfect autograph of the second volume, described above by Dr. Nicolson,—and placed by him (Dr. Leland) in the College Library, where the group may now be seen together. It is fortunate that we actually have still in existence a copy of the printed catalogue of the books of the patriotic Doctor O'Fergus, which is preserved along with several other memorials of him, by his worthy great-grandson, my esteemed friend, James Marinus Kennedy, Esq. (of 47, Lower Gloucester-street, in this city), who has kindly permitted me to consult this interesting catalogue. On examining it, I found included in it the Annals of Ulster,—a transcript of the first volume of the Annals of the Four Masters, by Hugh O'Mulloy, an excellent scribe, in two volumes,—and the imperfect autograph copy of the second volume,—among several other MSS. of less value, set down for sale; but no account of the Annals of the Abbey of *Inis Mac Nerinn*, mentioned by John Conry in his communication to Dr. Nicolson. So far indeed we have lost the direct evidence of the volume being that which Conry had mentioned to the bishop; but the fact of its having been purchased by the College along with the other books and transcripts belonging to Conry's collection, the identity in the years of its beginning and ending, and the original locality to which it was referred, which, though erroneous, was approximately correct, can leave no rational doubt of its being the reputed Annals of the Abbey of *Inis Mac Nerinn* in *Loch Cé*, though the internal evidences clearly prove it to be the Annals of the *Rock* of *Loch Cé*, or Mac Dermot's Rock, the residence of the owner and part-compiler, Brian Mac Dermot, in 1590. Indeed, even the wanting link above alluded to is supplied in a contemporary list or catalogue of the Irish books sold at Dr. O'Fergus' sale, which is preserved in (pasted into) a MS. volume in the Library of the Royal Irish Academy (commonly known by the name of " Vallancy's Green Book "), and contains the names of the persons to whom, and the prices at which, the various Irish MSS. there were sold. For in that list I find it mentioned that Dr. Leland bought 'No. 2427, Annals of the Four Masters, three vols. [the two volumes of transcription and one of autograph before mentioned], a fine MS., £7 19s.;' and also, '2410, Annals of Ulster, by the Four Masters [sic], a very ancient MS. on vellum;' and '2411, Continuation of the Annals of Tigernach, very ancient, on vellum,' both together for £18. The last mentioned MS. was, I have no doubt, the one of which I have been speaking, mistaken by the maker of the catalogue for a 'Continuation of Tigernach,' probably only because he could make no better guess at what it really was. And it is singular that this volume is now lettered 'Tighernaci Continuator' on the back: (H. 1. 19, T.C.D.)

"I have thus, I think, conclusively identified the MS. spoken of by Dr. O'Donovan as the 'Annals of Kilronan,' and I have identified it as one different from the original Book of the O'Duigenans of Kilronan, referred to by the Four Masters. Whether that MS. is or is not the same as the Annals of *Loch Cé*, referred to by Sir James Ware, does not, however, appear to me to be by any means clearly settled[1] by Nicolson, the accuracy of whose descriptions of Irish MSS. is not always implicitly to be depended on. Certainly, Sir James Ware does quote from what he calls the Annals of *Loch Cé* at the year 1217, as we shall presently see, though in the passage before quoted from Nicolson, that writer positively says that 'all he (Ware) ever saw was a fragment of them, beginning at 1249, and ending at 1408.'

" The references by Ware to these Annals are in his 'History of the Bishops.' In the first volume of this important work (as edited by Walter Harris, pp. 84, 250, 252, 271), we find it

---

[1] Vid. *infra*, pp. xxxii-xxxiv.

stated on the authority of the Annals of 'Lough Kee' (*Loch Cé*), that Adam O'Murg (*Annadh O'Muireadhaigh*), Bishop of Ardagh (*Ard-achadh*), died in the year 1217; Cairbre O'Scoba, Bishop of Raphoe (*Rath Bhotha*), in the year 1275; William Mac Casac, Bishop of Ardagh, in the year 1373; and John Colton, Archbishop of Armagh, in the year 1404. On reference to our volume of Annals, we find the death of *Annadh O'Muireadhaigh* and *Cairbré O'Scoba* under the respective years of 1217[1] and 1275. The other years, 1373 and 1404, are now lost, though these lost sheets were probably in existence in Ware's time.

"The following little note, written in the lower margin of the eleventh page of the fragment in the British Museum, is not without interest in tracing this very volume[2] of Annals to the possession of the family of Sir James Ware.

"'Honest, good, hospitable, Robert Ware, Esq., of Stephen's Green; James Magrath is his servant for ever to command.'

"This Robert was the son of the very candid writer on Irish history just mentioned, Sir James Ware; and it is pretty clear that this entry was made in the book, of which the fragment in the British Museum formed a part,[2] while it was in the hands of either the father or the son.

"Having thus endeavoured, and I trust successfully, to identify for the first time this valuable book of Irish Annals, I now proceed to consider the character of its contents, so as to form a just estimate of its value, as a large item in the mass of materials which still exist for an ample and authentic History of Ireland.

"These Annals of *Loch Cé*, as I shall henceforth call them, commence with the year of our Lord 1014, containing a very good account of the Battle of Clontarf; the death of the ever memorable *Brian Boroimhé*; the final overthrow of the whole force of the Danes, assisted as they were by a numerous army of auxiliaries and mercenaries; and the total destruction of their cruel and barbarous sway within the 'Island of Saints.'

"The first page of the book is nearly illegible, but it was restored on inserted paper in a very good hand, at *Carn Oilltriallaigh* in Connacht, on the 1st of November, 1698, by *S. Mac Conmidhe*.

"The account of the Battle of Clontarf just alluded to, is especially interesting, because it contains many details not to be found in any of the other annals now remaining to us.

"In chronology as well as the general character, the Annals

---

[1] This is an error; the death of Annadh O'Muiredhaigh is entered in this Chronicle under the year 1216.   [2] Vid. *infra*, p. xxxii.

of Loch Cé resemble the Annals of Tighernach, the Annals of Ulster, and the Chronicum Scotorum ; but they are much more copious in details of the affairs of Connacht than any of our other annals, not excepting even perhaps the Chronicle now known as the Annals of Connacht. And as all these additional details involve much of family history and topography, every item of them will be deemed valuable by the diligent investigator of our history and antiquities.

"The dates are always written in the original hand, and in Roman numerals, represented by Irish letters.

"The text is all in the ancient Gaedhlic characters, and mainly in the Gaedhlic language, but mixed occasionally with Latin, particularly in recording births and deaths, when sometimes a sentence is given partly in both languages."

The conclusions to be derived from the foregoing disquisitions are briefly :—

Results of the foregoing descriptions.

1. That both Dr. O'Donovan and the Rev. Dr. Todd considered the MS. to be a copy of the "Book of the O'Duigenans of Kilronan," which the Four Masters used when compiling their annals ; and

2. That Professor O'Curry, whilst inclining to the same opinion, concluded that the Chronicle should be called the "Annals of Inis-Mac-Neirinn, in Loch-Cé," or rather the "Annals of Loch-Cé."

The name "Annals of Loch-Cé" given to the MS. H. 1. 19, by Professor O'Curry.

The great respect justly entertained for Professor O'Curry's opinion on such subjects has led to the general adoption of the title which he has given to the present Chronicle, although the evidence on which he bases his opinion is not conclusive. He seems to have merely followed Dr. Nicolson in connecting the MS. with the monastery of Inis-Mac-Neirinn; but the name of that monastery occurs only thrice throughout the Chronicle, a circumstance which appears to conflict with the notion that it was compiled therein.

In discussing Dr. O'Donovan's suggestion, that the MS. was a copy of the "Book of the O'Duigenans" which the Four Masters used, and which commenced with the year 900, Professor O'Curry lays too much stress on the fact that the present Chronicle commences with the year 1014, for it is most likely, as O'Donovan says[1], that it has "lost several pages at the beginning." The first page begins with a capital of the usual size, not with an enlarged or ornamental letter, as manuscripts generally do; and the usual indications with which Irish scribes signified the beginning of a work are also wanting.

Although the MS. was unquestionably copied for, and was the property of, Brian MacDermot, whose chief residence was on an island in Loch-Cé; yet the appropriateness of the title which Professor O'Curry has given to it remains a subject of considerable doubt. A portion of it, at least, seems to have been copied in a different place;[2] and Sir James Ware (or rather Walter Harris, the editor of his works), quotes frequently from a chronicle called the "Annals of Loughkee," which it is very certain, as will presently be made apparent, was not the same compilation as that which is now in question.[3] The Chronicle so called by Ware and Harris, is also frequently referred to by Archdall;[4] but the source from which he derived his references is really a list of entries contained in a paper MS. in King's collection, in the Library of the Royal Dublin Society. These entries are entitled "Annals of Loughkee," and stated to have been taken from "MS. Clogher, No. 10." The latter MS. is included in the Clogher Manuscripts in the Library of Trinity College, Dublin, its present classification being F. 1, 18. The entries referred to occupy four pages, commencing at p. 319 of the volume, and are headed "Ex Annalibus Loghkeensibus." But it appears, on comparing these entries with the original of the present Chronicle, that they must have been taken

[marginal note:] Doubts as to the appropriateness of the name.

---

[1] Vid. *supra*, p. xiii.

[2] Namely, at *Cluain Hi Bhrain*, now Cloonybrien, in the parish of Ardcarne, barony of Boyle, county Roscommon, not far from Loch Cé. Vid. *supra*, p. xxiii., and vol. ii., p. 224, n. [2].

[3] O'Curry's opinion (*supra*, p. xxix), that the MS. was in the possession of the Ware family was founded on a misconception. Vid. *infra*, p. xxxii; and also p. lv.

[4] Monasticon Hibernicum; *passim.*

from a different source, most likely from a compilation made in the Monastery of Trinity Island[1] in Loch-Cé, or Lough-Key, not far from the Rock of Lough-Key, Mac Dermot's residence.

The original of the present Chronicle not used by Ware.

Taking into account Ware's remarkable accuracy in dealing with the historical materials at his disposal, it may be concluded that he never had the use of the original of these volumes, from the omission in his works of numerous important entries which appear in the present work, and which he certainly would not have passed over, had they come under his notice. A few instances will serve to render this apparent.

Contains entries not found in Ware's account of Irish Bishops.

In his account of the Archbishops of Armagh, when speaking of Tomaltach (or Thomas) O'Conor,[2] Ware makes no allusion to the connexion of this prelate with the see of Elphin, although it is evident from the entry within given (p. 219; at the year 1201), that Tomaltagh had held the bishopric of Elphin, or Sil-Muiredhaigh,[3] as it is there called, either before his first occupation of the primatial chair, or between the date of his resignation of it, in 1184, and his resumption in 1185.

In his list of the Bishops of Cork, Ware omits the name of Bishop O'hAedha, or O'Hea, whose death is recorded in the present Chronicle, at the year 1182.[4]

---

[1] In a list of Irish Historical Materials contained in Vallancey's "Green Book," a MS. in the Royal Irish Academy, a fragment of a Chronicle answering to the above is described as follows: "Annals of Ireland (of Lough-kee), partly Latin, partly Irish, ab anno 1249 ad annum 1356, in [the Bishop of] Clogher's MSS., T. C. Dublin." Another MS. is also thus described by the same writer; "Annalium (pars) coenobii S. Trin. de Lough-kee, incipiens ab anno 1249, et desinens an. 1381, ex hibernico idiomate in Anglicanum versa. Bibl Chand. No. 35. These are translated by Con. MacGeoghegan, are imperfect, and now in the possession of the Rev. Richard Archdall. They are defective in the beginning, middle, and end. The original in Irish, compleat, is in my possession, beginning 1244, and ending 1562." But the Irish original here referred to by Vallancey is no other than the so-called "Annals of Connacht."

[2] Ware's Works (ed. Harris), vol. i, p. 62.

[3] Vid. infra, p. 218, n. 1.

[4] Id., p. 163.

Under the head of Bishops of Clonfert, he has no mention of the name of Celechair O'hAirmhedhaigh (or O'Harvey), whose obit is given *infra*, at the year 1186 ; but in his place, Ware has Maelcallainn O'Cleirchen, who is called "Bishop of Glenn-da-locha "[1] in the present chronicle, and who was perhaps the same as the "Malchus alias Macrobius" referred to by Ware,[2] who "did not know when he died."

The name of Echthighern, son of Maelchiarain, whose death is entered *infra*,[3] under the year 1191, is omitted from Ware's list of the Bishops of Cluain-Iraird, or Clonard ; and that of David O'Gillapatraic (ob. 1253),[4] from among the Bishops of Clonmacnois ; the name of Echmilidh, who died in 1204,[5] is not included in the catalogue of Bishops of Ulidia, or Down ; nor is that of O'Dobhailen[6] (O'Devlin) among the Bishops of Cenannus, or Kells, of whom Ware may be said to have given no account. Gilla-Isa O'Maeilin, Bishop of Mayo,[7] is omitted from the catalogue of that ancient diocese, as is also Bishop O'Selbhaigh, who died in 1182,[8] from the list of the diocese of Port-Lairge, or Waterford.

In his account of the Bishops of Elphin, Ware makes no allusion to the curious dispute regarding the election of Bishop John O'hUghroin, so quaintly related in the present Chronicle under the year 1244 ;[9] in reference to whom he says[10] "I do not find whether he was actually consecrated or not," though his consecration is recorded within at the year 1245.[11] Neither does he seem to have known anything of the election of Marian O'Donnabhair in 1297,

---

[1] In transferring this Maelcallain O'Cleirchen from Glendalough to Clonfert, Ware seems to have been misled by Colgan (*Act. SS.*, p. 153, n. 2) ; and the latter by the Four Mast. See their Annals at the year 1186, first entry.

[2] Works (ed. Harris), vol. i, p. 375.

[3] Vid. p. 185.

[4] *Infra*, p. 401.

[5] *Ib.*, p. 233.

[6] *Ib.*, p. 245.

[7] *Ob.* 1185 ; *infra*, p. 171.

[8] *Infra*, p. 163.

[9] *Ib.*, p. 367.

[10] Works (ed. Harris), vol. i, p. 629.

[11] *Infra*, p. 371.

who "went to Rome, to contest the bishopric, and died
on that journey."[1] The appointment of Andrew O'Crean,
" by the Council of Ireland," in 1582,[2] and his removal in
1584, in favour of John Lynch, are also unnoticed.

In his catalogue of the Archbishops of Tuam, also, when
writing of Maelmaire (or Marian) O'Laghtnan, Ware says
that "immediately upon his election, he hastened to Rome
to solicit the Pope's confirmation; where he was approved
of by Gregory the IX., and invested with the pall."[3] But
it is stated in this Chronicle, at the year 1236[4] (not 1235,
as in Ware), that he went to England, " and was consecrated by virtue of the letters of the comarb of Peter, and
the consent of the king of the Saxons"; and the trans-
mission of the pallium to him from Rome is also noticed
within under the year 1237,[5] although apparently unknown to Ware.

It is evident from the foregoing that Ware could not
have used the present Chronicle. Had he done so, his
works would have been enriched with much additional
information on the History and Antiquities of Ireland,
which he laboured with so much zeal to illustrate.

Hence, we can only accept the title "Annals of Loch-
Cé" as a somewhat arbitrary designation; and possibly
as being in derogation of the better claim of another now
lost MS. to that title. The "Annals of the Rock of
Loch-Cé," or the "Annals of Carrick-MacDermot," would
be a more appropriate name.

Loch-Cé, or Lough-Key, the name of which is thus associated with the present Chronicle, is a beautiful lake in the
county of Roscommon, near the town of Boyle. The Rock

Loch-Cé,
co. Ros-
common.

---

[1] *Infra*, p. 519. The Four Masters
say that it was his competitor, Malachy
MacBrian, who died on the journey to
Rome; and O'Donovan, in a note to
his ed. of the F. M. (at A.D. 1297,
note ²) corrects the Annals of Ulster,
which agree with the present Chronicle.

But O'Donovan was wrong, as the
death of Bishop Malachy is recorded
by the Four M. under the year 1303.

[2] *Infra*, p. 455.

[3] Works (ed. Harris), vol. i, p. 605.

[4] *Infra*, p. 335.

[5] *Ib.*, p. 345.

of Loch-Cé, MacDermot's chief residence, so frequently mentioned in the Chronicle under the name of Carraig-Mic-Diarmada, is a small island situated in the southern corner of the lake, close to the demesne of Rockingham. Within a few perches of that fine structure, the seat of Lord Kingston, may be seen the site of the ancient abode of the MacDermots, previous to the erection of the old castle which covered "the Rock." The more ancient residence, which was called "Longphort Mic Diarmada," must have been constructed of perishable materials, as no traces of masonry are now discernible. Even before the MacDermots established their superiority over the territory of Moylurg, the site was one of note; stories of its ancient importance still linger in the traditions of the neighbourhood; and old men point out there the secluded spot nightly visited by the spirit of "Lady Magreevy," the wife of a chieftain of the older sept of Magreevy, or Mac Riabhaigh,[1] its former possessors.

As in the case of other Irish lakes, the origin and history of Loch-Cé have occupied the inventive minds of bards and *shenachies*, whose accounts are still remembered in the locality. According to one account, taken down by O'Donovan, the name of Loch-Cé is derived by the people from a woman named Cé, or Céibh (*Ceiv*), who was the daughter of Manannan Mac Lir (the Irish Neptune), and whom they call *Ceib ni Manannain*, i.e. Ceib, daughter of Manannan. "She belonged," as O'Donovan relates the tradition, "to the giants of Keish (Keshcorran, county Sligo); was disfigured and rendered insane by some enchantment; fled towards Loch-Cé, and remained at [where now is] Rockingham, where she was taken care

Legendary accounts of its origin.

---

[1] The tribe name of the family of Mac Riabhaigh was Feara-Scene, or Feara-Skene (vid. *infra*, sub an. 1238; p. 349); and this tradition may help to fix their situation, which O'Donovan could not point out. *See* his ed. of the Four Mast., A.D. 1238, n. [1], where he incorrectly says that no other reference to the tribe occurs in the Irish Annals than the single entry given by the Four Masters.

of by a family of the Keeltys for twelve months. To this family, for their kindness to her, she gave the privilege that none of the name should ever be drowned in the lake. By the laws of the enchantment she could not remain in any place where her ugliness would be remarked. After twelve months she went back to Kesh, where all refused to admit her, except Oisin, who gave her an asylum. On the following day, she became a beautiful woman, and, for his kind treatment, took Oisin with her to *Tír na hóige* (*patria juventutis*), the situation of which is not known; but it is the Elysium of the Irish, lying somewhere under ground; and many caves in Ireland are said to lead to it."[1]

Dinnsenchus account of Loch-Cé, and site of the battle of Moytura-Cunga.

Another, and older, account represents the name of the lake as derived from a man named Cé, one of the Druids of Nuada, king of the mystic race known as the Tuatha De Danann. This account is contained in the copy of the curious legendary tract entitled *Dinnsenchus,* preserved in the Book of Lecan; and as it is of peculiar interest to the historian and antiquary—inasmuch as it indicates a different locality as the site of the battle of Magh-tuiredh-Cunga, from that which has hitherto been generally recognised[2] as the scene of the overthrow of the Firbolg dynasty by the Tuatha De Danann race—it is here printed from the original MS.[3]

Loch Cé canar ɼo hainmniʒeꝺ. NĪ. Ꝺia ʈucaꝺ caʈ Muiʒi ʈuiɼeaꝺ Cunʒa eꝺiɼ Eochaiꝺ mac Eiɼc ocuɼ Nuaꝺa aiɼceꝺlam, ɼi Ʈuaiʈi ꝺe ꝺanann, ꝺia ɼo moiꝺ foɼ feaɼaiƀ ƀolʒ, ocuɼ ꝺiaɼ benaꝺ a lam ꝺo Nuaꝺa anꝺ la Sɼenʒ mac Senʒaimꝺ, ꝺia nꝺechaiꝺ ꝺɼai Nuaꝺaꝺ .i. Cé ꝺo ꝺecain an áiɼ, co ɼo moiꝺ foɼ ꝺaɼachʈ ocuɼ foɼ ꝺeɼʒmiɼe ɼaiɼɼꝺeɼ, conaɼ an ꝺon ꝺaɼachʈ co ɼanic co caɼnn Coiɼɼɼleibe, ocuɼ ɼo ʒaƀ ac ɼiƀal in maiʒi no co fuaiɼ caɼnn cloch aɼ in maiʒ; coɼ ʈhoiʈ ɼuan coꝺalʈa faiɼ, co moiʒ in loch na

[1] Vid. Ordnance Survey Letters (R. I. Acad.); Sligo, pp. 412-13.

[2] See Wilde's Lough Corrib, p. 210, sq.

[3] Book of Lecan, fol. 236, b 2.

τhimcheall, coɲ baιoeo he; coñao uao ιτa ιn loch .ι. loch
Cé. Unoe oιcιτuɲ—

    lóch Cé cιo ιmaɲ mebaιo,
      Oιambaι na moιჳ mιn lebaιɲ;
      Inτ uɲჟι ιoan, a ḟιɲ
      Ca hιnao aɲ aɲ eɲιch.

    Fιaɲɲaιoιm oιb cuιch ιn Ce
      O ɲloιnoιo cach uιle hé;
      Cιa cambaι aɲ banba comblaιo,
      In oɲaι amɲa caɲ ɲoɲbaιɲ.

    Cɲaeo he ιnτ aobaɲ am aɲ ḟaɟ
      In loch uaιne can uaτhɟaɟ;
      Inτ uιɟqι ɟaιlιch ჳlan ჳlaɟ,
      Raιoιo oam a oιnoɟenċaɟ.

    Oɲaι Nuaoao ɲo neɲτao baιo
      Mac Echτaιch mιc Eoaɲlaιm
      Iɟ o ḟeɲτ aιnm ιn lacha,
      Aɲ τechτ a maιòm moɲ caċa.

    Τaιnιc o Muιჳ τuιɲeao τhe
      O ɲo ჳaeoɲao ჳaι neme;
      Iaɟ na ჳuιn oaɟιm conoene,
      Coɲ ḟuιo ι caɲn choιɟɲɟlebe.

    Sul oo eɲιch Ce aɟιn chaɟn
      Oo moιo ιn loch na τιmċeall;
      Oo lιn cach ooιɟι naɟ ċaιɟ
      Iɟ claɟ ιn moιჳι mιnჳlaιɟ.

    Iɟ oe ɟιn ιτa loch Cé,
      Aoeɲιm can ιmaɲჳae;
      O oɲaι Nuaoao nιamoa a ჳaιl,
      Aτa loċ oɟ na lochaιb.

                      l. o. c. h.

"Loch Cé; from what was it named? Not difficult to tell.
When the battle of Magh-tuiredh-Cunga was given between

Eochaidh, son of Erc, and Nuada Airgetlam, king of the Tuatha De Danann, on which occasion the Feara-Bolg were routed, and his hand was cut off Nuada there, by Sreng son of Sengann, Nuada's druid, i.e. Cé, went to see the slaughter; whereupon he rushed in madness and red lunacy towards the south-east; and he ceased not from the madness until he came to the carn of Corr-sliabh; and he commenced traversing the plain until he found a heap of stones on the plain, where a deep sleep fell upon him; and the lake burst up around him, so that he was drowned; and therefore it is from him the lake is, i.e. Loch Cé. Unde dicitur—

> Loch Cé, wherefore did it burst forth,
> When it was a smooth wide plain?
> The pure water, O man!
> From what place did it arise?
>
> I ask of you, who was the Cé
> From whom all name it?
> Who, in famous Banba, possessed him?
> The illustrious druid, where did he increase?
>
> What is the cause from which proceeded
> The green, unruffled lake?
> The clear blue, glad water—
> Relate to me its *dinnsenchus*.
>
> The druid of Nuada, who strengthened valour,
> Son of Echtach, son of Edarlam:
> The name of the lake is from his grave,
> After his coming from the rout of a great battle.
>
> He came from the hot Magh-tuiredh,
> When poisoned lances had wounded him—
> After being wounded by fierce weapons—
> Until he sat on the carn of Corr-sliabh.
>
> Before Cé got up from the carn,
> The lake burst forth around him,
> It filled each thick wood,
> And the surface of the smooth green plain.

It is from this that Loch Cé is,
I say it, without falsehood ;
From Nuada's druid, bright his valour,
Is this loch above the lochs.

L. O. C. H.

The MS. from which the foregoing legend has been taken was compiled in the year 1416, in the present county of Sligo, by Gilla-Isa Mor MacFirbisigh, one of the most eminent antiquaries of his time, who probably quoted the story from some ancient authority, although it is not found in the copies of the Dinnsenchus Tract contained in the other principal Irish MS. compilations. But whether his authority for the legend was written, or oral, it would seem that MacFirbisigh considered the battle of Magh-tuiredh-Cunga—a battle much celebrated in the legendary history of Ireland—to have been fought in some place to the north-west of Loch-Cé, since the druid Cé, from whom the name of the lake has here been derived, is represented as proceeding from the battlefield in a south-eastern direction, to the carn around which the waters of the lake subsequently burst forth. There are extensive sepulchral remains in the townland of Magh-tuiredh, or Moytirra, in the parish of Kilmactranny, and county of Sligo, about ten miles to the north-west of Loch-Cé, which was apparently the place implied in the account of Gilla-Isa Mor MacFirbisigh; but they are considered to be the remains of a battle different from that of Magh-tuiredh-Cunga ; and another member of the same learned family, Dubhaltach MacFirbisigh, agrees[1] with the Four Masters, O'Flaherty, and other Irish writers of the seventeenth century, in fixing the site of the battle of Magh-tuiredh-Cunga near Cong, in Conmaicne-Culi-Tolaidh, now the barony of Kilmaine, county Mayo.

Two battles of Moytura.

It is difficult to conceive how Dr. O'Donovan, a scholar

---

[1] See his Geneal. Work (R. I. Acad. copy), p. 76.

no less remarkable for his extensive acquirements than his scrupulous regard for accuracy, should have hazarded the assertion[1] that "the Four Masters have all the entries in this Chronicle." It is a statement entirely without foundation, as he himself virtually confesses in another passage already quoted.[2] It is true that in the earlier portions a general correspondence is noticeable in the arrangement and contents of both chronicles. This observation, however, applies to most of the Irish Annals, and in an especial manner to the more ancient compilations. The Irish annalists who succeeded Tighernach, down to the time of the Four Masters, with few exceptions, seem to have borrowed their materials principally from his chronicle, as far as it went. This formed the skeleton of each body of annals, to which was subsequently added such information as could be gleaned from the registers of local monasteries, from tradition, and sometimes from those historical poems which formed the substitute for annals among the Irish in ancient times.

General correspondence among ancient Irish Annals.

The Annals of the Four Masters. The correspondence occasionally observable between the present chronicle and the Annals of the Four Masters, not only in the arrangement and contents of the earlier entries, as already remarked, but also in the use of peculiar phraseology, tends to strengthen Dr. O'Donovan's conjecture that this chronicle is an imperfect copy of the "Book of the O'Duigenans," cited by the Four Masters. Even if this were conclusively proved, it would, nevertheless, be extremely improbable that the Four Masters would have incorporated with their compilation the entire contents of the original MS. The nature of the work on which they were engaged, namely, a digest of the Irish Annals, necessarily precluded them from doing more than making a selection from the various collections at their disposal; and in too many instances this work of selection was performed in a very unsatisfactory manner.

[1] Vid. *ante*, p. xv.   [2] *See* note [1], p. xv, *ante*.

The value and authority of the Annals of the Four Events recorded in this Chronicle, unnoticed by the Four Masters. Masters have been seriously diminished by the disingenuous practice, too frequently followed by the compilers,[1] of omitting or suppressing entries which may have seemed to them to exhibit the character of ecclesiastics in a questionable light, or to cast discredit on the Church of which they were zealous members. The compilers of the Annals of Loch-Cé are less open to censure in this particular, and seem to have made their entries irrespectively of such considerations. Numerous transactions of this nature are recorded in the present chronicle. To select a few examples :—the Four Masters have no notice of the conflict "of the relic-house" related in this work, under the year 1055, between the comarb of Patrick (*i.e.* the Archbishop of Armagh), and the comarb of SS. Finian and Colum Cille, nor of the "great war in Armagh, between Cumuscach O'hEradhain and Dubhdhaleithe," regarding "the abbacy," recorded under the year 1060. Neither do they notice the sacrilegious attack on the Archbishop of Armagh by Tighernan O'Ruairc, in the year 1128, denounced in such strong language in this Chronicle; the capture of the abbey house of Kildare, by the Hy-Kinsellagh, in 1132, when the abbess was subjected to outrageous treatment; nor the battle mentioned in the latter year, between the community of Scrin (Ballinaskreen, county Londonderry) and Lochlainn O'Boylan.

The Four Masters are also silent regarding the violence practised towards Irish abbots (Cistercians?), in England, in 1217, on their way to a general chapter of their order; and regarding the simony within attributed to "Jacobus Pencial," the Roman legate to Ireland,[2] at the year 1221. They have no notice of the singular transaction related

---

[1] Vid. Reeves's ed. of Adamnan's Life of St. Columba, pp. 250, 254, 255.

[2] And also to Scotland. "Magister Jacobus canonicus S. Victoris Parisiis Apost. sedis pœnitentialis, Scotiæ et Hiberniæ 'legatus, convocatis totius regni prelatis apud Perth tenuit generale concilium quatuor continuis diebus." *Fordun; Scot. Chron.,* A.D. 1221; ed. Goodall; lib. ix., c. 37 vol. ii., p. 46.

in this Chronicle under the year 1244, in connexion with the election of a Bishop of Elphin; nor of the "great war" between the Archbishop of Armagh and the Bishop of Meath, in 1263, so briefly recorded in this work. Examples of the omission of transactions of this class[1] by the Four Masters might be multiplied; but the foregoing will perhaps suffice to disprove O'Donovan's statement that these otherwise industrious compilers had copied all the entries in this Chronicle, and at the same time justify the remarks which Dr. Reeves (*Adamnan*, pp. 250, 254, 255, 401) has made in condemnation of their unwise partiality.

Character of Roderick O'Conor, the last monarch of Ireland.

The remarkable statement contained in the present Chronicle at the year 1233 (*infra*, p. 315,) regarding the profligate character of Roderick O'Conor, the last monarch of Ireland, and the fruitless attempt alleged to have been made to reform him, with the offer of five wives, if he abstained from "the sin of the women," may well have been omitted by the Four Masters, as incredible; but other important events in his life, such as his retirement to Cong Abbey in the year 1183,[2] and his resumption of the sovereignty of Connacht in 1185,[3] are also unnoticed by them.[4]

The present Chronicle nearly agrees with the Annals of Ulster, in the early portion.

The contents of this Chronicle from the year 1015 to the year 1138, where the first hiatus occurs, and again from 1170 to 1220, are very much in accord with the Annals of Ulster. This accordance, in some places so close as to suggest the idea that the original compilers of both works had drawn their materials from a common

---

[1] Some of the preceding entries are also in the Annals of Ulster, which the Four Masters used when making their compilation. *See* O'Donovan's ed. of the Four M.; Int, p. xii.

[2] *Infra*, p. 165.

[3] *Ib.*, p. 169.

[4] The Four Masters naturally paid more attention to the history of Ulster than to that of any other province of Ireland. It cannot be matter for surprise, therefore, that the affairs of Connacht (especially during the 13th century, when the Burks established their power over that province, and during the 16th century, when the descendants of William Fitz Aldelm, with the aid of the native Irish, endeavoured to shake off English supremacy), should be, as they are, more fully detailed in this Chronicle.

source, is especially noticeable in certain peculiarities of language and orthography ; and also in numerous entries relating to English and foreign affairs, which are not found in other Irish annals.

In the old translation of the Annals of Ulster, preserved in the British Museum,[1] there are some notices of events which are contained in this Chronicle, but do not occur in either of the original Irish copies of the Annals of Ulster at present known. One important entry, namely, the account of the murder[2] of the eminent Irish poet, Cuan O'Lochain, recorded *infra* under the year 1024, appears to have caused some difficulty to Dr. O'Donovan, who, in quoting it, confesses[3] that he was "not prepared to say where the translator found authority for it." But it is contained in the Bodleian MS. of the Annals of Ulster, although not in the Dublin copy ;[4] and also in the Annals of Inisfallen, but in somewhat different phraseology.

In his account of the Annals of Ulster, Professor O'Curry observes[5] that "throughout the entire MS. blank spaces had been left by the original scribe at the end of each year, and that in these spaces there have been added, by a later hand,[6] several events and *aliases,* or corrections of dates." This practice, which is in keeping with the custom[7] of ancient annalists, has been followed throughout

---

[1] Clarend. Coll., vols. xx. and xlix.; Ayscough, Nos. 4784 and 4795.

[2] By the Sinnachs, or Foxes, whose family name is stated to have been derived from the remarkable retribution which followed the commission of the crime. See also a reference to the same circumstance in the Chron. Scotorum, at the year 1022=1024.

[3] *Miscell. of the Irish Archæological Society;* Dublin, 1846; vol. i., pp. 187-8.

[4] H. 1. 8, Trin. Coll., Dublin.

[5] *Lectures,* p. 92.

[6] It may be remarked that many entries, and clauses of entries, which are included in the text of the origi-nal of the present volumes, are inter-lined in the Dublin MS. of the Annals of Ulster.

[7] "The Chronicle in its earliest form," as Sir T. Duffus Hardy ob-serves, "was little more than a bar-ren register of dates. The wants of the historian were supplied by a few sheets of parchment stitched together, with blank spaces, in which successive annalists might enter, from time to time, a brief record of events which fell especially beneath their notice, or immediately affected the welfare of the brotherhood." *Descript. Cat. of Materials relating to the Hist. of Great Britain and Ireland;* vol. i., part 1; Pref., p. xiii.

d 2

the greater portion of the MS. H. 1. 19. Down to the
year 1221, a space of from six to eight lines has been left
after the entries for each year; from 1462 to 1496 the
same thing is noticeable; and again, from 1542 to the
end; (the blanks in the last division being utilized by
Brian Mac Dermot).

**Entries re-
lating to
foreign
affairs.**
I have alluded to the numerous entries relating to foreign affairs which appear in the present Chronicle. Some
of these entries are, no doubt, taken from the early Irish
annalists; but others seem to have been derived from different sources, not now traceable. The obit of the Emperor Henry II. (whom the chronicler calls "king of
the world"), and the succession of Conrad II., recorded
infra under the year 1023, appear to have been borrowed
from Tighernach, as well as the notice of the battle between
Conrad II. and Eudes, Count of Champagne, referred to
under the year 1038, and the poisoning of the Pope,
recorded at the year 1048.

**The sources
from which
they were
probably
obtained.**
The notice of the earthquake in Sliabh-Elpa (the Alps),
recorded *infra* at the year 1118, is also contained in the
Annals of Ulster, which add that the event was "related
by pilgrims," thus indicating, perhaps, the nature of the
authority for many references to such foreign events mentioned in the present Chronicle as are not noticed in the
other Irish annals, nor in the contemporary chronicles of
England.

**Retreat of
the waters
of the
Muir-Tor-
rian.**
Two of these entries are worthy of more than a passing
remark, considering that they appear solely in an Irish
chronicle compiled in a remote part of Connacht. I refer
to the drying up of "fifteen *giurneisi*[1] on each side of the
Muir-Torrian,"[2] recorded under the year 1215, and to the
**Death of a
Roman
Emperor
Charles.**
statement that the "Roman Emperor Carolus (Carrthalus)
was slain by the Saracens, whilst defending Christendom," which is given at the year 1268. The retreat of the
waters of the Muir-Torrian, (possibly here used as desig-

[1] *See* note *, p. 253 *infra.*
[2] The Tyrrhene Sea, Mare Inferum, or Tuscan, as distinguished from the Mare Superum, or Adriatic Sea.

nating the Ligurian, as well as the Tuscan sea), may reasonably be referred to the effects of an earthquake ;[1] and the account of the phenomenon may have been communicated to the chronicler by some one of the Irish ecclesiastics who attended the Lateran Council, held in the month of November, 1215. But it is difficult to suggest the authority for the entry relating to the " Roman Emperor Charles," or to indicate the person alluded to by that title.[2]

The notice of the death of Hakon, king of Norway, under the year 1263, affords an illustration of the singular meagreness sometimes observable in entries by our early annalists of events of real historical importance. It is merely stated that " Ebhdhonn (it is thus the name is written) died in Innsi-Orc (the Orkneys), on the way whilst coming to Ireland ;" but for what purpose he was coming is left unexplained. The object of King Hakon's visit to Ireland, on this occasion, is related in Munch's History of Norway, as follows :— *Important entry regarding King Hakon's project of invading Ireland in 1263.*

" Whilst King Hacon lay near Gude, whence there is but a short distance over to the north coast of Ireland, it happened, as we have mentioned above, that embassies came to him from the Irish, who gave him to know that they were ready to become subject to him, in case he would come and liberate them from the oppressive dominion of the English !"[3]

It is hardly possible, after the lapse of so many cen-

---

[1] An earthquake is recorded as having occurred in Burgundy and Limousin, on the 3rd of March, 1215; but it cannot be more closely synchronized with the event above noticed, as the Irish chronicler, with a characteristic disregard for preciseness in the detail of dates, has not given the day of the week or month. Vid. *Chron. Cluniac.*; Dom Bouquet, tom. xviii., p. 743.

[2] The entry is not contained in any of the other Irish chronicles, and may involve some confusion of person or date; but other references to affairs in the east (the return from Palestine of Louis IX., in 1254, and his death in 1270; and the battle of Damascus in 1299, for example), are given with enough of exactness to make it worth the consideration of those who desire to investigate this obscure period of German history. Under the same year (1268) the annalist Clyn records that "Karolus vicit Coradellum imperatorem Grecorum."

[3] Det Norske Folks Historie, fremstillet af P. A. Munch, Christiania, 1868; vol. IV., pt I., p. 407.

turies, and considering the silence of English and Irish historians on the subject, to ascertain by what authority these embassies were despatched to King Hakon; but Munch assumes that they were sent by the native chieftains of Ulster, and not by the inhabitants of Ireland of Norse descent.

Again he says :—

"His (Hakon's) loss was rather not so great but that he could contemplate immediately to go over to Ireland from thence; for whilst he was lying still in Lamlash harbour, there came to him Sigurd the South Islander, back from Ireland, with his following, and brought him the proposal from the Irish that they would maintain his whole army during the next winter, if he would come and liberate them from their English masters."[1]

Munch's chief authority for the foregoing statements was probably the *Saga Hakonar Hakonarsonar*, which thus refers to the subject :—

"Then, whilst King Hakon was in the southern islands, there came embassies to him from Ireland, that the Irish would give themselves under his dominion if he liberated them from the misfortune which the Englishmen had inflicted, for they held then all the best places in sight. Then sent the King to Ireland Sigurd, the South Islander, with light ships, and to ascertain on what condition (*meot hversju*) the Irish would solicit him to go thither. After that King Hakon sailed southwards in front of Satiris Mula, with the whole army, and lay to at Hereyjarsund."[2]

"A little later the king sailed along Cumry out to Melasey; then came to him those men whom he had sent to Ireland, and told him that the Irish offered to maintain his whole army till this, that he freed them from under the dominion of the English. King Hakon was very desirous to sail to Ireland; but the whole army objected to that. Then the king declared that he would sail to the Southern Islands, since the army had but little provisions. After that the king sailed under Gude, and thence out into Ilarsund; and he lay there two nights, and imposed a tribute on the Island of 300 neats."[3]

---

[1] *Det Norske Folks Historie*, vol. I., p. 418.

[2] *Saga Hakonar Hakonarsonar*; Fornmanna Sögur, Kaupmannahöfn, 1835; vol. X., p. 131.

[3] *Ib.*, p. 142.

It is difficult to suppose that the general purport of these negotiations was unknown to the annalist; and we are justified in concluding that he has either observed a studied reticence regarding them, or, possibly, passed them by as of no account, in his estimation, in comparison with the petty feuds of the chieftains of Connacht, which he frequently details with so much of circumstance. When it is considered that two hundred and fifty years had passed since the expulsion of the Danes, and that the subjugation of the most warlike part of the island, to which Hakon's attention seems to have been specially directed, had been well nigh completed by the defeat and death of Brian O'Neill in the battle of Downpatrick, the enterprise of Hakon assumes a character of daring and magnitude, which makes the omission of all direct reference to it in the other Irish annals the more remarkable.

Silence of Irish annalists respecting King Hakon's project of invading Ireland.

The entries relating to English affairs are not devoid of interest, although couched in such brief terms. The account of the death of Harold Harefoot, correctly given under the year 1040, is limited to the bare statement that " Aralt, king of the Saxons *givas*,[1] moritur;" but the use of the word *givas*, a term which does not appear in any of the English chronicles, in connexion with the name of Harold, is curious as indicating the annalist's idea of the extent of King Harold's sovereignty, which he evidently did not regard as embracing the whole of England. The notice of the battle in which Siward, Earl of Northumberland, defeated MacBeth, in 1054, is also very brief; but it gives the loss in round numbers on each side, and supplies the name of " Dolfinn, son of Finntar," as among

English affairs.

Harold Harefoot.

Battle between Earl Siward and MacBeth.

---

[1] The word *givas* occurs also in the notice of Harold's death contained in the Annals of Ulster; but Dr. O'Conor (in his edition of those Annals) prints it *guiais*, and erroneously translates it "ferorum." But it really represents the "Occidentales Saxones qui antiquitus Gevissæ vocabantur." *Beda*, iii. 7. *See* also Lappenberg's *Hist. of England*, ed. Thorpe; London, 1845; vol. I., p. 109, n. 3. I am indebted to my learned friend, William J. O'Donnavan, esq., LL.D., for pointing this out to me.

the slain—particulars, it may be observed, that are not found in the record of this battle contained in the Anglo-Saxon chronicle.[1]

Death of King John.   In the short notice of the death of King John, at the year 1216 (*infra,* p. 254), he is stated to have died "*do reacht,*" an expression which has been translated " of a fit." The words *do reacht* also signify "of a law;" but this could hardly have been the meaning intended by the annalist; whilst the correctness of the interpretation within given is supported by the present use of the word *reacht,*[2] to signify "a fit," in those districts of Connacht where the Irish language is still spoken.

Expedition to the Continent.   Under the year 1254, the chronicler states that " the king of the Saxons went to Spain on a hosting;" but it is uncertain whether the expedition of King Henry III. to Gascony, in 1253, or that of Prince Edward to Spain in 1254, is spoken of, especially as Edward is confounded with his father in the notice of the battle of Lewes, and the war between " the king of the Saxons and the king of Britain " (or Wales), given under the year 1264.

Simon de Montford.   The war waged by the barons against King Henry III., in 1265, is briefly characterized as a " great war between the king of the Saxons and Simon Mufford (*i.e.* De Montford)." Equally brief is the further reference to the same war under the year 1267, where the name of De Montford is written " Suforn."[3] Regarding the expedition

---

[1] Dr. O'Conor was wrong in stating that the battle in question was not mentioned in the Anglo-Sax. Chron. See note [1], p. 52 *infra*; and *Rer. Hib. Script.,* tom. ii., p. 299, note.

[2] This word, in the form *racht*, is also explained " a fit" by O'Brien and O'Reilly. In Macgeoghegan's version of the Annals of Clonmacnois, which generally agrees with the present Chronicle, King John is said to have been " poyson'd by drinking of a cup of ale, wherein there was a toad pricked with a broach." But this account was manifestly taken from some English authority. See note [6], p. 254 *infra.*

[3] The attempts of the chronicler to represent English names in an Irish dress, are sometimes very rude. A curious instance occurs under the year 1582 (vol. ii. p. 457), where Thomas Ratcliffe, 4th Lord Fitz-Walter and 3rd Earl of Sussex, who had been

of Edward I. to Flanders, in 1297, it is stated that "a Expedition to Flanders. great expedition was led into France by Edward, *i.e.* the king of the Saxons, with cheerfulness and great spirits; but he came out of it, nevertheless, without obtaining sway or power on that occasion." In recording the war between Edward II. and Queen Isabella, in 1297, the Edward II. and Queen Isabella. chronicler is a little more explicit; but the brevity with which English affairs are referred to throughout the work renders it probable that the chronicler obtained his information from sources similar to those from which he seems to have derived his knowledge of continental events.[1]

The entry respecting John de Curci, in which it is Entry respecting John De Curci. stated (sub anno 1204) that De Laci set him at liberty *iar na crossad do dol co hIiarrusalem*, "after having been crossed (*cruce signatus*) to go to Jerusalem," taken in connexion with other entries of a like nature in reference to the crusades[2] in these Annals, means, beyond question, that De Laci imposed on his powerful rival the obligation of going to the Holy Land, as a condition of setting him at liberty.

This entry has been quoted by Dr. O'Donovan, in his edition of the Four Masters,[3] but by an unwonted error has been by him rendered, in the reverse sense, "after having been *prohibited* from going to Jerusalem," as if

---

Lord Deputy of Ireland, is called "Thomas-in-uisgi," or "Thomas of the water." The name Fitz-Walter was not unfrequently written Fitz-Water, which latter form the chronicler seems to have understood as signifying "of the water." Under the year 1332, where "the nobles of Alba" are stated to have been slain by Baliol, the name of the latter is written "Bailldelbhach," as if the writer considered it to be a compound formed of the words *ball*, "a spot," and *delbhach*, "figurative."

[1] Vid. *supra*, p. xliv·

[2] Under the year 1216 (p. 254 *infra*), two persons, named Mac Cargamhna and O'Celli, are stated to have been "crossed," to go "to the River (Jordan)," the words used being *ar na crossadh aroen, ocus ar ná chinnedh dhoibh dul dont sruth*; and under the year 1231 (p 306 *infra*), Flahertach O'Flanagan is represented as dying in the abbey of Boyle, *ocus é ar na crossadh*, "after having been crossed."

[3] O'Donovan's ed. F. M., ad an. 1204, note ⁿ.

"crossed" were used in the sense of *cross*, a hindrance, instead of *cross*, a sign.

This misconception had hitherto left the movements of De Curci, after his liberation, in the same obscurity which surrounded them while the native annals were still unpublished, save in so far as the publication of the Tower Records below referred to may be considered to have dispelled it. It might be thought that, as he obtained licence[1] in 1207 to come into England, a probable mode of accounting for his disappearance from local history after that time was to be found in the romantic tale of his imprisonment in the Tower of London, related with much detail by the Anglo-Irish annalists, and recorded as authentic by Grace in his "Annals of Ireland;"[2] but it would seem more probable that the silence of contemporaries about this period of his life is to be accounted for by his absence, now seemingly well authenticated, in the Holy Land.

Story of De Curci's imprisonment in the Tower of London.

The tale of his imprisonment has been repeated by later historians, and it is characteristic of the tone adopted towards the native Irish writers, that, in treating it as a

---

[1] " Rex omnibus, &c. Sciatis quod concessimus Johanni de Curci quod salvo et secure veniat in terram nostram Anglie, et moretur in ea cum amicis suis quamdiu nobis placuerit." *Rot. Litt. Pat. in Tur. Lond. asservat.* ; accurante T. Duffus Hardy; vol. i. pt. 1, p. 77 a (A.D. 1207).

[2] The legend represents De Curci, after his capture by De Laci, as having been conveyed to England, where he was condemned to perpetual imprisonment. " When he had endured for a long time the most squalid life of a prison," writes the annalist Grace, summarizing the tale, " he was at length set at liberty by King John, being chosen as champion against a certain man of gigantic stature whom the king of France had appointed the defender of his right to a certain castle; when the Frenchman, afraid of his great strength, had refused the combat, in the presence of both kings he gave noble proof of his vigour, having cut through a helmet at one stroke. Wherefore, by both he was gifted with large presents, and was restored by John to the earldom of Ulster; but having endeavoured fifteen times, always with great danger and contrary winds, to return to Ireland, and having sojourned some time with the monks at Chester, he returned to France, and there [ended] his life." Grace's *Annales Hiberniæ*, ad an. 1204.

fabrication, it is represented as the "narrative of Irish bards and romancers;"[1] whereas, in truth, the Irish alluded to are they who, in the present entry, have preserved one of the few facts now authentically known concerning De Curci.

The Tower Rolls, however, which preserve the evidence of his leave to return to England in 1207, also contain a mandate of King John, addressed to his constables and officers, in the year 1216, in favour of De Curci. They likewise contain directions for the payment of an annuity to John de Curci in the years 1212, 1213, and 1214, as well as the assignment of dower to Affrica, his widow, in 1219;[2] so that, if this be the same person, it can no longer be said that we are without reliable notices of him after the year 1205; but in that case the received opinion that the *Expugnatio Hibernica* of Giraldus Cambrensis was published prior to the year 1209,[3] may possibly be liable to correction; for Gerald seems to speak of De Curci as of one deceased.[4]

The references to the affairs of Alba, or Scotland, are also numerous; but not more so than might be expected, considering the relations that existed between Ireland and Scotland during the middle ages. The intimate nature of this relationship was sustained by the identity of national sentiment between the two countries, resulting from the possession of common traditions and a common literature, and the practice of a common system of education. Evidences of this community of social and intellec-

Affairs of Scotland.

[1] See Leland's *History of Ireland;* Dublin, 1814; vol. i., p. 181.

[2] The Patent Roll (Tower), of the 15th year of King John, contains a direction to the Irish Government to provide a portion of land in Ireland for the maintenance of Affrica, wife of John de Curci. *See* also Gilbert's *History of the Viceroys of Ireland;* Dublin, 1865; p. 63.

[3] Vid. *Giraldi Cambrensis Opera*, vol. 5, ed. Dimock; London, 1867; Introd. p. 59.

[4] *Ib.*, pp. 344-5. "Erat itaque Johannes vir albus et procerus," &c. and "legitimam ex sponsis prolem suscipere nondum meruere [scil. FitzStephen, Hervey, Reimund, and De Curci; of whom the first three were then certainly dead]."

tual culture are exhibited in many entries in the present Chronicle. At the year 1061, for instance, Dubhtach Albanach, or Dubhtach the Scotchman, is described as " chief anmchara (*i.e.* soul-friend, or confessor) of Ireland and Alba." Under the year 1181, Tadhg O'Dalaigh is called "ollamh (or chief poet) of Ireland and Alba." Again, under the date 1185, a similar title is given to Maelisa O'Dalaigh, chieftain of Corca-Raidhe, now the barony of Corkaree, in the county of Westmeath; whilst Brian O'Higgin, another Irishman, whose obit is recorded under the year 1476, is called "head of the schools of Ireland and Alba."

Defects in H. 1. 19, supplied from other sources. The Irish text of the present work from p. 584, vol. i., to p. 144, vol. ii., the original of which is wanting in the MS. H. 1. 19, has been supplied from a copy of the so-called Annals of Connacht, in two vols., preserved in the Library of Trinity College, Dublin, (class H. 1, 1 and 2),[1] Annals of Connacht. collated with another copy of the same Annals in the collection of the Royal Irish Academy (class 23, F. 8-9).[2] The Trinity College MS. appears to have been transcribed in the year 1764, by one Maurice O'Gorman, who states, in a memorandum on the last page of vol. ii., that he copied it from *sean leabhar meamraim,* "an old parchment book." Dr. O'Donovan was of opinion that the "old parchment book" in question was the same as the "*Annales Connaciæ Hibernicè,* formerly in the Stowe Library, but now in Lord Ashburnham's possession, described by Dr. O'Conor in his Stowe Catalogue.[3]

"The chronology," observes O'Donovan,[4] "is very minutely detailed in this work, the day of the week on which the calends of January of each year fell, the age of the moon on that day, the cycle of the moon, the cycle of the sun, and the indiction, being invariably marked."

---

[1] Signified by the letter B in the notes appended to the supplemental text.

[2] Denoted by the letter C.

[3] *Bibliotheca Stowensis,* vol. i. p. 73.

[4] *Catalogue of the Irish MSS. in the Library of Trinity College, Dublin,* p. 104.

"It appears," he says, "from several private letters from old Charles O'Conor of Belanagare, to the Chevalier Thomas O'Gorman, that the transcriber of this MS. (Maurice O'Gorman) was employed by the latter to copy several MSS. in the possession of the former; and it is more than probable that this is a copy of the *parchment* MS. described in the Stowe Catalogue by Dr. O'Conor, who deposited all his grandfather's MSS. in the Stowe Library." "This is the most curious historical record," he adds, "now extant of the province of Connaught."

These "Annals of Connacht," for such they must still continue to be called, have also been fully described by Professor O'Curry,[1] who considered the Royal Irish Academy copy to have been made by the same hand that transcribed the Trinity College copy, although the character of the handwriting in both is different. The Trinity College copy is, for a modern MS., unusually free from aspirate signs, while the text of the R. I. Academy transcript is overlaid with these signs. Both transcripts seem to have been certainly made from the same original; but what that original was it is not easy now to decide. "There is reason to believe," O'Curry says,[2] "that they are [it was] a fragment of the book of Annals of the O'Duigenans of Kilronan," which the Four Masters made use of.[3] But it is not at all certain that the MSS. B and C are copies of the "Annales Connaciæ" described by Dr. O'Conor, as some entries which he quotes from those Annals, in the description[4] already referred to, are not found in either B or C.

The contents of these MSS. agree so closely with the

[1] *Lectures,* &c. pp. 104, 113 sq. See also O'Curry's *Catalogue of Irish MSS. in the R. I. Academy;* Series i., vol. ii., p. 426.

[2] *Lectures,* p. 113

[3] A memorandum added by the late

Theophilus O'Flanagan, in the R. I. Acad. copy, at the year 1378, tends to support this conclusion. *See* note 9, vol. ii., p. 54, of the present work.

[4] *Bibl. Stowensis,* vol. i. pp. 74, 76.

corresponding text of the present work, as to make it probable that the MS. from which they were transcribed, and the MS. H. 1. 19, were independent copies of a common original—óne (the original of B and C) made for the family of O'Conor Donn, by the O'Mulconrys, the hereditary historians and antiquaries of the sept ; and the other (H. 1. 19), for Brian MacDermot, chiefly by members of the family of O'Duigenan, the historiographers of the MacDermots. The connexion of the O'Mulconrys with the original of B and C appears from memoranda transcribed into those copies ;[1] and it is very certain that the transcribers of the greater portion of H. 1. 19 were members of the O'Duigenan family.[2]

Other evidences of identity between the contents of the MSS. B and C, and H. 1. 19, are furnished by some marginal entries in an original volume of the Four Masters preserved in the Library of Trinity College, Dublin, (Class H. 2. 11). The entries in question, which are in the handwriting of Roderick O'Flaherty, the author of *Ogygia*, (who had the MS. H. 1. 19 in his possession, as already observed), profess to have been taken from "O'Mulconry's MS.," and from a MS. indicated by the letter L (*i.e.* the Annals of Lecan) ; and all the entries quoted from "O'Mulconry's MS.," with scarcely an exception, are to be found in the MS. H. 1. 19.

These considerations weighed so strongly with my much lamented friend, the late Rev. Dr. Todd,[3] who had atten-

---

[1] The memorandum mıԜı Ⅿıoⴑuⴗ O Ⅿɑoⴑconɑⴗe ("I, Miles O'Mulconry"), occurs in the MSS. B and C, at the end of the year 1543, apparently transcribed from the original. At the conclusion of the entries for 1410, the note pɑⴒın quı ⴗⴄⴗıpⴒⵑ, occurs also in both, similarly transcribed. This Patin, or Padeen (little Patrick), was undoubtedly another member of the family of O'Mulconry, and the father of Maurice O'Mulconry, who transcribed the copy of the old *Book of Fenagh*, at present in the possession of the Rev. Richard Slevin, P.P., Gortlitteragh, co. Leitrim.

[2] Vid. p. xxiii *supra*, and p. lvi *infra*.

[3] Dr. Todd contemplated publishing the present Chronicle, with the assistance of Professor O'Curry, who made a copy of that portion of the MS. end-

tively studied the subject, that he urged the advisability of supplying from B and C the large hiatus in H. 1. 19, extending from the year 1316 to 1413. It was his opinion, also, that the MS. B was more correct than C. It has therefore been made the basis of the supplemental text.

The text of the present work, from the end of the first line on p. 420, vol. II. (A.D. 1577), to the conclusion on .p. 514, has been taken from a fragment of an Irish chronicle, contained in a MS. volume in the British Museum, Clarendon coll., vol. xlv.; Add. 4792. This fragment comprises fourteen folios of the volume, viz., from folio 27 to folio 40, inclusive. Four of these folios (29, 30, 31, and 32) consist of vellum, the rest of paper. This fragment has been described by Professor O'Curry[1] as "a part of the continuation" of the MS H. 1. 19, and a copy of it, made by him, is now attached to the latter MS. But it is difficult to understand how it could have formed a portion of H. 1. 19, as the contents of the two first folios of the fragment are contained in the MS. of which it is stated to be a part. The vellum leaves in the Clarendon fragment differ[2] so much in size and character from the material on which the MS. H. 1. 19 is written, as to render it improbable that both MSS. ever formed portions of the same volume. Nevertheless, it is certain that the Clarendon fragment was written for, and partly by,[3] the same Brian MacDermot for whom the MS. H. 1. 19 was transcribed; and if not a part of the MS. H. 1. 19, which, for the

Fragment of MS. in the British Museum.

---

ing with the transactions of the year 1240. This transcript Dr. Todd, with characteristic kindness, placed at my disposal. But it came to my hands too late to be of use, as the corresponding portion of the work had been already printed. It was a cause of satisfaction to me, however, to know that my copy of the original MS. agreed literally with that of the lamented O'Curry.

[1] *Lectures*, &c., p. 95.

[2] The vellum in H. 1. 19 is of a uniform size throughout; is very thick, and ruled for writing, each leaf being 11 × 9 inches, whereas the vellum in the Clar. fragment is not ruled, and measures only 9½ inches in length, by 7 in breadth.

[3] The portions of the fragment in the handwriting of Brian MacDermot are indicated in the notes at foot of pages 420 to 514, vol. ii., of the present work.

reasons stated, it could hardly have been, it must have formed portion of a copy of the same MS., made while in a more perfect state than it is at present. Its authority is equally as good as if it actually formed an integral part of the MS. H. 1. 19; and the affairs of Connacht, from the year 1577 to 1590, a momentous period in the history of that distracted province, are recorded in it with an unusual degree of precision and detail.

Transcribers of H. 1. 19.

It appears from the differences observable in the character of the handwriting, that no less than six scribes were engaged in the transcription of the MS. H. 1. 19. That portion ending with the year 1241 seems to have been copied by a person who wrote his name "Philip Badl.'"[1] The abbreviated part of the name has been read "Badley;"[2] but it is doubtful whether it represents a surname. It was probably a cognomen of "Philip," who was evidently a member of the family of O'Duigenan, in which family the Christian name "Philip" was a very common one. The remainder of the MS. down to the year 1315 was copied by the same Philip,[3] a person Dubhthach[4] (apparently an O'Duigenan also), and a scribe who signs his name "Conairi, son of Maurice,"[5] and who was most likely another member of the same family. The entries from 1413 to 1461, inclusive, are in the handwriting of Brian MacDermot.[6] The contents of the MS. from 1462 to 1542 have been copied by Brian MacDermot and Philip "Badley," in conjunction with two other scribes, one of whom was named Donnchadh Mac-an-filedh, or Donough MacAneely;[7] the rest of the volume being in the handwriting of Dubhthach O'Duigenan, with the exception of some entries added by Brian MacDermot.

---

1 *See* vol. i., p. 58, note [4].

2 Vid. *supra*, pp. xiii., n. [2], xviii., xxiii.

3 *Infra*, p. 542, note [1].

4 *Ib.*, p. 274, note [2].

5 *Ib.*, p. 286, n. [3].

6 Vol. ii., p. 144, note [8].

7 *Ib.*, p. 312, note [8]; and see also 328, note [2].

The unenviable condition of persons who practised the transcription of Irish historical books, as a profession, in the latter part of the sixteenth century, may be inferred from some of the occasional notes added by the scribes. One of them complains of being "fatigued from Brian MacDermot's book "[1] (*i.e.* the MS. H. 1. 19). Another observes that he desists from his labours "until morning,"[2] probably for want of the nourishment of which he declares himself, further on,[3] to stand in need; whilst a third entreats the reader to overlook a slight error, because his "pulse shrank through excess of labour."[4]

A work transcribed under such circumstances could hardly be expected to present a text altogether acceptable to the philologist. The Irish of the present Chronicle is, nevertheless, fully up to the standard of the period in which it was written. The text in the original is very much abbreviated, the system of abbreviation practised by the scribes being frequently of an unusually complex nature. In extending the abbreviations, care has been taken to produce each word in the actual form in which the scribe would have written it; and where any attempts have been made to correct obvious errors, such attempts will be found indicated in the foot notes.

The translation is entirely literal, and may therefore appear somewhat rugged; but it seemed desirable, having regard to the character of the work, to adhere as closely as possible to the original. The necessity for a glossary has been obviated by the explanation, in foot notes, of difficult or obsolete words, as they occur.

The Provost and Fellows of Trinity College, Dublin, through their obliging Assistant Librarian, W. B. Hunt, Esq., afforded me free access to their valuable collection

---

[1] Vol. i., p. 58, note [4]. The writer uses the word *barc* (Eng. bark) for book, apparently confounding its Lat. equivalent (*liber*) with *liber*, " a book."

[2] *Ib.*, p. 342, note [4].

[3] *Scuirim do thachu pruinne;* " I cease for want of a dinner" (or of food). Vol. i., p. 572, n. [1].

[4] Vol. ii., p. 328, n. [2].

of Irish MSS.; and the President and Council of the Royal Irish Academy were no less indulgent. The facilities afforded to me by these bodies served in no small degree to lighten labours which would otherwise have been much more onerous.

During the progress of the work I was deprived, by the death of my revered friend, the late Rev. Dr. Todd, of the generous assistance and friendly counsel, so freely accorded to me on all occasions (and they were many) when I found it necessary to avail myself of his mature judgment, and intimate acquaintance with the materials of Irish History. Those who have been associated with him in his favourite pursuit—the study of the native records of Ireland—know with what unselfish earnestness he strove to imbue others with his own zealous devotion to the subject. Of one of his masterly essays on Irish archæology,[1] it has been justly said by an eminent writer, that it was "the signal of the awakening of hagiography in Ireland."[2] His death has left a blank in the list of Irish scholars, which time will not soon or easily fill.

My thanks are due to the Rev. Eugene Murphy, C.C., of Dromod, near Waterville, county Kerry, an accomplished Celtic scholar, for much valuable assistance; and to Dr. Carl Lottner, for supplying me with the translations above printed from the Norse.

In the preparation of the Index (a work which has entailed much labour), I derived material aid from the extensive acquaintance of my friend, D. H. Kelly, Esq., of Castle Kelly, with the topography of Connacht.

I am under special obligations to Samuel Ferguson, Esq., Q.C., LL.D., Deputy Keeper of the Public Records in Ireland, for many useful suggestions to which I have had regard in the translation of obscure passages, and in the preparation of this Preface.

[1] Pref. to *Obits and Martyrol. of Christ Church, Dublin.*

[2] R. P. De Buck. *L'Archeologie Irlandaise,* &c.; Paris, 1869; p. 27.

The proof sheets have been carefully read by my generous friend, the Rev. Dr. Reeves, without whose zealous co-operation the work would not be so free from errors as I trust it is. For his great kindness in this, as well as for many other like favours, I owe him an amount of gratitude which I should in vain endeavour to express.

W. M. HENNESSY.

DUBLIN,
     February, 1871.

annala locha cé.

ANNALS OF LOCH CÉ.

Annala Locha Cé.

Klt. Ináir for aoine, ui. xx.ⁱᵗ. L.; xu.; ceiṫre bliadna x. ocus mile aoís an Tigerna in tan sin. Slúaigheḋ lá mac Aṁlaoiḃ ocus lá Máolmórḋa, ocus Galla, ocus Laiġne, a Miḋe ocus a mBreghaiḃ, ocus iársin go termann Féichín, go ruccsat bú díarṁiḋe ocus broide adbal leó. Féil Griġóir ría nInid is in ḃliaḋoinsi, ocus mionċáisc a samraḋ, ionnus na haiċeis ó ċéin ṁáir.

Mór ṫionól fer Muman ocus Miḋe, ocus deiscert Connacht lá mBrían mBóroṁa mac Cinnéidiġ .i. rí Ereann, for ġallaiḃ Atha cliaṫ, ocus for Laiġnaiḃ, día ttaḃairt fó a réir amail dus rucc ríaṁ, óir ro aġain ocus ró áirdéiriġ cogaḋ coṁḟúasmadaċ etir Brían ocus ġallaiḃ Aṫa cliaṫ, ocus Laiġniḃ, an tan sin. Gaḃais Brían longport ig Clúain tarḃ, i sen Muiġ ealta, ré hAth cliaṫ atthúaiḋ. Nír ḃo bern báoghail aghaiḋ for Ath cliaṫ an ionbuḋsin; bá láṁ i nead gríḃe aghaiḋ fair. Nír ḃo hiomgaḃail deaḃṫa, seoċ ba ċuingeḋaiḃ gleiṫne ocus uġra móire saiġin ar an soċroide do rocht ann an ionbuḋ sin, óir do rochtatar ann tréinḟir ṫoghaiḋe ocus áirsiġe

---

[1] *Kalends of January on Friday*: *i.e.* the kalends, or first of January, fell in this year on a Friday, the twenty-sixth day of the moon's age; but read "28th" (although the Annals of Ulster have "26th").

[2] *The 15th.* The numerals xu. indicate that the year 1014 was the fifteenth year of the Solar Cycle; and the Sunday letter C.

[3] *Shrovetide.* Inid (inid), MS. The name is from the Lat. *initium*, and signifies the beginning of Lent. The Welsh form is *ynyd*.

ANNALS OF LOCH CÉ.

THE kalends of January on Friday,[1] the 26th of the moon, the 15th;[2] the age of the Lord, at that time, fourteen years and a thousand. A hosting by the son of Amhlaibh, and by Maelmordha, and the Foreigners and Lagenians, into Midhe and Bregha, and afterwards to Termann-Feichin; and they carried off innumerable cows, and a great number of captives. The festival of Gregory before shrovetide[3] in this year, and Little Easter[4] in summer, which had not been noticed from a remote time.

A.D.

[1014.]

A great assemblage of the men of Mumha, and Midhe, and the South of Connacht, by Brian Boromha, son of Cenneidigh, *i.e.* the King of Erinn, against the Foreigners of Ath-cliath, and against the Lagenians, to bring them under his obedience, as he had previously brought them; for a mutually aggressive war kindled and arose, at that time, between Brian and the Foreigners of Ath-cliath and the Lagenians. Brian took up a position in Cluain-tarbh in old Magh-Ealta, to the north of Ath-cliath. To attack Ath-cliath on this occasion was not *to attack* a "neglected breach."[5] It was *like putting* a hand into a griffin's nest to assail it. It would not be evading[6] conflict, but seeking great battles and contests, to advance against the multitude that had then arrived there; for the choicest brave

---

[4] *Little Easter:* mіonĉáіṛc, or Low Sunday. The word caіṛc (or caṛc) = pascha, the *k* sound made *p*, according to a well known law.

[5] *Neglected breach.* beṛn baoġhaіl (beṛn báoghail); lit. "gap of danger," but signifying a place left exposed to attack.

[6] *Evading.* hіonġabaіl, for hіomġabaіl, MS.

B 2

ⲓⲛⲛⲣⲓ ⲃⲣⲉⲧⲁⲛ, ó Ⲥⲁóⲓⲣ Ⲉⲁⲃⲣⲟⳟ, ocuⲣ ó Ⲥⲁóⲓⲣ Ⲉⳟⲓⲣⲧ, ocuⲣ ó Ⲥⲁóⲓⲣ Ⳟⲟⲛⲓⲁⲕ. Ⲇⲟ ⲣúⲁⲕⲧⲁⲇⲁⲣ ⲁⲛⲛ ⲣóⲣ ⲣⲟⲣⳟⲗⲁ ⲣⲓóⳟ ocuⲣ ⲧⲁⲟⲓⲣⲉⲁⲕ, cuⲣⲁⲃ ocuⲣ cⲁⲓⲧ ⲙⲓⳑⲓⲃ, ocuⲣ ⳑⲁ́ⲧ ⲛⳟⲟⲓⳑⲉ, ocuⲣ ⲧⲣⲉⲓⲛⲣⲓⲣ ⲕⲩⲁⲓⲣⲥⲉⲣⲧ ⲓⲛ ⲇⲟⲙⲁⲓⲛ, ⲉⲧⲓⲣ ⲇⲩⲃ Ⳑⲟⲕⳑⲟⲛⲛⲁⲕ ocuⲣ ⲣⲓⲟⲛⲛ Ⳑⲟⲕⳑⲟⲛⲛⲁch, ⲁ ⲣⲟⲕⲣⲁⲓⲇⲉ ocuⲣ ⲁ ⲙⲃⲁ́ⲓⲃ ⳟⲁⳑⳑ, ⳟⲟ ⲣⲁⲃⲁⲇⲁⲣ ⲁ ⲛⲟⲧⲕ cⳑⲓⲁⲕ ⲁⳟ ⲙⲁⲥ Ⲟⲙⳑⲁⲟⲓⲃ, ⲁⳟ ⲣⲣⲓⲕⲉóⳑⲁ́ⲙ ⲕⲟⳟⲁⲓⲃ ocuⲣ ⲕⲁⲧⲁⲓⳟⲧⲉ ⲇⲟ Ⳟⲁⲟⲓⲇⲉⲁⳑⲁⲓⲃ. Ⲇⲟ ⲣⲟⲕⲧⲁⲇⲁⲣ ⲁⲛⲛ Ⲥⲓóⳟⲣⲁⲇ ⲣⲓⲟⲛⲛ ocuⲣ Ⲥⲓóⳟⲣⲁⲇ ⲇⲟⲛⲛ, ⲇⲁ́ ⲙⲁⲥ Ⳑⲟⲕⲁⲓⲣ ⲓⲁⲣⳑⲁ ⲓⲛⲛⲣⲓ hⲟⲣⲥ, cⲟ ⲣⳑúⲁⳟⲁⲓⲃ ⲓⲛⲛⲣⲓ hⲟⲣⲥ ⲓⲙⲁⲓⳑⳑⲉ ⲣⲣⲓú. Ⲇⲟ ⲣⲟⲕⲧⲁⲇⲁⲣ ⲁⲛⲛ, ⲓⲙⲟⲣⲣⲟ, ⲣⳑóⳟ ⲇⲓⲙóⲣⲁ ⲁ hⲓⲛⲛⲣⲓⲃ ⳟⲁⳑⳑ, ocuⲣ ⲁ Ⲙⲁⲛⲩⲓⲛⲛ, ocuⲣ ⲁⲣ ⲛⲁ Ⲣⲉⲛⲛⲟⲓⲃ, ocuⲣ ⲁ ⲃⲣⲉⲁⲧⲛⲟⲓⲃ, ocuⲣ ⲁ Ⲡⳑⲉ́ⲙⲉⲛⲛⲟⲓⲃ. Ⲇⲟ ⲣúⲁⲕⲧⲁⲇⲁⲣ ⲁⲛⲛ ⲣóⲣ ⲃⲣⲟⲇⲁⲣ .ⲓ. ⲓⲁⲣⳑⲁ Ⲥⲁⲟⲓⲣⲉ Ⲉⲁⲃⲣⲟⳟ, ⳟⲟ ⲣⳑⲩⲁⳟⲟⲓⲃ ⲇⲓⲙóⲣⲁ, ocuⲣ Ⲩⲓⲧⲓⲣ ⲇⲩⲃ .ⲓ. ⲙⲓⳑⲓⲃ [Ⲥⲁⲟⲓⲣⲉ] Ⲉⳟⲓⲣⲧ, ocuⲣ Ⳟⲣⲓⲣⲓⲛⲉ cⲟⲣⲁⲇ Ⲡⳑⲉ́ⲓⲙⲓⲟⲛⲛⲁⲓⲃ, ocuⲣ Ⳟⲣⲉⲓⲣⲓⲁⲙ á Ⲛⲟⲣⲙⲁⲛⲛⲁⲓⲃ. Ⲇⲟ ⲣúⲁⲕⲧⲁⲇⲁⲣ ⲁⲛⲛ, ⲇⲟⲛⲟ, ⲙⲓⳑⲉ ⳑⲁ́ⲟⲕ ⲇⲟ ⲇⲩⲃ Ⲇⲁⲛⲁⲣⲟⲓⲃ ⲇⲁ́ⲛⲁ, ⲣóⲓⲕⲣⲉ́ⲛⲁ, ⲣⲟ ⲕⲁⳑⲙⲁ, ⳟⲟ ⲣⲥⲓⲁⲕⲟⲓⲃ ocuⲣ ⳟⲟ ⲣⲧⲁⲣⳟⳟⲁⲓⲃ, ocuⲣ cⲟ ⳑúⲓⲣⲉⲕⲟⲓⲃ ⲓⲟⲙⲇⲁ ó ⲧⲁ́ⲣⲓⲛⲛ ⳑⲉó. Ⲣⲟⲃⲁ́ⲇⲁⲣ ⲁⲛⲛ, ⲓⲙⲟⲣⲣⲟ, ⲣⳑóⳟ ⲇⲓⲙóⲣⲁ ocuⲣ ⳟⲁⲣⲣⲁⲃ óⳟ ⲁⳑⳑⲁⲧⲁ Ⲣⲓⲛⲉ ⳟⲁⳑⳑ, ocuⲣ ⲛⲁ cⲉⲛⲇⲁⲓⳟⲉ ⲧⲁⲛⳟⲁⲇⲁⲣ ⲁ ⲧⲓⲣⲓⲃ Ⲣⲣⲁⲛc, ocuⲣ ⲁ Ⲥⲁⳟⲣⲟⲓⲃ, ocuⲣ ⲁ Ⲃⲣⲉⲧⲟⲓⲛ, ocuⲣ Ⲣóⲙⲁ́ⲛ. Ⲇⲟ ⲣúⲁⲕⲧ ⲁⲛⲛ, ⲇⲟⲛⲟ, Ⲙⲁ́ⲟⳑⲙóⲣⲣⲟⲧⲁ ⲙⲁⲥ Ⲙⲩⲣⲕⲁⲇⲧⲁ ⲙⲓⲥ Ⲣⲓⲛⲛ .ⲓ. ⲁ́ⲓⲣⲇⲣⲓⳟ ⲕúⲓⳟⲉⲇ Ⳑⲁⲓⳟⲉⲛ, ⳟⲟ ⲣⲓóⳟⲁⲓⲃ, ⳟⲟ ⲇⲧⲁⲟⲓⲣⲉⲕⲁⲓⲃ, ocuⲣ ⳟⲟ ⲧⲧⲣⲉ́ⲓⲛⲣⲉⲣⲟⲓⲃ Ⳑⲁⲓⳟⲉⲛ; ⳟⲟ ⲙⲁⲥⲁ́ⲟⲙⲁⲓⲃ, ocuⲣ ⳟⲟ ⲛⳟⲓⲟⳑⳑⲁⲛⲛⲣⲁⲓⲃ ⲙⲁⲣ· ⲁ́ⲟⲛ ⲣⲓú ⲓⲣⲓⲛ ⲣⲟⲕⲣⲁⲓⲇⲉ ⲕⲉ́ⲇⲛⲁ.

Ⲃⲁ́ ⲙóⲣ ⲧⲣⲁ́ ⲁⲛ Ⲥⲟⲕⲣⲁⲓⲇⲉ ocuⲣ ⲓⲛ ⲧⲓⲟⲛóⳑ ⲧⲁ́ⲛⲓc ⲁⲛⲛ. Ⲃⲁ́ ⲃⲁ́ⲇⲁⲕ ocuⲣ ⲃⲁ́ ⲃⲟⲣⲣⲣⲁⲇⲁⲕ ⲁⲛ ⲕⲟⲓⲙⲉ́ⲓⲣⳟⲉ ⲇⲟ ⲣóⲛⲣⲁⲧ

---

1 *Caer-Eabhrog:* i.e. York.

2 *Caer-Eighist.* Not identified.

3 *Caer-Goniath.* Probably Caer-Gwent, or Caerwent.

4 *Black Lochlonnachs.* Ⲇⲩⲃ Ⳑⲟⲕⳑⲟⲛⲛⲁⲕ (dubh Lochlonnach). This was the name given by the Irish to the Danes to distinguish them from the *Finn* ("*fair*") *Lochlonnachs,* or Norwegians.

5 *Fair Lochlonnachs.* See last note.

6 *Siograd Finn:* i.e. "Siograd (or Sigurd) the Fair."

7 *Siograd Donn.* "Siograd (or Sigurd) the Brown."

men and heroes of the island of Britain had arrived there, from Caer-Eabhrog,[1] and from Caer-Eighist,[2] and from Caer-Goniath.[3] There arrived there, still, the principal kings and chieftains, knights and warriors, champions of valour and brave men of the north of the world, both Black Lochlonnachs[4] and Fair Lochlonnachs,[5] in the following and friendship of the Foreigners, until they were in Ath-cliath, with the son of Amhlaibh, offering war and battle to the Gaeidhel. Thither came Siograd Finn,[6] and Siograd Donn,[7] two sons of Lothar, Jarl of Innsi-hOrc, accompanied by the armies of Innsi-hOrc. Thither came, moreover, great hosts from Innsi-Gall, and from Manainn, and from the Renna,[8] and from the Britons, and from the Flemings. There arrived there also Brodar, *i.e.* the Jarl of Caer-Eabhrog, with very great hosts, and Uithir the Black, *i.e.* the warrior of [Caer-]Eighist, and Grisine, a knight of the Flemings, and Greisiam from the Normans.[9] There arrived there, likewise, a thousand bold, brave, powerful heroes of the black Danars, with shields and targets, and with many corslets, from Thafinn.[10] The great armies and famous young bands of Fine-Gall were also there, and the merchants who had come from the lands of France, and from the Saxons, and from Britain, and from the Romans. There arrived there, moreover, Maelmordha, son of Murchadh, son of Finn, *i.e.* the chief king of the province of Laighen, with the kings, and chieftains, and brave men of Laighen, with youths and servants accompanying them in the same multitude.

Great, indeed, was the multitude and assemblage that came thither. Warlike and haughty was the uprising they

---

[8] *Renna.* By the name *Renna* (pl. of *rinn*, "a point,") are probably meant the Rinns of Galloway, in Scotland.

[9] *From the Normans.* α hoɼmannaιb, for α noɼmaιɼnaιb, MS.

[10] *Thafinn.* This is probably an error, as the word is nearly oblitera-

ted in the MS. The Editor has followed Professor O'Curry's reading, which agrees with that of John MacConmidhe (see note [1], next page); but the original seems rather to read o ɫa ɼιnnɫoċɫ...from "Finn Lochl[ainn]," or Norway.

ɼυɴɴ .ı. αɴɴɼαꝺ օϲυɼ αɴᵹʟυıɴɴ ᵹαʟʟ օϲυɼ ᵹαօíꝺeαʟ
ʟαıᵹհeɴ, αɴ αᵹհαıꝺ ċαċα ɴα Ϻυıṁɴeϲհ, օϲυɼ ꝺօ ꝺıօɴᵹ-
ṁáıʟ ꝺօϲɼօıꝺe Ḃɼíαıɴ ḃóɼօṁα ꝺıóꝺ; ϲօɴαꝺ .uı. ϲαċα
ϲօṁóɼα ϲօıṁʟıօɴ ɴα ɴꝺαɴáɼ .ı. ϲαċ αᵹ ϲօıṁéꝺ αɴ
ꝺúıɴıꝺ αʟʟá αɼτıᵹհ, օϲυɼ ϲúıᵹ ϲαċα αᵹ ʟáṁαϲհ ıɴαᵹհαıꝺ
ɴα ɴᵹαօíꝺıօʟ.

Níóɼ ċıօɴóıʟ, ıɱօɼɼօ, Ḃɼíαɴ ɼʟóıᵹհ ıɴáıꝺ ɼօċɼαıꝺe
ıɴꝺαᵹհαıꝺ αɴ ɱօɼ ɼʟυαıᵹհeꝺ ɼıɴ íαɼċαıɼ ċօɱαıɴ օϲυɼ
ᵹαʟʟ, αϲհτ Ϻυıṁɴıᵹ αṁáıɴ, օϲυɼ Ϻօeıʟɼeϲհʟαıɴɴ ϲօ
ḃɼeɼαıꝺ Ϻıꝺe; υαıɼ ɴı τօɼɼαϲհταꝺαɼ ċυıᵹe Uʟαꝺ,
ıɴáıꝺ Αıɼᵹıαʟʟαı, ɴα Ϲıɴeʟ ɴeօᵹαıɴ, ıɴα Ϲıɴeʟ Ϲօɴαıʟʟ,
ıɴα Ϲօɴɴαϲհτα, αϲհτ հı Ϻαıɴe օϲυɼ հı ḃɼıαϲɼαċ, օϲυɼ
Ϲeɴeʟ Oeꝺα, υαıɼ ɴíɼ ꝺօ ɱαıċ αɴɴɼıɴ eτıɼ Ḃɼıαɴ օϲυɼ
Ταꝺᵹ αɴ eıϲհ ᵹıʟ, ɱαϲ Ϲατհαıʟ, ɱıϲ Ϲօɴċօḃαıɼ, ɼí
Ϲօɴɴαϲհτ. Ϲօɴıꝺ αıɼe ɼıɴ ɼօ eɼıᵹ Ταꝺϲ ꝺυʟ ʟα Ḃɼıαɴ
ıɼıɴ ϲαċ ɼıɴ Ϲʟυαɴα ταɼꝺ.

Αꝺϲı, ıɱօɼɼօ, Iɴꝺeıɼᵹe ɱαϲ Uɼαꝺαıɴ .ı. ᵹıʟʟα ᵹɼαꝺα
ꝺօ Ḃɼıαɴ, α ɴαıɼʟıɴᵹ αɴ αᵹհαıꝺ ɼıαɼ αɴ ċατհ, ɼeɴαꝺ
ϲʟeíɼeϲհ ɴıօɱꝺα, ıɴꝺαɼ ʟαıɼ, ꝺօċυɱ αɴ ʟօɴᵹρυıɼτ,
օϲυɼ ɼíαꝺ αᵹ ϲαɴταıɴ ċɼαıʟɱċeꝺαıʟ օϲυɼ ċɼαօɼʟeıᵹıɴɴ;
օϲυɼ ɼօ ɼıαɼɼαıꝺ Iɴꝺeıɼᵹe ϲıα ɴα ϲʟeıɼıᵹ. Séɴáɴ ɱαϲ
ᵹeıɼɼċıɴɴ ɼıɴ, αɼ ɴα ϲʟeıɼıᵹ. Ϲıꝺ ꝺυɼ ɼυϲ αʟʟe ó ɴα
eᵹʟαıɼ ɼeıɴ ϲօɴıϲϲe ɼօ հé, օʟ Iɴꝺeıɼᵹe. Ɍeıϲհ ꝺʟıᵹeɼ
ꝺօ Ḃɼıαɴ, օʟ αɴ ϲʟeıɼeαċ; ꝺα ɴıαɼɼαꝺ τáɴıϲ ɼυɴɴ.

---

1 *Multitude.* The first page of the
original having become very obscure,
and now quite illegible, the preceding
text has been taken from a transcript
of it, made in the year 1698, at Carn-
Oilltriallaigh, now Heapstown, co.
Sligo, by one John MacConmidhe, or
MacNamee, under the circumstances
which he has explained in the following note :—

"Ḃıօꝺ α ɼıօɼ αᵹ ᵹαċ αóɴ ʟeıᵹɼeɼ
αɴ ḃeᵹáɴ ɼıɴ ᵹυɼ αḃ í ϲıαʟʟ ɼíɴe
ɴα ταօíḃe ꝺαıʟʟe ɼօ ꝺօɴ ταօıḃ
αɱυıᵹ ꝺօɴ ʟeαḃαɼ, ꝺօ ɼᵹɼıօḃυɼα
αɴɴɼօ, ꝺeϲϲʟα α ꝺυʟ ɼ ɴꝺαıʟʟe
ɴí ɼα ṁó ꝺı; ı ɱḃαıʟı ċαıɼɴ օıʟʟ-
τɼıαʟʟαıᵹ ꝺαṁ αɴıօᵹ αɴ ꝺeαċṁαꝺ
ṁαꝺ ʟá ꝺօ Noueɱḃeɼ, 1698. S.
ɱαϲ Ϲօɴɱıꝺe."

"Be it known to every one who
reads this fragment, that it is the
true sense of the obscure page of the
outside of the book I have written
here, for fear it should become more
obscure. In the village of Carn-
Oilltriallaigh am I to-day, the tenth
day of November, 1698. S[ean]
Mac Conmidhe." Mac Conmidhe's
copy, which follows the first folio
of the MS., is accompanied by a

made, viz.:—the warriors and champions of the Foreigners, and of the Gaeidhel of Laighen, against the battalions of the men of Mumha, and to ward off from them the oppression of Brian Boromha. The muster of the Danars was, therefore, six great battalions, *i.e.* one battalion guarding the fortress within, and five battalions contending against the Gaeidhel.

Brian, however, assembled neither host nor multitude[1] against this great army of the west of the world, and of Foreigners, but the men of Mumha alone, and Maelshechlainn with the men of Midhe; for there came not to him the Ulidians, nor the Airghialla; nor the Cenel-Eoghain, nor the Cenel-Conaill; nor the men of Connacht, save the Hi-Maine, and Hi-Fiachrach,[2] and Cenel-Oedha; for goodwill existed not then between Brian and Tadhg-an-eich-ghil,[3] son of Cathal, son of Conchobhar, king of Connacht; and hence it was that Tadhg refused to go with Brian to that battle of Cluain-tarbh.

Moreover, Indeirghe, son of Uradhan, *i.e.* Brian's orderly-servant,[4] saw in a vision, the night before the battle, a synod of many clerics, as he thought, coming towards the camp, singing psalms and reading aloud; and Indeirghe asked who the clerics were. "That is Senan,[5] son of Gerr-chinn," said the clerics. "What has brought him hither from his own church?" asked Indeirghe. "Debts[6] that are due to him from Brian," replied the cleric, "and it is to

---

transcript thereof made by Professor O'Curry.

[2] *Hi-Fiachrach: i.e.* the Hi-Fiach-rach-Aidhne, a sept descended from Fiachra, brother of Niall of the Nine Hostages, who occupied a district co-extensive with the present diocese of Kilmacduagh, in the co. Galway.

[3] *Tadhg-an-eich-ghil: i.e.* "Tadhg (or Thaddeus) of the white steed."

[4] *Orderly-servant.* ᵹilla ᵹꞃaꝺa. ᵹilla (gilla) means a lad, or servant,

(gillie), and ᵹꞃaꝺa is the gen. of ᵹꞃaꝺ—Lat. *gradus.*

[5] *Senan: i.e.* St. Senan of Inis-Cathaigh, now Scattery Island, in the Shannon.

[6] *Debts.* By the debts here referred to is probably meant an atonement for the profanation of Inis-Cathaigh (St. Senan's establishment) committed by Brian in the year 977. See Ann. Four Mast., and Chron. Scotorum, at the year 975 = 977.

Ro ιoⳅ̃αιⲇιⲣ ⲣιⲣ ιꝫα ⳅ̃ιꝫ, oⲗ Iⲛⲇειⲣꝫⲉ, ⲥειⲛoⳅ̃ ⲣoιⳅ̃ⲣⲉⲇⲏ
ⲗαιⲣ α ⳅ̃oⳅⳁⳅ ⲣⳙⲛⲛ. Αⳙⳙⲙⲁⲣⲁⳅ̃ ⳅιꝫ αⲙⲙ α ⲛιoⲥⲁⲇ ⲣⲉ
Sénⲁⲛ, oⲗ αⲛ ⲥⲗⲉⲣⲉⳅ̃, oⲥⳙⲣ ιⲣ ⲉιꝫιⲛ ⲣⳙιⲣⲣ. Ⳅιⲁꝫⳙιⲇ ⳙⲁⳇ
ιⲁⲣⲣιⲛ. Iⲛⲇιⲣⲣⲉⲣ, ιⲙoⲣⲣo, Iⲛⲇⲉⲣꝫⲉ ⲇo Ḃⲣιⲁⲛ αⲛⳅ
αιⲣⲗιⲛꝫ αⳅ ⲥoⲛⲇⲁιⲣⲥ, oⲥⳙⲣ ⲃⳇ ⲙⲉⲣⲣⲁιⲇⲉ α ⲙⲉⲛⲙⲁ ⲗⲁιⲣ
α ⳅ̃ⲗⳙιⲛⲣιⲛ.

Αⳅ ⲥoⲛⲛⲁιⲣⲥ, ⲇⲛⲁ, Ⲇιⲁⲣⲙⲁιⲇ .h. Ⲥoⲣⲥⲣⲁιⲛ .ι. ⲣⲉⲣ
ꝫⲣⲁⳇⲁ Ⲇoⲙⲛⲁιⲗⲗ ⲙιⲥ Ⲇιⲁⲣⲙⲁⲇⲁ, oⲥⳙⲣ ⲣo ⲃoιⲣιⳙⲙ αꝫ
ⲙⲁⲣⲃⲁⳇ ⲛⲁⲛ ꝫⲁⲗⲗ αⲛ ιⲛιⲣ Ⲥⲁⳅ̃ⲁιꝫ αιⳇⳅⲉ αιⲛⲉ ⳅ̃αⲣꝫ,
αⲛⲇ αιⲣⲗιⲛꝫ ⲥⲉⲇⲛⲁ ⲇo Ḃⲣιⲁⲛ, oⲥⳙⲣ ⲣⲉⲁⳅⳅ ⲙⲃⲗιⲁⲇⲛⲁ
ⲇⲏⲉⲥ αⲣ xxⁱⳅ ⲣιⲁⲣⲁιⲛ αιⳇⳅⲉ oⲉιⲛⲉ ⲣιⲛ ιⲛⲁⲣ ⲙⲁⲣⲃⲁⲇ
Ḃⲣιⲁⲛ αⲇ ⲥoⲛⲛⲥⳙⲣ ιⲛⲇ αιⲣⲗιⲛꝫ ⲣιⲛ.

Ⳅⳇⲛιⲥ Oⲉⲃιⲛⲛ, ιⲛꝫⲉⲛ Ⲇⳙιⲛⲛ oιⲗⲉⲛ, ⲣⲉⲁⲗ ⲃⲉꝫ ⲣιⲁ ⲛιⲁⲣ-
ⲙⲉιⲣꝫⲉ ιⲛⲇ αιⳇⳅⲉ ⲣιⲛ, ó ⲣⳇⲇ Ⲥⲣⲁιꝫⲉ ⲗⲉιⳅ̃ⲉ, ⲇⲁꝫⲁⲗⲗⲁⲙ
Ḃⲣιⲁⲛ, ꝫⳙⲣ ιⲛⲛιⲣ ⲇo ꝫo ⲇⳅιoⳅⲣⲁⲇ αⲣ ⲛⲁ ⳅ̃αⲣⲁⳅ̃. Ro
ⲣιⲁⲣⲣⲁιⲇ Ḃⲣιⲁⲛ ⲇι ⲥιⲁ ⳇⲁ ⲙⲁⲥⲁιⲃ ⲃⳙⳇ ⲣι ⳇⲁ ⲉιⲣ,
oⲥⳙⲣ ⲥιⲁ ⲗⳇⲛ ⲇιⳇ ⲛo ⲙⲁⲣⳇⲣιⳇⲉ ιⲣιⲛ ⲥⲁⳅ̃ ιⲙⲁⲣoⲉⲛ ⲣⳙⲣιⳙⲙ.
Iⲛ ⲥⲉⲇ ⲙⲁⲥ ⲇo [ⳅ̃ιⳇⲣιⲛ ιⲣⲉ] ⲃⳙⲣ ⲣⳇ αⲣ ⲏⲉιⲣⲣ, αⲣ ⲣι.
Ⲥoⲛιⳇ ⳙιⲙⲉ ⲣιⲛ ⲣo ⳅ̃ⳙιⲣⲣιⳙⲙ ⲣιoⲣ αⲣ ⲥⲉⲛⲇ Ⲙⳙⲣⳅⲁⳇⲁ,
ⲥo ⲇⳅιoⲣⲣⲁⲇ ⲇιⲁ αꝫⲁⲗⲗⲁⲙ ⲣιⲁ ꝫⲥⲁⳅ̃ ⲣⳙⲗ αⲇ ⲣιⲣⲣⲁⲇ αⲛ
ⲣⲗⳙⲁιꝫ. Nι ⳅ̃ⳇⲛιⲥ Ⲙⳙⲣⳅⲁⲇ αⲛⲛ ⲥoⲛⲣⳙⲣꝫⲁιⳇ α ⲗⲉιⲛⲉ
ⳙιⲙⲉ. Iⲣ αⲛⲛⲣιⲛ ⲇo ⳅ̃ⲗⳙιⲛ Ⲇoⲛⲛⳅⲁⲇⲏ ⲙⲉⲇⲁ Ḃⲣιⲁιⲛ
αꝫ ιoⲙⲁꝫⲁⲗⲗⲁⲙ ⲣⲉ α ꝫιⲗⲗⲁ ꝫⲣⲁⳇⲁ, oⲥⳙⲣ ⲛιⲣ αⲛ ⲣⲉ α
ⲉⲇⲁⳅ̃ ⳙιⲗⲉ ⲇo ꝫⲁⳇⳇⲁⲗ ⳙιⲙⲉ, αⳅⳅ ⳅⲁιⲥ ⲥo ⲏoⲣoⲛⲛ ⲥo
ⳅⳙⲥ α ⲗⲁⳍ αⲣ ⲥⳙⲁιⲗⲗⲉ ⲛⲁ ⲏιⲙⲇⲏⲁιⲇⲉ α ⲣⲁιⳇⲉ αⲛ ⲣⳇ
'ιⲛⲁ ⲣⳙⲣⳙιⲗⲗ, ꝫⳙⲣ ⲣιⲁⲣⲣⲁιⲇ ⲇo Ḃⲣιⲁⲛ ⲥιⳇ ⲇo ꝫⲉⲛⳙⲙ;
ιⲛ αⲣ ⲛⲁ ⲥⲣⲉⳅⲁιⲃ ⲛo ⲣⲁꝫⲏⲁⲇ, ⲛo ιⲣιⲛ ⲗoⲛꝫⲣoⲣⳅ ⲛo

---

[1] *Killing of the Foreigners.* This event took place in the year 977. See last note.

[2] *For Brian.* ⲇo Ḃⲣιⲁⲛ. That is to say, he had a vision *concerning* Brian.

[3] *Oebhinn;* now Aoibhill (pron. Eevill), the familiar sprite of the Dal-gCais, or sept of the O'Brien's of Thomond. See *Danish Wars,* ed. Todd, cxi., *n*².

[4] *Sidh,* pron. *Shee;* a name applied by the Irish to a supposed fairy residence. "Viros Sidhe vocant Hiberni aerios Spiritus, aut phantasmata; ex eo, quod ex amœnis collibus quasi prodire conspiciantur, in quibus vulgus eos habitare credit: quæ collium talium ficta habitacula à nostris *Sidhe* vel *Siodha* dicuntur." O'Flaherty's *Ogygia,* pars iii., cap. xxii. See

demand them he has come here." "They would be paid to him at his house," said Indeirghe, "even though he had not come here." "To-morrow the time for paying them to Senan arrives," said the cleric, "and they must be paid." They afterwards departed from him. Indeirghe told Brian, moreover, the vision that he had seen, and his (Brian's) mind was the worse for hearing it.

Diarmaid Ua Corcrain, *i.e.* the orderly-man of Domhnall, son of Diarmaid, and who had been at the killing of the Foreigners[1] in Inis-Cathaigh, saw the same vision, on the night of Easter Friday, for Brian;[2] and thirty-seven years before that Friday night in which Brian was slain this vision was seen.

Oebhinn,[3] daughter of Donn-Oilen, came a short time before nocturns on that night, from the Sidh[4] of Craig-liath,[5] to converse with Brian, and told him that he would fall on the morrow. Brian enquired of her which of his sons should be king after him, and how many of them would be slain in the battle along with himself. "The first son [whom thou shalt see[6]] shall be king after thee," said she. Wherefore it was that Brian sent for Murchadh, in order that he might come to speak with him before all, ere the multitude would arrive. Murchadh came not until he put on his garment. Then it was that Donnchadh heard the voice[7] of Brian, conversing with his orderly-servant, and he waited not to put on all his clothes, but came quickly and placed his hand on the post of the bed in which Brian was, in his tent, and asked Brian what he should do, whether he should go on the

---

also O'Donovan's supplt. to O'Reilly's Dictionary, in *voc.* ꞅꞁꞇ.

[5] *Craig-liath.* Now Craiglea, near Killaloe, co. Clare.

[6] *See.* The words within brackets are conjecturally supplied, the corresponding space in the original MS.

being blank, some words having apparently been erased.

[7] *Voice.* ᵹₑₒₐ. This word is not found in any Glossary accessible to the Editor. It is probably a mistake for ᵹₑₒₐₙᵣ, or ᵹₑₐₒₐₙᵣ, explained ᶜₐᵢₙ ₙₒ ᵤᵣₗₐᵦᵣₐ, "speech, or eloquence," in O'Clery's Glossary.

anpad. Adubairt Brian, imorro, ó do tuc aichne ar ξut nDonnchada, uair rob olc lair a comrachtuin chuige ar tur; ir cuma lem, ar ré, cid be ní do néir, oir ni dot iarrad roba. Tanic Donnchad, imorro, arin pupuill tria luinne iarrin, ocur dorala Murchad do i ndorur na puirple, ocur ni tuc nech did taimthech di aroile.

O ro riacht, imorro, Murchad co raibe aξ iom-aξallam re Brian, ro ráid imorro Brian rrir: eirξ, ar ré, ic leabaid co ti an la, ocur an ni ro bud mian lemra nir chedaiξ dia duit e. Ro buí trá ξach micel-main a cinn a celi doib amlaid rin no ξo tanic maiden an laoi cona lan roillri .i. oeine chaξ. Ir annrin ro cuired caχ croda comoirderc etorra dibliniub, da ná rrith indramail a nErinn. Maiξid ror ξallaib ocur ror laiξnib a torraξ, conrordileξuid uile co leir, in quo bello cecidit ex aduerra caterua ξallorum, Maolmorda mac Murchada, airdriξ Laiξen, ocur Domnall mac Ferξaile, rí na bForthuaθ, ocur Broξarban mac Conchobair, ri .h. bFailξe. Cecidit uero a ξallir, Dubξall mac Amlaib, ocur Siξrud mac Lodair, iarla inri hOrc, ocur ξilla Ciaráin mac ξlúin iaruinn, riξdamna ξall, Uiθir dub, ocur Suairtξair, ocur Donnchad .h. hEruilb, ocur ξrirríne, ocur Luimne, ocur Amlaib mac Laξ-mainn, ocur Brodar .i. toirrech na luinξri Lochlainne, qui occidit Brian, et re mile etir marbad ocur badhad. Do rorchuir ann, din, a brriθξuin in chaθa rin ó ξoeidelaib, Brian mac Ceindeidiξ mic Lor-cain, airdriξ ξoeidel Erenn ocur ξall Brettan, ocur Augurt iarthair tuaircert Eorpa uile, ocur a

---

*Gallorum; i.e. of the Foreigners (Galli.)

2 *Son of Conchobhar.* The text has mc Cor mc Conch. "son of Cor . . . son of Conchobhar," as if the tran-scriber had intended to represent Brogarban as the son of Cormac, but observing his mistake, substituted "Conchobhar," omitting to erase the letters "mac Cor."

foraging excursions, or remain in the camp. Brian said, however, when he recognized Donnchadh's voice, (for he liked not his being the first to come to him), "I care not what thou doest," said he, "as it was not for thee I was seeking." Donnchadh, moreover, left the tent after that, in anger, and Murchadh met him in the door of the tent, and neither of them saluted the other.

When Murchadh, also, came and was conversing with Brian, Brian said to him : "go to thy bed," said he, "until the day comes, and that which I should wish, God has not permitted to thee." All evil omens were thus crowding upon them until the morning of the day came with its full brightness, i.e. Easter Friday. It was then that a brave, noble battle was fought between them on both sides, for which no equal was found in Erinn. The Foreigners and Lagenians were first defeated and entirely routed, in quo bello cecidit ex adversa caterva Gallorum,[1] Maelmordha, son of Murchadh, chief king of Laighen, and Domhnall, son of Ferghal, king of the Fortuatha, and Brogarbhan, son of Conchobhar,[2] king of Ui-Failghe. Cecidit vero a Gallis, Dubhgall, son of Amhlaibh, and Sighrud,[3] son of Lothar, Jarl of Insi-hOrc, and Gillaqiarain, son of Gluniarainn, royal heir of the Foreigners ; Uithir the Black, and Suairtghair, and Donnchadh, grandson of hErulbh, and Grisine, and Luimne, and Amhlaibh, son of Lagmann, and Brodar, (i.e. the captain of the Lochlann fleet, who slew Brian) ; and six thousand, either by killing or drowning.[4] There fell there, also, in the mutual wounding of that battle, of the Gaeidhel, Brian, son of Cenneidigh, son of Lorcan, supreme king of the Gaeidhel of Erinn, and of the Foreigners of Britain, and the Augustus of the whole north-west of Europe, and his son,

---

[3] *Sighrud;* i.e Sigurd, son of Lodver. See Todd's *Danish Wars,* Gen. Table VI. (A), p. 264, n. 11.

[4] *Either by killing or drowning.* The expression eⱃip ṁaⱃbaⱃ ocuⱃ baⱃhaⱃ lit. signifies "between killing and drowning."

mac .i. Murchaꝺ, ocuſ a macſiꝺe .i. Toiſſꝺhelbach mac Murchaꝺa, ocuſ Conaing mac Ꝺuinncuan, mic Ceinꝺeiꝺiᵹ, ſiꝺaṁna Muman, ocuſ Moᵹla mac Ꝺoṁnaill, mic Paolain, ſí na nꝺéiſi Muman; Eochaiꝺh mac Ꝺunaꝺhaiᵹh, ocuſ Niall mac Cuinn, ocuſ Cuꝺuiliᵹ mac Ceinneꝺiᵹ, tſi coeimte bſiain; ocuſ Taꝺc mac Murchaꝺa hi Ceallaiᵹ, ſi .h. Maine; Moelſuanaiꝺ .h. heiꝺin, ſi Eiᵹne; ᵹeiḃenꝺach .h. Ꝺuḃaᵹain, ſí Feſaṁaiᵹe, ocuſ mac Bethaiꝺ mic Muiſeᵹhaiᵹh Cloein, ſí Ciaſſaiᵹhe Luacſa, ocuſ Ꝺoṁnall mac Ꝺiaſmaꝺa, ſi Coſca baiſcinn; Sᵹannlan mac Cathail, ſí Eoᵹanachta Loca Léin, ocuſ Ꝺomnall mac Eiṁin mic Cuinniᵹ ṁóiſ, móſṁaoſ Maiſ in Albain, et alii multi nobileſ.

Iſ ann boi apt aiſꝺſiᵹ .i. bſian mac Ceinneiꝺiᵹ, ocuſ Conaing mac Ꝺuinncuan, aſ cúl na caᵹ aᵹ cantain a ſalm, ocuſ aᵹ ꝺenam iſnaiꝺe, conſuſteſno feaſ ꝺian ꝺaſſochtach Ꝺanmaſᵹach aſ iomᵹaḃail an ḃaiſſ aſ an maiꝺṁ, ᵹo ſainic ᵹuſ an maiᵹin amboí an ſi. O ꝺo aiſiᵹ an Ꝺanmaſᵹach an ſí ambaoᵹal ſoſnoᵹᵹ a cloiꝺeiṁ, ocuſ ſo ꝺiᵹenꝺ aiſꝺſi Eſenn ocuſ ſoſ ꝺiᵹenꝺ Conaing muſ an ceꝺna, ocuſ toſᵹuiſ féin a bſſiᵹᵹuin in coṁſuic ſin.

Luiꝺ, tſá, Maolmuiſe mac Eochaꝺa .i. comſoſba Patſaic, co ᵹſuiᵹiꝺ ocuſ mionnuiꝺ conic[e] Soſꝺ Coluim Cille, co ttuc aſſ cuiſſ bſiain ocuſ Muſchaꝺa a mic, ocuſ cenꝺ Conaing, ocuſ cenꝺ Moᵹhla, conſoſaꝺnocht a nAſꝺ Maᵹa a moluiꝺ nuí. Ꝺí aiꝺᵹe, umoſſo, ꝺóſum ocuſ ꝺo ᵹſamaꝺ Paꝺſaiᵹ aᵹ aiſe na ᵹcoſſ ſſopteſ honoſem ſeᵹiſ ſoſiti.

Ꝺúnlaing mac Tuathail, ſí Laiᵹen, ꝺhéc. Caᵹ eꝺiſ Cian mac Maoilṁuaiꝺ ocuſ Ꝺomnall mac Ꝺuibꝺáboiſenꝺ, co toſchaiſ ann Cian, ocuſ Cathal, ocuſ

---

¹ *Feara - Maighe.* Feſṁaiᵹe, | mhaighe-Feine, but the distinctive
MS.; *rectè* Feſaṁaiᵹe (Fera- | portion (Feine) was often dropped,
Maighe). The name in full is Feara- | and continues so in the modern form,

i.e. Murchadh, and his son, viz. Toirrdhelbhach, son of Murchadh; and Conaing, son of Donncuan, son of Cenneidigh, royal heir of Mumha ; and Mothla, son of Domhnall, son of Faelan, king of the Deisi-Mumhan ; and Eochaidh, son of Dunadhach, and Niall, son of Conn, and Cuduiligh, son of Cenneidigh—Brian's three guards; and Tadhg, son of Murchadh Ua Ceallaigh, king of Ui-Maine ; Maelruanaidh Ua hEidhin, king of Aighne; Geibhendach Ua Dubhagain, king of Fera-Maighe;[1] and Mac-Bethaidh, son of Muiredhach Claen, king of Ciarraighe-Luachra ; and Domhnall, son of Diarmaid, king of Corca-Bhaiscinn ; Sgannlan, son of Cathal, king of Eoghanacht-Locha-Léin ; and Domhnall, son of Eimhin, son of Cainnech Mór, great steward of Marr in Alba ; et alii multi nobiles.

The supreme king, *i.e.* Brian, son of Cenneidigh, and Conaing, son of Donncuan, were behind the battalions, chaunting their psalms, and performing prayers, when a vehement, furious, Danmarkian escaped from the battle, avoiding death, until he came to the place where the king was. As soon as the Danmarkian perceived the king unguarded, he unsheathed his sword, and beheaded the supreme king of Erinn, and he beheaded Conaing likewise ; and he himself fell in the mutual wounding of that fight.

Maelmuire, son of Eochaidh, *i.e.* the comarb of Patrick, came, truly, with seniors and relics, to Sord-Choluim-Chille, and bore from thence the bodies of Brian and his son Murchadh, and the head of Conaing, and the head of Mothla, which he buried at Ard-Macha, in a new grave. Two nights, moreover, was he, with the congregation of Patrick, waking the bodies, propter honorem regis positi.[2]

Dunlaing, son of Tuathal, King of Laighen, died. A battle between Cian, son of Maelmhuaidh, and Domhnall, son of Dubhdabhoirenn, in which Cian, and Cathal, and

---

Fermoy, the name of a barony and town in the co. Cork.

[2] *Regis positi.* ꞃeꞇᵹıꞅ poꞃꞃıcı, MS.

Raᵹallach, τρι mic Mailṁuaiᵭ, ocuτ άρ áᵭbail impa. Caτhal mac Ꝺomnaill, ρί .ħ. nԐchach, ꝺo maρbaꝺ la Ꝺonnchaꝺ mac Ꝺριain. Maiᵭm ρία Ταꝺᵹ mac Ꝺριain ꝛορ Ꝺonnchaꝺh mac Ꝺριain, ꝺú naρ ꝛaρᵹbaꝺ Ruaiꝺρι mac Ꝺonnaᵹan, ρί αραꝺh. Sloiᵹeꝺ la .ħ. Maolꝺoρaiꝺ ocuτ la .ħ. Ruaiρc a Maᵹ nαόι, ᵹo ρο ṁaρbτaτ Ꝺomnall mac Caτhail, ocuτ ᵹuρ innρaiꝛꝛeτ in maᵹ, ocuτ ᵹo ρucτaτ ᵹialla Connachτ, liceτ non in eaꝺem uice. Maiᵭm ꝛορ Ꝺál nαραiꝺe ρία nUllταιb, ubi mulτi occiꝛι ꝛunτ. Ꝼlaiᵶbeρταch mac Ꝺomnaill, comaρba Ciáρain ocuτ Ꝼinnén, ocuτ Ronán, comaρba Ꝼeᵶin, ocuτ Conn .ħ. Ꝺiᵹράιᵭ in Cριτꞇo ꝺoρmieρunτ. αꝺ imᵭa τρά aιꝛιꝛι na bliaꝺnai ꝛa.

Ꝁlt. Enaiρ .uii. ꝛ.; L. iiii.; coiᵹ bliaꝺna ꝺhéc [aρ] mile aiꝛ in Τιᵹeρna. Ꝺomnall mac Ꝺuiᵭᵭaboiρenꝺ ꝺo ṁaρbaꝺ la Ꝺonnchaꝺ mac Ꝺριain i caᵶ. Ꝼlaiτbeρταch .ħ. Neill ꝺo τochτ a Miᵭe ꝺo caᵭaiρ Maoilτꝛeclainn. Mailꝛeclainn iaꝛum aρ ꝛloiᵹeaꝺ a Laiᵹne, ᵹuρ ꝛo oρτ Laiᵹne, ocuτ ᵹo ꝺτuc bóꝛuiṁe ocuτ eiꝺiꝛe Laiᵹen laiꝛ. Niall mac Ꝼeꝛᵹaile mic Connaiᵶ a ꝛuo ᵹeneꝛe occiꝛuτ eꝛτ, o Uiᵭ Τuiꝛτꝛe. Muiꝛceρταch .ħ. Loꝛcáin, aiꝛcinnech Loτꝛa, [ꝺhéc]. αoᵭ .ħ. Ruaiꝛc, ρί Ꝺꝛeꝛꝛne, ꝺo maꝛbaꝺ la Ταꝺc an eich ᵹil mac Caτhail, ρί Connachτ, ꝺolóꝛe .ι. aᵹ Loᵶ Neill a Maꝺ Oi, ꝺo ꝛoeꝛꝛam na baᵶla ioꝛꝛa, conιꝺ eꝺh o ꝛin τallaꝺ ꝛiᵹe aρ a clainꝺ, ᵶenmoᵶá Oeᵭ aṁáin.

---

[1] *Ui-Echach;* *i.e.* the Ui-Echach of Munster, a tribe settled in the S.W. of the co. Cork, and descended from Eochaidh, son of Cas, son of Corc, King of Munster in the fourth century. On the adoption of surnames by the Irish the principal family of this tribe took the name of O'Mahony. There were other tribes in Ulster called Ui-Echach, or *Nepotes Eochadii.*

[2] *Ruaidhri, son of Donnagan.* In the Ann. Four Mast. and Chron. Scotorum the name is "Ruaidhri *Ua* Donnagain (or O'Donnagain)."

[3] *Killed.* ꝛaꝛcbaꝺ, lit. "was left."

[4] *Ubi.* ube, MS.

[5] *Occisi.* occiꝛꝛι, MS.

[6] *Ronan.* ꝛonain (the gen. form of the name), MS.

[7] The 4th. The numerals iiii are evidently in mistake for uii; although the Ann. Ult. have also iiii.

Raghallach—the three sons of Maelmhuaidh—were slain, and a prodigious slaughter about them. Cathal, son of Domhnall, king of Ui-Echach,[1] was slain by Donnchadh, son of Brian. A victory by Tadhg, son of Brian, over Donnchadh, son of Brian, in which Ruaidhri,[2] son of Donnagan,[2] king of Aradh, was killed.[3] A hosting by Ua Maeldoraidh and Ua Ruairc into Magh-Aei, and they slew Domhnall, son of Cathal, and devastated the plain, and carried off the pledges of Connacht, licet non in eadem vice. A victory over the Dal-Araidhe by the Ultonians, ubi[4] multi occisi[5] sunt. Flaithbhertach, son of Domhnall, comarb of Ciaran and Finnen; and Ronan,[6] comarb of Fechin; and Conn Ua Digraidh, in Christo dormierunt. Numerous are the events of this year.

The kalends of January on the 7th feria, the 4th[7] of the moon; the age of the Lord fifteen years [over] a thousand. Domhnall, son of Dubhdabhoirenn, was slain in a battle by Donnchadh, son of Brian. Flaithbhertach Ua Neill came into Midhe, to assist Maelsechlainn. Maelsechlainn *went* afterwards on a hosting into Laighen, and he plundered Laighen and carried off a borumha,[8] and the pledges of Laighen. Niall, son of Ferghal, son of Connach, a suo genere occisus[9] est, *i.e.* by the Ui-Tuirtre. Muirchertach Ua Lorcain, airchinnech of Lothra, [died]. Aedh Ua Ruairc, king of Breifne, was slain, dolose,[10] by Tadhg-an-eich-ghil, son of Cathal, king of Connacht, viz.:—at Loch Neill in Magh-Aei, against the protection of the Bachal-Isa; wherefore it was that kingship was taken from his children, except Aedh[11] alone.

---

[8] *Borumha; i.e.* a prey of cows.

[9] *Occisus.* occirrur, MS.

[10] *Dolose.* vo lórre (dolósse), MS.

[11] *Except Aedh.* The meaning is, that in consequence of the great transgression committed by Tadhg, in slaying O'Ruairc, who was protected by oaths sworn upon the Bachal-Isa (Baculus Jesu), his descendants were excluded from the right of succeeding to the sovereignty of Connacht, with the exception of his son, Aedh, or Hugh ("of the broken spear"), who succeeded his father, and transmitted the succession to his posterity.

ḟclt. Ǫnαιρ ι.f; l. xuιιι.; ρe bliαọnα ọhec ocuρ
mile αιρ ιn Τιʒeρnα. Mac Líaʒ, αρọ ollam Ǫρenn,
moρtuuρ eρτ. Caċ eọιρ Ullτoιb ιρ Ọál Αραιọe, ʒuρ
ṁuιʒ ρoρ Ọαl nΑΑραιọe; ọo ρuιτ αnn Ọomnαll .h.
Loιnʒριʒ, ρí Ọál nΑΑραιọe, ocuρ Nιαll mac Ọuιḃċuιnne,
ocuρ Conchoɓaρ .h. Ọomnαllαιn, ρí .h. Τuιρτρι.
Nιαll mac Ǫochαọα, ocuρ Coρcραċ [mac] Muιρeʒhαιʒ
mιc Ϝlαιnn, ρí Ϝeρα Mαιʒe hÍċα, a ρuιρ occιρι ρunτ.
Ọonncuαn mac Ọúnlαιnʒ, ρí Lαιʒen, ocuρ Ταọc .h.
Rιαιn, ρí .h. n'Oρonα, ọo ṁαρɓαọ lá Ọonnchαọ mac
Ʒιllα Ϝατραιc ρoρ láρ Leιċʒlιnne. Ọún Leċʒlαιρρι
ọo uιle loρcαọ. Cluαιn ʒeρτα ocuρ Cenαnτuρ ọo
loρcαọ. ΑΑιρbeρταc mac Coιρρọóɓρán, αιρċιnnech Roιρ
ΑΑιlιτρeαċ, ọo eʒ. Síċ αn Ǫριnn.

ḟclt. Ǫnαιρ ιιι.f; l. xxuιιι.; ρeαchτ mblιαọnα
ọhéc ocuρ mile αιρ ιn Τιʒeρnα. ΑΑonʒuρ mac Cαιρρe
ċαlmα, ρíọαmnα Τempαch, moρtuuρ eρτ. Ϝeρʒαl mac
Ọomnαιll mιc Conchoɓαρ, ρíọαmnα ΑΑιlιʒ, ọo ṁαρɓαọ
o Cénel Ǫoʒαιn ρéιn. Ϝlαnn .h. ɓeιce, ρι .h. méċ,
a ρuιρ occιρuρ eρτ. Coρmαc .h. Loρcáιn, ρí hι nǪchαch,
ọo mαρɓαọ o Uιɓ Τρenα. Ọonnchαọ mac Ọonnchαọα
hι Conʒαlαιʒ, ρíọαmnα Ǫρenn, a ρuιρ occιρuρ eρτ.
Muιρeọαch .h. Ọuιɓeoιn, ρí .h. mιc Cuαιρ ɓρeʒh, ọo
ṁαρɓαọ lα Ϝlαιċbeρταch .h. Neιll. ΑΑρ ʒαll ocuρ
Lαιʒen ιmm Oɓɓα lα Mαeιlρeclαιn. Oenʒuρ mac
Ϝlαιnn, αιρchιnnech Lαιnne Léιρe; Coρmαc .h. Mαoιl-
mιọe, αιρchιnnech Oρommα ράιċι, moρtuι ρunτ. Ʒιllα-
coluιm mac Muιρeọhαιʒ .h. Mαιlτρeα, ocuρ Oeọh .h.
hǪραọáιn, ρí [h.]mɓeρραιl Mαċα, moρtuι ρunτ.
Ʒιllα Cριρτ .h. Loρcαιn, τιʒeρnα Cαιlle Ϝαllαmαιn, ọo
mαρɓαọ α Cenαnτuρ.

1 *Mac Liag.* The bard of king
Brian Boromha. See Hardiman's
Irish Minstrelsy, vol. ii., p. 361.

2 *Son.* mac. Omitted in MS.;
supplied from the Ann. Ult.

3 *Feara-Maighe-Itha.* ϝeρ.ρṁαιʒe

híτα(Fern-mhaighe-hItha), MS. The
"Feara-Maighe-Itha" ("men of Magh
Itha") were the people inhabiting Magh
Itha, or "the plain of Ith," a district
in the co. Donegal, between the rivers
Finn and Mourne, and now the barony

The kalends of January on the 1st feria, the 18th of the moon; the age of the Lord sixteen years and a thousand. Mac Liag,[1] chief poet of Erinn, mortuus est. A battle between the Ulidians and the Dal-Araidhe, and the Dal-Araidhe were defeated; in which fell Domhnall Ua Loingsigh, king of Dal-Araidhe, and Niall, son of Dubh-thuinne, and Conchobhar Ua Domhnallain, king of Ui-Tuirtre. Niall, son of Eochaidh, and Coscrach, [son][2] of Muiredhach, son of Flann, king of Feara-Maighe-Itha,[3] a suis occisi sunt.[4] Donncuan, son of Dunlaing, king of Laighen, and Tadhg Ua Riain, king of Ui-Drona, were killed by Donnchadh, son of Gillapatraic, in the middle of Leith-ghlinn. Dun-leth-glaise was entirely burned. Cluainferta and Cenannus were burned. Airbhertach, son of Cosdobh-ran, airchinnech of Ros-ailitrech, died. Peace in Erinn.

The kalends of January on the 3rd feria, the 28th[5] of the moon; the age of the Lord seventeen years and a thousand. Aenghus, son of Carre Calma,[6] royal heir of Temhair, mortuus est. Ferghal, son of Domhnall, son of Concho-bhar, royal heir of Ailech, was slain by the Cenel-Eoghain themselves. Flann Ua Beice, king of Ui-Méith, a suis occisus est. Cormac Ua Lorcain, king of Ui Echach, was slain by the Ui-Trena. Donnchadh, son of Donnchadh Ua Conghalaigh, royal heir of Erinn, a suis occisus est. Muiredhach Ua Duibheoin, king of Ui-mic-Uais-Bregh, was slain by Flaithbhertach Ua Neill. A slaughter of the Foreigners and Lagenians, near Odhbha, by Maelsechlainn. Oengus, son of Flann, airchinnech of Lann-leire; Cormac Ua Maelmidhe, airchinnech of Druim-raithe, mortui sunt. Gillacoluim, son of Muiredhach Ua Maeltrea, and Oedh Ua hEradháin, King of [Ui]-mBresail-Macha, mortui sunt. Gillachrist Ua Lorcain, lord of Caille-Follamhain, was killed in Cenannus.

---

of Raphoe; to be distinguished from Magh-Itha-Fothairt, a district in the co. Wexford.

[4] *Occisi sunt.* occıruı̣ eṙc, MS.

[5] *The 28th; rectè 29th.*

[6] *Carre Calma.* "Carrach Calma" ("Carrach the powerful") in the other chronicles.

C

Ictt. Enaιp ɪɪɪɪ. p.; l. x.; ochτ mbliαɔnα ɔhéc ocup
mɪle αɪp ɪn Τɪʒepnα. Ͻpoen mac Moelṁópɔα, pí
Lαɪʒen, ɔo ɔαllαɖ ɪ nαₓ clιαch lα Sɪτpeac mac
αṁlαɪbh. Moelαn mac Eιcnɪʒ .h. Lopcαɪn, pí ʒαɪlenʒ
ocup Τuατ Luɪʒne uɪle, ɔo mαpbαɔ ɔo Sαɪₓnɪɓ. Slóɪʒeɖ
lα Cénel Eoʒαɪn ʒo Cιll pαɓpιc, ʒup mαpɓpατ ɔpoιnʒ
ṁóɪp, ocup co bₑₐpʒuιɓpατ ʒιllα Cpιpτ mac Conαɪnʒ
mιc Conʒαlαɪʒ, muιpe Cloιnne Sιnαιɓ. Ͻoṁnαll .h.
Coeιnɔelɓαιn, pι Loɓʒαιpe, ocup Cαιpṁιɖe .ɪ. pechταιpe
Moeιlτpeclαιn, ɔo mαpbαɔ lα pιpα Ceαll ocup Ele
ταιppιuʒ cpeιce. In péτlα ṁonʒach ɔo αₓpuʒαɔ ιn
hoc anno, ppια pe coeιcιɔιp, ιn αιmpιp poʒṁαιp.

Ictt. Enαιp u. p.; l. xxι.; nóι mblιαɔnα ɔhéc ocup
mɪle αɪp ɪn Τɪʒepnα. αιlén mac Oιppéιn, pí Muʒopn,
ocup Oιppeιn .h. Cαₓupαɪʒ [τιʒep]nα Sαιₓne, ɔo mαpbαɔ
lα ʒαιlenʒαιb. Cιll ɔαpα uιle ɔo lopcαɔ ɔo τeneɖ
ɔαιɓ. Ͻomnαll mac Mαιlτpeclαιnn, coṁαpbα pιnnen
ocup Mocolmóʒ, ιn Cpιpτo quιeuιτ. αpɔʒαp ocup αpɓú,
meιc Mάιlτpechlαιnn mιc Moelpuαnαιʒ, ɔα pιʒɔαṁnα
Oιlιʒ, α puιp occιpι punτ. Mατʒαmαιn mac Conαιnʒ
mιc Ͻuιnncuαn, pιɔαṁnα Mumαn, ɔo éʒ. plαιɓbep-
ταch .h. Neιll ɔo ₓeαchτ α τιp Conαιll, ʒup po opτ
τιp nEnnα ocup τιp Lúʒɔech. Ruαιɔpι .h. hαιllel-
lαιn, pι .h. nEchαch, ɔo mαpbαɔ lα pιpα peppmαιɖe.
Ro mαpbαɖ, ιmoppo, ɔά mac Cιnnéɔιɓ .ι., Conʒαlαɓ
ocup ʒιllαmuιpe, ιnά ɔιʒuιl pó céɔóιp. Epɓʒ ɔo
ταbαιpτ ɔo Uιɓ Cαιpréιn ɔo Ͻonnchαɔ mac ɓpιαιn,
ʒup po τepcαɔ α ɓop ɔep ɔe. Ͻαṁlιαʒ Ͻepmuιʒe ɔo
bpιppeɖ lα Muιpcepταch .h. Cαppαιʒ pop Moelṁuαιɔ,

---

[1] *Ua Lorcain.* This is the name in the Annals of Ulster also, but Tighernach and the Four Masters write it Ua Leochain, which is probably the correct form, as the family of Ua Leochain, now anglicised "Loughan" (and incorrectly translated "Duck"), were, in the eleventh century, chiefs of Gailenga-Mora, a district comprising the present barony of Mor-gallion, co. Meath, and a part of the adjoining co. of Cavan.

A.D.
[1018.]

The kalends of January on the 4th feria, the 10th of the moon; the age of the Lord eighteen years and a thousand. Braen, son of Maelmordha, king of Laighen, was blinded in Ath-cliath by Sitric, son of Amhlaibh. Maelan, son of Eicnech Ua Lorcain,[1] king of Gailenga and all Tuath-Luighne, was slain by the Saithne. A hosting by the Cenel-Eoghain to Cill-Fabhrich, when they killed a great number, and lost Gillachrist, son of Conaing, son of Conghalach, steward of Clann-Sinnaigh. Domhnall Ua Caindelbhain, king of Laeghaire, and Caismidhe, _i.e._ Maelsechlainn's lawgiver, were slain by the Feara-Ceall and Ele, _whilst_ taking a prey. The hairy star[2] was seen in this year, during the space of a fortnight, in harvest time.

[1019.]

The kalends of January on the 5th feria, the 21st of the moon; the age of the Lord nineteen years and a thousand. Ailén, son of Oissén, king of Mughorna, and Oissen Ua Cathusaigh, lord of Saithne, were killed by the Gailenga. Cill-dara was all burned by lightning. Domhnall, son of Maelsechlainn, comarb of Finnen and Mocholmog, in Christo quievit. Ardghar and Archú, sons of Maelsechlainn, son of Maelruanaidh—two royal heirs of Oilech—a suis occisi[3] sunt. Mathghamhain, son of Conaing, son of Donncuan, royal heir of Mumha, died. Flaithbhertach Ua Neill went into Tir-Conaill, and he destroyed Tir-Enna and Tir-Lughdech. Ruaidhri Ua hAillelain, king of Ui-Echach, was slain by the men of Fernmhagh. The two sons of Cennedigh, viz.:—Conghalach and Gillamuire, were likewise slain, immediately after, in revenge of him. An attack was made on Donnchadh, son of Brian, by the Ui-Caisin, and his right hand was cut off. The stone-church of Dermhagh was broken open by Muirchertach, grandson of Carrach, against

---

[2] _Hairy Star; i.e._ a comet. The appearance of this comet is also recorded in the Annals of Ulster, under this year, but is not noticed in any of the other Irish Chronicles.

[3] _Occisi._ Occissus, MS.

rí bɼeɼ Cell, ocuɼ a ʒabaiɼʒ aɼɼ aɼ éiȝin, ocuɼ a
maɼbaᵭ iaɼum.

Jctt. Gnaiɼ .ui. ɼ.; l. ıı.; ɼiʒe bliaᵭna aɼ mile aiɼ
ın Ʒiȝeɼna. Ceall ᵭaɼa cona ᵭeɼʒiȝiᵭ ᵭo loɼcaᵭ.
Ȝlionn ᵭa loʒa cona ʒeɼʒoiȝiᵭ ᵭo loɼcaᵭ. Cluaın
Íɼaiɼᵭ ocuɼ Cluaın mic nóiɼ, ocuɼ Soɼᵭ Coluim Cille,
ʒeɼʒiaɼaɼʒe cɼematae ɼunʒ. Ílaiʒbeɼʒach .h. hGochaᵭa
ᵭo ᵭallaᵭ la Nıall mac Gochaᵭa. Ȝillacíaɼuın mac
Oiɼeine, ɼí Muȝᵭoɼna ɼɼi ɼé oen laoı, ᵭomaɼbaᵭ la .h.
mic Cuaıɼ Ụɼeȝ. Cɼᵭ maʒa uile co léiɼ ᵭo loɼcaᵭ .ı.
ın ᵭaɱliaȝ móɼ cona ʒuıȝe ᵭo luaıᵭe, ocuɼ an cloıȝʒech
cona ʒloȝaıb, ocuɼ an Sabáll, ocuɼ an Ʒoaı, ocuɼ caɼbaᵭ
na nabaᵭ, ocuɼ anʒ ɼenʒaʒaɼ ɼɼociuɼʒu ɼ̄ᶜ a ʒeiɼʒ
Jctt. luın, an luan ɼıa Cinȝciɼ. Moelmuıɼe mac
Gochaᵭa, comaɼba Íaʒɼaıc, cenᵭ cleiɼech iaɼʒaɼ
Goɼɼa uile, ın .xx. anno ɼɼıncıɼaʒuɼ ɼuı, ı ʒeiɼʒ noın
Iúın, ᵭıa hoeıne ɼıa Cinȝciɼ, ın Cɼıɼʒo quieuıʒ. Cmal-
ȝaᵭ a ȝcomɼoɼbuɼ Íaʒɼaıc, ᵭo ɼeıɼ ʒuaıʒı ocuɼ eȝlaıɼe.
Íınnlaoʒ mac Ruaıᵭɼı, ɼı Clban, a ɼuıɼ ὄcciɼuɼ eɼʒ.
Oeᵭh .h. hínnɼechʒaıȝ, ɼí .h. Méʒ, ᵭo maɼbaᵭ ᵭo Uıᵭ
Niallaın.

Jctt. Gnaiɼ .ı. ɼ.; l. xııı.; bliaᵭaın aɼ ɼıchıʒ aɼ mile
aıɼ ın Ʒiȝeɼna. Maıᵭm ɼıa nUȝaıɼe mac Dúnlaınȝ,
ɼí Laıȝen, ɼoɼ Siʒɼıoc mac Cɱlaıᵭ, ɼí Cʒa cliaʒ ocon
Oeılȝne Moȝoɼóȝ. Íɼoıɼ cɼuıʒnechʒa ᵭo ɼeɼʒhaın ın
Oɼɼɼaıȝıᵭ ın hoc anno. Cɼeaʒ la mac Oeᵭa hı Neıll
ᵭaɼ Uıᵭ Doɼʒaınn. Ụaᵭaɼ a Muıȝ aʒechʒa, ocuɼ ɼo
maɼbʒaʒ ın leʒ ᵭeɼȝ ıconʒaıɼɼechʒ, coniᵭ ʒaiɼʒeᵭaɼ

<hr>

¹ *Tertia.* ʒeɼicıa (tercia), MS.

² *Crematæ.* cɼematʒe (crematte),
MS.

³ *Ui-mic-Uais.* The MS. has .h.
mıc Cuaıɼ (Ui-mic-Cuais), a form in
which the name is frequently written;
but the proper form is Ui-mic-Uais,
the tribe name of one line of the descendants of Colla Uais, king of Ireland in the 4th century.ⁿ The name

of Ui-mic-Uais is still preserved in
that of the barony of Moygoish, co.
Westmeath.

⁴ *Carbad-na-nAbadh* ; lit. " the
chariot of the Abbots."

⁵ *The 3rd.* C ʒeiɼʒ. These words
are preceded by the characters " ɼ̄ᶜ,"
which are probably an abbreviation
of the word ɼcıliceʒ (scilicet).

⁶ *Occisus.* Occissus, MS.

Maelmhuaidh, king of Feara-Ceall, who was taken out of it by force, and afterwards slain.

The kalends of January on the 6th feria, the 2nd of the moon; the age of the Lord twenty years and a thousand. Cill-dara, with its oratories, was burned. Glenn-da-locha, with its oratories, was burned. Cluain-Iraird, and Cluain-mic-Nois, and Sord-Choluim-Chille, tertia[1] parte crematæ[2] sunt. Flaithbhertach, grandson of Eochaidh, was blinded by Niall, son of Eochaidh. Gillaciarain, son of Oisen, king of Mughdhorna during the space of one day, was slain by the Ui-mic-Uais[3]-Bregh. Ard-Macha was altogether burned, viz.:—the great stone-church with its roof of lead; and the belfry with its bells, and the Sabhall, and the Toai, and Carbad-na-nAbadh,[4] and the old preaching chair, on the 3rd[5] of the kalends of June, the Monday before Whitsuntide. Maelmuire, son of Eochaidh, comarb of Patrick, head of the clerics of the entire West of Europe, in the 20th year of his government, on the 3rd of the nones of June, on Friday before Whitsuntide, in Christo quievit. Amhalghaidh *placed* in the comarbship of Patrick, with the consent of laity and clergy. Finnlaech, son of Ruaidhri, king of Alba, a suis occisus[6] est. Oedh Ua hInn-rechtaigh, king of Ui-Meth, was slain by the Ui-Niallain.

The kalends of January on the 1st feria, the 13th of the moon; the age of the Lord twenty-one years and a thousand. A victory by Ughaire, son of Dunlaing, king of Laighen, over Sitric, son of Amhlaibh, king of Ath-cliath, at Deilgne-Moghorog. A shower of wheat[7] was shed in Osraighe in hoc anno. A predatory excursion by the son of Oedh Ua Neill through Ui-Dortain; they were in Magh-atechta, and they killed the Lethderg[8]

---

[7] *Shower of Wheat.* The words cαοιτε cꞃuιτnechτα, signifying the same thing, are written in the margin.

[8] *Lethderg;* i.e. "the half-red." This seems to have been the agnomen of some chieftain of the Ui-Dortain; but the person meant has not been identified. The text of the clause is corrupt and not very intelligible.

.h. Méth, ocur Mugorna, ocur na Saitne, ocur rir
Fernmaide, ocur .h. Dortonn, cona ríguib. Ro bói dna
.h. Celechain ocur .h. Lorcain, con Uib mbrearrail,
ocur con Uib Niallain, ar a gcinn a noenach Maca, co
compangadar uile uime, co ruc mac Oeda a gabáil
tairrrib uile, ocur ni raibe acht dá .xxit. dhéc óglaech,
ocur do cer rochaide etorra ar lár Aird Maca;
ric in libro Duibdáleite. Dranacan .h. Moeluidir,
airre Mide, do marbad dia belltaine illoc Ainninn.
Aed mac Floinn mic Mailtrechlainn, rídamna Tempac,
ocur Domnall .h. Murchada, occiri runt.

Ktt. Enair .ii. r.; l. xxiiii.; dá bliadain ar xxit. ar
mile air in Tigerna. Mac Cerbaill, rí Eli, ocur
Domnall .h. Cellaig, rí Fotart, ocur Sitrec mac
Imair, ri Puirt Lairge, occiri runt. Macleiginn
mac Cairill, rí Oirgiall, ocur Flann .h. Tadcáin,
airchinnech Dermaide, ocur Lachtnán comarba Innri
cainnega, in Cristo dormierunt; in Ard Maca adbat.
Moeilrechlainn mór mac Domnaill, airdrig Erenn,
tuir ordain ocur oirechuir iarthair domuin, do ég ir in
trerr bliadain .xl. regni rui, ir in trer bliadain .lxx.
aetatir ruae, in .iiii. a nonar Septembrir, die uidelicet
dominico, recunda lúnae.

Murcomrac rorran Ufairrge etir Gulla Ata cliac
ocur Niall mac Eochada, rí Ulad, gur ro muig ror na
Gallaib, ocur gur láad a nderg ár, ocur gur ro doerta

---

1 *Ua Celechain.* h. Celechair
(Ua Celechair), MS.; but this is a
mistake, as the ruling family at this
period in Ui-Breasail, (now the bar.
of O'Neilland East, co. Armagh),
was that of Ua Celechain, or O'Cal-
laghan.

2 *In libro Dubh-da-leithe.* This
book is also quoted in the Ann. Ult.,
under the years 962 and 1021. It is
supposed to have been compiled by
Dubhdaleithe, abbot of Armagh, whose

death is recorded in the Chron. Scotorum under the year 1061=1063.
Nothing else is known regarding the
book at present.

3 *Murchadh;* i.e. Murchadh Glun-
ilair, king of the Northern Hy-Neill,
who was slain in the year 972=974,
according to the Chron. Scotorum.

4 *He,* i.e. Lachtnan, the last mentioned of the three.

5 *Of his Reign.* regni rui, MS.
King Maelsechlainn (or Malachy) II.

in a conflict, but the Ui-Meith, and the Mughdhorna, and the Saithne, and the men of Fernmhagh, and the Ui-Dorton, with their kings, overtook them. Ua Cele-chain[1] and Ua Lorcain, with the Ui-Breasail and Ui-Niallain, were, moreover, before them in Oenach-Macha, so that they all surrounded him; but the son of Oedh Ua Neill carried his preys through them all, and he had only twelve score warriors; and many were slain be-tween them in the middle of Ard-Macha. Sic in libro Dubh-da-leithe.[2] Brannacan Ua Maeluidhir, a chief of Midhe, was slain on May-day in Loch-Ainninn. Aedh, son of Flann, son of Maelsechlainn, royal heir of Temhair, and Domhnall, grandson of Murchadh,[3] occisi sunt.

The kalends of January on the 2nd feria, the 24th of the moon; the age of the Lord twenty-two years and a thousand. The son of Cerbhall, king of Eile, and Domhnall Ua Ceallaigh, king of Fotharta, and Sitric, son of Imhar, king of Port-Lairge, occisi sunt. Macleighinn, son of Cairell, king of Oirghiall, and Flann Ua Tadhgain, airchinnech of Dermhagh, and Lachtnan, comarb of Inis-cain-Degha, in Christo dormicrunt; in Ard-Macha he[4] died. Maelsechlainn the Great, son of Domhnall, supremo king of Erinn, pillar of the dignity and nobility of the west of the world, died in the 43rd year of his reign,[5] in the 73rd year of his age,[6] on the 4th of the nones of Sep-tember,[7] viz. :—on Sunday, the 2nd of the moon.[8]

A naval battle on the sea, between the foreigners of Ath-cliath and Niall, son of Eochaidh, king of Uladh; and the foreigners were defeated, and slaughtered; and some of

obtained the sovereignty of Ireland in A.D. 980, and reigned until the year 1002, when he was deposed by Brian Boromha, after whose death, in 1014, Malachy resumed the sovereignty, which he held until his demise. The chronicles generally include the 12 years of Brian's usurpation in the regnal period of Malachy, thus in-dicating their opinion of the illegiti-macy of Brian's title to the sovereignty.

[6] *Of his age.* etatir ꞃua (etatis sua), MS.

[7] *Of September.* Septimbꞃiꞃ (Sep-timbris), MS.

[8] *The 2nd of the moon.* ꞃ. Luna, MS.; the ꞃ. being probably a mistake for ꞃ, an abbrev. for ꞃecunꝺa.

αpoile τíᵬ αꝑᴄena. Muιꝑᴄeꝑᴛαᴄ .h. Cαꝑꝑα, ꝑíᵬamna Ceṁꝑαch, vo ṁαꝑbαv on ᵹuᴄ .ι. la Moeιlꝑeᴄlaιnn. Maιᵬm α Sleιᵬ Fuαιv ꝑoꝑ αιꝑᵹιalla, la Nιall maᴄ Θoᴄαvα, ᵹuꝑ ᴄuιꝑeᵬ veꝑᵹ αꝑ Oιꝑᵹιall ann. Maᴛᵹαmaιn maᴄ Laιᵹnén, ꝑí Feꝑnmαιve, vo maꝑbαᵬ vo ᴄαᴛhal .h. Cꝑíᴄán ꝑoꝑ láꝑ Cluana Θoαιꝑ.

ⱪᴄᴛ. Θnáιꝑ .ιιι. ꝑ.; L. .ιι.; ᴛꝑι blιavna .xx.eᴛ αꝑ mιle αιꝑ ιn Cιᵹeꝑna. Θꝑᴄꝑα ι .xιιιι. eꝑᵹαι Ienáιꝑ, .ιιιι. ᴛo Θnáιꝑ, vια Ꝺαꝑvaoιn; eꝑᴄꝑα ᵹꝑéιne, ιmoꝑꝑo, ι .xxιιι. an éꝑᴄαι ᴄevna, vια Ꝺαꝑvaoιn, ᴄιnn ᴄoeιᴄιᵬιꝑ, ι nóι ⱪᴄᴛ. [Feᵬꝑα]. Ꝺomnall maᴄ Oevha bιᵹ hí Máιlꝑeᴄlaιnn vo ṁαꝑᵬαv o maᴄ Senán .h. leoᴄán. Ꝺonnᴄhαv .h. Ꝺuιnn, ꝑí ᵬꝑeᵹ, vo ᵹαᵬáιl vo ᵹallaιb ιna naιꝑeᴄhᴛ ꝑéιn, oᴄuꝑ α ᵬꝑeιᴛ ᴛαꝑ muιꝑ. loᴄlaιnn maᴄ Maιlꝑeᴄlaιnn vo maꝑbαv α ꝑuιꝑ. Cαᵬᴄ maᴄ ᵬꝑιaιn vo maꝑbαv o Θιlιᵬ. Conᴄhobαꝑ .h. Cαꝑꝑα vo maꝑbαv lαꝑ na ᵹuᴛa. leoᵬaιlιn, ꝑι ᵬꝑeαᴛᴛan, vo·éᵹ. Oenꝑeᴄ, ꝑι an vomaιn, vo éᴄ ιn pαᴄe; vαꝑ α éιꝑꝑι ꝑo ᵹαᵬ ꝑιᵹe an vomaιn .ι. Cuana. Ꝺomnall .h. hΘᵹꝑα, ꝑí luιᵹne Connaᴄhᴛ, vo maꝑbαv lá .h. Conᴄobαιꝑ .ι. ꝑí Connaᴄhᴛ.

ⱪᴄᴛ. Θnαιꝑ .ιιιι. ꝑ.; L. xuι.; ᴄeιᴛꝑι blιavna xx.eᴛ αꝑ mιle αιꝑ ιn Cιᵹeꝑna. Uᵹaιꝑe maᴄ Ꝺunlaιnᵹ, ꝑí laιᵹen, oᴄuꝑ Moelmoꝑᵬa maᴄ loꝑᴄáιn, ꝑí.h. Cιnnꝑelaιᵹh; ᴛeαᴄ vo ᵹαᵬáιl ꝑoꝑꝑa αᵹ Ꝺuᵬloᴄ la Ꝺonnꝑleιᵬe maᴄ Maolmóꝑᵬa, ꝑι. h. ᵬFaoláιn, oᴄuꝑ α ᴛuιᴛιm ann. Ꝺonnꝑléιbe ꝑeιn vo maꝑᵬαᵬ ᵹo ᵹαꝑ ιαꝑꝑιn la híᵬ Muιꝑeᵹhaιᵹh. Cαᴄ αᵬa na ᴄꝑoιꝑꝑι α Coꝑann, evιꝑ .h. Moelvoꝑαιᵬ .ι. ꝑí Ceneoιll Conaιll, oᴄuꝑ .h. Ruaιꝑᴄ, ᵹuꝑ ꝑo ṁuιᵹ ꝑoꝑ

---

¹ *The Guth,* i.e. the stammerer, a nickname of Maelsechlain, which attached to his descendants. See under the years 1023 and 1025.

² *The 2nd.* Read 5th; the 11 of the MS being a palpable mistake for υ.

³ *Eclipse;* i.e. an eclipse of the Moon. Vid. *L'Art de verif. les Dates,* tom. I., pag. 71.

⁴ *The Guths.* See note ¹.

⁵ *Leobhailin.* leoᵬαιlιm (Leobhailim), MS. Llewellyn, or Llywelyn, son of Seisil, is meant, whose death is entered in the *Annales Cambriæ* under the year 1023, but in *Brut y Tywysogion* at the year 1021.

⁶ *Oenric;* i.e. the Emperor Henry II.

⁷ *Cuana.* The Emperor Conrad II.

them were enslaved, moreover. Muirchertach, grandson of
Carra, royal heir of Temhair, was slain by the Guth,[1] *i.e.*
by Maelsechlainn. A victory was gained at Sliabh-Fuaid,
over the Airghialla, by Niall, son of Eochaidh; and a
terrible slaughter of the Airghialla was committed there
Mathghamhain, son of Laighnén, king of Fernmhagh, was
slain by Cathal Ua Crichain, in the middle of Cluain-Eois.

The kalends of January on the 3rd feria, the 2nd[2] of the
moon; the age of the Lord twenty-three years and
a thousand. An eclipse[3] on the 14th of the January
moon, the 4th of the ides of January, on Thursday. An
eclipse of the sun, also, on the 27th of the same moon, on
Thursday, at the end of a fortnight, on the ninth of the
kalends [of February] Domhnall, son of Oedh Bec Ua
Maelsechlainn, was slain by the son of Senan Ua
Leochain. Donnchadh Ua Duinn, king of Bregha,
was apprehended by the Foreigners, in their own assembly, and taken beyond the sea. Lochlainn, son
of Maelsechlainn, was slain a suis. Tadhg, son of
Brian, was slain by the Eile. Conchobhar, grandson of Carra, was killed by the Guths.[4] Leobhailin,[5]
king of Britain, died. Oenric,[6] king of the world, died
in pace; after him Cuana[7] assumed the sovereignty
of the world. Domhnall Ua hEghra, king of Luighne
of Connacht, was slain by Ua Conchobhair, *i.e.* the king
of Connacht.

The kalends of January on the 4th feria, the 16th
of the moon; the age of the Lord twenty-four years
and a thousand. Ugaire, son of Dunlaing, king of
Laighen, and Maelmordha, son of Lorcan, king of Ui-
Ceinnsealaigh, had a house captured against them, at
Dubhloch, by Donnsleibhe, son of Maelmordha, king of
Ui-Faelain, and they fell there. Donnsleibhe was himself
slain, soon afterwards, by the Ui-Muiredhaigh. The battle
of Ath-na-croisi, in Corann, between Ua Maeldoraidh, *i.e.*
king of Cenel-Conaill, and Ua Ruairc; when Ua Ruairc was

.h. Ruairc, gur ro láadh derg ár fer mBreiffne ocus Connacht la Cenel Conaill. Cúan .h. Lóċáin .i. príṁéigess Erenn, do ṁarbaḋ lá Teṫḃa. Do ríġne Dia firt fileḋ co follus ar an lucht ro ṁarḃ, óir ro bássaiged a ndroċ oighed iad, ocus ni ro haḋnuiced a cuirp gur ḟoġuil foeil ocus foluámain iad. Domnall mac Aoḋa, ríḋaṁna Oiliġ, do marḃaḋ do Ġilla ṁúgra mac ógáin. Maoldúin .h. Concaille, rí .h. Niallain, do marbad do Uíḃ Dorṫaind. Moelruanaiḋ .h. Ciarḋa .i. rí Cairpri, a suis occisus est. Crech la mac hI Neill, gur ro ort .h. Méth ocus .h. Dorṫainn.

Kll. Enáir .ui. f.; l. ii.; coic bliadna .xx. ar mile air in Tigerna. Muiredhach mac Mugróin, comarba Ciaráin; Maoileoin .h. Toráin, comarba Doire, [dormierunt]. Niall .h. Conchobair, ríḋamna Connacht; Geirgaola, rí Bregh, occisi sunt. Moeilsecluinn Got, rí Miḋe, do éc. Sloiged la Flaiṫbertach .h. Néill a mBreaghaib ocus a nGallaiḃ, co ṫuc gialla Goeideal ó Gallaiḃ. Creaċ la Cathalán, rí Fernmaide, for feruiḃ Manach. Creaċ la fira Manach fó cédóir co Loċ nUaiṫne, gur ro loiscset, ocus gur ro marḃsat .uii. bfir dhég for brú an loċa. Termonn Feiċín do argain do Caṫalán .h. Criċán.

Kll. Enair .uii. f.; l. xui.; sé bliadna. xx. ar mile air in Tigerna. Sloiged la mac Briain a Miḋe, ocus a mBreaghaib, go Gollaib ocus go Laiġnib, ocus go

---

[1] *Terrible Slaughter.* derg ár; lit. "red slaughter."

[2] *Died.* ro bássaiged; lit. "were put to death."

[3] *Gillamughra.* In the Ann. Ult. and Four Mast. the name is written Gillamura, or "servant of Mura," which is probably the correct form, as the name was apparently derived from St. Mura of Othan, or Fahan, co. Donegal.

[4] *Sixth feria.* The MS. has uii (7th); but this is clearly a mistake, as the feriæ for the four preceding years were respectively, 1, 2, 3, and 4, and the year 1024 being a leap year, the 1st of January in the year 1025 fell on the 6th feria, or Friday.

[5] *The 2nd.* This is wrong. The Ann. Ult. correctly read xxuii (27).

[6] *Which;* i.e. the habitation on the lake. Loch-Uaithne, now called Lough-Ooney, is near the village of

defeated, and a terrible slaughter[1] of the men of Breifne and Connacht was committed by the Cenel-Conaill. Cuan Ua Lochain, *i.e.* the chief poet of Erinn, was slain by *the men of* Tethfa. God performed a "poet's miracle," manifestly, on the party that killed him, for they died[2] an evil death, and their bodies were not buried until wolves and birds preyed upon them. Domhnall, son of Aedh, royal heir of Oilech, was slain by Gillamughra,[3] son of Ogan. Maelduin Ua Conchaille, king of Ui-Niallain, was killed by the Ui-Dorthainn, Maelruanaidh Ua Ciardha, *i.e.* king of Cairpre, a suis occisus est. A predatory expedition by the son of Ua Neill, so that he ravaged Ui-Meth and Ui-Dorthainn.

[1025.] The kalends of January on the 6th feria,[4] the 2nd[5] of the moon; the age of the Lord twenty-five years and a thousand. Muiredhach, son of Mughron, comarb of Ciaran; Maeleoin Ua Torain, comarb of Doire, [dormierunt]. Niall Ua Conchobhair, royal heir of Connacht; Geirgaela, king of Bregha, occisi sunt. Mael-sechlainn Got, king of Midhe, died. A hosting by Flaithbhertach Ua Neill into Bregha, and to the Foreigners, and he took the hostages of the Gaeidhel from the Foreigners. A predatory expedition by Cathalan, king of Fernmhagh, against the Feara-Manach. A predatory expedition by the Feara-Manach, immediately after, to Loch-nUaithne, which[6] they burned, and they slew seventeen men on the margin of the lake. Termon-Feichin was plundered by Cathalan Ua Crichain.

[1026.] The kalends of January on the 7th feria,[7] the 16th[8] of the moon; the age of the Lord twenty-six years and a thousand. A hosting by the son of Brian[9] into Midhe and Bregha, and to the Foreigners[10] and Lagenians, and

---

Smithsborough, in the barony of Dartry, co. Monaghan. The chiefs of Dartraighe-Coininnse, or Dartry, had their principal residence at this lake, whence they were sometimes called "lords of Loch-Uaithne."

[7] *Seventh feria*; �misᴜ. ꝑ. (4th feria),

MS.; but the numerals ᴜ are by mistake for ᴜ.

[8] *The* 16*th.* *Rectè* 9th, as in the Ann. Ult.

[9] *Son of Brian;* i.e. Donnchadh.

[10] *Foreigners.* The foreigners of Dublin are here meant.

hOrrραιζιb, ζο ρυc α ηζιαλλα. Slóιζeδ λα Flαιτbερταch
.h. Neιλλ α Mιδe, ζο τυc α ηζιαλλα, ocυρ ζοηδeαchαιδ
ρορ λeιc οιζριδ α ηιηιρ Mochτα, ζυρ ρο ιηδιρ αη ιηιρ.
Slóιζheδ λα mαc Eochαδα ιριη úαιρ ceδηα ζο Ζυλλαιb,
ζυρ ρο λοιρc, ocυρ co τυc bροιδ mορ υαιδιδ, ocυρ ρeoδα
δίρίήé. Moeλρυαηαιδh .h. Mαολδοραιδh δο δυλ ιηα
αιλιτρι. Αιmeρζιη .h. Mόρδα, ρί λαιζρι, ιητeρρecτυρ
eρτ. Feαλλ λα Domnαλλ .h. Ceλλαιζ ρορ Mυιρeδhαch
.h. Céλe, ζυρ ρο mαρδ ιηα αιρeαchτ ρeιριη.

Kʟ. Eηαιρ ι. ρ.; λ. xx; ρeαchτ mbλιαδηα .xx. αρ mιλe
[αιρ ιη Τιζeρηα]. Rιαιορι mαc Foζαρταιζ, ρί δeιρceρτ
Ͳρeζ, δο éζ ιη αιλιτρι. Ταδc mαc Ζιλλα Ρατραιζ δο
δαλλαδ λα ρί Ορρραιζe .ι. Donnchαδ mαc Ζιλλα Ραδραιζ.
Slόιζeδ λα mαc Ͳριαιη αη Ορρραιζιδ, ζυρ ρο λάρατ Ορρ-
ραιζeάρ α mυιηητeρι ιm Dόζρα mαc nDunchαδα, ocυρ ιm
Domnαλλ mαc Senčάιη, ocυρ ιm ρochαιδe mόιρ αιρčeηα.
Cατčαλάη .h. Cριočάη, ρί Feρnmαιδe, ocυρ Cúλoča .h.
Ζαιρčéιč, ρί .h. Méιč, δο comčυιτιm λeροιλe α ηιρζαιλ.
Cρeč λα Céηeλ nEoζαιη α nUλλτοιb, co τυcρατ bόρομα mόιρ
λeό. Dún Cυιλλιηδ α nΑλbαιη δο υιλe λορcαδ ιη hoc αηηo.

Kʟ. Eηαιρ .ιι. ρ.; λ. ι.; ochτ mbλιαδηα xx.et αρ mιλe
αιρ ιη Τιζeρηα. Ταδc mαc Echαch, αιρchιηηech Cιλλ
Dάλúα; Ͳριαη .h. Cončoͳαιρ, ocυρ Cορηάη .h. Ruαιρc,
ocυρ Flαιčbeρταč .h. hEραδάιη, ocυρ Cončoͳαρ mαc
Eochαδα, occιρι ρυητ. Moeλmochτα, ρί bρeρ Roιρ, o
Conαιλλιb occιρυρ ρυηeρτ. Oρζαιη Dαιmλιαζ λα ριηα
Mαηαch. Mαc Concυαιζηe, ρί hí nEchαch, δο éc.
Sιτρeαc mαc Αήλαιδ, ρί Ζαλλ, ocυρ Flαηηάζαη .h.

---

1 *Doghra.* The name is also thus
written in the Annals of Ulster; but
in Tighernach, the Chron. Scotorum,
and the Four Mast., it is written
" Gadhra, son of Dunadhach," which
is probably the correct form.

2 *Dun-Cuillind;* i.e. Dunkeld.

3 *Occisi.* occιρρι, MS.

4 *Was slain.* occιρρι r̄c, MS.;
a mere blunder of the scribe. The
Annals of Ulster, the contents of
which are at this period almost iden-

tical with the entries in the present
chronicle, have o. e. for "occisus est."

5 *Son.* The MS. has m̄. m̄. for
"mαc mαιc" ("son of the son,")
with which the Annals of Ulster
agree; but this is a mistake, as the
Sitric in question was the son of
Amhlaibh, Amlaff, or Olaf (son of
another Sitric), who was slain in
Munster in 1013. See Todd's *Danish
Wars,* p. 288, note 16.

Osraighe, and he carried off their pledges. A hosting by Flaithbhertach Ua Neill into Midhe, whose pledges he took; and he went over the ice into Inis-Mochta, so that he plundered the island. A hosting by the son of Eochaidh, at the same time, to the Foreigners; and he burned *their territory* and carried off from them a great spoil, and countless jewels. Maelruanaidh Ua Maeldoraidh went on his pilgrimage. Aimhergin Ua Mordha, king of Laighis, interfectus est. Muiredhach Ua Céle was betrayed by Domhnall Ua Ceallaigh, who slew him in his own assembly.

The kalends of January on the 1st feria, the 20th of the moon; [the age of the Lord] twenty-seven years and a thousand. Ruaidhri, son of Fogartach, king of the South of Bregha, died in pilgrimage. Tadhg Mac Gillapatraic was blinded by the king of Osraighe, *i.e.* Donnchadh Mac Gillapatraic. A hosting by the son of Brian into Osraighe, when the Osraighe committed a slaughter of his people, including Doghra,[1] son of Dunchadh, and Domhnall, son of Senchan, and a great multitude besides. Cathalan Ua Crichain, king of Fernmhagh, and Culocha Ua Gairbheith, king of Ui-Meith, fell by each other in a conflict. A predatory expedition by the Cenel-Eoghain into Ulidia, and they brought with them a great prey of cows. Dún-Cuillind,[2] in Alba, was altogether burned in hoc anno.

The kalends of January on the 2nd feria, the first of the moon; the age of the Lord twenty-eight years and a thousand. Tadhg, son of Eochaidh, airchinnech of Cill-Dalua, *died.* Brian Ua Conchobhair, and Cornán Ua Ruairc, and Flaithbhertach Ua hEradhain, and Conchobhar, son of Eochaidh, occisi[3] sunt. Maelmochta, king of Feara-Ross, was slain[4] by the Conaille. Plundering of Daimhliag by the Feara-Manach. The son of Cu-Cuailgne, king of Ui-Echach, died. Sitric, son[5] of Amhlaibh, king of the Foreigners, and Flannagan Ua Ceallaigh, king of Bregha,

Cellαιᵹ, ʀí Ḃʀeᵹ, ᴅo ᴅul ᴅo Róıṁ. Cʀeć lá Cénel
Eoᵹaın a τíʀ Conaıll, co τucʀaτ ᵹaḃála moʀa leó.

Ḱττ. Enáıʀ ıııı. ꝼ.; ʟ. xıı.; noı mḃlıaᴅna .xx. aʀ mıle
aıʀ ın Τıᵹeʀna. ᴅonnꝛleıḃe .h. Ḃʀoᵹaʀḃáın, ʀí .h.
ḃꝼaılᵹe, a ꝛuıꝛ occıꝛuʀ eʀτ. ᴅonnchaᴅ .h. ᴅonnacáın,
ʀí Ꝼeʀnmaıᴅe, ocuꝛ mac hı Ᵹeıʀʀce, ʀí Conaılle, ᴅo
comτuıτım a Cıll Sleıḃe. Ḃʀıan .h. Conchoḃaıʀ,
ʀíᴅamna Connachτ, a ꝛuıꝛ occıꝛuʀ eʀτ. Oeᴅh .h.
Ruaıʀc ocuʀ Oenᵹuꝛ .h. hᴁonᵹuꝛa, ocuʀ aıʀchınnech
ᴅʀoma clıaḃ, ocuʀ τʀı ꝼıćτ ᴅuıne elı ᴅo loꝛcaᴅ
maılle ꝼʀıu, a nınᴅıʀ na laınne. Muıʀceʀτach .h.
Canannán, no .h. Maolᴅoʀaıḃ, ᴅo maʀbaᴅ ᴅo Uıḃ
Canannán. Aṁlaıḃ mac Sıτʀec, ʀí Ᵹall, ᴅo eʀᵹaḃáıl
ᴅo Maťᵹaṁaın·.h. Rıaᵹáın, ʀí Ḃʀeaᵹ, ᵹo ḃꝼaʀᵹaıḃ ᴅa
ceᴅ ᴅhéᵹ ḃo, ocuʀ .ıı. xxτ eoć mḃʀeτnach, ocuʀ τʀı
xxτ uınᵹe ᴅo óʀ, ocuʀ cloıᴅem Caʀluꝛa, ocuʀ aıτıʀe
ᵹaoıᴅel eᴅıʀ Laıᵹnıḃ ocuʀ leτ Cuınn, ocuʀ τʀı ꝼıćτ
uıncce ᴅaıʀᵹeᴅ ᵹıl ına huınᵹe ᵹeıṁlıᴅe. Maolcoluım
mac Maılḃʀíᵹᴅe, mıc Ruaıᴅʀı, ocuʀ Maolḃʀıᵹᴅe .h.
Ḃʀolćáın, ꝛʀíṁ τꝛaoʀ Eʀenn na aımꝛıʀ, moʀτuı ꝛunτ.

Ḱττ. Enaıʀ .u. ꝼ.; ʟ .xxııı.; τʀíća ḃlıaᴅna aʀ mıle aıʀ
ın Τıᵹeʀna. Ꝼlaıτḃeʀτach ᴅo τeachτ o Róıṁ. Aʀᴅ
mḃʀeacáın ᴅo loꝛcaᴅ ocuʀ ᴅaʀᵹaın ᴅo Ᵹallaıḃ Aťa
clıaḃ, ocuʀ ᴅa ceᴅ ᴅuıne ᴅo loꝛcaᴅ ıꝛın ᴅaıṁlıaᵹ, ocuʀ
ᴅa ceᴅ elı ᴅo ḃʀeıḋ amḃꝛoıᴅ. Cıll ᴅaʀa ᴅo loꝛcaᴅ
τꝛe anḃꝼaıτćeꝛꝛ mná. Sloıᵹeᴅ la mac Eochaᴅa co

---

[1] *Son of Ua Geirrche.* He is called
"Cinaeth," or Kenneth, in Tighernach and the Four Mast.; but in the
latter Annals the name Ua Geirrche
is incorrectly written "Angeirrce."

[2] *Oengus.* The MS. has Oenᵹuꝛo
(Oenguso), the gen. form of the
name.

[3] *Ua Maeildoraidh.* This is the
correct name according to the other
Irish Chronicles in which the event

is recorded. Tighernach adds that
Muirchertach Ua Maeildoraidh, or
O'Muldory, was "king of Cenel-
Conaill."

[4] *Fetter ounce.* uınᵹe ᵹeıṁlıᴅe
(uinge geimhlidhe). The Irish word
geimhel, or *geimhen* pron. *géven* (bonds,
fetters), from which *geimhlidhe* is
formed, seems to be the origin of the
English word *gyves.*

[5] *Flaithbhertach;* i.e. Flaithbhertach

went to Rome. A preying expedition' by the Cenel-Eoghain into Tir Conaill, when they carried off great spoils.

The kalends of January on the 4th feria, the 12th of the moon; the age of the Lord twenty-nine years and a thousand. Donnsleibhe Ua Brogarbhain, king of Ui-Failghe, a suis occisus est. Donnchadh Ua Donnacain, king of Fernmhagh, and the son of Ua Geirrche,[1] king of Conaille, fell by each other at Cill-sleibhe. Brian Ua Conchobhair, royal heir of Connacht, a suis occisus est. Oedh Ua Ruairc, and Oengus[2] Ua hAenghusa, and the airchinnech of Druim-cliabh, and sixty other persons along with them, were burned in Inis-na-lainne. Muirchertach Ua Canannain, or Ua Maeldoraidh,[3] was slain by the Ui-Canannain. Amhlaibh, son of Sitric, king of the Foreigners, was taken prisoner by Mathghamhain Ua Riagain, king of Bregha, until he (*Amhlaibh*) gave twelve hundred cows, and six score British horses, and three score ounces of gold, and the sword of Carlus, and the hostages of the Gaeidhel, both of Laighen and Leth-Chuinn; and three scores ounces of white silver, as his fetter ounce.[4] Maelcoluim, son of Maelbrighde, son of Ruaidhri, and Maelbrighde Ua Brolchain, chief artificer of Erinn in his time, mortui sunt.

The kalends of January on the 5th feria, the 23rd of the moon; the age of the Lord thirty years and a thousand. Flaithbhertach[5] came from Rome. Ard-Breacain was burned and plundered by the Foreigners of Ath-cliath, and two hundred men were burned in the stone-church, and two hundred more carried off in captivity. Cill-dara was burned through the negligence of a woman. A hosting by the son of Eochaidh to

---

O'Neill, called " an trostain " " of the [pilgrim's] staff," from his pilgrimage to Rome. There is probably an error in the text, however, as the other

Irish Chronicles record Flaithbhertach's departure for Rome in this year, and his return therefrom in the succeeding year.

Telaiġ noc, ocur nocha ʋtáppaiġ ní. Eochaʋh .h. Cethenén, comapba Tiġepnaiġ, ápʋ ṕoí Epenn an eġna, a nApʋ Macha quieuit. Taʋc an eit́ ġil mac Cathail mic Conchobaip, .i. aippiġ Connacht, ocur an ġot, pi Miʋe, occipi ṕunt. Ruaiʋpi .h. Canannan ʋo mapbaʋ la hOeʋ Ua Néill. Taʋc .h. Lopcáin, pí .h. Cennrelaiġ, ʋo éġ ina ailitri a nġlinn ʋa laċa. Cú ṁapa mac Mic Liaġ, apʋ ollam Epenn, ʋo ʋul ʋéc.

[Ctt. Enaip .ui. p.; l. iiii.; bliaʋain ap tríċa ocur mile aip in Tiġepna. Oeʋh .h. Neill ʋo ċocht ṕluaġ mór atimćell mic Eochaʋa ṕoip, co tuc tri ṁíle ʋo ḃuaiḃ, ocur ʋá ceʋ ap ṁíle ʋo ḃpoiʋ. Sloiġeʋ la mac Eochaʋa a níḃ Echach, ġup po loircret Cill Combaip cona ʋepċoiġ, ocur ġup po mapb seṫ́ap ʋo cleipchaib, ocur ġo puc tríċa ʋo ḃpoiʋ. Sloiġeʋ la mac Ḃpiain an Oppṕaiġib, ġup po láḃ áp a ṁuinntipe im Maolcoluim Caonpaiġech, et alii multi. Caʋuṫ́aċ, comapba Caoimġin, ʋo ḃallaʋ la Ʋomnall mac Ʋunlaing. Cpeaċ int ṕneachta la hOeʋ [Ua] Neill a típ Conaill, ġup po ṁapḃ .h. Canannán, pi Cineoil Conaill. O Ʋonnacán, pí Apaʋ ṫ́ípe, ʋo mapbaʋ la .h. mḂpiain .i. Toippʋhelbach.

[Ctt. Enaip .uii. p.; l. xu.; ʋá bliaʋain .xx. ocur mile aip in Tiġepna. Maṫ́ġaṁain .h. Riaġain, pi Ḃpeaġ, ʋo mapbaʋ ʋo Ʋomnall .h. Ceallaiġ, per ʋolum. Ġilla Comġáin mac Maolbpíġʋe, mop ṁáop Muipebe, ʋo loipcaʋ co coecait ʋo ʋoeinḃ imme. Ʋoṁnall .h. Maolʋopaʋ, pi Ceneoil Conaill, ʋ'ṕaġḃail ḃáip an bliaʋain pin. Mac Maṫ́ġaṁna mic Muipeġhaigh, pi Ciappaiġhe, ocur Ʋonnġal mac Ʋuinncothaiġ, pí

₁ *Tadhg-an-eich-ghil;* lit. "Tadhg (Thady, or Thaddeus), of the white steed."

₂ *Died.* ʋo ʋul ʋéc; lit. "went to death."

₃ *Around the son of Eochaidh.* This

is another mode of saying that Oedh marched round the territory of the son of Eochaidh, i.e. Ulidia.

₄ *The son of Brian;* i.e. Donnchadh, son of Brian Boromha.

₅ *Caenraighech.* This is an epithet

Telach-og, but he obtained nothing. Eochaidh Ua Cethenén,
comarb of Tighernach, chief sage of Erinn in wisdom,
in Ard-Macha quievit. Tadhg-an-eich-ghil,[1] son of Cathal,
son of Conchobhar, *i.e.* chief king of Connacht, and the Got,
king of Midhe, occisi sunt. Ruaidhri Ua Canannain was
slain by Oedh Ua Neill. Tadhg Ua Lorcain, king of Ui-
Ccinnsealaigh, died on his pilgrimage at Glenn-da-locha.
Cumhara, son of Mac-Liag, chief poet of Erinn, died.[2]

The kalends of January on the 6th feria, the 4th of [1031.]
the moon; the age of the Lord thirty-one years and a
thousand. Oedh Ua Neill went with a large army eastwards, around the son of Eochaidh,[3] when he carried off
three thousand cows, and one thousand and two hundred
captives. A hosting by the son of Eochaidh into Ui-
Echach, when they burned Cill-Combair with its oratory,
and killed forty clerics, and carried off thirty captives.
A hosting by the son of Brian[4] into Osraighe, when
a slaughter of his people was committed, including
Maelcoluim Caenraighech,[5] et alii multi. Cathusach,
comarb of Caeimhghen, was blinded by Domhnall, son
of Dunlaing. "The prey of the snow"[6] by Aedh [Ua]
Neill, in Tir-Conaill, when he killed Ua Canannain, king
of Cenel-Conaill. O'Donnagain, king of Aradh-thire, was
slain by Ua Briain, *i.e.* Toirdhealbhach.

The kalends of January on the 7th feria, the 15th of [1032.]
the moon; the age of the Lord thirty-two years and
a thousand. Mathghamhain Ua Riagain, king of Bregha,
was slain by Domhnall Ua Ceallaigh, per dolum. Gilla-
comghain, son of Maelbrighde, great steward of Murebhe,[7]
was burned, together with fifty persons. Domhnall Ua
Maeldoraidh, king of Cenel-Conaill, died in this year.
The son of Mathghamhain, son of Muiredhach, king of
Ciarraighe, and Donnghal, son of Donncothaigh, king of

signifying "of Caenraighe," or Kenry,
a district now forming the barony of
Kenry, in the co. of Limerick.

[6] *Prey of the snow.* So called from

the quantity of snow that fell during
the expedition.

[7] *Murebhe;* i.e. Moray, in Scotland.
The name is written mebe in the MS.

D

ζαιλεηζ, occiρι ρuητ. Eττρú .h. Coηαιηζ, ριδαμηα Muμαη, occiρuρ eρτ o ṁuiηητeρ Iμλecha. Μαιδṁ Όρομμα δeηδcaiρ ροη Uλλταιb ρια ηΑιρζιαλλα. Μαιδṁ ιηbeρ Bóiηηe ρια Sιτρec μαc Αṁλαιδ, ροη Coηαιλλιδ, ocuρ ροη Uιδ Όορτ̇uiηη, ocuρ ροη Uιδ Μέιch, iη ρο λάδ iηηáρ. Μoeλτuiλe, eρροζ Αιρδ Μαcha, iη Cρiρτo [quieuiτ]. Αodh .h. Ρuρρeiδ δο ζαbáiλ ηα heρροcóiδe iαρρiη.

Κtt. eηáiρ .ii. ρ.; l. αx.uii.; τρι bλιαδηα τρícα αρ ṁíλe áiρ iη Τιζeρηα. Μαιδṁ ρια Μuρchaδ .h. Μαiλτρecλαiηη ροη Coηcobaρ .h. Μáiλρecλαiηη, ζuρ ρuρ μαρbαδ Μαoλρuαηαiδ Ua Caρρα Caλμα, ocuρ Loρcáη .h. Caoiηδeλbáiη, ρι Loeζuiρe, eτ αλii μuλτι. Coηcobaρ .h. Μuiρeζhaiζh, ρí Ciaρρaiζhe, occiρuρ eρτ. Αoηαch Caρμαη λα Όoηηchaδ μαc ζιλλαραδραiζ, iaρ ηζαbáiλ ρiζe λaiζheη δό. Αimeρζiη .h. Ceρbαiλλ, ρi Eλi, [ocuρ] Cuṁuμαη μαc Ruaiδρi hi Ceδρaδα, μορτui ρuητ. Μαiδṁ λé heiλe, i τoρcραδαρ Βραoη hUa Cleiρiζ, ocuρ Μuiρeδach μαc μιc ζιλλαραραiζ, eτ αλii μuλτι. Scρíη Ρeδαiρ ocuρ Ρóiλ αζ τeρeρρiη ρoλa ροη αλτóiρ Ραδραιc i ηΑρδ Μacha, coρam omηibuρ uiδeητibuρ. Oeδh μαc Ρλαiτ̇beρταiζ hi Neiλλ, ρí Oiλiζ, ocuρ ριδαμηα Eρeηη, ροητ ρeηiτeητiam μορτuuρ eρτ, oiδ̇ce ρéλe Αiηδρiaρ. Αodh O Neiλλ μορτuuρ eρτ.

Κtt. eηαiρ iii. ρ.; l. uii.; ceτρι bλιαδηα τρícα αρ ṁíλe áiρ iη Τιζeρηα. Μαoλcoλuiμ μαc Ciηαoδα, ρι Αλbaη,

---

1 Occisi. occιρι, MS.

2 Occisus. ococciρρuρ, MS.

3 Community. μuiηητeρ (muinn-ter.) This word generally signifies "people," but, as here, frequently denotes a monastic family or community. In this sense Mr. Whitley Stokes has compared it with the N. H. Germ. münster, Eng. minster. See Goidilica; Calcutta, 1866, p. 31.

4 Grandson. The MS. has mac "son;" but this is probably a mistake, as Carra (or Carrach) Calma, "Carrach the powerful," was slain in 967, according to the Chron. Scotorum. The Annals of Tighernach, of Ulster, and the Four Masters, have "ua," or "grandson."

5 Alii. αλi, MS.

6 Occisus. occiρρuρ, MS.

7 Fair of Carman; i.e. the fair, or public sports, of Carman, or Loch-Carman, now Wexford.

8 Son of Mac Gillapatraic. So also

Gailenga, occisi[1] sunt. Edru Ua Conaing, royal heir of Mumha, occisus[2] est by the community[3] of Imlech. The victory of Druim-Bennchair *was gained* over the Ulidians, by the Airghialla. The victory of Inbher-Boinne *was gained* by Sitric, son of Amhlaibh, over the Conaille, and the Ui-Dorthainn, and the Ui-Meith, in which they were put to slaughter. Maeltuile, bishop of Ard-Macha, in Christo [quievit]. Aedh Ua Furreidh assumed the bishoprick afterwards.

A.D.
[1032.]

The kalends of January on the 2nd feria, the 26th of the moon; the age of the Lord thirty-three years and a thousand. A victory by Murchadh Ua Maelsech-lainn over Conchobhar Ua Maelsechlainn, in which Maelruanaidh, grandson[4] of Carrach Calma, and Lorcan Ua Caindelbhain, king of Laeghaire, et alii[5] multi, were slain. Conchobhar Ua Muiredhaigh, king of Ciar-raighe, occisus[6] est. The fair of Carman[7] *was celebrated* by Donnchadh Mac Gillapatraic, after he had assumed the kingship of Laighen. Aimhergin Ua Cerbhaill, king of Eile, [and] Cu-Mumhan, son of Ruaidhri Ua Cedfadha, mortui sunt. A victory *was gained* by the Eile, in which Braen Ua Clerigh, and Muiredhach, son of Mac Gilla-patraic,[8] et alii[9] multi, were slain. The shrine of Peter and Paul dropped[10] blood on the altar of Patrick, in Ard-Macha, coram omnibus videntibus.[11] Aedh, son of Flaithbhertach Ua Neill, king of Oilech, and royal heir of Erinn, post poenitentiam mortuus est, on the night of Andrew's festival. Aedh Ua Neill mortuus est.[12]

[1033.]

The kalends of January on the 3rd feria, the 7th of the moon; the age of the Lord thirty-four years and a thousand. Maelcoluim, son of Cinaeth, king of Alba,

[1034.]

---

in the Ann. Ult. The Four Mast. call him "Muiredhach Mac Gilla-patrick;" but the Ann. of Tigher-nach have "Muiredhach, son of Muirchertach Mac Gillapatraic."

[9] *Alii.* αιℓιι, MS.

[10] *Dropped.* αᵹ τeρeηᵹιη; lit. "dropping."

[11] *Videntibus.* uιᴅenτιρuιᴘ, MS.

[12] *Mortuus est.* This is a repetition of the preceding entry, and is in a different but contemporary hand.

D 2

obiit. Aṁlaib mac Sitrec do marbad do tSaxanachaib, ag dul do Róiṁ. Gillareclain, mac Gillamoconna, occiṛuṛ eṛt. Dubdaingen, ṛi Connacht, a ṛuiṛ occiṛuṛ eṛt. Donnchad mac Briain do innṛed Oṛṛaiẑe co léiṛ. Cathal Maiṛtiṛ, aiṛcinneč Coṛcaiẑe, ocuṛ Conn mac Maolṛadṛaiẑ, aiṛcinneč Munẑaiṛde, in Cṛiṛto doṛmieṛunt. Macnia .h. hUchtáin, ṛeṛ léiẑinn Cenannṛa, do Báthad aẑ tiachtain a hAlbain, ocuṛ cuilebad Coluim Cille, ocuṛ tṛi mionna do ṁionnaib Padṛaiẑ, ocuṛ tṛiča ṛeṛ iṁṛaib. Suibne mac Cinoetha, ṛi Gall Ẑoeidil.

Ktt. Enaiṛ .iiii. ṛ.; L. xuiii.; coiẑ bliadna .xxx. aṛ mile aiṛ in Tiẑeṛna. Cnut mac Sain, ṛi Saxan, dhéc. Cathal mac Aṁalẑaid, ṛi iaṛtaiṛ Laiẑen, ocuṛ a Ben .i. inẑen mic Gillačaimẑin, mic Cinoeta, ocuṛ a ču, do marbad an aoinṛeacht do mac Cellaiẑh mic Dunchada. Flaitbeṛtač .h. Muṛchada, ṛi Cenel mBoẑuine, cum multiṛ occiṛuṛ eṛt. Iaṛnán .h. Flannchada .i. Cú na naom ocuṛ na bṛiṛén do ẑaiṛči Be, do teacht ṛoṛ cṛeič a n'Delbna, coná táiṛčedaṛ uaite do Delbna a nimaiṛeẑ, ẑo dtaṛdṛat cliachaṛ ndó, ocuṛ co taṛdṛat áṛ a muintiṛe, ocuṛ ṛo marbad tṛe neṛt na noem. Raẑnall .h. hiṁaiṛ, ṛi Puiṛt Laiṛẑe, do marbad in Ač cliač la Sitṛec mac Aṁláib. Aṛd mBṛeacáin do

---

[1] *Saxons;* i.e. the Saxons of England, probably.

[2] *Cuilebhadh.* cuilebad. The Four Mast., who give this entry, seem to have misunderstood the meaning of the word cuilebad, for they divide it into two words, cu lebad, which Dr. O'Donovan (Ann. Four Mast., A.D. 1034), has translated "with the bed," in the endeavour to represent the meaning of the text, although he must have been aware that lebad was not the abl. case of lebad, a bed. The *cuilebhadh* of Colum Cille was a relic, either an altar-cloth, or canopy, as appears from an ancient tract cited in Professor O'Curry's *Lectures*, pp. 333-5. See Reeves's *Adamnan*, pp. 321-3, where many references to this *cuilebhadh* are collected; but the suggestion (loc. cit.), that cuilebhadh is the Irish form of *colobium* is hardly admissible, as according to the ancient tract referred to, it seems to have been an altar-cloth. See another reference to *cuilebhadh* under the year 1128, *infra.*

[3] *Gall Gaeidhel;* lit. "foreign Gaeidhel," and understood to signify the descendants of Irish who settled in, or intermarried with the natives of Scotland, the Hebrides, and the Isle of

obiit. Amhlaibh, son of Sitric, was slain by Saxons,[1] in going to Rome. Gillasechlainn, son of Gillamochonna, occisus est. Dubhdaingen, king of Connacht, a suis occisus est. Donnchadh, son of Brian, plundered Osraighe entirely. Cathal Martyr, airchinnech of Corcach, and Conn, son of Maelpatraic, airchinnech of Mungairit, in Christo dormierunt. Macnia Ua hUchtain, lector of Cenannus, was drowned while coming from Alba; and the cuilebhadh[2] of Colum-Cille, and three reliquaries of the reliquaries of Patrick, and thirty men along with them, *were also drowned.* Suibhne, son of Cinaeth, king of the Gall-Gaeidhel,[3] *mortuus est.*

The kalends of January on the 4th feria, the 18th of the moon; the age of the Lord thirty-five years and a thousand. Cnut, son of Sain,[4] king of the Saxons, died. Cathal, son of Amhalghaidh, king of the West of Laighen,[5] and his wife, *i.e.* the daughter of the son of Gillacaeimghin, son of Cineath, and his dog, were slain together by the son of Cellach, son of Dunchadh. Flaithbhertach Ua Murchadha, king of Cenel-mBoghuine, cum multis occisus est. Iarnan Ua Flannchadha, *i.e.* he who was called "Cú na naem ocus na bhfiren,"[6] went on a predatory excursion into Delbhna; but a small number of the *men of* Delbhna overtook his band, and gave him battle, and committed a slaughter of his people; and he was slain through the power of the saints. Raghnall, grandson of Imhar, king of Port-Lairge, was killed in Ath-cliath, by Sitric, son of Amhlaibh. Ard-Breacain was plundered by Sitric, son

---

Man. The name has also been translated Dano-Irish. See Reeves's *Adamnan,* p. 306, note [1].

[4] *Sain,* for Svain, or Svein; an instance of the tendency in the Irish to change a primitive *sv* into *s.* See *Zeuss, Gram. Celt.,* vol. I., p. 145; and *Revue Archéologique, Avril,* 1867, p. 287.

[5] *West of Laighen.* The Four Mast. call Cathal "king of Ui-Ceallaigh-Cualann," a territory in the north-east of the present co. of Wicklow, which would indicate that the words ιαμτaιμ Laιšen of the text should be aιμτeμ Laιšen, "east of Leinster." The word aιμτeμ (east), usually abbreviated μτeμ, is frequently misunderstood for ιαμταμ.

[6] *Cú na naem ocus na bhfiren;* i.e. "the dog of the saints and the faithful." *Cú* is generally, in composition, a complimentary title.

αρξαιη ℓα Sιτρεc mac αⅿ̇ℓαιɓ.　Soρⅾ Coℓυιm Cιℓℓε ⅾo
ℓoρcαⅾ ocυρ ⅾo αρξαιη ⅾo Conċoɓαρ .h. Mάιℓρeċℓαιηη
ηα ⅾίξαιℓ.

Ktt. Enάιρ .υ. p.; ℓ. αxυιιι.; ρe ɓℓιⅾoηα xxx. αρ mιℓe
αιρ ιη Cιξeρηα.　Ⅾomηαℓℓ O hUαⅿ̇αραιη, ρί ɓρeρ ℓί,
occιρυρ eρτ o Ⅾάℓ αραιⅾe.　Sξoℓόc O Fℓαηηαξάιη, ρί
ɓρeρ ⅾCeⅮρα, α ρυιρ [occιρυρ eρτ].　Ⅾomηαℓℓ mac
Fℓαιηη, ρίⅾαⅿ̇ηα Ceⅿραċ, ⅾo mαρɓαⅾ o ρeρυιɓ ɓρeιρfηe.
Mυρcαⅾ .h. αηċαραιℓℓ, ocυρ Nιαℓℓ mac Mυιρξeρρα,
ⅾα ρίⅾαⅿ̇ηα ιαρταιρ Conηαċτ, omηeρ occιρι ρυητ.
Cυċίċe mac Eιξηeċάη, ρί ċeηeόιℓ ηEηηα, oɓιιτ.　Ⅾonη-
cαⅾ mac Ⅾύηℓαιηξ, ρί ℓαιξeη, ⅾo ⅾαℓℓαⅾ ℓα Ⅾoηηcαⅾ
mac ξιℓℓαρατραιξ, conⅾeρɓαιℓτ ⅾe.　FℓαιⅮɓeρταċ ιη
τρορⅾαιη .h. Néιℓℓ, αιρορίξh Oιℓιξ, ρoρτ ρeηeτeητιαm
oρτιmαm, ιη Cριρτo qυιeυιτ.　Rυαιⅾρι mac Cαιⅾξ, mιc
ℓoρcαιη, ⅾo ⅾαℓℓαⅾ ℓα mac Mαιℓ ηα mɓό.

Ktt. Eηαιρ υιι. p.; ℓ. .x.; ρeċτ mɓℓιⅾoηα αρ τρίċα
αρ ⅿ̇ίℓe αίρ ιη Cιξeρηα.　CαⅮαℓ mac Rυαιⅾρι, ρι
ιαρⅮαιρ Conηαċτ, ⅾo ⅾυℓ ⅾα oιℓιⅮρι ξo hαρⅾ Maċα.
Fℓαηη .h. Mαιℓρecℓαιηη ⅾo ⅾαℓℓαⅾ ℓα Conchoɓαρ hUα
Mαoιℓρecℓαιηη.　αρċύ .h. Ceℓeċάη, ρί .h. mɓeρραιℓ,
ocυρ Rυαιⅾρι .h. ℓoρcάιη, ρί .h. Nιαℓℓάιη, occιρι ρυητ
ιc Cραoιɓ ċαιℓℓe ό Mυιρeⅾhach O Rυαⅾαċάιη, ocυρ
ό Uιɓ Echαcċ.　Cύιηⅿ̇αιη .h. Roɓαηη, ρί ρυιρτ ℓαιρξe,
α ρυιρ occιρυρ ρτ̅.　Cρι .h. Moeℓⅾoραιⅾ ⅾo mαρɓαⅾ.
Ⅾoιηeηⅾ αⅾɓαιℓ ocυρ fℓιυċηυρ mόρ ιη ɓℓίαⅾαιη ρι.

Ktt. Eηάιρ ι. p.; ℓ. xxι.; ochτ mɓℓιⅾoηα αρ .xxx. αρ
mιℓe αιρ ιη Cιξeρηα.　Coℓmάη cαm .h. Conξαιℓe,
c̅omαρɓα Moℓαιρρι, ιη Cριρτo qυιeυιτ.　ξιℓℓα Cριρτ,

---

1 *The 28th.* Should be 29th.

2 *Occisus est.* occιρυρ ρτ̅, for
occιρυρ ρυητ, MS.

3 *Omnes.* oιⅿ̅ρ, MS. The Ann. Ult.
read o̅e̅ρ, which Dr. O'Conor reads
"a suis." The Four Masters have ⅾo
mαρɓαⅾ, "were slain."

4 *Cuchiche;* lit. "canis mamillæ."

5 *Flaithbhertach In - trostain;* i.e.
"Flaithbhertach of the [pilgrim's]
staff," in allusion to his journey
to Rome, mentioned under the year
1030.

6 *Est.* ρτ̅, for ρυητ (sunt), MS.

of Amhlaibh; *and* Sord-Choluim-Cille was burned and plundered by Conchobhar Ua Maeilsechlainn, in revenge thereof.

The kalends of January on the 5th feria, the 28th[1] of the moon; the age of the Lord thirty-six years and a thousand. Domhnall O'hUamharain, king of Feara-Lí, occisus est[2] by the Dal-Araidhe. Sgolóc O'Flannagain, king of Feara-Tethfa, a suis [occisus est]. Domhnall, son of Flann, royal heir of Temhair, was slain by the men of Breifne. Murchadh Ua Anchapaill, and Niall son of Muirghes, two royal heirs of the West of Connacht, omnes[3] occisi sunt. Cuchiche,[4] son of Eignechan, king of Cenel-Enna, obiit. Donnchadh, son of Dunlaing, king of Laighen, was blinded by Donnchadh Mac Gillapatraic, and he died thereof. Flaithbhertach In-trostain[5] Ua Neill, chief king of Oilech, post pœnitentiam optimam in Christo quievit. Ruaidhri, son of Tadhg, son of Lorcan, was blinded by the son of Mael-na-mbó.

The kalends of January on the 7th feria, the 10th of the moon; the age of the Lord thirty-seven years and a thousand. Cathal, son of Ruaidhri, king of the West of Connacht, went on his pilgrimage to Ard-Macha. Flann Ua Maelsechlainn was blinded by Conchobhar Ua Maelsechlainn. Archú Ua Celechain, king of Ui-mBresail, and Ruaidhri Ua Lorcain, king of Ui-Niallain, occisi sunt at Craebh-chaille by Muiredhach O'Ruadhachain, and by the Ui-Echach. Cúinmhain Ua Robhann, king of Port-Lairge, a suis occisus est.[6] Three *of the family* of Ua-Maeldoraidh were slain. Prodigious tempests and great moisture in this year.

The kalends of January on the 1st feria, the 21st of the moon; the age of the Lord thirty-eight years and a thousand. Colman Cam[7] Ua Conghaile, comarb of Molaise, in Christo quievit. Gillachrist, son of Cathbharr

---

[7] *Cam*; i.e. "the crooked." The Four Mast. call him *caech*, (=Lat. cæcus), or "blind," but the Ann. Ult. read *cam*.

mac Caṫḃapp h1 Ꝺoṁnaill, ʒaḃal ċoʒaiꝺ ocuꝛ coꝛnuma Cénil Conaill, ꝺo maꝛbaꝺ la mac Cuinn h1 Ꝺomnaill. Caṫ eꝺiꝛ Cuanna, ꝛí Ꝩaxan, ocuꝛ Oꝁa, ꝛi Fꝛanc, 1 ꝺꝛoꝛcaiꝛ míle ꝼeꝛ imm Oꝁa. Oꝛcallaꝺ O Rúaꝺaċán, ꝛí .h. neachach, ꝺo maꝛbaḋ la cloinn ꞇꝱíonaiʒ 1 nⱭꝛꝺ Maċa, lá ꝼéli an Ullꞇain, anꝺiʒuil maꝛḃꞇa Ꝋochaꝺa mic an Ⱥbaꝺ, ocuꝛ anꝺiʒuil ꞇꝛápꝛaiʒꞇe Ⱥiꝛꝺ Macha. Maiꝺṁ ꝛoꝛ Uiḃ Maine ꝛia nꝊelḃna, ꝛoꝛ laꝛ Cluana mic Nóiꝛ, áine ꝼeile Ciaꝛáin, in quo mulꞇi occiꝛi ꝛunꞇ. Cúꝺuiliʒ .h. Ꝺonnchaꝺa, ꝛíꝺaṁna Caiꝛil, ꝺo maꝛbaꝺ ꝺo 1ḃ Faoláin.

Ⱪꞇꞇ. Enáiꝛ .11. ꝼ.; L. 11. Noí mbliaꝺna ꞇꝛíċa aꝛ míle aiꝛ in Ꞇiʒeꝛna. 1áco, ꝛí Ꝺꝛeaꞇan, a ꝛuiꝛ; Ꝺomnall mac Ꝺonnchaꝺa, ꝛí .h. bꝼáolain, ó Ꝺomnall .h. Feꝛʒaile; Ꝺonnchaꝺ ꝺeꝛʒ .h. Ruaiꝛc, ó .h. Conchobaiꝛ; Ruaꝺꝛi, ꝛí Feꝛnṁaiʒe, a ꝛuiꝛ; Oeꝺh .h. Flannaʒán, ꝛí Luiꝛʒ ocuꝛ .h. bꝼiacꝛaċ, omneꝛ occiꝛi [ꝛunꞇ]. Ꝺonnchaꝺ mac ʒillaꝛaꞇꝛaiʒ, aiꝛꝺꝛíʒ Laiʒen eꞇ Oꝛꝛꝛaiʒe, [ꝺo éc]. Muiꝛeꝺhach mac Flaiꞇḃeꝛꞇaiʒ h1 Neill ꝺo maꝛbaꝺ ꝺo Leiꞇꝛenꝺuiḃ. Ceꝛḃall mac Faolain occiꝛuꝛ eꞇ ó ʒalloiḃ.

Ⱪꞇꞇ. Enaiꝛ .111. ꝼ.; L. .x111. Ceꞇhꝛaċa bliaꝺna aꝛ míle aiꝛ in Ꞇiʒeꝛna. hic eꝛꞇ annuꝛ milleꝛimuꝛ eꞇ quaꝺꝛaʒeꝛimuꝛ annuꝛ ab Incaꝛnaꞇione Ꝺomini. Coꝛcꝛan Cleiꝛech, cenꝺ Ꝋoꝛꝛa im cꝛabaꝺ, ocuꝛ im eʒna, in Cꝛiꞇꞇo ꝛauꝛauiꞇ. Ꝺonnchaꝺ mac Cꝛíonán, ꝛi Ⱥlban, a ꝛuiꝛ occiꝛuꝛ eꞇ. Ⱥꝛalꞇ, ꝛí Ꝩaxan, ʒiuaꝛ moꝛiꞇuꝛ. Cell ꝺaꝛa

---

[1] *Cuana*; i.e. the Emperor Conrad II. See under the year 1023, *supra*, where the name is similarly written. The Emperor Henry III. is called "Cona" in the Ang. Sax. Chron. See Thorpe's ed., vol. ii., p. 159.

[2] *Ota*. Odo, or Eudes, Comte de Champagne, slain in the battle of Bar le Duc, 17 Dec., 1037.

[3] *Ua Conchobhair*; i.e. Aedh Ua Conchobhair, or Hugh O'Conor.

[4] *Ruaidhri*. The Ann. of Tighern.

and the Four Mast. read mac Ruaꝺꝛi, "son of Ruaidhri (or Rory.)"

[5] *Ui-Fiachrach*; i.e. Ui-Fiachrach of Ard-Sratha.

[6] *Omnes*. oṁeꝛ (oimnes), MS.

[7] *Leithrenna*. Tighernach writes the name Ui-Labhradha, in which he is followed by the Four Mast. See O'Donovan's ed., p. 836, *n. z*, where the editor adds, "the O'Laverys (Ui-Labhradha), a family still numerous in the barony of Iveagh, county of

Ua Domhnaill, the prop of battle and defence of the Cenel-Conaill, was slain by the son of Conn Ua Domhnaill. A battle between Cuana,[1] king of the Saxons, and Ota,[2] king of the Franks, in which a thousand men were slain along with Ota. Orcallaid O'Ruadhachain, king of Ui-Echach, was slain by Clann-Sionaigh in Ard-Macha, on the festival of Ultan, in revenge for the killing of Eochaidh Mac-an-Abaidh, and for the profanation of Ard-Macha. A victory gained over the Ui-Maine by the Dealbhna, in the middle of Cluain-mic-Nois, on the Friday of Ciaran's festival, in quo multi occisi sunt. Cúdhuiligh, grandson of Donnchadh, royal heir of Caisel, was slain by the Ui-Faelain.

The kalends of January on the 2nd feria, the 2nd of the moon; the age of the Lord thirty-nine years and a thousand. Iaco, king of Britain, a suis; Domhnall, son of Donnchadh, king of Ui-Faelain, by Domhnall Ua Ferghaile; Donnchadh Derg Ua Ruairc, by Ua Conchobhair;[3] Ruaidhri,[4] king of Fernmhagh, a suis; Oedh Ua Flannagain, king of Lurg and Ui-Fiachrach,[5]—omnes[6] occisi [sunt]. Donnchadh Mac Gillapatraic, chief king of Laighen and Osraighe, [died]. Muiredhach, son of Flaithbhertach Ua Neill, was slain by the Leithrenna.[7] Cerbhall, son of Faelan, was slain by Foreigners.

The kalends of January on the 3rd feria, the 13th of the moon; the age of the Lord forty years and a thousand. Hic est annus millesimus[8] et quadragesimus annus ab Incarnatione[9] Domini. Corcran Cleirech,[10] the head of Europe as regards piety and wisdom, in Christo[10] pausavit. Donnchadh, son of Crínán, king of Alba, a suis occisus est. Aralt, king of the Saxons, givas[11] moritur. Cill-dara was

---

Down." The Ann. Ult., however, have the name as in the text.

[8] *Millesimus.* miłṙemuṙ (milsemus), MS.

[9] *Incarnatione.* ūcaṙnácīõe (ancarnacione), MS.

[10] *Corcran Cleirech;* i.e. "Corcran the Cleric."

[11] *Givas.* This word is written

ṡuaıṙ in the Ann. Ult., but Dr. O'Conor prints it ṡuaıṙ, and translates "ferorum." The old English transl. of the Ann. Ult. (in Brit. Mus.) has "Aralt, king of Saxons of Gills." The Editor is unable to explain the word. The death of Aralt (Harold "Harefoot") is entered in the Anglo-Sax. Chron. also under the year 1040.

uile do lorcad im ḟeil Míchíl. Cenanntur do lorcad. Dún da leṫglas do lorcad, ocur il ċella airchena.

Ktt. Enáir .u. f.; L. xxiiii.; bliadain æt. ar mile air in Tigerna. Ad imḋa trá na hairirre etir marbad ocur crechad, ocur ċaṫaib, irin mbliadain ri. Ni cumaing nech a ninnirin co léir, acht mad uaitte do iliḃ ḋíḃ, ar dáiġ oérra na ndoeineḃ do innirin treoṫa. Mac Beṫaid, mic Beṫaid, mic Ainmire, ard ollam Airo Maċai ocur Erenn airchena, [do éc]. Domnall reṁar, mac Mail na mbó, do marbad do Laiġniḃ. Muircertach mac Gillapadraig do marbad do Uiḃ Cáolluiḋe, a mebail. Creċ la hAirġiallaib a Conaillib, co rucrat Conaille forra, gur brirred ḋíḃ a Muiġ dáċuinnech. Creċ la .h. Nell a niḃ Echach Ulad, co tuċrat creiċ ṁóir leo. Gilla Comġaill mac Duinncuan, mic Dúnlaing, do ḃreṫ a Cill dara ar éigin, ocur a ṁarbad iarum.

Ktt. Enair .ui. f.; L. u.; ḋá bliadain æl. ar mile áir in Tigerna. Ferna mór Moeḋóg do lorcad la Donnchad mac Briain. Glend uinrinn do lorcad do mac Mail na mbó, ocur an dairṗtech do brirreḃ, ocur ced duine do marbad, ocur ceitri ced do ḃreiṫ eirde a nóiġuil Ferna móire. Murchad mac Dúnlaing, rí Laigen, ocur Domnall mac Aoḋa, rí [h.] dairċe, do ṫitim la Gillapadraig mac nDonnchada, rí Orrraige, ocur la Macraiṫ .h. nDonnchada, rí Eoganachta. Flann mac Maoilreclainn, ríḋamna Erenn, do marbad tre ṁeaḃuil.

Ktt. Enair .uii. f.; L. xiii.; tri bliadna .æl. ar mile air in Tigerna. Caṫal mac Ruaidri, rí iarṫair

---

1 *Son of Bethadh*. Mic Beṫaid. Omitted in Tighernach, the Ann. Ult., and the Four Mast. Probably a repetition of the name mac Beṫaid.

2 *Glenn-Uissen*. glend uinrinn (Glend uinsinn, i.e. Ash-glen), in the text; but the name is generally written Glenn-Uissen in old texts, which is now changed to Killeshin, the name of an old church, and parish, in the barony of Slievemargy, Queen's co.

3 *Eoghanachta*; i.e. Eoghanachta-Chaisil, "the Eoghanachts of Cashel," a sept descended from Eoghan-Mór, king of Munster in the 3rd century, anciently seated in the district around Cashel, co. Tipperary.

entirely burned about the festival of Michael. Cenannus
was burned. Dún-da-leth-ghlas was burned, and many
churches besides.

· The kalends of January on the 5th feria, the 24th of
the moon; the age of the Lord forty-one years and
a thousand. Numerous, truly, are the events in this year,
between slayings and plunderings, and battles. No one
could relate them all, but only a few of many of them are
related, on account of the dignity of the people mentioned
in them. Mac Bethaidh, son of Bethadh,[1] son of Ainmire,
chief poet of Ard-Macha, and likewise of Erinn, [died].
Domhnall Remhar, son of Mael-na-mbó, was slain by the
Lagenians. Muirchertach Mac Gillapatraic was slain by
the Ui-Caelluidhe, in treachery. A preying expedition
by the Airghialla into Conaille, but the Conaille overtook
them, and they were defeated in Magh-dha-chuinnech.
A preying expedition by the Ui-Neill into Ui-Echach-
Uladh, and they carried off a great prey. Gillacomghaill,
son of Donncuan, son of Dunlaing, was forcibly taken
from Cill-dara, and afterwards killed.

The kalends of January on the 6th feria, the 5th of
the moon; the age of the Lord forty-two years and a
thousand. Ferna-mór-Maedhóig was burned by Donnchadh, son of Brian. Glenn-Uissen[2] was burned by the
son of Mael-na-mbó, and the oratory broken, and one
hundred persons were slain, and four hundred taken out
of it, in retaliation for Ferna-mór. Murchadh, son of
Dunlaing, king of Laighen, and Domhnall, son of Aedh,
king of [Ui]-Bairche, fell by Gillapatraic, son of Donnchadh, king of Osraighe, and by Macraith, grandson of
Donnchadh, King of Eoghanachta.[3] Flann, son of
Maelsechlainn, royal heir of Erinn, was slain through
treachery.

The kalends of January on the 7th feria, the 16th
of the moon; the age of the Lord forty-three years and a
thousand. Cathal, son of Ruaidhri, king of the West of

Connacɦc, ꝺo eᵹ ın αılıcꝑı α ɴȢꝛꝺ ꝳαċα. Ꝺoṁnαll .ɦ. Ƒeꝑᵹαıle, ꝛí Ꝑoꝑċuαċ Lαıᵹen, ꝺo ꝳαꝑȢαꝺ ꝺíα Ȣóeınıb ꝛeın. Ƒlαnn .ɦ. ɦȢnbꝶécɦ, ꝛí .ɦ. ꝳecɦ, ꝺo ṁαꝑȢαꝺ ó UıȢ CeꝑȢαıll, ó ꝛí Ƒeꝑnmαıᵹe. Oeꝺɦ .ɦ. Conꝛıαclα, ꝛí ꝳecȼꝛα, ꝺo mαꝑȢαꝺ o ꝳuıꝛceꝑcαcɦ O ꝳαoılcꝛeċlαınn. Ceınnéıꝺıᵹ O Cuıꝛc, ꝛí ꝳúꝛcꝛαȢe, occıꝛuꝛ eꝛc. Ᵹıllα- moconnα O ꝹuıȢȢıoꝑmα ın ꝑαce ꝺoꝑmıuıc. ꝳαıȢm ꝳαıle Cαonṁαıȼ ꝛoꝑ bꝛú Sıuıꝛe, ꝛoꝑ OꝛꝛꝛαıᵹıȢ, ocuꝛ ꝛoꝑ Eꝑṁumαn, ꝛıα Cαꝑcαcɦ mαc SoeꝑȢꝛecɦαıᵹ, ꝺú α bƒαꝑᵹbαꝺ .ɦ. Ꝺonnαᵹáın, ꝛí Ȣꝛαꝺ. ꝳαıȢm ꝛoꝑ Cenel ᵹConαıll lα Cenél nEoᵹαın α ꝺceꝑmonn ȢáȢeoóᵹ.

Ƙcc. Enαıꝑ .ı. ꝼ.; L. xxuıı.; ceıcꝛı blıαꝺnα αꝑ .xc. αꝑ mıle αıꝛ αn Cıᵹeꝑnα. Cumuꝛcαcɦ .ɦ. ɦȢıllelán, ꝛı .ɦ. nEcɦαcɦ, ꝺo mαꝑbαꝺ ó UıȢ Cαꝑꝛαcáın. Ꞁıαll .ɦ. Celeɦán, ꝛí .ɦ. mȢꝛeαꝛꝛαıl, ocuꝛ α bꝛácɦαıꝛ .ı. Cꝛénꝼeꝑ, ꝺo Ȣαllαꝺ ꝺo mαcuıȢ ꝳαcαꝺán cꝛe ṁebαıl. Ꝺomnαll .ɦ. Cuıꝛc, ꝛí ꝳúꝛcꝛαȢe, ꝺo mαꝑbαꝺ ꝺo .ɦ. [Ƒ]lαȢlén, ocuꝛ ꝺo .ɦ. Oıꝛın. Cꝛeċ lα Ꞁıαll mαc ꝳαılꝛeċlαınn .ı. bα ꝛí nOılıᵹɦ αn cαn ꝛın, ꝛoꝑ UıȢ ꝳécɦ ocuꝛ ꝛoꝑ Cuαılᵹne, ᵹo ꝛuᵹ ꝺα ceꝺ ꝺɦéᵹ bó, ocuꝛ ꝛoċαıꝺe ꝺo bꝛαıꝺ, α nꝺíᵹuıl cꝛáꝑαıᵹȼe ċluıᵹ nα neȢαcɦcα. Cꝛeċ elı ꝺno lα ꝳuıꝛceꝑcαcɦ ɦUα Ꞁeıll ꝛoꝑ ꝳuᵹȢoꝑnα, co cuc bóꝛumα ocuꝛ bꝛoıꝺ α nꝺíᵹuıl cꝛáꝑαıᵹȼe αn ċluıᵹ ceꝺnα. ın Cleıꝛeɦ .ɦ. Concɦobαıꝑ ꝺo ṁαꝑbαꝺ.

Ƙcc. Enαıꝑ .ııı. ꝼ.; L. .ıx.; coıᵹ blıαꝺnα .xc. αꝑ mıle αıꝛ ın Cıᵹeꝑnα. Conᵹαlαċ .ɦ. loċlαınn, ꝛí

---

[1] *Muscraidhe.* There were anciently many territories in Ireland called Muscraidhe, or Muskerry. The district here referred to, formerly known by the names of Muscraidhe Treithirne, Muscraidhe Breogain, and Muscraidhe Chuirc, is comprised in the present barony of Clanwilliam, in the S. of the co. Tipperary.

[2] *Occisus est.* occıꝛı ꝛunc, MS.

[3] *Dormivit.* ꝺoꝑmıeꝛꝯ̄ for dor- mierunt, MS.

[4] *In which . . was slain.* ꝺú α bƒαꝑᵹbαꝺ (dú a bfhargbad); lit. "where was left."

[5] *Muscraidhe;* . i.e. Muscraidhe- Chuirc. See note[1] *supra.*

[6] *Clog-an-edachta.* The "Bell of the Bequest," otherwise called *Clog- udachta-Phadraig,* or the "Bell of

Connacht, died in pilgrimage at Ard-Macha. Domhnall Ua Ferghaile, king of Fortuatha-Laighen, was slain by his own people. Flann Ua hAnbhfheth, king of Ui-Meth, was slain by the Ui-Cerbhaill, *i.e.* by the king of Fernmhagh. Oedh Ua Confhiacla, king of Tethfa, was killed by Muirchertach O'Maelsechlainn. Cennedigh O' Cuirc, king of Muscraidhe,[1] occisus est.[2] Gillamochonna O'Duibhdhiorma in pace dormivit.[3] The victory of Mael-caenmhaigh, on the brink of the Siuir, *was gained* over the men of Osraighe and Er-Mumha, by Carthach, son of Saerbrethach; in which Ua Donnagáin, king of Aradh, was slain.[4] A victory *was gained* over the Cenel-Conaill, by the Cenel-Eoghain, at Termon-Dábheóg. A.D. [1043.]

The kalends of January on the 1st feria, the 27th of the moon; the age of the Lord forty-four years and a thousand. Cumuscach Ua hAillelain, king of Ui-Echach, was slain by the Ui-Carracain. Niall Ua Cele-cháin, king of Ui-Breasail, and his brother, *i.e.*, Trénfer, were blinded by the sons of Matadhan, through treachery. Domhnall Ua Cuirc, king of Muscraidhe,[5] was slain by Ua [F]ladhlén, and Ua Oisin. A preying expedition by Niall, son of Maelsechlainn, *i.e.*, who was at that time king of Oilech, against the Ui-Meth and Cuailgne, when he carried off 1,200 cows, and a multitude of captives, in revenge for the profanation of Clog-an-edachta.[6] Another preying expedition, moreover, by Muirchertach Ua Neill, against the Mughdhorna; and he carried off a prey of cattle, and captives, in revenge for the profanation of the same bell. The Cleirech[7] Ua Conchobhair was slain. [1044.]

The kalends of January on the 3rd feria, the 9th of the moon; the age of the Lord forty-five years and a thousand. Conghalach Ua Lochlainn, king of [1045.]

Patrick's Bequest," because it was believed to have been bequeathed by St. Patrick. The text reads *Clog-nanedachta*, or "Bell of the Bequests;" but the other Irish Chronicles in which it is mentioned, have ınᴅ eᴅachᴛa "of the Bequest." See Reeves's *Adamnan*, p. 323, *n.* [d].

[7] *The Cleirech*; i.e. the Cleric.

Copcumpuaiꝺ; Ꝣlúmiapainn .h. Cléipćén,   pi   .h.
ꝁCaippi; flaitbeptach .h. Canannán, pi Ceneoil
Conaill; Ꝺomnall .h. Ceꝺpaꝺa, opꝺan Muman, mopꞇui
punꞇ. Aipchinnech Leitꝁlinne ꝺo mapbaꝺ a nꝺopuip na
cille. Cpeć la Muipceptach .h. Néll a bpepaib Dpeaꝁ,
conup ꞇappaiꝺ Ꝣaipbeiꞇ .h. Caċupaiꝁ, pí Dpoꝁ, ic Cappán
Linne, ocup an ṁuip lán ap a ćinn, ꝁo ꞇopchaip Muipceptach ann, eꞇ alii mulꞇi. Capptach, mac 8aoip-
Dpeꞇhaiꝁ, pí Eoꝁanachꞇa Caipil, ꝺo lopcaꝺ a ꞇiꝁ
ċeineꝺ ꝺo .h. Lonꝁapꝁáin mic Ꝺuinncuan, cum mulꞇip
nobilibup upꞇip. Caċ eꞇip Albanchaib eꞇoppa ppein, a
ꞇopchaip Cponán, ab Ꝺúin cuilleꝺ.

Ƙꞇꞇ. Enaip .iiii. p.; L .xx. Sé bliaꝺna .xꞇ. ap mile
aip in Tiꝁepna. Muipeꝺhach mac flaitbeptaiꝁ hi
Neill, piꝺamna Oiliꝁ, ocup Aíꞇéꝺh .h. hAíꞇéꝺh, pí .h.
nEchach, ꝺo lopcaꝺ a ꞇiꝁ ċeneꝺ lá Conulaꝺh mac
Conꝁalaiꝁ, pí Uáchꞇaip ċipe. Apꞇ Uallaċ O Ruaipc
ꝺo mapbaꝺ ꝺo Cenel Conaill. fepꝁal .h. Ciapꞇa, pi
Caippi, ꝺo mapbaꝺ ꝺo .h. flannaꝁáin, pí Teċpa.

Ƙꞇꞇ. Enáip .u. p.; L i. Seachꞇ mbliaꝺna ap .xꞇ. ap
mile aip in Tiꝁepna. Snechꞇa mop ipin mbliaꝺain pi
o ḟéil Muipi ꝁo féil Paꞇpaiꝁ, ꝺo ná fpíꞇ pamail,
conpuplá áp nꝺaoine ocup inꝺele, ocup fiaꝺṁiol an
ṁapa, ocup énlaiꞇhe. Muipceptach .h. Maꝺaꝺáin,
pí .h. mDpeppail, ꝺo mapbaꝺ a nApꝺ Macha, ꝺo
Maꝺaꝺán .h. Céleaċán, pep ꝺolum. Niall .h. Ruaipc
ꝺo ṁapbaꝺ la .h. Conchobaip. Cpeć pluaiꝁeꝺ lá Niall
mac Mailꞇpeclainn a mDpeꝁhaib, ꝁu popmapꝺ .h.
nifepnáin.

Ƙꞇꞇ. Enáip .ui. p.; L .xii. Ochꞇ mbliaꝺna ap .xꞇ. ap

---

1 *Others.* ali, MS.
2 *On fire.* ċeineꝺ; lit. "of fire,"
MS.
3 *Multis.* mulꞇipp (multiss), MS.
4 *Uallach;* i.e. the proud.
5 *Snow.* pneꝼa, for pnechꞇa, MS.

The form pneꝼa has been altered to
pneapa (for pneachꞇa), by Roderick
O'Flaherty, who has added several
marginal notes throughout the volume.
6 *Ua Conchobhair;* i.e. Aedh, or
Hugh O'Conor.

Corcomruaidh ; Glún-iarainn Ua Cleirchén, king of Ui-
Cairpre; Flaithbhertach Ua Canannáin, king of Cenel-
Conaill; Domhnall Ua Cedfadha, the glory of Mumha,
mortui sunt. The airchinnech of Leithghlinn was killed in
the door of the church. A predatory expedition by Muirchertach Ua Neill into Feara-Breagh ; but Gairbheith Ua
Cathusaigh, king of Breagha, overtook him at Cassán-
Linne, when the sea was full in before him, and Muirchertach and many others[1] were slain there. Carthach,
son of Saerbhrethach, king of Eoghanacht-Caisil, was
burned in a house on fire,[2] by the grandson of Longhar-
gan, son of Donnauan, cum multis[3] nobilibus ustis. A
battle between the men of Alba, among themselves, in
which Cronan, abbot of Dun-Cuillend, was slain.

[1046.] The kalends of January on the 4th feria, the 20th of
the moon ; the age of the Lord forty-six years and a
thousand. Muiredhach, son of Flaithbhertach Ua Neill,
royal heir of Oilech, and Aitedh Ua hAitedh, king of
Ui-Echach, were burned in a house on fire, by Cu-Uladh,
son of Conghalach, king of Uachtar-thire. Art Uallach[4]
O'Ruairc was slain by the Cenel-Conaill. Ferghal Ua
Ciardha, king of Cairpre, was slain by Ua Flannagain,
king of Tethfa.

[1047.] The kalends of January on the 5th feria, the 1st of
the moon ; the age of the Lord forty-seven years and a
thousand. Great snow[5] in this year from the festival of
Mary to the festival of Patrick, for which no equal was
found, so that it caused a destruction of people, and cattle,
and the wild animals of the sea, and of birds. Muirchertach, grandson of Madadhan, king of Ui-Bresail, was
killed in Ard-Macha, by Madadhan Ua Celechain, per
dolum. Niall Ua Ruairc was slain by Ua Conchobhair.[6]
A predatory hosting by Niall, son of Maelsechlainn, into
Bregha, when he slew Ua hIffernain.

[1048.] The kalends of January on the 6th feria, the 12th
of the moon ; the age of the Lord forty-eight years

mile αιρ ιn Τιξερna.   Γερξαl .h. mαιlṁuαιṡ, ρí bγερ
ξCeαll; ξιllαcoluιm .h. hειcnιč αιρṽρι Οιρξιαlla;
Cenṽραοlaṽ Ο Cuιll, αρṽ οllαm mumαn; mαοlγάṫαιll
.h. hειṽιn ρι .h. bγιαcραč Αιṽne, mορτuι ρunτ.
Comαρbα Ρεṽαιρ .ι. ιn Ράρα, ocuρ ṽα ρερ ṽhéc ṽα αορρ
ξράιṽ, ṽγαξαιl ṫáιρ mαιlle γριρ, ιαρ nόl neιṁe ṽο ραττ
ṽόιṽ ιn comαρbα ρο hιοnnαρbaṽ αρρ ρeṁe.

ʞcɫɫ. Enαιρ .ι. γ.; ɫ. xxιιι. Νοι mbliaṽna αρ xɫ.
αρ mile αιρ ιn Τιξερna.   mαοlcοιnnιč .h. Ταιčlιξ,
comαρbα Ṽαιmιnnρι, [ṽο éc].   muιρcερταch mαc
mαιlτρεclαιnn ṽο ṁαρbαṽ la Conchοbαρ .h. mαιlρεch-
lαιnn, ṽαρ ραρuξαṽ Ṽé ocuρ ṽαοιne.   Conchοbαρ .h.
Cιnnγαοlaṽ, ρí .h. Conαιll ξαbρα; ιοṁαρ .h. béιce, ρí
.h. méṫ, occιρι ρunτ.

ʞcɫɫ. Enαιρ .ιι. γ.; .ɫ. ιιιι.; coecα bliaṽna αρ mile
αιρ ιn Τιξερna.   mαοlρuαnαṽ .h. Concoιρne, ρí Ele;
Ṽοnnchαṽ mαc ξιllαγαοláιn, ρí .h. bγαιlξe, occιρι
ρunτ.   Cιll ṽαρα cοnα ṽαmliaξ ṽο lορcαṽ. Cleιρčén
.h. muιneόc, τuιρ cραbαṽ nα hEρenn, [quιeuιτ ιn
Cριρτο].   Scαιnṽeρ eṽιρ γιορα muιξe hιčα ocuρ
Οιρξιαlla, α τορchαιṽh Eochαιṽh .h. hΟρρene.

ʞcɫɫ. Enαιρ .ιιι. γ.; ɫ. xu.; bliaṽαιn αρ. ɫ. αρ mile
αιρ ιn Τιξερna.   muιρcερταch mαc bριc, ρι nα nṼéιρι,
ṽο lορcαṽ ṽο Uιṽ Γαοláιn.   mαc buατán mιc bριc ṽο
mαρbαṽ α nṽαṁliaξ lιρ ṁόιρ, ṽο mάιlτρεclαιnn Ο bριc.
Αṁαlξαιṽ mαc Cαṫαιl, ρí ιαρṫαιρ Connαchτ, ṽο
ṫαllαṽ la hΑcοṽ .h. Conchοbαιρ.   Lαιξnén mαc mαοláιn,
ρí ξαιlenξ, cum ρuα ρεξιnα .ι. ιnξen αn ξαιτ, ṽο ṫul

---

and a thousand. Ferghal Ua Maelmhuaidh, king of Feara-Ceall; Gillacoluim Ua hEighnigh, chief king of Oirghiall; Cendfaeladh O'Cuill, chief poet of Mumha; Maelfabhaill Ua hEidhin, king of Ui-Fiachrach-Aidhne, mortui sunt. The comarb of Peter, i.e., the Pope, and twelve of his men of grade along with him, died after drinking poison which the comarb who had previously been expelled thence (i.e., *from the Papacy*) gave to them.

The kalends of January on the 1st feria, the 23rd of the moon; the age of the Lord forty-nine years and a thousand. Maelcainnigh Ua Taichligh, comarb of Daimh-inis, [died]. Muirchertach, son[1] of Maelsechlainn, was slain by Conchobhar Ua Maelsechlainn, to the profanation of God and of men. Conchobhar Ua Cinnfhaeladh, king of Ui-Conaill-Gabhra, *and* Imhar Ua Béice, king of Ui-Méth, occisi[2] sunt.

The kalends of January on the 2nd feria, the 4th of the moon; the age of the Lord fifty years and a thou-sand. Maelruanaidh, grandson[3] of Cucoirne, king of Eile, *and* Donnchadh, son of Gillafhaelain, king of Ui-Failghe, occisi sunt. Cill-dara, with its stone-church, was burned. Cleirchen Ua Muineóc, tower of the piety of Erinn, [quievit in Christo]. A conflict between the men of Magh-Itha and the Oirghialla, in which Eochaidh Ua hOssene was slain.

The kalends of January on the 3rd feria, the 15th of the moon; the age of the Lord fifty-one years and a thousand. Muirchertach, son of Brec, king of the Deisi, was burned by the Ui-Faelain. Mac Buatan,[4] son of Brec, was slain in the stone-church of Lis-mór, by Maelsechlainn, grandson of Brec. Amhalghaidh, son of Cathal, king of the West of Connacht, was blinded by Aedh Ua Concho-bhair. Laighnén, son of Maelan, king of Gailenga, cum sua regina, *i.e.*, the daughter of the Gut,[5] went on their

---

Ann. Ult.; but Tighernach and the Four Mast. have it more correctly "Faelan, son of Brattan."

[5] *The Gut*; i.e. "the stammerer;" one of the O'Melaghlins, whose death is recorded under the year 1030, *supra*.

E

día aiitzu do Róiṁ, ocuf a ég. Mág Laċlaiṁ do
ionnaṗbaḋ a ṙiġe Tealċa óg, ocuf Aoḋ .h. Ferġail do
ṙíġhaḋ na ionaḋ.

Ktt. Enaiṙ .iiii. f.; l. xx.iiii; ḋá bliaḋain aṙ .l. aṙ
mile aiṙ in Tiġeṙna. Domnall bán .h. Ḃṙiain do
maṙbaḋ la Connachtaiḃ. Ḃṙaon mac Maolṁóṙḋa, ṙí
laiġen, [do ec] i Colaiṅea. Macṙaiċ .h. Donnchaḋa,
ṙí Eoġanachta Caiṙil, do ég.

Ktt. Enaiṙ .iii. f.; l. iii.; tṙi bliaḋna .l. aṙ mile
aiṙ in Tiġeṙna. Mac na hoiḋċe .h. Ruaiṙc, ríḋamna
Connacht, do maṙbaḋ do Diaṙmaiḋ .h. Cuinn a niṁṙi
Loċa hArbech. Flaitḃeṙtach .h. Maolfaḃaill, ṙí
Caiṙṙġe Ḃṙachaiḋe; Muṙchaḋ .h. Ḃeolláin, aiṙchin-
nech Dṙoma cliaḃ; omneṙ in pace doṙmieṙunt. Cṙeċ
lá mág Laċluinn ocuf la feṙuiḃ ṁoiġe hIṫa foṙ Cenel
mḂinniġ Loċa Dṙoċaiṫ, go ṙuġfat tṙi ceḋ bó, ocuf guṙ
ṙo ṁaṙḃfat Duiḃeṁna mac Cinoeċa .i. feġnaḃ Cluana
Fiaċna, ocuf Cúmaċa mac Claiṙċén, maeṙ Dál gCaiṙ.
Moelcṙón mac Cathail, ṙi Ḃṙeġh, do maṙbaḋ do .h.
Ṙiacáin. Donnchaḋ .h. Cellaċáin, ríḋamna Caiṙil, do
ṁaṙbaḋ dOṙṙṙaiġiḃ. Niall .h. hEicniċ, ṙí feṙ Manach,
do maṙbaḋ dfeṙuiḃ Luiṙg.

Ktt. Enaiṙ .iii. f.; l. xiii.; ceitṙi bliaḋna .l. aṙ
mile aiṙ in Tiġeṙna. Ioṁaṙ mac Aṙailt, ṙí Ġall, do
ég. Aoḋ .h. Ferġail, ṙí Tealċa óg, ocuf mac Aṙċon
.h. Celeċán, ṙí .h. mḂṙeṙṙail, do maṙbaḋ dfeṙuiḃ
Feṙnmaiġe. Maiḋm Finnṁaiġe foṙ Uiḃ Méiṫ ocuf
foṙ Uachtaṙ ṫíṙe, ṙia nUiḃ Eċaċ, dú atoṙchaiṙ
an cṙoiḃḋeṙg, ríḋamna Uachtaiṙ ṫíṙe. Aoḋ mac

---

1 *He died.* Tighernach adds that
he died taiṙ iaṙ tiachtain o Ṙoim,
"in the east, after coming from Rome."
The Four Mast. represent both Laighnén and his wife as having died on
their journey homewards.

2 *[Died].* [do ec]. Supplied from
the Ann. Ult.

3 *Colainea*; i.e. Cologne

4 *Mac-na-hoidhche;* lit. *filius noctis.*

5 *Loch-h.Arbhech;* now Loch-Arrow,
on the borders of the cos. of Sligo
and Roscommon.

6 *Omnes.* oiṁṙ (for oimneṙ), MS.

7 *Dormierunt.* doṙṙieṙṫ, MS.

8 *Mac Lachlainn.* mag claċluinn,
MS.

pilgrimage to Rome, and he died[1]. Mac Lachlainn was
expelled from the sovereignty of Tealach-óg, and Aedh,
grandson of Ferghal, was made king in his place.

The kalends of January on the 4th feria, the 27th of
the moon; the age of the Lord fifty-two years and a
thousand. Domhnall Bán Ua Briain was slain by the
men of Connacht. Braen, son of Maelmordha, king of
Laighen, [died][2] in Colainea.[3] Macraith, grandson of
Donnchadh, king of Eoghanacht-Chaisil, died.

The kalends of January on the 6th feria, the 7th of
the moon; the age of the Lord fifty-three years and a
thousand. Mac-na-hoidhche[4] Ua Ruairc, royal heir of
Connacht, was slain by Diarmaid Ua Cuinn on an island of
Loch-hArbhech.[5] Flaithbhertach Ua Maelfhabhaill, king
of Carraig-Brachaide, *and* Murchadh Ua Beollain, airchinnech of Druim-cliabh, omnes[6] in pace dormierunt.[7] A
preying expedition by Mac Lachlainn[8] and the men of
Magh-Itha, against the Cenel-Binnigh of Loch-Drochait,
when they carried off three hundred cows, and killed
Duibhemhna, son Cinaeth, viz.:—the vice-abbot of Cluain-
Fiachna, and Cúmacha, son of Clairchen, steward of Dal-
Cais. Maelcrón, son of Cathal, king of Bregh, was slain
by Ua Riacain. Donnchadh Ua Cellachain, royal heir of
Caisel, was slain by the Osraighe. Niall Ua hEighnich,
king of Feara-Manach, was slain by the Feara-Luirg.

The kalends of January on the 7th feria, the 18th of
the moon; the age of the Lord fifty-four years and
a thousand. Imhar, son of Aralt, king of the Foreigners,
died. Aedh, grandson of Ferghal, king of Tealach-óg, and
the son of Archu[9] Ua Celechain, king of Ui-Bresail, were
slain by the men of Fernmhagh. The victory of Finn-
mhagh *was gained* over the Ui-Meith and the men of
Uachtar-thire, by the Ui-Echach, in which fell the
Croibhdherg,[10] royal heir of Uachtar-thire. Aedh, son of

---

[9] *Archu*; lit. "slaughter hound,"
from aṛ, slaughter, and cu, a hound.

[10] *The Croibhdherg*; i.e. "the red-
handed," or, more literally, "red fist."

E 2

Ceϻϻéϼϫ mϲ Duϻϻϲυαϻ, muϻϼe Cloϻϻe Coϻϼϼϫhelϼaϫ,
ϼo maϼϼaϼ ϼo Conϻachταϫ. Caϲ eϼϼ ϼϼϼa αλϼaϻ ocuϼ
Saxϼaϻaϫ, ϻ ϲoϼϲϼaϼaϼ ϲϼϻ mϻle ϼϼeϼaϫ αλϼaϻ, ocuϼ
mϻle ϫo leϲ ϼo Saxϼaϻaϫ, ϻm Dolϼϻϻ mac Ϸϻϻϲaϻϼ.[1]
Loϲ Suϼϫe Oϼϼáϻϻ a Sléϫ ϫuaϼeaϼa ϼo élúϫ a ϻϼeϼeϼh
oϫϲe Ϸéle Mϻchϻl, conϼeachaϻϼ ϻϼϻϻ Ϸáϼaϻll, quoϼ non
auϼϻϲum eϼϲ ab anϲϻquϻϼ.

Kϲϲ. enáϻϼ .ϻ. Ϸ.; Lxxϻx. Coϻϲ blϻaϼna .l. aϼ mϻle
aϻϼ ϻϻ Cϻϫeϼϻa. Domnall ϼuaϼ O bϼϻaϻϻ ϼo maϼϼaϼ
la .h. ϻθϻϼϻϻ. ϫϻllaϼaϲϼaϻϲ ϼí Oϼϼϼaϻϫe [ϼo ecc].
Maϼϻ ϼϻa Coϻϼϼϼealbaϲ .h. mbϼϻaϻϻ ϼoϼ Muϼchaϼ
.h. mbϼϻaϻϻ, ϼú aϼϲoϼϲϼaϼaϼ ceϻϲϼϻ ceϼ ϻϻ ceϲϼϻ
ϲóϻϼϼechaϫx. Caϲ maϼϲaϼϲϫe ϼϻa ϻDuϼϼáleϻϲe,
comaϼba Ϸaϲϼaϻc, ϼoϼ mac Loϻϻϫϻϲ hϻ Maoϻlϲϼeaϲlaϻϻϻ
.ϻ. comaϼba Ϸϻϻϻéϻ ocuϼ Coluϻm Cϻlle, ϼú ϻϼϲoϼϲϼaϼaϼ
ϻle.

Kϲϲ. enaϻϼ .ϻϻ. Ϸ.; L. x. Sé blϻaϼna .l. aϼ mϻle aϻϼ
ϻϻ Cϻϫeϼϻa. Caϲuϼaϲ mac ϫϻϼϼϫaϼϲáϻϻ, comaϼba Cuϻϻϻϲ ϻ
Cϻaϻachϲa; Ceϲϼaϼh, ceϻϼ cleϻϼech Muman, quϻeueϼuϻϲ.
Cϼeϲ lá Nϻall mac Maoϻlϲϼeclaϻϻϻ ϼoϼ Dál ϻαϼaϻϫe, ϫo
ϼϲuc .xx. ceϼ ϼo ϼuaϫ, ocuϼ ϲϼϻ .xx. ϼuϻϻe ϼo bϼaϻϼ.
Ϸlann Maϻϻϻϼϼeach, aϻϼo ϼϻle ocuϼ aϻϼ[ϼ]ϼeϼ léϫϻϻϻ,
ocuϼ ϼoí ϼenϲuϼa eϼenn, ϻϻ uϻϲa eϲeϼna ϼequϻeuϻϲ.

---

[1] *Dolfinn.* There is no mention of
this Dolfinn in the account of this
battle given in the Anglo-Saxon
Chronicle, which has it under the
same year; the only person of the
name occurring in the Chronicle being
Dolphin, Earl of Cumberland, expelled by William in 1092. The battle is briefly recorded in the Annals
of Tighernach. See O'Conor's ed.,
Rerum Hibernicarum Scriptores, tom.
II., p. 299, where the editor incorrectly adds, "silet de hoc prælio
Chron. Sax."

[2] *[Died].* The corresponding expression in the text, [ϼo ecc], is supplied from Ann. Ult.

[3] *Relic-house,* maϼϲaϼϲϫe; i.e.,
the house (at Armagh?) in which
the *martra,* or relics of the martyrs
were kept. The Annals of Tighernach record the event in a more
intelligible manner: caϲh eϲϻϼ
Duϼϼaleϲhe, comaϼba Ϸaϲϼaϻc,
oϲuϼ Muϼchaϼ h. Maelϼechlaϻϻ,
comaϼba Ϸϻϼeϼ ocuϼ Coluϻm
Cϻlle, ac coϼϻum maϼϲϼaϻϫe:
"a battle between Dubh-da-lethe,
comarb of Patrick, and Murchadh
Ua Maelséchlain, comarb of Finnen
and Colum Cille, contending for relics
(*martraige*)." Murchadh Ua Maeil-
sechlain is not included in the list of
the successors of Colum Cille pub-

Cennedigh, son of Donncuan, steward of Clann-Toir-dhealbhaigh, was slain by the men of Connacht. A battle between the men of Alba and the Saxons, in which fell three thousand of the men of Alba, and one thousand and a half of the Saxons, together with Dolfinn,[1] son of Finntar. Loch-suidhe-Odhrain, in Sliabh-guaire, stole away in the end of the night of the festival of Michael, and went into the Fabhall, quod non auditum est ab antiquis.

The kalends of January, on the 1st feria, the 29th of the moon; the age of the Lord fifty-five years and, a thousand. Domhnall Ruadh O'Briain was slain by Ua hEidhin. Gillapatraic, king of Osraighe, [died].[2] A victory was gained by Toirdhelbhach Ua Briain over Murchadh Ua Briain, in which four hundred were slain, together with fourteen chieftains. The battle of the relic-house[3] was gained by Dubh-da-leithe, comarb of Patrick, over the son of Loingsech Ua Maelsechlainn, i.e. the comarb of Finnén and of Colum Cille, in which many were slain.

The kalends of January on the 2nd feria, the 10th of the moon; the age of the Lord fifty-six years and a thousand. Cathusach, son of Gerrgarbhan, comarb of Cainech in Cianachta,[4] and Cetfadh, head of the clerics of Mumha, quieverunt. A predatory expedition by Niall, son of Maelsechlainn, against the Dál-Araidhc, when he carried off two thousand cows, and three score men as prisoners. Flann Mainistrech, chief poet, and chief lector, and professor of the history of Erin, in vita æterna requievit.[5] Lightning came and killed three

---

lished by Dr. Reeves in his ed. of *Adamnan's* life of the Saint, and therefore it is to be presumed that Murchadh was only abbot of Cluain-Iraird and Kells, founded respectively by Sts. Finnen and Colum Cille. The event has been omitted by the Four Masters.

[4] *Cianachta;* i.e. Cianachta of Glenn Geimhin, now the bar. of Keenaght, co Londonderry, in which St. Cainnech was born, and founded the church of Drumachose or Termon-kenny.

[5] *Requievit,* ɼeꞯuieꞏꞅꞇ, MS.

Tene ġeláin do ṫocht ġur ro ṁarḃ triar aġ Oirṫert
Tóla ocus mac leiġinn aġ Suird, ocus ġurro bris
 inoile. Creċ do chuaid Eochaid .h. Flaiṫeṁ i Maġ-
ioṫa, oiḋċe nodlac mór, ġo dtuc .u. ced bó conuice
uirrse .i. co hoḃuinn Maiġe Uaṫa, ocus rorṡágrat na
bú irin aḃuinn, ocus ro báite ochtar ar da richait
díḃ, im Cuilend mac Derġain.

Ḳlt. Enair .iiii. p.; l. xx.i. Seacht mbliadna .l. ar
mile air in Tiġerna. Niall .h. hEcnechán, rí Cenel
nEnda, a suis occisus est. Dúnġal .h. Donnchada, ri
Eoġanachta Caisil, do ṫuitim la Murchad .h. Briain.
Finnġuine .h. Finnġuine, róaṁna Muman, dó
ṫuitim la Maolseclainn mac mBric. Maolruanaid
.h. Roċartaiġ, rí deirscrit Eli, do ṫuitim la Donnchad
mac Briain. Duḃṫúleiṫe .h. Sinaoṫa, airchinnech
Corcaiġe, ocus Roḃartaċ mac Ferḋomnaiġ, comarba
Coluim Cille, in Domino dormierunt. Domnall .h.
Ruairc do ṁarḃaḋ la Domnall mac Maolruanaid, rí
fer Manach.

Ḳlt. Enair u. p.; l. íi.; ocht mbliadna .l. ar mile
air in Tiġerna. Imlech Iubair do lorcad co leir,
edir ḋaimliaġ ocus ċloictech. Lulaċ mac Ġilla
Comġáin, airdríġ Alban, do ṁarbad la Maolcoluim
mac Donnchada i caṫ. Maiḋm Sleiḃe Crott rian
Diarmaid mac Maoilnambó, for Donnchadh mac
mBriain, dú i torchair Cairpri .h. Líġḋa, airchinneċ
Imliġ Iḃair, ocus Riḋardan mac Concoirne, rí Ele,
et alii multi. Mac Beṫad mac Finnlaoiċ, airdriġ

---

¹ *Fastnesses*. indile. This word
is probably a mistake. The Ann. Ult.
(Dublin copy) has "in mbile," "the
tree." In Dr. O'Conor's ed. of the Annals referred to, the words in mbile
are incorrectly printed in mbaile, i.e.
"the place."

² *Magh-Uatha*. So in Four Mast.
and in the Annals of Ulster. Dr.

O'Donovan is wrong in saying (Four
Mast., p. 872, note ⁿ), that the name
is written Abhainn-Maighe-nItha in
the Ann. Ult. It is printed so in
Dr. O'Conor's text, but the Dublin
MS. has the name aḃainn Maiġe
hUatha.

³ *Of them;* i.e. of the predatory
band.

persons at Disert-Tola, and a student at Sord, and broke
fastnesses.[1] Eochaidh Ua Flaithemh went on a preying
expedition into Magh-Itha, on the night of great Christmas, and he brought five hundred cows to the water, i.e.
to the river of Magh-Uatha;[2] and they left the cows in
the river, and forty-eight of them[3] were drowned, along
with Cuilend, son of Dergan.

The kalends of January on the 4th feria, the 21st of
the moon; the age of the Lord fifty-seven years and
a thousand. Niall Ua hEgnechain, king of Cenel-Enna,
a suis occisus est. Dunghal Ua Donnchadha, king of
Eoghanacht-Caisil, fell by Murchadh Ua Briain.[4] Finnghuine, grandson of Finnghuine, royal heir of Mumha,
fell by Maelsechlainn, son of Brec. Maelruanaidh Ua Fogartaigh, king of the South of Eile, fell by Donnchadh,
son of Brian. Dubhdhaleithe Ua Cinaetha, airchinnech
of Corcach, and Robhartach, son of Ferdomhnach, comarb of Colum Cille, in Domino dormierunt. Domhnall
Ua Ruairc was slain by Domhnall, son of Maelruanaidh,
king of Feara-Manach.

The kalends of January on the 5th feria, the 2nd[5] of
the moon; the age of the Lord fifty eight years and a
thousand. Imlech-Ibhair was entirely burned, both stone
church and steeple. Lulach, son of Gillacomghain, chief
king of Alba, was slain by Maelcoluim, son of Donnchadh, in battle. The victory of Sliabh-Crot was gained
by Diarmaid, son of Mael-na-mbó, over Donnchadh, son
of Brian, in which fell Cairpre Ua Lighdha, airchinnech
of Imlech-Ibhair, and Ribhardan, son of Cucoirne, king
of Eile, et alii multi. Mac Bethad, son of Finnlaech,

---

[4] Ua Briain; i.e. O'Brian, grandson
or descendant of Brian. The MS. has
mac Ḃṛiain, son of Brian, but this is
a mistake, as Murchadh, son of Brian,
was slain in the battle of Clontarf in
1014. The Murchadh here referred
to was Murchadh sgiath gearr (Murrough "short shield"), whose death
is recorded under the year 1068, infra,
and who was the second son of
Donnchadh, or Donogh, son of Brian
Boromha.

[5] The 2nd. The MS. erroneously
reads xii (12).

Αlbαn, do mαrbαd lα Mαolcoluim mαc n'Donnchαdα
ι cατ̆.

Ϳclτ. Enαιr ιιι. ꝑ.; l. xιιι. Nαοι mblιαdnα .l. αꝛ mιle
αιꝛ ιn ΤιƷeꝛnα. Cꝛeαc̆ lα Mαοιꝛeclαιnn .h. Mαdαdαιn
α nΑιꝛꝛτeꝛαιḃ, co ꝛuƷ τꝛι ced bó uel paulo pluꝛ,
ocuꝛ Ʒuꝛꝛo mαꝛb Ʒιllαmuιꝛe mαc ΑιꝛechταιƷ, muιꝛe
cloιnne Sιonαιch. Mαοιꝛechlαιnn .h. bꝛιc do muchαd
α nuαιm lα Mαοιꝛechlαιnn .h. bꝼαolάιn. Αοḋ .h.
Dubdα, ꝛι .h. nΑmαlƷαdα, α ꝼuιꝛ occιꝛuꝛ eꝛτ. Cꝛeαc̆
lα hΑꝛdƷαꝛ ṁάƷ lαc̆lαιnn co Cenel EoƷαιn, α n'Dαl
Αꝛαιde, co dτucꝛατ boꝛuṁα ṁoꝛ, ocuꝛ dα ced duιne
edιꝛ ṁαꝛbαd ocuꝛ eꝛƷαbαιl. Cαthαl mαc ΤιƷeꝛnάιn,
ꝛί ιαꝛthαιꝛ Connαcht; ConƷαlαc̆ .h. RίαƷαιn, ꝛίdαmnα
Τempαch; Duαꝛcαn .h. heƷꝛα, ꝛί luιƷne; Ʒιllα
CoeṁƷιn mαc Ʒιllα CoṁƷαιll, ꝛίdαṁnα lαιƷen, occιꝛ
ꝛunτ. Τomαlταch .h. Mαοιlḃꝛénuιnn, muιꝛe ꝼιl
MuιꝛeꝷhαιƷh, moꝛτuuꝛ eꝛτ.

Ϳcτt. Enαιꝛ .uίί. ꝑ.; l. xx.ιιιι. Seꝛcατ blιάdαn αꝛ mιle
αιꝛ ιn ΤιƷeꝛnα. Mιlleꝛιmo αc .lx. αnno Domιnιce ιn-
cαꝛnατιonιꝛ. CoƷαd móꝛ ι nΑꝛd Mαc̆α edιꝛ Cumuꝛcαch
.h. neꝛαdαιn ocuꝛ Duḃḋάleιc̆e, comαꝛbα Pατꝛαιc, ιmón
αbḋuιne. Cenαnτuꝛ do loꝛcαd co leιꝛ conα ḋαmlιαƷ.
leιꝷꝷlend do loꝛcαd co huιlιƷe Ʒénmoτά αn deꝛτech.
Domnαll Déιꝛꝛec̆, ꝛꝼίṁ αnṁc̆αꝛα Eꝛenn, ocuꝛ Conn nα.

---

[1] *Ua Bric.* See next note.

[2] *Mortuus est.* m. ꝛ. (for mortni
sunt), MS. The Ann. Ult. have also
m. ꝛ. In the Annals of the Four
Masters, Tomaltagh Ua Maeilbhren-
uinn (or O'Mulrennin) is incorrectly
stated to have been put to death with
Maelsechlain Ua Bric, as above referred to.

[3] *Millesimo.* mιllιꝛιmo, MS.

[4] *Ac.* αƷ, MS.

[5] *Incarnationis.* ιncαꝛnαcιonιꝛ,
MS.

[6] *Ua nEradhain.* h. neꝛαꝛdαιn,

MS. The Ann. Ult. have this entry,
word for word with the present chronicle; but it is not given in Tighernach,
or the Four Masters. It appears from
the Chron. Scotorum that Cumuscach
was successful in the contest, as the
record in the latter authority (1058=
1060) is "a change of abbots at Ard-
Macha, viz.:—Cumuscach Ua Eradh-
ain in the place of Dubhdalethe."

[7] *Dertech.* This word, which is also
written *dairtech, deartech, durtech,* and
duirtech, is supposed to mean "domus
penitentiæ." It is usually translated "oratory." See Petrie's *Round*

chief king of Alba, was slain by Maelcoluim, son of
Donnchadh, in battle.

The kalends of January on the 6th feria, the 13th [1059.]
of the moon; the age of the Lord fifty-nine years
and a thousand. A preying expedition by Maelsechlainn Ua Madadhain into Airthera, when he carried off
three hundred cows, vel paulo plus, and killed Gillamuire Mac Airechtaigh, steward of Clann-Sionaigh.
Maelsechlainn Ua Bric[1] was smothered in a· cave by
Maelsechlainn Ua Faelain. Aedh Ua Dubhda, king of
Ui-Amhalghadha, a suis occisus est. A preying expedition by Ardghar Mac Lachlainn, with the Cenel-Eoghain,
into Dal-Araidhe, when they carried off a great cattle
spoil, and killed or captured two hundred persons. Cathal,
son of Tighernan, king of the West of Connacht; Conghalach Ua Riagain, royal heir of Temhair; Duarcan Ua
hEghra, king of Luighne; Gillacaeimhghin, son of Gilla-
comghaill, royal heir of Laighen, occisi sunt. Tomaltach
Ua Maelbhrenuinn, steward of Sil-Muiredhaigh, mortuus
est.[2]

The kalends of January on the 7th feria, the 24th of [1060.]
the moon; the age of the Lord sixty years and a
thousand; millesimo[3] ac[4] sexagesimo anno Dominicæ
Incarnationis.[5] A great war in Ard-Macha, between Cumuscach Ua nEradhain[6] and Dubhdhaleithe, comarb of
Patrick, regarding the abbacy. Cenannus was altogether
burned, together with its stone church. Leithghlenn was
completely burned, with the exception of the dertech.[7]
Domhnall Deissech,[8] chief anmchara[9] of Erinn, and Conn-

Towers, Trans. R. I. Acad., vol. xx.,
pp. 119, 120, 341, where many references to the nature and use of the
dertech will be found.

[8] *Deissech*; i.e. of the Deise, a tribe
name still preserved in those of the
baronies of Decies-within-Drum, and
Decies - without - Drum, in the co.

Waterford, and Deece, in the co.
Meath.

[9] *Anmchara*; i.e. confessor; lit.
"soul friend;" the word being a compound of the Lat. *animæ carus*. See
Dr. Reeves's Tract on *The Culdees of
the British Islands* (Trans. R. I.
Acad., vol. xxiv), p. 88.

mbochτ Cluana mic Nóιη, ατ Chηιγτum uocaτι ηunτ.
Flannaᵹán .h. Cellaιᵹ, ηι bηeᵹ, τo héc ina ailiτηι.

Kττ. Enáιη ιι. γ.; l. u.; bliaτain γeγcaτ aη mile
aoιη ιn Τιᵹeηna Muιηeτach. h. Maolcoluιm, aιηcιn-
nech Ɗoιηe, [τo ec]. Ɗomnall .h. Maolτoηaιτ τo
maηbaτ la Ruaιτηι .h. Canannán a caτ. Cúulaτ
mac Conᵹalaιᵹ, ηι Uachτaιη τίηe, ιn peniτenτιa
moητuuη eητ. Niall mac Maoιlγeclainn moητuuη
eητ. Slúaιᵹeτ la hccoτ .h. Concobaιη co Cenτ τoηaτ,
ᵹuηηo bηιγγ ιn ᵹcaτηaιᵹ, ocuη ᵹuη ῖῖuᵹ ιn τιηηaιτ.
Ᵹlenτ τá laca τo loηcaτ ᵹo leιη.

Kττ. Enáιη .ιιι. γ.; l. xιι. Ɗa bliaτain .lx. aη
mile aoιη ιn Τιᵹeηna. Ruaιτηι h. Flaιτbeητaιᵹ, ηι
ιaηταιη Connachτ. Ɗomnall .h. Moelτoηaιτ τo
ῖaηbaτ la hccoτ .h. Concobaιη ι caτ. Ᵹιlla Cηιoγτ
.h. Moelτoηaιτ, comaηba Coluim Cille eτιη Eηinn ιγ
Albain, [γuιeuιτ]. Cηeaτ la hccηoᵹaη ῖáᵹ Laclainn
ι Connachτoιb, co τucγaτ γé mile τo buaιτ, ocuη
mile τo τaoιnιτ. Ruaιτηι mac Concaιηηᵹe, ηιτamna
Feηumaιτe, τo ῖaηbaτ τo mac Neιll hi Ruaιηe.

Kττ. Enáιη .ιιιι. γ.; l. xx.uιι.; τηι bliaτna .lx. aη
mile aιη ιn Τιᵹeηna. Caτhal .h. Ɗonnchaτa, ηι .h.
nEchach Mumaιn, [τo maηbaτ]. Cúτuιlιᵹ .h. Τaτᵹ,
ηι bηeη Lí; Moeιlηechlainn .h. Moτaτáιn, ηιτaῖna

---

¹ *Conn-na-mbocht.* In English, "Conn of the poor."

² [*Died*]. [τo ec]. Supplied from the Four Mast.

³ *Mortuus est.* moητuι ηunτ, MS.; from which it would appear that some other names, intended to have been recorded, were omitted by the transcriber of the Chronicle.

⁴ *Burned.* At the end of the entry for this year one of the transcribers of the Chronicle has added the following memorandum:—"Iγ ιm ηᵹιταc τo τáηc bηιαιn mic Ɗιαηmατα. cc⁰.Ɗ⁰. 1589. Mιη Pιlιp bατοτ."

"I am fatigued from the book of Brian Mac Diarmada. A.D. 1589. I am Philip Badlaigh." The last figure has been mutilated and reduced to a 0, so that the date has been read 1580 by O'Curry. See *Lectures*, &c., p. 94. Four leaves of paper follow, all blank except a few verses scribbled on the back page of the 2nd leaf.

⁵ *Ua Flaithbhertaigh.* See next note.

⁶ *Domhnall Ua Maeldoraidh.* This is evidently an incorrect repetition of the entry under the preceding year, recording the death of Domhnall Ua

na-mbocht[1] of Cluain-mic-Nois, ad Christum vocati sunt. Flannagan Ua Cellaigh, king of Bregh, died on his pilgrimage.

The kalends of January on the 2nd feria, the 5th of the moon; the age of the Lord sixty-one years and a thousand. Muiredhach, grandson of Maelcoluim, air-chinnech of Doire, [died].[2] Domhnall Ua Maeldoraidh was slain by Ruaidhri Ua Canannain, in a battle. Cu-uladh, son of Conghalach, king of Uachtar-thire, in pœni-tentia mortuus est.[3] Niall, son of Maelsechlainn, mortuus est. A hosting by Aedh Ua Conchobhair to Cenn-coradh, when he demolished the fortress, and filled up the well. Glenn-da-locha was completely burned.[4]

The kalends of January on the 3rd feria, the 16th of the moon; the age of the Lord sixty-two years and a thousand. Ruaidhri Ua Flaithbhertaigh,[5] king of the West of Connacht; Domhnall Ua Maeldoraidh[6] was slain by Aedh Ua Conchobhair, in battle. Gillachrist Ua Maeldoraidh, comarb of Colum Cille both in Erinn and Alba, [quievit].[7] A predatory expedition by Ardghar Mac Lachlainn into Connacht, when they carried off six thousand cows, and a thousand persons. Ruaidhri, son of Cu-cairrge, royal heir of Fernmhagh, was killed by the son of Niall Ua Ruairc.

The kalends of January on the 4th feria, the 27th of the moon; the age of the Lord sixty-three years and a thousand. Cathal Ua Donnchadha, king of Ui-Echach-Mumhan, [was slain].[8] Cudhuiligh Ua Taidhg, king of Feara-Li; Maelsechlainn Ua Madadhain, royal heir

---

Macildoraidh (or O'Muldory), at the hands of Ruaidhri Ua Canannain. The words which follow, viz.:—"was slain by Aedh Ua Conchobhair, in battle," belong properly to the previous entry, which should there-fore read "Ruaidhri Ua Flaithbher-taigh, king of the West of Connacht, was slain by Aedh Ua Conchobhair, in battle."

[7] [*Quievit*]. Supplied from the Ann. of Tighernach.

[8] [*Was slain*]. [Do marbad]. Sup-plied from the Ann. Four Mast., which add that Cathal was slain by his own son, Finnshuilech, or the "fair eyed."

Oiliᵹ, α ɼuıɼ ınımıcıɼ occıɼı ɼunᴄ, [.ı.] o Cénel Conαıll.
Coınnṁeᴅh móɼ lα máᵹ Lαċlαınn oᴄá ᵹlenᴅ Suılıᵹe
ɼıαɼ co hıαɼᴄhαɼ Luıᵹne, ocuɼ ᵹo Muαıᴅ O nΑmαlᵹαᴅα,
ᴅu αᴄαnᵹαᴅαɼ ɼıᵹɼαıᴅe Connαchᴄ ınα ċech, ım Αoᴅ .h.
Conchobαıɼ, ocuɼ ım Αoᴅ mαc Neıll 1 Ruαıɼc, ocuɼ ım
mαc Αıɼᴄ h1 Ruαıɼc. Uαıṁ Αllα α ᵹCeɼα ᴅo ᵹαbαıl
o Connαchᴄαıᴃ ɼoɼ muınᴄeɼ Αoᴅα h1 Concobαıɼ, ın ɼo
muchαᴅ .lx. αɼ ceᴅ. Nıαll mαc Eochαᴅα, αıɼᴅ ɼı Ulαᴅ,
α éᵹın ıᴅ Nouembıɼ, ın Ɔαɼᴅαoın, ocuɼ ın xuıı. [eɼcα].

ᴊᴄᴄ. Enαıɼ .u. ꝝ.; L .ıx.; ceıᴄɼı blıαᴅnα .lx. αɼ
mıle αıɼ ın Ꞇıᵹeɼnα. Ɔoılᵹén .h. Sonα, αıɼchınnech
Αıɼᴅ Sɼαċα; ın Ɔαll .h. Lonαın ɼɼıméᵹeıɼ ɼeɼ
Mumαn; Eochαıᴅ .h. Ɔoɼéıᴅ, αıɼchınnech Ɔoṁnαᵹ
ṁóıɼ Moıᵹe h1ᴄα, ın Ɔomıno ᴅoɼmıeɼunᴄ. Muıɼ-
ceɼᴄαch .h. Neıll, ɼı Ꞇeαlċα óᵹ, ᴅo mαɼbαᴅ; o Uıᴃ
Cɼemᴄhαınn occıɼuɼ eɼᴄ. Ɔonnchαᴅ mαc Bɼıαın
Bóɼoıṁe, αıɼᴅɼíᵹ Mumαn, ᴅo eᵹ α Róıṁ ınα αılıᴄɼı.
Ɔıαɼmαıᴅ .h. Loɼcαın, ɼíᴅαmnα Lαıᵹen, ᴅo ṁαɼbαᴅ lα
Cenel Eoᵹαın α nUllᴄoıb. Αɼᴅᵹαl ṁáᵹ Lαċlαınn, ɼí
Oılıᵹ, ᴅo eᵹ α Ꞇeαlαıᵹ oᵹ, eᴄ ɼeɼulᴄuɼ eɼᴄ ın Αɼᴅ
Mαchα ın mαuɼoleo ɼeᵹum. Leobeléın, ɼí Bɼeᴄαn, ᴅo
mαɼbαᴅ lα mαc ıαcoıɼ. Echmαɼcαch, ɼí ᵹαll, ᴅo eᵹ.

ᴊᴄᴄ. Enαıɼ. uıı. ꝝ.; L. xx. Coıᵹ blıαᴅnα .lx. ocuɼ mıle
αıɼ ın Ꞇıᵹeɼnα. Ɔuᴃᴄαch Αlbαnαch, ɼíṁ αnmċαɼα
Eɼenn ocuɼ Αlbαn, α nΑɼᴅ Mαchα quıeuıᴄ. Ɔonnchαᴅ
h. Mαċᵹαṁnα, ɼí Ulαᴅ, ᴅo ṁαɼbαᴅ α mBennċαɼ α

---

1 *Muaidh*; i.e. the river Muaidh, or Moy, in the territory of the Ui Am-halghadha, or Tirawley, between the counties of Mayo and Sligo.

2 *Came into his house*; or, in other words, "submitted to him."

3 *Connachtmen.* So also in the Ann. Ult.; but the Four Masters say the "Conmaicni," which is more likely to be correct.

4 *The 9th.* The MS. erroneously reads x.ıx. (19th).

5 *Ardghal.* Called Ardghar under the year 1062.

6 *Mausoleo.* αuɼoʟıo(ausolio), MS.

7 *Leobhelin.* The Annals of Ulster more correctly read "MacLeobelın," "the son of Leobhelin," i.e. Grifud, or Gruffudd, son of Llewelyn, whose death is recorded in the *Brut y Tywyso-gion* at the year 1061, but under 1063

of Oilech, a suis inimicis occisi sunt, [viz. :]—by the Cenel-
Conaill. A great coigne by Mac Lachlainn from Glenn-
Suiligh westwards to the west of Luighne, and to Muaidh[1]
of Ui-Amhalghadha, when the chieftains of Connacht
came into his house,[2] with Aedh Ua Conchobhair, and
with Aedh, the son of Niall Ua Ruairc, and with the son
of Art Ua Ruairc. The cave of Alla, in Cera, was captured by the Connachtmen,[3] against the people of Aedh
Ua Conchobhair, in which one hundred and sixty persons
were suffocated. Niall, son of Eochaidh, chief king of
Uladh, died on the ides of November, on a Thursday, and
on the 18th [of the moon].

The kalends of January on the 5th feria, the 9th[4] of
the moon ; the age of the Lord sixty-four years and
a thousand. Doilghen Ua Sona, airchinnech of Ard-
Sratha ; the blind Ua Lonain, chief poet of the men of
Mumha ; Eochaidh Ua Doreidh, airchinnech of Domh-
nach-mór of Magh-Itha, in Domino dormierunt. Muirchertach Ua Neill, king of Tealach-óg, was slain ; by the
Ui-Cremthainn occisus est. Donnchadh, son of Brian
Boromha, chief king of Mumha, died in Rome, on his
pilgrimage. Diarmaid Ua Lorcain, royal heir of Laighen,
was slain by the Cenel-Eoghain, in Uladh. Ardghal[5]
Mac Lachlainn, king of Oilech, died at Tealach-og, et
sepultus est in Ard-Macha, in mausoleo[6] regum. Leobhelin,[7] king of Britain, was slain by the son of Iacop. Echmarcach, king of the Foreigners, died.

The kalends of January on the 7th feria, the 20th of
the moon ; the age of the Lord sixty-five years and
a thousand. Dubhthach Albanach,[8] chief anmchara[9] of
Erinn and Alba, quievit in Ard-Macha. Donnchadh Ua
Mathghamhna, king of Uladh, was slain at Bennchair a

---

in the *Annales Cambriæ*; in neither of
which Chronicles, however, is the
name of his slayer given.

  [8] *Dubhthach Albanach*; i.e. Dubhthach Albanicus, or the Scotchman.

See Dr. Reeves's interesting note regarding this Dubhthach, *Adamnan*, p.
401, note *.

  [9] *Anmchara*; i.e. confessor. See
note [9], p. 57, *supra*.

ꞃuıꞃ. Ꞛoð .h. hUꞇꞇꞃꞇıꞃcc ꝺo ꞡꞇbꞇıꞁ ꞃıꝣe Ceneoıꞁ
Eoꞡꞇın. Mꞇc Ꞇꞇıꝋꞡ hı Ceꞁꞁꞇıꝣ, ꞃí O Mꞇıne, ocuꞃ
Fꞁꞇıꞇbeꞃꞇꞇch O Fꞁꞇıꞇbeꞃꞇꞇıꝣ, ꞃı ıꞇꞃꞇhꞇıꞃ Connꞇchꞇ,
occıꞃı ꞃunꞇ ꞁꞇ hꞛoð .h. Concobꞇıꞃ. Domnꞇꞁꞁ .h.
Loınꞡꞃıꝣ, ꞃí Dꞇꞁ nꞛꞃꞇıꝺe, ocuꞃ Muıꞃceꞃꞇꞇch .h.
Mꞇoꞁfꞇꝧuıꞁꞁ, ꞃı Cꞇıꞃꞃꞡe ꝺꞃꞇcꞇıꝣe, ꝺo ṁꞇꞃbꞇꝺ o Uíꞇ
Méꞇh. Leoꞡán mꞇc Lꞇıꝣnén, ꞃí Lꞇıꝣne, ꝺo mꞇꞃbꞇꝺ ꞁꞇ
Conchobꞇꞃ .h. Mꞇoıꞁꞃeꞇꞁꞇınn. Eꞇṁıꞁıð .h. hꞛꞇıꞇheıꝺ,
ꞃı .h. nEchꞇch, ꝺo mꞇꞃbꞇꝺ ꝺo Ceneꞁ Eoꞡꞇın.

Kꞁꞇ. Enꞇıꞃ ı. ꞃ.; ꞁ. ı. Se bꞁıꞇꝺnꞇ .ꞁꝉ. ꞇꞃ mıꞁe ꞇıꞃ
ın Ꞇıꝣeꞃnꞇ. Ꞛoð .h. Ruꞇıꞃc, ꞃı .h. mꞅꞃuın, moꞃꞇuuꞃ
eꞃꞇ ꞃꞇꞇım ıꞇꞃ noꞃꞡuın Scꞃíne Pꞇꝺꞃꞇıc. Ꞡıꞁꞁꞇbꞃꞇıꝺe,
ımoꞃꞃo, ꞃí .h. mꞅꞃuın, ocuꞃ mꞇc Senáım, ꞃí Ꞡꞇıꞁenꝣ,
occıꞃı ꞃunꞇ. Cnó meꞃ móꞃ ı nEꞃınn uıꞁe, uꞇ ꞃebeꞁꞁꞇꞇ
fꞁumınıbuꞃ.

Kꞇꞇ. Enꞇıꞃ .ııı. ꞃ.; ꞁ. ꝩꝩ.ııı. Seꞇchꞇ mbꞁıꞇꝺnꞇ .ꞁꝉ.
ꞇꞃ mıꞁe ꞇıꞃ ın Ꞇıꝣeꞃnꞇ. Sꞁoıꝣeꞇꝺ ꞁꞇ Ꞇoıꞃꞃꝺheꞇꞁbꞇch
.h. mꞅꞃíꞇın co Loꞇ Cıme, coꞃꞃuꞃ mꞇꞃꝧ ꝺon ꞇꞃꞁóıꝣeꝺ
ꞃın .h. Conchobꞇıꞃ, ꞃí Cıꞇꞃꞃꞇıꝣe Luꞇcꞃꞇ. Ceꞁꞁ ꝺꞇꞃꞇ
conꞇ ꞇemꞁꞇıb ꝺo uıꞁe ꞁoꞃcꞇꝺ. Ꞛoꝺh ın ꝣꞇı ꝧeꞃnꞇıꝣ,
mꞇc Ꞇꞇıꝋꞡ ın eıch ꝣıꞁ mıc Cꞇꞇhꞇıꞁ .ı. ꞇıꞃoꞃí ꞇoıꝣeꝺ
Connꞇchꞇ ocuꞃ Luꞇm ꞡꞇıꞃcıꝺ nꞇ nꝣꞇoıꝺeꞇꞁ, ꝺo mꞇꞃbꞇꝺ
ı cꞇꞇ Ꞇuꞃꞁꞇıꝣ Ꞛꝣnꞇ ꞁꞇ hꞛoð mꞇc Ꞛıꞃꞇ Uꞇꞁꞁꞇıꝣ hı
Ruꞇıꞃc, ocuꞃ Ꞛoð .h. Concenuınn, ꞃí .h. nDıꞇꞃmꞇꝺꞇ,
eꞇ ꞇꞁíí muꞁꞇı.

---

[1] *Luighne.* Lꞇıꝣne (Laighne), MS.
In the Annals of Tighernach, of
Ulster, and the Four Mast., the name
of the territory is "Gailenga," a district partly represented at present by
the barony of Morgallion, in the co.
Meath. The name of Laighne, or
more properly Luighne, is now preserved in that of the barony of Lune,
in the same county.

[2] *Was slain.* ꝺo mꞇꞃbꞇꝺ (do
marbad). These words are erroneously
repeated in the MS.

[3] *Immediately.* ꞃꝺꞇıꞇım (sdaitim)
for ꞃꞇꞇım MS.

[4] *Ut rebellat fluminibus.* fꞁumın-
ebuꞃ, MS. This expression is intended to denote that the nuts shed
by the trees choked the rivers, or, as
the Four Masters paraphrase it, "that
the course of brooks and streamlets
was impeded."

[5] *The 3rd feria, 23rd of the moon.*
There is here a double mistake. The
first of January in the year 1067
occurred on Monday, the Dom. Letter
being G, and coincided with the 12th
day of the moon's age. But the nota-
tion seems to be that of the next year.

[d] *Ua Conchobhair.* Dr. O'Donovan,

suis. Aedh, grandson of Ualgharg, assumed the kingship of Cenel-Eoghain. The son of Tadhg Ua Ceallaigh, king of Ui-Maine, and Flaithbhertach Ua Flaithbhertaigh, king of the West of Connacht, occisi sunt by Aedh Ua Conchobhair. Domhnall Ua Loingsigh, king of Dal-Araidhe, and Muirchertach Ua Maelfabhaill, king of Carraig-Brachaighe, were slain by the Ui-Méth. Leogan, son of Laighnen, king of Luighne,[1] was slain[2] by Conchobhar Ua Maelsechlainn. Echmhilidh Ua hAitheidh, king of Ui-Echach, was slain by the Cenel-Eoghain.

The kalends of January on the 1st feria, the 1st of the moon; the age of the Lord sixty-six years and a thousand. Aedh Ua Ruairc, king of Ui-Briuin, mortuus est, immediately[3] after the plundering of the shrine of Patrick. Gillabraide, moreover, king of Ui-Briuin, and the son of Senan, king of Gailenga, occisi sunt. A great nut crop in all Erinn, ut rebellat fluminibus.[4]

The kalends of January on the 3rd feria,[5] the 23rd of the moon[5]; the age of the Lord sixty-seven years and a thousand. A hosting by Toirdhelbhach Ua Briain to Loch Cime, on which hosting Ua Conchobhair,[6] king of Ciarraighe-Luachra, was slain. Cill-dara, with its churches, was entirely burned. Aedh "of the gapped spear," son of Tadhg "of the white steed," son of Cathal, i.e. the high-king of the province of Connacht, and the helmsman of the valour of the Gaeidhel, was slain in the battle of Turlach-Aghna by Aedh, son of Art Uallach Ua Ruairc; and Aedh Ua Concenainn, king of Ui-Diarmada, et alii[7] multi.

---

in a note to his ed. of the Four Mast. (p. 891, note*), observes "according to the Annals of Tigernach and those of Boyle, which correspond in recording his death in this year (1067), his name was Hugh." There is no such statement in either of the authorities referred to. Dr. O'Donovan seems to have confounded Ua Conchobhair, or O'Conor, of Ciarraighe-Luachra, with Aedh Ua Conchobhair, king of Connacht, whose death in the battle of Turlach-Aghna is recorded by Tighernach at the year indicated, but in the Annals of Boyle under the year 1064.

[7] *Alii.* ꝏ, MS.

Ictt. Enaip .iiii. p.; l. xx.iii.; ocht mbliαona .lx.
ap mile aip in Cizepna. Maiom pitbe oo tabaipt
oαcoo .h. Maoiltpeclainn ap a oepbpathaip bin̄ein .i.
Oomnall mac Neill mic Maoiltpeclainn, pi Oiliz,
zup mapbαo ann Oomnall pein, ocup oon Oomnall,
impppo, oo zaipt Oomnall na mbocht. Mupchαo .h.
bpiain, piōaṁna Muman, oo mapbαo la pipa Cerpa.
Plaitbeptach .h. Pepzail, pi Celcα óz, oo zuin la Cenel
mbinniŏ.

Iclt. Enaip .u. p.; l. iiii.; .ix. mbliαona .lx. ap mile
aip in Cizepna. Oún oá letzlap ocup αpo gpαtα, ocup
Lupcα, ocup Supo Coluim Cille, ab izne oippipate punt.
h. hαcoōa, pi .h. bpiαčpαč αpoa gpαtα, moptuup ept.

Iclt. Enáip. ui. p.; l. xu. Seachtṁoōαo bliαoan ap
mile aip in Cizepna. .h. Plaitpi, pi Ulαo, oo atpízhαo
la .h. Moelpuanαo ocup la uUllta; acht chena po
mapbαo ant .h. Moelpuanαo pin po ceoóip i cαč, la
Oonnpletbe .h. nEochαoa. Mupchαo mac Oiapmaoα,
pi Laizen ocup Zall, [moptuup ept], et pepultup ept
in αč cliαč. αb la .i. mac mic boečαin, oo mapbαo
oo mac in abαo hi Maoloopαo. Cepmann Oáōeóc
oo apzuin oo Ruaiōpi O Canannáin; et uinoicauit
Oeup et Oαōeoz, ante plenum annum.

Iclt. Enaip .uii. p.; l. xxui.; bliαoain peachtṁoōαo
ap mile aip in Cizepna. Cill oapa, ocup Zlenn oa
lαčα, ocup Cluain Oulcáin cpemate punt.

Iclt. Enaip. i. p.; l. uiii.; ōá ōliαoain .lxx. ap mile

---

[1] *Memorable defeat.* Maiōm
pitbe. Dr. O'Donovan (Four Mast.
ad. an.) considered pitbe to be the
name of a place, and translates "the
battle of Sithbhe." But the word
pitbe is in many glossaries explained
"pichbeo .i. pot a cbú," "perpetual;" i.e., "its fame is long."

[2] *Domhnall na mbochi*; i.e. "Domhnall (or Daniel) of the poor.

[3] *Dissipatæ.* oippipαtta (disipatta),
MS.

[4] *Hi*; i.e. III (or I) Coluim Cille, or
Iona.

[5] *Mac-in-abaid*; i.e. "the son of the
abbot." There was an abbot of Hi
called Gillachrist Ua Maeldoraidh,
whose death is recorded under the
year 1062, *supra*; and Dr. Reeves
supposes that he was the father of
the individual who is here called

The kalends of January on the 3rd feria, the 23rd of the moon; the age of the Lord sixty-eight years and a thousand. A memorable defeat[1] was inflicted by Aedh Ua Maelsechlainn on his own brother, viz.:—Domhnall, son of Niall, son of Maelsechlainn, king of Oilech, in which Domhnall himself was slain; and this Domhnall, moreover, was usually called "Domhnallnambocht."[2] Murchadh Ua Briain, royal heir of Mumha, was slain by the men of Teffa. Flaithbhertach, grandson of Ferghal, king of Tealach-óg, was *mortally* wounded by the Cenel-Binnigh.

The kalends of January on the 5th feria, the 4th of the moon; the age of the Lord sixty-nine years and a thousand. Dún-da-lethglas, and Ard-Sratha, and Lusca, and Sord-Choluim-Chille, ab igne dissipatæ[3] sunt. Ua Aedha, king of Ui-Fiachrach of Ard-Sratha, mortuus est.

The kalends of January on the 6th feria, the 15th of the moon; the age of the Lord seventy years and a thousand. Ua Flaithri, king of Uladh, was dethroned by Ua Maelruanaidh and the Ulidians; but this Ua Maelruanaidh was slain in battle immediately after, by Donnsleibhe Ua hEochadha. Murchadh, son of Diarmaid, king of Laighen and of the Foreigners, [mortuus est], et sepultus est in Ath-cliath. The abbot of Hi,[4] i.e. the grandson of Baethan, was slain by Mac-in-abaid[5] Ua Maeldoraidh. Termonn-Dabheog was plundered by Ruaidhri O'Canannain, et vindicavit Deus et Dabheog ante[6] plenum annum.

The kalends of January on the 7th feria, the 26th of the moon; the age of the Lord seventy-one years and a thousand. Cill-dara, and Glenn-da-locha, and Cluain-Dolcain crematæ[7] sunt.

The kalends of January on the 1st feria, the 7th of the moon; the age of the Lord seventy-two years and a

---

"son of the abbot Ua Maeldoraidh." See Reeves's *Adamnan*, p. 401, note [b].

[6] *Ante.* 7, for et, MS. The word ante is supplied from the Annals of Ulster. Ruaidhri O'Canannain's death is entered under the next year.

[7] *Cremata.* cṗemaṫṫe (crematte), MS.

aoir in Tigerna. Diarmaid mac Maoilnambó, rí
Laigen ocur Gall, do tuitim i cat la Conchobar .h.
Maoilrechlainn .i. rí Tempac, ocur ár Gall ocur
Laigen uime; in reachtmað la oßebra, mairt illaít
reachtmuine mar ßerað in cat rin. .h. Rógarta, rí
Eli, do marbað la .h. mbrian. Ruaidri O Canannain,
rí Cenel Conaill, do marbad la .h. Maoldoraid .i.
Conžur. Franca do dul i nCClbain, co tucrat mac ríž
CClban i neroirecht leó.

Ktt. Enair .111. ß.; L. xuiii.; tri bliadna ar lxx. ar
mile aoir in Tigerna. Conchobar .h. Maoilrechlainn, rí Tempac, do marbað do mac Flainn mic
Maoiltrechlainn, dar rárugað Bacla Iorra, baculo
prerente. Sloiged la Toirrdealbac i Leit Cuinn, conderna creic ndiairmide i nGaileng, ocur gurro marb
Maolmórda O Caturuiž, rí Bregh. Sitrec mac CCin-
laoib do marbad a Manuinn.

Ktt. Enáir .1111. ß.; L. xxix. Ceitri bliadna .lxx.
ar mile aoir in Tigerna. CCrd macha do lorcad in
mairt íar mbelltaine, cona huilib templaib ocur
clogaib, etir rait ocur trian. Ražnall .h. Madadain,
rídamna Oiliž, occirur ert a ruir.

Ktt. Enair .11. ß.; L. x.; coic bliadna .lxx. ar mile
aoir in Tigerna. Gorßraið mac Ražnuill, rí CCta
cliat; Cinoet .h. Conbethaið .i. toírrech Cenel mbinniž,

---

[1] *Seventh day of February.* The
Ann. Ult. and the Four Mast. say
"the seventh of the Ides of February;" but this comes to the same
thing, as the seventh of the Ides coin-
cides with the seventh of this month.

[2] *As a hostage.* i neroirecht (i
neidirecht); lit. "in hostageship."

[3] *The 3rd feria, the 18th of the
moon.* The MS. has 1111 ß. l. uiii
(quarta feria, lunae viii), but this is
a mistake, as the 1st of January in
1073 (the Domin. Letter being F) co-

incided with Tuesday, the 18th day of
the moon that began on the 15th of
December, 1072.

[4] *Baculo.* bacolo (bacolo), MS.
For an interesting account of the
Bachall-Iosa (Baculus Jesu), see
*Obits and Martyrology of Christ
Church,* Dublin; ed. by the Rev. Dr.
Todd, for the Irish Archæol. Soc.;
Dublin, 1844; Introd., p. vi., *sq.*

[5] *Toirdhealbach;* i.e. Toirrdheal-
bhach (or Turlough) O'Brien, the
grandson of king Brian Boromha.

thousand. Diarmaid, son of Mael-na-mbó, king of Laighen and of the Foreigners, fell in a battle by Conchobhar Ua Maelsechlainn, i.e. king of Temhair, and a slaughter of the Foreigners and Lagenians *was committed* about him. It was the 7th day of February,[1] and Tuesday the day of the week, on which this battle was fought. Ua Fogarta, king of Eile, was slain by Ua Briain. Ruaidhri O'Canannain, king of Cenel-Conaill, was slain by Ua Maeldoraidh, i.e. Aenghus. The French went into Alba, and carried off with them the son of the king of Alba as a hostage.[2]

The kalends of January on the 3rd feria,[3] the 18th[3] of the moon; the age of the Lord seventy-three years and a thousand. Conchobhar Ua Maelsechlainn, king of Temhair, was slain by the son of Flann, son of Maelsechlainin, in profanation of the Bachall-Iosa, baculo[4] præsente. A hosting by Toirdhealbhach[5] into Leth-Chuinn, when he committed countless depredations in Gailenga, and when he slew Maelmordha Ua Cathusaigh, king of Bregh. Sitrec, son of Amhlaibh, was slain in Manainn.

The kalends of January on the 4th feria, the 29th of the moon; the age of the Lord seventy-four years and a thousand. Ard-Macha was burned on the Tuesday after May-day, with all its churches and bells, both Rath[6] and Trian.[6] Raghnall Ua Madadhain, royal heir of Oilech, occisus est a suis.

The kalends of January on the 5th feria, the 10th of the moon; the age of the Lord seventy-five years and a thousand. Goffraidh, son of Raghnall,[7] king of Ath-cliath, *and* Cinaeth Ua Conbhethaidh, i.e. chieftain of

---

[6] *Rath and Trian.* The *Rath* was the central enclosure of the place; and the wards, three in number, which formed the outer belt of habitation, were called *Trians.* See *The Ancient Churches of Armagh*, by the Rev. Dr. Reeves, 1860, p. 14.

[7] *Son of Raghnall.* The Ann. Ult. say that Goffraidh, or Godfrey, was the grandson of Raghnall, which is more likely to be correct, as Raghnall was slain in the battle of Tara, in A.D. 980.

moptui puinc. Sloigeao la Toippioealbach ocup la Leč
moča i Leč Cuinn, co puachtatap co hCCč Pipõeazha,
coocapopat CCipzialla maiõm CCpoa Monann pop
Muipceptach .h. mõpiain, ou aotopcpaoap ile. Donnchao O Canannán, pi čenel Conaill, occipup ept. Domnall mac Mupchaoa, pí CCča cliač, ohéc oo zalap tpi
noičče.

Jctt. Enaip .ui. p.; L. xxii. Se bliaona .lxx. ap mile
aip in Tizepna. Zilla Cpipt O Duiõoapa, pí Pep
Manach i nDaiminip la pepuiõ Manach occipup ept.
Domnall .h. Cpičán, pi .h. bpiačpach CCpoa zpača, ocup
áp imme, [oo mapbao] oo Uiõ oTuiptpi ocup oo čenél
mõinniõ Zlinne. Mupchao mac Plainn hi Mailtpech-
lainn, pí Teihpach ppi pé čpí noičče, oo mapbao a
zcloictech Cenannpa oo mac Maoláin, pi Zaileng.
Slóizeao la Toippohealbach .h. mõpiain aConnachtaiõ,
co táinc pí Connacht ina čech .i. Ruaiopi .h. Conchobaip.
Maiõm bélat pía nCCoõ .h. Mailpechlainn ocup pía
bpepuiõ Muiže hIča, pop Ciannachta, zup po láõ a
noepz áp. Zopmlaič inzen hi Pózapthaiž, ben Toipp-
ohealbaiz hi Bpian, ohéc.

Jctt. Enaip .i. p.; L. ii. Seacht mbliaona .lxx. ap
mile aip in Tizepna. Sloizeao la Toippohealbach .h.
mõpiain a niõ Cennpelaiž, zuppo čuiõpiž mac Domnaill pehaip, pi .h. Cennpelaiž. Mac mic Maoláin .i.
pí Zaileng, oo mapbaõ lá Mailpechlain, lá pí Teihpach.
Mupchao O Mailpechlainn oo mapbao ó pepuiõ Teppa.

---

[1] *Occisus est.* occippi pt (for occisi
sunt), MS.

[2] *Was slain.* The words oo map-
baō, apparently omitted by the
copyist through mistake, are supplied
from the Annals of Ulster, the contents of which, at this period, are
nearly identical with the entries in
the present chronicle.

[3] *Cloicteach;* i.e. "bell-house,"
steeple, or round tower.

[4] *Son.* Under the next year this
person is said to be the "grandson"
of Maelan, which is probably correct,
as Maelan, son of Conghalach, king
of Gailenga, his ancestor, was slain in
978, in the battle of Tara, gained by
king Maelsechlain (or Malachy) II.
over the Danes. See note [6].

[5] *Came into his house;* i.e. submitted
to him.

Cenel-Binnigh, mortui sunt. A hosting by Toirdhealbhach and Leth-Mogha into Leth-Chuinn, until they
reached Ath-Fhirdheagha, when the Airghialla gained the
victory of Ard-Monainn over Muirchertach Ua Briain, in
which many were slain. Donnchadh O'Canannain, king
of Cenel-Conaill, occisus est. Domhnall Mac Murchadha,
king of Ath-cliath, died of three nights' disease.

The kalends of January on the 6th feria, the 22nd of
the moon; the age of the Lord seventy-six years and a
thousand. Gillachrist O'Duibhdara, king of Feara-Manach,
occisus est,[1] in Daimhinis, by the Feara-Manach. Domhnall Ua Crichain, king of Ui-Fiachrach of Ard-Sratha,
[was slain],[2] with a havoc about him, by the Ui-Tuirtre
and the Cenel-Binnigh of the valley. Murchadh, son of
Flann Ua Maelsechlainn, king of Temhair during the
space of three nights, was slain in the cloicteach[3] of
Cenannus by the son[4] of Maelan, king of Gailenga. A
hosting by Toirdhealbhach Ua Briain to Connacht, when
the king of Connacht came into his house,[5] viz.:—Ruaidhri
Ua Conchobhair. The victory of Belat was gained by
Aedh Ua Maelsechlain, and by the men of Magh-Itha,
over the Cianachta, who were put to slaughter.[6] Gormlaith, daughter of Ua Fogartaigh, wife of Toirdhealbhach
Ua Briain, died.

The kalends of January on the 1st feria, the 2nd of the
moon; the age of the Lord seventy-seven years and
a thousand. A hosting by Toirdhealbhach Ua Briain
into Ui-Cennselaigh, and he put the son of Domhnall
Remhar,[7] king of Ui-Cennselaigh, in chains. The grandson[8] of Maelan, i.e. the king of Gailenga, was slain by
Maelsechlainn, king of Temhair. Murchadh O'Maelsechlainn was slain by the men of Teffa. The victory of the

---

[6] *Slaughter*; ꝺeᴘᵹ áᴘ (derg ár),
lit. "red slaughter."

[7] *Domhnall Remhar*; i.e. "Domhnall (or Daniel) the fat."

[8] *Grandson.* See note [4]. According to the Chron. Scotorum (1073)
and the Four Mast. (1076), his name
was Amhlaibh, or Olaf.

Maðm na Maoile ðerge ror repuið Manach ria Cénel nEogain Tealċa óg, ðú i torcraðar ile.

Ictt. Enair íi. r.; l. xiii. Ocht mbliaðna .lxx. ar mil air in Tigerna. Lorcán .h. bríain ðéc. Leꞇlobar .h. Laignén .i. airðríg Oirgíalla, ðo marbað la Ruaiðri .h. Ruaðaċán. Conchobar .h. bríain, rí Telċa óg ocur ríðaṁna Erenn, ðo marbað ðo ċenel mbinniċ Glinne. Oomnall mac mic Tigernáin, rí Conmaicne, ðo ṁarbað. Cathal mac Oomnaill, rí ċénel nEnða, ðo ṁarbað la Cénel Eogain na hinnri.

Ictt. Enair .iii. r.; l. xxiii.; .ix. mbliaðna .lxx. ar mile air in Tigerna. Ceallaċ O Ruanaða, arð ollaṁ Erenn, [ðo éc]. Cúṁðe mac mic Lorcáin, rí Ferṁuige, [ðo éc].

Ictt. Enair .u. r.; l. u. Ochtṁoða bliaðan ar mile air in Tigerna. Oonn .h. Leꞇlobair, rí Ferṁuige, ðo ṁarbað ðo Uiñ Laiꞇen a rleiñ Ruaið. Maðm Aċa Ergail a taoñ Cloċair, ror repuið Manach rian Oomnall ṁág Laċlain ocur ría brepuið Muige hIċa, i torchair Sitrec .h. Caoṁáin ocur mac Neill hi ꞇꞏeppraich, et alíi multi.

Ictt. Enair .iii. r.; l. xiii.; bliaðain ochtṁoða ar mile air in Tigerna. h. Maꞇgamna, rí Ulað, ðo ṁarbað la Oonnrleiñe .h. nEochaða, a nOún ðá leꞇ glar. Corcach cona templaib, ocur Cell Oálúa, ab igne ðirriraꞇe runt.

Ictt. Enáir .uii. r.; l. xxiii.; ðá ñliaðain .lxxx. ar mile [air in Tigerna]. Gilla Crirt .h. Maolraðaill, rí Cairrge braċaiñe, ðéc. Oomnall mac Conchobair hi bríain mortuur ert. Cathal mac Aoða hi Conchobair

1 *Of the Island*; i.e. of the island or peninsula of Inishowen, in the co. of Donegal.

2 *Grandson.* So also read the Ann. Ult., but the Four Mast. have "son."

3 *The 4th.* The MS. has u (5th): but this is a mistake.

4 *Sixteenth.* ui. (for 6th), MS., which is a mistake, as the 1st of January, 1081, coincided with the 16th day of the moon that commenced on the 17th of December, 1080.

5 *Ab igne dissipatæ.* ab igne ðirriraꞇe, MS.

Maelderg was gained over the Feara-Manach, by the
Cenel-Eoghain of Telach-og, in which many were slain.

The kalends of January on the 2nd feria, the 13th of [1078.]
the moon; the age of the Lord seventy-eight years and
a thousand. Lorcan Ua Briain died. Lethlobhar Ua
Laighnén, i.e. chief king of Oirghiall, was slain by
Ruaidhri Ua Ruadhachan. Conchobhar, grandson of
Brian, king of Telach-og, and royal heir of Erinn, was
slain by the Cenel-Binnigh of the valley. Domhnall,
grandson of Tighernan, king of Conmaicne, was slain.
Cathal, son of Domhnall, king of Cenel-Enna, was killed
by the Cenel-Eoghain of the Island.[1]

The kalends of January on the 3rd feria, the 24th of [1079.]
the moon; the age of the Lord seventy-nine years and
a thousand. Ceallach O'Ruanadha, chief poet of Erin,
[died]. Cumhidhe, grandson[2] of Lorcan, king of Fernmhagh, [died].

The kalends of January on the 4th[3] feria, the 5th of the [1080.]
moon; the age of the Lord eighty years and a thousand.
Donn Ua Lethlobhair, king of Fernmhagh, was slain
by the Ui-Laithen on Sliabh-Fuaid. The victory of
Ath-Ergail, by the side of Clochar, was gained over the
Feara-Manach by Domhnall Mac Lachlainn, and by the
men of Magh-Itha, wherein Sitric Ua Caemhain and the
son of Niall Ua Serraigh, et alii multi, were slain.

The kalends of January on the 6th feria, the 16th[4] of [1081.]
the moon; the age of the Lord eighty-one years and a
thousand. Ua Mathghamhna, king of Uladh, was slain
by Donnsleibhe Ua hEochadha, in Dun-da-lethghlas.
Corcach, with its churches, and Cill-Dalua, ab igne
dissipatæ[5] sunt.

The kalends of January on the 7th feria, the 27th of [1082.]
the moon; [the age of the Lord] eighty-two years and a
thousand. Gillachrist Ua Maelfhabhaill, king of Carraig-
Brachaidhe, died. Domhnall, son of Conchobhar Ua
Briain, mortuus est. Cathal, son of Aedh Ua Conchobhair,

mórcuuſ eſc. Plaicbeſcach .h. Maolaoúin, ſí Luiſg,
ohéc.

Kct. enaiſ ı. ſ.; L. ıx.; cſı blıaona .lxxx. aſ mıle
[aıſ ın Cıʒeſna]. Domnall .h. Canannán, ſí čenel
Conaıll, a ſuıſ occıſuſ eſc. Ccoő .h. Maoılſechluınn, ſí
Oılıʒ, [oo éc]. Muıſceſcach .h. Caıſıll, aıſcınneč Oúın,
ſaoı bſeıčemnachca ocuſ cſenčuſa, mórcuuſ eſc.
Domnall .h. Ločlaınn oo ʒaőaıl ſıʒe čénel Eoʒaın.
Cſech ſíʒ laıſ aſ Conaıllaıb Muıſčeımne, co cuc
bóſuma móſ, ocuſ ʒo ocáſſaő cuaſuſoal moſ oon
čſeıch ſın oſeſuıő Peſnmuıʒe.

Kct. enaıſ ıı. ſ.; L. xx. Ceıčſe blıaona .lxxx. aſ
mıle [aıſ ın Cıʒeſna]. Donnchaő .h. Maolſuanaő,
peſſecucoſ ecclesıaſum, oo maſbaő oſeſuıő Luıſg.
Ʒlenő oá lača cum ſuıſ cemplıſ oo loſcaő. Sloıʒeaő
la Donnſleıbe, ſí Ulaő, ʒo Oſoıčec áča, co ocaıſo
cuaſuſoal oo mac ın čaılıʒ hı Ruaıſc. Cſeač la
Domnall maʒ Lačlaınn caſ a éıſ a nUllcaıb, ʒo ocucſa
bóſuma móſ. Sloıʒeaő la ſıſu Muman a Mıőe, ocuſ
ıſ ſoſ an ſloıʒeaő [ſın] aobač Conchobaſ .h. Ceoſaőa;
ocuſ oo čuaoaſ Conmaıcne a Cuaőmumaın caſ a néıſı,
ʒuſſo loıſcſec oúıne ocuſ cella, ocuſ ʒo ſucſac cſeıč
móıſ. Maıőm Mónaıő Cſuınneóıʒe ſıa Leč Moőa
ſoſ Donnchaő O Ruaıſc, [ı coſchaıſ .h. Ruaıſc] ocuſ
Cınnéıoıč O Őſıan, ec alıı pluſımı. Domnall Ua
Ʒaıſmleʒhaıʒh oo maſbaő oo Domnall maʒ Lačlaınn.

1 *Occisus.* occıſſuſ, MS.
2 *Son;* i.e. Donnchadh, whose death is recorded in the Annals of the Four Masters at the year 1084. See note 5.
3 *Caillech;* or "the cock." His proper name was Art. His death is entered under the year 1046, *supra,* where he is called "Art Uallach," or "Art the proud."
4 *In their absence;* i.e. whilst the men of Mumha, or Munster, were engaged in the expedition to Midhe, or Meath.
5 *In which fell Ua Ruairc.* Some words being manifestly omitted from the text, the clause within brackets has been supplied from the Annals of Ulster, the phraseology of which, as regards this entry, is otherwise pre-

mortuus est. Flaithbhertach Ua Maelduin, king of Lurg, died.

The kalends of January on the 1st feria, the 9th of the [1083.] moon; [the age of the Lord] eighty-three years and a thousand. Domhnall Ua Canannain, king of Cenel Conaill, a suis occisus[1] est. Aedh Ua Maelsechlainn, king of Oilech, [died]. Muirchertach Ua Cairill, airchinnech of Dún, professor of jurisprudence and history, mortuus est. Domhnall Ua Lochlainn assumed the sovereignty of Cenel-Eoghain, and made a royal predatory expedition into Conaille-Muirtheimhne, whence he carried off a great spoil of cattle; and liberal pay was given to the men of Fernmhagh on this expedition.

The kalends of January on the 2nd feria, the 20th of [1084.] the moon; [the age of the Lord] eighty-four years and a thousand. Donnchadh Ua Maelruanaidh, persecutor ecclesiarum, was slain by the Feara-Luirg. Glenn-da-locha, cum suis templis, was burned. A hosting by Donnsleibhe, king of Uladh, as far as Droichet-atha; and he gave pay to the son[2] of the Caillech[3] Ua Ruairc. A predatory expedition by Domhnall Mac Lachlainn, in his (*Donnsleibhe's*) absence, into Ulidia, and he carried off a great spoil of cattle. A hosting by the men of Mumha into Midhe; and it was on [that] expedition Conchobhar Ua Cedfadha died. And the Conmaicne went into Tuadh-Mumha in their absence,[4] when they burned forts and churches, and carried off great spoils. The victory of Moin-Cruinnoige by Leth-Mogha, over Donnchadh O'Ruairc; [in which fell Ua Ruairc],[5] and Cennedigh O'Briain, et alii plurimi. Domhnall Ua Gairmleghaigh was slain by Domhnall Mac Lachlainn.

---

cisely the same as that of the present chronicle. This was the person referred to a few lines before, as having received pay from Donnsleibhe, king of Uladh, on the occasion of an expedition to Droichet-atha, or Drogheda. See note [1], last page, and also note [3], page 76.

Ịcꞇꞇ. Ꞇnꞁꞃ ꞁꞁꞁꞁ. ꞃ.; ꞁ. ꞁ.; ꞇ. bꞁꞁꞇꞁnꞇ ocꞇ꞊ꞇꞇꞁꞇ ꞇꞃ ꞁꞁꞁꞁe ꞇꞁꞃ ꞁꞁ Ꞇꞁꞁꞃꞁnꞇ. Ꞁꞁꞃcꞁꞇꞇ .ꞁ. ꞁꞇoꞁꞇoꞃꞇꞁꞇ, ꞃꞁ Ceneꞁ Conꞇꞁꞁꞁ, ꞇꞁꞃ oꞃꞇꞁꞁn, ocꞁꞃ oꞁꞃecꞁꞁꞁꞃ, [ocꞁꞃ] oꞁꞁꞁ꞊, ꞇꞃꞇ꞊ꞇꞁꞁ bꞇꞁꞃ ꞇꞁ bꞁꞁꞇbꞇꞁn ꞃꞁ. Ꞇomnꞇꞁꞁ mꞇc Ꞁꞇoꞁco꞊ ꞁꞁꞁm, ꞃꞁ Ꞇꞁbꞇn, moꞃꞇꞁꞁꞁꞃ eꞃꞇ. ꞁꞇꞁ꞊ꞇꞃ꞊ O Ꞃꞁꞇꞁꞃc, ꞃꞁꞇꞇꞁꞁnꞇ Connꞇcꞁꞇ, ꞇꞁéc.

Ịcꞁꞇ. Ꞇnꞇꞁꞃ .ꞁꞁ. ꞃ.; ꞁ. ꞇꞁꞁ.; ꞁꞁ. bꞁꞁꞇbꞇ ocꞁꞇmꞇꞇꞇ ꞇꞃ ꞁꞁꞁe ꞇꞁꞃ ꞁꞁ Ꞇꞁꞃꞁꞃꞇ. Ꞁꞇoꞁꞁꞃꞇ ꞁꞇ bꞃoꞁꞇꞇn, ꞃoꞁ Ꞇꞃenn ꞁ neꞁꞁꞇ ocꞁꞃ ꞇ ꞁcꞃꞇbꞇꞇꞇ, ocꞁꞃ ꞇ bꞃꞁꞁꞁꞇecꞁꞇ ꞁꞁ bꞇꞃꞁꞇ ꞇꞇꞇcꞁꞇꞃꞃꞇꞇ, ꞃꞁꞁm ꞃꞃꞁꞃꞁꞇꞁm énꞁꞃꞁꞇ. Ꞇoꞁꞃꞃ꞊ ꞇeꞇꞁbꞇcꞁ O bꞃꞁꞇꞁn, ꞃꞁ Ꞇꞃenn, ꞇo é꞊ ꞇ ꞁCꞁnn ꞇoꞃꞇꞇ ꞁꞇꞃ mꞁꞃ mꞇꞃꞇꞃꞇ, ocꞁꞃ ꞁꞇꞃ nꞇꞇꞃꞁ꞊e ꞃoꞇꞇ, ocꞁꞃ ꞁꞇꞃ ꞇoꞇꞇꞁꞇꞇ ꞇꞁꞃꞃ Cꞃꞁoꞃꞇ ocꞁꞃ ꞇ ꞃoꞁꞇ, ꞁ ꞃꞃꞁꞇ [ꞁꞇ] ꞁꞁꞁꞁ, ꞁꞃꞁn .ꞁꞁꞁ. mꞇꞇ bꞁꞁꞇꞇꞇꞁn .ꞁꞁꞁ. ꞇ ꞇꞁꞃꞁ. Ꞇꞇꞁ꞊ .ꞁ. bꞃꞁꞇꞁn, ꞇ mꞇc, ꞇo ꞁéc ꞇ ꞁcꞁnn ꞁꞁꞁꞃ ꞁꞇꞃꞃꞁn. Ꞁꞇꞁꞁm nꞇ Cꞃꞁoncꞁꞇ ꞃoꞃ Ꞁꞇoꞁꞁ꞊ ꞃecꞁꞁꞇꞁnn, ꞃꞁꞇ ꞁꞇꞁ꞊nꞁꞇ ocꞁꞃ ꞃꞁꞇ n꞊ꞇꞁꞁoꞁꞇ, ꞁ ꞇoꞃcꞇꞁꞃ Ꞁꞇoꞁcꞁꞇꞃꞇꞁn .ꞁ. Cꞇꞇꞁꞃꞇ꞊, ꞃꞁ bꞃe꞊, eꞇ ꞇꞁꞁꞁ mꞁꞁꞇꞁ. Ꞁꞇꞁꞁm ꞃꞁꞇ nꞇꞇꞁꞃꞃꞇeꞃꞇꞁꞇ ꞃoꞃ ꞁꞁꞁ Ꞇcꞁꞇcꞁ, ꞁ ꞇoꞃcꞇꞁꞃ Ꞇomnꞇꞁꞁ .ꞁ. ꞁꞇꞇꞇꞁꞇ.

Ịcꞇꞇ. Ꞇnꞇꞁꞃ ꞁꞁꞁ. ꞃ.; ꞁ. ꞇꞁꞁꞁꞁ. Ꞇeꞇcꞁꞇ mbꞁꞁꞇꞇꞇꞇ .ꞁꞁꞁꞁ. ꞇꞃ ꞁꞁꞁe ꞇꞁꞃ ꞁꞁ Ꞇꞁꞃꞁꞃꞇꞇ. Ꞇomnꞇꞁꞁ mꞇc ꞊ꞁꞁꞁꞇꞃꞇꞇꞃꞇꞁc, ꞃꞁ Oꞃꞃꞃꞇꞁ꞊e, ꞇo é꞊. Ꞁꞇoꞁꞁꞃeꞇꞁꞇꞁnn mꞇc Concꞁobꞇꞁꞃ, ꞃꞁ Ꞇemꞃꞃꞇcꞁ, ꞇo ꞁꞇꞃbꞇꞇ ꞁꞇ ꞃꞁꞃꞇ Ꞇeꞇꞃꞇ ꞇ meꞇꞁꞁꞁ. Ꞇom꞊ nꞇꞁꞁ .ꞁ. ꞁꞇꞇen ꞇo mꞇꞃbꞇꞇ ꞇo Ꞇomnꞇꞁꞁ ꞁꞇ꞊ ꞁꞇꞇꞁꞇꞁnn. Cꞇꞇ Conꞇꞇꞁꞇ, ꞇ cꞃꞁꞇ Coꞃꞁꞁnn, ꞁꞇ Ꞃꞁꞇꞁꞇꞃꞁ nꞇ ꞃꞇ꞊ bꞁꞁꞇe mꞇc Oeꞇꞇ ꞁꞁ ꞊ꞇ beꞃnꞇꞁ꞊, ꞃoꞃ Ꞇꞁoꞇ mꞇc Ꞇꞁꞃꞇ ꞁꞇꞁꞁꞇ꞊ ꞁꞁ Ꞃꞁꞇꞁꞃc, ꞃꞁ Connꞇcꞁꞇ ocꞁꞃ Conmꞇꞁcne; ꞇcꞁꞇ cꞁenꞇ ꞇoꞃcꞇꞁꞃ Oeꞇꞁ mꞇc Ꞇꞁꞃꞇ ꞁꞁꞁ Ꞃꞁꞇꞁꞃc, ocꞁꞃ mꞇꞇꞇe

---

[1] *The 4th.* ꞁꞁꞁ. MS.; a mistake arising from the similarity between the numerals ꞁꞁꞁ (7) and ꞁꞁꞁꞁ (4) as written in old MSS.

[2] *Either language;* i.e. Latin and Irish, doubtless. A curious Latin-Irish poem, attributed to a person named Máilisa, apparently this Maelisa Ua Brolchain, is preserved in the *Leabhar Breac,* a 14th cent. MS. in the library of the R. I. Academy, p. 501. The bilingual character of the poem has probably something to do with the title of "sage . . . in the poetry of either language." See also *Mailisu's Hymn,* published by Mr. W. Stokes; *Goidilica,* Calcutta, 1866, p. 94.

The kalends of January on the 4th[1] feria, the 1st of the
moon; the age of the Lord eighty-five years and a
thousand. Murchadh Ua Maeldoraidh, king of Cenel-
Conaill, pillar of dignity, nobility, [and] hospitality, died
in this year. Domhnall, son of Maelcoluim, king of Alba,
mortuus est. Ualgharg O'Ruairc, royal heir of Connacht,
died.

The kalends of January on the 5th feria, the 12th of
the moon; the age of the Lord eighty-six years and
a thousand. Maelisa Ua Brolchain, the sage of Erinn
in wisdom and in piety, and in the poetry of either language,[2] suum spiritum emisit.[3] Toirdhealbhach O'Briain,
king of Erinn, died at Cenn-coradh, after great suffering,
and after long penance, and after receiving the body of
Christ and His Blood, on the day before [the ides[4]] of July,
in the 77th year of his age. Tadhg Ua Briain, his son, died
before the end of a month afterwards. The victory of the
Crionach was gained over Maelsechlainn, by the Lagenians
and by the Foreigners, in which fell Maelciarain Ua
Cathusaigh, king of Bregh, et alii multi. A victory by
the Airthera over the Ui-Echach, in which Domhnall Ua
hAitheidh was slain.

The kalends of January on the 6th feria, the 23rd of
the moon; the age of the Lord eighty-seven years
and a thousand. Domhnall Mac Gillapatraic, king of
Osraighe, died. Maelsechlainn, son of Conchobhar, king
of Temhair, was slain by the men of Tethfa, in treachery.
Domhnall Ua Laithen was slain by Domhnall Mac Lachlainn. The battle of Conachail, in the territory of Corann,
was gained by Ruaidhri "of the yellow hound," son of
Aedh "of the gapped spear," over Aedh, son of Art
Uallach Ua Ruairc, king of Connacht and Conmaicne.
Moreover, Aedh, son of Art Ua Ruairc, was slain; and the

Cóηηαιcne uιle ιυζυλᾱτι ϼunτ eτ occιϼι. Ͽτt. ηατυϼ
eϼτ hoc anno ΤοιϼϼϷealbach .h. Conchobaιϼ.

Ͽτt. Εηαιϼ .ιιιι. ϼ.; L. ιιιι. Ochτ mbλιαϷηα ochτmaϷa aϼ mιλε aιϼ ιη Τιξεϼηα. SλοιξeϷ la Ϸomηall
ṁᾱξ Lachlaιηη .ι. lᾱ ϼí 11laϷ, a Conηachτοιϼ, co ϼιαchτ
RuaιϷϼι .h. Conchobaιϼ ιηα čeηϷ, coηϷeαčϷaϼ Ϸιϐ-
λιηιϐ ιϼιη Mumaιη, ξυϼϼο λοιϼceτ CeηϷ čoϼaϷ ocuϼ
Lυιmηech, ocuϼ aη mačaιϼe co Ϸúη aιčeϷ, co τιcϼoτ leo
ceηϷ mιc Caιlιč 1 Ruaιϼe. aϼ moϼ ϼoϼ ξallaιϐ ατha
cliač, ocuϼ Ϸuιϼτ Lᾱιϼξe, ocuϼ Loča Caϼmaη, ϼια ηℓιϐ
Εchach Mumaη, ιϼιη lό ϼo ṁιϷϼaϷaϼ Coϼcαιξ Ϸo
oϼξuιη. Moeιλιϼa .h. Maoιlξeϼιc, ollam Εϼeηη, Ϸhéc.

Ͽτt. Εηαιϼ ιι. ϼ.; L. χιι. ℓoí mbλιαϷηα ochτmaϷa
aϼ mιλe aιϼ ιη Τιξεϼηα. Lυϼca Ϸo loϼcaϷ, ocuϼ .ιχ.
bϼιčτ Ϸuιηe Ϸo loϼcaϷ ιηα Ϸaṁλιᾱξ, o ϼeϼuιϐ Mumaη.
Cιll Ϸaϼa Ϸo loϼcaϷ ιη hoc anno. ϷoηηchaϷ mac
Ϸomηaιll ϼeṁaιϼ, ϼí Laιξeη, a ϼuιϼ occιϼuϼ eϼτ. ϷoηηchaϷ mac ξιllaϼaτϼαιc, ϼí Oϼϼαιξe, occιϼuϼ eϼτ.

Ͽτt. Εηαιϼ .ιιι. ϼ.; L. χχuι. ℓόčaτ bλιαϷaη aϼ mιλe aιϼ
ιη Τιξεϼηα. Coṁξᾱl eτιϼ Ϸomηall ṁᾱξ Lachlaιηη ocuϼ
Muιϼceϼτach O bϼιαιη, ϼι Caιϼιl, ocuϼ Mac Floιηη hì
Maoιlτϼechlaιηη, ϼí Τeαmϼα, ξo ϷταϼϷϼατ a mbϼαιξϷe
ocuϼ a ηξιalla uιle Ϸo ϼí Oιlιξ, .ι. Ϸomηall ṁᾱξ Lachlaιηη.

Ͽτt. Εηαιϼ .ιιιι. ϼ.; L. uιι.; bλιαϷaιη aϼ ηόčaτ ocuϼ
mιλe aιϼ ιη Τιξεϼηα. MuϼchaϷ mac Ϸomηaιll ϼeṁaιϼ
Ϸo maϼbaϷ a mebaιl la hΕηηa mac ϷιαϼmαϷa. 1η

---

[1] *Hoc.* oc, MS. This record is
preceded by the characters Ͽℓt, for
kalends, which, however, are not intended to indicate a distinct year.
Roderick O'Flaherty, who, as already
remarked, seems to have possessed the
MS., has added the marginal note
".ι. ϼι Conηachτ, giallas an choiged
uιℓe Ϸo;" "i.e. king of Connacht;
the entire province submitted to him
(Toirdhealbhach)."

[2] *The 4th.* xxiiii. MS.

[3] *Son of Cailech Ua Ruaire;* i.e.
Donnchadh Ua Ruairc, who was slain
in the year 1084, in the battle of Moin-
Cruinneoige (now Monecronock, near
Leixlip, co. Kildare). The Annals of
the Four Mast. state that his head
was carried to Luimnech, or Limerick.
The surname, 1 Ruaιϼc, has been interlined by Roderick O'Flaherty. *See*
notes [2], [3], and [5], p. 72.

[4] *They;* viz. :—the two last named
persons, Muirchertach O'Briain, and
the son of Flann Ua Maelsechlainn.

nobles of Conmaicne all jugulati sunt et occisi. Natus est hoc[1] anno Toirdhealbhach Ua Conchobhair.

The kalends of January on the 7th feria, the 4th[2] of the moon; the age of the Lord eighty-eight years and a thousand. A hosting by Domhnall Mac Lachlainn, i.e. the king of Uladh, into Connacht; and Ruaidhri Ua Conchobhair came to meet him; and they both went to Mumha, when they burned Cenn-coradh, and Luimnech, and the Machaire as far as Dun-Aiched; and they brought with them the head of the son of Cailech Ua Ruairc.[3] A great slaughter *was inflicted* on the Foreigners of Ath-cliath, and Port-Lairge, and Loch Carman, by the Ui-Echach-Mumhan, on the day on which they resolved to plunder Corcach. Maelisa Ua Maelgeric, poet of Erinn, died.

The kalends of January on the 2nd feria, the 15th of the moon; the age of the Lord eighty-nine years and a thousand, Lusca was burned, and nine score persons were burned in its stone-church, by the men of Mumha. Cill-dara was burned in hoc anno. Donnchadh, son of Domhnall Remhar, king of Laighen, a suis occisus est. Donnchadh Mac Gillapatraic, king of Osraighe, occisus est.

The kalends of January on the 3rd feria, the 26th of the moon; the age of the Lord ninety years and a thousand. A convention between Domhnall Mac Lachlainn, and Muirchertach O'Briain, king of Caisel, and the son of Flann Ua Maelsechlainn, king of Temhair; and they[4] delivered all their hostages and pledges to the king of Oilech, i.e. Domhnall Mac Lachlainn.

The kalends of January on the 4th feria, the 7th[5] of the moon; the age of the Lord ninety-one years and a thousand. Murchadh, son of Domhnall Remhar, was slain in treachery by Enna, son of Diarmaid. The southern half[6]

---

[5] *The 7th.* The MS. has xun (17); but this is a mistake, as the 1st of January, 1091, was the 7th day of the moon that commenced on the 26th of the previous month of December.

[6] *Southern half.* Leṫ anꝺeṗṗ. The Ann. Ult. and Four Mast. have leṫ iapṫapach (leth iartarach), "western half."

leɫ anꝺeɩrr ꝺo ꞃaiɫ Cꞃꝺa Macha ꝺo Loꞃcaꝺ. Ꝺonnꞃleiꞃe .h. heochaꝺa ꝺo maꞃbaꝺ la mac mic Lacꞃlainn .ı. la ꞃí Oiliẑ, a mbél ẑuiꞃꞇ in ioꞃaiꞃ, ı caɫ. Maoilíꞃa comaꞃba ꝑaꞇꞃaic .u. Ct. Enaiꞃ in peniꞇenꞇia quieuiꞇ. Mac Oeꝺha mic Ruaiꝺꞃi, ꞃi iaꞃꞇhaiꞃ Connachꞇ, moꞃꞇuuꞃ erꞇ. blíaꝺuin ꞇꞃuꞇhach ꞇꞃocꞃaiꝺ ʒo nꝺeiẑ ɫꞃín in blíaꝺain rı.

Ctt. Enaiꞃ .u. ꞃ.; L. xuiii. Ꝺá blıaꝺain nócaꞇ aꞃ mile aiꞃ in Ꞇiʒeꞃna. Cluain mic Nóir ꝺo milleꞃ la rꞃa Muman. Ruaiꝺꞃi .h. Concobaiꞃ, aiꞃꝺrí Connachꞇ, ꝺo ꞃallaꝺ a mebail la .h. bꝼlaiꞃꞃeꞃꞇaiẑ, ꞃi iaꞃꞇhaiꞃ Connachꞇ. Muiꞃeꝺhach ꞃáẑ Caꞃꞃꞇhaiẑ, ꞃi Eoʒanachꞇa Caiꞃil, moꞃꞇuuꞃ erꞇ. Raɫ Cꞃꝺa Macha cona ꞇemplaib ꝺo Loꞃcaꝺ ı Ct. Sepꞇimbiꞃ, ocur rꞃeꞃ ꝺo Ꞇꞃiun ꞃóꞃ ocur rꞃeꞇh ꝺo Ꞇꞃiún ꞇSaxan. In craiꞃꝺech .h. ꝼallamain ꝺo ꞃáꝺhaꝺ aꞃ Loɫ Caiꞃꞃʒin ꞇꞃe ercuine Ruaiꝺꞃi hi Concobaiꞃ. Cb Incaꞃnaꞇione Ꝺomini urque aꝺ [ꝺ]allaꝺ Ruaiꝺꞃi ꝼluxeꞃünꞇ anni M. xc. ıı. Cb iniꞇio munꝺi. uı. millia. cc.xc.ı.

Ctt. Enaiꞃ .uıı. ꞃ.; L. xxıx.; ꞇꞃi blıaꝺna nócaꞇ aꞃ mile aiꞃ in Ꞇiʒeꞃna. Cꝺ O baiẑellán, ꞃı ꝼeꞃnmaiꝺe, ꝺhéc. Cꝺ mac Caꞇhail hi Conchobaiꞃ, ꞃíꝺaꞃna Connachꞇ, omner occiri runꞇ. Sil Muiꞃeʒhaiẑ ꝺinnaꞃbaꝺ a Connachꞇuiꞃ ꝺo Muiꞃceꞃꞇach O bꞃiain. Cꝺ .h. Canannáin, ꞃí Cenel Conaill, ꝺo ꞃallaꝺ la Ꝺomnall mac Loclainn, ꞃı Oiliẑ. Maolcoluim mac Ꝺonnchaꝺa, aiꞃꝺríẑ Clban, ocur Eꝺꞃaꝺ a mac, ꝺo maꞃbaꝺ ꝺo

---

1 *Bél-ghuirt-an-iobhair.* Lit. "the mouth of the field of the yew." The Ann. Ult. and also the Four Mast. (1094) have Belach-ghuirt-an-iobhair ("the pass of the field of the yew.") The place referred to was near Gortinure, in the parish of Killelagh, barony of Loughinsholin, co. Londonderry.

2 *Pænitentia.* peniꞇencia, MS.

3 *Rath;* i.e. the inclosure. See note 6, page 32, and note 6, page 67.

4 *Kalends.* The Annals of Ulster and the Four Mast. say "the fourth of the kalends."

5 *Trian-mór;* i.e. the "great third," or ternal division of Armagh.

6 *Trian-Saxan.* The "third" of the Saxons; that division of Armagh

of the Rath of Ard-Macha was burned. Donnsleibhe
Ua hEochadha was slain by the son of Mac Lachlainn,
i.e. the king of Oilech, at Bél-ghuirt-an-iobhair,[1] in battle.
Maelisa, comarb of Patrick, on the 5th of the kalends of
January, in pœnitentia[2] quievit. The son of Aedh, son
of Ruaidhri, king of the West of Connacht, mortuus est.
A sappy, plentiful year, of good weather, was this year.

A.D.
[1091.]

The kalends of January on the 5th feria, the 18th of
the moon; the age of the Lord ninety-two years and a
thousand. Cluain-mic-Nois was devastated by the men of
Mumha. Ruaidhri Ua Conchobhair, chief king of Connacht, was blinded in treachery by Ua Flaithbhertaigh,
king of the West of Connacht. Muiredhach Mac Carthaigh,
king of Eoghanacht-Caisil, mortuus est. The Rath[3] of
Ard-Macha together with its churches, was burned on the
kalends[4] of September, and a row of Trian-mor,[5] and a
row of Trian-Saxan.[6] The Devotee Ua Fallamhain was
drowned in Loch Cairgin, through the malediction of
Ruaidhri Ua Conchobhair. Ab Incarnatione[7] Domini to
the blinding of Ruaidhri fluxerunt anni m.xcii; ab initio
mundi,[8] ʉ mılƚıɑ, cc.xc.ı.

[1092.]

The kalends of January on the 7th feria, the 29th of
the moon; the age of the Lord ninety-three years and a
thousand. Aedh O'Baighellain, king of Fernmhagh, died.
Aedh, son of Cathal Ua Conchobhair, royal heir of Connacht, omnes[9] occisi sunt. The Síl-Muireghaigh were
expelled from Connacht by Muirchertach O'Briain. Aedh
Ua Canannain, king of Cenel-Conaill, was blinded by
Domhnall Mac Lachlainn, king of Oilech. Maelcoluim,
son of Donnchadh, chief king of Alba, and Edward his

[1093.]

---

where the Saxon students resided.
See Dr. Reeves's Tract on the *Ancient
Churches of Armagh*, p. 14.

[7] *Incarnatione.* ıncɑ́ɼnɑcıone, MS.

[8] *Initio mundi.* ınıcıo ꞧ, MS.

[9] *Omnes.* oımneꞧ, MS. It would
seem from the expression "omnes
occisi sunt," that some other names in
the original authority from which
he transcribed were omitted by the
copyist of this chronicle.

Ꝼrancaib, .i. ꞇ nInḃer Alḃa ꞇ Saxanaiḃ. A ꞃꞁġan ꞇmoꞃꞃo .i. Maꞃġaréꞇa, ꝺhcc ꝺꞇa ċuꞇaꞇ̇ ꞃꞇa cꞇnn nómaꞇꝺe. Sꞇl Muꞇꞃeġhaꞇġ ꝺoꞃꞇ̇ꞇꞁ a Connachꞇa ġan ċeꝺuġhaḋ. Meꞃꞁ móꞃ ꞇn hoc anno.

Kꞇꞇ. Enaꞇꞃ .i. ꝼ.; l. x.; cceꞇ̇ꞃe blꞇaꝺna nóċuꞇ aꞃ mꞇle aꞇꞃ ꞇn Ꞇꞇġeꞃna. Ꝼlaꞇ̇ḃeꞃꞇach .h. hAꞇ̇eoh, ꞃꞁ .h. nEchach, ꝺo ḃallaḋ la Ꝺonnchaꝺ .h. nEochaꝺa, la ꞃꞁ Ulaḋ. Sloꞇġeaꝺ la Muꞇꞃceꞃꞇach O mḂꞃꞇaꞇn co hAꞇ̇ clꞇaꞇ̇, ꞃuꞁꞃo ꞇnnoꞃḃ Ꞹoꞃꞃꞁaꞇ̇ Meꞃanach a ꞃꞇġe Ꞹall, ocuꞃ ꞃuꞁꞃo maꞃḃ Ꝺomnall O Maoꞇlꞃechlaꞇnn, ꞃꞁ Ꞇeꞃꞁa. Aꞃ ꝺaꞷ ḃaoꞇneḋ Aꞇꞃꞃꞁꞇꞃ ꝺo ċoꞃ la hUllꞇoꞇb. Ꞃuaꝺꞃꞁ O Ꝺonnacaꞇn, ꞃꞁ Aꞃaḋ, moꞃꞇuuꞃ eꞃꞇ. Conchobaꞃ O Conchobaꞇꞃ, ꞃꞁ Cꞇannachꞇa, ꞇn penꞇꞇenꞇꞇa moꞃꞇuuꞃ eꞃꞇ. Maꞇ̇ḃ ꞃꞇa Sꞇl Muꞇꞃeġhaꞇġ ꞃoꞃ Ꞇuaḋ Muman, aꝺꞇoꞃ̇ ċꞃaꝺaꞃ ꞇꞃꞁ ceꝺ uel paulo pluꞃ. Ꝺonnchaḋ mac Máꞇlcoluꞇm, ꞃꞁ Alban, ꝺo maꞃbaḋ o a bꞃáꞇ̇ꞃꞁḃ ꝼꞃéꞇn, ꝼeꞃ ꝺoluꞇm .i. ó Ꝺomnall ocuꞃ ó Eꝺmonꝺ. Ꝺoꞇneꝺ móꞃ a nEꞃꞁnn ꞇꞇle, ꝺꞇa ꞃo ꝼaꞇꞃ ꝺomaꞇuꞃ.

Kꞇꞇ. Enaꞇꞃ ꞇꞇ .ꝼ.; l. xxꞇ. Cóꞇꞃ blꞇaꝺna nóċaꞇ aꞃ mꞇle aꞇꞃ ꞇn Ꞇꞇġeꞃna. Snechꞇa móꞃ ꝺoꝼeꞃꞇ̇aꞇn ꞇn Ceꝺaoꞇn ꞇaꞃ Kꞇꞇ. Enaꞇꞃ, ꞃuꞁꞃo ꞇ̇aꞃḃ áꞃ ꝺáꞇne, ocuꞃ ceꞇ̇ꞃa, ocuꞃ én. Cenannꞇuꞃ cona ꞇ̇eꞁ̇ꞁlaꞇb, ocuꞃ Ꝺeꞃꞁꞇ̇aꞃ̇ cona leḃꞃaꞇḃ, ocuꞃ Aꞃꝺ ꞃꞃaꞇ̇a cona ꞇempall, ocuꞃ ꞇl ċella elꞇ aꞃꞁchena, cꞃemaꞇe ꞃunꞇ. h. heꞇꞃꞁnꞇꞃ̇, ꞃꞁ ꝼeꞃ Manach, ꝺo maꞃbaꝺ a ꞃuꞇꞃ. Maꞇ̇ḃ Aꞃꝺachaꝺ ꞃꞇa n'Ꝺal Aꞃaꞇ̇e ꞃoꞃ Ullꞇoꞇb, ꝺú ꞇꝺꞇoꞃꞃchaꞇꞃ Ꞹꞇlla comġaꞇll O Caꞇꞃꞁll. Ꞇeꞇ̇ḃ móꞃ ꞇn nEꞃꞁnn, ꞃuꞃ ꞃoꞃ maꞃḃ áꞃ móꞃ ꝺaoꞇnꞇḃ o Kꞇꞇ. Auꞃuꞇꞃꝺ co ḃellꞇaꞇnꞇ aꞃ cꞇnn .i. blꞇaꝺaꞇn aꞃꞇac ꝺo ġaꞇꞃꞇ̇ ḋꞇ. Muꞇꞃ̇ceꞃꞇach

[1] *Inbher-Alda.* Now Alnwick, in Northumberland.

[2] *Nomaid.* Some period of time, the exact duration of which has not been ascertained; but probably signifying a period of twenty-four hours. Matthew Paris states that on hearing of the death of Malcolm, Margaret— "faciens sacerdoti de omnibus plene confessionem, accepto salutis viatico, animam felicem Deo statim destinavit."

[3] *Cianachta;* i.e. Cianachta-Glinne-Geimhin, now the barony of Keenaght, co. Londonderry.

[4] *Pœnitentia.* peneꞇꞇncꞇa, MS.

[5] *Mortuus est.* m (moꞃꞇuꞇ) ꞃunꞇ, MS.

son, were killed by Franks, viz.:—in Inbher-Alda,[1] in
Saxon-land. His queen, moreover, i.e. Margareta, died of
grief for him before the end of a nomaid.[2] The Síl-
Muireghaigh *appeared* again in Connacht, without permission. Great fruit in hoc anno.

The kalends of January on the 1st feria, the 10th of the
moon; the age of the Lord ninety-four years and a thousand. Flaithbhertach Ua hAitheidh, king of Ui-Echach,
was blinded by Donnchadh Ua hEochadha, king of Uladh.
A hosting by Muirchertach O'Briain to Ath-cliath, when
he expelled Goffraigh Meranach from the kingship of the
Foreigners, and killed Domhnall O'Maelsechlainn, king of
Temhair. A slaughter of the good men of the Airthera
was committed by the Ultonians. Ruaidhri O'Donnacain,
king of Aradh, mortuus est. Conchobhar O'Conchobhair,
king of Cianachta,[3] in pœnitentia[4] mortuus est.[5] A
victory[6] by the Síl-Muireghaigh over *the men of* Tuadh-
Mumha, in which three hundred were slain, vel paulo
plus. Donnchadh, son of Maelcoluim, king of Alba, was
slain by his own brothers, per dolum, viz.:—by Domhnall
and by Edmond. Great inclemency of the weather in all
Erinn, from which grew scarcity.

The kalends of January on the 2nd feria, the 21st of
the moon; the age of the Lord ninety-five years and a
thousand. Great snow fell on the Wednesday after
the kalends of January, which killed a multitude of
men, cattle, and birds. Cenannus with its churches, and
Dermhagh with its books, and Ard-Sratha with its church,
and many other churches besides, crematæ[6] sunt. Ua
hEighnigh, king of Feara-Manach, was slain a suis. The
victory of Ard-achadh *was gained* by the Dal-Araidhe
over the Ulidians, in which Gillacomghaill O'Cairill was
slain. A great pestilence in Erinn, which killed a large
multitude of people, from the kalends of August to the
May following, viz.:—it was called a " mortal year."

---

[6] *Victory.* See note [1], next page. | [7] *Crematæ.* cꞃemaꞇe, MS.

h. Caippe, muipe Cenel Ccongupa, ocup pigairina Oiligh, ofagail báip. Goffpaig Mepánach, pí Gall, moptuup ept. Cat Fidnacha in quo ceciderunt multi diaptap Connacht ocup do Copcumpuaid, la Tadc mac Ruaidpi hí Conchobaip.

Ktt. Enaip .iii. f.; l. ii. Sé bliadna nocat ap mile aip in Tigepna. Flann .h. hCCnbpet, pí deipcept CCipgiall, ofagail báip in bliadain pin. Matgamain .h. Ségda, pí Copca duibne, dhéc. Conchobap .h. hCCinniapaid, pí Ciannachta, ocup .h. Céin pí .h. mic Caipptinn, do comtuitim a gcliathap. Uaman móp pop fepuid Epenn uile pia bfeil Eoin na bliadna pin, guppo tepaip Día ocup Patpaic tpe tpoipctib comapba Patpaic ocup cleipech nEpenn aipchéna. Muipceptach .h. Dubda, pí .h. nCCmalgaid, do mapbad a puip. Madadán O Madadán, pí tpíl nCCnmchada, moptuup ept. Cuulad .h. Celecáin, pídomna Oipgiall, do mapbad la hUltuid. Eogan .h. Cepnaig, aipchinnech Doipe, hi noidecim Ktt. Enáip, quieuit. Flaitbeptach .h. Flaitbeptaig, pí iapthaip Connacht, do mapbad do Madadán O Cuanna, ocup do Sil Muipeghaig, a noíguil tpúl a dtigepna. Domnall .h. hEnna, aipdeppug Caipil, quieuit.

Ktt. Enaip .u. f.; l. xiii. Seacht mbliadna nocat ap mile aip in Tigepna. Tadc mac Ruaidpi hí Conchobaip, pídamna Connacht, dhec. Slúaiged la Muipceptach .h. mbpiain ocup la let Moda, co Mag Muiptemine. Slúaiged la Domnall mag Laclainn a dtuaipcept Epenn, co Fid Conaille, do tabaipt cata

---

¹ *Battle of Fidhnacha.* This battle is given by the Four Masters under the year 1094; and the present entry seems to be a repetition, in somewhat altered phraseology, of the "victory" recorded above under the same year.

² *The 2nd.* The MS. has xii (12th); but this is wrong, as there was new

moon on the 31st of December, 1095.

³ *Their lord's eyes.* The blinding of Ruaidhri Ua Conchobhair, lord or king of Connacht, by Ua Flaithbhertaigh, is recorded above under the year 1092. The death of Ua Flaithbhertaigh is entered in the Annals of Ulster

A.D.

Muirchertach Ua Cairre, steward of Cenel-Aenghusa, and royal heir of Oilech, died. Goffraigh Meranach, king of the Foreigners, mortuus est. The battle of Fidhnacha,[1] in quo ceciderunt multi of the West of Connacht, and of Corcumruaidh, *was gained* by Tadhg, son of Ruaidhri Ua Conchobhair.

[1095.]

The kalends of January on the 3rd feria, the 2nd[2] of the moon; the age of the Lord ninety-six years and a thousand. Flann Ua hAnbfheth, king of the South of Oirghiall, died in this year. Mathghamhain Ua Seghdha, king of Corca-Dhuibhne, died. Conchobhar Ua hAinniaraidh, king of Cianachta, and Ua Cein, king of Ui-mic-Cairthinn, fell by each other in combat. Great terror over the men of all Erinn before the festival of John of this year; but God and Patrick saved them through the fastings of the comarb of Patrick and the clerics of Erinn besides. Muirchertach Ua Dubhda, king of Ui-Amhalghaidh, was slain a suis. Madadhan O'Madadhain, king of Síl-Anmchadha, mortuus est. Cu-uladh Ua Celechain, royal heir of Oirghiall, was slain by the Ulidians. Eoghan Ua Cernaigh, airchinnech of Doire, on the 19th of the kalends of January, quievit. Flaithbhertach Ua Flaithbhertaigh, king of the West of Connacht, was slain by Madadhan O'Cuanna and the Síl-Muireghaigh, in revenge for their lord's eyes.[3] Domhnall Ua hEnna,[4] arch-bishop of Caisel, quievit.

[1096.]

The kalends of January on the 5th feria, the 13th of the moon; the age of the Lord ninety-seven years and a thousand. Tadhg, son of Ruaidhri Ua Conchobhair, royal heir of Connacht, died. A hosting by Muirchertach Ua Briain and by Leth-Mogha, to Magh-Muirtheimhne. A hosting by Domhnall Mac Lachlainn from the north of Erinn to Fidh-Conaille, to give them battle; but the

[1097.]

and Four Mast. at the year 1098, which is probably the correct date.
[4] *Ua hEnna.* This entry seems also to be misplaced. The Ann. Ult. and the Four Masters have it at the year 1098.

δόιb, co ρυιγταιρπιγc coṁαρba ρατραιc, .ι. Ὀoṁnall, ρó ᵹne ρίṫe. Loclaιnn .h. Ὀυιḃḋαρα, ρι Ḟeρṁⱶαιᵹe, ᴅo ṁαρbαᴅ ᴅo Uιḃ Ḃρυυιn Ḃρeιϝne. Cnó ṁeρ móρ ιϝιn mbℓíαᴅαιn ϝιn, .ι. bℓιαᴅαιn nα ᵹcnó bϝιnn ; xxx. bℓιαᴅnα on cno meρ ϝo ᵹυρ αn ᵹcno meρ ϝoṁuιn.

Ⱪtt. Ɛnαιρ .uι. ϝ.; ℓ. xx.ιιιι. Ochτ mbℓιαᴅnα nóċατ αρ míle αιϝ ιn Τιᵹeρnα. Τρι ℓonᵹα ᴅo ℓonᵹuιḃ ᵹαll nα nInnγeḃ ᴅo τϝℓατ ᴅo Uℓℓτoιb, ocuγ α bϝoιρenᴅ ᴅo mαρbαᴅ, .ι. xx. αρ ceᴅ, uel paulo pluγ. Ὀιαρmαιᴅ mαc Ɛnᴅα mιc Ὀιαρmαᴅα, ρί Lαιᵹen, ᴅo ṁαρḃαᴅ ᴅo clαιnn Μuρchαᴅα mιc Ὀιαρmαᴅα. Ὀoṁnαll .h. Roḃαρταιᵹ, coṁαρbα Coluιm Cιlle ϝρι ρé ϝoᴅα, ιn pαce ᴅoρmιuιτ. Μαιḋṁ Ϝeρϝᴅe Súιlιḃe ϝoρ Cenel Conαιll ρια Cenél nɛoᵹαιn, ᴅú ιᴅτoρchαιρ Ɛceρταch .h. Ταιρceρτ, eτ αlιι mulτι.

Ⱪtt. Ɛnαιρ .uιι. ϝ.; ℓ. u.; ιx. mbℓιαᴅnα nóċατ αρ míle αιϝ ιn Τιᵹeρnα. Αϝcolτ móρ ρó Ɛριnn uιle ιn ḃℓιαᴅαιn ϝι. Cenαnτυγ αb ιᵹne ᴅιϝϝιρατα eϝτ. Cιll ᴅαρα ᴅιmιᴅια ραρτe cρeṁατα eϝτ. Sℓoιᵹeᴅ lα Muιρceρταch .h. mḂριαιn ocuγ lα Leṫ Μoᵹα, co Sℓιαb Ϝuαιᴅ, conᴅeρnα Ὀoṁnαll, coṁαρbα ρατραιc, ρíṫ ḃℓιαᴅnα eτuρρα ocuγ τuαιρceρτ Ɛρenn. Sℓoιᵹeᴅ lα Ὀoṁnαll ṁάᵹ Lαċlαιnn ocuγ lα τuαιρceρτ Ɛρenn ι nUℓℓτoιḃ. Uℓαιḃ ᴅono ιᵹ Cρoιḃ ċelċα αρ α ᵹcιnn, α bϝoϝlonᵹρuιρτ. Cóṁϝoιcιτ α nᴅí ṁαρcϝlúαᵹ. Μαιḋιρ ϝoρ ṁαρcϝlúαιᵹ Uℓαḃ, ocuγ mαρḃταρ .h. hαƇṁράin αnn. Ϝάᵹḃuιᴅ Uℓαιᴅ ιαϝϝιn αn Lonᵹρoρτ, ocuγ loιϝcιτ Cenel nɛoᵹαιn é, ocuγ τeρcuιτ cρoιḃ ċelċα. Ὀo beραρ δόιḃ δά eιᴅιρe ιαϝϝιn, ocuγ coṁαρbα Coṁᵹαιll α lαιṁ ϝρια δá αιᴅeρe cle.

<hr>

¹ *Before us.* ϝoṁuιn; i.e. *supra.* Under the year 1066 there is an entry of a great nut crop in Erinn.

² *Dormivit.* ᴅoρmιeρū̄τ, MS. Hence it would appear that some other names occurring in the original

authority from which he copied had been here omitted by the transcriber of this chronicle.

³ *Dimidia.* ᴅémeᴅια (démedia), MS.

⁴ *Craebh-thelcha;* i.e. "the spread-

comarb of Patrick, i.e. Domhnall, prevented them, under the guise of peace. Lochlainn Ua Duibhdhara, king of Fernmhagh, was slain by the Ui-Briuin-Breifne. A great nut crop in this year, viz. : the year of the white nuts; thirty years from this nut crop to the nut crop before us.[1]

The kalends of January on the 6th feria, the 24th of the moon; the age of the Lord ninety-eight years and a thousand. Three ships of the ships of the Foreigners of the Islands were plundered by the Ultonians, and their crews slain, viz. :—one hundred and twenty *men*, vel paulo plus. Diarmaid, son of Enna, son of Diarmaid, king of Laighen, was killed by the sons of Murchadh, son of Diarmaid. Domhnall Ua Robhartaigh, comarb of Colum Cille during a long period, in pace dormivit.[2] The victory of Fersad-Suilidhe *was gained* over the Cenel-Conaill by the Cenel-Eoghain, in which fell Ecertach Ua Tairchert, et alii multi.

The kalends of January on the 7th feria, the 5th of the moon; the age of the Lord ninety-nine years and a thousand. Great famine throughout all Erinn in this year. Cenannus ab igne dissipata est. Cill-dara dimidia[3] parte cremata est. A hosting by Muirchertach Ua Briain, and by Leth-Mogha, to Sliabh-Fuaid; but Domhnall, comarb of Patrick, made a year's peace between them and *the men of* the North of Erinn. A hosting by Domhnall Mac Lachlainn and *the men of* the North of Erinn, into Ulidia. The Ulidians, however, were before them at Craebh-thelcha,[4] in a camp. Their two cavalry hosts engage. The cavalry host of Ulidia is defeated, and Ua hAmhrain is slain there. The Ulidians afterwards abandon the camp, and the Cenel-Eoghain burn it, and cut down Craebh-thelcha.[4] Two hostages are subsequently given to them,[5] and the comarb of Comhghall as security for two other hostages.

---

ing tree of the hill." This tree, under which the kings of Ulidia were inaugurated, gave name to the place which is now known as Crewe, a townland in

the parish of Glenavy, barony of Massereene, and county of Antrim.

[5] *To them*; i.e. to Mac Lachlainn and his companions.

Daimliaᵹ Αpoα Spαċα oo Lopcαo opepuiᵬ nα Cpoiᵬe
pop iᵬ Piαcpαċ.

Ictt. Enaip .i. p.; L. xiii. Ceo bliαoαn αp mile αip in
Ciᵹepnα. Oonnchαo mαc Gochαoα, pí Ulαo, ocup opem
oo ṁαiċiᵬ Ulαᵬ ime, oo ᵹαbáil le Ooṁnαll ṁαᵹ
Loċlαinn, pí Oiliᵹ, i quincτ Ictt. Iuin. Sloiᵹeᵬ lα
Oomnαll ṁáᵹ Lαċlαinn ᵹuppo ṁil pip ᵬpeαᵹ, ocup
pine ᵹαll. Sloiᵹeᵬ lα Muipcepταch .h. mᵬpíαin co
hGppuαᵬ. Loinᵹep Αċα cliαċ co hInír Goᵹαin, ᵹuppo
lá i náp eoip ᵬáċαo ocup mαpbαo. Mαc mic ᵹillα-
ċoluim hi Oomnαill, pí Ciniuil Lúiᵹoec, α puip occípup
epτ. Αppiᵬ .h. hΑṁpαᵬáin, muipe Oál bPíαταċ, oᵬéc.
ᵹillαbpíᵹoe .h. Cuipc, pí Muſpαioi ᵬpeoᵹuin, moptuup
epτ. ᵹillα nα nαom .h. heiᵹin, pi .h. bPiαcpαċ Αiᵹne,
moptuup epτ. Gċpí .h. Mαolmuipe, pí Ciαnnαchτα, oo
mαpbαo ohUlα Conchobαp Ciαnnochτα.

Ictt. Enaip .iii. p.; L. xxiii.; bliαoαin αp ceo αp
mile αip in Ciᵹepnα. Oonnchαo mαc Αooα hi Ruαipc
oo ṁαpbαo opepuiᵬ Mαnαch. Sloiᵹeᵬ lá Muipcepταċ
.h. mᵬpíαin ocup lα Leċ Moᵬα i Connαchταᵬ, ocup
oαp Gppuαᵬ i Cíp Conuill, ocup αpiᵬein α Cíp Goᵹαin,
ᵹuppo pᵹαilpeτ Oileċ, ocup ᵹup loipcpeτ, ocup ᵹup
τpápαiᵹpeτ il ċellα, im Pαċαin ṁóip Muρα ocup im
Αpo Spαċα, Oo looαp αppin ταp Peppαiτ Cαmpα,
ᵹuppo loipcpeτ Cuil Rαċαin, ocup conoepipατ ouineᵬáiτ
αnn. ᵹαbαio ᵹeill Ulαᵬ iαppin, ocup oo luio ταp
pliᵹio Míᵬluαċpα oiα [ċiᵹ], iαp mbuαiᵬ inτ Plóiᵹio pin.
Cpeαċ lα Oonnchαo .h. Mαoilpechlαinn α bPepnmαᵹ,

---

1 *Ui-Fiachrach.* The Ui-Fiachrach
of Ard-Sratha are here referred to.
See Index.

2 *Ua hEochadha.* The MS. has
mαc Gochαoα, with which the Ann.
Ult. agree. But the Ann. Inisfal.
(Bodleian copy) and the Four Mast.
have Ua hEochadha (O'Haughey,

Houghy, or Hoey), which is the correct
form, as appears from the entry under
the year 1101, regarding his release.

3 *Went.* According to the Four
Mast. the fleet of Ath-cliath (i.e. the
naval force of the Danes of Dublin)
was "brought by Muirchertach Ua
Briain, till he arrived at Doire

The stone-church of Ard-Sratha was burned by the men of Craebh, against the Ui-Fiachrach.[1]

The kalends of January on the 1st feria, the 16th of the moon; the age of the Lord one hundred years and a thousand. Donnchadh Ua hEochadha,[2] king of Uladh, and a number of the chieftains of Uladh along with him, were taken prisoners by Domhnall Mac Lachlainn, king of Oilech, on the fifth of the kalends of June. A hosting by Domhnall Mac Lachlainn, so that he destroyed Feara-Breagh and Fine-Gall. A hosting by Muirchertach Ua Briain to Eas-Ruaidh. The fleet of Ath-cliath went[3] to Inis-Eoghain, where they were cut off both by drowning and killing. The grandson of Gilla-Choluim Ua Domhnaill, king of Cenel-Luighdech, a suis occisus est. Assidh Ua hAmhradhain, steward of Dal-Fiatach, died. Gillabrighde Ua Cuirc, king of Muscraidhe-Breoghain, mortuus est. Gilla-na-naemh Ua hEighin, king of Ui-Fiachrach-Aighne, mortuus est. Echri Ua Maelmuire, king of Cianachta, was slain by Ua Conchobhair of Cianachta.

[1100.]

The kalends of January on the 3rd feria, the 27th of the moon; the age of the Lord one hundred and one years, and a thousand. Donnchadh, son of Aedh Ua Ruairc, was slain by the Feara-Manach. A hosting by Muirchertach Ua Briain, and by Leth-Mogha, into Connacht, and across Eas-Ruaidh into Tir-Conaill, and from thence into Tir-Eoghain; and they demolished Oilech, and burned and profaned many churches, including Fathan-mor-Mura and Ard-Sratha. They proceeded thence across Fersat-Camsa, and they burned Cúil-Rathain, and committed a massacre there. They took the hostages of Uladh afterwards, and he (*Muirchertach*) proceeded by Slighe-Midhluachra to his [house],[4] after the triumph of that hosting. A predatory incursion by Donnchadh Ua Maelsechlainn into Fernmhagh,

[1101.]

(Derry);" but as Muirchertach seems to have conducted an expedition by land to Eas-Ruaidh (the falls at Ballyshannon, co. Donegal), it is probable that this naval expedition was conducted to support him.

[4] *House.* tig (abl. of teg, or tec); supplied from the Ann. Ult.

conur ταrναιo .h. Cerᵬuill, ocur ᵹurror marᵬ ᵵá ceo
uel paulo plur.   Oonnchαo .h: hЕochαᵭα, rí Ulαo,
το ᵮuαrlucαo α cuiᵬrec lα Oomnall ṁáᵹ Lαᵭlαinn,
lá rí nOiliᵹ, ταr ceno α mic ocur α comᵬαlτα, .i.
α noαimliαᵹ Ⱥroα Mαchα, ᵵre imριᵭe comαrbα
ρατrαιc ocur ᵵrαṁᵵα ρατrαιc αrchenα, ιαr comluᵹα
ron mᵬαᵭuill irrα, ocur ró ṁionuiᵬ uαιrle eli in .xι.
kt. Еnαιr.

ktt. Еnαιr .ιιιι. r. ; l. ιx.; οá blιαoαιn αr ceo αr
mιle, αιr ιn Τιᵹernα.   Sορο Coluιm Cιlle το loρcαo.
Oonnchαo mαc Еᵵρι hι Ⱥιᵵιᵬ, ρíοαṁnα .h. nЕchαch, το
mαrbαo το Ulltοιᵬ ιrιn ᵭuiᵹeo mír ιαr rúruᵹαo
muιnτιre ρατrαιc τó.   Oοṁnαll mαc Τιᵹernαιn hι
Ruαιrc το mαrbαᵭ το Conmαιcnιᵬ, ocur το buᵭ rí αr
Conmαιcnιᵬ, ocur coιmrιᵹᵵeóιr αr Connαchτuιᵬ αn
Oomnαll rιn.   ᵮlαιᵵᵬerταch mαc ρoτhαιo, rí .h.
bᵮιαcrαᵭ Ⱥroα Srαᵭα, το ṁαrbαo το rεruιᵬ Luιrᵹ.
Slοιᵹeo lá Cenel nЕoᵹαιn co Mαᵹ Coᵬα · Oo loᵭαr
Ulαιo αn οιᵭᵭe rιn ᵭon lonᵹρuιrτ, ᵹur mαrᵬrαo
Sιτρec .h. Mαolᵮαᵬuιll, rí Cαιrρᵹe ᵭrαchαιοe, ocur
Sιτρec mαc Conραιᵹ, mιc Еoᵹαιn, eτ αlιι.   Mαᵹnur,
rí Loᵭlαιnn, το ᵵeαchτ loιnᵹer mór co Mαnuιnn,
ocur ríᵵ ᵬlιαᵭnα το ᵭenum ᵵó ρe rεruιᵬ Еrenn.
Еιoεrеᵭα rer nЕrenn α láṁ Oοṁnαll comαrbα
ρατrαιc, ρe ríᵵ ᵬlιαᵭnα eoιr O mᵬrιαιn, .i. Muιr-
ᵭerταch, ocur máᵹ Lαᵭlαιnn, .i. Oomnαll. Ror
Οιlιᵵρι οαrᵹuιn, .i. cum rατρe rιιo, το Uιᵬ Еchαch, α
nοíᵹuιl ṁαrᵬᵵα hι Oonnchαoα.   Cαιrιol το loρcαo το
Еιlιᵬ.

ktt. Еnáιr u. r.; l. xx.; ᵵrí blιαᵭnα αr ceo αr
mιle αιr ιn Τιᵹernα. Sᵹαιnοer cruαιᵭ cróᵭα eᵵιr

---

¹ *Mutually.* The meaning is that
Donnchadh Ua hEochadha and Domhnall Mac Lachlainn pledged mutual
oaths by the relics in question.

² *That night.* αn οιᵭᵭe rιn; i.e.

the night after the Cenel-Eoghain had
entered Magh-Cobha.

³ *Patre.* ρᵱe, MS. The abbot of
a monastery was sometimes called
pater, or *pater monasterii.*

A.D.

but Ua Cerbhaill overtook him, and slew two hundred *of his band,* vel paulo plus. Donchadh Ua hEochadha, [1101.] king of Uladh, was released from bondage by Domhnall Mac Lachlainn, king of Oilech, in exchange for his son and his foster-brother, viz. :—in the stone-church of Ard-Macha *he was released,* through the intercession of the comarb of Patrick, and the congregation of Patrick likewise—after mutually[1] swearing by the Bachall-Isa, and by other principal relics—on the 11th of the kalends of January.

[1102] The kalends of January on the 4th feria, the 9th of the moon; the age of the Lord two years, and a hundred, and a thousand. Sord-Choluim-Chille was burned. Donnchadh, son of Echri Ua hAitheidh, royal heir of Ui-Echach, was slain by the Ulidians, in the fifth month after he had profaned the community of Patrick. Domhnall, son of Tighernan Ua Ruairc, was slain by the Conmaicne; and this Domhnall was king over the Conmaicne and an arbitrator over the Connachtmen. Flaith-bhertach, son of Fothadh, king of Ui-Fiachrach of Ard-Sratha, was slain by the Feara-Luirg. A hosting by the Cenel-Eoghain to Magh-Cobha. The Ulidians proceeded on that night[2] to the camp, and slew Sitrec Ua Mael-fhabhuill, King of Carraig-Brachaidhe, and Sitrec, son of Conrach, son of Eoghan, et alii. Maghnus, king of Loch-lann, came with a large fleet to Manainn, and made a year's peace with the men of Erinn. The hostages of the men of Erinn in the hands of Domhnall, comarb of Patrick, for a year's peace between O'Briain, i.e. Muirchertach, and Mac Lachlainn, i.e. Domhnall. Ros-Oilitri was plundered, i.e. cum patre[3] suo, by the Ui-Echach, in revenge for the killing of Ua Donnchadha. Caisel was burned by the Eile.

[1103.] The kalends of January on the 5th feria, the 20th of the moon; the age of the Lord three years, and a hundred, and a thousand. A severe, fierce conflict between the

ξερμιὅ λμιρξ ocμρ Τμαἔ Rαἔα, ι τορchαιρ άρ ceach-
ταρὅe. h. Cαnαnnαn, .ι. ρί Ceneoιλ ξConαιλλ, τo
ιonnαρὅατ αρρ α ρίξe λα Ὀomnαλλ mάξ λαἔλαιnn.
Coξατ mor eτιρ Cenel nEoξαιn ocμρ Ulλτα, co τάnιc
Mμιρceρταch O bριαιn co ρερμιὅ Mμmαn, ocμρ λαιξen,
ocμρ Orρραιξe, ocμρ ξο mαιἔιὅ Connαchτ, ocμρ ξo
bρερμιὅ Mιὅι, ιm α ρίξμιὅ, ξο Mαξ Coὅα, τρόιρμὅιn
Ulαὅ. Ὀολοταρ μιλe τιβλίnμιὅ ξο mαἔαιρe Cιρτ
Mαἔα, .ι. co Cιλλ nα coρnαιρe, comβαταρ ρechτihμιn
α bρορὅμιρι ρoρ Cρτ Mαcha. Ὀomnαλλ ihάξ λαἔλαιnn
ξο τμαιρceρτ Eρenn ρμιρ in ρé α nιὅ bρερραιλ
Mαcha, αξhατ in αξhατ ρμμ. Ο ροβ τμιρρρech
ἔρά ριρ Mμmαn, τo λμιὅ Mμιρceρταch co hConαἔ
Mαἔα, ocμρ co hehμιn Mαἔα, ocμρ τιmἔeλλ τo Cρτ
Mαἔα, co bράρξμιὅ ochτ nμιnξe όιρ ρoρραn αλτόιρ,
ocμρ ξμρρο ξeαλλ ochτ .xx. bó; ocμρ ιnnταιρ αρίρ co
Mαξ Coὅα, ocμρ ραξὅμρ λαιξmιξ ocμρ ρochαιτe τρερμιὅ
Mμmαn αnn; ocμρ τo ἔόιὅ ρéιn, ιmoρρo, αρ cρeιch
α nὈάλ Cρaιὅe, co bραρξμιὅ Ὀonnchατ mαc Τοιρρ-
τheαλβαιξ αnn, ocμρ mαc hι Concoβαιρ, ρί Cιαρραιξe,
ocμρ .h. beόαιn, eτ αλιι oρτιmι. Ὀo λμιὅ Ὀomnαλλ
ihάξ λαἔλαιnn, co mαιἔιβ Ceneoιλ Conμιλλ ocμρ Eoξαιn,
ocμρ αn τμαιρceιρτ μιλe ιme, co Mαξ Coὅα, ρoρ αmμρ
λαιξen. Τeξμιτ ιmoρρo λαιξne, ocμρ Orρραιξe, ocμρ
ριρ Mμmαn, ocμρ ξαλλ αihαιλ ροὅάταρ, ιnα nαξhαιτ;
ocμρ ρερμιτ caἔ, .ι. α nόιn Cμξμρτ, ocμρ α Ceταoιn αρ
αoí λαιἔe ρechτihμιne, ocμρ in nomατ .xx. τéρcα, ocμρ
αnτ ochτmατ λο ιαρ τοιξechτ τo Mαἔα ρo ρeραὅ in caἔ
ριn. Mαιτhιτ τρά ρoρ λeth Moὅα, ocμρ λάιττeρ α
nάρ, ocμρ άρ λαιξen ιm Mμιρἔeρταἔ mαc ξιλλαἔολmόξ,
ocμρ ιm ἔά .h. λορτάιn, ocμρ ιm Mμιρceρταch mαc mιc
ξορmαιn, eτ αλιι; ocμρ άρ .h. Cιnnρeαλαιξ ιm ἔα ihαc

<hr />

₁ *Machaire-Aird-Macha*; i.e. the
plain of Ard-Macha, a level district
lying round Armagh.

₂ *Magh-Cobha*. Over the name
Magh-Cobha are written the words

ιτ ₂ nὅ ιmρeτραταρ (for ,"ut est
non impetratur"); but probably they
should have followed the preceding
words "7 ξμρ ρo ξeαλλ ochτ .xx.
bo," "and promised eight score cows."

men of Lurg and Tuath-Ratha, in which fell a multitude on both sides. Ua Canannain, i.e. the King of Cenel-Conaill, was expelled from his sovereignty by Domhnall Mac Lachlainn. A great war between the Cenel-Eoghain and the Ulidians, when Muirchertach O'Briain came with the men of Mumha, and Laighen, and Osraighe, and with the nobles of Connacht, and with the men of Midhe, together with their kings, to Magh-Cobha, to assist the Ulidians. They all went, respectively, to Machaire-Aird-Macha,[1] i.e. to Cill-na-Cornaire, where they were a week laying siege to Ard-Macha. Domhnall Mac Lachlainn, with *the men of* the North of Erinn, *was* during the time in Ui-Bresail-Macha, confronting them. When, however, the men of Mumha were weary, Muirchertach proceeded to Aenach-Macha, and to Emhain-Macha, and round to Ard-Macha, when he left eight ounces of gold upon the altar, and promised eight score cows; and he turned back to Magh-Cobha,[2] and left there the Lagenians, and a multitude of the men of Mumha; and he himself went, moreover, on a predatory expedition into Dal-Araidhe, where he lost Donnchadh, son of Toirdhealbhach, and the son of Ua Conchobhair, king of Ciarraighe, and Ua Beóain, et alii optimi. Domhnall Mac Lachlainn, accompanied by the chieftains of Cenel-Conaill and *Cenel*-Eoghain, and of the whole North, went to Magh-Cobha, to attack the Lagenians. The Lagenians, however, and the Osraighe, and the men of Mumha, and the Foreigners, such as they were, came to meet him, and a battle was fought: viz., on the nones of August, and on Wednesday, as regards the day of the week, and on the 29th of the moon, and on the eighth day after coming to Macha, this battle was fought. *The men of* Leth-Mogha were defeated, and a slaughter of them was committed, and a slaughter of the Lagenians, with Muirchertach Mac Gillacholmog, and with two Ua Lorcains, and with Muirchertach, son of Mac Gormain, et alii; and a slaughter of the Ui-Ceinnsealaigh, with two sons of

Máilhorða, ocur im .h. Riain .i. rí .h. nOróna, et alíí; ár Orrraiξe, im ξillaρatραιc rúað, rí Orrραιξe, ocur im riξραιð Orrραιξe airchena; ár ξall Αǎa cliác im Τρορðán mac Epec, ocur im pol Αǒmann, ocur im beollán Αrmann, et alιι; ár rer Muman im ðá .h. bric .i. ðá rióahna na nOéιρι, ocur im .h. bfaιlðe, .i. rióahna Corca ðuιðne, ocur erre Laιξen, .i. im .h. Muιρeξhaιξ, .i. rι Cιαρραιξe, cona mac, et alιι multi ortimi quor caura breuιtatιr reribere rretermιrιmur. Τerρataρ Cenél nEoξaιn ocur maιte Cenél Conaιll ocur an τuaιrceιrt árchéna, co corcur mór, ocur co réðuιb ιmðhaιb, ιmón rupuιll riξða, ocur ιmon camlιnne, ocur im réðuιð ιmðuιð aιrchena. Maξnur, rí Loǎlaιnn, ðo marbað ar creιǎ ι nUlltaιð.

κττ. Enáιr .uι. r.; .l. ι.; ceιτρι blιaðna ar ceð ar mιle aιr ιn Τιξerna. O Concobaιr Corcumruaιð, .i. Concobar mac Maoιlτreǎlaιnn, morτuur ert. Mac na hoιðce .h. Ruaιre a ruιr rratrιbur occιrur ert. Sloιξeð la Muιrcertǎ .h. mðρiaιn co Maξ Muιrǎemne, ξur hιll τreaðaιre an maιðe co huιlιðe; ocur ðon τrloιξeð rιn ro herξrað Cuulað O Caιnðelðáιn, rι Loeξaιre, conðerðaιlt ðe. Sloιξeð la Ðomnall háξ Laǎlaιnn co Mað Coða, co tuc ξιalla Ulað, ocur conðechaιð co Τemραιξ, ocur ξur loιrc bloιð hór ð[o] .h. Laeξaιre, ocur co ðtarð termann ðóιð aιrchena. Ðunchað .h. Concobaιr, rι Cιanachta, ðo marbað ða ðaonιð rféιn.

κττ. Enaιr ι. r.; l. xιι. Coιξ blιaðna ar ceð ar

<hr/>

1 *Pol Adhmann.* In the Ann. Four Mast. and Ann. Ult. this individual is called pol mac Αmaιnð, "Pol (or Paul) son of Amand."

2 *Beollan Armann.* "Beollan, son of Armann," Four Mast.

3 *Dynast of Laighen.* Erre Laιξen. These words are seemingly misplaced, and should probably follow after some one of the names enumerated in the slaughter of the Lagenians a few lines before. The phraseology of the whole sentence is rather loose and rugged.

4 *Quos.* quorr (quoss), MS.

5 *Causa.* quárra (quússa), MS.

Maelmordha, and with Ua Riain, i.e. king of Ui-Drona, et alii; a slaughter of the Osraighe, with Gillapatraic Ruadh, king of Osraighe, and with the chieftains of Osraighe likewise ; a slaughter of the Foreigners of Ath-cliath, with Trosdan, son of Eric, and with Pol Adhmann,[1] and with Beollan Armann,[2] et alii; a slaughter of the men of Mumha, with two Ua Brics, i.e. two royal heirs of the Deisi, and with Ua-Failbhe. i.e. royal heir of Corca-Dhuibhne, and a dynast of Laighen,[3] i.e. with Ua Muire-ghaigh, i.e. king of Ciarraighe, together with his son, et alii multi optimi quos[4] causa[5] brevitatis scribere[6] præter-misimus.[7] The Cenel-Eoghain, and the nobles of Cenel-Conaill and of the North likewise, returned with great spoils, and with numerous treasures, including the royal pavilion, and the standard, and many precious things besides. -Maghnus, King of Lochlann, was slain on a predatory expedition in Ulidia.

The kalends of January on the 6th feria, the 1st of the moon ; the age of the Lord four years, and a hundred, and a thousand. O'Conchobhair of Corcumruaidh, i.e. Conchobhar, son of Maelsechlainn, mortuus est. Mac-na-hoidhche Ua Ruairc a suis fratribus occisus est. A hosting by Muirchertach Ua Briain to Magh-Muirthemhne, and he totally destroyed the tillage of the plain; and it was on this hosting that Cuuladh O Caindelbhain, King of Laegh-aire, was thrown *from his horse,* of which he died. A host-ing by Domhnall Mac Lachlainn to Magh-Cobha, when he obtained the hostages of Ulidia; and he proceeded to Temh-air, and burned a large part of Ui-Laeghaire, but gave protection to *some of* them[8] however. Donnchadh Ua Con-chobhair, King of Cianachta, was slain by his own people.

The kalends of January on the 1st feria, the 12th of the moon ; the age of the Lord five years, and a hundred,

---

[6] *Scribere.* ꞃcꞃ1b1, MS.
[7] *Prætermisimus.* p̄mı꞉꞉ımuꞃ, MS.

[8] *Some of them;* i.e. some of the inhabitants of the district of Ui-Laeghaire.

mile αιρ ιη Τιξεриα. Conchobαρ mαc Mαοιλτρεᴄlαιηη, ríδαm̃ηα Τεmραch, occiρυρ ερτ. Dom̃ηαll, comαρbα Ρατραιc, το τοchτ co hΑᴄ cliαᴄ το δεηυm ríδα ιδιρ Mυιρceртαch O m̃bρίαιη ocυρ Dom̃ηαll m̃áξ Lαᴄlαιηη, ξυρροξαδ ξαlαρ αηη é, ocυρ co ττυcαδ αηη α ξαlαρ ρéιη co Dom̃ηαch Oιρρτεр Εm̃ηα, ξυρρο hoηξαδ αηη; co ττυcαδ ιαρριη co Dαιmliαξ, coητερbαιlτ αηη; ξο ττυcαδ α coρρ ξο hΑρτο Mαchα. Ceαllαᴄ mαc Αοδα, mιc Mαοιlιoρρα, το οιρηεδ ηα ιοηαδ α comαρbυρ Ρατραιc, α τοξα ρερ ηΕρεηη; ocυρ το chóιδ ρο ξράδhαιb α lo ρéιle Αδumηáιη. Slοιξεδ lα Mυιρceртαch O m̃bρίαιη, ξυρρο ιηηαρb Doηδchαδ .h. Mαοιlτρεclαιηη α ρίξε ιαρτhαιρ Mιδε.

Ιctt. Εηαιρ .ιι. ρ.; l xxιιι. Sé blιαδηα αρ cεδ αρ mile αιρ ιη Τιξεриα. Cρεαᴄ ρlóιξεδ lα Dom̃ηαll m̃áξ Lαᴄlαιηη τροιρίξιη Doηηchαδα hι Mαóιlτρechlαιηη, ξυρρο oρταδαρ ιαρταρ Mιδε, ocυρ ξο ττáρρυρ Doηηchαδ ρéιη αηη ρορ ρceιm̃lιδ, ocυρ ξυρρο m̃αρbαδ é. Cellαᴄ, comαρbα Ρατραιc, ρορ cυαιρτ Cenel Εoξαιη, cεδηα cυρ, ξο ττυc α óξρéιρ, .ι. bó ξαchα ρειριρ, ηo αξ ηδάρα ξαchα τρίρ, ηo leᴄ υηξα ξαchα ceαᴄραιρ, lα ταoδ ηίδbαρτ ηιm̃δα olchεηα. Cαᴄδαρρ O Dom̃ηαιll, τυιρ ᴄορηαmα ocυρ coιηξlecα, ορδυιη ocυρ eιηιξ Ceneoιl Lúιξδεᴄ, τραξαιl δáιρ. Cellαᴄ ρορ cυαιρτ Mumαη, cεδηα cυρ δεóρ, ξο ττυc α lαη ᴄυαιρτ, .ι. υιι. mbα ocυρ .υιι. cαοιριξ ocυρ leᴄ υιηξe ξαchα ρυιηη τρίοᴄα cεδ α Mumαιη, lα ταoδ ρéδ ηιm̃δα olchεηα, ocυρ

---

[1] *Occisus est.* occιρι ρυητ, MS. There were probably some other names included in the corresponding entry in the original MS. from which the transcriber of this chronicle copied, and which he omitted from his copy, without altering the expression *occisi sunt.* Many similar instances of negligence are observable in the MS.

[2] *Daimhliag.* Now Duleek, co.

Meath. The Four Mast. say "Daimhlaig-Arda-Macha;" i.e. the stone-church of Ard-Macha (or Armagh); but the statement in this chronicle, which agrees with the Ann. Ult., is apparently more correct, as Domhnall seems to have been too ill to bear the journey to Armagh.

[3] *Half an ounce;* i.e. of silver.

[4] *Triocha-ced.* The extent of the

and a thousand. Conchobhar, son of Maelsechlainn, royal heir of Temhair, occisus est.[1] Domhnall, comarb of Patrick, came to Ath-cliath, to make peace between Muirchertach O'Briain and Domhnall Mac Lachlainn, where sickness seized him, and he was carried in his sickness to Domhnach-oirther-Emhna, where he was anointed; and he was afterwards carried to Daimhliag,[2] where he died; and his body was taken to Ard-Macha. Ceallach, son of Aedh, son of Maelisa, was ordained in his place, in the comarbship of Patrick, by the choice of the men of Erinn; and he received orders on the day of Adhamnan's festival. A hosting by Muirchertach O'Briain, when he expelled Donnchadh Ua Maelsechlainn from the sovereignty of the West of Midhe.

The kalends of January on the 2nd feria, the 23rd of the moon; the age of the Lord six years, and a hundred, and a thousand. A predatory hosting by Domhnall Mac Lachlainn, to assist Donnchadh Ua Maelsechlainn, when they injured the west of Midhe; and Donnchadh himself was met there on a scouting party, and slain. Ceallach, comarb of Patrick, went on the visitation of Cenel-Eoghain, for the first time, and he obtained his full demand, viz.:—a cow for every six persons, or an in-calf heifer for every three, or half an ounce[3] for every four, in addition to many offerings besides. Cathbharr O'Domhnaill, pillar of the defence and warfare, of the glory and hospitality of the Cenel-Luighdech, died. Ceallach *went* on a visitation of Mumha, the first time also; and he obtained his full tribute, viz.:—seven cows, and seven sheep, and half an ounce[3] for every triocha-ced[4] in Mumha, in addi-

---

triocha-ced, (literally "thirty hundreds"), or cantred, as it is sometimes rendered, has not been accurately defined; but it seems to have comprised about twice the extent of an ordinary barony. See Dr. Reeves's valuable paper on the *Townland Distribution of Ireland*; Proceedings of the Royal Irish Academy, vol. vii., p. 475.

aṗroéḋ, umorro, Cellaċ gráḋa uasal erpuic a comairle fer nEṗenn don dul sin.

Kal. Enair .iii. f.; .l. iiii. Seacht mbliadna ar ced ar mile air in Tigerna. Snechta lói co noiḋċe dfertḣain in Cedaoin ria ḃféil Patraic, gurro lá ár cetra Eṗenn. Cend ċoraiḋ do loscad etir ḋá ċáisc, go roscuid ndabach etir ṁiḋ ocus brogóid. Conċobar O Duinnsleḃe, ríḋaṁna Ulaḋ, do ṁarbad dferuiḃ Fernṁuiġe. Maiḋm ría nUíḃ Ḃreṡiul for Uíḃ Méth, i torchair i nár imm á rí, .i. Aoḋ .h. hInnreachtaiġ. Fliuċ ḋoinend ṁór isin mbliadain sin, gurro mill na harḃanna uile. Sith ḃliadna do ḋenum do Ceallaċ, comarba Patraic, etir Muircertach .h. mBriain ocus Domnall ṁág Laċlainn.

Kal. Enair .iiii. f.; l. xu.; ocht mbliadna ar ced ar mile air in Tigerna. Luimnech do loscad. Domnall .h. Ruairc, ri .h. mBriuin, occisus est. Cellach, comarba Patraic, for cuairt Connacht, cedna cor, co dtuc a óġréir. Teċ do ġaḃáil do .h. Maṫġamna, ocus do .h. Maelruanaiḋ, for Goll nGarḃraiġe, .i. for rí Ulad, .i. Eochaid mac Duinnsleiḃe hI Eochaḋa, ocus a

[1] *Received.* aṗroéḋ. In his edition of the Annals of the Four Masters, Dr. O'Donovan has rendered the word aṗroéḋ by "conferred;" but the meaning is "received," as appears from several ancient authorities quoted by Zeuss, *Grammatica Celtica*, vol. i., p. 493, where the word is glossed *accepit* and *recepit*. See Reeves's *Adamnan*, p. 326, note q. The word "primate" appears in the margin in a hand somewhat more modern than the original. Roderick O'Flaherty has also added the word "primate" in the margin, to signify that the primacy of Armagh was acknowledged in the person of Ceallach, or Celsus.

[2] *On that occasion.* don dul sin; lit. "on that going." Another form of the same expression, in dul so, "on this occasion," has been misunderstood by the learned Zeuss, who translates it *hoc opus*. See *Gram. Celt.*, Introd., p. xvi.

[3] *The 4th.* The MS. has xxiiii (24th), but this is a mistake, as new moon occurred on the 29th of December, 1106, and the 1st of January, 1107, was consequently the fourth day of the moon's age.

[4] *Between the two Easters;* i.e. between Easter Sunday and "Little Easter," or Low Sunday.

[5] *Puncheons.* dabac. Roderick O'Flaherty translates this word "keeves" in a marginal note: "sixty keeves of beere and meade burnt."

[6] *Beer.* brogóid (brogóid)=Welsh *bragawd*, the drink called in English *bragget*.

tion to many presents besides; and Ceallach, moreover received[1] the dignity of a superior bishop, by the consent of the men of Erinn, on that occasion.[2]

The kalends of January on the 3rd feria, the 4th[3] of the moon; the age of the Lord seven years, and a hundred, and a thousand. Snow fell for a day and night, the Wednesday before the festival of Patrick, which caused a great destruction of the cattle of Erinn. Cenn-coradh was burned between the two Easters,[4] with sixty puncheons[5] of mead and beer.[6] Conchobhar, grandson[7] of Donnsleibhe, royal heir of Uladh, was slain by the men of Fernmhagh. A victory by the Ui-Bresail over the Ui-Meth, in which they[8] were slaughtered, together with their king, i.e. Aedh Ua hInnreachtaigh. Very wet weather in this year, which destroyed all the corn crops. A year's peace was made by Ceallach, comarb of Patrick, between Muirchertach Ua Briain and Domhnall Mac Lachlainn.

The kalends of January on the 4th feria, the 15th of the moon; the age of the Lord eight years, and a hundred, and a thousand. Luimnech was burned. Domhnall Ua Ruairc, king of Ui-Briuin, occisus est.[9] Ceallach, comarb of Patrick, *proceeded* on a visitation of Connacht *for the* first time, and obtained his full demand. A house was taken by Ua Mathghamhna and Ua Maelruanaidh over Goll Garbraighe, i.e. the king of Uladh, i.e. Eochaidh, son of Donnsleibhe Ua hEochadha, and he was beheaded

---

[7] *Grandson.* The Ann. Ult. and the Four Mast. call Conchobhar "son of Donnsleibhe," which is doubtless correct; and it is probable that his father was Donnsleibhe Ua hEochadha (Donlevy O'Hoey), king of Uladh, whose death is given by the Four Mast. under the year 1094.

[8] *They*; i.e. the Ui-Meth.

[9] *Occisus est.* The MS. has *occisi sunt*, from which it appears that the name of some other person, occurring in the authority from which the entry had been copied, was omitted by the transcriber of the chronicle. The Annals of Ulster have the entry as follows:—Ꝺomnall .h. Ꝼnbeiꞇ ꝛı .h. Mꞁeiꞇ; Ꝺomnall .h. Ruaiꝛc, ꝛı .h. mⱵꝛuin, o. ꝛ.;" i.e. "Domhnall Ua hAinbheith, king of Ui-Meith, *and* Domhnall Ua Ruairc, king of Ui-Briuin, occisi sunt."

H

ჽიɔenɔaᵬ leó. 'Oaɾmeɾɾ móɾ ɾó Eɾınn uıle. ᵬlıaᵭaın
cɾuᵵhach ჽo nɔeıჽɾín, ocuɾ ჽo nımaɔ aɾᵬa ocuɾ meɾɾa,
ın ᵬlıaɔaın ɾın.

Ᵽcᵵᵵ. Enaıɾ .uı. ɾ. ; l. xxuı. ; ıx. mblıaɔna aɾ ceɔ aɾ
mıle aıɾ ın Cıჽeɾna. ín Cáıɾc ɾoɾ .uıı. Ᵽcᵵᵵ. Máoı
ocuɾ Mınᵵaıɾc ala laıᵵe ɔo cɾámɾaᵬ. Sloıჽeɔ lá
Muıɾceɾcach .ᴏ. mᵬɾıaın ɔɾóıɾıᵭın Muɾchaɔa ᴏı
Maoılcɾechlaınn, ჽuɾɾo aıɾჽ ɔɾeım ɔo Uıᵬ ᵬɾúın.
Sloıჽeɔ lá 'Oomnall ṁáჽ Laᵵlaınn ჽo ɔcuaıɾceɾc Eɾenn
uıme, co Slıaᵬ ɾuaıɔ ; ჽonɔeɾna Cellach, comaɾba
ɾacɾaıc, ɾíᵵ ᵬlıaᵭna ecıɾ O mᵬɾıaın ocuɾ ṁáჽ
Laᵵlaınn, ჽonɔeaᵵaɔaɾ cuaıɾceɾc Eɾenn ıaɾɾın, ım
Conall ocuɾ ım Eoჽan, ჽo Maɔ .ᴏ. mᵬɾɾaıl, ɾoɾ
ammuɾ Ulaᵬ baɔaɾ a Maჽ Coᵬa, ჽo ɔcaɾɔɾac
Ulaᵬ na ceoɾa ჽıalla ɾo ᵵoჽɾaɔ ɾeın ɔoıᵬ. αcaᵭ
.ᴏ. Ruaıɾc ɔo ᵵochc a lonჽɾoɾc Muɾchaɔa ᴏı
Moeılcɾechlaınn, ɾá ᵭó, ჽuɾɾo lá aɾ cɾe eɾcuıɾe
ᵵɾáṁᵵa ɾacɾaıc. Mac ჽıllaɾacɾaıc, [ɾí] Oɾɾɾaıჽe
.ı. 'Oomnall ɾuaᵬ, ɔo ṁaɾbaᵬ ɔo macaoṁ uıle aჽ cuɾ
ᵵluıce.

Ᵽcᵵᵵ. Enaıɾ .uıı. ɾ. ; l. uıı. ; x. mblıaɔna aɾ ceɔ aɾ
mıle aıɾ ın Cıჽeɾna. ჽılla Coluım O Maolṁuaıᵬ,
ɾí bɾeɾ Ceall, ıuჽulacuɾ eɾc. Muɾchaɔᴏ mac Caıᵬc
ᴏı ᵬɾıaın, ɾíɔaṁna Muman, moɾcuuɾ eɾc. ᵬéᵬınn,
ınჽen Ceınnéıɔıჽ ᴏı ᵬɾıaın, ben 'Oomnaıll ṁéჽ Laᵵlaınn, .
ɾí Oılıჽ, ɔhéc. Cɾeᵵ la 'Oomnall ṁáჽ Laᵵlaınn ı
Connachcuıᵬ, co ɔcuc ṁıle ɔo ᵬɾaıɔ, ocuɾ ıl ṁıle ɔo
ᵵeᵬɾuıᵬ. Cellaᵵ, comaɾba ɾacɾuıᵬ, ceɔna coɾ ɾoɾ
cuaıɾc Mıᵬe, ჽo ɔcuc a óıჽɾeıɾ eıɾɔe. Maıᵬm ɾıa
ჽConmaıcnıᵬ ɾoɾ Sıol Muıɾeჽhaıჽh .ı. maıᵬm Moıჽe

---

1 *Little Easter*; i.e. Low Sunday.

2 *Curse.* The Four Masters imply
that the curse of the "congregation of
Patrick [i.e. of Armagh]" was in-
curred by Murchadh Ua Maelsechlainn through his profanation of the
Bachall-Isa [Baculus Jesu] and the

successor of Patrick, in slaying Ua
Finn, lord of Feara-Rois, who was
under their protection.

3 *Thousand.* ṁıle, MS. The aspiration of the first letter of the word
mıle indicates that it must have been
preceded by a word terminating in a

by them. A great crop of oak *fruit* throughout all Erinn.
A sappy year, with good weather, and with much corn
and produce, *was* this year.

The kalends of January on the 6th feria, the 26th of
the moon ; the age of the Lord nine years, and a hundred,
and a thousand. Easter on the 7th of the kalends of
May, and Little Easter[1] on the second day of summer. A
hosting by Muirchertach Ua Briain, to aid Murchadh Ua
Maelsechlainn, and he plundered a section of the Ui-Briuin.
A hosting by Domhnall Mac Lachlainn accompanied by *the
men of* the North of Erinn, to Sliabh-Fuaid ; but Ceallach,
comarb of Patrick, made a year's peace between O'Briain
and Mac Lachlainn ; and *the men of* the North of Erinn,
together with the *Cenel*-Conaill and *Cenel*-Eoghain, went
afterwards to Magh-Ui-Bresail, to attack the Ulidians
who were in Magh-Cobha ; but the Ulidians gave them
the three hostages whom they themselves selected. Aedh
Ua Ruairc came twice into the camp of Murchadh Ua
Maelsechlainn, and committed a slaughter through the
curse[2] of the congregation of Patrick. Mac Gillapatraic,
[king] of Osraighe, i.e. Domhnall Ruadh, was killed by
another youth whilst playing a game.

The kalends of January on the 7th feria, the 7th of the
moon ; the age of the Lord ten years, and a hundred, and
a thousand. Gillacoluim O'Maelmhuaidh, king of Feara-
Ceall, *jugulatus est*. Murchadh, son of Tadhg Ua Briain,
royal heir of Mumha, *mortuus est*. Bébhinn, daughter of
Cenneidigh Ua Briain, wife of Domhnall Mac Lachlainn,
king of Oilech, died. A predatory expedition by Domhnall
Mac Lachlainn into Connacht, whence he carried off a
thousand[3] prisoners, and several thousand cattle. Ceallach, comarb of Patrick, *went for the* first time on a visitation of Midhe, and carried off from it his full demand, A
victory by the Conmaicne over the Síl-Muireghaigh, i.e.

vowel ; and in the Four Masters the
number of prisoners is stated to | have been ꞇꞃí míle (trí mhíle) "three
thousand."

bpénġaip. Maiḋm lá Sil Muipeġaiġ pop Connaicniḃ .i. maiḋm an Roip, ap bélaiḃ Cpuaċna, ατopcpaḋap τpi .h. Pepġaile, ocuſ maiṫi imḋa ele áipċena.

Ktt. Enaip i.f.; l. xuiii; aon bliaḋain ḋéc ap cet ap mile aiṗ in Τιżeṗna. Popτ laiṗże ḋo loṗcaḋ. Cenannτuſ ḋo loṗcaḋ. Slóiżeḋ la hUllτoiḃ co Τelaiż óż, żuṗṗo ṫeṗcṗaτ a bileḋa. Cpeċ la Niall ṁáż laċlainn, żo τuc τṗi ṁile ḋo ḃuaiḃ ina noíżuil. Τene ḋaiṫ ḋo loṗcaḋ Ḋúin ḋa leṫżlaſ, eḋiṗ ṗáiṫ ocuſ τṗían. Senaḋ ċléipeċ nEpenn a bṗiaḋ mic nOenżuṗa, a nUiṗneċ, im Cellaċ comaṗba Paτṗaic, ocuſ im Maolmuiṗe .h. nDúnán .i. uaṗſul ſenóiṗ na hEpenn, żo coicaiτ neſṗoż, uel paulo pluſ, żo τṗíü ceḋaiḃ ſażaṗτ, ocuſ żo τṗi ṁile maic neżalṗa, im Muiṗceṗτaċ .h. mḂṗíain żo maiṫiḃ leiṫe Moḋa, oſuṗáil ṗiażla ocuſ τṗoiḃéṗ ſoṗ ċáċ eτiṗ τuaiṫ ocuſ eżluiſ. Ḋonnċaḋh .h. hOCnluain, pí .h. Niallán, ḋo maṗbaḋ ḋia bṗáiṫṗiḃ a meaḃuil. Na bṗaiτṗi híṗin ḋo maṗbaḋ ḋo Uiḃ Niallán ina ḃiżuil ṗia żcinn .xx. aiḋċe iaṗṗin. Comḋál eτiṗ Ḋomnall ṁáż laċlainn ocuſ Ḋonnċaḋh .h. nEoċaḋa, żonḋeṗnṗaτ lán ſíṫ, ocuſ żo τaṗḋṗaτ Ulaḋ eiḋepeḋa a ṗiaṗa ſein ḋo Ḋomnall.

Ktt. Enaip .ii. f.; l. xx.ix.; ḋá bliaḋain ḋéc ap cet ap mile aiṗ in Τιżeṗna. Ṗáiṫ Olṗḋ Maċa cona τempall ḋo loṗcaḋ in .x. Ktt. Olppil, ocuſ ḋá ſṗeiτh ḋo τṗiun Maṗṗán, ocuſ an τṗeſſ ſṗeiṫh ḋo τṗiun móṗ. Cpeċ la Ḋomnall ṁáż laċlainn ḋaṗ Pine żall, co ḋτuc bṗaiḋ áḋbal ocuſ bópuma ṁóṗ.

---

[1] *Sacred trees.* bileḋa. The kings of Cenel-Eoghain were inaugurated under certain remarkable trees at Telach-og (now Tulloghoge, or Tully-hog), parish of Desertcreat, barony of Dungannon, county of Tyrone.

[2] *For them;* i.e. for the cutting down of the sacred trees (*biledha*).

[3] *Rath;* i.e. the fort. Dr. Reeves has pointed out to me that the local name *Rath-Righbhaird*, which occurs in the Tripartite (Irish) Life of St. Patrick is represented by *Fossa-Rig-bairt* in the Book of Armagh, fol. 15[aa], whence it would appear that *rath* originally meant the ditch surrounding a fort. Ultimately, however, the name of *rath* was applied to the

the victory of Magh-Brénghair. A victory by the Sil-Muireghaigh over the Conmaicne, viz.:—the victory of the Ros, opposite Cruachan, in which fell three Ua Ferghails, and many other nobles besides.

The kalends of January on the 1st feria, the 18th of the moon; the age of the Lord eleven years, and a hundred, and a thousand. Port-Lairge was burned. Cenannus was burned. A hosting by the Ulidians to Telach-og, when they cut down its sacred trees.[1] A predatory excursion by Niall Mac Lachlainn, who carried off three thousand cows in revenge for them.[2] Dun-da-lethghlas was burned by lightning, both Rath[3] and Trian.[4] A synod of clerics at Fiadh-mic-Aenghusa, in Uisnech, including Cellach, comarb of Patrick, and including Maelmuire Ua Dunain, i.e. the noble senior of Erinn, with fifty bishops, vel paulo plus, with three hundred priests, and with three thousand students, together with Muirchertach Ua Briain, attended by the nobles of Leth-Mogha, to impose rules and good customs on all, both laity and clergy. Donnchadh Ua hAnluain, king of Ui-Niallain, was slain by his brothers, in treachery. These brothers were slain by the Ui-Niallain, in revenge for him, before the end of twenty nights thereafter. A convention between Domhnall Mac Lachlainn and Donnchadh Ua hEochadha, when they made a full peace; and the Ulidians gave hostages to Domhnall, for *the payment of* his own demand.

The kalends of January on the 2nd feria, the 29th of the moon; the age of the Lord twelve years, and a hundred, and a thousand. The Rath[3] of Ard-Macha, with its church, was burned on the 10th of the kalends of April, and two rows of Trian-Massan, and the third row of Trian-mór. A predatory expedition by Domhnall Mac Lachlainn across Fine-Gall, and he carried off an immense number of captives, and a great spoil of cattle.

---

entire surface circumscribed by the *fossa.*

[4] *Trian.* This word signifies "third part." See note [6] page 67.

|ctt. enaıp .ıııı. p.; L. x.; τρı blıaona ohéc ap ceo ap
mıle aıp ın Tıʒepna.　Coepτeneo oo τeachτ oıoτe péle
Paτpaıc pop Cpuaτán Ccıʒle, ʒuppo mıll .xxx. oon óepp
τpoıpτe.　MaoıLpechLaınn O Conchobaıp, pí Copcum-
puaıo, ohéc.　Oonn O Taıpcepτ, τóıppech Cloınne
Sneıoʒıle, oo mapbao La Nıall máʒ LaτLaınn.　SlóıʒeO
La Oomnall maʒ LaτLaınn ʒo maτıO Ceneóıl ConaıLL
ocup Eoʒaın, ocup CcıpʒıaLL, ʒo ʒlıonn pıʒe, ʒuppo
ıonnapbpaτ Oonnchao a pıʒe nUlao, ocup ʒuppo
pannpaτ ULLτu eτıp .h. Maτʒamna ocup maca Ouınn-
pleτe.　Oál nCcpaıoe, ımoppo, ocup ı Echach aıʒe
péın.　Sloıʒeo La Muıpceptach .h. mUpıaın, ʒo pepuıo
Muman, ocup ʒo Laıʒnıo ocup Connachτaıo, ʒo Maʒ
Coba, opóıpıoın Oonnchaoa.　Slóıʒeo ele La Oomnall
máʒ LaτLaınn, ʒo ʒConallchaıo ocup Eoʒanchaıo ocup
CcıpʒıaLL, ʒo Maʒ Coba mup an ceona, opóıpıoın Ulao,
ʒo paıoe ımneppa caτa eτoppa, ʒuppo eoappcap
comapba Paτpaıc po ʒné píτe.　Oonnchao .h. hEochaoa
oo oallao La hEochaıo .h. Maτʒamna, ocup La
hULLτoıo.　Slóıʒeo La Muıpceptach .h. mUpíaın, ocup
Lá Leτ Moba, eτıp laoτ ocup τléıpeτ, ʒo ʒpenoıc.
Oomnall máʒ LaτLaınn ʒo maτıO τuaıpcepτ Epenn
.ı. Conaıll ocup Eoʒaın ocup CcıpʒıaLL, co Cluaın
Caoın a bpepuıo Roıp, ʒo mbaoap pıu pé míopp cınn
comaıp pıu poıle, conoepna Cellaτ, comapba Paτpaıc,
ʒup an mbaτuıll ıoppa, píτ blıaona eτoppa.　Sʒaınoep
cpóba eτıp pepuıo Pepnmaıoe póoéın, oú ıτopépaoap
oa píoamna Pepnmaıoe .ı. .h. Cpoτáın ocup .h.
Oonnacán.

|ctt. enaıp .u. p.; L. xxı.; ceıτpı blıaona oéc ap ceo

---

1 *Donn*. The Ann. Ult. and the Four Mast. write the name Donnchadh.

2 *Donnchadh;* i.e. Donnchadh Ua hEochadha, or O'Hoey.

3 *Danger.* ımneppa, anc. written ımnepı. This word is usually trans-

lated "challenge;" but it really seems to be a loan word from the Latin *imminentia*, the *n* preceding the *i* in the Latin, disappearing in the Irish, as is frequently the case in Irish words borrowed from the Latin.　See a paper

The kalends of January on the 4th feria, the 10th of the moon; the age of the Lord thirteen years, and a hundred, and a thousand. A thunderbolt fell on Cruachan-Aighle, on the night of the festival of Patrick, which destroyed thirty of the fasting people. Maelsechlainn O'Conchobhair, king of Corcumruaidh, died. Donn[1] O'Tairchert, chieftain of Clann-Sneidhghile, was slain by Niall Mac Lachlainn. A hosting by Domhnall Mac Lachlainn, with the nobles of Cenel-Conaill and *Cenel*-Eoghain, and the Airghialla, to Glenn-Righe; and they expelled Donnchadh[2] from the sovereignty of Uladh, and divided Uladh between Ua Mathghamhna and the sons of Donnsleibhe; but Dal-Araidhe and Ui-Echach *were retained* by himself. A hosting by Muirchertach Ua Briain, with the men of Mumha, and the Lagenians and Connacht-men, to Magh-Cobha, to aid Donnchadh.[2] Another hosting by Domhnall Mac Lachlainn, with the men of *Cenel*-Conall and of *Cenel*-Eoghain, and the Airghialla, to Magh-Cobha likewise, to aid the Ulidians; and there was a danger[3] of battle between them, until the comarb of Patrick separated them under the semblance of peace. Donnchadh Ua hEochadha was blinded by Eochaidh Ua Mathghamhna and the Ulidians. A hosting by Muirchertach Ua Briain and *the people of* Leth-Mogha, both laics and clerics, to Grenog. Domhnall Mac Lachlainn, with the nobles of the North of Erinn, viz. :—of the *Cenel*-Conaill and *Cenel*-Eoghain, and Airghialla, *proceeded* to Cluain-caein, in Feara-Rois; and they were during the space of a month confronting one another, until Ceallach, comarb of Patrick, with the Bachall-Isa, made a year's peace between them. A fierce conflict between the men of Fernmhagh themselves, in which two royal heirs of Fernmhagh, viz., Ua Crichain and Ua Donnagain, were slain.

The kalends of January on the 5th feria, the 21st of

" On the affinities of certain Irish and Latin words," by Bishop Graves; | *Proceedings* of the R. I. Academy, vol. v., p. 337.

αρ míle αιρ ιn Τιζερηα. Τειδm ζαλαιρ mόιρ oo ζαβάιλ
Μυιρcερταιζ Ι Βρίαιn, ρί Ερεnn, ζυρρο ρcαρ ρρί α ρίζε.
Οιαρμαιο .Ϡ. Βρίαιn, ιmορρο, oo ζαβάιλ ρίζε Μυμαn
ιnα ριαδnυρε ζαn cέουζαο. Sλοιζεο λα Οοmnαλλ mάζ
Λαčλαιnn co Ράιč Cεnoαιζ, co τάnιc Εοchαιο .Ϡ. Μαč-
ζαmnα co nΥλλτοιβ ιnα čech, ocυρ Οοnnchαο .Ϡ.
Λοιnζριζ co nΟάλ Αραιδε, ocυρ Αοδ .Ϡ. Ρυαιρc ζο
βρερυιδ Βρειρρne, ocυρ Μυρchαο .Ϡ. Μαοιλρεčλαιnn
ζο βρερυιδ Μιδε. Οο λοταρ υιλε οιδλίnυιδ ταρ Αč
Λυαιn co Ούn Λεόδα, ζο οτάnιc Τοιρρδhεαλbαch .Ϡ.
Conchobαιρ ζο ζConnαchτυιδ, ocυρ Νιαλλ mαc Οοm-
nαιλλ mάζ Λαčλαιnn, ocυρ μαιčε Cλοιnnε Conυιλλ, ιnα
αιρechτ. Τιαζυιο αρρ ιαρρin ζο Τελαιζ .Ϡ. nΟεζhαιδ α
nΟάλ ζCαιρ, conoερnγατ ορραδ bλίαδnα ocυρ ριρ
Μυμαn, ocυρ oo chύαιο Οοmnαλλ mάζ Λαčλαιnn αρ
ρυο Connαchτ, ocυρ αρρin οία čιζ. Αοδ mαc Οοnn-
chαoα hΙ Εοchαoα, ρίζoαmnα Υλαo, μορτυυρ ερτ.
Ρυαιορι .Ϡ. Cαnαnnάn, ρίδαmnα Cιnεοιλ Conαιλλ, oo
μαρbαo λα Cεnέλ Εοζαιn. Μυιρcερταch mάζ Λαch-
λαιnn, ρίδαmnα Οιλιζ, ιnιυρτε ιnτερρεcτυρ ερτ.

Κtt. Εnαιρ .ιιι. ρ.; λ. ιι.; cόιζ bλιαonα δhέc αρ cεo
αρ míle αιρ ιn Τιζερηα. Οοιnεno oερmάιρ, ocυρ
ρεοδ, ocυρ ρnechτα, o .xυ. Κt. Εnαιρ ζο .xυ. Κt. Μαρ-
τιι, υel παυλο ρλυρ, ζυρρολά άρ έn ocυρ cεčρα, ocυρ
oαοιnε, ocυρ οία ρο ραρ τερcα mόρ ocυρ οοmmαττα
ρό Ερinn υιλε, ocυρ α Λαιζnιδ ρech cάč. Οιαρμαιο

---

[1] *King of Erinn.* ρι Ερ, for ρι
Ερεnn, MS. The words have been
altered to ριδαmnα Ειριοnn ("royal
heir of Erinn") by a later hand than
that of the original transcriber. The
emendator was evidently a supporter
of the view held by the northern
(Irish) historians, that Domhnall Mac
Lachlainn, the contemporary and rival
of Muirchertach O'Brien, was the real
monarch of Ireland in his time, whereas his opponent was only second in

dignity. See *Cambrensis Eversus*, ed.
Rev. Matt. Kelly, Dublin, 1850, vol.
ii., p. 55.

[2] *Removed.* The meaning is that the
disease was the cause of his being removed from the sovereignty. In the
Chron. Scotorum (1110–1114) it is
stated that "the men of Erinn turned
against him."

[3] *Came into his house;* or, in other
words, "submitted to him."

[4] *Clann-Conaill;* or Cenel-Conaill,

the moon; the age of the Lord fourteen years, and a hundred, and a thousand. A great fit of sickness seized Muirchertach Ua Briain, king of Erinn,[1] and removed[2] him from his sovereignty. Diarmaid Ua Briain, moreover, assumed the sovereignty of Mumha, in his presence, without permission. A hosting by Domhnall Mac Lachlainn to Rath-Cennaigh, when Eochaidh Ua Mathghamhna, with the Ulidians, came into his house,[3] and Donnchadh Ua Loingsigh, with the Dal-Araidhe, and Aedh Ua Ruairc, with the men of Breifne, and Murchadh Ua Maelsechlainn, with the men of Midhe. They all proceeded across Ath-Luain to Dun-Leodha, where Toirdhealbhach Ua Conchob-hair, with the Connachtmen, and Niall, son of Domhnall Mac Lachlainn, with the chieftains of Clann-Conaill,[4] came into his assembly. They all went thence, afterwards, to Telach-Ui-Deghaidh in Dal-Cais, where they and the men of Mumha made a year's peace; and Domhnall Mac Lachlainn went through Connacht, and from thence to his house. Aedh, son of Donnchadh Ua hEochadha, royal heir of Uladh, mortuus est. Ruaidhri Ua Canannain, royal heir of Cenel-Conaill, was slain by the Cenel-Eoghain. Muirchertach Mac Lachlainn, royal heir of Oilech, injuste[5] interfectus est.[6]

The kalends of January on the 6th feria, the 2nd of the moon; the age of the Lord fifteen years, and a hundred, and a thousand. Very severe weather, with frost and snow, from the 15th of the kalends of January[7] to the 15th of the kalends of March,[8] vel paulo plus, which made great havoc of birds, and cattle, and people; and from which arose great scarcity and want throughout all Erinn, and in Laighen especially.[9] Diarmaid O'Briain, king of Mumha,

---

as in the Annals of Ulster and the Four Mast.

[5] *Injuste.* ꟷ (injuiste), MS.

[6] *Interfectus est.* ꟷ (interfecti sunt), MS.

[7] *The 15th of the Kalends of January;* i.e. the 18th of December, 1114.

[8] *Of March.* ꟷ (Marcius), MS.

[9] *Especially.* ꟷ (sech cách), lit. "beyond all."

O Bríain, rí Muman, do ġaḃáil la Muircertach O mBríain. Ionnraiged grerri do ṫabairt do macuiḃ mic Aoḋa mic Ruaiḋri, ar Toirrḋealbach .h. Conchobair, ar rí Connacht, gurro loited, ocur gurḃó crólige ḋó. Maiḋm ria nDoṁnall .h. mBríain ocur ria ngallaiḃ Aṫa cliaṫ, ar Laiġniḃ, i torchair Donnchaḋ O Maoilnambó, rí .h. gCinnrelaiġ, ocur Conchobar O Conchobair, rí .h. bḟailġe, cona macuiḃ, ocur rochaide airchena. Doṁnall mac Taiḋġ hí Bríain, ríḋaṁna Muman, do marbaḋ la Connachtuiḃ. Muircertach .h. Bríain do ġaḃáil a riġe féin do ríḋír, ocur teacht rlóiġeḋ a Laiġniḃ, ocur a mBreḃġuiḃ. Daṁliag Airḋ mBrecáin cona lán do ḋaoiniḃ do lorcaḋ dḟeruiḃ Muman, ocur cella imḋa airchena a bḟeruiḃ Breġh. Creċ mór la Toirrḋealbach O Conchobair ocur la Connachtuiḃ, gurro airgret Tuaḋmuma go Luimnech; go rucrat bóruma ḋiairṁiḋe, ocur braid imḋa. Maoilrechlainn .h. Maoilrechlainn, ríḋaṁna Temraċ, occirur erṫ.

Ktt. enáir .uii. f.; l. .xiii. Sé bliaḋna ḋéc ar ced ar mile air in Tiġerna. Cellaċ, comarba Patraic, ror cuairt Connacht don ḋarna cor, go dtuc a lan ċuairt. Cill Dalúa cona tempall do lorcaḋ. Corcach mór Muman, ocur Imleċ Iḃair, ocur dairṫech Moeilíra hí Bríoláin, ocur bloḋ do Lior mór, do lorcaḋ irin mbliaḋain céona. Achaḋ mbó Cainniġ [do lorcaḋ]. Cluain Iraird cremata erṫ. Teċ abaḋ mór Airḋ Maċa, go .xx. teġh uime, do lorcaḋ i torach corġuir na bliaḋna ra. Laḋmann mac Doṁnaill, rí Alban, do marbaḋ do ḟeruiḃ Móiraḃ. Derḃáil, ingen Toirrḋealbaiġ hí Bríain, mortua erṫ.

---

1 *Extreme agony.* crólige; lit. "gore bed," from *cro*, or *cru*, "gore," and *lige*, "a bed." The expression is frequently translated "agonies of death," but incorrectly.

2 *Occisus.* Occirrur, MS.

3 *Ladhmann.* The name of this person is not included in the usual lists of the kings of Scotland. He was the son of Domhnall, son of Donnchadh king of Scotland, sl. A.D. 1040.

was captured by Muirchertach O'Briain. A murderous attack was made by the grandsons of Aedh, son of Ruaidhri, on Toirdhealbhach Ua Conchobhair, king of Connacht, and he was wounded so that he was in extreme agony.[1] A victory by Domhnall Ua Briain and the Foreigners of Ath-cliath, over the Lagenians, in which Donnchadh, grandson of Mael-na-mbo, king of Ui-Ceinnsealaigh, and Conchobhar Ua Conchobhair, king of Ui-Failghe. with his sons, and a multitude besides, were slain. Domhnall, son of Tadhg Ua Briain, royal heir of Mumha, was slain by the Connachtmen. Muirchertach Ua Briain assumed his own sovereignty again, and went on a hosting into Laighen and Bregh. The stone-church of Ard-Brecain, with its full of people, was burned by the men of Mumha, and many churches besides in Feara-Bregh. A great predatory excursion by Toirdhealbhach O'Conchobhair and the Connachtmen, and they plundered Tuadh-Mumha as far as Luimnech, and carried off countless cattle spoils and numerous prisoners. Maelsechlainn Ua Maelsechlainn, royal heir of Temhair, occisus[2] est.

The kalends of January on the 7th feria, the 13th of the moon; the age of the Lord sixteen years, and a hundred, and a thousand. Cellach, comarb of Patrick, *went* on a visitation of Connacht, for the second time, and obtained his full tribute. Cill-Dalua, with its church, was burned. Corcach-mor of Mumha, and Imlech-Ibhair, and the oratory of Maelisa Ua Brolchain, and a part of Lis-mór, were burned in the same year. Achadh-bo-Chainnigh [was burned]. Cluain-Iraird cremata est. The Abbot's great house of Ard-Macha, with twenty houses about it, was burned in the beginning of the Lent of this year. Ladhmann,[3] son of Domhnall, king of Alba, was slain by the men of Moray.[4] Derbhail, daughter of Toirdhealbhach Ua Briain, mortua est.

---

[4] *By the men of Moray.* ᴅᴏ ꜰᴇꝛᴜɪꝃ ᴍᴏɪꝛɪᴀꝃ. Dr. O'Conor (ed. Ann. Ulst., sub an.) translates these words | "a prædonibus maritimis." But he has mistaken the meaning.

Ктt. enaip .11. ꝼ. L. xxiiii. Seachт mbliaѡna ѡhec aп ceѡ aп mile aiп in Tiзeпna. Conchobaп .h. Caипellán ѡo maпbaѡ la ꝼeпuiѡ Manach. Caᵵ Lecaoín ѡo ᵵabaiпт ѡo Bпian mac Muпchaѡa ocuꞅ ѡo macaiѡ Caᵵail hi Conchobaiп, зo зConnachтuiѡ impa, ꝼпi Toiппѡhealbach mac nѡiaпmaѡa ocuꞅ ꝼпi ѡál зCaiꞅ, зuппo ᵯuiᵹ ꝼoп ѡál зCaiꞅ, ocuꞅ зuппo láaѡ in náп. Maiѡm ꝼoп Cenel neoзain na hinnꞅi la Cenél Conuill, зuп láaѡ i náп, ocuꞅ зuп maпbaѡ moпán ѡá maiᵵib.

Ктt. enaip .iii. ꝼ.; L. [u].; xuiii. mbliaѡna ѡhéc aп ceѡ aп mile aiп in Tiзeпna. Laiѡзnén .h. ѡuiѡѡaпa, пí ꝼeпmanach, ѡo maпbaѡ ѡo Ulᵵ bꝼiaᵵпaᵵ ocuꞅ ѡꝼeпuiѡ na Cпoiѡe. ѡiaпmaiѡ .h. bпíain, пí Muman ocuꞅ Leiᵵe Moѡa aipchena, ѡhéc i Copcaiз ᵯóiп Muman, iaп nonзaѡ ocuꞅ naiᵵпiᵹe. Meꞅꞅ ceѡ nuinзe ѡo eiѡeaѡ ioѡbaпт ocuꞅ aiꝼꝼпenѡ Cellaiᵹ, comaпba Paᵵпaiꞅ, ѡo ᵵáѡhaѡ i nѡaᵵall, ocuꞅ bíѡᵹaѡ ѡó ꝼéin. Paпchaliꞅ, comaпba Peᵵaiп, ꝼeпuuꞅ peliзioꞅuꞅ, cum ѡilecтione ѡei eт pпoximi aѡ Cпiꞅтum miзпauiт. Maпia, inзen Maoilcoluim .i. inзen пí ᵫlban, ben пí Saxan, moптua eꞅт. Sloiзeѡ la Toiппѡhealbach .h. Conchobaiп, пí Connachт, ocuꞅ la Muпchaѡ O Maoilꞅechlainn, пí Tempach, imaille ꝼпiꞅ, ocuꞅ lá hᵫloѡ O Ruaiпc, iꞅin Mumain зo зlenѡ Maᵹaiп, ocuꞅ зo ѡтaпѡ ѡeпmuᵯa ѡo ᵯáз Caпптhaiᵹ, ocuꞅ Tuaѡmuᵯa ѡo macuiѡ ѡiaпmaѡa hi bпíain, ocuꞅ зo тuc a nзíalla ѡibᵫlinuiѡ.

---

[1] *Murchadh.* The Ann. Four Mast. call him Murchadh Ua Flaithbhertaigh (Murrough O'Flaherty).

[2] *Toirdhealbhach;* i.e. Toirdhealbhach Ua Briain, or Turlough O'Brien.

[3] *Of the Island;* i.e. of Inis-Eoghain, or Inishowen, so called to distinguish them from the other branch of the Cenel-Eoghain inhabiting the district forming the present county of Tir-Eoghain, or Tyrone.

[4] *Ui-Fiachrach.* The Ui-Fiachrach of Ard-Sratha are here meant. See Index.

[5] *The value.* This entry is contained in the Annals of Ulster, almost in the same words; yet Dr. O'Conor, in his edition of these Annals, translates it "Catinus centum unciarum (auri, aut argenti) pro oblationibus Missarum. Celsus Vicarius Patricii demersus in Lacu Dabal, et ereptus propriis viribus." "This translation, which quite misrepresents the meaning of the original, also errs in the introduction of the word *lacus;* for though there is a Loch Dabhaill mentioned in the Four Mast. at A. M.

The kalends of January on the 2nd feria, the 24th of the moon ; the age of the Lord seventeen years and a hundred, and a thousand. Conchobhar Ua Cairellain was slain by the Feara-Manach. The battle of Lecain was given by Brian, son of Murchadh,[1] and by the sons of Cathal Ua Conchobhair, having the Connachtmen along with them, to Toirdhealbhach[2] son of Diarmaid, and to the Dál-Cais; and the Dál-Cais were defeated and put to slaughter. A victory over the Cenel-Eoghain of the Island,[3] by the Cenel-Conail, when they were put to slaughter, and many of their chieftains slain.

A.D. [1117.]

The kalends of January on the 3rd feria, [the 5th] of the moon ; the age of the Lord eighteen years and a hundred, and a thousand. Laidhgnén Ua Duibhdhara, king of Feara-Manach, was slain by the Ui-Fiachrach,[4] and by the men of the Craebh. Diarmaid Ua Briain, king of Mumha, and of all Leth-Mogha, died at Corcach-mór of Mumha, after unction and penitence. The value[5] of one hundred ounces of the offering and mass cloths of Cellach, comarb of Patrick, were submerged in the Dabhall ; and he himself was endangered. Paschalis, comarb of Peter, servus religiosus, cum dilectione[6] Dei et proximi, ad Christum migravit.[7] Maria,[8] daughter of Maelcoluim, i.e. daughter of the king of Alba, wife of the king of the Saxons, mortua est. A hosting by Toirdhealbhach Ua Conchobhair, king of Connacht, and by Murchadh O'Mael-sechlainn, king of Temhair, along with him, and by Aedh O'Ruairc, into Mumha, as far as Glenn-Maghair ; and he gave Des-Mumha to Mac Carthaigh, and Tuadh-Mumha

[1118.]

3581, the name here denotes the river anciently called Dabhall, and now known as the Blackwater, on the south side of which is a large tract of archiepiscopal property, in the parish of Eglish, formerly called Clonaul (Cluain ôabaill), which name is still preserved in the corrupt form Glenaul, as applied to a farm in the parish, and more widely to an electo-ral division in the Poor Law Union of Armagh." *Note* by Dr. Reeves.

[6] *Dilectione*. ɔilexioni (dilexioui), MS.

[7] *Migravit* miᵍuⱱ (for migravid), MS.

[8] *Maria*; i.e. Queen Matilda. Her name is written *Mahald* in the Anglo-Sax. Chron.

Sloiʒeꝺ eli leiꞃ co hⱭⱦ cliaꞇh, ʒo ꞇuc mac ꞃí Tempach boí a laim ʒall, ocuꞃ ʒialla ʒall buꝺéin, ocuꞃ ʒialla Laiʒen ocuꞃ Oꞃꞃꞃaiʒe. Sʒél inʒnaꝺ iꞃin mbliaꝺain ꞃi .i. ꞇalaṁcuṁꞃcuʒaꝺ aꝺbal i ꞃleiꞃ ⱷlpa, ʒuꞃꞃuꞃ muʒhaiꝺ il caꞇꞃaⱦa, ocuꞃ áꞃ ꝺaoiniꝺ innꞇiꝺ. Sʒél inʒnaꝺ eli in nⱷꞃinn ꞃéin beóꞃ .i. muꞃꞃꝺúꞇconn ꝺo ʒaꝺáil ꝺiaꞃʒaiꞃiꝺ liꞃ Ɑꞃʒlionn a nOꞃꞃꞃaiʒiꝺ, ocuꞃ aꞃoile a Poꞃꞇ Laiꞃʒe. Ꝺomnall mac Ruaiꝺꞃi hI Conchobaiꞃ moꞃꞇuuꞃ eꞃꞇ. Ruaiꝺꞃi O Conchobaiꞃ, ꞃi Connaꞇhꞇ ꞃe heꝺh ʒcían, ꝺo éʒ i nailiꞇꞃi iꞃ in ꞇꞃeiꞃeꝺ bliaꝺain ꞇꞃioⱦa iaꞃ ná ꝺallaꝺ ; in cleꞃicaꞇu uiꞇam ꞃeliciꞇeꞃ i ʒCluain mic Nóiꞃ ꞃiniuiꞇ.

Ꝉꞇꞇ. ⱷnaiꞃ. iiii. ꝼ. ; L. ꭓui. ; ix. mbliaꝺna ꝺhéc aꞃ ceꝺ aꞃ mile aiꞃ in Tiʒeꞃna. Cenn ⱦoꞃaꝺ ꝺo ꞃʒaoileꝺ ꝺo Connachꞇuiꝺ. Muiꞃceꞃꞇach O bꞃiain, ꞃí ⱷꞃenn, ꞇuiꞃ oꞃꝺuin ocuꞃ oiꞃechuiꞃ iaꞃꞇhaiꞃ ⱷoꞃꞃa, iaꞃ mbuaiꝺ ꞃíʒe ocuꞃ aiꞇꞃiʒe, a bꝼeil Moⱦaomóʒ, iꞃin ꞃeiꞃeꝺ ꞇo Maꞃꞇii, in bono ꝼine uiꞇam ꞃiniuiꞇ. Cúⱦollⱦaille O baiʒelláin, aꞃꝺ ollam ⱷꞃenn ꞃe ꝺán, ocuꞃ ꞃói a nꝺéiꞃc ocuꞃ a noinech, ocuꞃ aꞃ ⱦonniꞃcle ⱦoiꞇⱦinn ꞃꞃi ꞇꞃuaʒa ocuꞃ ꞇꞃéna, ꝺo maꞃbaꝺ ꝺꞃeꞃuiꝺ Luiꞃʒ, ocuꞃ ꝺo ⱦuaiꝺ Ráꞇa, cum ꞃua uⱦoꞃe eꞇ ꝺuobuꞃ ꝼiliꞃ ꞃuiꞃ boniꞃ, eꞇ cum .ꭓꭓu. aliiꞃ, eꝺiꞃ ṁuinnꞇeꞃ ocuꞃ aoiꝺeʒha i naoin ꞇiʒ, Saꞇaꞃn minⱦaꞃʒ, ocuꞃ a bꝼéil bécáin mic Cula. Ruaiꝺꞃi O Toꞃmaiꞃ, aiꞃchinnech Ꝑaⱦna móiꞃe, quieuiꞇ. Conchobaꞃ O ʒaiꞃmleʒhaiʒh, ꞇoíꞃꞃech Ceneoil

---

[1] *Son.* The Chron. Scotorum and the Four Mast. call him "Domhnall, son of Murchadh Ua Maelechlainn."

[2] *Story.* In the Ann. Ulst. this event, or "story," is stated to have been reported by pilgrims: "ꞃcel inʒnaꝺ inꝺiꞃiꝺ na hailiꞇꞃiʒ," "a wonderful story which the pilgrims relate." The Anglo-Sax. Chron. records this earthquake under the year 1117.

[3] *Cities.* Ꝅꞃⱦa, for · caꞇꞃaⱦa (cathracha), MS. Caꞇꞃaⱦa is the acc. pl. of caꞇhaiꞃ, which usually signifies *civitas*; but it is also sometimes used to denote a monastery or ecclesiastical establishment. The Anglo-Sax. Chron. states that many "monasteries and towers" were destroyed.

[4] *Clericatu.* The words *in clericatu* are here put in apposition with the expression in ailiꞇꞃi, "in pilgrimage." See Chron. Scotorum, Introd., p. liii.

[5] *The 6th.* ui. eꝺ, for ꞃeiꞃeꝺ, MS. The festival of Mochaemhóg (of Liath-

to the sons of Diarmaid Ua Briain, and carried off the hostages of each. Another hosting by him to Ath-cliath, when he carried away the son[1] of the king of Temhair, who was in the hands of the Foreigners, and the hostages of the Foreigners themselves, and the hostages of Laighen and Osraighe. A wonderful story[2] in this year, viz.: a very great earthquake in Sliabh-Elpa, which extinguished many cities,[3] and a multitude of people in them. Another wonderful story also in Erinn, viz.:—a mermaid was caught by the fishermen of Lis-Airglinn, in Osraighe, and another at Port-Lairge. Domhnall, son of Ruaidhri Ua Conchobhair, mortuus est. Ruaidhri O'Conchobhair, king of Connacht for a long time, died in pilgrimage in the thirty-sixth year after he was blinded—in clericatu[4] vitam feliciter finivit at Cluain-mic-Nois.

The kalends of January on the 4th feria, the 16th of the moon; the age of the Lord nineteen years and a hundred, and a thousand. Cenn-coradh was demolished by the Connachtmen. Muirchertach O'Briain, king of Erinn, prop of the glory and magnificence of the West of Europe, after the triumph of sovereignty and penance, on the festival of Mochaemhóg, on the 6th[5] of the ides of March, in bono[6] fine vitam[7] finivit. Cúchollchaille O'Baighelláin, chief ollamh of Erinn in poetry, and a man distinguished for charity and hospitality, and for universal benevolence towards the needy and the powerful, was slain by the Feara-Luirg and Tuath-ratha, cum sua uxore et duobus filiis suis[8] bonis, et cum xxxv. aliis, consisting both of his family and guests, in the same house, the Saturday before Little Easter, on the festival of Becan,[9] son of Cula. Ruaidhri O'Tormair, airchinnech of Fathan-mor, quievit. Conchobhar O'Gairmleghaigh, chief of Cenel-Moain, was slain

---

Mochaemhog, or Lemakevoge, barony of Eliogarty, co. Tipperary) is on the 3rd of the ides, or 13th of March.

[6] Bono. buno, MS.

[7] Vitam. uittam (vittam), MS.

[8] Suis. ruir, MS.

[9] Festival of Becan; i.e. the 5th of April, on which day the saint was commemorated at Imlech-Fiaich, now the par. of Emlagh, bar. of Lower Kells, co. of Meath, formerly called, after the patron saint, Imlechbeggan.

Móain, do maṗbaḋ do Uiḃ Dúḃda, ocuṗ do ċlainn Flaiṫḃeṗtaiġh. Niall mac Domnall még Laċlainn, ríḋaṁna Oiliġ ocuṗ Eṗenn, ocuṗ teṫṗa Eṗenn aṗ cṗuṫ ocuṗ aṗ ċeill, aṗ einech ocuṗ aṗ eṗgna, do ṫuitim la Cenel Móain iṗin ochtmaḋ bliaḋain .xx. a aóiṗi, an Luan a laiṫi ṡeachtmaine, iṗin deiċmaḋ daoiṗ éṗga, a bṗéil na tṗi maic neṅdac, in decimo octauo Kalendaṗ Ianuaṗii.

Kll. Enaiṗ .u. f.; l. [xx.uii.]; xx. bliaḋna aṗ ced aṗ mile aiṗ in Tiġeṗna. Sloiġed lá Domnall még Laċlainn dṗoiṗiḋin Muṗchada 1 Maoilṭṗechlainn, go hCC Luain i naġaiḋ Connacht, go dtaṗd Toiṗṗḋhealbach O Conchobaiṗ bṗéġ ṡiṫ impa. Maiḋm maċaiṗe Cille moíṗe h1 Nialláin ṗia Raġnall mac mic Riabaiġ, foṗ Uiḃ Echach, guṗṗo laḋ i náṗ. Cellach, comaṗba Patṗaic, foṗ cuaiṗt Muman, go tuc a óġṗeiṗ, ocuṗ guṗ ṡáġuiḃ bennachtuin. Bṗanán mac Ġillacṗiṗt, tóiṗṗech Coṗca CClann, ḋéc. Eaċṁaṗcach mac Uiḋṗén, tóiṗṗech Cenéóil bḟeṗaġhaiġh, do maṗbaḋ dḟeṗuiḃ Manach. Dṗoiċet CCṫa Luain do ḋénum.

Kll. Enaiṗ. uii. f.; l. ix.; bliaḋain aṗ .xx. aṗ ced aṗ mile aiṗ in Tiġeṗna. Domnall mac CCṗdġaiṗ még Laċlainn, deṗṗṡaiġṭech Ġoeiḋel Eṗenn, aṗ cṗuṫ ocuṗ aṗ ċenél, aṗ ċeill ocuṗ ġaiṗced, aṗ tṗonuṗ ocuṗ aṗ ṡoṁaṗtain, aṗ ṫiḋnacal ṗeod ocuṗ biḋ, do éġ a nDoiṗe Coluim Cille iṗin ochtmaḋ bliaḋain aṗ .xxx. a ṗiġe, ocuṗ iṗin tṗeṡ bliaḋain .lxx. a aoiṗi, oiḋċe Cedaoine do ṡunnṗad, ocuṗ a ceṫṗomaḋ id ṗeabṗa, a bṗéil Mocuaṗóġ ind eġna. Sloiġed la Toiṗṗḋhealbach .h. Conchobaiṗ, go gConnachtuiḃ uime, a nDeṗṗ Mumuin, guṗ indiṗṗet óṫa maġ Feiṁin go Tṗáiġ Li, ediṗ ċill ocuṗ tuaiṫ, .i. ṗeachtṁoḋa cill, uel paulo pluṗ. Cṗeċ

---

[1] *Decimo octavó.* decimoṗ octauuṗ (decimos octavus), MS. The "Three Innocent Sons," (Ananias, Misahel, and Azariah), are commemorated on the 16th of December. The death of Niall occurred probably on the *eve* of the festival, i.e. the 15th of December, or 18th of the kalends of January.

[2] *The 4th of the ides.* The festival of Mochuarog "the Wise" was observed on the 5th of the ides, i.e. the 9th of February, which in the year 1121, coincided with the 4th feria, or Wednesday.

[3] *Church and territory;* i.e. ecclesiastical and secular lands.

by the Ui-Dubhda, and by the Clann-Flaithbhertaigh
Niall, son of Domhnall Mac Lachlainn, royal heir of
Oilech and Erinn, and the paragon of Erinn for figure
and sense, for honour and learning, fell by the Cenel-
Moain, in the 28th year of his age, on Monday *as regards*
the day of the week, on the tenth of the moon's age, the
festival of the "Three Innocent Sons," in decimo octavo[1]
kalendas Janu[a]rn.

The kalends of January on the 5th feria, [the 27th]
of the moon; the age of the Lord twenty years, and a
hundred, and a thousand. A hosting by Domhnall Mac
Lachlainn to Ath-Luain, to assist Murchadh Ua Maelsechlainn against Connacht, and Toirdhelbhach O'Conchobhair made a false peace with them. The victory of the
plain of Cill-mór in Ui-Niallain *was gained* by Raghnall,
son of Mac Riabhaigh, over the Ui-Echach, who were put
to slaughter. Cellach, comarb of Patrick, *went* on a visitation of Mumha, when he obtained his full demand, and
left a blessing. Branan, son of Gillachrist, chief of Corca-
Achlann, died. Echmarcach Mac Uidhrén, chief of Cenel-
Feraghaigh, was slain by the Feara-Manach. The bridge
of Ath-Luain was made.

The kalends of January on the 7th feria, the 9th of the
moon; the age of the Lord twenty-one years, and a hundred, and a thousand. Domhnall, son of Ardghar Mac
Lachlainn, the most distinguished of the Gaeidhel of
Erinn for figure, for family, for sense and prowess, for
prosperity and for constancy, for the bestowing of jewels
and food, died in Doire-Choluim-Chille in the 38th year
of his reign, and in the 73rd year of his age, on the night
of Wednesday particularly, and on the 4th of the ides[2] of
February, the festival of Mochuarog "the Wise." A
hosting by Toirdhelbhach Ua Conchobhair, accompanied
by the men of Connacht, to Des-Mumha, and they plundered from Magh-Feimhin to Traigh-Lí, both church and
territory,[3] viz.:—seventy churches, vel paulo plus. A

I

ꞃloiꝾeᷘ la Coiꞃꞃᷘhealbach O Conchobaiꞃ ᷘoꞃiᷘiꞃ
a nᷘeꞃ Mumaiꞃ, ꞅo ꞃuachꞇ ꞇeꞃmonn Liꞃ ṁóiꞃ, ocuꞃ ꞅo
ᷘꞇáꞃꞃaiᷘ bóꞃuma ᷘiaiꞃṁiᷘ, ocuꞃ ꞅo bꝼáꞃꞅuiᷘ Muiꞃe-
ᷘach O ꝼlaiᷘbeꞃꞇaiꝾ, ꞃí iaꞃꞇhaiꞃ Connachꞇ, ocuꞃ CCoᷘ
.h. heiᷘiṅ, ꞃí .h. bꝼiacꞃaᷘ EiꝾne. Cloicꞇech Celᷘa
niꞃmuiꞃne i nOꞃꞃꞃaiꝾe ᷘo ᷘluiꝾe ᷘo ᷘaoiꞃ ᷘeniᷘ, ocuꞃ
cloᷘ ꞃo ꞃꝾeinᷘ aꞃꞃ ꞅuꞃꞃo maꞃᷘ mac leiꝾinn iꞃ in cill.
Cellach, comaꞃba Paꞇꞃaic, ᷘo Ꝿaᷘáil eꞃꞃocoiᷘe CCeᷘ
cliaꞇh a ꞇoꝾa Ꝿall ocuꞃ Ꝿoeiᷘeal. CCꞇhach nꞅoeiᷘe ᷘo
ᷘochꞇ i noiꞃ ᷘecimbiꞃ, ꞅuꞃꞃo lá a benncobaꞃ ᷘo Cloicꞇec
CCiꞃᷘ Maᷘa, ocuꞃ ꞅonᷘeꞃna ꞃiᷘhaꞃ móꞃ ꞃó Eꞃinn uile.

‖cꞇꞇ. Enaiꞃ i. ꝼ. ;.l. xx.; ᷘá bliaᷘain aꞃ .xx. aꞃ ceᷘ aꞃ
mile aiꞃ in CiꝾeꞃna. CCoᷘ .h. Ruaiꞃc, ꞃí Conmaicne,
ᷘo ᷘuiꞇim la ꞃeꞃuiᷘ Miᷘe aꞅ bꞃeiᷘ cꞃeiᷘe uaꞇha.
Scꞃíṅ Colmáin mic Luaᷘain ᷘꞃaꝾᷘáil i nailiꝾ Lainne,
ꞃeꞃ ᷘuᷘacꞇ i ꞇalmain, ᷘia Ceᷘaoin in bꞃaiᷘ. Sloiꞅeᷘ la
Coiꞃꞃᷘhealbach hi Conchobaiꞃ ꞅo loᷘ Sailech. a Miᷘe,
ꞅo ꞇániᷘ mac Muꞃchaᷘa, ꞃi Laiꞅen ocuꞃ Ꝿall, ina ᷘech.
Móꞃ, inꞅen ᷘomnaill ṁéꝾ Laᷘlainn, ben Coiꞃꞃᷘhel-
baiꝾh hi Concobaiꞃ, ᷘhéc. Cꞃeᷘ móꞃ la Conchobaꞃ
ṁáꝾ Laᷘlainn ocuꞃ la Cenel nEoꞅain, ꞅo ꞃanꞅaᷘaꞃ
Cill ꞃuaiᷘ i nUllꞇoib, co ꞇucꞃaꞇ boꞃuma ᷘiaiꞃṁiᷘe.
CCoᷘ O ᷘuiᷘᷘiꞃma, ꞇoiꞃech na bꞃéᷘa, ocuꞃ cenn oiniꝾ
in ꞇuaiꞃceꞃꞇ, ocuꞃ ᷘomnall a bꞃáꞇhaiꞃ, moꞃꞇui ꞃunꞇ.

‖cꞇꞇ. Enaiꞃ ii. ꝼ. ; l. i. Cꞃi bliaᷘna .xx. aꞃ ceᷘ aꞃ
mile aiꞃ in CiꝾeꞃna. Ꝿaileng ᷘo Ꝿaᷘáil ꞇiꝾe i nᷘaiṁ-
liaꞅ Cianáin, ꞃoꞃ Maoilꞃechlainn .h. Maoilꞃechlainn

---

[1] *Lost.* ꞅo bꝼáꞃꞅuiᷘ; lit. "when
he left."

[2] *Thunderbolt.* caoiꞃ ᷘeniᷘ; lit.
"a fire-brand," from caoꞃ, a brand,
and ꞇeneᷘ, fire.

[3] *Student.* mac leiꝾinn ; i.e. "son
of learning."

[4] *Gale.* aꞇhach (athach). This
word, which so frequently occurs
in old Irish as a synonym for "a
strong gale," seems cognate with the
German *athem.*

[5] *In the tomb.* i nailiꝾ (i nailigh).
ailiꝾ is the abl. of ailech (ailech),
which means "a stony place." The
Four Mast. have iolaᷘ, and the Ann.
Ulst. ailaᷘh, different forms of the
word otherwise written ulaᷘ, and
signifying a burial place, which seems
to have been intended in the present
entry, and is translated so accordingly.

predatory hosting by Toirdhelbhach O'Conchobhair again into Des-Mumha, until he reached the termon of Lis-mór; and he obtained countless cattle spoils, and lost[1] Muiredhach O'Flaithbhertaigh, king of the West of Connacht, and Aedh Ua hEidhin, king of Ui-Fiachrach-Eighne. The steeple of Telach-nInmuinne, in Osraighe, was cleft by a thunderbolt;[2] and a stone flew from it, which killed a student[3] in the church. Cellach, comarb of Patrick, assumed the bishopric of Ath-cliath by the choice of Foreigners and Gaeidhel. A gale[4] of wind occurred on the nones of December, which knocked off the conical cap of the steeple of Ard-Macha, and caused a great destruction of trees throughout all Erinn.

The kalends of January on the 1st feria, the 20th of the moon; the age of the Lord twenty-two years, and a hundred, and a thousand. Aedh Ua Ruairc, king of Conmaicne, fell by the men of Midhe, whilst taking a prey from them. The shrine of Colman, son of Luachan, was found in the tomb[5] of Lann, a man's cubit in the earth, on Spy Wednesday. A hosting by Toirdhelbhach Ua Conchobhair to Loch-Sailech in Midhe, when Mac Murchadha, king of Laighen and the Foreigners, came into his house.[6] Mor, daughter of Domhnall Mac Lachlainn, wife of Toirdhelbhach Ua Conchobhair, died. A great predatory expedition by Conchobhar Mac Lachlainn and the Cenel-Eoghain, until they arrived at Cill-ruaidh in Ulidia, and they carried off countless cattle spoils. Aedh Ua Duibhdhirma, chief of the Bredach, and head of the hospitality of the North, and Domhnall his brother, mortui sunt.

The kalends of January on the 2nd feria, the 1st of the moon; the age of the Lord twenty-three years, and a hundred, and a thousand. The Gailenga captured a house at Daimhliag-Cianain, against Maelsechlainn Ua Maelsech-

---

[6] *Came into his house.* This is an idiomatic way of saying that Mac ┃ Murchadha (Mac Murrough) submitted to O'Conor.

.i. rí Miḋe ocur Temrach, zurro loirc in tech ambói,
ocur reachtṁoḋa ro tiżiḃ eli ime, ocur zurro marḃrat
rochaiḋe ria muinter. Térnaoí Maoilrechlain réin
ḋeinech Dé ocur Cianain, zan lorcaḋ, zan ṁarḃaḋ.
Ammur anaiċniḋ ro ṫaḃairt ror comarba Ailḃe, .i.
Maolmórḋa mac mic Cloċna, .i. tech ro ża̋áil rair ror
lár a Imliż réin, ocur ror mac Cerḃaill hI Ciarmaic, rí
Ane, zurro marḃaḋar moirḟeirer ann; ocur térnaḋur,
imorro, na ḋaoine maiċ arr tre raiċ Ailḃe ocur na
hecluire, ocur ra loirceḋ ann, imorro, bernan Ailḃe.
Ro marḃaḋ, imorro, ria zcinn ṁiór iarrin, an tí ro
żaḃ in tech rin, .i. in Żilla caoċ .h. Ciarmaic; ocur
ḋeoċuin iar nainmniuzaḋ éiriḋéin; ocur ro benaḋ a
ċenḋ ḋe a ráruzaḋ Dé ocur Ailḃe. Donnrleiḃe mac
Caṫaláin, ronur ocur romarċuin Ulaḋ uile, mortuur
ert. Donnchaḋ mac Żilla Patraic ruaḋ, rí Orżraiże,
a ruir occirur ert. Conżalaċ .h. Laiċbertaiż [riḋaṁna]
Oiliż, occirur ert.

Ktt. Enair .iii. r.; L. xii.; ceitri bliaḋna .xx. ar ceḋ
ar mile air in Tiżerna. Toirḟinn mac Turcuill, príṁ
oiz tiżern Żall nErenn, rubita morte reriit. Taḋz
mac ṁéz Carrthaiż, rí Der Muman, ḋéc. bíḋzaḋ
mór ro rí Temrach ria Domnaiz Carz, .i. a ṫeċ ṫárz ro
tuitim rair ocur ror a ṫeżlaċ. Luimnech ro lorcaḋ
uile achtmaḋ bez. Alaxanḋair mac Maolcoluim, rí
Alban, in bona penitentia mortuur ert. Żeill Der
Muman ro marḃaḋ la Toirrḋhealbach O Conchobair,

---

¹ *Unprecedented.* αnαiṫniḋ; lit.
"unknown."

² *His own Imlech.* Properly *Im-
lech-Ibhair,* "the *Imlech* (or marsh)
of the yew." The place is now called
Emly, and gives name to the diocese
of Emly. By the words "his own
Imlech" is to be understood, simply,
that Maelmordha was then the possessor of the place, in virtue of his
position as comarb, or successor, of

St. Ailbhe, the founder, who died
about A.D. 541.

³ *Bernan-Ailbhe;* i.e. the gapped,
or broken, bell of Ailbhe; from *berna,*
a gap. The old translator of the Annals of Ulster (Cod. Clarend., Brit.
Mus., tom. 49) translates this "the
mitre" of Ailbhe; and Dr. O'Conor,
in his edition of the same Annals,
understands the word *bearnan* to
mean "cathedra," although elsewhere

lainn, i.e. king of Midhe and Temhair, and they burned the
house in which he was, and seventy other houses around it,
and killed a multitude of his people. Maelsechlainn himself
escaped through the protection of God and Cianan, without
being burned or slain. An unprecedented[1] attack was
made on the comarb of Ailbhe, i.e. Maelmordha, grandson
of Clothna, viz. :—a house was captured against him in the
middle of his own Imlech,[2] and against the son of Cerbhall
Ua Ciarmhaic, king of Ane; and seven persons were
killed there. The good men escaped therefrom, however,
through the grace of Ailbhe and the Church; but the
Bernan-Ailbhe[3] was, indeed, burned there. The person
who captured this house, viz. :—the Gilla-caech[4] Ua
Ciarmhaic, (and he was by title a deacon), was slain
before the end of a month afterwards, and his head was
cut off, for the profanation of God and Ailbhe. Donnsleibhe Mac Cathalain, the prosperity and happiness of all
Uladh, mortuus est.[5] Donnchadh Mac Gillapatraic
Ruadh, king of Osraighe, a suis occisus est. Conghalach
Ua Laithbhertaigh [royal heir][6] of Oilech, occisus est.

The kalends of January on the 3rd feria, the 12th of
the moon; the age of the Lord twenty-four years, and a
hundred, and a thousand. Toirfhinn Mac Turcuill, principal young lord of the Foreigners of Erinn, subita morte
periit. Tadhg, son of Mac Carthaigh, king of Des-Mumha,
died. A great alarm was given to the king of Temhair
on Easter Sunday, viz. :—his Easter house[7] fell on him
and on his household. Luimnech was all burned, except
a little. Alexander, son of Maelcoluim, king of Alba, in
bona pœnitentia mortuus est. The hostages of Des-

(ed. Tighern., ad an. 1043) he renders
the word by "cithara." It is also
erroneously represented as a "mitre"
by Colgan (*Trias Thaumaturga*, p.
633), Ware (Harris's ed., vol. i., p.
493), and Archdall (*Monasticon Hibernicum*, p. 656).

[4] *Gilla-caech*; lit. "blind fellow."

[5] *Mortuus est.* m. ꞃꞇ. for moꞃꞇuı
ꞃunꞇ, MS.

[6] *Royal heir.* ꞃıꝺamna. Omitted
in MS. Supplied from the Ann. Ult.

[7] *Easter house.* ꞇeꝺ ꝺaꞃꞡ; meaning the house in which the king celebrated the festival of Easter.

.ı. Maoılṙechlaınn mac Coṙmaıc ṁég Caṙṙtaıġ, ṙí Caıṙıl, ocuṙ .h. Cıaṙmaıc, ocuṙ Acaıne .h. Coṫtaıġ oıḃ Cuanach Cnamċaılle. Aṙoġaṙ, mac mıc Aoḃa hı Maoıltṙechlaınn, oo maṙbao la muınteṙ Ooıṙe ı noınech Coluım Cılle.

Ictt. Enaıṙ .u. ṗ.; l. xxııı.; u. blıaona .xx. aṙ ceo aṙ mıle aıṙ ın Tıżeṙna; quınt ıo Enáıṙ, ımoṙṙo, ṙoṙ ao[ın]ṫoen, ocuṙ ṗṙím ṙuıṙṙe, ocuṙ ıṙ ınnte tuaṙġabao a ḃuınne oíoın ṙoṙ ḃaṁlıaż moṙ Aṙo Maċa, ıaṙ ná lán eżaṙ oo ḟlınntech la Cellach comaṙba Paṫṙaıc, ıṙın .xxx.mao blıaoaın aṙ céo ó ná ṙaḃa ṙlınntech ṙaıṙ co comlán ṙoıme ṙın. Żıllabṙaıoe .h. Ruaıṙc oo ḃátao a loċ Aıllınne. Sloıżeao la Toıṙṙoealbach O Conchobaıṙ a Mıḃe, żuṙṙo ıonnaṙb Muṙchao .h. Maoılṙechlaınn aṙṙ a ṙíże, ocuṙ żonoeṙna tṙı ṙıża ṙoṙ ṙeṙuıḃ Mıḃe. Maṙbaṙ, ımoṙṙo, Oomnall mac Muṙchaoa ın tṙeṙ ṙí, ṙıa żoınn nómaıoe, .ı. Maoılṙechlaınn mac Oonnchaoa. Sloıżeo la Muıṙceṙtach O Ceṙḃuıll, ṙı oeıṙceṙt Ṙeṙnmaıoe, a bṙeṙuıḃ Ḃṙeż, conuṙ taṙṙaıo Oıaṙmaıt .h. Máoılṙechlaınn żo bṙeṙuıḃ Mıḃe, ocuṙ żo bṙeṙuıḃ Ḃṙeaż, żuṙṙo maṙbao Muıṙceṙtach ann, ocuṙ áṙ a tṙfluaıż ımme.

Ictt. Enaıṙ .uı. ṗ.; l. ıııı. Se blıaona .xx. aṙ ceo, aṙ mıle, aıṙ ın Tıżeṙna. Enná mac Muṙchaoa, ṙí laıżen, moṙtuuṙ eṙt. Slóıżeo la Toıṙṙoealbach O Conchobaıṙ a laıżneıḃ, żuṙṙo żaḃ ı nżıalla. h. Maolṙuanaıżh, ṙí Ṙeṙmanach, a ṙuıṙ occıṙuṙ eṙt. Maoılıṙa.h. Conne, ṙóı żaoıoel Eṙenn a mḃṙeıṫemnuṙ ocuṙ a nUṙo Paṫṙaıc, ıaṙ naıṫṙıże ṫożaıoe ın Cṙıṙto

---

[1] *In revenge;* i.e. for some offence committed against the community of Doire (Derry), an establishment founded by St. Colum Cille.

[2] *Fifth of the ides.* quıncıt for quınt ıo, MS.

[3] *Protecting ridge.* buınne oíoın, lit. "ring (or clasp) of protection." The ridge line is evidently meant, although Dr. O'Donovan translates the words "roof" (Four Mast. ad an.), and Dr. O'Conor (Ann. Ult.), renders them by "operimentum."

[4] *Nomaidh.* This word is explained "time, season" by O'Reilly, who writes it noḃhao. But it seems to signify some specific period of time. See note [2], p. 80, *supra.*

Mumha were slain by Toirdhelbhach O'Conchobhair, viz. :—Maelsechlainn, son of Cormac Mac Carthaigh, king of Caisel, and Ua Ciarmhaic, and Achaine Ua Cobhthaigh of the Ui-Cuanach of Cnamchaill. Ardghar, grandson of Aedh Ua Maelsechlainn, was slain by the people of Doire, in revenge[1] for Colum-Cille.

The kalends of January on the 5th feria, the 23rd of the moon; the age of the Lord twenty-five years, and a hundred, and a thousand. The fifth of the ides[2] of January, moreover, *was* on Friday, the first of the moon, and on it the protecting ridge[3] was raised over the great stone-church of Ard-Macha, after it had been fully covered with shingling by Cellach, comarb of Patrick, in the one hundred and thirtieth year since it had a complete shingle roof before. Gillabraide Ua Ruairc was drowned in Loch-Aillinne. A hosting by Toirdhelbhach O'Conchobhair into Midhe, when he expelled Murchadh Ua Maelsechlainn from his sovereignty, and placed three kings over the men of Midhe. Domhnall, son of Murchadh, however, killed the third king, viz. :—Maelsechlainn, son of Donnchadh, before the end of a "nomaidh."[4] A hosting by Muirchertach O'Cerbhaill, king of the South of Fernmhagh, to the men of Bregh; but Diarmait Ua Maelsechlainn, with the men of Midhe and the men of Bregh, met him, and Muirchertach was slain there, and a slaughter of his host *was committed* about him.

The kalends of January on the 6th feria, the 4th of the moon; the age of the Lord twenty-six years, and a hundred, and a thousand. A hosting by Toirdhelbhach O'Conchobhair to the Lagenians, and he received their pledges. Ua Maelruanaigh, king of Feara-Manach, a *suis occisus est.* Maelisa Ua Conne, the most learned of the Gaeidhel of Erinn in jurisprudence, and in the Ord-Patraic,[5]

---

[5] *Ord-Patraic*; i.e. the Ordo of Patrick; some ecclesiastical ordinance of which no exact account has survived.

qᴜɪeᴜɪᴛ. Coɼcać ṁóɼ ᴍᴜmαɴ, coɴα ᴛempʟαɪb, ᴅo ʟoɼcαᴅ. ᴅoṁɴαʟʟ .ɦ. ᴅúḃᴅα ᴅo ḃáᴛɦαᴅ ɪαɼ ɴᴅeɴαm cɼeɪće α Ṫíɼ Coɴαɪʟʟ. Rɪ̇ᴛᴜɼᴜɼ Ṫoɪɼɼᴅɦeαʟbαɪ̇ɡ ɦı Coɴcɦobαɪɼ co ɦαꞓ clíαᴛɦ, ɡo ᴅᴛαɼᴅ ɼɪ̇ɡe αᴇα clíαꞓ ocᴜɼ ʟαɪɡeɴ ᴅíα mαc, .ı. ᴅo Coɴcɦobαɼ. ` Coɡαᴅ móɼ ɪ ɴeɼɪɴɴ, ɡᴜɼḃó ɦeɪɡeɴ ᴅo ćomαɼbα Pαᴛɼαɪc beɪꞓ mí ɼoɼ bʟɪαᴅαɪɴ ɼɼı ɦαɼᴅ ᴍαcɦα αɴecɦᴛαɪɼ, αɡ ɼı̇ḃᴜɡɦαᴅ ɼeɼ ɴeɼeɴɴ, ocᴜɼ αɡ ᴛαbαɪɼᴛ ɼɪαɡʟα ocᴜɼ ᴛɼoḃéɼ ɼoɼ ćáꞓ eᴛɪɼ ᴛᴜαꞓ ocᴜɼ eɡʟᴜɼ. Cɼeꞓ ṁeḃʟα ʟα Rᴜαɪᴅɼı .ɦ. Ṫᴜαćαɪɼ ı ɴαɪɼɼ‑ ᴛeɼαɪḃ, ɡo ᴅáɼɼαᴅαɼ αɪɼɼꞓɪɼ áɼ ᴛɼʟᴜαɪɡ Rᴜαɪᴅɼı, ocᴜɼ ɡᴜɼɼᴅ ᴅɪćeɴᴅαḃ eɪɼɪḃéɪɴ αɴɴɼɪɴ. Sʟoɪɡeαᴅ ʟα Ṫoɪɼɼ‑ ᴅɦeαʟbαcɦ O Coɴcɦobαɪɼ ɡo ɼocɦᴛ Ɡʟeɴɴ [ᴍαɡɦαɪɼ] α ɴᴅeɼ ᴍᴜmᴜɪɴ, ocᴜɼ ɡo ᴅᴛᴜc bóɼᴜmα ᴅɪαɼmɪḃe.

Ⱪᴄᴛᴛ. Єɴαɪɼ .ᴜıı. ꜰ.; ʟ. xᴜ. Seαcɦᴛ mbʟɪαᴅɴα .xx. αɼ ceᴅ αɼ mıʟe αɪɼ ıɴ Ṫıɡeɼɴα. Sʟoɪɡeḃ ʟα Ṫoɪɼɼᴅɦeαʟ‑ bαcɦ O Coɴcɦobαɪɼ α ɴᴅeɼ ᴍᴜmαɪɴ, ɡo ɼocɦᴛ Coɼcać ṁóɼ ᴍᴜmαɴ, ɡo ᴅᴛᴜc ɡɪαʟʟα ᴍᴜmαɴ ɡo ʟéɪɼ. αɪɼꞓɪɼ ᴅo ɡαḃáɪʟ ᴛɪɡe Ꝼʟoɪɴɴ mıc Sıɴαɪꞓ α ᴅᴛɼúɴ ᴛɼαxαɴ ı ɴαɼᴅ mαcɦα, ɼoɼ Rαɡɴαʟʟ mαc mıc Rɪαbαɪ̇ɡ, αɪᴅće ʟᴜαɪɴ Іɴeᴛı, ocᴜɼ α ḃɪćeɴᴅαḃ ʟeó. Cαꞓ eᴛɪɼ Ꙋʟᴛoɪb ɼeɪɼɼıɴ, ᴅᴜ ı ᴛoɼɼɼαᴅαɼ ḃá ɼí Ꙋʟαḃ, .ı. Nıαʟʟ mαc ᴅᴜɪɴɴɼʟeɪḃe, ocᴜɼ αɼ Ꙋʟαᴅ ımme, ocᴜɼ Єocɦαɪᴅ .ɦ. ᴍαᴛ̇ɡαmɴ[α], α bꝼɼɪᴛ̇ɡᴜɪɴ ıɴ ṁαḃṁα ɼɪɴ. Ɡɪʟʟα Cɼɪɼᴛ .ɦ. ɦeɪcɴɪ̇ɡ, ɼı ꝼeɼ ᴍαɴαcɦ ocᴜɼ αɪɼᴅɼí Oɪɼɡíαʟʟ, ᴅɦéc ıɡ Cʟocɦαɼ .ɦ. ɴᴅoɪṁíɴ, ıαɼ ɴαɪᴛɼıɡꞓ ᴛ̇oɡαɪᴅe. Ꝼıɼ

---

[1] *And committed.* The original text is here slightly inaccurate, owing apparently to the omission of some word or words before άɼ (ár), "slaughter"; but the sense of the passage is correctly given in the translation.

[2] *Glenn-Maghair.* ɡʟeɴɴ (Glenn), MS. The portion of the name within brackets [Maghair] has been supplied from the Annals of Ulster. Glenn-Maghair is now called Glanmire, a place situated near the city of Cork.

[3] *Of the Monday of Shrovetide.* ʟᴜαɪɴ Іɴeᴛı; Іɴeᴛı being for Іɴıᴛı, gen. of Іɴıᴛ (init) = Lat. *initium*, from which it is borrowed, and signifying the "beginning" of Lent.

[4] *Mutual wounding.* Ꝼɼıᴛ̇ɡᴜıɴ (frithghuin), which is generally translated "heat of battle," literally means "counter - wounding," being compounded of ꝼɼıꞓ, *against*, and ɡᴜıɴ, a *wound*.

[5] *Clochar - Ui - nDaimhin;* i.e. "the rocky place of the descendants of

after choice penance, in Christo quievit. Corcach-mor of Mumha, with its churches, was burned. Domhnall Ua Dúbdha was drowned after committing a depredation in Tir-Conaill. Royal journey of Toirdhelbhach Ua Conchobhair to Ath-cliath, when he gave the sovereignty of Ath-cliath and Laighen to his son, i.e. to Conchobhar. Great war in Erinn, so that the comarb of Patrick was obliged to be a month and a year absent from Ard-Macha, pacifying the men of Erinn, and imposing rules and good customs on all, both laity and clergy. A treacherous depredation by Ruaidhri Ua Tuachair, in Airthera; but the *men of* Airthera overtook, *and committed*[1] a slaughter of, the army of Ruaidhri; and he himself was there beheaded. A hosting by Toirdhelbhach Ua Conchobhair until he reached Glenn-[Maghair],[2] in Des-Mumha, and he carried off countless cattle spoils.

The kalends of January on the 7th feria, the 15th of the moon; the age of the Lord twenty-seven years, and a hundred, and a thousand. A hosting by Toirdhelbhach O'Conchobhair into Des-Mumha, until he reached Corcach-mor of Mumha, and he carried off the hostages of all Mumha. The *men of* Airthera captured the house of Flann, son of Sinach, in Trian-Saxan, in Ard-Macha, against Raghnall, son of Mac Riabhaigh, on the night of the Monday of Shrovetide,[3] and he was beheaded by them. A battle between the Ulidians themselves, when two kings of Ulidia, viz.:—Niall, son of Donnsleibhe (and a slaughter of the Ulidians about him), and Eochaidh Ua Mathghamhna, were slain in the mutual wounding[4] of the battle. Gillachrist Ua hEighnigh, king of Feara-Manach, and chief king of Oirghiall, died in Clochar-Ui-nDaimhin,[5] after choice penance. The men of Mumha

---

Daimhin," now Clogher, in the co. Tyrone. The Ann. Ult. and the Four Mast. have "Clochar-maic-Daimhine" ("Clochar of the son of Daimhin"). The death of Daimhin, from whose descendants the name of Clochar-Ui-Daimhine is derived, is entered in the Annals of Tighernach under the year 566. See Reeves's *Adamnan*, p. iii., note [c].

Muman ocuγ Laiʒen do ιmpóᵹ áγιᵹιγ γογ Τοιγγᵭhealbach O Conchobaiγ, ocuγ α nʒeill do ᵹíγliuʒαᵭ dóíᵭ, ocuγ α mac do αᵹγιʒαᵭ do Ʒallaιb, ocuγ do Laiʒnechaιb; ocuγ do γαᵭγατ γί Eli γογγα, .ι. Domnall mac mιc γaolaιn. Ceγᵭall mac mιc γaolaιn, ocuγ áγ .h. bγaolaιn ιmme, do ᵭuιτιm la híᵭ bγaιlᵹe aγ láγ Cille daγa, αʒ coγnum ᵭoᵭoγbuιγ Bγιᵹᵭe. Τaιllτι ιnʒen Muγchaᵭa hι Maoιlτγechlaιnn, ben Τοιγγᵭhealbaιᵹ 1 Conchobaιγ, ᵭéc. Ʒilla Bγιᵹᵭe .h. γoγannáιn, aιγchιnnech Αγᵭa γγatha, moγτuuγ eγτ.

Kɬ. Enaιγ .ι. γ.; L. xx.uι. Ochτ mbliαᵭna .xx. aγ ceᵭ aγ mile aιγ ιn Τιʒeγna. bιγγexτuγ eτ embolιγmuγ annuγ. Fιγ Muιᵹe híᵭa, .ι. Domnall .h. Ʒαιγmleʒhaιʒh, do ᵹαᵭáιl τιᵹe aγ γí γeγ Manach, .ι. γoγ γaolán .h. Duιᵭᵭaγa, ocuγ α ᵭuιτιm leo, ocuγ γochaιde do ᵭaιᵭιᵭ γeγ Manach uιme. Maιᵭm για maγcγluaᵹ mιc ᵭéʒ Lachlaιnn, .ι. Conchobaγ mac ᵭéʒ Laᵭlaιnn, γoγ ᵭaγcγluaᵹ Τιʒeγnaιn 1 Ruaιγc, 1 τoγcaιγ .h. Cιaγᵭa, γí Caιγbγe, ocuγ Cathal .h. Raιᵹιlliᵹ, ocuγ Sιτγec .h. Maoιlbγιᵹᵭe, ocuγ mac Αoᵭa hι Duᵭᵭa, γí .h. nΑmalʒaᵭa, eτ alιι mulτι. Ʒnιom ʒγánna, aιnιaγmaγτach, anaιᵭnιᵭ, γo ᵭuιll eγcuιne γeγ nEγenn eτιγ laoᵭ ocuγ ᵭleιγeᵭ, da ná γγιᵭ mac γaᵭla 1 nEγιnn γιam, do ᵭenum do Τιʒeγnán .h. Ruaιγc ocuγ do h. mᵭγιuιn, .ι. comaγba γaτγaιc do nochτ τγaγuʒαᵭ na γιaᵭnuγe γéιn, ocuγ α ᵭuιᵭechτa do γlaτ, ocuγ dγem do maγbaᵭ ᵹíᵭ, ocuγ mac cleιγech dιa muιnτeγ γeιn do ᵭí γa cuιlebaᵭ do ᵭaγbaᵭ ann. Iγγé, ιmoγγo, aнιaγmaιγτ

---

1 *His son*, viz.:—Conchobhar, or Conor, whom his father is stated to have made king of Ath-cliath (Dublin) and Laighen, in the preceding year.

2 *Bissextus.* bιγexmuγ (bisexmus), MS.

3 *Embolismus.* emboleγmuγ (embolesmus), MS.

4 *Against.* aγ, MS.; lit. "upon," or "over."

5 *Unprecedented.* αnaιᵭnιᵭ; lit. "unknown."

6 *Cuilebadh.* See note 2, p. 36, *supra.* The expression cleιγech . . . . . . do ᵭí γa cuιlebaᵭ, "a cleric who was under a Cuilebadh," seems to imply that *cuilebadh* does not

and of Laighen again turned against Toirdhelbhach O'Conchobhair, and their hostages were withdrawn by them, and his son[1] was dethroned by the Foreigners and Lagenians; and they placed over themselves the king of Eile, i.e. Domhnall, grandson of Faelan. Cerbhall, grandson of Faelan, (and a slaughter of the Ui-Faelain about him), fell by the Ui-Failghe in the middle of Cill-dara, defending the comarbship of Brigid. Taillti, daughter of Murchadh Ua Maelsechlainn, wife of Toirdhelbhach Ua Conchobhair, died. Gillabrighde Ua Forannain, airchinnech of Ard-Sratha, mortuus est.

The kalends of January on the 1st feria, the 26th of the moon; the age of the Lord twenty-eight years, and a hundred, and a thousand. Bissextus[2] et embolismus[3] annus. The men of Magh-hItha, i.e. *with* Domhnall Ua Gairmleghaigh, captured a house against[4] the king of Feara-Manach, i.e. against Faelan Ua Duibhdhara, who fell by them, and many of the nobles of Feara-Manach along with him. A victory *was gained* by the cavalry of the son of Mac Lachlainn, i.e. Conchobhar, son of Mac Lachlainn, over the cavalry of Tighernan Ua Ruairc, in which were slain Ua Ciardha, king of Cairbre, and Cathal Ua Raighilligh, and Sitric Ua Maelbrighde, and the son of Aedh Ua Dubhda, king of Ui-Amhalghadha, et alii multi. An ugly, ruthless, unprecedented[5] deed, which earned the malediction of the men of Erinn, both lay and clerical—for which no equal was found previously in Erinn—was committed by Tighernan Ua Ruairc, and by the Ui-Briuin, viz.:—the comarb of Patrick was openly profaned in his own presence, and his retinue were plundered, and a number of them slain; and a young cleric of his own people, who was under a cuilebadh,[6] was killed there. The evil consequence, moreover, that

---

mean simply a *colobium*, as Dr. Reeves thought (*Adamnan*, p. 323), but rather some kind of vestment or altar-cloth.

Dr. O'Conor (Ann. Ult. ad an.) translates the clause "clericus qui fuit sacris vestibus indutus."

do ḟáp don 'ṁiġnioṁpa conáč bḟuil in nEpinn comaipce
iṗ caipiṗi do ḋuine óṗin amač no ʒuppo ḋiġuilc ó Dia
ocuṗ ó ḋaoiniḃ inc olc ṗa.   1n ḋinṗeṁ ṗa, cṗá, cucaḃ ṗoṗ
čomaṗba Pacṗaic iṗṗ amail ocuṗ ḋinṗeṁ in Coiṁḃeʒ, óiṗ
iḋubaiṗc in Coiṁḃe ṗein iṗin Soiṗʒél, qui uoṗ ʒpeṗnic
me ʒpeṗnic, qui me ʒpeṗnic, ʒpeṗnic eum qui miṗic
me.   Cpečṗlóiʒeḃ lá Coippḋhealbach .h. Conchobaiṗ a
laiʒniḃ ʒo ṗuachc Loč Capman ; aṗṗiéic ciṁčell
laiʒen co hⱰč cliač, ocuṗ do ṗiʒne boḋiʒbaḋ móṗ in
čonaiṗ ṗin ; o Ɒč cliač ḋia čiʒ doṗuḋiṗ.   Doṗala,
imoṗṗo, mičlú inc ṗlóiʒeḃ ṗin ṗoṗ Ciʒeṗnan O Ruaiṗc
cona muincer.   Cpeč la ṗṗa Peṗṗmaiḋe a čiṗ .h.
mḂṗúin, co cucṗac ʒaḃála moṗa.   ḃeiṗiḃ Ciʒeṗnán .h.
Ruaiṗc co nUi mḂṗuin, ocuṗ co ṗochaiḋe móṗ ele,
ṗoṗṗa aʒ Ɒč Ṗiṗḋeʒhaiḋ.   Peṗchuṗ cač ecoṗṗa diḃli-
nuiḃ.   Meabaḃ, imoṗṗo, ṗoṗ Ciʒeṗnan ocuṗ ṗoṗ 1ḃ
ḃṗúin, ʒuppo maṗbaḃ .cccc. ḋiḃ i coṗach [a nḋíoʒail]
oiṗiʒ muincire Pacṗaic.   Slóiʒeḃ la Conchobaṗ .h.
Ločlainn, ocuṗ la Cénel nEoʒain, ocuṗ la Dal nⱰpaiḋe,
ocuṗ la hⱰiṗʒialla, i Maʒ Coḃa, ʒo cucṗac ʒialla .h.
nEchach.   Impáiḋ iaṗṗin ṗoṗ a laiṁ člí a bṗeṗuiḃ
ḃṗeʒh, ʒuṗ ṗáʒuiḃṗec oṗoṗʒ dia muincep ann, ocuṗ
ʒonḋeṗṗac col móṗ ṗía Dia ocuṗ ḋaoiniḃ, .i. loṗcaḋ
Ɒča Cṗuim cona cemplaiḃ, ocuṗ ṗochaiḋe do ḋul a
maṗcṗa innciḃ.   Non impecṗaca pace Dei uel hominum ṗecṗo ambulaueṗunc.   Siḋ blíaḋna ʒo leiḃ, uel
paulo pluṗ, do ḋenum do čomaṗba Pacṗaic ecip Connachca ocuṗ ṗiṗ Muman.

---

[1] *That there was not.* The text
has "conáč bḟuil," lit. "that there
is not." But the use of the subj.
pres. is certainly wrong, as appears
from the context, although the same
phraseology occurs in the Annals of
Ulster. The Four Masters omit the
entire passage.

[2] *Vos.* uoṗṗ (voss), MS.

[3] *Round Laighen;* i.e. round by the
sea coast, from Loch-Carman (Wexford) to Ath-cliath, or Dublin.

[4] *Ath-Fhirdheghaidh.* Otherwise
written "Ath-Fhirdhiaidh" ("ford of
Firdhiadh," a chief slain there by
Cuchullain, in the 1st century), now
Ardee, in the co. of Louth.

[5] *In vindication.* a nḋíoʒail.
Supplied from the Annals of the Four
Masters, it appearing that some words,

grew from this misdeed, was, that there was not[1] in Erinn any enduring protection for a man thenceforth, until this injury was avenged by God and men. This contempt, truly, which was shown to the comarb of Patrick, was like the contempt of the Lord, for the Lord Himself said in the Gospel, qui vós[2] spernit me spernit; qui me spernit, spernit eum qui misit me. A predatory hosting by Toirdhelbhach Ua Conchobhair into Laighen, until he reached Loch-Carman; from thence round Laighen[3] to Ath-cliath, (and he committed a great destruction of cows along that route); and from Ath-cliath to his home again. The infamy of this hosting, moreover, rested on Tighernan O'Ruairc, with his people. A depredation by the men of Fernmhagh in the territory of the Ui-Briuin, and they carried off great spoils; *but* Tighernan Ua Ruairc, with the Ui-Briuin, and with another large army, overtook them at Ath-Fhirdheghaidh.[4] A battle was fought between them on both sides. Tighernan and the Ui-Briuin were defeated, however, and four hundred of them were slain in the beginning, [in vindication][5] of the honour of Patrick's people. A hosting by Conchobhar Ua Lochlainn and the Cenel-Eoghain, and the Dal-Araidhe and Airghialla, into Magh-Cobha, when they carried off the hostages of the Ui-Echach. They afterwards turned to the left, into Feara-Bregh; and they lost a number of their people there, and committed a great outrage before God and men, viz.:—the burning of Ath-truim with its churches; and a great number *of persons* suffered martyrdom in them. Non impetrata[6] pace Dei vel hominum[7] retro[8] ambulaverunt. A peace of one year and a half, vel paulo plus, was made by the comarb of Patrick between the Connachtmen and the men of Mumha.

---

probably of identical meaning, had been omitted from the text, as the word that follows, oiniʒ (oinigh), is in the gen. case. A similar omission occurs in the Annals of Ulster.

[6] *Impetrata.* impeτρατ (impetrat), MS.

[7] *Hominum.* oimnium (oimnium), MS.

[8] *Retro.* peℭ, for peτρo, MS.

Ictt. Enaip 111. p. ; l. u11. ; 1x. mbliaoan .xx. ap ceo ap mile aip in Cizepna. Cellač, comapba Pατpαιc, .1. aipoerpuc iapthaip Eoppa, ocur mac oiže annaz, oippoepc, ocur aoinceno po piapaižeroap zaill ocur zaioel, loeich ocur cléipiž; iap noipneô, imoppo, erpuc ocur racapt ocur áor zacha zpáiô aipchena; ocur iap zcoirrerzaô il imao tempal ocur pelzeo; iap tíônacul réo ocur maoiniô, ocur iap bpupáil creioim ocur tpoôér ror čáč etip ťuaiô ocur eziur; ocur iap mbethaio čeleôapthaio aipprennuiž, aointiž, irnaížtiž; ocur iap nonzao ocur naitpiže ťozaroe, po raoiô a anum a nucht aingel ocur ápčaingel i nΑpo Pατpαιc irin Mumain, i Ict. Αppil, in recunoa [repia], ocur irin .1111.mao bliaoain .xx. in aôuine, ocur irin .l.mao bliaoain a aoiri. Rucao, tpa, a čopp hi .111. noin Αppil zo ler móp Močuoa, po reir a ťimna rein, ocur po rpičaireô zo pralmuiô ocur iomnaô ocur čainntiziô, ocur po haônaiceo zo honópach i miolaiô na nerpuc, i ppiô noin Αppil, in quinta repia. Muirceptach mac Domnaill po roirneô i comporbur Pατpαιc in noin Αppil. Teč Coluim Cille a Cill mic nEnáin po žaôáil oó Taircert ror Αoô mac Catôapp Uí Domnaill, ocur a lorcaô oó. Cairlón Αťa luain po ôenam la Toirr-ohealbach O Conchobair. Zillacrirt mac mic Uiôrín, tóirrech čénel bƒeraohaiž, po lorcao a tiž a altronn i Tír Manach, a meôuil. Niall .h. Cričán, rí .h. bƒiacpač Αroa rrača, po marbaô po Uiô Ceinoéioiž.

Ictt.Enaip .1111. p. ; l. xu111. ; xxx. bliaoan ap ceo ap

The kalends of January on the 3rd feria, the 7th of the moon; the age of the Lord twenty-nine years, and a hundred, and a thousand. Cellach, comarb of Patrick, i.e. the chief bishop of the West of Europe; a pure, illustrious virgin; the only head whom Foreigners and Gaeidhel, *both* laics and clerics, obeyed; after having, moreover, ordained bishops and priests, and persons of every degree besides; and after having consecrated very many churches and cemeteries; after having bestowed jewels and wealth; and after having imposed faith and good manners on all, both laity and clergy; and after a life of mass-celebration, fasting, *and* praying, and after unction and choice penance, resigned his soul into the bosom of angels and archangels, in Ard-Patraic, in Mumha, on the kalends of April, the 2nd [feria], in the twenty-fourth year of his abbotship, and in the fiftieth year of his age. His body was conveyed, truly, on the 3rd of the nones of April, to Lis-mór-Mochuda, according to his own will; and it was waked with psalms, and hymns, and canticles, and was honourably interred in the tomb of the bishops, on the day before the nones of April, on the 5th feria.[1] Muirchertach, son of Domhnall, was ordained in the comarbship of Patrick, on the nones of April. The house of Colum-Cille, in Cill-mic-Nenain, was captured by Tairchert[2] against Aedh, son of Cathbhar Ua Domhnaill; and it was burned by him. The castle of Ath-Luain was built by Toirdhelbhach O'Conchobhair. Gillachrist, son of Mac Uidhrin,[3] chief of Cenel-Feradhaigh, was burned in the house of his fosterer, in Tir-Manach, in treachery. Niall Ua Crichain, king of Ui-Fiachrach of Ard-sratha, was slain by the Ui-Ceinneidigh.

The kalends of January on the 4th feria, the 18th of the moon; the age of the Lord thirty years, and a hun-

---

is Mac Uidhrin, or Mac Uidhrén, as appears from the entry under the year 1120, *supra*, and under the same year also in the Ann. Four Mast.; and the Ann. Ult.

mile air in Tigerna. Sord Coluim Cille, cona templaib ocur mionnuibh, do loscad. Cúaibne .h. Conchobair, rí .h. bFailghe, dhéc. Cath etir fira Alban ocur fira Muiriebh,[1] i torcradar .iiii. míle drerubh Moiriébh im a rígh, .i. Aonghur mac ingine Lulaigh, ocur mile drerubh Alban, a bfrithghuin. Sloiged la Mág Lachlainn ocur la tuaircert nErenn a nUlltoib, gur thinóilret Uladh do thabairt chatha dóib, gurro mheabadh for Ulltoib, gur ro láadh in nár, im Aodh .h. Loingrich, rí Dál nAraidhe, ocur im Gilla Patraic mac Serridh, rí Dál mBuinne, ocur ím Dubhrailbhe mac Cartáin,[2] ocur im fochaide airchena. Indrit, imorro, in tír go hoirrter na hArda,[3] etir thuaith ocur chill,[4] go tucrat míle do braid, uel paulo[5] plur, ocur il mhile do buaibh ocur deachaib. Teguid maithe Ulad, imorro, imó a righ, iarrin go hArd Macha, i comhdáil Conchobair, gondernrat rích ocur comluidhe, ocur gur fargrat giallа. Merr mór gacha toradh go coitchend i nErinn uile in bliadain rin.

Kal. Enair .u. f.; l. xxix.; bliadain ocur .xxx. ar ced ar mile air in Tigerna. Crech rlóighedh la Toirrdhealbach O Conchobair ocur la cuicedh[6] Connacht i Mumuin, gurro airgret hI Conuill Gabra. Sloighedh la Conchobar .h. mBriain ocur la fira Muman i Laighnibh, gurro ghabh a ngialla, ocur arrein a Midhe, gurro airgret inir Locha Seimhdidhe. Cómraicid a marcrlúag ocur marcrluagh Connacht annrin, gurro mhebadh for marcrluagh Connacht, go torchair mac Conconnacht hI Concobair,

[1] *Muiriebh;* i.e. Moray, in Scotland. The Annals of Ulster have the record of this battle under the same year, but the Editor of these Annals, Dr. O'Conor, understood fera moreb (as the name is written in his text), to mean "pirates," for he renders the words "bellum etir firu Alban ocur fera moreb," by "Bellum inter Albanenses et prædones maritimos."

[2] *Mac Cartain.* Anciently written "Mac Artain," but "Mac Cartain" in later texts, the *c* of *Mac* being attracted over to *Artain*, as in the case of Loch Coirb, originally Loch Oirbren.

[3] *Ard.* Now the Ards, in the east of the county of Down.

[4] *Both territory and church;* i.e. both lay and ecclesiastical lands.

[5] *Paulo.* pablo (pabhlo), MS.

[6] *Province.* cuicedh (cuicedh), lit. "the fifth," Ireland being anciently divided into five provinces. Even at

dred, and a thousand. Sord-Choluim-Chille, with its churches and relics, was burned. Cúaibhne Ua Conchobhair, king of Ui-Failghe, died. A battle between the men of Alba and the men of Muiriebh,[1] in which 4,000 of the men of Muiriebh,[1] with their king, i.e. Aenghus, son of Lulach's daughter, and 1,000 of the men of Alba, fell in the mutual wounding. A hosting by Mac Lachlainn and the *men of the* North of Erinn, into Ulidia, and the Ulidians assembled to give them battle; but the Ulidians were defeated and slaughtered, together with Aedh Ua Loingsigh, king of Dal-Araidhe, and with Gillapatraic Mac Serridh, king of Dal-Buinne, and with Dubhrailbhe Mac Gartain,[2] and many besides. They plundered the country, moreover, as far as the east of the Ard,[3] both territory and church,[4] and carried off a thousand captives, vel paulo[5] plus, and many thousands of cows and horses. The chief men of Ulidia, however, came afterwards, with their king, to Ard Macha, to meet Conchobhar, and they made peace and took mutual oaths, and they (*the Ulidians*) left hostages. A great crop of every kind of produce generally in Erinn this year.

The kalends of January on the 5th feria, the twenty-ninth of the moon; the age of the Lord thirty-one years, and a hundred, and a thousand. A predatory hosting by Toirdhelbhach O'Conchobhair and the *men of the* province[6] of Connacht, into Mumha, when they plundered Ui-Conaill-Gabhra. A hosting by Conchobhar Ua Briain, and by the men of Mumha, into Laighen, and they took their hostages;[7] and *they proceeded* from thence into Midhe, and plundered the island of Loch-Seimhdidhe. Their cavalry and the cavalry of Connacht met there, and the cavalry of Connacht were defeated, and the son

---

the present day the Irish-speaking people call each of the four provinces a *cuicedh*, or "fifth."

[7] *Their hostages*; i.e. the hostages of the men of Laighen, or Leinster.

ocur in rervánca .h. Carrchaish, .i. ollam Connachc.
Sloished la Conchobar mág Lačlainn, ocur la hUllcoib,
go ocuaircepc Erenn leo, i gConnachca, go ocaporac
Connachca ammur ror vered in crlóis a bráil na Sexra,
i corchravar Conn .h. Maoilgaoič ocur an garvánach
.h. baoisill, ocur rochaive mór eli. Ar a oive rin,
imorro, comváilic iar na várach ag Loč Cé, ocur vo
gníav ríč bliavna. Creč la Tigernán .h. Ruairc, ocur
la rira Breirrne, var éiri inc rlúaiš a Cuailgne, gurro
airgrec .h. Meich. Ag imróv voiv imorro .i. vo Ullcoib,
ocur vo veircepc Airgiall, var Ač Luain vía cigiv,
comraicic a mois Conalle rurin gcreič noile. Feruic
cač i corchair Rágnall .h. hEochava, rí Ulav, ocur
Cúmive .h. Criočáin, rí Fernmaive, ocur a mac, ocur
Vonnrleive .h. hInnrechcaix, rí .h. Méč, ec alii
multi. Maoilira .h. Foglava, erruc Cairil, in renec-
cúce bona quievic.

Kct. Enáir .iii. r.; l x.; va bliavain críča ar ceo
ar mile air in Tigerna. Teač navav Gille vara vo
gaváil viv gCeinnrelaix ror čomarba mBrigvi, ocur a
lorgav, ocur blav mór vón čill, ocur rochaive vo
marbav ann, ocur an caileč réin vo breič a mbroiv,
ocur a cavairc a leabaiv rir. Veabav vo venum
vo muincer na Scrine Colum Cille, ocur vo Ločlainn
.h. baigellán, i corchair airchinnech na Scrine, .i.
Macraič .h. Niallán, ocur Ločlainn réin. Sloished
la Conchobar mág Lačlainn co hAč rirveghaiv, co
vcánic Tigernán .h. Ruairc ina čech, ocur go vcaro
braigve vó.

Kct. Enair i. r.; l. xxi.; cri bliavna críča ar ceo ar

---

[1] *Ferdána;* i.e. "the man of song,"
or poet.

[2] *Garbhanach.* This is a sobriquet
signifying "the fierce," or "the
rough," from garv (garbh), coarse,
or rough.

[3] *Left;* i.e. after the northern
armies had left on the expedition
to Connacht.

[4] *An engagement was fought.* Veav-
bav vo venum (deabadh do
dhenum); lit. "a dispute was made."

[5] *Came into his house;* or, in other
words, "submitted to him."

of Cuchonnacht Ua Conchobhair, and the Ferdána[1] Ua
Carthaigh, i.e. the *chief* poet of Connacht, were slain.
A hosting by Conchobhar Mac Lachlainn and the Ulidians, the *men of the* North of Erinn being with them,
into Connacht; but the Connachtmen made an attack on
the rear of the army, in the vicinity of the Seghais, in
which Conn Ua Maelgaeithi, and the Garbhanach[2] Ua
Baeighill, and a great many more, were slain. Notwithstanding this, however, they met together on the morrow
at Loch-Cé, and made a year's peace. A depredation
by Tighernan Ua Ruairc and the men of Breifne, after
the army had left,[3] in Cuailgne, and they plundered
Ui-Meith. On their return, however, (*i.e. the return of
the* Ulidians and the men of the South of Airghiall),
across Ath-Luain, to their houses, they met with the
other depredators in Magh-Conaille. A battle was fought,
in which Raghnall Ua hEochadha, king of Uladh, and
Cumhidhe Ua Crichain, king of Fernmhagh, and his son,
and Donnsleibhe Ua hInnrechtaigh, king of Ui-Meith, et
alii multi, were slain. Maelisa Ua Foghladha, bishop of
Caisel, in bona senectute quievit.

The kalends of January on the 6th feria, the 10th of
the moon; the age of the Lord thirty-two years, and a
hundred, and a thousand. The abbot's house of Cill-dara
was captured by the Ui-Ceinnselaigh against the comarb of Brighid, and burned, and a large part of the church
was burned, and a great many were slain there; and the
nun herself was carried off a prisoner, and put into a man's
bed. An engagement was fought[4] by the people of Scrín-
Choluim-Chille and Lochlainn Ua Baeighellain, in which
the airchinnech of the Scrín, i.e. Macraith Ua Niallain, and
Lochlainn himself, were killed. A hosting by Conchobhar
Mac Lachlainn to Ath-Fhirdheghaidh, when Tighernan
Ua Ruairc came into his house,[5] and gave him hostages.

The kalends of January on the 1st feria, the 21st of
the moon; the age of the Lord thirty-three years, and a

[1132.]

[1133.]

K 2

mile aiṙ in Ꞇiᵹeṙna. Slóiᵹeṫ la Coṙmac ṁáᵹ Caṙṙ-
ċaiᵹ, ocuṙ la Conchobaṙ .h. mḃṙiain, ı Connachtuiḃ,
ᵹuṙṙo maṙḃṙat Caṫal mac Caṫail hı Conchobaiṙ,
ṙíṫamna Connacht, ocuṙ ᵹuṙṙo ṙᵹaoilṙet Ꝺún Muᵹṙṙn
ocuṙ Ꝺún móṙ, ocuṙ ᵹuṙṙo ınꝺıṙṙet móṙán ꝺon tíṙ.
Cṙeċ ṙlóiᵹeṫ la Ꝺonnchaꝺ .h. ᵹCeṙḃuill ocuṙ la
ṙıṙa Ꝼeṙnmaıꝺe, a ḃṙıne ᵹall, conuṙ táiṙṫe Ꞇoṙcaill
aᵹ Ꝼınnaḃaıṙ, ocuṙ ᵹonꝺeṙṙᵹat ꝺebaıṫ ı toṙchaiṙ
Ráᵹnall mac Ṗóil, ocuṙ ꝺṙonᵹ ṁóṙ·ꝺo ᵹalloıḃ ımme ;
ocuṙ ᵹıꝺ ıaꝺ ṙıṙa Ꝼeṙnmaıꝺe ṙein, túcaꝺ ṙoncaṫ ṙoṙṙa.
Conchobaṙ mac Muṙchaꝺa hı Maoıltṙeclainn, ṙí
ṫaṁna Ꞇempaċ, ꝺo ᵹuın la Laıᵹnıḃ, ocuṙ a ṁaṙḃaṫ ꝺo
ᵹallaıḃ ıaṙṙın. Ꝺonnchaꝺ mac ᵹıllaċolmóᵹ, ṙíꝺamna
Laıᵹen, ꝺo maṙḃaꝺ ꝺṙeṙuıb Mıꝺe. Ꝼıne ᵹall ꝺo loṙcaꝺ
ḃéoṙ ꝺṙeṙuıḃ Mıꝺe. Luṙca, cona tempall lán ꝺo ꝺaoınıḃ
ocuṙ ꝺo ċaıṙᵹeꝺhaıḃ, ꝺo loṙcaꝺ ꝺon lucht ceꝺna. Ḃó
ṫıḃaꞇ aṙ ꝺteacht ı nԐṙınn co huılıꞇe, ꝺá ná ṙṙıꞇ ṙamaıl
ó ꞇanıc ın bóꝺıḃaꞇ móṙ ṙoıme ṙın ı naımṙıṙ Ꝼlaıꞇḃeṙtaıᵹ
mıc Loınᵹṙıᵹ, ocuṙ ꝺá blıaꝺaın .xxx. aṙ .cccc. etoṙṙa.

Ktt. Ԑnaıṙ .ıı. ꝼ. ; l. ıı. ; ceıṙṙı blıaꝺna .xxx. aṙ ceꝺ
aṙ mıle aıṙ ın Ꞇıᵹeṙna. 1n bóꝺıḃaꞇ ceꝺna ḃóṙṙ aᵹ
ınṙeꝺh na hԐṙenn, conıꝺ lan aıṙᵹnıᵹ ṙochaıꝺe ın ᵹach
aıṙꝺ ı nԐṙınn. Aṙċú .h. Ꝼlaıꞇḃeṙtaıᵹ, ṙíꝺaṁna
Oılıᵹ, ꝺo ċuıtım la Cenél Conaıll a ṙaoı ṁaꝺma.
Ꝺonnchaꝺ .h. Conchobaıṙ, ṙí .h. ḃṙaıᵹe, ocuṙ Maoılṙechlaınn mac a aṫaṙ, ꝺo coımꝺebaıꝺ, ᵹo toṙcṙaꝺaṙ
comꞇuıtım. Sloıᵹeꝺ la mac Muṙchaꝺa ocuṙ la Laıᵹnıḃ,
ı nOṙṙaıᵹıḃ, conuṙ táṙṙaꝺaṙ Oṙṙaıᵹe, ocuṙ ᵹuṙṙo

---

1 *Gillacholmóg.* This name is more
correctly written Gillamocholmóg,
(i.e. "servant of Mocholmóg,") in the
Annals of the Four Masters.

2 *Occurred.* aṙ ꝺteacht; lit.
"after coming."

3 *Flaithbhertach.* See next note.

4 *432 years.* The great cow mortality here referred to is stated in the
Ann. Ult. and Chron. Scotorum to
have broken out in the year 699,
which was not in the time of
Flaithbhertach, king of Ireland, but
in that of his father, Loingsech,
who reigned from A.D. 695 to 704,
according to O'Flaherty's chronology.
See *Ogygia*, p. 432, and Wilde's *Table
of Cosmical Phenomena* (Census of

hundred, and a thousand. A hosting by Cormac Mac
Carthaigh and Conchobhar Ua Briain, into Connacht,
when they killed Cathal, son of Cathal Ua Conchobhair,
royal heir of Connacht, and demolished Dun-Mughorn
and Dun-mór, and plundered a great part of the country.
A predatory hosting by Donnchadh Ua Cerbhaill and the
men of Fernmhagh into Fine-Gall; but Torcaill overtook them at Finnabhair, and they fought a battle, in
which Raghnall, son of Pol, was slain, and a great number of Foreigners along with him; and as regards the
men of Fernmhagh themselves, they were subjected to
great danger. Conchobhar, son of Murchadh Ua Maelsechlainn, royal heir of Temhair, was wounded by the
Lagenians, and afterwards slain by Foreigners. Donnchadh Mac Gillacholmóg,[1] royal heir of Laighen, was
slain by the men of Midhe. Fine-Gall was again burned
by the men of Midhe. Lusca, with its church full of
people and treasures, was burned by the same party. A
great cow mortality occurred[2] throughout all Erinn, for
which no likeness was found since the great cow mortality came before that in the time of Flaithbhertach,[3] son
of Loingsech; and 432 years[4] *elapsed* between them.

The kalends of January on the 2nd feria, the 2nd of
the moon; the age of the Lord thirty-four years, and a
hundred, and a thousand. The same cow mortality again
devastating Erinn, so that numbers of people were quite
impoverished in every locality in Erinn. Archu Ua Flaithbhertaigh, royal heir of Oilech, fell by the Cenel-Conaill
in a battle-breach. Donnchadh Ua Conchobhair, king
of Ui-Failghe, and Maelsechlainn, his father's son, engaged
in conflict, and fell by each other. A hosting by Mac
Murchadha and the Lagenians, into Osraighe; but the
Osraighe encountered them and committed a slaughter of

Ireland, 1851, part v., vol. i.), p. 54.
O'Flaherty, who appears to have had
the MS. in his possession, as already

observed, has added the note "great
dearth of cows" in the margin.

áiγαt áp inτ fluaiᵹ, oú i τορchαiρ Uᵹαiρe O Τuαthαil, píᵭαmnα Lαiᵹen, eτ αlii mulτi. αρ Oᵳᵳραiᵹe ocuᵳ ᵹαll puiρτ Láiρᵹe oo ̌cuρ lα mαc Muρchαoα ocuᵳ lα Lαᵹniᵬ, i noíᵹuil in áiρ ρéᵐρáiτe. Ioᵐαρ .ḣ. ḣαoᵭαcαn, αn ᵳeρ lαᵳ ρo cumoαiᵹheo ρeᵹléᵳ Póil ocuᵳ Peταiρ i nαρo Mαᵭα, oo éᵹ inα αiliτρi α Róiᵐ. Oonnchαo mαc Muρchαoα hi bρiαin oo mαρbαᵭ, conα mαc, oo ᵭeᵳ Mumαin. Mαolᵹαρᵬ móρ in hoc αnno.

Kττ. Enáiρ .iii. f.; L. xiii. ; cóiᵹ ᵬliαonα .xxx. αρ ceo αρ mile αiρ in Τiᵹeρnα Mαolmóρᵬα .ḣ. Conchobαiρ, pí .ḣ. bᵳαilᵹe, oo mαρbαo oiα oeρbρáτhαiρ ᵳéin. Eᵭρí .ḣ. Ταᵭᵹ, ᵳi bᵳeᵳ Li, conα bρατhαiρ ocuᵳ conα ᵐnαoí, oo ᵐuchαo in nuαiᵐ oo Uíᵬ Τuiρτρi. Ruαioρi O Cαnαnnán, ᵳí ̌cénel Conαill, ᵳeρ coᵹταᵭ, coρnαmαᵭ, co noeᵳeρc ocuᵳ nooenoαchτ, oo mαρbαo oᵳeρuiᵬ muiᵹe híᵭα, .i. oo Mαolρuαnαiᵭ O Cαρellαn ocuᵳ oo ̌cloinn Oiαρmαoα. Ooiρe Coluim Cille conα τemplαib oo loρcαo i τeρτ Kττ. αρρíl. Cluαin iραiρo ocuᵳ Raiᵭ Luραiᵭ, ocuᵳ Cenαnτuᵳ, ocuᵳ il ̌cellα αiρchenα, αb iᵹne oiᵳᵳiρατe ρunτ. Sochαioe ᵐóρ oo ᵭeᵳ Mumαin oo ̌cuiτim lα τuαᵭ Mumαin ᵳoρ τochuρ Cluαnα cαoin Moᵬimoᵹ, i τορchαiρ Finnᵹuine.ḣ. Cαini, ᵳí Ꝣlenoαmnαᵭ, ocuᵳ Mαᵭᵹαᵐαin .ḣ. Oonnchαoα, ᵳí ̌cenel Lαoᵹαiρe, ocuᵳ αoᵬ .ḣ. Conchobαiρ, ᵳí Coρcumρuαiᵭ, ocuᵳ Mαolᵹoρm .ḣ. Rinn, ocuᵳ mαc Loᵭlαinn hi Cinαoᵭα oo 1ᵬ mic Cαille, eτ αlii pluᵳimi. Cúᵐαρα, imoρρo, mαc Conmαρα mic Oomnαill, ᵳí .ḣ. Cαiᵳᵳín, oo ̌cuiτim α bᵳριᵭᵹuin. hαnρico mαc Uillilim, ᵳí Fραnc, ocuᵳ Sαxαn, ocuᵳ bρeταn, oo éᵹ. Coiᵳρeᵹαo τempαil Coρmαic.

---

1 *Regles.* The name "Regles" is usually applied to an abbey church.

2 *Murrain;* mαelᵹαρᵬ(maelgarbh), i.e. a cattle distemper.

3 *Igne.* inᵹne (ingne), MS.

4 *Dissipatæ.* oiᵳιρατe(disipate),MS.

5 *Hanrico.* Henry I., king of England.

6 *Saxons;* i.e., the English.

7 *Cormac's church.* This is the remarkable example of early Norman

the host, in which fell Ughaire O'Tuathail, royal heir of Laighen, et alii multi. A slaughter of the Osraighe, and of the Foreigners of Port-Lairge, was committed by Mac Murchadha and the Lagenians, in revenge for the afore- said slaughter. Imhar Ua hAedhagain, the man by whom the Regles[1] of Paul and Peter at Ard-Macha was erected, died on his pilgrimage at Rome. Donnchadh, son of Murchadh Ua Briain, was slain, together with his son, by *the people of* Des-Mumha. A great murrain[2] in hoc anno.

The kalends of January on the 3rd feria, the 13th of the moon; the age of the Lord thirty-five years, and a hundred, and a thousand. Maelmordha Ua Conchobhair, king of Ui-Failghe, was killed by his own brother. Echri Ua Taidhg, king of Feara-Lí, with his brother, and with his wife, was smothered in a cave by the Ui-Tuirtre. Ruaidhri O'Canannain, king of Cenel-Conaill, a war- like, defensive man, of charity and humanity, was slain by the men of Magh-Itha, viz., by Maelruanaidh O'Cairellan, and by Clann-Diarmada. Doire-Choluim- Chille, with its churches, was burned on the 3rd of the kalends of April. Cluain-Iraird, and Rath-Luraigh, and Cenannus, and many other churches, ab igne[3] dissipatæ[4] sunt. A great number of *the men of* Des-Mumha fell by *those of* Tuadh-Mumha, on the causeway of Cluain-caein- Modhimog, where Finghuine Ua Caeimh, king of Glenn- namnach, and Mathghamhain Ua Donnchadha, king of Cenel-Laeghaire, and Aedh Ua Conchobhair, king of Cor- cumruaidh, and Maelgorm Ua Rinn, and the son of Loch- lainn Ua Cinaedha of the Ui-Maccaille, et alii plurimi, were slain. Cumara, moreover, the son of Cumara, son of Domhnall, king of Ui-Caisin, fell in the mutual wounding. Hanrico,[5] son of William, king of the French, Saxons,[6] and Britons, died. Consecration of Cormac's church.[7]

architecture erected on the Rock of Cashel, of which Dr. Petrie has given | a description; *Round Towers*, pp. 286– 289.

Aoḋ .h. Cellaiġ, rí .h. Maine, mortuus ert. Aoḋ ṁáġ
Coċlain mortuur ert.

Ktt. enair iiii. f.; l. xxiiii. Sé bliaḋna .xxx. ar
ced ar mile air in Tiġerna. biṛṛextilir annuṛ et
embolirmur annuṛ; poṛitur huiur anni non fṛequen-
ter accedit, .i. i nomaḋ lá don eṛṛach Domnach Ineḋe;
undecim Ktt. Aṗṛil Domnach Cárc; an la ṛia mbelltaine Dardaoin ṛṛerġaḃala; in deaċmaḋ lá do
tṛámṛaḋ Domnach Cincíre. Roḃartaċ .h. Cellaiġ,
aiṛchinnech Faċna móiṛe, in penitentia mortuur ert.
Domnall mac Muircertaiġ hi Ḃriain ḋéc i nailitṛi a
Lir ṁór. Conchobar mac Domnaill ṁeġ Laċlainn, rí
Oiliġ, ocur ríḋaṁna Erenn, do marbaḋ dṛeṛuiḃ muiġe
hIĊa a meaḃail aṛechta, dia Luain et octauur Kalen-
daṛ Iunii. Aoḋ mac Toiṛṛḋhealbaiġ hi Conchobair do
ḋallaḋ lé a braṫair ṛéin. Maiḋm Finnabraċ aṛ
Aoḋ mac Domnaill hi Conchobair, ocur ṛoṛ Taḋc .h.
Ceallaiġ ocur aṛ iḃ Maine, ubi cecidit Conchobar
.h. Cellaiġ, aṫair Taḋc, et alii multi. Conchobar
mac Toiṛṛḋhelbaiġ ocur Síl Muiṛeġhaiġ uictoṛer
ṛueṛunt.

Ktt. enair .ui. f.; l. u. Seacht mbliaḋna .xxx. ar ced
ar mile air in Tiġerna. Aṫhach ġaoiṫe déṛṁaiṛe
in lá ṛia bḟéil imberta uṛce, ġuṛṛo tṛaṛcar ṛeḋa
ocur templa imḋa i nErinn. Domnall .h. Conaing,
aiṛoeṛ puic Leiṫe Moḋa, tuiṛ craḃaḋ ocur hecna, ocur
iṛnaiġṫe, ocur toiṛberta bíḋ ocur ṛeod do tṛuaġ ocur
do tṛén, in bona ṛenectute dormiuit. Teiḋm tṛeaġuid
ṁór i nErinn ġo coitċeno, ġuṛṛo ṁarḃ ṛochaide.

1 *Bissextilis.* biṛextil (bisextil), MS.

2 *Embolismus.* embleṛmur, MS.

3 *Shrove Sunday.* Domnach Ineḋe, (Domnach Inede), "the Sunday of the commencement (of Lent)."

4 *Pœnitentia.* peninci (peninci), MS.

5 *Mortuus est.* m. r̄c (for mortui sunt), MS.

6 *Brother.* The Ann. Four Mast. state that the deed was committed by Aedh's father, with which the Annals of Clonmacnoise agree.

7 *Ubi.* ube, MS.

Aédh Ua Cellaigh, king of Ui-Maine, mortuus est. Aedh Mac Coghlan mortuus est.

The kalends of January on the 4th feria, the 24th of the moon; the age of the Lord thirty-six years, and a hundred, and a thousand; bissextilis[1] annus, et embolismus[2] annus; positus hujus anni non frequenter accidit, viz.:— Shrove Sunday[3] *fell* on the 9th day of spring; Easter Sunday on the 11th of the kalends of April; Ascension Thursday on the day before May-day, *and* Whit Sunday on the tenth day of summer. Robhartach Ua Cellaigh, airchinnech of Fathan-mór, in pœnitentia[4] mortuus est.[5] Domhnall, son of Muirchertach Ua Briain, died in pilgrimage at Lis-mór. Conchobhar, son of Domhnall Mac Lachlainn, king of Óilech, and royal heir of Erinn, was slain by the men of Magh-Itha, in treachery, at an assembly, on Monday, the 8th of the kalends of June. Aedh, son of Toirdhelbhach Ua Conchobhair, was blinded by his own brother.[6] The victory of Finnabhair *was gained* over Aedh, son of Domhnall Ua Conchobhair, and over Tadhg Ua Cellaigh, and over the Ui-Maine, ubi[7] cecidit Conchobhar Ua Cellaigh, father of Tadhg, et alii multi. Conchobhar, son of Toirdhelbhach, and the Sil-Muiredhaigh victores fuerunt.

The kalends of January on the 6th feria, the 5th of the moon; the age of the Lord thirty-seven years, and a hundred, and a thousand. A tremendous storm of wind on the day before the festival óf the Sprinkling of Water,[8] which prostrated many forests and churches in Erinn. Domhnall Ua Conaing, chief bishop of Leth-Mogha, pillar of piety, and wisdom, and prayer, and of the presentation of food and treasures to the poor and mighty, in bona senectute dormivit.[9] A great colic disease in Erinn generally, which killed many. A hosting by the

---

[8] *Festival of the Sprinkling of Water;* i.e. Rogation Sunday.

[9] *Dormivit.* ꝺoꞃmıeꝺꞇ (for dormierunt), MS.

Sloiṁeḋ la Laiġniḃ ocuṗ la ṁallaiḃ ḋḟóiṗiḃin tṗíl
mḃṗiain, ṁo poṗt Laiṗṁe, ṁo tucṗat ṁialla aṗ. Cṗeć
ṗlóiṁeḋ la Sil mḃṗiain i ṁCiaṗṗaiṁiḃ, ṁuṗṗo aiṗṁṗet
[tua]ćtá ocuṗ cealla. Domnall .h. Maoilṗeclainn,
ṗíḋaṁna Eṗenn, a ṗuiṗ occiṗuṗ eṗt. Móṗ inṁen Muiṗ-
ćeṗtaiṁ hI bṗiain, ben Muṗchaḋa hí Maoiltṗeclainn,
aiṗḋ ṗíṁan Eṗenn, in penitentia moṗtua eṗt. Taća móṗ
a coiceḋ Connacht, et multi moṗtui ṗunt ab ea. Aoḋ
mac Domnaill hí Conchobaiṗ occiṗuṗ eṗt. Domnall
.h. Dubtaiṁ, Eleṗinenṗiṗ epiṗcopuṗ, ocuṗ comaṗba
Ciaṗán Cluana mic Nóiṗ, aṗuḋ Cluain ṗeṗta bṗénuinn
quieuit in Cṗiṗto.

Ktt. Enaiṗ .uii. ṗ.; l. xui. Ocht mbliaḋna .xxx. aṗ
ceḋ aṗ mile aiṗ in Tiṁeṗna. Matṁamuin O Conocobaiṗ,
ṗí Ciaṗṗaiṁe, tuiṗ oṗḋuin ocuṗ oiṗechuiṗ Leiće Moḋa
aṗ ṁiḋnacal ṗéḋ ocuṗ maoiniḃ, ḋoṗmiuit. Lioṗ móṗ,
ocuṗ Cill ḋaṗa, ocuṗ Tech Moling, ocuṗ Soṗḋ Coluim
Cille, ḋo loṗcaḋ. Maolṗuanaiḋ .h. Caiṗellain, coinnel
aḋanta ćuaiṗciṗt Eṗenn aṗ cṗuth, aṗ ćeill, aṗ ṁaiṗceḋ,
ḋo maṗbaḋ la Cenel Móain. Inḋṗeḋ tuaiṗceṗt tSaxan
o ṗeṗuiḃ Alban, ṁo tucṗaḋ bṗaiḋ nḋiáiṗṁiḋe ocuṗ
ṁaḃála imḋa. Coṗmac mac ṁéṁ Caṗṗthaiṁ, aiṗḋ ṗíṁ
Deṗ Muman, ocuṗ eṗṗuc ṗíṁ nEṗenn ina ṗeiṁeṗ, aṗ
cṗabaḋ, aṗ ṁiḋnacul ṗéḋ ocuṗ maoine ḋo ćleiṗćiḃ
ocuṗ ćellaiḃ, ocuṗ aṗ iaṗmaṗt neṁluṗḋaṁḋa a leḃṗuiḃ,
ocuṗ a naiḋmiḃ, ḋo Dia ocuṗ . . . . . ḋo ćuitim

---

1 *Síl Briain;* i.e. the descendants
of Brian Boromha.

2 *Territories.* The MS. has ćṫá,
evidently a mistake for tuaṫa, acc.
and nom. pl. of tuaiṫh, a territory
or district.

3 *North of Saxan;* i.e. the north of
England, or Northumberland.

4 *Bishop-king.* eṗṗuc ṗíṁ. This
designation has been the source of

much misconception with writers on
Irish history, some of whom, including the late Dr. Petrie (*Round Towers,*
pp. 306, 307), were of opinion that
Cormac Mac Carthaigh was really
both a bishop and a king, whilst
others, with Dr. O'Brien and Dr.
Lanigan, considered him as having
only been honoured with the title of
"bishop-king" for his piety, and liber-

Lagenians and Foreigners, in aid of Síl-Briain,[1] to Port-
Lairge, from which they brought pledges. A predatory
hosting by Síl-Briain[1] to the Ciarraighe, and they plundered territories[2] and churches. Domhnall Ua Maelsechlainn, royal heir of Erinn, a suis occisus est. Mór,
daughter of Muirchertach Ua Briain, wife of Murchadh
Ua Maelsechlainn, chief queen of Erinn, in pœnitentia
mortua est. A great scarcity in the province of Connacht, et multi mortui sunt ab ea. Aedh, son of
Domhnall Ua Conchobhair, occisus est. Domhnall Ua
Dubhthaigh, bishop of Elphin, and comarb of Ciaran of
Cluain-mic-Nois, apud Cluain-ferta-Brenainn quievit in
Christo.

The kalends of January on the 7th feria, the 16th of
the moon; the age of the Lord thirty-eight years, and a
hundred, and a thousand. Mathghamhain O'Conchobhair,
king of Ciarraighe, pillar of the dignity and glory of
Leth-Mogha in presenting jewels and valuables, dormivit. Lis-mór, and Cill-dara, and Tech-Moling, and Sord-
Choluim-Chille, were burned. Maelruanaidh Ua Cairellain, kindling lamp of the north of Erinn as regards
figure, understanding, and valour, was slain by the Cenel-
Moain. Plundering of the North of Saxan[3] by the men
of Alba, who carried off countless captives, and numerous
spoils. Cormac, son of Mac Carthaigh, chief king of Des-
Mumha, and bishop-king[4] of Erinn in his time as regards
piety, and the presentation of jewels and valuables to
clerics and churches, and ecclesiastical riches, in books and
utensils, to God and . . . . fell in treachery

---

ality to the Church. There is no
other proof of his having been a
bishop save this title, which is otherwise written ᚱᚔᚌ ᚓᚄᚉᚑᚚ, "king-
bishop," in a MS. of the Gospels, preserved in the Brit. Museum (Harl.
1802), transcribed in the year 1138;
of which see an account by Rev. Dr.
Reeves; *Proceedings* of the *R. I.
Academy*, vol. 5, p. 45, *sq.*

α meαburl lα τυαᵭ Mumαin; ocur bennαchτ le α αnmuin.

```
*     *     *     *     *     *     *     *
   *     *     *     *     *     *     *
 *     *     *     *     *     *     *     *
   *     *     *     *     *     *     *
 *     *     *     *     *     *     *     *
   *     *     *     *     *     *     *
 *     *     *     *     *     *     *     *
```

Kt. Θnáip .u. p.; l. x. Seachτmoᵭα αp ceᵭ αp mile αip αn τιᵹepnα. Conchobαp mαc Muipcepταiᵹ meᵹ Lαčlαinn, pí Cinel Θoᵹαin, ocur píᵭαᵐnα Θpenn uile, ᵭo mαpbαᵭ ᵭccoᵭ beᵹ mαc Cαnα, ocur ᵭo Uiᵭ Cαppαcán, ᵭé Sαᵵαpn Cápᵭ, αp láp τpín ᵐóip α nᵭppᵭ Mαᵭα. ᵭonnchαᵭ Cennpealαᵭ O Ceallaiᵹh ᵭo mαpbαᵭ ᵭo Laiᵹniᵭ. Cᵭ cliαᵭ ᵭo milleᵭ ᵭo ᵭiapmaiᵭ mαc Mupchαᵭα, ocur ᵭallmuppαchiᵭ τuc leip αnoip ᵭo ᵐilleᵭ nα hΘpenn, α nᵭiᵹail α ionnαpbᵭα ταp muip αpp α ᵭepαnn pein, ocur α mαc ᵭo ᵐαpbαᵭ. τucpαᵭ ᵭαnα áp pop Ᵹαllαiᵭ Cᵭᵭ cliαᵭ ocur Puipτ Láipci, ocur τucᵭα, τpá, αp ᵭiáipᵐe poppα pum. Ro millτi ᵭonα Laiᵹin ocur pip Mιᵭe, eᵭip ceallα ocur τuαᵭα, leo; ocur po ᵹαᵭpαᵭ Cᵭ cliαᵭ ocur Popτ Laipce ᵭon ᵭol pin. Ᵹnioᵐ móp αinbᵭiαl ᵭo ᵭenum ᵭon ᵐαnαch mαc comαpbα Ꝼinᵭein Moiᵹe bile, ocur ᵭo Mαᵹnup mαc ᵭuinnpleibe, ᵭo piᵹ Ulαᵭ, co τóippiᵹiᵭ Ulαᵭ, ocur co nUllτoib αipᵭenα, cenmóᵭα Mαoilpα eppuc, ocur Ᵹiollα ᵭomuinᵹuipτ

---

[1] Soul. The entries from this to the year 1170 are unfortunately missing from the MS. At the bottom of the page, which forms fol. 16 b., Roderick O'Flaherty has added the note "I finde this Booke wantes 32 years in this place." The space intervening between the foregoing entry and the next is occupied by six blank leaves of paper.

[2] Kalends. The text of the present entry is in a different hand from the preceding. On the top margin, fol. 17 a, where the entry begins, the scribe has added the memorandum "ι nαinm ᵭé αn τιonnpcnα po," i.e. "in the name of God, this beginning."

[3] The Monk. His name was Amhlaibh (Amlaf, or Olaf), according to the Four Masters. See also Colgan's

by *the people of* Tuadh-Mumha; and a blessing be with his soul.[1]

* * * * * * * *

   * * * * * * *

* * * * * * * *

   * * * * * * *

* * * * * * * *

   * * * * * * *

* * * * * * * *

   * * * * * * *

The kalends[2] of January on the 5th feria, the 10th of the moon; the age of the Lord seventy *years*, and a hundred, and a thousand. Conchobhar, son of Muirchertach Mac Lachlainn, king of Cenel-Eoghain, and royal heir of all Erinn, was slain by Aedh Bec Mac Cana, and by the Ui-Carragain, on Easter Saturday, in the middle of Trian-mór, at Ard-Macha. Donnchadh Cennsealach O'Ceallaigh was slain by Lagenians. Ath-cliath was spoiled by Diarmaid Mac Murchadha, and by pirates whom he brought with him from the east, to spoil Erinn, in retaliation for his expulsion beyond the sea from his own territory, and for his son having been slain. They inflicted a slaughter, moreover, on the Foreigners of Ath-cliath and Port-Lairge, and a countless slaughter was, however, inflicted on them. Laighen, indeed, and Feara-Midhe were wasted by them, both churches and territories; and they occupied Ath-cliath and Port-Lairge on that occasion. A great, ungenerous deed was committed by the monk,[3] son of the comarb of Finnen of Magh-bile, and by Maghnus, son of Donnsleibhe, king of Uladh, with the chieftains of Uladh, and the Ulidians besides—except Bishop Maclisa, and Gilladomhaingairt, son of Cormac,

---

Acta SS.,v. I., p. 650, where it is incorrectly stated that Amhlaibh was abbot of Magh-bile (Moville, in the co. Down). The mistake has been repeated by Archdall (*Monasticon Hibernicum*, p. 125).

mac Copmaic, comapba Coingaill, ocup Maolmapcain, comapba Finnén, cona muinncepaibh .i. coimčinóil cananach piagalca co napav, po opvaig Maolmaoóóc .h. Mopgaip, legáiv comapba Peccaip a Saball Pacpaic, vo ionnapba app an mainipvip po cumvaigpec péin, ocup a napguin co léip evip libpa ocup aivmebú, vaoine, eoča, ocup čaopča, ocup na huile po cinoilpec ann o aimpip an legáiv pénpaíce conuige pin, cenmóčác na hionaip ocup na cábaivče bavap iompa ipin uaip pin, cpia fopmav ocup čáiv collaigi, ocup paince onopa vó péin, óip po víčuippec manaig Dpočaiv áča é app a navóuine cpia čúipiv vligčecha. Uc uč cpa, maipg vo poine, ocup ip maipc víp a nvepnav an gniom; achc amáin ní vechaiv a bpav cen invechaiv ón Coimviv, uaip po mapbuiv a naoinpechc o uaiccib namav na coippig vo poine; ocup po gonav an pí [ocup] po mapbav gap bic iapcain, co hainbpeachcnač, ipin čaile a nvepnav an comaiple anpipén pin, .i. a nDún. Dia Maipc, cpa, po víčuipev an coimčinól; via Maip[c] cpa, a gcinn bliavna, po mapbaic maičі Ulav ocup po gonav a pí. Dia Maipc, gaipiv iapcain, po mapbav hé péin o [a] vepbpachaip a nDún. Diapmaiv .h. hαinbpech, pí .h. Méč ocup coippech mapepluaig píg Oiliš, vo mapbav vo Longup cánic a hinnpiv Opc ipin innpi po cumvaigev aca péin fop Loč Ruive .i. Inip Lačain. Iapla O Sopangvó vo ceachc a nEpinn le Diapmaiv mac Mupchava, a nvigail a ionnapbča vo Ruaivpi mac Coippvealbaig hl Concohbaip; ocup cuc Diapmaiv a ingen péin ocup cuiv vá ôuchaiv vó; ocup acaiv goill cfacpon a nEpinn ó pin.

1 *Himself*; i.e. the monk Amblaibh.
2 *Himself slain*. This emphatic form would seem to indicate that the monk Amblaibh was meant. The Four Masters say po mapbav é, "he was killed," which Dr. O'Donovan (Ann. Four Mast. ad eund. an.) and

Colgan (*Acta SS.*, vol. I., p. 651) understood, doubtless with justice, as referring to Eochaidh, king of Ulidia.

3 *Loch-Ruidhe*. There is no lake in Ireland known now by this name. There is a little island called "the Loughans" in the Bann, a little to

comarb of Comhgall, and Maelmartain, comarb of Finnen, with their fraternities—viz., a community of regular
canons, with their abbot, whom Maelmaedhog Ua Mor-
ghair, legate of the comarb of Peter, had ordained at
Sabhall-Patraic, were expelled from the monastery which
they themselves had erected; (and they were entirely
plundered both in books and utensils, people, horses,
and sheep, and all things which they had collected there
from the time of the aforesaid legate until then, except
the tunics and the capes which were about them in that
hour), through envy and carnal love, and greed of honour
for himself;[1] as the monks of Droiched-Atha had expelled
him from their abbacy for lawful reasons. Alas! alas!
truly; woe *to them* who committed it; and woe to the
land in which the deed was committed; but, however, it
did not escape long without the vengeance of the Lord, for
the chieftains who committed it were slain together by a
few enemies; and the king was wounded, [and] unluckily
slain a short time after, in the place where this unjust
resolution had been adopted, viz., in Dún. On Tuesday
the community was expelled; on Tuesday, also, before
the end of a year, the chieftains of Uladh were slain,
and the king was wounded. On Tuesday, soon after,
he was himself slain[2] by [his] brother, in Dún. Diarmaid O'hAinfheth, king of Ui-Meith, and leader of the
cavalry of the king of Oilech, was killed by *the men of* a
fleet which came from Innsi-hOrc, in the island which
had been constructed by themselves in Loch-Ruidhe,[3] i.e.
Inis-Lachain. Earl Strongbow came into Erinn with
Diarmaid Mac Murchadha, to avenge his expulsion by
Ruaidhri, son of Toirdhealbhach O'Conchobhair; and
Diarmaid gave him his own daughter, and a part of his patrimony; and Saxon Foreigners have been in Erinn since then.

the south of Coleraine (where the
river is rather dilated), which has all
the appearance of having been arti-
ficially constructed. But see O'Donovan's *Four Mast.*, note *, page 1179,
and note b, p. 1486, at the year 1544.

Ḱt. eпaip .iii. ꝼ.; [l.] .xxii.; bliaꝼaiп aꝛ ꝛeaċtmoꝼa, aꝛ ceꝺ, aꝛ ṁíle, aiꝛ aп Ꞇiʒeꝛпa. Ꝺiaꝛmaiꝺ mac Mupċaꝺa, ꝛí coiʒeꝺ Laiʒeп, iaꝛ milleꝺ čeall пiomꝺa, ocuꝛ ꞇuač, ꝺo éʒ a bꝼeꝛпa ceп coꝛp cꝛiꝛꞇ, ceп aiꞇꝛiʒe, ceп ꞇioппa, a пeiпeċ Coluim Cille ocuꝛ Ꝼiппéiп, ocuꝛ пa пaom aiꝛčéпa iꝛ a cealla ꝛa ṁill. Ꝏxoll mac Ꞇoꝛcaill, ꝛí Ꝏᴄa cliač, ocuꝛ hꝋoiп a hiппꝛiꝺ Oꝛc, ꝺo ṁaꝛbaꝺ ꝺoпa ʒallaib ceꝺпa. Saꝺꝺ, iпʒeп Ꝫluiпiaꝛaiпп mic Mupċaꝺa, comaꝛba bꝛíʒꝺe, ꝺeʒ a пaiꞇꝛiʒhe. Maiꝺṁ ꝛoꝛ Ꞇiʒeꝛпaп .h. Ruaiꝛc ocuꝛ aꝛ ꝼeꝛuiꝺ Miꝺe, ocuꝛ aꝛ ꝼeꝛuiꝺ Ꝼeꝛпṁoiʒe imalle, .i. maiꝺṁ aп luaiꞇꝛiʒ ꝛecuпꝺum quoꝛꝺam, aꝛ ꝛaiččе Ꝏᴄa cliač, ꝛia Miloiꝺ Coʒaп coпa ṁuiпꞇeꝛ, i ꝺꞇoꝛċaiꝛ ꝛoċaꝺe ṁóꝛ im Ꝏꝏꝺ .h. Ruaiꝛc, .i. ꝛí .h. mꝺꝛuiп, ocuꝛ maċaiꝛe Ꝫaileпʒ, ocuꝛ Coпmaicпe. Ro maꝛꝺꞇa aпп, ꝺoп, cóiʒ ꞇoiꝛꝛiʒ ꝺꝼeꝛuiꝺ Ꝼeꝛпṁoiʒe, .i. Maolmoċꞇa mac Coпꝛeaꝺla ocuꝛ Coпcobaꝛ a ꝺeꝛbꝛaꞇhaiꝛ, ꝺá čóiꝛꝛeċ Ciпeoil bꝼeꝛaꝺhaiʒ. Ꝼeiпꝺiꝺ O Coпʒaile, coiппeal ʒaiꝛceꝺ ocuꝛ eпʒпama Oiꝛʒiall, moꝛꞇuuꝛ eꝛꞇ.

Ueпiꞇ iп hibeꝛпiam heпꝛicuꝛ ꝛoꞇeпꞇiꝛꝛimuꝛ ꝛex Ꝏпʒliae, eꞇ iꝺem ꝺux Noꝛmaппiae eꞇ Ꝏquiꞇaпiae, eꞇ comeꝛ Ꝏпꝺeʒauiae eꞇ aliaꝛum mulꞇaꝛum ꞇeꝛꝛaꝛum ꝺomiпuꝛ, cum ꝺuceпꞇiꝛ .xl. пauibuꝛ; ocuꝛ ꞇaпic a ꞇíꝛ aʒ Poꝛꞇ Laiꝛʒe ocuꝛ ꝛo ʒaꝺ ʒialla Mumaп ; ocuꝛ ꞇaпic iaꝛꝛiп co hꝎᴄ cliaꞇ, ocuꝛ ꝛo ʒaꝺ ʒialla Laiʒeп ocuꝛ ꝼeꝛ Miꝺe, ocuꝛ .h. mꝺꝛuiп, ocúꝛ Oiꝛʒialla, ocuꝛ Ulaꝺ. Ꝼeꞇꝛuꝛ eꝛꝛuc O Maiпe Coппaċꞇ, maпaċ cꝛaiꝛꞇeċ, ocuꝛ ꝼeꝛ úʒꝺaꝛꝛꝺa, ꝺo baꞇhaꝺ aꝛ Siпuiпп a .iii. Ḱt. ieпaiꝛ.

---

¹ *Axall.* The Four Mast. write the name more correctly "Asgall," and add that he was the son of Raghnall, i.e. Raghnall Mac Torcaill, *mor maer,* "great steward" or "earl," of Dublin, who was slain by the people of East Meath in 1146. Giraldus Cambrensis calls him Hasculphus.

² *hEvin*; i.e. Hoan, or John, whom

Giraldus calls "Insanus." See *Hibernia Expugnata*, lib. 1, cap. 21, and *Harris's Hibernica*, pp. 33–36, for an interesting account of the deaths of Hasculf, and Hoan, or John *Le Devé.*

³ *The same.* This record is perhaps transposed, and should follow the second next entry; or it may be that

The kalends of January on the 6th feria, the 22nd of the moon; the age of the Lord seventy-one years, and a hundred, and a thousand.   Diarmaid Mac Murchadha, king of the province of Laighen, after spoiling numerous churches and territories, died at Ferna—without the body of Christ, without penitence, without *making* a will—through the merits of Colum-Cille, and Finnen, and the other saints whose churches he had spoiled.   Axall[1] Mac Torcaill, king of Ath-cliath, and hEoin[2] from Innsi-hOrc, were slain by the same[3] Foreigners.   Sadhbh, daughter of Gluniarainn Mac Murchadha, comarb of Brigid, died in penitence.   A victory was gained over Tighernan O'Ruairc, and the men of Midhe, and the men of Fernmhagh together, (viz. :—the "victory of the ashes" secundum quosdam), on the green of Ath-cliath, by Milo de Cogan with his people, in which a great number were slain along with Aedh O'Ruairc, i.e. the king of Ui-Briuin, and Machaire-Gaileng, and Conmaicne. There were also slain there five[4] chieftains of the men of Fernmhagh, viz. :—Maelmochta Mac Confeabhla, and Conchobhar, his brother, two chieftains of the Cenel-Feradhaigh.   Feindidh O'Conghaile, lamp of valour and bravery of Oirghiall, mortuus est.

Venit in Hiberniam Henricus potentissimus rex Angliæ,[5] et idem dux Normanniæ[6] et Aquitaniæ,[7] et comes[8] Andegaviæ,[9] et aliarum multarum terrarum dominus, cum ducentis .XL. navibus; and he came on shore at Port-Lairge, and took the hostages of Mumha; and he came afterwards to Ath-cliath, and took the hostages of Laighen, and of the men of Midhe, and the Ui-Briuin, and Oirghi-alla, and Uladh.   Petrus, bishop of the Ui-Maine of Con-nacht, a pious monk, and a man of authority, was drowned in the Sinuinn on the 6th of the kalends of January.   A

some other entry intended to be copied has been omitted by the scribe.

[4] *Fire.*   The names of only two are given, and these belonging to a different territory.   There is probably some corruption of the text.

[5] *Angliæ.*   anʒlie, MS.

[6] *Normanniæ.*   nopmanie, MS.

[7] *Aquitaniæ.*   aquitanie, MS.

[8] *Comes.*   comepp, MS.

[9] *Andegaviæ.*   anvegaine, MS.

T.

Ⲥⲣⲉⲁⲥ̆ móⲣ la Maᵹnuⲣ mac Ⲃⲟⲓⲛⲛⲣⲗⲉⲓⲃⲉ, ᵹo nⲓⲗⲧⲁⲓⲃ
ⲓⲗⲉ, a ccúⲓl an ⲧ̇ⲩⲁⲓⲣⲥⲉⲓⲣⲧ, ᵹo ⲣⲟ aⲓⲣᵹⲣⲉⲇ Cúl ⲣⲁⲧ̆ⲁⲓⲛ
ocⲩⲣ cⲉⲁⲗⲗⲁ ⲟⲓⲗⲉ, ᵹo ⲣⲩᵹⲣⲁⲇ ⲩⲁⲧ̆ⲁⲇ ⲃⲉᵹ ⲇⲟ Cⲓⲛⲉⲗ
Ⲉⲟᵹ̆ⲁⲓⲛ ⲣⲟⲣⲣⲁ ⲩⲙ Conchoⲃⲁⲣ .ⲏ. Cⲁⲧ̆ⲁⲓⲛ, ocⲩⲣ ⲧⲩᵹⲣⲁⲇ
clⲓⲁⲧⲏⲁⲇ̆, ocⲩⲣ ⲣⲟ ⲙⲁⲣⲃⲣⲁⲇ ⲣⲉⲣ aⲣ .ⲭⲭ. ⲉⲧⲓⲣ ⲧⲁⲟⲓⲣⲉⲥ̆ⲁⲓⲃ,
ocⲩⲣ ⲙⲁⲥⲁ ⲧⲟⲓⲣⲉⲥ̆, ocⲩⲣ ⲣⲟⲥ̆ⲁⲓⲃⲉ ⲉⲓⲗⲉ ⲙⲁⲓⲗⲗⲉ ⲣⲣⲓⲩ; ocⲩⲣ
ⲣⲟ ᵹoⲛⲁⲇ̆ Maᵹnⲩⲣ ⲣⲉⲓⲛ, ocⲩⲣ an Maᵹnⲩⲣ ⲣⲓⲛ ⲇⲁⲛ ⲇⲟ
ⲙⲁⲣⲃⲁⲇ̆ ᵹⲁⲓⲣⲓⲇ ⲓⲁⲣ ⲣⲉⲓⲛ ⲇⲟ Ⲃⲟⲓⲛⲛⲣⲗⲉⲓⲃⲉ, .ⲓ. ⲇⲁ ⲇⲉⲣⲃⲣⲁⲧⲏⲁⲓⲣ
ⲣⲉⲓⲛ, ocⲩⲣ ⲇⲟ Ᵹⲓⲟⲗⲗⲁ Ⲁⲟⲛᵹⲩⲣⲁ ⲙⲁⲥ Ᵹⲓⲟⲗⲗⲁ ⲉⲁⲣⲣⲩⲓⲥ,
.ⲓ. ⲇⲟ ⲣⲉⲁⲥ̆ⲧⲁⲓⲣⲉ Monⲁⲓᵹ̆ an Ⲃⲩⲓⲛ, ⲓⲁⲣ noⲗⲥⲁⲓⲃ ⲙⲟⲣⲁⲓⲃ
ⲓⲟⲙⲇⲁⲓⲃ ⲇⲟ ⲇⲉⲛⲁⲙ̇ ⲇⲟ, .ⲓ. ⲓⲁⲣ ⲗⲉⲥⲁⲇ̆ a ⲙⲛⲁ ⲣⲟⲣⲧⲁ ⲣⲉⲓⲛ,
ocⲩⲣ ⲓⲁⲣ ⲙⲃⲣⲉⲓⲧ̆ a ⲙⲛⲁ o a ⲟⲓⲇⲉ, .ⲓ. o Coⲓⲙⲙⲩⲓᵹⲉ .ⲏ.
Ⲫⲗⲟⲓⲛⲛ, ocⲩⲣ ⲣⲓ́ aᵹ á ⲇⲉⲣⲃⲣⲁⲧⲏⲁⲓⲣ ⲣⲉⲓⲛ aⲣⲧⲩⲣ, .ⲓ. aᵹ
Ⲁⲟⲇ̆; ⲓⲁⲣ ⲧⲧⲁⲃⲁⲓⲣⲧ ⲉⲓⲥⲓⲛ ⲇⲟ ⲣⲟⲣ ⲙⲛⲁⲟⲓ a ⲇⲉⲣⲃⲣⲁⲧⲏⲁⲣ
ⲉⲓⲗⲉ, .ⲓ. Ⲉⲟⲥ̆ⲁⲇⲁ; ⲓⲁⲣ ⲣⲁⲣⲩᵹⲁⲇ̆ cloⲥ ocⲩⲣ ⲃⲁⲥ̆ⲁⲗⲗ, cⲗⲉⲓⲣⲉⲥ̆
ocⲩⲣ cⲉⲁⲗⲗⲁ.

Ⲕⲧ. Ⲉⲛⲁⲓⲣ .ⲩⲓⲓ. ⲣ.; ⲗ. ⲓⲓ. Ⲃⲁ́ ⲃⲗⲓⲁⲇⲁⲓⲛ .ⲗⲭⲭ. aⲣ cⲉⲇ aⲣ
ⲙⲓⲗⲉ aⲓⲣ ⲓⲛ Ⲧⲓᵹⲉⲣⲛⲁ. Ⲣⲓ́ Ⲥⲁⲭⲣⲁⲛ ⲇⲟ ⲇ̆ⲩⲗ a ⲏⲈⲣⲓⲛⲛ ⲇⲓⲁ
Ⲃⲟⲙⲛⲁⲓᵹ Cⲁ́ⲥⲥ, ⲓⲁⲣ cⲉⲗⲉⲃ̆ⲣⲁⲇ aⲓⲣⲣⲣⲓⲛⲛ. Ⲧⲓᵹⲉⲣⲛⲁⲛ Ⲟ
Ⲣⲩⲁⲓⲣⲥ, ⲣⲓ Ⲃⲣⲉⲓⲣⲛⲉ ocⲩⲣ Conⲙⲁⲓⲥⲛⲉ, ocⲩⲣ ⲣⲉⲣ cⲩⲙⲁⲥⲏⲧⲁ
ⲙⲟⲓⲣ ⲣⲣⲓ ⲣⲉ́ ⲣ̇oⲇⲁ, ⲇⲟ ⲙⲁⲣⲃⲁⲇ ⲇⲟ Ⲥⲁⲭⲁⲛⲩⲓⲃ cⲉⲇⲛⲁ, ocⲩⲣ
Ⲃⲟⲙⲛⲁⲗⲗ ⲙⲁⲥ Ⲁⲛⲛⲁⲇ ⲇⲓⲁ cⲉⲛⲉⲗ ⲣⲉⲓⲛ ⲙⲁⲓⲗⲗⲉ ⲣⲣⲓⲩ. Ⲁ
ⲇⲓⲥⲉⲛⲇⲁⲇ ⲇⲁⲛⲁ ⲇⲟⲓⲃ, ocⲩⲣ a cⲉⲛⲇ ocⲩⲣ a coⲣⲣ ⲇⲟ ⲃⲣⲉⲧ̆
co ⲇⲟⲥ̆ⲣⲁⲓⲃ co ⲏⲀⲧ̆ⲏ cⲗⲓⲁⲧⲏ. Ⲁⲛ cⲉⲛⲇ ⲇⲟ ⲧⲟⲥⲃⲁⲓⲗ ⲣⲟⲣ
ⲇⲟⲣⲩⲣ ⲓⲛ ⲇⲩⲓⲛⲉ ⲓⲛⲁ ⲣⲉⲁⲧⲏⲇⲉⲣⲥⲥ ⲧⲣⲓⲁᵹ̆ ⲇⲟ Ᵹⲁⲓⲇⲉⲗⲁⲓⲃ.
Ⲁⲛ coⲣⲣ, ⲇⲟⲛⲟ, ⲇⲟ cⲣoⲥⲏⲁⲇ ocⲩⲣ a ⲥ̆oⲣⲣ ⲣⲩⲁⲣ. Maⲓⲇⲙ
ⲣⲟⲣ Cⲉⲛⲉⲗ nⲈoᵹⲁⲓⲛ [ⲗⲁ] .ⲏ. Maoⲗⲇⲟⲣⲁⲓⲇ̆ ocⲩⲣ ⲗⲁ Cⲉⲛⲉⲗ
Conⲁⲓⲗⲗ, ocⲩⲣ aⲣ lⲁⲛ ⲙⲟⲣ ⲇⲟ cⲩⲓⲣ ⲣⲟⲣⲣⲁ; ⲓ ⲙⲓⲣⲃⲁⲓⲗ,
ⲧⲣⲁ, ⲇⲟ ⲛⲁoⲙⲁⲓⲃ an Coⲓⲙⲇⲉⲇⲏ a ⲛⲓ́ ⲣⲓⲛ, .ⲓ. ⲇⲟ Ⲫⲁⲧⲣⲁⲓⲥ

---

[1] *Son.* Roderick O'Flaherty has written "O Ⲃⲩⲛ̄ⲣⲗⲉⲓⲃⲉ" in the margin, to signify that Maghnus was the grandson of Donnsleibhe; i.e. of the Donnsleibhe O'hEochadha (or Donlevy O'Hoey), who is stated by the Four Masters, under the year 1094, to have been slain by the king of Ailech.

[2] *Donnsleibhe.* The note "Ⲃⲟⲛⲛⲣⲗⲉⲓⲃⲉ ⲇⲟ ᵹⲁⲃ̆ⲁⲓⲗ ⲣⲓᵹⲉ ⲇⲁ ⲉⲓⲣ,"

"Donnsleibhe assumes kingship after him," has been written in the margin by the original hand; as also the word ⲗⲟⲣⲧⲁⲛⲉⲥⲏⲧ, "lust."

[3] *Bachalls;* i.e. croziers, or Pastoral staves. The word ⲃⲁⲥ̆ⲁⲗⲗ is of course a loan from the Lat. baculus.

[4] *King of the Saxons.* Henry II. of England.

[5] *Saints of the Lord.* The clause

great preying expedition by Maghnus, son[1] of Donnsleibhe, with all the Ulidians, into Cuil-an-tuaisceirt, when they plundered Cul-rathain and other churches; but a small party of the Cenel-Eoghain, with Conchobhar Ua Cathain, overtook them, and gave *them* battle, and killed twenty-two persons, between chieftains and sons of chieftains, and many others along with them; and Maghnus himself was wounded; and this Maghnus, moreover, was slain soon after by Donnsleibhe,[2] i.e. his own brother, and by Gilla-Aenghusa, son of Gilla-Espuic, viz.:—the rector of Monach-an-Dúin, after he had committed many great crimes; i.e. after abandoning his own married wife, and after carrying off the wife of his tutor, i.e. Cumhuighe Ua Floinn, (and she *had been possessed* by his own brother, Aedh, at first); after having offered violence to the wife of his other brother, i.e. Eochaidh; after profaning bells and bachalls,[3] clerics and churches.

A.D.
——
[1171.]

The kalends of January on the 7th feria, the 2nd of the moon; the age of the Lord seventy-two years, and a hundred, and a thousand. The king of the Saxons[4] departed from Erinn on Easter Sunday, after the celebration of mass. Tighernan O'Ruairc, king of Breifne and Conmaicne, and a man of great power for a long time, was slain by Saxons, truly; and Domhnall, son of Annad of his (*Tighernan's*) own tribe, *was* along with them. He was also beheaded by them, and his head and body were ignominiously carried to Ath-cliath. The head was placed over the door of the fortress, as a miserable spectacle for the Gaeidhel; the body was suspended, moreover, with his feet upwards. A victory *was gained* over the Cenel-Eoghain, [by] O'Maeldoraidh and the Cenel-Conaill, and a great slaughter was inflicted on them. This event was, indeed, as a miracle on the part of the saints of the Lord,[5] viz.:—

[1172.]

"ı mıɼbaıl, τɼα, ɒo naomaıḃ an Coımɒeɒh α ní ɼın" ("i mirbail, tra, do naomaibh an Coimdedh a ni | sin"), literally rendered, would read "as a miracle, indeed, for the saints of the Lord, this thing."

ocur ᴅo Colum Cille, ocur ᴅona naomaiḃ aircena ir a
cealla ro millric. Lán cuaircᴄ·cóigiᴅ Connachc, an
cecramaᴅ reachc, la gillamoliac comarba Pacraic,
.i. la primraᴅ Eirenn, co hCCrᴅ Macha. ᴅomnall O
Fergail, coireć Conmaicne, ᴅo marbaᴅ la muincer righ
Saxan. gilla CCoᴅa, erpuc Corcaighe, rer lán ᴅo rach
ᴅe, in bona reneccuce quieuic.

ĸᴄ. Enair ii. r.; L. xiii.; cri bliaᴅna reachcmaᴅa ar ceᴅ
ar mile air in Tigerna. Muireᴅach O Cobchaigh, erpuc
ᴅoire ocur Raca ḃoᴄ, ocur cuaircerc Erenn uile, an
mac óiᵹe, ocur an leᵹ loᵹmar, ocur an ᵹem ᵹloine, ocur
an réᴅla roluria, ocur cirᴅe cairceᴅa na heᵹna, ocur
craoḃ cnuarraiᵹ na cánóine, iar cióᴅnacul ḃiᵭ ocur
éᴅaiᵹ ᴅo ḃochcaiḃ, iar nᴅail il ṁaoine ᴅéiᵹriḃ, iar
mbuaᴅ ᵹcrabaᴅ ocur oilicri, ocur aicriᵹe, ro ṗáiᴅ a
ᵹripaᴅ ᴅocum nime a nᴅuiḃ reiᵹler Coluim Cille a
nᴅoire, in quarca iᴅ Febra, in reaca reria. ᴅo ronaᴅ
mirbuile mora ir in aᵹhaiᴅ aᴅbaᴄ, .i. an aᵹhaiᴅ ᴅo
roillriuᵹhaᴅ óca iarmeirᵹe co ᵹairm an ćailiᵹ, ocur
in calaṁ uile ror larraᴅ, ocur caor ṁór ćeiniᴅ ᴅo
eirᵹe ór an mbaile, ocur a cochc roirrᴅer, ocur eirᵹe
ᴅo ćáᴄ uile, inᴅar leo robe an lá acu ; ocur ro ḃói
aṁlaiᴅ rin co himeal in aieoir inᴅar leo. Creć ṁór la
hCCoᴅ mac CConᵹura, ocur la clann CCoᴅa, co ro airᵹrec
crian mor ; ocur ro marbaᴅ an rer rin a ᵹcinn cri
míor iar narᵹuin CCirᴅ Macha ᴅó.

---

1 *Visitation.* Cuaircᴄ· This word,
which literally means *circuit*, is applied not alone to the circuit, or visitation, but also, as in the present case, to
the fees obtained during the visitation.

2 *Gillamoliag.* gillamoliac (gil-
lamoliac), MS. The name is written
Gilla-Mac-Liag ("servant of Mac
Liag"), in the Annals of the Four
Masters (ad eund. an.), and in the lists
of abbots of Armagh published in the
Rev. Dr. Todd's *St. Patrick,* pp. 179,

182. Perhaps the name gillamoliag
is but a mistranscription of gillamc-
liag, although the form Gillamoliag
appears also under the years 1174,
1175.

3 *Primate.* Incorrectly written
primraᴅ in the MS. But prim-
raiᴅ (primfaidh) properly means
"chief prophet," being comp. of
prim=primus, and raiᴅ=vates.

4 *King of the Saxons*; i.e. the
King of England, (Henry II).

of Patrick, and Colum-Cille, and the other saints whose
churches they had spoiled. The full visitation[1] of the
province of Connacht *was brought*, for the fourth time,
by Gillamoliag,[2] comarb of Patrick, i.e. the primate[3] of
Erinn, to Ard-Macha. Domhnall O'Ferghail, chief of
Conmaicne, was slain by the people of the king of the
Saxons.[4] Gilla-Aedha, bishop of Corcach, a man full of
the grace of God, in bona senectute quievit.

The kalends of January on the 2nd feria, the 13th of
the moon; the age of the Lord seventy-three years, and a
hundred, and a thousand. Muiredhach O'Cobhthaigh,
bishop of Doire and Rath-both, and of all the north of
Erinn; the son of chastity, and the precious stone, and the
bright gem, and the brilliant star, and a treasury of
wisdom, and a fruitful branch of the canon; after having
bestowed food and clothes upon the poor; after having
distributed numerous gifts to poets; after the triumph
of devotion, and pilgrimage, and penitence—resigned his
spirit to heaven in the Dubh-regles[5] of Colum-Cille in
Doire, on the 4th of the ides of February, in sexta feria.
Great miracles were wrought in the night on which he
died, viz.:—the night was illumined from nocturns until
cock-crow, and the ground was all in flames; and a large
mass of fire ascended over the town, and proceeded
towards the south-east; and all persons arose *from their
beds*, imagining that it was day; and it was thus[6] as far
as the horizon,[7] they thought. A great depredation *was
committed* by Aedh Mac Aenghusa and the Clann-Aedha,
and they plundered Trian-mór;[8] and this man was killed
before the end of three months after he had plundered
Ard-Macha.

---

[5] *Dubh-regles.* By "Dubh-regles"
is meant "black-regles," or "black
abbey-church."

[6] *Thus;* i.e. "the air was illumined."

[7] *Horizon.* co himeal in aieoir

(co himeal in aieoir); lit. "to the border of the air."

[8] *Trian-mór.* Lit. "the great
third;" a division of Ard-Macha, or
Armagh. See note [6], p. 67, *supra*.

ʞt. εnαιρ .ıııı. ρ.; ι. xx.ıııı.; ceıτρı bιıαɒnα ocuγ
ρeacнτmoɒαɒ αρ ceɒ, αρ mıιe, αιρ ın Τıʒeρnα. Pιann
O Ʒoρmaın, αıρɒ ρeριeıʒınn Αıρɒı Mαсα ocuγ Cρenn
uıιe, γeρ eoιας comαρταmuıι ıγ ın eʒnα Ɒıαɒα ocuγ
ɒomαnɒα, ıaρ mbeıτ bιıαɒaın αρ γıcıτ α bʄρanʒcaıb
ocuγ α Sαсραnαıb αʒ ʄoʒιuım, ocuγ γıce bιıαɒaın αʒ
ʄoιιαmnuʒ γʒoι nCρenn, αɒbατ co γıταmaıι α .xııı. ʞt.
[Αρριι], ɒıα Ceɒαoın ρıα ʒCαıρc, .ιxx. αeτατıγ γuαe
αnno. Mαoιρατραıc O Dαnáın, eγρuıc Conneρe ocuγ
Ɒáι nΑραıɒe, γeρ αıρmıɒneτ ιán ɒo noıme, ocuγ ɒo
τennγα, ocuγ ɒo ʒιoıñe τρıɒe, ɒhéc co ιαn ʄeacнτnαch α
nı Coιuım Cıιιe, ıaρ ρenταıʒ τoʒhαıɒe. Ʒıoιιαmoιıαʒ
mαc Ruαıɒρı, comαρbα Pατραıc, αıρɒeρuıc ocuγ
ρρımʄαıɒ Αıρɒ Mαcha ocuγ Cρenn uıιe, mαc óıʒe ιαn
ɒo ʒιoıne τρıɒe, ocuγ ɒo γıταmια, ɒo éʒ co ʄeacнτnach α
.ıı. ʞt. Αρριι, ɒıα Ceɒaın ıaρ Cαıρcc, ıγγın ρeacнτmαɒ
bιıαɒaın .ιxxx.ατ α αıρı, ocuγ ıaρ mbeτ .uıı.mbιıαɒnα
.xxx. γαn αıρɒeρuıcoıτ; eτ ρo bαı αn γeρ uαραι ρın
.uı. bιıαɒnα .x. co ιαn onóρach α nαbɒaıne Coιuım Cıιιe
α nɒoıρe, ρıα comαρbuγ Pατραıc. Ʒıιιαmocαıbɒeo, αb
mαınıγτρeτ Pεταıρ ocuγ Poıι α nΑρɒ Mαcha, moʒ
τρeʄαıρ ταıρıγı ɒon Coımɒıch, ɒo éc .ıı. ʞt. Αρριι,
.ιxx.ατ αeτατıγ γuαe.

ʞt. Iαnαıρ .ıııı. ρ.; ι. u. Cuıc bιıαɒnα .ιxx. αρ ceɒ
αρ mıιe, αıρ ın Τıʒeρnα. Fιαıτhbeρταch O Dρoιταn,
comαρbα Coιuım Cıιιe, τuıρ eccnα ocuγ eınıʒ, γeρ
ɒıα τuʒαταρ cιeıρıʒ Cρenn cατhαıρ eγbuıc αρ eccnα
ocuγ αρ α γeʄuρ, ocuγ ɒıα ταρccuρ comαρbuγ Iαe,
ɒo écc co ρeacнτnach ıaρ τρebιoıτ τoʒαıɒe α nɒuıῆ

---

1 *Peacefully.* ɒo ρıταmaıι (do
sithamail), MS.; apparently a mistake
for co ρıταmaıι (co sithamail), as
in the Ann. Ult.

2 [*Of April*]. Easter Sunday falling on the 24th of March in the year
1174, the Wednesday preceding it

coincided with the 20th of March, or
13th of the kalends of April; which is
also the date in the Annals of Ulster.

3 *Ætatis suæ.* eτατıρ γuαe, MS.

4 *Gillamoliag.* "Gillamacliag" in
the Four Mast. See note 2, p. 148,
supra.

A.D.

[1174.]

The kalends of January on the 3rd feria, the 24th of the moon; the age of the Lord seventy-four years, and a hundred, and a thousand. Flann O'Gormain, chief lector of Ard-Macha, and of all Erinn, a learned, observant man in the Divine and worldly wisdom—after having been twenty-one years learning in France and in Saxon-land, and twenty years governing the schools of Erinn—died peacefully[1] on the 13th of the kalends [of April],[2] the Wednesday before Easter, .lxx. ætatis suæ[3] anno. Maelpatraic O'Banáin, bishop of Condere and Dal-Araidhe, a venerable man full of sanctity, and of meekness, and of purity of heart, died full happily in Hi-Coluim-Cille, after a choice old age. Gillamoliag,[4] son of Ruaidhri, comarb of Patrick, archbishop and primate[5] of Ard-Macha, and of all Erinn, a son of chastity, full of purity of heart, and of meekness, died happily on the 6th of the kalends of April, the Wednesday after Easter, in the 87th year of his age, and after having been thirty-seven years in the archiepiscopate; and this same illustrious man had been sixteen years very honourably in the abbacy[6] of Coluim-Cille, at Doire, before *he obtained* the comarbship of Patrick. Gillamochaibheo, abbot of the monastery of Peter and Paul at Ard-Macha, a diligent, faithful servant of the Lord, died on the 2nd of the kalends of April, in the 70th *year* ætatis suæ.[3]

[1175.]

The kalends of January on the 4th feria, the 5th of the moon; the age of the Lord seventy-five years, and a hundred, and a thousand. Flaithbhertach O'Brolchain, comarb of Colum-Cille, tower of wisdom and honour; a man to whom the clerics of Erinn gave a bishop's chair for his wisdom and goodness, and to whom the comarbship of Hi had been presented, died happily, after

---

[5] *Primate.* ᵱᴘiṁᵱaiᴅ (primh-fhaid); lit. "chief prophet." See note [3], p. 148.

[6] *In the abbacy.* i naḃᴅaine; i.e. in the abbacy, or government of the monastery, founded by Colum-Cille.

ρecleρ Coluim Cille.   ჳillamoliac .h. bρanán vo
oiρneჃ ina inavh i comaρbuρ Coluim Cille.   Maivm
aρ Cenel Enva ρia neჃmaρcach O Cathain, ocuρ
ρia Niall O nჳaiρmleჃaich, ocuρ áρ móρ vo chuρ
ρoρρa.

ჸct. ianaiρ .u. ρ.; l. xiii.   Se bliavna ρeachtṁovav
aρ cev aρ mile aiρ in Tiჳeρna.   Saxuin vinnaρbav
vo Vomnall O bρiain a Luimnech, tρé ρoρbaiρi vo
Ⴣenam ρoρρa.   Inჳen ρí Oiρჳall, .i. benmiჃe ინჳen
Vonnchava i Ceρbaill, ben ConmuiჃe i [f]lainv, ρiჳan
.h. Tuiρtρi ocuρ ρeρ li, vo éc.   Inჳen Ruaivρi i
Concobaiρ, .i. ben flaჃbeρtaჳ hi MaoilvoraiჃ, vo
maρbav vo macuib .h. Caiρeallán.   ρabuρ ocuρ
Cenantuρ vρaρρuჳav vo ჳallaib, ocuρ vo U bρuin.
Luჳmaჳ vρaρρuჳav vona Saჳρanaib.   Caiρlén ჳall ocuρ
Cenantuρ aჳ a nvenum.   αnt iaρla Saჳρanach vo
éჳ a nαჃ cliaჃ vo bainne aillρe ρo ჳaჃ ρoρ a Ⴀoiρ,
tρi ṁiρჃuilib bριჃve ocuρ Coluim Cille, ocuρ na naom
áιρჃena iρa cealla ρo ṁill.   Caiρlén Slaine aρaiჃe
Ricarov flémenn cona ρúaiჳ, aρρ a ρaჃuρ aჳ millev
Oiρჳall ocuρ .h. mbρuin ocuρ ρeρ MiჃe, vo ṁillev
la Maolρeclainn mac mic LaჃlainN, la ρi Cenél
nEoჳain, ocuρ la hOiρჳialla, vú inaρ maρbav cev nó
niρa ṁó vo ჳalloib, cenmoჃáჃ mna ocuρ leinim, ocuρ
eiჃ an caiρléin, cona teρno vuine a mbethaiv aρρ an
ჳcaiρlen; ocuρ ρo ρaρρaჳev tρí caiρleán a MiჃe
aρ na ṁaρach aρ oṁan Ceneoil Eoჳain, .i. caiρlén
Cenannρa, ocuρ caiρlén Calatρuim, ocuρ caiρlén Vaiρe
ρatρaic.   Cuṁuიჳe O floinn, ρí .h. Tuiρtρi ocuρ ρeρ

---

1 *Dubh - regles*; i.e. "the black
abbey church."

2 *Gillamoliac.*   This name is more
usually written Gilla-Mac-Ling, which
is Latinized *Gelasius.*   See Reeves's
Adamnan, p. 403, and note 8, p. 148,
supra.

3 *Benmidhe;* lit. "the woman of
Midhe (or Meath)."

4 *Gall.*   There is probably some
mistake in the text, as there is no
trace of any "castle of Gall."   The
expression aჳ a nvenum ; lit. "at
their making," implies that more than

choice suffering, in the Dubh-regles[1] of Colum-Cille. Gillamoliac[2] O'Branain was ordained in his place, in the comarbship of Colum-Cille. A victory was gained over the Cenel-Enna, by Echmarcach O'Cathain and Niall O'Gairmledhaigh, and a great slaughter was inflicted on them.

The kalends of January on the 5th feria, the 16th of the moon, the age of the Lord seventy-six years, and a hundred, and a thousand. The Saxons were expelled from Luimnech by Domhnall O'Briain, by laying siege to them. The daughter of the king of Oirghiall, i.e. Benmidhe,[3] daughter of Donnchadh O'Cerbhaill, wife of Cumhuighe O'[F]loinn, queen of Ui-Tuirtre and Feara-Lí, died. The daughter of Ruaidhri O'Conchobhair, i.e. the wife of Flaithbhertach O'Maeldoraidh, was killed by the sons of O'Cairellain. Fabhar and Cenannus were wasted by the Foreigners, and by the Ui-Briuin. Lughmhagh was wasted by the Saxons. The castles of Gall[4] and Cenannus in process of construction. The Saxon Earl[5] died in Ath-cliath of an ulcer which attacked his foot, through the miracles of Brighid and Colum-Cille, and the other saints whose churches he had spoiled. The castle of Slane, in which was Richard Fleming with his forces, from which they were ravaging Oirghiall, and Ui-Briuin, and Feara-Midhe, was spoiled by Maelsechlainn, son of Mac Lachlainn, king of Cenel-Eoghain, and by the Oirghialla; on which occasion a hundred, or more, of the Foreigners were slain, besides the women, and children, and horses of the castle; so that no man escaped alive from the castle; and three castles in Midhe were deserted on the morrow, through fear of the Cenel-Eoghain, viz.:— the castle of Cenannus, and the castle of Calatruim, and the castle of Daire-Patraic. Cumhuighe O'Floinn, king

one castle is referred to; but the entry in Ann. Ult. and the Four Mast. is caiṗlen ᵹaᄔ ᵹá ᵭenaᵯ ı cCenannuᵲ; i.e. "a castle of the foreigners in process of construction at Cenannus (Kells)," which is doubtless the correct reading.

[5] *Saxon Earl*; i.e. Strongbow.

Lí ocup Dal Apaide, do mapbad do Coinṁide, .i. da
bpaṫaip péin, ocup do pepuiḃ Lí.

Ict. Enaip .uii. p. ; L. xxiii. Seacht mbliadna peacht-
mada ap ced ap mile aip in Ṫizepna. Dún da
Leṫżlaip do milled do tSeon do Cúippi ocup dona
pidepuiḃ tancadap maille ppip, ocup caiplén do denam
dóiḃ ann app a tucpad maiḋm pá dó pop Ullzoiḃ,
ocup maiḋm pop Cenél nEożain ocup pop Oipżiallaiḃ,
dú nap mapbad Conchobap O Caipellén, .i. toipech
Clainni Diapmada, ocup in po mapbad maiti iomḋa eli.
Do pad, dana, Conchobap O Caipellán maiḋm pop O
Maoldopaid ocup pop čenél Conaill, dú in po mapbad
áp čenél Enna im mac hi Seppuż, ocup im maiṫib
iomḋa eli aipchena. Milid Żócan, cona pidepiḃ, do
bpeiṫ do Muipceptach mac Ruaidpi hi Cončobaip co
Rop Comáin, do milled Connacht, ap ulca pé naṫaip.
Ro loipced umoppo, Connachta po cedóip. Tuaim,
dono, ocup cella an tipe do milled ap ulca pip na
Żallaiḃ, ocup tucpat maiḋm popp na Żallaiḃ, .i.
Ruaidpi O Conchobaip co bpepuiḃ Connacht maille
pip; ocup po dičuippet ap eicin app an tip amač iad.
Ro ḋall, dono, Ruaidpi O Conchobaip a mac iappin a
ndiżail an tupuip pin. Oeḋ O Neill, .i. pí Ceneoil
Eożain pe haṫaid, ocup píḋaṁna Epenn uile, do
mapbad le Maolpeclainn ṁáz Lačlainn, ocup la
hApożal ṁáz Lačlainn. Apożal pein, dono, do ṁapbad do Neill aza mapbad anpein. An Timpanach .h.

<hr/>

[1] *Muirchertach.* The name Murchadh (Murrough), as written in the
Annals of the Four Mast. and of
Ulster, and in the Dublin Annals of Inisfallen, appears to be the correct form.

[2] *Burned.* There is apparently
some confusion between this entry
and the next, the events of both of
which form only one entry in the
Annals of Ulster and of the Four Masters. The record in the latter chronicle
runs thus:—" po loippced donā

Connaċtaiż po cedóip Tuaim da
żualann ocup cealla an tipe
aipčena, ap na haippdoíp Żoill
inntiḃ," i.e. "The Connachtmen,
however, burned Tuaim-da-ghualann
(Tuam) and the other churches of
the country, in order that Foreigners
should not rest in them." The Dublin Annals of Inisfallen, compiled
by the late Dr. O'Brien, Titular
Bishop of Cloyne, and his co-labourer
the Abbé Conry, represent the English

of Ui-Tuirtre, and Feara-Lí, and Dal-Araidhe, was killed
by Cumhidhe, i.e. his own brother, and by the Feara-Lí.

The kalends of January on the 7th feria, the 27th of
the moon; the age of the Lord seventy-seven years, and
a hundred, and a thousand.   Dun-da-lethghlais was
spoiled by John de Curci and the knights who came
along with him; and they built a castle there, from which
they gained a victory twice over the Ulidians, and a
victory over the Cenel-Eoghain and over the Oirghialla,
in which Conchobhar O'Cairellain, i.e. the chief of Clann-
Diarmada, was slain; and in which many other nobles
were slain.   Conchobhar O'Cairellain, indeed, gained a victory over O'Maeldoraidh and the Cenel-Conaill, in which
a great number of the Cenel-Enna were slain, along with
the son of O'Serrigh, and many other chieftains likewise.
Milo de Cogan, with his knights, was brought by Muirchertach,[1] son of Ruaidhri O'Conchobhair, to Ros-Comain,
to spoil Connacht, through hatred towards his father.
Connacht, truly, was thereupon burned.[2]   Tuam, moreover, and the churches of the country, were destroyed,
through hatred towards the Foreigners; and they, i.e.
Ruaidhri O'Conchobhair and the men of Connacht along
with him, gained a victory over the Foreigners, and
drove them by force out of the country.   Ruaidhri O'Conchobhair, moreover, blinded his son afterwards, in revenge
for this expedition.   Aedh O'Neill, i.e. king of Cenel-
Eoghain for a time, and royal heir of all Erinn, was slain
by Maelsechlainn Mac Lachlainn, and by Ardghal Mac
Lachlainn.   Ardghal himself, also, was slain by O'Neill
when he (O'Neill) was being killed there.   The Timpanach[3]

---

as having burned the territory of
Connacht in their progress.

[3] *Timpanach;* i.e. the tympanist.
The Irish would seem to have anciently
had a stringed musical instrument
called a ᴄɪmpαn, or tympanum.   In
the Book of Leinster (MS. Trin. Coll.,

Dublin, 12th cent.) one is referred to
having only three strings: ꝑeꝛ bec
ꝼꝛɪ ᴄhéᴄ ɪnα ᴄhɪmpαn (*fer bec tri
thét ina thimpan*), "a little man with
three strings in his timpan."   See H.
2. 18, T. C., D.; fol 206, b. 2.

Coɪппɪcéп, ollam ᴄuaɪꞃceɪꞃᴄ Єꞃeпп, ᴅo ṁaꞃbaᴅ ᴅo čeпél Conaɪll, cona mnaoɪ ocuꞃ cona ṁuɪппᴄeꞃ. Sluaɪʒeᴅ la Seon ᴅo Cúɪꞃꞃɪ ocuꞃ laꞃ na ꞃɪᴅeꞃɪḃ a п'Ꝺal ᴀꞃaɪᴅe, ᴅáꞃ ṁaꞃḃꞃaᴄ 'Ꝺomnall mac ṁɪc Caᴄuꞃaɪʒ, ꞃí 'Ꝺal ᴀꞃaɪᴅe. Táпɪc, ᴅono, Seon ᴅon ᴄuꞃuꞃ ceᴅna a пɪḃ Tuɪꞃᴄꞃɪ ocuꞃ a bꞃeꞃaɪḃ Lí, coꞃo loɪꞃc Cuṁuɪʒe O Floɪnn ᴀɪꞃꞃᴄeꞃ Maɪʒe ꞃeṁe, ocuꞃ co ꞃo loɪꞃc Cul ꞃaᴄaɪn, ocuꞃ cealla ɪṁᴅa elɪ.

Ɉcl. Єпaɪꞃ ɪ. ꞃ.; l. ɪx.; ochᴄ mblɪaᴅna .lxx. aꞃ ceᴅ aꞃ mɪle aɪꞃ ɪn Tɪʒeꞃna; céᴅ blɪaᴅaɪn noɪᴅecᴅa. Uɪlc ṁoꞃ ᴅo čenum á Cenel Móáɪn an ḃlɪaᴅaɪn ꞃɪn, .ɪ. muɪппᴄeꞃ 'Ꝺomnaɪll 1 ʒaɪꞃmleʒhaɪʒ ᴅo maꞃbaᴅ Concobaɪꞃ mɪc Conallaɪʒ 1 Luɪnɪč aꞃ láꞃ ᴄɪʒe 'Ꝺomnaɪll 1 ʒaɪꞃmleʒhaɪʒ ꞃeɪn, a meabaɪl, aꞃ comaɪꞃce aɪꞃčɪnᴅɪʒ na hЄꞃnaɪᴅe. ᴀᴄᴄóɪꞃꞃech ᴅo čenum ᴅo 'Ꝺomnall O ʒaɪꞃmleʒhaɪʒ, ocuꞃ Cenel Móaɪn ᴅo ᴄabaɪꞃᴄ ᴄoɪꞃꞃɪʒechᴄa ᴅo Ruaᴅꞃɪ O Flaɪᴄḃeꞃᴄaɪʒ. 'Ꝺomnall mac 'Ꝺomnaɪll 1 ʒaɪꞃmleʒhaɪʒ ᴅo maꞃbaᴅ a meabaɪl le claɪnn 1 Flaɪᴄḃeꞃᴄaɪʒ ocuꞃ le claɪnn n'Ꝺomnaɪll aɪꞃčena; ocuꞃ Tɪʒeꞃnan mac Raʒnaɪll mɪc 'Ꝺomnaɪll, ocuꞃ očᴄaꞃ laɪn ḃɪaᴄach ᴅo Cenél Móeɪn aꞃ aon ꞃú. ʒaoᴄ aᴅbaɪl ᴅo čoɪʒechᴄ ɪꞃɪn mblɪaᴅaɪn ꞃɪ, co ꞃo ᴄꞃaꞃcaɪꞃ ḃloɪḃ ṁoɪꞃ ᴅo čoɪllᴄɪb, ocuꞃ ᴅꞃɪḃbaᴅaɪḃ ocuꞃ ᴅo ꞃaɪlʒɪḃ ꞃa móꞃaɪḃ ꞃꞃɪ láꞃ, ocuꞃ co ꞃo ᴄꞃaꞃcaɪꞃ ꞃóꞃ ꞃe .xx. ꞃalaᴄ, uel paulo pluꞃ, a п'Ꝺoɪꞃe Coluɪm Cɪlle. 1ꞃ an mblɪaᴅaɪn ꞃɪn, ᴅono, ᴄaɪnɪc Seon ᴅo Cúɪꞃ[ꞃɪ] coꞃa ꞃɪᴅeꞃɪḃ co 'Ꝺún, aꞃ cꞃechaɪb co maᴄaɪꞃe Conaɪlle, co

---

[1] *He burned*; i.e. O'Floinn. The Annals of the Four Masters represent De Curci as the incendiary, which is more likely to be correct.

[2] *First year of nineteen*; i.e. the first year of the Cycle of 19.

[3] *Under the protection.* The meaning is, that when Conchobhar O'Luinigh, or Conor O'Looney, was slain, he was under the protection, or guarantee, of the Airchinnech (Herenach) of the

Ernaidhe, a church which gave name to the parish of Ernaidhe, now Urney, situated in the counties of Donegal and Tyrone, to the south of Lifford.

[4] *Was deposed.* The phrase "aᴄ-ᴄóɪꞃech ᴅo čenum ᴅo 'Ꝺomnall O ʒaɪꞃmleʒhaɪʒ," literally translated, would read "an ex-chieftain was made of Domhnall O'Gairm-leghaigh, (or Daniel O'Gormley)."

[5] *Biatachs.* The *Biatach* was an

O'Connicén, *chief* poet of the North of Erinn, was slain by the Cenel-Conaill, together with his wife and family. A hosting by John de Curci and the knights, into Dal-Araidhe, on which occasion they slew Domhnall, grandson of Cathusach, king of Dal-Araidhe. John went also, on the same expedition, into Ui-Tuirtre and Feara-Lí; but Cumhuighe O'Floinn burned Airther-maighe before him; and he burned[1] Cul-rathain, and many other churches.

A.D.
[1177.]

The kalends of January on the 1st feria, the 9th of the moon; the age of the Lord seventy-eight years, and a hundred, and a thousand; the first year of nineteen.[2] Great crimes were committed by the Cenel-Moain in this year, viz.:—the people of Domhnall O'Gairmleghaigh killed Conchobhar, son of Conallach O'Luinigh, in the middle of Domhnall O'Gairmleghaigh's own house, in treachery, *though he was* under the protection[3] of the airchinnech of the Ernaidhe. Domhnall O'Gairmleghaigh was deposed[4] from being chief, and the Cenel-Moain gave the chieftainship to Ruaidhri O'Flaithbhertaigh. Domhnall, son of Domhnall O'Gairmleghaigh was slain, in treachery, by the sons of O'Flaithbhertaigh and the other sons of Domhnall; and Tighernan, son of Raghnall, son of Domhnall, and eight full biatachs[5] of the Cenel-Moain, *were slain*, along with them. Very great wind came in this year, which prostrated large tracts of woods and forests, and huge trees; and it moreover prostrated six score large trees, vel paulo plus, in Doire-Choluim-Chille. It was in this year, also, that John de Curci, with his knights, came to[6] Dún, on a preying expedition to Machaire-Conaille, when they plundered several

[1178.]

---

extensive farmer who held his land subject to the condition of having to supply a certain amount of food (*biad*) to his lord, as well as to strangers and guests quartered on him by his chieftain. Instead of *lán biatach*, the Four Masters employ the term maithib (dat. pl. of maith, "good"), and conventionally signifying "nobles," or "gentlemen."

[6] *To.* co. The Annals of Ulster read "o" ("from"), which is more correct, as De Curci was at this time residing at *Dún*, or Downpatrick.

ro airgret muintera iomda, ocur co rabadar aiδce a
longpuirτ a nglinn Rige. Tanic dono Murchad O
Cerbaill, rí Oirgiall, ocur mac Duinnrlebi, .i. rí
Ulaδ, čuca an oiδce rin ; ocur tucrat telcaδ δó. Ro
meabad ror gallaib ocur ro cuired a nderg ár.
Tanic dona an Seon cedna ar crechaiδ a nDál
Araide, ocur a nUiδ Tuirtri. Tuc, dona, Cúmoige O
Flóinn, rí .h. Tuirtri ocur brer Li telcaδ δoiδ. Ro
moiδ, dono, an caτ rin ror galloiδ, ocur ro cuired a nár.

Kt. Enáir 11. r.; L. xx. Noi mbliadna reachtmada
ar ced, ar mile, air an Tigerna; .i. an dara bliadain
noiδegda, in trear bliadain ror birex. Siδ do δenum
do Donnchaδ .h. Caipellán, ocur do clainn Diarmada
uile, re Cenel Móien ocur re .h. nGairmleghaiδ, .i.
re hAmlaib mac mic Máien, .i. derbrathair mna
Donnchada 1 Caipellén, ar lár tempail Arda graδa,
rá mionnuiδ Domnaig moir ocur na hErnaide, ocur
Arda graδa. h. Gairmleghaiδ, dono, do δoiδechτ irin
ló ar na marach do gabáil tuilled rlána co teδ
Donnchada 1 Caipellán. Meabal ainbδial do δenum
ar lár an airechτa a ndopur τige 1 Caipellan, a
bδiaδnure a derbδrethar rein, .i. mna Donnchada, .i. é
rein ocur triar δá muinnter maille rir [do marbaδ].
Ard Maca do lorcad ex maiore parte, .i. na huile
regléra ocur na huile templa, cenmoδá regler Briδde,
ocur tempal na Ferta. Cealla τíre hEogain o τrleiδ
δuδ δer drolmugad tria δogad ocur tria δoδmataiδ an

---

1 *Gave him battle;* i.e. gave battle to
De Curci. The word τelcuδ, translated battle, literally means a " cast-
ing," or " hurling," being the infinit.
sub. of the verb τoilgim (do-oilg-
im), "I cast loose." or "hurl." In
the Annals of Ulster the word is
written in two different ways, τael-
cad and τailcaτ, both incorrect.

2 *Nineteen;* i.e. the Cycle of the
moon, or Cycle of 19.

3 *Domnach-Mór.* There are a great

many churches of this name in Ireland, but the church here meant was
that of Domhnach-mor-Maighe-Itha,
now Donaghmore, in the parish of
the same name, barony of Raphoe,
co. Donegal.

4 *Ernaidhe.* See note 3, p. 156.

5 *His;* i.e. Amhlaibh O'Gairmledhaigh's.

6 *Were slain.* The corresponding
words in the text, (do marbad), are
supplied from the Annals of Ulster.

families, and were for a night encamped in Glenn-ri͠ghe. Murchadh O'Cerbhaill, king of Oirghiall, and Mac Duinn-sleibhe, i.e. the king of Uladh, came to them, however, on that night, and gave him battle.[1] The Foreigners were defeated, and put to great slaughter. The same John went also on a preying expedition into Dal-Araidhe, and into Ui-Tuirtre. But Cumhuighe O'Floinn, king of Ui-Tuirtre and Feara-Lí, attacked them. This battle was, moreover, gained over the Foreigners, and they were put to slaughter.

The kalends of January on the 2nd feria, the 20th of the moon; the age of the Lord seventy-nine years, and a hundred, and a thousand, viz.:—the 2nd year of nine-teen;[2] the third year after a bissextile. Peace was made by Donnchadh O'Cairellain, and by all the Clann-Diarmada, with the Cenel-Moain, and with O'Gairmleghaigh, i.e. with Amhlaibh, grandson of Maen, i.e. the brother of the wife of Donnchadh O'Cairellain, in the middle of the church of Ard-sratha, before the reliquaries of Domh-nach-mór[3] and the Ernaidhe,[4] and Ard-sratha. O'Gairm-leghaigh, moreover, came on the day following to the house of Donnchadh O'Cairellain, to obtain additional guarantees. A wicked treachery was committed in the middle of the meeting, in the doorway of the house of O'Cairellain, in the presence of his[5] own sister, i.e. the wife of Donnchadh, viz.:—he himself, and three of his people along with him, [were slain].[6] Ard-Macha was burned ex majore parte, i.e. all the regleses, and all the churches, except Regles-Brighde[7] and Tempul-na-ferta.[8] The churches of Tir-Eoghain, from the mountain south-wards, were evacuated this year through war and distress.

The persons slain were, of course, O'Gairmleghaigh, or O'Gormley, and his companions.

[7] *Regles-Brighde;* i.e. the abbey-church of Brigid.

[8] *Tempul-na-ferta.* "The church of the graves (of the reliquaries)." The earliest church founded at Ar-magh. See Reeves's *Ancient Churches of Armagh* (Lusk, 1860), p. 7, sq.

bliaōain ɼi. ƵillaōomnaiƷ O Ɽoɼannáin, aiɼċinn-
neċ Aɼōa ɼɼaċa, eτ Moelmuiɼe mac ƵillacománI,
ɼeɼnaɼaō an baile ceōna, in Cɼιɼτο quieuɼɼunτ.
Cluana ocuɼ Aɼō ɼɼaċa, ocuɼ Domnaċ móɼ, ocuɼ an
Eɼnaiōe oɼolṁuƷaō o ɼeɼaιƀ ṁoiƷe hiċe.

|Ct. Enáiɼ .ιιι. ɼ.; l. ι. Oċτmaōa aɼ ceo aɼ mile
aoiɼ an ΤιƷeɼna. Ƶilla an Coimōheō .h. Caɼán,
comaɼba Ɽατɼaιc, oo éƷ. RaƷnall .h. Caiɼellán oo
maɼbaō oo ċenel Móéin a neineċ Coluim Cille, aɼ
láɼ Doiɼe. Macɼaιċ .h. DaiƷɼι, aiɼċinneċ [Doiɼe],
oo écc. Donnċaō .h. Caiɼellán oo ṁaɼbaō oo ċenél
Conaill, a noiƷuil a ṁeaƀla aɼ O nƷaiɼmleƷhaiƷ, ocuɼ
a neineċ Coluim Cille. Caċ na Conchobaɼ a Connaċτ, oáɼ ṁaɼƀuɼτaɼ Conċobaɼ MoenṁoiƷe Conchobaɼ .h. CeallaιƷ, .ι. ɼι .h. Maine, ocuɼ ΤaƀƷ a mac,
ocuɼ Diaɼmaιō .h. CeallaιƷ, ocuɼ maιċ .h. Maine uile,
a moiƷ Sɼuιƀe Ƨealáin a Ƨcínn Daiɼe na Ƨcaɼall.
MuιɼƷeɼ .h. heiōin oo maɼbaō. Domnall .h. Cin-
néιōιƷ, ɼι Uɼmuman, moɼτuuɼ eɼτ.

|Ct. Enaiɼ .u. ɼ.; l. xιι. bliaōain oċτmaōaō aɼ
ceō aɼ mile aiɼ an ΤιƷeɼna. Caċ moiƷe Diú͡Ƨƀa
ɼoɼ clainn ΤoiɼɼohealbaιƷ ṁóiɼ hι Conchobaiɼ, le
Ƒlaιċbeɼτaċ .h. Móeloɼaιō, ɼι ċenel Conaill, ocuɼ
iɼ oe Ƨoiɼτeɼ caċ na ɼíōaṁna, anoorċuιɼ bɼian
luιƷneċ ocuɼ MaƷnuɼ, ocuɼ τɼι mιc Aoōa mιc
ΤoiɼɼohealbaιƷ hι Conchobaiɼ, .ι. MaoilɼeċhLuinn
ocuɼ Muιɼeōaċ ocuɼ Muιɼceɼτaċ; ocuɼ Aoō mac

---

[1] *Cluana.* cluūa, MS. The name of
this church is written "Cluane" in the
Annals of Ulster. The church of Cluain
-I, or Clooney, in the parish of Clon-
dermot, co. Londonderry, (where there
are still some ruins), is apparently
meant.

[2] *Domhnach-mor.* See note [3], p. 158.

[3] *Ernaidhe.* See note [4], p. 156.

[4] *Gilla-an-Choimdedh.* This name
signifies "Servus Domini."

[5] *In defence.* ι neineċ. The word
neineċ has several meanings. It is
used to express "protection," "hospitality," and "honour." The sense
of the passage is that Raghnall
O'Cairellain was slain in revenge for
some offence committed by him against
the community of Doire (Derry),
originally founded by St. Colum
Cille.

[6] *Of Doire.* Doiɼe; om. in MS.,

Gilladomhnaigh O'Forannain, airchinnech of Ard-sratha, and Maelmuire, son of Gillacomain, vice-abbot of the same place, in Christo quieverunt. Cluana,[1] and Ard-sratha, and Domhnach-mór,[2] and the Ernaidhe[3] were emptied by the men of Magh-Itha.

The kalends of January on the 3rd feria, the first of the moon; the age of the Lord eighty years, and a hundred, and a thousand. Gilla-an-Choimdédh[4] O'Carán, comarb of Patrick, died. Raghnall O'Cairellain was slain by the Cenel-Moain, in defence[5] of Colum-Cille, in the middle of Doire. Macraith O'Daighri, airchinnech [of Doire],[6] died. Donnchadh O'Cairellain was killed by the Cenel-Conaill, in revenge of his treachery[7] towards O'Gairmleghaigh, and in defence of Colum-Cille. The battle of the Conchobhars, in Connacht, in which Conchobhar Maenmaighe killed Conchobhar O'Ceallaigh, i.e. the king of Ui-Maine, and his son Tadhg, and Diarmaid O'Ceallaigh, and all the nobles of Ui-Maine; at Magh-sruibhe-gealain, at the head of Daire-na-capall, *this battle was fought.* Muirghes O'hEidhin was slain. Domhnall O'Cennedigh, king of Ur-Mumha, mortuus est.

The kalends of January on the 5th feria, the 12th of the moon; the age of the Lord eighty-one years, and a hundred, and a thousand. The battle of Magh-Diughbha *was gained* over the sons of Toirdhelbhach Mór O'Conchobhair, by Flaithbhertach O'Maeldoraidh, king of Cenel-Conaill, (and of it is said "the battle of the royal heirs"); in which were slain Brian Luighnech,[8] and Maghnus;[9] and the three sons of Aedh, son of Toirdhelbhach O'Conchobhair, viz. :—Maelsechlainn, and Muiredhach, and Muirchertach; and Aedh, grandson of Aedh,

---

and supplied from the Annals of Ulster. The preceding word airchinnech is written twice in the MS.

[7] *His treachery.* As related under the year 1179.

[8] *Brian Luighnech.* Son of Turlough O'Conor, called Toirdhelbhach mór, or "the great."

[9] *Maghnus.* Another son of Turlough O'Conor.

M

mic Oeða mic Ruaiðri, rí iartair Connacht, ocur
Donnchað mac Briain hi Fallamain, et alii nobiler
et iġnobiler cum eir. Donnchað mac Domnaill
Miðiġ hi Conchobair ro tairrinġ Flaitbertach .h.
Moelдorað дo tornum críce Cairpri ðó feirin; ocur
rucað cuirp na riġraiðe rin iar ná noiġeð co Cluain
mic Nóir, a nothár liġe riġraiðe a rinnrer. Dunlainġ
.h. Caollaiġi, erpuc Leitġlinne, quieuit. Alaxandair
pápa in Críro quieuit. Tаðġ O Dálaiġ, ollam Erenn
ocur Alpan, in Críro quieuit. Sittric .h. Cuinn,
toirech muinteri Ġilláin, дo marbað дo mac Oeða
.h. Ferġail. Donnfleiðe O Ġадra mortuur ert.
Sloiġeð lá Domnall mac Aoða méc Laťlainn, ocur
le Cenél nEoġain Tealťa óc, a nUlltaið, ocur дo
Brireдоr cať ar Ultaið ocur ar Uíð Tuirtri, ocur
ar feraið Li, im Ruaiðri mac Duinnrlebi, ocur im
Coimmoiġe .h. Floinn. Tomaltach O Conchobair дo
ġaðail comarbuir Patraic, ocur conderna cuairt
Ceneoil Eoġain, ocur co тuc bennachtain.

Kt. Enair iii. f.; L. xxiii.; дa bliaдain ochtmoдa
ar ceд, ar mile, air in Tiġerna. Sloiġeð la Domnall
mac Laťlainn co Dún mbó a nDáil Ríatta, ocur cať
дo tabairt дóið дo ġalloib annrein; ocur maiðm ar
ťenel nEoġain, ocur Raġnall O Breirlén дo marbað
ann, ocur Ġilla Críst .h. Caťán, et alii multi, ocur
rórcéla Martain дo ðreť дo ġalloib leo. Aeð .h.
Caellaiġi, erpuc Airġiall, ocur cend canánach, quieuit.
Ġilla in Coimдeдh mac Inlertair .h. hAinliġe, тurrech
Ceneoil Dofра, mortuur ert. Domnall .h. hUallaťan,
airдerpuc Muman; Auġuртín .h. Sealbaiġ, erpuc
puirt Láirce, ocur .h. hAeða, erpuc Corcaiġe, mortui
runt. Miliд Ġocán ar nġaðáil дó riġe Corcaiġe ocur

<hr>

1 *Ruaidhri.* Ruaidhri O'Flaithbhertaigh, (or O'Flaherty).

² *Alii.* ali, MS.

³ *Eis.* erit, MS.

⁴ *Gospel of Martin.* A MS. copy
of the Gospels alleged to have belonged to St. Martin of Tours, and to
have been brought to Ireland by St.

son of Ruaidhri,[1] king of the West of Connacht; and Donnchadh, son of Brian O'Fallamhain, et alii[2] nobiles et ignobiles cum eis.[3] (Donnchadh, son of Domhnall Midhech O'Conchobhair, *it was* that brought Flaithbhertach O'Maeldoraidh, to defend the territory of Cairpre for himself). And the bodies of those nobles were conveyed, after their deaths, to Cluain-mic-Nois, *and interred* in the sepulchre of the nobles of their ancestors. Dunlaing O'Caellaighe, bishop of Leithghlinn, quievit. Alexander papa quievit in Christo. Tadhg O'Dalaigh, *chief* poet of Erinn and Alba, in Christo quievit. Sitric O'Cuinn, chieftain of Muinter-Gillcán, was slain by the son of Aedh O'Ferghail. Donnsleibhe O'Gadhra mortuus est. A hosting by Domhnall, son of Aedh Mac Lachlainn, and by the Cenel-Eoghan of Telach-óg, into Ulidia; and they gained a battle over the Ulidians, and over the Ui-Tuirtre, and the Feara-Lí, together with Ruaidhri Mac Duinn-sleibhe and Cumhuighe O'Floinn. Tomaltach O'Conchobhair assumed the comarbship of Patrick, and made a visitation of Cenel-Eoghain, and gave a blessing.

The kalends of January on the 6th feria, the 23rd of the moon; the age of the Lord eighty-two years, and a hundred, and a thousand. A hosting by Domhnall Mac Lachlainn to Dún-bó in Dal-Riada, and they gave battle there to the Foreigners; and the Cenel-Eoghain were defeated, and Raghnall O'Breslen was slain, and Gillachrist O'Cathain, et alii[2] multi; and the Gospel of Martin[4] was carried off by the Foreigners. Aedh O'Caellaighe, bishop of Oirghiall, and head of canons, quievit. Gilla-an-Choimdedh, son of Inlestar O'hAinlighe, chieftain of Cenel-Doffa, mortuus est. Domhnall O'hUallachan, chief bishop of Mumha; Augustin O'Sealbhaigh, bishop of Port-Lairge; and O'hAedha, bishop of Corcach, mortui sunt. Milo de Cogan, after assuming the kingship of Corcach and Des-Mumha;

Patrick. See O'Donovan's ed. of the *Four Masters*, note [d], under A.D. 1182; | and Reeves's *Adamnan*, pp. 324-6.

M 2

Oeṙṁuman, ocuṙ aṙ naṙẑaıṅ ꝺó Œꞇa clıaꞓ ocuṙ
puıṙꞇ Láıṙce ocuṙ Coṙcaıẑe, ocuṙ aṙ mılleꝺ Eṙeṅṅ
uıle, eꞇıṙ ꞓıll ocuṙ ꞇuaıꞓ, ꝺo ṁaṙbaꝺ ꝺo Mac Cıṙe,
ꝺo ṙıẋ .h. mıc Caılle, ocuṙ áṙ Ẑaıll ımmaıllı ꝼṙıṙṙ,
[.ı.] mac Sleımne, ocuṙ Comaṙ ṙuẑaꞓ, ocuṙ Ceṅṅ cuılıṅṅ,
ocuṙ Remuṅṅ, ocuṙ ꝺa mac Sꞇeṁıṅ, ocuṙ moṙaṅ elı.
Maıꝺṁ ṙe Ruaıꝺṙı .h. Conchobaıṙ, ocuṙ ṙe Conchobaṙ
Moeṅṁoıẑe, ṙoṙ Oonnchaꝺ mac Oomnaıll Mıꝺıẋ, ocuṙ
ṙoṙ .h. Moelꝺoṙaıꝺ, ubı mulꞇı cecıꝺeṙuṅꞇ.

Ꝃꞇ. Enaıṙ .uıı. ꝼ.; L. ıııı. Cṙı blıaꝺnа ochꞇmaꝺaꝺ
aṙ ceꝺ, aṙ mıle, aıṙ ın Cıẑeṙna. Ruaıꝺṙı .h. Conchobaıṙ, ṙı Eṙeṅṅ, ꝺo ꝺul ꝺa aılıꞇṙı ꝺo Connẑa Ꝼeıꞓın,
ocuṙ a ṙıẋe ꝺꝼáẑbaıl aẑá na mac, .ı. aẑ Conchobaṙ
ṁoeınnaıꝺe. henṙıc mac na hımpeṙeıṙe, ṙı Saxṙan,
moṙꞇuuṙ eṙꞇ. Ióṙeꝺ .h. hOeꝺa, eṙꞃuc .h. Ceınṙealaıẑ,
quıeuıꞇ. Oomnall mac Ẑılla Enáın, ꝺux claıṅṅı
Ꝼlaıꞓemaıl, occıṙuṙ eṙꞇ. Cachaṙ ıꞇıṙ an nẑılla
ṙıabach .h. [Ꝼ]laıꞓbeṙꞇaıẋ ocuṙ mac hı Ẑaıṙmleẑhaıẋ,
ocuṙ .h. Ꝼlaıꞓṙeṙꞇaıẋ ꝺo ṁaṙbaꝺ aṅṅ, ocuṙ ꝺṙeam
ꝺo ꞓenel Móeın ꝺo maṙbaꝺ aṅṅ. bécc .h. heẑṙa
moṙꞇuuṙ eṙꞇ.

Ꝃꞇ. Enáıṙ .ı. ꝼ.; L. xu.; ceıꞇṙı blıaꝺna ochꞇmaꝺa,

1 *Mac Sleimne.* "Son of Sleim-in." The Four Mast., at the year 1212, record the killing of the "sons of Sleimhin" in the battle of Coill-na-crann, or Kilmore, in the King's county. And under the year 1227, *infra*, a "Master Sleimhin (or Slevin)" is mentioned.

2 *Thomas Sugach*; i.e. "Thomas the Merry." Not mentioned in the other chronicles; nor is anything else known to the Editor regarding him.

8 *Cenn-cuilinn.* This name lit. signifies "Holly-head." It may be a corrupt way of writing the name Cantitunensis (Reimundus Kantitunensis) in Irish. See Cambrensis, *Expugnatio Hibernica*, (ed. Dimock), lib. ii., cap. xxxv.

4 *Remunn.* In reference to this passage, Dr. O'Donovan (Four Mast., A.D. 1182, note e) understands Reimund de la Grose to be the person here alluded to; but it is more probable that Reimund Fitz-Hugh (Reimundus Hugonides) is meant, as Cambrensis (*Expug. Hib.*, lib. ii., cap. xxxv.) represents the latter as having been slain in Olethan (Ui-Liathain), a territory now represented by the barony of Barrymore, co. Cork, and adjoining the district of Ui-Mac-Caille, the present barony of Imokilly, in the same county.

5 *Two sons of Stephen;* or two Fitz-Stephens. Giraldus Cambrensis (*Expug. Hib.*, lib. ii., cap. xx.) mentions only one, Radulphus, or

and after plundering Ath-cliath, and Port-Lairge, and Corcach; and after destroying all Erinn, both church and territory, was slain by Mac Tire, king of Ui-Mac-Caille, and a slaughter of Foreigners along with him, [viz.] :— Mac Sleimne[1] and Thomas Sugach,[2] and Cenn-cuilinn,[3] and Remunn,[4] and two sons of Stephen,[5] and a great many more. A victory was gained by Ruaidhri O'Concho-bhair, and by Conchobhar Maenmhaighe, over Donn-chadh, son of Domhnall Midhech, and over O'Mael-doraidh, ubi[6] multi ceciderunt.

The kalends of January on the 7th feria, the 4th of the moon; the age of the Lord eighty-three years, and a hundred, and a thousand. Ruaidhri O'Conchobhair, king of Erinn, went on a pilgrimage to Cunga-Feichin, and left his sovereignty to his son, i.e. to Conchobhar Maenmhaighe. Henry, son of the Empress,[7] king of the Saxons, mortuus est. Joseph O'hAedha, bishop of Ui-Ceinnsealaigh,[8] quievit. Domhnall, son of Gilla-Enain, dux of Clann-Flaithemhail, occisus est. A conflict between the Gilla-riabhach O'Flaithbhertaigh and the son of O'Gairm-leghaigh; and O'Flaithbhertaigh was slain there, and a number of the Cenel-Moain were slain there. Becc O'hEghra mortuus est.[9]

The kalends of January on the 1st feria, the 15th of the moon; the age of the Lord eighty-four years, and a hun-

---

Ralph, the son-in-law of Milo de Cogan. In the Annals of Ulster the names of the persons slain on this occasion are added to the original entry for the year 1182, in a later hand, thus:—Miliꝺ Ꝣocan ocuꝛ Remonn, ocuꝛ Cenn Cuilino, ocuꝛ ꝺa mac Steimni, et alii multi; i.e. "Milo de Cogan, and Reimund, and Cenn-Cuilind, and the two sons of Stephen, et alii multi." Mageoghegan, in his translation of the so-called Annals of Clonmacnoise, says "Miles Cogann, Raymond de la Grose, Kean-Koyleann, and the two sons of Ffitz-

Steeven, were killed by Mac Tire, prince of Imokilly."

[6] *Ubi.* ube, MS.

[7] *Son of the Empress.* mac na peꝛeiꝛe, MS.; the last word being altered to hImpeꝛeiꝛe, by a later hand.

[8] *Bishop of Ui-Ceinnsealaigh.* The territory of Ui-Ceinnsealaigh was nearly co-extensive with the present diocese of Ferns.

[9] *Mortuus est.* The Four Masters observe that Becc O'hEghra (or Beg O'Hara) was "treacherously slain."

αρ ceδ, αρ mile, αιρ ιη Τιχερηα. Ωρτ .h. Moeιλρechλαιηη, ρí Mιδe, δο ṁαρbαδ δο Διαρmαιδ .h. bριαιη
α cοηηe αc Δρυιm ċυιλιηη, ιαρ δτοιχeċτ δó δο λαρ α
αιρechτα ρéιη, δο λαbρα ρe mαc hι bριαιη α οeηαρ,
οcυρ mαc ι bριαιη δο ρeαλλ ραιρ. Ωṁλáιb mαc Ρeρχαιλ
hι Ruαιρc, ρι bρeιρηe, ιητeρρecτυρ éρτ. Δeιċ τιχe
ριċeτ δο ṁαιτhιb ṁυιηητιρe Ωρδα Mαċα δο αρχυιη δο
χαλλαιb ηα Mιδe. Mαολιορρα .h. Cεροbαιλ δο χαbáιλ
cοṁαρbυιρ Ρατραιc, ιαρ ηá ράcbáιλ δο Τοmαλταch
.h. Conchοbαιρ. Mαολρechλαιηη bec .h. Moeιλρechλαιηη δο χαbáιλ ριχe Mιδe α hαċλe báιρ Ωρτ.
Cαιρλéη δο τóχbáιλ λα χαλλαιb α Cιλλ ράιρ. Cαιρλéη
eλι δο ṁιλλeδ αηη λα Moeιλρechλαιηη οcυρ λα Conchοbαρ Moeηmαιχe .h. Conchοbαιρ, cο ροchαιδe mοιρ
δα χαλλαιb mαιλλe ριυ. Τεmραλλ mορ Τυαmα δα
χυαλαηη δο ċυιτιm α ηαéη λó eδιρ ċeηδ οcυρ ċλοιċ.
Cαρραιχ λοċα Ce δο λορcαδ δο ċeηe báιċ, .ι. ρí ρορτ
ρο οιρρδeρc mυιητeρι Mαολρυαηαιδ, bαιλe ηα ραηιc
αηαcαλ mαοιηe ιηá δαοιηe δα ραιb αηη, δú ιη ρο mιλλιτ
ρe ριċιτ ηο α ρeċτ bρiċιτ δο δαοιηιb ρυαιċeητα, ιm ċúιχ
δυοιηe δéχ δο ρíολ ριχ οcυρ ταοιρρeċ, ιm ṁηαοι mιc
Διαρmαδα, .ι. ιηχeη hι Εδιη, οcυρ ιm ṁηαοι α mιc, .ι.
ιηχeη Δοṁηαιλλ hι Conchοbαιρ, οcυρ ιm ιηχeη hι Δυbδα,
οcυρ ιm mαc Δοηηchαδα hι Mαοιλbρeηυιηη, οcυρ ιm

---

[1] *Slain.* In the Annals of Ulster it is stated that he was slain " in treachery, at the instigation of the Gaill (English)."

[2] *Druim-Chuilinn.* The MS. has Δρυιm ċυιλm̄, the last letter being so written as to represent either an m or ιη. But the reading in the text is the most probable. There is a place called Druim-Chuilinn (now Drumcullen), in the south of the barony of Eglish, King's co., which was very likely the place of meeting between O'Melaghlin and O'Brien, as

it is on the boundary between the ancient territories of Meath and Munster.

[3] *Cill-Fair.* Owing to the aspiration of the ρ in the last syllable, Cιλλ-ράιρ is now called Cill-úir, or Killare.

[4] *There.* This seems to be a mistake. It does not appear that there was any castle at Cill-Fair before the one erected in this year, as above recorded; and it certainly is not likely that the English were at this time in alliance with Maelsechlainn and

dred, and a thousand. Art O'Maelsechlainn, king of Midhe, was slain[1] by Diarmaid O'Briain, at a meeting at Druim-Chuilinn,[2] after having come from the midst of his own assembly to speak apart with the son of O'Briain, and the son of O'Briain deceived him. Amhlaibh, son of Ferghal O'Ruairc, king of Breifne, interfectus est. Thirty houses of the principal persons of the community of Ard-Macha were plundered by the Foreigners of Midhe. Maelisa O'Cerbhaill assumed the comarbship of Patrick, after it had been resigned by Tomaltach O'Conchobhair. Maelsechlainn Bec O'Maelsechlainn assumed the kingship of Midhe after the death of Art. A castle was erected by the Foreigners at Cill-Fáir.[3] Another castle was destroyed there[4] by Maelsechlainn and Conchobhar Maenmhaighe O'Conchobhair, and a great multitude of Foreigners along with them. The great church of Tuaim-da-ghualann fell in one day, both roof and stone. The Rock of Loch-Cé[5] was burned by lightning, i.e. the very magnificent, kingly residence of Muinter-Maelruanaidh, where neither goods nor people of all that were there found protection; where six score, or seven score, of distinguished persons were destroyed, along with fifteen men of the race of kings and chieftains, with the wife of Mac Diarmada, i.e. the daughter of O'hEidhin, and his son's wife, i.e. the daughter of Domhnall O'Conchobhair, and the daughter of O'Dubhda, and the son of Donnchadh

O'Conor—much less that they assisted those Irish chieftains to destroy a castle presumably belonging to some Englishman. The Four Masters state that "another castle was plundered by Maelsechlainn and Conchobhar Maenmhaighe O'Conchobhair (Conor Moinmoy O'Conor)," and that "many Englishmen were slain there." The Annals of Ulster also record the plundering of the "other castle" in nearly the same words as the Four Masters use, and add "co ʀoċaιꝺe moιn ꝺo ᵹalloιb anꝺ," i.e. "with a great multitude of Gaill (English) there."

[5] The Rock of Loch-Cé; i.e. the chief residence of Mac Dermot, where the MS. from which the present collection has been printed is supposed to have been transcribed. See Introduction. This catastrophe is also entered, in an abridged form, under the year 1187.

mac Ɖuınn hı Mannacháın, ocuɼ ım ɖá ınᵹen hı
Manɖacháın, ocuɼ ım mac Maonuıᵹ, ım ċaoıɼech Cınel
mɓuılᵹ, ocuɼ ımon ɼaᵹaɼꞇ .h. Maoılbeallꞇoıne, ocuɼ
ım ᵹıllaċıapáın .h. Connachꞇáın, .ı. mac óıᵹe, ocuɼ
coınɖel cɼabaɖ, ocuɼ ım áɼ ɖıaıɼḟıɖı elı ɖo ċaoımɓ
maıċı ; ocuɼ ᵹach aon nach aɼ loıɼceɖ ɖıɓ ɼo baıɖıꞇ
ıɼın mɓloɼc maıɖm buaıɖeɼċa ɼın a nɖoɼuɼ an ċaıle,
conα ɼıachꞇ a mbeċaıᵹ aɼɼ achꞇ Conchobaɼ mac Ɖıaɼ-
maɖa co nuaꞇaɖ beᵹ ɖo ᵹleɼe a muınnꞇıɼı. Iɼın
CCoıne ıaɼ nınıꞇ ċoɼᵹuıɼ ɖo ɼıᵹneɖ an ᵹnıom ɼın.

Ꝃꞇ. Enáıɼ ꞁꞁꞁ. ꝼ. ; L. xxuı. ; u. blıaɖna ochꞇmaɖa
aɼ ceɖ aɼ mıle aıɼ ın Ꞇıᵹeɼna. Meɼɼ moɼ ıɼın
blıaɖaın ɼ. Þılıp Unɼeɼɼɼa, ᵹo nᵹalloıb Eɼenn
uıme, a nCCɼɖ Maċa co cenɖ .uı. la ocuɼ .uı. noıɖċe
a ceɼꞇ ṁeɖón an ċoɼᵹuıɼ. Ruaıɖɼı .h. Conchobaıɼ,
ɼí Eɼenn, ɖo ꞇeachꞇ aɼ a aılıꞇɼı, ocuɼ Ꝛaıll ocuɼ ꝼıɼ
Muman ɖo bɼeıċ leıɼ ɖó, .ı. Ɖomnall O Ɓɼıaın, ᵹuɼ
mıllɼeꞇ ıaɼꞇaɼ Connachꞇ, eꞇıɼ ċıll ocuɼ ꞇuaıꞇh. Sıċ
ıaɼɼın ɖo ɖenam ɖó ꝼeın ocuɼ ɖá mac, ocuɼ Connachꞇ ɖo ɼoınn eꞇoɼɼa. Ceall Ɖálua ɖaɼᵹuın ocuɼ
ɖo loɼcaɖ ɖo Caꞇhal ċaɼɼach mac Conchobaıɼ
Moenṁaıᵹe, ocuɼ ɖo Connachꞇaıɓ, ꞇaɼéıɼ ꝼıɼ Muman,
a nɖıᵹuıl a ceall ɖo loıɼcɼeꞇ ꝼıɼ Muman, ocuɼ
áɼ a ᵹcleıɼech ocuɼ a mban ɖo ṁaɼbaɖ ocuɼ ɖo
loɼcaɖ ına ꞇemplaıb ocuɼ ına ꞇıᵹıɓ, ocuɼ a lıoɖaıɼ,
ocuɼ a naıɖme, [ocuɼ] a ɼeoıɖ ɖo bɼeıċ leó. Maelıɼa
O Ɖalaıᵹ, ollam Eɼenn ocuɼ CClban, ocuɼ aɼɖ ɖuıx
Coɼcaɼaoıɖe, ocuɼ aon ɼoᵹa Eɼenn aɼ ɼaꞇ, aɼ ɖeılɓ,
ocuɼ aɼ maıċ, ɖo éᵹ a ᵹCluáın Iɼaıɼɖ aᵹá aılıꞇɼı.

---

¹ *Burned.* The text of the re-
mainder of this sentence is written in
the margin, a mark of reference being
added.

² *Fruit.* The Annals of Ulster
have ɖaıɼ meɼɼ (dair mess), i.e.
"oak crop," or acorn crop.

³ *Philip Unsessra.* Philip of Wor-
cester. Giraldus Cambrensis gives
an account of this foray of Philip's,
Topog. Hib., cap. 1., and *Expug.
Hib.*, lib. ii., cap. xxv.

⁴ *After the men of Mumha;* i.e.
after the men of Mumha (or Munster)

O'Maelbhrenuinn, and the son of Donn O'Mannachain, and the two daughters of O'Mannachain, and Mac Mae-naigh, chieftain of Cenel-Builg, and the priest O'Mael-bealtaine, and Gillachiarain O'Connachtain, (i.e. a son of chastity and lamp of piety), and a countless destruction besides of good men; and every one of them who was not burned[1] was drowned in this tumultuous consternation, in the entrance of the place; so that there escaped not alive therefrom but Conchobhar Mac Diarmada with a very small number of the multitude of his people. On the Friday after Shrovetide this event occurred.

The kalends of January on the 3rd feria, the 26th of the moon; the age of the Lord eighty-five years, and a hundred, and a thousand. Great fruit[2] in this year. Philip Unsessra,[3] accompanied by the Foreigners of Erinn, *remained* at Ard-Macha during six days and six nights, in the very middle of Lent. Ruaidhri O'Conchobhair, king of Erinn, came from his pilgrimage; and he took with him the Foreigners, and the men of Mumha, i.e. Domhnall O'Briain *and his party*; and they destroyed the West of Connacht, both church and territory. Peace was afterwards made by himself and his son, and Connacht was divided between them. Cill-Dalua was plundered and burned by Cathal Carrach, son of Conchobhar Maenmhaighe, and the men of Connacht, after the men of Mumha,[4] in retaliation for their churches which the men of Mumha had burned; and *for* the slaughter of their clerics and women who were slain and burned in their churches, and in their houses; and for carrying off their books, and utensils, [and] precious things. Maelisa O'Dalaigh, *chief* poet of Erinn and Alba, and principal dux of Corca-Raidhe, and the single choice[5] of Erinn as regards grace, form, and good-ness, died at Cluain-Iraird on his pilgrimage. Amh-

---

had returned home from their foray into the West of Connacht.

[5] *Single choice.* aon ṗoġa (aon rogha); lit. "one choice."

Aṁláiḃ .h. Muireḋaiġ, erpuc Cenel Eoġain, quieuit.
Iohannep mac pi Saxan [ɔo ċeaċt] ɔo ġaḃáil piġe
nEpenn, luċt tpi piċit long, pe taoḃ apoiḃe ɔo
ġalloiḃ Saxan a nEpinn pompa, gup ġaḃrat Aṫ
cliaṫ, ocur coiʒeɔ Laiʒen, ocur conɔepnaɔap caipléin
aʒ tippaiɔ Paċtna ocur aʒ Apɔ Pínáin. Maiḋm pia
nɔomnall .h. mḃpiain pop muintep mic piʒ Saxan,
inap mapḃaɔ iol imaɔ ʒall anɔ, um comalta mic
piʒ Saxan. Ruaiḋpi .h. ʒpaɔa, ocur Ruaiɔpi .h.
Conaing, ɔo mapḃaɔ le ʒalloiḃ acc ap ċaiplen tippait
Paċtna. Mac piʒ Saxan ɔo ɔul taipir iappin ɔo
copait Uʒa ɔe Láci pe a aṫaip, uaip irre Uʒa ɔe Láci
pa piʒ Epenn ap cinɔ mic piʒ Saxan, ocur ni ro leiʒ
ɔrepuiḃ Epenn cir na bpaiʒɔe ɔorrum. Ɔonnċaɔ
mac Ɔomnaill Miɔiċ occirur ert. ʒilla irá .h.
Maoilín, erpuc Maiʒe hEó, quieuit. Ḃpian Ḃpeirneċ,
mac Toipɔhelḃaiʒ .h. Conċobaip, moptuur ert. Planɔ
.h. Pinnecta, ɔux cloinne Mupċaɔa, moptuur ert.
Mac Copmaic meic meic Caprṫaiʒ, pi Ṁuman, ɔo
mapḃaɔ ɔo ʒallaiḃ Copcaiʒi. Ɔomnall .h. ʒilla-
patpaic, pi Orraiɔe, moptuur ert. Maoilreċlainn
mac mic Loċlainn, pi Cenel Eoʒain, intepfectur ert
tpe meḃail, o Saxanaiḃ. Ɔiapmaiɔ, mac Toipɔhelḃaiʒ
.h. Ḃpiain, ɔo ɔallaɔ la bpaṫaip pein, heɔon la
Ɔomnall. Maṫʒamain, mac Conċobaip Maonmaiʒe,
ɔo ʒaḃail la Mupċaɔ mac Taiḃcc .h. Cellaiʒ, ocur

---

[1] *Bishop of Cenel-Eoghain.* The
Annals of Ulster and the Four Masters call him "bishop of Ard-Macha
(Armagh) and Cenel-Feradhaigh."
In the former Annals, (and also in the
present chronicle under the next
year), he is stated to have been
buried in Derry "po copaiḃ a aṫap,
.i. an erpuic .h. Coḃṫaiʒ" "at
the feet of his father, the bishop
O'Cobhthaigh (or O'Coffey)." But, as
Dr. O'Donovan remarks (*Four Mast.,*
note [2], A.D. 1185), "it looks very
odd that a Bishop O'Murray should

be the son of a Bishop O'Coffey."
His mother may have been of the
family of O'Murray, which name he
may have adopted.

[2] *Came.* ɔo ċeaċt. Supplied
from Ann. Ult.

[3] *Tipraid-Fachtna;* lit. "Fachtna's
well." Giraldus Cambrensis (*Expug.
Hib.,* lib. ii., cap. xxxv., ed. Dimock)
writes the name "Tibraccia." Tib-
beraghny, in the parish of the same
name, barony of Iverk, and co. of
Kilkenny, is the place referred to.

[4] *Ard-Finain.* In the barony of

laibh O'Muiredhaigh, bishop of Cenel-Eoghain,[1] quievit.
John, son of the king of the Saxons, [came][2] to assume
the sovereignty of Erinn, with a fleet of three score
ships, (besides what there were of Saxon Foreigners in
Erinn before them); and they took possession of Ath-
cliath and the province of Laighen, and erected castles at
Tipraid-Fachtna[3] and Ard-Finain.[4] A victory was gained
by Domhnall O'Briain over the people of the son of the
king of the Saxons, in which very many Foreigners were
slain, along with the foster-brother[5] of the son of the
king of the Saxons. Ruaidhri O'Gradha and Ruaidhri
O'Conaing were slain by Foreigners in the slaughter of the
castle of Tipraid-Fachtna.[3] The son of the king of the
Saxons went across afterwards to complain of Hugo de
Laci to his father; for it was Hugo de Laci that was king of
Erinn when the son of the king of the Saxons came, and he
permitted not the men of Erinn *to give* tribute or hostages
to him.[6] Donnchadh, son of Domhnall Midhech, occisus est.
Gilla-Isa O'Maeilin, bishop of Magh-Eó, quievit. Brian[7]
Breifnech, son of Toirdhelbhach O'Conchobhair, mortuus
est. Flann O'Finnechta, dux of Clann-Murchadha, mor-
tuus est. The son of Cormac,[8] son of Mac Carthaigh,
king of Mumha, was slain by the Foreigners of Corcach.
Domhnall O'Gillapatraic,[9] king of Osraighe, mortuus
est. Maelsechlainn, son of Mac Lachlainn, king of
Cenel-Eoghain, interfectus est, through treachery, by
Saxons. Diarmaid, son of Toirdhelbhach O'Briain,
was blinded by his own brother, viz.:—by Domhnall.
Mathghamhain, son of Conchobhar Maenmhaighe, was
taken prisoner by Murchadh, son of Tadhg O'Cellaigh,

Iffa and Offa, co. Tipperary. The
MS. from this down to 1190, with
the exception of some of the entries
for 1188, is in a different hand from
the preceding.

[5] *Foster-brother.* comalta; i.e.
nursed together, from com = Lat. co,
and alta = altus.

[6] *To him;* i.e. to John.

[7] *Brian.* Ꝑꞁan, MS.

[8] *Son of Cormac.* His name was
Diarmaid (or Dermot) Mac Carthy.

[9] *O'Gillapatraic.* The Four Masters call him Mac Gillapatraic, the
more usual Irish form of the name
which is now anglicised Fitzpatrick.

α τιοnαcαl το Ďomnαll .h. bruαin. Ríże Connαcht
το żαbαil το Conchobαp Mαonmαiże.

Ict. Iαnαip .iiii. p.; L. iiii. Se bliατnα .lxxx. αp ceτ
αp mile αip in Τiżepnα. Ταchαipi mop i τuαipcept
Epenn αn bliαταin pin. Αiτpiżατ Ďomnαill mic Αοτα
mec Lαclαinn, ocup piżατ Ruαiτpi i Lαiτbepthαich ic
τpeim το Cenel Eoγαin τelcα oγ. Conchobαp .h.
flαiτbeptαich το mαpbατ lá Ruαiτpi .h. flαiτbeptαich, lα α τepbpαthαip feippin, α nΑpαinτ.
Ďepbopcαill, inżen Mupchατα .h. Mάoilpeclαinn, το
τul co Ďpoceτ Αthα, τα αiliτpi. Ruαiτpi .h. Conchobαip τinταpbατ τiα mαc fein, .i. το Conchobαp
Mαonmαiże. Ďonnchατh mαc Ταiτcc .h. Cellαiż
moptuup ept. Mαolcαlαinτ O Cleipcen, eppuc Żlinτ
τά lαchα, in Cpipτo quieuiτ. Celechαip .h. Αpmeταiż,
eppuc Cluαnα feptα bpenαinn, quieuiτ. Conchobαp
Mαonmαiże το τecht co Mucαpτ, ocup Αοτ .h.
Ruαipc το τecht inα τech, ocup bpαiżτe το thαbαipτ
το Conchobαp, ocup Τíp Τuαthαil το żαbαipτ το
Connαchτuip. Uγα τe Lάci το Ďupmαż Coluim Cille,
το τenαm cαiplein inτi, ocup fluαż τiαipmiτe το
żαllοiβ lαip, uαip ipp e pα piż Miτe ocup bpefni, ocup
Αipżiαll, ocup ip το τo bepτα cip Connαcht, ocup po żαβ
Epinn uile το żαllοiβ. Ro ţo lάn, τonα, Miτi o
Sinαinn co fαipci το čαiplenαiβ ocup το żαllοiβ. Iαp
τταipepin το inτ fαοταp pin, .i. cαiplen Ďupmαiże το
τenαm, ταnic αmαch το fechαin αn cαiplein, occup

and delivered to Domhnall O'Briain. The sovereignty of Connacht was assumed by Conchobar Maenmhaighe.

The kalends of January on the 4th feria, the 7th of the moon; the age of the Lord eighty-six years, and a hundred, and a thousand. Great contentions in the North of Erinn this year. Dethronement[1] of Domhnall, son of Aedh Mac Lachlainn, and installation as king of Ruaidhri O'Laithbhertaigh, by a section of the Cenel-Eoghain of Telach-óg. Conchobhar O'Flaithbhertaigh was slain by Ruaidhri O'Flaithbhertaigh, his own brother, in Ara. Derbhorcaill,[2] daughter of Murchadh O'Maelsechlainn, went to Droiched-atha, on a pilgrimage. Rúaidhri O'Conchobhair was expelled by his own son, i.e. by Conchobhar Maenmhaighe. Donnchadh, son of Tadhg O'Cellaigh, mortuus est. Maelcalainn O'Cleirchen, bishop of Glennda-locha, in Christo quievit. Celechair O'Airmhedhaigh, bishop of Cluain-ferta-Brenainn,[3] quievit. Conchobhar Maenmhaighe came to Mucart, and Aedh O'Ruairc went into his house,[4] and gave hostages to Conchobhar, and gave Tir-Thuathail to the Connachtmen. Hugo de Laci *went* to Durmhagh-Choluim-Cille, to build[5] a castle in it, having a countless number of Foreigners along with him; for he was king of Midhe, and Breifne, and Airghiall, and it was to him the tribute of Connacht was paid; and he it was that won all Erinn for the Foreigners. Midhe, from the Sinainn to the sea, was full of[6] castles and of[6] Foreigners. After the completion by him of this work, i.e. the erection of the castle of Durmhagh, he came out to look at the castle, having three Foreigners

---

therefore, between the elopement of Derbhorcaill and the advent of Strongbow and his companions, during which period many other causes occurred to provoke the hostility which led to Dermot's expulsion, and to his subsequent appeal for assistance to Henry II. Her death is recorded under the year 1193, *infra.*

[3] *Brenainn.* p̄ī. for Pꞃenaınn (Prenainn), MS.

[4] *Went into his house.* This is another way of saying that O'Ruairc submitted to O'Conchobhair.

[5] *To build.* ꝺo ꝺenaım, for ꝺo ꝺenam, MS.

[6] *Of.* ꝺo. The MS. should probably read ꝺa (da=do a), "of his."

cριαρ ρο ξαΙΙοιɓ Ιαιρ. Ταιηικ ρονα εη οκκΙαεκ ρο
ρεριιɓ Mιɓε ρα ιηρραιξε, οκυρ α τυαξη ρα ηα κοιη, .ι.
ξιΙΙα ξαη ιηατηαιρ .h. Mιαɓαιξ, ραΙτα αη τριηηαιɓ
ρειρριη, οκυρ τυκ εη ρυιΙΙε ρο κκυρ ɓεη α κεηρ ρε,
οκυρ ξυρ τυιτ ειτιρ κεηρ οκυρ κοΙαιηρ α κΙορη αη
καιρΙειη. Cριρáη .h. Connορκhι, ερρυκ Ιιρ móιρ
οκυρ Ιεξαιτ κοмαρρα ρεταιρ, ιη Cριρτο ρυιειιιτ. Οιαρ-
маιρ маκ Cαρρξαмηα οκκιρυρ ερτ. Mυρκhαρ .h.
CεΙΙαιξ, ρι .h. Mαιηε, οκκιρυρ ερτ. ξιΙΙα ɓεραικh .h.
CιΙΙιη, ρεκηαρ 8ιΙ Mυιρεραιξ, мορτυυρ ερτ. CcмΙáιɓ
.h. Mυιρεξhαιξh, ερρυκ. Ccιρρ Mακhα οκυρ CεηεοιΙ
ɓρεραραιξh, Ιοκραηη ροΙυρτα ηο ροιΙΙριξερ τhúαιτh
οκυρ εξΙυιρ, ιη Cριρτο ρυιειιιτ, α η'Ουη Cριιτηε, οκυρ α
τɓαɓαιρτ κο honóρακh κο Οαιρε CοΙυιm CιΙΙε, οκυρ α
αɓηακυΙ α ταοɓ αη τεαмρυιΙ ρο τορραιɓ α αταρ.
ροξαρτακh .h. CερɓαΙΙáη ρο οιρ[ρ]ηερ ηα ιοηαρ.
ξιΙΙα Cριρτ маκ CατɱοειΙ, ρí τοιρρεκh τεηεοιΙ ρερ-
αραιξh οκυρ ηα κΙαηη, .ι. κΙαηη Οεηξυρα, οκυρ κΙαηη
Ουιɓιηρρεκhτ, οκυρ κΙαηη ροξαρταιξ, οκυρ .h. Cεηρ-
ραρα οκυρ κΙαηηι τοΙΙα ρο ρεριιɓ Mαηακh, οκυρ
κεηη κοмαιρΙε τυαιρκερτ Eρεηη, ρο ɱαρɓαρ Ια .h.
ηεικηιɓ, οκυρ Ια Mυιητερ τοεɱáιη, οκυρ α κεηρ ρο
ɓρεɓ Ιεó ɓοιɓ κο ρρíɓ υατhαιɓ α ξκιηη ɱíρ íαρταιη.
MοειΙρεκhΙαιηη маκ Mυιρκερταιξ ɱéξ ΙακτΙαιηη ρο
маρɓαρ ρο ξαΙΙαιɓ. Conn .h. ɓρειρΙéη, τοιρρεκh
ραηαρ, ρυιειιιτ.

)cτ. ιαηαιρ υ. ρ.; .Ι. κυιιιι. 8εακhτ мɓΙιαρηα οκhτ-
маρα αρ κερ, αρ мιΙε, αιρ ιη Τιξερηα. Rυαιρρι O
Ιαιɓɓερταιξh, ρí CεηεοιΙ Eoξαιη, ρο маρɓαρ αρ κρεκhαιɓ
α τíρ CοηαιΙΙ. Ορυιm κΙιαɓ ρο αρξυιη ρο маκ MαοιΙ-

---

1 *The Sinnach* ; lit. "the fox;" a name by which the chief of the family of O'Caharny of Teffia was known. The circumstances attending the murder of Hugo de Laci have been much misrepresented by writers. Dr. O'Donovan (*Four Masters*, A.D. 1186, notes ' ') has collected many interesting references to the event.

2 *Occisus.* οκκιρρυρ, MS.

8 *Amhlaibh O'Muiredhaigh* ; or Auliffe O'Murray. This is the same

along with him. There came towards him then a youth
of the men of Midhe, having his axe concealed, viz. :—
Gilla-gan-inathair O'Miadhaigh, the foster son of the
Sinnach[1] himself; and he gave him one blow, so that he
cut off his head, and he fell, both head and body, into
the ditch of the castle. Christian O'Connorchi, bishop
of Lis-mór, and legate of the comarb of Peter, in Christo
quievit. Diarmaid Mac Carghamhna occisus est. Murchadh O'Cellaigh, king of Ui-Maine, occisus[2] est. Gilla-
beraigh O'Cillin, vice-abbot of Sil-Muiredhaigh, mortuus
est. Amhlaibh O'Muiredhaigh,[3] bishop of Ard-Macha and
Cenel-Feradhaigh, a brilliant lamp that used to enlighten
laity and clergy, in Christo quievit, in Dun-Cruithne;
and he was honourably brought to Doire-Choluim-Cille,
and interred in the side of the church, at his father's feet.[4]
Fogartach O'Cerbhallain was ordained in his place.
Gillachrist - Mac Cathmhail, king-chieftain of Cenel-
Feradhaigh and the Clanns, (viz. :—Clann-Aenghusa, and
Clann-Duibhinrecht, and Clann-Foghartaigh; and Ui-
Cendfada and Clann-Colla, of the Feara-Manach), and
head of counsel of the North of Erinn, was slain by
O'hEighnigh and Muinter-Caemhain; and they carried
off his head, which was obtained from them at the end of
a month afterwards. Maelsechlainn, son of Muircher-
tach Mac Lachlainn, was slain by Foreigners. Conn
O'Breislén, chieftain of Fanad, quievit.

The kalends of January on the 5th feria, the 18th of
the moon; the age of the Lord eighty-seven years, and
a hundred, and a thousand. Ruaidhri O'Laithbhertaigh,
king of Cenel-Eoghain, was slain while on a predatory
excursion in Tir-Conaill. Druim-cliabh was plundered by

---

ecclesiastic who is called "bishop
of Cenel-Eoghain" under the year
1185.

   [4] *His father's feet.* See note [1],

p. 170. This entry and the three next
are given under the year 1185 in the
Annals of Ulster and the Four Masters.

τrechlaınn 1 Ruaırc, ꝺo rı .h. mbrıúın ocuʀ Conmaıcne,
ocuʀ ꝺo mac Cathaıl 1 Ruaırc, ocuʀ ꝺo ʒallaıb na Mıꝺe
maılle rú. Acht ᵭena, ꝺo róıne Ꝺıa ocuʀ Colum Cılle
fırτ ampa oʀʀa annrın, .ı. ʀo maʀbaꝺ mac Moéılτrech-
laınn 1 Ruaırc rıa cıonn ᵭaoıcıꝺırı ıaʀrın a Conmaıcne,
ocuʀ ʀo ꝺallaꝺ mac Cathaıl 1 Ruaırc le .h. Móelꝺo-
raıꝺ, .ı. flaıᵭbertach, a neınech Coluım Cılle, ocuʀ ʀo
maʀbaꝺ ʀé .xx. ꝺoer ʒráꝺa mıc Moeılτrechlaınn aʀ
fuτ Conmaıcne ocuʀ ᵭaıʀʀrı Ꝺruma clíab, τre ṁírbaıl
Ꝺé ocuʀ Coluım Cılle. Carʀaʒ Loᵭa Cé ꝺo loʀcaꝺ a
meꝺón lóı, ꝺu ın ʀo báıꝺheꝺ ocuʀ ın ʀo loırceꝺ ıl ımaꝺ
ꝺoeınıꝺ, ım ınʒen .h. Eıꝺın, .ı. Ꝺuıꝺerra ınʒen Ruaıꝺrı
hı Eıꝺın, ben Conchobaır mıc Ꝺıaʀmaꝺa, rı ṁoıʒe
Luırʒ.

Ꝁτ. ıanaır .uı. f.; L. xxıx.; ochτ mblıaꝺna ochτmaꝺa
aʀ ceꝺ, aʀ mıle, aır ın Τıʒeʀna. Ruaıꝺrı .h. Canannan,
rí ᵭeneoıl Conaıll re heꝺ, ocuʀ ríꝺaṁna Erenn ꝺór,
ꝺo maʀbaꝺ ꝺo [f]laıᵭbertach .h. Moelꝺoraıꝺ τrıa
meabaıl, ac ꝺroıᵭeτ Slıcıᵹ, .ı. ıaʀ na ꝺréʒaꝺ ꝺo láʀ
Ꝺruma clíab amaᵭ, ocuʀ braτhaır ꝺó ꝺo ṁarbaꝺ
maılle rır, ocuʀ ꝺrem ꝺá ṁuınnτer. h. ʒaırꝺ,
τoırrech fer Ꝺroma, ırré ʀo ımmır láṁa aʀ .h.
Canannáın, ocuʀ ʀo maʀbaꝺ é reın le muınnτer
Echṁaʀcaıᵹ 1 Ꝺoᵭaʀτaıʒh a ꝺoıʒaıl hı Canonnáın.
Ꝺomnall .h. Canannaın ꝺo leꝺraꝺ a ᵭoırrı ꝺıa ᵭuaıꝺ
reın a nꝺoıre, aʒ buaın arclaını connaıᵹ, ocuʀ a éᵹ ꝺe
τrıa ercaıne τráṁτa Coluım Cılle. Maʀτaın .h.

---

1 *The son.* In the Annals of Ulster
he is called Aedh, or Hugh.

2 *Cathal.* The MS. has mac
Moeılτrechlaınn, "son of Maelsech-
lainn," but it should be "son of
Cathal," as in the Annals of Ulster.

3 *Were slain.* The words ocuʀ ʀo
maʀbaꝺ ʀé .xx. ꝺoer ʒraꝺa, "and
six score of the favorites . . . ."

were slain," are written twice in the
MS., i.e. at the bottom of one page and
the beginning of the next.

4 *Burned.* This seems to be an
abridged repetition of the catastrophe
recorded under the year 1184.

5 *Ua Gairbh.* The Four Masters
call him Maghnus O'Gairbh, or Manus
O'Garve.

the son[1] of Maelsechlainn O'Ruairc, king of Ui-Briuin and Conmaicne, and by the son of Cathal O'Ruairc, and the Foreigners of Midhe along with them. But God and Colum-Cille wrought a remarkable miracle against them there, viz.:—the son[1] of Maelsechlainn O'Ruairc was killed in Conmaicne before the end of a fortnight afterwards, and the son of Cathal[2] O'Ruairc was blinded by O'Maeldoraidh, i.e. Flaithbhertach, in revenge of Colum-Cille; and six score of the favorites of the son[1] of Maelsechlainn were slain[3] throughout Conmaicne and Cairpre-Droma-cliabh, through the miracle of God and Colum-Cille. The Rock of Loch-Cé was burned[4] at mid-day, where a great many people were drowned and burned, along with the daughter of O'hEidhin, i.e. Duibhessa, daughter of Ruaidhri O'hEidhin, wife of Conchobhar Mac Diarmada, king of Magh-Luirg.

The kalends of January on the 6th feria, the 29th of the moon; the age of the Lord eighty-eight years, and a hundred, and a thousand. Ruaidhri O'Canannáin, king of Cenel-Conaill for a time, and also royal heir of Erinn, was slain by [F]laithbhertach O'Maeldoraidh, through treachery, at the bridge of Sligech, i.e. after being enticed out from the middle of Druim-cliabh; and a brother of his was slain along with him, and a number of his people. O'Gairbh,[5] chieftain of Feara-Droma, it was that laid hands on O'Canannáin; and he was himself slain by the people of Echmarcach O'Dochartaigh, in revenge of O'Canannáin. Domhnall O'Canannáin wounded his foot with his own axe, at Doire, while cutting[6] a piece of wood; and he died thereof through the curse of the community of Colum-Cille. Martin O'Brolaigh, chief sage

---

[6] *While cutting;* ᴀᵹ ƀᴜᴀın (ag buain). In the Dublin copy of the Annals of Ulster the expression is ı ᵹᴀıᴄ, which Dr. O'Donovan (*Four Masters,* note P, A.D. 1187) translates "while stealing." But the primary meaning of ᵹᴀıᴄ is to "cut off," or "sever." See O'Donovan's *Supplt. to O'Reilly's Irish Dictionary,* under ᵹᴀᴄᴀım.

N

bpolaiġ, apd egnaiġ Ṡoeidil uile, ocur aird ſepleiġinn
Apd Macha, do éc. Aṁláib .h. Daiġri do tocht co
hí dá oilitri, ocur a éc a nhí iar naitriġe toġaide.
Ṡaill ċairlen Muiġe Caba, ocur drem do Uiḃ Echaċ
Ulad, do toiġeċt ap creic a tír Eoġain co torrachc-
adar co leim Neill, ocur ġo ro ġaḃrat bú annrin.
Teid Doṁnall ṁáġ Laċlainn na ndeġaid, ocur ruc
orra aġ Caḃán na ġrann ard, co tardrat deabaid
dóiḃ, ocur ġurro ṁuiġ ſor na Ṡalloib, ġur cuired a
ndeiġ ár, ocur co tardad ſádhaḃ do ġall ġai irin ſí
a aonur, co torcair annrin a bſritġuin an ṁádṁa, .i.
Domnall mac Aoda ṁéġ Laċlainn, ri Oiliġ, ocur riḋamna Erenn ap cruṫ, ocur ap ċeill, ap tiġeḋur, ocur ap
treaḃaire; ocur rucaḃ an la rin fein co hApd Macha,
ocur ro haḃnacaḃ co honorach. Sluaiġed la Seon na
Cúirti ocur la Ṡalloib Erenn uile, a Connachta, maille
re Conchobar .h. nDiarmada, ocur mac Ruaidri hi
Conchobair mur oen rú. Tinoilir rí Connacht, .i.
Conchobar Moenṁoiġe, maẛt Connacht uile, ocur tic
Domnall .h. Briain ġo ndreim do ſeruiḃ Muman
[i roċſraide rí Connacht. Ro loircret na Ṡaill cuid
do cellaib Connacht, ocur ni ro leiġret na Ṡoeidhel
rṡoeiled oroile doiḃ. Imrait, umorro, na Ṡaill tar a
nair a hiarthur Connacht co rangadur Err dara, do
dul a tír Conaill. Cruinniḃer .h. Moeldoraid, .i.

<hr>

[1] *Leim-Neill;* lit. "Niall's Leap."
The Annals of Ulster and the Four
Masters have Leim-mic-Neill ("the
son of Niall's Leap"), which seems to
be the correct form. It was the name
of some place in the neighbourhood
of Dungannon, co. Tyrone, called
after Donnagan, son of Niall, son of
Maelduin, son of Aedh Oirdnighe,
monarch of Ireland, who died in the
year 819. See O'Donovan's *Four
Mast.,* A.D. 1188, note 2.

[2] *Royal heir.* riḋamna. This

word which means literally "materies
regis," is usually translated royal heir,
for want of a better synonyme; but the
context implies only that Domhnall
Mac Lachlainn, on account of the
qualities attributed to him, was
worthy to be king of Erinn.

[3] *In the host.* . . . . ſaide,
MS. Some letters erased. The read-
ing i roċſaide is restored from the
Annals of Ulster.

[4] *Of some others.* Instead of the clause
in the text, "7 ni ro leiġret na

of all the Gaeidhel, and chief lector of Ard-Macha, died. A.D.
Amhlaibh O'Daighri went to Hi on a pilgrimage, and [1188.]
he died in Hi after select penance. The Foreigners of the castle of Magh-Cobha, and a party of the Ui-Echach-Uladh, went on a preying excursion into Tir-Eoghain, until they arrived at Leim-Neill,[1] where they seized cows. Domhnall Mac Lachlainn went after them, and overtook them at Cabhán-na-crann-ard, and gave them battle; and the Foreigners were defeated and put to great slaughter; and a thrust of a foreign spear was given to the king alone, who fell there in the heat of the battle, viz.:—Domhnall, son of Aedh Mac Lachlainn, king of Oilech, and royal heir[2] of Erinn as regards figure, intelligence, hospitality, and wisdom; and *his body* was conveyed on the same day to Ard-Macha, and honourably interred. A hosting into Connacht by John de Curci and the Foreigners of all Erinn, accompanied by Conchobhar O'Diarmada and the son of Ruaidhri O'Conchobhair. The king of Connacht, i.e. Conchobhar Maenmhaighe, assembles the chieftains of all Connacht, and Domhnall O'Briain, with a number of the men of Mumha, comes in the host[3] of the king of Connacht. The Foreigners burned some of the churches of Connacht, and the Gaeidhel did not allow them *to effect* the demolition of some others.[4] The Foreigners, moreover, turned back from the West of Connacht, until they reached Es-dara, to go into Tir-Conaill. O'Maeldoraidh, i.e. Flaithbhertach, assembles

---

Goeidhel sgoeiledh oroile doib," "and the Gaeidhel did not allow them *to effect* the demolition of some others," the Annals of Ulster and the Four Masters read "7 ni ro leicset scoiliudh doib," which Dr. O'Donovan freely translates "but they [i.e. English] made no delay," but which should be rendered "and they did not allow them [the English] to disperse." Possibly the word oroile, considered by the Editor to be a mistake for aroile, and translated "some others" is meant for o aroile, "from each other," in which case the translation should be "and the Gaeidhel did not allow them [the English] to disperse."

plaiτbeρτach, maiτe čenel Conaill na gcoinne co Oρuim čliaϋ; ocuρ óτ čualaϖaρ na ʒaill ρin ρo loiρcτeτ eρρ ϖaρa co léiρ, ocuρ cloaiϖ ταρ a naiρ a gCoρρρliab, ocuρ τucρaτ Connachταiʒ ammuρ ρoρρa a gCoρρρliab, ocuρ ρo čuiρρeτ a náρ. Ro maρbaϖ, ϖona, moρán ϖá maiτib. Τoρčuiρ ann, ϖona, Muρchaϖ mac Feρʒail .h. Moeilρuanaiϖ, ocuρ Maelρechlainn .h. Maταϖain, eτ alii mulτi cum eiρ. ʒilla Cρiρτ mac Conʒalaiʒ .h. Muiρeϖaiʒ moρτuuρ eρτ; ocuρ ρaʒbuiϖ na ʒaill in τíρ can a bec ϖo milleϖ ϖon cuρ ρin. Eταin inʒen .h. Cuinn, ρiʒan Muman, ϖo bi ʒa hailiτρi ic Ooiρe, ϖo eċ iaρ mbuaiϖ o ϖoman ocuρ o ϖeman. Muiρceρταch mac Uaϖa .h. Concennaiϖ, ρi .h. nOiaρmaϖa, moρτuuρ eρτ. Oomnall mac Lochlainn .h. Maolρuanaiϖ, ocuρ Feρccal .h. Τaϖc in τechlaiʒ, ocuρ Plaiτϖeρταch mac Siτρica .h. Finnachτa occiρi ρunτ. Muiρceρταch .h. bρain, ρi bρeʒmaicče, occiρuρ eρτ. Τaiτhleč mac Conchobaiρ, mic Oiaρmaϖa, mic Τaϖc .h. Maelρuanaiϖ, occiρuρ eρτ.

ct. ianaiρ i. p.; l. x.; .ix. mbliaϖna ochτmoʒaϖ aρ ceϖ, aρ mile, aiρ in Τiʒeρna. Oomnall mac Muiρceρταich meʒ Laċlainn [ϖo maρbaϖ] ϖo ʒalloiϋ Oal Aρaϖi acu ρein. Muρchaϖ O Ceρϋail, aiρϖρi Oiρʒiall, ϖo eċ iρin mainiρτiρ móiρ iaρ naiτρiʒe τoʒaiϖe. Aρϖ Macha ϖo loρcaϖ o cρoρρa bρiʒϖe co ρecleρ bρiʒϖe, iτiρ ρaiτh, ocuρ τρian, ocuρ τempall. Echmiliϋ mac mic Cana, ρonuρ ocuρ ρoϋaρταin Τiρe hEoʒain uile, ϖo eċ. Mac na hoiϖče O Maolρuanaiϖ, ρi bρeρ Manach,

---

[1] *Left the country.* The Annals of Ulster add aρ eicin (ar eicin), "by compulsion." This clause is evidently misplaced, and should follow the expression "et alii multi cum eis" in the preceding sentence.

[2] *Breghmhaighe.* The Annals of Ulster read bρeʒṁuine (Breghmhuine), which is the correct form. The name is still preserved in that of the barony of Brawny, co. Westmeath.

[3] *Was slain.* The corresponding expression in the text, [ϖo maρbaϖ], is supplied from the Annals of Ulster.

[4] *With themselves.* The MS. has aċa for aca (with them), as in the Annals of the Four Masters. The Annals of Ulster read acu.

[5] *The great monastery;* i.e. the Abbey of Mellifont, in the co. of Louth.

[6] *Crossa-Brighde,* i.e. "Brigid's

the chieftains of Cenel-Conaill to Druim-cliabh, to meet them; and when the Foreigners heard this they burned Es-dara entirely, and turned back into Corr-sliabh; and the men of Connacht made an attack on them in Corr-sliabh, and put them to slaughter. Many of their principal men were slain. Murchadh, son of Ferghal O'Maelruanaidh, and Maelsechlainn O'Matadhain, fell there also, et alii multi cum eis. Gillachrist, son of Congalach O'Muiredhaigh, mortuus est; and the Foreigners left the country[1] without injuring much of it on this occasion. Etain, daughter of O'Cuinn, queen of Mumha, who was on a pilgrimage at Doire, died after triumphing over the world and the devil. Muirchertach, son of Uada O'Concennain, king of Ui-Diarmada, mortuus est. Domhnall, son of Lochlainn O'Maelruanaidh, and Ferghal O'Taidhg-in-Teghlaigh, and Flaithbhertach, son of Sitric O'Finnachta, occisi sunt. Muirchertach O'Brain, king of Breghmhaighe,[2] occisus est. Taithlech, son of Conchobhar, son of Diarmaid, son of Tadhg O'Maelruanaidh, occisus est.

The kalends of January on the 1st feria, the 10th of the moon; the age of the Lord eighty-nine years, and a hundred, and a thousand. Domhnall, son of Muirchertach Mac Lachlainn, [was slain][3] by the Foreigners of Dal-Araidhe, *whilst staying* with themselves.[4] Murchadh O'Cerbhaill, chief king of Oirghiall, died in the great monastery,[5] after choice penance. Ard-Macha was burned from Crossa-Brighde[6] to Recles-Brighde,[7] including Rath and Trian,[8] and churches. Echmilidh, son of MacCana, the happiness and prosperity of all Tir-Eoghain, died. Mac-na-hoidhche[9] O'Maelruanaidh, king of Feara-Manach, was

---

crosses." "These crosses probably marked boundaries and limits of certain jurisdiction; but where they stood it is impossible now to pronounce." Reeves's *Ancient Churches of Armagh*, p. 20.

[7] *Regles – Brighde.* The abbey church of St. Brigid. *Ib.*, p. 25.

[8] *Rath and Trian.* See note [6], p. 67.

[9] *Mac-na-hoidhche*; which signifies "son of the night."

ꝺo αιꞇριꞡαꝺ, ocuꞃ ι ꝺuL ꝺoᓉum ι CeꞃꞃαιL, ocuꞃ ꞃLuαꞡ
ꞡαLL ꝺo ꞇeαchꞇ ιꞃ [ιn] ꞇιꞃ; ocuꞃ compαιcιꝺ .h. CeꞃꞃαιLL
ocuꞃ .h. maoLꞃuαnαιꝺ ꞃιu, ocuꞃ mαιꞡιꞃ ꞃoꞃ .h. CeꞃbαιLL,
ocuꞃ mαꞃbꞇαꞃ O maoLꞃuαnαιꝺ. Conchobαꞃ maonmαιꞡe,
mαc Ruαιꝺꞃι, αιꞃꝺꞃι Connαchꞇ, ocuꞃ ꞃιꝺαmnα Eιꞃenn
uιLe, ꝺo mαꞃꞃαꝺ ꝺα Luchꞇ ꞡꞃαꝺhα ꞃeιn, heꝺon, muιꞃ-
ceꞃꞇαch mαc CαꞇhαιL, mιc Ꝺιαꞃmαꝺα, ocuꞃ ꝺU Ꝼιnn-
αchꞇα, .ι. ιn cꞃoꞃαch ꝺonn .h. Ꝼιnnαchꞇαιꝺ, ocuꞃ αn
menꝺꞇαch O CιmLιꝺcαιn, ꞇꞃια eꞃαιL α bꞃαꞇhαꞃ ꞃeιn, .ι.
Conchobαιꞃ .h. n'Ꝺιαꞃmαꝺα. α mbeoL Ꞇoᓉαιꞃ ꞡιbhꞃι
ꞃoꞃ mαꞃꞃαꝺ. Conchobαꞃ .h. n'Ꝺιαꞃmαꝺα, mαc Ruαιꝺꞃι
ι Conchobαιꞃ, ꞃιꝺαmnα Connαchꞇ, ꝺo mαꞃbαꝺ ꝺo CαꞇhαL
ᓉαꞃꞃαch, mαc Conchobαιꞃ maonmαιꞡe, α nꝺιꞡαιL α
αꞇhαꞃ. αꞃꝺ machα ꝺo αꞃccαιn ꝺo Seoιn nα Cúιꞃꞇe
ocuꞃ ꝺo ꞡαLLoιb. mαc nα hΙmꞃeꞃαꞃι, ꞃí Sαxαn, ꝺo éc.
maoLcαιnnιch .h. Ꝼeꞃcomαιꞃ, ꞃeꞃLeιꞡιnn Ꝺoιꞃe, ꝺo
bαꞇhαꝺ eꞇιꞃ αιꞃꝺ ocuꞃ ιnnιꞃ Eoꞡhαιn. Ꝺιαꞃmαιꝺ
mαc ꞆoιꞃꝺheαLbαιꞡh .h. Conchobαιꞃ occιꞃuꞃ eꞃꞇ.
Ꝺonꝺchαꝺ .h. ꝼαιLαmαιn, uαꞃαL ꞃαcαꞃꞇ, ocuꞃ ꞃꞃuꞇh
ꞃenoιꞃ cLαιnnι Uαꞇαch, quιeuιꞇ. muꞃchαꝺ O ꝼLαn-
ꝺαꞡαιn, ꝺux cLαιnne CαꞇhαιL, moꞃꞇuuꞃ eꞃꞇ.

Kl. Enáιꞃ .ιι. ꞃ.; [L.]xxι. Nóᓉαꞇ [bLιαꝺαn] αꞃ ceꝺ
αꞃ mιLe αb ιncαꞃnαꞇιone Ꝺomιnι noꞃꞇꞃι ιeꞃu Cꞃιꞃꞇι,
eꞇ ꞃecunꝺuꞃ αnnuꞃ ꞃꞃeꞃαꞃαꞇιonιꞃ bιꞃꞃexꞇι, αc .xιιιι.
αnnuꞃ cιcLι ꝺecennoueαLιꞃ, αꞇque .c.xxιιιι. αnnuꞃ
unꝺecιmι cιcLι mαꞡnι ꞃαꞃcαLιꞃ αb ιnιꞇιo munꝺι. Lonꞡ
CαꞇhαιL cꞃoιbꝺeꞃꞡ hι Conchobαιꞃ, ꞃí Connαchꞇ, ꝺo
ᓉαꞇhαꝺ αꞃ Loᓉ Rιb, ocuꞃ ꞃo báꞇheꝺ xxxuι. uιꞃι ιm
αιꞃechꞇαᓉ .h. Rαꝺuιb, ꝺux cLαιnnι ꞇomαLꞇαιꞡh, ocuꞃ

---

1 *Into the country*; i.e. into Feara-
Manach, or Fermanagh, then the
territory of O'Maelruanaidh (O'Mulroney).

2 *The Crosach Donn.* This sobriquet signifies the "brown-streaked."
The word cꞃoꞃαch means cross-
streaked, or seamed, and was some-

times applied to persons having scars
across the face.

3 *The Mendlach*; i.e. "the crafty."

4 *O'Diarmada.* In the Annals of
Ulster (Dublin copy) the words mαc
Coꞃmαιc ("son of Cormac") are
added over the name O'Diarmada.

5 *Son of the Empress.* Henry II.

dethroned, and he went to O'Cerbhaill ; and a Foreign army came into the country;[1] and O'Cerbhaill and O'Maelruanaidh encountered them, and O'Cerbhaill was defeated, and O'Maelruanaidh slain. Conchobhar Maenmhaighe, son of Ruaidhri, chief king of Connacht, and royal heir of all Erinn, was killed by his own favorites, viz. :—Muirchertach, son of Cathal, son of Diarmaid, and O'Finnachta, i.e. the Crosach Donn[2] O'Finnachta, and the Mendtach[3] O'Cimlidhcain, through the instigation of his own brother, viz. :—Conchobhar O'Diarmada. In the entrance of Tochar-Gibhsi he was slain. Conchobhar O'Diarmada,[4] son of Ruaidhri O'Conchobhair, royal heir of Connacht, was killed by Cathal Carrach, son of Conchobhar Maenmhaighe, in revenge of his father. Ard-Mácha was plundered by John de Curci and the Foreigners. The son of the Empress,[5] king of the Saxons, died. Maelcainnigh O'Fercomhais, lector of Doire, was drowned between Ard[6] and Inis-Eoghain. Diarmaid, son of Toirdhelbhach O'Conchobhair, occisus est. Donnchadh O'Fallamhain, noble priest, and illustrious senior of Clann-Uadach, quievit. Murchadh O'Flannagain, dux of Clann-Cathail, mortuus est.

The kalends of January on the 2nd feria, the 21st [of the moon] ; ninety [years], and a hundred, and a thousand ab Incarnatione Domini nostri Jesu[7] Christi, et secundus annus præparationis bissexti,[8] ac xiiii. annus cicli decennovenalis,[9] atque cxxuii. annus undecimi[10] cicli magni paschalis ab initio mundi. The ship of Cathal Crobhderg O'Conchobhair, king of Connacht, was drowned in Loch-Ribh, and thirty-six men were drowned, including Airechtach O'Radhuibh, dux of Clann-Tomaltaigh, and

---

[6] *Ard;* i.e. Ardmagilligan, or Tamlaghtard, in the N. of the co. of Londonderry.

[7] *Jesu.* ıhƃu, MS.

[8] *Præparationis bissexti.* ꝑꝑꝓ cıonıꞃ bıꞃeꞓꞇı, MS.

[9] *Decennovenalis.* ꝺecınoũnꝺꞇ, MS.

[10] *Undecimi.* unꝺecım, MS.

ım Conchobaṗ, mac Caċaıl mıʒaṗán, mıc Ꞇoıṗṗ○hel-
baıʒh hı Conchobaıṗ, ocuṗ ım Ꞇⁿuıṗceṗꞇach mac n'Oıaṗmaꝺa mıc Ꞇaıꝺc hı Ꞇⁿoelṗuanaıꝺ, ocuṗ ım Ꞇⁿuıṗʒeṗ
mac Uaꞇa hı Conċenuınn. 'Ouıꝺeṗṗa, ınʒen 'Oıaṗmaꝺa
mıc Ꞇaıꝺʒ, ben an Coṗnamaıċ hı 'Ouꝺꝺa, moṗꞇua eṗꞇ.
Ꞇⁿóṗ, ınʒen Ꞇoıṗṗꝺhelbaıʒ hı Conchobaıṗ, moṗꞇua
eṗꞇ. 'Oıaṗmaıꝺ .h. Ꞃabaṗꞇaıʒ, abb 'Oúṗⁿhaıʒe Coluım
Cılle, quıeuıꞇ. Ꞓıllenꝺ, ınʒen Ꞃıacáın .h. Ꞇⁿoelṗuanaıꝺ, .ı. ben Ꞓıṗechꞇaıʒ .h. Ꞃaꝺuıꝺ, moṗꞇua eṗꞇ.
Ꞇⁿaolṗechlaınn .h. Nechꞇaın ocuṗ ʒıllabeṗaıʒ .h.
Sluaıʒeꝺhaıʒ ꝺo ⁿhaṗbaꝺ la Ꞇoıṗṗꝺhelbach mac
Ꞃuaıꝺṗı hı Conchobaıṗ. Sımón Ꝑueṗ.

|Cꞇ. Ꞑnáıṗ ııı. ꝼ.; L. ıı.; blıaꝺaın aṗ noċaꞇ aṗ ceꝺ, aṗ
mıle, aıṗ an Ꞇıʒeṗna. Ꞃuaıꝺṗı .h. Conchobaıṗ ꝺꝼáʒbáıl
Connachꞇ, ocuṗ a ꝺul ı Cenel Conaıll. 'Oomnall, mac
Ꞇⁿoeılıṗṗa meıc ınꝺ abaıꝺ, moṗıꞇuṗ. In ʒaıllıⁿh ꝺo
ꞇṗáʒhaꝺ an ꝺlıaꝺaın ṗı, ocuṗ ꝼṗıꞇ ꞇuaꝺ ınnꞇe, ocuṗ
láⁿh ón ċuıṗṗ ʒo ċéle ꝺı; ocuṗ ꝼṗıꞇ ṗleʒ ınnꞇe, ocuṗ ꞇṗí
ꝺuıṗn ocuṗ ꞇṗí meoıṗ ılleıꞇeꝺ ṗlenna ná ṗleıʒe ṗın,
ocuṗ láⁿh on nʒualuınn a ṗaꝺ. Ꞑaċċıʒeṗn mac Ꞇⁿáoıl-
ċıaṗáın, aıṗꝺꝼenoıṗ Ꞑṗenn, eṗṗuc ċluana hΙṗaıṗꝺ,
moṗıꞇuṗ. Caıṗlén Ꞃaċa Cuanaṗꞇaıʒ ꝺo ꝺenum. ʒaoꞇ
ⁿhóṗ ıṗın blıaꝺaın ṗı.

|Cꞇ. Ꞑnaıṗ .ıııı. ꝼ.; L. xııı.; ꝺa blıaꝺaın noċaꞇ aṗ
ceꝺ, aṗ mıle, aıṗ ın Ꞇıʒeṗna. 'Oa mac mıc Caṗṗʒamna,
ocuṗ ꝺa mac Ꞇaıꝺc mıc Ualaıṗʒ, ocuṗ .h. hꞒaıṗꞇ, ocuṗ

---

[1] *Son of Cathal Migaran.* The
Four Masters simply say mac
Caċaıl; "son of Cathal." Dr.
O'Donovan (*Four Mast.*, A.D. 1190,
note ⁿ) thought that the Cathal
meant was Cathal Crobhderg, or
"Cathal red-fist," who was the
brother of Cathal Migaran.

[2] *Son of Tadhg*; i.e. son of Tadhg
O'Maelruanaidh. O'Donovan (*Four
Mast.* ad an.) is incorrect in making

mac Ꞇaıꝺʒ a family name (Mac
Teige) at this period.

[3] *The Cosnamhach Ua Dubhda*, or
Protector O'Dowda. The words ben
an Coṗnamaıċ hı 'Ouꝺꝺa (wife of
the Cosnamhach O'Dubhda) have
been interlined by the orig. hand.

[4] *Aillenn.* The obit of this woman
is given by the Four Mast. under the
year 1191.

[5] *Simon Puer.* This entry has

Conchobhar, son of Cathal Migaran,[1] son of Toirdhelbhach O'Conchobhair, and Muirchertach, son of Diarmaid, son of Tadhg O'Maelruanaidh, and Muirghes, son
of Uada O'Concennain. Duibhessa, daughter of Diarmaid, son of Tadhg,[2] wife of the Cosnamhach O'Dubhda,[3]
mortua est. Mor, daughter of Toirdhelbhach O'Conchobhair, mortua est. Diarmaid O'Rábhartaigh, abbot
of Durmhagh-Choluim-Chille, quievit. Aillenn,[4] daughter
of Riacan O'Maelruanaidh, i.e. wife of Airechtach
O'Radhuibh, mortua est. Maelsechlainn O'Nechtain and
Gillaberaigh O'Sluaighedhaigh were slain by Toirdhelbhach, son of Ruaidhri O'Conchobhair. Simon Puer.[5]

The kalends of January on the 3rd feria, the 2nd of the
moon; the age of the Lord ninety-one years, and a hundred, and a thousand. Ruaidhri O'Conchobhair left
Connacht and went[6] into Cenel-Conaill. Domhnall, son
of Maelisa Mac-ind-abaid,[7] moritur. The Gaillimh[8] became dry this year, and an axe was found in it *measuring*
a hand from one point of it to the other; and a spear was
found in it, and the breadth of the blade of this spear was
three hands and three fingers; and its length was a hand
from the shoulder. Echthighern, son of Maelciarain,
chief senior of Erinn, bishop of Cluain-Iraird, moritur.
The castle of Rath-cuanartaigh was built. Great wind
in this year.

The kalends of January on the 4th[9] feria, the 13th[10] of
the moon; the age of the Lord ninety-two years, and a
hundred, and a thousand. The two sons of Mac Carghamhna, and two sons of Tadhg Mac Ualairg, and

---

been left unfinished. The name of
Simon Puer (Poer, or De la Poer)
does not occur in the usual lists of
the early English colonists of Ireland.

[6] *Went*. The Four Masters add
that the object of Ruaidhri's journey
was to obtain assistance to recover
his kingdom of Connacht.

[7] *Mac-ind-abaid*; i.e. "son of the
abbot."

[8] *Gaillimh*; pron. *Gailleeve*; i.e.
the Galway river.

[9] *The 4th*. The MS. has ııı (3),
which is wrong.

[10] *The 13th*. The MS. reads xxıı
(23), but incorrectly.

bρανάn mac bρανάin, eτ αlιι cum eιρ, το mαρbατ το ξαlloib αξ Ráτ Αοτα, ocuρ τρeαm το ξαlloib ρein το τuιτim ann. Ταιτlech .h. Τuττα, ρι .h. nΑmαlξαιτ ocuρ .h. bριαcρατ Μuαιτe, το mαρbατ το τá mac a mic ρein. Μαιτm ιc Cαρραιτ eτcαραιτ ρορ ξαlloib, ρια muιnτeρ Μαοιlρinna. Νa ξιúρnαρραιξ το mαρbατ ιρ in Μumain, ocuρ áρ móρ immαιlle ρριu. Cαιρlén áτα in Uρτuιρ ocuρ cαιρlen Cιlle bιαριξe το τenum ιρ in bliατain ρι. Οeτh .h. Ρloinn, τux ρíl Μοelρuαin, mορτuuρ eρτ. Εοchατ .h. bοeiξιll το mαρbατ το Uιτ bριαcρατ Αρτα ρρατα.

Κt. Εnαιρ .u. ρ.; Λ.xxιιιι.; τρι bliατnα nοτατ aρ ceτ, aρ mile, aιρ in Τιξeρna. Τomnαll Ο bριαin, lοcραντ ροluρτα ρíτα ocuρ coξτα, ocuρ ρella aτanτα einιτ Λeιτe Μοτα ocuρ na Μuιτhnech, το τul τéc. Ξοιll το τeachτ aρ Innιρ .h. Ρinnταin, ocuρ a cuρ aρ eιξin τι. Cúmιτe Ο Ρloinn το mαρbατ το ξαlloib. 8nechτa móρ eτιρ τá τáιρc ιρ in mbliατain ρι. Τιαρmαιτ mac Conbροξα hι Τímuραιξ, τux Clαinnι Μáιlιξρa, ocuρ ρι .h. bραιlξe ρρι ρo ρoττα, mορτuuρ eρτ. Cαthαl oταρ mac meιc Cαρρthαιξ occiρuρ eρτ. Τeρτορξαll, ιnξen Μuρchατα hι Μαeιlρechlαinn, mορτuα eρτ a nαιlιτρι immαιnιρτιρ Τροcαιτ áτα. Μuιρceρtach, mac Μuρchατα [mic] Μuρchατα, ρι .h. Cιnnρeαlαιξ, mορτuρ. Οeτ .h. Μοeιlτρénuinn, τux clαinnι Con-chobαιρ, occiρuρ eρτ. Μαcbethαιτ .h. Τοταιlén, aιρτinnech Cαmτα, mορτuuρ eρτ ι nαιlιτρι a nInιρ Clοτρann. Ξιllαcριρτ .h. Μuccαράn, eρρuc Αιρξιall, quιeuιτ. Cαιρlen Τomnαιξ Μαιξen το τenum ιρ in

1 *Alii.* alí, MS.
2 *Giurnassaigh.* This entry is not contained in any of the other Irish chronicles; and the Editor has not been able to identify the persons whose names are disguised under the form " Giurnassaigh."
3 *Cill-Bixsighe.* Rectè Cill-Big-
sighe, or "church of St. Bigsech;" now Kilbixy, a village in the barony of Moygoish, co. Westmeath.
4 *The 5th.* The MS. reads uιι (7th); but the original figure was u (5th), which has been altered to uιι by a later hand.

O'hAirt, and Branan Mac Brànain, et alii[1] cum eis, were slain by Foreigners at Rath-Aedha; and a number of the Foreigners themselves fell there. Taithlech O'Dubhda, king of Ui-Amhalghaidh and Ui-Fiachrach-Muaidhe, was killed by the two sons of his own son. A victory was gained at Carraidh-echaraidh, over the Foreigners, by Muinter-Maelsinna. The Giurnassaigh[2] were slain in Mumha, and a great slaughter along with them. The castle of Ath-in-urchair, and the castle of Cill-Bixsighe,[3] were erected in this year. Aedh O'Floinn, dux of Sil-Maelruain, mortuus est. Eochaidh O'Baeighill was slain by the Ui-Fiachrach of Ard-sratha.

The kalends of January on the 5th[4] feria, the 24th of the moon; the age of the Lord ninety-three years, and a hundred, and a thousand. Domhnall O'Briain, brilliant lamp of peace and war, and kindling star of the honour of Leth-Modha and the men of Mumha, died.[5] The Foreigners went upon Inis-Ui-Finntain, and were driven therefrom by force. Cumhidhe O'Floinn was slain by the Foreigners. Great snow between *the* two Easters[6] in this year. Diarmaid, son of Cubrogha O'Dimusaigh, dux of Clann-Maclughra, and king of Ui-Failghe for a long time, mortuus est. Cathal Odhar, son of Mac Carthaigh, occisus est. Derbhorcaill, daughter of Murchadh O'Maelsechlainn, mortua est in pilgrimage, in the monastery of Droichet-atha. Muirchertach, [son][7] of Murchadh Mac Murchadha, king of Ui-Ceinnsealaigh, moritur. Aedh O'Maelbhrenainn, dux of Clann-Conchobhair, occisus est. Macbethaidh O'Dobhailen, airchinnech of Camach, mortuus est in pilgrimage, in Inis-Clothrann. Gillachrist O'Muccaran, bishop of Airghiall,[8] quievit. The castle of Domhnach-Maighen was erected in this year. Maelsech-

---

[5] *Died.* ᴅᴏ ᴅᴜʟ ᴅéᴄ; lit. "went to death." This entry and the two following are given by the Four Masters under the year 1194.

[6] *Between the two Easters;* i.e. Easter Sunday, and Low Sunday, which

is usually called "Little Easter." The entry is repeated in the MS.

[7] [*Son.*] [ᴍᴀᴄ]; supplied from the Annals of Ulster.

[8] *Bishop of Airghiall;* i.e. bishop of Clogher.

mbliadain ṁ. Moelṛechlainn mäc Ḋonnchaḋa, ṁ Oṛṛaiʒhe, ꝺo éʒ. Iniṛ Cloṭṛann ꝺo aṛcuin ꝺo Ʒilliṗeṛṫ mac Ʒoiṛꝺealb, cona ʒalloiḃ, ocuṛ ꝺo macaiḃ Ʒillecṗiṛṫ mic Caṗṗʒamna, .i. Ʒillacṗoiḃeṛṗáṫ ocuṛ Aṁlaiḃ, co muinṫeṛ Maeilṛinna inmaille ṛṛiu. Muiṛceṛṫach .h. Ceṛbaill ꝺo ḋallaꝺ. Oenʒuṛ, mac Ʒoṛmán .h. Ailʒiuṛa, quieuiṫ [in] Cṗiṛṫo aʒ ú ailiṫṛi a nIniṛ Cloṭṛann. ū.ccc.xcuiii.

Kt. enaiṛ uii. ṗ.; l. u.; ceiṫṛe bliaꝺna nočaṫ aṛ ceꝺ, aṛ mile, aiṛ in Ṫiʒeṛna. Ečmaṛcach .h. Caṫán ꝺo éʒ a ṛecleṛ Poil. Sacaṛṫ moṛ Ia ꝺo éʒ. Siṫṛec .h. Ʒaiṛmleʒhaiʒ ꝺo maṛbaꝺ ꝺo mac Ꝺuinnṛleḃe. Ab iniṫio munꝺi iuxta .lxx. Inṫeṗṗṛeṫeṛ, ūi. ꝺc.xluii.; iuxta ueṛo Eḃṛeoṛ, ū.ccc.xcuiii. Ab Incaṛnaṫione auṫem iuxta Eḃṛeoṛ, ṁ.ccc.xluii.; ṛecunꝺum Ꝺioniṛium, ṁ.c.xciiii.; iuxta ueṛo Ḃeꝺam ab Incaṛnaṫione, ṁ.c.lxxxuii. Solaṗiṛ quiꝺem cicli, .i. cicli .xxuii. annoṛum, xix. annuṛ; cicli inꝺicṫioniṛ .xii. annuṛ. Secunꝺuṛ annuṛ ṗṛeṗaṛaṫioniṛ biṛṛexṫi; cxxxi. annuṛ unꝺecimi cicli maʒni ṗaṛcaliṛ ab iniṫio munꝺi. Mac Conchobaiṛ mic Ꝺomnaill ʒeṗṗlámaiʒ .h. Ḃṛiain ꝺo ḋallaꝺ ocuṛ ꝺo ṛṗochaꝺ lá ʒalloiḃ. Mac Maʒnuṛa mic Ꝺuinnṛleḃi ꝺo maṛbaꝺ ꝺúa Aṅluain. Sluaiʒeꝺ le Ʒilliṗeṛṫ mac Ʒoiṛꝺealb co hEṛṛ Ṛuaiḃ, ocuṛ ṛo imṗó ó Eṛṛ Ṛuaiḃ ʒan ṛoṫaṗḃa ꝺonṫ ṛluaiʒeꝺ ṛin. Conṛꝺuinṫín .h. Ḃṛiain, eṛṗuc Cill Ꝺalua, ꝺo éʒ. .ū.ccc.xcix.

---

1 *Osraighe.* oṛṛṅe, MS.

2 *Mac Goisdealbh.* The Four Masters say "la macaiḃ Oiṛꝺealb," "by the sons of Osdealbh." In the Dublin copy of the Annals of Inisfallen the name is written Gillibert (or Gilbert) de Nangle; which is correct, as Nangle was the original name of the family subsequently called Mac Goisdelbh, and now Costello.

3 *Gilla-Croichefraich;* i.e. "servant of Croichefraich," or Cruimther-Fraech, founder and patron of the ancient monastery of Cloone, in the co. Leitrim. For an account of Cruimther-Fraech (i.e. Presbyter Fraechus), see, in Colgan's *Acta Sanctorum Hib*, the places indicated under "Fraichus Magister S. Berachi," 3rd index. His festival was on the 20th of December.

lainn, son of Donnchadh, king of Osraighe,[1] died. Inis-
Clothrann was plundered by Gilbert Mac Goisdealbh,[2]
with his Foreigners, and by the sons of Gillachrist Mac
Carghamhna, viz.:—Gilla-Croichefraich[3] and Amhlaibh,
having Muinter-Maelsinna along with them. Muircher-
tach O'Cerbhaill was blinded. Aenghus, son of Gorman
O'Ailghiusa, quievit [in] Christo on his pilgrimage in
Inis-Clothrann. v̄.ccc.xcviii.[4]

The kalends of January on the 7th feria, the 5th of the
moon; the age of the Lord ninety-four years, and a hundred,
and a thousand. Echmarcach O'Cathain died in Recles-
Poil.[5] The great priest of Hi died. Sitric O'Gairmleghaigh was slain by Mac Duinnsleibhe. Ab initio mundi
juxta lxx. Interpretes, v̄i.dc.xlvi.; juxta vero Ebræos,
v̄.ccc.xcviii.[6] Ab Incarnatione[7] autem juxta Ebræos,
M.ccc.xlvii.; secundum Dionysium, M.c.xciiii.; juxta vero
Bedam, ab Incarnatione M.c.lxxxvii. Solaris quidem cycli,
i.e. cycli xxviii. annorum, xix. annus; cycli indictionis xii.
annus. Secundus annus præparationis[8] bissexti;[9] cxxxi.
annus undecimi cycli magni paschalis ab initio mundi.
The son of Conchobhar, son of Domhnall Gerrlamhach
O'Briain, was blinded and emasculated by Foreigners.
The son of Maghnus Mac Duinnsleibhe was slain by
O'hAnluain. A hosting by Gilbert Mac Goisdealbh to
Es-Ruaidh; and he returned from Es-Ruaidh without
having obtained much profit on this hosting. Constantine
O'Briain, bishop of Cill-Dalua, died. v̄.ccc.xcix.[10]

---

[4] v̄.ccc.xcuiii. These numerals,
though added at the end of the entry
for A.D. 1193, belong to the next
year. They represent the year of the
world (5398) corresponding to the
A.D. 1194, according to the chronicler's notion of the Hebrew computation.

[5] *Recles Poil.* The abbey church
of St Paul, at Derry.

[6] v̄.ccc.xcviii. The MS. has
v̄.ccc.xviii (5318).

[7] *Incarnatione.* incapnacione, MS.
[8] *Præparationis.* ppapacioịp, MS.
[9] *Bissexti.* bipexti, MS.
[10] v̄.ccc.xcix. These numerals,
which refer to the next year, represent
the age of the world (5399) corresponding to A.D. 1195, according to
the Hebrew computation.

Ӄt. Enαιρ. ι. ρ.; l. xuι.; u. blιαᲗnα nóċατ αρ ceᲗ αρ
mιle αιρ ιn TιƷeρnα, ρecunᲗum Თιonιριum. Ꮯb ιnιτιο
munᲗι ιuxτα .lxx. Ιnτeρρρeτeρ, ū̄.Თc.xluιιι; ιuxτα
Ebρeoρ .ū̄.ccc.xcιx. Ꮯb ιncαρnατιone ιuxτα Ebρeoρ,
m̄.cccc.xluιιι; ρecunᲗum Თιonιριum, m̄.c.xcu; ρecun-
Თum ƄeᲗαm, m̄.c.lxxxuιιι. Solαριρ cιclι .xx. αnnuρ;
τeρτιuρ αnnuρ ρρeραρατιonιρ bιρρexτι; c.xxxιι. αnnuρ
unᲗecιmι cιclι mαƷnι ραρcαlιρ αb ιnιτιο munᲗι.
Flοριnτ .ħ. Rιαcαιn hι moeιlρuαnαιᲗ, eρρuc Olειnn,
ιn Cριρτo quιeuιτ. Ꮯᵹ clιαᵹ o Თροιᵹeτ ᵹuᵹ ᵹuαιᵹ Თο
lορcαᲗ. SlοιƷeᲗ lα hEóαn nα Cúιρτe, ocuρ lα mαc UƷá
Თe lαcí, Თo ᵹαbáιl neιρτ ρορ ᵹαllοιb lαιƷen ocuρ
mumαn. mαc ƷοιρᲗelb Თo ᵹαb[áιl] . . . . CαᲗhαl
CροιᵹᲗeρƷ .ħ. Conchobαιρ, ρí Connαchτ, co ρocραιττe
Connαchτ, Თo Თul ιριn mumαιn, ocuρ ρo ṁιllρeτ
cαιρρléιn ocuρ bαιleᵹα ιomᵹα ιιnτe, ocuρ Თo ρonρατ
cρeᵹα mórα, ocuρ τanƷαᲗαρ ιmᶂlán. Ιn Ʒιllα ρρonṁαol
O ᲗοᲗαρταᵹ, ocuρ Cenél Conαιll áιρᵹenα, Თo ιmρó αρ
.ħ. mαoιlᲗοραιᲗ. CαᲗhαl CροιᵹᲗeρƷ .ħ. Conchobαιρ,
ρí Connαchτ, Თo chuρ ᵹuαιρceρτ Connαchτ Თá ᶂuρταchτ,
ocuρ cαᵹ ρeρρénαch mαιlle ρριú. mórᵹιnól Connαchτ
lα CαᲗhαl ƷCροιᵹᲗeρc co háᵹ luαιn, Თú ιρραᵹαᲗαρ Თá
ceᲗ Თéƻ uel αmρlιuρ, co τáιnιc Eoαn nα Cúιρτe, ocuρ
mαc UƷα Თé lαcí, ocuρ mαᵹι Ʒαll nα coιnne, con-
Თeρnρατ α ρíᵹ. CαᲗhαl, mαᵹ ᲗιαρmαᲗα, mιc Tαιᵹƻ hι
moeιlρuαnαιᲗ, ᲗιnnορραᲗ α Connαchταιᵹ ιριn mumáιn,
ocuρ α ᵹeαchτ ιριn mblιαᲗαιn ceᲗnα τρe neρτ α lαṁα
α Connαchταιᵹ, co ραnιc cαιρρlén nα Cαιllιƻι, ocuρ ρο
mαρᵹ Თαoιne ιomᵹα ροιme αnᲗeρ conuιƷe ριn, ocuρ Თο

---

1 *Præparationis bissexti.* ρραραιρ
bιρexτι, MS.

2 *Grandson.* ħ. for Uα (Ua or O'),
'nepos,' MS. The Four Masters say
that Florence was the son of Riacan
O'Maelruanaidh, or O'Mulroney.

3 *Was apprehended.* Თο ᵹαᵹ, for
Თο ᵹαbáιl, MS. The entry is in-

complete. The Four Masters represent the matter differently, for they
say that Mac Goisdelbh, or Mac
Costello, joined Cathal Crobhderg,
king of Connacht, in the foray into
Munster, which forms the subject of
the succeeding entry.

4 *Safely.* ιmᶂlán. This word,

The kalends of January on the 1st feria, the 16th of the moon; the age of the Lord ninety-five years, and a hundred, and a thousand, secundum Dionysium. Ab initio mundi, juxta lxx. Interpretes, vi.dc.xlvii.; juxta Ebræos, v̄.ccc.xcix. Ab Incarnatione juxta ·Ebræos, M.cccc.xlviii; secundum Dionysium, M.c.xcv.; secundum Bedam, M.c.lxxxviii.; solaris cycli xx. annus; tertius annus præparationis bissexti;[1] cxxxii. annus undecimi cycli magni paschalis ab initio mundi. Florence, grandson[2] of Riacan O'Maelruanaidh, bishop of Oilfinn, in Christo quievit. Ath-cliath from the bridge northwards was burned. A hosting by John de Curci and the son of Hugo de Laci, to assume power over the Foreigners of Laighen and Mumha. Mac Goisdealbh was apprehended[3] . . . . . Cathal Crobhderg O'Conchobhair, king of Connacht, with the army of Connacht, went into Mumha; and they destroyed many castles and towns therein, and committed great depredations; and they returned safely.[4] The Gilla-sron-mhael[5] O'Dochartaigh, and the Cenel-Conaill likewise, turned against O'Maeldoraidh. Cathal Crobhderg O'Conchobhair, king of Connacht, sent *the men of* the North of Connacht to assist him,[6] and a battalion of mercenaries along with them. A great gathering of *the men of* Connacht by Cathal Crobhderg, to Ath-Luain, where there were twelve hundred men, vel amplius; and John de Curci, and the son of Hugo de Laci, and the nobles of the Foreigners, came to meet him, when they made their peace. Cathal, son of Diarmaid, son of Tadhg O'Maelruanaidh, was expelled from Connacht into Mumha; and he came again in the same year, through the strength of his hands, into Connacht, until he reached Caislen-na-Caillighe;[7] and he killed many persons on his way from the south as far as

---

owing to the omission of the aspirated letter'(ḟ), is now generally written ımⱡán (imlán.)

[5] *The Gilla-sron-mhael*; i.e. "the pug-nosed fellow."

[6] *Him*; i.e. O'Maeldoraidh, or O'Muldory.

[7] *Caislen-na-Caillighe*. The Hag's Castle, in Lough Mask.

róne creċa móra, ocus oirgne, ó nach dernad a ríṫ.
Domnall .h. Finn, comarba Brénuinn a gCluain
ferta, quieuit. ū.cccc. Reclér Póil ocus Petair,
cona templaib, ocus co mbloid dona ráṫaib, do lorcad.
Sloiged la Ruaidri mac Duinnsleibe co ngalloib, ocus
go macaib rig Connacht, do cum cenel nEogain ocus
Airrter. Tancatur, dono, Cenel Eogain Telċa óc
ocus Airrter co maċaire Aird Maċa, co tucsat cat
dóib, ocus gurro marbad derg ár a ndoeinib; ocus
ro marbad drong do macaib rig Connacht irin maidm
sin. Muircertach mac Muircertaig meic Laclainn,
rí ceneoil Eogain, ocus ridamna Erenn uile, tuir
gairciḋ ocus engnama Leiṫe Cuinn, dírgoeiltir Gall
ocus cairlén, tocḃáil[id] ceall ocus caḋur, do marbad
do Donnchad mac Blorcaid i Caċáin a comairle cenel
Eogain uile, .i. iar tabairt na tri repíne ocus cánoine
Patraic fris a tempul tuaircertach Aird Maċa
reiṁe; ocus rucad a corp co Doire Coluim Cille,
ocus ro haḋnaiced co honorach é ann. Mac Blorcaid
i Cuirrín do argain termuinn Dáḃeóg, ocus ro marbad e fein ind, co nderg ár a muinteri, ría cinn mhíor
tria mhirḃuiliḃ Dáḃeooc. Is in mbliadain sin, dono, ro
ḃrig Domnall mac Diarmada meg Carrthaig cat ar
galloib Muman ocus Luimnig, in ro marbad a nderg

---

[1] *As peace was not made with him.*
The words ó nach dernaḋ a ríṫ (ó
nach dernadh a sith), literally translated, means "since their (or his) peace
was not made."

[2] v̄.cccc. The compiler of this
chronicle seems to have intended
adding here the year of the world
(v.cccc.xlix), corresponding to the
year A.D. 1196, according to his
notion of the Hebrew chronology, in
token of the completion of the records
for the year; but did not carry out
his intention. This conjecture is confirmed by the fact that some of the
following entries under this year are
given in the Annals of Ulster, and
also by the Four Masters, under A.D.
1196.

[3] *Recles.* A *Recles* is generally
understood to signify an "abbey
church," though sometimes apparently
denoting a cemetery. That above
referred to was at Armagh.

[4] *Raths.* See note 6, p. 67. In the
Four Masters the expression is "ɣo
mbloiḋ ṁoir don Ráiṫ," "with a
great part of the Rath"; but the word
ráṫaib (abl. pl. of ráṫ), in the text,
would imply that there was more than
one enclosure, or building enclosed by
a fosse.

that; and he committed great depredations and plunderings, as peace was not made with him.[1] Domhnall O'Finn, comarb of Brenainn at Cluain-ferta, quievit. v̄.cccc.[2] The Recles[3] of Paul and Peter, with its churches, and a part of the Raths,[4] was burned. A hosting by Ruaidhri Mac Duinnsleibhe, with the Foreigners, and with the sons of the king of Connacht, to the Cenel-Eoghain and Airthera. The Cenel-Eoghain of Telach-óg and the Airthera came, however, to the plain of Ard-Macha, and gave them battle, when a great multitude[5] of their people were slain; and a number of the sons of the king of Connacht were killed in this defeat. Muirchertach, son of Muirchertach Mac Lachlainn, king of Cenel-Eoghain, and royal heir of all Erinn, tower of the valour and bravery of Leth-Chuinn, destroyer of Foreigners and of castles,[6] founder of churches and sanctuaries,[7] was slain by Donnchadh, son of Bloscadh O'Cathain, by the advice of all the Cenel-Eoghain, viz.:—after having previously sworn to him[8] by the three shrines, and the Canoin-Patraic,[9] in the northern[10] church of Ard-Macha; and his body was conveyed to Doire-Choluim-Chille, and there honourably interred. The son of Bloscadh O'Cuirrin plundered Termonn-Dabheóg, and he himself was killed on account thereof, with a dreadful slaughter of his people, before the end of a month, through the miracles of Dabheóg. In this year, moreover, Domhnall, son of Diarmaid Mac Carthaigh, gained a victory over the Foreigners of Mumha and Luimnech, in which a great multitude[5] of

A.D.
[1195.]

---

[5] *Multitude.* áp (ár); lit. "slaughter."

[6] *Destroyer of Foreigners and of castles.* The Four Masters say "destroyer of the cities and castles of the Foreigners."

[7] *Sanctuaries.* The word caɒuf (cadhus), translated "sanctuaries," actually means "respect," or "veneration;" but the corresponding expression used by the Four Masters is caoiṁ neiṁeaɒ(caoimh-neimheadh),

which Colgan (*Trias Thaumat.,* p. 504; col. 2) renders by "sanctuarium."

[8] *To him;* i.e. after Donnchadh O'Cathain (or Donough O'Kane) had pledged his friendship to Mac Lachlainn, in presence of the sacred things referred to.

[9] *Canoin-Patraic;* i.e. the canon of St. Patrick, supposed to mean the Book of Armagh.

[10] *Northern.* Cuaıfceftach. The Annals of Ulster have ɒoıfceftach (deiscertach), "southern."

áp, ocur in po óicuip a Luimnech iαꝺ íappin; ocur po
óbpir ꝺá ṁαıóṁ eli óeor an bliαꝺαin rin.

Ƈt. Enaip 11. p.; L. xxuii.; ui. bliαꝺnα noċατ αp ceꝺ, αp
mile, αb 1ncαpnατione Ꝺomini [recunꝺum] Ꝺioniriṁ;
recunꝺum Beꝺαm, αb 1ncαpnατione Ꝺomini .m.c.lxxxix.
Ccb 1ncαpnατione iuxtα Ebreor .m. cccc. xlix. Ccb inıτıo
munꝺı iuxtα .lxx. 1ɴτeppρeτep, .ui. ꝺc. xluıı. Ccb inıτıo
munꝺı iuxtα Ebreor, ū.cccc. Solαpır cıclı .xxı. αnnur;
cıclı inꝺıcτıonır .xiiii. αnnur; cıclı lunαpır .xuı. αnnur,
αtque birreaτılır αnnur; c.xxx[ııı]. αnnur unꝺecımı cıclı
mαᵹnı pαpcαlır αb inıτıo munꝺı. . . . . αıᵹ hı Cαταpnαıᵹ,
rαcαpτ mop Cluαnα mıc Noır, quıeuıτ α mαınırτıp ċılle
Ꝺécαın, ı nouıcı ṁαnαıᵹ. 1n bαnαb mop ınᵹen hı
Mαeılpechlαınn ꝺhec. Cpeċρluαıᵹeꝺ lα ᵹαllαıb nα
Mıꝺe α τıp .h. mbρıuın, co po compuıc .h. Ruαıpc
conα muınτıp rpıú, ocur ᵹuppo moıᵹ rorr nα ᵹαlloıb,
cup mαpbαꝺ áp ꝺıáırmı ꝺıb. Ruαıꝺpı .h. rlαıτbepταıᵹ,
rí ıαpċαıp Connαchτ, ꝺo óul αp muıp αp τeıcheꝺ
Cαthαıl Cpoıbꝺepc ocur Connαchτα αıpchenα, ocur
α óul ꝺocum hı bρıαın. h. Conchobaıp ꝺá óıchup o
.h. mbρıαın ꝺopıóırı, ocur α ċup αp muıp mαp αn ceꝺnα.
Cpeċα mopα ꝺo óenım óó α Conmαıcne mαpα, ocur
α nUṁαll. Cαthαl .h. rlαıτbepταıᵹ ꝺo mαpbαꝺ.
Ruαıꝺpı mαc Ꝺuınnrleıóe ꝺo óreċ hρocραıꝺe moıpe
α Connαchταıᵹ, ım mαc Moeılírα hı Conchobaıp, ocur
ım mαc mıc Mupchαꝺα hı Mαeılnαmbó, ocur ım bρıàn
buıóe .h. rlαıċbepταıᵹ; conꝺepnrατ Ccıpᵹíαllα, ocur .h.
hCcnluαın, ocur rorclα ċeneóıl Eoᵹαın ınneαll αp α
ᵹcınn, .ı. ꝺα cατ ṁópα, co τucrατ cατ ꝺá ċéle, ᵹup

---

1 *Two other defeats.* According to
the Annals of the Four Masters, in
which the entry occurs under the year
1196, the two additional defeats were
inflicted by Mac Carthy on the English.

2 *Atque.* αıτque (aitque), MS.

3 *Bissextilis.* bırreaτılır (bisex-
tilis), MS.

4 *Undecimi.* unꝺexımı (undeximi),
MS.

5 *Magni.* mαı⅕ (for mαıᵹnı), MS.

6 . . *aigh.* The MS. is defective;
but the defect extends only to the
Christian name of O'Catharnaigh.

7 *Number.* áp (ár); lit. "slaughter."

8 *Expelled him.* ꝺá óıchup (da
dhichur). The expression is intended
to convey that Cathal Crobhderg

them were killed, and through which he afterwards expelled them from Luimnech; and he inflicted two other defeats[1] also in this year.

The kalends of January on the 2nd feria, the 27th of the moon; ninety-six years, and a hundred, and a thousand ab Incarnatione Domini [secundum] Dionysium. Secundum Bedam ab Incarnatione Domini, M.c.lxxxix. Ab Incarnatione juxta Ebræos, M. cccc. xlix. Ab initio mundi juxta lxx. Interpretes, vi.dc.xlvii. Ab initio mundi juxta Ebræos, v.cccc. Solaris cycli xxi. annus; cycli Indictionis xiiii. annus; cycli lunaris xvi. annus, atque[2] bissextilis[3] annus; cxxx[iii]. annus undecimi[4] cycli magni[5] paschalis ab initio mundi . . . aigh[6] O'Catharnaigh, great priest of Cluain-mic-Nois, quievit in the monastery of Cill-Becain, in the noviciate of a monk. The great abbess, daughter of O'Maelsechlainn, died. A predatory hosting by the Foreigners of Midhe, into the territory of Ui-Briuin; but O'Ruairc, with his people, encountered them, and the Foreigners were defeated, and a countless number[7] of them slain. Ruaidhri O'Flaithbhertaigh, king of the West of Connacht, went on the sea, to escape from Cathal Crobhderg, and from the men of Connacht also, and went to O'Briain. O'Conchobhair again expelled him[8] from O'Briain, and he was driven to sea as before. Great depredations were committed by him (*O'Flaithbhertaigh*) in Conmaicne-mara, and in Umhall. Cathal O'Flaithbhertaigh was killed. Ruaidhri Mac Duinnsleibhe conducted a large army from Connacht,[9] including the son of Maelisa O'Conchobhair, and the son of Mac Murchadha, grandson of Mael-na-mbó, and Brian Buidhe O'Flaithbhertaigh; but the Airghialla, and O'hAnluain, and the chief men of the Cenel-Eoghain assembled to meet them, viz.:—two large battalions; and they gave one another battle, when

O'Conor *procured* the expulsion of O'Flaherty from the house of O'Brien.

[9] *From Connacht.* The Four Masters state that the object of the expedition was to attack the Cenel-Eoghain and the Airthera (or Oriors).

mapbaʋ ann ant ʄocpaiʋi ʄin uile, im mac 1 Conchobaiʄ, ocuʄ im mac mic Muʄchaʋa, ocuʄ im mac h1
Plaitʄeʄtaiʒ; co nach teʄnó óiʓ aʄʄ acht mac Ouinn-
ʄleiʓe uachaʋ aʄ echaib, ocuʄ beʒan ʋont ʄocʄaiʋe.
Socʄaiʋe móʄ ʋo muinteʄ Eoluiʄ ʋo ṁapbaʋ lá
hUalʒaʄʒ .h. Ruaiʄc, ʄi bʄeiʄʄne. Ruaiʋʄi .h.
Plaitbeʄtaiʒ ʋo ʋul 1 tiʄ Conaill, ocuʄ a teacht
aʄ ʄin ʄe coiʄ comaʄba Patʄaic a teć h1 Conchobaiʄ,
ocuʄ ʄit ʋo ʋenum ʄʄiʄ, ocuʄ a ʄeʄonn ʋo ćabaiʄt ʋó.
1n ʒilla ʄuaʓ mac ṁéʒ Raʒnuill, toiʄʄech muintiʄe
hEoluiʄ, ʋo maʄbaʋ la Oiaʄmaiʋ mac Maʒnuʄa h1
Conchobaiʄ, tʄia ʄuʄáil mic Cathail h1 Ruaiʄc, [laʄ]
ʄo maʄbaʓ muinnteʄ Eolaiʄ ʄeṁi. Oeʓ .h. ʄeʄʒail,
ʋux muintiʄe Anʒaile, ʋo maʄbaʋ ʋo macaiʓ Sitʄeaca
h1 Cuinn. Matʒaṁuin mac Conchobaiʄ Maonmaiʒe
ʋo ṁaʄbaʋ le ʄeʄʄénach ʋo muinteʄ Oomnaill .h.
Moʄʋa. Oomnall O Moʄʋa ʄein ʋo ćuitim iʄin uaiʄ
ceʋna ʋo laim Cathail ćaʄʄaiʒ mic Conchobaiʄ
Moenmuiʒi, a noiʒail a ʋeʄbʄathaʄ, i. Matʒaṁna.
Sloiʒeʋ la Seon na Cuiʄti co nʒalloib Ulaʋ, co hEʄʄ
Cʄaiʓe, conʋeʄnʄat ćaiʄlen Cille Santail, co ʄo
ʄolṁaiʒeʋ tʄića ceʋ Ciannachta leó aʄʄ an caiʄlén

---

1 *This army*; i.e. the army of Mac
Duinnsleibhe, or Mac Donlevy.

² *All slain.* The entry concludes
by stating that a very few out of the
army escaped.

³ *Muinter-Eolais.* The Four Masters say "the nobles (maite) of
Muinter-Eolais." "Muinter-Eolais"
was the tribe name of the sept of
Mac Raghnaill, or Reynolds, whose
territory comprised the southern half
of the present county of Leitrim.

⁴ *The Gilla-ruadh*; i.e., "the red
fellow."

⁵ *Son of Cathal.* His real name
was Ualgharg O'Ruaire, or Ulrick

O'Rorke, as appears from the entry
a few lines before.

⁶ [*By whom*]. The expression ʄo
maʄbaʋ being the pass. form of the
verb maʄbaʋ, to kill, it would seem
that some word had been omitted before it. The text has therefore been
corrected from the Ann. Four Mast.,
by the insertion of the word laʄ, "by
whom."

⁷ *Muinter-Eolais.* See note ³ on this
page.

⁸ *Mercenary.* ʄeʄʄénach. This
word is frequently translated "archer"
by Dr. O'Donovan, in his edition of
the Annals of the Four Mast, but

this army[1] was all slain[2] there, along with the son of O'Conchobhair, and the son of Mac Murchadha, and the son of O'Flaithbhertaigh; so that there escaped of them only Mac Duinnsleibhe with a few on horses, and a very few of the army. A great number of Muinter-Eolais[3] were slain by Ualgharg O'Ruairc, king of Breifne. Ruaidhri O'Flaithbhertaigh went into Tir-Conaill, and came from thence, along with the comarb of Patrick, into the house of O'Conchobhair, and made peace with him; and his territory was given to him. The Gilla-ruadh,[4] son of Mac Ragnaill, chieftain of Muinter-Eolais, was killed by Diarmaid, son of Maghnus O'Conchobhair, at the instigation of the son of Cathal[5] O'Ruairc, [by whom][6] the Muinter-Eolais[7] had previously been slain. Aedh O'Ferghail, dux of Muinter-Anghaile, was slain by the sons of Sitric O'Cuinn. Mathghamhain, son of Conchobhar Maenmhaighe, was slain by a mercenary[8] of the people of Domhnall O'Mordha. Domhnall O'Mordha fell himself at the same time by the hand of Cathal Carrach, son of Conchobhar Maenmhaighe, in revenge of his brother, i.e. Mathghamhain. A hosting by John de Curci, with the Foreigners of Ulidia, as far as Es-craeibhe, when they erected the castle of Cill-Santail;[9] and the cantred of Cianachta was wasted by them from this

---

sometimes also "auxiliary." It is explained "hireling" in the valuable Irish Dictionary compiled by Peter Connell, which is at present preserved in the British Museum. The words, .i. coġ obū are added in the margin, apparently to indicate the name of the person who slew Mathghamhain, or Mahon, which may be written Congobann; but they may also represent the words coġaḋ obann, and signify that Mahon's death arose from a "sudden quarrel."

9 *Cill-Santail.* In the Annals of Ulster (Dublin copy), which have this and the following entries for this year under the year 1197, the name is written Cill-Santan; but in the old translation of the Annals in question it is called Kilsandle. The Four Masters also (1197) have Cill-Sanctain. Dr. O'Donovan (Four Mast., A.D. 1197, note ⁿ) says that the castle was situated on the east side of the river Bann, not far from Coleraine, near which there is a remarkable mound called Mountsandall, anciently Dún-da-bhenn, or the "Fort of the two peaks." See Reeves's *Ecclesiastical Antiquities of Down and Connor*, p. 74.

rin. Ir annra cairlen rin ro rácbað Ruirtel ritún
co rocraiðe maille rir. Tanic, ðono, Ruirtél ritún
ar creiŏ co port Ðoire, ocur ro airc Cluain hí, ocur
Enach, ocur Ðerg bruač. Ruc, ðono, Flaitbertach .h.
Máeilðoraið, .i. rí Conaill ocur Eogain, co nuathað to
conallaiŏ ocur ðEoganchaiŏ rorra, co tucrat maiŏm
ror traiŏ na h. congmála orra, co ro marbað a
nár ann, im mac Aroŏail mec Lačlainn, tria ŏírb-
bailiŏ Coluim Cille, ocur Cainniŏ, ocur Brecáin ro
aircretor ann. Mac Gilla Eiðiŏ ðo Ciannachta ðo
rlat altóra tempail ŏoir ðoire Coluim Cille, ocur
ðo breiŏ ceitri corn ir ferr ðo boi i nErinn eirðe, .i.
im mac riabach ocur im mac rolur ocur im ŏorn .h.
Maeilðoraið, ocur im cam coruinn, .i. corn i Ðoŏar-
taiŏ; ocur ro brir iat, ocur tall a ninnŏura ŏíŏ: rriŏ,
umorro, ir in trer lá iar ná ngaið na reoit rin, ocur
an tí ro ŏaið, ocur ro crochað e ag croir na riaŏ a
neinech Coluim Cille ra haltoir ro ŏáraiŏeð. Conchobar .h. Catáin ðo éc. Flaitbertach .h. Maeil-
ðoraiŏ, rí Ceneoil Conaill ocur Eogain, ocur Airgíall,
ocur cornamach Tempach, ocur riðamna Erenn uile,
.i. Conall ar loechŏacht, Cuŏullain ar ŏairceð, ocur
Guaire ar einech, a éc iar treaŏlaið ŏoŏhaiðe a ninir
Saimér i quart noin Februa, irin triŏatmað bliaðain a
flaiterra, ocur irin noimað bliaðain ar caogaið a oéiri;

---

[1] *Harbour.* port (port)=Latin
portus.

[2] *Of the Nua-congmhail.* na .h.
congmála, MS. This seems to be a
corrupt way of writing nua congbála,
the gen. of nua congbail, which
Colgan (*Actt.* SS., p. 141, note [8])
translates "nova habitatio." There
were many places in Ireland so called.
The place above referred to is now
known as Faughanvale, in the county
of Londonderry. The Irish name
nua congbail has assumed various

forms in the course of its adoption as
an English name. See a very learned
and interesting paper on *Changes and
corruptions in Irish topographical
names,* by P. W. Joyce, A.M.; Proceedings of the R. I. Acad., vol. ix.,
p. 225, *sq.*; and Dr. Reeves's *Colton's
Visitation,* p. 79.

[3] *Mac-riabhach;* i.e. "the swarthy
son."

[4] *Mac-solus;* lit. "son of light."

[5] *Defender.* cornamach (cosnam-
ach). This word also signifies "con-

castle. It was in this castle Rustel Pitun was left, together with a large force. Rustel Pitun came, moreover, on a preying expedition to the harbour[1] of Doire, and he plundered Cluain-Hí, and Enach, and Derg-bruach. But Flaithbhertach O'Maeldoraidh, i.e. the king of *Cenel*-Conaill and *Cenel*-Eoghain, with a small number of the *Cenel*-Conaill and *Cenel*-Eoghain, overtook them, and defeated them on the strand of the Nua-congmhail,[2] where they were slaughtered, along with the son of Ardghal Mac Lachlainn, through the miracles of Colum-Cille, and of Cainnech, and of Brecan, whom they had plundered there. Mac Gilla-Eidigh of Cianachta robbed the altar of the great church of Doire-Choluim-Chille, and took therefrom the four best goblets that were in Erinn, viz. :—Mac-riabhach,[3] and Mac-solus,[4] and the goblet of O'Maeldoraidh, and the Cam-coruinn, i.e. the goblet of O'Dochartaigh ; and he broke them, and took off their precious things. These articles were found on the third day after being stolen ; and the person who stole them was discovered, and he was hanged at Cros-na-riagh in revenge of Colum-Cille, whose altar had been profaned Conchobhar O'Cathain died. Flaithbhertach O'Maeldoraidh, king of Cenel-Conaill, and *Cenel*-Eoghain, and Airghiall, the defender[5] of Temhair, and royal heir of all Erinn—viz. :—a Conall[6] in heroism, a Cuchullain[7] in valour, and a Guaire[8] in hospitality—died after great suffering, in Inis-Saimer, on the fourth of the nones of February, in the thirtieth year of his reign, and the nine and fiftieth year of his age;

---

tender," and may mean that Flaithbhertach O'Maeldoraidh was worthy to dispute the monarchy of Ireland with all comers.

[6] *A Conall.* The Conall here referred to was Conall Cernach, a warrior much celebrated in early Irish romances, who is alleged to have lived in the first century of the Christian era. See O'Flaherty's *Ogygia*, part III., cap. xlvii

[7] *Cuchullain.* The Cuthullin of Macpherson.

[8] *Guaire.* Guaire Aidhne, king of Connacht, who died in the year of our Lord 659 = 663, according to the Chron. Scotorum, and who was celebrated for his hospitality.

ocur ro haðnacht a n'Oruim ċuama co honorach; ocur ʒaƀur Eċmarcach .h. 'Oočartaiʒ riʒe ċeneóil Conaill ro ceðóir; ocur ní raiðe acht coeicíðir a riʒe an tan tainic Seón na Cúirti, co rocraiðe moir maille rir, tar Tuaim a tír Eoʒain; arriðéin co hẮrð grata; iarrin timchell co 'Ooire Coluim Cille, co raƀaðar coic aiðče ann. Imċiʒit iarrin co Cnoc narcain, ða niomorchor ċairir. Teʒaið ðono Cenél Conaill, im Eċmarcach .h. n'Oočartaiʒ, ða niinnroiʒeð, ocur ðo ratrat caċ ðoiƀ ðú in ro marbað ðá ceð ðiƀ im a rí, .i. Eċmarcach .h. n'Oočartaiʒ, ocur im 'Oonnchað .h. Taircert, riċoirech ċlainni Sneiðʒile, ocur im Ʒilla-briʒðe .h. n'Oočartaiʒ, ocur im ṁaʒ 'Ouƀán, ocur im maʒ Fergail, ocur im macuiƀ .h. mƀaiʒill, et aliir nobilibur; ocur ro airʒret Inir Eoʒain, ocur ðo rárʒrat ðoruma moir eirðe.

|ct. Enair .iiii. r.; L. ix. Seacht mbliaðna noċat ar ceð, ar mile, ab Incarnatione recunðum 'Oioni-rium; ab Incarnatione recunðum ƀeðaṁ .ṁ.c.lxxxx. Ắb Incarnatione iuxta Eƀreor .ṁ.cccc.l. Ắb initio munði iuxta Eƀreor .ū.cccc.i. Ắb initio munði recun-ðum .lxx. Interpretter .ūi.ðc.xlix. Solarir cicli .xxii. annur; cicli inðictionir .xu. annur; cicli lunarir .xuii. annur; rrimur annur rreparationir birrexti; c.xxx.iiii. annur cicli maʒni rarcalir unðecimi ab initio munði. Ruaiðri .h. Flaiċbertaiʒ, rí iarthair Con-nacht, ðo ʒaƀail ðo Cathal croiƀðerʒ .h. Conchobair, ri Connacht. Int erruc .h. Moelciarán, .i. erruʒ Ắirʒíall, ocur manaċ rri ré faða, ocur ab 'Oroiċit áċa, mortuur ert. 'Oomnall mac ṁeʒ Raʒnaill, ðux muintire hEoluir, ðo marbað. Concoƀar mac 'Oiar-

1 *To transport themselves.* ða niomochor, for ða niomorchor, MS.
2 *Aliis nobilibus.* aliorr nobiler, MS.
3 *Incarnatione.* ācar, MS.

4 xxii. The MS. has xxu.
5 *Præparationis bissexti.* rraparciōir birrexti, MS.
6 *Bishop of Airghiall;* i.e. bishop of Clogher.

and he was honourably intérred at Druim-thuama. And Echmarcach O'Dochartaigh assumed the sovereignty of Cenel-Conaill immediately after; and he was only a fortnight in the sovereignty when John de Curci, accompanied by a large army, went across Tuaim into Tir-Eoghain, and from thence to Ard-sratha, and afterwards round to Doire-Choluim-Chille, where they remained five nights. They went afterwards to Cnoc-Nascain, to transport themselves[1] across it. The Cenel-Conaill, however, with Echmarcach O'Dochartaigh, came towards them, and gave them battle, when two hundred of them (the Cenel-Conaill) were slain, together with their king, i.e. Echmarcach O'Dochartaigh, and Donnchadh O'Tairchert, king-chieftain of Clann-Sneidhghile, and Gillabrighde O'Dochartaigh, and Mac Dubhán, and Mac Ferghail, and the sons of O'Baighill, et aliis nobilibus;[2] and they (the Foreigners) plundered Inis-Eoghain, and carried off therefrom a great cattle-spoil.

The kalends of January on the 4th feria, the 9th of the moon; ninety-seven years, and a hundred, and a thousand ab Incarnatione secundum Dionysium. Ab Incarnatione[3] secundum Bedam, m̄.c.lxxxx. Ab Incarnatione juxta Ebræos, m̄.cccc.l. Ab initio mundi juxta Ebræos, v̄.cccc.i. Ab initio mundi secundum lxx. Interpretes, v̄i.dc.xlix. Solaris cycli xxii.[4] annus; cycli Indictionis xu. annus; cycli lunaris xvii. annus; primus annus præparationis bissexti;[5] cxxxiiii. annus cycli magni paschalis undecimi ab initio mundi. Ruaidhri O'Flaithbhertaigh, king of the West of Connacht, was apprehended by Cathal Crobhderg O'Conchobhair, king of Connacht. The bishop O'Maelciarain, i.e. bishop of Airghiall,[6] and a monk for a long time, and abbot of Droiched-átha, mortuus est. Domhnall, son of Mac Raghnaill, dux of Muinter-Eolais, was slain. Conchobhar, son of Diarmaid, son of Tadhg

mada mic Taiḋg .h. Maeilruanaiḋ, ri Ṁoiġe Luirg, mortuus est a mainistir na Buille i nouici ṁanaiġ. Gillamoliac O Branan do aċċor a comḟorbuis uaḋa, ocus Gillacrist .h. Cernaiġ do oirdneḋ na ionaḋ ar ṫoġa [laech] ocus ċleirech tuaisceirt Erenn, a nabḋaine Coluim Cille. ū.cccc.ii.

Kl. Enair u. f.; l. xx. Ab Incarnatione Domini, secundum Dionisium, ocht mbliadna noċat ar cet, ar mile, ais in Tigerna. Ab Incarnatione secundum Bedam, .m̄.c.lxxxxi. Ab Incarnatione secundum Ebreos, m̄. cccc. li. Ab initio mundi iuxta Ebreos, ū. cccc. ii.; ab initio mundi iuxta .lxx. Interpretes, .ūi. dc.l. Solaris cicli .xxiii. annus; cicli indictionis primus annus; cicli lunaris .xiiii. annus; secundus annus preparationis bissexti; c.xxxu. annus undecimi cicli magni pascalis ab initio mundi. Goffraid mac Goffrada hI Raiġilliġ do marbad dúa Donnchada, a meaḃuil. Ruaidri mac Toirrdhelbaiġ móir hI Conchobair, .i. rí Erenn uile, itir Ġulla ocus Ġoeidela, cen ḟressarra, do éc a Cunga Feiċin, iar mbúaiḋ ó doṁan ocus ó ḋeman. Oeḋ, mac Briain Breiḟniġ, mic Toirrdhealḃaiġ hI Conchobair, do ṁarbad la Cathal gcarrach .h. Conchobair. Cnó ṁes mór is in

---

[1] *Gillamoliac.* Written "Gillamacliac" in the Annals of the Four Masters, which, as well as the Annals of Ulster, have the event at the year 1198.

[2] v̄.cccc.ii. These figures are intended to represent the year of the world's age corresponding to A.D. 1198, according to the Hebrew computation, and therefore belong to the next entry.

[3] *The age of the Lord.* ais in tigerna (ais in Tigerna). These words are of course redundant.

[4] *Initio.* īicio (inicio), MS.

[5] *Bissexti.* bisexti (bisexti), MS.

[6] *Without dispute.* cen ḟressarra. Roderick O'Flaherty, who seems to have carefully examined the MS., has drawn his pen through the word cen, "without," and underlined it with dots, in token of expunging it. He has also substituted the word co, "with," to signify that Ruaidhri, or Roderick O'Conor, was not the undisputed king of Ireland; but he is called "king of Connacht, and of all Ireland, both the Foreigners and

O'Maelruanaidh, king of Magh-Luirg, mortuus est in the monastery of Buill, in the noviciate of a monk. Gilla-moliac[1] O'Branan resigned his comarbship; and Gillachrist O'Cernaigh was ordained in his place, by the election of [the laity] and clergy of the North of Erinn, in the abbacy of Colum-Cille. v̄.cccc.ii.[2]

The kalends of January on the 5th feria, the 20th of the moon; Ab Incarnatione Domini secundum Dionysium, ninety-eight years, and a hundred, and a thousand, the age of the Lord.[3] Ab Incarnatione secundum Bedam, m̄.c.lxxxxi. Ab Incarnatione secundum Ebræos, m̄. cccc.li. Ab initio mundi juxta Ebræos, v̄.cccc.ii.; ab initio[4] mundi juxta lxx. Interpretes, v̄i.dc.l. Solaris cycli xxiii. annus; cycli Indictionis primus annus; cycli lunaris xviii. annus; secundus annus præparationis bissexti;[5] cxxxv. annus undecimi cycli magni paschalis ab initio mundi. Goffraidh, son of Goffraidh O'Raighilligh, was slain by O'Donnchadha, in treachery. Ruaidhri, son of Toir-dhealbhach Mór O'Conchobhair, i.e. the king of all Erinn, both of Foreigners and Gaeidhel, without dispute,[6] died at Cunga-Feichin, after triumphing over the world and the devil. Aedh, son of Brian Breifnech, son of Toirdhelbhach O'Conchobhair, was slain by Cathal Carrach O'Conchobhair. A great nut crop in this year,

---

Gaeidhel," by the Four Masters, who generally supported the pretensions of the northern princes to the title of kings of Ireland, on occasions when the right of being so considered formed a subject of dispute between the partisans of the north and south. But O'Flaherty seems to have in view the dissensions which are recorded above, under the years 1185 and 1186, as having taken place between Ruaidhri and his own son, Conor Maenmhaighe, not indeed regarding the sovereignty of Ireland, but in

reference to the government of Connacht; for after his submission to Henry II., in 1175, Ruaidhri could have but little pretensions to the crown of Ireland. The death of Ruaidhri is entered under the year 1199 in the Annals of Ulster (Dublin copy); but at the year 1198 the following note occurs:—"no ᵹumao aṅ an ℟ ꞃo buò ċoiꞃ Ruaioꞃi Ua Concobaiꞃ ꞅo ḃeiṫ;" "or perhaps on this kalend [i.e. in this year] the *death of* Ruaidhri O'Conchobhair should be *recorded*."

bliαὸαιn ṙιn, conά ταṙṙαιὸ ὸυιne ιṙιn αιmṙιṙ ὸειᵹenαch
meṙ buὸ mo nάṙṙ. Sloιᵹeὸ lα Seón nα Cúιṙτι αṙ fuὸ
čeαll Ulαὸ, .ι. Αṙὸ ṙṙατα ocuṙ Rατ ὸoč, ocuṙ α mιlleὸ
ὸó no co ṙoαchτ Ὸoιṙe, co ṙαιὸe αnnṙιn ὸά oιὸče αṙ
ṙechτṁuιn αᵹ mιlleὸ Ιnnṙι hEoᵹαιn, ocuṙ αn τιṙe
αιṙčenα; ocuṙ nι ὸechαιὸ αṙ ḟṙι ṙe ṙoὸα, no co
nὸechαιὸ Oeὸh .h. Ueιll luchτ .u. lonᵹ co cιll α
Lαταṙnα, ᵹo ṙo loιṙc [ní] ὸon Ὸαιlι, ocuṙ ᵹuṙ mαṙb
ὸιṙ τeṙτα ὸo ὸα .xx. αnn. Ιṙ αnnṙιn ὸo bαὸαṙ Ᵹαιll
moιᵹe Lιne ocuṙ nα Ὸαl nΑṙαιὸe τṙι ceὸ αṙ α cιnn,
eτιṙ ιαṙαnn ocuṙ ᵹαn ιαṙonn, ocuṙ níṙ αιṙιᵹeὸoṙ αon ní
no cuṙ ὸoιṙτeὸoṙ nα ᵹcenn, ocuṙ τucṙατ ὸeαbαιὸ αṙ lαṙ
ιn Ὸαιle, ᵹuṙ ṙo ṁuιᵹ ṙoṙṙ nα Ᵹαllαιb, ocuṙ co τucṙατ
coιc ṁαὸmαnnα ό ṙιn αmαč, no ᵹonὸečoταṙ ιnα lonᵹuιὸ
ṙoṙṙα; ocuṙ níṙ ṙαᵹbαὸ αčτ coιᵹeṙ ὸo muιnnτιṙ h1
Ueιll. Ro ιmčιᵹ Seon oτ čuαlα ṙιn, ṙoṙτeα.

Ɉcτ. En αιṙuι. ṙ.; l. ι. Αb Ιncαṙnατιone ṙecunὸum
Ὸιonιṙιum, ṁ.c.xcιx.; αb Ιncαṙnατιone ṙecunὸum
Ὸeὸαm, .ṁ. c. xcιι.; αb Ιncαṙnατιone ṙecunὸum Eṙṙeoṙ,
.ṁ. cccc. lιι.; αb ιnιτιo munὸι ṙecunὸum Eṙṙeoṙ, ū.
cccc.ιιι.; αb ιnιτιo ṙecunὸum .lxx. Ιnτeṙṙṙeτeṙ, ūι.
ὸc.lι. Cιclι ṙolαṙιṙ .xxιιιι. αnnuṙ; cιclι ιnὸιcτιonιṙ
.ιι. αnnuṙ; cιclι lunαṙιṙ .xιx. αnnuṙ; τeṙτιuṙ αnnuṙ
ṙṙeṙαṙατιonιṙ bιṙṙexτι; c.xxxuι. αnnuṙ unὸecιmι cιclι
mαᵹnι ṙαṙcαlιṙ αb ιnιτιo munὸι. Sιč ὸo ὸenum ὸo
Cατhαl cṙoιbὸeṙc ocuṙ ὸo Cατhαl čαṙṙαch, ocuṙ Cατhαl
cαṙṙαch ὸo ταbαιṙτ ὸon τιṙ, ocuṙ ṙeṙonn ὸo čαbαιṙτ

---

[1] *Cill . . . in Latharna.* The
name of the church (Cill . . .)
is also incomplete in the Annals of
Ulster and the Four Masters. Dr.
O'Donovan (*Four Mast.*, A.D. 1198,
note [1]) suggests that Cill-ruadh, now
Kilroot, in the parish of the same name,
barony of Lower Belfast, and county of
Antrim, was meant. But Dr. Reeves
rightly objects (in a note to the Edi-

tor) that Kilroot is too far south,
whereas it would appear that some
church between Glenarm and Larne
was indicated.

[2] *[A part].* [ní]. Supplied from
the Ann. Four Mast.

[3] *Thirty-eight.* ὸιṙ τeṙτα ὸo ὸα
.xx.; lit. "two wanting of two score."

[4] *Both in iron and without iron.*
eτιṙ ιαṙαnn ocuṙ ᵹαn ιαṙonn (etir

so that no man in the later time witnessed a greater
crop than it.   A hosting by John de Curci among the
churches of Ulidia, i.e. Ard-sratha and Rath-bhoth, and
they were destroyed by him until he reached Doire,
where he remained two nights over a week, devastating
Inis-Eoghain' and the country besides; and he departed
not for a long time, until Aedh O'Neill went with five
ships to Cill . . . . in Latharna,[1] and burned [a part][2] of
the town, and killed thirty-eight[3] persons there.   At this
time the Foreigners of Magh-line and Dal-Araidhe, *to the
number of* three hundred, both in iron and without iron,[4]
were before them, and they observed nothing until the
Foreigners poured in upon them; and they delivered
battle in the middle of the town, when the Foreigners
were defeated; and they (*the Irish*) inflicted five defeats on
them in addition, and went to their ships in spite of them;
and only five of the people of O'Neill were lost.   John
departed when he heard this, postea.

The kalends of January on the 6th feria, the 1st[5] of [1199.]
the moon.   Ab Incarnatione[6] secundum Dionysium,
m̅.c.xcix.; ab Incarnatione[6] secundum Bedam, m̅ c.xcii;
ab Incarnatione[6] secundum Ebraos, m̅.cccc.lii.; ab initio
mundi secundum Ebraos, u̅.cccc.iii.; ab initio secundum
lxx. Interpretes, u̅i.dc.li.; cycli solaris xxiiii. annus; cycli
Indictionis ii. annus; cycli lunaris xix. annus; tertius[7]
annus præparationis bissexti;[8] cxxxui. annus undecimi
cycli magni paschalis ab initio mundi.   Peace[9] was
made by Cathal Crobhderg and Cathal Carrach; and
Cathal Carrach was brought into the country,[10] and land

---

iarann ocus gan iaronn), lit. "between
iron and without iron;" i.e. "both
clad in mail and without mail."

[5] *The 1st.* The MS. erroneously
reads xi (11th).

[6] *Incarnatione* incapnacione (in-
carnacione), MS.

[7] *Tertius.* τερciuγ (tercius), MS

[8] *Bissexti.* biγeαcι (bisexti), MS.

[9] *Peace.* This entry is given by
the Four Masters at the year 1198.
It is added in the Annals of Ulster
(Dublin copy) under the year 1199,
by a later hand.

[10] *Country;* i.e., Connacht.

ró. Ruaſlucaó oo Ruaıoſı .h. Flaѣbeſtaıᵹ. Cſech
oo ѣenum oo Caѣal cſoıboeſᵹ aſ ᵹalloıb, cuſ loıſc
bóóúın Cѣa, ocuſ ᵹuſſo maſѣ oaıne ıomѣa, ocuſ co
tucſat ѣú ımѣa leo oá tıᵹ. Ꝥoſmᵹal .h. Cuınn, oux
muıntıſe Ꝥıllcān, oo ᵹabáıl oo ᵹalloıb, ocuſ a muınteſ
oo chuſ aſ anſó oo ѣıѣ bıѣ ocuſ ѣoaıᵹ, ıaſ na naſᵹuın
oo ᵹalloıb. Caıſſlen Ꝥſanaıſo oo ѣenum ıſ ın mblıa-
oaın ſı. Oeo .h. Cuınn ocuſ mac Ocѣa na namuſ,
ocuſ oſem elı oo Conmaıcnıѣ, oo maſbao oo tſeſſén-
chaıb Connacht. Oo ponſat Ꝥaıll ın blıaoaın ſı tſı
ſloıᵹeѣa ḿoſa a tıſ Eoᵹaın, ocuſ an tſeaſ ſloıᵹeѣ oo
ponſat oo ᵹaѣſat Lonᵹpoſt aᵹ Oomnach ḿoſ Muıᵹe
Imѣláıſ, ocuſ oo ѣuıſſet ſluaᵹ móſ amaѣ oo mılleo
ın tıſe. Támıc Oeѣ .h. Neıll a naıſſćıſ anſ ſlúaıᵹ
ſın cuſſo compuıc ſſıſ na Ꝥalloıb, ocuſ co taſo
áſ oıáıſmıѣe ſoſſa; ocuſ ſo élóѣ an ćuıo elı oona
Ꝥalloıb ıſın oıѣće, conoeѣaouſ taſ Tuaım. Sanctuſ
Mauſıcıuſ .h. boeoan ıı hí Coluım Cılle ıı pace
quıeuıt. Sloıᵹeѣ la Ruaıoſı O nOuınnſlébı ѣo ᵹcuıo
oo Ꝥalloıb Mıѣe, co ſo aıſᵹſet maınıſtıſ Póıl ocuſ
Reoaıſ, co náſ ſáᵹaıѣſet ınntı acht aon ѣoın. Oomnall .h. Ooćaſtaıᵹ, ſí Ceneoıl Enna ocuſ Cſoa Mıѣaıſ,
ıı pace quıeuıt. Rolant mac Uchtſaıѣ, ſí Ꝥall ᵹoeıoel,
quıeuıt.

 Kt. Enaıſ.uıı.ſ.; L.xıı.; oa ceo ocuſ mıle blıaoan aoıſ
ıı Tıᵹeſna. Oonnchaoh, mac Ruaıoſı hı Conchobaıſ,

[1] *Set free.* The capture of O'Flaithbhertaigh, by Cathal Crobhderg, is
recorded under the year 1197, *supra.*

[2] *The bódhún of Ath.* bóóúın Cѣa.
The word bóóúın means an enclosure
for cattle, being composed of *bó*, a
cow, and *dún*, a fortress. It is also
written bóóún, whence the word *bawn*
in English. By Cѣ (gen. Cѣa) is
probably meant Ath-Luain, or Athlone. See note [5], p. 213.

[3] *Built.* In the Dublin copy of

the Annals of Inisfallen, the castle of
Granard is stated to have been erected
by Richard Tuit, against O'Reilly.

[4] *Aedh - na - namus;* i.e. "Aedh
(Hugh) of the soldiers, or mercenaries."

[5] *Mercenaries.* ſeſſénchaıb, abl.
pl. of ſeſſénach (sersénach). In
O'Reilly's Irish Dictionary the word
sérsenach, (written *séirseanach*), is explained "an auxiliary, an unhired

was given to him. Ruaidhri O'Flaithbhertaigh was set free.[1] A depredation was committed on the Foreigners by Cathal Crobhderg, who burned the bódhún of Ath,[2] and killed many persons; and they carried with them many cows to their homes. Gormghal O'Cuinn, dux of Muinter-Gillcan, was taken prisoner by the Foreigners; and his people were reduced to great distress from want of food and clothing, after being plundered by the Foreigners. The castle of Granard was built[3] in this year. Aedh O'Cuinn, and the son of Aedh-na-namus,[4] and some more of the Conmaicne were slain by the mercenaries[5] of Connacht. The Foreigners performed three great hostings to Tir-Eoghain this year, and on the third hosting which they performed they encamped at Domhnach-mor of Magh-Im-chlair, and they sent out a great army to devastate the country. Aedh O'Neill came to meet this army, and he encountered the Foreigners, and inflicted on them a count-less slaughter; and the remainder of the Foreigners escaped in the night, and went across Tuaim. Sanctus Mauricius O'Baedan in Hi-Choluim-Chille in pace quievit. A hosting by Ruaidhri O'Duinnsleibhe, with some of the Foreigners of Midhe; and they plundered the monastery of Paul and Peter,[6] so that they left only one cow in it. Domhnall O'Dochartaigh, king of Cenel-Enna and Ard-Midhair, in pace quievit. Roland Mac Uchtraigh, king of Gall-Gaeidhel, quievit.

The kalends of January on the 7th feria, the 12th of the moon; the age of the Lord two hundred years, and a thousand. Donnchadh, son of Ruaidhri O'Conchobhair,

---

workman, a free labourer." But Conell Mageoghegan, the translator of the so-called Annals of Clonmacnois, renders it (A D. 1200) by "souldier." See note [6], p. 196, *ante.* The remaining events for this year comprise all the entries for the same year in the Annals of Ulster, which give the age of the

moon on the 1st of January as "xi.," like this chronicle.

[6] *The Monastery of Paul and Peter;* i.e. at Armagh. The death of Ruaidhri O'Duinnsleibhe (Rory O'Donlevy), at the hands of the English, is entered under the year 1201, where he is called Mac Duinnsleibhe, or Mac Donlevy.

dá ngoiréi Donnchav Uaithnech, do marbav dona Zalloib bavar illuimnech. Crech mór la Cathal croibverc ocur la Connachtaib i niarthar Miᵭe, co tucrat creic ndérmair leo do buaib, ocur dechaib, ocur do mucaib, ocur do choerchaib; co tángavor imrlán, cen lamhachtain beime friú, reᵭ bruiᵹin alle, acht triar no cethar do marbav ar fireᵭ ᵭib. Impuᵭ do ᵹallaib uathaib annrin, acht begán doeinib ro fazaibret ac rethav forro. Od conncavar, immorro, Connachta Zaill do impuᵭ uavhaib, do imᵭiᵹ zach oen le névail ᵭib, acht .h. Conchobair ocur .h. Flaichbertaiᵹ, ocur mac Zoirvealb, uathav rluaiᵹ dia néir. Od connccavar in lucht raifcri ro fazrat Zaill rin, do imráᵭar invezhav Zall, ocur ro inniret ᵭóib in rluaᵹ do imᵭecht lé na névalaib, acht uathav rluaiᵹ bói illurᵹ dia néir. Ro impavar na Zaill invezaiᵭ int rluaiᵹ. Rucrat forra ro cevóir, ocur ro meabav rompa ror ᵹoivelaib, ocur ro marbav ann Ruaivri O Flaichbertaiᵹ, ri iarthair Connacht, ocur Amláib .h. Cuinn, ocur do muinter Zillán ror marb é. Ro marbav ann Cathal .h. Coinᵭenuinn, ri .h. nDiarmava, et alii multi cum irtir interfecti funt do macaib ócloech ocur do zilliᵭ; rev tamen non multi rev pauci interfecti funt ibi, ri uerum ert ut nunciatum ert nobir. Ro facbav .h. Conchobair cin duine na farrav acht Muircertach mac Merain, .i. a ᵭoirreoir, ocur oen

---

[1] *Donnchadh Uaithnech;* i.e. Donn-chadh "of Uaithne;" so called from having been fostered in the territory of "Uaithne," now Owneybeg, a barony in the N.E. of the county of Limerick. The death of this Donnchadh (or Donough) has been added by a later hand to the entries for the year 1200 in the (Dublin) Annals of Ulster.

[2] *Past the Bruighin hither.* reᵭ bruiᵹin alle. This form of ex-pression would of itself suggest the quarter in which the original of the present chronicle was compiled, if other evidence was wanting, as the "Bruighin" mentioned was the place anciently called *Bruighin Da Choga,* one of the five Bruighins, or palaces, celebrated in ancient Irish romance. See O'Curry's *Lectures,* &c., p. 260. The name of *Bruighin Da Choga,* (the little Brug, or palace, of Da Choga), is still preserved in that of Breen, the name of a fort, or rath, in the townland of Bryanmore Upper, parish

who was called Donnchadh Uaithnech,[1] was slain by the Foreigners who were in Luimnech. A great depredation by Cathal Crobhderg and the Connachtmen, in the West of Midhe; and they carried off an enormous spoil of cows and horses, and pigs, and sheep; and they came safely past the Bruighin hither,[2] without a blow being struck against them, saving that three or four of them were killed on scouting parties. The Foreigners turned back[3] from them then, except a few men whom they left watching them. When the Connachtmen, however, saw the Foreigners turning back from them, each one of them went off with his prey, except O'Conchobhair, and O'Flaithbhertaigh, and Mac Goisdealbh, who remained after them with a very small company. When the watching band left by the Foreigners saw this, they went back after the Foreigners, and informed them that the host had departed with their preys, except a very small company that remained in their track.[4] The Foreigners pursued the host, and overtook them immediately, and routed the Gaeidhel before them; and Ruaidhri O'Flaithbhertaigh, king of the West of Connacht, was slain there; and Amhlaibh O'Cuinn, of the Muinter-Gillcán,[5] *was the person* that slew him. Cathal O'Conçennuinn, king of Ui-Diarmada, was slain there, et alii multi cum istis interfecti sunt, of the sons of warriors, and attendants; sed tamen non multi sed pauci interfecti sunt ibi,[6] si verum est ut nunciatum est nobis. O'Conchobhair was left without a man in his company, except Muirchertach Mac Merain, i.e. his doorkeeper,

of Drumraney, barony of Kilkenny West, and county of Westmeath. The expedition was led by Cathal Crobhderg, from Connacht, across the Shannon, into Westmeath, and the chronicler, in recording the return of the band towards Connacht, uses the word alle, "hither."

[3] *Turned back.* From this it appears that O'Conor's band was pursued by the English of Midhe, or Meath.

[4] *Remained in their track.* The text has bói illurg oia néir, "who were in (the) track after them;" i.e. acting as a rear guard.

[5] *Of the Muinter-Gillcán.* The MS. has 7 oo muinter Ʒillcán "and of the Muinter-Gillcán," from which it would appear either that the sign 7 (for ocur) is wrongly added, or that some name has been omitted after it.

[6] *Ibi.* ibe, MS.

P

ócloech eli, .i. mac Ceitennach .h. Cepín; ocur tennó
arr amlaid rin. Ro Lenrat Ʒaill in maiḃm co hĊẽ
Luain, ocur ro impátar annrin, ocur rucrad α creiĊ
leó, ocur monán dechaiḃ Connacht. Tinol la Cathal
cnoiḃdenʒ co ranic tin Fiacrać Ọiʒni, man buḋ dana-
cail α ẽine ẽéin nó rachad. Ni heḃ, ón, achт tinól
meaḃla ocur miḃneitri, dá тanic milled Connacht
ocur α milled ẽéin, .i. dinnroiʒed Cathail ẽannaiʒ mic
Conchobain ṁoenmaiʒe hi Conchobain, dá ẽíchun α
Connachтaiḃ, nó dá ʒabáil, no dá ṁanbaḃ. Ọt ẽuala
Cathal cannach rin do ẽuin α muinтen irin ẽonḃan,
ocur ro boi ẽéin Lín α ẽocraide dá néir. Ro innroiʒ
Cathal cnoiḃdenʒ aniar α tin Fiacrać cuice rium, ocur
ó nánic α Lán ẽenainn Cathail ẽannaiʒ do ẽuin rluaiʒ
món ina ḋeʒaid, im Toinnḋhealbach mac Ruaidri, ocur
im macaiḃ eli Ruaidri, ocur im Maolẽulaid .h.
Flaiẽbentaiʒ, ri iantain Connacht, ocur im macuiḃ
mic Taiḋʒ .h. Cellaiʒ, ocur im an ridire .h. Mael-
rechlainn, ocur im an rúta Midhech; ocur o rancodan
irin caille ro heinʒeḃ ḋoiḃ, ocur тucaḃ ḋeabaid ḋóiḃ,
ocur ro ṁeabad an muinтen Cathail cnoiḃdenʒ, ocur
ro manbad ann Moelẽulaid .h. Flaiẽhbentaiʒ, ocur
an ridire .h. Moelrechlainn, ocur iuʒaláid mac
Conmeḋa, ocur Domnall mac in ʒilla ḋuiḃ .h. Loeḋóc.
Ianrin cuirir Cathal cannach techтa co Luimnech,
docum Uilliam Ḃunc, ocur do benaiт mac Cathail
ẽannaiʒ ina laiṁ α nʒill re тuanurdal na nʒall.
Ianrin ro ẽinóil Uilliam Ḃunc rluaʒ món ó Ọẽ cliaḃ,
ocur ó Laiʒniḃ, ocur Ʒaill Luimniʒ ocur Muṁan
áirchena, ocur dα .h. Ḃniain, .i. Muircentach ocur
Conchoban ruaḃ, cona ẽocraide, α bẽóinrithin Cathail

---

1 *The Midhe band.* αn rúta
Mrohech (an rúta Midhech). The
word *rúta* is doubtless the same as *rout*,
and is intended to signify a company of
soldiers, although explained " a tribe of
people" by O'Reilly (*Irish Dictionary*).

2 *William.* Roderick O'Flaherty
has written the name Uillᵏ. (for
Ulick) in the margin; but the form
in the text is correct.

and one other warrior, i.e. the son of Ceithernach Ua Cerin; and he escaped thus. The Foreigners followed up the rout as far as Ath-Luain, and they turned back then, and brought their preys with them, and a great number of the horses of Connacht. A hosting by Cathal Crobhderg until he reached Tir-Fiachrach-Aighne, as if he went to protect his own land. It was not so in reality; but it was a treacherous and malicious hosting, of which came the destruction of Connacht, and his own destruction, viz.:—to attack Cathal Carrach, son of Conchobhair Maenmhaighe O'Conchobhair, to expel him from Connacht, or to capture him, or to kill him. When Cathal Carrach heard this, he sent his people into the woods, and he was himself behind them with all his army. Cathal Crobhderg advanced towards him from the west, from Tir-Fiachrach; and when he reached the middle of the territory of Cathal Carrach, he sent a large army in pursuit of him, with Toirdhelbhach son of Ruaidhri, and other sons of Ruaidhri; and with Maelchulaird O'Flaithbhertaigh, king of the West of Connacht; and with the grandsons of Tadhg O'Cellaigh; and with the knight O'Maelsechlainn, and with the Midhe band.[1] And when they arrived in the wood they were opposed, and battle was given to them, and the people of Cathal Crobhderg were defeated; and Maelchulaird O'Flaithbhertaigh, and the knight O'Maelsechlainn, and Iughuláid Mac Conmedha, and Domhnall, son of the Gilla-dubh O'Laedhóc, were slain there. Cathal Carrach afterwards sent messengers to Luimnech, to William Burk, and they delivered the son of Cathal Carrach into his hands as a pledge for the pay of the Foreigners. William[2] Burk subsequently assembled a large host from Ath-cliath, and from Laighen, and the Foreigners of Luimnech and Mumha besides, and the two O'Briains, viz.:—Muirchertach and Conchobhar Ruadh, with their armies, to the assistance

P 2

čarraiʒh. Ra ʒoiριο οόιƀ ιριn τíρ an τan οo ιmτiʒ
Caτhal cροιƀοerʒ erτe, ιaρ ʒclor οo bραιʒοe Τomal-
ταιʒ mιc Conchobaιρ mιc Οιαρmαοa, ocur meιc
Οιρechταιʒ ocur τρíl Μuιρeʒhaιʒ áιρčena, ocur na
Τuaτ, ocur hι Ʒαορa, ocur hι Eʒρa, ocur .h. Οuƀοa,
οo ʒαбáιl οo Caτhal čαρρach. Ιrreο οo ριnne Caτhal
cροιƀοeιρc οul ιριn τuαιρceρτ co τeč hι Eιcniʒ, ρι
ρeρ Manach, ocur αρριοeιc οocum 1 Νeιll, .ι. Οeƀ .h.
Νell, ocur οocum Eoaιn na Cúιρτι a nΥllτoιb. Cιƀ ριl
ann τρa, achτ, níρ ράʒuιƀ Caτhal cαρρach ocur Uιllιam
bυρc, ocur an οa .h. bρíaιn, cona nʒαlloιb ocur cona
nʒoeιοelαιƀ, cιll ιna τuaτ ó Echτʒe co Οún Rορρá-
pach, ocur ó ριnuιnn ρíαρ co ραιρρʒe, naρ αιρʒρeaτ
ocur náρ ṁιllρeτ, ιonnur naρ ƀín τempul ná alτóιρ, na
ραʒαρτ ná manach, na canánach ná ab, ιná erρuc, aρ
an ρloιʒ noemnaƀοa ριn, co nochταoιρ na ραcαρτa ιρ na
τempluιb, comberοíρ na mná ocur caƀ cρoƀ ocur caƀ
eallaƀ nó ƀíƀ ιρ na τempluιb leo, cen čáƀuρ οo noem
ιná οo neιmιο, na οo αιcṁeιl aρ ταlmaιn; conach
τucaƀ aρ Connachταιb ρíam ρoιme οíʒαιl ʒορτa ocur
nochτa, ocur αιρʒne maρ an οιʒαιl ριn. Ρορlonʒρορτ
ac Connachτuιƀ ac áτ lιac ó ρeιl bριʒοι co coeιcιƀíρ
ρíα mbeallταιnι, ʒuρρo αιρʒeτ muιnτeρ Ʒιllcán
uιle achτ bec, ocur ʒuρρo maρbρατ .h. Οuιƀιοíρ οo
muιnτeρ Αnʒαιle, ocur ʒuρρo αιρcρeτ. Ροelán .h.
Οonnchαοa οo maρbαο οo Οαρτραιʒιƀ. blιαοaιn
ρuaρ aρcalτach, nach ταρραιο οuιne ιρ ιn αιmριρ ριn
a macραmla. Cρeƀ ρluαιʒeο la Connachτuιƀ ιρ ιn
Μumaιn, ʒuρ loιρcρeτ boƀún Luιmnιʒ ocur caρlen

---

of Cathal Carrach. They were but a short time in the district when Cathal Crobhderg left it, after hearing that the hostages of Tomaltach, son of Conchobhar Mac Diarmada, and of Mac Oirechtaigh and all the Sil-Muireghaigh, and of the Tuatha,[1] and of O'Gadhra, and of O'hEghra, and of O'Dubhda, were taken by Cathal Carrach. What Cathal Crobhderg did was to go into the North, to the house of O'Eighnigh, king of Feara-Manach, and from thence to O'Neill, i.e. Aedh O'Neill, and to John de Curci in Ulidia. However, Cathal Carrach and William[2] Burk, and the two O'Briains, with their Foreigners and Gaeidhel, left neither church nor territory from Echtghe to Dún-Rossárach, and from the Sinuinn westwards to the sea, that they did not pillage and destroy, so that neither church, nor altar, nor priest, nor monk, nor canon, nor abbot, nor bishop, afforded protection against this demoniacal host; and they used to strip the priests in the churches, and carry off the women, and every kind of property and stock found in the churches, without regard to saint or sanctuary, or to any power[3] on earth; so that never before was there inflicted on the Connachtmen any punishment[4] of famine, nakedness, and plundering like this punishment.[4] The Connachtmen had an encampment at Ath-liac from the festival of Brigid until a fortnight before May-day, and they plundered nearly all Muinter-Gillcan, and slew and plundered O'Duibhidhir of Muinter-Anghaile. Faelan O'Donnchadha was slain by the Dartraighe. A cold, foodless year, the equal of which no man witnessed in that age. A predatory hosting by the Connachtmen into Mumha, and they burned the bodhún[5] of Luimnech, and Caislen-Ui-Conaing, and

---

usually means vengeance, revenge, or retaliation.

[5] *Bodhún.* The Four Masters, who give this entry under the year 1201, instead of boδún have maɼᵹaδ (margadh), "market." The word

boδún, which would literally mean "cow fort," being comp. of bó, a cow, and δún, a fort, is also generally translated "market" by Mageoghegan, in his version of the Annals of Clonmacnoise.

.h. Conuing, ocur baile imða eli; ocur ðá crec eli lar na Connachtaið ceðna, cur aircreð iartar Miðe ocur .h. bfaiľge. Cúcocrič̌e m̃ág Eoč̌agáin ðo marbað ðo 1ð failʒe. Mebal ðo ðenum ðo ʒalloib Ulað ar Airteraib, ocur a marbað uli acht bec. Slóiʒeð eli la Cathal carrach ocur la ʒalloib Mum̃an a Connachtaið, cur loircret cealla Connacht uili achtmað bec, ocur cur m̃illret Connacht uili.

Kt. Enair .ii. f.; l. xxiii.; bliaðain ar ða ceð ar mile air in Tiʒerna. Ruaiðri mac Duinnr̃lébi, r̃i Ulað, .i. coinneal ʒaircið ocur enʒnum na nʒoeiðel uile, ðo marbað ðo ʒalloib Eoain na Cuirti, iar na č̌eʒmail ðoib a mboeʒal a aonur, ðo m̃irbailib f̃oil ocur Pettair, ocur Patraic, ro ·r̃araiʒ. Crec la Cathal ʒcroibðerʒ .h. Conchobair, ocur .h. Neill maroen fr̃ir, ocur .h. heicnič̌ r̃i fer Mánach uachað r̃lóiʒ, ʒur aircret Cuil cnama, .i. muinter Diarmaða, mic Conchobair, mic Taiðʒ hi Maelruanaiʒ. Crec ele le Cathal croibðerʒ lin a focraoi fein, a tir n̄Aililla, cur airc ðaoine iomða ðo muinter Tomaltaiʒ, mic Conchobair, mic Diarmaða, mic Taiðʒ hi Maelruanaiʒ, riʒ moiʒe Luirc. Caðla .h. Dubthaiʒ, airðerruc č̌oiceð Connacht, in Crirto quieuit. Cathal croibðerʒ .h. Conchobair lin a focraoi, ocur .h. Neill lin a focraoi, ocur Č̌enel Eoʒain, ocur rochaoe ðo č̌enel Conaill, ocur .h. heicnič̌, r̃i bfer Manach, cona focraoiðe uile;

---

[1] *Cúcocriche.* This name literally means "border hound," from *cú*, a dog or hound, and *cocriche*, gen. of *cocrich*, a border.

[2] *Nearly all.* achtmað bec; lit. "excepting little."

[3] *Lamp.* The word coinneal, translated "lamp," is merely a loan word from the Latin *candela*.

[4] *Whom he profaned.* The profanation here referred to is doubtless the

proceeding recorded above under the year 1199, where Ruaidhri O'Duinnsleibhe (or Rory O'Donlevy) is stated to have plundered the monastery of Paul and Peter, at Armagh.

[5] *Diarmaid.* He was the son of Conchobhar Mac Diarmada, or Conor MacDermot. The note "M'Dermott pread (sic) by Cahal Crobhderg and O'Neill," has been added in the

many other places; and two other predatory expeditions
were led by the same Connachtmen, and they plundered the West of Midhe, and Ui-Failghe. Cúcocriche[1]
Mac Eochagain was slain by the Ui-Failghe. An act of
treachery was committed by the Foreigners of Uladh
against the Airthera, who were nearly all slain. Another
hosting by Cathal Carrach and the Foreigners of Mumha,
into Connacht, when they burned nearly all[2] the churches
of Connacht, and devastated all Connacht.

The kalends of January on the 2nd feria, the 23rd of
the moon; the age of the Lord one year, and two hundred, and a thousand. Ruaidhri Mac Duinnsleibhe, king
of Uladh, i.e. the lamp[3] of valour and prowess of all the
Gaeidhel, was slain by the Foreigners of John de Curci,
after they had met him alone, undefended, through
the miracles of Paul and Peter, and of Patrick, whom he
profaned.[4] A predatory expedition by Cathal Crobhderg O'Conchobhair, accompanied by O'Neill, and by
O'hEighnigh, king of Feara-Manach, with a small army;
and they plundered Cuil-cnamha, i.e. the people of
Diarmaid,[5] son of Conchobhar, son of Tadhg O'Maelruanaidh. Another predatory expedition by Cathal
Crobhderg, with all his own army, into Tir-Aililla, when
he plundered many persons of the people of Tomaltach,
son of Conchobhar, son of Diarmaid, son of Tadhg O'Maelruanaidh, king of Magh-Luirg. Cadhla O'Dubhthaigh,
archbishop of the province of Connacht, in Christo
quievit. Cathal Crobhderg O'Conchobhair, with all
his army; and O'Neill, with all his army; and the
Cenel-Eoghain; and a multitude of the Cenel-Conaill;
and O'hEighnigh, king of Feara-Manach, with all
his forces, *went* into Connacht until they reached

---

margin by O'Flaherty. Under this
year the Annals of Ulster have the
entry "ɪnnαꞃbα Cα̇αɪl cꞃoɪḃ̇oeꞃ̄ɡ,
ocuꞃ ꞃɪ̇̄ɡαɔ̇ Cαɫαɪl cαꞃꞃαɪ̇̄ɡ ɪnα

ɪnαꞇo;" "expulsion of Cathal Crobhderg, and Cathal Carrach was made
king in his place." The Four Masters
refer these events to the year 1199.

α Connachtuiƀ co pancotap teč mƀóeitin ı nαιptech,
conꝺepnꝛat cpeιč moıp ap muıntep Tomaltaıᵹ mıc
Ꝺιapmaꝺa, ocuꝛ cuꝛ mapƀꝛat ꝺaıne ımƀa ꝺa muıntep.
Iapꝛın tapla ꝺebaıꝺ etıp Cathal cpoıbꝺepᵹ ocuꝛ maıčı
an tuaıpceipt. Ropé, ꝺono, aƀbap na ꝺeaƀča ꝛın, .ı.
ıꝛꝛeꝺ pob áıl la Cathal cpoıbꝺepᵹ, ınꝛoıᵹeꝺ Cathaıl
čappaıᵹ ocuꝛ Uıllıam ɓuꝛc; ocuꝛ aꝺubꝛaꝺoꝛ ın lucht
elı nač paᵹꝺaoıꝛ ꝺočum ᵹall, oıp ıꝛꝛeꝺ aꝺubꝛaꝺ ꝛıú ın
tan tancotap ó tıᵹıƀ, nach paƀaꝺap ᵹaıll ı ꝛocpaıꝺe
Cathaıl čappaıᵹ. Ro ꝺeılıᵹ cač ꝛe čelı ꝺıƀ uımı ꝛın,
ocuꝛ ꝺo chúaıꝺ Cathal cpoıbꝺepᵹ ı maptoꝛ Connacht,
ocuꝛ ꝺo čuaꝺap ın lucht elı ꝺınnꝛoıᵹeꝺ a tıpe ꝛeın;
ocuꝛ ıꝛꝛı ꝛlıᵹe ꝛo ᵹaƀꝛat ꝺo Sleıƀ Luᵹa, ocuꝛ α
ᵹCoꝛonn. Ro hınnıꝛꝛeꝺ an ní ꝛın ꝺo Cathal cappach,
ocuꝛ ꝺUıllıam ɓuꝛc. Iꝛꝛı comaıple ꝺo ꝛónꝛat ꝺul
anꝺeᵹhaıꝺ lucht an tuaıꝛceıpt, ocuꝛ ıꝛ ann ꝛucꝛat
ꝛoꝛpa ac ꝺul tap ꝺpoıcet Eꝛꝛa Ꝺapa. Ro lenꝛat
ꝺocum ꝺpoıčıt Maptpa. Ro ımpaꝺap lucht ın tuaıꝛceıpt ꝺo taƀaıpt ꝛuaca ꝺoıƀ, ocuꝛ nı ꝛo ꝛoemaꝺ uatha
ın ꝛuaıc. Ro ımpaꝺap ꝺono Connachtaıᵹ ıaptaın, ocuꝛ
ꝛucꝛat ap .h. neıcnıč, ꝛı ꝛeꝛ Manach, ocuꝛ ꝛo mapƀaꝺ
é; ocuꝛ ní heıꝛıum nach ꝺepna maıč, acht an ıomaꝛ-
cpaıꝺ ꝺo bꝛeč ꝛaıp. Ro ımpo .h. Neıll ına ꝛꝛučınᵹ ꝛa
laım, ocuꝛ níp leıᵹeꝺ aꝛ tempul Eꝛꝛa Ꝺapa hé no co
taꝺ bpaıᵹꝺı ocuꝛ ꝛıč ꝺo Cathal čappach. Ro map-
ƀuıꝺ, ımoꝛꝛo, ꝛochaıꝺe moꝛ ꝺıƀ o ꝛın co Ꝺpuım člıaƀ,

---

[1] *Tech-Bacithin in Airtech.* The
Annals of Ulster and the Four Mast.
(1199) read τeč ɓαoıτın αιpτıᵹ
"Tech-Bacithin of Airtech." The
place is now called Tibohine, and is
a townland in the parish of the same
name, barony of Frenchpark, and co.
of Roscommon.

[2] *Depredation.* This seems to be a
repetition, in somewhat altered phraseology, of the depredation recorded a
few lines before.

[3] *They proceeded.* Ro ᵹaɓꝛat
(ro gabhsat); lit. "they took."

[4] *They;* i.e. the northern marauders.

[5] *Droichet - Martra.* This name,
which signifies either the "bridge of
relics," or the "bridge of martyrdom,"
seems partly preserved in that of Bell-
adrehid, in Irish bél an ꝺꝛoıchıꝺ,
"the mouth of the bridge," a hamlet
on a small stream a mile to the north
of Ballysadare, on the road to Sligo.

[6] *Battle.* Ruαcα; gen. of ꝛuaıc,

Tech-Baeithin, in Airtech;[1] and they committed a great depredation[2] on the people of Tomaltach Mac Diarmada, and slew many men of his people. A dispute arose afterwards between Cathal Crobhderg and the chieftains of the North. The cause of this dispute was *as follows*, viz.:—what Cathal Crobhderg wished was to go against Cathal Carrach and William Burk; and the other party said that they would not go towards the Foreigners, because they had been informed, when they left their homes, that there were no Foreigners in the army of Cathal Carrach. On this account they separated one from the other, and Cathal Crobhderg went into the west of Connacht, and the other party went towards their own country; and the way they proceeded[3] was to Sliabh-Lugha, and into Corann. This fact was told to Cathal Carrach, and to William Burk. The resolution they adopted was to go after the Northern party; and they came up with them *as they*[4] *were* crossing the bridge of Es-dara, and followed *them* to Droichet-Martra.[5] The Northern party turned to give them battle;[6] but battle was not accepted from them. The Connachtmen afterwards returned, and caught O'hEighnigh, king of Feara-Manach, and he was slain; and not because he did not act bravely,[7] but because he was outnumbered. O'Neill turned back in his path, in subjection,[8] and he was not allowed to leave the church of Es-Dara until he gave hostages and peace to Cathal Carrach. Great numbers of them[9] were slain, moreover, from thence to Druim-cliabh, and to

---

which, although interpreted by O'Reilly altogether in the sense of defeat, means properly an attack, or onset.

[7] *Bravely.* The words ocuꝛ ní heiꝛꝼum nach ꝺeꝛna maiꞇ, literally translated, would read "and it was not he that performed not good."

[8] *In subjection.* ꝼa ꞁaim; lit. "under [the] hand." The meaning is that

O'Neill voluntarily returned as a prisoner to Es-Dara, or Ballysadare. The word ꝛꝛuꞇinᵹ, translated path, signifies literally the way by which a person has come, being comp. of ꝼꝛuꞇ, against, and ınᵹ or enᵹ, a track or footstep.

[9] *Of them;* i.e. of the northern party.

ocur co Ðún .h. nÐipṁeðaiᵹ, ocur co Sáil mbeinne.
Tomaltach mac Oeða mic Toippdhealbaiᵹ hI Conchobaip, comꝼopba Ꝓatpaic, ocur ppíṁaitt na hEpenn,
ocur erpuc Sil Muipeðhaiᵹ, in Cpirto quieuit; im
maiᵹ Mupa na heċloirce uitam ꝼinitit, ac ðul co
hArð Maċa. Oeð mac Taiċliᵹ I Ðuðda, pi .h.
nAmalᵹaið, occirur ert.

Mórrluaiᵹed la hEoain na Cuirti ocur la hUᵹa oᵹ
mac Uᵹa ðe Láci, co rocpaide moip do ᵹalloib na
Miðe laip, mapoen re Cathal cpoibðepᵹ, a Connachtaib, do copnum piᵹe re Cathal cappach; ocur irri
pliᵹe [po ᵹaḃrat] ðerr Ruaid ocur a Caippri Ðroma
cliaḃ, a Copann, a ᵹCopprliaḃ na Seᵹra, a maᵹ Luipᵹ
an Ðaᵹða, a maᵹ Nói, a maiᵹiḃ ꝼinna, do ðún Leoða,
a Moenṁaᵹ, a tir ꝼiaċpaċ Aiᵹne, co pancodar Cill
mic Ðuaċ; ocur ir aire po innroiᵹret an ꝼad rin
roċer, anðeᵹhaid ðó ocur muintipe rer Connacht ocur
Cathail ċappaiᵹ, ar na mbpeiċ laip do Cathal ċap-
pach a Tuaðṁuṁuin, ocur a Cenél Oeða na hEchtᵹe,
etir ðoéiniḃ ocur innliḃ; ocur po ḃói ꝼéin lín a
rocpaide tapeir a ṁuintepi. Ro hinnired, imorro,
dona rluaᵹaiḃ rin in ċoill ꝼor a poiḃe rorlonᵹport
Cathail ċappaiᵹ ocur Connacht; ocur irrí comaiple do
ronrat an rorlonᵹport ðinnroiᵹed; ocur o pancottar
in ċoilled po reiðiᵹret hí, ocur do ronrat rliᵹed
móir rempa co pancodar in Lonᵹport; ocur ir amlaid
ruaradar an Lonᵹport rolam, ar na ꝼáᵹbáil do Cathal

1 *Magh-Mura-na-hechloisce.* "The plain of Mura of the Spring (or Pool)." The situation of this plain has not been discovered. In the Annals of Boyle, and also in the Dublin Annals of Inisfallen, Tomaltach (who is incorrectly called Thomas in the latter chronicle), is stated to have been buried in the abbey of Mellifont, county of Louth, from which it would seem probable that Magh-Mura was somewhere to the south of Armagh, and on the way from Elphin thereto. The

word eċloirc (echloisc) means a spring, or pool, and was anciently applied as a name to many places in Ireland. Tomaltach O'Conor's name is not found in the usual lists of the bishops of Sil-Muiredhaigh, or Elphin; and this entry leaves it uncertain whether he became bishop of Elphin before he occupied the see of Armagh, or after he resigned it.

2 *Corrsliabh-na-Seghsa.* The Curlieu hills, in the county of Roscommon.

3 *Magh-Luirg-in-Daghda;* i.e. "the

Dun-Ui-Airmhedhaigh, and to Sáil-Beinne. Tomaltach, son of Aedh, son of Toirdhelbhach O'Conchobhair, comarb of Patrick, and primate of Erinn, and bishop of Síl-Muiredhaigh, in Christo quievit. In Magh-Mura-na-hechloisce[1] vitam finivit, whilst going to Ard-Macha. Aedh, son of Taichlech O'Dubhda, king of Ui-Amhal-ghaidh, occisus est.

A great hosting to Connacht by John de Curci and Hugo the younger, son of Hugo de Laci, accompanied by a great number of the Foreigners of Midhe, together with Cathal Crobhderg, to contest the sovereignty with Cathal Carrach; and the way [they went] was to Es-Ruaidh, and into Cairpre-Droma-cliabh, into Corann, into Corrsliabh-na-Seghsa,[2] into Magh-Luirg-in-Daghda,[3] into Magh-Nai, into Maighe-Finna, to Dun-Leodha, into Maenmhagh, into Tir-Fiachrach-Aighne, until they reached Cill-Mic-Duach. And the reason they proceeded so far southwards was in pursuit of the cows and people of the Connachtmen, and of Cathal Carrach, which had been carried off by Cathal Carrach to Tuadh-Mumha and to Cenel-Aedha of Echtghe, both men and cattle; and he himself was behind his people, with all his forces. These hosts were informed of the wood in which was the camp of Cathal Carrach and *the men of* Connacht; and the resolution they adopted[4] was to move towards the camp. And when they reached the wood they cut it down, and made a great road before them until they arrived at the camp, which they found empty,[5] after having been abandoned

---

plain of the Daghda's track," so called, according to an ancient legend, from the Daghda, one of the principal personages of the Tuatha-De-Danaans. This plain, the name of which is usually anglicised Moylurg, comprised the plains of the present barony of Boyle, south of the river Boyle, in the county of Roscommon.

[4] *The resolution they adopted.* The

expression iʀʀí comaiρle ꝺo ꝑonꝑaꞇ, which occurs so frequently in this chronicle, and is usually translated as above, literally rendered would read "it is the counsel they made."

[5] *Which they found empty.* The clause "oċuʀ iʀ amlaiꝺ ꝼuaʀaꝺaʀ an longꝑoʀꞇ ꝼolam" literally means "and the condition in which they found the camp was—empty."

čarpach gairid reimi rin, ap na innirin dó an rluag rin do beič čuici; ocur po tói a monað eli irin coillid, gairid ón longpopt, agá bpeičeam rum. Irri comaiple do ponrat Goill, o pancodar an longpopt, dul ap cend a ngilla, ocur a nech, po fágrat alla muiᵹ don čoillid, ocur an méide po fágrat da rluaiᵹ. Od čonnaipc Cathal carpach ocur Connachtaiᵹ rin, .i. iadrum aᵹ impúð amač dorưðiri, po éipiᵹret na ndeᵹhaid, ocur pucrad roppa irin peiðechad do ponrat buðéin. O po cumaipc cač ap a čéli ðíb po meabad re Cathal ᵹcarpach ocur re Connachtaið, ocur po marbad .lx. uel ampliur do máčib muintire Eoain na Cuipti ann, .i. do máčib Gall moiᵹe Line ocur Ulad aipčena, da mbarưnaib ocur dá ridiriȝ, ocur po buailed Eoain rein do čloič gur čuit dá eč. O rangadar amač ap an coillid docum a muintire do rcuip an ruaic ðíb, ocur irri comaiple do ponrat impúð ina brpičing, ocur lotar an aghaid rin co hArd Račuin; ap na bárach co Tuaim da ᵹualann; ocur irred do ráiðret óṙṙ aird gurab a Túaim do beiðír an oiðče rin; ocur ni heð do ponrat, acht imčecht ó čanic inn aghaid co pancodar Cill Dáčonne a cind tóčaip Monad Coinneða, ocur do bádar annrin no co tánic in máiden. O čanic an máiden do imðiᵹetar, ocur do čuadar in lá rin co Ror Comáin; ap na bárach co Rinn dúin ap Loč Ri; ocur do badar rechtmuin ac imluchtad ant rluaiᵹ, ocur a nech ocur a neallað, tar Loč Ri roip; ocur ní čuala Cathal carpach na Connachtaiᵹ rin co tánic la deiᵹenach in immluchtaiᵹ. O po cualadar Cathal carpach ocur Connachtaiᵹ rin, po lenrat iat co Rinn

---

¹ *The attack ceased.* do rcuip an ruaic ðíb (do scuir an ruaic dhíbh). Lit. "the attack ceased off them." The particle do is written | twice, viz.:—at the end of one page and beginning of the next. The word ruaic here also signifies a conflict, or attack, and not a retreat,

by Cathal Carrach a short time previously, when he was informed that this host was approaching him. And he was in another place in the wood, a short distance from the camp, awaiting them. The resolution the Foreigners adopted, when they reached the camp, was to go towards their horse-boys and horses, whom they had left outside the wood, and those of their host whom they had left behind. When Cathal Carrach and the Connachtmen saw this, viz.:—the others turning out again, they went after them, and overtook them in the clearing which they (*the Foreigners*) had themselves made. When they mingled, one with the other, the battle was won by Cathal Carrach and the Connachtmen, and sixty, vel amplius, of the nobles of John de Curci's people were slain there, i.e. of the nobles of the Foreigners of Magh-Line, and of all Uladh, of their barons and knights; and John himself was struck with a stone, so that he fell from his horse. As soon as they came out of the wood to their people the attack ceased,[1] and the resolution they adopted was to turn back in their track; and they proceeded that night to Ard-rathain. On the morrow they went to Tuaim-da-ghualann; and what they said publicly was, that they would remain[2] in Tuaim that night; but they did not do so, for they departed as soon as the night came, *and marched* until they arrived at Cill-Dachonne, at the head of Tochar-mona-Coinnedha, where they remained until the morning came. When the morning came they departed, and they went that day to Ros-Comain. On the morrow they proceeded to Rinn-dúin on Loch-Rí, and they were a week transporting the army, and their horses, and their property, eastwards across Loch-Rí. And neither Cathal Carrach nor the Connachtmen heard of this until the last day of the transportation. When Cathal Carrach and the Connachtmen heard of it, they

as O'Reilly explains it. See note [6], p. 216.

[2] *They would remain.* no beirír (no bheidís); lit. "they would be."

δúin, cuɲ ṁaɲḃɲaꞇ an ṁéiꝺ aɲ a ɲucɲaꞇ, ocuɲ ɲo
baiꝺiꝺ an ṁeiꝺ aɲ naċ ɲucɲaꞇ ac ꞇeiċeꝺ; ocuɲ ɲo
báꝺiꝺ imaꝺ ꝺoeiniḃ aɲ a nimluċꞇaḋ ɲe heꝺ na
ɲeaċꞇṁuine ɲeme ɲin. O ɲancoꞇaɲ Ʒaill iɲin Miꝺe
ɲo ʒaḃɲaꞇ Caꞇal cɲoiḃꝺeɲʒ a nʒell ɲo ꞇuaɲuɲꝺal,
ocuɲ ɲucaꝺ Eoain co hαꞇ cliaċ no ʒuɲ ꝼáʒuiḃ bɲaiʒꝺi
aɲɲ ꝼein ꝼe ꝼeiɲ ɲí Saxɲan. Conċobaɲ na ʒlaiɲꝼeine,
mac Caꞇail Í Ruaiɲc, ꝺo ḃáꝺhaꝺ. Ʒaill ꝺꝼuaɲlucaꝺ
ꝺo Caꞇal cɲoiḃꝺeɲʒ. Conċobaɲ bec ṁec Laċlainn
ꝺo ṁaɲbaꝺ la Cenel Conaill. Oeꝺh .h. Neill ꝺaꞇɲiʒaꝺ
lá Cenel nEoʒain iɲin mbliaꝺain ɲin. Niall .h. Ꝼloinn
ꝺo maɲbaꝺ ꝺo ʒalloiḃ, a meaḃail. Maʒnuɲ mac Ꝺiaɲ-
maꝺa mec Laċlainn ꝺo maɲbaꝺ ꝺo Muiɲceɲꞇaċ .h.
Néill. Muiɲceɲꞇaċ .h. Néill ꝼein ꝺo maɲbaꝺ ann.

 Kt. Enaiɲ .iii. ꝼ.; l. iiii.; ꝺa bliaꝺain aɲ ꝺá ceꝺ aɲ
mile aiɲ in Ꞇiʒeɲna. Ꝼelix O Ꝺuḃláin eɲꝑuc Oɲɲaiʒe,
moɲꞇuuɲ eɲꞇ. Inꞇ eɲꝑuc .h. Mellaiʒ moɲꞇuuɲ eɲꞇ.
Caꞇal cɲoiḃꝺeɲʒ ꝺo ꝺul iɲin Mumain, iaɲ bꝼuaɲlucaꝺ
ꝺe aɲɲ a ċuibɲiʒiꝺ, ꝺocum Uilliam ḃúɲc. Iohanneɲ
ꝑɲeɲbiꞇeɲ caɲꝺinaliɲ ꝺe Monꞇe Celio, qui eꞇ leʒaꞇuɲ
aꝑoɲꞇolice ɲeꝺiɲ eɲaꞇ, in hiḃeɲniam ueniꞇ. Slóiʒeꝺ

---

1 *Those whom they did not overtake;*
i.e. the parties who were on the western
side of Loch-Ri, on the coming up of
Cathal Carrach and the Connachtmen, but whom the pursuers did not
succeed in catching.

2 *John.* Eoain. Interlined in original hand. As the text stood before
this emendation, it would represent
Cathal Crobhderg as the person who
had been conveyed to Ath-cliath, or
Dublin; and such seems to have been
Roderick O'Flaherty's opinion, for he
has added the marginal note, "John
de Coarcy after his fateege att
Lanesborow takes Cahal Crobhderg
prisoner, for his army's pay; O'Connor
gives him hostages in Dublin to give

him yᵉ k[ing] of England's saying."
The Dublin Annals of Inisfallen
represent the transaction as follows:—
"Seaʒan ꝺe Couɲci ocuɲ ḃalꞇeɲ
ꝺe Laci ʒo bɲeɲaiꝺ Miꝺe ꝺo
ꞇeaċꞇ a Connaċꞇa, a cúnʒnaṁ
le Caꞇal cɲoiḃꝺeɲʒ. Maꝺm moɲ
ꝺoiɲ iaꝺ ꝼein ocuɲ Caꞇal caɲ-
ɲaċ, ocuɲ ṁuinꞇeɲ Uilliam ꝺe
ḃúɲc aʒ Cill mic Ꝺuaċh, áiꞇ aɲ
bɲiɲeaꝺ ꝺo Seaʒan ꝺe Couɲci,
ʒuɲ buꝺ héiʒion ꝺo ꝺol ꞇaɲ Loċ
ɲíaɲ [recte ɲaiɲ], aiꞇ aɲ ʒaḃaꝺ
le clainn hUʒo ꝺe Laci é, ꝺo
ċoṁaiɲle ɲiʒ Saʒɲan, ʒuɲ ḃéiʒin
bɲáiʒꝺe maiċe ꝺꝼáʒail aɲ."
"John de Curci and Walter de
Laci, with the men of Midhe, went to

A D.
[1201.]

followed them to Rinn-dúin, and killed as many as they overtook, and those whom they did not overtake[1] were drowned while escaping; and a great many men were drowned whilst being conveyed across during the preceding week. As soon as the Foreigners arrived in Midhe they arrested Cathal Crobhderg as a pledge for *the payment of* wages; and John[2] was taken to Ath-cliath until he gave pledges from himself that he would obey the king of the Saxons. Conchobhar-na-Glaisfheine, son of Cathal O'Ruairc, was drowned.[3] The Foreigners released Cathal Crobhderg. Conchobhar Bec Mac Lachlainn was slain by the Cenel-Conaill. Aedh O'Neill was dethroned by the Cenel-Eoghain in this year. Niall O'Floinn was slain by the Foreigners, in treachery. Maghnus, son of Diarmaid Mac Lachlainn, was killed by Muirchertach O'Neill. Muirchertach O'Neill was himself slain there.

[1202.] The kalends of January on the 3rd feria, the 4th of the moon; the age of the Lord two years, and two hundred, and a thousand. Felix O'Dubhláin, bishop of Osraighe, mortuus est. The bishop O'Mellaigh[4] mortuus est. Cathal Crobhderg went into Mumha, to William Burk, after being released from his bonds. Johannes, Presbyter Cardinalis de Monte Celio, qui et legatus Apostolicæ sedis erat, in Hiberniam venit. A hosting by

---

Connacht to assist Cathal Crobhderg. A great breach between themselves and Cathal Carrach and the people of William de Burk, at Cill-Mic-Duach, where John de Curci was defeated, so that he was forced to go across the lake [Loch Ree] westwards, [*recte* eastwards], where he was taken prisoner by the sons of Hugo de Laci, by the advice of the king of England, and good pledges had to be obtained from him." The expression in the text "no ᵹᴜᴩ ꝼáᵹᴜɪb bᴩᴀɪᵹᴏɪ αᴩᴩ ꝼᴇɪɴ,"

"until he gave pledges from himself," evidently refers to De Curci.

[3] *Drowned.* The Four Masters, who give this event at the year 1200, state that Conor-na-Glaisfheine O'Ruanc was drowned on the occasion of a defeat which he and the Ui-Briuin suffered at the hands of O'Donnell, near Ballyshannon.

[4] *O'Mellaigh*; i.e. Conn O'Mellaigh (or O'Melly), bishop of Eanach ᴅúɪɴ, or Annaghdown, in the county of Galway.

λα Caṫal ocuр λα hUilliam buрc, ocuр λα claiηη Ꝺomηail hi bρíaiη, [.i.] Muiрċeрτaċ ocuр Conċóbaρ ρuaḃ, ocuр λα Fiηġiη mac meg Caρρṫaiġ, a Connaċ-τuiḃ, co рaηcovaр maiηiрτiр Aṫa va λaрac ꝛoр buill, conav iητi vo̍ ꝛoηꝛaτ a bꝼoꝛλoηgꝑuiꝛτ, ocuр ꝛo ḃavaρ τꝛi τꝛaḃ iηητe, cuр elηevaρ ocuр cuр ꝼalcovaρ iη maiηiꝛviр uile; ocuр ꝛobé mév iη elηiḃ, co ꝛavavuр ηa mηa ag ꝛeꝛꝛeηcaib aητ ꝛlúaig a τiġ ġalaiꝛ ηa maηaċ, ocuр a τiġiḃ iη claḃτꝛa, ocuр iη gaċ ioηav aiρċeηa iꝛiη maiηiꝛτiꝛ uile. Niꝛ ꝼacbav, vono, veητa iꝛiη maiηiꝛτiꝛ ciη bꝑiꝑꝼev ocuр ceη loꝛcav, aċτ cꝛeτa ηa τiġeḃ ηamá; ocuр ciḃ iaτ ꝛiη, ꝛo-bꝑiꝑꝛiτ ocuр ꝛo loiꝛciτ moꝛáη viḃ. Niꝛ leiceo ní vꝼoiꝛꝛeηem ηa maiηiꝛoꝛeċ uile voηa maηċaib ocuр voηa bꝛaiτꝛiḃ, aċτ covailτeċ ηa maηaċ ηamá, ocuр τeḃ ηa ηouici. Caiꝛꝛel vo ċiηηꝛeηa λα hUilliam buꝛc voη τuꝛuꝛ ꝛiη im ċeḃ cloiċi móꝛ ηa ηáiveḃ, ocuр oꝛaiꝛ ḃá λá vo ċaḃaiꝛτ aꝛ a ṫoḃailτ. Caṫal caꝛꝛaċ, mac Conċóbaiꝛ ṁoeηmaive, ꝛí. Connaċτ, vo maꝛbav le Ꝣalloib iꝛ iη τꝛeꝛ λα τoḃalτa iη ċaiꝛil. Caiꝛmeꝛcτaꝛ, imoꝛꝛo, iη caiꝛel iaꝛ maꝛbaḃ Caṫail ċaꝛꝛaiċ. Ꝛo maꝛḃaiτ vono aꝛoeη ꝛiꝛiη ꝛíġ, .i. Ꝺiaꝛmaiτ, mac Ꝣillacꝑiꝛτ, mic Ꝺiaꝛmava, mic Caiḃc hi Maelꝛuaηaiḃ, ocuρ Comalτaċ mac Caiċliġ .h. Ꝺuḃva, eτ alii multi. Ꝛo ꝼacꝛaτ iη maiηiꝛτiꝛ iaꝛꝛiη, ocuр aꝛ ηa ꝼacḃáil vóib vo leic · Uilliam buꝛc imċeċτ vo claiηη hi bꝛiaiη, ocuρ vo mac ṁég Caꝛꝛṫaigh, coηa ꝛoꝛꝛaive. Iꝛꝛí comaiꝛle, imoꝛꝛo, vo ꝛiηηe Caṫal cꝛoibveꝛc ocuρ Uilliam buꝛc,

1 *Cathal*. Cathal Crobhderg.

2 *Roofs*. cꝛeτa. The word cꝛeτ (pl. cꝛeτa) properly means a frame formed of hurdles, and is probably borrowed from the Latin *crates*, or English *crate*. O'Reilly (*Irish Dictionary*) has the word cꝛeiτ, which he translates "a ridge."

3 *Killed*. The Four Masters (at the year 1201), as translated by Dr. O'Donovan, state that Cathal Carrach "went forth to view a contest [be-

Cathal[1] and William Burk, and by the sons of Domhnall O'Briain, [i.e.] Muirchertach and Conchobhar Ruadh, and by Finghin, son of Mac Carthaigh, into Connacht, until they reached the monastery of Ath-da-larag, on the Buill, in which they fixed their residence; and they were three days in it, so that they polluted and defiled the entire monastery; and such was the extent of the defilement that the mercenaries of the army had the women in the hospital of the monks, and in the houses of the cloister, and in every place in the entire monastery besides. No structure in the monastery was left without breaking and burning, except the roofs[2] of the houses alone; and even of these a great portion was broken and burned. No part of the buildings of the entire monastery was allowed to the monks and brothers, excepting only the dormitory of the monks, and the house of the novices. A stone wall was commenced by William Burk, on this occasion, round the great stone house of the guests, and two days' work was devoted to its erection. Cathal Carrach, son of Conchobhar Maenmhaighe, king of Connacht, was killed[3] by the Foreigners on the third day of the building of the stone wall. *The erection of* the stone wall, moreover, was interrupted after the killing of Cathal Carrach. There were *others* also slain along with the king, viz.:—Diarmaid, son of Gillachrist, son of Diarmaid, son of Tadhg O'Maelruanaidh, and Tomaltach, son of Taichlech O'Dubhda, et alii multi. They subsequently left the monastery; and after they had left it William Burk permitted the sons of O'Briain, and the son of Mac Carthaigh, to depart with their forces. The resolution that Cathal Crobhderg and William Burk adopted,

tween his own army and the forces of Cathal Crobhderg and William de Burgo]; but a body of his own people being violently driven towards him, he became involved in the crowd, and was killed."

Q

.i. a ρεηρεναιξ do ρξοειλεд ρο Connachταιъ, do ταbach
a τυαρυρдαιl; et do chúαιд Uilliam Ьυρс cona ραъ
maille ριρ, ocυρ Cathal crοιbдερξ, co Cunξα Ϝειċín.
Do ρala τρα ρξέl miorьάlдα ιαρριn, ocυρ ni ϝερρ ιn τρε
ъυιne, no an τρε ρριραιд Dé a nдelb ъυιne, ταnic ριn,
.i. ιρρεд ρο hιnniρεъ Uilliam Ьυρc do marbaд, conach
ραъ a Connachταιъ conáιρ nach ρanic ιn ρcέl ριn. Iρρí
comaιρle do ρonρατ na haιρechτa aρ ξcluιnριn ιn
ρξεοιl ριn, amaιl do neτíρ oen comaιρle, .i. ξach oen
do marbaд a ċonme; ocυρ ιρ amlaιд ριn do ροnaъ, .i.
ξach oιρechτ do marbaд a ρanic ċuca; ocυρ ιρρεд ιn
erbυд do ρειρ ρξέl a nдáιneъ ρϝέιn .ix. ceд uel ampliυρ.
Od ċuala Uilliam Ьυρc a muιnτερ do marbaд, do
caξραд .h. Conchobaιρ aιξe. Ranic ιn ρabaъ docum
.h. Conchobaιρ, ocυρ ρο ϝaξυιъ an áιτ ambóι Uilliam.
Téιд Uilliam don Mumaιn ιaρ ϝaξbaιl uρmóιρ a
muιnτιρε. Sénaъ cleιρech Erenn, eτιρ ξulla ocυρ
Ξοειдela, ιn Αъ cliaъ ιmon Caιρдιnáιl, .i. Iohanneρ
Pρερbιτερ de Monτe Celio. Senaъ Connachτ, loechaιb
ċleιρċιb, ιc áъ Luaιn ιmon ξcaιρдináł ceдna, a ξcιnn
coeιcιъιρι. Taъc .h. Ьραιn, ρι Luιξne, do éc. Τοιρρ-
дhealbach mac Ruaιдρι mιc Τοιρρдhealbaξ hí
Conchobaιρ do ξαъáιl la Cathal ξcrοιbдερc, ocυρ
ιρριαд ρορ ξαъ hé, .i. Donnchaд .h. Duъдa, ρι .h.
nΑmalξαιд, ocυρ Conchobaρ ξοτ .h. hEξρα, ρι Luιξ̃ι
Connachτ, ocυρ Dιαρmαιд mac Ruaιдρι hí Conchobaιρ,

1 *Mercenaries.* ρεηρεναιξ. Mageoghegan, the translator of the
Annals of Clonmacnois, at the year
1200, renders the word ρεηρεναιξ
(pl. of ρεηρεναch) by "souldiers."
See note [8], p. 196, *supra.*

2 *Event.* ρξέl. Lit. "story."

3 *The tribes.* na haιρechτα.
The word aιρechτ (airecht) is generally employed in the Brehon Laws
to signify an assembly, or court of
law. See the MS. H. 3. 18., Trin.
Coll. Dublin, pp. 25 and 57 *b.* But
it also means a tribe or district; and
in this sense it has given name to the
barony of Αιρechτ-i-Conchobhaιρ,
or Iraghticonnor, in the county of
Kerry. The territory, as well as the
sept, of Ui-Cathain (or O'Kane), in
the county of Londonderry, was also
called Αιρechτ-i-Cathain. See
O'Donovan's ed. of the Four Mast.,
A.D. 1376, note [d].

4 *His guest.* a ċonme; i.e. the
person quartered on him.

A.D.
[1202.]

moreover, was to despatch their mercenaries[1] throughout Connacht, to levy their wages; and William Burk, together with all who were with him, and Cathal Crobhderg, went to Cunga-Feichín. After this a miraculous event[2] happened, and it is not known whether it occurred through a man, or through the spirit of God in the shape of a man, viz.:—it was reported that William Burk had been killed; and there was not a road in Connacht by which this report did not come. The resolution adopted by the tribes[3] on hearing this news, was, as if they had taken counsel together, viz.:—each man to kill his guest.[4] And thus it was done, viz.:—each tribe[5] killed all that came to them; and the loss, according to the report of their own people, was nine hundred, vel amplius. When William Burk heard that his people had been slain, he plotted against O'Conchobhair;[6] but timely notice reached O'Conchobhair, and he left the place where William was; and William went to Mumha, after losing the majority of his people. A synod of the clerics of Erinn, both Foreigners and Gaeidhel, in Ath-cliath, with the Cardinal, i.e. Johannes Presbyter de Monte Celio. A synod of Connacht, both laics and clerics, at Ath-Luain, with the same Cardinal, at the end of a fortnight. Tadhg O'Brain, king of Luighne, died. Toirdhelbhach, son of Ruaidhri, son of Toirdhelbhach O'Conchobhair, was taken prisoner by Cathal Crobhderg; and they who arrested him were these, viz.:—Donnchadh O'Dubhda, king of Ui-Amhalghaidh, and Conchobhar Got O'hEghra, king of Luighne of Connacht, and Diarmaid, son of Ruaidhri

---

[5] *Tribe.* oɩɼeċτ. Another mode of writing the word aɩɼeċτ. See note [3], last page.

[6] *Plotted against O'Conchobhair.* The expression ꝺo caſɼaꝺ .ħ. Conchobaɩɼ aɩʒe, literally rendered, would read "O'Conchobhair was whispered by him." The word caſɼaꝺ is the 3rd sg. imperf. pass., and also the infin. pres. of the verb coʒaɼ, or caʒaɼ (con-gair), to whisper, or talk together; from the root *gar*; Sanskrit grî. See Stokes's *Goidilica*, p. 15, n. 13. It has made its way into the English slang vocabulary, in the form "coggering," vulgarly used to express "whispering," or "plotting."

mac a αταιη ϝéin, ocuγ Dιαηmαιδ mac Rυαιδηι mιc Μαᵹηυηα, .ι. mac mιc δεηbηαταιη a αταιη. Μoelϝιннειн mac Colmαιн, αηδ ϝεнoιη τoᵹαιδε, ιн pαce quιεuιτ. Domναll cαηηαch .h. Dochαηταιᵹ, ηí τóιηηech Cηδα Μιδαιη, δo mαηbαδ δo ṁυιннτεη Dúιᵹιll αη нαηᵹυιн čeαll нιmδα, ocuγ τυαιč. Domναll .h. Bηolčán, ηηóιη ocuγ uαηαl ϝεнoιη τoᵹαιδε αη cηuč, αη čeιll, αη ṁíne, αη moηδαchτ, αη ecнα, αη αηδ cηαbαδ, ηoητ mαᵹнαm τηιbulατιoнem eτ oητιmαm ηeнιτeнτιαm, ιн quιнτα kαleнδαη Μαιι [quιεuιτ].

kt. Eнáιη .ιιιι. ϝ.; l. xu.; τηí blιαδна αη δá ceδ αη mιle αιη ιн τιᵹeηнα. Slυαιᵹeδ la hUιllιαm Dυηc, ocuγ ᵹoιll Μhumαн ocuγ Μhιδe lαιη, α Connαchταιδ, coнδeηнα cαιηlén αᵹ Μιlec α Sιl нCнιmchαδα; ocuγ ιηηe ιoнαδ αнδeηнαδ, ιoṁóн τempul moη ιн δαιle, cuη lιнαδ δo cηιαδ ocuγ δo člochαιδ uιme ᵹo δeнδuιδ; ocuγ ηo ṁιllηατ ιαηταη Connαchτ eτιη čιll ocuγ τυαιč. ᵹoητα ṁóη ι нEηιнн uιle co coιτčeнδ ιγ ιн δlιαδαιн γι, co mčóιη на cleιηιᵹ ιн ϝeoιl .ιγ ιн čoηᵹuη. Clυαιн ϝeητα Bηénuιнн ocuγ Μιlec ocuγ Clυαιн ṁιc Nóιγ δαηᵹuιн δo Uιllιαm Dυηc. Conchobαη ηuαδ .h. Bηιαιн δo mαηbαδ la a δeηbηαταιη ϝeιн, .ι. Μuιηceηταch mac Domναιll mιc τoιηηδheαlbαιᵹ hí Bηιαιн. τoιηηδheαlbach mac Rυαιδηι hí Conchobαιη δo élυδ αηη a ᵹειṁιl, ocuγ ηιč δo δeнum δo Cαταl cηoιbδeηᵹ ϝηιγ, ocuγ ϝeηoнн δo čαbαιητ δó. Slυαιᵹeδ lαη αн нᵹιúηδíη, .ι. la Μαoιlϝeη,

---

[1] *King-chieftain of Ard-Midhair.* In the Annals of Ulster, (Dublin copy, which has the entry at the year 1203), Domhnall Carrach O'Dochartaigh is called ηí τιηe Conαιll, "king of Tir-Conaill," of which territory Ard-Midhair, or Ardmire, was a sub-district.

[2] *Tribulationem.* τηιbulαcιoнιm, MS.

[3] *Pœnitentiam.* peнeτιнcιαm, MS.

[4] [*Quievit*]. The Annals of Ulster, in which the death of Domhnall O'Brolchán is given at the year 1203,

say "ingressus est viam universæ carnis."

[5] *Meiler.* The compiler of the chronicle, following in the footsteps of many Irish etymologists who endeavoured to give an Irish complexion to words and names of which they did not know the origin, writes this name mαoιlϝeη, as if it meant "servant man," from mαol, *servant*, and ϝeη, a *man*. Regarding this predilection on the part of Irish writers, Conell Mageoghegan observes, in his translation of the Annals of Clonmacnoise, at the

O'Conchobhair, the son of his own father, and Diarmaid, son of Ruaidhri, son of Maghnus, i.e. the grandson of his father's brother. Maelfinnein, Mac Colmain, a high, choice senior, in pace quievit. Domhnall Carrach O'Dochartaigh, king-chieftain of Ard-Midhair,[1] was slain by Muinter-Buighill, after plundering many churches and territories. Domhnall O'Brolchán, a prior, and an illustrious, choice senior for figure, for sense, for gentleness, for dignity, for wisdom, and for great piety, post magnam tribulationem[2] et optimam pœnitentiam,[3] in quinta kalendas Maii [quievit].[4]

The kalends of January on the 4th feria, the 15th of the moon; the age of the Lord two hundred and three years, and a thousand. A hosting by William Burk, accompanied by the Foreigners of Mumha and Midhe, into Connacht, when he erected a castle at Mílec, in Sil-Anmchadha; and the place where the castle was erected was round the great church of the place, which was lined round with earth and stones to the pinnacles; and they devastated the West of Connacht, both church and terri-tory. Great famine in all Erinn generally in this year, so that the clergy used to eat meat in Lent. Cluain-ferta-Brenuinn, and Mílec, and Cluain-mic-Nois were plundered by William Burk. Conchobhar Ruadh O'Briain was slain by his own brother, i.e. Muirchertach, son of Domhnall, son of Toirdhelbhach O'Briain. Toirdhel-bhach, son of Ruaidhri O'Conchobhair, escaped from his bonds; and Cathal Crobhderg made peace with him, and gave him land. A hosting by the Justice, i.e. by Meiler,[5]

---

year 1182—"There are soe many leaves lost or stolen out of the ould Irish booke which I translate, y^t. I doe not know how to handle it; but to satisfie y^r. request, I will translate such places in the booke as I can read; and yet in the mean time I shall intreat you to hould me excused for not nameing the K^s. Deputies and Englishmen therein contained by theire right names, for I goe by the wordes of the ould booke, and not by my owen invention, which [i.e. the nomenclature of the original] is soe ill-favouredly and confusedly handled that mine author could not gett his penn to name the K^s. of England or other foraigne contryes by theire pro-per names, but by such Ir. names as he pleased to devise out of his owen head, although he was a great Latinist and scholler."

ocur la bhaldar de Laci ir in Mumain, do ionnarbad
Uilliam burc. O do cuala Uilliam rin do cuaid in a
conne, ocur ro fácuib drem da muinter ir in cairlen
rempáici. Do cuaid Moeilrer ocur bhaldar docum
Luimnig, ocur ó rancodar co Luimnech do cuir Uilliam
teachta ar cenn na rocraide ro fágaib ir in cairlen.
Iarrin ro élodar ocur ro facrat in cairrlen rolam
ar forcongra a tigerna, ocur ar terce bid, ocur
ar egla Connacht. Ro múrrat Connachta in cairlen
iarrin. Do fácaib Uilliam Luimnech. Tucaid tri
cairléna dó, ocur da braigit dég uada do maicib a
muintire, imo a mac rein, ocur imón ingin. Do fill
Moeilrer iarrin a Luimnech. Toirrdhealbach mac
Ruaidri dionnarbad a Connachtuib do Cathal
croibderg, ocur a chur ir in Mide, ocur rit do denum
rír a cedóir ar impide na ngall, .i. Máilrer ocur
baldar. Sluaiged la macaib Goirdelb ocur la Maoilrer
mbec, maroen re Domnall carrach .h. Moeildoraidh,
a tir Conaill, do tabach rige do Domnall carrach;
ocur Domnall carrach féin do marbad do cenel
Conaill don turur rin. Tuaim dá gualann dfolmachad,
ocur Cunga Feicín do delatriuchad cen tech cen tempul,
ocur cealla Connacht uile dfolmachad achtmad beg.
Doire Coluim Cille do lorcad óta reilic Mártain co
tiprait Adomnáin. Diarmait mac Muircheartaig mec
Laclainn, co ngalloib, do teacht ar creic a tir Eogain,
curro aircret Scrín Coluim Cille, co rucrat orra
dream do cenel Eogain, curro muig ar galloib, gurro
marbad Diarmait mác Laclainn tre mirbuilib na

---

1 *Walter.* baldar, MS.

2 *The aforesaid castle;* i.e. the castle of Milec, or Meelick, in the barony of Longford, county of Galway, and on the banks of the river Shannon.

3 *Meiler.* moeilrer, MS. See note 5, p. 228.

4 *Three castles.* In Mageoghegan's translation of the Annals of Clonmacnoise it is stated that "William Burk was banished from Limerick by Meyler, who refused to give him one castle there."

5 *Relic-Martain.* The cemetery of St. Martin.

and by Walter[1] de Laci, into Mumha, to expel William
Burk. When William heard this he went to meet them,
and he left a number of his people in the aforesaid castle.[2]
Meiler[3] and Walter[1] went towards Luimnech; and when
they had arrived at Luimnech, William sent messengers
for the forces which he had left in the castle. They
afterwards escaped and left the castle empty, at the
command of their lord, and through scarcity of food, and
through fear of the men of Connacht. The Connachtmen
levelled the castle after that. William left Luimnech.
Three castles[4] were given to him, and twelve hostages of
the nobles of his people were given by him, together with
his own son and daughter. Meiler[3] afterwards returned
from Luimnech. Toirdhelbhach, son of Ruaidhri, was
banished from Connacht by Cathal Crobhderg, and sent
into Midhe; and peace was immediately made with him
through the intercession of the Foreigners, viz.:—Meiler
and Walter. A hosting by the sons of Goisdelbh and by
young Meiler, together with Domhnall Carrach O'Maeldoraidh, to Tir-Conaill, to recover the sovereignty for
Domhnall Carrach; and Domhnall Carrach himself was
slain by the Cenel-Conaill on this expedition. Tuaim-dha-
ghualann was emptied, and Cunga-Feichín was rased, *so
that it was* without a house or church, and the churches
of nearly all Connacht were emptied. Doire-Choluim-
Chille was burned, from Relic-Martain[5] to Tiprait-
Adhomnain.[6] Diarmaid, son of Muirchertach Mac Lachlainn, accompanied by the Foreigners, went on a predatory expedition to Tir-Eoghain; and they plundered
Scrin-Choluim-Chille; but a number of the Cenel-Eoghain
came up with them, and the Foreigners were defeated, and
Diarmaid Mac Lachlainn was slain, through the miracles

---

6 *Tiprait-Adhomnain;* i.e. the well
of Adomnan. This entry is given
under the year 1204 in the Annals of
Ulster; but by the Four Masters at
the year 1203.

rcpíne. Sloigeð la mac Uga ðé Laci go ngalloib Mıðe
Laır, a nUllToıb, curro ðícuırret Seon na Cúırtı a
hUllToıb.

Ct. Enaır .u. p.; l. xxm.; ceıtre blıaðna ar ðá
ceð, ar mıle, aoır ın Tıgerna; ocur ın .um. blıaðaın
.x. a nóıðécðu. Caırc a gert Ct. mái ır ın blıaðaın
rı, ocur mıncaırc a ramrað. Tıgernán mac an
abað ðo éc a Sruthaır bracáın agá aılıtrı cona
manchaıb. Muırcertach Teptach, mac Conchobaır
mocnmaıge, mıc Ruaıðrı hı Conchobaır, ðo marbað
ðo Ðıarmaıð mac Ruaıðrı ocur ðOeð mac Ruaıðrı, .ı.
ðá ðerbrátar a athar. Maıðm la Ðomnall mac
meg Carrthaıg ocur la Ðermumaın ror galloıb, ubı
cecıðerunt .c.lx. uırı uel amplıur. In glaırrıan ðo
marbað la Cathal croıbðerc ocur la Connachtaıb,
ocur rí na glaırféıne, .ı. Mant na mulcán .h.
Ruaırc ðo gabáıl leó, ocur a ðallað. ben ðo
tabaırt cuıge ocur ó anothur a ðallta ocur a ðenð
ðo at ocur e réın uıle, treran lánramnur; ocur
a éc arra haıtle. Eacmılıð mac comorba Fınðéın,
erruc Ulað, ðo ec. Meabal ðo ðenum ðo Connachtaıb ar mac hı Ruaırc, ocur ar macuıb .h.
Moeılmıaðhaıg, ocur a marbað. Cat etır Uga óg
mac Uga ðé Lacı co ngalloıb na Mıðe, ocur Eoan
na Cuırtı co ngalloıb Ulað. Eoan na Cúırtı ðo

---

1 *The shrine;* i.e. a shrine preserved
in the church called from it Scrin-
Choluim-Chille, "the Shrine of
Colum-Cille;" the name of which is
still preserved in that of the parish
of Ballynascreen, in the barony of
Loughinsholin, county of Londonderry, where the remains of an old
church still exist. See Reeves's
Adamnan, p. 282.

2 *The* 18*th.* The MS. incorrectly
reads .xum. blıaðaın .x., for .um.
blıaðaın .x.

3 *Of the Nineteen.* .ıx.ðécðu, for
noıðécðu; i.e. the Decennovenalian
cycle, or cycle of 19.

4 *Little Easter.* Low Sunday.
The 25th of April was therefore
Easter Sunday, and the 2nd of May
Low Sunday.

5 *Tephtach;* i.e. the Tephian, or
Teffian; so called, probably, from

of the shrine.[1] A hosting by the son of Hugo de Laci, with the Foreigners of Midhe, to Ulidia; and they banished John de Curci from Ulidia.

The kalends of January on the 5th feria, the 26th of the moon; the age of the Lord two hundred and four years, and a thousand; and the eighteenth[2] year of the Nineteen.[3] Easter on the seventh of the kalends of May in this year, and Little Easter[4] in summer. Tighernan Mac-an-abaidh died at Sruthair-Bracain, on his pilgrimage with his monks. Muirchertach Tephtach,[5] son of Conchobhar Maenmhaighe, son of Ruaidhri O'Conchobhair, was slain by Diarmaid, son of Ruaidhri, and by Aedh, son of Ruaidhri, his father's two brothers. A victory by Domhnall, son of Mac Carthaigh, and *the men of* Des-Mumha, over the Foreigners, ubi ceciderunt clx.uiri, vel amplius.[6] The Glasfhian[7] were slain by Cathal Crobhderg and the Connachtmen and the king of the Glasfhian, i.e. Mant-na-mulchán O'Ruairc, was captured by them, and blinded. A woman[8] was brought to him whilst he lay suffering from the operation, and shared his company; and he died soon after. Echmhilidh, son of the comarb of Finnen, bishop of Uladh, died. Treachery was practised by the Connachtmen against the son of O'Ruairc and the sons of O'Maelmhiadhaigh, who were slain. A battle between young Hugo, son of Hugo de Laci, with the Foreigners of Midhe, and John de Curci with the Foreigners of Uladh. John de Curci was taken prisoner,

---

having been fostered in Teffia. His death is given by the Four Masters at the year 1203.

⁶ *Amplius.* ꝺmpliuꞃ, MS.

⁷ *Glasfhian.* This seems to have been the name of some sept of foreign descent. The word *Glasfine* is explained as signifying "a foreign tribe," by Dr. O'Donovan; who adds that "the son of an Irish girl by an

Albanach, or Scotchman, would be so called." See *Supplement to O'Reilly's Irish Dictionary,* in voce.

⁸ *Woman.* The liberty has been taken of using some licence in the translation of this sentence, as the sense of the original passage, if literally interpreted, would scarcely be fit for publication.

ʒαϐáιl, ocup a lecuɒ αpp ιap na cpoppaɒ ɒó ɒul co
hιαppupαlem. Ɒá mac ⱰuιnnꝂleιϐe ɒo ṁαpϐαɒ ɒo
Uιϐ Єchach a meαϐuιl. Sιτpeac O Spóιτén, αιpcιn-
nech na Conʒṁálα, quιeuιτ.

ƒƈτ. επαιp .ιιιι. p.; Ł. uιι.; u. blιαɒna ap ɒá ceɒ, ap mιle,
αoιp ιn Tιʒepna. Uιllιam ϐupc, mιllτιʒeoιp Єpenn uιle
ɒuαple ocup ɒo ƈcnɒup pеɒnα, mopτuup epτ. Loƈlαιnn,
mac Ɒoṁnαιll mιc Ꝝepʒαιl hι Ruαιpc, ɒo ṁαpϐαɒ ɒo
muιnτеp Ꝝеoɒαƈáιn. Sιc móp ocup pnechτα ó ƒƈτ. επαιp
co Ꝝéιl Ꝑατpαιc ιp ιn mblιαɒαιn pι. Ʒιllα Cpιpτ .h. Moeιl-
mιαɒhαιʒ, τúppech muιnτιpe hЄoluιp, ɒo mαpϐαɒ ɒo
Connachτuιϐ. Lonʒup lα hЄoαn na Cuιpτe a hιnnpιϐ
Ʒαll, ɒo ƈopnum Ulαɒ pе mαcαιϐ Uʒα ɒé Lacι, ocup pе
Ʒαllοιϐ na Mιɒе; achτ chenα nιp Ꝝápp ταpϐα ɒon
lonʒαp pιn achτ ιn τíp ɒo ṁιlleɒ ocup ɒαpcuιn; ocup
ιmτeachτ ɒóιϐ ιαppιn ʒαn nepτ ɒo ʒαϐáιl. Ɒo pone
Єoαn a ƈopαιɒ ocup a ṁuιnnτepup pе .h. Neιll ocup pе
Cenel Єoʒαιn.

ƒƈτ. επαιp pop ɒomnach, ocup ochτmαɒ .x. puιppе.;
uι.blιαɒnα ap ɒá ceɒ, ap mιle, αιp ιn Tιʒepna. Αϐ
Incαpnατιone Ɒomιnι nopτpι lhepu Cpιpτι pecunɒum
Ɒιonιpιum, m̄.cc.uι.; pecunɒum auτem ϐeɒαm, m̄.c.xcιx.;
aϐ Incαpnατιone pecunɒum Єϐpeop, m̄.cccc.lιx; aϐ
ιnιτιo munɒι pecunɒum Єϐpeop ū.cccc.x.; aϐ ιnιτιo
munɒι pecunɒum .lxx. Inτepppeτep, ū.ɒc.luιι. Muιpʒepp
.h. hЄnnα, αιpɒepuc Muman, ocup léʒαιɒ comαpϐα
Ꝑαταιp ꝼpι pе ꝼoɒα, quιeuιτ. Mupchαɒ .h. hOeɒα,
еppuc Copcαιʒe, quιeuιτ. Ɒomnαll mac ṁéʒ Cαppτhαιʒ,

---

¹ *Crossed.* The expression ιαp nα
cpoppαɒ ɒó ɒul co hιαppupαlem
has been translated "having been
prohibited from going to Jerusalem"
by Dr. O'Donovan (*Four Mast.*, A.D.
1204, note ⁿ). But as the name of
John de Curci does not appear in
any of the Irish Annals after the

year 1205, the interpretation above
given seems to be the correct one.

² *O'Sroithen.* The name is written
O'Sruithen in the Ann. Four Mast.,
which have his death at the year
1204, and in the Annals of Ulster,
in which the obit is entered under
1205.

and released after having been crossed[1] to go to Jeru- [1204.]
salem. Two sons of Donnsleibhe were slain by the Ui-
Echach, in treachery. Sitric O'Sroithen,[2] airchinnech of
the Congbhail,[3] quievit.

The kalends of January on the 7th feria, the 7th of the [1205.]
moon; the age of the Lord two hundred and five years,
and a thousand. William Burk, destroyer of all Erinn, of
nobility and chieftainship, mortuus est. Lochlainn, son
of Domhnall, son of Ferghal O'Ruairc, was slain by
Muinter-Pheodhacháin. Great frost and snow from the
kalends of January to the festival of Patrick in this year.
Gillachrist O'Maelmhiadhaigh, chieftain of Muinter-
Eolais, was slain, by the Connachtmen. A fleet *was
brought* by John de Curci from Innsi-Gall, to contest
Uladh with the sons of Hugo de Laci and the Foreigners of
Midhe. No good resulted from this expedition, however;
but the country was destroyed and plundered; and they[4]
afterwards departed without obtaining power. John
made[5] his covenant and amity with O'Neill and the
Cenel-Eoghain.

The kalends of January on Sunday, the 18th of the [1206.]
moon; the age of the Lord two hundred and six years,
and a thousand. Ab Incarnatione Domini nostri Jesu
Christi, secundum Dionysium, m̄.cc.vi; secundum autem
Bedam, m̄.c.xcix: ab Incarnatione[6] secundum Ebræos,
m̄.cccc.lix; ab initio[7] mundi secundum Ebræos, v̄.cccc.x.;
ab initio mundi secundum lxx. Interpretes, v̄.dc.luii.
Muirghes O'hEnna, archbishop of Mumha, and legate ot
the comarb of Peter during a long time, quievit. Murchadh
O'hAedha, bishop of Corcach, quievit. Domhnall, son

---

[3] Of the *Congbhail.* na Cong-
rhala, MS.; but na Congbala in
Ann. Ult. and the Four Mast. At
the year 1196, *supra*, the name of
Faughan-vale, in the co. of Londonderry, is written na hua Congbala,
which is corrupt. The place here

referred to is Conwal, in the barony
of Kilmacrenan, county of Donegal.

[4] *They*; i.e. the fleet.

[5] *Made.* vo ro ú, for vo rone,
MS.

[6] *Incarnatione.* ācarrnacīōe, MS.

[7] *Initio.* ınıcıo, MS.

ɼι Ɗeɼṁuman, moɼτuuɼ eɼτ. Ccnɗιleɼ ṁáȝ ɼιnnɓaɼɼ
moɼτuuɼ eɼτ. Ɗonατ .h. ɓecɓα, eɼρuc .h. nCcmαlȝαιɗ,
quιeuιτ. Mαolɼeταιɼ .h. Cαlmáιn, comαɼɓα Cαιnnιȝ,
τuιɼ cɼαɓαɓ ocuɼ eιnιȝ τuαιɼceɼτ Eɼenn, ιn ραce
quιeuιτ. Ɗιɫ ṁóɼ αɼ ɓαοιnιɓ ocuɼ αɼ ιnnιlιɓ ιɼ ιn
mɓlιαɗαιn ɼι. Comαɼɓα ρατɼαιc ɗo ɫul co τech ɼι
Sαxɼαn ɗo τɼochɼαɗ ɫeαll Eɼenn, ocuɼ ɗo ɫoɼɼαοιɗ αɼ
ȝαlloιɓ.

Ƙτ. enαιɼ ɼoɼ Luαn, ιιι.ɼ.; L. xx.; ɼeαɫτ mɓlιαɗnα
αɼ ɗα ceɗ, αɼ mιle, αιɼ ιn Τιȝeɼnα. Τomαlταɫ nα
cαιɼɼȝe, mαc Conɫoɓαιɼ, mιc Ɗιαɼmαɗα, mιc Ταιɓȝ hι
Mαοιlɼuαnαιɓ, ɼι muιȝe Luιɼȝ, moɼτuuɼ eɼτ. Ruαιɓɼι
.h. ȝαɓɼα, ɼι ɼleιɓe Luȝα, moɼτuuɼ eɼτ. Cατhαl, mαc
Ɗιαɼmαɗα, mιc Ταιɓc hι Mαιlɼuαnαιɓ, ɗo ȝαɓáιl ɼιȝe
ṁuιȝe Luιɼȝ ιɼ ιn ɓlιαɗαιn ɼι. Cɼeαɫ lα hEιcneαchán
.h. nɗoṁnαιll α ɓɼeαɼαιɓ Mαnαch; ocuɼ ɼucɼατ ɼιɼ
Mαnαɫ ɼoɼɼα lιn ɓuɓ αιɓɓle ιnáιτ ɼéιn, ocuɼ ɼo mαɼ-
ɓαɗ .h. Ɗoṁnαιll, ɼι τιɼe Conαιll, αnn, τuιɼ enȝnumα,
ocuɼ eιnιȝ, ocuɼ cαlmαταιɼ τuαιɼceιɼτ Eɼenn ȝo ɼιn;
ocuɼ ɗo ɫuιτ αnn ɗɼeαm ɗá ɓeȝ ɓαοιnιɓ ɓuɓéιn mαιlle
ɼɼιɼ, .ι. αn ȝιllα ɼιαɓαɫ mαc Ceαllαιȝ hι ɓαοιȝιll, Mαɫ-
ȝαṁαιn mαc Ɗoṁnαιll ṁιɓιɫ hι Concoɓαιɼ, Ɗonnchαɓ
Conαllαɫ mαc Conɫoɓαιɼ Moenmuιɓe hι Concoɓαιɼ, eτ
αlιι mulτι nobιleɼ eτ ιȝnobιleɼ cum eιɼ occιɼι ɼunτ.
Mαc méȝ Mαɫȝαṁnα, ocuɼ ɼιɼ Mαnαch, ocuɼ Ccιɼȝιαllα
ιιcτoɼeɼ ɼueɼunτ. Ccṁlαιɓ .h. Ɽeɼȝαιl, ɼι ɫuιɼɼeαɫ
muιnnτιɼe hCcnȝαιle, quιeuιτ. Cαιɼlén Ccɓα αn uɼɫαιɼ
ɗo ȝαɓáιl ɗo ɓαlɗαɼ ɗe Lαcí ocuɼ ɗá ɓɼαɫαιɼ, .ι. ɗo
Uȝα ɗe Lαcí.

---

1 *Ui-Amhalghadha.* By the title
"bishop of Ui-Amhalghadha" is
meant "bishop of Killala."

2 *Comarb of Cainnech.* He was
probably abbot of Drumachose, in the
barony of Keenaght, co. of Londonderry, founded by St. Cainnech, or
Canice.

3 *Of the Rock*; i.e. of the Rock of
Loch-Cé, or Mac Dermot's Rock, the
principal residence of Mac Dermot,
chieftain of Moylurg. See page 167,
supra.

4 *Them*; i.e. the forces of Eignechán
O'Domhnaill.

5 *Chieftains.* ɗα ɓeȝ ɓαοιnιɓ
(da dheagh dhaoinibh); lit. "of his
good men."

of Mac Carthaigh, king of Des-Mumha, mortuus est. Andiles Mac Finnbhairr mortuus est. Donat Ua Becdha, bishop of Ui-Amhalghadha,[1] quievit. Maelpetair O'Calmáin, comarb of Cainnech,[2] pillar of the piety and honour of the North of Erinn, in pace quievit. A great destruction of men and cattle in this year. The comarb of Patrick went to the house of the king of the Saxons, on behalf of the churches of Erinn, and to complain of the Foreigners.

The kalends of January on Monday, the 3rd feria, the 20th of the moon; the age of the Lord two hundred and seven years, and a thousand. Tomaltach of the Rock,[3] son of Conchobhar, son of Diarmaid, son of Tadhg O'Maelruanaidh, king of Magh-Luirg, mortuus est. Ruaidhri O'Gadhra, king of Sliabh-Lugha, mortuus est. Cathal, son of Diarmaid, son of Tadhg O'Maelruanaidh, assumed the sovereignty of Magh-Luirg in this year. A depredation was committed by Eignechán O'Domhnaill in Feara-Manach; but the Feara-Manach, in greater force than they were, overtook them,[4] and O'Domhnaill, king of Tír-Conaill, till then the tower of valour, and honour, and strength of the North of Erinn, was slain there; and a number of his own chieftains[5] fell along with him, viz.: the Gilla-riabhach,[6] son of Ceallach O'Baighill; Mathghamhain, son of Domhnall Midhech[7] O'Conchobhair; Donnchadh Conallach, son of Conchobhar Maenmhaighe O'Conchobhair; et alii[8] multi nobiles et ignobiles[9] cum eis occisi[10] sunt. The son of Mac Mathghamhna and the Feara-Manach, and the Airghialla, victores fuerunt. Amhlaibh O'Ferghail, king-chieftain of Muinter-Anghaile, quievit. The castle of Ath-an-urchair was captured by Walter de Laci and his brother, i.e. Hugo de Laci.

---

[6] *The Gilla-riabhach;* i.e. "the brown fellow."

[7] *Domhnall Midhech;* or Daniel the Meathian; so called, apparently, from having been fostered in Meath.

[8] *Alii.* αlı, MS.

[9] *Ignobiles.* ıꞅnobılıꞃ (ignobilis), MS.

[10] *Occisi.* occıꞃꞃı (occissi), MS.

Ict. Θnαιρ ρορ ṁαιρτ, ί. x. Ocht mbίιαṙηα αρ ᵭα cec
αρ mιίe αιρ ιη Τιζερηα. Cαταί mαc Ⴁιαρmαᵭα mιc
Ταιᵭᵹ hι Mαoιίρυαηαᵭ, ρι mυιᵹe ίυιρc, cο ᵹαᵬάιί ία
Cαταί Cροιᵬᵭεαρc, cαρ ραρυᵹαᵭ ηα ηερρuc cο ᵭαᵭαρ
α ρίάηοιᵹεαᵭτ ετορρα, .ι. Αρᵭᵹαί .h. Conchoᵬαιρ, ocυρ
Mυιρεᵭhαᵭ .h. Ⴁυᵬthαιᵹ, ocυρ Cίeιmeητ .h. Snιαᵭhαιᵹ.
ρυαρίυcαᵭ cε α cιηη ρεαίαιτ τρé ρίάηοιᵹεcht ηα ηερρuc
ριη, ᵹαη ᵹιαίί ᵹαη ειcιρe. Ⴁυί cό αρ ιη τιρ αmαᵭ
ιαρριη, ocυρ cρεαᵭ ṁόρ cο ᵭéηαṁ ᵭό, ocυρ α bρειᵭ ίειρ
cο ράηιc ίoᵭ mιc Néη. Τοιᵹεαᵭτ cό cοριᵭιρ α cιηη
ρεαchτṁυιηe αρ cρειᵭ α τιρ ηOιίιοίία, ocυρ α bρειᵭ ίαιρ
ιρ ιη ᵹCοιρρριαᵭ, ocυρ cαρ Cορρριαᵭ α mαᵹ ίυιρc.
Socραιce mόρ cο ᵭρειᵭ ραιρ αηηριη, .ι. Ⴁιαρmαιc,
mαc Mαᵹηυρα, mιc Τοιρρᵭεαίᵬαιᵹ hι Conchoᵬαιρ, ocυρ
Mαᵹηυρ, mαc Mυιρcεαρταιᵹ, mιc Τοιρρᵭεαίᵬαιᵹ hι
Conchoᵬαιρ, ocυρ Cορmαc mαc Τοmαίταιᵹ ηα cαιρcι,
ocυρ Mυιρεcαch mαc Τοmαίταιᵹ ηα cαρρcι, ocυρ
Ⴁοηηρίéιᵬe mαc Ṙυαιᵭρι hι ᵹαᵭρα, ρι ρίειᵬe ίυᵹα, ocυρ
ρίαιᵭᵬερταᵭ .h. ρίαηηαcάη, τυιρρεαᵭ cίοιηηe Cαᵭαιί,
ocυρ ᵹιίία ηα ηech .h. Mαηηαᵭαιη, ρι .h. mᵭριυιη ηα
Snιηηα. Οc ᵭοηηcαcαρ ηα ρεmρεηαᵹ bρειρρηεᵭα ιητ
ρocραιce ρο ṁόρ αρ mᵭρειᵭ ρορρα, ό ραηcοcαρ cαρ ίειc
η'Ⴁαṁαιᵹe αηοηη ρο ᵭειᵭρετ. Ορ ηαch ραιᵬe, ιmορρο,
αcht α ṁυιηητερ ρéιη α bραρραᵭ mιc Ⴁιαρmαᵭα, ρο
ίιηᵹεc ραιρ ocυρ ρο mαρᵬαc α mαc, .ι. Mυιρᵹερ, ocυρ
ρο mαρᵬαιτ cαοιηe eίι cα mυιηητιρ, ocυρ ρο ᵹαᵬαc é
ρéιη ρα ᵭεόιᵹ. Ιαρ ρcοειίec ηα ρocραιce mοιρe ριη ιρρí
comαιρίe cο ροηρατ cίαηη Τοmαίταιᵹ ηα cαιρρce mαc
Ⴁιαρmαᵭα cο ᵭαίίαc. Ṙο cαίίαc, ιmορρο, αcα hé,
ocυρ ρο mαᵭṁαιᵹhec α mυιηητιρ. Coᵹαᵭ mόρ ετιρ
ᵹαίίαιᵭ Θρεηη ιρ ιη mbίιαcαιη ρι, .ι. ετιρ mαcυιᵭ Uᵹα
ce ίαcí, ocυρ Moειίρερ, ocυρ Serρραιᵭ Mαρéιρ.

---

1 *District.* τιρ, lit. country,=
Lat. terra.

2 *Tomaltach of the Rock;* i.e. Tomaltach Mac Diarmada, or Mac Dermot.
See note 3, page 236. This entry is

given by the Four Masters, but rather
imperfectly, under the year 1207.

3 *Gilla-na-nech;* lit. "the boy
(gillie) of the horses."

4 *Mercenaries.* ρᵭρρεηαᵹ. This

A.D.
[1208.]

The kálends of January on Tuesday, the 10th of the moon; the age of the Lord two hundred and eight years, and a thousand. Cathal, son of Diarmaid, son of Tadhg O'Maelruanaidh, king of Magh-Luirg, was taken prisoner by Cathal Crobhderg, in violation of the bishops who were guarantees between them, viz.:—Ardghal O'Conchobhair, and Muireadhach O'Dubhthaigh, and Clement O'Sniadhaigh. He was released after some time, through the guarantee of those bishops, without pledge or hostage. He departed out of the district[1] afterwards, and took a great prey, which he carried with him until he reached Loch-mic-Nén. At the end of a week he came again on a predatory expedition to Tir-Oiliolla, and he carried the prey into the Corr-sliabh, and over Corr-sliabh into Magh-Luirg. A great force overtook him there, viz.:—Diarmaid, son of Maghnus, son of Toirdhelbhach O'Conchobhair; and Maghnus, son of Muirchertach, son of Toirdhelbhach O'Conchobhair; and Cormac, son of Tomaltach of the Rock;[2] and Muiredhach, son of Tomaltach of the Rock;[2] and Donnsleibhe, son of Ruaidhri O'Gadhra, king of Sliabh-Lugha; and Flaithbhertach O'Flannacain, chief of Clann-Cathail; and Gilla-na-nech[3] O'Mannachain, king of Ui-Briuin-na-Sinna. When the Breifnian mercenaries[4] perceived that they had been overtaken by this immense force, as soon as they had passed over Lec-Damhaighe they fled. When only his own people, therefore, were with Mac Diarmada, he was rushed upon, and his son, i.e. Muirghes, was slain; and other men of his people were slain, and he himself was ultimately captured. After the dispersion of this great force the counsel which the sons of Tomaltach of the Rock[2] adopted was to blind Mac Diarmada. He was blinded by them, truly, and his people were routed. A great war between the Foreigners of Erinn this year, i.e. between the sons of Hugo de Laci, and Meyler, and Geoffroi Mareis. A great predatory

word properly means hirelings, or mercenaries; but in some cases it is | used to signify "archers." See note[8], p. 196, and note[1], p. 226, *supra.*

Cρeαć ſluαιξeờ móρ lα hOeờh .h. Néιll α nInιſ Eοξαιn;
οcuſ ſuc .h. Doṁnαιll, .ι. Doṁnαll móρ ſορρα, cο τucαờ
mαιờm eτορρα ιn ρο mαρbαờ áρ ờιαιſṁờe ờοeιnι αρ
ξαch Leτ; uαιl ιn ρο ſαξbαờ Doṁnαll mαc Muρchαờ,
cο náρ αờ̃αl ờΘοξαnchαờ mαιlle ſ̄ιſ, οcuſ Γeρξαl
.h. bóιξιll, οcuſ Cορmαc .h. Doṁnαιll, οcuſ Dαờιờ
O Dοċαρταιξ, οcuſ ờρeαm ờο ṁαιτιờ Čenel Cοnαιll
mαιlle ſιu. Cατ τucſατ mιc Rαξnαιll ṁιc Sοṁαιρle
ſορ ſeραιờ Scιαờ, ờu ιn ρο mαρbαờ áρ ờιαιſṁờe.

|ct. Enáιρ ſορ Ceờαοιn, L. xxι. Nαοι mblιαờnα αρ
ờá ceờ αρ mιle αιſ ιn Τιξeρnα. Rι Sαxραn ờο ċοιξeċτ
α nEριnn cο lοιnξeρſ nαờ̃αl lαιſ. ξιllα Cρ̄ιſτ .h.
Ceρnαιξ, cοmαρbα Cοnờeρe, ιn bοnα ρenιτenτια quιeuιτ.
Dαuιờ, eſρuc Lοċα ξαρmαn, ờο mαρbαờ ờ̃ Γοeláιn nα
nDeιρſι Mumαn. Cατ eτιρ Cοnαllαιờ οcuſ Eοξαnċαιờ,
ubι ιnτeρſecτι ſunτ mulτι ờe uτροque exeρcιτu. Γιnξιn,
mαc Dιαρmαờα, mιc Cορmαιc ṁeξ Cαρρτhαιξ, ſι ờeſ
Mumαn, ιnτeρſecτuſ eſτ α ſuιſ. Uαlξαρc .h. Ruαιρc
ờο αċſιξhαờ, οcuſ Cρτ mαc Doṁnαιll mιc Γeρξαιl hι
Ruαιρc ờο ſιξαờ nα ιοnαờ.

|ct. Enαιſ ſορ ờαρờαοιn; L. ιι.; x. mblιαờnα αρ ờá
ceờ αρ mιle αιſ ιn Τιξeρnα. Cρτ mαc Doṁnαιll mιc
Γeρξαιl ι Ruαιρc, ſι bρeιſſne, ờο mαρbαờ τρια
ṁeαờ̃ιl lα Cορmαc mαc Cιρτ hι Mαοιlρeċlαιnn.
Céle .h. Dubthαιξ, eſρuc Mοιξe hΕó, quιeuιτ. Γlαιτ-
ờeρταċ .h. Γlοιnn, cοmαρbα Dαċοnnα Eρρα mιc nEιſc,
ιn Cρ̄ιſτο quιeuιτ.

   Ιοhαnneſ mαc mιc nα Γeρeιſι, ſι Sαcſαn, ờο ċeαċτ

---

[1] *Multitude.* áρ; lit. "slaughter,"
or "havoc."

[2] *In which fell.* uαιl ιn ρο ſαξbαờ; lit. "where was (or were)
left." The word uαιl is negligently
written for bαιl, "a place," which
is the root of bαιle, or "bally," a
word entering into the composition
of many typographical names in
Ireland.

[3] *Came.* This is an error. The
second visit of King John to Ireland
is correctly entered under the next
year. The Four Masters have the
record at the year 1209.

[4] *Comarb of Condere;* i.e. bishop
of Condere, or Connor.

[5] *Loch-Garman.* This is the Irish
name of Wexford, which never was
a bishop's see. Probably David was

hosting by Aedh O'Neill into Inis-Eoghain, and O'Domhnaill, i.e. Domhnall Mór, overtook them, when a battle
was fought between them, in which a countless multitude[1] of people were slain on either side ; in which
fell[2] Domhnall, son of Murchadh, with an enormous
slaughter of the *Cenel*-Eoghain along with him, and
Ferghal O'Baighill, and Cormac O'Domhnaill, and David
O'Dochartaigh, and a number of the chieftains of Cenel-
Conaill along with them. A battle was gained by the
son of Raghnall, son of Somhairle, over the men of Sciadh,
in which a countless multitude were slain.

The kalends of January on Wednesday, the 21st of the
moon ; the age of the Lord nine years, and two hundred,
and a thousand. The king of the Saxons came[3] to Erinn,
accompanied by an immense fleet. Gillachrist O'Cernaigh, comarb of Condere,[4] in bona pœnitentia quievit.
David, bishop of Loch-Garman,[5] was killed by O'Faelan
of the Deisi-Mumhan. A battle between the *Cenel*-
Conaill and the *Cenel*-Eoghain, ubi interfecti sunt multi de
utroque exercitu.[6] Finghin, son of Diarmaid, son of Cormac
Mac Carthaigh, king of Des-Mumha, interfectus est a suis.[7]
Ualgharg O'Ruairc was dethroned, and Art, son of Domhnall, son of Ferghal O'Ruairc, was made king in his place.

The kalends of January on Thursday,[8] the 2nd of the
moon ; the age of the Lord ten years, and two hundred,
and a thousand. Art, son of Domhnall, son of Ferghal
O'Ruairc, king of Breifne, was slain through treachery by
Cormac, son of Art O'Maelsechlainn. Céle O'Dubhthaigh,
bishop of Magh-hEó, quievit. Flaithbhertach O'Floinn,
comarb of Dachonna of Es-mic-Eirc, in Christo quievit.

Johannes, grandson of the Empress,[9] king of the Saxons,

---

bishop of Ferns. His name is not
mentioned by the Four Masters.

[6] *Exercitu.* exꞇꞇꞇu, for exꞇep-
cꞇu, MS.

[7] *A suis.* áꞇꞇuiꞇ, MS.

[8] *Thursday.* The feriæ for the years

1209 and 1210 should be Thursday and
Friday, respectively ; the Dominical
Letter for 1209 being D, and for 1210 C.

[9] *Of the Empress.* nɑ ᵱeᵱeiᵱi,
MS. Better nɑ hImpeᵱeiᵱi, as under
the year 1189, *supra.*

R

co hEpinn, coḃlaċ móp, ir in mḃliaḋain ri. Iap
τορραchτain ᴅó ρο ḟógaip rloigeᴅ móp rop ḟeραiḃ
Epenn i nUllτaiḃ, ᴅo ġaḃail Uga ᴅé Laci, nó ᴅa ḃichup a
hEpinn, ocur ᴅo ġaḃail ċaipce Ḟepgura. Ro ḟáġaiḃ Uga
Epinn, ocur in lucht ro báᴅap ac coiméᴅ na caippce ro
ḟaġáiḃret hí, ocur τancoᴅap ᴅinnrοigeᴅ in rí ; ocur ᴅo
cuip in rí ᴅoeine ᴅá ṁuinnτip ḟéin innτi. Do ċuip
iappin coḃlaċ ᴅa ṁuinnτip a Manainn, gup aipcret,
ocur ro ṁápḃrat a ᴅaine.

Caτal croiḃᴅepc .h. Conchoḃaip, rí Connaċτ, ocur
Connaċτa ap an rluaigeḃ rin. Αp τορραċτain ᴅóiḃ
aτuaiḃ aᴅuḃaipτ rí Saxan re rí Connaċτ ᴅul a gcinn
ċoeisτíre ᴅá innrοigeᴅ. Aᴅuḃaipτrium co rachaᴅ, ocur
gomḃeραḃ á mác laip, .i. Oeᴅh mac Caτhail croiḃᴅepc ;
ocur ní he in rí ᴅo boi ag á iappaᴅ. Τaḃaip, ap an rí,
no co bḟaġa caipτ ap τrian Connaċτ. O ρanic .h.
Conchoḃaip ina ionaᴅ ḟéin, irrí comaiple ᴅó ρoine ḟéin
ocur a ḃen ocur a ṁuinnτip, gan an mac ᴅo ḃpeτ a
gcenn an rí, gep ḃi rin comaiple ba meᴅa. Aċτ
ċena, ó ρanic .h. Conċoḃaip ᴅoċum rí Saxan, ocur naċ
ρuc a mac leir, ρo gaḃaᴅ le rí Saxan ᴅiapmaiᴅ mac
Conċoḃaip mic ᴅiapmaᴅa, rí ṁuiġe Luipg, ocur
Conchobap .h. hEġpa, rí Luiġne Connacht, ocur Finᴅ .h.
Capmacan, ḟep gáḃa ᴅU Conchoḃaip, ocur Τoipbepᴅ
mac Ġall ġoeiᴅil, ρeaċtaipe ᴅo ρeaċtaipiḃ hí Conchoḃaip. Do ċuaiᴅ rí Saxan τaipir iappin, ocur ρuc
laip ná maiṫi rin a Saxanaiḃ. Ro ḟáġaiḃ cenᴅur
Epenn ag an ngaill erρuc, ocur aᴅuḃaipτ ḟrir τrí

***

1 *The Carraic*; i.e. Carrick-Fergusa
("the rock of Fergus"), now Carrick-
fergus.

2 *Who requested this.* ᴅo bói ag á
iappaᴅ ; lit. "who was asking him."

8 *For.* ap ; lit. "on."

4 *Adopted.* ᴅo ρoine ; lit. "made."

5 *Son of a Gall-Gáeidhel*; i.e. " son
of a foreign Gaeidhel." The Four Mast.

(1209) say mac rí Ġall gaoiḋeal,
"son of the king of Gall-Gaeidhel ;"
but in the Annals of Clonmacnoise
(1208) he is called "Mac Gall-goyle."
Of the people called Gall-Gaeidhel Roderick O'Flaherty writes as follows :—
"Gall-gaidelios vero existimo Gaide-
lios insulas Britanniæ adjacentes tum
incolentes. Nam Donaldum filium Tha-

came to Erinn, with a great fleet, in this year. After
arriving he commanded a great hosting of the men of
Erinn to Ulidia, to apprehend Hugo de Laci, or to expel
him from Erinn, and to capture Carraic-Fergusa. Hugo
left Erinn, and the persons who were defending the
Carraic[1] abandoned it, and came to the king; and the
king put men of his own company into it. He afterwards sent a fleet of his people to Manainn, and they
plundered it, and killed its people.

Cathal Crobhderg O'Conchobhair, king of Connacht, and
the Connachtmen *were* on this hosting. On their return
from the north the king of the Saxons told the king of
Connacht to come to meet him at the end of a fortnight. He
promised that he would, and that he would bring his son
with him, i.e. Aedh, son of Cathal Crobhderg; (and it
was not the king who requested this).[2] "Bring *him*,"
said the king, "that he may receive a charter for[3] the
third part of Connacht." When O'Conchobhair arrived
at his own place, the counsel which he, and his wife, and
his people adopted[4] was, not to take the son to the king,
although this was the worst counsel. However, when
O'Conchobhair went to the king of the Saxons, and did
not take his son with him, Diarmaid, son of Conchobhar
Mac Diarmada, king of Magh-Luirg, and Conchobhar
O'hEghra, king of Luighne of Connacht, and Find
O'Carmacan, a man of trust to O'Conchobhair, and
Toirberd, son of a Gall-Gaeidhel,[5] one of O'Conchobhair's
stewards, were apprehended by the king of the Saxons.
The king of the Saxons went across afterwards, and took
these chieftains with him to Saxon-land. He left the
government of Erinn with the Foreign Bishop,[6] and ordered

---

dæi O Brian, quem Anno Christi 1075
Manniæ, ac Insularum proceres regni
súi Protectorem acceperunt, Inse-gall,
et Gallgædelu regem Hibernicè dic-
tum reperio. Hebrides vero sunt, quas
nostri Inse-gall dixerunt." *Ogygia*,

p. 360. But see Reeves's *Adamnan*,
p. 306, note [i], and p. 390, note [b].

[6] *The Foreign Bishop*; i.e. John de
Gray, bishop of Norwich. See Gilbert's *Viceroys of Ireland*; Dublin,
1865; p. 76.

R 2

caiṗléin ꝺo ꝺenam a Connachtaiḃ. Ro oṗꝺuiẓ an Ʒaill
eṗꝼuc ṗluaiẓeḋ ꝺinnṗoiẓeꝺ Connaċt, .i. ṗé ꝼein ocuṗ
ṗoċṗaiꝺi na Miꝺe ocuṗ Laiẓen, co háṫ Luain, conꝺeṗnaḋ
ꝺṗoiċeꝺ taṗ áṫ Luain laiṗ, ocuṗ caiṗlén a nionaꝺ
caiṗléin i Conċoḃaiṗ.

Ꝺonnchaḋ Caiṗṗṗech .h. Ḃṗiain cona ṗoċṗaiꝺi, ocuṗ
Seꝼꝼṗaiḋ Maiṗeiṗ cona ṗoċṗaitti ꝺo ẓallaiḃ Muman,
ocuṗ Oeḋ mac Ruaiꝺṗi i Conċoḃaiṗ ocuṗ mac hi
Flaiṫḃeṗtaiẓ maṗ oen ṗṗiú, i Connaċtuiḃ co ṗancoꝺaṗ
Tuaim ꝺá ẓualann, ocuṗ ꝺo ṗonṗat cṗeċa moṗa aṗṗin
co Loċ na naiṗne i Ciaṗṗaiẓe, ocuṗ ꝺo ṗonṗaꝺ cṗeċa
moṗa annṗin; ocuṗ ꝺo ḃaꝺaṗ coeciꝺiṗ, no ṗiciꝺ oiꝺċe
aċt bec, i Ciaṗṗaiẓe, ocuṗ Connaċta ṗe naẓaiꝺ. Ꝺo
ṗonṗat ṗiṫ iaṗṗin, .i. .h. Conchoḃaiṗ ocuṗ Ꝺonnchaḋ
Caiṗṗṗeċ ocuṗ Seꝼꝼṗaiḋ Máṗeiṗ. Iṗṗi ṗiṫ ꝺo ṗonṗat,
.i. ṗliẓe ꝺo Lecuꝺ ꝺoiḃṗium co háṫ Luain ꝺinnṗoiẓeꝺ
an ẓaill eṗṗuic, ocuṗ ṗiaꝺṗum ꝺo ꝺenam ṗiꝺa etiṗ .h.
Conċoḃaiṗ ocuṗ in Ʒaill eṗṗuic. Ꝺo ṗónṗat ṗiṫ etoṗṗa;
ocuṗ iṗṗi ṗiṫ ꝺo ṗonṗat, .i. Toiṗṗꝺelḃaċ mac Caṫail
cṗoiḃꝺeṗc, ocuṗ mac ꝺeẓ ꝺuine eli ꝺo Connachtuiḃ,
ꝺo taḃaiṗt i laiṁ in ẓaill eṗṗuic.

Kt. Enaiṗ [ꝼoṗ ṗaṫaṗn], L. xiii.; en bliaꝺain ꝺéc
aṗ ꝺá ceꝺ aṗ mile aiṗ in Tiẓeṗna. Toiṗṗꝺelḃaċ mac
Ruaiꝺṗi ꝺo ꝺenum cṗeċi a maẓ Luiṗc, co ṗuc iṗ in
Seẓuiṗ hí ꝺocum Ꝺiaṗmaꝺa, .i. a ḃṗaṫaṗ; ocuṗ ꝺo
Len Oeḋ mác Caṫail hé conꝺechaiꝺ iṗ in tuaiṗceṗt
aṗ a ṫeicheꝺ. h. Ꝺoḃailén, eṗpuc Cenannṗa, quieuit.
Ʒalo mac Manċáin, aiṗꝺ ecnaiꝺ Eṗenn uile, occiṗuṗ
eṗt. Ricoṗꝺ ꝺe Ꝺiuiꝺ ꝺo maṗbaꝺ ꝺo Ċloiċ i nAṫ

---

¹ *The Foreign Bishop.* John de Gray, bishop of Norwich, Lord Justice of Ireland.

² *The conditions were.* iṗṗi ṗiṫ ꝺo ṗonṗat; lit. "it is the peace they made."

³ *They;* i.e. Donnchadh Cairbrech O'Brien and Geoffroi Mareis.

⁴ *Delivered;* i.e. as hostages.

⁵ *Son of Ruaidhri;* i.e. the son of Ruaidhri O'Conchobhair, or Rory O'Conor, king of Connacht.

⁶ *Occisus est.* occiṗṗuṗ eṗtt, MS.

him to erect three castles in Connacht. The Foreign Bishop[1] commanded a hosting towards Connacht, viz. :—himself and the forces of Midhe and Laighen, as far as Ath-Luain, when a bridge was constructed by him across Ath-Luain, and a castle instead of O'Conchobhair's castle.

Donnchadh Cairbrech O'Briain, with his army, and Geoffroi Mareis, with his army of the Foreigners of Mumha, and Aedh, son of Ruaidhri O'Conchobhair, and the son of O'Flaithbhertaigh along with them, *proceeded* into Connacht, until they reached Tuaim-da-ghualann, and committed great depredations from thence to Loch-na-nairne, in Ciarraighe, where they committed great depredations; and they were a fortnight, or nearly twenty nights, in Ciarraighe, and the Connachtmen before them. They made peace afterwards, i.e. O'Conchobhair, and Donnchadh Cairbrech, and Geoffroi Mareis. The conditions were,[2] i.e. that they[3] should be allowed a passage to Ath-Luain, to meet the Foreign Bishop,[1] and should make peace between O'Conchobhair and the Foreign Bishop. They made peace between them; and the conditions were that Toirdhelbhach, son of Cathal Crobhderg, and the son of another noble, should be delivered[4] into the hand of the Foreign Bishop.

The kalends of January [on Saturday], the 13th of the moon; the age of the Lord eleven years, and two hundred, and a thousand. Toirdhelbhach, son of Ruaidhri,[5] took a prey in Magh-Luirg, and carried it into the Seghais, to Diarmaid, i.e. his brother; and Aedh, son of Cathal, pursued him until he (*Toirdhelbhach*) went into the North, to escape from him. O'Dobhailen, bishop of Cenannus, quievit. Galo Mac Manchain, chief sage of all Erinn, occisus est.[6] Richard de Tuit was killed by a stone[7]

---

[7] *By a stone.* The Four Masters, who record the accident under the year 1210, state that the stones of the castle of Athlone fell on Richard Tuit, and killed him on the spot, together with his priest and some of his people.

Luáin. bpaiξϭe Connacht ϭo τοιξeᴇτ ɪ ɴЄpɪɴɴ, .ɪ.
Оɪарmаɪϭ mac Conċoбaɪp ṁɪc Оɪарmаϭa, pí Muɪξe
Luɪpξ, ocup Conchoбap .h. hЄξpa, pí Luɪξnɪ, ocup pɪɴϭ
.h. Capmacáɴ, ocup Τoɪpbepϭ mac ξall ξaoɪϭeɪl.
Ⲁɪpechτaċ mac Ᵽuɪɴɴċaτhaɪξ occɪpup epτ. Τomap
mac Uchτpaɪξ, co macuɪб Raξnuɪll ṁɪc Ѕomaɪpliċ, ϭo
τoɪξɪechτ co Ᵽoɪpɪ Colum Cɪlle co pechτ lonξa
peaċτṁoϭaτ, ocup ɪn baɪle ϭo mɪlleϭ ϭoɪб co mόp.
h. Ᵽoṁnaɪll ocup ɪaϭféin ϭo ϭul apoen a ɴlɴɪp
Ꮯoξaɪn, ocup an τíp ϭo ṁɪlleб co huɪlɪбe.

Ꝃt. enaɪp pop ϭomɴaċ; ϭa blɪaϭaɪn ϭeξ ap ϭa ceϭ,
ap mɪle, aɪp ɪn Τɪξepɴa. Ѕluaɪξeб la Connaċτa τpé
τoξaɪpm ɪn ξaɪll epbuɪc ocup ξɪllɪbepτ mɪc ξoɪpϭelb,
co hЄpp Ruaɪб, conϭepɴaϭ caɪpplen Cháɪl upce leό.
Ѕluaɪξeб elɪ la ξallaɪб Ꮯpenn ocup lap an ɴξaɪll
epbuɪc ceϭna, ϭo ξaбáɪl τuaɪpcɪpτ Ꮯpenn, conϭepɴpaτ
caɪpplén Cluana hЄoɪp; ocup τucτaϭ pɪp Мanaċ ocup
mac meξ Маτξaṁna áp mόp poppa ϭon leɪτ aτuaɪϭ ϭo
ċluaɪn Ꮯoɪp. Маɪϭm mόp ap Ꮯoan ϭe ξhpéɪ, .ɪ. ɪúpϭíp
na hЄpenn, la mac Ⲁɪpτ hɪ Маoɪlpeċlaɪnn, cup páguɪб
a ɪnɴṁup uɪle ann. ɪmap .h. Ᵽepξaɪl, ϭux muɪnτɪpe
hⲀɴξaɪle, occɪpup epτ a ppaτpe puo. ξɪllacpɪpτ mac
Оɪарmаϭa ϭo ṁapbaϭ la Мupchaб cappaċ .h. bᵽepξaɪl.
Cpeaċ ϭo ϭenam ϭon ξɪlla pɪaclaċ .h. бόɪξɪll, ocup ϭo
ϭpeɪm ϭo ċenel Conaɪll, pop Cenel Ꮯoξaɪn, ocup ɪaϭ ap
comaɪpce hɪ Τaɪpcepτ. Ruc O Τaɪpcepτ poppa, ocup
pepaɪб ϭeabaɪϭ ppɪú. Маpbτap, umoppo, ɪn ξɪlla
pɪaбaċ O Τaɪpcepτ, .ɪ. pí ċoɪppeċ cloɪnɴɪ Ѕneɪϭξɪle ocup

<hr>

1 *The hostages of Connacht.* Who had been taken to England by King John in the preceding year.

2 *Occisus.* occɪppup, MS.

3 *Foreign Bishop;* i.e. John de Grey, Lord Justice of Ireland.

4 *Son of Art.* His name was Cormac O'Maelsechlainn, or O'Melachlin. Under the next year this

Cormac is stated to have obtained another victory over the Foreigners.

5 *The Gilla-fiaclach.* This sobriquet signifies "the fellow of the teeth."

6 *A battle.* The word ϭeabaɪϭ, translated "battle" here and elsewhere, although used in this sense generally by the Irish annalists,

in Ath-Luain. The hostages of Connacht[1] arrived in Erinn, viz.:—Diarmaid, son of Conchobhar Mac Diarmada, king of Magh-Luirg, and Conchobhar O'hEghra, king of Luighne, and Find O'Carmacan, and Toirbherd son of a Gall-Gaeidhel. Airechtach Mac Duinncathaigh occisus[2] est. Thomas Mac Uchtraigh and the sons of Raghnall, son of Somhairle, came to Doire-Choluim-Chille with seventy-seven ships, and the town was greatly injured by them. O'Domhnaill and they went together to Inis Eoghain, and they completely destroyed the country.

The kalends of January on Sunday; the age of the Lord twelve years, and two hundred, and a thousand. A hosting by the Connachtmen, at the command of the Foreign Bishop[3] and Gillibert Mac Goisdelbh, to Es-Ruaidh, when the castle of Cael-uisce was erected by them. Another hosting by the Foreigners of Erinn and the same Foreign Bishop, to take possession of the North of Erinn, when they erected the castle of Cluain-Eois; and the Feara-Manach, and the son of Mac Mathghamhna, inflicted a great slaughter on them on the northern side of Cluain-Eois. A great victory was gained over John de Grey, i.e. the Justice of Erinn, by the son of Art[4] O'Maelsechlainn, in which he lost all his treasure. Imhar O'Ferghail, dux of Muinter-Anghaile, occisus est a fratre suo. Gillachrist Mac Diarmada was slain by Murchadh Carrach O'Ferghail. A depredation was committed by the Gilla-fiaclach[5] O'Baighill and a party of the Cenel-Conaill, on the Cenel-Eoghain, who were under the guarantee of O'Tairchert. O'Tairchert overtook them, and fought a battle[6] against them. The Gilla-riabhach[7] O'Tairchert, i.e. the king-chieftain of

---

originally meant "disceptatio," as appears from the *Book of Armagh*, in which (fol. 178, a. 2) the verb, in the form *nu debthi[tis]*, is glossed "disceptabant." See Stokes's *Irish Glosses*, p. 166.

[7] *The Gilla-riabhach;* i.e. "the swarthy fellow."

cloiṅne Finᵹin, ιc cornum a oiniᵹ. Druim čoein cona
templuiḃ do lorcad do Cenel Eoᵹain, can cead dUa
Neill. Ferᵹal .h. Cačain, .ı. rí Ciannačta, ocur fer na
Craoiḃe, do ṁarḃad do ᵹallaiḃ. Domnall O Dáiṁin do
marḃad do mac ṁéᵹ Lačlainn a ndorur reclera Coluim
Cille.

Ḱt. Enaιr ror Maιrt, l. u. Trí bliadna deᵹ ar da
ced, ar mile, aιr in Tiᵹerna. Caιrlén Cluana Eoιr do
milled la .h. Neill. Ᵹillibert mac Ᵹoιrdelḃ do
marḃad a caιrrlen Coeil urce, ocur in caιrrlen rein
do lorcad. Donnchad .h. Eιᵹin do ᵹallad la hOedh
mac Cathail croιḃdeirc. Maιᵹm Coille na ᵹcrann la
Cormac mac Aιrt hı Maoιlrečloιnn ror ᵹallaιḃ, du a
torchaιr rochaιde ṁór do ᵹallaιḃ ιmó Feιrrur Merráτ,
ocur ιmó Ualdar Dunél. Domnall mac Domnaιll
ḃrecaıᵹ hı Maoιlrečlaιnn do marḃad do ᵹallaιḃ.
Tomar mac Uchτraıᵹ ocur Ruaιdrı mac Raᵹnaιll
do arcuιn Doιre Coluim Cille, ocur do ḃreᵹ réd
muιnnτιre Doιre ocur τuaιrcerτ Erenn dó[ıb] aιrčéna,
do lár τempaιl moιr in reclera amač. h. Cačan ocur
rır na Craιḃι do τechτ co Doιre do ᵹaḃáιl τıᵹe ar
macaιḃ ṁéᵹ Lačlaιnn, ᵹu ro ṁarḃτaτ ceallóιr ṁór
recléra Doιre eτorra. Do roιne Dıa ocur Colum
Cille, τra, mιrḃuιl ṁór annrın, .ı. fear τınóıl ın
τoιcerτuιl rın, Maᵹamaın maᵹ Aιčne, do marḃad é
a noιnech Coluım Cille a ndorur ᵹuιḃ reclérra Coluım
Cille reın. Caιrlén Cula račaın do ᵹenum do Tomarr

---

1 *Without licence.* An idiomatic mode of expression signifying "in despite of."

2 *Recles-Choluim-Chille*; i.e. the Recles (or abbey-church) of Colum-Cille, at Derry.

3 *Coill-na-gcrann;* i.e. "the wood of the [great] trees;" now Kilmore, or the great wood, in the parish of Killoughy, barony of Ballyboy, King's county. This victory is perhaps a repetition of the victory recorded under the last year, as having been gained over the Foreigners by (Cormac) the son of Art O'Maelsechlainn.

4 *Perris Messat.* The Four Masters call him Piarus Masan, or Piers Mason; but in Mageoghegan's version of the Annals of Clonmacnoise the name is written "Ferrus Mersey." He is called "Petrus Meset, Baro Delvinii," in Grace's Annals.

Clann-Sneidhghile and Clann-Finghin, was slain, moreover, defending his honour. Druim-chaein, with its
churches, was burned by the Cenel-Eoghain, without
licence[1] from O'Neill. Ferghal O'Cathain, i.e. king of
Cianachta and Feara-na-Craeibhe, was killed by the Foreigners. Domhnall O'Daimhin was slain by the son of
Mac Lachlainn in the doorway of Recles-Choluim-Chille.[2]

The kalends of January on Tuesday, the 5th of the
moon; the age of the Lord thirteen years, and two
hundred, and a thousand. The castle of Cluain-Eois was
destroyed by O'Neill. Gillibert Mac Goisdelbh was
killed in the castle of Cael-uisce, and the castle itself was
burned. Donnchadh O'hEidhin was blinded by Aedh,
son of Cathal Crobhderg. The victory of Coill-na-gerann[3]
was gained by Cormac, son of Art O'Maelsechlainn, over
the Foreigners, in which a great multitude of the Foreigners
were slain, along with Perris Messat[4] and Walter Dunel.
Domhnall, son of Domhnall Bregach[5] O'Maelsechlainn,
was slain by the Foreigners. Thomas Mac Uchtraigh and
Ruaidhri Mac Raghnaill plundered Doire-Choluim-Chille,
and carried off the precious things of the community of
Doire, and of the North of Erinn besides, from the middle
of the great church of the Recles.[6] O'Cathain and Feara-
na-Craeibhe came to Doire, to capture a house against
the sons of Mac Lachlainn, when they killed the
great butler[7] of the Recles[6] of Doire between them. God
and Colum-Cille, however, performed a great miracle there,
viz.:—the man who had assembled this muster, Mathghamhain Mac Aithne, was killed in vindication of Colum-
Cille, in the very doorway of the Dubh-Recles[8] of Colum-
Cille. The castle of Cul-rathain was erected by Thomas

---

[5] *Domhnall Bregach;* i.e. Domhnall
(Daniel) "the deceitful," or "the
false."

[6] *Recles;* i.e. the Recles of Colum-
Cille. See note [2], last page.

[7] *Butler.* cealloip (cealloir). This
word is explained "superior of a cell,

or monastrey" in O'Brien's *Irish Dictionary;* and Dr. O'Donovan translates
it "great prior," (Four Mast., 1213);
but it means "butler," or *cellarius.*
See Reeves's *Adamnan,* pp. 46, 367.

[8] *Dubh-Recles.* "Black Recles," or
Black Abbey-church.

mac Uᴄꞇꞃꭺꞁꞡ, ocuꞃ ꞁe ꞡꭺꞁꞁꭺꞛ Uꞁꭺꞝ ; ocuꞃ ꞃꞝ ꞡꞃáꞁꞃeꞇ
ꞃeꞁꞡe ocuꞃ cꞁocꭺnꭺ ocuꞃ cumꞝꭺꞡe ꞟn bꭺꞁꞁe uꞟꞁe,
cénmoꞇá ꞟn ꞇempꭺꞁꞁ ꞟꞝáꞟn, ꞝocum ꞟn cꭺꞟꞃꞁeꞟn ꞃꞟn.
Rꞟ ꭺꞁbꭺn ꞝo éc, .ꞟ. Uꞟꞁꞁꞟꭺm ꞡꭺꞃm. Oeꞝ O Neꞟꞁꞁ ꞝo
ꞇꭺbꭺꞟꞃꞇ ꞝꭺꞝmꭺ ꞃoꞃ ꞡꭺꞁꞁꭺꞛ, ocuꞃ ꞝeꞃc áꞃ ꞡꭺꞁꞁ ꞝo
chuꞃ ꭺnn, ocuꞃ ꭺn Cꭺꞃꞃꞁonꞡꞃoꞃꞇ ꞝo ꞁoꞃcꭺꞝ ꞟꞃ ꞟn ꞁó
céꞝnꭺ, eꞇꞟꞃ ꞝꭺꞟnꞟꞛ ocuꞃ ꞟnnꞟꞁe.

Ꞁcꞇ. Gnꭺꞟꞃ ꞃoꞃ Céꞝꭺꞟn ; ꭣuꞟ. ꞃuꞟꞃꞃe. Cꭺꞟꞃꞁen ꞔꞁuꭺnꭺ
mꞟc Nóꞟꞃ ocuꞃ cꭺꞟꞃꞁen Uuꞃꞝꭺꞟꞡe ꞝo ꞝenum ꞝo
ꞡꭺꞁꞁꭺꞛ. Uꞟꞔuꞃ mꞟc ꭺꞟꞃꞇ ꭺ Ueꭺꞁꞛnꭺ ꞝo ꞡꭺꞁꞁꭺꞛ
ocuꞃ ꞝo ꞡoꞟꞝeꭺꞁꭺꞛ Gꞃenn uꞟꞁe. Coꞃmꭺc mꭺc ꭺꞟꞃꞇ ꞝo
ꞝuꞁ ꭺ n'Ueꞁꞛnꭺ ꭺꞃꞟꞃ, ocuꞃ ꞃuꭺꞝꭺch bó ꞝo bꞃeꞟꞇh ꞝꭺ
ꞝuꞟnnꞇꞟꞃ ó ꞔꭺꞟꞃꞃꞁen Chꞁuꭺnꭺ, ocuꞃ mꭺꞟꞝm ꞝo ꞇꭺbꭺꞟꞃꞇ
ꞝoꞟb ꭺꞃ ꞡꭺꞁꞁꭺꞛ ꞟn ꞔꭺꞟꞃꞃꞁéꞟn. Ꞟꞝꭺꞃ mꭺc ꞡꭺꞃꞃꞡꭺꞝnꭺ
ꞝo mꭺꞃbꭺꞝ ꞝo ꞡꭺꞁꞁꭺꞟb Mꭺoꞟꞁꞟꞃ. Mꭺc ꭺꞟꞃꞇ ꞝo ꞝuꞁ co
cꭺꞟꞃꞃꞁen áꞇꭺ ꞛuꞟꞝe ꭺ ꞃeꞃꭺꞟꞛ Ceꭺꞁꞁ, ocuꞃ ꭺ ꞛóꞝun ꞝo
ꞁoꞃcꭺꞝ, ocuꞃ ochꞇꭺꞃ ꞝꭺ ꞝoeꞟnꞟꞛ ꞝo ꞝꭺꞃbꭺꞝ, ocuꞃ ꞟnnꞟꞁe
ꞟomꞛꭺ ꞝo ꞛꞃeꞟꞇ ꞁeꞟꞃ. Uꭺꞁꞡꭺꞃc .h. Ruꭺꞟꞃc, ꞃí ꞛꞃeꞟꞃꞃnꞟ,
ꞝo ꞝuꞁ ꭺꞃ cꞃeꞟc ꭺ ꞃeꞃonn Ꞃꞟꞁꞟꞃ mꞟc ꞡoꞟꞝꞝeꞁꞛ, ocuꞃ bꭺ
ꞟmꞛꭺ ꞝo ꞇꭺꞛꭺꞟꞃꞇ ꞝo ꞁꭺꞟꞃ, ocuꞃ ꭺ ꞇoꞟꞡeꭺchꞇ ꞃꞁáꞟ. Coꞃmꭺc
mꭺc ꭺꞟꞃꞇ ꞝo ꞇeꭺchꞇ ꭺꞃꞟꞃ ꭺ n'Ueꭺꞁꞛnꭺ, ocuꞃ cꞃeꭺꞔ ꞛíꞡꞁꭺ
ꞝo ꞝenum ꞛó ꭺꞃ Moeꞟꞁꞃeꞔꞁꭺꞟnn mbec .h. Moeꞟꞁꞃeꞔꞁꭺꞟnn,
ocuꞃ ꭺ ꭺꞃꞡuꞟn uꞟꞁe, ocuꞃ ꭺ ꞔuꞃ ꭺ Ueꞁꞛnꭺ ; ocuꞃ mꭺc
Uꞟꞁꞁꞟꭺm Muꞟꞁꞟnꞝ ꞝo mꭺꞃbꭺꞝ ; ocuꞃ Moeꞟꞃechꞁuꞟnn óꞡ
ꞝo ꞝuꞁ ꭺꞃꞃ ꭺ ꞇoꞃꭺꞝ ꭺ ꞃeꞔꭺ. Coꞃmꭺc mꭺc ꭺꞟꞃꞇ ꞝo
ꞝuꞁ co cꭺꞟꞃꞃꞁén mꞛꞟꞃꞃꭺ, ocuꞃ ꭺ boꞝun ꞝo ꞁoꞃcꭺꞝ, ocuꞃ
ꞟn ꞔeꭺꞁꞁ uꞟꞁe ꞝo ꞁoꞃcꭺꞝ, ocuꞃ ꭺ bꞟꭺꞝ ꞝo bꞃeꞟꞇ eꞃꞇe co
ꞁéꞟꞃ, ꭺꞃ ꞝꭺꞟꞡ nꭺ ꞃuꞟꞡoꞟꞃ ꞡoꞟꞁꞁ ꞟn cꭺꞟꞃꞁéꞟn bꞟꭺꞝ ꞟnꞇꞟ.

---

1 *Clochans.* Small stone buildings.

2 *The Carlongphort.* Carlingford.

3 *The son of Art;* i.e. Cormac, the
son of Art O'Maelsechlainn, or O'Melachlin.

4 *Delbhna.* There were several
districts in Ireland anciently called
Delbhna, for an account of which see
O'Flaherty's *Ogygia,* part iii., cap. 82,
and O'Donovan's edition of O'Dubhagain's *Topographical Poem,* App.,
p. vii. The district here referred to
seems to have been Delbhna-Eathra,
or Delvin Mac-Coghlan, which was
nearly co-extensive with the present
barony of Garrycastle, King's county,
and in which the castle of Cluain, or
Cluain-mic-Nois, was situated.

5 *Cluain.* Cluain-mic-Nois, or Clonmacnoise. See last note.

Mac Uchtraigh and the Foreigners of Ulidia; and they threw down all the tombs, and clochans[1], and structures of the town, excepting the church alone, in order to *build* this castle. The king of Alba died, i.e. William Garm. Aedh O'Neill inflicted a defeat on the Foreigners, and committed a great slaughter of the Foreigners there; and the Carlongphort[2] was burned on the same day, both people and cattle.

The kalends of January on Wednesday, the 16th of the moon. The castle of Cluain-mic-Nois and the castle of Durmhagh were built by Foreigners. Expulsion of the son of Art[3] from Delbhna, by the Foreigners and Gaeidhel of all Erinn. Cormac, son of Art, went into Delbhna[4] again, and his people carried off a prey of cows from the castle of Cluain,[5] and defeated the Foreigners of the castle. Imhar Mac Garghamhna was killed by Meiler's Foreigners. The son of Art went to the castle of Ath-buidhe in Feara-Ceall, and burned its bawn,[6] and slew eight of its inhabitants, and carried off a great number of cattle. Ualgharg O'Ruairc, king of Breifne, went on a predatory incursion into the territory of Philip Mac Goisdelbh, and brought away a great number of cows, and returned safely. Cormac, son of Art, came again into Delbhna, and committed a retaliatory depredation on Maelsechlainn Bec O'Maelsechlainn, and plundered him, and expelled him from Delbhna, and killed the son of William Muilinn:[7] and Maelsechlainn the younger[8] escaped by virtue of his running. Cormac, son of Art, went to the castle of Birr, and burned its bawn,[6] and burned the entire church, and took all its food out of it, in order that the Foreigners of the castle should not get

---

6 *Bawn.* bóóun, boóun. See note 5, p. 213, *supra.*

7 *William Muilinn.* Dr. O'Donovan (Four Mast. A.D. 1213) calls him "William of the Mill;" but Mageoghegan (Annals of Clonmac-

noise ad eund. an.) says "the knight called William Moylyn."

8 *Maelsechlainn the younger.* Moelṛechluinn óᵹ. Called Maelsechlainn Bec, or Melachlin "the Little," two lines before.

ʒillα nα nαeṁ .h. Ruαḃán, eppuc Luʒni, in Cpipτo
quieuiτ. O Muipicen, eppuc Cluαnα mic Noip, [in
Cpipτo quieuiτ]. Muipcepταč mαc bpiαin το
ṁαpbατ το ʒαllαiḃ. Iṗ in mbliαταin pi, umoppo,
το boi αnτ Ccoḃ bpeici ppipṗ αpαiττi in cαḃopταč.
Cpeαč το ṫenum τCcoḃ mαc Mαoilpečluinn ṁéʒ
Lαčlαinn pop comαpbα Coluim Cille, ocup Oeḃ ṗéin
το mαpbατ το ʒαllαiḃ, iṗ in mbliαταin ceτnα, τpiα
ṁipbuil Coluim Cille. benṁiḃe inʒen hi Eicnič, .i.
ben Oeḃα hi Néill, .i. pí Oiliʒ, in bonα peniτenτiα
quieuiτ. Sluαiʒeḃ lα hOeτh .h. Neill α nullταiḃ,
ocup τuc mαiḃm móp αp ʒαllαiḃ. Clαxαnταip mαc
Uilliαm ʒαpm το pighαḃ pop Clbαin.

Kt. Enáip pop τ'αpταin, ocup α peαčτmατ .xx. puippe.
Coiʒ ḃliατnα τhéʒ αp τá čeτ, αp mile, αip in Tiʒepnα.
bliαταin τepiḃ noiτecτα, ocup pi nα bliαταin conτpαpḃα. Cpτʒαl .h. Conchoḃαip, eppuc Soil Muipe-
ʒhαiʒ, in pαce quieuiτ. Inτ eppuc .h. Ceαllαiʒ Rαṫαin
in Cpipτo quieuiτ. Coṁḋál eppuc nα Cpipταiʒečτα co
Róim α nαmpip Innociτ pαpα τepτii. Iṗ pi po umip
nα neppuc bαταp αnn, cccc.xii., inτep quop puepunτ ταm
ppimατep quαm αpchiepipcopi .lxxi.; numepuṗ αbbατum
eτ ppiopum, τccc.; α ṗéil Mαpταin το punnpατ. Cuiʒ
ʒiupneipi τéc τα ʒαc leṫ το τpáʒhατ το ṁuip Toppiαn
ipin mbliαταin pi. Cαṫαl mαc τ'iαpmατα mic Tαiḃʒ
hi Mαoilpuαnαiḃ, pí muiʒe Luipʒ, in Cpipτo quieuiτ.
Τpατ .h. Moelṗαḃuill, τóippech čeneóil Pepʒupα, co náp

---

1 *The false Aedh.* Probably some
person who pretended to be one of the
many characters mentioned in the
so-called prophecies, as destined to
deliver Ireland from oppression.

2 *Of the Nineteen.* xix.τα, MS.; i.e.
of the cycle of 19, or cycle of the moon.

3 *Contrary.* conτpαpḃα; meaning opposed to a bissextile year.

4 *Bishop of Sil-Muiredhaigh.* That
is to say, bishop of Elphin.

5 *Rathan.* Now Rahan, in the
parish of the same name, barony of
Ballycowan, King's county. In the
Annals of the Four Masters (A.D.
1214) the Bishop O'Cellaigh
(O'Kelly) is called "bishop of Ui-
Fiachrach," which Dr. O'Donovan
understood to mean Ui-Fiachrach-
Aighne, a territory co-extensive with
the present diocese of Kilmacduagh,
county Galway.

food in it. Gilla-na-naemh O'Ruadhan, bishop of Luighne, in Christo quievit. O'Muiricen, bishop of Cluain-mic-Nois, [in Christo quievit]. Muirchertach, son of Brian, was slain by Foreigners. In this year, moreover, appeared the false Aedh,[1] who was called "the Aider." A depredation was committed by Aedh, son of Maelsechlainn Mac Lachlainn, on the comarb of Colum-Cille; and Aedh himself was slain by the Foreigners in the same year, through a miracle of Colum-Cille. Benmhidhe, daughter of O'hEighnigh, i.e. the wife of Aedh O'Neill, i.e. king of Oilech, in bona pœnitentia quievit. A hosting by Aedh O'Neill into Ulidia, and he inflicted a great defeat on the Foreigners. Alexander, son of William Garm, was made king over Alba.

The kalends of January on Thursday, the 27th of the moon; the age of the Lord fifteen years, and two hundred, and a thousand; the last year of the Nineteen;[2] and it was a contrary[3] year. Ardghal O'Conchobhair, bishop of Sil-Muiredhaigh,[4] in pace quievit. The bishop O'Cellaigh of Rathan[5] in Christo quievit. A congress of the bishops of Christendom at Rome, in the time of Pope Innocent the Third.[6] This is the number of the bishops that were there, viz.:—cccc.xv., inter quos fuerunt[7] tam primates quam archiepiscopi lxxi.; numerus abbatum et priorum, d.ccc. On the festival of Martin, in particular, *the congress met.* Fifteen giurneisi[8] on each side of Muir-Torrian[9] became dry in this year. Cathal, son of Diarmaid, son of Tadhg O'Maelruanaidh, king of Magh-Luirg, in Christo quievit. Trad O'Maelfhabhuill, chieftain

---

[6] *Third.* cenċii, for cenċii, MS

[7] *Fuerunt.* puaepūc(fuaerunt),MS.

[8] *Giurneisi.* The Editor is unable to say what measure is intended to be expressed by the word *giurneisi,* which is not properly Irish, unless it may be that signified by *jorneus,* or *jornetum,* Fr. *journèe.* (See Du Cange, sub voce *jornale*). But this is properly not a measure of *length.* The event is not recorded in any other authority accessible to the Editor; nor is it easy to say where the chronicler obtained his information, unless from some of the Irish ecclesiastics who attended the council held at Rome in the year 1215.

[9] *Muir-Torrian.* The Adriatic sea is apparently meant.

móṙ ⁊ia bṙaiṫṙiḃ maille ṙiṡ, ⁊o maṙḃa⁊ ⁊o Muiṙé⁊haċ
mac moṙṁaiṙ Leṁña.   ⁊onnċaḃ O ⁊uiḃ⁊iṙma,
⁊óiṙṙeċ ña ḃṙé⁊cá, ⁊ó héc a n⁊uiḃ ṗecléṙ Coluim Cille
i n⁊oiṙe.   Muṙċaḃ mac Caṫṁáil, ṙi ⁊oiṙeċ Cenel
ḃḟeṙaḃaiẓ, ⁊héc ⊤ṙe miṙbail Coluim Cille.   Ruai⁊ṙi
.h. Flainn, ṙi ⁊uṗluiṙ, ⁊héc.

Ḱt. enaiṙ ṙoṙ ⁊eine, ⁊ocuṙ .ix. úaṫa⁊ ṙuiṙṙe.
Ḃlia⁊ain ⊤oṙṙaċ ṅói⁊ec⁊a, ocuṙ ṙí ña ḃlia⁊ain ⁊iṙiẓ.
Sé ḃlia⁊na ⁊héc aṙ ⁊á cé⁊, aṙ míle, aiṙ in ⊤iẓeṙna.
Ẓillaṫuṙc .h. Mannaċain ⁊héẓ iṙ iñ Roim in ḃlia⁊ain
ṙi.   Señaḃ Ċleiṙeċ in ⁊omuin uile iṙ in Roim in ḃlia⁊ain
ṙi; icc La⁊eṙum imón papa Innoceñ⊤iuṙ, ocuṙ a hai⁊le
in⊤ ṙena⁊ṡ ṡiñ Innocen⊤iuṙ papa quieui⊤ in Cṙiṡ⊤o.
Seoan, ṙí Saxṙan, aṙ na ai⊤ṙiẓaḃ ⁊o ṡaxṙanċaiḃ iṙ iñ
ḃlia⁊aiñ ṙi, ocuṙ a héẓ ⁊o ṗeaċ⊤.   Mac ṙiẓ Fṙanc ⁊o
ẓaḃáil ṙiẓe Saxṙan, ocuṙ ⁊ṙaẓáil a ḃṙaẓ⁊.   Ẓilla-
ċṙoiceṙṙaiċ ṁac Caṙṙẓaṁna ⁊héẓ, ocuṙ in ṙacaṙ⊤ .h.
Celli moṙ⁊uuṡ eṡ⊤, aṙ na cṙoṡṙa⁊ aṙoen; ocuṙ aṙ ná
ċiññéṡ ⁊oiḃ ⁊uil ⁊on⊤ ṡṙuṫ.   In⊤ aṙ .h. Ló⁊an, ṙói
cṙaḃa⁊ ocuṙ leiẓinn, iñ pace quieui⊤.   Ẓṙiẓaiṙ mac
Ẓilla ná náṅẓeal, aṙ maña͘ċ Eṙenn, in pace quieui⊤ iṙ
iñ ⁊omuñ ⊤oiṙ, aṙ ña innóṙba⁊ ⁊o ṁañċaiḃ ⁊ṙoiċi⁊
a⊤á, aṙ ⊤ñū⁊ ocuṙ ṙoṙṁa⁊.   Pṙimái⊤ Eṙenn, .i. Mac
Ẓillauiḃiñ, ⁊ó éc iṡ in Roim iaṙ ṙena⁊ cleṗeċ Eṙeñn
⁊ó, ocuṙ ⁊o ní⊤eṙ ṙeṙ⁊á ṙia⁊naċa ⊤ṙi⁊ iṙiñ Roim.   In⊤
aiṙ⁊eṙṗuc .h. Ruana⁊a ⁊o ẓaḃáil ⁊o Connaċ⁊aiḃ ocuṙ
⁊o Moeiliṙa .h. Conċoḃaiṙ co ⁊ocṙaċ, ocuṙ co ṙoṙeiẓñeċ,
ocuṙ a ċuṙ a ñẓlaṙuiḃ, in ní ñaċ cualamaṙ ṙiaṁ ṙoime,
.i. aiṙ⁊eṙṗuc ⁊o ẓeiṁleċa⁊.   Añña⁊ .h. Muiṙeẓhaiẓ,

.¹ *Lemhain.* The name of a district
in Scotland co-extensive with Dum-
bartonshire, and deriving its name
from the river Leamhain, or Leven ;
now Lennox.

² *Of the Nineteen.* .ix. ec⁊a, for ṅoi-
⁊ec⁊a, MS. The year 1216 was the first
year of the cycle of 19, or Lunar cycle.

³ *Synod.* This is apparently a repetition of the entry under the preceding year.

⁴ *Innocentius.* iñnocénciuṙ, MS.

⁵ *Innocentius.* innocen⁊iuṙ, MS.

⁶ *Of a fit.* ⁊o ṗeaċ⁊ (which
seems written for ⁊ó ṙac⁊), MS.
In Mageoghegan's version of the An-

of Cenel-Ferghusa, with a great slaughter of his brethren along with him, was killed by Muiredhach, son of the Great Steward of Lemhain.[1] Donnchadh O'Duibhdirma, chieftain of the Bredach, died in the Dubh-recles of Colum-Cille, in Doire. Murchadh Mac Cathmhail, king-chieftain of Cenel-Feradhaigh, died through a miracle of Colum-Cille. Ruaidhri O'Floinn, king of Durlus, died.

The kalends of January on Friday, and the 9th of the moon; the first year of the Nineteen,[2] and a bissextile year; the age of the Lord sixteen years, and two hundred, and a thousand. Gillachrist O'Mannachain died in Rome this year. A synod[3] of the clerics of the whole world in Rome this year, at the Lateran, with the Pope Innocentius;[4] and soon after this synod Innocentius[5] papa quievit in Christo. John, king of the Saxons, was deposed by the Saxons in this year; and he died of a fit.[6] The son of the king of France assumed the sovereignty of the Saxons, and obtained their pledges. Gilla-Croichefraich Mac Carghamhna died, and the priest O'Celli mortuus est; after they had both crossed themselves,[7] and determined to go to the river.[8] The abbot O'Lotan, a paragon of piety and learning, in pace quievit. Gregory, son of Gilla-na-naingel, abbot of the monks of Erinn, in pace quievit, in the eastern world, after having been expelled by the monks of Droiched-atha, through envy and jealousy. The primate of Erinn, i.e. Mac Gillauidhir, died in Rome, after holding a synod of the clerics of Erinn; and manifest miracles are performed through him in Rome. The archbishop O'Ruanadha was cruelly and violently taken prisoner by the Connachtmen and Maelisa O'Conchobhair, and put in chains; a thing that we never heard of before, viz.:—an archbishop being manacled. Annadh O'Muiredhaigh,

---

nals of Clonmacnoise, King John is stated to have died from "drinking of a cup of ale wherein there was a toad pricked with a broach." The Annals of Bermondsey say that he died "ut quidam ferunt, venenatus cum cerusis per quendam monachum nigrum Wigorniæ." See also *Chronica Monasterii de Melsa*, ad an. 1216.

[7] *Crossed themselves*; i.e. assumed the sign of the cross, or became Crusaders.

[8] *The river*; i.e. the river Jordan.

erpuc Αρדαchαιד, quιeuιτ. ρατριςιυρ, erpuc Cnuιc Μuαιδe, quιeuιτ. Ματξαṁαιn .h. Lαιτbερταιξ; ρí čloιnnι ΟοṁnαιLL, דhéξ.

Ісτ. Θnαιρ ροn Οοṁnαch, L. xx; blιαדαιn bιρρεch. Ѕεαčτ mblιαדnα דεξ αρ δα čεד, αρ mιLe, αιρ ιn Τιξερnα. Оιρριn, αρ cαnαnαč Μαιnιρορεč דερc, quιeuιτ. Ѕcατ- ánαιξ Θρεnn ulε o· ρuρτ Lαιρce ιneρρ, ocuρ o loč Cαρmαn, co Οοιρe ·Coluιm CιLle ροτhúαιד, דo דúL co Μαnαιnn דo ιαρcαιρεčτ. Θcen דo דεnum דoιδ ιnτι, ocuρ α mαρbαד ulι α níc α neιcιn α Μαnuιnד. Ϲραιδ Θρεnn ulε דo דúL ταιριρ ροιρ αρ αn cαιριτιL coιτčιnn ιρ ιn mblιαדαιn ρι, ocuρ α nξιLle דo δíρcαιleד, ocuρ α ρορclα דo mαρbαד α Ѕαxαnuιδ, ocuρ α αρδαιne דo δuαιn דo αραιδ Οροιčιד áčα αρ αn cαιριτιL ριn. Ϲ lán τoραδ ρορ cαč cραnn דáρ δú ˙meρρ ραιρ ιριn mblιαדαιn ρι. Ϲρεčρluαιξεδ דo ξαLLαιδ ULαד דo δúL ξo hΟρד Μαčα, ocuρ α hαρcαιn ule דoιδ, ocuρ .h. ροčuelán ρo ρדιuραρταρ íαד, uαιρ ρo ξεαLLαρταρ דo ṁuιnnτιρ Ορדα Μαčα nαch αιρξριδíρ ·ξoιLL ιαד αn ξceιn דo δíαδρum αξ ξαLLαιδ. Ϲ cιnn ρεαčτ- ṁuιne ιαρριn ταnιc .h. NéLL· ρuαδ ocuρ mαc meξ Ματξαṁnα, ocuρ דo ρonρατ cρειč ṁóιρ αρ ξαLLαιδ .ι. דá čεד ocuρ mιLe bó. Ταncoταρ ξoιLL ocuρ .h. ροčuelán nα nדιαιδ. Ro ιmραדαρ Θoξαnαιξ ρριι, ocuρ ρo ṁαρδτατ ceιδρι ξoιLL .x. ρα ραιδe luιρεčα, ιm cónρδáρlα n·ΟεαLξαn, ocuρ ρo mαρbαד .h. ροčuelán α nenεch ραδραιc. ξιLLατιξερnαιξ mαc ξιLLαρonáιn, erpuc ϹιρξιαLL ocuρ cenn cαnαnαč Θρεnn, ιn bonα ρenιτεnτια quιeuιτ.

---

[1] *Bissextile.* bιρρεch. This is of course a mistake, as the preceding year (1216) was a bissextile.

[2] *Mainistir-derg.* "Red Abbey;" now Abbeyderg, in the parish of Taghsheenod, barony of Moydow, and county of Longford.

[3] *The general chapter.* This was apparently a chapter of the Cistercian order, as Mellifont Abbey, referred to in the entry under the name of Droi-chet-atha, or Drogheda, was the chief Cistercian house in Ireland.

[4] *Eoghanachs;* i.e. the Cenel-Eogh-ain, or "descendants of Eoghan," son of Niall of the Nine Hostages.

bishop of Ard-achadh, quievit. Patricius, bishop of Cnoc-
Muaidhe, quievit. Mathghamhain O'Laithbhertaigh, king
of Clann-Domhnaill, died.

The kalends of January on Sunday, the 20th of the
moon; a bissextile[1] year; the age of the Lord seventeen
years, and two hundred, and a thousand. Oissin, abbot
of the canons of Mainister-derg,[2] quievit. All the fishermen of Erinn from Port-Lairge, from the south, and from
Loch-Carman northwards to Doire-Choluim-Chille, went
to Manainn to fish. They committed violence in it, and
were all slain in punishment for their violence in Manainn.
All the abbots of Erinn went across eastwards, to the
general chapter,[3] in this year; and their attendants were
dispersed, and the choice of them were slain, by Saxons;
and the abbot of Droichet-atha was deprived of his
abbacy in this chapter. Every tree the nature of which
it was to bear fruit had its full crop in this year. A predatory host of the Foreigners of Uladh went to Ard-Macha,
which was all plundered by them; and O'Fothuelan
was the person who guided them; for he had promised
to the community of Ard-Macha that the Foreigners
would not plunder them whilst he would be with
the Foreigners. At the end of a week afterwards
O'Neill Ruadh and the son of Mac Mathghamhna came
and took a great prey from the Foreigners, viz.:—one
thousand and two hundred cows. The Foreigners and
O'Fothuelan went after them. The Eoghanachs[4] turned
against them, and killed fourteen Foreigners who
were clad in coats of mail, including the constable of
Dealgan;[5] and O'Fothuelan was slain in revenge of
Patrick. Gilla-Tighernaigh Mac Gilla-Ronain, bishop of
Airghiall,[6] and head of the canons of Erinn, in bona
pœnitentia[7] quievit.

---

[5] *Dealgan;* otherwise written Dun-
Dealgan; now Dundalk, in the county
of Louth.

[6] *Bishop of Airghiall;* that is to
say, bishop of Clogher.

[7] *Pœnitentia.* penincıά, MS.

S

|ct. enαιp pop Luαn; L. 1; bliαɒαin ταnαιpe puip[pe].
Ochτ mbliαɒnα ɒéᵹ αp ɣá céɒ, αp mile, αιp in Τιᵹepnα.
Ᵹillαepnáin .h. Mαpταιn, ollαm Epenn, ocup pói
ilɒánαchτα, ιαp cinneɒ α ɓeɣα αᵹ nα mαnchαιɓ, in pαce
quιeuιτ. Ιn pepɒánα .h. Máilpíoc, pói α ɣánα pein o
hib Ɒαlαιᵹ píop, mopτuup epτ. Ταɓc .h. Pepᵹαιl, ɒux
muιnnτιpe hᴁnᵹαιle, ɒo mαpbαɒ ɒo Mupchαɒ ɣαppαɓ
.h. Pepᵹαιl. Ɒιαpmαιɒ, mαc Concoɓαιp mic Ɒιαpmαɒα,
pí moιᵹe Luιpc, ɒéᵹ ιp in mbliαɒαin pι, ocup Copmαc mαc
Τomαlταιᵹ [nα Cαιppᵹe], mic Concoɓαιp, ɒo ᵹαɓáιl
pιᵹe ɒeιp Ɒιαpmαɒα. Ɒonnchαɒ .h. Mαoιlɓpenuιnn
ɒo éᵹ in hoc αnno. Mop, inᵹen Ɒomnαιll hι Ɓpιαιn,
ben Cαthαιl Cpoιɓɒepc hι Concoɓαιp, oen pιᵹαn Connαchτ,
ɒo ec in bliαɒαin pι. Spαɒɓαιle áɣα Luαιn ɒo Lopcαɒ
ɒo Leιɣ nα Mιɓι. .h. Níoc, αb ɓille ɓecαn, ɒo éᵹ ιαp
mbuαιɒ mαnɓine ocup ᵹcpαɓαɒ. Ɒomnαll .h. ᵹαɒpα
mopτuup epτ. Muιpcepταɓ .h. Ploιnn, pí .h. Τuιpτpι,
ɒo mαpbαɒ ɒo ᵹαllαιɓ. Conᵹαlαɓ .h. Cuιnn, coιnnιul
ᵹαιpceɒ ocup enᵹnumα ɣuαιpcιpτ Epenn, píɒoιpeɓ
Muιɓe Luᵹhαɒ ocup τpíol Cαɓupαιᵹ ule, ɒo mαpbαɒ ιpιn
τó céɒnα. Mαιlιpα .h. Ɒαιᵹpι; αpɓιnneɓ Ɒoιpe Coluιm
Cιlle, in bono pine quιeuιτ in pαce.

|ct. enαιp pop Mαιpτ, ocup αl.ι.x. puιppe, ocup in
τpep bliαɒαιn puιphí; epατ pluuια pep τoτum αnnum
pαucιp ɒιebup excepτιp. Νoι mbliαɒnα .x. αp ɣá ceɒ,
αp mile, αιp in Τιᵹepnα. Comαpbα Peιɓin Pobαιp

---

¹ *After a bissextile.* The MS. has merely puιp[pe] (fuirre), lit. "on it;" the usual form of expression in Irish MSS., to indicate the moon's age, but in this case the number of the year after a bissextile.

² *The Ferdána;* lit. "the man of song."

³ *Chief professor.* The word pói (soi) is variously understood as signifying a chief professor, sage, paragon, or eminent person. It is a word of obscure origin, as Mr. Whitley Stokes observes; *Irish Glosses,* p. 37.

⁴ *From the O'Dalaighs down;* i.e. the best poet after the O'Dalaighs, or O'Dalys, a family much celebrated for the proficiency of several members in poetry. See O'Donovan's historical sketch of the family of O'Daly; *Tribes of Ireland;* Dublin, John O'Daly, 1852.

⁵ *Queen.* oen pιᵹαn (oen righan); lit. "the one queen," or sole queen.

⁶ *Town.* Spαɒɓαιle (Sradbhaile). This word properly signifies a village, or town, consisting of one street, not

The kalends of January on Monday, the 1st of the moon; the second year after a bissextile;[1] the age of the Lord eighteen years, and two hundred, and a thousand. Gilla-Ernain O'Martain, *chief* poet of Erinn, and professor of many arts, after spending his life with the monks, in pace quievit. The Ferdana[2] O'Maelrioc, the chief professor[3] of his own art from the O'Dalaighs down,[4] mortuus est. Tadhg O'Ferghail, dux of Muinter-Anghaile, was killed by Murchadh Carrach O'Ferghail. Diarmaid, son of Conchobhar Mac Diarmada, king of Magh-Luirg, died in this year; and Cormac, son of Tomaltach [of the Rock], son of Conchobhar, assumed sovereignty after Diarmaid. Donnchadh O'Maelbhrenuinn died in hoc anno. Mor, daughter of Domhnall O'Briain, wife of Cathal Crobhderg O'Conchobhair, queen[5] of Connacht, died this year. The town[6] of Ath-Luain was burned on the Midhe side.[7] O'Nioc, abbot of Cill-Becan, died after the triumph of diligence and devotion. Domhnall O'Gadhra mortuus est. Muirchertach O'Floinn, king of Ui-Tuirtre, was slain by the Foreigners. Conghalach O'Cuinn, torch[8] of valour and bravery of the North of Erinn, king-chieftain of Magh-Lughach and all Sil-Chathusaigh, was slain on the same day. Maelisa O'Daighri, airchinnech of Doire-Choluim-Chille, in bono fine quievit in pace.

The kalends of January on Tuesday, the 12th of the moon;[9] and the third year after a bissextile;[10] erat pluvia per totum annum paucis diebus exceptis. The age of the Lord nineteen years, and two hundred, and a thousand. The comarb of Feichin of Fobhar mortuus est. Murchadh

---

defended by a castle; and is comp. of *srad*=street, and *baile*, a village or town. It sometimes becomes a proper name, in the form "Stradbally."

[7] *Midhe side.* That is to say, the portion of the town of Ath-Luain, or Athlone, which lay on the Meath side of the river Shannon.

[8] *Torch.* coinniul; lit. "candle;" a loan from the Lat. *candela*.

[9] *Moon.* The words ali .x. puippe (ali dec fuirre) signify lit. "twelve on it." See note [1], last page.

[10] *After a bissextile.* puippi, another form of puippe. See note [1], last page.

moμτυυμ eμτ. Muμchαδ cαμμαč .h. Feμgαil δο δul αμ
cμeič α Connαchτιδ, ocuμ α neιμξe δó, ocuμ μochαιδι δο
Connαchτιδ δο mαμδαδ αnn; ocuμ mαιδm αμ Muμchαδ
cαμμαch, ocuμ δμém móμ δά muιnnτιμ δο ṁαμδαδ αnn,
ocuμ α τeαchτ μeιn αμ eιcιn αμμ. Cluαιn Coμμčι δο
loμcαδ, conα τιξιδ ocuμ conα τempαll, ιμ ιn δlιαδαιn
μι, ocuμ Dμočeτ Δτα δο δul μe μμuč. Clemenμ, eμμuc
Luιξnι, ιn Cμιμτο quιeuιτ. Fonαčδαn .h. δμónαn, comoμbα
Coluιm Cιlle, ιn pαce quιeuιτ. Flαnn .h. δμolčαn δο
oιμδneδ ιnα ιonαδ.

ḳt. Θnαιμ μομ Ceδáιn, ocuμ τμeαμμ .xx. μuιμμe;
ocuμ blιαδαιn bιμexμα hí, ocuμ ιn coιceδ blιαδαιn
δon nαιecδα, ocuμ ταιμcι ιn .lxx. ιnδáμ μιče blιαδαn
αμ δα čéδ, αμ mιle, αιμ ιn Τιξeμnα. Dubδαμα mαc
Muιμeδαιξ hí Mαιlle δο mαμδαδ α congαιμ lá Cατhαl
Cμοιδδeμc ιnα lonξμομτ μeιn, δαμ μáμuξαδ Connαčτ
uιle; ocuμ bα τμuαξ αn ξnιom μιn, ξιδ ιαδ α ṁιξnιm-
μαδα μeιn τáιnιc μμιμ. Coιμecμαδ čempuιl mαιnιμ-
δμeč nα δuιlle α Connαčτιδ ιn δlιαδαιn μι. Oeδ .h.
Mαοιleοιn, eμμuc čluαnα, δο δατhαδ. Moeιlμechluιnn,
mαc Concoδαιμ Mαenṁuιξe, moμτυυμ eμτ. Ζιllαcμιμτ
ṁάc Ζομmán, μαξαμτ móμ τιξe Sιnchι, ιn μenoιμ ιμ mo
δeιμc ocuμ cμáδαδ ocuμ eξnα, leιξιnδ ocuμ μcμιδιnn,
ocuμ ταcταιμ ξαch neιč μαncuμ α leμ δο δoeιnιδ ocuμ
δο leαδμuιδ ιμιn eξluιμ, ιαμ mbuαδ ξcμαδαδ ocuμ
αιlιτμι, ιn neιmeδ ιnnμι Cločμαnn quιeuιτ ιn Cμιμτο.
Uαlδμα δé Lαcí δο čeαchτ ι nEμιnn, ocuμ μluαιξeδ móμ
δο δenuṁ δó δocum cμαnδοιξe .h. Rαιξιllιξ. Δ δul

---

[1] *Rose up against him.* α neιμξe
δo; lit. "their rising up to him."

[2] *Droichet-atha;* i.e. the bridge over
the Boyne, called Droichet-átha, or
"the bridge of the ford," from which
the name of Drogheda is derived.

[3] *Was carried away.* δο δul μe
μμuč; lit. "went with the stream."

[4] *Bishop of Luighne;* i.e. bishop of
Achonry.

[5] *Of the Nineteen.* The cycle of

19, or Lunar Cycle. The statement
which follows in the text seems un-
intelligible, probably owing to the
omission of some words.

[6] *Cluain;* i.e. Cluain-mic-Nois, or
Clonmacnoise.

[7] *Mac.* ṁάc for ṁác, MS.

[8] *Crannog.* A crannog (so called
from being constructed of *crann*, trees)
means a stockaded island in a lake, of
the nature of the Swiss pfahlbauten.

Carrach O'Ferghail went on a predatory expedition into Connacht, and they rose up against him;[1] but a multitude of the Connachtmen were slain; and Murchadh Carrach was defeated, and a great number of his people were slain there; and he himself escaped with difficulty. Cluain-Coirpthe was burned, with its houses, and with its church, in this year; and Droichet-atha[2] was carried away[3] by the flood. Clemens, bishop of Luighne,[4] in Christo quievit. Fonachdan O'Brónan, comarb of Colum-Cille, in pace quievit. Flann O'Brolchan was ordained in his place.

A.D. [1219.]

The kalends of January on Wednesday, and the 23rd of the moon; and it was a bissextile year, and the fifth year of the Nineteen[5]; and the Seventy are earlier than the age of the Lord twenty years, and two hundred, and a thousand. Dubhdara, son of Muiredhach O'Maille, was killed in a dispute by Cathal Crobhderg, in his own camp, in violation of all Connacht; and this was a grievous act, although it was his own misdeeds that recoiled on him. Consecration of the church of the monastery of Buill, in Connacht, in this year. Aedh O'Maeleoin, bishop of Cluain,[6] was drowned. Maelsechlainn, son of Conchobhar Maenmhaighe, mortuus est. Gillachrist Mac[7] Gormain, great priest of Tech-Sinche, the senior of greatest charity, and devotion, and knowledge of reading and writing; and the promoter of everything necessary to men and books in the church, after the triumph of devotion and pilgrimage, in the sanctuary of Inis-Clothrann quievit in Christo. Walter de Laci came to Erinn, and performed a great hosting to the crannog[8] of O'Raighilligh. He went upon it, and

[1220.]

The site of the one here referred to has not been previously pointed out, but it appears to have been situated in Lough Oughter, county of Cavan, where the old castle of Cloch-Uachtair (or Cloch-Oughter) now stands. In a letter from Guy de Chatillon to Henry III., dated July, 1224, Grennoch Oraely, as the name is written, is stated to have been captured from William de Lascy by Oraely, Walter de Riddelsford, and Richard Tuit, on the same day on which the castle of Kilmore [co. Cavan] was taken, from which it appears to have been in the neighbourhood. See *Royal and other Historical Letters, illustrative of the reign of Henry III.*, ed. Shirley, London, 1862; vol. i., p. 499.

uippe, ocur bpaiʒoe do ʒaßail oó, ocur neapt móp.
Cpeaĉ móp do denum do Mupchad ĉappach .h. Pepʒail
ap muinntip ʒepadain, ocur Tadc do .h. Conaĉ do
mapbad; ocur Maʒnur mac Toippdealßaiʒ .h. Con-
choßaip, ocur loan Maippín do denum cpeach pluaiʒed
docum Mupchaid ina diaid. Moelmichil .h. Tomaid,
aipo aipĉindech tiʒe Sinĉe, ocur ʒilla in Coimded mac
Pepdomuin, quieuepunt in Cpiʒto. Lúcapr de Letpeuille[1]
do teacht i nЄpinn, ocur ppimáitecht Єpenn uile do
tabaipt do lair; ocur ir hé rin ced ʒall po ʒaß
ppimáitecht Єpenn ap túr.[2]

Ket. enaip rop Aine, ocur cetramad uathad puippe.
Bliadain ap piĉit ap dá ced, ap mile, aip in Tiʒepna.
In Caipneĉ riaßac[3] máʒ Plannchaid do mapbad doed,
mac Domnaill, mic Pepʒail .h. Ruaipc. ʒilla na
noeim mac Conmeda, dux muinntipe Laodaĉáin, do
mapbad den upchup raiʒde do macaib .h. Plannacáin
doippxep Theppa, ac teacht ón caiplén núa.[4] Moeilreĉ-
luinn óc O Moeilpeĉluinn do ßadhad, ocur mac Conmeda, .i. mac Uʒolóid mec Conmeda. Caiplen Aĉa
liaʒ do puabaipt do denum do Ualopa de Laci ocur do
rluaʒ na Miɓe uile. Oo ĉualadap imoppo Connachta
rin, tancodap taipir i níap co rancodap tri láp muinntipe hAnʒole, ocur a Maʒ mbreaʒmuide, ʒup loircedap
daingen hI Cuinn, ocur ʒondeĉadap tpemit riap ir in
calaid, cur racbad dóiß in caiplen ap éicin, ocur tpe
cóip rĩa.

lacób Penciail do ĉeacht i nЄpinn map leʒáid ó Róim,
do rédduʒad ocur doroduʒad dál eʒlardada, ocur eipeʒa

---

[1] *De Letreville.* A mistake for De Netterville.

[2] *The first.* The clause "ocur ir hé rin céd ʒall po ʒaß ppimáitecht Єpenn ap túr," signifies literally "and he is the first foreigner who obtained the primacy of Erinn at first."

[3] *The Cairnech Riabhach;* lit. "the swarthy priest." The word cairnech is explained raʒapt (sagart = sacerdos), in O'Clery's Glossary.

[4] *The Caislén-núa;* i.e. "the new castle." Newcastle, in the parish of Forgney, barony of Shrule, county of Longford, is probably the place re-

obtained hostages and great power. A great depre- A.D.
dation was committed by Murchad Carrach O'Ferghail [1220.]
on Muinter-Geradhain, and Tadhg O'Conaith was slain;
and Maghnus, son of Toirdhelbhach O'Conchobhair, and
John Maissin led a predatory force afterwards against
Murchadh. Maelmichil O'Tomaidh, high airchinnech of
Tech-Sinche, and Gilla-in-Choimdedh Mac Ferdomhuin,
quieverunt in Christo. Lucas de Letreville[1] came to Erinn,
and brought with him the primacy of all Erinn; and he
was the first[2] Foreigner who obtained the primacy of
Erinn.

The kalends of January on Friday, and the fourth of [1221.]
the moon; the age of the Lord twenty-one years, and two
hundred, and a thousand. The Cairnech Riabhach[3] Mac
Flannchaidh was slain by Aedh, son of Domhnall, son of
Ferghail O'Ruairc. Gilla-na-naemh Mac Conmedha, dux of
Muinter-Laodhacháin, was killed with one cast of an arrow
by the sons of O'Flannagan of Eastern Teffa, whilst coming
from the Caislén-núa.[4] Maelsechlainn O'Maelsechlainn,
the younger, was drowned, and Mac Conmedha, i.e. the
son of Ugholoid Mac Conmedha. The castle of Ath-Liag
was attempted to be made by Walter de Laci and all the
forces of Midhe. When the Connachtmen heard this,
however, they came across from the west, and proceeded through the middle of Muinter-Anghaile, and
into Magh-Breghmhuidhe, when they burned Daingen-
Ui-Chuinn, and went through it westwards into the
Caladh; and the castle was abandoned to them, through
force, and on conditions of peace.

Jacobus Penciail came to Erinn[5] as Legate from Rome,
to settle and arrange ecclesiastical affairs; and he collected

---

ferred to, as the district in which it is
situated was known as Eastern Teffia.

[5] *Came to Erinn.* The arrival of
this Legate is entered under the year
1220 by Mageoghegan, in his trans-

lation of the so-called Annals of
Clonmacnois, and also by the Four
Masters; but they are silent as to
the simony attributed to him in this
chronicle.

nα nech vóp ocuṛ vaiṛẓev vo timṛuẓav vó ó ċleiṛċiḃ
Eṛenn tṛe ṛímóntacht, ocuṛ imteaċt vó a hEṛinn iṛin
mbliavain cévna. Viaṛmaiv, mac Ruaivṛi, mic Thoiṛṛ-
vealḃaiẓ ṁóiṛ hi Conċoḃaiṛ, vo ṁaṛbav vo Tomáṛṛ macc
Uchtṛaiḃ aẓ teacht a hinnṛiḃ Ẓall, ocuṛ é aẓ tinol ċaḃ-
laiẓ vo ẓaḃail ṛiẓe Connacht; ocuṛ ba móṛ in ṛcél ṛin,
.1. aḃḃaṛ ṛiẓ Eṛenn vo ċuitim amluiv ṛin aṛ belaiḃ a
inmhe. Maolṛuanaiv .h. Vuḃva, ṛí .h. nαmalẓaiv, vo'
baohav ac tinól in caḃlaiẓ cevna. Viaṛmaiv .h. Culech-
áin, ṛói ṛenchuṛa ocuṛ ṛcṛiḃinn, vo éc iṛ in ḃliavain
ṛin, .1. ṛeṛ ṛa mó gṛṛeaṛtṛa ocuṛ eoluṛ tanic na aimṛiṛ
ṛein; ocuṛ iṛṛé ṛo gṛṛiov leabaṛ oiṛṛṛinn in ċnuic,
ocuṛ leabaṛ oiṛṛṛinn eli a ṫinẓṁála vo Viaṛmaiv mac
Oiṛeachtaiẓ, vá oive, ocuṛ vo Ẓhillaṛaopaic vá comḃa-
lta, vo comaṛbuiḃ αchaḃ Ṛabaiṛ viaiḃ a noiaiḃ. Mac
Uẓa vé Laci vo ċoivečt i nEṛinn vo nemṫoil ṛí Saxan, co
tanic co hOevh .h. Neill, co tancovaṛ aṛoen i naẓhaiḃ
ẓall Eṛenn, ocuṛ ẓuṛ millṛet moṛán a Mṛḃe, ocuṛ a
laiẓniḃ, ocuṛ a nUlltaiḃ; ẓuṛṛuṛṛcaoilṛet caiṛlén
Cula ṛathain, ocuṛ co ṛo tinoilṛev Ẓoill Eiṛenv co
Vealẓain cečṛi catα .xx., ẓu ttainic αov O Neill ocuṛ
mac Uẓa ve Laci cečṛi catα na naẓhaiḃ, ẓo tuẓṛav Ẓaill
a bṛeṫ ṛein vUa Neill annṛiḃe.

ḳtt. Enaiṛ ṛoṛ ṛaċaṛn, ocuṛ cuiceḃ .x. ṛuiṛṛe;
M.cc.xxii.　Int ab Mac Suala in pace quievit.
Ẓillamoċoinne .h. Caṫail, ṛí Ceneoíl αova tiaṛ ocuṛ toiṛ,
vo maṛḃav vo Sheċnaṛaċ mac Ẓilla na naom .h. Sheċ-
naṛaiẓ, iaṛ na bṛaṫ va ṁuinntiṛ ṛein. Ẓaoṫ moṛ,
tṛéṛ aṛ milleo vénta, ocuṛ cumvaiẓe, ocuṛ lonẓa in
bliavain ṛin. Moṛ, inẓion hi ḃaoiṫill, ben αmlaoiḃ
hi ḃeollain, moṛtua eṛt. Ṅiall O Neill vo ṛaṛuẓav

---

[1] *Pity.* ṛcél; lit. "story."

[2] *Without the consent.* The words vo neṁtoiL signify lit. "by non-consent."

[3] *Cenel-Aedha.* There were many territories in Ireland called Cenel-Aedha; but the one here referred to was Cenel-Aedha-na-hEchtghe, or Kinelea, a district in the barony of Kiltarton, co. Galway, the patrimony of the O'Shaughnessys. See the map prefixed to O'Donovan's *Hy-Many.*

horseloads of gold and silver from the clerics of Erinn, through simony, and departed from Erinn in the same year. Diarmaid, son of Ruaidhri, son of Toirdhelbhach Mór O'Conchobhair, was slain by Thomas Mac Uchtraigh as he was coming from Insi-Gall, whilst collecting a fleet for the purpose of acquiring the sovereignty of Connacht; and this was a great pity,[1] viz. :—the materies of a king of Erinn to fall so before his time. Maelruanaidh O'Dubhda, king of Ui-Amhalghaidh, was drowned whilst assembling the same fleet. Diarmaid O'Culechain, a professor of history and writing, died in this year, i.e. a man who had more writings and knowledge than any one that came in his own time; and it was he that wrote the Mass book of Cnoc, and another Mass book the equal of it for Diarmaid Mac Oirechtaigh, his tutor, and for Gillapatraic, his foster-brother—the comarbs of Achadh-Fabhair in succession. The son of Hugo de Laci came to Erinn without the consent[2] of the king of the Saxons, and proceeded to Aedh O'Neill; and they both went against the Foreigners of Erinn, and committed great injuries in Midhe, and in Laighen, and in Ulidia, and demolished the castle of Cul-rathain; and the Foreigners of Erinn collected twenty-four battalions to Delgan; but Aedh O'Neill and the son of Hugo de Laci came with four battalions against them, and the Foreigners gave his own award to O'Neill there.

The kalends of January on Saturday, and the 15th of the moon; M.CC.XXII. The abbot Mac Suala in pace quievit. Gillamochoinne O'Cathail, king of Cenel-Aedha[3] east and west, was slain by Sechnasach, son of Gilla-na-naemh O'Sechnasaigh, after having been betrayed by his own people. Great wind, through which structures, and buildings, and ships were destroyed in this year. Mor, daughter of O'Baighill, wife of Amhlaibh O'Beollain, mortua est. Niall O'Neill profaned Doire

Ꝺoıꞃe ım ınꞁen hı Chαᵵάın, ocuꞃ ᵵάınıc ꝺo mıꝛᵬuılαıᵬ
Ꝺé ocuꞃ Coluım Cılle ꞁuꞃ bo ꞁeαꞃꝛꝼαoꞁlαᵵ Nıαll ıαꞃꞃın.
Ꞇαᵭꞁ O ᵬαoıᵬıll, ꞃonuꞃ ocuꞃ ꞃαıᵭᵬꞃeαꞃ ᵵuαıꞃcıꞃᵵ
Eıꞃenꝺ, ꞃeꞃ ꞃcαoılᵵe ꞃéꝺ ocuꞃ mαoıne ꝺo luchᵵ ꞁαᵵα
ceıꞃꝺe, moꞃᵵuuꞃ eꞃᵵ.

ƈᵵᵵ. enάıꞃ ꝛoꞃ Ꝺomnαᵵ, ocuꞃ .uı.xx. ꞃuıꞃꞃe.
ℳ.cc.xxııı. Œlꞃín .h. ℳαolᵯuαıᵬ, eαꞃᵬoꞁ ꝛeꞃnα, ın
Cꞃıꞃᵵo quıeuıᵵ. 1nᵵ eαꞃꞃoꞁ ℳαꞁ ꞁeαlαın, eꞃꞃoꞁ Cılle
ꝺαꞃα, eoꝺem αnno [quıeuıᵵ]. Clúαın mıc Noıꞃ ꝺo
loꞃcuᵬ, ocuꞃ ꞃeóıꝺ ımᵬα, mαꞃ αen ꞃe ꝺα ᵵempoll, ın
blıαꝺαın ꞃın. Uıllıαm ꝺe Lαcı ꝺo ᵵeᵵᵵ ı nEıꞃınn, ocuꞃ
cꞃαnnoꞁ 1nnꞃı Lαoꝺαᵵαın ꝺo ᵬénum ꝺó; ocuꞃ Connαᵵ-
ᵵαıꞁ ꝺo ᵵeᵵᵵ uıꞃꞃe αꞃ eıꞁın, ocuꞃ nα ꝺαıne ꝺo bı ınnᵵe
ꝺo Leꞁαᵬ αmαᵵ αꞃ ᵬꞃeıᵵıꞃ. Se ᵵꞃαıꞁᵵe .xx. ꝺo cuꞃ αꞃ
ᵵempul ᵵıꞁe Sınᵵe ꝺo ꝛαꞁαꞃᵵ ın bαıle, .ı. ℳαel mαꞁ
ꞁoꞃmαın. ꞁαoᵵ moꞃ ıꞃ ın lo ıαꞃ bꞃeıl ℳαᵵα, ꞁuꞃꞃo
ꞃoıꞃıꞃᵵαıꞃ coıꞃce eꞃenn uıle ꝺo neoᵵ ᵵαꞃꞃuıᵬ αꞃ lάꞃ ᵬe.
ℳuꞃchαꝺ cαꞃꞃαch .h. ꝛeꞃꞁuıl ꝺo mαꞃbαꝺ ᵬén uꞃchuꞃ
ꞃoıꞁꝺe αc ꞁαbάıl ꞁꞃeıꞃı αꞃ Œoᵬ mαc Œmlαıᵬ 1 ꝛeꞃꞁuıl.
Seᵵnuꞃαᵵ mαc ꞁıllα nα nαoᵯ .h. Sheᵵnuꞃαıꞁ ꝺo mαꞃbαꝺ
ꝺo cloınn Cuıleın, ocuꞃ ꞃαꞃαchαꝺ nα bαclα moꞃe ℳıc
Ꝺuαᵵ ımme, ocuꞃ α mαc cleıꞃeᵵ ꝺo mαꞃbαꝺ. ℳαolíꞃu
mαc Ꞇoıꞃꞃꝺheαlᵬαıꞁ .h. Concuᵬαıꞃ ꝺo éc α nımıꞃ meᵭóın.
Ꝺuᵬᵵαᵵ .h. Ꝺubᵵhαıꞁ, αb Cunꞁα, [quıeuıᵵ] ın hoc αnno.
ꝛınn .h. Cαꞃmαcαın, ꞃeꞃ ꞃeꝺmα ocuꞃ ꞃeꞃαnnuıꞃ moıꞃ
ꝺo ꞃıꞁ Connαᵵᵵ, moꞃıᵵuꞃ.

---

[1] *On account of.* ım. The meaning is that Niall O'Neill acted towards the daughter of O'Cathain, or O'Cane, in such a way as to profane the right of asylum pertaining to the church of Derry, or to violate some compact entered into by him in the presence of the reliquaries or community of Derry.

[2] *Crannog.* By a crannog is meant a stockaded island. See note [6], p. 260, and next note; and also *The War of the Gaedhil with the Gaill*, ed. by the Rev. Dr. Todd; Introduction, p. clx, note [1].

[3] *Inis-Laodhachain;* i.e. "the island of Laodhachan." In Mageoghegan's version of the Annals of Clonmacnoise, under the year 1222, De Laci is said to have "founded a *castle* at Logh-Loygeachan." The statement in the text, which represents the Connachtmen as having "entered forcibly upon it," [i.e. the structure erected by De Laci,] points rather to a crannog than a castle. The names

on account of[1] the daughter of O'Cathain; and it happened, through a miracle of God and Colum-Cille, that Niall was afterwards short-lived. Tadhg O'Baighill, the happiness and opulence of the North of Erinn, the distributor of jewels and riches to men of every profession, mortuus est.

The kalends of January on Sunday, and the 26th of the moon; M.cc.xxiii. Alpin O'Maelmhuaidh, bishop of Ferna, in Christo quievit. The bishop Mac Gelain, bishop of Cill-dara, eodem anno [quievit]. Cluain-mic-Nois was burned, and many jewels, together with two churches, in this year. William de Laci came to Erinn, and constructed the crannog[2] of Inis-Laodhachain;[3] and the Connachtmen entered forcibly upon it, and let out on parole the people who were in it. Twenty-six feet *in height* was added to the church of Tech-Sinche, by the priest of the place, i.e. Mael Mac Gormain. Great wind on the day after the festival of Matthew, which injured all the oats of Erinn that it found standing. Murchadh Carrach O'Ferghail was killed by the discharge of an arrow, whilst making an attack on Aedh, son of Amhlaibh O'Ferghail. Sechnasach, son of Gilla-na-naemh O'Sechnasaigh, was slain by the Clann-Cuilein, and the great bachal[4] of Mac Duach was profaned[4] regarding him, and its cleric[5] was slain. Maelisa, son of Toirdhelbhach O'Conchobhair, died in Inis-medhóin. Dubhthach O'Dubhthaigh, abbot of Cunga, [quievit] in hoc anno. Finn O'Carmacain, agent and great landholder to the king of Connacht, moritur.

Inis-Laodhachain and Loch-Laodhachain are now obsolete. They were probably applied to a lake and island in the county of Westmeath, or county of Cavan.

[4] *Bachal . . . profaned.* The sense of the passage is that O'Sechnasaigh, or O'Shaughnessy, was slain in violation of some oath or pledge taken on the great bachal (baculus) of Mac Duach, patron of Kilmacduagh, county Galway, which was thereby profaned. The bachal in question is preserved in the museum of the late Dr. Petrie.

[5] *Its cleric.* α mαc cleipeč; i.e. the cleric who had charge of the bachal.

Ctt. Enáip pop Luan, ocup .uıı. uatḣao puıppı.
M.cc.xxıııı. Cıḃ po pepapoaıp a nınaouıḃ a ʒConnachtuıḃ,
.ı. a ττíp Maıne, ocup a Soʒaın, ocup a nUıb Oıapmaoa,
ocup a claınn Taıḃʒ, oap páp teıḃm mop ap ḃúaıb ıap
ʒcaıteṁ peoıp ocup ouılleḃaıp, ocup na oaoıne oo
caıteḃ allacht ocup a bpeoıl oo nıḃ ʒallpa exomla
ḃoıḃ. Catal Cpoıḃoepcc .ꞕ. Concobaıp, pí Connaćt, ocup
pí ʒoeıḃel Eıpenn ıap totacht, opaʒáıl baıp a maınıptıp
Cnuıc Muaıḃe, a cuıcceoh callaınn Iúın; ant oen ʒaeıoel
ap pepp tanaıc o Ḃpıan Ḃopaıme anuap, ap uaıplı
ocup ap onoıp; toccbalach tpepaʒmap totachtać na
tuać; pobaptan paıḃbep poıneṁaıl na pıtćana; ooıḃ
ıp pé peıṁıop oo ʒabaḃ oećmaḃ ap tup a nıać Eıpenn;
colaṁuın connaıl cpaıḃoeć cpeıoṁe ocup Cpıptaıʒ-
eachta; cepttoıʒteoıp na cıntać ocup na coıḃoenać;
muḃaıʒteoıp na mepleć ocup na maloptać; coıṁeut-
taıo coıttceno catbuaḃać an peachta pıoʒ, oa tucc Oıa
oeʒ onoıp a talmaın, ocup an plaıtear nemoa ćall,
ap neucc a naıbıo ṁanaıʒ oó, ap mbpeıt buaḃa o
ooman ocup o oeaman oo. Αοo O Concobaıp, a mac
peın, oo ʒabaıl pıʒe Connacht le a péin ocup le a polaıo
oap a éıpe; uaıp ba pı ap totacht pe laıṁ a atop peıṁe;
ocup oo baoap bpaıʒoe Connacht na upláıṁ; ocup ıp e
Oıa po ćeoaıʒ ın píʒe oopum amluıo pın, uaıp nı
oepnao oulc a ʒConnachtuıb pe paoḃap ʒabala pıʒe
oopuṁ achtmaḃ aon plao ap plıʒeḃ na Cpúaıće, ocup po·
benuıo a láṁa ocup a ćopa oon tí oo poıne, ocup aon
ben oo pápachao oo mac ḣı Mannachaın; ocup po oallao

---

[1] *The best.* ant oen : . . . ap
peapp; lit. "the one . . . that
is best."

[2] *Beyond.* The MS. has tallo,
which is a mistake for tall.

[3] *His luck.* a péın; i.e. the luck
of Cathal Crobhderg, Aedh's father.

[4] The words pe laıṁ a atop,
translated "near his father," signify

literally "by the hand of his father,"
but conventionally "by the side of his
father."

[5] *Speedy.* It is not easy to render
into appropriate English the expression in the text, pe paoḃap ʒabala
pıʒe oopum, which actually means
"with the edge of the taking of
sovereignty by him." The sense of
the clause is that such was the severity

The kalends of January on Monday, and the 7th of the moon; M.CC.XXIIII. A shower fell in places in Connacht, viz. :—in Tir-Maine, and in Soghan, and in Ui-Diarmada, and in Clann-Taidhg, from which grew a great distemper among cows after eating grass and foliage; and their milk and flesh produced various diseases in the persons who partook of them. Cathal Crobhderg O'Conchobhair, king of Connacht, and king of the Gaeidhel of Erinn according to merit, died in the monastery of Cnoc-Muaidhe on the 5th of the kalends of June; the best[1] Gaeidhel for nobility and honour that came from *the time of* Brian Borumha down; the battle-prosperous, puissant upholder of the people; the rich, excellent maintainer of peace; (for it was in his time that tithes were first received in the land of Erinn); the meek, devout pillar of faith and Christianity; the corrector of the culprits and transgressors; the destroyer of the robbers and evil-doers; the general battle-victorious defender of the royal law, to whom God gave good honour on earth, and the heavenly kingdom beyond,[2] after dying in the habit of a monk, after triumphing over the world and the devil. Aedh O'Conchobhair, his own son, assumed the government of Connacht, with his luck[3] and happiness, after him; for he was a king in dignity near[4] his father previously, and the hostages of Connacht were at his command; and it was God who granted the sovereignty to him thus, for no crime was committed in Connacht through the speedy[5] assumption of sovereignty by him, but one act of plunder on the road to Cruach,[6] and his hands and feet were cut off the person who committed it; and one woman was violated by the son of O'Mannachain, who was blinded for his

---

with which Aedh O'Conchobhair exercised the law at the time of his assuming the sovereignty, that acts of violence and rapine were prevented; and it appeared, therefore, that the

sovereignty had been destined to him by God.

[6] *Cruach*; i.e. Cruach-Patraic, or Croagh-Patrick, a mountain in the county of Mayo.

nα činuιὃ ό. Muιρξeρ cαnαnαč, mαc Ruαιὃρι .h. [Con-
čoϐαιρ], ὃuιne ιρ comὃeιρι ταιnιc ὃo Zαοιὃeαlαιὃ ριαm
ιlleιξenὃ ocuρ ι cαnταιρechτ, όcuρ hι ueρρ ὃéninuιὃechτ,
ὃo éξ ιρ ιn blιαbαιn ρι, ocuρ α αϐlúcαὃ α Cunξα ℓeιchιn
ιαρ mbuαιὃ onξτα ocuρ αιτριξe. Ὀomnαll Ꝋ Cellαιξ, ρí
.h. mαιne, ὃo éξ ιn hoc αnno. Cúcenαnn .h. Concenuιnn
ὃo éξ ιn blιαὃαιn ριn. mατξαmuιn .h. Ceιρín, ρí Cιαρραιξe Ꝇoča nα nαιρne, ὃo éξ. mαelιρu mαc ιn eρριιc
ι mαeιlℓαξmαιρ, ρeρρún .h. ℓιαčραch ocuρ .h. nɑnhαl-
ξαιὃ, ocuρ αὃαρ eρριιc, ὃo mαρϐαὃ ὃo mαc Ὀonnchαὃα
ι Ὀubὃα, αρ ξcαιčen α bιὃ ocuρ α čeιnιὃ nα čιξh ρeιn.
ɑeὃ mαc Concubαιρ moenhuιξe ὃo éξ αξ τοιξecτ onτ
ρρuč ocuρ ο ιeρuραlem ιn blιαὃαιn ρι. mαc ιn Uξα
ὃo τeαchττ α nꝊιριnn ὃαιnὃeoιn ρíξ Sαxαn, ocuρ
ρoρbuιρe cocαιὃ ocuρ eρραιn ὃo ℓάρ eττoρραι ocuρ
Zoιll Ꝋιρenn, no ξuρ eιρξeὃαρ Zoιll Ꝋιρenn ιnα αξuιὃ,
ocuρ ξuρ hιnὃαρbuιὃ ι nuč ɑoὃα ι Neιll, ρíξ ɑιlιξ,
ocuρ ξuρ τιnoιleὃαρ Zoιll ocuρ Zαοιὃel Ꝋιρenn ὃα
nιnnραιξιι, .ι. ɑoὃ mαc Cαhαιl cροιὃὃeρξ, ρι Connαchτ,
ocuρ Ὀonnchαὃ Cαιρρρech .h. bριαιn, ρí mumαn, ocuρ
Ὀιαρmαιτ cluαραch mαξ Cαρτhαιξ, ρι Ὀeαρmumαn, ocuρ
mαιče Ꝋρenn αρčenα cenmoča Cenel Conuιll ocuρ
Ꝋοξαιn, co ριαchταὃαρ muρτemne ocuρ Ὀun Ὀelξαn,
ocuρ ξuραρ αρ ρο ιαρραὃ ξιαllα ocuρ eτeρe ο mαcuιb
ιn Uξα ocuρ ο ɑoὃ .h. Neιll. ιρ αnnριn ταιnιc .h. Neιll
conα ξαllαιὃ ocuρ conα Zαοιὃeluιὃ, co ρο ροιnnριτ ιαὃ
αρ ρlιξčhιὃ Slebe ℓuαιὃ, ocuρ αρ ὃοιρριὃ Ꝋnhnα,
ocuρ αρ ℓιὃ Conαιlle, ξuρ ξρeαnnuιξριm Zullu ρα α
ιnὃραιξeὃ ιρ nα ιnατuιὃ ριn. Cιὃ τραchτ, οὃ conncαὃαρ
Zoιll Ꝋιρenn ξuρ uρϐαlτα ιn ιmὃeαξuιl ριn ὃραξϐáιl

---

[1] *His*; i.e. O'Dubhda's.

[2] *The river.* The river Jordan.

[3] *Hugo.* The MS. reads mαc ιn
Uξα; lit. "the son of the Hugo."

[4] *Cluasach.* A sobriquet, signifying
"of the ears," from *cluas*, an ear.

[5] *The doors of Emhain.* Ὀοιρριὃ
Ꝋnhnα, i.e. the approaches to Emhain,
now the Navan fort, near Armagh,
the ancient residence of the kings of
Ulster. There are five townlands
called "Dorsy," in the barony of
Fews Upper, co. of Armagh, which

offence. Muirghes Cananach, son of Ruaidhri O'[Conchobhair], the most expert man that ever came of the Gaeidhel in reading, and in psalm-singing, and in verse-making, died in this year, and was interred in Cunga-Feichin, after the triumph of unction and penitence. Domhnall O'Cellaigh, king of Ui-Maine, died in hoc anno. Cucennainn O'Concennainn died in this year. Mathghamhain O'Ceirín, king of Ciarraighe-Locha-na-nairne, died. Maelisu, son of the bishop O'Maelfhaghmhair, parson of Ui-Fiachrach and Ui-Amhalghaidh, and materies of a bishop, was killed by the son of Donnchadh O'Dubhda, after enjoying his[1] food and his fire in his[1] own house. Aedh, son of Conchobhar Maenmhaighe, died while coming from the river,[2] and from Jerusalem, this year. The son of Hugo[3] came to Erinn against the will of the king of the Saxons, and causes of war and contention grew up between him and the Foreigners of Erinn, until the Foreigners of Erinn rose up against him, and he was banished to Aedh O'Neill, king of Ailech; and the Foreigners and Gaeidhel of Erinn, viz. :—Aedh, son of Cathal Crobhderg, king of Connacht, and Donnchadh Cairbrech O'Briain, king of Mumha, and Diarmaid Cluasach[4] Mac Carthaigh, king of Des-Mumha, and the chieftains of Erinn besides, excepting the Cenel-Conaill and *Cenel-Eoghain*, assembled to proceed against them, until they reached Muirthemhne and Dun-Delgan; and from thence they demanded pledges and hostages from the sons of Hugo,[3] and from Aedh O'Neill. It was then that O'Neill came with his Foreigners and Gaeidhel, whom he distributed on the passes of Sliabh-Fuaid and the doors of Emhain,[5] and on Fidh-Conaille, when he challenged the Foreigners to attack him in those places. However, when the Foreigners of Erinn saw that this protection[6] was assured to them,

Dr. Reeves thinks may represent the ᴠoɪᴘᴘɪ Eᴛʜnᴀ of the text.

[6] *This protection;* i.e. the protection from attack secured to O'Neill by the skilful distribution of his forces in the passes leading from Dun-Delgan, or Dundalk, across the Fews, into the neighbourhood of Armagh.

ʋoιb ιr ι comαιρle ʋo ροηρατ ριԺ ʋo ʋenum re clαηʋαιb
ιη Uʒα, ocυr bρeԺ ρ1ʒ Sαχαη ριρ ηα ρίԺυιb ριη; ocυr
ρo rcαoιlρeʋαρ ʒoιll Eιρenn ʒαη cίρ ʒαη coṁα o Ccoʋ
O Neιll.

Slυαιʒeʋ ṁόρ le hOeʋ mαc Cατhαιl cρoιʋeρʒ co
cαιρlen Ccιρʋ αblα ι cριch Bρéρne, conʋeԺαταρ αρ
αη ʒcαιρlen, cυρ loιρceαʋαρ, ocυr ʒυρ mαρbαʋαρ cαԺ
oeη rαρυταρ αηη ʋo ʒαllαιb ocυr ʋo ʒαoιʋeαlαιb.
Dυαρcαη O hEʋρα, ρι Lυιʒne, moρτυυρ erτ. Moρ-
rlυαιʒeʋ ʋo ʋénum ʋo Ccoʋ Uα Neιll α ʒConnαԺτα,
lα mαccα Rυαιʋρι hι Concυbαιρ, ocυr le τoʒαιρm
τρι Mυιρeʋυιʒ υιle αchτ mαc Dιαρmατα αṁάιη,
.ι. Coρmαc mαc Tomαlταιʒ, conʋeαԺαιʋ αρ rυʋ Connαchτ bυʋ ʋer co ρeʋυιb CcԺα Lύαιη, co ραιbe ʋα
oιʋce αʒ Mυιllιb UαnαԺ, ocυr ʒυρ αιρʒreτ Loc Nen,
ocυr co τυʒ reoιʋ hι Conchoʋαιρ αρ leιr. Tάnιc ηα
ʋιαιʋ co Cαρη ρραoιԺ, ocυr ʋo αιρʒeρταιρ ToιρρʋheαlbαԺ
mαc Rύαιʋρι αηη, ocυr ʋo chυαιʋ ηα lυαԺcéιm ʋα τιʒ αρ
ʒccloιρτιη τρlόιʒ moιρ ʋo ʒαlloιb ocυr ʋo Mυιmnechαιb,
ρά Donncchαʋ CαιρbρeԺ .h. mbριαιη, ocυr ρρα Séρρυιʋ
Mαιρeιr, αʒ Ccoʋ .h. Concoʋαιρ ocυr αʒ mαc Dιαρmατα
cυιʒe; ocυr o ηαc rυcrαταρ αρ O Neιll ρo lenρατ
meιc Rυαιʋρι, ʒυρ ταιρρeʋαρ α ηuchτ ι Neιll ιαʋ αρίρ.
Ro mαρbαʋαρ Mυιṁnιʒ ʋon τυρυr ριη EchmαρcαԺ
mαc bραηαιη, ταoιρԺ Coρcα Eαclαnn, αʒ Cιll Cellαιʒ,
αρ ηʋίԺυρ cloιnne Rυαιʋρι α Cunnαchτα αmαԺ. ʒoιll
ocυr Mυιṁnιʒ ʋo ʋol ρα Tερmαnn Cαoιlριηn, ocυr ʋo
cυιρeʋ άρ ηα ηʒαll τρé ρeρτυιb Cαιlριηʋ. Ccρ moρ
αρ ʋαoιnιb αη blιαʋαιη ριη. Ccητ αρbαρ ʒα bυαιη α

¹ *Request.* The Four Masters (1225) say that O'Neill led a great force into Connacht, at the request of Donn Og Mac Airechtaigh, who wanted to be revenged of Aedh O'Conor, for having deprived him (Donn) of his lands.

² *Fedha-Atha-Luain;* i.e. the woods of Ath-Luain, a district in the barony of Athlone, county of Roscommon, the patrimony of the sept of O'Nechtain, or O'Naghten.

³ *Plundered.* ʋo αιρʒeρταιρ. Thus also in the Annals of Ulster. The Four Masters have "ριοʒταρ ToιρρʋeαlbαԺ mαc Rυαιʋρι αηηριη," "Toirdhelbhach, son of

A.D.

[1224.]

the resolution they adopted was to make peace with the sons of Hugo, and to leave the conditions to the award of the king of the Saxons; and the Foreigners of Erinn separated, without *obtaining* tribute or conditions from Aedh O'Neill.

A great hosting by Aedh, son of Cathal Crobhderg, to the castle of Ard-abhla in the territory of Breifne, when they entered the castle, and burned it, and killed every one whom they found in it, both Foreigners and Gaeidhel. Duarcan O'hEghra, king of Luighne, *mortuus est.* A great hosting to Connacht was performed by Aedh O'Neill, with the sons of Ruaidhri O'Conchobhair, and at the request[1] of all the Sil-Muiredhaigh, excepting only Mac Diarmada, i.e. Cormac, son of Tomaltach; and he (*Aedh O'Neill*) proceeded along Connacht, southwards, to Fedha-Atha-Luain,[2] and remained two nights at Muille-Uanach, and pillaged Loch-Nen, and carried off thence the treasures of O'Conchobhair. He came afterwards to Carn-Fraich, where he plundered[3] Toirdhelbhach, son of Ruaidhri; and he proceeded at a quick pace to his house on hearing that a large army of Foreigners and Momonians, under Donnchadh Cairbrech O'Briain and Geoffroi Mareis, was coming against him, led by Aedh O'Conchobhair and Mac Diarmada. And as they did not overtake O'Neill they pursued the sons of Ruaidhri, whom they banished again to O'Neill. The Momonians killed Echmarcach Mac Branain,[4] king of Corca-Achlann, at Cill-Cellaigh, on this expedition, after driving the sons of Ruaidhri out of Connacht. The Foreigners and Momonians attacked Termann-Caelfhinn; and a slaughter of the Foreigners was committed through the miracles o Caelfhinn. A great mortality of people this year. The

Ruaidhri, was made king there," which appears the more correct, inasmuch as the object of Aedh O'Neill's journey was to support the sons of Ruaidhri O'Conchobhair. The text

should probably read "ɼo ɼɩʒeɼταɩɼ," "he made . . . . king."

[4] *Mac Branain.* The killing of this chieftain is entered under the next year also.

T

haicle na ꝼele Ḃꞃiᵹꝺe, ocuꞅ an cꞃeaḃaꝺ ꝺa ꝺenum an
áineᵹ. ᴛaḃᵹ O hEḃꞃa ꝺo éᵹ in bliaꝺain ꞅin.

Ιᴄᴛ. Enaiꞃ [.ıııı.ꝼ.], ocuꞅ .u. bliaꝺna .ᴄᴄ. aꞃ ꝺa céꝺ,
aꞃ mile, aoiꞅ in ᴛiᵹeꞃna. ꝼelim O Concubaiꞃ ꝺo ᵹabail
ᴛiᵹe aꞃ ꝺoṁnall O ꝼlaiᵹbeꞃᴛuiᵹ, ᵹuꞃ maꞃḃ ocuꞅ ᵹuꞃ
loiꞅc e ꝼein ocuꞅ a bꞃaᵹaiꞃ. Ced mac hi ꝼlaiᵹbeꞃᴛuiᵹ
ꝺo ᵹabail ꝺo Ceꝺ .h. Concubaiꞃ, ocuꞅ a ᵹabaiꞃᴛ a láiṁ
ᵹall. ᴛiᵹeꞃnan mac Caᵹuil i Concubaiꞃ ꝺo ṁaꞃbaꝺ
le ꝺonnchaꝺ Ua n'ꝺuḃꝺa. Caiꞃlén Cille moiꞃe ꝺo
bꞃiꞅeꝺ le Caᵹal O Raiᵹilliᵹ. Muiꞃᵹeꞅ mac ꝺiaꞃmaꝺa
ꝺo maꞃbaꝺ. Cṁláoiḃ O ḃeollain, aiꞃcinneᵹ ꝺꞃoma
cliaḃ, ꞃái einiᵹ ocuꞅ ᴛiᵹe aoiꝺeꝺ Eiꞃenn, ꝺo éᵹ an
bliaꝺain ꞅin. h.Maoilbꞃénuinn, ab mainiꞅꝺꞃeᵹ ḃúille,
ꝺo éᵹ ꝺo cuꞃlinn. Coṁeꞃᵹe cocᵹa ꝺéiꞃᵹe iꞅ in bliaꝺain
ꞅi la ᴛoiꞃꞃꝺelḃaᵹ mac Ruaiꝺꞃi mic ᴛoiꞃꞃꝺelḃaiᵹ
moiꞃ, ocuꞅ le hCeꝺ mac Ruaiꝺꞃi, ꞃí [Connachᴛ], ocuꞅ
le hCeꝺ O Neill, ꝺo coꞃnum cuiciꝺ Connaᵹᴛ ꞃe hCeꝺ
mac Caᵹuil cꞃoibꝺeꞃᵹ, ᴛꞃe ꝼoꞃconᵹꞃa ꝺuinn oiᵹ meᵹ
Oiꞃeaᵹᴛuiᵹ, ꞃiᵹ ᴛáoiꞃiᵹ Sil Muiꞃeꝺuiᵹ, a nꝺiᵹuil a
ꞃeꝼuinn ocuꞅ a aiciꝺeaᵹᴛa ꝺo buain ꝺe ; ocuꞅ ó ꞃo
impa ꞃum ꞃo impaꝺaꞃ Connachᴛaiᵹ, .i. Sil Muiꞃeꝺhaiᵹ,
ocuꞅ iaꞃᴛaꞃ Connaᵹᴛ um Ceꝺ O ꝼlaiᵹbeꞃᴛuiᵹ, ꞃi iaꞃᴛaꞃ
Connachᴛ. Ciꝺ ᴛꞃá aᵹᴛ, ᴛainic Ceꝺ O Neill leo ᵹo láꞃ
ꞃil Muiꞃeꝺhaiᵹ, ocuꞅ ꞃo ꞃíᵹeꝺaꞃ annꞅin ᴛoiꞃꞃꝺelḃaᵹ
mac Ruaiꝺꞃi, ocuꞅ ꝺo imᴛiᵹ Oeꝺ .h. Neill ꝺia ᴛiᵹ, uaiꞃ
ꞃo ba ᴛaiꞃiꞅi le macaiḃ Ruaiꝺꞃi a naiꞃeᵹ ꝼein aꞃ na
ᵹcuiꞃeꝺ ꝺo ᵹaᵹ oen ꞃo leiᵹ ꝺiḃ, aᵹᴛmaꝺ Coꞃmac mac
ᴛomalᴛaiᵹ na Caiꞃꞃᵹe mic ꝺiaꞃmaꝺa, ocuꞅ ꝺáuiꝺ Ua
ꝼloinn, ocuꞅ aeꞃ ᵹꞃáꝺa aꞃᵹena. ꝺala, imoꞃꞃo, Ceꝺa
mic Caᵹail cꞃoibꝺeꞃᵹ, ꝺo ᵹuaiꝺ a nuᵹᴛ ᵹall, ocuꞅ ꝺo

---

1 *At the same time*; i.e. when the
corn was in process of being reaped.

2 *Year.* At the end of this entry the
scribe who copied this portion of the
MS. has added the note "Meꞃe ꝺuḃ-
ᴛhach qui ꞃcꞃibꞃiᴛᴛ (sic)," "I am
Dubhthach qui scripsit." See Introduction.

3 *King.* Aedh (or Hugh) O'Conor,
son of Ruaidhri, was not at this time
king of Connacht; the sovereignty
having been first assumed by him in
the year 1228, "by the election of the
Justiciary and chiefs of Connacht, in
preference to Turlough, his elder
brother," as the Four Masters observe.

corn was reaped immediately after the festival of Brigid; and the ploughing was going on at the same time.[1] Tadhg O'hEghra died this year.[2]

The kalends of January [on the 4th feria], and the age of the Lord twenty-five years, and two hundred, and a thousand. Felim O'Conchobhair captured a house against Domhnall O'Flaithbhertaigh, and killed and burned himself and his brother. Aedh, son of O'Flaithbhertaigh, was apprehended by Aedh O'Conchobhair, and delivered into the hands of the Foreigners. Tighernan, son of Cathal O'Conchobhair, was killed by Donnchadh O'Dubhda. The castle of Cill-mór was broken down by Cathal O'Raigh-illigh. Muirghes Mac Diarmada was slain. Amhlaibh O'Beollain, airchinnech of Druim-cliabh, principal upholder of the hospitality and guest-houses of Erinn, died in this year. O'Maelbhrenuinn, abbot of the monastery of Buill, died of *the opening of* a vein. A commotion of war was raised in this year by Toirdhelbhach, son of Ruaidhri, son of Toirdhelbhach Mór, and by Aedh, son of Ruaidhri, king[3] [of Connacht], and by Aedh O'Neill, to contest the province of Connacht with Aedh, son of Cathal Crobhderg, through the solicitation of Donn Og Mac Oirechtaigh, king-chieftain of Síl-Muiredhaigh, in retalia-tion for having been deprived of his land and patrimony; and when he rebelled the Connachtmen rebelled, viz.:— the Síl-Muiredhaigh, and *the men of* the West of Con-nacht, with Aedh O'Flaithbhertaigh, king of the West of Connacht. However, Aedh O'Neill came with them to the middle of Síl-Muiredhaigh; and they then made Toirdhelbhach, son of Ruaidhri, king; and Aedh O'Neill went home, because the sons of Ruaidhri preferred their own assemblies, which had been summoned by them res-pectively, with the exception of Cormac, son of Tomaltach Mac Diarmada of the Rock, and David O'Floinn, and other men of trust. As regards Aedh, son of Cathal Crobhderg, moreover; he repaired to the Foreigners,

T 2

ṗala ʒo roṫánaċ ṿoṗuṁ, uaiṗ iṗ ann ṿo ḃaṫaṗ Ʒaill
Eiṗenṿ i náṫ Luain an ṗin, a ʒcúiṗt, ocuṗ ba caṗa
ṿoṗum ʒaċ aon ṿiḃ tṗé na aṫaiṗ ocuṗ tṗeiṁiṿ ṗéin,
uaiṗ ṗo ba ṗoacmuinʒeċ tuaṗuṗṿuil eiṗiṁ ocuṗ a
aṫaiṗ ṗeiṁe ṿoiḃ. Tucṗaṁ leiṗ tṗa an Ʒiuiṗtiṗ ocuṗ
Ʒaill Eṗenn, an méṿ ṗo ba loṗ leiṗ ṿiḃ, ocuṗ ṿo eiṗiʒ
ṗóṗ leiṗ Ṿonnċaṿ Caiṗbṗeċ O Ḃṗiain co na ṗoċṗuiṿe,
ocuṗ O Maoileċluinn co na ṗoċṗuitte. Iṗ annṗin ṿo
teiċṗeṿ luċt ṁoiʒe hAei ocuṗ na Tuaṫa a Luiʒniḃ
ocuṗ a ttíṗ nAmulʒuiʒ, le a mbúaiḃ, ocuṗ ṗo ṗaʒbuit
meic Rúaiṿṗi ʒan tṗocṗaite, ʒan tinol aiṗeċta; ocuṗ ni
ṗaibe na bṗaṗṗaṿ aċt uaṫaṿ ṗíṿamnaṿ ocuṗ taoiṗiċ,
ocuṗ ʒille eċ, ocuṗ ʒille ṗṗiċeolṁa. Tanʒaṿaṗ mic
Rúaiṿṗi ṗompa ʒu Cill Cellaiʒ, beʒ ṗlúaʒ ocuṗ ṗíṿamnaṿ
maille ṗṗiú, ṿo ḃeṫ aṗ cúl a mbo ocuṗ a muinntiṗe.
Ṿo innṗuiʒ Aeṿ mac Caṫuil cṗoiḃṿeṗʒ, co na Ʒallaiḃ,
Toiṗṗṿelḃaċ mac Rúaiṿṗi maṗ aṗaibe co na taoiṗiċ-
aiḃ, ocuṗ ni moṗ ʒu ṗaiḃe aċt ʒille eaċ ocuṗ ṗoṗlúaʒ
maille ṗṗiṗ, uaiṗ ṿe ċuaiṫ Aeṿ mac Rúaiṿṗi, ocuṗ
mac Muiṗceṗtuiʒ, ocuṗ Ṿomnall Ua Ḟlaiṫḃeṗtaiʒ,
ocuṗ Tiʒeṗnan mac Caṫail, ócuṗ mic Toiṗṗṿelḃuiʒ mic
Rúaiṿṗi, ṿanacal bó ocuṗ muinntiṗe Ḟeṗʒuil i Taiṿʒ
tuʒ comluiʒe ṗṗiu; ocuṗ iṗ amluiṿ taṗla conaṿ é céṿ
Connaċtaċ ṗo bṗiṗ aṗ a comluiʒe ṗe macuiḃ Rúaiṿṗi
é; ocuṗ tuʒaṿaiṗ mac Caṫail co na Ʒallaiḃ ṿanacal a
bó ocuṗ a muinntiṗe leiṗ ina cenn ṗuṁ. Iṗ annṗin ṿo.
ṗala Ʒaill a cenṿ Toiṗṗṿelḃaiʒ mic Rúaiṿṗi. Ro
eṗiʒṗium ocuṗ a taoiṗiʒ, ocuṗ ṿo ċuiṗeṿaṗ a ṗoṗlúaʒ
ṗompa, ocuṗ tanʒaṿaṗ aṗ ʒo haluinn ʒan ṿaoine ṿo
ṁaṗbaṿ ṿiḃ; uaiṗ tainic Ṿonn oʒ maʒ Aiṗeċtuiʒ ocuṗ
Ḟlaiṫḃeṗtaċ O Ḟlannaʒáin, ocuṗ beʒan ṿon ṗút Eoʒanaċ,

---

[1] *Muirchertach.* Called Muirchertach Muimhnech, or Murtough the
Momonian, from having been fostered
in Munster. He was son to Turlough
Mór O'Conor, king of Ireland.

[2] *Cathal;* i.e. Cathal Migaran, another son of Turlough Mór O'Conor.

[3] *Oath.* By "pledging a mutual
oath" is meant entering into an
offensive and defensive treaty.

and it happened fortunately for him, as the Foreigners of Erinn were then at Ath-Luain, holding a court, and every one of them was a friend of his, for his father's sake and his own; for he and his father before him were very liberal of wages to them. He brought with him the Justiciary, and as many of the Foreigners of Erinn as he thought sufficient; and Donnchadh Cairbrech O'Briain, with his army, and O'Maelechlainn, with his army, went also with him. The people of Magh-hAei and the Tuatha fled then into Luighne and Tir-Amhalghaidh, with their cows; and the sons of Ruaidhri were left without an army, without a tribe-assemblage, there being in their company only a few royal heirs, and chieftains, and horse-boys, and attendants. The sons of Rauidhri proceeded to Cill-Cellaigh, accompanied only by a small band and a few royal heirs, to protect their cows and people. Aedh, son of Cathal Crobhderg, with his Foreigners, advanced towards Toirdhelbhach, son of Rauidhri, where he was with his chieftains; and there were hardly any others than horse-boys and a rabble along with him, for Aedh, son of Ruaidhri, and the son of Muirchertach,[1] and Domhnall O'Flaithbhertaigh, and Tighernan, son of Cathal,[2] and the sons of Toirdhelbhach son of Ruaidhri, went to protect the cows and people of Ferghal O'Taidhg, who had pledged a mutual oath[3] with them. And it so happened that he was the first Connachtman who violated his mutual oath with the sons of Ruaidhri; and he brought the son of Cathal, with his Foreigners, to protect his cows and people, in opposition to them. It was then that the Foreigners encountered Toirdhelbhach, son of Ruaidhri. He and his chieftains arose, and they placed their rabble before them, and retreated excellently without any of their men being slain; for Donn Og Mac Airechtaigh, and Flaithbhertach O'Flannagain, and a small number of the Eoghanach band[4]

---

[4] *Eoghanach band.* ρύτ Θοζαnαċ; i.e., the rout, band, or company of the Cenel-Eoghain, or people of Tir-Eogh- ain (Tyrone), descended from Eoghan, son of Niall of the Nine Hostages, monarch of Ireland in the fifth century.

ταρ α ɴéɪρ. Iρ αɴ ló ρɪɴ ᴅο ραλα ɼɪρeᵬ α ᵹceɴɴ
Eαᴄmαρcuɪᵹ mɪc Ḃραɴαɪɴ, ocuρ ρe uαᴄɦαᴅ ɼoᴄɼuɪᴄe αρ
λαρ ᴅoɪρe ᴄoɪλλe ɪᴄɪρ α mucαᵬ ocuρ α ḃú, ocuρ ᴅο
ρoɪɴe ɼuᵯ eɴᵹɴuᵯ mαɪᴄ αᵹ α ᵯαρḃαᴅ, αᴄᴄ ɪmαρcαɪᵹ
ᴅο ᴅeᵹ ᴅαoɪɴɪᵬ ᴅο ḃρeᴄ ɼαɪρ. Iρ αɴɴɼɪɴ ᴅο λeɴ Ⱥoᴅ
mαc Cαᴛɦαɪλ cρoɪᵬᴅeρᵹ, coɴα ᵹαλλαɪᵬ, mɪc Rúαɪᴅρɪ ɪɴ
αɪᴅᴄe ρɪɴ ᵹo Mílɪuc, ocuρ ᴅο ḃɪ ᴛρɪ ɦαɪᴅᴄe αɴɴρɪɴ αᵹ
αρᵹuɪɴ Luɪᵹɴe αρ ᵹαᴄ λeᴄ ɪmme. Iρ ɪɴᴅocoɴⱥɪᵹ ᴅο
ραλα ᴅⱡλα Eᴅρα ρɪɴ, ɼíᴄ ᴅο ᴅéɴαᵯ ɪαρ ɴα αρᵹuɪɴ, ᴅαρ
ceɴɴ αɴ ᵬeᵹαɪɴ ᴅο ɼαᵹḃαᴅ α Luɪᵹɴɪᵬ. Iρ αɴɴ ᴅο
ḃαᴅαρ meɪc Rúαɪᴅρɪ ocuρ α ɴᴅρuɪm ρe Loᴄ mɪc
Oρeᴅuɪᵹ α ɴᵹλɪɴᴅ ɴα Moᴄαρᴛ. Iɼɼɪ comαɪρλe ᴅο ρoɪɴe
mαc Cαᴛɦαɪλ cρoɪᵬᴅeρᵹ, ᴅuλ ocuρ ᵹoɪλλ α 'ɴᴅɪαɪᴅ ḃo ɴα
ᴛᴛuαᴄ ocuρ Sɪλ Muɪρeᴅɦɪᵹ, ocuρ cλoɪɴɴe Tomαλᴛαɪᵹ,
ɼλɪᵹe ɴαc αρ ᵹαᵬ mαc ᵹoɪλλ ρoɪme ɼɪαᵯ, .ɪ. α ɼɪᴅ
ᵹαᴅλαɪᵹ, ᵹo ɼɪαᴄᴄαᴅαρ áᴄ ᴛɪᵹe ɪɴ Meɼαɪᵹ, ocuρ ɴɪ
ɼuαραᴅαρ ḃɪoρ ɴα ḃuɴɴɼαɪᵹ ɪɼ ɪɴ ɼλɪᵹeᵬ ρɪɴ. Ꝺo
αɪρᵹeᴅαρ Cuλ Ceρɴαᴅα, ocuρ ᴛuᵹαᴅαρ ᴅɪλᵹeɴᴅ αρ
ḃuαɪᵬ ocuρ αρ ᴅαoɪɴɪᵬ αɴɴρɪɴ. Ⱥɴᴅeαᴄɦαɪᴅ ᴅɪᵬ ρɪɴ
mḃαc, ɪɴ ᵯeɪᴅ ɴαᴄ αρ ḃαɪᴅɪᴄ, ρο αɪρᵹɪᴅ ocuρ ρο ᴛαρḃuɪᴅ.
Tρuαᵹ αᵯ ρɪɴ, ᵹαcɦ oeɴ ρο ᵹαḃ ᵹu Ꝺuḃ ᴄuɴᵹα ρο ḃάɪᴅɪᴄ,
ocuρ ɪɼ αᵯλuɪᴅ ᴅο ᵹeɪᵬɪ́ ɴα cαρραɴɴά co ɴα ceɼcαɴᴅαɪᵬ
ocuρ α λάɴ ᴅο λeɴḃuɪḃ αρ ɴα mḃαᴛɦαᴅ ɪɴɴᴛα. Iɴ méɪᴛ
ᴛéρɴα ó ᵹαλλαɪᵬ ᴅο ɪmeρcɪᵬ cλoɪɴɴe Tomαλᴛαɪᵹ, ocuρ
ɴαc αρ ḃάɪᴛɦɪᵬ ᴅɪᵬ, ᴅο cɦuαɪᴅ ᴅρoɴᵹ ᴅɪᵬ α ᴛᴛíρ Ⱥᵯαλᵹαɪᴅ,
ocuρ ᴅο cɦúαɪᴅ O Ꝺuḃᴅα ɼúᴄuɪᵬ, ocuρ ɴíρ ɼαᵹuɪḃ eɴ
ḃoɪɴ αcα Ꝺαλα, ɪmoρρo, cλoɪɴɴe Rúαɪᴅρɪ, ɪɼɪ comαɪρλe
ᴅο ρoɴɼαᴅ αᵹ Loᴄ mɪc Ⱥɪρeᴅuɪᵹ, ɼcαoɪλeᴅ ɴo ᵹo
ɼᵹαoɪλᴛɪρ α ᵹoɪλλ o mαc Cαᴛɦαɪλ cρoɪᵬᴅeρᵹ, .ɪ. ᴅα mαc
Rúαɪᴅρɪ, Toɪρρᴅeλḃαᴄ ocuρ Ⱥoᴅ, ocuρ mαc Mαᵹɴuρα,
ḃcuρ Ꝺoɴɴ oᵹ, ᴅο ᴅuλ α ᵹceɴɴ ɦɪ Ḟλαᴛḃeρᴛuɪᵹ α ɼɪρ

---

1 *Mac Branain.* The death of
Echmarcach Mac Branain is entered
under the previous year also. The
words αᵹ α ᵯαρḃαᴅ, translated
"when they were killing him," actually means "at his killing."

2 *In front of.* α ɴᴅρuɪm ρe;
lit. "their back to;" MS.

3 *Foreigner.* mαc ᵹoɪλλ; lit. "son
of a foreigner."

4 *Donn Og.* Donn Og (Donn the
younger) Mac Airechtaigh, or Mageraghty.

followed them. In that day a scouting party encountered Echmarcach Mac Branain,[1] who was with a
small force in the middle of an oak wood, amongst his
pigs and his cows; and he performed great valour when
they were killing him, but a superior number of brave men
overtook him. Then Aedh, son of Cathal Crobhderg, with
his Foreigners, followed the sons of Ruaidhri that night
to Milic; and he remained there three nights, plundering
Luighne on every side. This thing was unfortunate for
O'hEghra, who had to make peace, after being plundered,
for the sake of the little that had been left in Luighne.
The sons of Ruaidhri were at this time in front of[2] Loch-
mic-Oiredhaigh in Glenn-na-Mochart. The resolution
adopted by the son of Cathal Crobhderg was to go, along
with the Foreigners, after the cows of the Tuatha, and of
Sil-Muiredhaigh, and of Clann-Tomaltaigh, by a route that
no Foreigner[3] ever took before, viz.:—into Fidh-Gadh-
laigh, until they reached Ath-tighe-in-Mesaigh; and they
received neither arrow nor dart in that route. They
plundered Cul-Cernadha, and inflicted vengeance on cows
and people there. Of those that went into the Bac,
all who were not drowned were plundered and killed.
Pity, alas! every one who went towards Dubh-Cunga
was drowned; and so the fishing weirs were found
with their baskets full of children, after being drowned
in them. Of all the droves of Clann-Tomaltaigh that
had escaped from the Foreigners, and that had not been
drowned, a number went into Tir-Amhalghaidh; and
O'Dubhda attacked them, and left not a single cow
with them. As regards the sons of Ruaidhri, moreover;
the resolution they adopted at Loch-mic-Airedhaigh
was, to disperse until his Foreigners should separate
from the son of Cathal Crobhderg, viz.:—the two sons
of Ruaidhri—Toirdhelbhach and Aedh—and the son
of Maghnus, and Donn Og,[4] were to go to meet
O'Flaithbhertaigh, their mutual ally; and the sons of

comluiġe; meιc Muιρceρτuιġ hι Concubaιρ ocuρ Τιġeρnan mac Caτhaιl το τul aρ cul a mbó ocuρ a muιnnτιρe, ocuρ ρίτ το τenum ταρ a ccenτ no ġo nιmτιġoιρ a Ġoιll ό mac Caτhaιl cρoιττeρġ.

Ϸαλα, ιmoρρo, ιn leιτe τeaρ το Connacητuιb, nιρ úαιġnιτe το, uaιρ ταnġaταρ Ġaιll Laιġen ocuρ Ϸonnchaτ (no Muιρceρτaċ) Ua Ϸριaιn ρompa. Ταnġaταρ Ġaιll Ϸeρmuman ocuρ ρeρριam Coρcaιġe ρompa maρ ιn ġceτna. Ϸo aιρġreτ ocuρ ρo maρϸρατ ceċ τen aρ a ρuġρατ. Ϸa holc la Oeτ mac Caτhaιl cρoιττeρġ a ττeċτ ριn τon τίρ, uaιρ nι he ρo ċuιρ ιaτ, aċτ το ċualaταρ a bρuaιρ an Ġιuρτίρ co na ġallaιτ τéταλαιτ, ρo ġaτ τnúτ ocuρ ρoρmaτ ιaτ. Ϸa τρuaġ, τρa, anτ olc το ceτuιġ Ϸιa τon ċúιġιτ ιρ ρeρρ το bι a nEιριnn τοιρ na τιαρ, τeρ na ċuαιτ; uaιρ nι caιcleτ ιn mac όġláeċ a ċele aġ cρeachaτ nó aġ aρġuιn achτ comaτ τρeιρι το. Ϸo cuιριτ mná, ocuρ leιmb, ocuρ όιġτιġeρn, ocuρ τρeoιn ocuρ eττρeoιn, ρe ρúachτ ocuρ ρe ġoρτα τon coġaτ ριn. Ϸαλα, ιmoρρo, Αeτα mιc Caτhaιl cρoιττeρġ, τάιnιc ρeṁe ġρ Maġ nEo, ocuρ το ċuaταρ meιc Muιρċeρτuιġ ιna ċeaċ aρ cumaιρcιτ, ocuρ aρ ρláηαιτ, ταρ cenn a mbo ocuρ a muιnnτιρe. Ϸo chúaιτ aρ na ṁáραċ ġo Cιll meτόιn, ocuρ το coṁραιceταρ na τρί ρlúαġ το Ġallaιτ annριn, ocuρ ιρ beġ naρ lan ιn τριcha uιle το na τρί ρlúαġuιτ ριn το ġallaιτ ocuρ το ġaoιτeλuιτ. Ιρ annριn τάιnιc Αeτ Ua Ϸλαιτϸeρτuιġ aρ coρuιb ocuρ aρ ρláηαιτ maιτeaτ nġall ocuρ Ϸonnchaτ Caιρbριġ ι Ϸριaιn, a caρτeρa Cρίρτ, hι τeaċ mιc Caτhaιl cρoιττeρġ ocuρ an Ġιuιρτίρ; το ριnne ρίτ ταρ cenτ a bό ocuρ a muιnnτιρe ριρ, ocuρ

<hr/>

[1] *Muirchertach O'Conchobhar*; i.e. Muirchertach Muimhnech. See note [1], p. 276.

[2] *Cathal.* Cathal Migaran. See note [2], p. 276.

[3] *More quiet.* nιρ uaιġnιτe τό; lit. "it was not more lonely."

[4] *Or Muirchertach.* The alias read-ing is correct, as appears from the Annals of Ulster, the Four Masters, and Mageoghegan's version of the Annals of Clonmacnoise.

[5] *Against them.* ρompa; lit. "before them."

[6] *Sheriff.* ρeρριam, MS.

[7] *Exposed.* το cuιριτ; lit. "were

Muirchertach O'Conchobhar,[1] and Tighernan, son of A.D.
Cathal,[2] to go to protect their cows and people, and to [1225.]
make peace for their sake, until his Foreigners should
depart from the son of Cathal Crobhderg.

As regards the southern half of Connacht, also, it was
not more quiet,[3] for the Foreigners of Laighen, and Donnchadh (or Muirchertach)[4] O'Briain, came against them.[5]
The Foreigners of Des-Mumha and the sheriff[6] of Corcach
came also against them.[5] They plundered and killed
every one whom they caught. Aedh, son of Cathal
Crobhderg disliked their coming into the district, for it
was not he who invited them ; but when they heard of all
the spoils the Justiciary with his Foreigners had obtained,
envy and jealousy seized them. Grievous, indeed, was the
misfortune God permitted to *fall on* the best province
in Erinn, east or west, south or north ; for the young man
would not spare his companion, in preying or in plundering,
provided that he was the stronger. Women and children,
and young lords, and the mighty and the weak, were
exposed[7] to cold and famine through this war. As to
Aedh, son of Cathal Crobhderg, however ; he advanced to
Magh-nEó, and the sons of Muirchertach[1] went into his
house,[8] under conditions and guarantees, for the sake of
their cows and people. He went on the morrow to Cill-
medhoin, and the three armies of Foreigners met there ;
and the entire cantred was nearly filled with these three
armies of Foreigners and Gaeidhel. It was then that Aedh
O'Flaithbhertaigh came, on the covenants and guarantees
of the nobles of the Foreigners, and of Donnchadh
Cairbrech O'Briain, his gossip,[9] into the house[8] of the son
of Cathal Crobhderg and the Justiciary, made peace with
him for the sake of his cows and people, and *engaged*

---

put." The same expression is incor-
rectly translated "perished" by Dr.
O'Donovan, in his ed. of the Four
Mast., ad eund. an.

   [8] *House.* The expression "going

into one's house" is used to signify
making "submission."

   [9] *Gossip.* A person who stands
sponsor to the child of another is still
called the "gossip" of the child's father.

meic Ruaiḋri ḋo iηηαρḃα uaḋ.   Ḋo imτiʒ mac Caṫail
cροiḃḋeρʒ co ηα ʒallaiḃ ʒu Ṫuaim ḋa ʒ́ualaηη, ocuρ ḋo
leiʒ imτecḣτ ḋo ʒallaiḃ laiʒeη ocuρ Ḋeρmumaη uaḋ,
ocuρ ḋo ḃí a ḋál ḟeiη ḋo ρḋlucaḋ iη ʒiuιρτίρ ταρ áṫ luaiη.
Ḋo ρoiηeρiṁ comaiρli aile aηηρiη, .i. impoḋ ḋoċum 1
Ḟlaiṫḃeρτuiʒ aρ cula, uaiρ ηiρ ṫaiρiρi leiρ maρ ḋo
ρáʒuiḃ é; uaiρ ḋo ḃaḋaρ meic Ruaiḋri alla aηiaρ ḋo
loċ aiʒe, ocuρ a cliamaiη ḟeiη, .i. Ḋoηη oʒ, máille ḟριu.
1ρ aηηρiη ρo ḋeiliʒ meic Maʒηuρa ρe macuiḃ Ruaiḋri,
ocuρ ḋo ċuaταρ a τoiρ ηαcmulʒαḋ aρ ceηη a mbo ocuρ
a muiηητiρe, ocuρ ρuaραḋαρ iατ ʒu ρoḋáηαċ, caη iuραḋ
caη aρʒuiη, ocuρ ρuʒρατ leo iατ a ηucḣτ 1 Ruaiρc, ocuρ
ḋo ρoηρατ cρeicḣ moiρ aρ Pḣilip mac ʒoiρḋealbḣ.
Ḋoηcḣαḋ Caiρbρecḣ, imoρρo, ḋo cuiρ maiṫe a muiη-
τiρe, ocuρ a oeρa ʒράḋα, ρeiṁe co ηéḋáluiḃ móρa.
Ḋo cuaḋ Oeḋ mac Ruaiḋri ocuρ Eoʒaη Ua ḣeiḋiη a
ciηḋ uρτaρρηα, uaṫaḋ ḋo ḋeʒ ḋaoiηiḃ, ocuρ ηiρ ḣaηaḋ
aηηρiη aʒ Muimηecḣaíb ρe ḣuραḋ meic iη aiρḋ ρíʒ,
ocuρ ḋo luiḋριṁ oρρa, ocuρ ḋo ʒaḃ aoρ ʒράḋα Ḋoηηcḣαḋα
Caiρbρicḣ, ocuρ ba τρom ηa ḣeḋala ḋo ρaʒḃuiτ aηηρiη
aʒ Oeḋ mac Rúaiḋri.   1ρ aηηρiη ḋo cḣuaiḋ Ḋoηηcḣαḋ
Caiρbρecḣ ḋá ṫiʒ, ocuρ ḋo ρiηηe ρíṫ ocuρ baiττe
coiηηell ρe ḣaccḋ mac Rúaiḋri, ocuρ ḋo ʒeall ʒaη
τoiʒecḣτ aηaʒ́haiḋ mic Rúaiḋri aρíρ, ḋαρ ceηḋ a
oeρa ʒράḋα ḋo léiʒeη aρ; ocuρ ηíρ comaillριṁ ριη,
uaiρ τáηic aρ iη ρluaiʒeḋ ρa ηeρa a céḋoiρ aηaʒ́haiḋ
mic Rúaiḋri.   1ρ aηηρiη, τρa, ταiηic mac Caṫail
cροiḃḋeρc ocuρ iη 1úρτιρ ʒu calaḋ 1ηηρι Cρeṁa, ταρeiρ
ʒall laiʒeη ocuρ Mumaη ḋimṫecḣτ, ocuρ ḋob eiʒeη
ḋu Ḟlaiṫḃeρτuiʒ 1ηιρ Cρeṁa ocuρ Oilen ηa ciρce, ocuρ
aρτραiʒe iη loċa aρíρ, ḋo ταḃaιρτ aρ ceηη a bo ocuρ a

---

¹ *The lake*; i.e. Loch Corrib.

² *Drowning of candles.* Instead of
the expression "ḋo ρiηηe ρíṫ 7
baiττe coiηηell," the Four Masters, who give these events under

the year 1225, say "ʒo ηḋeaρηa
ρíṫ báiττe coiηḋel," "made a
peace of drowning of candles;" i.e.
a peace solemnized by the drowning
of candles, or one the violation of

to banish the sons of Ruaidhri from him. The son of Cathal Crobhderg went with his Foreigners to Tuaim-da-ghualann, and permitted the Foreigners of Laighen and Des-Mumha to depart from him; and it was his own duty to escort the Justiciary across Ath-Luain. He adopted another resolution then, viz.:—to turn back towards O'Flaithbhertaigh; for he liked not the way in which he left him, as the sons of Ruaidhri were at the west side of the lake[1] with him, and his own son-in-law, i.e. Donn Og, along with them. Then the sons of Maghnus separated from the sons of Ruaidhri, and went into Tir-Amhalghaidh in quest of their cows and people, and found them there, happily, without being plundered or molested; and they carried them with them under the protection of O'Ruairc; and they committed a great depredation on Philip Mac Goisdelbh. Donnchadh Cairbrech, moreover, sent the nobles of his people, and his men of trust, on before him with great spoils. Aedh, son of Ruaidhri, and Eoghan O'hEidhin intercepted them with a small band; and the Momonians awaited not the attack of the son of the chief king; but he went after them and captured the men of trust of Donnchadh Cairbrech; and heavy were the spoils left with Aedh, son of Ruaidhri. Then Donnchadh Cairbrech went home, and made peace and "drowning of candles"[2] with Aedh, son of Ruaidhri; and he promised that he would not again go against the son of Ruaidhri, in return for the release of his men of trust; but he kept not this, for he came immediately on the next hosting against the son of Ruaidhri. It was then, moreover, that the son of Cathal Crobhderg and the Justiciary came to the port of Inis-cremha, after the Foreigners of Laighen and Mumha had departed; and O'Flaithbhertaigh was obliged to give Inis-cremha, and Oilen-na-circe, and also the boats of the lake, for the sake of his cows and people. Aedh,

---

which would involve the terrors of excommunication, of which cere- | mony the extinguishing of candles formed a part.

muinntipe. Tánic Oeð mac Cαthαil cpoiðvepc apíp ʒu
Tuαim vα ʒúαlαnn, ocuf vo chuαiv peiṁe vo iðlucαv
αn lúiptíp, ocuf vo fαʒbαv uαthαv vo ṁαithib ʒαll,
ocuf peippéαnuiʒ imðα αiʒe, uαip nip ταifipi leif
Connαchτuiʒ, αchτmαv uαthαv viʒ. Tuʒfum αnnfin
mαiðe αn αipeðτα illαiṁ ʒαll α nʒill pe ττúαpufvul,
.i. flαiτbepταch .h. flαnnαʒαin ocuf fepʒαl .h. Tαiðʒ,
ocuf pochαive αile vo Connαchτuiʒ; ocuf if vαib pein
vob eiʒen α bpuαfluʒαv. If αnv fin vo eipiʒh Uα
flαiτhbepτuiʒ apíp, ocuf mic Muipcepταiʒ ocuf nα
piʒvαmnα αpchenα, vocum mic Ruαiðpi, ταpéif α ʒαll
vimτeðτ o αoð mαc Cαthuil cpoiðvepc; ocuf vo cuip
Oév τechτα ocuf pepibenvα vinnpαiʒev ʒαll, vo innfin
in αthimpáið, ocuf viαppαv τuilleαð pofpuive. Do
fpeccpαv co poinnib eipium, uαip fα τuillmech vo ʒαll-
loib nα τupuif fin; vo ʒeiðτíp éταlα, ocuf ní fαʒvαif ʒáv
nα himefαpcαin. Tucαv ʒαll Lαiʒen ocuf Vepmumαn
vopum von vulα fin fα Uilliαm Cpαf ocuf fα mαcuib
ʒpifin, pochαive mop; ocuf o ταnʒαvαp vinnpαiʒev
mic Cαthαil cpoiðvepʒ τáinic ταp τochαp αnoif, ocuf
vo ʒαð peiṁe fúαf mαp α ʒcúαlα meic Ruαiðpi vo beiτ,
.i. α niʒ Viαpmαvα, ʒαn pochαive, ʒαn luchτ comluiʒe
vo pochτuin ðucα. If αnnfin vo ðuip αov mαc Cαthαil
cpoiðvepʒ félim, α bpαthαip, ocuf mαiðe vα muinnτep
vo ʒαll feippénchαib, αp cpeið Θoʒαin 1 Θiðin α niʒ
fiαcpαð αiðne, ocuf vo báταp α τiʒ Lonʒpuipτ α nαpv
pαðuin αp ðí nα cpeiðe moð τpáð αp nα ṁápαð. Do ðuαlα
O flαiτhpepτuiʒ ocuf meic Muipcepτuiʒ, ocuf fiατ αʒ

---

¹ *Mercenaries.* feipféαnuiʒ. The
Four Masters (1225) employ the term
feinnuð, "soldiers."

² *William Cras.* The form of the
name in the Four Mast. is ccpαf,
which is the same as ʒpαf, Gras.
"Cras, or Gras, was the sobriquet of
Raymond le Gros, and afterwards
became a family name, which is now

always incorrectly written Grace. It
is derived from the French *gras*, or
gros." O'Donovan, *Four Mast.*, A.D.
1225, note ^m.

³ *The Tochar*; i.e. the causeway.
The full form of the name is Tochar-
mona-Coinnedha, "the causeway of
the moor (or bog) of Coinnidh." It
is situated in the parish of Temple-

son of Cathal Crobhderg, went again to Tuaim-da-ghualann, and proceeded on to escort the Justiciary; and a few of the chiefs of the Foreigners, and many mercenaries,[1] were left with him, for he liked not the Connachtmen with the exception of a few of them. He then delivered the nobles of the community into the hands of the Foreigners, as a pledge for wages, viz.:—Flaithbhertach O'Flannagain, and Ferghal O'Taidhg and many more of the Connachtmen, who were obliged to release themselves. It was then that O'Flaithbhertaigh and the sons of Muirchertach, and the other royal heirs, went again to the son of Ruaidhri, after the Foreigners had departed from Aedh, son of Cathal Crobhderg; and Aedh despatched messengers and writings to the Foreigners, announcing the revolt, and requesting additional forces. He was cheerfully responded to; for these expeditions were profitable to the Foreigners, who used to obtain spoils, and used not to encounter danger or conflict. The Foreigners of Laighen and Des-Mumha were furnished to him on this occasion, in great force, under William Cras[2] and the sons of Griffin; and when they came towards the son of Cathal Crobhderg, he came from the east across Tochar,[3] and proceeded on southwards to where he heard the sons of Ruaidhri were, (viz.:—in Ui-Diarmada), without an army, without allies having arrived to them. Then Aedh, son of Cathal Crobhderg, sent his brother Felim and the chiefs of his people, with Foreign mercenaries, to plunder Eoghan O'hEidhin in Ui-Fiachrach-Aidhne; and they were in a house-camp[4] at Ard-rathain, with a view to committing the depredation early on the morrow. O'Flaithbhertaigh and the sons of Muirchertach, as they

---

togher ("church of Tochar,") barony of Ballimoe, and county of Galway.

[4] *In a house-camp.* α τιγ Longpuirc. Probably a camp established around some houses. The Four Mast.

(1225) say αὀαιγ Longpuirc, "a night camp." The word Longpopc, translated camp, is also explained "castrum." See Stokes's *Irish Glosses*, Dublin, 1860; p. 24.

innraigeo meic Ruaiópi, Ʒaill oo oul ap cpeich oo cum
Eoʒain 1 Eiỗin a pip comluiʒe, ocup a mbeᵹ a nꞒpo
pathuin. 1p 1 comaiple oo pónpaᵹ innraigeo Ꞓpoa
paᵹuin, ocup oul a ʒcenn Ʒall ipin maicin moᵹ cpaᵹ ap
na ᵹapaᵹ, ocup in baile oo lopcaỗ ina ʒceno. Ꝺo
innraigeoap co maicin, ʒu pabuᵹap moᵹ cpáᵹ ap paicᵹe
an baile. 1p hi comaiple oo ponpao, Cuaᵹal mac
Muipcepcuiʒ ocup a nʒaill oo ᵹup ap cúp oon baile,
ocup an neaᵹ oo pipᵹeỗ oo Ʒaoioeluiỗ map aon pip;
Ua Flaᵹbepcuiʒ ocup mec Muipcepcuiʒ um an mbaile
amuiʒ. 1p laioip, oana, oo cóp ipin mbaile annpin.
1p he Ʒaoioeal oo ppeʒaip mapóen pe Cuaᵹal .i.
Caiᵹleᵹ mac Ꞓoỗa 1 Ꝺuỗoa; ocup o oo cuaoap co
mepỗana ipin baile oo ceiᵹeoap Ʒoill poip píap ap in
mbaile, ocup in maiỗm paip ap ʒallaib. Na Ʒaill oo
cuaᵹap píap a maiỗm ap in mbaile ip iac cuʒ in maiỗm
ap a paibe oo Ʒaoioeluiỗ ap cul an baile. Ni paib
Ʒaoioel buo beooa ina in lucht ap a cuccao in maiỗm
pin píap, acht nachap ᵹecaiʒ Ꝺia pooán oppa. 1n opong
oo cuaᵹup paip oo len Cuaᵹal ocup Caiᵹlech .h.
Ꝺuỗoa iao; oo cecloic Cuaᵹal conp[o]upla na nʒall,
ocup oo choic pe la Caiᵹlech. ba pooan mop oo
macaib Ruaiỗpi can beᵹ ipin maiỗm pin. 1p oon
maiỗm pin píap oo mapbao Maᵹʒaᵹain, mac Oéoa,
mic Conchobaip Maenmaiʒe, ocup mac Ʒillicpipᵹ mic
Ꝺiapmaoa, ocup mac mic Ꞓmlaib mic Ꞓipechcaiʒ, ocup
Niall mac Fepʒail .h. Caioʒ; ocup po mapbao in ci
po mapb é .i. bpathaip Culen .h. Ꝺimupaiʒ.

Ꝺala meic Ruaiỗpi, po compuiceoap ap na ᵹapaᵹ pi

1 *The sons of Ruaidhri;* who were at this time in Ui-Diarmada, as already explained.

2 *Him;* i.e. Niall, son of Ferghal O'Taidhg.

3 *O'Dimusaigh.* After this name (which is now commonly written, as pronounced, O'Dempsey, or Dempsey without the O'), the scribe of this portion of the MS. has added the observation, (at the end of fol. 68, b.), "bíỗ pin aʒaᵹ a Ꝺuỗᵹaiʒ o Conaipi mac Muipip;' i.e. "have that O'Dubhthach, from Conairi, son of Maurice." The Dubhthach addressed was one of the learned family of O'Duigenan of

were marching to the sons of Ruaidhri, heard of the
Foreigners having gone on a plundering expedition to
Eoghan O'hEidhin, and of their being at Ard-rathain.
The resolution they adopted was to march towards Ard-
rathain, and to attack the Foreigners early the next morning,
and to burn the town against them.   They marched until
morning, and were early on the green of the town, when
they determined to send first to the town Tuathal, son of
Muirchertach, and their Foreigners, and whomsoever of
the Gaeidhel would desire to go with him—O'Flaithbhertaigh and the *other* sons of Muirchertach remaining
outside the town.   Bravely, indeed, was the town then entered.   The Gaeidhel who offered to go with Tuathal was
Taichlech, son of Aedh O'Dubhda.   And when they went
boldly into the town the Foreigners fled eastwards and
westwards out of the town; and the Foreigners were
driven in rout eastwards.   The Foreigners who fled
westwards out of the town inflicted a defeat on those
of the Gaeidhel who were in the rear of the town.   There
were no Gaeidhel more vigorous than the company on
whom this defeat westwards was inflicted; but God did
not grant that good fortune should attend them.   Tuathal
and Taichlech O'Dubhda pursued the party that went
eastwards; and Tuathal first wounded the constable of
the Foreigners, who fell by Taichlech.   It was very fortunate for the sons[1] of Ruaidhri that they were not in this
defeat.   It was in this defeat westwards that Mathghamhain,
son of Aedh, son of Conchobhar Maenmhaighe, and the
son of Gillachrist Mac Diarmada, and the grandson of
Amhlaibh Mac Airechtaigh, and Niall, son of Ferghal
O'Taidhg, were slain; and the person who slew him[2] was
killed, viz.:—the brother of Culen O'Dimusaigh.[3]

As regards the sons of Ruaidhri: they met on the

Kilronan, for some account of whom
see the Introduction.   "Conairi (or
Conaire) son of Maurice," the writer
of the note, seems to have been another
member of the same industrious family
of Irish scholars and historians.

.h. Flaichbepcuiż ocup pe macuiḃ Muipcepcuiż, ocup
pe Cizepnan mac Conchobaip, ocup pe Oonn óż, ocup
canzaoap pompa aneap zo Opuim Cenannain. Ir
annpin cainic Αοο mac Cachail cpoiboepc cona żalloiḃ
ina noeżhaio. Ir hi comaiple oo pónao aca cec neach
oiḃ oo innpaizeo a ḃó ocup a muincipe, ocup meic
Rúaiopi opáżbáil. Canzaoap meic Rúaiopi ap in cíp,
uaip ni paḃucap żaill na pocpaice acca a ppaipe; ocup
oo chúaio Oonn apír a nucht Αοḃa 1 Néill. Ocup níp
páp oonc pluaizeo pin oaibpiṁ acht an cip ir pepp oo
ḃi a nEipinn oo lot ocup oo milleo cpeampa. Oala,
imoppo, Αeḃa mic Cachail cpoiboepc, oo innpuiż .h.
Flaichḃepcaiż, ocup tuc żeill ocup bpaizoe uaoa oon
oulaḃ pin. Cainic poime anúap zu Cill meooin, ocup
zu Maż nEo, anoiaio meic Muipcepcuiż ocup Cizepnain,
ocup oo ponpao píc oap cenn a mbó ocup a muinncipe,
ocup oo cuacap a cech Oeḃa mic Cachail cpoiboepc ap
planaizecc Oonnchaoa Caipbpiż ocup maiti na nżall.
Ir cumpanaḃ panzup a leap pin, uaip ni paiḃe ceall na
cuaic zan ṁilleo in la pin a Connachcuiḃ.

Iap naipzniḃ, ocup iap mapbao bo in cipe ocup a
oaoine, ocup ap cup caic uile pe púachc ocup pe żopca,
oo páp ceioṁ mop żaluip ipin cip uile, .i. cenel ceapca
cpépa bpolṁuizce na baileḃa zan ouine beo opacbail
innciḃ, ocup oo epnacíp apaile oon ceioṁ pin, ocup ba
úachao. Flann mac Aṁlaoiḃ 1 Fhallumain, caipec
clainne hUacaċ, oo ṁapbao le Felim macCachail cpoib-
oepz pan čożao pin. Aṁlaoib mac Fepčuip 1 Fhallu-
ṁain, caoipec a oúčcupa ir pepp cainic pe haimpep im-
cein, oo ez, ocup a mac oo ṁapbao an aon ṁí, .i. in
Flann peṁpáicce. Caḋż O Finnachta, pep zpaoa oOeḃ

---

1 *With.* pup for pu, MS.

2 *Muirchertach;* i.e. Muirchertach
Muimhnech, or Murtough the Mo-
monian, son of Turlough Mór O'Conor.
See note 1, p. 276, *supra.*

3 *Son of Conchobhar.* The Four

Mast. say "son of Cathal;" i.e. of
Cathal Migaran, a younger brother of
Cathal Crobhderg. See note 2, p. 276.

4 *Went into the house.* By this
expression is implied that they submitted to Aedh.

morrow with[1] O'Flaithbhertaigh, and with the sons of Muirchertach,[2] and with Tighernan, son of Conchobhar,[3] and with Donn Og; and they proceeded on from the south to Druim-Cenannain. It was then Aedh, son of Cathal Crobhderg, with his Foreigners, went in pursuit of them. The resolution they adopted was—each of them to go towards his cows and his people, and to abandon the sons of Ruaidhri. The sons of Ruaidhri went out of the district, as they had no Foreigners or forces in readiness, and Donn went again under the protection of Aedh O'Neill; and there resulted nothing to them from this hosting but that the best territory in Erinn was injured and destroyed through them. Regarding Aedh, son of Cathal Crobhderg, however; he went to O'Flaithbhertaigh, and brought pledges and hostages from him on this occasion. He proceeded downwards to Cill-medhoin, and to Magh-Eo, in pursuit of the sons of Muirchertach,[2] and of Tighernan; and they made peace for the sake of their cows and people, and went into the house[4] of Aedh, son of Cathal Crobhderg, under the guarantee of Donnchadh Cairbrech and the chiefs of the Foreigners. This was a necessary tranquility, for there was not a church or territory in Connacht on that day without being destroyed.

After plunderings; and after killing the cows and people of the country, and exposing every one to cold and famine, a great plague prevailed in the whole district, viz.:—a species of fever, by which the towns used to be emptied, without a living man being left in them; and some would recover from this plague, but they were few. Flann, son of Amhlaibh O'Fallamhain, chieftain of Clann-Uatach, was slain by Felim, son of Cathal Crobhderg, in that war. Amhlaibh, son of Ferchar O'Fallamhain, the best chieftain of his nation that had come for a long time, died; and his son was slain in the same month, viz.:—the aforesaid Flann. Tadhg O'Finnachta, a man of trust to Aedh, son of

U

mac Rúaiḋpi, ꝺo maṗbaꝺ le muinnṫep mic Ꝺoꝺaȝain
aṗ ṗpeẜ cpeiᴄe pin coȝaꝺ ceꝺna. Muiṗeꝺaᴄ .h.
Finnachᴛa, ᴛáipech cloinne Finnachᴛa, no Muṗchaꝺa,
ꝺo éȝ a naṗᴛṗach aṗ Loᴄ Oiṗbpin, ocuṗ ṗe ṗlán aȝ ꝺul
inᴛe. Moelbpiȝꝺe .h. Maicin, aṗ Copuiṗ Paᴛpaic, in
Cpiṗᴛo quieuiᴛ; mac oiȝe ocuṗ ecnaiꝺ; ocuṗ iṗ leiṗ ṗo
ᴛinnṗcnaꝺ ᴛempoll Copuiṗ Paᴛpaic, ocuṗ ṗo ṗopbaꝺ a
ṗanᴛoiṗ ocuṗ a cpiceꝺa co moṗ ṗoéᴛṗaᴄ, in onoip
Paᴛpaic, ocuṗ Muiṗe, ocuṗ Eoin appuil.

M.cc.xx.ui. Kt. Enaip aṗ ꝺapꝺaoin, ocuṗ .ix.xx. ṗuippe.
Ꝺomnall mac Rúaiꝺpi hi Fhlaiᴄbepᴛuiȝ ꝺo ṁaṗbaꝺ ꝺo
maᴄuiꝺ Muiṗcepᴛaiȝ hi Flaiᴄbepᴛuiȝ, aṗ nȝabáil ᴛiȝe
ṗaiṗ. Cpuaȝ, ᴛpa, in ȝnim ꝺo ṗonaꝺ annṗin, aꝺbuṗ ṗiȝ
iapᴛhaiṗ Connachᴛ ꝺo maṗbaꝺ, ȝan ᴛiṗ ȝan ꝺúᴛᴄuṗ
ꝺṗaȝḃáil ᴛaṗ a cenꝺ. Ciȝepnan, mac Conchobaiṗ, mic
Caᴛháil Miȝapan .h. Conchobaiṗ, ꝺo maṗbaꝺ le
Ꝺonnchaꝺ Ua n'Ouꝺꝺa, ocuṗ la a maᴄuiꝺ; ṗíꝺamna iṗ
mo einech ocuṗ enȝnuṃ ᴛáinic ꝺo cloinn Conchobaiṗ,
ocuṗ iṗ mó ꝺo ṗoine ꝺo neiᴄiꝺ ṗiaᴄᴄinᴛa ṗoꝺanaᴄa.
Feṗȝul .h. Caiꝺȝ, ꝺux lochᴛa ᴛiȝe Caᴛháil cpoibꝺeṗȝ
ocuṗ a mic na ꝺiaiꝺ, ꝺo ṁaṗbaꝺ le Ꝺonnṗlebe .h.
nȝaꝺṗa; ṗeṗ apꝺ ṗaiᴄ moiṗ, ocuṗ ṗiṗi mo ꝺo ᴛuiᴛ
ꝺa eaṗcaiṗꝺiꝺ. Αeꝺ mac Ꝺuinnṗléiꝺe i Shoᴄlaᴄain,
aipcinneaᴄ Cunȝa, ṗai cannᴛaiṗechᴛa ocuṗ cpoᴛȝleṗa,
maṗoen ṗe ȝleṗ ꝺo ꝺenum ꝺo ṗein naᴄ ꝺeṗnaꝺ ṗeṁe,
ocuṗ ba ṗai in ȝac ceiṗꝺ, iꝺiṗ ꝺan ocuṗ ȝṗiꝺꝺaᴄᴄ ocuṗ
ṗcṗiꝺenꝺ, ocuṗ aṗ ȝach nealaꝺuin ꝺo niꝺ ꝺuine, ꝺo éȝ
an bliaꝺain ṗin. Núalaꝺ inȝen Rúaiꝺpi hi Conchobaiṗ,
banṗiȝan Ulaꝺ, ꝺo éȝ a Cunȝa Fheiᴄin, ocuṗ a haꝺlucaꝺ

---

[1] *Clann-Murchadha.* This was the
tribe name of a branch of the once
powerful sept of O'Finaghty, who
were seated on the eastern side of the
river Suck, in the county of Galway.

[2] M.cc.xvi. The MS. has m.cc.xx.u.
(1225), which is so apparent an error
that the liberty has been taken of
correcting it. The mistake here committed by the scribe has been repeated
at the years 1227, 8, and 9.

[3] *Future king.* The words αꝺbuṗ
ṗiȝ signify literally "materies regis."

[4] *Son of Conchobhar.* Tighernan is
also called "son of Conchobhar" under

A.D.
[1225.]

Ruaidhri, was killed by the people of Mac Aedhagain, while on a scouting party in the same war. Muiredhach O'Fmnachta, chieftain of Clann-Finnachta (or *Clann-Murchadha*),[1] died in a vessel on Loch-Oirbsen; and he was quite well when going into it. Maelbrighde O'Maicin, abbot of Tobur-Patraic, in Christo quievit. *He was* a virgin and sage; and it was by him the church of Tobur-Patraic was begun, and its sanctuary and crosses were diligently finished, in honour of Patrick, and Mary, and the Apostle John.

[1226.]

M.cc.xxvi.[2] The kalends of January on Thursday, and the 29th of the moon. Domhnall, son of Ruaidhri O'Flaithbhertaigh, was slain by the sons of Muirchertach O'Flaithbhertaigh, after capturing a house against him. Pity, alas! the deed that was there committed—the killing of a future king[3] of the West of Connacht, without obtaining land or patrimony thereby. Tighernan, son of Conchobhar,[4] son of Cathal Migaran O'Conchobhair, the royal heir of greatest honour and bravery that came of the sons of Conchobhar, and who performed the most renowned, successful exploits, was killed by Donnchadh O'Dubhda and his sons. Ferghal O'Taidhg, dux of the household of Cathal Crobhderg, and of that of his son after him—a man of great prosperity, and by whom his enemies fell in greatest numbers—was slain by Donnsleibhe O'Gadhra. Aedh, son of Donnsleibhe O'Sochlachain, airchinnech of Cunga, a professor of singing, and of harp-making—who made, besides, an instrument for himself, the like of which had never been made before, and who was distinguished in every art, both in poetry and engraving, and writing, and in every science that a man could exercise—died in this year. Nualadh, daughter of Ruaidhri O'Conchobhair, queen of Uladh, died at Cunga-Feichin, and was interred in the Canons' church of

the year 1224; but the Four Masters say that he was son of Cathal Migaran, who was the son of Turlough Mór O'Conor, and consequently the brother of king Ruaidhri, and of Cathal Crobhderg.

U 2

α ττempall canánach Cunʒa. Ccѣ .h. ꝑlaiѣberταiʒ το ʒabáil το Ccѣ mac Caτhail croibτerʒ, ocur a ταbairτ illaim ʒall. Muirʒer mac Όiarmaτα το marbaѣ. Cairlen Cille moire το brireѣ le Caτhal .h. Raiʒilliʒ.

m.cc.xx.uii. Ḱτ. Enair ꝼor Ccine, ocur τѣmaτ uaτhaτ ꝼuirre. Cuirττ το τenuṁ το Ʒallaib Ccѣa cliaѣ occur Erenn α nCcѣ cliaѣ, occur Ccѣ mac Caτail croibτerʒ το ʒairm ꝼuirre, occur ꝼell ꝼair ꝼorran cuirττ rin, no ʒo ταnaic Uilliam Maꝑurccal, a ꝼer carατραiѣ ꝼein, cona rocraiττe, ar lar na cúirττe, ʒo riʒ lair ar éicin erτi amaѣ hé, ocur ro τѣlaic iomlan τia τir ꝼein. Όála Ccѣa mic Caτhail croibτerʒ, ar a haiѣli rin το ꝛone conne ic Laταiʒ ѣaeiѣ τuaiѣѣil ꝛe hUilliam Maiꝛéir, mac Serꝛaiѣ, ocur ní τechaiτ riṁ ταr Laτhach anonn achτmaѣ uaτhaτ beʒ .i. Cormac mac Tomalταiʒ na Cairʒe mic Όiarmuτa, ocur Όiarmaiτ mac Maʒnura, ocur Maʒnur mac Muirѣerταiʒ hI Conѣobair, ocur Taτʒ mac Maτʒaṁna hI Cheiꝛín, ocur Ruaiτꝛí hUa Maoilbꝛenaiτ; ocur ταnaic Uilliam Maꝛér ochταr marѣaѣ ar an laταir rin, ocur το cuimniʒ mac Caτhail croibτerʒ an ꝼeall ocur an meabul το ꝛinτeτ aiꝛ i nCcѣ cliaѣ, ocur το eiꝛiʒ ꝛeꝛu το τoiꝛꝛlinʒeτar na Ʒoill, ocur το cuir laiṁ a nUilliam Maiꝛéiꝛ, ocur το ꝼreʒꝛaѣ ʒu boeѣa ꝼeramail ó a muinτer é, uaiꝛ ꝛo ʒabaτ Uilliam Maiꝛeir ocur maiʒirτir Sleiṁne ocur Uʒa Ccꝛoin, ocur το marbaτ conrταꝛla Ccτa Luain ; ocur το ѣuir na Ʒoill rin a láiṁ ταꝛ Laτhaiʒ rúar, ocur ταinic riṁ ocur a ꝛaibe το Connachτiiѣ na ꝼocair, ocur ꝛo aiꝛʒeτar an marʒaѣ, ocur το loirceτar an baile, ocur ba ʒnim roѣair το

---

1 *Broken down.* This is probably a repetition of the entry under the year 1225, to the same effect.

2 **m.cc.xxvii.** The MS. has m.c.xxui. (1226). which is wrong. See note 2, p. 290.

3 *Was established.* το τeneṁ, for το τenuṁ, MS. Lit. " was made."

4 *Lathach - caech - tuaithbhil.* This name signifies the "northern blind slough," or pool. It was situated immediately to the west of Athlone,

Cunga. Aedh O'Flaithbhertaigh was taken prisoner by Aedh, son of Cathal Crobhderg, and delivered into the hands of the Foreigners. Muirghes Mac Diarmada was slain. The castle of Cill-mor was broken down[1] by Cathal O'Raighilligh.

M.cc.xxvii.[2] The kalends of January on Friday, and the 10th of the moon. A court was established[3] by the Foreigners of Ath-cliath and Erinn at Ath-cliath; and Aedh, son of Cathal Crobhderg, was summoned before it; and he was betrayed in that court until William Mareschal, his own friend, came with his forces into the midst of the court; and they carried him out of it by force, and conveyed him safely to his own country. As regards Aedh, son of Cathal Crobhderg; he appointed a meeting immediately after at Lathach-caech-tuaithbhil,[4] with William Mareis, son of Geoffroi; and he went across the Lathach with only a very few, viz.:—Cormac, son of Tomaltach Mac Diarmada of the Rock, and Diarmaid, son of Maghnus, and Maghnus, son of Muirchertach O'Conchobhair, and Tadhg, son of Mathghamhain O'Ceirin, and Ruaidhri O'Maelbhrenainn. And William Mareis came to the place with eight horsemen. And the son of Cathal Crobhderg remembered the deception and treachery practised against him in Ath-cliath, and he advanced before the Foreigners dismounted, and laid a hand on William Mareis. And he was seconded actively and bravely by his people; for William Mareis, and Master Sleimhne, and Hugo Arden were taken prisoners, and the Constable of Ath-Luain was slain; and he (*Aedh*) sent the Foreigners in captivity southwards across Lathach; and he and all the Connachtmen who were with him went and plundered the market, and burned the town. And this was a felicitous act for all the Connachtmen, for they

and the name is still preserved in that of the village and townland of Bellaugh, or *Beal-lathaich* ("mouth of Lathach"), in the parish of St. Peter, near Athlone.

Connachtuiḃ uile ṙin, uaiṙ ṙuaiṙ ṙiṁ a meic ocuṙ a
ningina, ocuṙ braiġde Connacht, ocuṙ ṙiṫ do Connachtuiḃ da éiṙ. Donnṡleiḃe .h. ġadra, ṙi Sléiḃe Luġa, do
maṙbad don Ḃilla ṙúad, do mac a deṙbraṫaṙ ṙein ; ocuṙ
ṙo maṙbad ṙuṁ ino tṙe imdeall mic Caṫail cṙoiḃdeṙg.
Loġaoiṙ, ṙi Ḟṙanc, do éc. Ḃoṙta móṙ in bliadain ṙi,
ocuṙ daoine aġ éġ di ocuṙ do ġalṙaiḃ exaṁluiḃ aṙċena.
Moṙṡluaiged la mac Uilliam i Connachta, ocuṙ le
hCCeḋ mac Ruaiḋṙi mic Toiṙṙdhelḃaiġ moiṙ, ġuṙ loiṙc-
ṙed Iniṙ meḋoin, ocuṙ ġuṙ aiṙġṙit in tiṙ uile, ocuṙ ġuṙ
ġabṙad bṙaiġde. Sluaiged la Seṙṙuiḋ Maiṙeiṙ ocuṙ
la Toiṙṙdhelḃaċ mac Rúaiḋṙi, hi Maġ Nae, condeṙṙat
caiṙlén a Rinn dúin, ocuṙ ġuṙ ġabṙat bṙaiġde Sil
Muiṙedhaiġ. CCeḋ mac Caṫail cṙoiḃdeṙg .h. Conchobaiṙ do dul hi Tiṙ Conuill, docum hi Domnuill.
Impod do atuaiḋ aṙiṙ, ocuṙ a ḃen do taḃaiṙt leiṙ.
Meic Toiṙṙdhelḃaiġ do ḟecḃail do, ocuṙ a eiḋ ocuṙ a
ben do buain de aġ teacht iṙin Seġaiṙ, ocuṙ an ben do
ċuṙ illaiṁ Ḃall. Sluaiged do ḋenum do Toiṙṙdhelḃaċ
mac Rúaiḋṙi ocuṙ do ġallaiḃ Miḋe, a níaṙṫaṙ Connacht,
condeṙṙat cṙeiċ moiṙ aṙ CCoḋ mac Rúaiḋṙi i
Ḟlaithḃeṙtaiġ. Dul doib aṙ ṙin a ġCeṙa, ocuṙ
bṙaiġde clainne Muiṙceṙtaiġ Muimniġ do ġabail doiḃ,
ocuṙ nuimiṙ ṁaṙt do taḃaiṙt dó[iḃ] aṙ ġach tṙicha.
Cṙeaċ hSliġiġ do ḋenum leiṙin nĠiúiṙtiṙ ocuṙ le Ḃṙian
mac Toiṙṙdhelḃaiġ, ġuṙ ġabudaṙ mná imḋa ambṙoid. ·

M.cc.xxuiii. ⟨kl⟩ Enaiṙ aṙ Saṫaṙn, ocuṙ a haon
.xx.ṙuiṙṙe; CCeḋ mac Caṫail cṙoiḃdeṙg i Conchobaiṙ
do maṙbad do Ḃalloiḃ a mebuil ġṙánna, aṙ na ḋiċuṙ

1 *The Gillaruadh*; lit. "the red
fellow."

2 *Loghais.* Lonis VIII.

3 *The Seghais.* This was the ancient
name of the Boyle river, in the county
of Roscommon; but it subsequently
came to be applied to the adjacent Curlieu hills, which were called in Irish
Corrsliabh-na-Seghsa, or the "round
hill of the Seghais." In Mageogho-
gan's version of the Annals of Clonmacnoise, the place where Aedh was
met by his enemies is called Gortin-
cowle-Luachra, "the field of the

obtained their sons and daughters, and the hostages of Connacht, and peace for the Connachtmen afterwards. Donnsleibhe O'Gadhra, king of Sliabh-Lugha, was slain by the Gillaruadh,[1] his own brother's son; and he was killed therefor through the device of the son of Cathal Crobhderg. Loghais,[2] king of the Franks, died. A great famine in this year; and people died of it, and of various diseases besides. A great hosting into Connacht by the son of William, and by Aedh, son of Ruaidhri, son of Toirdhelbhach Mór; and they burned Inis-medhoin, and plundered the entire country, and took hostages. A hosting by Geoffroi Mareis, and by Toirdhelbhach, son of Ruaidhri, into Magh-Nai, when they erected a castle at Rinn-dúin, and took the hostages of Sil-Muiredhaigh. Aedh, son of Cathal Crobhderg, went into Tir-Conaill, to O'Domhnaill. He returned from the north, and brought his wife with him. The sons of Toirdhelbhach met him, and took from him his horses and his wife, as he was coming into the Seghais;[3] and the wife was surrendered to the Foreigners. A hosting was performed by Toirdhelbhach, son of Ruaidhri, and by the Foreigners of Midhe, into the West of Connacht, and they committed a great depredation on Aedh, son of Ruaidhri O'Flaithbhertaigh. They went from thence into Cera, and took the hostages of the sons of Muirchertach Muimhnech, and brought a number of beeves from each cantred. A depredation was committed in Sligech by the Justiciary, and by Brian, son of Toirdhelbhach, when they took many women prisoners.

M.cc.xxviii.[4] The kalends of January on Saturday, and the 21st of the moon. Aedh, son of Cathal Crobhderg O'Conchobhair, was slain[5] by the Foreigners in an ugly

---

rushy corner;" and it is added that he was betrayed by his porter.

[4] M.cc.xxviii. The MS. has m.cc.xxun (for 1227), which is incorrect. See note [2], p. 290.

[5] *Slain.* The murder of Aedh O'Conchobhair (or Hugh O'Conor), is entered under the year 1228 in the Annals of Ulster and the Four Masters.

oo Connachtuiƀ úαthαιƀ. Ʒιuιrtιr nα hEιρenn oo
ʒαbáιl oo mαc Uιllιαm ƀuρc. Αeo mαc Rúαιoρι oo
ʒαbαιl ριʒe Connαcht, ocur α bραιƀreƀα mαροen ριρ;
ocur ρο hαιρʒeƀ tuαtα ocur ceαllα Connαcht leo, ocur
ρο oιcuιρeƀ cleιριʒ ocur αor eαlαƀαn αn tιρe α ʒcριchαιb
cιαnα coιmιʒƀeƀα. Ƥeρʒαl mαc Sιtριc 1 Ruαιρc oo
mαρbαo oo mαcuιƀ Neιll mιc Conʒαlαιʒ 1 Ruαιρc.
Nιαll mαc Conʒαlαιʒ 1 Ruαιρc oo ṁαρbαo oo Αρt mαc
Αιρt 1 Ruαιρc.

Ʃctt. Enáιρ ρορ Oomnαch, ocur αιle uαthαo ρuιρρe.
M.cc.xxιx. Ʒιllα ιn Coιmƀeƀ .h. Ouιlenoαιn, comαρbα
Ƥeιčιn, oo eʒ αn blιαoαιn ριn. Cρeαč Rennα oúιn oo
ƀénum lα Ƥelιm .h. Concubαιρ, ocur Concubαρ buιoe
mαc Toιρρohelƀαιʒ oo ṁαρbαo, ocur Tαoʒ mαc Coρmαιc; et táιnιc ιn Ʒιuιρoιr ʒu Teρmαnn Cαoluιnn,
ocur oo loιρʒeƀ ιn bαιle, ocur oo loιρceƀ tempull
1mlιʒ Uρčαoα. Mαιom Cluαnαčα tuʒ Ƥelιm αρ mαcuιƀ
Rúαιoρι, ocur αρ Conchobαρ mαc Coρmαιc.

Ʃctt. Enαιρ ρορ Mαιρt; bírex, ocur tρeρ .x. ρuιρρe.
M.cc.xxx. 1nntóƀ oΑeƀ mαc Rúαιoρι ocur oo Conn-
αchtuιƀ αρcenα, αρ mαc Uιllιαm .ι. Rιcαρo ƀúρc, ocur
αρ ʒαlloιb, tρe αρluč Ouιnn oιʒ mιc Ouιnncαthαιʒ mιc
Αιρečtαιʒ, ocur Coρmαιc mιc Tomαltαιʒ nα Cαιρρʒe
mιc Oιαρmαoα, ocur α oeρα ʒραƀα; uαιρ oo ραoαtuρ
ριoe bρéιčιρ nαč beιtιρ αʒ αn ριʒ oo béραƀ α tech
nʒαll ιαt. Oo ρonραt, tρα, cρechα moρα ρορ ʒαllαιb
.ι. Oeƀ mαc Rúαιoρι ocur ιαρthαρ Connαcht oo αρʒuιn
mιc oιʒ Uιllιαm ocur Αoáιm ƀuιƀ. Oonn oʒ, ιmoρρo,

---

[1] *Son of William Burk*; i.e. Richard
Burk, or De Burgh, son of William
Fitz-Adelm de Burgh, viceroy of
Ireland under king Henry II.

[2] m.cc.xxix. The date in the MS.
is m.cc.xxviii (1228); a mistake
arising from the error committed by
the scribe at the year 1226, and repeated from that year to 1230, inclusive. See note [2], p. 290.

[3] *Cormac*; i.e. Cormac Mac Diarmada, or Mac Dermot. Roderick
O'Flaherty has added the marginal
note "O'Conor against O'Conor."

[4] *The 18th of the moon.* The MS.
has tr̄ .xx., for tρeρ .xx., "23rd,"
which is wrong, as the 1st of January
in 1230 coincided with the 13th day of
the moon's age. Instead of the year

treachery, after having been expelled by the Connachtmen.
The Justiciaryship of Erinn was assumed by the son of
William Burk.[1] Aedh, son of Ruaidhri, assumed the
sovereignty of Connacht, and his brothers along with
him ; and the territories and churches of Connacht were
plundered by them, and the clerics and men of science of
the land were banished to remote, foreign countries.
Ferghal, son of Sitrec O'Ruairc, was killed by the sons
of Niall, son of Conghalach O'Ruairc. Niall, son of Conghalach O'Ruairc, was killed by Art, son of Art O'Ruairc.

The kalends of January on Sunday, and the 2nd of the
moon ; M.cc.xxix.[2] Gilla-in-Choimdhedh O'Duilendain,
comarb of Feichín, died this year. The plundering of
Rinn-dúin was effected by Felim O'Conchobhair ; and
Conchobhar Buidhe, son of Toirdhelbhach, and Tadhg, son
of Cormac, were slain ; and the Justiciary came to Termann-
Caeluinn, and the town was burned, and the church of
Imlech-Urchadha was burned. Felim gained the victory
of Cluain-acha over the sons of Ruaidhri, and over Conchobhar, son of Cormac.[3]

The kalends of January on Tuesday ; a bissextile *year*,
and the 13th of the moon ;[4] M.cc.xxx. Aedh, son of
Ruaidhri, and the Connachtmen also, turned against the
son of William, i.e. Richard Burk, and against the Foreigners, through the persuasion of Donn Og, son of
Donncathaigh Mac Airechtaigh, and of Cormac, son of
Tomaltach Mac Diarmada of the Rock, and his favourites ;
for they had pledged their word that they would not
belong to any king who would bring them into the
house[5] of the Foreigners. They committed, moreover,
great depredations on the Foreigners, viz. :—Aedh, son of
Ruaidhri, and *the men of* the west of Connacht plundered
the young son of William, and Adam Dubh ;[6] Donn Og,

M.cc.xxx. the MS. has m.cc.xxix.
See note [3], on last page.

[5] *Bring them into the house;* i.e. make
them tender their submission.
[6] *Adam Dubh.* "Adam the Black."

ocuṛ meic Maṡnuıṛ, ocuṛ ʒlaṛláıℭ ṛıl Muıṛeⱱaıʒ, ⱱo
aṛʒuın mıc Ʒoıṛⱱelℭ ocuṛ cıṛe Maıne. Cıℭ cṛa achc ṛo
cınoıl mac Uıllıam uṛmoṛ Ʒall Éıṛenn, ocuṛ Ʒaoıⱱel
ımℭa, ocuṛ caınıc ı Connachca, ocuṛ Ƒeılım mac Cachaıl
cṛoıⱱⱱeṛʒ leıṛ, ⱱo cabaıṛc ṛíʒe Connachc ⱱó, ocuṛ ⱱo
ınnaṛbaⱱ Ɑoⱱa mıc Rúaıⱱṛı ocuṛ caℭ Connachcuıʒ ṛo
ımṗó ṛaıṛ. Canʒaⱱaṛ aṛ cúṛ ṛompa co caıṛlen ⱱona
Ʒaıllṁe, ⱱocum Ɑoⱱa ı Ƒhlaıℭbeṛcaıʒ. Iṛ ann ṛın ⱱo
chuaıⱱ Ɑoⱱ mac Rúaıⱱṛı ⱱo ṗoıṛıchın Ɑoⱱa hı Ƒhlaıℭ-
beṛcaıʒ, ocuṛ Connachcuıʒ leıṛ ṛa macuıℭ Muıṛceṛcaıʒ ı Conchobaıṛ, ocuṛ ⱱo ⱱáⱱaṛ Connachcuıʒ
alla aníaṛ ⱱo Ʒaıllṁ ocuṛ Ʒaıll alla anaıṛ; ocuṛ
ⱱeaⱱℭa moṛa ecuṛṛa caℭ láoı. Do bacaṛ cṛa Ʒaıll
aṁlaıℭ ṛın, ocuṛ nı ṛuaṛ ṛíℭ, na ʒeıll, na eıcıṛe o
Connachcuıℭ. Iṛṛí comaıṛle ⱱo ṛónṛac Ʒaıll ceℭc
anⱱıaıⱱ na mbó ocuṛ na muınnceṛa ṛo ceıℭṛec a
ṛleıⱱℭıℭ ocuṛ a nıaṛʒculaıb ın cíṛe, ocuṛ a noılenaıb
ṁaṛa; ocuṛ canʒaⱱaṛ ın oıⱱℭe ṛın o caıṛlen ⱱona
Ʒaıllme co Ɗṛoıceⱱ ınʒıne Ʒoıllın. Iṛ annṛın ṛo ba
maıⱱen ⱱoıℭ. Iṛ annṛın ⱱo ṛıaṛṛaıʒ mac Uıllıam ın
bṛuıl ṛlıʒe ecṛaınn ocuṛ loℭ accıcṛaıⱱıṛ cuıⱱ ⱱo
Connachcuıℭ anuaṛ. Do ṛṛeaʒṛaⱱaṛ na heolaıʒ é:
aca aṛṛíaⱱ. Do coṛuıʒṛım maṛcṛlúaıʒ ṛa Cunʒa
ṛıaṛ ocuṛ ṛa Cıll (no ṛa Inıṛ) méⱱoın. Iṛ annṛın ⱱo
ṛala ⱱo ⱱṛeım ⱱıaıṛṁe ⱱo Connachcuıℭ beℭ aʒ ceℭc
o Cunʒa moℭ cṛaℭ aṛ ná ṁáṛuℭ, aṛ na ʒcuṛ ℭaıṛıṛ ın
oıⱱℭe ṛeṁe ṛın, na nⱱeıṛıb ocuṛ na ccṛíaṛuıℭ, co
hamʒlıc, anbṛaıcech; ocuṛ ṛo maṛbuıⱱ uachaⱱ
ⱱo ⱱeʒ ℭaınıb ṛa oeṛ ʒṛaⱱa Muıṛceṛcaıʒ mıc
Maʒnuıṛ ı Conchobaıṛ .ı. Ɗıaṛmaıⱱ O hEıⱱⱱneℭaın,

---

1 *Against him*; i.e. against the son of William, Richard de Burgh.

2 *Gaillimh.* The Galway river.

3 *Droiched-inghine-Goillin*; i.e. "the bridge of Goillin's daughter." This name, which is now obsolete, was probably that of some bridge over the Black River, which flows into Lough Corrib, a few miles to the south-east of Cong.

4 *The lake.* Loch-Oirbshen, or Lough Corrib.

5 *Cill-(or Inis-)medhoin.* Cill-medhoin, or Kilmaine, is a townland

also, and the sons of Maghnus, and the young soldiers of Sil-Muiredhaigh, plundered Mac Goisdelbh and Tir-Maine. The son of William, however, assembled the greater part of the Foreigners of Erinn, and many Gaeidhel, and came into Connacht, accompanied by Felim, son of Cathal Crobhderg, to give him the sovereignty of Connacht, and to expel Aedh, son of Ruaidhri, and every Connachtman who had turned against him.[1] They proceeded at first to the castle of Bun-Gaillmhe, to Aedh O'Flaithbhertaigh. Then Aedh, son of Ruaidhri, went to assist Aedh O'Flaithbhertaigh; the Connachtmen accompanying him, under the sons of Muirchertach O'Conchobhair; and the Connachtmen were on the west side of Gaillimh,[2] and the Foreigners on the east side; and great conflicts *occurred* between them every day. The Foreigners were in this wise, and they obtained neither peace, nor pledge, nor hostage from the Connachtmen. The resolution the Foreigners adopted was to go after the cows and the people that had fled to the hills and fastnesses of the country, and into the islands of the sea; and they went that night from the castle of Bun-Gaillmhe to Droiched-inghine-Goillin,[3] where it was morning with them. Then the son of William asked "is there a passage between us and the lake,[4] by which some of the Connachtmen could come down?" The guides answered him: "there is," said they. He disposed a party of horse to the west towards Cunga, and towards Cill-(or Inis-)medhoin.[5] It happened then that a countless number of Connachtmen were coming from Cunga early on the morrow, having been unwisely, and unwarily, transported across *the lake* the night before, in parties of two and three; and a few good men were slain together with the men of trust of Muirchertach, son of Maghnus O'Conchobhair,

---

in the parish of Kilmainemore, barony of Kilmaine, county Mayo, situated about ten miles to the north-east of

Cong. Inis-medhoin, or Inishmaine, is an island in Lough Mask, near the eastern shore.

ocur Lochlainn mac Clerain, ocur Tαog mac Ʒillacpipt
1 Mháoilbpenuinn. Ɗαλα imoppo Ʒαll, tαngαtαp α
hαitle αnt poðαin pin ɡo Mαg néo nα Sαxαnαč. Tαngαtαp αp nα ḿάpuč co Tobup Pátpαic, ocur ɗo eipgeɗαp
cαnánαiʒ ocur Lucht cinnte bečαð in bαile ɗocum mic
Uilliαm, ocur ɗo fipeɗαp αp ɗepeipc αp mac Uilliαm
cαn beč αcα in oiɗče pin. Ɗo pαtαð ɗoibpiḿ pin, ocur
tαngαtαp Ʒαill pompα píp ɡo Muine Mαicin. Ro bα
lepc le Ʒαlloið, tpα, tect o Mαiʒ Eo conuiʒe pin, αcht
nαč puαputαp bpαiɡɗe nα oitipe o Mαʒnup mac
Muipceptαiʒ Muimniʒ. O nαč bpuαputαp bpαiɡɗe
tαngαɗαp αp nα tαpuč ɡu hᴀᴄhαɗ Fhαbαip, ocur ɗo
gαbαɗαp Lonʒpopt ipin bαile, αllα αniαp ɗon čill .i. α
Mαpʒenαnα αp bpú Lochα Cpíchαn. Tαinic Mαʒnup
mac Muipceptαiʒ inα tech, ocur tuʒ ʒeill ɗoið. Ɗαλα
imoppo Ʒαll, tαngαɗαp αp ná tάpuč ɡo Muine Mαicín
αpíp, ocur ɗo bαtαp αðhαiʒ αnn. Ɗo cuαɗαp αp nα
tάpαch ɡo Mαʒ Sine, ocur αppin inα nuiðeðuið αp
pαt Luiʒne co Ceip Chopuinn. Ɗo cuαɗαp αppein ipin
Copfliαð, ocur ɗo leiʒeɗαp nα heolαiʒ in ɡnát pliʒeɗ
uαthαib, ocur tαngαɗαp ipin pliαð uile ɡαn toippčim.
Ɗαλα imoppo Oeðα mic Ruαiðpi, ocur Copmαic, mic
Tomαltuiʒ nα Cαippʒe, mic Conchobαip mic Ɗiαpmαɗα,
ocur Ɗuinn oiʒ méʒ Oipechtuiʒ, ocur fil Muipeðhαiʒ,
ɗo bαɗαp ip in coilliô; ip i comαiple ɗo ponpαt cαn
uið ɡαn upán ɗo ɗenum αp ʒαlloið, o ɗo piαčtαɗαp α
mbα ocur α muintepα leo α nɗαinʒniô muintipe hEoluip
ocur Slebe in íαpuinn. ᴀɗubαipt Ɗonn oʒ nαch
ɗinʒneð in comαiple pin. Ip i comαiple ɗo poine piḿ,
ɗul leč αniαp ɗo Ʒαlloið co píαcht Finnčαpnn, ocur α
bpαthαip fein, ocur oʒbαthα fil Muipeðhαiʒ, ocur
α Ʒoill fein, ocur mac Ɗomnαill bpeʒuiʒ .h.

---

1 *Devout people.* Lucht cinnte
bečαð; lit. "people of devoted life;"
i.e. people who had devoted their lives
to religion.

2 *Went into their house;* i.e. made
his submission to the Foreigners.

3 *Crossed.* The expression tαngαɗαp ipin pliαð uile, which has
been rendered "they crossed the entire
mountain," literally translated, would
read "they came into all the mountain."

viz.:—Diarmaid O'hEidhnechain, and Lochlainn Mac   A
Clesain, and Tadhg, son of Gillachrist O'Maelbhrenainn.   [12
As regards the Foreigners: they went after this success
to Magh-Eo of the Saxons. They proceeded on the
morrow to Tobur-Patraic, where the canons and devout
people[1] of the place came to the son of William, and
requested the son of William, for charity, not to remain
with them that night. This request was granted to them;
and the Foreigners proceeded down to Muine-Maicin.
The Foreigners were loth, indeed, to go from Magh-Eo
thither; but they had not obtained either hostages or
pledges from Maghnus, son of Muirchertach Muimhnech.
As they had not obtained hostages they went on the morrow
to Achadh-Fabhair, and encamped in the town, to the
west of the church, viz.:—at Margenana, on the brink
of Loch-Crichan. Maghnus, son of Muirchertach, went
into their house,[2] and gave them pledges. As to the
Foreigners, moreover; they came again on the morrow to
Muine-Maicin, and remained a night there. They proceeded the next day to Magh-Sine, and from thence,
by marches, through Luighne to Ceis-Corainn. They
went from thence into the Corr-sliabh, and the guides
abandoned the usual path; and they crossed[3] the entire
mountain without being met. With reference to Aedh,
son of Ruaidhri, and to Tomaltach of the Rock, son of
Conchobhar Mac Diarmada, and Donn Og Mac Airechtaigh, and the Sil-Muiredhaigh, who were in the wood—
the resolution they adopted was not to bestow attention or regard on the Foreigners, since their cows, and
their people with them, had reached the fastnesses of
Muinter-Eolais and of Sliabh-an-iarainn. Donn Og said
that he would not observe this resolution. The course he
decided on was to go to the west side of the Foreigners
until he reached Finn-charn, accompanied by his own
brother, and the young men of Sil-Muiredhaigh, and by
his own Foreigners, and by the son of Domhnall Bregach

Mháilṡeclainn cona ġalloiḃ, ocus Brian mac Toirr-dhelḃaiġ; ocus do ċuir Donn lucht deaḃṫa ċuca, ocus do ḃí deabaiḋ maiṫ ga coṫachad ar Galloib, ocus do biriṁ fein ag costaḋ ar mullaċ an ċairn, ocus a sbéis isin deabaiḋ. Is annsin do cuiredar Goill slúaig timċill imun gcarn, do ḟersenchaib ocus do ṁarcachaib diarṁiṫiḃ, ocus nír airigedar iad no gur ṫimċillsed aníar um carn, ocus do fágbad Donn a oenar annsin achtmad began da braitriḃ, ocus Brian mac Toirrdhelḃaiġ; ocus is gairid do leiged an oén inat iat aṁlaid sin. Do fograḋ, tra, ocus do haiṫneḋ Donn óg ann sin ocus se a oenar, ocus do luiġedar serrenaiġ imḋa, ocus do cuireḋ .u. faiġde annsuiṁ; ocus rug oen marcach fair fadeóiḋ, ocus ni raibe darm aige siṁ acht túaġ, ocus nir leigsim in marcaċ fair; ocus do ċuired in marcaċ in ga ind gac núaire. Tangadar na serrénaiġ uile ina timcell sum anoir ocus aníar, ocus do ṫuit leis an anforlonn ruc air annsin. Dala imorro Aoda mic Rúaidri, bui don leṫ anoir do Galloiḃ ag a feiṫem; ocus ni tug deabaid doiḃ, ocus ni da deóin tug Donn; ocus ro siachd in maidm soir ina ċend, ocus ni ḟitir Donn do marbad annsin; ocus do chuaid Aeḋ allos a laṁa as gan doṁaire; ocus einfer diḃ do bi ag luiḋe fair do iomparaṁ ris ocus tucc urcor dó don ġai boei ina laim, cor gaḃ a crand trid, ocus do leicceḋram as iartain. Ciḋ tra acht o tarrla sodan do Galloib, ocus o ro marbad Donn ócc, do cuiredar Gaill creċa mora amaċ go riachtadar Sliaḃ an iarainn, ocus is soċaide do cuiredar re fuacht ocus re gortta annsin, ocus ro marḃaitt mna ocus leiniṁ, ocus ro nochtaid in meid nar marḃaid, ocus tuccadar creċa mora

[1] *Fell.* In the Dublin copy of Mageoghegan's version of the Annals of Clonmacnoise, the slaying of Donn Mac Airechtaigh, or Mageraghty, is stated to have occurred "at the mount called Slieu Leysie." But *Leysie* is probably a mistake for Seysie, i.e. Seghais, a name applied to the Curlieu hills in the counties of Roscommon and Sligo.

[2] *Sliabh-an-iarainn,* "the hill of the iron," a mountain in the north of the county of Leitrim.

O'Maelsechlainn with his Foreigners, and by Brian, son of
Toirdhelbhach; and Donn sent a fighting party to them,
and a good conflict was being waged against the Foreigners, and he himself was stationed on the summit of
the carn, and his hope in the conflict. Then the Foreigners
sent a countless host of mercenaries and cavalry around
the carn, and they (*Donn's party*) observed them not
until they passed from the west around the carn; and
Donn was left alone there, with the exception of a few
of his kinsmen, and of Brian, son of Toirdhelbhach; and
only for a short time were they allowed to remain
thus in one spot. Donn Og, being then alone, was
proclaimed and recognised; and many soldiers took aim,
and five arrows were lodged in him; and one horseman came up with him afterwards; and though he
(*Donn*) had no weapon but an axe, he did not allow
the horseman to close with him; and the horseman
would drive his lance into him occasionally. The other
soldiers surrounded him from the east and west, and he
fell[1] by the superior power that overtook him there.
Regarding Aedh, son of Ruaidhri, moreover; he was on
the east side of the Foreigners, awaiting them; and he did
not give them battle, and it was not with his consent
that Donn had done so. And the rout extended eastwards
towards him; and he knew not then that Donn had been
slain; but Aedh escaped uninjured through the strength
of his hand; and he turned upon one man of them who
was taking aim at him, and cast the lance which
was in his hand at him, so that the shaft went
through him; and he was afterwards allowed to depart.
However, as success attended the Foreigners, and as Donn
Og was slain, the Foreigners sent out great predatory
bands as far as Sliabh-an-iarainn,[2] and subjected multitudes to cold and hunger on this occasion. And women
and children were killed; and all that were not killed
were stripped; and they carried off great, fruitful preys

τοιρτͤϲηα λͤο ϧο λοιηϧροϧτ ηα ηϧαλλ. Ⱥρ ριη ρο
ιητιξͤναρ Ϧαιλλ αρ ηα μαραϲ, οϲυρ νο ϧαϧβαναρ ριξͤ
αϧ Ϝͤινλιμμ μαϲ Ϲατηαλ ϲροιβνͤρϧ, οϲυρ ρο ηιηηαρ-
βυιν Ⱥͤν μαϲ Ruαινρι α ηυϲητ Ⱥͤνα ηι Νͤιλλ. Ⱥͤν
.η. Νͤιλλ νο ͤϲ ιρριη βλιαναιη ριη; ρι Ϲͤηͤλ Εοϧαιη αρ
ϲλυ οϲυρ αρ μαιϲͤρ; ρι ηα τυϲϲ ϧιαλλ ηα ͤιττιρͤ νο ϧαλλ
ηα νο Ϧαͤινιλ; ρι νο ραν μανμοηηα οϲυρ μαρβτα
μορα αρ ϧαλλοιβ; ρι νο βα ϲοϲαϲ ͤνο Ϧοͤινͤλαιβ υιλͤ
ηͤϲ ρο βιϲ αρ ιηναρβαν ηο αρ ρͤϲραη; ρι ροβ ϝͤιλι οϲυρ
ροβ ιηηνͤϧουιηͤ ταηιϲ νο ρͤραιβ Ειρͤηη ιαρ ϲͤημαιρ.
Ϧιλλα Ιορρα Uα Ϲλͤιριϧ, ͤρϧυϲ Λυιϧηͤ, ϧυιͤυιτ ιη Ϲριρτο.
Ιορͤϲ μαϲ Τͤιϲͤϧαιη, ͤρϧυϲ Ϲοημαιϲηͤ, ϧυιͤυιτ ιη Ϲριρτο.
Ϧιλλα Ϲαρρτηαιϧ .η. ηͤλϧιραη, ϲαηαηαϲη οϲυρ αηϲαιρͤ,
ϧυιͤυιτ. Ϣοηηρλͤιϧͤ .η. ηιημαιηͤη, μαηαϲη ηαομ, οϲυρ
αρν μαιϧιρνοιρ ραορ μαιηιρνρͤϲη ηαϧυιλλͤ, μορτυυρͤρτ.
Ϣαολμοιρͤ. η. Ϣαοιλͤοιη, ϲομρορβα Ϲιαραιη Ϲλυαηα
μιϲ Νοιρ, ϧυιͤυιτ. η.Ϲͤρϧαλλαιη, ͤρϧυϲ Ϲͤηͤοιλ Εοϧαιη,
ϧυιͤυιτ ιη Ϲριρτο. Rοολ Ϸͤιτιτ, ͤρϧυϲ ηα Ϣιϧͤ, υιρ
ρͤλιϧιορυρ ͤτ ϲαριτατιυυρ, ͤτ Ϣͤι ϝαμυλυρ, ιη Ϲριρτο
ϧυιͤυιτ. Ϣαολρͤϲλαιηη μαϲ Ϸηιρͤνιηη, υαϧαλ ϝαϲαρτ
οϲυρ μαιϧιρτιρ λͤιϧιηη, ιη Ϲριρτο ϧυιͤυιτ, ιηα ηοβιτρι
ϣαηαιϧ α μαιηιρτοιρ ηαϧυιλλͤ. Ⱥρτ μαϲ Ⱥιρτ ηι ρυαιρͤ
νο ϣαρβαν νο Ραϧηαλλ .η. Ϸηιηη, ρͤρ νολυμ. Ϣαϲραιϲ
μαϧ[ϸ]ͤιριϧ, ͤρϧυϲ Ϲοημαιϲηͤ, ϧυιͤυιτ ιη Ϲριρτο. Ϣαοιλ-
ρͤϲλαιηη.η.Ϣαηναϲαιη νο μαρβαν να βραιϲͤριβ ϝͤιη.
Ϣυιβͤρρα, ιηϧͤη Ruαινρι ηι Ϲοηϲηοβαιρ, βͤη Ϲατηαιλ
μιϲ Ϣιαρμανα, νο ηͤϲ ιηα ϲαιλλͤϲ ϧυιϧ. Ϣυιρͤνηαϲη

---

[1] *An exile or wanderer.* αρ ιηναρβαν ηο αρ ρͤϲραη; lit. "on exile
or on wandering."

[2] *Bishop of Luighne;* i.e. bishop of
Achonry. The name of Luighne, the
ancient patrimony of the sept of
O'Hara, is still preserved in that of
the barony of Leyny, in the county of
Sligo.

[3] *Conmaicne.* By "bishop of Conmaicne" is meant "bishop of Ardagh."

[4] *Carpenters.* ραορ. The expression αρν μαιϧιρνοιρ ραορ may
mean "chief, noble master," as well
as "chief master of the carpenters,"
the word ραορ being an adjective
("cheap, free, noble"), and also the
nom. sg. and gen. pl. of ραορ, "a
carpenter."

[5] *O'Cerbhallain.* The Four Masters

to the camp of the Foreigners. The Foreigners departed after this, on the morrow, and left the sovereignty with Fedhlim, son of Cathal Crobhderg; and Aedh, son of Ruaidhri, was banished to Aedh O'Neill. Aedh O'Neill died in this year—the king of Cenel-Eoghain through fame and goodness; a king who gave neither pledge nor hostage to Foreigner or Gaeidhel; a king who inflicted great defeats and killings on Foreigners; a king who was a protector to every one of the Gaeidhel who might be an exile or wanderer;[1] who was the most generous king, and the very best man, that had come of the men of Erinn for a long time. Gilla-Isa O'Clerigh, bishop of Luighne,[2] quievit in Christo. Joseph Mac Teichedhain, bishop of Conmaicne,[3] quievit in Christo. Gilla-Carthaigh O'hEilghisan, a canon and anchorite, quievit. Donnsleibhe O'hInmhainén, a holy monk, and chief master of the carpenters[4] of the monastery of Buill, mortuus est. Maelmuire O'Maeleoin, comarb of Ciaran of Cluain-mic-Nois, quievit. O'Cerbhallain,[5] bishop of Cenel-Eoghain,[6] quievit in Christo. Rool[7] Petit, bishop of Midhe, vir religiosus et caritativus, et Dei famulus, in Christo quievit. Maelsechlainn Mac Firedinn, a noble priest and master of reading, in Christo quievit in his monastic noviciate in the monastery of Buill. Art, son of Art O'Ruairc, was slain by Raghnall O'Finn, per dolum. Macraith Mac Seirigh,[8] bishop of Conmaicne,[3] quievit in Christo. Maelsechlainn O'Mannachain was killed by his own brethren. Duibhessa, daughter of Ruaidhri O'Conchobhair, wife of Cathal Mac Diarmada, died a black nun.[9]

(1230) give his Christian name as Ꝼꞁoꞃenꞇ, or Florence.

[6] *Bishop of Cenel-Eoghain;* i.e. bishop of Derry.

[7] *Rool.* Ralph, or Radulphus.

[8] *Mac Seiridh.* mᴀᴈ eiꞃin, MS. The name is written Mᴀᴈ Seꞃꞃᴀiᴈ by the Four Masters, and Mᴀc ꞃeꞃꞃᴀiᴈ

in the Annals of Ulster. The inaccurate form of the name in the text is owing to the omission of the letter ꞃ, which, being aspirated and consequently silent in the pronunciation, was left out by the scribe.

[9] *A black nun;* i.e. doubtless, after having assumed the black veil.

O Ζορμγτιιlιζ ρρίοιρ ρεζλέρρα lιιιρι mιc Νέιριn, τιιιηε
ιγ εζηαιτε οcuγ ιγ cραιϐϐιξε το ϐι α cuιcεϐ Chonnαchτ,
ιn Cριγτο quιειιτ. Τιαρμαιτ mάξ Cαρρτhαιξ, ρί
Τερμυmαn, quιειιτ ιn Cριγτο.

M.cc.xxx. ρριμο. Κtt. Εnαιρ ρορ Cετιαοιn, οcuγ cεthαρ
ριchιτ γιιιρρι, οcuγ αn γειγεϐ ϐλιατιαιn τhéc τιοn čιcιl
ναοιϐεcϐα, οcuγ ιn ηomατι τhεc τιοn cιcιl ρολαιρ, οcuγ
αn cεthραματι ϐλιατιαιn ιnτιcτιοnιρ hí. ρεčγαιξε,
ιnzεn Conchoϐαιρ mιc Τιαρματια, ϐεn Muιρcερταιξ
Muιmnιξ mιc Τοιρρϐhελϐαιξ μοιρ hι Conchoϐαιρ, τιο
éξ ιριn mϐλιατιαιn ριn .ι. ϐεn ιγ μο οcuγ ιγ άιllε, οcuγ ιγ
ρέλι, οcuγ ιγ ιnηραcα, οcuγ ιγ ρερρ clú τιαnιc τιο Lειč
Cuιnn; οcuγ τιοϐ í ριn ματčαιρ Mhαξηυρα mιc Muιρcερταιξ Muιmnιξ, οcuγ Conchoϐαιρ ρυαιτι, οcuγ Τuαthαιl,
οcuγ Τοιρρϐhελϐαιξ ραcαιρτ .ι. ρρίοιρ ρεζλέρα ρετιαιρ
οcuγ ρόιl. Τυϐčαϐλαιξ, ιnzεn Conchoϐαιρ mιc Τιαρματια, τιο éξ α μαιnιγτιρ ηα ϐúιllε ιn hoc αnηο.
Τυιnηίn .h. Μαοlconαιρε, ollαm ρίl Muιρεξhαιξ
Muιllεthαιn mιc Ρερξυρα, τιο éξ ιn hoc αnηο. Ρlαnη
.h. Connαchταιξ, εγρuc .h. mϐριuιn, quιειιτ. Ρετιlιm,
mαc Cαthαιl cροιϐτιερc, τιο ξαϐάιl lα mαc Uιllιαm α
ϐúρc α Mιlιuc, ταρ γlάnαιξεchτ μαιčhι Ζαll Ερεηη.
Ρlαιčϐερταch .h. Ρlαnηαξάn, τιux člαιnηι Cαthαιl mιc
Mhuιρεϐhαιξ mhuιllεthαιn, τιο éc α ηoιlιčρε, α μαιnιγτιρ
ηα ϐúιllι, οcuγ é αρ ηα cρορραϐ. Slóιξετι μοιρčιnóιl
lα Τομnαll .h. nΤομηαιll, ρι τιρε Conαιll, οcuγ lα
hΟΟοnξuρ mαc Ζιllαριnnéιn, αρ Chαthαl .h. Ραιξιllιξ,
co ρυcρατι lοιnzερ lεο ρορ Loč Uαchταιρ, ξuρ αιρccρετ
Εο ιnιρ, οcuγ ξuρ μαρϐρατ αn ρτιέτι ξεαl ιγ ρερρ ϐόι

---

1 *O'Gormshuiligh*; pron. O'Gormooly. In the Four Masters he is
called Uα Ζορμξαιlε, or O'Gormally.

2 *Kalends.* The letters .čε. are
added in the margin. The writer probably intended to signify that the Dominical Letter for the year 1231 was E.

3 *Regles of Peter and Paul.* The "abbey church" of Saints Peter and Paul.

4 *Race of Muiredhach Muillethan.*
Sιl Muιρεξhαιξ muιllεthαιn.
"Sil-Muiredhaigh," (pron. Sheel-
Murray), was the tribe name of the
family of O'Conor of Roscommon, and

Muiredhach O'Gormshuiligh,[1] prior of the Regles of Inis-
Mic-Neirin, the most learned and devout man that was
in the province of Connacht, in Christo quievit. Diarmaid
Mac Carthaigh, king of Des-Mumha, quievit in Christo.

M.cc.xxx. primo. The kalends[2] of January on Wednesday, and the twenty-fourth of the moon ; and it was
the sixteenth year of the Decennovenalian cycle, and
the nineteenth of the solar cycle, and the fourth year
of the Indiction. Fethfailghe, daughter of Conchobhar
Mac Diarmada, wife of Muirchertach Muimhnech, son of
Toirdhelbhach Mor O'Conchobhair, died in this year, viz. :
the greatest, and most beautiful, and most generous, and
most virtuous, and most famous woman that came of
Leth-Chuinn ; and she was the mother of Maghnus, son
of Muirchertach Muimhnech, and of Conchobhar Ruadh,
and of Tuathal, and of the priest Toirdhelbhach, i.e. the
prior of the Regles of Peter and Paul.[3] Dubhchabhlaigh,
daughter of Conchobhar Mac Diarmada, died in the
monastery of Buill in hoc anno. Duinnin O'Maelconaire,
chief poet of the race of Muiredhach Muillethan[4] son of
Fergus, died in hoc anno. Flann O'Connachtaigh, bishop
of Ui-Briuin,[5] quievit. Fedhlim, son of Cathal Crobhderg,
was apprehended by the son of William Burk, at Milic,
in violation of the guarantee of the principal Foreigners
of Erinn. Flaithbhertach O'Flannagain, dux of the descendants of Cathal son of Muiredhach Muillethan, died
in pilgrimage in the monastery of Buill, after having
been crossed.[6] A great hosting-assemblage *was led* by
Domhnall O'Domhnaill, king of Tir-Conaill, and by
Aenghus Mac Gillafhinnéin, against Cathal O'Raighilligh;
and they brought vessels with them upon Loch-Uachtair,
and plundered Eo-inis, and killed the best white steed

---

their correlatives, who were descended
from Muiredhach Muillethan (Mured-
achus Latus-vertex), king of Connacht, who died A.D. 701.

[5] *Bishop of Ui-Briuin;* i.e. bishop
of Kilmore.

[6] *Crossed.* That is, having been
enrolled amongst the crusaders.

in Erinn, ocur co rucrat Cacht ingen mec Phiacrach, ben hi Raigilligh leo, ocur co rucrat reoid ocur ionnmur ocur maiter in baile uile leo. Dioinir .h. Morda, erpuc Oilerinn, iar cur errocóide de ar dégerc[1], ocur ar cricnoghud a betha in Oilén na Trinóide ar Loc Cé, do Dhia ocur do Chlárur mág Mhaoilín, doircidechain Oilerinn, ocur don urd canánac an inaid cetna, xliii. Kt. Ianuarii[2] in eadem inrola quievit in Crirto. Dubtemprac, ingen hi Chuinn, ben Phlaitbertaigh hi Phlannacáin, mortua ert. Concobar gود[3] .h. hEghra, ri Luighne, mortuur ert. Tinnrcna baile marccaid do denum la Cormac mac Tomaltaig a Port na Cairrge[4]. Mac Neill hi Ghairmleghaigh, dux cineoil Móain, mortuur ert. Donnchad .h. Connchobair do gabáil errucoide Oilerinn tairéir Dioinir hi Mhordai. Gilla Ira mág Shamradain, dux Teallaigh Echac, quievit. Ualgarg .h. Ruairc, ri breffne, do eg in oilitri ar rliged ant rroca.

Ktt. Enair for Dardaoin, ocur cuiced huathad ruirre, ocur in reachtmad dhec don cicil noidecda hí, ocur an ricetmad bliadain don cicil foluir, ocur an cuiced bliadain indictionir; anno Domini M.cc. xxxii. Aod, mac Aimlaid, mic Domnaill, mic Murchada, mic Gilla na naom, mic Ohrain, mic Shenlaic, mic Eochada, mic Ferghail, o nabartar hi Ferghail, do lorcad ar innri Loca Cúile la cloinn Aoda ciabaigh, mic Murchada, mic Gilla na naom hi Ferghail, iar caitem noi mbliadna a toirighecht na hAngaile dó tairéir Murchada charraigh hi Pherghuil. Gilla na naom .h. Dálaigh, rói ndána ocur tighe aided ocur cotaige caic a coitcinne

---

that was in Erinn; and they carried away with them Cacht, daughter of Mac Fiachrach, wife of O'Raighilligh, and carried away with them the jewels, and treasures, and goods of the entire place. Dionysius O'Mordha, bishop of Oilfinn, after resigning the bishopric with a view to ending his life in Trinity Island on Loch-Cé, through love[1] for God, and for Clarus Mac Mailin, archdeacon of Oilfinn, and for the order of Canons of the same place, xviii. kalendas Januarii[2] in eadem insula quievit in Christo. Dubh-themhrach, daughter of O'Cuinn, wife of Flaithbhertach O'Flannagain, mortua est. Conchobar Got[3] O'hEghra, king of Luighne, mortuus est. The erection of a market town at Port-na-Cairge[4] was commenced by Cormac, son of Tomaltach. The son of Niall O'Gairmleghaigh, dux of Cenel-Moain, mortuus[5] est. Donnchadh O'Conchobhair assumed the bishopric of Oilfinn after Dionysius O'Mordha. Gilla-Isa Mac Shamhradhain, dux of Tellach-Echach, quievit. Ualgharg O'Ruairc, king of Breifne, died in pilgrimage on the way to the river.[6]

The kalends of January on Thursday, and the fifth of the moon; and it was the seventeenth of the Decennovenalian cycle, and the twentieth year of the solar cycle, and the fifth year of the Indiction. Anno Domini M.CC.XXXII. Aedh, son of Amhlaibh, son of Domhnall, son of Murchadh, son of Gilla-na-naemh, son of Brian, son of Senlacch, son of Eochaidh, son of Ferghal (from whom the O'Ferghails are named), was burned on the island of Loch-Cuile by the sons of Aedh Ciabhach, son of Murchadh, son of Gilla-na-naemh O'Ferghail, after having spent nine years in the chieftainship of the Anghaile, in succession to Murchadh Carrach O'Ferghail. Gilla-na-naemh O'Dalaigh, a distinguished professor of poetry, and *keeper* of a house

---

county of Roscommon, and is the seat of Viscount Lorton. Roderick O'Flaherty has added the marginal note "a market in Carig Mac Dermott."

[5] *Mortuus.* ᵐᵒᵖᵗᵘᵖ, MS.

[6] *The river;* ᵃᵖ ᵖᵘᵹᵉᵈ ᵃᵑᵗ ᵖᵖᵒᵗᵃ; lit. "on the way of the River," i.e. the River Jordan.

ıcıp cpuaჳ ocup cpén, do éჳ ın hoc anno. Rıჳe do
ċabaıpc d'Aoძ mac Ruaıძpı do pıძıp, ocup pıჯ do ძenum
ძó pe mac Uıllıam buppc ıap nჳábaıl Peıძlım mıc
Caċaıl cpoıბძepჳ ძó. Caıplen bona ჳaıllṁe do
ძenum do Rıcapძ de buppჳ, ocup caıplen ძúın ımძaın
do cınnpcna la hAძam Sდonძún. Concobap mac
Aoძa mıc Ruaıძpı do élúძ ó ჳalloıb, ocup mıc pıჯ
Connacḣc do ċınól do uıme, ocup a ძul ıp na Cuaċaıb
ap ınnpaıჳıძ, ocup a mapbძძ láp na Cuaċaıb, ocup
ჳıllacellaıჯ O heıძın, ocup ჳıllacpıpc mac Donnċaძa
mıc Dıapmada, ocup pochaıde ımძa maılle ppıú; ocup
ıppé an lá pın do ჳealpac na Cuaċa a pamċaca uıle
an can aoußpaძ [ჳup] pep pamċaıჯe ჳıle po ṁapძ
mac Aoძa. Donnċaძ ṁac Comalcaıჯ mıc Dıapmada
mopcuup epc. Maჯnup mac Amláıb mıc Caıძჳ mıc
Maolpuanaıძ, coınnel eınıჯ ocup enჳnuma ocup cpabaძ,
ın Cpıpco quıeuıc. Pachcna .h. hAllჯaıძ, comapba
Dპomma Mucaძa, ocup oıppıძel Ua bṗhıaċpach,
pep ċıჯe aıძheძ ocup Luძpa, ocup Leıჯınn, ocup Leppuıჯძı
cıpe ocup calman, ın hoc anno quıeuıc. Maoıleoın
boძap .h. Maolċonaıpe do ჳaძáıl Ċlúana bolcáın ın
hoc anno. Cpı mıc Duınn I Mhannaċáın do ṁapbaძ do
Dhonnċaძ mac Muıpcepcaıჳ, a Cepmann Chaolaın,
ın hoc anno. Coıppecpaძ cempuıll Cılle moıpe a Cıp
bpıuın na Sınna, do Donnċaძ .h. Conchobaıp, eppuc
Olepınn, ocup canánaıჯ do ძenum ıpın mbaıle cedna la
Conn.h.bṗhlannacáın, do boı na ppıoıp ann an can pın.

---

[1] *Hoc.* oc, MS.

[2] *Again.* Under the year 1230,
supra, it is stated that the sovereignty
of Connacht was given to Aedh's cou-
sin, Fedhlim O'Conor, son of Cathal
Crobhderg, and that Aedh was banished to O'Neill.

[3] *Bun-Gaillmhe.* The mouth of the
Galway river. The Chron. Scotorum
at the year 1120=1124, and the Four

Masters, under 1124, record the erec-
tion of a castle by the Irish at Dun-
Gaillmhe, " the fort of Galway," or
Galway town.

[4] *Whitened.* The object of whiten-
ing the handles of the battle-axes was
to prevent the discovery of the person
who had slain Conchobhar, son of
Aedh.

[5] *Torch.* coınnel; lit. " candle."

of hospitality and maintenance for all in general, both poor and rich, died in hoc[1] anno. The sovereignty was again[2] given to Aedh, son of Ruaidhri, who made peace with the son of William Burk, after he had apprehended Fedhlim, son of Cathal Crobhderg. The castle of Bun-Gaillmhe[3] was erected by Richard de Burgh, and the castle of Dun-Indhain was begun by Adam Staunton. Conchobhar, son of Aedh, son of Ruaidhri,* escaped from the Foreigners, and assembled the sons of the king of Connacht about him; and he went into the Tuatha on an incursion, when he and Gillacellaigh O'hEidhin, and Gillachrist, son of Donnchadh Mac Diarmada, and a great multitude along with them, were slain by the Tuatha. And it was on that day the *men of the* Tuatha whitened[4] all their axe-handles, when it was said [that] a man with a white axe-handle had slain the son of Aedh. Donnchadh, son of Tomaltach Mac Diarmada, mortuus est. Maghnus, son of Amhlaibh, son of Tadhg Mac Maelruanaidh, torch[5] of honour, and bravery, and piety, in Christo quievit. Fachtna O'hAllghaith, comarb of Druim-mucadha, and official of UiFiachrach; keeper of a house of hospitality for guests and invalids; and the promoter of learning and improver of country and land, in hoc[1] anno quievit. Maeleoin Bodhar[6] O'Maelconaire took possession of Cluain-Bolcain in hoc[1] anno. The three sons of Donn O'Mannachain were slain by Donnchadh, son of Muirchertach, at Termon-Caelain, in hoc[1] anno. Consecration of the church of Cill-mor, in Tir-Briuin-na-Sinna,[7] by Donnchadh O'Conchobhair, bishop of Oilfinn; and Canons were established in the same town by Conn O'Flannagain,

---

[6] *Bodhar;* i.e. "the deaf."

[7] *In Tir-Briuin-na-Sinna.* This clause (ı Ṫıρ Ḃρıuın nα Sınnα) is transposed in the orig., being written after the name Oᴌeρınn in the succeeding line. Tir-Briuin-na-Sinna "the country of the Ui-Briuin of the Shannon," was one of the districts called the "three Tuatha," and included the parishes of Aughrim and Kilmore, to the east of Elphin, in the county of Roscommon.

Peڤlim mac Cαthαil cpoibꝺepᵹ ꝺo leiᵹen αmαc̓ ꝺo ᵹαlloib in hoc αnno.

Ktt. Onαip-pop pαt̓αpn, ocup peipeꝺ ꝺhéc puippe; int ochtmαꝺ bliαꝺαin ꝺhec ꝺon cicil noiecꝺα hí; xx. ppimo αnno cicli polαpip; pexto αnno inꝺictionip; αnno Ꝺomini m.cc.xxx. tepcio.¹ Sluαiᵹeꝺ lα Peꝺlim mac Cαthαil cpoibꝺepᵹ i Connαchtα, ᵹo tαnic Copmac mac Tomαltαiᵹ, pí Muiᵹe Luipᵹ, inα c̓oinni, ᵹo tuc leip α Mαᵹ Luipᵹ, ocup ᵹonꝺeppαt poplonᵹpopt αᵹ Ꝺpuim Ᵹpeαcpαiꝺe, .i. .h. Conchobαip ocup Copmac, ocup Conchobαp α mac, ocup nα tpi Tuαt̓α, ocup ꝺá mac Muipceptαiᵹ mic Ꝺiαpmαꝺα, .i. Ꝺonnchαꝺ ocup Muip-ceptαch; ocup ippí comαiple ꝺo ponpαt ꝺiꝓlinuiꝺ, tocht αnꝺiαiꝺ Oeꝺα mic Ruαiꝺpi, pi Connαcht, ocup clαinni Ruαiꝺpi αipchenα, co tucpαꝺ ᵹpαonc̓αoiꝺm peꝓαnαch poppα, ᵹup benαꝺ piᵹe ocup cenꝺup Connαcht ꝺo clαinn Ruαiꝺpi mic Thoippꝺelꝓαiᵹ ipin ló pin, oip po mαpbαꝺ Oeꝺ mac Ruαiꝺpi, pi Connαcht, αnn, ocup αoꝺ Muimnech mac Ruαiꝺpi, ocup α mac, ocup Ꝺonnchαꝺ mac Ꝺiαpmαꝺα mic Ruαiꝺpi, ocup ꝺαoine imꝺα eli mαille ppiú nαch αippꝓiꝺtep punn; iαp pápuᵹαꝺ t̓iᵹe ꝓαoit̓ín ocup iαp ná plαt ꝺOeꝺ Muimnech mac Ruαiꝺpi, ocup iαp plαtt chéαll ocup eᵹlup nimꝺα eli ꝺoiꝓ, po tuitpet pein i neinech nα ceαll ocup noem Connαcht ꝺo pápuᵹαꝺ. Raᵹαllac̓ O Plαnnαᵹáin ꝺo mαpbαꝺ ipin lo ceꝺnα pin, ocup po mαpbαꝺ Tomαp bipíp, conpꝺáplα nα hOpenn, ocup Ooαn α bpαt̓αip, ocup Ooαn Sᵹuiép,² ocup Ᵹoill imꝺα eli αnn ꝓeop, iαp nα nepcoine, ocup iαp mbαꝺαꝺ α conniol³ ꝺo c̓léipc̓iꝓ Connαcht peme pin. Coic

---

¹ *Tertio.* tepcio, MS.

² *Sguier.* Sᵹuiep (Sguier), MS. The Four Mast. write the name Ᵹuep (Guer).

³ *Extinguished.* The words iαp mbαꝺαꝺ α conniol, signify literally "after drowning their candles;" i.e. after they had been excommunicated. See note ², p. 282, *supra*.

who was prior there at that time. Fedhlim, son of Cathal Crobhderg, was set at large by the Foreigners in hoc anno.

The kalends of January on Saturday, and the 16th of the moon; the eighteenth year of the Decennovenalian cycle; xx. primo anno cycli solaris; sexto anno Indictionis; anno Domini M.CC.XXX. tertio.[1] A hosting into Connacht by Fedhlim, son of Cathal Crobhderg, when Cormac, son of Tomaltach, king of Magh-Luirg, came to meet him, and took him with him into Magh-Luirg; and they established a camp at Druim-Gregraidhe, viz.:—O'Conchobhair, and Cormac, and his son Conchobhar, and the three Tuatha, and the two sons of Muirchertach Mac Diarmada, i.e. Donnchadh and Muirchertach. And the resolution they respectively adopted was to go in pursuit of Aedh, son of Ruaidhri, king of Connacht, and the other sons of Ruaidhri, whom they totally defeated and dispersed; and the sons of Ruaidhri, son of Toirdhelbhach, were deprived of the sovereignty and supremacy of Connacht on that day, for Aedh, son of Ruaidhri, king of Connacht, and Aedh Muimhnech, son of Ruaidhri, and his son, and Donnchadh, son of Diarmaid, son of Ruaidhri, were slain there, and many other persons along with them who are not enumerated here. After the profanation and pillaging of Tech-Baeithin by Aedh Muimhnech, son of Ruaidhri; and after many other churches and ecclesiastical establishments had been plundered by them, they fell themselves in revenge for having profaned the churches and saints of Connacht. Raghallach O'Flannagain was slain on the same day; and Thomas Biris, constable of Erinn, and his brother John, and John Squier,[2] and many other Foreigners also, were slain there, after they had been cursed, and after their candles had been extinguished,[3] by the clerics of Connacht before that. Five years, moreover, was Aedh,

bliαdnα, ımoppo, dOedh mac Ruaıdpı α pıże Connacht,
amaıl ıpbept :—

   Αod mac Ruaıdpı an puathaıp mıp,
   Coıg bliadna op cınn an dúıżıd,
   Żup túıt, epbud żach ımıl,
   Αn pep poın la Feıdlımıd.

Dedh flaıtıup claınnı Ruaıdpı hı Conchobaıp, pı
Epenn, ınnpın. Uaıp tapccaıd an Papa cept ap Epınn
dó peın ocup dá fıol na dıaıd żo bpát, ocup peıppep do
mnaıb pópda, ocup tżup do pecad na mban o pın amac;
ocup nıp żab Ruaıdpı pın; ocup ó nap żab do ben Dıa
pıże ocup flaıtemnup dá fıol co ppát ı ndıżoltup
pecaıd na mban. Ro żab Feıdlım mac Cathaıl cpoıb-
depc pıże ocup flaıtemnup pop Connachtaıb app α
haıtle, ocup na caıpléın do pónad le nept claınnı
Ruaıdpı hı Conchobaıp ocup mıc Uıllıam bupc, po
pcaoıled la Feıdlım ıad .ı. caıplén bona żallme
ocup Caıplén na cıpce, ocup Caıplén na caıllıżı, ocup
caıplen Duın ımdáın. Sıt ocup pmacht ap cetepnaıb,
ocup ap macaıb mallachtan, do eıpże po cedóıp pe
Lınn ın pıż óıg pın ın bliadaın pın, żo paıb na típeı na
teıżle pe peımep. Sloıżed la hUıllıam de Lacı .ı. mac
Uża ocup ıngıne Ruaıdpı mıc Thoıppdelbaıż moıp
hı Conchobaıp, ocup la żalloıb na Mıde maılle ppıp,
condechadap pocpaıde mop ıpın mbpeıppne docum
Chathaıl hı Raıżıllıż, ocup docum Chonconnacht a

---

[1] *Said.* The stanza which follows is from a poem by a person called (*infra*, at A.D. 1278) Donn Losc O'Maelchonaire (Donn the Lame O'Mulconry), beginning Eıptıż α eıgpı Danba, "Listen, ye learned of Banba," copies of which are preserved in several Irish MSS. See MSS. 23, G, 12, R. I. Acad., p. 120; and 23, G, 8, fol. 57 *b.*

[2] *To himself;* i.e. to Ruaidhri O'Conchobhair, or Rory O'Conor.

[3] *For ever.* co ppát for co bpát, MS. The expression co bpát, conventionally signifying "for ever," literally means "to judgment;" i.e. 'to the day of judgment." The use of p for b is frequently noticeable in the text of this chronicle. The observations "Roger's children extinguished," and "the Pope offers Roger O'Conor six wives," have been added in the margin by Roderick O'Flaherty.

son of Ruaidhri, in the sovereignty of Connacht, as was said :—[1]

> Aedh, son of Ruaidhri, of the quick onset
> *Was* five years over the province,
> Until fell, a loss to every feast,
> This man by Fedhlimidh.

This was the termination of the sovereignty of the descendants of Ruaidhri O'Conchobhair, king of Erinn: for the Pope had offered right over Erinn to himself[2] and his seed after him for ever, and six married wives, provided that he desisted from the sin of the women from thenceforth; but Ruaidhri did not accept this. And as he did not accept, God took kingship and sovereignty from his seed for ever,[3] in punishment of the sin of the women. Fedhlim, son of Cathal Crobhderg, immediately assumed sovereignty and government over the Connachtmen; and the castles that had been erected through the power of the sons of Ruaidhri O'Conchobhair and the son of William Burk were demolished by Fedhlim, viz. :—the castle of Bun-Gaillmhe,[4] and Caislen-na-circe,[5] and Caislen-na-caillighe,[6] and the castle of Dun-Imdhain. Peace, and correction over kernes and sons of malediction,[7] grew up immediately in the time of this young king, in this year, so that the districts were orderly during his reign. A hosting by William de Laci, (i.e. the son of Hugo and the daughter of Ruaidhri, son of Toirdhelbhach Mor O'Conchobhair), and by the Foreigners of Midhe along with him; when they went in great force into the Breifne, to Cathal O'Raighilligh, and to his brother Cuconnacht,

---

[4] *Bun-Gaillmhe;* i.e. the mouth of the Gaillimh, or Galway river, which gives name to the town of Galway. See note *, p. 310, *supra.*

[5] *Caislen-na-circe;* (pron. Kashlén-na-Kirké); literally "the Hen's Castle," a name still applied to the ruins which are to be seen on a rocky island in the N.W. of Lough Corrib. See Sir William Wilde's *Lough Corrib,* &c., p. 271.

[6] *Caislen-na-caillighe.* "The Hag's Castle," in Lough Mask, county Mayo.

[7] *Sons of malediction.* Outlaws, or persons who had been excommunicated.

bµαṫαµ, conveµηµατ cµeċα móµα.   Oµonʓ, ιmoµµo, vo
muιnnτιµ hι Rαιʓιllιʓ vo ċeʓṁαιl Uιllιαm vé Lαcí ocuµ
vocum mαιċιι αnτ µlóιʓ αµ veµeḃ nα ʓcµeċ, ocuµ
ταċuµ vo ċαḃαιµτ vαµoιlι ṽoιḃ, ocuµ Uιllιαm ḃµιτ vo
mαµḃαv αnnµιn, ocuµ ʓαιll ṁαιċι elι mαιlle µµιµ, ocuµ
Uιllιαm ve Lαcí vo loτ αnn, ocuµ Séµluµ mαc Cαṫαιl
ʓαιll, ocuµ µoċαιve elι mαµαon µιú; ocuµ α nιmµúṽ
ιαµµιn ʓαn ʓeιll ʓαn evιµe αµ ιn τíµ; ocuµ Uιllιαm ve
Lαcí, αcuµ Seµluµ mαc Cαṫαιl ʓαιll hι Conċoḃαιµ,
ocuµ Ḟeoµuµ µιnv mαc nα ʓαιll µιʓnα, ocuµ Oιαµmαιv
beµnαċ. h. Mαoιlµeċluιnn, vo héc ιnα τιʓιḃ µeιn µo
cevóιµ vo nα loτταιḃ τucαv µoµµα α Mónαι ċµαnvċαιn.
Oonncαṫαιʓ, .ι. αιµċιnveċ Αċαιv Ṝαḃαιµ, xuιιι. Ḱτ.
Ιαnuαµιι ιn Cµιµτo quιeuιτ; µeµ co nαιµmιvιn ċellι ocuµ
cµoċα α τuαιċ ocuµ α neʓluιµ, vuιne vob µeµµ ocuµ vob
µeιle ιm cµoṽ ocuµ ιm bιuṽ ταnιc ι ʓcomαιmµιµ µιµ,
víven τµuαʓ ocuµ τµén, αιµmιvιn αn τíµe ocuµ αn
ταlmαn, µoιuµαιṽ ocuµ µéṽʓαιv cαċα válα ιvιµ α
muιnτιµ µeιn ocuµ cαċ α ʓcoιτċιnne.   Mαιlíµα .h.
Mαonαιʓ, .ι. uαµαl µαʓαµτ vo ʓαḃαv α ḟαlταιµ ʓαċ láι
αċτ vια Oomnαιʓ nαmá, ιn Cµιµτo quιeuιτ. Ḟeµʓαl
mαc Coµmαιc moµτuuµ eµτ.

Ḱτ. Enαιµ µoµ Oonmαċ, ocuµ .xxιιι. µuιµµe; blια-
vαιn veµιṽ noιecvα hí; xxᵒ.ιιᵒ. αnno cιclι µolαµιµ;
µeµτιmo αnno ιnvιcτιonιµ; αnno Oomιnι m.cc.xxx.
quαµτo.   Αċṽ .h. heʓµα, µí Luιʓne, vo ṁαµḃαv vo
Oḣonnċαv mαc Ouαµcáιn hι Eʓµαι, ocuµ τeċ vo
loµcαv αιµ, ocuµ α ṁαµḃαv α nvoµuµ αn τιʓe ιαµ
τeαċτ αµ vó, α nvóιʓαιlτ α bµαιτµeċh ocuµ coιʓ mαc

---

[1] *Brit.* Roderick O'Flaherty writes the name "Brett," in a marg. note.

[2] *Cathal Gall.* "Cathal (or Charles) the Foreigner;" so called from his connexion with the English, or speaking the English language.

[3] *Charles.* Ceµluµ, MS.; but written Seµluµ two lines before.

[4] *Feorus Finn.* "Pierce the Fair."

[5] *Foreign Queen;* i.e. Isabella, mother of Henry III.

[6] *Diarmaid Bernach;* "Diarmaid the gapped;" i.e. of the gapped teeth; from beµnα, "a gap."

[7] *Januarii.* ιenuαµιι, MS.

and committed great depredations. A party of the
people of O'Raighilligh, however, encountered William de
Laci and the chieftains of the host, who were behind the
preys; and they gave each other battle, and William
Brit[1] was slain there, and other good Foreigners along
with him; and William de Laci was wounded there, and
Charles, son of Cathal Gall,[2] and many more along with
them; and they (the Foreigners) afterwards returned
from the district, without pledges or hostages; and
William de Laci; and Charles,[3] son of Cathal Gall[2] O'Conchobhair; and Feorus Finn,[4] son of the Foreign Queen;[5]
and Diarmaid Bernach[6] O'Maelsechlainn, died in their own
houses immediately after from the wounds inflicted on
them at Mona-crand-chain. Donncathaigh, i.e. airchinnech
of Achadh-Fabhair, xviii. kalendas Januarii[7] in Christo
quievit: a man held in high repute for sense and figure, in
country and church; the best and most generous man of
his contemporaries regarding cattle and food; the protector of the poor and mighty; the object of esteem of
the country and land; the guide and settler of every
affair between his own people and all in general. Maelisa
O'Maenaigh, i.e. a noble priest who was wont to recite his
psalter every day excepting Sunday alone, in Christo
quievit. Ferghal Mac Cormaic mortuus est.

The kalends of January on Sunday, and the 27th of
the moon. It was the last year of the Nineteen; xx°.ii°.
anno cycli solaris; septimo anno Indictionis; anno Domini
M.CC.XXX. quarto. Aedh O'hEghra, king of Luighne,
was killed by Donnchadh, son of Duarcan O'hEghra—(a
house was burned over him, and he was killed in the
door of the house, after coming out of it)—in revenge for
his having first killed his[8] brother[9] and the five sons of

---

[8] His; i.e. Donnchad's or Donough's. In the Annals of Boyle it is stated that Donnchadh was the brother of Aedh O'hEghra, or Hugh O'Hara.

[9] His brother. α bρατc[c]ρ for α bρατcρech, MS. The Four Masters say α δеарιbρатαρ, which is the more usual form. The correct gen. sg. of bρατhαρ is bρατhαρ, not bρατρech. See Stokes's Irish Glosses, pp. 80, 120.

oeρbρατhαρ α ατhαρ oo mαρbαo ŏóραm αρ τúρ, ocuρ α
oeρbρατhαρ eli oo ŧαllαo. Rιcαρo mαc Uιllιαm
Mαρuρξál oo ŧoξbáιl coξαιo [ιn αξαιo] ριξ Sαχραn α
Sαcραιb, ocuρ τοιξeϲhτ oo ταιριρ αnoιρ ξonoeϲhαιo α
Lαιξnιb; ocuρ τιnolαιτ ξαιll Eρenn ιnα αξαιo α huϲhτ
ριξ Sαϲραn, .ι. mαc Muιριρ, ξιuιρoíρ nα hEρenn mun
αm ριn, ocuρ ιαρlα Ulαo, .ι. Uξα oe Lαcí, ocuρ Uαloαρ
oé Lαcí, .ι. τιξeρnα nα Mιŏe; ocuρ ταncoταρ ριn uιle
ξo Cuιρρeϲh Lιρρe α Lαιξnιb, ξuρ ϲuιρρeτ cατ ριϲ̆oα
ρορnιατα ρριρn Mαραρξál, ξuρ mαρbαo Rιcαρo
mαc Uιllιαm Mαρuρξál αnn, ocuρ ξuρ ξαbαo Seρ-
ρραιξ Mαρuρϲál; ocuρ nι ραιbe αξ cuρ αn cατα ριn
ραoeóιŏ αchτ eιριom α αonαρ, ιαρ ná τρeιξen oα muιnτeρ ŭŏeιn; ocuρ oonα heϲhταŏ ιρ mó oo ρónαo ιριn
αιmριρ[ριn] ιnτ eϲhτ ριn. Oenξuρ .h. Mαoιlαξ̆ḿαιρ,
eρρuc .h. nαmαlξαιo, quιeuιτ ιn Cρ̆ιρτo. Snechτα moρ
ιτιρ oα nooluιc, ocuρ ριc ιαρριn, co nιmξíoιρ oαoιne
ocuρ eιϲ ρο neρeohαιb ρριḿ Locα ocuρ αιbne Eρenn.
αonξuρ mαc ξιllαριnnén, ρι Locα hEιρne, oo oul oo
ŏenum cρeιϲe αρ Oomnαll .h. nOomnαιll, ρí τιρe
Conαιll; ocuρ ρuc .h. Oomnαιll ραιρ, ocuρ α mαρbαo
oonτ ριbαl ριn. ξιllα nα nαom mαc αιρτ hι Dρáιn,
ταιρϲιnoeϲh Roρρα Comáιn, ιn Cρ̆ιρτo quιeuιτ. Mαιl-
ρeταιρ .h. Coρmαcán, mαιξιρτeρ Roρρα Comáιn, ιn
Cρ̆ιρτo quιeuιτ. Oιαρmαιo .h. Cuιnn, ouχ muιnτeρι
ξιllξán, moρτuuρ eρτ. Mαιlρα mαc Oαnιel hι
ξoρmρ́uιlξ, ρριóιρ Innρι mιc Néιριn αρ Loϲ Cé, moρτuuρ

---

1 *His*; i.e. Donnchadh O'hEghra's.
See note 8, p. 317.

2 [*Against*]. [ιn αξαιo]. Apparently omitted by the scribe, and supplied from the Annals of Boyle.

3 *Mac Maurice.* His proper name
was Maurice FitzGerald, but as his
grandfather's name was Maurice, he
may have been called Mac Maurice
by way of patronymic. See the *Earls
of Kildare*, by the Marquess of Kildare, 1st series, p. 11, *sq*.

4 *Cuirrech-Liffe.* Now called the
Curragh of Kildare.

5 *Himself alone*; i.e. Richard
Maréchal. The Four Masters mention this defection of the forces of
Richard Maréchal in nearly the same
words, but the clause has been wrongly
translated by Dr. O'Donovan, who
represents Geoffroi Maréchal (*rectè* De
Marisco or De Marreis) as the person
abandoned by his own people.

his[1] father's brother, and having blinded his[1] other
brother.　Richard, son of William Maréchal, raised a war
[against][2] the king of the Saxons, in Saxon-land, and
came across from the east, and went into Laighen; and
the Foreigners of Erinn assembled against him on behalf
of the king of the Saxons, viz. :—Mac Maurice,[3] Justiciary
of Erinn at that time, and the Earl of Uladh, i.e. Hugo
de Laci, and Walter de Laci, i.e. the Lord of Midhe.　And
all these proceeded to Cuirrech-Liffe[4] in Laighen, and
fought a fierce, obstinate battle against the Maréchal; and
Richard, son of William Maréchal, was slain there, and
Geoffroi Maréchal taken prisoner.　And there was no one
fighting this battle towards the end but himself alone,[5]
after he had been abandoned by his own people.　And
this deed was one of the greatest deeds committed in
[that] time.　Aenghus O'Maelaghmhair,[6] bishop of Ui-
Amhalghaidh,[7] quievit in Christo.　Great snow between
the two Christmasses,[8] and frost afterwards, so that men,
and horses under burthens, would pass over the principal
lakes and rivers of Erinn.　Aenghus Mac Gillafinnen,
king of Loch-Erne,[9] went to commit a depredation on
Domhnall O'Domhnaill, king of Tir-Conaill; and O'Domhnaill caught him, and he was slain on this journey.
Gilla-na-naemh, son of Art O'Brain, airchinnech of Ros-
Comain, in Christo quievit.　Maelpetair O'Cormacán,
master of Ros-Comain, in Christo quievit.　Diarmaid
O'Cuinn, dux of Muinter-Gilgan, mortuus est.　Maelisa,
son of Daniel O'Gormshuiligh,[10] prior of Inis-Mic-Neirin

[6] *O'Maelaghmhair.* h. Maoilaġ-
ṁaip. The name is usually written
Maoilḟaġṁaip, but the ḟ and other
aspirated consonants are frequently
omitted in the text of this chronicle.
See note [8], p. 305, *supra.* The name
would be pronounced O'Mullover.

[7] *Bishop of Ui-Amhalghaidh;* i.e.
of Killala.

[8] *Two Christmasses.*　Great Christmas, or the 25th of December, and
Little Christmas, or Twelfth Night.

[9] *King of Loch-Erne.*　The king of
Feara-Manach, or Fermanagh, was
also sometimes called king of Loch-
Erne, by way of distinction.

[10] *O'Gormshuiligh.* This name, which
would be pronounced O'Gormooly, is
written O'Gormghaile (O'Gormally)
by the Four Masters. See note [1], p. 306.

eɼc. Ʒillαιɼα .h. Ʒibillαιn, mαnαch, αnαcoɼιτα ιnɼole
ɼαncτe Τɼινιτατιɼ, ιn Cɼιɼτo quιeuιτ. Ɖomnαll mαc
Ccoδα hι Néιll, ɼί čenél Eoʒαιn, ocuɼ ɒeɼ αδbuɼ ɼι
Eɼenn, ɒo mαɼbαɒ ɒo mάʒ Lαčlαιnn ocuɼ ɒo čenél
Eoʒαιn ɼαδeιɼιn.

ʃcτ. Enαιɼ ɼoɼ Luαn, ocuɼ ochτmαɒ uατhαɒ ɼuιɼɼe;
ɼɼιmuɼ αnnuɼ cιclι ɒecennouenαlιɼ; xxιιι. αnno cιclι
ɼolαɼιɼ; uιιι. αnno ιnɒιcτιonιɼ; αnno Ɖomιnι .m.cc.
xxx.quιnτo. Mαɒαδαιn .h. Mαɒαδαιn, ɼι ɼιl nCcnm-
chαɒα, moɼτuuɼ eɼτ. ιɼααc .h. Mαιlαʒmαιɼ, αιɼčιn-
ɒech Cιlle hCclαιδ, ɒo héc ιn hoc αnno. Ločlαιnn,
mαc mιc Echτιʒeɼn .h. Chellαιʒh, ɒo mαɼbαɒ ɒo
mαcαιδ αn ʒιllα ɼιαbαιʒ hι Bhαιʒιll ιn hoc αnno.
Ταιčleč mαc Ccoδα hι Ɖuδɒα, ɼι .h. nCcmαlʒαιɒ ocuɼ
.h.bɼιαcɼαč, ɒo mαɼbαɒ ɒαon uɼchuɼ ɼoιʒɒe αc
euɒαιn α Lonʒɼuιɼτ Ɉheδlιm mιc Cατhαιl cɼoιbɒeɼʒ,
ɼιʒ Connαchτ. Sloιʒeɒ moɼ lα Ʒαlloιb Eɼenn αɼ nα
τιnόl ɒo Rιcαɼɒ mαc Uιllιαm Buɼc; ocuɼ ταncαɒαɼ
ταɼ Cč Luαιn co Roɼ Comαιn, ocuɼ ɼo loιɼceɒ Roɼ
Comάn leo, ocuɼ αɼɼιeιn co hOιlɼιnn, ocuɼ ɼo loιɼceτ
τempαll mόɼ Oιleɼιnn; ocuɼ ταncαɒαɼ αɼɼιδé co mαιnιɼɒιɼ Cčα ɒα lααɼαc ɼoɼ Buιll; ocuɼ ιɼɼιαɒ bα hαɼɒ
αιɼιʒ ocuɼ bα huɼɼunταιʒ ɒonτ ɼluαιʒeɒ ɼιn, .ι. Mαc
Muιɼιɼ, .ι. Ʒιuιɼόιɼ nα hEɼenn, ocuɼ Uʒα ɒé Lαcί ιαɼlα
Ulαɒ, ocuɼ Rιcαɼɒ mαc Uιllιαm Buɼc, ocuɼ Uαlɒαɼ
Rιταδαɼɒ, αɼɒ Bαɼún Lαιʒen, co nʒαlloιb Lαιʒen
mαɼoen ɼιɼ, ocuɼ ɼιταδα Eɼenn uιle mαɼαon ɼú, ocuɼ
Eoαn Ʒocάn co nʒαlloιb nα Mumαn mαιlle ɼιɼ; ocuɼ
ταncαɒαɼ αʒh[αιɒ] Ɖomnαιʒ nα Τɼιnoιɒe ʒo mαιnιɼɒιɼ

1 *Anacorita.* ιncoɼιτα, MS.

2 *Trinitatis.* τɼιneτάτιɼ, MS.
Trinity Island, in Loch-Cé, is the
place meant.

3 *Decennovenalis.* ɒecιnouατ, MS.

4 *Quinto.* quιncτo, MS.

5 *O'Maelaghmhair.* h. Mαιlαʒmαιɼ, for h. Mαιlɼαʒmαιɼ. See
note 6, last page.

6 *In hoc.* αn oc, MS.

7 *Mac Maurice.* Maurice FitzGerald.
See note 3, p. 318.

8 *Walter Ritabard.* Giraldus Cambrensis writes his name Gualterus de
Ridenesfordia (*Expugnatio Hibernica*,

on Loch-Cé, mortuus est. Gilla-Isa O'Gibillain, a monk, anacorita[1] insulæ Sanctæ Trinitatis,[2] in Christo quievit. Domhnall, son of Aedh O'Neill, king of Cenel-Eoghain, and the good material of a king of Erinn, was slain by Mac Lachlainn and the Cenel-Eoghain themselves.

The kalends of January on Monday, and the eighth of the moon; primus annus cycli Decennovenalis;[3] xxiii. anno cycli solaris; viii. anno Indictionis; anno Domini M.cc.xxx. quinto.[4] Madadhan O'Madadhain, king of Sil-Anmchadha, mortuus est. Isaac O'Maelaghmhair,[5] airchinnech of Cill-Alaidh, died in hoc[6] anno. Lochlainn, grandson of Echtighern O'Cellaigh, was slain by the sons of the Gilla-riabhach O'Baighill in hoc anno. Taichlech, son of Aedh O'Dubhda, king of Ui-Amhalghaidh and Ui-Fiachrach, was killed by the discharge of an arrow, whilst interfering (to *quell a dispute*) in the camp of Fedhlim, son of Cathal Crobhderg, king of Connacht. A great hosting by the Foreigners of Erinn, who were assembled by Richard, son of William Burk; and they went across Ath-Luain to Ros-Comain, when Ros-Comain was burned by them; and *they went* from thence to Oilfinn, and burned the great church of Oilfinn; and they proceeded from thence to the monastery of Ath-da-laarc on the Buill. And the persons who were the principal chieftains and the boldest on this hosting were Mac Maurice,[7] i.e. the Justiciary of Erinn, and Hugo de Laci, Earl of Uladh, and Richard, son of William Burk, and Walter Ritabhard,[8] high baron of Laighen, with whom were the Foreigners of Laighen; and the routs[9] of all Erinn were along with them; and John Gocan,[10] having the Foreigners of Mumha along with him. And they went on the night of Trinity Sunday to the monas-

---

Lib. II., cap. xxi., ed. Dimock); but the more correct form is De Ridelisford, as Mr. Gilbert has it. *Irish Viceroys*, passim.

[9] *Routs;* i.e. bands, companies, or troops.

[10] *Gocan.* A corrupt way of writing the name of Cogan, apparently begun in Munster, where the name is pretty general at present under the form of Goggan, or Goggin.

ɴα ḃúıƚƚe, ocuſ ɗo ċuαɗαſ α ſeſſénαıʒ ſon mαıɴıſɗıſ
ocuſ ɗo ḃſıſeɗαſ αɴ ſcſıoſɗα, ocuſ ɽucαıɗ α ıɴɴṁuſ
uıƚe, ocuſ α coıƚıʒ αſſſıɴɴ ocuſ α éɗαıʒe αƚɗoſα αſſ ;
ocuſ ɓα ʒſαıɴ ṁóſ ƚα mαıċıḃ Ʒαƚƚ αɴ ɴı ſıɴ, ocuſ ɗo
cuıſıc αſ cúƚα ʒαcɦ ɴı ɗıḃ ɗá mɓóı αſ ſαʒαıƚ, ocuſ ɗo
hícαıc ɴα ɴeıcɦe ɴαcɦ ḃſſıḃ ; ocuſ ɗo ċuıſeɗαſ α ſıſıḃ
ocuſ α ſeſſénαıʒ αſ α ɓαſαcɦ, ocuſ α ſıcαɗα ceıceſɴe,
ʒo Cſeıc ocuſ co Cαıſċı Muıƚċe, ocuſ αſſıɴ co Coſ
ʒƚıɴɴe Ɫeſɴα, co cucſαɗ cſeċα móſα ƚeo co hÓſɗ
ċαſɴα α coıɴɴe αɴ ʒuıſɗıſ. Ɗo ſoɴſαc Ʒαƚƚ comαıſƚe
ıɴʒɴαɗ αɴɴſıɴ ɴαſ ſmuαıɴ Coɴɴαcɦcαcɦ ɴα Muımɴecɦ
ɗo ɗenum ɗoıḃ, cſe ſαſƚαċ Eoʒαıɴ hı Eıʒıɴ, ɗo ɗíʒαıƚ
α ċɴeɗ αſ Muımɴecɦαıḃ ocuſ αſ Ɗoɴɴcɦαɗ Cαıſbſecɦ
.h. ɓſıαıɴ, .ı. coıʒecɦc αſ cúƚα ıſıɴ ſƚıʒeɗ ceoɴα α Cıſ
Mhαıɴe, ocuſ α Mαoɴṁoıʒ, ocuſ αſſıeıʒ α Cuαɗṁumuıɴ,
ʒαɴ ſαḃαɗ ʒαɴ ſáċuʒαɗ, co ḃſſıḃ Muımɴıʒ ʒαɴ ceıcɦeɗ
ʒαɴ αıſċıƚƚ ; ocuſ ɗo ſóɴſαɗ cſecɦαı móſα ɗıαıſṁıɗeı
ſoſſα αɴɴſıɴ. Ɗαƚα Coɴɴαcɦc, ımoſſo, ocuſ Ɫeɗƚım
mıc Cαċαıƚ cſoıḃɗeſʒ, cαɴcoɗαſ αɴɗıαıɗ Ʒαƚƚ αſ
ɴéƚúḃ ɗóıḃ, ɗo comαƚƚ α mḃſeıcſı ſe Muımɴecɦαıḃ,
ocuſ ɗo cαḃαıſc α ƚá ɓáʒα ƚeo, ocuſ ɗo ɓeſċe [ɗeαḃċα]
ɗeſṁáſαı ɗıṁoſα ecuſſα ʒαcɦ ƚoı. Iɴ ƚá ɗeıʒeɴαcɦ,
ımoſſo, ɗo eſʒeɗαſ Coɴɴαcɦcαıʒ ocuſ Muımɴıʒ ɗocum
ɴα ɗeαḃċα, ocuſ cucſαc co beoɗα bıċɴeſcmαſ, ocuſ co
ſeſαmαıƚ ſeoċαıſ hí. Αcɦc cɦeɴα, ſo ƚuıɗſeɗ ıƚ ıomαɗ
Ʒαƚƚ ɴéıɗıʒeı ocuſ cſomƚαıḃ mαſcſƚuαıʒ oſſα, ocuſ ɗo
mαſbαɗ ſocɦαıɗe ɗſeſuıḃ Mumαɴ αɴɴſıɴ, cſe αımʒƚıcuſ
comαıſƚe ɗo ſαƚα ɗo Ɗoɴɴcɦαɗ Cαıſſſeċ .h. mɓſıαıɴ ;
ocuſ cαɴcoɗαſ Coɴɴαcɦcαıʒ αıſɗe ſo ſceıṁ eɴʒɴumα
ocuſ ſoṁαıſı, ʒαɴ ɗuıɴe ſuαıcɦeɴcα ɗo ṁαſbαɗ ɗıḃ.
Iſſí comαıſƚe ɗo ſoıɴe .h. ɓſıαıɴ αſ ɴá ɓαſαċ, ſıċ ɗo

---

¹ [*Contests*]. The word ɗeαḃċα, omitted in the text, has been supplied from the Four Masters.

² *Between them*; i.e. between the

Foreigners and Eoghan O'hEidhin (Owen O'Heyne) on the one side, and the Momonians and Conacians on the other.

tery of Buill; and their soldiers attacked the monastery, and broke open the sacristy; and all its valuable things, and its mass-chalices and altar-cloths, were taken out of it. And this was very hateful to the chieftains of the Foreigners, who returned every article of them that was to be found; and they paid for the things that were not found. And on the morrow they sent their scouts and soldiers, and their routs of kernes, to Creit, and to Cairthe-Muilche, and to Tor-Ghlinne-Ferna, when they brought great preys with them to Ard-carna, to meet the Justiciary. The Foreigners then adopted an extraordinary resolution, (which no Conacian or Momonian contemplated that they would adopt), at the request of Eoghan O'hEighin, who wished to revenge his injuries on the Momonians, and on Donnchadh Cairbrech O'Briain, viz. :— to go back in the same path into Tir-Maine, and into Maen-magh, and *they went* from thence to Tuadh-Mumha, without being noticed or observed; and the Momonians were found without having escaped or made preparations; and they then committed great *and* countless depredations on them. As regards the Conacians and Fedhlim, son of Cathal Crobhderg, however, they followed the Foreigners, after they had stolen away, to keep their engagement with the Momonians, and to afford them succour; and vehement, great [contests][1] were fought between them[2] each day. On the last day, moreover, the Conacians and Momonians went to the contest, and fought it actively, strenuously, manfully, and fiercely. Nevertheless, too many mail-clad Foreigners and a great multitude of cavalry pressed upon them, and a large number of the men of Mumha were slain there through indiscretion of counsel on the part of Donnchadh Cairbrech O'Briain. But the Conacians came out of it with the credit of bravery and glory, without any notable man of them having been slain. The resolution O'Briain adopted, on the morrow, ṫenum ꞃe Ꞅalloiḃ, ḃꞃaiᵹṽe ocuꞅ cíꞃ ꞇo ṫaḃaiꞃꞇ ꞇoiḃ ; ocuꞅ ꞃo ḃuṽ ꞃoꞇa ṽóꞃuim conꞇeꞃnaꞇ an coṁaiꞃle ꞃin, uaiꞃ ꞃo cꞃeċaꞇ ocuꞅ ꞃo loiꞃceꞇ uꞃṁoꞃ a muinꞇeꞃi conice ꞃin. Ꝺala Ꞅall, imoꞃꞃo, ꞇancaꞇaꞃ ꞃempu ꞇoċum Cónnaċꞇ, ocuꞅ ꞇucaꞇaꞃ a naiᵹhiꞇ aꞃ ꞇúꞃ aꞃ Ccṽ .h. ḃꝉlaiṫḃeꞃꞇaiᵹ, ocuꞅ ꞇo ꞃoine ꞃiṫ ꞃe Ꞅalloiḃ ꞇaꞃ cenꞇ a ḃo ocuꞅ a muinꞇiꞃe, ꞇaꞃ cenn a ꞇiꞃe ocuꞅ a ṫalman. Ꝺala Ꝑeṽlim mic Caṫail cꞃoiḃꞇeꞃᵹ, imoꞃꞃo, iꞃꞃí comaiꞃle ꞇo ꞃoine in neoċ ꞃuaiꞃ ꞇo ḃuaiṽ a Conmaicne Maꞃa, ocuꞅ a Conmaicne na Cúile, ocuꞅ ꞇo ᵹaċ neoċ ꞇo ꞃoine a comaiꞃle, ocuꞅ mac Maᵹnuiꞃ ocuꞅ Conċoḃaꞃ ꞃuaṽ mac Muiꞃceꞃꞇaiᵹ ṁuiṁniᵹ, a mḃꞃeiṫ leiꞅ ı nuċꞇ hı Ꝺhomnaill, ocuꞅ an ꞇíꞃ ꞇo leiᵹen ꞇo ᵹalloiḃ ꞇiaꞃꞃaꞇ. ıaꞃꞃin ꞇꞃa ꞇancaꞇaꞃ Ꞅoill ᵹo Ꝺún Moṽoꞃꞇ, ocuꞅ ꞇo ċuiꞃeꞇaꞃ ꞇeċꞇa ꞇoċum Maᵹnuꞃa mic Muiꞃceꞃꞇaiᵹ Muimniᵹ, ꞇiaꞃꞃaꞇ ꞃiꞇe ocuꞅ ḃꞃaᵹaꞇ ꞃaiꞃ, ocuꞅ nı ꞇuc Maᵹnuꞃ ꞃiṫ ına ḃꞃaiᵹꞇi ꞇoiḃ. Ꝺo ċuiꞃeꞇaꞃ, ꞇꞃa, Ꞅoill cꞃeċa móꞃa o ṽún Muiᵹṽoꞃꞇ ına macaiḃ Ruaiṽꞃi, co · ꞃeꞃꞃénaċaiṽ ꞇiáiꞃṁiṽṫi, ᵹuꞃ aiꞃceꞇaꞃ Ꞇccuill, ocuꞅ ꞇucaꞇaꞃ ꞇainꞇi móꞃa leo ᵹo Ꝺꞃuimne a còinne ᵹall. Ꝺala, imoꞃꞃo, Ccṽa hı Ꝑhlaiṫḃeꞃꞇaiᵹ ocuꞅ Ꞇoᵹain hı Ꞇṽin, ꞇancaꞇaꞃ ꞃloiᵹ móꞃ ꞇimċell, ocuꞅ aꞃꞃꞇꞃaiᵹe iaꞃ na ꞇaiꞃḃeꞃꞇ co liónán ċinn ṁaꞃa. Ꞇancoꞇaꞃ na haꞃꞇꞃaiᵹe cona ꞃoċaiꞇiḃ, ocuꞅ ꞇanic an Ꞅiúꞃꞇiꞅ ına coinne co Ꝺꞃuimne, ᵹo calaꞇ ınnꞅi Cconaiᵹ. Ꝺo ḃói Maᵹnuꞃ ocuꞅ a lonᵹa aꞃ ꞃꞃuṫ na hinnꞅi, ocuꞅ ꞇeaḃꞇa móꞃa ocuꞅ imꞃiaᵹa ına naiᵹiṽ imáꞃeċh. Ro ꞃᵹiꞇaiᵹiꞇ ꞇꞃa Ꞅoill in uaiꞃ ꞃin, ocuꞅ iꞃꞃí coṁaiꞃle ꞇo ꞃónꞃaꞇ lonᵹꞃoꞃꞇ ꞇo ᵹaḃáil, ocuꞅ a naꞃꞇꞃaiᵹe ꞇo ṫaꞃꞃinᵹ cuca a cúil ꞇon ꞇꞃaiᵹ ꞃo

---

¹ *Dun-Modhord—Dun-Mughdhord.* Different forms of the same name. The place is now called Doon, and is situated a little to the east of Westport, co. of Mayo.

² *Had been brought.* ıaꞃ na ꞇaiꞃꞇeꞃꞇ. The Four Mast. say aꞃ ná ꞇꞇaꞃꞃainᵹ, "having been drawn."

³ *Callow.* calaꞇ. This word, the original meaning of which is "hard," "firm," is explained as also signifying "fields on the banks of a river; a holm, or landing place for boats, a ferry," by Dr. O'Donovan. *Supplt. to O'Reilly's Irish Dictionary.*

⁴ *Sound of the island;* i.e. the sound,

was to make peace with the Foreigners, and, to give them hostages and tribute; and it was too long for him until this resolution was adopted, for the greater part of his people had been plundered and burned up to that time. With regard to the Foreigners, moreover, they proceeded on towards Connacht, and advanced first against Aedh O'Flaithbhertaigh, who made peace with the Foreigners for the sake of his cows and people, for the sake of his country and land. As to Fedhlim, son of Cathal Crobh-derg, however, the resolution he adopted was to take with him towards O'Domhnaill all the cows that he found in Conmaicne-Mara, and in Conmaicne-na-Cúile, and those belonging to all who had obeyed his counsel—and the son of Maghnus, and Conchobhar Ruadh, son of Muirchertach Muimhnech—and to leave the country wasted for the Foreigners. After this, truly, the For-eigners came to Dun-Modhord,[1] and sent messengers to Maghnus, son of Muirchertach Muimhnech, to demand peace and hostages from him; and Maghnus gave them neither peace nor hostages. The Foreigners then sent great predatory bands from Dun-Mughdhord,[1] under the sons of Ruaidhri, with innumerable mercenaries; and these plundered Eccuill, and brought great herds with them to Druimne, to meet the Foreigners. As regards Aedh O'Flaithbhertaigh and Eoghan O'hEidhin, however, they went round with a large army, and with boats which had been brought[2] to Linan-Chinn-mhara. The boats came with their forces, the Justiciary having gone to meet them to Druimne, to the callow[3] of Inis-aenaigh. Magh-nus was at this time, with his vessels, on the sound of the island;[4] and great contests and conflicts were waged by them[5] in turn. The Foreigners were at this time fatigued, and the resolution they adopted was to occupy a camp, and to withdraw their boats to a corner of the

---

or stream, between Inis-aenaigh and the shore.

[5] *By them.* By the crews of Magh-nus's boats, and his enemies on shore.

ṁóιρ ɔo ƀí αΝΝ ριΝ. Oɔ coΝΝαιρc MaᵹΝυρ' αΝ Νí ριΝ
ταΝιc ɔoΝτ ρρυɣ ρecha ρoιρ, ocυρ ɔo cυαιƀ α ΝlΝιρ
RaɣαιΝ, ocυρ ɔo ċυαɔαρ cυιɔ ɔá ṁυιΝΝτερ α ΝlΝιρ
αoΝαιᵹ, ocυρ ρυcρατ cαoιριᵹ αιρɔe ɔí α Νιɣe. Oɔ
coΝΝcoɔαρ [ᵹαιll], ιmoρρo, MaᵹΝυρ coΝα mυιΝΝτερ,
ɔυl ɔoιƀ ρρeιΝ ρóΝ oιléΝ ocυρ ɔυl ɔoιƀ ι ΝoιléΝ elι,
ocυρ Να ραιƀ ρeιchem Να ρoρcomυρ αcα αρ ᵹαlloιb,
ocυρ αΝτ oιléΝ ɔo ƀeιɣ eτoρρα ocυρ Να ᵹoιll; αΝ ταΝ ρo
αιριᵹρeτ Να ᵹoιll ριΝ ρo éριᵹρeτ co hαɣlαm ιmóιρcιρ,
ocυρ co hoᵹυl éρcαιɔ, ocυρ ɔo ɣoᵹƀαɔαρ α Ναρρτραιᵹe
co hobαΝΝ αρ ραɔ Να τράᵹα, ocυρ ɔo ċυιρeɔαρ αρ mυιρ
ιαɔ, ocυρ ρoρ líΝυιɔ co hαɣlαm ɔo ῤlυαᵹαιb ocυρ ɔo
ρeρρéΝchαιb αρmɣα éιɔιᵹɣι ιαɔ; ocυρ ɔo ċυαɔαρ αΝ ɔá
oιléΝ, ocυρ ɔo mαρbαɔαρ ιΝ bῤυαραɔαρ ɔo ɔαoιΝιb
ιΝΝτιƀ. Ɔo éριᵹ MaᵹΝυρ ocυρ ιΝ Νeoċ bóι ɔα mυιΝτιρ
α ΝlΝιρ RaιɣιΝ, ocυρ ɔo ċυαɔαρ ιΝα loΝᵹαιb; ocυρ ɔα
mαɔ ταιριρe le MaᵹΝυρ mυιΝτερ Mhαιlle ɔo cυιρρeɔ
ρe α loΝᵹα α ceΝɔ Να Νᵹαll ocυρ α Ναρρτραċ. Cιɔ τρα
αchτ, ᵹιɔ ᵹαιριɔ ɔo lá bοι αΝΝ ιΝɔ υαιρ ριΝ, Νι ραιƀe bó
αρ oιléΝ ρια Νoιɔɣe αρ ιΝΝριƀ Moɔ ᵹαΝ ċυρ αρ cαlαɔ, ocυρ
ɔo ραɔɔαoιρ [mυιΝΝτερ Να ṁbo] ρeιΝ ρeme mυΝα beιɣ
ᵹαƀαιl ρoρρα, ρe hίτταιᵹ ocυρ ρe ᵹoρτα; ocυρ ρo mαρbαιɔ
ɔροɔ ɔαoιΝe ιmɔα ιΝ oιɔɣe ριΝ eτoρραι. ΙΝ αoιΝe,
ιmoρρo, αρ α ƀαραch ɔo cυαρρ leo αρ oιléΝαιb τυαιρceρτ
Uṁαιll, ocυρ τυcαɔαρ mαιᵹιρɔρeαɔα Να ρeρρéΝαch
ρmαchτ ᵹαΝ ɔυιΝe ɔo ṁαρbαɔ ιΝ oΝóιρ ιΝ ċéρɔα.
O ταιρΝιc, τρα, ɔo ᵹαlloιb ρlαɔ ocυρ cρechαɔ Uṁαιll
ɔo ṁυιρ ocυρ ɔo ɣíρ, ταΝcαɔυρ ρompα, ocυρ α mbú

---

[1] *Large strand.* "This strand lies
to the north of Murresk Lodge, and
extends from Bartŕaw ('strand top')
Point to Annagh island, near the foot
of Croaghpatrick." O'Donovan, *Four
Mast.*, A.D. 1235, note [1].

[2] [*The Foreigners*]. [ᵹoιll]. Supplied from the Annals of Connacht,
the text of which is almost identical
with that of this chronicle; but the

phraseology of the present entry is
rather loosely given in both authorities. Indeed the version of the sentence in the Annals of Connacht, in
which the name of Maghnus (inter-
lined in the original of this text) does
not occur, reads "when the Foreigners,
moreover, saw that they themselves
could go towards the island, and then
to the other island," &c., which pro-

large strand[1] which was there. When Maghnus perceived
this thing he proceeded from the sound eastwards, and
went upon Inis-rathain; and some of his people went
upon Inis-aenaigh, and took sheep therefrom to eat.
When [the Foreigners][2] observed, moreover, that Maghnus
and his people had gone towards the island, and then to
another island, and that they had neither watch nor ward
over the Foreigners, and that the island was between them
and the Foreigners—when the Foreigners perceived this
they arose readily, furiously, terribly, and quickly; and
they suddenly lifted their boats along the strand, and put
them on the sea, and filled them promptly with forces,
and with armed, mail-clad soldiers, who went upon the
two islands, and killed all the people they found in them.
Maghnus, and all of his people who were in Inis-rathain,
arose and went into their vessels; and if O'Maille's
people had been esteemed[3] by Maghnus, he (O'Maille)
would have sent his vessels against the Foreigners and
their boats. However, though short the period of the
day remaining at this hour, there was not a cow on any
island of Innsi-Modh[4] that was not transferred to the
shore before night; and [the owners of the cows][5] would
have themselves previously gone away, through thirst and
hunger, if they had not been captured; and many inferior
persons were slain between them this night. On Friday,
moreover, the day following, they went upon the islands
of the North of Umhall, and the masters of the mercenaries,
in honour of the Passion, imposed a restriction that no
man should be killed. When the Foreigners had succeeded in robbing and plundering Umhall, by sea and
land, they proceeded with their cows and preys to

---

bably gives the correct sense. The note
"the islands of yᵉ Oulles preæed by
yᵉ English" has been added in the
margin by Roderick O'Flaherty.

³ *Esteemed.* The MS. has ⲧⲁⲓⲣⲓⲣ
for ⲧⲁⲓⲣⲣⲉ (as in the Annals of Connacht), dear, prized, or esteemed.

⁴ *Innsi-Modh.* A general name for
the islands in Clew bay, county Mayo.

⁵ *Cows.* The words within brackets,
which seem to have been omitted by
an oversight, although they are also
wanting in the Annals of Connacht,
are supplied from the Four Masters.

ocus a creċa leo, co Lúġḃurtán, ocus tiaġaid Goill asseiġ ina núiġedhaib imṫechta co hEs dara, condernadar creich ar .h. nDoṁnaill ar daiġin innarbṫa Feḋlim mic Cathail croibdeirg ċuige. Tancatar Goill assiḋéin á Coirrsliab na Seġsa, ocus do ċuadar go calad puirt na Cairrge ar Loċ Cé, dá ġaḃail ar ṁuintir Cormaic mic Tomaltaiġ, ocus ar cuid do ṁuintir Phéḋlim hI Conċobair bói ag á coiméd. Tucsat Goill Erenn, imorro, ocus an Giusdís comairce ċoitċend, ocus tearmonn tairisi, do Clarus ṁág Mhailín, dairċindechain Oilefin, ocus do ċanánchaib na Trinóide ar an oilén, ocus do chúaid an Giuisdís féin ocus maiṫi na nGall d'féguin an inaid sin, ocus do denum irnaiġṫi ann, ocus do ṫabairt ċaḃair dó in onóir na naom Trinóide. Tanic, imorro, loinges go ngaillesiḃ ocus co pirrélaiḃ docum an loċa annsiḋé, ocus do tógbad pirrél a crésalaḃ beg léo, ocus do diobruiced imorro cloċa imḋa ar in pirrél sin isin Cairric; ocus o nar ḟédsad ní di forran seol sin do ronsat Goill airrtraiġe imḋa do tiġiḃ Arda Carna, ocus tucsat áṫanna in tíre uile co natuiġidh lasamuin leo; ocus ro ceanglaadar tunnaḃa folṁa atimceall na réthed sin dá conġṁail edarḃuas ós uisce; ocus do seolsat long ṁor ocus tech claraḃ ors a cionn do tairring na reithed docum na Cairrge dia loisced tréran seolaḃ sin. Do ġaḃ, imorro, egla an lucht do ḃoi innti roim na seoltaiḃ sin, ocus tancadar aisde ar breiṫir, ocus ar comadhaib, ocus do cuir an Giuisdis lucht a coiméta innti do ġalloib arṁṫa éidiġṫi, ocus do ċuir a lán do

---

[1] *On account of the banishment;* i.e. on account of the asylum afforded by O'Domhnaill to Fedhlim O'Conchobhair, on the retirement of the latter into the North, a short time previously, as stated at p. 325.

[2] *With implements and engines.* co ngaillesiḃ ocus co pirrélaiḃ. The word gaillesiḃ, abl. pl. of gailles, seems to signify "foreign implements," but their exact nature is uncertain; while pirrélaiḃ is apparently a mistake for pillesaiḃ, abl. pl. of pilles, a missile, or instrument for discharging missiles.

Lughbhurtan ; and the Foreigners went from thence by regular marches to Es-dara, when they committed a depredation on O'Domhnaill, on account of the banishment[1] to him of Fedhlim, son of Cathal Crobhderg. The Foreigners proceeded from thence to Corrsliabh-na-Seghsa, and went to the callow of Port-na-Cairge on Loch-Cé, to take it from the people of Cormac, son of Tomaltach, and from some of the people of Fedhlim O'Conchobhair, who were guarding it. The Foreigners of Erinn, however, and the Justiciary afforded a general protection and friendly shelter to Clarus Mac Mailin, archdeacon of Oilfinn, and to the Canons of the Trinity on the Island ; and the Justiciary himself, and the chiefs of the Foreigners, went to see that place, and to pray there, and to show respect to it, in honour of the Holy Trinity. A fleet came then, also, with implements and engines[2] to the lake, and an engine[3] was raised by them on a small earthen wall,[4] and many stones were projected, truly, from this engine into the Rock.[5] And as they were not able to accomplish anything against it in this way, the Foreigners made several boats of the houses of Ard-carna, and brought with them the ignitible materials of the district that a flame might be enkindled by them ; and they tied empty tuns round this ram[6] to keep it afloat on the water ; and they sailed a large vessel surmounted by a house of boards, to tow this ram to the Rock,[5] to burn it by this means. The people who were in it[7] were seized with fear at these stratagems, and they came out of it on parole and conditions ; and the Justiciary put therein a garrison of armed, mail-clad Foreigners, and

---

[2] *Engine.* pinnél. See last note.

[4] *Earthen wall.* cпéпat for cпéпa-taò, MS.; cпebanach, Annals of Connacht.

[5] *The Rock;* i.e. the fortress of the Rock of Loch Cé.

[6] *Round this ram.* a timceatt na péch (pécheò) pin ; i.e. the ram or raft made by uniting the boats made of the houses of Ard-carna, a village in the neighbourhood of Loch Cé.

[7] *In it;* i.e. the Rock.

biaᵭ ocuʃ ᵭo linn innṫi áiʃchena. Ro ḟáᵹḃaᵭaʀ Ƶoill
Connachṫ iaʀʃin ᵹan ḃiaᵭ, ᵹen éᵭaċ, ᵹen eallaċ, ocuʃ
ni ʀucaᵭaʀ ᵹeill ina eoiʀe leo ᵭon ċuʀ ʃin; ocuʃ mʀ
ḟáᵹḃaᵭaʀ ʀíṫ, ina ʃaime, na ʀóinṁiᵭe innṫi, achṫmaᵭ
na Ƶaoiᵭel ḟéin aᵹ ʃlaṫ ocuʃ aᵹ maʀbaᵭ a ċeli imón
ḃʀuiᵹeall ᵭo ḟáᵹaiḃʀeṫ Ƶoill innṫe ᵭon ᵭul ʃin.
ᵭála Ḟeᵭlim, imoʀʀo, ᵭo ʀoine ʀíṫ ʃiʃin nƵiuiʃᵭiʀ, ocuʃ
.u. ṫʀiuċa ceᵭ an ʀíᵹ ᵭó, ocuʃ cíʃ ocuʃ béʃʃ ᵭo eiʀoiṫ;
ocuʃ ṫanic Coʀmac mac Ṫomalṫaiᵹ mic ᵭiaʀmaᵭa
maʀ oen ʃiʃ. ᵭala lochṫa coiméṫa na Caiʀʀᵹe,
imoʀʀo, ᵭo ḃaᵭaʀ ʃice oiᵭċe innṫi on ᵭaʀᵭaoin ᵹó
ʀoile; ocuʃ ᵭo ċuaiᵭ cónʃᵭapla na Caiʀʀᵹe amaċ ṫaʀ
ᵭoʀuʃ, ocuʃ ʀo an ʃeʀ ᵭia muinnṫiʀ ʃéin, .i. .h. hOiʃʀo,
allaʀṫiᵹ ᵭon comlaᵭ ᵭaʀ a néiʃ, ocuʃ ʀo iaᵭ an
ᵹcomlaᵭ ʃoʀʀa; ocuʃ ʀo ċeiċʀeᵭ na Ƶoill co hoilen na
Ṫʀinóiᵭe aʀ comaiʀce Claʀuiʀ ṁéᵹ Mhaoilín, ocuʃ
ᵭo ioᵭluic íaᵭ iaʀʃin. Aʀ nᵹabail na Caiʀʀᵹe ᵭo
Coʀmac, imoʀʀo, iʃʃí comaiʀle ᵭo ʀoine an ċaiʀʀiᵹ
ᵭo ṫʀaʃcʀaᵭ ocuʃ ᵭo ʀcaoileᵭ, conaċ ᵹabᵭaoiʀ Ƶoill
hí ᵭoʀiᵭiʃ. ᵭa mac Muiʀeᵹhaiᵹ hi Mhaille, [.i.]
ᵭomnall ocuʃ Muiʀceʀtach, ᵭó ṁaʀbaᵭ la ᵭomnall,
mac Maᵹnuiʃ, mic Muiʀceʀtaiᵹh hi Choncobaiʀ, ocuʃ
la Niall ʀuaᵭ mac Caṫail hi Conchobaiʀ, a Cliaʀa,
ocuʃ a niᵭlucaᵭ innṫi ᵭeóʀ. Ṫuaṫal, mac Muiʀceʀtaiᵹ
hi Conchobaiʀ, ᵭo maʀbaᵭ la Conchobaʀ mbuiᵭe mac
Ṫoiʀʀᵭelḃaiᵹ hi Conchobaiʀ, ocuʃ la Conchobaʀ mac
Oeᵭa Muimniᵹ, in hoc anno. Seʃʃénaiᵹ ocuʃ ceteʀna
ᵭo ḃaᵭaʀ aʀ Ḟinnloċ Ceʀa, aᵹ ᵭíċoiʀce a huchṫ mic
Ruaiᵭʀi, ᵭo ṁaʀbaᵭ la Maᵹnuʀ mac Muiʀceʀtaiᵹ hi
Conchobaiʀ in hoc anno. Maṫheuʃ, pʀioʀ inʃole
Ṫʀiniṫaṫiʃ, quieuiṫ in Cʀiʃṫo. Ƶillacoimᵭeᵭh .h.

Came with him; that is, made his
peace with the Justiciary at the same
time.

Island. The words co hoilen na
Ṫʀinoiᵭe are repeated in the MS.

Away. The Four Masters add

that they were conveyed aʀ an ṫíʀ,
"out of the country."

Aedh Muimhnech; i.e. Aedh (or
Hugh) O'Conchobhair, called "Muimhnech," or "Momonian," from
having been fostered in Munster.

he also put its full of food and drink into it. The Foreigners afterwards left Connacht without food, clothes, or cattle; and they did not carry off with them either pledges or hostages on this journey; and they left neither peace, nor quietness, nor tranquillity, nor happiness in the country; but the Gaeidhel themselves were robbing and killing one another regarding the residue which the Foreigners left in it on this occasion. As regards Fedhlim, however, he made peace with the Justiciary, and obtained the king's five cantreds, out of which he was to receive rent and customs; and Cormac, son of Tomaltach Mac Diarmada, came with him.[1] As to the warders of the Rock, moreover, they were twenty nights in it, from one Thursday to another, when the constable of the Rock went outside the door, and one of his own people, i.e. O'Hoist, who remained inside the door after them, closed the door on them; and the Foreigners fled to Trinity Island,[2] *to place themselves* under the protection of Clarus Mac Mailin, who subsequently conveyed them away.[3] After the occupation of the Rock by Cormac, moreover, the resolution that he adopted was to raze and demolish the Rock, so that the Foreigners should not again occupy it. The two sons of Muiredhach O'Maille, [viz.] Domhnall and Muirchertach, were slain by Domhnall, son of Maghnus, son of Muirchertach O'Conchobhair, and by Niall Ruadh, son of Cathal O'Conchobhair, in Cliara, where they were interred also. Tuathal, son of Muirchertach O'Conchobhair, was killed by Conchobhar Buidhe, son of Toirdhelbhach O'Conchobhair, and by Conchobhar, son of Aedh Muimhnech,[4] in hoc anno.[5] The mercenaries and kernes who were on Finn-loch of Cera, acting oppressively on the part of the son of Ruaidhri, were slain by Maghnus, son of Muirchertach O'Conchobhair, in hoc anno. Mattheus, prior Insulae Trinitatis, quievit in Christo. Gillacoimdedh

---

[5] *Hoc anno.*   oc αno, MS.

Cuilin, pṗepoṗiṫuṗ ṫe inṗoṫa mic Ṅeṗin, ṗaṫeṗ Cláṗi Elṗeneṅiṗ aiṗchiṫiacoṅi, ṗeliciṫeṗ in Cṗiṫo quieṁiṫ, eṫ in inṗoṫa Sancṫe Cṗiniṫaṫiṗ eṗṫ ṗepulṫuṗ ṫie Sancṫi Ṗinniani, cuiṗ aniṁa ṗequieṗcaṫ in pace. Cliaṫḃaċ ṫuc Ṫonnchaṫ mac Muiṗceṗṫaiġ ṫiḃ Ḃṗuin na Sinna, ġuṗ maṗbaṫ ṗoṗġla .h. mḂṗuin annṗin. In ṗacaṗṫ moṗ .h. hαṄnainn ṫo éġ α Cill m[oiṗ]. Caiṗṗlen Milic ṫo bṗiṗṗeṫ la Ṗeṫlim .h. Conchobaiṗ. Ecluṗ Ṫṗuimne αḃα Liaġ ṫo Loṗcaṫ, ocuṗ quaṗṫa ocuṗ libeṗna.

Kll. Enaiṗ ṗoṗ ṁaiṗṫ, ocuṗ nomaṫ ṫhec ṗuiṗṗe; xx°. quaṗṫo cicli ṗolaṗiṗ; nono anno inṫicṫioniṗ; anno Ṫomini .M.cc.xxx°. ṗexṫo. Maileċlainn .h. Máille ṫo maṗbaṫ i nOilén Ṫacṗunṫe la Ṫomnall, mac Maġnuiṗ, mic Muiṗceṗṫaiġ Muiṁniġ hi Conchobaiṗ, in hoc anno. Ṗeṫlim mac Caṫail cṗoibṫeṗġ ṫo innaṗbaṫ ṫon ġiuiṗṫiṗ .i. ṫo Mac Muiṗiṗ, ṫa caiṗṫiṗ Cṗiṫo, aṗ nimṫeachṫ ṫo Mac Uilliam a Saxṗanaib, ocuṗ aṗ eiġin ṫo ṗiachṫ aṗṗ uaṫha cona ṁaṗcṗluaiġ, aṗ bṗaġail ṗabaṫ ṫó, ocuṗ ṫo ṗonaiṫ cṗeċa moṗa aṗ a ṁuinṫeṗ iaṗ na imṫeachṫ ṗein. Ceiṫ aṗṗ iaṗum i nuchṫ hi Ṫomnaill; ocuṗ ṫo ṗonaṫ caiṗlén Muille Uanach ṫon ṫul ṗin aṗ Connachṫ; ocuṗ iṗ amlaiṫ ṫo ṗónaṫ an ṗeall ṗin, .i. coinne ċelġe ṫo ṗoġṗaṫ ṗoṗ .h. Conchobaiṗ a mbeol áḃα Ṗeoṗuinne, ocuṗ Ṡoill Eṗenn ṫo ċinól ṫon ġiuiṗṫiṗ ṫocum na coinne ṗin; ocuṗ Ṗeṫlim ṫo

---

[1] *Cujus.* cuiṗ, MS.

[2] *Requiescat.* ṗequieṗcanṫ, MS.

[3] *Cill-m[or].* The MS. has Cill m.; but Cill-mor (Kilmore) in the county of Roscommon was, in all probability, the place meant.

[4] *Inclosures and offices.* q̄ṫ (for quaṗṫa, or cuaṗṫa) ocuṗ libeṗna. Cuaṗṫa is the nom. plur. of cuaiṗṫ, a circle, or circular inclosure, and libeṗna signifies small wooden structures. Instead of libeṗna, the

Annals of Connacht (Dublin copies) read libuṗ na cañ, for libuṗ na cananach, "the books of the monks;" but the alteration is probably owing to the transcriber's ignorance of the meaning of the word libeṗna.

[5] *Oilen-Dacrunde.* "The island of Dacrunde," a small island to the north of Rinville, in the barony of Ballinahinch, off the coast of the county of Galway.

[6] *Hoc anno.* oc. α., for oc anno, MS.

O'Cuilin, præpositus de Insula Mic-Nerin, pater Clari Elfinensis archidiaconi, feliciter in Christo quievit, et in Insula Sanctæ Trinitatis est sepultus die Sancti Finniani ; cujus[1] anima requiescat[2] in pace.   Donnchadh, son of Muirchertach, gave battle to the Ui-Briuin-na-Sinna, when the principal men of the Ui-Briuin were slain.   The great priest O'hAnain died in Cill-m[or].[3]   The castle of Milic was broken down by Fedhlim O'Conchobhair.   The church of Druimne-Atha-Liag was burned, and the inclosures and offices.[4]

The kalends of January on Tuesday, and the nineteenth of the moon ; xx°.quarto cycli solaris ; nono anno Indictionis ; anno Domini M.cc.xxx°.sexto.   Maelechlainn O'Maille was killed on Oilen-Dacrunde[5] by Domhnall, son of Maghnus, son of Muirchertach Muimhnech O'Conchobhair, in hoc anno.[6]   Fedhlim, son of Cathal Crobhderg, was banished by the Justiciary, i.e. Mac Maurice,[7] his gossip,[8] after the departure of Mac William to Saxon-land ; and with difficulty he escaped from them, with his cavalry, after having received forewarning ; and they committed great depredations on his people after his (*Fedhlim's*) own departure. He went off afterwards to seek the protection of O'Domhnaill ; and the castle of Muille-Uanach[9] was erected on this occasion against Connacht.   The way in which this treachery was practised was thus, viz. :—O'Conchobhair was summoned to a deceitful meeting at Bel-Atha-Feoruinne ;[10] and the Foreigners of Erinn were assembled by the Justiciary to this meeting ; and they pursued Fedhlim

---

[7] *Mac Maurice;* i.e. Maurice Fitz-Gerald. See note 8, p. 318.

[8] *Gossip.* carroer Crirτ; lit. "Christ-friend." A person standing sponsor to the child of another was called the "gossip" of the child's father. But gossip=God-sib, "God-related."

[9] *Muille-Uanach.* In Mageoghegan's version of the Annals of Clon-macnoise the name is written Uilleinne-Uanach, and Ulluinnie-Wonagh.

[10] *Bel-Atha-Feoruinne.* "The mouth of Ath-Feoruinne," or the ford of Feorann, now Afeoran, a townland on the east side of the river Suck, in the parish of Taghboy, barony of Athlone, and county of Roscommon. The place of meeting is called Mowney-myne in the last quoted authority.

lenmain co Ror Comáin voiḃ, ocur a lenmain arrvé
ʒo vroiċev Sliciʒ; ocur o nach rucrav rair vo ronrav
crecha móra ar Thaḋʒ .h. Conchobair, ocur ro ʒaḃavur
morán vo mnaiḃ maiċi annrin, co rucrav a mḃroiv
leo íav. Táncovar na ʒoill, imorro, cona creċaiḃ
ocur cona mḃroiv leo ʒo Vruimm nʒreaʒraive a Muiʒ
Luirʒ, oir ir annrin vo ḃí an ʒiurvír rein aʒ á ḃurr-
naive. Vo imċiʒ an ʒiurvír ocur na ʒoill iarrin, ocur
vo ráʒaiḃriov reċem ocur rorláṁur in tíre aʒ Ḃrian
mac Toirrvhelḃaiʒ. Creċa móra vo ḋenum vo Ḃrian
ocur vo trerrénachaiḃ an ʒiurvír ar ċlainn Ccoḋa
mic Cathail croiḃvErʒ, ocur ar rochaive eli vo ṁuinter
Fheḋlim. Creċa móra ocur ʒrerra imḋa vo ḋenum vo
macaiḃ Oeḋa ar ʒalloiḃ, ocur ar a nercairoiḃ ʒaoivil,
ʒur loiteD ocur ʒur milleD an tír ocur in talam
eaturra imórech. Conchobar mac Ccoḋa Muimniʒ vo
ṁarbaD la Maʒnur mac Muirċertaiʒ hi Conċobair in
hoc anno. Moelmuiri .h. Lachtnain, toʒa Thuama,
vo [vul] a Saranaiḃ ocur ʒraḋa vo tabáirt rair tre
rcribenvuiḃ comarba Pevair, ocur comaonta riʒ
Saxran. Mac Uilliam vo ċoiʒeacht arr Sacranaiḃ,
ocur ni mor vo maiḃ na hErenn vo rinne vá ċoirc.
Vala Feḋlim mic Cathail croiḃvErʒ, imorro, tánic
i Connachtuiḃ vorír ré cuireḃ ċova vo Connachtaiḃ
rein, imo O Ceallaiʒh ocur imó .h. bFhloinn, ocur imo
macaiḃ Ccoḋa mic Cathail croiḃvErʒ, ocur má mac
Ccirt hi Mhaoilrechlainn, ʒo raḃavar viblinuiḃ cetri
caċa commóra; ocur vo innroiʒevar co Rinn vúin,
ocur vo ċuavar ʒo neṁuirr niatta naimveṁuil, ocur
ʒo bruʒṁar borrravach, tar an mbáḋun ocur tar

---

[1] *Son of Toirdhelbhach*: i.e. of
Toirdhelbhach, or Turlough, son of
Roderick O'Conor, King of Con-
nacht.

[2] *Hoc.* oc, MS.

[3] *The elect*; i.e. the bishop elect. Sir
James Ware, who refers the succession

of this bishop to the year 1235, states
that "immediately upon his election
he hastened to Rome, to solicit the
Pope's confirmation; where he was
approved of by Gregory the IXth, and
invested with the Pall."—Harris's ed.
of *Ware*; Bishops, at *Tuam*. See p.

to Ros-Comain, and pursued him from thence to the bridge of Sligech; and as they did not overtake him they committed great depredations on Tadhg O'Conchobhair; and they then seized a great number of noble women, whom they carried away with them in captivity. The Foreigners came, moreover, with their spoils and captives, to Druim-Gregraidhe in Magh-Luirg; for it was there the Justiciary himself was awaiting them. The Justiciary and the Foreigners afterwards departed, and left the guardianship and government of the country with Brian, son of Toirdhelbhach.[1] Great depredations were committed by Brian, and by the soldiers of the Justiciary, on the sons of Aedh, son of Cathal Crobhderg, and on several others of Fedhlim's people. Great depredations, and numerous outrages, were committed by the sons of Aedh on the Foreigners, and on their Gaeidhelic enemies, so that the country, and the land, were injured and destroyed between them respectively. Conchobhar, son of Aedh Muimhnech, was killed by Maghnus, son of Muirchertach O'Conchobhair, in hoc[2] anno. Maelmuire O'Lachtnain, the elect[3] of Tuaim, [went] to Saxon-land, and was consecrated by virtue of the letters of the comarb of Peter, and the consent of the king of the Saxons. Mac William returned from Saxon-land; and little of[4] Erinn's benefit did he effect by his journey. As regards Fedhlim, son of Cathal Crobhderg, moreover; he came again into Connacht, at the invitation of some of the Connachtmen themselves, including O'Cellaigh and O'Floinn, and including the sons of Aedh, son of Cathal Crobhderg, and the son of Art O'Maelsechlain—who numbered altogether four large battalions. And they advanced to Rinn-duin, and went boldly, bravely, hostilely, vigorously, and furiously across the bádhun,[5] and over the ditch of

---

345, *infra*, where it is stated (A.D. 1237) that the pallium was sent to him "from Rome."

[4] *Of.* ᴅᴏ.; repeated in the MS.

[5] *Bádhun.* This word, otherwise written bóᴏun, signifies an inclosure for cows. See note [5], p. 213.

claᵹᵹaiᵹ an oilen a ᵲabaᴅaᵲ ba ın τiᵲe uile, ocuᵲ ᴅo
ᵹaᴆ ᵹach τuiᵲᵲeč buıᴆne, ocuᵲ ᵹach cenᴅ ᵲlúaiᵹ ᴅiᴆ
anᴅıaıᴆ na mbó; ocuᵲ ᴅo beᵲᴅíᵲ na ba leo muᵲ a
τeᵹᵯaᴅíᵲ ᵲempu. Τᵲuaᵹ, aᵯ, an ní ᴅo ᵲonaᴆ annᵲın,
.ı. ᵲo τᵲeicᵲeτ a τiᵹeᵲna, ocuᵲ a nenech, ocuᵲ a
nenᵹnum, aᵲ na héᴅalaib τaᵲla ᴆóıᴆ annᵲın, maᵲ naᵲ
ᵳoᵹuın; oiᵲ ᴅo ᵲáᵹᴆaᴅaᵲ a τᵲiaᴆ ocuᵲ a τiᵹeᵲna na
αοnaᵲ, conaᴆ ᵲaiᴆe achτ aon ceᵵᵲaᵲ maᵲcach ına
ᵳoᴆaiᵲ ᴅona ceiτᵲi cóiᵲiᵹᵵhib ᵲo baı maᵲoen ᵲiᵲ,
ᵹuᵲ ᵯeabaᴅ aᵲ ᵹuᴆ an aiᵲᴅᵲiᵹh oᵹ á bᵳoᵲᴅaᴅ, ocuᵲ oᵹ
á bᵳuıᵲech. Ɔala, ımoᵲᵲo, Θoᵹaın hi Θiᴆın, ocuᵲ
ᵬᵲuaın mıc Τoiᵲᵲᴅelᴆaiᵹ, ocuᵲ Concobaiᵲ ᵬuiᴆe mıc
Τoiᵲᵲᴅhelbaiᴆ, ocuᵲ mıc Ꝫoiᵲᴅealᴆ; óᴅ conncaᴅaᵲ an
ᵲluaᵹ aᵹ ᵲcaoileᴅ ocuᵲ aᵹ ᵲᵹannᵲaᴅ o ᵲoile ᵲe
neᴅálaıb, co haimᵹlıc, éᵹcoᴆᵲaıᴅ, anbᵳaıτeᴆ, ᴅo eᵲᵹeᴅaᵲ
co héᵲcaıᴅ, aᵵlam, uᵲmıᵲnech, uaᵵhaᴅ maᵲcᵲluaᵹ
ocuᵲ ᵲeᵲᵲénaiᵹ ımᴆa ımaille ᵳᵲiú, ocuᵲ ᴅo ᵵuaᴅaᵲ
maᵲ a bᵳacaᴅaᵲ .h. Conchobaiᵲ, uaᵵhaᴅ ᵲluaᵹ ocuᵲ
ᵲochaıᴅe na ᵳaᵲᵲaᴅ. Iᵲ annᵲın ᴅo ᵲala Conchobaᵲ
buıᴆe mac Τoiᵲᵲᴅhelbaiᵹ aᵲ ᴅᵲuım mıc nαᴅoᴆa mıc
Caτhaıl cᵲoiᴅᴅeᵲᵹ, ocuᵲ ᴅo. chúaıᴅ ına cenᴅ co
huᴅmall anbᵳaıτech, ı ᵲichτ ᴅᵲuınᵹe ᴅá muınnτeᵲ ᵳeın,
ocuᵲ ᴅo ᵵuıτᵲıom le Ꝛuaıᴅᵲı mac Oeᴆa mıc Caτhaıl
cᵲoiᴆᴅeᵲᵹ annᵲın. Ꝛo maᵲbaᴅ ᵲochaıᴅe ᴅonτ ᵲluaᵹ
ıᵲın oilén, ocuᵲ allamoiᵹ ᴅon oilén, ᴅo ᴆaoınıᴆ
ᵯallaıᵹᵵe conmıolᴆaıτcı, ıᵲın maᴆm ᵲın, achτmaᴆ
Τaᴅc mac Coᵲmaic mıc Τomalτaıᵹ mıc Ɔiaᵲmaᴅa
nama. Oᴅ ᵵuala, ımoᵲᵲo, Mac Uilliam an maᴆm
ᵲın ᴅo ᵵabaıᵲτ aᵲ ᵹach óen ᴅa ınnτó ᴅia muınnτeᵲ
ᵳaıᵲ, ᴅo eiᵲıᵹ le .h. Conchobaiᵲ, ocuᵲ τánic ᴅá ᵲuaᵹaᴅ

---

¹ *Foot soldiers.* ᵲeᵲᵲénaiᵹ. This
word, which occurs very frequently in
the present chronicle, has been elsewhere generally translated mercenaries; but it seems here to mean in-
fantry, as it is apparently used to
distinguish the force so named from
maᵲcᵲluaᵹ, "cavalry." The Four

Masters employ the word amᵲaıᴆ,
abl. pl. of amuᵲ, "a hireling soldier."

² *Candle extinguished*; i.e. excommunicated; the extinguishment of
candles forming a part of the cere-
mony of excommunication. See note ²
p. 282, *supra.*

the island in which all the cows of the country were; and every captain of a company, and every chief of a host went after the cows; and they took the cows away with them as they met them. Lamentable, alas! was the deed committed then, viz.:—they abandoned their lord, their honour, and their reputation, for the preys which they met there, as became them not; for they left their king and lord alone, so that there were along with him only four horsemen out of the four battalions that had accompanied him, and the chief king's voice was strained stopping and detaining them. With regard, however, to Eoghan O'hEidhin, and to Brian, son of Toirdhelbhach, and Conchobhar Buidhe, son of Toirdhelbhach, and Mac Goisdelbh—when they observed the host unwisely, weakly, unwarily scattering and dispersing from each other with preys, they arose quickly, actively, courageously, having a small number of cavalry and many foot soldiers[1] along with them, and went to where they saw O'Conchobhair attended only by a very small band and company. Then it happened that Conchobhar, son of Toirdhelbhach, came behind the son of Aedh, son of Cathal Crobhderg, and went towards him quickly, heedlessly, taking him for one of a party of his own people; and he fell there by Ruaidhri, son of Aedh, son of Cathal Crobhderg. A multitude of the host—of cursed, candle-extinguished[2] people—were slain in the island, and outside the island, in this defeat, excepting only Tadhg,[3] son of Cormac, son of Tomaltach Mac Diarmada. When Mac William heard, moreover, that this defeat had been inflicted on all of his people who had turned against him,[4] he joined with O'Conchobhair, and came

---

[3] *Excepting only Tadhg.* The sense is that Tadhg, son of Cormac, son of Tomaltach Mac Diarmada, was the only person of the number slain who had not been cursed and "candle-extinguished," or excommunicated.

[4] *Against him;* i.e. against Fedhlim, son of Cathal Crobhderg O'Conor.

z

no dia čendugad. Tanic, tra, Diarmaid mac Maǧnuir
hI Conchobair a nucht mic Muircheptaiǧ hI Conchobair. Ir annrin tanic Mac Uilliam, gan pabad
can patugad, co Tuaim da gualann; aǧǧidé co Maǧ
néó na Saxranach; ocur nip págbad cruač fil no arba
da paiǧe a pelic ṁoip Moiǧe héó, na a pelic Tempuil
Mičil Cpčaingel, gan tócǧail do lathaip an áoinpecht;
ocur tucad tri picid no ceṫpa pichid cliaǧ aǧǧ na
templaiǧ rin, maille pe ǧach milled oili, ocur rciamčendaig tap a néipe, ocur ni paiǧe poinn annreic. Ocur
tancadap aǧǧéic co Turloč, ocur tucaǧ in arađain
cetna poippe; ocur do čuipedap crecha mora amač
dinnpoiǧed muintepi mic Mhaǧnuir, ocur do pala
muintep Conchobaip puaiǧ ocur Turlaiǧ doiǧ, ocur
do haipcid a cumurc a čeli iad uile. Rob écen, trá,
do Mhaǧnur muintep mic Mhaǧnuir hI Conchobaip do
ǧíchup uaǧa do neoč po piacht čuiǧe diǧ, no do bérǧa
ant amur cedna rair mup tucaǧ ap a ǧrathaip.
Dala Conchobaip puaiǧ, imoppo, do chuaid ap a ǧarach
a tech Mic Uilliam, ocur do pone riǧ ann, ocur do
hicaid a crecha rir dona buaiǧ tremit ap haipcedh
hé, ocur in nech ruapadap muinntep na cille beo dá
croǧ tucaǧ doiǧ hé. Dala mic Maǧnura, imoppo, do
chúaid a tech Gall tap cend a ǧó ocur a ṁuintipe, do
neoč po págbad aiǧe dá ǧuaiǧ. Ir annrin do čuaid

---

[1] *To attack him, or to pacify him.* The
Four Masters say dia cceennrucchad
"to pacify them," i.e. Fedhlim and his
subjects. But the Four Masters, who
seem to have copied their account of
these transactions from the original of
the present chronicle, probably misunderstood the object of Mac William's
journey, which was, apparently, to attack and subdue Fedhlim O'Conor, if
he found it practicable to do so, or to
pacify him if he found that Fedhlim
could not be attacked with safety.

[2] *Relig.* Cemetery or churchyard.
[3] *Disorder.* This translation is
merely conjectural, as the meaning of
the word rciamčendaig is not certain.
It does not occur elsewhere in the
chronicle, nor is it found in any
dictionary or glossary accessible to
the editor.
[4] *The son of Maghnus*; i.e. Diarmaid
(or Dermot), son of Maghnus—namely,
Maghnus O'Conchobhair, or O'Conor.
[5] *Thrlagh.* The name of this place,
which is situated in the barony of

to attack him, or to pacify him.[1] Diarmaid, son of Maghnus O'Conchobhair, went under the protection of the son of Muirchertach O'Conchobhair. Then it was that Mac William proceeded, without notice, without being observed, to Tuaim-dá-ghualann, and from thence to Magh-Eó of the Saxons; and not a stack of seed or corn of all that was in the great relig[2] of Magh-Eó, or in the relig[2] of the church of Michael the Archangel, was left without being taken away together; and three score, or four score baskets were brought out of these churches, besides every other injury and disorder[3] committed after them; but this was of little consequence. And they went from thence to Turloch, on which the same punishment was inflicted. And they sent out[*] great predatory bands against the people of the son of Maghnus,[4] who met the people of Conchobhar Ruadh and of Turlagh,[5] and plundered them all indiscriminately. Maghnus,[6] indeed, was obliged to send away from him such of the people of the son of Maghnus[4] O'Conchobhair as had come to him, or else the same treatment would have been inflicted on him as had been inflicted on his brother.[7] As to Conchobhar Ruadh, moreover, he went on the morrow into the house[8] of Mac William, and made peace there; and his preys of the cows of which he had been plundered were restored to him; and what the people of the church[9] found alive of their stock was given to them. Regarding the son of Maghnus,[4] also, he went into the house[8] of the Foreigners for the sake of his cows and people, i.e. of all that had been left to him of

Carra, county of Mayo, is written Turloch three lines before.

[6] *Maghnus*. Maghnus, son of Muirchertach Muimhnech O'Conchobhair, under whose protection Diarmaid, son of another Maghnus O'Conchobhair, had previously placed himself, as related in the first sentence of this page.

[7] *His brother*. Conchobhar Ruadh,

son of Muirchertach Muimhnech, son of Turlough Mór O'Conchobhair.

[8] *Went into the house*. The expression "going into the house" of a person signifies making submission to him.

[9] *Of the church*; i.e. of the church of Turlagh. See note [5]. last page.

Mac Uilliam co balla, ocuſ do bí dá oidce innti, ocuſ do
čuaid arríde co Tuaim dá gualann, ocuſ do ṗagaib Connachta iarrin gan biad, gan édač, a cill ina tuaiṫ; gen
ríḡ, gen raime, gen rocra; achtmad cáč ſa čeli, achtmad
111 tiġernuſ do beirbír mic Muirčertaiġ dó. Iſ don
dula ſin do loircedar muinter Briain mic Thoirr-
dhealbaiġ tempul Imḟliċ Brocada, a cend muinteri
h1 Ḟloinn, ocuſ a lán do mnaib ocuſ do lenbaib ocuſ do
caillečaib duba, ma tri ſagartaib ann; ocuſ do loirced
Termann Chaoluinn beoſ lár an nGiurdír. Oed .h.
Ḟlaithbertaiġ, ſi iarthair Connacht, do éc in hoc anno;
ſer iſ mó ocuſ iſ indeġduine tanic diarthar Connacht
ſiam, ocuſ iſmo aġ á ſaib dáil ġach duine čuiġe, ocuſ gan
a ḋailſiom co duine. Ḟlechad mór ocuſ doinenn ocuſ
cocad iſin mbliadain ſin; gorta ocuſ terca bíḋ ocuſ
édaiġ, ocuſ ceterna ocuſ mic mallachtan cen čáduſ do
čill ina do neimiḋ, ar ná coinnel batháad do lamuib
errpuc; ocuſ uaſal graḋ eġailſech Cathoileġba gan
beiċ la ná aġaid gan oman no imhecla ſorra. Teiċte
imḋa, ocuſ madmanna mence do cum na templaib ſia
nGalloib ocuſ ġoeidelaib, ocuſ tiġe lerča do ḋenum do
templaib ocuſ dáſaraib noem iſin mbliadain ſin, ocuſ
ſria ſé da bliadain dhéc o čocad h1 Neill anúaſſ Goill
ocuſ ġoeidel aġ ſlat imórech, gan ſiġe gen cenduſ do
neoč ſeoč aroile, acht comuſ a loit aġ Galloib cač uaiſ
ticdíſ innte. Ri Connacht ocuſ a riġḋaṁna aġ arccain
ocuſ aġ ſáruġad th[úath], ocuſ ceall taſ a néiſi.
Diarmaid mac Neill h1 Ruaiſc do ḋallad la Coincon-
nacht .h. Raiġilliġ. Cathal ſiabach, mac Gillabroide

---

1 *Conceded to him.* The meaning
of this clause is not very clear, and
it is probable that the entry is not
fully given.

2 *Imlech-Brochadha.* "The marsh
of Brochaidh." The etymology of
the word *Imlech*, which is usually
thus written, and signifies a marsh,

appears from the form in the text,
imḟliċ, gen. of imḟleċ, "very wet."

3 *Hoc.* oc, MS.

4 *Candle-extinguished*; i.e. excommunicated.

5 *The war of O'Neill.* The expedition of O'Neill to Connacht, recorded
under the year 1225, *supra.*

his cows. Then Mac William went to Balla, where he remained two nights, and proceeded from thence to Tuaim-da-ghualann; and he left Connacht afterwards without food or clothing in church or territory, without peace, or quiet, or prosperity, but each man attacking his fellow, excepting the supremacy which the sons of Muirchertach conceded to him.[1] It was on this occasion the people of Brian, son of Toirdhelbhach, burned the church of Imlech-Brochadha[2] against the people of O'Floinn, and its full of women, children, and black nuns, and three priests, in it. And Termann-Caeluinn was also burned by the Justiciary. Aedh O'Flaith-bhertaigh, king of the West of Connacht, died in hoc[3] anno; the greatest and most excellent man that had ever come of the West of Connacht; a man to whom everybody had recourse the most frequently, whilst he had recourse to no man. Great rain, and bad weather, and war in this year; famine, and scarcity of food and clothing; and kernes and sons of malediction, who had been candle-extinguished[4] by the hands of bishops, without respect for church or sanctuary; and superior dignitaries of the Catholic church were neither day nor night without suffering from fear or terror. Numerous retreats and frequent headlong routs to the churches *took place*, before Foreigners and Gaeidhel, and lodging-houses were made of churches and the residences of saints, in this year; and during the period of twelve years down from the war of O'Neill[5] were the Foreigners and Gaeidhel plundering in turn, without sovereignty or supremacy being possessed by one beyond another, but the Foreigners able to destroy it (*Connacht*) every time they came into it; the king and royal heirs of Connacht pillaging and profaning territories and churches after them. Diarmaid, son of Niall O'Ruairc, was blinded by Cuconnacht O'Raighilligh. Cathal Riabhach, son of Gillabroide O'Ruairc, king of

hi Ruaιpc, pι .h. mОpιúιn, mopτuup epτ. Μαcpαἐ
ṁáᵹ Μhoιlín, ραcepᴅop Cιlle mιc Τpená, mopτuup epτ.
Θeᴆ .h. ᵹιbellán, ραcepᴅop ċιlle Roᴅán, ocup cananach
hé ᵹoᴆeoιᴅ an ᴅιlén na Τpιnóιᴅe, mopτúúp epτ aoιne
Νoᴅluc, ocup ᴅo ᵬí ιpιn ċopaιᴅ ιn oιᴆċe pιn aᵹá ᵮαιpe
co haιpᵮpenᴅ ap ná ᵬαpach; ocup ᴅo hannluιceᴅ co
honopach hé ιappιn. Μαιᴅm Cluána caᵵa ᴅo ᵵabaιpτ
ᴅᵮheᴆlιm .h. Conchobaιp ap claιṅṅ Ruαιᴅpι ocup ap
Conchobap mac Copmaιc mιc Ðιαpmaᴅá.

ĸt. Θnaιp ᵮop Ðapᴅaιn, ocup ᴅechmaᴅ ᵮιcheᴅ
ᵮuιppe; xx°. qúιnᴛo áṅno cιclι ᵮolapιᵮ; τepᴛιup annup
[cιclι] ᴅecennouenálιᵮ; xx°. anno ιnᴅιcᴛιonιᵮ. Μ.cc.τpι-
cepιmo ᵮepᴛιmo. Sloιᵹeᴅ lá Ꝑeᴆlιm mac Cαᵵaιl cpoιbᴅepᵹ, ι Connachτa; Cúcoṅṅachᴛ .h. Raᵹιllιᵹ ocup .h.
mОpιúιṅ úιle maιlle ᵮpιp, ocup Cαᵵál ṁáᵹ Raᵹnuιll
ocup Conmaιcnιᵹ maιlle ᵮpιp, ocup τpι mιc Θeᴆa
mιc Caᵵaιl cpoιbᴅepᵹ, ᴅιnnpaιᵹeᴅ mac Ruαιᴅpι .ι.
ᵬpιαιn mιc Τhoιppᴅhelbaιᵹ, ocup Μhuιpċepᴛaιᵹ, ocup
Ðomnaιll mιc Ðιαpmaᴅα mιc Ruαιᴅpι, ocup Conchobaιp mιc Copmaιc mιc Ðιαpmaᴅα, mup a paᴆaᴅap,
conᴅechaᴅap ᴛap Coιppᵮlιab na Šeᵹpa buᴆ ᵵuaιᴆ ιna
noeᵹhaιᴆ, co pancaᴅap co Ðpuιm Raιᴛᴛe; ocup ᴅo
ᵵuιpeᴛap ᵮlιchᴛ Ruαιᴅpι ᵮeppénaιᵹ an ᵹιuιpᴅίp ᴅo
baᴅap ιna ᵬᵮochaιp ᴅo ᴛabaιpτ ᵵeaᴆᵵa ᴅᵮheᴆlιm.
Ðo ᵮóᵹaιp Ꝑeᴆlιm ᵹan upchup ᴅo ᵵabaιpτ ᴅóιᴆ,
achᴛ na cιnn ᴅo cpomaᴅ ocup cup cuca co ᴅίᵹaιp ᴅap-
pachaᵵ. Νιp ᵮuιlnᵹeᴅap ṅa ᵮeppénaιᵹ pιn, achᴛ po
ṁeabaᴅ ᴅιᴆ a cenᴅ a muιnᴛιpe, ocup ᴅo mapbaᴅ
ᵮeppénaιᵹ ιmᴆa ᴅιᴆ, má Μαc Μίᵬpιc, ᴅon puαιc pιn.
Оᴅ conncoᴛap mιc Ruαιᴅpι cen baιl oppa, ocup na

[1] *Sacerdos.* pocepᴅop, MS.
[2] *Sacerdos.* pocepᴅόpp, MS.
[3] *Christmas Friday;* i.e. the Friday before Christmas Day. Instead of aoιne Νoᴅluc, the Four Masters have oιᴆċe Νoᴅlac, i.e. Christmas Eve, which is probably correct.

[4] *Afterwards.* At the end of this entry, which concludes fol. 40 *b* of the MS., the scribe has added the note pᵹuιpιm co ᴅίa, i.e. "I desist until morning."

Ui-Briuin, mortuus est. Macraith Mac Mailin, sacerdos[1] of Cill-mic-Trena, mortuus est. Aedh O'Gibellan, sacerdos[2] of Cill-Rodan, and subsequently a canon in Trinity Island, mortuus est on Christmas Friday;[3] and he was waked in the choir that night, and until mass on the morrow, and was honourably interred afterwards.[4] The defeat of Cluain-catha was inflicted by Fedhlim O'Conchobhair on the sons of Ruaidhri, and on Conchobhar, son of Cormac Mac Diarmada.

The kalends of January on Thursday, and the 30th of the moon; xx°. quinto anno cycli solaris; tertius annus [cycli] Decennovenalis; x°. anno Indictionis. M.cc. tricesimo[5] septimo. A hosting into Connacht by Fedhlim, son of Cathal Crobhderg, accompanied by Cuconnacht O'Raighilligh and all the Ui-Briuin, and by Cathal Mac Raghnaill and the Conmaicne, and by the three sons of Aedh, son of Cathal Crobhderg, to attack the descendants[6] of Ruaidhri where they were, viz.:— Brian, son of Toirdhelbhach, and Muirchertach and Domhnall, sons of Diarmaid, son of Ruaidhri, and Conchobhar, son of Cormac, son of Diarmaid; and they went northwards across Corrsliabh-na-Seghsa[7] in pursuit of them, until they arrived at Druim-raithe. And the descendants of Ruaidhri sent the mercenaries of the Justiciary, who were along with them, to give battle to Fedhlim. Fedhlim ordered *his men* not to shoot at them, but to stoop the heads and rush fiercely, furiously at them. The mercenaries did not sustain this, but were driven in rout towards their people; and many mercenaries of them were slain in this onset, including Mac Mibhric. When the descendants of Ruaidhri perceived

---

[5] *Tricesimo.* ̇ciṗṗio for ṫṗıcıṗ-ṗımo, MS.

[6] *Descendants.* mac (gen. pl.), lit. "sons," MS.

[7] *Corrsliabh - na - Seghsa.*   "The round hill of the Seghais," now the Curlieu hills, on the borders of the counties of Roscommon and Sligo.

reppénaiξ ap pcaoiled, ocup ap pcainnped, do ṗácḃadap
anc inaḃ a paḃadap ξan duine do mapbad ḋiḃ ; ocup
do pcaoilpic a haiċle in ṁaḋma pin ξan aicpeaḃ a Síl
Muipeξhaiξh oppa; ocup po haipccio a muincepa uile,
ocup do pónaḃ cpeċa mópa ap Conchobap mac Copmaic
a Típ nOilella, ocup cucpad iappin loinξep ap Loċ Cé,
ξup ḃċuippio de Conchobap mac Copmaic, pi Mhoiξe
Luipc, ocup po aipcpec Maξ Luipc uile, ocup po
ṗáξaiḃpec ciξepnup an cípe ocup in Loċa ac Donnchad
mac Muipcheptaiξ luaċṗuiliξ. Donáic .h. Piḃubpa,
compopba Pacpaic, quieuic. Siḋ do ḋenum don ξiup-
díp pe Peḋlim mac Cachail cpoiḃdepξ, ocup cucaḃ .u.
cpiuċa an piξ ḋó ξen cpoḃ ξen ċípp oppa. ḃapuin na
hEpenn do ċeachc a Connachcaiḃ ocup cinnpcedal
caiplen do ḋenum doiḃ innci. Céd ṗenaḃ Mhaol-
muipe hi Lachcnain, .i. aipdeppuic Cuama, ac Aċ
Luain, iap cochc a ṗaillium ċuiξe ón Roim. Maξnup,
mac Diapmada, mic Mhaξnuip, do ṁapbad do
Domnall, mac Diapmada, mic Ruaidpi hi Conchobaip
in hoc anno. Muipceptach, mac Diapmada, mic
Ruaidpi hi Conchobaip, do ṁapbad la macuiḃ
Maξnuip mic Muipceptaiξ Muimniξ hi Conchobaip,
ipin mbliadain pin. Cinnpcedal ṁainipdech cananach
do ḋenum do Chlápup máξ Mhoeilín i noilén na
Cpinóide ap Loċ Uachcaip, cpia ċḋnacal Cachail hi
Raiξilliξ, in hoc anno. Comáp .h. Ruaḃain, eppuc..
Lúiξni, in Cpipco quieuic. ξilla Ippa, mac an Scélaiξi

---

1 *Son of Cormac*; i.e. son of Cormac
Mac Diarmada.

2 *Muirchertach Luath-shuilech*; i.e.
"Muirchertach (or Murtough) the
quick-eyed," of the family of Mac
Diarmada, or Mac Dermot.

3 *Rent.* Under the year 1235 a
similar grant is stated to have been
made to Fedhlim O'Conchobhair; and
the present entry is doubtless a repeti-

tion of the former, unless it may be
inferred that the events recorded under
the year 1236 led to the revocation
of the previous grant; but as Dr.
O'Donovan remarks, it is scarcely
true that Fedhlim obtained the five
cantreds "free from cattle-tribute or
rent," for it appears from a Pipe Roll
quoted in Hardiman's *History of Galway*, p. 48, note ˣ, that in A.D. 1262

that they had not good fortune, and that the mercenaries were scattered and dispersed, they left the place
in which they were without a man of them being slain;
and they separated after this defeat, so that they had
no residence in Sil-Muiredhaigh; and all their people
were plundered; and great depredations were committed on Conchobhar, son of Cormac,[1] in Tir-Oilella.
And they afterwards brought a fleet upon Loch-Cé,
from which they expelled Conchobhar, son of Cormac,[1]
king of Magh-Luirg; and they left the sovereignty of
the district and the lake with Donnchadh, son of Muirchertach Luath-shuilech.[2]   Donat O'Fidhubhra, comarb
of Patrick, quievit. Peace was made by the Justiciary
with Fedhlim, son of Cathal Crobhderg; and the five
cantreds of the king were given to him, free from cattle-
tribute or rent.[3] The barons of Erinn came into Connacht, and commenced to build castles in it.   First
synod of Maelmuire O'Lachtnain, i.e. archbishop of
Tuaim, at Ath-Luain, after the coming of his pallium
to him from Rome.[4] Maghnus, son of Diarmaid, son of
Maghnus,[5] was killed by Domhnall, son of Diarmaid, son
of Ruaidhri O'Conchobhair, in hoc anno.   Muirchertach,
son of Diarmaid, son of Ruaidhri O'Conchobhair, was killed
by the sons of Maghnus, son of Muirchertach Muimhnech
O'Conchobhair, in this year. The erection of a monastery for canons was commenced by Clarus Mac Mailin,
in Trinity Island on Loch-Uachtair, through the gift of
Cathal O'Raighilligh, in hoc[6] anno.   Thomas O'Ruadhain, bishop of Luighne,[7] in Christo quievit. Gilla-Isa,

---

Ffethelmus O'Konechor owed 5,000
marks and 2,000 cows for three
cantreds of land in Connacht, in fee
farm. See O'Donovan's ed. of the
Ann. Four Mast., A.D. 1235, note ¹,
and A.D. 1237, note ².

⁴ *From Rome.* See note ³, p. 334,
supra.

⁵ *Maghnus;* i.e. Maghnus, son of

Muirchertach Muimhnech O'Conchobhair, who was the son of Turlough
Mór O'Conchobhair, king of Ireland.

⁶ *Hoc.* oc, MS. Under the year
1250, *infra,* the removal of " White
Canons" from Trinity Island in Loch
Cé to this new foundation is recorded.

⁷ *Bishop of Luighne;* otherwise
bishop of Achonry.

hi Thopmaiᵹ, eppuc Conmaicne, in Cpipto quieuic.
ᵹilla na nech .h. Manoachain oo´éc a maimiptip na
búille, in hoc aňno. Cpeč oo ᵹenum oo Conchobap
mac Copmaic ap Ruaiopi .h. nᵹaopa, ocup a bpathaip
oo ṁapbao. Opaiᵹoe Conchobaip mic Copmaic oo
ṁapbao la Feolim mac Cathail cpoiboepᵹ ipin
mbliaoain pin. Opumann iapčaip ocup o lathach
Cille Opaoin co loč, ioip čoill ocup móin ocup ṁačaipe,
oo čabaipt oo Ohonnchao mac Muipceptaiᵹ oo
coimčinól na Tpinóioe pop Loč Cé, ocup oo Chlápup
ṁáᵹ Mhaoilin, a naimpip a piᵹe ocup a flaičiupa;
ocup ᵹioeoh nip čó paoa pemep a piᵹe, óip ni paiče
acht mí a tiᵹepntup, ocup po ᵹač Conchobap pein an
piᵹe oopioip.

Kt. Enáip pop Aoine, ocup aonmao ohéc puippe;
xx°. pexto aňno cicli polapip; quaptup annup oe-
cennouenalip [cicli]; xi°. aňno inoictionip; aňno ab
incapňatione Oomini, M.cc. xxx. octauo. Oonnchao
Uáičnech, mac Aooa, mic Ruaiopi hi Conchobaip, oo
ṁapbao la Taoc mac Oeoa mic Cathail cpoiboepᵹ, in
hoc aňno. Oonnchao mac Ouapcáin hi Eᵹpa, pi Luiᵹne,
oo ᵹaváil la Taoc mac Oeoa mic Cathail cpoiboepc,
ocup aň tán pucao oia coimét hé, po mapčpat a
bpaičpi péin é .i. mec Aooa hi Eᵹpa, ap an pliᵹeo a
Típ Opiuin na Sinna. Oonnchao mac Muipčeptaiᵹ oo
oul ipin mOpeppne oocum hi Raiᵹilliᵹ, co po leicpet
cpeč ṁóp i Connachta, ᵹup aipccpeo muintep čluana
Coippči, ᵹup ṁapbao maiče Muinňtepi hEoluip, ocup
mópán oona Tuathaib, a tópaiᵹecht na cpeice pin.

<hr>

1 *The Scelaighe*; lit. "the story-
teller."

2 *Conmaicne.* By bishop of Conmaicne is meant "bishop of Ardagh."

3 *Hoc.* oc, MS.

4 *Son of Cormac*; i.e. of Cormac,
son of Diarmaid, son of Ruaidhri
O'Conchobhair, king of Connaught.

5 *Son of Muirchertach*; i.e. of
Muirchertach Mac Diarmada, or
Murtough Mac Dermot. Roderick
O'Flaherty has added the marginal
note "lands given to yᵉ clergy by
M'Dermott."

6 *Decennovenalis.* oecinouemalip,
MS.

son of the Scelaighe[1] O'Tormaigh, bishop of Conmaicne,[2] in Christo quievit. Gilla-na-nech O'Mannachain died in the monastery of the Buill in hoc[3] anno. A depredation was committed by Conchobhar, son of Cormac,[4] on Ruaidhri O'Gadhra, whose brother he killed. The hostages of Conchobhar, son of Cormac[4] were slain by Fedhlim, son of Cathal Crobhderg, in this year. Drumann-iarthar, and from Lathach-Cille-Braein to the lake, both wood and bog, and plain, was given by Donnchadh, son of Muirchertach,[5] to the community of the Trinity on Loch-Cé, and to Clarus Mac Mailin, in the time of his reign and sovereignty; but nevertheless, the duration of his reign was not löng, for he was only a month in the lordship, and Conchobhar himself assumed the sovereignty again.

The kalends of January on Friday, and the eleventh of the moon; xx°. sexto anno cycli solaris; quartus annus Decennovenalis[6] [cycli]; xi°. anno Indictionis; anno ab Incarnatione[7] Domini, M.CC. XXX. octavo. Donnchadh Uaithnech,[8] son of Aedh, son of Ruaidhri O'Conchobhair, was killed by Tadhg, son of Aedh, son of Cathal Crobhderg, in hoc[3] anno. Donnchadh, son of Duarcan O'hEghra, king of Luighne, was taken prisoner by Tadhg, son of Aedh, son of Cathal Crobhderg; and when he was taken away to be confined his own kinsmen, i.e. the sons of Aedh O'hEghra, slew him on the way in Tir-Briuin-na-Sinna. Donnchadh, son of Muirchertach,[9] went into the Breifne to O'Raighilligh, when they sent a great predatory band into Connacht, who plundered the community of Cluain-Coirpthe; and the principal men of Muinter-Eolais, and several of the Tuatha, were slain in pursuit of

---

[7] *Incarnatione.* ᴀnᴄᴀpnᴀᴄıoınıp, MS.

[8] *Donnchadh Uaithnech.* Donnchadh the Uaithnian, so called from having been fostered in the territory of Uaithne, or Owney. See note [1]. p. 208, *supra.*

[9] *Donnchadh, son of Muirchertach.* See note [5], last page.

Maolρuαnαιɔ mαc Ɔonnchαɔα hι Ɔhuƀɔα ɔo mαρbαɔ
lα Mαιlρechlαιnn, mαc Conchobαιρ ρuαιƀ, mιc Mhuιρ-
čeρtαιᵹ Mhuιmnιᵹ hι Conchobαιρ, ocuρ lα mαcTιᵹeρnáιn
mιc Cαthαιl ṁíᵹαρáιn hι Conchobαιρ. Cαιρléna ɔo
ƀenum α Muιnnteρ Muρchαɔα, ocuρ α Conmαιcne
Cúιle, ocuρ α Ceρα, láρ nα bαρúnαιƀ ρempáιtι.
Ruαιɔρι, mαc Ⱥoƀα hι Fhlαιthbeρtαιᵹ, ɔo ᵹαƀαιl ɔo
ᵹαlloιƀ. Cloιctech Enαιᵹ ɔúιn ɔo ƀenum. Slαιᵹeɔ
lα Mαc Muιριρ .ι. ᵹιúρɔíρ nα hEρenn, ocuρ lα hUᵹα
ɔe Lαcí, ιαρlα Ulαɔ, α Cenél Eoᵹαιn ocuρ α Cenel
Conαιll, ᵹuρρo αιƀριᵹɔαɔ Máᵹ Lαčlαιnn, ocuρ ᵹuρ
ιnnαρbραɔ αρρ α číρ ρeιριn, ocuρ tucραɔ ριᵹe ɔo mαc
hι Neιll, ocuρ ρo ᵹαƀραɔ ρeιn bραιᵹɔe čeneóιl Conαιll
ocuρ Eoᵹαιn. Felιx .h. Ruαnαɔα, αιρɔeρρuc Tuαmα, α
hαιčle α coρα ƀe αρ ᵹρáƀ ɔo Ɔhíα, ɔo héc ιαρ nᵹαbáιl
αιbιɔe mαιnčeρρα uιmo α Cιll Muιρe ι nⱭč clιαƀ.
Cαthαl ṁáᵹ Rιαbαιᵹ, túιρρech Feρ Scéne, moρtuuρ
eρt. Flαιčbeρtαch mαc Cαčṁαoιl, αρɔ toιρech čenél
bFeραɔhαιᵹ, ocuρ αρɔ toιρech ɔαnα clαιnnι Conᵹαιle
ocuρ O Cenɔρoɔα α Tíρ Mhαnαch, bαρρ ᵹαιρcιɔ ocuρ
enιᵹ čιρe hEoᵹαιn, ɔo ṁαρbαɔ ɔo Ɔonnchαɔ mαc
Cαčṁαoιl, ɔα bραthαιρ ρeιn, α meαƀαιl.

Ict. Enáιρ ρoρ ραčαρn, ocuρ αlι ριcheɔ ρuιρρe;
xxᵒ. uιιιᵒ. αnno cιclι ρolαριρ; quιnto αnno cιclι ɔecen-
nouenαlιρ; xιιᵒ. αnno ιnɔιctιonιρ. Mᵒ. ccᵒ. tριceριmo
nono. Muιρceρtαch mαc Ɔomnαιll hι bριαιn ɔo héc
ιn hoc αnno. Toιρρɔhelbαč mαc Ruαιɔρι hι Conchobαιρ, ρι Connαcht, ɔo éᵹ. Cαč Chαιρn tριαɔαιl ɔo
čαbαιρt ɔo Ɔomnαll ṁáᵹ Lαčlαιnn, ɔú αρ mαρbαɔ

---

¹ *The aforesaid barons.* The English
barons mentioned under the year 1237
as having proceeded into Connacht.

² *Cloictech*; i.e. "bell house," steeple, or round tower.

³ *Mac Lachlainn.* Domhnall (or
Daniel) Mac Lachlainn.

⁴ *The son of O'Neill.* Brian O'Neill,
who was called Brian Catha-an-
Dúin, or "Brian of the battle of

Down." See under the year 1260,
infra.

⁵ *Cill-Muire.* "Mary's Church,"
or Mary's Abbey, Dublin.

⁶ *Brother.* The word bραthαιρ
signifies "brother" and "kinsman,"
in which latter sense it has been
understood in the present case by
Dr. O'Donovan (Ann. Four Mast.,
sub an.). In translating "brother"

this predatory band. Maelruanaidh, son of Donnchadh
O'Dubhda, was slain by Maelsechlainn, son of Conchobar
Ruadh, son of Muirchertach Muimhnech O'Conchobhair,
and by the son of Tighernan, son of Cathal Migaran
O'Conchobhair. Castles were erected in Muinter-Mur-
chada, and in Conmaicne-Cúile, and in Cera, by the
aforesaid barons.[1] Ruaidhri, son of Aedh O'Flaithbhertaigh, was taken prisoner by the Foreigners. The
cloicthech[2] of Enach-dúin was erected. A hosting by
Mac Maurice, i.e. the Justiciary of Erinn, and by Hugo de
Laci, earl of Uladh, into Cenel-Eoghain and Cenel-Conaill,
when they dethroned Mac Lachlainn[3] and expelled him
from his own land, and gave the sovereignty to the son
of O'Neill;[4] and they themselves obtained the hostages of
the Cenel-Conaill and *Cenel*-Eoghain. Felix O'Ruanadha,
archbishop of Tuaim, after resigning the archiepiscopate through love of God, and after assuming a monastic habit, died in Cill-Muire[5] in Ath-cliath. Cathal
Mac Riabhaigh, chieftain of Feara-Scene, mortuus est.
Flaithbhertach Mac Cathmhail, high chieftain of Cenel-
Feradhaigh, and high chieftain also of Clann-Conghaile,
and of Ui-Cendfhoda in Tir-Manach, head of the valour
and honour of Tir-Eoghain, was slain by Donnchadh Mac
Cathmhail, his own brother,[6] in treachery.

The kalends of January on Saturday, and the twenty-
second[7] of the moon; xx°.vii°. anno cycli solaris; quinto
anno cycli Decennovenalis;[8] xii°. anno Indictionis; M.CC.
tricesimo nono. Muirchertach, son of Domhnall O'Briain,
died in hoc[9] anno. Toirdhelbhach, son of Ruaidhri
O'Conchobhair, king of Connacht, died. The battle of
Carn-tShiadhail was given by Domhnall Mac Lachlainn,
in which were slain Domhnall Tamhnaighe O'Neill,

---

the Editor has followed Roderick
O'Flaherty, who has added the marginal note "Mac Cathfil kilt by his
brother."

[7] *Twenty-second.* aϧ ρicheꝺ. aiϧ
ρicheꝺ, MS.

[8] *Decennovenalis.* ꝺecιaϧ, MS.

[9] *Hoc.* oc, MS.

Oomnall Taṁnaɪᵹe O Neɪll, ocuʀ Mᵹ́ᵹ Maᵹᵹamna, ocuʀ Ṡomaɪʀle .h.ᵹaɪʀmleᵹhaɪᵹ, ocuʀ Caoᵹ ḃeʀnuɪʀ .h.ᵹaɪʀmleᵹhuɪᵹ, ocuʀ maɪᵹɪ ᵹenel Móáɪn, ocuʀ ʀochaɪᴅe aɪʀchena; ocuʀ ʀo ᵹaᵹ aʀɪʀ an ʀɪᵹe ᴅo benaᵹ ᴅe ɪn blɪaᴅaɪn ʀoɪme ʀɪn, ᵹaʀéɪʀ an ṁaᵹma moɪʀ ʀɪn ᵹuc aʀ ᵹenel Móáɪn, ocuʀ aʀ Aɪʀᵹɪallaɪḃ. Feʀᵹal mac Conconnacht hɪ Raɪᵹɪllɪᵹ, ʀí Oaʀᵹʀaɪᵹe ocuʀ ᵹlaɪnnɪ Feʀnṁuɪᵹe, ocuʀ ʀɪ na Ḃʀeɪ̇ʀne o Slɪaḃ ʀoɪʀ maᴅ ɪaʀ leaḃaʀ ele, ᴅo ṁaʀbaᴅ la Maolʀuanaɪᴅ mac Feʀᵹaɪl, ocuʀ la Conchobaʀ mac Coʀmaɪc, aʀ nᴅula ᴅó aʀ cʀeɪᵹ ᴅocum mac Neɪll mɪc Conᵹalaɪᵹ, ᵹuʀ aɪʀᵹ ɪaᴅ, ocuʀ ᵹuʀ ᵹaᵹ ᵹech uṁʀa; co ᵹanɪc Muɪʀceʀᵹach mac Neɪll aʀ bʀeɪ̇ɪʀ aʀɪʀ ᵹɪᵹ amaᵹ, ocuʀ ʀo ᵹabaᵹ é, ocuʀ ᴅo ṁaʀbaᴅ aca é ᵹaʀéɪʀ mɪc hɪ Raɪᵹɪllɪᵹ ᴅo ṁaʀbaᴅ. Cʀeᵹ móʀ ᴅo ᵹenum ᴅo ᵹalloɪḃ Éʀenn aʀ .h. nᴅomnall, ᵹuʀ aɪʀcᵹeᵹ Caɪʀʀʀe, ᵹo ʀaɪḃe an ᵹɪúʀᴅɪʀ ʀeɪn a nÉʀʀ ᴅaʀa ᵹá nuʀnaɪᴅe, ocuʀ conᴅechaᴅaʀ a ʀɪʀᵹɪ co Oʀuɪm ᵹlɪaḃ. Laʀʀaɪʀʀínaɪ, ɪnᵹen Chaᵹhaɪl cʀoɪbᴅeʀᵹ, uxoʀ hɪ Ohomnaɪll, ᴅo ᵹaḃaɪʀᵹ leᵹḃaɪle ᴅo ʀeʀonn ḃuʀᵹa, .ɪ. leᵹḃaɪle Roʀ Ḃɪʀn, ᴅo Chlaʀuʀ Mᵹ́ᵹ Mhaoɪlɪn, ocuʀ ᴅo coɪmᵹɪnól canánach oɪleɪn na Tʀɪnóɪᴅe aʀ loᵹ Cé, a nonóɪʀ na Tʀɪnóɪᴅɪ ocuʀ Mhuɪʀe Ḃaɪnᵹɪᵹeʀna, ɪn hoc anno. Coʀmac mac Aɪʀᵹ hɪ Mhaoɪlᵹʀechlaɪnn moʀᵹuuʀ eʀᵹ.

Kl. Enaɪʀ ʀoʀ Oomnach, ᵹʀeʀ uaᵹhaᴅ ʀuɪʀʀe;

<hr/>

[1] *Caech-Bernais.* This is a sobriquet signifying "the blind [man] of Bernas," or Bernas-mór, a well known mountain in the south of the county of Donegal.

[2] *He;* i.e. Domhnall Mac Lachlainn. The concluding part of this entry is incorrectly given by the Four Masters.

[3] *Clann-Fernmhaighe.* This name is written Clann-Fermhaighe under the year 1274, *infra.* But Clann-Fernmhaighe would seem to be the correct form, as the name is now anglicised "Glanfarne." The district in question is in the barony of Dromahaire, county of Leitrim. See O'Donovan's ed. of O'Dubhagain's *Topographical Poem;* Dublin, 1862, app. p. xxxvii.

[4] *The mountain;* i.e. Slieve-aniarainn, a mountain in the north of the county of Leitrim.

[5] *Son of Cormac.* Cormac Mac Diarmada, or Mac Dermot.

and Mac Mathghamhna, and Somhairle O'Gairmleghaigh, and Caech-Bernais[1] O'Gairmleghaigh, and the chieftains of Cenel-Moain, and great numbers besides; and he[2] assumed again the sovereignty which had been taken from him the year before, after this great defeat which he inflicted on the Cenel-Moain and the Airghialla. Ferghal, son of Cuconnacht O'Raighilligh, king of Dartraighe and Clann-Fernmhaighe,[3] (and king of the Breifne from the mountain[4] eastwards, according to another book), was slain by Maelruanaidh, son of Ferghal, and by Conchobhar, son of Cormac,[5] after he had gone on a predatory expedition against the sons of Niall, son of Conghalach, when he plundered them, and captured a house about them; and Muirchertach,[6] son of Niall, came out of the house on parole, and was made prisoner and killed by them,[7] after the son of O'Raighilligh had been slain. A great depredation was committed on O'Domhnaill by the Foreigners of Erinn, who plundered Cairbre; and the Justiciary himself was at Es-dara, awaiting them, his scouts having gone as far as Druim-cliabh. Lassairfhina, daughter of Cathal Crobhderg, uxor of O'Domhnaill, gave a half-bally of her marriage portion,[8] i.e. the half-bally of Ros-Birn, to Clarus-Mac Mailin[9] and the community of Canons of Trinity Island on Loch-Cé, in honour of the Trinity and Lady Mary, in hoc[10] anno. Cormac, son of Art O'Maelsechlain, mortuus est.

The kalends of January on Sunday, the third of the [1240.]

---

[6] *Muirchertach, son of Niall*; i.e. Muirchertach, son of Niall, son of Conghalach O'Ruairc.

[7] *By them.* That is, by the friends of Ferghal O'Raighilligh, or Farrell O'Reilly.

[8] *Marriage portion.* ꞅepoɴɴ ꞅuꞃꞇa; lit. "marriage land."

[9] *Clarus Mac Mailin.* This ecclesiastic, whose name occurs so frequently in these annals, is stated in the O'Reilly pedigree, (MS. in the office of the Ulster King at Arms, Dublin Castle), to have been bishop of Kilmore; but his name does not appear in any list of the bishops of that diocese accessible to the editor. See note under the year 1251, *infra.*

[10] *Hoc.* oc, MS.

bliaᵭaiɴ ᵭeꞃiꞃ aɴ ċicil ꞃoluꞃᵭa; ꞃeꭗꞇo aɴɴo cicli ᵭe-
ceɴɴouenaliꞃ; ꭗiiii. aɴɴo iɴᵭicꞇioɴiꞃ; ᷃.cc.ꭗl. Cꞃeċ
ᵯóꞃ la Coiɴcoɴɴaċꞇ .h. Raiᵹilliᵹ ꞃoꞃ Coꞃmac ᷃ac
ɴᵭiaꞃmaᵭa, ᵹuꞃ aiꞃᵹeꞃᵭaiꞃ co hᵓꞃᵭ ċaꞃna iɴ ꞇíꞃ
uile, ocuꞃ ᵹuꞃ ᵯaꞃᵬuꞃᵭaiꞃ ᵭaoine iᵯᵭa a ɴᵓiᵹalꞇuꞃ a
mic. Feᵭlim .h. Conchobaiꞃ ᵭo ᵭul co ꞇech ꞃí Saꭗan,
ᵭo ċoꞃꞃaoiᵭ ᵹall ocuꞃ ᵹaoiᵭel Eꞃenn ꞃꞃiꞃ; ocuꞃ ꞃuaiꞃ
onoiꞃ ᵯóꞃ on ꞃiᵹ ᵭon chuꞃ ꞃin; ocuꞃ ꞇáɴic ꞃlán ᵭía
ꞇiᵹ, co ꞃubach ꞃomenmnach. Oeᵭ mac ᵹilla na noem
cꞃuim h1 Sechnuꞃaiᵹ ᵭo ᵯaꞃbaᵭ la Conchobaꞃ, mac
Oeᵭa, mic Caꞇhail cꞃoibᵭeꞃᵹ, ocuꞃ la Fiacꞃa.h.
bᶠhloinn. Saᵭᵬ, inᵹen h1 Chinneꞇiᵹ .i. ben ᵭonn-
chaᵭa Chaiꞃꞃꞃiᵹ h1 ᵬꞃiain, moꞃꞇua eꞃꞇ. ᵹilla na
noem .h. ᵭꞃeain, aiꞃċinnech ᵓꞃᵭa caꞃna, ᵭo héc in
hoc anno.

ꝃꞇ. Enaiꞃ ꞃoꞃ ᵯaiꞃꞇ, ocuꞃ .ꭗiiii. ꞃuiꞃꞃe; ꞃꞃimuꞃ
annuꞃ cicli ꞃolaꞃiꞃ; ꞃeꞃꞇimo anno ᵭecennouenaliꞃ
cicli; ꭗiiii. cicli inᵭicꞇioɴiꞃ. ᷃.cc.ꭗl. ꞃꞃimo. ᵹꞃiᵹoꞃiuꞃ
nonuꞃ papa quieuiꞇ in Cꞃiꞃꞇo. Cꞃeċ ᵯóꞃ ᵭo ᵭenam
ᵭon ᵹiuꞃᵭíꞃ, .i. ᵭo ᷃uiꞃiꞃ ᷃ac ᵹeꞃailꞇ, a ᷃aᵹ nᵓoi,
ᵹuꞃ aiꞃᵹeꞃᵭaiꞃ Fiaċꞃa .h. Floinn ocuꞃ ᵭonnchaᵭ
᷃ac ᵭiaꞃmaᵭa; co ꞃucꞃaꞇ uaꞇhaᵭ ᵭo muinꞇeꞃ h1
Conchobaiꞃ ꞃoꞃꞃo, ᵹuꞃ maꞃbaᵭ leo Náꞃ ᷃ac ᵹilla-
ċeallaiᵹ, eꞇ alii mulꞇi. Comoꞃba Paᵭꞃaic ᵭo ċoiᵹeċꞇ
iɴᵭ Eꞃinn .i. anꞇ ᵓlmánach, ocuꞃ ꞃꞃuuileᵭ leiꞃ ón
Papa aꞃ ċellaib Paᵭꞃaic i nEꞃinn. ᵭoᵯnall móꞃ
.h. ᵭomnaill, .i. mac Eᵹnecháin h1 ᵭomnaill, ꞃí ċíꞃe
Conaill, ocuꞃ Feꞃ ᷃anach, ocuꞃ iochꞇaiꞃ Connachꞇ co
Coiꞃꞃꞃliaᵬ, ocuꞃ Oiꞃᵹiall o ċláꞃ anuaꞃ, ᵭaᵯ comaiꞃ
Cuinn Ceᵭochaꞇaiᵹ aꞃ ċlóᵭ ᵹach cliaꞇċai, meᵭh

---

¹ *Decennovenalis.* ᵭecīaꞇ, MS.

² *By Cuconnacht.* la coī ᵭí ᵭnꞃ̄,
for la Coiɴcoinnconnachꞇ, MS.,
which is incorrect.

³ *His son;* i.e. Ferghal O'Raighilligh, who had been slain by Con-

chobhar, son of Cormac Mac Diarmada, in the preceding year.

⁴ *Gilla-na-naem Crom.* Gilla-na-
naemh "the stooped," or literally
" the stooped servant of the angels."

moon; the last year of the solar cycle; sexto anno cycli Decennovenalis;[1] xiii°. anno Indictionis: M.cc.xl. A great depredation *was committed* by Cuconnacht[2] O'Raighilligh on Cormac Mac Diarmada, when he plundered the entire country to Ard-carna, and killed several people, in revenge for his son.[3] Fedhlim O'Conchobhair went to the house of the king of the Saxons, to complain to him of the Foreigners and Gaeidhel of Erinn; and he received great honour from the king on this occasion, and came home safely, joyfully, contentedly. Aedh, son of Gilla-na-naemh Crom[4] O'Sechnusaigh, was killed by Conchobar, son of Aedh, son of Cathal Crobhderg, and by Fiachra O'Floinn. Sadhbh, daughter of O'Cennedigh, i.e. the wife of Donn-chadh Cairbrech O'Briain, mortua est. Gilla-na-naemh O'Dreain, airchinnech of Ard-carna, died in hoc anno.

The kalends of January on Tuesday, and the 14th of the moon; primus annus cycli solaris; septimo anno Decennovenalis cycli; xiiii°. cycli Indictionis; M.cc.xl. primo. Gregorius nonus, papa, quievit in Christo. A great depredation was committed in Magh-Noi by the Justiciary, i.e. Maurice Fitz-Gerald, when he plundered Fiachra O'Floinn and Donnchadh Mac Diarmada; but a few of the people of O'Conchobhair overtook them, and Nár Mac Gillacellaigh was slain by them, et alii[5] multi. The comarb of Patrick, i.e. the Almanach,[6] came to Erinn, having privileges from the Pope over the churches of Patrick in Erinn. Domhnall Mór O'Domhnaill, i.e. the son of Egnechan O'Domhnaill, king of Tir-Conaill, and of the Feara-Manach, and of the lower part of Connacht as far as Corr-sliabh, and of Oirghiall from the plain[7] downwards—a man like Conn Ced-chathach[8] for

---

[5] *Alii.* ᵃᵇᵃ, MS.

[6] *The Almanach;* i.e. the German. His name was Albert of Cologne, al-though Matthew Paris calls him An-delm.

[7] *The plain.* cláp. The plain of

Oirghiall or Oriel, or the level part of the county of Louth.

[8] *Conn Cedchathach.* "Hundred-battled Conn," monarch of Ireland; slain A.D. 157.

comϲϲꞃom Coꞃmαιc Uι Cuιnn αꞃ ѕeαꞃϲ bꞃeαϲɦαιb, ocuꞃ
ιmeċϲꞃαιꝺ Cιꞃϲ Cιoιnꝼιꞃ αꞃ ιonnαꞃbαꝺ α eꞃcαꞃαꝺ;
ʒuαιllιʒe Ѣꞃιαιn Ѣɦoꞃomα αꞃ ċoʒαꝺ ocuꞃ cꞃαbαꝺ, ꝺéc
ꞃe ɦαꝼαꞃϲ, αꞃ mbꞃeιϲ buαꝺα o ꝺomαn ocuꞃ ó ꝺemαn, α
nαιbíꝺ αn uιꞃꝺ leιϲ α mαιnιꞃꝺιꞃ Eꞃꞃα Ꞃuαιꝺ, ocuꞃ α
αꝺɦnαcαl co ɦonoꞃαcɦ ιnnϲι ꝺóꞃ, ιαꞃ nα ꝺeιϲ ceϲꞃι
blιαꝺnα ꝺɦéc α ꞃιʒe ꝺó; ιꞃιn ꝼoʒmαꞃ ꝺo éc. Mαoιl-
ꞃeċlαιn ꝺo ʒαbáιl ꞃιʒe α ɱιonαꝺ α αϲɦαꞃ, .ι. α mαc
ꞃeιꞃꞃιn. ɦ. Neιll ꝺo ċoιʒecɦϲ nα ċenn ιαꞃ ná ιnnαꞃbαꝺ
ꝺo Mɦáʒ Lαċlαιnn αꞃꞃ α ꞃιʒe. Ꝺulα ꝺo Mɦαιlꞃeċlαιnn
.ɦ. Ꝺomnαιll le Ѣꞃιαn .ɦ. Neιll, ocuꞃ α ϲeαcɦϲ
ꝺιɓlínαιꝩ α Cenel Eoʒαιn ꝺoꞃιꝺιꞃ, ocuꞃ cαϲ ꝺo ϲαbαιꞃϲ
ꝺoιꝩ ꝺo Ꝺomnαll Mɦáʒ Lαċlαιnn ιn ϲαn ꞃιn .ι. cαϲ
Cαιmeꞃʒe, ocuꞃ Ꝺomnαll Mɦáʒ Lαċlαιnn, ꞃιʒ Cenιuιl
Eoʒαιn ꝺo ɱαꞃbαꝺ αnnꞃιn, ocuꞃ ꝺeċneαbαꞃ ꝺα
ꝺeιꞃɓꝼιne mαιlle ꞃιꞃ, ocuꞃ ϲáιꞃιʒ Cenιuιl Eoʒαιn uιle
ꝺo mαꞃbαꝺ αnn; ocuꞃ ꞃιʒe Cénιuιl Eoʒαιn ꝺo ʒαbáιl
ꝺo Ѣꞃιαn .ɦ. Neιll ιαꞃꞃιn; ocuꞃ ꝺo mαꞃbαꝺ Sιαꝺαιl
ιꞃιn ċαϲ, ocuꞃ ꝺαoιne mαιϲe ιɱꝺα ꞃoꞃ. Sιϲꞃιuc Mɦαʒ
Oιꞃecɦϲαιʒ, ϲoιꞃecɦ Cɦloιnnι Ꞇomαlϲαιʒ, ꝺo ɦéc ιꞃιn
mblιαꝺαιn ꞃιn. Uαlϲꞃα ꝺé Lαcí, ϲιʒeꞃnα nα Mιꝺe,
ocuꞃ cenꝺ comαιꞃle ʒαll Eꞃenꝺ, ꝺo éʒ α Sαꭓαnαιb ιn
hoc αnno. Coιꞃecꝺαꝺ ϲempuιl nα mbꞃáϲɦαꞃ mιnúꞃ ιn
Cϲ Luαιn lα comαꞃbα Ꝑαϲꞃαιc. Mαc Muιꞃιꞃ Mιc
ʒeꞃuιlϲ, ʒιúꞃꝺιꞃ nα ɦEꞃenn, ꝺo ϲeαcɦϲ ꞃlúαʒ moꞃ co
ɦCϲ leϲɦαn α Luιʒne, ocuꞃ ꝺo ꞃóιne ꞃιϲ ꞃe Ꞇαꝺc .ɦ.
Conchobαιꞃ αnn, ocuꞃ ꝺo ιmꞃúꝩ ϲαꞃ αιꞃ ιαꞃꞃιn. Ꞇαꝺc
.ɦ. Conchobαιꞃ ꝺo αꞃccαιꞃ Ꝺαꞃϲꞃαιʒe, ocuꞃ ċlαιnnι
Ꝼeꞃnɱuιʒe. Sιϲ ꝺo ċenum ꝺo ċomαꞃbα Ꝑαϲꞃαιc ꞃe
ɦαιꞃꝺeꞃꞃuιc Connαcɦϲ, ocuꞃ ꞃιꞃ nα ɦeꞃꞃocuιb elι

---

1 *Cormac.* Cormac Mac Airt, king of Ireland, grandson of the monarch Conn, and the alleged compiler of some of the Irish legal institutes.

2 *Art Aenfher.* "Art the Lonely," father of Cormac Mac Airt.

3 *Siadhail.* There is no reference to this person in any of the other Irish Chronicles, excepting the so-called Annals of Connacht; nor can the editor say to what family or sept he belonged. From some person

winning every battle; the equal of Cormac,[1] grandson of Conn, for just judgments; the rival of Art Aenfher[2] for banishing his enemies; the fellow of Brian Borumha in warfare and piety—died on his pillow, after triumphing over the world and the demon, in the habit of the Grey Order, in the monastery of Es-Ruaidh; and he was also honourably interred in it, after he had been fourteen years in the sovereignty. In the autumn he died. Maelsechlainn, i.e. his own son, assumed the sovereignty in the place of his father. O'Neill came to him, after he had been expelled from his sovereignty by Mac Lachlainn. Maelsechlain O'Domhnaill joined Brian O'Neill, and they both went again into Cenel-Eoghain, and then gave battle to Domhnall Mac Lachlainn, viz. :—the battle of Camerghe, where Domhnall Mac Lachlainn, king of Cenel-Eoghain, was slain, and ten of his kinsmen along with him. And all the chieftains of the Cenel-Eoghain were slain there; and the sovereignty of Cenel-Eoghain was afterwards assumed by Brian O'Neill. And Siadhail[3] was killed in the battle, and many more good men. Sitric Mac Oirechtaigh, chief of Clann-Tomaltaigh, died in this year. Walter de Laci, lord of Midhe, and head of counsel of the Foreigners of Erinn, died in Saxon-land in hoc[4] anno. Consecration of the church of the Friars Minor in Ath-Luain, by the comarb of Patrick. Mac Maurice Fitz-Gerald, Justiciary of Erinn, went with a great army to Ath-lethan in Luighne, and made peace there with Tadhg O'Conchobhair, and afterwards returned. Tadhg O'Conchobhair plundered Dartraighe and Clann-Fernmhaighe.[5] Peace was made by the comarb of Patrick with the archbishop of Connacht, and with the

---

of this name has probably been derived that of Carn-tSiadhail, (now Carnteel, in the barony of Dungannon, county of Tyrone), where Domhnall Mac Lachlainn defeated the Cenel-

Moain and Airghialla in the year A.D. 1239, as above recorded.

[4] *Hoc.* oc, MS.

[5] *Clann-Fernmhaighe.* See note [8], p. 350, *supra.*

2 A 2

áipchena, ap lop ſepainn Paopaic a Connachtaiḃ. Diapmaio, mac Maġnuip, mic Thoippoheḃaiġ ṁoip hI Chonchobaip, ſaoi neiṁġ ocuſ nenznama, moptuuſ eſt. Aonġuſ Mháġpaiḃ, ſacapt Copmaic mic Diap- maoa, ante natale Domini, moptuuſ eſt. Maġnuſ mac Feṛġail poſt natale Domini moptuuſ eſt. Int eſpuc .h. Flaithbeptaiġ, .i. eſpuc Enaiġ Dúin, quieuit in Cṛiſto. Taḋc mac Ruaioṛi hI Ġhaoṛa oo éc in hoc anno. Sueſṛán pápa quieuit in Cṛiſto.

Ḱt. Enaiṛ ſoṛ Ceoaoin; xxu.ſuiṛṛe; ſecunouſ annuſ cicli ſolaṛiſ; octauo anno oecennouenaliſ cicli; xu. anno inoictioniſ cicli; M.cc.xl.ſecunoo. Donnchao Caiṛḃṛech .h. Ḃṛiain, ṛi Tuaḋṁuṁan, ocuſ a mac .i. Toiṛṛoheḃach mac Donnchaoa Caiṛṛuiġ, moptui ſunt; ocuſ oob e in Donnchao ſin .h. Ḃṛiain congṁalaiġ cṛeioṁe ocuſ clú leiḃi Moḋa, ocuſ tuiṛ oṛoain ocuſ aiṛeċuiſ oeiſcept Eṛenn. Móṛ, inġen Donnchaoa hI Feṛġail, quieuit in Cṛiſto. Aoḃ .h. Conchobaip .i. ant aiḃċléiṛeċ, mac Aoḋa mic Ruaioṛi hI Conchobaip, oo ṁaṛbao la Toiṛṛoheḃach mac Aoḋa mic Cathail cṛoiḃoeṛg. Conchobaṛ .h. Ḃṛiain oo ġaḃáil ṛiġe Tuaḋṁuman. Ḃṛian mac Donnchaoa hI Dhuḃoa, ṛí .h. bFhiacṛaċ ocuſ .h. nAṁalġaio, ocuſ Iṛṛuiſ, oo ṁaṛbao aṛ ſliġeo aġ oul oa ailiṭṛe co mainiſtiṛ na Ḃúille. Caiṛioil móṛ la Pṛimſáiḃ Aṛoa Macha ocuſ la haṛaoaiḃ canánach Eṛenn uile; oo commoṛaḃ a nuiṛo, a luġṁaḋ, oiaṛ tóġbao ann moṛ oo ċaiṛiḃ oo ċinól Moḋta on Roim. Sloiġeo móṛ laṛ an nĠiuṛoiſ ocuſ la Ġalloib Eṛenn aiṛchena, ocuſ la Feḋlim mac Cathail cṛoiḃoeṛg hI Conchobaip, a Cénel Conaill a noiġuil Taiḋc hI Conchobaip, ġuṛ

<hr>

1 *Natale.* natali, MS.

2 *Hoc.* oc, MS.

3 *Stephen.* Sueſṛán, MS.; which is a mistake for Celestine IV.

4 *Decennovenalis.* oecinoũali, MS.

5 *Primate.* The MS. has pṛimſáiḃ,

which properly means "chief prophet." See note 3, p. 148, *supra.*

6 *In revenge of.* a noiġuil. The text is here incorrect. The Four Masters more accurately say inoiaiḃ "after," or "in pursuit of" Tadhg

other bishops likewise, on account of Patrick's land in Connacht. Diarmaid, son of Maghnus, son of Toirdhelbhach Mor O'Conchobhair, a man distinguished for hospitality and valour, mortuus est. Aenghus Magraith, Cormac Mac Diarmada's priest, ante Natale[1] Domini mortuus est. Maghnus, son of Ferghal, post Natale[1] Domini mortuus est. The Bishop O'Flaithbhertaigh, i.e. bishop of Enach-dúin, quievit in Christo. Tadhg, son of Ruaidhri O'Gadhra, died in hoc[2] anno. Stephen,[3] papa, quievit in Christo.

The kalends of January on Wednesday, the twenty-fifth of the moon; secundus annus cycli solaris; octavo anno Decennovenalis[4] cycli; xv°.anno Indictionis cycli; M.cc.xl.secundo. Donnchadh Cairbrech O'Briain, king of Tuadh-Mumha, and his son, i.e. Toirdhelbhach, son of Donnchadh Cairbrech, mortui sunt; and this Donnchadh O'Briain was the maintainer of the faith and renown of Leth-Modha, and the pillar of the dignity and nobility of the south of Erinn. Mór, daughter of Donnchadh O'Ferghail, quievit in Christo. Aedh O'Conchobhair, i.e. the ex-cleric, son of Aedh, son of Ruaidhri O'Conchobhair, was killed by Toirdhelbhach, son of Aedh, son of Cathal Crobhderg. Conchobhar O'Briain assumed the sovereignty of Tuadh-Mumha. Brian, son of Donnchadh O'Dubhda, king of Ui-Fiachrach, Ui-Amhalghaidh, and Irrus, was killed on the way, as he was going on a pilgrimage to the abbey of the Buill. A great chapter *was held* at Lughmhagh by the Primate[5] of Ard-Macha and the abbots of the Canons of all Erinn, to advance their Order; on which occasion many of the relics which Mochta had collected from Rome were taken up. A great hosting to Cenel-Conaill by the Justiciary, and by the Foreigners of Erinn likewise, and by Fedhlim, son of Cathal Crobhderg O'Conchobhair, in revenge of[6]

O'Conchobhair, who had fled to Cenel-Conaill. The Tadhg in question was the son of Aedh, son of Cathal Crobh-derg, and consequently the nephew of king Fedhlim O'Conchobhair.

ʒαḃγατ ʟoɴʒpopτ ɪ ɴ'Ɗpuɪm τɦuαmα, co ταɴcoταp mαɪτe Chénel Conaill ɪɴα τeαċ, co τucγατ ḃpαɪʒɖe ɓóɪḃ. Spɪɖeʟ Sʟɪcɪʒ ɖo ėɪɴɖʟucαɖ ɖoɴ ʒɪuɪpóɪp ɖo Chláρuρ Ϻɦáʒ Ϻɦαɪʟíɴ α ɴoɴóɪp ɴα Τpɪɴóɪɖe. Ταḃc .ɧ. Conchobaɪp ɖo ʒαḃáɪʟ ʟe Coɪɴcoɴɴαcɦτ .ɧ. Ꞃαɪʒɪʟʟɪʒ, αp popʒαʟʟ Ϝɦéɖʟɪm mɪc Cατɦαɪʟ cpoɪḃɖepʒ, ɪpɪɴ mḃʟɪαɖαɪɴ pɪɴ. Ϻαʒɴuρ .ɧ. Ϻuɪpeʒɦαɪʒ ɖo ṁαpḃαɖ ɖo Τɦomαp mαc Ϻupcɦαɖα. Ηɪαʟʟ, mαc Ɗomɴαɪʟʟ mūp, mɪc Ꞃuαɪɖpɪ ɦɪ Choɴcɦobαɪp, ɖo ʟopcαɖ, ocuρ τpɪ .ɧ. Seċɴuραɪʒ, ɪɴ óeɴ τɪʒ α Ϻuɪʒ ɴϹó ɴα Sαχαɴαcɦ ʟα ʟoʒḃαoɪp ɖo ṁuɪɴτep Ϻɪc Ϻɦuɪpɪp. Ccoḃ .ɧ. Ϻαɴɖαcɦαɪɴ ɖo éʒ α ɴαɪḃío ċαɴáɴαċ α Cɪʟʟ ṁóɪp. Ɗomɴαʟʟ Ϻαc Ccɪpτéɴ ɖo éc ɪɴ hoc αɴɴo. Ϻɪc Oeḃα ɦɪ Coɴcɦo-bαɪp ɖo ḃuʟ αp ċαɪppʟeɴ Ϻɪc Ʒoɪpɖeʟḃ ɪpɪɴ mḃpeɪppɴe.

Ӄ.ᴛ. Θɴáɪp ɼop ḃαpɖαoɪɴ, ocuρ peɪppeɖ uαcɦαɖ ɼuɪppe; τepτɪuρ αɴɴuρ cɪcʟɪ ɼoʟαpɪp; ɴoɴuρ αɴɴuρ ɖeceɴɴoueɴαʟɪp [cɪcʟɪ]; ppɪmuρ αɴɴuρ ɪɴɖɪcτɪoɴɪp; Ϻ.cc.χτ.τepτɪo. Ταḃc, mαc Oeḃα, mɪc Cατɦαɪʟ cpoɪḃɖepʒ, ɪαp ɴá ʟéʒeɴ αmαcɦ ɖ∪α Ꞃαɪʒɪʟʟɪʒ, ɖo ḃoɪʒecɦτ co mαɪɴɪpτɪp ɴα ḃuɪʟʟe ocuρ poċpαɪɖe ɖo ḃαḃαɪpτ ʟαɪp ʒo τecɦ Ϻɪc Ɗɪαpmαɖα, .ɪ. Copmαɪc mɪc Τomαʟταɪʒ, ocuρ Ϻαc Ɗɪαpmαɖα ɖo ʒαḃαɪʟ ɖó αɴɴ, ocuρ α ṁατɦαɪp ɼéɪɴ ɖo ḃpeɪτ ʟαɪp ɖó ɪαppɪɴ, .ɪ. Θɖαoɪɴ ɪɴʒeɴ Ϻɦéʒ Cαppτɦαɪʒ, .ɪ. ɪɴʒeɴ Ϝɦɪɴʒɪɴ ṁóɪp Ϻɦeʒ Cαppτɦαɪʒ, beɴ Ϻɪc Ɗɪαpmαɖα, ocuρ α ταḃαɪpτ ɖo Choɪɴcoɴɴαcɦτ .ɧ. Ꞃαɪʒɪʟʟɪʒ ɴα mɴαoɪ, αρρ α ɼuαpʟucαɖ pɼéɪɴ. Ταḃc ɖo ḃuʟ αpíp ɼó ɼéɪʟ Ϻápταɪɴ, uαcɦαɖ ɖo ḃαoɪɴɪḃ, α coɪɴɴe ɦɪ Ꞃαɪʒɪʟʟɪʒ, ocuρ Ταḃʒ ɖo ʒαḃáɪʟ ɖó α ḃpɪoʟʟ ocuρ α meαḃαɪʟ, ɪɴ ɖαpɴα peαcɦτ, ocuρ α ṁuɪɴɴτep ɖo ṁαpḃαɖ, ocuρ α ḃeɪτ α ʟáɪṁ co ɼéɪʟ ḃepαɪʒ ɪɴ eppαcɦ ɪαppɪɴ. Sʟoɪʒeɖ

---

1 *Domhnall Mūr.* The letters *Mūr* represent the abbrev. form of some sobriquet of Domhnall.

2 *Went.* ɖo ɖuʟ. The infin. part. ɖo is repeated in the MS.

3 *Tertius.* τcɪuρ (tercius), MS.

4 *Tertio.* τcɪo (tercio), MS.

5 *The festival of Martin;* i.e. Saint Martin of Tours. Martinmas, or the 11th of November.

Tadhg O'Conchobhair; and they encamped at Druim-Thuama, when the chieftains of Cenel-Conaill came into their house, and gave them hostages.   The hospital of Sligech was presented by the Justiciary to Clarus Mac Mailin, in honour of the Trinity.   Tadhg O'Conchobhair was apprehended by Cuconnacht O'Raighilligh at the instigation of Fedhlim, son of Cathal Crobhderg, in this year.   Maghnus O'Muiredhaigh was slain by Thomas Mac Murchadha. Niall, son of Domhnall Mūr,[1] son of Ruaidhri O'Conchobhair, was burned, together with three O'Sechnasaighs, in a house in Magh-Eó of the Saxons, by Loghbhais of the people of Mac Maurice.   Aedh O'Mannachain died in the habit of a canon, in Cill-mór.   Domhnall Mac Airten died in hoc anno.   The sons of Aedh O'Conchobhair went[2] upon the castle of Mac Goisdelbh in the Breifne.

The kalends of January on Thursday, and the sixth of the moon; tertius[3] annus cycli solaris; nonus annus Decennovenalis [cycli]; primus annus Indictionis; M.cc.xl.tertio.[4]   Tadhg, son of Aedh, son of Cathal Crobhderg, after having been released by O'Raighilligh, came to the monastery of the Buill, and brought a force with him to the house of Mac Diarmada, i.e. Cormac, son of Tomaltach; and he took Mac Diarmada prisoner there, and afterwards carried off his own mother, (i.e. Etain, daughter of Mac Carthaigh, i.e. daughter of Finghin Mór Mac Carthaigh, wife of Mac Diarmada), whom he gave to Cuconnacht O'Raighilligh as his wife, for his own release.   Tadhg went again about the festival of Martin,[5] with a few men, to meet O'Raighilligh, who apprehended Tadhg, in treachery and deceit, a second time, and killed his people; and he himself was kept in confinement until the festival of Berach[6] in the following Spring.   A

---

[6] Berach.   Saint Berach, or Barry, patron of Cluain-Coirpthe, now Kilbarry, in the parish of Termonbarry, barony of Ballintober North, county of Roscommon.   The festival of Saint Berach was celebrated annually on the 11th of February.

mór la ri Saxan vocum rí Franc, ocur techta vo
tocht on rí viarrav Zall Erenn cuize. Ricarv mac
Uilliam búrc vo vul cuize ar in rloizev rin, ocur a éz
toir. Uza vé Laćí, iarla Ulav, mortuur ert; ocur ni
hé in ceo Uza ro maro Zilla zan ionathar a n'Ourmaiz
Choluim Cille, acht int Uza véizenach. Petrur Mház
Craić ar zcinnevh a beća a canánchoib oilen na
Trinóive ar Loć Cé, mortuur ert, et repultur ert
in vie rancti Martini. Maoileoin .h. Crechán,
aircivecain Tuama, ar techt tairir ina maizirtir, vo
éc in ΑΙ cliać. Finvachta .h. Luzava, comarba
beneoin ocur vezánach mór Tuama, vo éz im féil
Martain. Caćarach .h. Snéviura, vezanach Muinteri
Maolruanaiv, vo éz a nΑΙrv ćarna im feil Lúirinc.
Cathal mac Αοvα hi Conchobair, valta Mhuintire
Raizilliz, vo innto orra, ocur creć vo vénam vó ar
Muirceptach mac Zillafúiliz a Maz Nirri, ocur
Muirceptach réin vo zaбail vó, ocur a marbav a
cuinzir a Cill tSheirín. Creć mór eli vo venam vó
ro cevóir ar ćlainn Fernmaize, ocur ar Oharzraiz.
Creć Mhoizе Réin la Cathal mac Αοvα vór, zur
épiz cozav etir fíol Conchobair ocur .h. Raizilliz.
Tempul Αrvα carna vaivбliuzav la Clárur Mház
Mhaoilín in hoc anno.

Ct. Enair ror Αoine, ocur xuiii. ruirrе; iiii. anno
cicli rolarir; xº. anno vecennouenalir [cicli]; ii. anno

---

¹ *The first Hugo.* The murder of
the elder Hugo de Laci is recorded under
the year 1186, *supra.* In place of the
present entry the so-called Annals of
Connacht describe the death of Hugo
de Laci the elder, in nearly the same
words used above, under the year 1186.

² *Gilla - gan - inathar.* This is a
sobriquet signifying the "fellow
without viscera." The name of the
individual was O'Miadhaigh. See p.
175, *supra.*

³ *Die Sancti Martini.* See note ⁵,
page 358.

⁴ *Coming across;* i.e. from England, or the Continent.

⁵ *Comarb of Benen;* i.e. successor
of Benen, or Benignus, who was one
of Saint Patrick's disciples, and patron
of several ecclesiastical establishments,
of which the most celebrated were
Drumlease, in the county of Leitrim,
and Kilbannon, in the county of Galway. Finnachta O'Lughadha must

great expedition by the king of the Saxons to the king of France, and messengers came from the king, summoning the Foreigners of Erinn. Richard, son of William Burk, went to him on this expedition, and died in the east. Hugo de Laci, earl of Uladh, mortuus est. (He was not the first Hugo,[1] whom Gilla-gan-inathair[2] killed at Durmhagh-Choluim-Chille, but the last Hugo). Petrus Mac Craith, after spending his life with the canons of Trinity Island on Loch-Cé, mortuus est, et sepultus est in die Sancti Martini.[3] Maeleoin O'Crechain, archdeacon of Tuaim, after coming across[4] as a master, died in Ath-cliath. Finnachta O'Lughadha, comarb of Benen,[5] and great dean of Tuaim, died about the festival of Martin. Cathasach O'Snedhiusa, dean of Muinter-Maelruanaidh,[6] died at Ard-carna about the festival of Laurence.[7] Cathal, son of Aedh O'Conchobhair, the foster-son of Muinter-Raighilligh, turned against them, and committed a depredation on Muirchertach Mac Gillashuiligh, in Magh-Nisse, and apprehended Muirchertach himself, whom he killed while in bonds at Cill-tSeisin. He committed another great depredation, immediately after, on Clann-Fernmaighe[8] and the Dartraighe. Magh-Rein was also plundered by Cathal, son of Aedh, when a war broke out between the race of Conchobhar[9] and O'Raighilligh. The church of Ard-carna was enlarged by Clarus Mac Mailin in hoc anno.

The kalends of January on Friday, and the 17th of the moon; iiii. anno cycli solaris; x°. anno Decennovenalis

---

have been the comarb of Benen in the latter place, as he is called "great dean of Tuaim," near which the church of Kilbannon is situated.

[6] *Muinter-Maelruanaidh.* This was the tribe name of the Mac Dermots of Magh-Luirg, or Moylurg, in the county of Roscommon, and was used as well to express the name of the district inhabited by the sept as that of the people. Moylurg was a rural deanery in the diocese of Elphin.

[7] *Festival of Laurence.* The 10th of August.

[8] *Clann-Fernmaighe.* Otherwise written Clann-Fermhaighe. See note [3], p. 350, *supra.*

[9] *The race of Conchobhar.* The O'Conchobhair or O'Conors.

ιηϲιϲτιοηιϝ. Μ.cc.xl.quαϝτο. Ταϫϲ, mαc Ccoϫα, mιc
Ccατhαιl cϝοιϫϫϵϝϫ, ϫο ϫαllαϫ ocuϝ ϫο ϝϝοchαϫ lα
Cοιηϲοηηαϲhτ .h. Rαιϫιlliϫ, ϝο ϝéιl ϫϵϝαιϫ, αϫ Ιηηϝι ηα
cοηαιϝϵ αϝ Loϫ Ccιllιηηϵ, ιαϝ ηά ϫϵιϲh α láιm ó ϝéιl
Μαϝταιηϲοϝιϲϵ ϝιη. Ruαιϫϝι mαc Ccoϫα hι Chοηchοϫαιϝ,
α ϫϵϝϫϝάϲαιϝ, ϫο ϫάϫhαϫ αϝ αη ϫCuιϝϝíη ϫConηαch-
ταch αϫ Ccϫ líαϫ ηα Sιηηα, ιη uιι°. ιϫuϝ Μαϝτιι, ocuϝ
α αϫlúcαϫ αmmαιηιϝτιϝ Chluαηα τuάιϝcϵϝτ co huαϝϝαl
οηοϝαch. Conchοϫαϝ, mαc Ccoϫα, mιc Ccατhαιl cϝοιϫϫϵϝϫ, ϫο éc α cιηη mίοϝ ϫοη ϵϝϝαch cϵϫηα. Sluαιϫϵϫ
αϫϫαl mόϝ lα Ϝϵϫlιm mαc Ccατhαιl cϝοιϫϫϵϝϫ, ιϝιη
mϫϝϵιϝϝηϵ ϝοιϝ ϫοcum hι Rαιϫιlliϫ, ϫο ϫίϫuιlτ α
ϫαlτα ocuϝ α ϫϝατhαϝ ϝαιϝ, .ι. Ταϫϫ hι Chοηchοϫαιϝ,
co ϝαϫαϫαϝ αϫhαιϫ α ϫϝοϝlοηϫϝuιϝϫ α ϫϝιϫηαchα
Μhοιϫϵ Rέιη, ocuϝ ηι ϝαιϫϵ cϵηϫ ϝοϝ ϫϵmϫuΙ ϝιϫηαchα
αη ταη ϝιη; ocuϝ ηι ϝαιϫϵ ιη cοmαϝϫα ιϝιη mϫαιlϵ αη
οιϫϫϵ ϝιη; ocuϝ ο ηαϫ ϝαιϫϵ, ϫο lοιϝcϵϫαϝ ϝυτατα αητ
ϝlúαιϫ ϫοτα ocuϝ ϫélϝcάláιη ϫο ϫαϫαϝ ιϝιη ϫϵmϫul
αϝτιϫ, ϫαη ϫϵϫ ϫα ηϫαοιηιϫ mαϫι; ocuϝ ϫο muchαϫ
ϫαlτα Ϋé ιη cοmαϝϫα αηη; ocuϝ ταηιc αη cοmαϝϫα
ϝéιη ϫucα αϝ α ϫάϝαϫ co ϫϝϵϝϫ ocuϝ lοηηuϝ mόϝ
αηϫιαιϫ α ϫαlτα, ocuϝ ϫο ιαϝϝ ϝé éϝαιc α ϫαlτα αϝ
.h. Conϫοϫαιϝ; ocuϝ αϫuϫαιϝτ .h. Conchοϫαιϝ co
τιϫϝϵϫh α ϫϝϵϫ ϝéιη ϫό. Ιϝ í mo ϫϝϵϫϝα, αϝ αη
cοmαϝϫα, άητ αοη ϫuιηϵ ιϝ ϝϵϝϝ αϫuιϫ ϫο lοϝcαϫ lιϫ α
ηéϝuιc mιc Ϋé. Μαϫηuϝ mαc Μuιϝϫϵϝταιϫ Μhuιϝmηιϫ

---

[1] *Emasculated.* ϫο ϝϝοchαϫ. The
Four Masters write ϫο chϝοchαϫh
"was hanged;" but the Dublin copy of
the Annals of Ulster and the Annals of
Connacht agree with this chronicle.

[2] *Festival of Berach.* See note [6],
p. 359, *supra.*

[3] *Festival of Martin.* The 11th of
November. See note [5], p. 358, *supra.*

[4] *Kinsman.* ϫϝατhαϝ, gen. sing.
of ϫϝατhαιϝ, which is used to express "brother" as well as "kins-

man." In the present case the person
represented as the *brathair* of Fedhlim,
son of Cathal Crobhderg, was the son
of his brother Aedh (or Hugh) O'Conor.

[5] *Foster-son.* He is called ϫαlτα
Ϋé, or "God-foster-son," in the text.
In explanation of this name the
following story, (characterized in the
margin as a ϝϫϵul ϫϝϵαηηmϝαϝ, or
"delightful story"), is included in
the account of the present transaction
contained in the Annals of Connacht,

[cycli]; ii. anno Indictionis; M.cc.xl.quarto. Tadhg, son of Aedh, son of Cathal Crobhderg, was blinded and emascu-lated[1] by Cuconnacht O'Raighilligh, about the festival of Berach,[2] in Inis-na-conaire on Loch-Aillinne, after having been in confinement from the festival of Martin[3] until then. Ruaidhri, son of Aedh O'Conchobhair, his brother, was drowned on the Cuirrin-Connachtach at Ath-Liag-na-Sinna, in vii°. idus Martii, and most honorably interred in the monastery of Cluain-tuaiscert. Conchobhar, son of Aedh, son of Cathal Crobhderg, died before the end of a month of the same Spring. A very great hosting by Fedhlim, son of Cathal Crobhderg, eastwards into the Breifne, to O'Raighilligh, to inflict punishment on him for his foster-son and kinsman,[4] i.e. Tadhg O'Conchobhair, when they encamped for a night in Fidhnacha of Magh-Rein. And there was no roof on the church of Fidnacha at that time; and the comarb was not in the place that night; and as he was not, the routs of the army burned the booths and huts that were inside in the church, without the permission of the chieftains; and the comarb's spiritual foster-son[5] was suffocated there. And the comarb himself came to them on the morrow, in great fury and rage on account of his foster-son, and demanded the eric[6] of his foster-son from O'Conchobhair. And O'Conchobhair said that he would give him his own award. "My award," said the comarb, "is that the best man amongst you shall be burned by you as the eric[6] of the son of God."[7] "Maghnus, son of Muirchertach

---

viz.:—"ocuʃ ıʃeò ınnıʃıð eoláıʒ conað aṁláıð ʃuáıʃ ın coṁaʃba an ðalca ʃın, a ʃaʒbáıl aʃ caʃʃáıʒ clóıcı baı ıʃın baıle, ocuʃ nı ʃeaðacaʃ mácáıʃ no acáıʃ occa ʃıaṁ; ocuʃ ʒʃáðáıʒıʃ an comaʃba he; ocuʃ áıchʃıʃceʃ co cuc lachc ðo aʃ a cıʒıb buðéın;" i.e. "and the learned relate that the way in which the comarb obtained

this foster-son was, that he found him on a stone rock which was in the town; and they know not that he had ever had a father or mother; and the comarb loved him; and it is reported that he suckled him from his own breast."

[6] *Eric.* A fine or compensation for bloodshed or injury.

[7] *Son of God.* See note [5], last page.

ɼın, aɼ .h. Conchobaɼ. Nı hé, ıʊıɼ, aɼ Maʒnuɼ, achʊ
anʊí ıɼ cenn aɼ an ɼlúaʒ. Nı ʒéɼaʊɼa ɼıʊ, aɼ an
coɱaɼba, no co bɼaʒbaɼ éɼuıc mo ʊalʊa uaıʊ. Ɗo
ımʊıʒ ın ɼlúaʒ ıaɼɼın aɼɼ an mbaıle amaʊ, ocuɼ ʊo
len an coɱaɼba ıaʊ co hꞹ na Cuıɼɼe ɼoɼɼan
nʒeıɼcʊıʒ, ocuɼ ʊo ʊí an ʊuıle ʊaɼ bɼuachaıb ʊı, ocuɼ
nı ɼancoʊaɼ ʊaıɼɼı conʊeɼnɼaʊ ʊech ɼbıʊél Єoın
baıɼʊe ʊo ʊáı a nımeal ın áʊa ʊo ɼcaoıleʊ, ʊa chuɼ
ʊaɼɼan aʊuınn ʊo ʊul ʊaıɼɼı ʊonʊ ɼlúaıʒ; conʊechaıʊ
mac Muıɼceɼʊaıʒ Muımnıʒ, .ı. Maʒnuɼ, ıɼın ʊech,
ocuɼ Concobaɼ mac Coɼmaıc Mıc Ɗıaɼmaʊa; conʊu-
baıɼʊ Maʒnuɼ ɼıɼın bɼeɼ ʊo ʊí ʊúaɼɼ aʒ ɼcaoıleʊ an
ʊıʒe, aʒ ɼínɼéɼe a cloıʊem uaʊa ɼúaɼ, aʒɼın an
ʊaıɼɼıʒe ʊonʒʊuɼ an maıʊe ʒan ʊuıʊım; leıɼın comɼáʊ
ɼın ʊo ʊuıʊ aıɼɼʒe an ʊıʒe a ʒcenʊ Mhaʒnuɼa mıc
Muıɼceɼʊaıʒ Muımnıʒ, ʒonʊeɼna bɼúlıʒ ʊía ʊınn, ʒuɼ
ʊó maɼʊ ʊe aɼ an laʊhaıɼ ɼın, ocuɼ ʒuɼ hıʊluıceʊ a
nʊoɼuɼ ʊempuıl Ɽhıʊnacha allamuıʒ; ocuɼ co ʊucaʊ
ʊɼí lán ʊluıʒ na ɼıʒ ʊoɼɼɼáıl aıɼʒıʊ leıɼ, ocuɼ ʊeıʊ neıʊ
ɼıʊeʊ; ʒuɼ ab amlaıʊ ɼın ɼuaıɼ coɱaɼba Caıllín éɼaıc
a ʊalʊa Ɗé ɼóʊeoıʊ uaʊhaıʊ. Ocuɼ ʊo ɼónaʊ leachʊ
lánɱaıɼech ʊo ʊlochaıb ɼnoıʊʊı, ocuɼ cɼoɼɼ caoın
ʊénɱaʊ ʊloıʊe óɼɼ a ʊınn ıaɼɼın; ocuɼ ʊo bɼıɼɼeʊaɼ
Muınnʊeɼ Ɽuaıɼc ın leachʊ ıaɼ ʊɼıoll ʊo ʊoɼaʊ na-
maʊuıɼ. Ɗonnchaʊ, mac Ɽınʒın, mıc Maoılɼechluınn,
mıc Ꞷʊa, mıc Ꞇoıɼɼʊhelbaıʒ hı Conchobaıɼ, una
ɼeɼʊımana anʊe Ꮶalenʊaɼ Maıı, ı.. eɼɼuc Oleɼınn, ʊo
éc an ınıɼ Cloʊɼann aɼ loʊ Ɽıʊ, ocuɼ a aʊlucaʊ a
manıɼoıɼ na búılle. Ɗonnchaʊ móɼ .h. Ɗálaıʒ, .ı.
ɼúı náɼ ɼáɼaıʒeʊ, ocuɼ nach ɼaıɼéʊaɼ ʊoıʊʊe ɼe ʊán, ʊo

---

[1] *Eric.* See note [6], last page.

[2] *Hospital-house.* ʊech ɼbıʊél.
The Four Masters read ʊeaʊ ɼeɼel,
"chapel-house;" but the latter is
probably incorrect. The word ɼɼıʊél,
which, under the form Spiddal, Spittal,
Spiddell, or Spittel, enters pretty

largely into the topographical nomenclature of Ireland, is a loan from
the Lat., *hospitalis.*

[3] *Pointing.* aʒ ɼínɼéɼe, properly
"extending." The Four Masters
employ the form ɼıneaʊ, which is
the more usual; but in the Annals of

Muimhnech, is he," answered O'Conchobhair. "No, truly," said Maghnus, "but the person who is chief over the army." "I shall not leave you," said the comarb, "until the eric[1] of my foster-son will have been obtained from you." The host went afterwards out of the town, and the comarb followed them to Ath-na-cuirre on the Geirctech; and the flood was over its banks, and they did not pass over it until they pulled down the hospital-house[2] of John the Baptist, which was on the margin of the ford, to place it across the river, that the host might pass over it. The son of Muirchertach Muimhnech, i.e. Maghnus, and Conchobhar, son of Cormac Mac Diarmada, went into the house, when Maghnus, pointing[3] up his sword, said to the man who was overhead throwing down the house, "there is the nail which prevents the beam from falling." At these words the rafter of the house fell on the head of Maghnus, son of Muirchertach Muimhnech, and fractured his skull, so that he died on the spot; and he was interred outside the door of the church of Fidhnacha; and thrice the full of Clog-na-righ of silver was given as an offering for him, and thirty horses; and thus it was that the comarb of Caillin ultimately obtained the eric of his spiritual foster-son from them. And a splendid monument of hewn stones, surmounted by a beautiful stone cross, was afterwards erected over him; but the O'Ruaircs broke down the monument after a while through hostility. Donnchadh, son of Finghin, son of Maelsechlainn, son of Aedh, son of Toirdhelbhach O'Conchobhair, i.e. the bishop of Oilfinn, died in Inis-Cloth-rann on Loch-Ribh, una septimana ante Kalendas Maii, and was interred in the monastery of the Buill. Donn-chadh Mór O'Dalaigh, an eminent man who was never surpassed,[4] and never will be surpassed, in poetry, died,

---

Connacht the expression is ᵹ ⱃⰵ ⱃⰵⱂⰵⱅⰵ ⰰ ⱍⰾⱁⰹⱅⰹⱞ, "extending the *sepete* (point?) of his sword."

[4] *Surpassed.* náⱃ ⱃáⱃⰰⰹⰶⰵⱅ for ná ⱃⱁ ⱃáⱃⰰⰹⰶⰵⱅ; lit. "was not pro-faned."

héc, ocus a aḋlucad a mainistir na Búille. Túaim dá gualann do loscad fo ċeiṫriḃ templaib, ocus tiġe in ḃaile uile maille friú. Airċindechain Tuama do ḃádhad ar glaislinn Chluana. Ferġal Mac Taḋcaḋain do marbad la Conċobar Mac Tigernáin, a bḟeall, a ninis Fraiċ ar Loċ Gile. Coinntinn ocus cendairc mór do ḟás a coraid Oilefinn taréis Donnchada hI Conchobair espuic tShíl Muireghaiġ, im ḋáiġin toġa do ḋenum acu, óir do ṫoġadar dream ḋíḃ Tomás .h. Cuinn. .i. ḃráthair minúr do ḃí ina ḟoidhech ṫoghaide ġlan ó ġniṁ; ocus do éiriġ don toġa sin Clárus Mhág Mháilín ocus Iohannes, da oirċindechain Oilefinn, et Malachias decanus, et sacrista Olefinensis, uolentes unum de coro eligere sicut ius fuit; quod audientes iuniores canonici elegerunt sibi comarb Comman .h. Conċobair; maiores uero predicti elegerunt sibi Iohannem airchidiaconum in plena sinodo apud Aṫ Luain per Clárum aircidiaconum Elfenensem, quia nunquam uoluit errori aliorum consentire. Cormac, mac Tomaltaiġ na cairrge, mic Conċobair Mic Diarmada, .i. riġ Ċlainni Mhaolruanaiḋ uile, do éc iar caiṫem sé mbliadan bḟiched ocus blaiḋe do bliadain eli for innairṁe ocus eniġ ocus ċoṫaiġṫi ċúiced Connacht re Gallaib ocus re Gaoideluiḃ ḃidís ina aighid, i naibíd ṁánaiġ leiṫ a mainisdir na Búille, a naimsir an ḟaġaṁair, iar mbreiṫ buaiḋe ó ḋeman ocus ó ḋoman.

Kal. Enair for Domnach, ocus xxiiii. fuirre; quinto anno cicli solaris; xi. anno decennouenalis [cicli];

---

[1] *Glaislinn-Chluana.* The "green pool of Cluain;" probably the name of an inlet of the Shannon, near Cluain, or Clonmacnoise. See O'Donovan's *Hy-Many*, p. 130, note [b]; and also his edition of the Four Masters, A.D. 1244, note [q], where Dr. O'Donovan supposes, but without sufficient authority, that the "Glaislinn" referred to was near Tuam.

[2] *Making an election.* toġa do ḋenum acu; lit. "to make a selection by them," the word acu, "by them," being represented by a q.

[3] *Decanus.* decanas, MS.

[4] *Unum.* unam, MS.

[5] *Fuit.* The MS. has fūit, as if the word fuerit was intended.

[6] *Audientes.* abdientes, MS.; an

and was interred in the monastery of the Buill. Tuaim-da-ghualann was burned, including four churches, and the houses of the whole town along with them. The arch-deacon of Tuaim was drowned in Glaislinn-Chluana.[1] Ferghal Mac Tadhgadhain was killed by Conchobhar Mac Tighernain, in treachery, in Inis-Fraich on Loch-Gile. A great contention and dispute grew up in the choir of Oilfinn after *the death of* Donnchadh O'Conchobhair, bishop of Sil-Muiredhaigh, on the subject of making an election;[2] for a number of them elected Thomas O'Cuinn, i.e. a Friar Minor, who was from his conduct a choice bright vessel; but this election was objected to by Clarus Mac Mailin and John, the two archdeacons of Oilfinn, et Malachias decanus,[3] et sacrista Oilfinensis, volentes unum[4] de choro eligere sicut jus fuit;[5] quod audienties[6] juniores canonici elegerunt sibi[7] Comarb Comman O'Conchobhair; majores vero prædicti elegerunt[8] sibi[7] Johannem archidiaconum in plena synodo apud Ath-Luain,[9] per Clarum archidiaconum Elfinensem, quia nunquam voluit[10] errori aliorum consentire. Cormac, son of Tomaltach of the Rock, son of Conchobhar Mac Diarmada, i.e. the king of all Clann-Maelruanaidh, after spending twenty-six years and a part of another year in maintaining *valour*[11] and hospitality, and defending the province of Connacht against the Foreigners and Gaeidhel who were opposed to him, died in the habit of a grey monk in the monastery of the Buill, in the harvest time, after triumphing over the devil and the world.

The kalends of January on Sunday, and the 28th of the moon; quinto[12] anno cycli solaris; xi. anno Decenno- [1245.]

---

instance of the substitution of b for u, frequently observable in Irish MSS.

[7] *Sibi.* ṁbe, MS.

[8] *Elegerunt.* eleᵹeꞃc, MS.; the ᵹ being aspirated through mistake.

[9] *Ath-Luain.* The MS. has Ctᴄɑ tuɑın, the gen. form of the name.

[10] *Voluit.* uotuıᴅ, MS.

[11] *Valour.* As this clause stands in the text, ꞃoꞃ ınnɑıꞃṁe ocuꞃ enıᵹ, "in rewarding and hospitality," it is apparent that some word has been omitted before ocuꞃ (and), probably ᵹɑıꞃᴄeᴅ, "valour" or "bravery."

[12] *Quinto.* quınᴄco, MS.

tertio indictionir; m.cc.xl.quinto. Conchobap puað,
mac Mhuircertaiξ Muimniξ, mic Toirroelbaiξ móir
hI Conchobair, do marbað olla Thimaiç, da maor
buóéin, do buille do rciain, tre iomaξallam pocail
tarla etorra a Purt na leice; ocur Ξilla Crird mac
Imáir hI Birn do marbað in máir iarrin; ocur Conchobar puad do breiç co mainirdir na buille, ocur a
éc innti don lot rin, ocur a aðlucað innte ðór ar buað
onξta ocur aiçriξe do Ohía. Cairlen Sliξiξ do ðenam
le Mac Muirir Mic Ξeralt, ξiúrdir na hErenn, ocur
le Sil Muirexðaiξ, uair a dúbrað re Fedlim a denam
ar a pinξinn rein, ocur cloca ocur aol tiξe rridél na
Trinóide do tocðáil cuiξe, iar tabairt an ionaið rin
reime don ξiúrdir, .i. Muirir Mac Ξeralt, do Chlarur
Mháξ Mháilín, a nonoir na naoim Trinoide. Oomnall
.h. Flannacán, ar Cunξa, mortuur ert. Sluaiξed mór
la rí Sacran a mbretnaib, conderna lonξport mór a
cairtel Enξannóc, ocur do cuired litri ocur leξáide co
hErinn leo co Ξallaib na hErenn, ocur. ξo Fedlim
mac Cathail Croibderξ, da raða riú dul a coinne an
riξ a mbretnaið, do ξaðail nert ar Bhretain. Oo
chúaid trá an Ξiúrdir ξo nΞallaib Erenn leir docum
an riξ, ocur do cuaið Fedlim mac Cathail croibderξ
hI Conchobair, ocur roçraide mór do ξaoiðealaið leir,
a bpurtacht an riξ a mbreatnaið; ocur ro millret
an cric co huiliξe; ocur nir ξaðrat ξeill iná eoire-
don chur rin ror Bhretnaið; ocur ba honórach Fedlim
aξ an riξ don dol rin, ocur ba buideach Fedlim aξ
teacht on riξ anoir. Cairlén Aça an cir ar bru
Moiξe Nirri do denam do Mhilið Mac Ξoirdelð.
Fiacra mac Oaud hI Fhloinn, tiξerna tShíl Maoil-
ruain, mortuur ert in die natalir Oomini. Cerðall

¹ *Tertio.* tercio, MS.

² *His own expense.* a pinξinn
rein; lit. "his own penny."

³ *Previously given.* See under the
year 1242, p. 358, *supra.*

⁴ *Britain*; i.e. Wales.

⁵ *Engannoc.* In other authorities
written Gannoch; now Digauway, in
Carnarvonshire.

A.D.
[1245.]

venalis [cycli] ; tertio[1] Indictionis. M.CC.XL.quinto. Conchobhar Ruadh, son of Muirchertach Muimhnech, son
of Toirdhelbhach Mor O'Conchobhair, was killed by
O'Timaith, his own steward, with a stab of a knife,
in a dispute which occurred between them at Port-
na-leice; and Gilla-Christ, son of Imhar O'Birn, killed
the steward afterwards; and Conchobhar Ruadh was
conveyed to the monastery of the Buill, and died in
it of this wound, and was buried in it also, after the
victory of unction and penitence towards God. The
castle of Sligech was built by Mac Maurice Fitz-Gerald,
Justiciary of Erinn, and by the Sil-Muiredhaigh; for
Fedhlim was told to erect it at his own expense,[2] and
to convey thereto the stones and lime of the hospital-
house of the Trinity, after this place had been previously
given[3] by the Justiciary, i.e. Maurice Fitzgerald, to Clarus
Mac Mailin, in honour of the Holy Trinity. Domhnall
O'Flannagain, abbot of Cunga, mortuus est. A great army
was led by the king of the Saxons into Britain,[4] when
they established a great camp at the castle of Engannoc;[5] and letters and ambassadors were sent by them to
Erinn, to the Foreigners of Erinn, and to Fedhlim, son
of Cathal Crobhderg, desiring them to go to meet the
king in Britain, to subdue Britain. The Justiciary, therefore, accompanied by the Foreigners of Erinn, went to
the king ; and Fedhlim, son of Cathal Crobhderg O'Conchobhair, accompanied by a great army of Gaeidhel, went
to the assistance of the king in Britain ; and they completely destroyed the country, but obtained neither
pledges nor hostages from the Britons on this occasion.
And Fedhlim was treated with honour by the king on
this journey ; and Fedhlim was thankful coming westwards from the king. The castle of Ath-an-chip, on the
border of Magh-Nisse, was built by Milidh Mac Goisdelbh.
Fiachra, son of David O'Floinn, lord of Sil-Maelruain,
mortuus est in die Natalis Domini. Cerbhall Buidhe, son

2 B

buıðe, mac Taıðc, mıc Cconξura Pınnaðраč hı Ohálaıξ, moρτuur erτ. Caırlén Suıcín do ðenam ır ın mbliaðaın rın.   Sneachτa neıme do chur oıðče félı rancτ[1] Nıcoláр, ocur do ðenaд a рála ocur a meoır don luchτ do ımðeξh ann ; ocur ní ðechaıd an rneachτa rın aр no co тaınıc Nodluıc móр.   Muırčeртach, mac Muır-ξıura, mıc Cathaıl Mhıc Oıaрmaдa, do ṁaрbaд do rерuıð Oреırnı.   Maıξırдer uero Iohanner, electur ın Elrenenrem epırcopum[2] per Claрum áірcıdıaconum eıurдem[3] redır, eτ per Malachıam[4] decanum[5] catheдralem, eτ per Ξelaрıum racrırτam, perрeхıτ aд дomınum papam urque aд Lıunr rur Róna ubı ruıτ ın exılıo a reдe Romana, deıecτur per Romanoрum ımperaτoрem ; eτ τanτam ξraτıam habuıτ ın oculır дomını pape eτ cuрıe romane quod carraτa electıone racτa de Comaрb Comán per ıunıorer Elrenenrır corı canonıcor, electıo de ırro racτa per maıorer lıceτ paucıorer reuerenτer obτınuıτ ; eτ quod дomınur papa mırıτ lıτerar ruar cum ırro aд Тuamenrem archıepırcopum, uτ ın epırcopum conrecреτur, ın nomıne Oomını Ieru Crırτı conrecraτur erτ rerpon-дenτıbur Crırτı rıdelıbur eτ uerıτaτem reruaрe cuрıenτıbur dıe conrecraτıonır eıur, Oeo ξraτıar. Raξnall .h. Maoılṁıaдhaıξ do ṁaрbaд la Connach-τuıð ın hoc anno.   Muırčeртach, mac Cathaıl, mıc Oıaрmaдa, mıc Тhaıðξ hı Mhaoılruanaıð, do ξaðáıl rıξe na Caıррξe τaréır Corṁaıc mıc Тhomalτaıξ, ocur a ðeıð blıaðuın ocur rıče co comlán a rıξe íarrın.

Ictt. Enáır ror Luan, .ıх. ruırре ; uı. anno cıclı

---

[1] *Saint.* ra, for ranτ, or rancτ, MS. ; an instance of corrupt transcription arising from phonetic influence ; as in pronouncing the words ranτ Nıcolár in Irish, the two last letters of ranτ would scarcely be sounded, for which reason they have been omitted by the scribe. The festival of Saint Nicholas is the 6th of December.

[2] *Archidiaconum.* aıрcıdıacunū, MS.

[3] *Ejusdem.* eırдem, MS.

[4] *Malachiam.* Malacıam, MS.

[5] *Decanum.* deccanam, MS.

of Tadhg, son of Aenghus Finnabhrach O'Dalaigh, mortuus est. The castle of Suicín was built in this year. Poisonous snow fell on the night of the festival of Saint[1] Nicholas, which took off the heels and toes of those who walked in it; and this snow did not disappear until Christmas arrived. Muirchertach, son of Muirghius, son of Cathal Mac Diarmada, was slain by the men of Breifne. Magister vero Johannes, electus in Elfinensem episcopum per Clarum archidiaconum[2] ejusdem[3] sedis, et per Malachiam[4] decanum[5] cathedralem,[6] et per Gelasium sacristam, perrexit ad dominum papam usque ad Liuns-[7] sur-Rhona ubi fuit in exilio[8] a sede Romana,[9] dejectus per Romanorum[9] imperatorem; et tantam gratiam habuit in oculis domini papæ et curiæ Romanæ quod cassata electione facta de Comarb Coman per juniores Elfinensis chori canonicos, electio[10] de ipso facta per majores licet pauciores reverenter obtinuit, et quod dominus Papa misit literas suas cum ipso ad Tuamensem[11] archiepiscopum, ut in episcopum consecretur; in nomine Domini Jesu Christi consecratus est respondentibus Christi fidelibus, et veritatem servare cupientibus die consecrationis ejus, Deo gratias. Raghnall O'Maelmhiadhaigh was slain by the Connachtmen in hoc anno. Muirchertach, son of Cathal, son of Diarmaid, son of Tadhg O'Maelruanaidh, assumed the sovereignty of the Rock[12] after Cormac, son of Tomaltach, and was fully twenty-one years in the sovereignty afterwards.

The kalends of January on Monday, the 9th of the

---

[6] *Cathedralem.* caṫpaṫalem, MS.

[7] *Liuns;* i.e. Lyons.

[8] *Exilio.* exelɪo, MS.

[9] *Romanorum.* Romonum, MS.

[10] *Electio.* elecṫo, MS.

[11] *Tuamensem.* Ꞇuamnenꞃem, MS.

[12] *Of the Rock;* i.e. of the Rock of Loch-Cé, in the county of Roscommon, the principal residence of Mac Dermot, chief of Magh-Luirg, or Moylurg. Irish chieftains were sometimes designated by a title derived from their principal residence, as in this instance, or from other places of note within their territories.

roláṗiṡ; xɪɪ.[anno] cɪclɪ ꝺecennouenaliṡ; ɪɪɪɪ. anno ɪnꝺɪcꞇɪonɪṡ; m.cc.[xl] uɪ. mɪl móṗ ꝺo ꞇeaċꞇ a ꞇíṗ a Cúɪl Iṗṗa a Caɪṗṗɪ Ꝺṗoma cliaḃ, co ꞇuc ṗoċma móṗ ocuṡ ṡoɪċeall ɪṡɪn ꞇíṗ uɪle. Oṡṗuc Oɪleṡɪnn, .ɪ. Eoɪn .ɦ. hUɪᵹṗóiṅ, .ɪ. mac comaṗba moċúa, ꝺo héc a Ráɪᵹ Cloḃa mɪc Ḃṗɪc ɪṡɪn mblɪaꝺaɪn ṡɪn. Ꝺṗuɪm leꞇaɪn ꝺo loṡcaꝺ ɪn hoc anno. maelṡechlaɪnn, mac Conchobaɪṗ ṗuaɪḃ, mɪc muɪṗceṗꞇaɪᵹ Mhuɪmnɪᵹ hɪ Conċobaɪṗ, ꝺo maṗbaꝺ la [muɪṗceṗꞇach] .ɦ.nꝺuḃꝺa ɪṡɪn ḃlɪaꝺaɪn ṡɪn. muɪṗceṗꞇach .ɦ. Ꝺuḃꝺa ꝺo ɪonnaṗba ꞇaṗ muɪṗ aṗ éɪṡ an ṁaṗḃꞇa ṡɪn. Ioan mac Iaᵹṗɪṡ ꝺo ꞇochꞇ na ᵹɪúṗꝺɪṡ ɪn Eṗɪnn, ocuṡ muɪṡɪṡ Mac Ꝣeṗaɪlꞇ ꝺo aɪꞇṗɪᵹhaꝺ. Coɪṗṗꝺhelbach mac Cloḃa hɪ Conċobaɪṗ ꝺo élúḃ a cṗannóɪᵹ Laċa Leɪṡɪ ɪṡɪn ṡaᵹaṁaṗ, ocuṡ a luchꞇ coɪméꝺa ꝺo ḃáꝺhaꝺ ꝺó, .ɪ. Coṗmac mac Muɪṗeᵹhaɪᵹ ocuṡ ꝺá .ɦ. Clɪnmɪṗech, ocuṡ a ḃuɪla ṡéɪn aṗ ɪaṗṡɪn. Cṗeaċ móṗ ꝺo ꞇenam ꝺo Mhuɪṡɪṡ Mac Ꝣeṗaɪlꞇ aṗ ꞇíṗ Chonaɪll, ocuṡ leꞇ ꞇɪṗe Conaɪll [ꝺo ꞇaḃaɪṗꞇ] ꝺó ꝺo Choṗmac mac Ꝺɪaṗmaꝺa mɪc Ruaɪꞇṗɪ, ocuṡ bṗaɪᵹꝺɪ hɪ Ꝺomnaɪll ꝺo ᵹaḃaɪl ꝺó aṗ an leɪꞇ aɪle; ocuṡ na bṗaɪᵹꝺe ꝺo ṡáᵹḃáɪl ꝺó a caɪṡlén Slɪᵹɪᵹ. ɦ. Ꝺomnaɪll ocuṡ maɪꞇɪ ċénel Conaɪll maṗoen ṡɪṡ ꝺo ċoɪᵹechꞇ lá Saṁna co Slɪᵹech, ocuṡ báꝺun an ḃaɪle ꝺo loṡcaꝺ léo, ocuṡ ᵹan ꝺul aṗ an caɪṡlen ꝺóɪḃ; ocuṡ ṗo cṗoċṡaꝺ na ḃaṗꝺa bṗaɪᵹꝺe hɪ Ꝺomnaɪll na ṡɪaꝺnuṡe aṗ mullaċ ɪn ċaɪṡléɪn, .ɪ. O Mɪanaɪn, oɪꝺe hɪ Ꝺomnaɪll; ocuṡ a comalꞇa. Cloḃ mac Cloḃa hɪ Conċobaɪṗ ꝺo ᵹaḃáɪl ocuṡ ꝺo aṗᵹaɪn. Coɪṗṗꝺealbach mac Cloḃa hɪ

---

[1] m.cc.[xl]vi. The MS. erroneously reads m.cc.uɪ. (1206.)

[2] *Whale.* mɪl móṗ; lit. "great animal." The more ancient name was blʌoach. See *Cormac's Glossary*, in voce ṗaṡu.

[3] *Hoc.* oc, MS.

[4] *Fitz-Geoffroi;* i.e. son of Geoffroi de Marisco. He was appointed Viceroy of Ireland in 1245. See Gilbert's *History of the Viceroys of Ireland*, p. 102.

[5] *Crannog.* For the meaning of *Crannog*, see note [6], p. 260, *supra*. According to Ḋr. O'Donovan, Loch-Leisi was the ancient name of Muck-enagh Lough, near the old church of Kilglass, in the parish of Kilmeane,

moon; vi. anno cycli solaris; xii. [anno] cycli Decennovenalis; iiii. anno Indictionis; M.cc.[xl]vi.[1] A whale[2] came
ashore at Cuil-irra in Cairpre of Druim-cliabh, which
brought great prosperity and joy to the entire country.
The bishop of Oilfinn, i.e. John O'hUghroin, i.e. the son
of the comarb of Mochua, died at Rath-Aedha-mic-Bric
in this year. Druim-lethan was burned in hoc[3] anno.
Maelsechlainn, son of Conchobhar Ruadh, son of Muirchertach Muimhnech O'Conchobhair, was killed by [Muir-
chertach] O'Dubhda in this year. Muirchertach O'Dubhda
was banished over sea after this killing. Jean Fitz-
Geoffroi,[4] came as Justiciary to Erin, and Maurice Fitz-
Gerald was deposed. Toirdhelbhach, son of Aedh O'Conchobhair, escaped from the crannog[5] of Loch-Leisi in the
autumn, and drowned his keepers—viz., Cormac Mac
Muiredhaigh[6] and two O'Ainmirechs; and he himself went
away afterwards. A great depredation was committed
by Maurice Fitz-Gerald in Tir-Conaill; and [he gave] the
half of Tir-Conaill to Cormac, son of Diarmaid, son of
Ruaidhri,[7] and received the hostages of O'Domhnaill for
the other half; and he left the hostages in the castle of
Sligech. O'Domhnaill, and the nobles of the Cenel-Conaill
along with him, went on Samhain-day[8] to Sligech; and
the bawn[9] of the town was burned by them, although
they did not enter the castle; and the warders hanged
O'Domhnaill's hostages, in his presence, on the top of the
castle, viz. :—O'Mianain, the tutor of O'Domhnaill, and his
foster-brother. Aedh, son of Aedh O'Conchobhair, was
taken prisoner, and plundered. Toirdhelbhach, son of Aedh

barony of Athlone, and county of
Roscommon. *Four Masters* (ed.
O'Donovan), A.D. 1246, note P.

[6] *Mac Muiredhaigh;* pron. Mac
Murray. The Four Masters write
the name Ua Muineaṁaiġ, or
O'Murray.

[7] *Ruaidhri;* i.e. Ruaidhri O'Conchobhair, or Rory O'Conor, the last
king of Ireland, who died A.D. 1178.

[8] *Samhain-day.* The 1st of November.

[9] *Bawn.* báóun. Also written
bóóun. See note [6], p. 213, *supra.*

Cončobaip vo ʒabáil apíp, ap comaipce eppuic Chluana, ocup a čabaipt a laim ʒall, ocup a chup a caiplen Ccta Luain. Tomaltach .h. Cončobaip vo toʒa vo cum eppocóive Oleṗinn. Mupchav .h. hCCnluain, pi Oipptep, vo ṁapbav tpé epáil bpiain Uí Neill.

Ict. enaip pop ṁaipt, ocup pichev puippe; peptimo anno cicli polapip: xiii. [anno] cicli vecennouenalip; quinto anno invictionip; M.cc.xl.uii. ʒpava eppuic an Oilṗinn vo ʒabáil vo Tomaltach, mac Toippvhelbaiʒ, mic Mhaoilpeclainn Uí Cončobaip, in Vomnach pia Septuaʒeipima, a Tuaim vá ʒualan. benevictup Mháʒ Oipechtaiʒ, aipčinneč CCchaiv Pabaip Umaill, vo ṁapbav a bṗeil na Cpoiče, an tpepp lá vo tṗaṁpav, vo mac Conchobaip puaiv mic Mhuipčeptaiʒ Mhuimniʒ, ocup vo mac Maʒnupa mic Mhuipceptaiʒ Mhuimniʒ hí Cončobaip, a bṗill ocup a meabail. Toippvhelbach vo élúv a caiplén CCta Luain. Miliʒ mac ʒoipvelb vo ʒabáil ṗeva Conmaicne, ocup Cathal Mhaʒ Raʒnuill vo ṗichup apva vó, ocup cpannóc Chlaon lača vo ʒabáil vó, ocup lucht a ʒabála vo ṗáʒbáil vó innti vá ṁuinntep ṗéin. Cathal ocup Toippvhelbach, vá mac CCova hí Cončobaip, vo coimepʒe le Máʒ Raʒnaill vo ṗichup Mic ʒoipvelb a piv Conmaicni, ʒup ʒabavap an cpannóc ocup an loč, ocup ʒup pʒaoilpev caiplén Leice veipʒe a ʒačapn Vomnaiʒ Chincípṗi, co tainic Toippvhelbach ap Oilén na Tpinóive ap cenv Chlapupa Mháʒ Mháilin in aipčivechain, ap na ṗeimʒev vo na ʒallaib teacht ap an caiplén imač no co tioṗvaoip leip in aipčivechain tap Sinainn anoip co Tuaim mná; ocup tancavap leip, ocup vo víčuipev

<hr />

1 *Cluain.* Cluain-mic-Nois, or Clonmacnois.

2 *Quinto.* quincto, MS.

3 *Festival of the Cross.* The 3rd of May.

4 *The castle of Ath-Luain ;* or castle of Athlone, in which he had been confined since the previous year.

5 *Fedha-Conmaicne;* i.e. "the woods of Conmaicne," written a few lines lower Fidh-Conmaicne, or the "*wood of C.*;" a district in the south-west of

O'Conchobhair, was again taken prisoner *whilst* under the guarantee of the bishop of Cluain,[1] and was delivered into the hands of the Foreigners, and placed in the castle of Ath-Luain. Tomaltach O'Conchobhair was elected to the bishopric of Oilfinn. Murchadh O'hAnluain, king of Oirthera, was slain at the instigation of Brian O'Neill.

The kalends of January on Tuesday, and the twentieth of the moon; septimo anno cycli solaris; xiii. [anno] cycli Decennovenalis; quinto[2] anno Indictionis; M.cc.xlvii. The grade of bishop of Oilfinn was assumed by Tomaltach, son of Toirdhelbhach, son of Maelsechlainn O'Conchobhair, on the Sunday before Septuagesima, in Tuaim-dá-ghualann. Benedictus Mac Oirechtaigh, airchinnech of Achadh-Fabhair of 'Umhall, was killed on the festival of the Cross,[3] the third day of summer, by the son of Conchobhar Ruadh, son of Muirchertach Muimhnech, and by the son of Maghnus, son of Muirchertach Muimhnech O'Conchobhair, in treachery and deceit. Toirdhelbhach escaped from the castle of Ath-Luain.[4] Milidh Mac Goisdelbh took possession of Fedha-Conmaicne,[5] out of which he expelled Cathal Mac Raghnaill; and he took possession of the crannog of Claen-loch, and left a garrison of his own people in it. Cathal and Toirdhelbhach, the two sons of Aedh O'Conchobhair, joined with Mac Raghnaill to expel Mac Goisdelbh from Fidh-Conmaicne; and they took possession of the crannog and lake,[6] and demolished the castle of Lecderg, on the Saturday before Whitsun-day. And Toirdhelbhach went upon Trinity Island to meet Clarus Mac Mailin, the archdeacon; for the Foreigners had refused to come out of the castle until they could go with the archdeacon across the Sinainn westwards[7] to Tuaim-mna; and they went

---

the county of Leitrim, belonging to the sept of Mac Raghnaill, or Mac Rannell (now Reynolds.)

[6] *Crannog and lake,* i.e. of Claen-loch, mentioned a few lines before.

[7] *Westwards.* The chronicler, writing in Connacht, uses the expression anoir, lit. "from the east," in reference to going across the Shannon from the county of Leitrim.

Claınn Ɀoıpᴅelḃ ap an ṫıp amaċ. Slúaıɀeᴅ móp lá
Muıpıp Mac Ɀepaılt, ocup lá Ɀallaıḃ maılle ppıp, co
pıachtaᴅap co Slıɀech ap túp, ocup appíᴅe co hEpp
Ruaıᴅ mıc Ḃhaᴅaıpn, ıpın Ceᴅaoın ıap bṗeıl Póıl ocup
Petaıp; ocup ᴅo ċuaıḃ Copmac mac Ďıapmaᴅa mıc
Ruaıᴅpı hı Choncċobaıp na ṫóıp ocup na ċınól annpíᴅe.
Ro ċınoıl .h. Ďomnaıll Cenél Conaıll ocup Cenél Eoɀaın
ap a ċınn a mbeol Œ̇a Senaıɀ, conáp léɀpeᴅ Ɀall ına
Ɀaoıᴅeal tap áṫ anunn pe heᴅh peachtṁuıne ón
tpáṫ ɀó apoıle; conıḃ hí comaıple ᴅo ponpaᴅ ıappın
Copmac .h. Conchobaıp ᴅo ᴅul mapcpluaɀ móp ap
puᴅ an ṁoıɀe poıp, ocup ᴅo ınnto ap puᴅ an ṁuıɀe
puap ap bopᴅ an ṁoıntıɀ; ocup ᴅo ɀaḃ annpíᴅe láṁ
pıp ın aḃaınn poıp co paınıc Œ̇ ċúıl uaıne pop Epne;
ocup nıp aıpıɀpet Cenél Conaıll én ní co ḃpacaᴅap
ċuca íaᴅ ᴅon leıṫ ᴅá paḃaᴅap peın ᴅon aḃuınn. Ocup
map aᴅċonncoᴅap Ɀoıll Cenél Conaıll ocup a naıpe
ımoppo poppan mapcpluaɀ ᴅo ḃí a leıṫ a nᴅpoma, po
lınɀpet peın ınt áṫ, co paḃaᴅap Cenél Conaıll etoppa
ᴅıḃlınaıḃ. Ro ppaoıneᴅ ap .h. nĎoṁnaıll cona ṗlúaıɀ,
ocup mapḃṫap ann Maoılpechlaınn .h. Ďomnaıll, pí
Cenéoıl Conaıll, annpın, ocup an Ɀılla muınélaċ .h.
ḃaoıᴅıll, ocup Mac Somaıple, pı Œıpıp Ɀaoıᴅel, ocup
maıṫı ċenéoıl Conaıll áıpċena; ocup po báıᴅıt mopán
ᴅo ṗlúaıɀ Mıc Ɀepaılt aɀ ᴅul tap Ṗınn buᴅ ċuaıᴅ, ocup
ᴅo mapbaᴅ mópan ᴅont ṗluaıɀ ceᴅna a Tepmann
Ďáḃeóoc a tópaıɀecht na ɀcpeaċ, ımá Uıllíam Ḃpıt
.ı. pıppıam Connacht, ocup pıᴅıpe óɀ aıpmech pa
bpaṫaıp ᴅó. Cıᴅ tpa acht po hınnpeᴅ ocup po

<hr>

1 *Es-Ruaidh-mic-Badhuirn.* "The
cataract of Ruadh, son of Badhurn,"
so called from Ruadh, or Aedh Ruadh
(Aidus Rufus), son of Badhurn, who
was drowned therein, A.M. 3603,
according to O'Flaherty's chronology.
The name of Es-Ruaidh, or Es-Aedha-
Ruaidh, is now written Assaroe, and
is applied to a cataract on the river

Erne, near Ballyshannon, county of
Donegal. See O'Flaherty's *Ogygia*,
part III., p. 258.

2 *They;* i.e. the invaders.

3 *Eastwards.* ρoıp. The Four
Mast., Ann. Ult., and Ann. Connacht
have ρıap, "westwards," which is
probably the correct reading.

4 *Upwards.* The word ρuap, which

with him ; and Clann-Goisdelbh were expelled out of the
district. A great hosting by Maurice Fitz-Gerald, and the
Foreigners along with him, until they reached Sligech in
the first instance, and from thence to Es-Ruaidh-mic-Badhuirn,[1] on the Wednesday after the festival of Paul and
Peter; and Cormac, son of Diarmaid, son of Ruaidhri O'Conchobhair, went there in his host and muster. O'Domhnaill assembled the Cenel-Conaill and Cenel-Eoghain to
meet him at Bel-atha-Senaigh, so that they allowed
neither Foreigners nor Gaeidhel to cross the ford during
the space of a whole week; when they[2] determined
that Cormac O'Conchobhair should go, with a large force
of cavalry, eastwards[3] along the plain, and then turn upwards[4] through the plain by the margin of the bog; and
he then proceeded eastwards along the river until he
reached Ath-Chuil-uaine on the Erne.   And the Cenel-
Conaill observed nothing until they saw them approaching
on their own side[5] of the river.   And when the Foreigners[6]
perceived the Cenel-Conaill watching the cavalry in their
rear, they themselves rushed across the ford, so that
the Cenel-Conaill were *placed* between both divisions.
O'Domhnall was defeated, with his army; and Maelsechlainn O'Domhnaill, king of Cenel-Conaill, was slain there;
and the Gilla-muinélach[7] O'Baoidhill, and Mac Somhairle,
king of Airer-Gaeidhel, and the nobles of the Cenel-
Conaill besides, *were slain*.   And many of Fitz-Gerald's
army were drowned going northwards across the Finn;
and many of the same army were slain at Termann-
Dabheog, in pursuit of the preys, including William Brit,
i.e. the sheriff of Connacht, and a young armed knight
who was his brother.   However, the entire country was

A.D.

[1247.]

---

literally means "upwards," relatively
signifies "southwards."

   [5] *Their own side;* i.e. the north side
of the river Erne.

   [6] *The Foreigners.* Those, namely,
who were on the southern side of
the river, unable to cross before the
execution of this flank march by
O'Conchobhair.

   [7] *The Gilla-muinélach;* lit. "the
[wry-]necked fellow."

haıpceŏ ıη cíp uıλe λεó ıαppıη, ocuſ ѕο ḟαʒαıbſec píʒe
Cheneóıλ Conαıλλ αʒ Ruαıѕpı .h. Chαηαηηáıη ѕon chup
pıη. Cocαѕ móp ѕo ŏenum ѕo Choıppѕheλbαch mαc
Αoŏα hı Conchobαıp, ocuſ ѕo Ðhonnchαѕ, mαc
Αnmchαѕα, .. mıc Ðonnchαѕα Mıc Ʒıλλαſáѕpαıc
ѕOppαıʒαıb, ſop ʒαλλαıb Connαchc, ʒup ŏınóıλ Coıppѕheλbαch mıc píʒ Connαchc ŏuıʒe co pıαchcαѕαp Ƒıŏ
.h. nÐıαpmαѕα ocuſ Muıncep Ƒhαchαıŏ, ocuſ po
mαpŏſαc ѕαoıne ımŏα ınncıŏ; ocuſ pαncαѕαp αppıŏé
co cαıſλén Ьonα Ʒαıλλṁe, ocuſ po λoıpcſec αn bαıλe
ocuſ αn cαıſλén, ocuſ po mαpbαѕ ocuſ po mıλλıѕ ѕαoıne
ımŏα αnn ; ocuſ ѕo mαpbαѕ mαc Eλʒéıѕ, .ı. ſenſcáλ
Connαchc, λα mαc Αnmchαѕα hı Ʒhıλλαſáѕpαıc
ѕOppαıʒıb; ocuſ po λenſαc Ʒoıλλ ıαѕ, ocuſ cucſαѕ
cαchup ѕóıŏ, ocuſ po mαpbαѕ ѕponʒ ѕo ʒαλλoıŏ αnnpıη,
ocuſ ѕo ımʒeѕαp uαchα ѕá nαımŏeóıη ; ocuſ ѕo ŏuαѕαp
α Cepα ıαppıη. Ro ŏınoıλ, ѕαnα, Sıupѕáη ѕe Execαp ocuſ
Cλαnn Αѕám ocuſ Ʒoıλλ Chepα, ocuſ ѕo ınnpoıʒeѕαp
Coıppѕheλbαch, ocuſ po ſáʒαıŏ Coıppѕheλbαch αn
cpíŏ ѕóıŏ o nαch pαıŏe λíη ceʒṁáλα ſpıú. Ьuıpʒéıp
Chınn cpáchcα ѕo λopcαѕ ѕo Cαŏc mαc Conchobαıp
puαıѕ, ocuſ ѕo Cαŏc mαc Cuαŏαıλ mıc Mhuıpcepcαıʒ
Mhuımnıʒ. Ηı heŏ αṁáın, αchc nı bſuαpαѕαp Ʒαıλλ
Connαchc pe cıαn ѕαımpıp poımepıη mαc pαṁλα αn
cocαıѕ ѕo ponſαѕ nα mıc píʒ pıη ſoppα ıpıη mbλıαѕαıη
pıη, uαıp nıp ſáʒαıŏſec cuαŏ nα cpıŏα ceѕ ѕo cpíŏ .
Chonnαchc ѕá pαıŏ αʒ Ʒαλλoıŏ ʒαn ŏpechαpʒαıη.
Ƒınnʒuαλα, ınʒen Ruαıŏpı hı Choncobαıp, ѕo éc α Cunʒα
Ƒheŏín ın hoc αnno. Roſ Chomáη ocuſ Αpѕ ŏαpnα
ѕo λopcαѕ ѕo ʒαλλoıb ın hoc αnno. Loınʒep móp ѕo
ŏeαchc ѕλλα Ðhuŏѕα ocuſ ѕλλα Ьháıʒıλλ ѕo αpʒαıη

---

[1] *Fidh-Ui-Diarmada.* "The wood
of Ui-Diarmada." The territory of
Ui-Diarmada, the patrimony of the
sept of O'Concannon, is comprised in
the present parish of Kilkerrin, barony
of Killian, and county of Galway.

[2] *Bun-Gaillmhe.* "The mouth of
the [river] Gaillimh," or Galway;
where now stands the town of Galway.

[3] *O'Gillapatraic.* Written Mac
Gillapatraic some lines before. The
name is now Anglicised Fitzpatrick.

afterwards devastated and plundered by them ; and they left the sovereignty of Cenel-Conaill with Ruaidhri O'Canannain on this occasion. A great war was waged by Toirdhelbhach, son of Aedh O'Conchobhair, and by Donnchadh, son of Anmchadh, son of Donnchadh Mac Gillapatraic of Osraighe, against the Foreigners of Connacht; and Toirdhelbhach assembled the sons of the kings of Connacht, until they reached Fidh-Ui-Diarmada[1] and Muinter-Fathaidh, where they killed many persons. And they proceeded thence to the castle of Bun-Gaillmhe,[2] and burned the town and castle ; and many persons were killed and plundered there. And Mac Elget, i e. the seneschal of Connacht, was killed by the son of Anmchadh O'Gillapatraic[3] of Òsraighe. And the Foreigners followed them and gave them battle, when a number of the Foreigners were slain ; and they[4] went away from them, in spite of-them, and went afterwards into Cera. Jordan de Exeter, and Clann-Adam, and the Foreigners of Cera assembled and proceeded against Toirdhelbhach ; and Toirdhelbhach left the country to them, as he had not forces enough to meet them. Burgheis-chinn-trachta[5] was burned by Tadhg, son of Conchobhar Ruadh, and by Tadhg, son of Tuathal, son of Muirchertach Muimhnech. Nor this alone ; but the Foreigners of Connacht had not experienced for a long time previously a war equal to that waged against them by these sons of kings in this year; for they left neither district[6] nor cantred of the territory of Connacht belonging to the Foreigners without pillaging. Finnghuala, daughter of Ruaidhri O'Conchobhair, died in Cunga-Feichin in hoc[7] anno. Ros-Comain and Ard-carna were burned by the Foreigners in hoc anno. O'Dubhda and O'Baighill came with a great

---

[4] *They* ; i.e. the Gaeidhel, or Irish.

[5] *Burgheis - chinn - trachta.* "The borough of the head of the strand," now probably Burriscarra, in the county of Mayo, as Dr. O'Donovan conjectures. Four Masters, A.D. 1247, note [m].

[6] *District.* ꞇh for ꞇhuaꞇ (*recté* ꞇuaꞇ), MS.

[7] *Hoc.* oc, MS.

Chαιρρρι, ocuρ Lucht Luıηζι δίᵬ το ᵬάτhατ αζ Ιηηρι Τυαᵭρραιρ ρα Mhaζηυρ hΙλα mᵬαιζιλλ. Conchobaρ .h. Μυιρεζhaιζh, eρρυc .h. bᵬhιαcραᵭ Ωιζηε, το ᵭζ α mᵬριρτομα. Ταᵬc mac Conchobaιρ ρυαιτ το Lορcατ Ιηηρι mόιρε Chλαοη Loᵭα, ocuρ ochταρ αρ ᵬιᵭιτ το ζαλλαιᵬ το Lορcατ ιηητι.

Ιct. Εηαιρ ρερ Cετάοιη, ocuρ ρριm ρυιρρε; octauo anno cιcλι ρολαριρ; xιιιι. cιcλι τεceηηουεηαλιρ; uι.anno ιητιcτιοηιρ; Μ.cc.xluιιι. Τιαρμαιτ .h. Cuαηηα, ρacαρτ mορ Οιλεᵬιηη, το héc, ocuρ α αᵬλυcατ α Cιλλ ᵬόιρ. Mac hι Sеᵭηυραιζ το ᵬαρbατ λα ζαλλοιb. Οιρεcιη ζυέρ το mαρbατ το ζhιλλαmοᵭοιηηe .h. Cαᵭhaιλ ιη hoc anno. Coιmερζε το ᵭеηυm το macaιb Mαζηυρα ocuρ το macaιb Conchobaιρ ρυαιᵬ, ocuρ ιmρόᵬ ᵭοιᵬ αρ ζhαλλοιb, ocuρ cαιρλéη mιc Εηρι το Lορcατ ᵭόιᵬ, ocuρ α ᵭοηρτάρλα το ζαᵬαιλ, ocuρ cρεαᵭα ᵭυαιρcερτ Uᵬαιλλ το bρeιᵭ Leo αρ Ιηηριᵬ Moᵬ. Ro ᵭιηόιλ, τaηa, Sιυρτάη τεxeταρ ocuρ Seoη ᵬυιτιλéη ocuρ Roιbíη Lαιζλeιρ, ocuρ ταοιηe ιmᵬα mαιλλe ρριú, ocuρ ταηcοταρ co ᵬαιλe ᵭορaιρ Ρατραιc, ocuρ αρριᵬe co hΩchατ ᵬαᵬaιρ, ocuρ ρο αιρζeτ Umαλλ uιλe ᵭηaιᵬ ocuρ τeρρ αρ ηα ᵬάραch. Ταηιc [mac] Εηρί τaηa ρλυαζ mόρ Leιρ α ηUᵬαλλ, uaιρ ρά Leιρ ρeιη hí, ocuρ ρο ᵭόι ιηητι ηα comηaιτe. Το ρόιηe τιη mac Εηρí ρíᵭ ρe Τomηαλλ mac Mαζηυρα ταρ ceητ α ᵭíρe, ocuρ ρο ζeαλλ Τomηαλλ co τíᵬρeτh ρocρaιτe ocuρ αρρτραιζe τοcυm α bρaᵭhaρ. Ταλa mac Conchobaιρ, ιmορρο, το ᵬατaρ αρ Ιηηριᵬ Moᵬ, ocuρ το hιηηιρρeτ τοιᵬ ρocρaιτe το ᵭυλ o mac Εηρí αρ céητ αρρτροιζe τοᵭom Τoᵬηaιλλ. Το ᵭuaταρ ρom αρ cιηη [an] ᵬuιᵬηe ριη, ocuρ ρο mαρbαταρ O Uaιη mac ηα

---

1 Inis-Tuathfrais. "The island of Tuathfrais." The name is written Ιηρι ᵬuaᵭ ρaρρ by the Four Masters; the difference between this form and that in the text being attributable to the omission, by the Four | Masters, of the letter ρ, which, although not marked in the text with the aspirate sign (ᵬ), should be aspirated according to the ordinary grammatical rules. Dr. O'Donovan was probably in error in identifying

fleet to plunder Cairpre; and the crew of one of the ships were drowned at Inis-Tuathfrais,[1] together with Maghnus O'Baighill Conchobhar O'Muiredhaigh, bishop of Ui-Fiachrach-Aighne,[2] died in Bristol. Tadhg, son of Conchobhar Ruadh, burned Inis-mór of Claen-locha, in which eight and twenty Foreigners were consumed.

The kalends of January on Wednesday, and the first of the moon; octavo anno cycli solaris; xiiii. cycli Decen-novenalis; vi. anno Indictionis; M.cc.xlviii. Diarmaid O'Cuanna, great priest of Oilfinn, died, and was interred in Cill-mór. The son of O'Sechnasaigh was slain by the Foreigners. Opecin Guér was slain by Gillamochoinne O'Cathail in hoc anno. The sons of Maghnus, and the sons of Conchobhar Ruadh, joined together, and turned against the Foreigners, and the castle of Mac Henry[3] was burned by them, and its constable taken prisoner; and the preys of the north of Umhall were taken by them to Innsi-Modh.[4] Iordan de Exeter, however, and John Butler, and Robin Lawless, and several persons along with them, assembled and went to Baile-tobair-Patraic, and from thence to Achadh-Fabhair; and they plundered all Umhall, north and south, on the morrow. Mac Henry[3] came also, with a large army, into Umhall, (for it belonged to himself, and he was residing in it). Mac Henry then made peace with Domhnall, son of Maghnus, for the sake of his territory; and Domhnall promised that he would furnish forces and boats to *attack* his brother. As regards the sons of Conchobhar, moreover; they were on Innsi-Modh,[4] and it was reported to them that a party had gone from Mac Henry to Domhnall, for boats. They advanced against this party, and killed O'hUain, the son

(Four Mast., A.D. 1247, note ᴾ) Tuathrass, or Tuathfrais, with the district of the Rosses in Donegal. But the examination of the evidences on the subject would occupy too much space here.

[2] *Bishop of Ui-Fiachrach-Aighne;* i.e. bishop of Kilmacduagh.

[3] *Mac Henry.* His name was Piers Poer, or De la Poer.

[4] *Innsi-Modh.* See note [4], p. 327, *supra.*

ʒαιλλριŏe, ocuρ 8eon mac an ʒαλλ ṙacαιρτ; ocuρ υo
mαρbαυ λα Όιαρmαιυ mac Μαʒnuιρ αρ an comαρc
ριn 8enóιυ ʒuéρ ocuρ ceṫρaρ υία muιnτιρ mαιλλe ρριρ.
Ccητ chena ρα hé ριn ιnτ áιṫeρ ʒo nαnáιṫeρ, óιρ ρo
mαρbαυ ιn cuιnʒιŏ cαλmα ocuρ ιn τaιρριʒ ιρʒαιλe, .ι.
Όιαρmαιυ mac Μαʒnuρα, αρ an λαṫαιρ ριn. Τaυʒ
mac Conchobaιρ ρuαιŏ υo ṁαρbαυ λα ʒαλλοιŏ ιριn
mbλιαυαιn ριn. Όα ṁoρ τρα eʒλα ocuρ αŏṁaṫ ιn mιc
ριn [ρoρ ʒαλλοιb] ocuρ ʒαoιυeλαιb ŏιṫíρ ιnα αʒhαιυ, co
bṙuαιρ a oιʒeυ ρα ŏeoιŏ. 8λoιʒeυ λα Μuιριρ Ριʒeρóιυ
a Τιρ Chonαιλλ. Cρeαċa móρa ocuρ uρṫa υo ŏenum
λeιρ ιnnτι, ocuρ .h. Cαnαnnan υo ιnnαρbαυ αριn τíρ
αmαċ ι nuchτ hι Néιλλ ocuρ Cheneóιλ Coʒαιn, ocuρ ριʒe
Cheneóιλ Conαιλλ υṙáʒbáιλ αʒ ʒoρρραιʒ mac Όomnαιλλ
ṁóιρ hι Όhomnαιλλ. 8λuαιʒeυ λα Cenéλ Coʒαιn ocuρ
λα .h. Cαnαnnán a Τιρ Conαιλλ υoριŏιρ, ocuρ τucρaτ
caṫ υá ċeλι αnnριn, ocuρ ρo mαρbαυ .h. Cαnαnnán ann,
ocuρ moρán υo υαoιnιŏ mαιċe mαιλλe ρριρ, λα Cenéλ
Conαιλλ, ocuρ λα ʒoρρραιʒ mac Όomnαιλλ hι Όhomnαιλλ;
ocuρ υo ʒαŏ ρeιn ριʒe Τhιρe Chonαιλλ ιαρριn. 8λuαιʒeυ
eλι λα ʒιúρυιρ na hCρenn a Cenéλ Coʒαιn υo ċum hι
Néιλλ, ocuρ ιρρι comαιρλe υo ρónρaυ Cenéλ Coʒαιn, o
ŏo ŏáι neρτ ʒαλλ ρoρ ʒhαoιυeλuιŏ Cρenn, bραιʒυe υo
ṫαŏαιρτ υo ʒhαλλοιŏ, ocuρ ριŏ υo ŏenum ρριú ταρ cenn
a τíρe. Conmαιcne Μαρα uιλe υo αρʒαιn υo ʒαλλοιŏ.
ʒóιλλ υo ŏuλ αρ ρλuαιʒeŏ υoċum hι Ρhλαιṫŏeρταιʒ,
ocuρ mαιŏm υo ṫαŏαιρτ υó ρoρρα, ocuρ moρán υo
mαρbαυ ŏó υιŏ. Μuιρceρταch .h. Όuŏυα .ι. anτ
αιṫċλeιρech, υo mαρbαυ λα mac Ρéŏλιm ι Chonċobαιρ.
Uιλλιαm Όuρc υo éʒ a 8αχuιŏ, ocuρ a coρρ υo ταŏαιρτ

1 *The foreigners.* ρoρ ʒαλλοιb;
omitted in MS., and supplied from the
Four Masters.

2 *From the country.* The MS. has
αρι τιρτιŏ, for αριn τιρτιŏ, which
is incorrect; for αριn is comp. of the

preposition αρ, and the sg. art. ιn;
whilst τιρτιŏ (*rectè* τιριŏ), is the
ablat. pl. of τιρ = Lat. *terra.* The
correct reading should be αριn τιρ,
or αρ na τιριŏ (out of the districts).

3 *They;* i.e. the Cenel-Eoghain, or

of the foreign woman, and John the son of the foreign priest; and Sinnott Guêr, and four of his people along with him, were slain by Diarmaid, son of Maghnus, in this encounter. However, this was the joy with sorrow, for the powerful champion and prop of battle, i.e. Diarmaid, son of Maghnus, was slain on the spot. Tadhg, son of Conchobhar Ruadh, was killed by the Foreigners in this year. Great, truly, was the fear and terror of this youth entertained by [the Foreigners][1] and Gaeidhel who were opposed to him, until he received his death ultimately. A hosting by Maurice Fitz-Gerald into Tir-Conaill. Great depredations and plunders were committed by him therein; and O'Canannan was expelled from the country[2] to O'Neill and the Cenel-Eoghain, and the sovereignty of Cenel-Conaill was left to Goffraigh, son of Domhnall Mór O'Domhnaill. A hosting by the Cenel-Eoghain, and by O'Canannain, again into Tir-Conaill, when they[3] gave battle to each other, and O'Canannain, and a great many nobles along with him, were slain by the Cenel-Conaill, and by Goffraigh, son[4] of Domhnall O'Domhnaill, who afterwards assumed the sovereignty of Tir-Conaill. Another hosting by the Justiciary of Erinn to Cenel-Eoghain, to O'Neill; and the resolution adopted by the Cenel-Eoghain was, since the power of the Foreigners was over the Gaeidhel of Erinn, to give[5] hostages to the Foreigners, and to make peace with them, for the sake of their country. Conmaicne-Mara was all plundered by the Foreigners. The Foreigners went on a hosting to O'Flaithbhertaigh, who defeated them, and killed a great number of them. Muirchertach O'Dubhda, i.e. the ex-cleric, was killed by the son of Fedhlim O'Conchobhair. William Burk died in Saxon-land, and his body was brought to Erinn,

inhabitants of the district subject to O'Neill, and the Cenel-Conaill, or O'Donnell's people.

[4] *Son.* mac. Repeated in MS.
[5] *To give.* ꝺo ꝫabaıꞃꞇ. Repeated in MS.

i nＥrinn, ocur a aＢlucaＤ in ＯＥ irriol. Rí Franc Ｄo
Ｄul co hIarurＡlém Ｄo Ｃornum na CríoＤaiＸechta
irin mbliaＤain rin. Comarba Paproic Ｄo Ｅeacht in
Ｅrinn, .i. peneＴincier in papa. Ióan Ｔirel Ｄo marbaＤ
Ｄon Ｚilla na naom .h. ＦerＧail. FeＤlim mac Cathail
croibＤerＧ Ｄo ＴabairＴ RaＥa na Románach Ｄo Ｃanán-
chaib Chille móire, ocur canＴarＣarＴa Ｄo rróll irin ló
ceＤna, Ｔre ＦurＡilem ocur Ｔre impiＤe ＴhaiＤc hi
ＭanＤachＡin, an onóir Muire ocur ＯＢＸurＤin, a br4aＢ-
nuire ṁórain Ｄo ṁaiＴＢ Connacht. ＯṁlＡiＢ mac
Cathail riabaＸ hi Ruaire Ｄo marbaＤ Ｄo ChonＣobar
Ｃarrach mac ＤonnchaＤa, per Ｄolum. FaＸartach .h.
ＤoＢoilén, rí an Choruinn, quieuit. MaiＸirＤir
ＺilleperＴ .h. CerＢuill quieuit in CrirＴo.

ct. Ｅnair ror ＯoIne, acur aile Ｄhéc rurre; nono
anno cicli rolarir; xu. anno Ｄecennouenalir cicli;
uii. anno inＤicＴionir; M.cc.xl. nono. SlúaiＸeＤ mór
la ＺiúrＤir na hＥrenn a LaＸniＢ Ｄo innroiＸeＤ na mac
riＸ no ＢＴóir aＸ lót ocur aＸ lán ṁilleＢ Ｚall; ocur ni
ＴucraＤ na mic riＸ LaＸneＢa ＴaoＢ rrir in nＺiúrＤir Ｄon
chur rin, ocur ó nach ＴucaＤar ＴucＴom laiṁ Ｔarran
Ｔír, ocur Ｄo lomaircＥＤ co leir lair hí. CoＸaＤ mór
ocur uilc imＤa Ｄo Ｄenum Ｄo FhinＸin MháＸ CarrＴhaiＸ
ar ＺhalloiＢ Ｄerṁuman in hoc anno. ＡＤＡm MinaＴúr
Ｄo ṁarＢaＤ Ｄo Mac ＺillamoＣoinne .h. ChaＴail, ocur
mórán aile maille rrir. Piarur Puér, .i. mac Ｅnri,
ocur ＤauiＤ Ｔriú ocur marcrlúaiＸ Ｄo ＸillaiＸib óＸa
maroen riú, Ｄo ＴoiＸecht roim Mic Fheoruir a Con-
nachtuiＢ, co cairlén SliciＸ; ocur aＤuar Ｄo mac
FeＤlim hi Conchobair an ní rin; ocur ó ＣualaiＢ
Ｔuc airrＣeirＴ rorra; ocur Ｄo marbaＤ annrin Piarur
Puér ocur ＤauiＤ Ｔriú, ocur cóiＸer Ｄo ＸillaiＸiＢ óＸa

1 *Pœnitentiarius.* The Four Masters write his name Raighned, but it should be Regnier or Reiner.

2 *Cuntarcupath.* Probably a vest-
ment, or cope, used in chaunting some offices. See Glossary.

3 *Augustin.* The MS. has ＯＢＸurＤin, another instance of the substitution of

and interred at Ath-issel. The King of France went to
Jerusalem, to defend Christendom, in this year. The
comarb of Patrick, i.e. the pœnitentiarius[1] of the Pope,
came to Erinn. John Tirrel was killed by Gilla-na-
naemh O'Ferghail. Fedhlim, son of Cathal Crobhderg,
gave Rath-na-Romanach to the canons of Cill-mór, and
a cantarcapath[2] of silk on the same day, at the persuasion
and request of Tadhg O'Mannachain, in honour of Mary
and Augustin,[3] in presence of several of the nobles of
Connacht. Amhlaibh, son of Cathal Riabhach O'Ruairc,
was killed by Conchobhar Carrach Mac Donnchadha, per
dolum. Foghartach O'Dobhailen, king of the Corann,
quievit. Master Gilbert O'Cerbhaill quievit in Christo.

The kalends of January on Friday, and the twelfth of
the moon; nono anno cycli solaris; xv. anno Decennovenalis cycli; vii. anno Indictionis. M.cc.xl.nono. A great
hosting by the Justiciary of Erinn into Laighen, to attack
the sons of kings who were injuring and totally destroying the Foreigners; and the Lagenian sons of kings
sided not with the Justiciary on this occasion; and as
they did not, he invaded[4] the country, which was entirely
wasted by him. A great war *was waged*, and numerous
injuries were committed, by Finghin Mac Carthaigh
against the Foreigners of Des-Mumha, in hoc[5] anno.
Adam Minatur was slain by the son of Gillamochoinne
O'Cathail, and many more along with him. Piers Poer,
i.e. the son of Henry, and David Treu, accompanied by a
mounted party of young men, proceeded before Mac
Feorais into Connacht, to the castle of Sligech. And this
was reported to the son of Fedhlim O'Conchobhair; and
when he heard it he laid an ambuscade for them, and
Piers Poer, and David Treu, and five young men along

---

an aspirated b (ḃ) for u. See note[6],
p. 366, *supra*.

[4] *Invaded.* The words ꞇuꞇꞃom

laṁ ꞇaꞃꞃan ꞇíꞃ literally signify
"he laid a hand over the country."
[5] *Hoc.* oc, MS.

2 C

mαρáon ρú ; ocuρ ρucαᵬ nα ϝιρ ριn ιnα coρραιᵬ co
hⱸρρ ᵭαρα ᵭια nαᵬͳucαᵬ. ιmᵹⱸρρ mιc ϝⱸᵭͳιm, ᵹánιc
ρⱸͫⱸ α Ϲíρ ϝͷιαϲ̃ραϲ̃ ιαρριn, ocuρ αρ ρuᵭ cριϲ̃ε Mιc
ϝⱸοͷuιρ, ocuρ ᵭο ͷommαιρᵹ hí ó Mhuαιᵭ co Ϲραιᵹ
nⱸᵬᵭοιͳε ροιρ ; ocuρ ρο ͳⱸn Ᵹεͷóιᵭιn Mαc ϝⱸοͷuιρ ιαᵭ,
ocuρ ρuc ρⱸ αρ ᵭhonnchαᵬ mαc Mαᵹnuρα, ocuρ ρο
ͳοιᵹεᵬ ͳαιρ hⱸ, ocuρ ρο ᵹαᵬαᵬ ᵹαρⱸιρ α ͳοιᵹ, ocuρ ρuc
ͳειρ co ᵭun Conᵹρεαᵹ hⱸ ιαρ ριn. Ro ͳⱸn mαc ϝⱸᵭͳιm
ιαᵭ ιαρ ριn, ocuρ ρο ᵬεn mαc Mαᵹnuρα ᵭíᵬ, ocuρ ρο
mαρᵬαᵭ Ᵹεͷóιᵭιn ρερ ᵭοͳum ; ocuρ ᵹερᵹα ᵭonnchαᵭ
mαc Mαᵹnuρα ᵭοn ͳοᵹ ριn ; ocuρ ᵬá moρ ιn ερᵬαᵬ
ᵭο ᵹαͳͳοιᵬ ocuρ ᵭο ᵹαοιᵭεͳαιᵬ ᵭιᵬͳίnιᵬ. Ro ͳínóιͳ
Mαc Muιρ̃ιρ ιαρρ̃ιn, ocuρ ᵹαnιc ροιͫε ι Connαchᵹαιᵬ,
ocuρ ᵭο ᵬεn ᵭο mαc ϝⱸᵭͳιm αn ͫⱸιᵭ αρ α ρuc αιᵹε
ᵭοnα cρεchαιᵬ ριn. Oᵭ ͳuαͳα ϝεᵭͳιm mαc Cαᵹhαιͳ
cροιᵬᵭερᵹ ᵹαιͳͳ ᵭο ᵬειᵹ ᵹιnοιͳᵹι nα ᵹomϝocuρ, ᵹαρⱸιρ
nα noͳc móρ ριn ᵭο ᵬεnum ᵭá mαc ορρα, ιρρí com-
αιρͳε ᵭο ρόιnε α ιmερcεchα ᵭο chuρ ᵹαρ Sιonuιnn
ροιρ ιρ̃ιn mᵬρειϝnε, ocuρ α ᵹuαιρcερᵹ ⱸρεnn. Ro ͳιnoιͳ
ᵭιn αn Ᵹιuιρᵭíρ ᵹαιͳͳ Mιᵭε ocuρ ͳαιᵹεn, ocuρ ᵹánιc
ρͳúαιᵹ móρ ρεͫε ᵹαρ Æᵹ ͳuαιn, ocuρ αρριᵬⱸ α Síͳ
Muιρ̃εᵹhαιᵹh, ocuρ Mαc Muιρ̃ιρ ᵭοn ͳειᵹ εͳι, ocuρ
Ᵹαιͳͳ Mhumαn ocuρ Chonnαchᵹ máροεn ϝρ̃ιρ ; ocuρ
ᵹαncoᵹαρ ιn ᵭá ᵹϝͳuαᵹ ριn co hOιͳϝιnn ιαρ mιͳͳεᵭ Shíͳ
Muιρ̃εᵭhαιᵹh ροmρu conuιᵹε ριn ; ocuρ ᵹucραᵹ Ϲοιρρ-
ᵭhεͳᵬαch mαc Oεᵭα mιc Cαᵹhαιͳ Cροιᵬᵭερᵹ ᵹucα, ocúρ
ᵭο ριᵹραᵹ αn ιnαᵭ ϝⱸᵭͳιm mιc Cαᵹhαιͳ cροιᵬᵭερᵹ hⱸ ;
ocuρ ρο αιρᵹρεᵹ cριᵹ̃ ᵬρⱸιϝnε ιαρ ριn, ocuρ ᵭο ρónραᵹ
uιͳc ιmᵬα ιnnᵹι ιn ᵹαch αιρᵭ, ocuρ ᵹucραᵹ α cρεαϲ̃α ͳεο
ιαρρ̃ιn, ocuρ ρο ᵬáᵭαρ ρ̃ιϲε οιᵬϲε ιmͳán α Sιοͳ Muιρ̃εᵹh-
αιᵹh αᵹ á mιͳͳεᵭ, ocuρ ρο αιρᵹρεᵹ ͳοϲ̃ Cⱸ conα

---

1 *Geroitin*; i.e. "Little Garrett."

2 *Them.* Fedhlim O'Conor and his forces.

3 *Dun-Contreat.* The Four Masters write the name ᵭún Conᵹρεαᵹαιn (Dun-Contreathain), which is the more correct form. The place is now called Donaghintraine, and is a town-land in the parish of Templeboy, barony of Tireragh, and county of Sligo.

with them, were slain there; and the bodies of these men were conveyed to Es-dara for interment. As regards the son of Fedhlim, he proceeded afterwards to Tir-Fiachrach, and through the country of Mac Feorais, which he entirely plundered from the Muaidh eastwards to Traigh-Eothaile. And Geroitin[1] Mac Feorais followed them[2] and overtook Donnchadh, son of Maghnus, who was wounded by him, and taken prisoner after having been wounded; and he subsequently took him with him to Dun-Contreat.[3] The son of Fedhlim pursued them afterwards, and rescued the son of Maghnus from them; and Geroitin was killed per dolum; and Donnchadh, son of Maghnus, died of this wound; and great was the loss to both Foreigners and Gaeidhel. Mac Maurice thereupon mustered, and proceeded into Connacht, and deprived the son of Fedhlim of as much of these preys as he found with him. When Fedhlim, son of Cathal Crobhderg, heard that the Foreigners were assembled in his neighbourhood, after his son had inflicted such great injuries on them, he adopted the resolution of sending his moveables across the Sinainn eastwards, into the Breifne, and to the North of Erinn. The Justiciary assembled the Foreigners of Midhe and Laighen, and advanced with a great army across Ath-Luain, and from thence into Sil-Muiredhaigh; and Mac Maurice advanced on the other side, accompanied by the Foreigners of Mumha and Connacht. And these two armies went to Oilfinn, after destroying Sil-Muiredhaigh before them so far; and they invited to them Toirdhelbhach, son of Aedh, son of Cathal Crobhderg, and made him king in the place of Fedhlim, son of Cathal Crobhderg. And they afterwards plundered the territory of Breifne, and committed numerous injuries in it in every direction, and subsequently brought their preys with them. And they were fully twenty nights in Sil-Muiredhaigh, devastating it; and they plundered Loch-Cé, together with its islands, and

2 c 2

oılénaıḃ, ocuʀ ın Chaıʀʀıg cona hımlıḃ. Do chúaıd, dana, ın Ɉıúʀdıʀ ıʀın Mıḋe ıaʀʀın, ocuʀ do chúaıd Mac Muıʀıʀ co Slıgech, ocuʀ ʀo ḟágaıḃʀıot Coıʀʀdhel-bach mac Ccoḋa aɉ coıméᴅ ḟıl Muıʀeɉhaıgh. Sloıged elı la mᾱcaıḃ ʀıɉ Connachᴅ co hCCᵹ na ʀıɉ, dá loʀcad ocuʀ da lomaʀgaın, ʀo ḟeıl Muıʀe ocuʀ ıommedóın ʀóɉṁaıʀ. Sluaɉ móʀ elı ʀa Choıʀʀdhelbach mac Oeḋa, ocuʀ ʀa CCoḃ óɉ mac Ccoḋa, ocuʀ do ḃı ıʀʀıam Connachᴅ aʀ a cınn ıʀın mbaıle, ocuʀ Ɉoıll ımḋa ḟaʀıʀ, ocuʀ ʀo ıaʀʀʀaᴅ na Ɉoıll caıʀde an láı ʀın a nonóıʀ Muıʀe ıʀa huaıʀle boı ḟaıʀ, ocuʀ nı ᴅucʀaᴅ na mıc ʀıɉ an caıʀde ʀın uaᴅhaıb a nonoıʀ Muıʀe ná na Cʀoıċe naım; achᴅ chena ʀo ınʀoıɉʀeᴅ ın baıle co dáʀʀachᴅ-ach do nemᴇoıl Coıʀʀdhelbaıɉ. Od ċonnaıʀc Sıuʀᴅán ocuʀ na Ɉoıll ʀın, ᴅancadaʀ aʀ an mbaıle amaċ acoınne na mac ʀıɉ ʀın, ocuʀ do ʀone Muıʀe mıʀbaıle ʀolluʀa annʀın; óıʀ ód conncodaʀ na mıc ʀıɉ cona muınᴅıʀ an maʀcʀluaɉ aḃuaᴅṁaʀ éıoıɉᴇı ċuca aʀ an mbaıle amaċ, ʀo ɉaḃ ɉʀáın ocuʀ eɉla aḋbaıl ıad aɉá᾽ ḃḟaıcʀın, ocuʀ ʀo ṁeabad ḋıḃ, ocuʀ ʀo maʀbad Ccoḃ mac Ccoḋa hı Chonċobaıʀ annʀın, ocuʀ Dıaʀmaıd ʀuad mac Coʀmaıc hı Mhóılʀeclaınn, ocuʀ dá mac hı Cheallaıɉ, ocuʀ ḃʀıan ın doıʀe mac Maɉnaʀʀa, ocuʀ Caʀʀach ınᴅ ʀıḃaıl mac Neıll hı Conchobaıʀ, ocuʀ ḃaoᴇɉalaċ Mac Ccoḋaɉáın, ocuʀ mac Dıaʀmada baċlaıɉ hı Conchobaıʀ, .ı. Maᴇɉamaın mac mıc Caıḋc, ocuʀ dá mac Loċlaınn hı Conchobaıʀ, ocuʀ Domnall Mac Coʀmaıc Mıc Dıaʀ-mada, ocuʀ an Ḟınnanach Mac ḃʀanáın, ocuʀ Cuṁuman Mac Caʀuʀlaıɉ, ocuʀ daoıne ımḋa elı mᾱlle ʀıu. Donnchad, mac Ccnmchada, mıc Donnchada hı Ɉhılla-ḟadʀaıc, .ı. anᴅ aon ċend ʀeḋna dob ḟeʀʀ enech ocuʀ

---

[1] *The Rock.* Mac Dermot's castle in Loch-Cé, near Boyle, in the county of Roscommon.

[2] *Festival.* The clause ıʀα huaıʀle

boı ḟaıʀ, which has been translated "whose festival it was," literally rendered would read "whose nobility was on it (the day)."

the Rock,[1] with its precincts. The Justiciary, moreover, went afterwards into Midhe, and Mac Maurice went to Sligech; and they left Toirdhelbhach, son of Aedh, guarding Sil-Muiredhaigh.   Another hosting by the sons of the kings of Connacht, on the festival of Mary in mid-autumn, to Ath-na-righ, to burn and plunder it. Another great army under Toirdhelbhach, son of Aedh, and Aedh Og, son of Aedh.   And the sheriff of Connacht was in the town before them, accompanied by many Foreigners; and the Foreigners requested a truce for that day in honour of Mary, whose festival[2] it was.   And the kings' sons did not grant this truce in honour of Mary or the Holy Cross; but they attacked the town furiously, against the will of Toirdhelbhach.   When Jordan[3] and the Foreigners observed this, they came out of the town against these kings' sons ; and Mary performed manifest miracles there ; for when the kings' sons, with their people, saw the terrible mail-clad cavalry coming towards them out of the town, prodigious fear and terror seized them at the sight, and they were routed ; and Aedh, son of Aedh O'Conchobhair, was slain there, and Diarmaid Ruadh, son of Cormac O'Maelsechlainn ; and two sons of O'Cellaigh; and Brian-in-doire,[4] son of Maghnus; and Carrach-ind-shibhail,[5] son of Niall O'Conchobhair ; and Baethghalach Mac Aedhagain; and the son of Diarmaid Bachlach O'Conchobhair, i.e. Mathghamhain, grandson of Tadhg ; and the two sons of Lochlainn O'Conchobhair ; and Domhnall, son of Cormac Mac Diarmada; and the Finnanach Mac Branain; and Cumumhan Mac Casarlaigh; and many other persons along with them.   Donnchadh, son of Anmchadh, son of Donnchadh O'Gillapatraic,[6] i.e. the captain of greatest honour and prowess that had

---

[3] *Jordan.* Jordan de Exeter, apparently the Sheriff of Connacht.

[4] *Brian-in-doire;* lit. "Brian of the oak wood." His family name was O'Conchobhair.

[5] *Carrach-ind-shibhail.* A sobriquet signifying "the rough man of the walking."

[6] *O'Gillapatraic.* See note [3], p. 378.

enᵹnum ⱰáⅿⒾⒸ ⱰΟⱤⱤⱮⱭⱫⅠⒷ ó Cholmán ⅿⱭⒸ ⒷⅠⒸⁿⒺ ̆ⒸαοⒾ̆Ⓒ
οⒸⓊⱤ Ɒ SⒸⱭⁿⅬáⁿ ⅿⱭⒸ ⒸⅠⁿⁿᖴⱭοⅼⱭⱰ ⱭⁿⓊⱭⱤ, [Ɒο ⅿⱭⱤⒷⱭ̆ⱱ] Ɒο
ꝽⱭⅼⅼοⅠⒷ ⅠⱤⁿ ⅿⒷⅼⅠⱭⱱⱭⁿ ⱤⅠⁿ; οⒸⓊⱤ ⱱο ⒷⱭ ⒸⓊⅿⱭοⅠⁿ ⱱο
ꝽⱭⅼⅼοⅠⒷ ⱤⅠⁿ ⱱⱳ̆Ᵹ ⅠⱤ ⅿóⱤ Ɽο ⅿⱭⱤⒷ, οⒸⓊⱤ Ɽο ⒸⱤⒺⱭ̆Ⓒ, οⒸⓊⱤ
Ɽο ⅼοⅠⱤⒸ ̆ⒷⅠⒷ ⱤⅠⱭⅿ ⒸοⁿⓊⅠⒸⒺ ⱤⅠⁿ; ⓊⱭⅠⱤ ⅠⱤⒻé ⱰοⁿⁿⒸⱳⱭⱱ
Ɑⁿ ⱰⱤⒺⱤⱤ ꝽⱭοⅠⱱⒺⅼ ⱱο ⒺⱤⅠ̆Ᵹ Ɑ ⁿⱭᵹⱳⱭⱳ ꝽⱭⅼⅼ ⅠⱭⱤ ⁿᵹⱭⒷáⅠⅼ
ⒺⱤⒺⁿⁿ ⱱóⅠⒷ, .Ⅰ. ConchoⒷⱭⱤ ⒽⓊⱭ MⱭοⅠⱤⒺⒸⅼⱭⅠⁿ, οⒸⓊⱤ
ConchoⒷⱭⱤ ⁿⱭ ꝽⒸⱭⅠⱤⅼéⁿ MⱭᵹ CŏⒸⅼáⁿ, οⒸⓊⱤ ⅿⱭⒸ Ɑⁿⅿ-
ⒸⱳⱭⱱⱭ; ⓊⱭⅠⱤ ⱰéⅠ̆ᵹⒺⱱⅠ ⅿⱭⒸ ⱭⁿⅿⒸⱳⱭⱱⱭ ᖴⒺⅠⁿ ⱱο ⒷⱤⱭ̆Ⓒ
ⁿⱭ ⅿⒷⱭⅠⅼⱰⅠ ⅿⱭⱤᵹⱭⱱ Ɑ ⱤⅠⒸⱳⱰ ̆ⱱⓊⅠⁿⒺ ̆ⒷοⅠⒸⱳⱰ, ⁿó ⱰⱤⱭⅠⒸⒺⁿⱱ,
ⁿο ̆ⱰοⱤⁿóⱤⱭ, ⁿο ⒺⱭⅼⱳ̆ⱲⁿⱭ ⒺⅠᵹⅠⁿ ⓊⅠⅼⒺ, ⓊⱰ ⱱⅠⱭⅠⱰⓊⱤ :—

ᵬⅠ̆ⱱ ⁿⱭ ⱰⱤοⒺⱤ ᵬⅠ̆ⱱ ⁿⱭ ̆ⱰοⱤⁿóⅠⱤ
ᵬⅠ̆ⱱ ⅿο ⅼⱭοᵹ ⁿⱭ ⅼⒸⱭᵬⱤóⅠⱤ
ᵬⅠ̆ⱱ Ɽé Ɑᵹ ⱤⒺⅠⒸ ᖴⅠοⁿⱭ ⅠⱤ ⒸⱤⱭⅠⒸⒺⁿⱱ,
MⓊⱤ ⱭⒷᖴⱭⅠⒸⒺⁿⱱ Ⅰⁿ ⱤⒺⱤⅿóⅠⁿ, Ɽⅼ̆.

ⱰⱭⱱᵹ .h.MⱭⁿⁿⱭ̆Ⓒáⁿ, ⱤⅠ .h. ⅿᵬⱤⅠⓊⅠⁿ ⁿⱭ SⅠⁿⁿⱭ, ⱱο
éⒸ Ⅰⁿ οⒸⱰⱭ̆Ⓑο ⅠⱱⓊⱤ ⅠⓊⁿⅠⅠ, οⒸⓊⱤ Ɑ Ɑ̆ⱱⅼⓊⒸⱭⱱ Ɑ CⅠⅼⅼ ⅿ̆ⱳóⅠⱤ ⁿⱭ
SⅠⁿⁿⱭ ⅠⱭⱤⱤⅠⁿ. Conn .h. ᖴⅼⱭⁿⁿⱭⒸⱭⁿ, ⱤⱤⅠóⱤ CⅠⅼⅼⒺ ⅿóⅠⱤⒺ
ⁿⱭ SⅠⁿⁿⱭ, ⱱο é̆Ᵹ Ⅰⁿ .ⓊⅠⅠ. ᖴⒸⱰⅼ. MⱭⅠⅠ. MⱭοⅼⅿⓊⅠⱤⒺ .h.
ⅼⱭⒸⱳⱰⁿáⅠⁿ, ⅿⱭⅠ̆ᵹⅠⱤⱰⅠⱤ Ɑ ⒸⱭⁿóⅠⁿ, οⒸⓊⱤ ᖴⱭⅼⅿⓊⅠⱤⒺ ᵹⱤο̆ⱰⱭ
ⒺóⱤ̆ⱰⱭⁿáⅠⁿ, οⒸⓊⱤ ⱭⅠⱤⱱⒺⱤⱤⓊⒸ ⱰⓊⱭⅿⱭ ̆ⱱá ᵹⓊⱭⅼⱭⁿⁿ οⒸⓊⱤ
ConnⱭⒸⱳⱰ ⓊⅠⅼⒺ, ⱱ̆ⒺⒸ ⅠⱤⅠⁿ ⁿᵹⒺⅠⅿⱤⒺ̆ⱱ, οⒸⓊⱤ ᵹⱭⅠⱤⅠⱱ ⒷⒺᵹ
ⱤⅠⱭ ⒽοⱱⅼⱭⅠⒸ. ⱭⅠⁿⱱⱤⅠⱭⱤ MⱭⒸ ᵹⅠⅼⅼⒺ̆ᵹéⅠⱤ, ⒸοⅿⱭⱤⱳⱭ
ᖴⒺⅠⒸⱳⅠⁿ, ⅿοⱤⱰⓊⓊⱤ ⒺⱤⱰ. MⱭοⅼⒸⅠⱭⱤáⅠⁿ .h. ⅼéⁿⱭ̆Ⓒáⁿ,
ⓊⱭⱤⱭⅼ ᖴⱭⒸⱭⱤⱰ ⅿóⱤ ⱰⱳⓊⱭⅿⱭ ⅿⁿá, ᖴⒺⱤ ⒸⅼⒺⅠⱤⒺⒸⱳ οⒸⓊⱤ
ⱭοⱤⱭ ᵹⱤⱳⅠ̆ⱱ ⱱο ⒸοⁿᵹⅿáⅠⅼ ⅠⁿⱭ ̆ⱰⅠ̆Ᵹ ᖴéⅠⁿ, οⒸⓊⱤ ᖴⒺⱤ ⱰⅠ̆ᵹⒺ

---

1 *Colman, son of Bicne Caech.* Bicne Caech, or "Bicne the Blind," was a chieftain of Ossory, who died about A.D. 700. He was the grandson of Scánlan, son of Cennfaeladh, mentioned in the succeeding line.

2 *Scanlan, son of Cennfaeladh.* The death of this Scanlan, chief of Ossory, called Scanlan Mór, or "Scanlan the Great," is recorded by the Four Masters at the year 640.

3 *The third Gaeidhel.* That is to say, he was the third Irishman, in point of distinction, who had risen against the English since the occupation of Ireland by the latter; the first and second being Conchobhar O'Maelsechlaiun and Conchobhar Mac Cochlain.

4 *Conchobhar-na-gcaislen.* "Conchobhar (or Conor) of the castles."

5 *Ut.* Ⓤⱱ, MS. The stanza which follows is written in what some Irish grammarians designate the present

come of the men of Osraighe down from Colman,[1] son of Bicne Caech,[1] and from Scanlan,[2] son of Cennfaeladh,[2] [was slain] by the Foreigners in this year. And this was a satisfaction for the Foreigners, as he had killed, and plundered, and burned many of them previously up to that time; for Donnchadh was the third Gaeidhel[3] who had risen against the Foreigners after they had occupied Erinn, viz. :—Conchobhar O'Maelsechlainn, and Conchobhar-na-gcaislen[4] Mac Cochlain, and the son of Anmchadh; for the son of Anmchadh was wont himself to reconnoitre the market towns in the guise of a pauper, or a carpenter, or a turner, or a person of some other trade, ut[5] dicitur:—

He is wont to be a carpenter; is wont to be a turner;
My nursling is wont to be a bookman;
He is wont to be selling wine and hides,
Where he sees the gathering, &c.

Tadhg O'Mannachain, king of Ui-Briuin-na-Sinna, died in octavo[6] idus[7] Junii, and was subsequently interred in Cill-mor-na-Sinna.[8] Conn O'Flannagain, prior of Cill-mor-na-Sinna,[8] died in septimo kalendas Maii. Maelmuire O'Lachtnain, a master in canon law, and a palmer of the river Jordan, and archbishop of Tuaim-dá-ghualann and of all Connacht, died in the winter, and a short time before Christmas. Andrias Mac Gillegheir, comarb of Feichin,[9] mortuus est. Maelciarain O'Lenachain, noble chief priest of Tuaim-mná; a man who maintained clerics and men of grade in his own house, and a man who kept a

---

tense of the consuetudinal mood, but what Zeuss calls the "secondary present." See *Gram. Celtic.*, pp. 412, 417. An Irish-speaking person in literally translating the language of the original, instead of the words "is wont to be" of the translation, would use the formula "does be," as there is no tense in English corresponding to the Irish "secondary present."

[6] *Octavo.* οϲταϋο, MS.; ϋ instead of u. See note [6], p. 366, *supra.*

[7] *Idus.* The word anno is written incorrectly before ꝺours in the MS.

[8] *Cill-mor-na-Sinna;* lit. "the great church of the Shannon," now Kilmore, about six miles east of Elphin, county of Roscommon.

[9] *Comarb of Feichin;* i.e. abbot of Cong, county of Mayo.

aoidhed coitcinn do cliaraib ocuş do comaiġtib, do éġ aş şligeḋ aġ dul co hArd Caşna, do éşdecht şenmora, işin Aoíne şia Luġnaşad; ocuş a aḋlucaḋ co huaşşal onoşach an Oilén na Tşinóide şoş Loċ Cé. Moş inġen Donnchaḋa hI Duḃda, ben in ġilla ṁuiné-laiġ hI Dhaoiġill, moştua eşt. Dún móş do loşcaḋ dona macaib şiġ in hoc anno. Da ḃliaḋain ḋéc ocuş şeacht ceḋ ḃliaḋan o ḋo chuaiḋ Colum Chille co hI ġuş an mbliaḋain şi.

ḳt. Enaiş şoş şaċoşn, ocuş tşeşş şichid şuişşe; x°. anno cicli şolaşiş; xui°. anno decennouenaliş cicli; uiii. anno indictioniş. M.cc.L. Feḋlim .h. Conchobaiş do ċeacht aş in tuaişceşt, ocuş şoşşaide ṁóş leiş a Cenél Eoġain, dinnşoiġeḋ na Dşeişşne, ocuş aşiḋé iş na Tuathaib, ocuş Conchobaş mac Tiġeşnáin maşḃen şiş, ocuş aşiḋé a Tiş Mhaine, ġuş ḋiċuişşeḋ Toişş-ḋhelbach a Connachtaib amach, condeachaiḋ in ucht ġall aşiş, ġuş ċinóil Feḋlim imeişcech Connacht leiş taş Sliaḃ Seġşa şiş, ġuş ċuişşet Ġoill teachta na ḋeġhaiḋ, condeşnaḋaş [şiḋ] şşiş, ocuş aişeac a şiġe şéin dó doşiḋiş. Dşaiġḋe Connacht do ḋallaḋ in Aċ Luain do ġall[oib], ocuş do Thoişşḋhelbach mac Aoḋa. Cşeaċ ṁóş do ḋenum do Fheḋlim aş Chaḋhal .h. Conchobaiş, ocuş a chuş aş innaşba a Connachtuib amaċ ḋó. Eşpuc Imliċ Iḃaiş do héc in hoc anno. Tomáş .h. Meallaiġ, eşpuc Enaiġ ḋúin, quieuit in Cşişto. Caişbşe hUa Maoilşechlainn do ṁaşbaḋ a şill a Dauiḋ Róiḋşi. Toişşḋhelbach mac Muişceştaiġ

---

1 *The Gilla-muinelach.* This is a sobriquet signifying "the [wry-] necked fellow." The individual so designated is stated, under the year 1247, to have been killed in a battle fought between Maurice Fitz Gerald and O'Donnell.

2 *Went to Ili.* There is an anachronism here, as St. Colum Cille proceeded to Ili in the year 563. The chronicler probably intended to say that the number of years that had elapsed since the Saint's departure were "twelve years *less* than seven hundred," which would refer the event to A.D. 561, or within two years of the actual date. See Reeves's *Adamnan*, Int., p. lxxv.

3 *Conchobhar, son of Tighernan.* O'Donovan (Four Mast., A.D. 1250)

general house of hospitality for ecclesiastics and strangers, died on the way whilst going to Ard-carna, to hear a sermon, on the Friday before Lammas; and he was nobly *and* honourably interred in Trinity Island on Loch-Cé. Mor, daughter of Donnchadh O'Dubhda, wife of the Gilla-muinelach[1] O'Baighill, mortua est. Dún-mór was burned by the kings' sons in hoc anno. Twelve years and seven hundred years since Colum-Cille went to Hi[2] until this year.

The kalends of January on Saturday, and the twenty-third of the moon; x°. anno cycli solaris; xvi°. anno Decennovenalis cycli; viii. anno Indictionis; M.cc.l. Fedhlim O'Conchobhair came from the North, with a large army from Cenel-Eoghain, and marched into the Breifne, and from thence into the Tuatha, accompanied by Conchobhar, son of Tighernan;[3] and *they went* from thence into Tir-Maine, and expelled Toirdhelbhach out of Connacht, who again went over to the Foreigners. And Fedhlim collected the herds of Connacht, *which he took* with him down across Sliabh-Seghsa; but the Foreigners sent messengers after him, and made [peace] with him, and his own kingdom was again restored to him. The hostages of Connacht were blinded in Ath-Luain by the Foreigners, and by Toirdhelbhach, son of Aedh.[4] A great depredation was committed by Fedhlim on Cathal O'Conchobhair, who was driven in exile out of Connacht by him. The bishop of Imlech-Ibhair[5] died in hoc anno. Thomas O'Meallaigh, bishop of Enach-dúin, quievit in Christo. Cairbre O'Maelsechlainn was slain in treachery by David Roche. Toirdhelbhach, son of Muirchertach Muimhnech

---

says that Conchobhar was the son of Tighernan O'Conor, called "Tighernan of Connacht;" but he was more probably the Conchobhar, son of Tighernan O'Ruairc, whose death is entered under the year 1257, *infra.*

[4] *Son of Aedh;* i.e. Aedh O'Conchobhair, or Hugh O'Conor.

[5] *The Bishop of Imlech-Ibhair.* Ware, who refers his death to the year 1249, calls him "Christian." *Bishops,* under Emly.

Muimniġ hi Conċobair, prióir reglera Petair ocur
Póil, do éɜ. Diarmaid .h. hEġra, ri Lúiġne, do éɜ
a prirún aɜ Mac Ꝫerailt. Sloiɜed mór la Muirir
Mac Ꝫerailt, ocur la Cathal Ua Raiɜilliġ, ocur lá
Cúconnacht .h. Raiɜilliġ, ocur maċ .h. mbriuin uile
maille riú, a Cenél Eoġain, co radadar tri hoiđċe a
Tolaiġ óɜ, ocur ruaradar morán dulc, ocur nír ġabrat
ɜéill ina edire ar .h. Neill don chur rin. Iar na
bpilleđ tar a nair a Cenél Conaill, hUa Canannán, ri
Cheneóil Conaill, do ġabáil do Muirir Mac Ꝫerailt,
ar comairce in erruic.hi Cerballáin, ocur a ṁarbad
doib iarrin, ocur ré aɜ triall dula arr ar éiɜin uatha.
Canánaiġ finna in uird Premonrtra, ɜairid ria
Nodluic, do ḃreiṫ do Chlárur Mháɜ Mhoilín leir ó
Ailén na Trinóide ar Loċ Cé co hAilén na Trinóide
ar Loċ Uachtair irin mbreifni, ocur ro ordaiɜ ann
canánaiġ in uird tre ċeoduɜad Cathail i Raiɜilliġ tuc
amaċ hi in rurrum et perpetuam elemorinam in honore
Sanctae Trinitatir; et idcirco Clarur hoc recit in
Domino quia Premonrtratenrer ɜaudeant conrimili
priuileɜio cum monacir ita quod ad ullam aliam
reliɜionem portea tranrire porrent. Conɜalaċ Mac
Iṫneoil, erpuc na Breifne, quieuit in Crirto. Flórint
Mac Floinn do ṫoɜađ docum errocoide Tuama dá
ġualann, ocur a ɜráđa do ṫabairt fair lá Nodlac a
Tuaim, ocur ro bo dinɜṁála cuiɜe hé ar ṁéd a eɜna,
ocur a eoluir an dliɜed.

Kt. Enáir for Domnach, ocur cethir uathad fuirre;
xi. anno cicli rolarir; xiii. anno decennouenalir cicli;
ix. anno indictionir. M.cc.l.primo. Clárur Mháɜ

1 *Regles.* This name properly signifies a church of Regular Canons,
as Dr. Reeves informs me, although
sometimes understood to mean an
"abbey church." The establishment
here referred to was doubtless in
either of the counties of Mayo or Roscommon.

2 *While imprisoned.* a prirún.
The lit. transl. is "in prison."

O'Conchobhair, prior of the ·Regles[1] of Peter and Paul, died. Diarmaid O'hEghra, king of Luighne, died while imprisoned[2] by Fitz-Gerald. A great hosting by Maurice Fitz-Gerald, and by Cathal O'Raighilligh, and by Cuconnacht O'Raighilligh, accompanied by all the chieftains of Ui-Briuin, into Cenel-Eoghain, when they were three nights at Tulach-óg; and they received many injuries, but obtained no hostages or pledges from O'Neill, on this occasion. After turning back into Cenel-Conaill, O'Canannain, king of Cenel-Conaill, was taken prisoner by Maurice Fitz-Gerald, whilst under the protection of the Bishop O'Cerbhallain;[3] and he was subsequently killed by them whilst endeavouring to escape forcibly from them. White Canons of the Premonstre Order were taken by Clarus Mac Mailin, a short time before Christmas, from Trinity Island in Loch-Cé, to Trinity Island in Loch-Uachtair, in the Breifne; and he established the canons of the order there through the permission of Cathal O'Raighilligh, who granted it (*Trinity Island*) in puram et perpetuam clemosinam[4] in honore Sanctæ Trinitatis;[5] et idcirco Clarus hoc fecit in Domino, quia Premonstratenses gaudeant[6] consimili privilegio cum monachis, ita quod ad ullam aliam religionem postea transire possent. Conghalach Mac Idhneoil, bishop of the Breifne,[7] quievit in Christo. Florence Mac Floinn was elected to the bishopric of Tuaim-dá-ghualann, and was consecrated on Christmas Day in Tuaim; and he was fit for it, on account of the extent of his learning, and his knowledge of law.

The kalends of January on Sunday, and the fourth of the moon; xi. anno cycli solaris; xvii. anno Decennovenalis cycli; ix. anno Indictionis. M.cc.l. primo. Clarus

---

[3] *Bishop O'Cerbhallain.* Bishop of Derry, 1230–1279.

[4] *Elemosinam.* eʟɪmoɪꝛɪɑɱ (elimoisinɑɱ), MS.

[5] *Trinitatis.* ꝼꝛɪnecɑꞇꝭꝛ, MS.

[6] *Gaudeant.* ᵹɑuoɪɑnꞇ, MS.

[7] *Bishop of the Breifne;* i.e. Bishop of the district now comprised in the diocese of Kilmore.

Mhaoilin, aincioiaconur Oilernenrir, uin ppouioun
et oircpetur, qui capnem ruam iemunir et opacioni-
bur macerabat, qui pauperer et oprannor oerenoe-
bat, qui pacientiam et coponam obreruabat, qui
perrecutionem a multir pnopten iurtitiam patiebatur, uenerabilir funoaton monarterionum Sancte
Cpinitatir pen totam hibenniam, et rpecialiten
funoaton monarteru Sancte Cpinitatir apuo Loé Cé,
ubi locum ribi repultune elegit, ibioem in Cpirto
quieuit rapato Oominice Pentecorter, cuiur anime ppo-
picietun Oeur Omnipotenr in celo cui ipre rerunit
in reculo, in cuiur honope eccleriam oe Rinn ouin et
monarterium rancte Cpinitatir apuo Loé Uachtair,
eccleriam rancte Cpinitatir [apuo] CCé inoige, eccleriam rancte Cpinitatir apuo Cill Rair eoiricauit.
Zillamochoinne, mac Zillamoéoinne h Chathail, oo
inanbao la Conchoban mac CCooa mic Cathail cpoib-
oerg. Caog, mac Tuathail, mic Muircertaig Muimnig
hi Conchobaip, oo manbao oo Zalloib irin ·mbliaoain
rin. Zilla Cpirt .h. Lachtnán, ab na Cpinóioe a
Cuaim, oo báohao an muin Epenn. Conchoban mac
Copmaic mic Chomaltaig, rói enig ocur engnuma a
aimreni, in Cpirto quieuit. Zepalt rucaé moptuur
ert Flaithbertach .h. Cepbaill, toirrech Callpaige,
oo inanbao la hCCprt mac CCirt hi Ruairc. Muireoh-
ach .h. Caog moptuur ert. Toirnech ocur tentecha
oo teacht a ramrao na bliaona ri, gup manbao oaoine
ocur inoile imba in Epinn. Ciaé mór oo rerthain lá
feli Poil ocur Petair, gup imthig etan moptimceal in

1 *Archidiaconus* aincioiacuur
for archidiaconus, MS. In the O'Reilly
pedigree, (MS. in the office of the
Ulster King at Arms, Dublin Castle),
Clarus Mac Mailin is said to have
been bishop of Kilmore, "monasterium
fundavit Cathaldus [O'Reilly, occisus
1256], in quadam insula sacra Sanctæ
Trinitatis (anglicè Trinity Island),

quæ lacu, ab Hibernis vocato Loch
Oughter, insidet, cui coenobio struendo
ac dotandose patronum præbuit Clarus
Mac Mailin *postea episcopus Kilmo-
rensis.*" But his name is not given
in any list of the bishops of that See
accessible to the Editor. He may have
succeeded Conghalach Mac Idhneoil,
whose death is above recorded under

Mac Mailin, archidiaconus[1] Oilfinnensis, vir providus et
discretus, qui carnem suam jejuniis et orationibus[2] macerabat; qui pauperes et orphanos defendebat; qui patientiam[3] et coronam observabat; qui persecutionem a multis
propter justitiam patiebatur;[4] venerabilis fundator[5]
monasteriorum[6] Sanctæ Trinitatis per totam Hiberniam,
et specialiter fundator[5] monasterii Sanctæ Trinitatis[7] apud
Loch-Cé, ubi locum sibi[8] sepulturæ elegit,[9] ibidem in
Christo quievit Sabbato Dominicæ Pentecostes; cujus
animæ propitietur Deus · omnipotens in cœlo, cui ipse
servivit in sæculo; in cujus honore ecclesiam de Rinn-
duin et monasterium Sanctæ Trinitatis apud Loch-Uachtair, ecclesiam Sanctæ Trinitatis [apud] Ath-Moighe,
ecclesiam Sanctæ Trinitatis apud Cill-Rais, ædificavit.
Gillamochoinne, son of Gillamochoinne O'Cathail was slain
by Conchobhar, son of Aedh, son of Cathal Crobhderg.
Tadhg, son of Tuathal, son of Muirchertach Muimhnech
O'Conchobhair, was killed by Foreigners in this year.
Gillachrist O'Lachtnain, abbot of the Trinity in Tuaim, was
drowned in the sea of Erinn. Conchobhar, son of Cormac,
son of Tomaltach, the most bountiful and valiant man of
his time, in Christo quievit. Gerald Sugach[10] mortuus est.
Flaithbhertach O'Cerbhaill, chieftain of Callraighe, was
slain by Art, son of Art O'Ruairc. Muiredhach O'Taidhg
mortuus est. Thunder and lightning came in the summer
of this year, by which many men and cattle were killed in
Erinn. A great shower fell on the festival day of Paul
and Peter, so that a boat sailed all round the town at

A.D.
[1251.]

1250, although the next in Ware's list
is Simon O'Ruairc, who obtained the
Royal assent on the 20th of June, 1251.

[2] *Orationibus.* opoinbuṗ, MS.

[3] *Patientiam.* paciencꞮam, MS.

[4] *Patiebatur.* pacꞮebaꞇuṗ, MS.

[5] *Fundator.* ꞅonꝺaꞇoṗ, MS.

[6] *Monasteriorum.* monaṗꞇeṗꞮꞮ, MS.

[7] *Trinitatis.* ꞇṗꞮneꞇaꞇꞮṗ, MS.

[8] *Sibi.* ṗꞮbe, MS.

[9] *Elegit.* eꞁeꞃꞮꝺ, MS.

[10] *Gerald Sugach;* i.e. "Gerald the
Merry." Apparently a member of
the noble family of Fitzgerald, and
possibly the son of Gerald, first Baron
of Offaly. See *The Earls of Kildare,*
by the Marquis of Kildare; Dublin,
1858, p. 11.

baile uile a Cill móin na Sinna, ocur co melpeoh muilionn an an rput do bí on rouaio co hCCt na raitte, fri re na herpartan do rada, a tempal Frónacha irin ló ceona. Tuimmilin Caipóin do ballad ocur a tenga do bein arr. Sic món irin ceo gempet gur teachtrat na Loča, ocur na móinte, ocur na huirceda uile. Senad món do denum do čleirčib Erenn a Tuaim. Arogal .h. Laitbertaig, rigdamna Oiliž, coinnel gairoi ocur enig tuaircert Erenn, mortuur ert. Gilla Crirt .h.Oreirr-len, tóirech Fánad, ocur bratair do, dó marbad la Ceallač mbalb .h. mbaigill. Donnchadh mac Catmaoil, tóirech Cheneóil bFeradaigh, do marbad dOirgiallaib.

Kt. Enáir for Luan, ocur cuiced dhec fuirre; xii. anno cicli rolarir; xuiii. anno decennouenalir cicli; x. anno indictionir. M.cc.L.ii. Monad nua dordugad do rig Saxan do denum an Erinn, ocur tréceď an airgid do bí roime air rin. Gaot món do tocht in octaid na hepifania, gur trarcair tige ocur templa imda in Erinn uile. Cairlén Caoil uirci do denum la Mac Muirir. Cairlen Mhuige Coba do denum leir beor. Moelmaodoc .h. beolláin, comarba Coluim Cille a nDruim cliab, .i. an fer ba mó rat ocur conáč ocur cáďur, ocur ba mó almra ocur enech, ocur onoir na aimrer fein in Erinn, do héc iar mbuaidh náirme ocur naitrige. Cúconnacht mac Conrnama, tóirech Mhuinteri Cinait, mortuur ert. Gilla Irra .h. Cer-baill, tóirech Callraighe Droma cliab, mortuur ert. Magnur Mac Gilladuib, toirrech Tellaig Ghairbet, quieuit. Terbach món ocur tirmač i rampad na bliadna rin, co teigóir tar Sinuinn gen fliuchad a cor, ocur an

---

¹ *Tuimmilin Carden.* This name is written Tui mil Caipoi in the orig.; but Tuimlin Caipoin in the so-called Annals of Connacht. Mageoghegan, in his version of the Annals of Clon-macnois, writes it Tom Miles Carden.

² *Balbh;* i.e. "the stammering;" Lat., balbus.

³ *Erinn.* The note tearbač món in hoc anno, i.e. "great heat in hoc anno," has been added in the margin by the scribe.

Cill-mor-na-Sinna, and that a mill could grind on the stream which ran from the arch to Ath-na-faithche, during the time the vespers were being chaunted in the church of Fidhnacha, on the same day. Tuimmilin Carden[1] was blinded; and his tongue was cut out. Great frost in the early winter, so that the lakes, and the bogs, and the waters were all frozen. A great synod was held by the clergy of Erinn at Tuaim. Ardghal O'Laithbhertaigh, royal heir of Oilech, lamp of valour and honor of the North of Erinn, mortuus est. Gillachrist O'Breislen, chieftain of Fánad, and a brother of his, were killed by Ceallach Balbh[2] O'Baighill. Donnchadh Mac Cathmhail, chieftain of Cenel-Feradhaigh, was killed by the Oirghialla.

The kalends of January on Monday, and the fifteenth of the moon; xii. anno cycli solaris; xviii. anno Decennovenalis cycli; x. anno Indictionis; M.CC.lii. New money was ordered by the king of the Saxons to be coined in Erinn; and the money previously in use was abandoned for it. Great wind came on the octave of the Epiphany, which prostrated several houses and churches throughout Erinn.[3] The castle of Cael-uisce[4] was erected by Mac Maurice.[5] The castle of Magh-Cobha was erected by him also. Maelmaedhoc O'Beollain, comarb of Colum-Cille in Druim-cliabh, i.e. the man of greatest prosperity, wealth, and esteem, of greatest charity, hospitality, and honor in his own time in Erinn, died after the triumph of devotion and penitence. Cuconnacht Mac Consnamha, chieftain of Muinter-Cinaith, mortuus est. Gilla-Isa O'Cerbhaill, chieftain of Callraighe of Druim-cliabh, mortuus est. Maghnus Mac Gilladhuibh, chieftain of Tellach-Gairbhith, quievit. Great heat and drought in the summer of this year, so that people used to cross the Sinuinn without

---

[4] *Cael-uisce.* "Narrow - water," between Warrenpoint and Newry, in the county of Down.

[5] *Mac Maurice*; i.e. Maurice Fitzgerald, second Baron of Offaly.

cruiṫnecht ag á buain fiche oiḋċe ria Luġnasad, ocus ant arbar uile ag á ḃuain in tan sin; ocus na croinn ag a loscad ag an ngréin. Sloiged mór la Gallaib Erenn i nUltoib, dá tarla imresain ḟorlongpuirt idir in rúta Midhech ocus in rutta Muimnech, gur marbad sochaide don rútai Muimnech annsin a nDún Dealgan. Murchad .h. Fallamain, ard ċonsdápla do Ċonnachtaiḃ, do marbad do seruiḃ Ḃreifni, per dolum, a bFhiḋnacha Mhoiġe Réin. Orlaiṫ, ingen Taiḋlig Mic Diarmada, mortua est. Conchobar Mac Caṫṁaoil, ri ṫoísech Chenecóil bFeradaig ocus ṫuaṫ nimḃa eli, ocus fer síṫe Conallaċ ocus Eoganaċ ocus Oirgíalla, do ṁarbad la rútaib Ḃríain hI Neill, ocus sé ag cosnum comairce friu, ocus é féin ar slanacus hI Ghairmleghaigh ocus hI Chaṫáin. Conchobar .h. Doċartaigh, rí ṫaissech Arda Miḋair, ocus tress rí ṫaissech na hErenn, tuir einiġ ocus engnuma in tuaiscert, dfagail ḃáis an ḃliaḋain sin.

Kt. Enáir for Cedaoin, ocus seiseḋ fiched fuirre; xiii. anno cicli solaris; xix. anno decennouenalis [cicli]; xi. anno indictionis. M.cc.l. tertio. Sloiged mór la Gallaiḃ Erenn fá Mac Muiris, i Cénel Eogain, dinnsoiged I Neill, ocus ní ro ġabsat geill iná edire don dula sin a Cénel Eogain, ocus tucaḋ ár díairṁe forra. Dáuid mac Ceallaig .h. Ghillaṗadraic, airdepsuc C[luana mic Nois], quieuit. Eogan .h. hEḋin, rí .h. bFhiacrach, mortuus est. Gilla Ceallaigh .h. Rúaiḋin, epsuc hUi bFhiacrach, mortuus est. Macraiṫ, mac Gillaċálma .h. Chónnachtaiġ, do marbad la mac Ua Galonn. Ingen in iarla Ultaiġ, .i. ben Mhílid Mic

1 *Defending his guarantee.* That is to say, defending persons whom he had engaged to protect.

2 *The third;* i.e. as regards reputation.

3 *Tertio.* tercio, MS.

4 *C[luain-mic-Nois].* This name is represented by the letter c in the MS.; but the Four Masters write the name in full. David O'Gillapatraic is not mentioned in Ware's list of the bishops of Clonmacnois.

5 *Ui-Fiachrach;* i.e. Ui-Fiachrach-Aidhne, in the county of Galway.

wetting their feet; and the wheat was reaped twenty nights before Lammas, and all the corn was reaped at that time; and the trees were burning from the sun. A great hosting by the Foreigners of Erinn to Ulidia, on which occasion a camp fight took place between the Meathian rout and the Momonian rout, when a great number of the Momonian rout were slain at Dun-Dealgan. Murchadh O'Fallamhain, a high constable of the Connachtmen, was killed by the men of Breifne, per dolum, at Fidhnacha of Magh-Rein. Orlaith, daughter of Taichlech Mac Diarmada, mortua est. Conchobhar Mac Cathmhail, king-chieftain of Cenel-Feradhaigh and many other territories, peacemaker of the *Cenel*-Conaill, *Cenel*-Eoghain, and Oirghialla, was slain by the routs of Brian O'Neill, whilst defending his guarantee[1] against them, he himself being under the protection of O'Gairmleghaigh and O'Cathain. Conchobhar O'Dochartaigh, king-chieftain of Ard-Midhair, and the third[2] king-chieftain of Erinn, pillar of the hospitality and bravery of the North, died this year.

The kalends of January on Wednesday, and the twenty-sixth of the moon; xiii. anno cycli solaris; xix. anno Decennovenalis cycli; xi. anno Indictionis; M.cc.l.tertio.[3] A great hosting by the Foreigners of Erinn, under Mac Maurice, to Cenel-Eoghain, to attack O'Neill; and they obtained neither pledges nor hostages in Cenel-Eoghain on this occasion; and a countless slaughter was inflicted on them. David, son of Ceallach O'Gillapatraic, archbishop of C[luain-mic-Nois],[4] quievit. Eoghan O'hEdhin, king of Ui-Fiachrach,[5] mortuus est. Gilla-Ceallaigh O'Ruaidhin, bishop of Ui-Fiachrach,[6] mortuus est. Macraith, son of Gillachalma O'Connachtaigh, was slain by the son of O'Galonn. The daughter of the Ultonian Earl

---

[6] *Bishop of Ui-Fiachrach.* That is to say, bishop of Killala, which diocese includes the territory anciently called Ui-Fiachrach-Muaidhe, or Hy-Fiach- rach of the Moy (now the barony of Tireragh, co. Sligo), which is to be distinguished from the Ui-Fiachrach in the line preceding.

Ʒoirdelḃ, do ég, et ṛepulta[1] eṛt a mainṛtiṛ na
buille. Mainṛtiṛ do ḋenum, ocuṛ ṛelic do ċoiṛeṛʒaḋ,
dona bṛaiṫṛiḃ ṗṛeiciúṛ a Sliʒech. Mainṛtiṛ oile
do ṫóṛainneḋ dona bṛaiṫṛiḃ aʒ Aṫ lethan a Luiʒni.
Coʒaḋ móṛ do ḋenum do Uṛían .h. Neill, do ṛíʒ
Cheneóil Eoʒain, aṛ Ʒhallaib, ocuṛ caiṛléna imḋa do
ṛcaoileḋ ḋó, ocuṛ ʒṛáid ḃaileḋa do loṛcaḋ, ocuṛ
Maċaiṛe Ulaḋ uile do ṛolṁuʒaḋ ḋó. Eṛpucoide
Chille hAlaiḋ do ʒaḃáil do Shean .h. Láidiʒ, .i.
bṛaṫaiṛ ṗṛeiciúṛ, ocuṛ a ʒṛáḋa eṛpuic do ṫabaiṛt a
Tuaim ḋá ʒualann an daṛa Domnach don ʒemċoṛʒuṛ.
Eṛpucoidi Chluana mic Noiṛ do ʒaḃáil do Thomaṛ .h.
Chuinn, .i. bṛaṫaiṛ minúṛ, ocuṛ a ʒṛáḋa do ṫabaiṛt a
cúiṛt in Pháṛa. Sluaiʒeḋ do ḋenum do Domnall .h.
Raiʒilliʒh, ocuṛ don ċaoċ .h. Raiʒilliʒh, ocuṛ do
Chaṫal .h. Conchobaiṛ, ocuṛ do Ʒhilla na naom .h.
Feṛʒuil, a Muintiṛ Eoluiṛ dinnṛoiʒed Chaṫail Mhéʒ
Raʒnuill, ʒuṛ aiṛʒred in tiṛ uile; ocuṛ do ḃadaṛ dá
oiḋċe a Tolaiʒ Alainn a bṛoṛlonʒpoṛt, ocuṛ an
tṛeṛṛ oiḋċe aʒ Enach ḋuiḃ, ocuṛ do ḋeliʒ Ʒilla na
naom .h. Feṛʒuil ṛṛiu annṛin, ocuṛ do ċuadaṛ Muinteṛ Raiʒilliʒh ocuṛ Caṫal .h. Conchobaiṛ co Cluain
Conmaicne, ocuṛ do ḃadaṛ aʒhaid a lonʒpoṛt innti.
Od ċuala, imoṛṛo, Aoḋ mac Feḋlim anní ṛin, do ṛóine
tinol co tinneṛnach, ocuṛ ṛo len ṛé Muinteṛ Raiʒilliʒh ocuṛ Caṫal Ua Conchobaiṛ ʒo Cluain Conmaicne,
ocuṛ tuc bṛeaṛṁaiḋm ṛoṛṛa, ʒuṛ maṛbad ann Donnchaḋ, mac Ʒilla Iṛa mic Donnchaḋa I Raiʒilliʒh,
ocuṛ Mac Ʒilla Thaoḋóc, ocuṛ .h. biḃṛaiʒ, et alii
multi. Uliadain iṛ ṛeṛṛ tanic ṛiam in ḃliadain ṛin
etiṛ meṛ ocuṛ toṛad talman ocuṛ eallaiʒ, ocuṛ ṛíḋ-
baide, ocuṛ luibe. Ailín .h. Súilleḃán, eṛpuc Leṛṛa

---

1 *Sepulta.* ṛepultuṛ, MS.

2 *Street-towns.* See note 6, p. 258, *supra.*

3 *Machaire-Uladh*; i.e., "the plain

of Uladh," the level part of the present county of Down.

4 *The Caech*; i.e. "the Blind;" caech =Lat. cæcus.

5 *Mac Gilla-Taedog and O'Bibh-*

i.e. the wife of Milidh Mac Goisdelbh, died, et sepulta[1] est in the monastery of the Buill. A monastery was erected, and a cemetery consecrated, for the Friars Preachers at Sligech. Another monastery was founded for the Friars at Ath-lethan, in Luighne. A great war was waged by Brian O'Neill, king of Cenel-Eoghain, against the Foreigners; and he demolished several castles; and street-towns[2] were burned, and Machaire-Uladh[3] was entirely desolated by him. The bishopric of Cill-hAlaidh was assumed by John O'Laidigh, i.e. a Friar Preacher; and his degree of bishop was conferred at Tuaim-dhá-ghualann, the second Sunday of Lent. The bishopric of Cluain-mic-Nois was assumed by Thomas O'Cuinn, i.e. a Friar Minor; and his degree was conferred at the Pope's court. A hosting was performed by Domhnall O'Raighilligh, and by the Caech[4] O'Raighilligh, and by Cathal O'Conchobhair, and by Gilla-na-naemh O'Ferghail, to Muinter-Eolais, to attack Cathal Mac Raghnail, when they plundered the whole country; and they were two nights encamped at Tulach-alainn, and the third night at Enach-dubh, where Gilla-na-naemh O'Ferghail separated from them; and Muinter-Raighilligh and Cathal O'Conchobhair went to Cluain-Conmaicne, where they were encamped for one night. When Aedh, son of Fedhlim, heard this thing, he suddenly assembled his forces, and followed Muinter-Raighilligh and Cathal O'Conchobhair to Cluain-Conmaicne, and inflicted a signal defeat on them, where Donnchadh, son of Gilla-Isa, son of Donnchadh O'Raighilligh, and Mac Gilla-Taedóg, and O'Bibhsaigh,[5] et alii[6] multi, were slain. This was the best year that had ever come for nuts, and the produce of the earth, and of cattle, and of trees and herbs. Ailin O'Suillebháin, bishop of Lis-mór, quievit.

saigh. By the omission of the conjunction ocur (and) the Four Masters convert these two names into one, "mac ᵹilla τaoδóc .h. biħraiᵹ," | "the son of Gilla-Taedog O'Bibhsaigh;" which is probably correct. See note 8, p. 405.

[6] Alii. alı, MS.

móip, quieuiт. Cuipт do denum do Comalтach .h.
Conchobaip, eppuc Olepinn, a Cill тSheipin in hoc anno.

Jctt. Enáip pop dapdaoin, ocup peachтmad hua-
тhad puippe; xiiii. annuр cicli polapiр; ppimuр
annuр decennouenaliр cicli; xii. annuр indicтioniр;
M.cc.l.quapтo. Piappuр Ppamiртеp, тigepna Conmaicni Dhúna móip, mopтuuр eрт. Mupchad .h.
Maoilpechlainn do mhapbad do Domnall mac anт Shin-
naig hi Chaтapnaig ipin bliadain pin. Iupóip na
hEpenn do dul a Saxanaib. Maniртip na mbpaтhap
ppeiciuр ag Cchт Leтhan a Luigne do lopcad uile.
Piappuр Riртubapd, тigepna тShil Maolpúain, ocuр
bapún uapal, do mapbad la Mupchad .h. Maoilpechlainn ap Loch Riъ. Siтpiuc Mhág Shenlaich do gabáil
do Phédlim mac Caтhail cpoibdepg, ocuр an pen puilech
Mhág Shenlaoich do dallad do ap lop anhlepра, .i.
apad piр guр peallpaт paip. Rí Saxan do dul ipin
Sbáin ap pluaiged in hoc anno. Maolbpígde mac in
eppuic .h. Maolpágmhaip mopтuuр eрт. Maolpinnén
.h. beolláin, comapba Dpoma cliab, mopтuuр eрт.
Donnchadh, mac Donnchadha mic Thomalтaig, ocuр
Cchláib .h. bibpaig do mhapbad a Cluain Conmaicne
la Connachтuib. Magnuр .h. gaдpa do mhapbad тpe
anpochain do muinтеp mic Pedlim hi Chonchobaip.
Ri Ppanc do doigechт тap aiр ó niapupolem ipin
Ppainc, iap ndenam pída тpi mbliadan idiр na Cpiр-
daigib ocuр na Saipipdinib. Bliadain po mhaiъ in
bliadain pin, co nimad daipmерpа ocuр co nimad
lachтa, ocuр gach maiъepai apchena. Cp móр do

¹ Hoc. oc, MS.

² Pramister. This is an unusually
corrupt form of the family name
"Bermingham."

³ The Sinnach; lit. "the Fox;" a
sobriquet by which the chiefs of the
sept of O'Catharnaigh (or O'Kearney)
of Teffia were known, and which
ultimately was adopted as the surname
of the principal branch of the family.

See Miscellany of the Irish Archæol.
Soc., pp. 184-9.

⁴ Ristubhard. Rectè de Ridelisford.
See note ⁸, p. 320, supra.

⁵ Sen-shuilech; lit. "old-eyed."

⁶ To Spain. The expedition of
Henry III. to Gascony, in 1253, is
probably referred to; or perhaps the
journey of Prince Edward to Spain
in the following year, to espouse

A mansion was erected by Tomaltach O'Conchobhair, bishop of Oilfinn, at Cill-tSheisin, in hoc[1] anno.

The kalends of January on Thursday, and the seventh of the moon; xiiii. annus cycli solaris; primus annus Decennovenalis cycli; xii. annus Indictionis; M.CC.L.quarto. Piers Pramister,[2] lord of Conmaicne of Dún-mór, mortuus est. Murchadh O'Maelsechlainn was slain by Domhnall, son of the Sinnach[3] O'Catharnaigh, in this year. The Justiciary of Erinn went to Saxon-land. The monastery of the Friars Preachers at Ath-lethan, in Luighne, was all burned. Piers Ristubhard,[4] lord of Sil-Maelruain, and a noble baron, was killed by Murchadh O'Maelsechlainn on Loch-Ribh. Sitric Mac Shenlaich was taken prisoner by Fedhlim, son of Cathal Crobhderg, and the Sen-shuilech[5] Mac Shenlaich was unnecessarily blinded by him; i.e. it was reported to him that they had acted treacherously towards him. The king of the Saxons went to Spain[6] on a hosting in hoc anno. Maelbrighde, son of the Bishop O'Mailfhaghmhair, mortuus est. Maelfinnen O'Beollain, comarb of Druim-cliabh, mortuus est. Donnchadh, son of Donnchadh,[7] son of Tomaltach, and Amhlaibh O'Bibhsaigh,[8] were slain in Cluain-Conmaicne by the Connachtmen. Maghnus O'Gadhra was slain without cause by the people of Fedhlim O'Conchobhair. The king of France returned from Jerusalem to France, after concluding a three years' peace between the Christians and the Saracens. This year was an excellent year, with abundance of oak-fruit, and with abundance of milk, and of all other good things besides. A great slaughter

Eleanor of Castile, is intended. Under the year 1264, *infra*, King Henry III. is called "Edward."

[7] *Son of Donnchadh.* This entry seems to be a repetition of the one under the preceding year, where Donnchadh is said to have been the son of

Gilla-Isa, son of another Donnchadh (O'Raighilligh).

[8] *Amhlaibh O'Bibhsaigh.* Apparently the person who is called " the son of Gilla-Taedog O'Bibhsaigh" by the Four Mast., under the year 1253. See note [5], p. 402.

čabaiṗc aṗ macaiḃ Mic Caṗṗgamna, ocuṗ aṗ Mhuin-
ceṗ Maoilḟinna, ꝺo Muinceṗ Ṡhillcan ocuṗ ꝺo Ṡhalloiḃ.

ⱪⱦ. Enaiṗ ꝼoṗ Aine, ocuṗ ochcmaꝺ ꝺhéc ꝼuiṗṗe; xu.
annuṗ cicli ꝼolaṗiṗ; ṗecunꝺuṗ annuṗ ꝺecennouenaliṗ
cicli; xiii. annuṗ inꝺiccioniṗ; M.cc.L.quinco. Innocen-
ciuṗ papa quieuiɫ in Cṗiṡco. Comaṡ mac Ꝺiaṗmaꝺa,
aiṗčiꝺiaconuṗ Oleꝼinn, in Cṗiṡco quieuiɫ. Aoꝺ mac
Ꝼeꝺlim hi Chonchobaiṗ ꝺo ꝺul a Cíṗ Eoɡain, ocuṗ ṗíč ꝺo
ꝺenum ꝺó eꞇiṗ a achaiṗ ꝼein ocuṗ ꞇuaiṗceṗc Eṗenn,
ocuṗ aṗaiḃe ꝼo Chonnachcaiḃ aṗ eiṗíčh a ꞇuaiṗceṗc
Eṗenn ó n[a] achaiṗ ꝺo čabaiṗc leiṗ ꝺo aꞇuaiꝺ, cona
nimiṗɡiḃ, cṗe láṗ a ꝺeṗɡ namaꝺ, .i. mec Ruaiꝺṗi i
Chonchobaiṗ ocuṗ Ṡaill, ocuṗ ni laṁḃaoiṗ na naimꝺe
ṗin achc ꝼaiṗeṗin inꞇ ꝼluaiɡ ocuṗ na nimiṗeio laiṁ
ṗiú. Aiṗꝺeṗpuꝼcoiꝺe Chaiṗṗil Mhuman ꝺo ɡaḃáil ꝺo
Mac Ceṗḃaill. Ceachꞇa Ꝼeꝺlim hi Conchobaiṗ ꝺo
ꝺul ꝺočum ṗi Sacṗan. Maꞇɡamain .h. Mannačán ꝺo
ṁaṗḃaꝺ aɡ ꝺuimlinn. Aiṗ[ꝺ]eṗpuc Cuama, .i.
Ꝼloiṗenꞅ Mháɡ Ꝼloinn, ꝺo ꝺul ꞇaiṗiṗ ꝼaiṗ ꝺaɡallam
ṗiɡ Saxan. Muiṗiꞅ Mac Ɡeṗailꞇ ꝺo ꝺul ꞇaiṗiṗ a cenꝺ
ṗiɡ Sacṗan. Ꝺiaṗmaiꝺ .h. Chuinn ocuṗ Aṁláiḃ a
mac ꝺo ṁaṗḃaꝺ, ocuṗ maiɫi Mhuinceṗi Ɡillcan maille
ꝼṗiú ꝺo ṁaṗḃaꝺ aɡ ꝼaṗaḃan Mhuiɡe Cṗeɡa, ꝺo
Ṡhilla na naom .h. Ꝼeṗɡail, ꝼeṗ ꝺolum; ocuṗ a
naṗɡain ꝺó iaṗṗin. Aiṗꝺeṗpuc Cuama ꝺo ceachc in
Eṗinn on ṗí, ocuṗ ɡach ní ꝺaṗ íaṗ ꝺṗaɡail ꝺó. Ceachꞇa
Ꝼeꝺlim ꝺo čeachc in Eṗinꝺ on ṗí muṗ an ceꝺna.
Oiṗčiꝺechain Enaiɡ ꝺúin, .i. .h. Láiꝺiɡ, quieuiɫ in
Cṗiṡco. Cṗeač ṁóṗ ꝺo ꝺenam ꝺo Ṡhalloiḃ aṗ .h.
ḃꝼhloinn. Conne ṁóṗ eꞇiṗ .h. Conchobaiṗ ocuṗ Mac
Uilliam ḃúṗc aɡ cochaṗ Mhónaꝺ Coinneaꝺa, ocuṗ
ṗíč ꝺo ꝺenum ꝺóiḃ annṗin, ocuṗ ɡach ꝺáil imá ṗaiḃe

---

1 *Innocentius.* innocencicuṗ, MS.

2 *Archidiaconus.* aiṗčiꝺiaconuṗ, MS.

3 *Mortal.* ꝺeṗɡ; lit. "red," MS.

4 *Caisel-Mumhan;* i.e. Caisel of Munster, or Cashel in the county of Tipperary.

5 *To the East.* That is, to England.

was inflicted on the sons of Mac Cargahmna, and on Muinter-Maelshinna, by Muinter-Gillgan and the Foreigners.

The kalends of January on Friday, and the eighteenth of the moon; xv. annus cycli solaris; secundus annus Decennovenalis cycli; xiii. annus Indictionis; M.cc.l. quinto. Innocentius[1] papa quievit in Christo. Thomas Mac Diarmada, archidiaconus[2] of Oilfinn, in Christo quievit. Aedh, son of Fedhlim O'Conchobhair, went into Tir-Eoghain, and made peace between his own father and the North of Erinn, and brought with him from the North all the Connachtmen who were in the North of Erinn in discord with his father, together with their chattels, through the midst of his mortal[3] enemies, viz. :—the sons of Ruaidhri O'Conchobhair and the Foreigners ; and these enemies dared no more than look at the host, and the chattels by their side. The archbishopric of Caisel-Mumhan[4] was assumed by Mac Cerbhaill. The ambassadors of Fedhlim O'Conchobhair went to the king of the Saxons. Mathghamhain O'Mannachain was slain at Buimlinn. The archbishop of Tuaim, i.e. Florence Mac Floinn, went across to the East,[5] to converse with the king of the Saxons. Maurice Fitz-Gerald went across to meet the king of the Saxons. Diarmaid O'Cuinn, and Amhlaibh his son, and the nobles of Muinter-Gillgan along with them, were slain at Faradhan-Muighe-Tregha by Gilla-na-naemh O'Ferghail, per dolum; and he afterwards plundered them (i.e. *Muinter-Gillgan*). The archbishop of Tuaim came to Erinn from the king, having obtained everything that he asked. The ambassadors of Fedhlim came to Erinn from the king, in like manner. The archdeacon of Enach-dúin, i.e. O'Laidigh, quievit in Christo. A great depredation was committed by the Foreigners on O'Floinn. A great meeting was held between O'Conchobhair and Mac William Burc, at Tochar-mona-Coinnedha; and they concluded a peace there, and all

.h. Conchobaiṗ ⁊o leᵹaⱱ leiṗ. Iuliana, inᵹen čomaṗba Chaillín, ocuṗ ᵹilla na noem, mac in čomaṗba, moṗtui ṗunt. Dṗían .h. Neill ocuṗ tuaiṗceṗt Eṗenn ⁊o čoiᵹecht ṗlóiᵹeⱱ móṗ aṗ Chathal .h. Raiᵹilliᵹh, ocuṗ ⁊ocum Chonconnacht hi Raiᵹhilliᵹh, ocuṗ ⁊o impáiṗiot ᵹan neṗt ᵹan ᵹialla ⁊o ṗⱱoiṗ. Raᵹnailt, inᵹen hi Pheṗᵹail, ⁊o éc i n⁊abaiᵹ ṗotṗaictí in hoc anno.

Ḱt. Enaiṗ ṗoṗ Sataṗn, ocuṗ .ix. ṗicheⱱ ṗuiṗṗe; xiii. anno cicli ṗolaṗiṗ; teṗtiuṗ annuṗ ⁊ecennouenaliṗ cicli; xiii. anno in⁊ictioniṗ; M.cc.l.ṗeato. Plann Mac Ploinn, aiṗⱱeṗpuc Tuama, ⁊o héc a mⱱṗioṗtoma. Aṗⱱeṗpuc Dhaile Ata cliat ⁊o héc in ⱱliaⱱain ceⱱna. Ruai⁊ṗi .h.ᵹa⁊ṗa, ṗiᵹ Sleⱱe Luᵹa, ⁊o ṁaṗbaⱱ ⁊á čaiṗⱱeṗ Cṗiṗt ṗein, .i. ⁊aui⁊ mac Ricaiṗ⁊ Cuiṗín, a ṗill ocuṗ a meⱱuil, ocuṗ a čaiṗlen ⁊o bṗiṗṗeⱱ in tan ṗin ⁊ó. Sloiᵹeⱱ aⱱⱱal ṁóṗ ⁊o ⱱenum la Uáteṗ mac Ricaiṗ⁊ mic Uilliam Dúṗc, ⁊ocum Peⱱlim mic Cathail cṗoiⱱ⁊eṗᵹ, ocuṗ ⁊ocom a mic, .i. Aoⱱ mac Péⱱlim, ocuṗ co mic Tiᵹeṗnáin i Ruaiṗc; ocuṗ iṗ imčian ṗoime ṗin ṗo tinólaⱱ a comliniṁaṗ ⁊it ṗlúaiᵹ ṗin an Eṗinn, oiṗ iṗeⱱh ṗo haiṗmeⱱh annṗin .i. ṗiche míle aṗ áiṗeṁ aoinṗiṗ; ocuṗ tanᵹa⁊aṗ na ṗluaᵹ lánṁóṗa ṗin ᵹo Maᵹ neó na Saṗanach, ocuṗ aṗṗiⱱe ᵹo Dalla, ocuṗ aṗṗiⱱe aṗ ṗu⁊ Luiᵹne, ocuṗ ṗo aiṗᵹṗeⱱ Luiᵹne aṗ ᵹach leit ina timčell; ocuṗ tanco⁊aṗ co hАcha⁊ Conaiṗe; ocuṗ ⁊o čuiṗṗet teachta aṗṗin uathaib ⁊innṗoiᵹeⱱ Mhuinnteṗi Raiᵹilliᵹh, ocuṗ a⁊uⱱṗa⁊aṗ ṗú tocht na coinne ᵹo cṗoiṗ ⁊oiṗe čaoin ṗoṗ cinn aiṗteṗach Dṗaitṗleⱱe a Tíṗ Thuathail; ocuṗ tanᵹa⁊aṗ Muinteṗ Raiᵹilliᵹh co Clachan mucaⱱa ṗoṗ Sleⱱ an iaṗain,

---

[1] *Mortui sunt.* m. e., for moṗtuuṗ eṗt, MS. Instead of mac in čoṁaṗba ("son of the comarb") the Four Mast. say a ⁊eṗbṗathaiṗ, "her brother," [i.e. the brother of the comarb's daughter], which

O'Donovan inadvertently translates "his [the comarb's] brother."

[2] *Tertius.* teṗtiuṗ, MS.

[3] *Flann.* The Christian name of this ecclesiastic is written Floirens (or Florence) under the last year.

A.D.

[1255.]

[1256.]

O'Conchobhair's conditions were conceded to him. Juliana, daughter of the comarb of Caillin, and Gilla-na-naemh, son of the comarb, mortui sunt.[1] Brian O'Neill and *the men of* the North of Erinn came on a great hosting against Cathal O'Raighilligh, and against Cuconnacht O'Raighilligh; and they turned back again without *obtaining* power or hostages. Raghnailt, daughter of O'Ferghail, died in a bath in hoc anno.

The kalends of January on Saturday, and the twenty-ninth of the moon; xvi. anno cycli solaris; tertius[2] annus Decennovenalis cycli; xiiii. anno Indictionis; M.cc.l. sexto. Flann[3] Mac Floinn, archbishop of Tuaim, died in Bristol. The archbishop of Baile-Atha-cliath[4] died the same year. Ruaidhri O'Gadhra, king of Sliabh-Lugha, was slain by his own gossip,[5] i.e. David, son of Richard Cuisin, in treachery and deceit; and his castle was broken down by him at the same time. A prodigious hosting was made by Walter, son of Richard, son of William Burc, against Fedhlim, son of Cathal Crobhderg, and against his son, i.e. Aedh son of Fedhlim, and to the sons of Tighernan O'Ruairc; and it was a very long time before since a host so numerous as this was assembled in Erinn, for it was reckoned that there were in it twenty thousand to a man. And these great hosts marched to Magh-Eó of the Saxons, and from thence to Balla, and from thence throughout Luighne; and they plundered Luighne on all sides about them. And they came to Achadh-Conaire, and despatched messengers from thence to Muinter-Raighilligh, and requested them to come to meet them to Cros-Doire-chaein, at the eastern end of Brat-sliabh in Tir-Tuathail. And Muinter-Raighilligh came to Clachan-mucadha on Sliabh-an-iarainn, and then

---

"Flann," which means "blood," and "red," has also been anglicised "Florence" in other Irish families. See *Martyrology of Donegal*, ed. Todd and Reeves, Int., p. lv.; and O'Donovan's ed. of *O'Dubhagain's, &c., Topog. Poems,* Int., p. [68].

[4] *Baile-Atha-cliath;* i.e. Dublin. The Archbishop's name was Luke.

[5] *Gossip.* See note [8], p. 333, *supra.*

ocúr ро impaоар Muinсер Raɩ̄ɩllɩɡh annrin ɡan
čoinne оḟaɡaɩl ó Ɉhalloɩb; ocur сanсоσar arrin со
Soɩlсen nɡarán; ɡurab ɩrin lo ceσna rin .ɩ. σɩa hꞼoine
σо funnraσ, ocur lá ḟéle croɩr сar ɡach lá, ро čɩnóɩl
Concobar mac Cɩɡernáɩn 1 Ruaɩre fɩr Ḃhreɩfne ocur
Conmaɩcne, ocur an ṁeɩσ ро ḟéσ maɩlle friú, fa Ꞽoσ
hUa Conchobaɩr ocur maɩči Connachс ocur сríl
Muɩreɡhaɩɡh áɩrchena; ocur irɩaσ ba ferr ar an
rlóɩɡeσ rin, .ɩ. Cončobar mac Cɩɡernáɩn 1 Ruaɩrc, .ɩ.
rɩ .h. mḂruím ocur Conmaɩcni, ocur Cachal .h. Ʞlaɩč-
berсaɩ̄, ocur Murchaσ finn .h. Ꞙerɡaɩl, ocur Ruaσ
in feσa .h. Ꞙloɩnn, ocur Ꞙlann Mháɡ Oɩrechсaɩ̄, ocur
Σonn óɡ Mháɡ Oɩrechсaɩ̄, ocur cuɩσ ṁór σо сríl
Ceallaɩɡ; ocur сrɩ mɩc Mɩc Σɩarmaσa, ocur Σɩarmaɩσ
.h. Ꞙlannaɡáɩn, ocur Cathaɩl mac Σuarcáɩn 1 Eɡhra,
ocur σá mac Cɩɡernáɩn 1 Conchobaɩr, ocur Ɉɩlla na
naom hUa Caɩσɡ. Rob ɩmσa сrá σóɡbaɩσ Chonnachс
ann órin amach. Ocur ɩr ann ruc соrach inс flúaɩɡ
rin для Mhuɩnсer Raɩ̄ɩllɩɡh aɡ Soɩlсen nɡarán, ocur
ро lenraс ɩaσ со hꞼlс сɩ̄e Mhéɡ Cuɩrrín. Ir annrin
ро impaоσar ɡlarláɩč Mhuɩnсɩre Raɩɡhɩllɩɡh frɩrɩn
flúaɩɡ cechсarrσa rin, ocur сucraс сrɩ maσmanna
forrа. Ir annrin rucraσ in fluaɡ mór forrа ɩar
marbaσ čoσa σɩa muɩnсer, ɩm Σhɩarmaɩσ .h. bꞘhlann-
aɡaɩn, ocur ɩm Mac Maonaɩ̄, ocur ɩmm Choɩcle .h.
Choɩcle, ocur ɩm fochaɩσe aɩle, ocur сancaσar uɩle na
fluaɡ čechсarrσa rin ɡo hꞼlс na hélсɩ, ocur ɡo Σoɩrín
crannča ɩσɩr Ꞽč na beɩčɩ̄e ocur ḃél ɩn bhealaɩɡ,
ocur Coɩll erra, ocur Coɩll aɩrrсer for Sleɩḃ in
ɩaruɩnn; ocur ɩr annrin ро ɩmráσar Muɩnсer Raɩɡhɩllɩɡh ɡo σúr ocur ɡo σɩchra, σarráchсach, σɩčeɩllɩσ,
σormachсaɩ̄čɩ, anaɡhaɩσ mɩc Ꞙhéσlɩm ocur ɩnam bóɩ

'1 *Soilten-gasan.* This name is more
correctly written by the Four Masters
Saɩlсen ua nɡarán, i.e. "the *saillen*
of the paths."

2 *Cross.* The criteria here given
indicate that the important battle so
fully described took place in the
year 1256-7, in which year the

turned back without having obtained a meeting from the Foreigners, and went from thence to Soilten-gasan.[1] And it was on the same day, viz. :—Friday in particular, and the festival of the Cross[2] above all days, that Conchobhar, son of Tighernan O'Ruairc, mustered the men of Breifne and the Conmaicne, and as many as he could secure along with them, including Aedh O'Conchobhair and the nobles of Connacht, and the Sil-Muiredhaigh besides. And the bravest on this hosting were these, viz. :—Conchobhar, son of Tighernan O'Ruairc, i.e. king of Ui-Briuin and Conmaicne, and Cathal O'Flaithbhertaigh, and Murchadh Finn O'Ferghail, and Ruadh-in-fhedha[3] O'Floinn, and Flann Mac Oirechtaigh, and Donn Og Mac Oirechtaigh, and a great number of Sil-Ceallaigh, and the three sons of Mac Diarmada, and Diarmaid O'Flannagain, and Cathal, son of Duarcan O'hEghra, and the two sons of Tighernan O'Conchobhair, and Gilla-na-naemh O'Taidhg. And great, indeed, was the number of the young men of Connacht there besides. And where the van of this host overtook Muinter-Raighilligh was at Soilten-gasan,[1] and they followed them to Alt-tighe-Mic-Cuirrin, where the recruits of Muinter-Raighilligh turned upon this separate host, and three times routed them. Then the great army came up with them, after some of their people[4] had been slain, along with Diarmaid O'Flannagain, and Mac Maenaigh, and Coicle O'Coicle, and many more ; and these several armies all marched to Alt-na-hélti, and to Doirin-cranncha, between Ath-na-beithighe and Bél-in-bhealaigh, and between Coill-essa and Coill-airther on Sliabh-an-iarainn, where Muinter-Raighilligh turned sternly, earnestly, furiously, wildly, irrepressibly, against the son of Fedhlim and all the Connachtmen

---

festival of the Exaltation of the Cross (14th Sept.) fell upon Friday, the Dominical Letter being G. The battle is briefly recorded by the Four Mast. under the year 1256.

[3] *Ruadh-in-fhedha;* lit. "the red [man] of the wood."

[4] *Their people;* i.e. the people of O'Ruairc and his allies, who were in the van of the army.

do Chonnachtuiḃ maille fris, do ḋíġuil a négcórach ocus a nanḃḟorrain forra; ocus ro ġreis cáċ ḋíḃ a muinter a cenn a celi, .i. caṫ .h. mBriúin ocus Connachtaiġ. Is annsin ro erġedair Connachtuiġ don leiṫ araill don ċaṫ, ocus rob iadsin an drong ḋánata, ḋaġṫaraid, ḋíscir, ḋenmnedach; ocus ro ċóirġedar ina laom loindrech, lasamail, lamṫaraid iad, ocus ina cipṫi ċoṁḋluṫ, ċoḃraiġ, ċenguilti, fan óigri nurrúnta narm laidir, .i. fa Aoḋ mac Feḋlim mic Cathail croibderg. Acht chena bá fergbruṫ flaṫa, ocus ba coḃraiġecht ċuraḋ, ocus ba laoċdacht leoman la mac an airdríġ isin lá sin; ocus ro feraḋ caṫ croḋa coscorach curata do ḋíḃ leiṫiḃ etorra isin úair sin; ro marḃait ocus ro gonait sochaide anunn ocus anall cechtar do ḋíḃ leiṫiḃ. Acht chena ro fágbad ann Concobar mac Tigernáin, ri Breifne, ocus Murchad finn .h.Ferġail, ocus Aoḋ .h.Ferġail, ocus Maolruanaiḋ Mac Donnchada, ocus daoine imḋa eli do lot ar an láṫair sin, ocus drem díḃ do ḋul dhéc dá ngonaiḃ ina tiġiḃ, má Murchad ḟinn .h. Ferġail, ocus fá Fhlann Mhág Oirechtaiġ, ro marbaḋ a friṫġuin in ċaṫa sin, ocus sochaide eli maille fris. Acht chena, isedh adeirid lucht eoluis an ṁor ċaṫa sin, conár ḟédsat laṫgaile na garsraiġe sin, iná miliḋ in ṁór maḋma, fechain in aghaid in ard ḟlaṫa, uair do ḃádar da rí ċoinnil ro ṁóra ruiscleṫna ar lassad ocus ar luamain ina ċinn; ocus ba haḋḟuaṫ la cáċ compáḋ fris in tan sin, uair do ḃai uiḋe iomagallṁa riar na sluagaiḃ ag dul a gcenn ċaṫa .h. mBriuin, ocus ro léic a ḟoċann airdriġ ocus a ġréċ curad órr aird a meḋón an ṁór ċaṫa, ocus nir'an don reim ocus don ruathar sin gur

---

[1] *Son of Tighernan;* i.e. of Tighernan O'Ruairc.

[2] *Were left.* ro fágbad. This expression usually signifies "were lost," or slain.

[3] *Murchadh Finn O'Ferghail.* The text seems here somewhat confused, as this chieftain has just been represented as having been lost, or "left," on the field of battle, unless the words

who were along with him, to avenge upon them their
wrongs and oppressions ; and each party then incited
their people against the other, i.e. the battalion of the Ui-
Briuin and the Connachtmen. Then the Connachtmen
arose on one side of the battle—a bold, expert, precipitate,
impetuous band—and arrayed themselves in a glistening,
flaming, quick-handed phalanx, and in close, steady,
united bodies, under the valiant, strong-armed heir, i.e.
Aedh, son of Fedhlim, son of Cathal Crobhderg. (And,
certainly, the son of the chief king had the glowing fury
of a prince, the firmness of a champion, and the valour
of a lion, on that day.) And a brave, destructive, heroic
battle was fought, between them respectively in that
hour ; and multitudes were killed and wounded, here
and there, on both sides. And Conchobhár, son of
Tighernan,[1] king of Breifne, and Murchadh Finn
O'Ferghail, and Aedh O'Ferghail, and Maelruanaidh Mac
Donnchadha, were left[2] there ; and many more persons
were wounded on the spot ; and a number of them died
of their wounds in their houses, including Murchadh
Finn O'Ferghail,[3] and including Flann Mac Oirechtaigh,
who was slain in the counter-wounding of the battle,
and many more along with him. However, the witnesses[4]
of this great battle say that neither the warriors of these
bands, nor the champions of the great victory, could gaze
at the face of the arch-prince, for there were two broad-
eyed, enormous, royal torches flaming and rolling in his
head ; and every one feared to address him at the time,
for he was as far as the voice could reach before the hosts,
advancing against the battalions of the Ui-Briuin. And
he raised aloud his battle-cry of a chief king, and his
champion's shout, in the middle of the great battle, and
desisted not from this career and onset until the battalion

---

ro fágbaḋ (lit. "were left") be understood as meaning "left wounded."

[4] *Witnesses.* luchṫ eoluir; lit.
"people of knowledge ;" i.e. persons

who witnessed the battle, or derived
their knowledge of it from those who
were present thereat.

ṁeaḃaḋ ḋo caṫ .h. mḃṗuin. Ciḋ ṫṗa acht ṗo maṗbaḋ
aṗ an laṫaiṗ ṗin Caṫal .h. Raiẑilliẑh, ṗi Mhuintiṗe Maoilṁóṗḋa ocuṗ ċaṫa Ccoḋa Pinn, ocuṗ a ḋá
mac maille ṗṗiṗ, .i. Ḋomnall ṗuaḋh ocuṗ Niall, ocuṗ
a ḋeṗḃṗaṫaiṗ, .i. Cuconnacht, ocuṗ ṫṗi mic Caṫail
ḋuiḃ hi Raiẑilliẑh, .i. Ẑoṗṗṗaiẑ, ocuṗ Peṗẑal, ocuṗ
Ḋomnall; ocuṗ Ccnnaḋ mac Ḋomnaill i Raiẑilliẑh ḋo
maṗbaḋ lá Conchobaṗ mac Tiẑeṗnain, ocuṗ an caoc
.h. Raiẑilliẑh, .i. Niall, ocuṗ Tiẑeṗnán Maẑ Ḃhṗáḋaiẑ,
ocuṗ Ẑilla Michil Mac Taiċliẑ, ocuṗ Ḋonnchaḋ .h.
biḃṗaiẑ, ocuṗ Maẑnuṗ Mac Ẑillaḋuiḃ, ocuṗ tuilleḋ
aṗ ṫṗi ṗiċtiḃ ḋo ṁaiṫiḃ a muinntiṗe maṗoen ṗiṗ;
ocuṗ ṗo maṗbaḋ ṗé ṗiṗ ḋéẑ ḋiḃ Raiẑilliẑh ann ḃeoṗ.
Caṫ Mhoiẑe Slecht aṗ bṗú Ccṫa ḋeṗẑ, aẑ Ccllt na
hellti, óṗ Ḃhealaiẑ na beiċiẑe, ainm in caṫa ṗin.

Moṗ ṗluaiẑeḋ eli la Peḋlim .h. Conchobaiṗ ocuṗ la
a mac, .i. Ccoḋ na nẐall, ocuṗ Connachta maille ṗṗiṗ,
ocuṗ Conn mac Tiẑeṗnain ocuṗ ṗiṗ Ḃṗeiṗne maṗoen
ṗiṗ, taṗéiṗ in ċaṫa ṗin; ocuṗ ṗanẑaḋaṗ imoṗṗo an
ḋá ṗluaẑ ṗin co Loċ an tṗéin, ocuṗ tiaẑuiḋ ṗo ċeallaiḃ
na Ḃṗéiṗne acht Piḋnacha namá, ocuṗ ḋo ċlóiṗet taṗ
a naiṗ ḋía tiẑiḃ ẑo mbṗaiẑḋiḃ ṗeṗ mḂṗeiṗṗne leó, .i.
Méic Phiaċṗach ocuṗ Meic Thiẑeṗnain, ocuṗ Méiẑ
Shamṗaḋáin, ocuṗ meic Cciṗt i Ruaiṗc; ocuṗ tucaḋ na
bṗaiẑḋe ṗin a laim i Ruaiṗc, .i. clann na taoiṗech hí ṗin;
ocuṗ tuc Máẑ Shaṁṗaḋain ocuṗ mac Cciṗt hi Ruaiṗc
a mbṗaiẑḋe ṗéin ḋOeḋ na nẐall. Téiḋ uaṫaḋ
maṗcṗlúaiẑ, ocuṗ beẑán coiṗiẑiḃ ocuṗ ṗeṗṗenach ḋo
Mhuinteṗ i Ruaiṗc ḋo ċuaṗtuẑaḋ ṗeṗuinn Mhuintiṗe
Maoilṁóṗḋa, oiṗ ḋo hinniṗeḋ ḋO Ruaiṗc ḋaine bṗoẑḋa
Mhuinteṗi Raiẑilliẑh ḋo timṗuẑaḋ a bṗuaṗaḋaṗ ḋo ṗocṗaiḋe ṗeṗṗénach Ẑhall ocuṗ Ẑhaoiḋel an aoin ionaḋ;

---

1 *Aedh Finn.* The common ancestor of the O'Ruaircs, O'Reillys, and
other families of Breifne.

1 *The Caech;* i.e. "the Blind;"
caech = Lat. cæcus.

2 *Aedh-na-nGall.* "Aedh (or Hugh)
of the Foreigners;" so called from his
relations with the Anglo-Normans,
called Gaill throughout this chronicle.

of the Ui-Briuin was routed. However, there were slain on that field Cathal O'Raighilligh, king of Muinter-Mael-mordha and the descendants of Aedh Finn,[1] together with his two sons, viz :—Domhnall Ruadh and Niall ; and his brother, i e. Cuconnacht , and the three sons of Cathal Dubh O'Raighilligh, viz. :—Goffraigh, and Ferghal, and Domhnall ; and Annadh, son of Domhnall O'Raighilligh, who was killed by Conchobhar, son of Tighernan ; and the Caech[2] O'Raighilligh, i.e. Niall ; and Tighernan Mac Bradaigh ; and Gillamichil Mac Taichligh ; and Donnchadh O'Biblisaigh ; and Maghnus Mac Gilladhuibh ; and over three score of the best of their people along with them ; and six-teen men of the Ui-Raighilligh were slain there besides. The battle of Magh-Slecht, on the brink of Ath-derg, at Alt-na-helti, over Bealach-na-beithighe, is the name of this battle.

Another great hosting, after this battle, by Fedhlim O'Conchobhair and his son, i.e. Aedh-na-nGall,[3] accom-panied by the Connachtmen, and by Conn, son of Tighernan,[4] with the men of Breifne , and these two hosts came, moreover, to Loch-an-trein, and attacked the churches of Breifne except Fidhnacha alone, and turned back to their houses, taking with them the hostages of the men of Breifne, viz. :—of Mac Fiachrach, and Mac Tighernain, and Mac Shamhradhain, and the son of Art O'Ruairc ; and these hostages, i.e. the sons of these chief-tains,[5] were delivered into the hands of O'Ruairc ; and Mac Shamhradhain and the son of Art O'Ruairc delivered their own hostages to Aedh-na-nGall.[3] A small force of cavalry, and a few footmen and mercenaries of O'Ruairc's people, went to patrol the territory of Muinter-Mael-mordha, for it had been reported to O'Ruairc that emis-saries of O'Raighilligh's people had collected to one place all the force that they found of Foreign and Gaeidhelic

---

[4] *Son of Tighernan ;* i.e. son of Tighernan O'Ruairc.

[5] *These chieftains,* viz.:—Mac Fiach-rach and the two others just named.

ocur a teacht do cuartochad Muinteri Mhaolmórda,
ocur docum Mheic Fhiacrac ar creic. Dála Muinnteri
Raigilligh, immorro, do fala da céli iad ocur muinter
hi Ruairc a bFarrnacht, ocur ó corncodar aigti a
céli do meabad do Muinter Raigilligh ocur riad tri
cóirigti commóra. Ni hed amáin, acht ro marbad re
cir déc ar fichid dib ar an láthair rin, ocur ochtar
dib rdéin ar arais rlonnad Muintire Raigilligh, ro
Amláib .h. Raigilligh, ocur ro Aod mac Cathail hi
Raigilligh, ocur tancodar muinter hi Ruairc dia
tigib co rubach romenmnach, gan brón gan breirium.
Conchobar mac Tigernáin hi Ruairc, ri Breifne, ocur
Gilla na noem Mhag Shampadáin, ocur Macraic mac
Tigernáin Mic Conbuide, ocur Mac na hoidce Mhág
Dhorchaid, ocur Cathal Mhág Rágnaill, ocur mic
rig ocur tuirrech .h. mbriuin cona rocraide, do teacht
go Fidnacha a coinne Domnaill hi Raigilligh, ocur ro
lenrat é arr an gcoinne rin, ocur ro marbrat a mac
gradac, .i. Annad .h. Raigilligh, ocur gilla Ira mac
an Crottaig, ocur rochaide maille friú; ocur tucrat
creic móir o Cruachan O Cúbrán ar ná bárach .i. la
féli brenainn, ocur ro airgret an tir rompu alle go
Fidnacha Moige Réin. Acht chena fa bainne ría
brfair do Muinter Raigilligh an lá rin, oir ro fárr
annridé torach imnid ocur uile móir orra orin amac,
oir ro cuirriot teachta dinnroiged Gall in tan rin, .i.
docum Mic Uilliam búrc ocur Mic Goirdelb, do milled
Connacht ocur na bréifne. Dála Ghall, immorro, ro

---

1 *Mac-na-hoidhche*; lit. "son of the night."

2 *Princes.* mic rig; lit. "sons of kings."

3 *Beloved son.* It must not be inferred from this expression that the person slain was the son of Domhnall O'Raighilligh, but rather a son by adoption, for Annadh, the son of

Domhnall O'Raighilligh, was slain in the battle of Magh-Slecht, as recorded in page 414.

4 *Mac-an-Crottaigh.* This name signifies "the son of the *crotach* (or hunch-back);" *crotach* being the adj. form of the word *cruit*, the Irish word for harp, and applied to a hump-backed person. An Irish speaker of

mercenaries, who had gone to make a circuit of Muinter-Maelmordha, and on a predatory expedition to Mac Fiachrach. As regards Muinter-Raighilligh, how- ever, they encountered O'Ruairc's people at Farnacht; and when they saw each other's faces, Muinter-Raighilligh gave way, although they were three great battalions. Not alone this; but thirty-six men of them were slain on the spot, eight of whom bore the family name of O'Raighilligh, including Amhlaibh O'Raighilligh, and Aedh, son of Cathal O'Raighilligh; and O'Ruairc's people went home joyously, contentedly, without sorrow, without reverse. Conchobhar, son of Tighernan O'Ruairc, king of Breifne, and Gilla-na-naemh Mac Shambradhain, and Macraith, son of Tighernan Mac Conbhuidhe, and Mac-na-hoidhche[1] Mac Dorchaidh, and Cathal Mac Raghnaill, and the princes[2] and chieftains of Ui-Briuin, with their forces, came to Fidhnacha to a meeting with Domhnall O'Raighilligh; and they followed him from this meeting, and killed his beloved son,[3] i.e. Annadh O'Raighilligh, and Gilla-Isa Mac-an-Crottaigh,[4] and many more along with them; and they carried off a great prey from Cruachan-O'Cúbhrán on the morrow, i.e. the festival day of Brenainn,[5] and plundered the district before them as far as Fidhnacha of Magh-Rein. This day, however, was but a "drop before a shower"[6] to Muinter-Raighilligh, as then grew the beginning of succeeding tribulation and injury to them; for they despatched messengers at that time to the Foreigners, viz.:—to Mac William Burk and to Mac Goisdelbh, *with a view* to devastating Connacht and the Breifne. As regards the Foreigners, moreover, they

---

the present day would say of one who assumed a stooping posture, ᴅo ċuıp ꞃe cꞃuıꞇ aıꞃ ꝼeın, i.e. "he put a *cruit* (harp) on himself."

[5] *Festival day of Brenainn.* Appa- rently the festival of St. Brenainn (or Brendan) of Clonfert, which fell on the 16th of May.

[6] *A drop before a shower.* This is as much as to say that the severe reverses already suffered by the O'Raighilligs were ominous of fur- ther great calamities, as the size of the drop that falls before a shower indicates the nature of the impending shower.

2 E

τιɴοιlγετ γlúαᵹ γο ṁóγ, ocuγ ταɴcαδαγ co Céιγ
Choγαιɴɴ, ocuγ γo ᵹαḃτατ loɴᵹγoγτ αɴɴ, ocuγ γo
ḃαδαγ ᵹoγᵹlα γechτṁuιɴe αɴɴγιɴ, ocuγ γo αιγᵹιοτ
cеαllα αɴ Choγαιɴɴ uιle. Ɔαlα ᴍuιɴτιγe Rαιᵹιllιᵹh,
ταɴcοδαγ γeɱπα co Loč Œιllιɴɴe ᵹo γoγτ ɴα hιɴɴγι
δαγαḃ αιɴm αɴ Fhuαγčoγγαch αγ Loč Œιllιɴɴe; ocuγ
ɴι τ̇αɴᵹαδαγ Ᵹαιll ιγιɴ ιοɴαδ čоιɴɴe γιɴ αγ еᵹlα Œοδα
hι Coɴčοḃαιγ, δο ḃι αɴ ταɴγιɴ α Cιll τ̇héιγιɴ αɴ
Uαchταγ τ̇ιγe, αᵹ éγδechτ γιγ ɴα γluαᵹαιḃ γιɴ αɴοιγ
ocuγ αɴιαγ, ocuγ αᵹ á γechαιɴ cια διḃ αγα τιḃγeḃ αmmuγ.
Ɔálα Œeδα hι Coɴčоḃαιγ, ổ čuαlα ᴍuιɴτeγ Rαιᵹιllιᵹh
δο čeαchτ αɴɴγιɴ, ιγγí comαιγle δο γóιɴe γé γéιɴ, ocuγ
.h. Ruαιγc mαιlle γγιγ ιɴταɴ γιɴ, .ι. α ɴeιč ocuγ α
ɴéιδιᵹ δγάᵹḃáιl α Cιll τ̇héιγιɴ, ocuγ δul δóιḃ γγеιɴ
δια coιγ ταγ Sιɴuιɴɴ γοιγ, δο τ̇αḃαιγč αmmuιγ αγ
ᴍuιɴτeγ Rαιᵹιllιᵹh; ocuγ δο čuαδαγ ιγ ɴα heɴᵹαιḃ,
ocuγ γo leιᵹγιοτ γιταδα ocuγ γeγγéɴαιᵹ γeɱπu δο
ḃγeιč αγ ᴍuιɴτeγ Rαᵹιllιᵹh, uτ γuγγαδιχιmuγ. Ro
ιmγáδαγ Ᵹαιll δια τιᵹ̇ιḃ ιαγγιɴ, ocuγ γo ḃαοι ιɴτ eγγuc
.h. ᴍαιcíɴ αᵹ ḃάδhαδ α coɴɴeαll ιm ɴóɴα comḃoγčα
γéγ γe γιḃδαδ. Œᵹhαιδ γeιle Cγοιγ, ιmmoγγo, γo
mαḃmαιᵹheδ [ᴍuιɴτeγ] Rαιᵹιllιᵹ, ocuγ ιγ αɴɴγαɴ
ιοɴαδ α τucαḃ αɴ ταčογ γιɴ δο ḃáι Œoḃ .h.
Coɴchoḃαιγ αɴ οιḃče γιɴ, ocuγ γo διčeɴδαḃ ᴍuιɴɴτeγ
Rαιᵹιllιᵹh αγ ɴα ḃáγach lαιγ ιγιɴ ιοɴαḃ γιɴ, ocuγ τuc
α cιɴɴα δocum Feḃlιm co Ɔúɴ Œιlle ιαγ mḃáḃɴα.
luγδíγ δο τ̇οιᵹechτ αɴ Eγιɴɴ ó γι Sαχαɴ δο ceγτuᵹαδ
γeγαιɴɴ ɴα hEγeɴɴ eδιγ ḃαγúɴαιḃ ocuγ γιδeγιḃ ɴα

---

[1] *O'Maicin.* Thomas O'Maicin,
bishop of Luighne, or Achonry, who
is called Thomas O'Miachan in Ware's
catalogue of the bishops of that See.
His death is entered under the year
1265 *infra.*

[2] *Drowning their candles;* i.e. ex-
communicating them (the English).
See note [2], p. 282 *supra.*

[3] *Festival of the Cross.* The festival
of the "Exaltation of the Cross," i.e.
the 14th of September, is doubtless
meant, as the date must have been
subsequent to the festival of St.
Brendan, which is the 16th of May.
See note [5], last page. This entry
seems to contain an account, taken
from a different authority, of the
great battle just before recorded.

assembled a very great host, and proceeded to Ceis-Corainn, where they encamped, and where they remained the greater part of a week; and they plundered all the churches of the Corann. As to Muinter-Raighilligh, they advanced to Loch-Aillinne, to the shore of the island which is called Fuar-chossach, on Loch-Aillinne; but the Foreigners came not to this rendezvous, through fear of Aedh O'Conchobhair, who was then at Cill-tSeisin in Uachtar-tire, observing these hosts from the east and from the west, and watching which of them he should attack. With regard to Aedh O'Conchobhair, when he heard that Muinter-Raighilligh had arrived at the place, the resolution which he and O'Ruairc (who was at this time with him) adopted, was to leave their horses and armour at Cill-tSeisin, and to go themselves on foot eastwards across the Shannon, to make an attack on Muinter-Raighilligh; and they went by the passes, and sent routs and mercenaries on before them, to catch Muinter-Raighilligh, ut supradiximus. The Foreigners returned home after this, and the Bishop O'Maicin[1] was "drowning their candles"[2] about nones, when it was equally dark in field and wood. On the night of the festival of the Cross,[3] truly, [Muinter][4]-Raighilligh were routed;[5] and it was on the spot in which this engagement was fought that Aedh O'Conchobhair passed that night; and Muinter-Raighilligh[6] were beheaded by him on the morrow in that place, and he brought their heads to Fedhlim, to Dun-Aille behind Badhna. A Justiciary came to Erinn from the king of the Saxons, to adjust the lands of Erinn between the

---

[4] *Muinter*. Omitted in MS.; supplied from Annals of Connacht.

[5] *Routed.* ṛo maḋmaıġh (for ṛo maḋmaıġheḋ), MS. The Annals of Connacht read ḋo maṛbaḋ, "were slain."

[6] *Muinter-Raighilligh.* Some words or names are here probably omitted,

as it is unlikely that the entire sept of Muinter-Raighilligh were decapitated on the occasion. But, as already observed (note [3], last page), this entry contains apparently a different version of the account of the battle so fully recorded above, pp. 409-415.

hepenn. Conne oo ḋenum oon Ᵹhiúroír ocur oᴀoḃ .h. Conchobair aᵹ Rinn oúin, ocur ríċ oo ḋénum re ċeli, ocur ᵹan laᵹouᵹao criċe na rerainn oo ḋenum ar .h. Conchobair in rao buḋ ᵹiúroír eiriom in Erinn. ᴀoḃ mac Feḋlim í Conchobair oarᵹain rerainn mic Ricairo Cuirrín a noíᵹailt hi Ᵹhaora [oo marḃao] ḋóram; ocur ro rcoeil a ċairlén iarrin, ocur ro marḃ araiḃe oo ḋaoiniḃ ann, ocur ro ᵹaḃurtar Loċ Teċet uile. Raᵹnall Mac brabáin, oux Corcc ᴀċlann, mortuur ert. Creaċ ṁor la Mac Uilliam búrc ar Ruaior .h. bḟlaiṫbertaiᵹ, ᵹur airᵹeroair Ᵹno ṁór, ocur Ᵹnó ḃeᵹ, ocur ᵹur ᵹaḃurtar Loċ Oirbrion uili iarrin. Conne ṁór aᵹ ᴀoḃ .h. Chonchobair ocur aᵹ ióan oe Ueroún, aᵹ ᴀċ Líaᵹ na Sinna, in hoc anno. Sitreac Ṁáᵹ Shenlaoiċ oo éluḃ, ocur a ḋul co mainiroir na búille ar comairce an uiro. Donncaṫaiᵹ Ṁáᵹ Shenloiċ oo éᵹ a mainiroir na búille in hoc anno. ᴀth Luain ocur Dún Daiᵹre oo lorcao an aon lo irin mbliaḋain rin. Ᵹilla an ċoimoeoh .h. Cinnḟaolaḋ, .i. ab Enaiᵹ ḋúin, quieuit. ᴀb na Trinoioe a Tuaim, .i. .h. Ᵹiollaráin, quieuit. Coᵹao mór oo eirᵹe eoir ᴀoḃ .h. Conċobair ocur Conn mac Tiᵹernáin hí Ruairc, ᵹer maiċ a cumann conuiᵹe rin. h. Ruairc oo ḋul a ᵹceno Ᵹhall, ocur ríċ ar leiċ oo ḋenum ḋó réin ᵹan ċeo oḟheiḋlim .h. Conchobair na ḋá mac. Creaċ ṁór oo ḋenum oo ᴀoḃ .h. Conchobair ar .h. Ruairc an ċéoaoin ria Nooluic mór, ocur oo rónrat ríċ iarrin.

℟ctt. Enair ror Luan, ocur .x. uaṫao ruirre; xuii. anno cicli rolarir; quarto anno oecennouenalir cicli; xu. inoictionir; M.cc.L.uii. Conn mac Tiᵹernáin hí

---

1 *Hoc.* oc, MS.

1 *Escaped*; i.e. from the hands of Fedhlim, son of Cathal Crobhderg O'Conor, by whom he had been taken

prisoner in the year 1254, as above recorded.

3 *The Order.* The community of the Cistercian Order established at Boyle in the year 1161.

barons and knights of Erinn.   A meeting was held by the Justiciary and Aedh O'Conchobhair at Rinn-dúin; and they made peace with one another, on condition that the territory or land of O'Conchobhair should not be diminished while he (*the Justiciary*) should be Justiciary in Erinn.   Aedh, son of Fedhlim O'Conchobhair, plundered the country of Richard Cuisin, in revenge [for his having killed] O'Gadhra; and he afterwards demolished his castle, and killed all the people who were in it, and took possession of all Loch-Techet.   Raghnall Mac Branain, dux of Corca-Achlann, mortuus est.   A great depredation *was committed* by Mac William Burk on Ruaidhri O'Flaithbhertaigh, when he plundered Gno-mór and Gno-beg; and he afterwards took possession of all Loch-Oirbsen. A great meeting was held by Aedh O'Conchobhair and John de Verdun, at Ath-Liag-na-Sinna, in hoc[1] anno. Sitric Mac Shenlaich escaped,[2] and went to the monastery of the Buill, to seek the protection of the Order.[3]   Donncathaigh Mac Shenlaich died in the monastery of the Buill in hoc anno.[4]   Ath-Luain and Dun-Daighre were burned on the same day in this year.   Gilla-an-Choimdedh O'Cennfhaeladh, i.e. abbot of Enach-dúin, quievit.   The abbot of the Trinity in Tuaim, i.e. O'Gillaráin, quievit. A great war arose between Aedh O'Conchobhair and Conn, son of Tighernan O'Ruairc, though their friendship was good until then.   O'Ruairc went to meet the Foreigners, and concluded a separate peace for himself, without the permission of Fedhlim O'Conchobhair, or of his son.   A great depredation was committed by Aedh O'Conchobhair on O'Ruairc, the Wednesday before Great Christmas; and they made peace afterwards.

The kalends of January on Monday, and the tenth of the moon; xvii. anno cycli solaris; quarto anno Decennovenalis cycli; xv. Indictionis; M.cc.lvii.   Conn, son of

---

[4] *Anno.* This entry concludes fol. 48 *b* of the MS. The next folio com- | mences in a different handwriting from the preceding.

Ruaıpc do ṫul a ṫeċh hı Conċhobaıp ocuṛ a mıc,
ocuṛ ṛíġ do ḋenum ḋó pṛıú; ocuṛ a mḃpeṫ ṛeın
do ṫabaıpṫ ḋóıḃ opepann na ḃpeıṗṗne, ocuṛ Cloċ
Innṛı na ṫopc ap Loċ Fınnṁuıġe do ṫabaıpṫ ḋóıḃ
ḋó, ocuṛ luċhṫ coıméṫa do ċhup ınnṫı dᴀoḋ mac
Feıḋlım mıc Caṫhaıl cpoıḃdepġ. Caṫhal cuıppceċh,
mac ᴀoḋa, mıc Caṫhaıl cpoıḃdepġ, ocuṛ ᴀoḋ mac
Conċhobaıp mıc ᴀoḋa mıc Caṫhaıl cpoıḃdepġ, do
ḋallaḋ le hᴀoḋ mac Feıḋlım mıc Caṫhaıl cpoıḃdepġ aḃpıoll, dap ṛápuġad laoḋ ocuṛ ċleıpeċh ocuṛ
ṁıonn Connaċhṫ, ṫpe ċnúḋ ocuṛ ṛopmad, ın hoc
anno.   Conn mac Caṫhaıl hı Raıġıllıġh, ṫáıṛṛeċh
Mhuınnṫıpe Maoılṁópḋa, do éġ.   Cloċ Innṛı na
ṫopc ap Loċ Fınnṁaıġe do lopcad dᴜα Ruaıpc, ocuṛ
luċhṫ a coıméṫa do leıġen ap a ḃpeıṫíp aıpde ḋó.
Sıṫpec mac Ualġaıpġ hı Ruaıpc do pıġhad do ᴀoḋ
.h. Conċhobaıp, a ġcend Conċhobaıp mıc Ṫıġepnáın hı
Ruaıpcc, ocuṛ Sıṫpıuc mac Ualġaıpġ do ṁapbad do
Ḋhoṁnall mac Conċhobaıp mıc Ṫıġepnaın hı Ruaıpc
ġoıpıd ıap ná pıġhad.   Muıpıp Mac Ġepaılṫ mopṫuur
epṫ ın hoc anno.   Coınne do ḋenum pe Ġıúpdíp na
hEpenn ocuṛ pe Mac Uıllıam Búpc, ocuṛ pe maıṫıḃ
Ġall Epenn áıpċena, ın ᴀṫ Luaın, do Feıḋlım mac
Caṫhaıl cpoıḃdepġ, ocuṛ ṛíġ do ḋenum ḋóıḃ dıḃlínaıḃ.
Cpeċh ṁóp do ḋenum dᴀoḋ .h. Conċhobaıp ap .h.
Ruaıpc pá ċáıpc.   Maolpádpaıc Mac hElı, aıpċhındeċh
Chılle hᴀClaıḋ, do ṁapbaḋ.   Caıṗlén Chaoıl uıpcı do
leġaḋ la Ġoṗṗpaḋ .h. nḊoṁnaıll ocuṛ la Cenél
Conaıll; ocuṛ luċhṫ a coıméṫa do ṁapbaḋ.   Uα
Ḋomnaıll ocuṛ Cenél Conaıll do ṫeaċhṫ ġo Slıġeċh,
ocuṛ mopán do Ġhalloıḃ ın ḃaıle do ṁapbad ḋóıḃ, ocuṛ
an ṛáṫḃaıle do lopgud leó, ocuṛ cpecha mópa do
ḃpeıṫ ḋóıḃ a Caıpḃpe; ocuṛ na Ġaıll dıa lenmaın

<hr/>

¹ *Cathal Cuircech.* The second word, │ is a sobriquet signifying purblind,
written caıpcech by the Four Masters, │ from cuıpce, or caıpce, explained in

Tighernan O'Ruairc, went into the house of O'Conchobhair and his son, and made peace with them, and gave them their own award of the land of Breifne; and he gave them Cloch-Innsi-na-torc on Loch-Finnmhuighe, and a garrison was placed in it by Aedh, son of Fedhlim, son of Cathal Crobhderg. Cathal Cuircech,[1] son of Aedh, son of Cathal Crobhderg, and Aedh, son of Conchobhar, son of Aedh, son of Cathal Crobhderg, were blinded by Aedh, son of Fedhlim, son of Cathal Crobhderg, in treachery, through envy and jealousy, in violation of the laics, and clerics, and reliquaries of Connacht, in hoc[2] anno. Conn, son of Cathal O'Raighilligh, chieftain of Muinter-Mael-mordha, died. Cloch-Innsi-na-torc, on Loch-Finnmhuighe, was burned by O'Ruairc, and its garrison was let out of it by him on parole. Sitric, son of Ualgharg O'Ruairc, was made king by Aedh O'Conchobhair, in opposition to Conchobhar, son of Tighernan O'Ruairc; and Sitric, son of Ualgharg, was slain by Domhnall, son of Conchobhar, son of Tighernan O'Ruairc, soon after his inauguration. Maurice Fitz-Gerald mortuus est in hoc anno. A meeting was held at Ath-Luain by Fedhlim, son of Cathal Crobhderg, with the Justiciary of Erinn, and with Mac William Burk and the other nobles of Erinn; and they made peace respectively. A great depredation was committed by Aedh O'Conchobhair on O'Ruairc, about Easter. Maelpatraic Mac hEli, airchinnech of Cill-Alaidh, was slain. The castle of Cael-uisce[3] was razed by Goffraidh O'Domhnaill and the Cenel-Conaill, and its garrison was slain. O'Domhnaill and the Cenel-Conaill proceeded to Sligech, and a great number of the Foreigners of the town were killed by them, and the street-town[4] was burned by them; and they carried off great preys into Cairbre. And the

---

an old Irish Glossary (MS., H. 3, 18, Trin. Coll., Dublin, p. 210) ꞃɩɴꞁᴅᴀ, i.e. a film on the eye, but it also signifies a hair.

[2] *Hoc.* oc, MS.

[3] *Cael-uisce.* The erection of this castle of Cael-uisce, by the English, is recorded above under the year 1212.

[4] *Street-town;* i.e. the street-town of Sligo. See note 6, p. 258 *supra.*

ʒo Cpeopán Choluim Chille ap Roʃ ʒéiðe a cpíc
Chaipbpi; ocuʃ maiðm vo ʈabaipʈ ap na ʒalloið
annʃin; ocuʃ .h. Oomnaill vo ʒuin ann; ocuʃ achʈ
muna ʒaðvaoiʃ a ʒona ʒpeim vlla Ohomnaill vo biað
maiðm poppa ʒo Muaið; ocuʃ vo iompúðʒav vía ʈiʒið
iappin ap aba ʒona hí Ohomnaill. Mainiʃvip Mhuipe
í Roʃ Chomáin vo čoipecʃav vo Thomalʈach .h. Conchobaip vona ðpaiʈpið ppeisiuʃ. Caipʈ vo ʈabaipʈ o
piʒh Saxan vo Pheðlim .h. Conchobaip ap čóiʒ ʈpiúča
an piʒ. Cocav móp evip Cončobap .h. mðpiain ocuʃ
ʒaill na Muman, ocuʃ áp móp vo ʈabaipʈ vlla ðpiain
ʃop na ʒalloið, ocuʃ cpeač móp vo ðenum vo Thaðʒ
.h. ðhpiain oppa ðeopʃ. Mac Oomnaill Connachʈaiʒ
hí ðpiain vo ṁapbað la ʒalloið ðeoʃ. Ap móp vo
ʈabaipʈ ap ʒhalloið Ulav vo Mac Ouinnʃlebe. Conchobap mac Tiʒepnain hí Ruaipc, pi ðpéipne, vo
ṁapbað aʒ Ať na ʃailme vo ʒhilla ðhepuiʒ .h. Laiṁ-
ðuiʒ, vo óʒlaoč vía ṁuinʈep ðuðéin, ocuʃ vo ṁuinnʈep
Mhača hí Raiʒilliʒ, a ðpeall. Cathal .h. Manvačáin
mopʈuuʃ epʈ a.ui. čallainv Oecimbip. Piónacha vo
ʃápuʒav vo Aoð mac Peiðlim hí Conchobaip im a
cpoð, .i. cev bó. Muipevhač mac Maoilðpiʒve hí
Phaipčeallaiʒ, comapba Maovóic, quieuiʈ. Cpeač
móp vo ðenum ap Mháʒ Shaṁpaðain vo ṁuinnʈep
Aoða mic Peiðlim hí Conchobaip. Tomaʃʃ .h. Maoil-
číapain, ʃaoi Epenn, quieuiʈ. Raʒnailʈ, inʒen hí
Pepʒail, quieuiʈ. ʒillapavpaic Mháʒ Phiacpač vo
ðallav la Mača .h. Raiʒilliʒh in hoc anno.

---

[1] *Credran - Choluim - Chille.* The *Credran* of Colum-Cille. The name of the place is written Credran-Cille in the Ann. Ult. and by the Four Masters. Ros-Geide, or Ros-Cede, in which Credran-Choluim-Chille was situated, is now known as the Rosses, in the parish of Drumcliff, barony of Carbury, county of Sligo; but *Credran* has not been identified.

[2] *Tomaltach O'Conchobhair.* Ware calls him Thomas O'Conor. He was at this time bishop of Elphin, from which See he was translated to that of Tuam in 1258.

[3] *Five cantreds.* The five cantreds here referred to were probably the same as are alleged to have been granted to Fedhlim in the year 1237. See note [2], p. 344 *supra*.

Foreigners pursued them to Credran-Choluim-Chille[1] in Ros-Geidhe, in the territory of Cairbre, where the Foreigners were routed, and O'Domhnaill was *mortally* wounded; but if his wounds had not disabled O'Domhnaill they would have been routed as far as Muaidh. And they (*the Cenel-Conaill*) returned home afterwards in consequence of O'Domhnaill's wound. The monastery of Mary, in Ros-Comain, was consecrated by Tomaltach O'Conchobhair[2] for the Friars Preachers. A charter was given by the king of the Saxons to Fedhlim O'Conchobhair for the king's five cantreds.[3] A great war between Conchobhar O'Briain and the Foreigners of Mumha; and a great slaughter was inflicted by O'Briain on the Foreigners; and a great depredation was committed on them by Tadhg O'Briain in addition. The son of Domhnall Connachtach O'Briain was, moreover, killed by the Foreigners: A great slaughter was inflicted on the Foreigners of Uladh by Mac Duinnslebhe. Conchobhar, son of Tighernan O'Ruairc, king of Breifne, was killed at Ath-na-Failmhe, in treachery, by Gillabcraigh O'Lamh-dhuibh, a young man of his own people, and by the people of Matthew O'Raighilligh. Cathal O'Mannachain mortuus est on the 6th of the kalends of December. Fidhnacha was profaned by Aedh, son of Fedhlim O'Conchobhair, regarding its stock, viz.:—one hundred cows.[4] Muiredhach, son of Maelbrighde O'Fairchellaigh, comarb of Maedhóg,[5] quievit. A great depredation was committed on Mac Shamhradhain by the people of Aedh, son of Fedhlim O'Conchobhair. Thomas O'Maelchiarain, the sage of Erinn, quievit. Raghnailt, daughter of O'Ferghail, quievit. Gillapatraic Mac Fiachrach was blinded by Matthew O'Raighilligh in hoc[6] anno.

---

[4] *One hundred cows;* which Aedh O'Conor apparently took away with him.

[5] *Comarb of Maedhóg;* i.e. abbot of Druim-lethan, or Drumlane, in the county of Leitrim.

[6] *Hoc.* hoꞇ, MS.

Klt. Enáin ron ṁaint acur .xxi. ruinne; xuiii. [anno]
cicli rolaṗir; quinto anno vecennouenalir cicli;
ṗrimur annur inoictionir; M.cc.Loctaio. Uáṫép oé
Sálepna, .i. aipvepuc Túama, ocur vecánach mór
Lunvainne, vo ég a Saxanaiḃ irin mbliavain rin; ocur
an bliavain reṁe rin vo toghav lá riġ Saxan hé.
Tomaltach .h. Conchobair, .i. erpuc Oilepinn, vo ṫóġa
na aipvepuc a Tuaim in hoc anno. Zoṗṗraiṡ .h.
Vomnaill, riġ Thíre Conaill, .i. lochrann aḃanta
einiġ ocur engnuma, ċoġaio ocur ċopnuma an ċúigiṡ
uile eirṡéin, vṗaġail ḃáir vo ġáiḃ ċpó ċaṫ Crevráin;
ocur nir ḃó bar iar mílaoċur achc ég iar mbuaiṡ rop
a ḃiṡbavuiḃ. Vomnall .h. Vomnaill vo riġhav na
ionaṡ; ocur tucrat Cenél Conaill uile braiġve ocur
tiġerntur vó. Vomnall mac Conchobair mic Tiġer-
náin i Ruaire, vo ḃoi a mbraiġvenur tar cenv a athar
aġ Feiṡlim hUa Conchobair ocur aġá mac, vo léġaṡ
amaċ ṡoiḃ, ocur riġe na Ḃreiṗne vo ṫabairt vó a
ninav a athar. Loinġer mór vo ṫochc a hinnriṡ
Zall la Mac Somairle, ocur vo ġaḃrat timċeall
Erenn ṫíar a Conmaicne Mara, ocur vo flatrat long
ċenvaiġe annrin ra na huile ṁaiċerraiḃ, evir fion
ocur évach, ocur uṁa ocur iarunn. Siṗriam Connachc,
.i. Siúptán vErrréiap, vo ṡul coblaċ mór vo Zhalloib
rop muir anveoiṡ Mic Somairle ocur na loinġri vo
roine rlat na luinge cennaiġ. Ir annrin vo ḃói Mac
Somairle ar oilén mara, ocur a longa a tir aca ann;
ocur ó conncovar coḃlaċ anc ṗipriam ċuca, téiv
Mac Somairle na éiveḃ ocur ina ċulaiv ċaṫa ocur
comlainn, ocur vo chúaiv a ṁuintep maille rir ina
néiveḃ an tan rin. Vala inc ṗipriam, imoppo, o panic
anc oilén vo ċuaiṡ a tír co hullam, ocur an ṁeiv rá

1 *Quinto.* quincto, MS.

2 *Of London.* Lunaiñe for Lunvainne, MS.

3 *Ashore.* a tír. The Four Masters state that Mac Somhairle's vessels were close by at anchor.

The kalends of January on Tuesday, and the twenty-first of the moon; xviii. [anno] cycli solaris; quinto[1] anno Decennovenalis cycli; primus annus Indictionis; M.CC.L.octavo. Walter de Salerna, i.e. archbishop of Tuaim, and great dean of London,[2] died in Saxon-land in this year; and the year before that he had been chosen by the king of the Saxons. Tomaltach O'Conchobhair, i.e. bishop of Oilfinn, was elected archbishop of Tuaim in hoc anno. Goffraidh O'Domhnaill, king of Tir-Conaill, i.e. who was the kindling torch of honour and valour, of warfare and defence of the entire province, died of the wounds *which he had received* in the battle of Credrán; and it was not death after cowardice, but death after triumphing over his enemies. Domhnall O'Domhnaill was made king in his place, and all the Cenel-Conaill gave him hostages and sovereignty. Domhnall, son of Conchobhar, son of Tighernan O'Ruairc, who was in captivity, for his father's sake, with Fedhlim O'Conchobhair and his son, was liberated by them; and the sovereignty of the Breifne was given to him in the place of his father. A great fleet came from Innsi-Gall with Mac Somhairle; and they passed round Erinn westwards to Conmaicne-Mara, where they robbed a merchant-vessel of all its goods, both wine and clothing, and copper and iron. The sheriff of Connacht, i.e. Jordan de Exeter, went on the sea, with a large fleet of Foreigners, after Mac Somhairle and the fleet that had robbed the merchant-vessel. Mac Somhairle was at this time on an island of the sea, having his vessels ashore;[3] and when they saw the sheriff's fleet approaching them, Mac Somhairle put on[4] his armour, and his dress of battle and combat; and his people then put on their armour along with him. As regards the sheriff, moreover, when he reached the island, he landed promptly, accompanied by all the Foreigners

---

[4] *Put on.* The text has ꞇóꞃo nα éꞇꝺẻ; lit. "goes into his clothes."

hullam leir ꝺona Ʒalloιb. Cιꝺ τɾα αchτ, ɾo ꝼɾeαɾlαꝺ
ocuɾ ɾo ꝼɾιτ́αιleꝺ αn ɾιɾ̄ιαm lα ɰαc Somαιɾle conα
ṁuιnnτeɾ. Ro mαɾbαꝺ αn ɾιɾ̄ιαm αnnɾιn ɾo ceꝺóιɾ,
ocuɾ Pιαɾɾuɾ Ꝗccαbαɾꝺ mαιlle ꝼɾιɾ, .ι. ɾιꝺιɾe ɾo
mαιτ̆ ꝺíα ṁuιnnτeɾ, ocuɾ ꝺαoιne mαιτ̆e elι mαιlle ꝼɾιú.
Ro ιmꝑó cαꝑlαc̆ nα nƷαll ιαɾ ɾιn, ιαɾ mαɾbαꝺ αn neoc̆
ꝺob ꝼeɾɾ αcu, ocuɾ ꝺo ιmꝉιƷ ɰαc Somαιɾle co hαιτeɾ-
ɾech, éꝺαlαch, ιαɾ mbuαιꝺ Ʒcoɾcαιɾ, ꝺια τ̆íɾ ꝼéιn íαɾ
ɾιn. Coιnne ṁóɾ αʒ Ꝗoꝺ .h.Conchobαιɾ, .ι. mαc Ꝟéꝺlιm
mιc Cατhαιl cɾoιꝺꝺeɾʒ, ocuɾ αʒ Cαꝉʒ .h.bɾίαιn mαιlle
ꝼɾιɾ, α Cαol uιɾce, ɾe bɾιαn.h.Néιll, ocuɾ ɾιꝉ ꝺo
ꝺenum ꝺοιꝉ ɾe c̆ele, ocuɾ ɾιʒe ꝺo τ̆αbαιɾτ ꝺo bɾιαn
.h.Neιll ꝼoɾ Ʒhαoιꝺelαιꝉ Eɾenn; ocuɾ τuc mαc Ꝟéꝺlιm
bɾαιʒꝺe ꝺo bɾιαn.h.Neιll, ocuɾ bɾαιʒꝺι ɰhuιnτeɾι
Rαιʒιllιʒh ocuɾ .h.mbɾιuιn uιle, ó Chenαnnuɾ ʒo Ꝺɾuιm
c̆lιαꝉ, ꝺꝗoꝺ .h.Chonchobαιɾ αnnɾιn. ɰαc̆α mαc Ʒιllα-
ɾuαιꝺ hι Rαꝺuιꝉ, .ι. αn ṁáιʒιɾꝺιɾ, ꝺo éʒ ιɾιn mblιαꝺαιn
ɾιn. ɰαcɾαιꝉ ɰháʒ Cιʒeɾnάιn, ꝺux Ceαllαιʒh Ꝺunchαꝺα, ꝺo ṁαɾbαꝺ lα Ꝺomnαll mαc Conchobαιɾ mιc
Cιʒeɾnαιn hι Ruαιɾc. Iɾ αnnɾιn ɾo ꝉenɾαꝺ ꝼιɾ
bɾeιꝼne ocuɾ Connαchτα uιle α ɾιʒe ꝺon Ꝺomnαll ɾιn
mαc Conchobαιɾ, ocuɾ ɾo ṁαɾꝑɾατ Ceαllαc̆ Ꝺunchαꝺα
α ꝺeɾbɾατhαιɾ, .ι. Cατhαl mαc Conchobαιɾ mιc Chιʒeɾ-
nαιn hι Ruαιɾc, ocuɾ τucɾατ ꝼιɾ bɾeιꝼꝼne ocuɾ Connαchτ ɾιʒe .h.mbɾιuιn ꝺo Ꝗɾτ mαc Cατhαιl ɾιαꝉαιʒ
1 Ruαιɾc. In mαnαch .h.Cuιɾnίn, .ι. ɾóι cɾαbαꝉ, quιeuιτ.
bɾιαn ɰháʒ Shάṁɾαꝺάιn, ꝺux Cheαllαιʒ Eαchαch, ꝺo
ṁαɾbαꝺ lα Connαchταιꝉ. Cocαꝺ móɾ ιꝺιɾ Ʒhαlloιb ocuɾ
Conc̆obαɾ.h.bɾιαιn, ꝺαɾ loιɾceꝺ Ꝗɾꝺ Rατ̆αιn ocuɾ
Cιll Cholʒαn, ocuɾ ʒɾάιꝺ ꝉαιlτe ocuɾ αɾbαnnα ιmꝉα
αɾ ʒαch leꝉ. Comάɾ.h.bιɾn moɾτuuɾ eɾτ. Coιnne
ṁóɾ eꝺιɾ Ʒhαlloιb ocuɾ Ʒhαoιꝺelαιꝉ Eɾenn α néʒmuιɾ
Ꝟheιꝺlιm hι Conchobαιɾ, α ɰúllαc̆ Lαιʒιꝺe, ocuɾ ɾιꝉ

---

¹ *Agabard.* αccαbαɾꝺ, MS. Mageoghegan writes this name "Caward."

² *To Aedh O'Conchobhair.* The Four
Masters state that the hostages of
Muinter-Raighilligh and all the Ui-
Briuin were given to Brian O'Neill.

But the Annals of Clonmacnoise
(Mageoghegan's version) agree with
the present chronicle. See note ⁶, p.
431.

³ *Street-towns.* See note ⁶, p. 258
supra.

who were ready. However, the sheriff was attended and served by Mac Somhairle and his people; and the sheriff was immediately killed there, together with Piers Agabard,[1] who was a brave knight of his people, and other good men along with them. The fleet of the Foreigners subsequently turned back, after their best men had been slain; and Mac Somhairle went afterwards exultingly, enriched with spoils, with the triumph of victory, to his own country. A great meeting was held at Cael-uisce by Aedh O'Conchobhair, i.e. the son of Fedhlim, son of Cathal Crobhderg, accompanied by Tadhg O'Briain, with Brian O'Neill, when they made peace with one another; and the sovereignty over the Gaeidhel of Erinn was given to Brian O'Neill; and the son of Fedhlim gave hostages to Brian O'Neill; and the hostages of Muinter-Raighilligh and all the Ui-Briuin, from Cenannus to Druim-cliabh, were then given to Aedh O'Conchobhair.[2] Matthew, son of Gilla-ruadh O'Radhuibh, i.e. "the Master," died in this year. Macraith Mac Tighernain, dux of Tellach-Dunchadha, was killed by Domhnall, son of Conchobhar, son of Tighernan O'Ruairc. It was then that the men of Breifne and all the Connachtmen took his sovereignty from this Domhnall, son of Conchobhar, and *the men of Tellach-Dunchadha* killed his brother, i.e. Cathal, son of Conchobhar, son of Tighernan O'Ruairc; and the men of Breifne and Connacht gave the sovereignty of Ui-Briuin to Art, son of Cathal Riabhach O'Ruairc. The monk O'Cuirnín, i.e. a most eminent devotee, quievit. Brian Mac Shamhradhain, dux of Tellach-Echach, was killed by the Connachtmen. A great war between the Foreigners and Conchobhar O'Briain, when Ard-rathain and Cill-Colgan, and many street-towns,[3] and much corn, were burned on every side. Thomas O'Birn mortuus est. A great meeting took place between the Foreigners and Gaeidhel of Erinn, in the absence of Fedhlim O'Conchobhair, at Mullach-Laighide, when peace was concluded

do ḋenum etoppa. Ꝣillacpiꝝo .h.Caꝛmacán, deꝣánach
Oileꝛinn, quieuit. Aꝛoꝣal.h.Conchobaiꝛ, .i. mac Comaꝛba Comáin, quieuit. Cuiꝛt in eꝛpuic a nOilꝛinn,
ocuꝛ cúiꝛt Chille Séiꝛin, do ꝛꝣaoileḋ do Aoḋ .h.Con-
chobaiꝛ in hoc anno. Aṁlaoiḃ mac Aiꝛt hi Ruaiꝛc,
.i. ꝛí Ḃꝛeiꝛꝛne o ꝼliaḃ ꝛiaꝛ, do éꝣ in hoc anno.

 Kt. Enáiꝛ ꝼoꝛ Cedaoin, ocuꝛ aile uathad ꝛuiꝛꝛe; xix.
[anno] cicli ꝛolaꝛiꝛ; ui. anno Decennouenaliꝛ cicli;
ꝛecundo anno indictioniꝛ; M.cc.L.ix°. Tomaltach, mac
Toiꝛꝛḋealbaiꝣh, mic Maoilꝛechlainn hi Conchobaiꝛ, do
ṫoiꝣecht ón Róiṁ an ḃliadain ꝛin, iaꝛ tabaiꝛt ꝣꝛáiḋ aiꝛd
eꝛꝛuic ꝼaiꝛ a cúiꝛt an ꝼaꝛa, ocuꝛ ꝼalliʉm do ṫabaiꝛt
laiꝛ cuiꝣe ꝼein, ocuꝛ ꝛochaiꝛ imḋa don eꝣluiꝛ áiꝛċena.
Coꝛmac.h.Luimlin, eꝛꝛuc Chluana ꝛeꝛta Ḃꝛénainn,
ocuꝛ aiꝛd eꝣnaiḋ na hEꝛenn, ocuꝛ ꝛenoiꝛ naom, quieuit.
Aoḋ.h.Conchobaiꝛ do ṫabaiꝛt ionaidh Aṁláiṁ do
Aꝛt Ḃeꝣ mac Aiꝛt hi Ruaiꝛc. Aꝛt mac Cathail
ꝛiaḃaiꝣ 1 Ruaiꝛc do ꝣabáil dAoḋ .h.Conchobaiꝛ. Aoḋ
.h.Conchobaiꝛ do ḋul ꝣo Doiꝛe Choluim Chille do
ṫabaiꝛt inꝣene Duḃꝣaill Mic Somaiꝛle, ocuꝛ ocht
ꝛichit óꝣlaoḋ máꝛaon ꝛía, ocuꝛ Ailín Mac Somaiꝛle
maille ꝛꝛiú. Cathal Mac Conꝼnama, taoiꝛech Mhuinn-
tiꝛe Cináiṫ, do ḋallaḋ la hAoḋ .h.Conchobaiꝛ, ocuꝛ
bꝛaiꝣde Domnaill 1 Ruaiꝛc do ḋallaḋ leiꝛ, .i. Niall
mac Donnchaḋa ocuꝛ Ḃꝛian mac Neill, iꝛin bliadain
cedna. Coinne etiꝛ Aoḋ .h.Conchobaiꝛ ocuꝛ Ḃꝛian
.h.Neill aꝣ Daiminiꝛ ꝼoꝛ Loċ Eiꝛne, ocuꝛ ꝛíṫ Domnaill
hi Ruaiꝛc do ḋenum ꝛe hAoḋ.h.Conchobaiꝛ, ocuꝛ
ꝛíꝣe na Ḃꝛeiꝛꝛne do tabaiꝛt dó. Taiċlech Mac
Diaꝛmada moꝛtuuꝛ eꝛt. Miliḋ Mac Ꝣoiꝛdelḃ moꝛ-

---

[1] *Breifne from the mountain west-wards* That part, namely, of Breifne, or the county of Leitrim, to the west of the mountain called Sliabh-in-iarainn.

[2] *Tomaltach.* This name has been anglicised "Thomas" by Ware. See note [2], p. 424 *ante*.

[3] *The place of Amhlaibh;* i.e. the kingship of Breifne, from Sliabh-in-iarainn westwards. See the last entry under the year 1258.

between them. Gilla-Christ O'Carmacan, dean of Oilfinn, quievit. Ardghal O'Conchobhair, i.e. the son of Comarb Comain, quievit. The bishop's palace at Oilfinn, and the palace of Cill-Seisin, were demolished by Aedh O'Conchobhair in hoc anno. Amhlaibh, son of Art O'Ruairc, i.e. the king of Breifne from the mountain westwards,[1] died in hoc anno.

The kalends of January on Wednesday, and the second of the moon; xix. [anno] cycli solaris; vi. anno Decenno-venalis cycli; secundo anno Indictionis; M.cc.lix°. Tomal-tach,[2] son of Toirdhelbhach, son of Maelsechlainn O'Con-chobhair, came from Rome in this year, after the degree of bishop had been conferred on him at the Pope's court; and he brought with him a pallium for himself, and great benefits for the church also. Cormac O'Luimlin, bishop of Cluain-ferta-Brenainn, and chief sage of Erinn, and a holy senior, quievit. Aedh O'Conchobhair gave the place of Amhlaibh[3] to Art[4] Beg, son of Art O'Ruairc. Art, son of Cathal Riabhach O'Ruairc, was taken prisoner by Aedh O'Conchobhair. Aedh O'Conchobhair went to Doire-Choluim-Chille to espouse the daughter of Dubhgall Mac Somhairle; and *he brought home* eight score young men with her, together with Ailin Mac Somhairle. Cathal Mac Conshnamha, chieftain of Muinter-Cinaith, was blinded by Aedh O'Conchobhair; and the hostages of Domhnall O'Ruairc, viz. :—Niall, son of Donnchadh,[5] and Brian, son of Niall,[6] were blinded by him in the same year. A conference *took place* between Aedh O'Con-chobhair and Brian O'Neill, at Daimhinis on Loch Erne, when peace was made with Domhnall O'Ruairc by Aedh O'Conchobhair, and the sovereignty of the Breifne was given to him. Taichlech Mac Diarmada mortuus est. Milidh Mac Goisdelbh mortuus est. Gilbert

---

[4] *Art.* The MS. has αιρτ, which is the genit. form of the name.

[5] *Donnchadh.* Donnchadh O'Ruairc.

[6] *Niall.* Niall O'Ruairc. The hos-tages here referred to were those given to Aedh O'Conchobhair in the preceding year. See note [2], p. 428.

cuur ert. Ʒillebert Mac Ʒoiroelḃ oo ɡáḃail la hꝗoḃ
.h.Conchobaiɲ, ocuɲ Sliaḃ Luɡa oo aɲɡuin oó uile.
Leiɡceɲ amaċ é iaɲ ɲin, ocuɲ ɡaḃcaɲ a cɲi mic a
mbɲaiɡoenuɲ caɲ a ċeno. ꝼlann ɲuaḃ .h. ꝼloinn
caoiɲech Shil Mhaolɲuain, ocuɲ Oonnchaoh .h.ꝼloinn
oo ɡaḃáil oꝗoḃ .h.Conchobaiɲ, ocuɲ Sil Mhaolɲuain
oo aɲɡuin oó uile. Sioḃaiḃ .h. baiʒill, .i. caoiɲech na
Cɲi Cúach, ꝼeɲ beoḃa oeiɡ einiɡ, oo ṁaɲbaḃ oia
bɲaiċɲiḃ ꝼein a bꝼioll in hoc anno. Caoɡ .h.bɲiain, .i.
aoḃaɲ ɲiɡ Muman, moɲcuuɲ erc. In Ʒilla cam Mac
Ʒillaċaɲán, ɲái noána ocuɲ léiɡinn, in Cɲiɲco quieuic.

Ιc. Εnaiɲ ꝼoɲ oaɲoaoin, cɲeaɲ oec ꝼuiɲɲe; xx. anno
cicli ɲolaɲiɲ; uii. anno Oecennouenaliɲ cicli; iii. anno
inoiccioniɲ. M.cc.lx. ꝗoḃ .h.Conchobaiɲ oo ḃul iɲin
cuaiɲceɲc oocum bɲiain hi Neill, ocuɲ moɲán oo
ṁaiċiḃ Connachc maille ꝼɲiɲ. Ua Neill ocuɲ Cenél
Εoɡain ocuɲ ꝗo .h.Conchobaiɲ ḃo oul oiḃlinaiḃ ɡo
Oún oá leċɡlaɲ, a coinne Ʒhall. Maioḃm aoḃail oo
ċabaiɲc oo Ʒhalloiḃ Oúin ꝼoɲɲa, ocuɲ bɲiɡn .h.Neill,
.i. ɲí Ʒaoioel Εɲenn, oo ṁaɲbaoh a ɡcaċ Oɲuma
oeɲɡ aɡ Oún oá leċɡlaɲ. Ro maɲbaḃ ann Oomnall
.h.Caiɲɲe, ocuɲ Oiaɲmaio Maɡ Laċlainn, ocuɲ Maʒnuɲ
.h.Caċán, ocuɲ Cian.h.hineiɲɡe, ocuɲ Oonnɲleiḃe
Mháɡ Cána, ocuɲ ꝗoḃ .h.Caċán, ocuɲ Muiɲceɲcach
.h.Caċán, ocuɲ Conchobaɲ .h.Ouiḃoíɲma, ocuɲ ꝗoḃ
.h.Ouiḃoíɲma a mac, ocuɲ ꝗmlaim .h. Ʒaiɲmleɡhaiɡh, .
ocuɲ Cú Ulaoh.h.hꝗnluain, ocuɲ Niall.h.hꝗnluain.
ꝗchc acá ní chena, ɲo maɲbaḃ .u. ꝼiɲ ohéc oo ṁaiċiḃ
Muinnceɲi Caċán aɲ an láchaiɲ ɲin. Ro maɲbao oono
oo Connachcaiḃ iɲin caċ láchaiɲ ceona ɲin Ʒilla Cɲiɲc,
mac Concobaiɲ, mic Coɲmaic, mic Comalcaiɡ Mic
Oiaɲmaoa, ocuɲ Cachal mac Ciɡeɲnáin hi Conċobaiɲ,
ocuɲ Maolɲuanaiḃ Mac Oonnchaoa, ocuɲ Cachal
mac Oonnchaoa mic Mhuiɲceɲcaiɡ, ocuɲ ꝗoḃ mac

---

1 *Mac Gillacharain.* The Four Masters write the name Mac Gillachiarain, which is apparently the more correct form.

Mac Goisdelbh was taken prisoner by Aedh O'Conchobhair, who plundered all Sliabh-Lugha. He (*Gilbert
Mac Goisdelbh*) was afterwards set at large, and his three
sons were taken as hostages in his place. Flann Ruadh
O'Floinn, chieftain of Sil-Maelruain, and Donnchadh
O'Floinn were taken prisoners by Aedh O'Conchobhair;
and Sil-Maelruain was all plundered by him. Sighradh
O'Baighill, i.e. the chieftain of the Three Tuatha, a
vigorous, most hospitable man, was killed by his own
brethren in treachery, in hoc anno. Tadhg O'Briain, i.e.
one fit to be king of Mumha, mortuus est. The Gilla-
cam Mac Gillacharain,[1] a distinguished professor of poetry
and literature, in Christo quievit.

The kalends of January on Thursday, the thirteenth of
the moon; xx. anno cycli solaris; vii. anno Decennovenalis
cycli; iii. anno Indictionis; M.cc.lx. Aedh O'Conchobhair
went into the North, to Brian O'Neill, accompanied by a
great many of the nobles of Connacht. O'Neill, and the
Cenel-Eoghain, and Aedh O'Conchobhair went together
to Dun-da-lethghlas against the Foreigners. A terrible
defeat was inflicted on them by the Foreigners of Dún,
and Brian O'Neill, i.e. the king of the Gaeidhel of Erinn,
was killed in the battle of Druim-derg at Dun-da-lethghlas. Domhnall O'Cairre, and Diarmaid Mac Lachlainn,
and Maghnus O'Cathain, and Cian O'hIneirghe, and Donnsleibhe Mac Cana, and Aedh O'Cathain, and Muirchertach
O'Cathain, and Conchobhar O'Dubhdhirma, and his son
Aedh O'Dubhdhirma, and Amhlaimh O'Gairmleghaigh, and
Cu-Uladh O'hAnluain, and Niall O'hAnluain were slain
there. In fact, fifteen of the principal men of Muinter-
Cathain were slain in that field. There were also slain
on the part of the Connachtmen in the same battle field,
Gilla-Christ, son of Conchobhar, son of Cormac, son of
Tomaltach Mac Diarmada, and Cathal, son of Tighernan
O'Conchobhair; and Maelruanaidh Mac Donchadha; and
Cathal, son of Donnchadh, son of Muirchertach; and

2 F

Muιρceρταιz ḟιηη, ocur Ταὁc mac Caṫaιl mιc Ḃριαιη
hι Maoιlρuaηαιὁ, ocur Dιαρmαιτ mac Ταὁz mιc
Mhuιρeὁhαιzh mιc Thomalταιzh hι Mhάιlρuαηαὁ,
ocur Conchoḃaρ Mac zιlla Θρράιτ, ocur Ταὁz mac Ceιη
hι zhaopa, ocur zιlla Ḃeραιz .h.Cuιηη, ocur Cαρṗṫaluṛ
mac aη eṛpuιc hι Mhuιρeὁhαιzh, eτ alιι multι ηoḃιler
eτ ιzηoḃιleṛ. Sluαιzeὁ la Mac Uιllιαm Ḃúρc ὁocum
Ḟeιὁlιm hι Conchoḃaιρ, zo τάηιc zo Ror Chommáη,
ocur ὁo leιz cρeaċ a zCρúṁτoηη, zuρ aιρz Claηη
Ccoḃazáιη; ocur ὁo leιz cρech elι a Τίρ Mhaιηe, zuρ
aιρz moράη ὁo ṁuιηητeρ aη eṛpuιc, oιρ ρo ḃaὁoρ az
Ρuρτ Ccιρeηaċ ιη ταη ριη. Ro aιρzρeτ Ror Comáη, ocur
ρo ṁιllριοτ a haρḃaρ; zιὁeὁ ηίρ laṁṛaτ ὁul ρech Ror
Comáιη ρíor ὁoη ὁul ριη, óιρ ὁo ḃόι Ḟeιὁlιṁ .h.Conchoḃ-
aιρ ocur a mac, .ι. Ccὁ ηa ηzall, ιρ ηa Τuaταιḃ, ocur
ba Connachτ aρ a cul ιριη ὁίċρuιὁ; coηιὁ hí comaιρle
ὁo ρoηρaτ ὁίḃlιηαιὁ ριċ ὁo ḃéηum ρe ρoιle, ocur Mac
Uιllιαm ὁo ḟιlleὁ ὁια ṫιz íαρριη. Sluαιzeὁ móρ la
Mac Muιριρ a Τuaὁṁumaιη ὁocum Conchoḃaιρ hι
Ḃhρίαιη, zo ταρla .h.Ḃριαιη aρ a zcιηη az Cόιll Ḃeρράιη,
ocur ὁo eρzeὁaρ Τúaὁṁuṅa ὁaὁ ὁá zach leιṫ ιριη
ċoιllιz, ocur ρo maὁṁaιzheὁ ηa zaιll aηηριη, ocur ρo
maρḃaὁ aηη Dauιὁ Ρριηὁeρράρ, .ι. ριὁιρe ρo uaρρal,
ocur ὁo maρḃaὁ aη Ḟaιlzech ocur ρeρρúη Ccρὁa
ραṫaιη, ocur Τomáρρ Ḃáρόιὁ, eτ alιι multι. Ccluxaη-
ὁaιρ ράρa quιeuιτ ιη Cριṛτo. Ccρραhám .h.Conalláιη,
eṛpuιc Ccρὁa Maċa, quιeuιτ. Roḃíη laιẑleιρ ὁo éz
Domηaċ cáρc aη Ḃlιαὁaιη ριη. Maẑηuρ Mac Oιρech-
ταιz ὁo ṁaρḃaὁ ὁo Domηall .h.Ḟhlaιṫιm ιη hoc aηηo.
loclaιηη mac Ccṁláὁ ṁιc Ccιρτ hι Rúaιρc, ocur

[1] *Alii.* alι, MS.

[2] *Ignobiles.* ιzηoḃιτ, MS.

[3] *The Bishop's people.* The bishop here referred to was apparently Thomas O'Kelly, bishop of Clonfert, who died in the year 1263, and who was the son of Domhnall Mor (or Daniel the Great) O'Kelly, chief of Hy-Maine, whose death is recorded under the year 1224 *supra.*

[4] *The Failgech.* This word, which

Aedh, son of Muirchertach Finn; and Tadhg, son of Cathal, son of Brian O'Maelruanaidh; and Diarmaid, son of Tadhg, son of Muiredhach, son of Tomaltach O'Maelruanaidh; and Conchobhar Mac Gilla-Erraith; and Tadhg, son of Cian O'Gadhra; and Gilla-Beraigh O'Cuinn; and Carthalus, son of the Bishop O'Muiredhaigh; et alii[1] multi nobiles et ignobiles.[2] A hosting by Mac William Burk against Fedhlim O'Conchobhair, when he went to Ros-Comain; and he sent a predatory band into Crumhthonn, who plundered Clann-Aedhagain; and he sent another predatory band into Tir-Maine, who plundered several of the Bishop's people,[3] for they were at that time at Port-Airenach. They plundered Ros-Comain, and destroyed its corn, but they dared not go northwards past Ros-Comain on this occasion, for Fedhlim O'Conchobhair and his son, i.e. Aedh na-nGall, were in the Tuatha, and the cows of Connacht were behind them in the wilderness. And the resolution both parties adopted was to make peace with one another; and Mac William afterwards returned home. A great hosting by Mac Maurice into Tuadh-Mumha, against Conchobhar O'Briain, when O'Briain met them at Coill-Berrain, and the people of Tuadh-Mumha opposed them on every side in the wood; and the Foreigners were then routed, and David Prendergast, i.e. a most noble knight, was slain there; and the Failgech,[4] and the Parson of Ard-rathain, and Thomas Barrett, et alii[1] multi, were slain. Alexander papa quievit in Christo. Abraham O'Conalláin, bishop of Ard-Macha, quievit. Robin Laighleis[5] died on Easter-Sunday in this year. Maghnus Mac Oirechtaigh was slain by Domhnall O'Flaithimh in hoc anno. Lochlainn, son of Amhlaibh, son of Art O'Ruairc, and his brother

---

means "the destitute," seems to have been the cognomen of one of the early Welsh settlers in Connacht, from whom the sept of Clann-an- Failghe descended. See O'Donovan's *Hy-Fiachrach*, p. 325.

[5] *Laighleis*. This name is now written "Lawless."

2 F 2

Tiʒeρnan a veρbρaṫaiρ maille ρριρ, vo ṁaρbav la
hACCoṁ.h.Conchobaiρ, iaρ ná τινnlucav vo Domnall
mac Neill mic Chonʒalaiʒ hi Ruaiρc. Domnall, mac
Conchobaiρ, mic Tiʒeρnáin hi Ruaiρc, .i. ρí Dρeiρne,
vo ṁaρbav la Teallach n'Dúnchava peρ volum, ocuρ
Muiρceρτach, mac Conchabaiρ, a veρbρaṫaiρ eli, vo
maρbav lá hACCoṁ .h. Conchobaiρ iaρριn. Aρτ beʒ mac
Aiρτ hi Ruaiρc vo maρbaṫ la hACCoṁ .h.Conċobaiρ maρ
an cevna. Tavʒ vuṫ, mac Neill mic Conʒalaiʒ, vo
ṁaρbaṫ la Maoilρeċlainn mac Aṁláib mic Aiρτ.
Cρeċ ṁóρ la hACCoṁ .h.Conchobaiρ aρ Thuaṫ Ráṫa,
váρ maρbaṫ Conchobaρ mac Dρanáin, vux Coρc AC̈-
lann, ocuρ Muiρceρτach.h.Maonaiʒ, ocuρ mac Dρiain
hi Phallamain, eτ alii mulτi. Cρeċ ṁóρ vo ḋenum
vo Mac Muιριρ aρ.h.n'Domnaill, ocuρ vρem vo
ṁuinnτeρ hi Domnaill vo ḋρeiṫ ρορρα a mDenván
Dρeċṁuiʒe, ocuρ vρeam vo loρcav ṫiṫ annριn, ocuρ
vρem eli ḋo ṁaρbav. Lonʒpoρτ Conchobaiρ hi Cheallaiʒ
vo loρcav vo ḋρeim vo muinnτeρ ACoṫ[a] hi Conchobaiρ.
Cιnaoṫ.h.Dιρn, .i. ρριóιρ Chille móιρ, quιeuιτ. Cρeċ
ṁóρ vo ḋenum vlla Domnaill aρ Mac Muιριρ, ʒuρ
aιρʒevaρ Caιρρρι uιle. Ʒρáḋa eρριc vo ṫabaιρτ vo
ċoṁaρba Pávραιc aρ Maoilρeaċlainn .h. Conchobaiρ,
aʒ Dún Dealʒain. Sιτρec Mḣáʒ Sheanláich vo
maρbaṫ an AC̈ Luaιn vo Dhonncaṫa Mac Oιρechταιʒ,
ocuρ vo Thomalτach Mac Oιρechταιʒ. Eóan vé
Ueρvún vo ṫochτ an Eριnn ιn hoc anno. Maolριnnén
.h.Mιṫiʒén quιeuιτ.

Kt. Enaιρ ρορ ḟaṫaρn, ocuρ ceṫaρ ριċev ρυιρρe;
anno Domini M.cc.lx. pριmo; [xx°.i°.]anno cιclι ρolaριρ;
ocτauo anno cιclι lunaριρ; quaρτo anno ινvιcτιονιρ.
Sé cleιριʒ ṫéc vo ṁaιṫιṫ ċleιρech Chenél Conaιll ρá

---

1 *Conghalach*; i.e. Conghalach
O'Ruairc.

2 *Art*. Another member of the
family of O'Ruairc.

3 *Alii*. alι, MS.

4 *Cill-mór*. Cill-mór-na-Sinna, or
Cill-mór of the Shannon, anciently
Cill-mor-Dithruibh, now Kilmore,

Tighernan along with him, were slain by Aedh O'Con-chobhair, after they had been surrendered by Domhnall, son of Niall, son of Conghalach O'Ruairc. Domhnall, son of Conchobhar, son of Tighernan O'Ruairc, i.e. the king of Breifne, was killed by the Teallach-Dunchadha per dolum; and Muirchertach, son of Conchobhar, his other brother, was afterwards killed by Aedh O'Con-chobhair. Art Beg, son of Art O'Ruairc, was killed by Aedh O'Conchobhair in like manner. Tadhg Dubh, son of Niall, son of Conghalach,[1] was killed by Maelsechlainn, son of Amhlaibh, son of Art.[2] A great depredation was committed by Aedh O'Conchobhair on *the people of* Tuath-ratha, on which occasion Conchobhar Mac Branain, dux of Corca-Achlann, and Muirchertach O'Maenaigh, and the son of Brian O'Fallamhain, et alii[3] multi, were slain. A great depredation was committed by Mac Maurice on O'Domhnaill; but a party of O'Domhnaill's people overtook them at Bendan-Brechmhuighe, where some of them were burned, and some more slain. The residence of Conchobhar O'Ceallaigh was burned by a party of Aedh O'Conchobhair's people. Cinaeth O'Birn, i.e. the prior of Cill-mór,[4] quievit. A great depredation was committed by O'Domhnaill on Mac Maurice, when he plundered all Cairpre. The degree of bishop was conferred by the comarb of Patrick on Maelsechlainn O'Conchobhair, at Dun-Dealgan. Sitric Mac Shenlaich was killed at Ath-Luain, by Donncatha Mac Oirechtaigh and Tomaltach Mac Oirechtaigh. John de Verdun came to Erinn in hoc anno. Maelfinnen O'Mithighén quievit.

The kalends of January on Saturday, and the twenty-fourth of the moon; anno Domini M.cc.lx.primo; [xx°.i°.] anno cycli solaris; octavo anno cycli lunaris; quarto anno Indictionis. Sixteen of the most distinguished of the clerics of Cenel-Conaill, together with Conchobhar

---

about six miles to the east of Elphin, | in the county of Roscommon.

Chonchobap.h.bᵹepᵹail, do ṁapbaᵭ la Conchobap
.h.Πeill ocup la Cenel nᴇoᵹain, a nᴅoipe Choluim
Chille.   Conchobap .h.Πeill do mapbaᵭ po ceᵭóip, τpe
ᵹipτaib Coluim Chilleᵭ, la ᴅomnall .h. mᵬᴇipᵹléin,
τaoipech ᵹánaᵭ.   Ccoᵭ mac Maoipechlainn hι Conchobaip do mapbaᵭ do. Mhaolᵹaᵭaill .h.ᴇιᵭin.   Cocaᵭ
móp ocup uile ιoṁᵭa do ᵭenum do ᵹhinᵹin mac ᴅomnaill Mhéᵹ Cappτhaiᵹ, ocup dá bpaiᵬpiᵬ, ap ᵹhalloιᵬ
ιpin mbliaᵭain pin.   Sloιᵹeᵭ móp la Clainn ᵹepailτ a
nᴅepṁumain, dinnpoιᵹeᵭ Mhéᵹ Cappτhaiᵹ, ocup do
innpoιᵹ Máᵹ Cappτhaiᵹ ιaᵭpum, ocup τuc maιᵭm
ᵹoppa; ocup do mapbaᵭ ann mac τomáp, ᴇoan ppoppιum nomen, ocup a mac, ocup cóιᵹ ᵹιᵭip ᵭhéc
maille ᵹpιú annpιn, ocup ochτ mbapúin ṁaιᵬι maille
pιú, ocup ᵹιllaιᵭ óᵹa ιmᵭa, ocup pepᵹénaιᵹ ᵭιáιpṁᵭι
opιn amaᵬ; ocup po mapbaᵭ an bappach móp ann
ᵭeóp.   ᵹιnᵹin Mháᵹ Cappτhaiᵹ do ṁapᵬaᵭ lá ᵹalloιᵬ
ιap pιn, ocup pιᵹe ᴅeppṁuman do ᵹaᵬáιl dá ᵭepbpáth-
aιp, .ι. don aιᵬᵬleιpech Mháᵹ Cappτhaiᵹ, dιa éιp.
Ccpτ mac Caτhaιl pιabaιᵹ hι Ruaιpc dó éluᵭ o Ccoᵭ
.h.Conchobaιp, ocup τaoιppιᵹ na ᵬpeιᵹne ocup Con-
maιcne do ᵬabaιpτ pιᵹe na ᵬpeιᵹne ᵭó.   Mac ᵹheopuιp
do ᵹápuᵹaᵭ τempaιl ṁóιp ᵹheιᵬιn an ᴇp dapa, ᵹup
mapᵬ cóιᵹep do Luιᵹnιᵬ ann, ιm Caτhal .h. neᵹpa.
Cpeᵬ la ᴅomnall .h.neaᵹpa ᵹop Chlainn ᵹheopuιp na
épuιc pᵭein, ᵹup mapᵬ Seιᵹᵹín Mac ᵹheopuιp, ocup
an τaτcluιᵹ τuc ᵹé a τempall ᴇppa dapa ιppé po ᵭóι
ιmó ᵬenᵭ aᵹ á mapbaᵭ.   ᵬpιan puaᵭ .h.ᵬpιan do
Lopcuᵭ ocup do pcaoιleᵭ ᵬaιᵹᵹléιn hι Chonaιnᵹ, ocup

---

1 *Colum-Cille.* This name is usually
understood as signifying "Columba
ecclesiæ." See Reeves's *Adamnan*,
Int., p. lxx. But the last member
of the name (*cille*, gen. of *cill*=
Lat. *cella*) is written ćιᵴᵗ in the
MS., for *chilledh*, probably through
mistake.

2 *Clann-Gerald;* i.e. the Geraldines.
3 *Proprium nomen.* ꝑ. noɱ̄., MS.
In the Annals of Connacht the words
ppoppιum nomen are plainly
written. The death of John Fitz-
Thomas is entered in Grace's Annals
at the year 1261, and also, incorrectly, under 1257.

O'Ferghail, were killed by Conchobhar O'Neill and the Cenel-Eoghain, in Doire-Choluim-Chille. Conchobhar O'Neill was immediately slain through the miracles of Colum-Cille,[1] by Domhnall O'Breisléin, chief of Fánad. Aedh, son of Maelsechlainn O'Conchobhair, was killed by Maelfhabhaill O'hEidhin. A great war *was waged*, and numerous injuries were committed, by Finghin, son of Domhnall Mac Carthaigh, and his brothers, against Foreigners in this year. A great hosting by the Clann-Gerald[2] into Des-Mumha, to attack Mac Carthaigh; and Mac Carthaigh attacked them, and defeated them, and Fitz-Thomas (John *proprium nomen*),[3] and his son,[4] and fifteen knights and eight noble barons along with them, were slain there, besides several young men, and soldiers innumerable. And the Barrach Mór[5] was also killed there. Finghin Mac Carthaigh was subsequently slain by the Foreigners, and the sovereignty of Des-Mumha was assumed after him by his brother, i.e. the Aithchleirech[6] Mac Carthaigh. Art, son of Cathal Riabhach O'Ruairc, escaped from Aedh O'Conchobhair; and the chieftains of the Breifne and Conmaicne gave him the sovereignty of the Breifne. Mac Fheorais profaned the great church of Feichin in Es-dara, where he killed five of the Luighne, together with Cathal O'hEghra. A depredation *was committed* by Domhnall O'hEghra on Clann-Fheorais in retaliation for this, when he killed Sefin Mac Fheorais, and what he had on his head when he was killed was the bell cover[7] which he had taken from the church of Es-dara. Brian Ruadh O'Briain burned and demolished Caislen-Ui-Chonaing,

---

[4] *His son;* i.e. Maurice FitzGerald.

[5] *The Barrach Mór.* The Barry Mór, Barrymore, or Barry the Great.

[6] *Aithchleirech.* Aithchleirech signifies ex-cleric, or rather quondam clericus; i.e. one who had resigned his clerkship, or been suspended.

[7] *Bell cover.* ꝏ꜀꜀ꞔꞀuꞀꝝ. Dr. O'Donovan translates this "bell" (*Four Mast.*, 1261); but ꝏ꜀꜀ꞔꞀuꞀꝝ is compounded of ꝏ꜀꜀ a covering, (also explained "a side," or "joint" by O'Reilly), and ꞔꞀuꝝ gen. of ꞔꞁoꝝ, a bell.

do marbaḋ a raibe do ḋáinib ann. Caisslen do tóirnneḋ ag Eóan dé Uerdún a Moiġ Duma a Muinntir Ghillgán in hoc anno. Longport Aoḋa hI Conchobair ag Snám in redaiġ do loscud dona Breiffnechaib. Loscud Chluana suilinn, .i. longpurt Feḋlim hI Conchobair. Mac Aoḋa hI Chonchobair do ṫabairt ar altrom dArt.h.Ruairc. Creaċ mór lá hAoḋ .h.Conchobair isin mBreifne go rainic Druim leṫan, ocus córtus maḋma do ṫaḃairt ar ḃlaiḋ dia rútadhaib, gur marbaḋ sochaide gan beiṫ suaiċniḋ ḋíb. Gilla Crist mac Edna hI Maoilċiaráin, taoisech Mhuintera Mhaoilċiarain ocus Theallaiġ Chonġusa, mortuus est. Aoḋ buiḋe .h.Neill expulsus est, ocus Niall cúlánach .h.Neill do rigad na ionad. Niall .h.Gairmleghaigh, taoisech Chenél Moáin, mortuus est.

Kl. Enáir for Domnach, ocus cúiged uathad fuirre; anno Domini M.cc.lxii; [xx°.ii°.]anno cicli solaris; nono anno cicli lunaris; u. anno indictionis. Maoilsechlainn mac Taiḋg hI Conchobair, espuc Shíl Muiredhaiġ, mortuus est. Slóiged adbal la Gallaib Erenn docum Pheiḋlim mic Cathail Croibderg, ocus doċum a mic, .i. Aoḋ na nGall, gur ċuir .h.Conchobair urṁór bó Connacht a Tír Conaill ar teiched na nGall; ocus do ḃí sé fein an Inis Saiṁér ar cúl a ḃó ocus a ṁuinntera. Dála Gall, imorro, tánic Mac Uilliam Burc tar tochur Mhónaiḋ Coinnedha aniar, ocus sluag mór maillefris, go hOilfinn, ocus Giúsdís na hErenn ocus Eóan de Uerdún tar Aṫ Luain anoir go Ros Comán; ocus do leigedar creaċa móra amaċ a gCenél Doḃṫa mic Aonġusa, gur airgedar an ṁéid ro an tar éis

---

[1] *Snamh-in-redaigh.* This name is written "Snamh-Muiredhaigh," or the "ford of Muiredhach," in the Annals of Connacht; but the Four Masters write it as in the next. Dr. O'Donovan conjectures (*Four Mast.*, A.D. 1261, note [y]) that it is "probably the place now called Druim-Snamha, Anglicè Drumsna, on the Shannon, on the boundary between the counties of Leitrim and Roscommon."

[2] *Bishop of Sil-Muiredhaigh;* i.e. bishop of Elphin.

[3] *Cenel-Dobhtha-mic-Aenghusa;* i.e.

and killed all the people who were in it. A castle was built by John de Verdun in Magh-dumha in Muinter-Ghilgan in hoc anno. The fortress of Aedh O'Conchobhair at Snamh-in-redaigh[1] was burned by the people of the Breifne. Burning of Cluain-Suilinn, i.e. the fortress of Fedhlim O'Conchobhair. The son of Aedh O'Conchobhair was given in fosterage to Art O'Ruairc. A great depredation *was committed* by Aedh O'Conchobhair in the Breifne, until he reached Druim-lethan, when a portion of his routs were defeated, and a great number of them were slain who were not distinguished. Gilla-Christ, son of Edna O'Maelchiarain, chieftain of Muinter-Maelchiarain and Tellach-Chonghusa, mortuus est. Aedh Buidhe O'Neill expulsus est, and Niall Culanach O'Neill was made king in his place. Niall O'Gairm-leghaigh, chieftain of Cenel-Moain, mortuus est.

The kalends of January on Sunday, and the fifth of the moon; anno Domini M.cc.lxii; [xx°.ii°.] anno cycli solaris; nono anno cycli lunaris; v. anno Indictionis. Maelsechlainn, son of Tadhg O'Conchobhair, bishop of Sil-Muiredhaigh,[2] mortuus est. A prodigious hosting by the Foreigners of Erinn against Fedhlim, son of Cathal Crobhderg, and against his son. i.e. Aedh-na-nGall, when O'Conchobhair sent the greater number of the cows of Connacht to Tir-Conaill, away from the Foreigners, and he himself remained in Inis-Saimer, in defence of his cows and people. As regards the Foreigners, however, Mac William Burc, accompanied by a great army, came from the west across Tochar-Mona-Coinnedha, to Oilfinn, and the Justiciary of Erinn and John de Verdun went westwards across Ath-Luain, to Ros-Comain; and they despatched great predatory bands into Cenel-Dobhtha-mic-Aenghusa,[3] who on that occasion plundered all that

the Cenel (kindred or sept) of Dobhtha, son of Aenghus. The territory formerly inhabited by the Cenel-Dobhtha is now better known as O'Hanly's country, a district in the east of the county of Roscommon.

hi Conchobaip a Connachta von oulaṁ rin; ocur vo
ṫoirneṁar inaṁ cairrlein a Rorr Comáin von toirc rin.
Dala Αοṁa hi Conchobaip, imorro, ro cinoil ríṁein rlúaġ
mór, ocur ro airġeṁar Ẓaill iarṫar Connacht uile,
ó Mhuiġ Éó na Saxanach ocur ó bhalla aníar, ocur
ro loirc a mbailti ocur a narṁanna orin ẓo Sliaṁ Luẓa,
ocur ro marṁurṁar vaoine imṁa etorra rin. Α haiċle
na ẓcreaċ mór rin vo ṁenum ṁó, vo ċuir a mic riġ ocur
táirriċ uaṁ an uachtar Connacht, ẓur loirceт ocur
ẓur airẓreт ó Thuaim ṁá ġualann co hΑċ Luain, ocur
ro marṁaṁar ina ḃfuaraṁar vo ṁaoiniṁ etorra rin
uile. Domnall .h.Mannaċáin vo márḃaṁ vo macaiṁ
Ruaiṁri ocur Taiṁġ hi Conchobaip. Dála Ẓall,
imorro, vo ċuireṁar techta uaṁa voċum hi Conchobaip
ocur a mic, vo ṫairrrin τrìṁa ṁóiṁ. Tanic imorro Αοṁ
.h.Conchobaip a coinne Ẓhall iarrin co hΑċ ṁoire
Chuirc, ocur vo róṁrat ríṫ annrin, ocur vo chúaiv an
oiṁċe rin a теċ Ẓall ẓan ḃraiġe ẓan eoire тар éiri;
ocur vo ḃi an aon ionaṁ ocur an aon leabaiv re Mac
Uilliam ḃúrc an oiṁċe rin ẓo ruḃach romeiṁnach;
ocur vo imċiġreт Ẓall ар a ḃárach тар éir ant ríṁa
rin vo ṁenum ṁóiṁ. Creċ mór vo ṁenum vo Ẓhalloiṁ
na Miṁe ар Ẓhilla na naom .h.Ferẓail, ар taoirech na
hΑnġaile, ocur a oirecht rein vo vul uaṁ anucht Ẓhall,
ocur aċtaoirech vo ṁenum ṁóiṁ ṁe, ocur taoirech vo
ṁenum vo mac Murchava ċarraiġ hi Ferẓail ina
ċenṁ. Uilc iomṁa vo creachaiḃ ocur vo ẓrearraiḃ,
vúrrṫhaiḃ ocur vairẓniḃ, ocur vo ṁarḃṫhaiḃ, vo ṁenum
vo Ẓilla na naom .h. Ferẓail ар Ẓhalloiṁ an ḃliaṁain
rin, ocur a ṫaoiriġecht ocur a ṫiẓernтur rein vo
ṫornum ар éẓin ṁó, ocur mac Murchava ċarraiġ vo
ṁíchur ар in тír amaċ ṁó. Sloiẓeṁ la Mac Uilliam
ḃúrc ocur la Ẓalloiṁ Erenn a nDermumain, vinnroiẓeṁ

---

[1] *All the men.* The Four Masters
say all who were inḟeaṁma, i.e.
"fit to bear arms."

[2] *Deposed.* The words aċtaoirech
vo ṁenum ṁóiṁ ṁe signify lit. "an ex-
chieftain was made of him by them."

remained in Connacht after O'Conchobhair; and they
marked out the site of a castle in Ros-Comain on this
expedition. With regard to Aedh O'Conchobhair, he
collected a large army, and plundered the Foreigners of
all the West of Connacht eastwards from Magh-Eó of the
Saxons, and from Balla, and burned their towns and corn
fields from thence to Sliabh-Lugha, and slew many
persons between those places. After he had committed
these great depredations he sent off his princes and
chieftains into Uachtar-Chonnacht, who burned and
plundered from Tuaim-dá-ghualann to Ath-Luain; and
they killed all the men[1] they found between those places.
Domhnall O'Mannachain was killed by the sons of
Ruaidhri and Tadhg O'Conchobhair. As to the Foreigners,
however, they despatched messengers to O'Conchobhair
and his son, to offer them peace. Aedh O'Conchobhair,
moreover, came subsequently to Ath-dhoire-Chuirc, to
meet the Foreigners; and they concluded peace; and he
went that night afterwards into the house of the Foreigners, without giving pledge or hostage; and he was
on that night in the same place, and in the same bed
with Mac William Burk, cheerfully, contentedly. And
the Foreigners departed on the morrow, after they had
concluded this peace. A great depredation was committed
by the Foreigners of Midhe on Gilla-na-naemh O'Ferghail,
chieftain of the Anghaile; and his own tribe forsook him,
and went over to the Foreigners; and he was deposed[2]
by them, and the son of Murchadh Carrach O'Ferghail
was made chieftain in opposition to him. Numerous
injuries *in the shape* of depredations, aggressions,
spoliations, plunderings and killings, were committed
by Gilla-na-naemh O'Ferghail on the Foreigners this
year; and he forcibly asserted his own chieftainship and
sovereignty, and expelled the son of Murchadh Carrach
O'Ferghail out of the district. A hosting by Mac
William Burk and the Foreigners of Erinn to Des-Mumha,

Ⅿhéᵹ Cáɼɼⴡhaiᵹ, ᵹo ɼaɴᵹaⴡaɼ aɴ Ⅿhaɴᵹaɼⴡach Loċa
Léiɴ, ocuɼ ɼo maɼbaⴡ Ʒeɼalⴡ Róiⴡɼi aɴɴɼiɴ lá Ⅿáᵹ
Caɼɼⴡhaiᵹ; ocuɼ a ⴡúⴡɼaⴡ ᵹuɼ ⴡé ɼiɴ aɴ ⴡɼeaɼɼ baɼúɴ
iɼ ɼeɼɼ ⴡo ⴡí aɴ Ɇɼiɴɴ. Ocuɼ ⴡobé ɼiɴ aɴⴡ áiⴡeɼ co
ɴaɴaiⴡeɼ ⴡo ⴤheɼɼⴞumaiɴ, oiɼ ɼo maɼbaⴡ mac ⴡomɴaill ᵹuiⴡ Ⅿeᵹ Caɼɼⴡhaiᵹ iɼiɴ lá ceⴡɴa ɼiɴ, .i. Coɼmac
mac ⴡoⴞɴaill, ocuɼ ɼob eɼⴡaⴡach Ʒaill ocuɼ Ʒáiⴡhel
aɴ lá ɼiɴ ɼoɴ Ⅿaɴᵹaɼⴡach. Comaɼba Ᵽaⴡɼaic ⴡo
ⴡeachⴡ aɴ eɼiɴɴ iɴ hoc aɴɴo.

Ƙⴡ. Ɇɴáiɼ ɼoɼ Luaɴ, ocuɼ ɼeiɼeⴡ ⴡhéc ɼuiɼɼe; aɴɴo
ⴡomiɴi Ⅿ.cc.lxiii.; xxiii. aɴɴo cicli ɼolaɼiɼ; x. aɴɴo
cicli luɴaɼiɼ; ui.aɴɴo cicli iɴⴡicⴡioɴiɼ. ⴡoɴɴ
.h.Ʋɼeiɼléiɴ ⴡo maɼbaⴡ la ⴡomɴall.h.ɴ'ⴡomɴaill
a ᵹcúiɼⴡ aɴ eɼɼuic a Raⴡ ⴡhoⴡ, a bɼeall. Slúaiᵹeⴡ
la Ⅿac Uilliam ⴞúɼc ⴡiɴɴɼoiᵹeⴡ Ꝑheiⴡlim hi Coɴchobaiɼ, ocuɼ ⴡiɴɴɼaiᵹeⴡ a mic, ᵹo ɼaɴᵹaⴡaɼ Roɼɼ
Comáɴ, ocuɼ ɼo ⴡeiⴡɼeⴡ Siol Ⅿuiɼeᵹhaiᵹh ɼompu a
ⴡuaiɼceɼⴡ Coɴɴachⴡ, ocuɼ ɴí bɼuaɼaⴡaɼ Ʒaill eɼecha
ɴa eⴡáil ⴡoɴ ⴡul ɼiɴ. ⴡoɴɴchaⴡ.h.Ꝑloiɴɴ ocuɼ
Taⴡᵹ a mac ⴡiɴɴɼoiᵹeⴡ ⴡɼoiɴᵹe ⴡoɴⴡ ɼlúaiᵹ ɼiɴ, ocuɼ
ⴡo maɼbaⴡ ceⴡ ⴡiⴞɼiɴ eⴡiɼ ⴞaiⴡ ocuɼ ɼaiⴡ, ɼo Ꝁiⴡíɴ
Ruiⴡɼél ocuɼ a mac, ocuɼ ɼo .u. macaiⴡ Choɴcoɴɴachⴡ
hi Coɴchobaiɼ, eⴡ alii multi; ocuɼ aɴ ɼluaᵹ ⴡo impó
ɼó ⴞéla ⴡia ⴡiᵹiⴡ iaɼɼiɴ. Tomáɼ .h.Ceallaiᵹ, eɼɼuc
Chluaɴa ɼeɼⴡa ⴞɼéɴaiɴɴ, quieuiⴡ iɴ Cɼiɼⴡo. Ɇⴡⴡoɴɴ,
ɼí Loⴡlaɴɴ, ⴡo éᵹ a ɴiɴɴɼiⴡ Oɼc aɼ ɼliᵹeⴡ aᵹ ⴡeachⴡ
aɴ eɼiɴɴ. ⴡáuiⴡ .h.Ꝑiɴɴ, ab maiɴiɼⴡɼech ɴa ⴡúille,
quieuiⴡ. ⴡiaɼmaiⴡ cleɼech, mac Coɼmaic Ⅿic
ⴡhiaɼmaⴡa, moɼⴡuuɼ eɼⴡ. αɴⴡileɼ Ⅿháᵹ Ꝑhiɴɴ-
ⴞaɼɼ, ⴡux Ⅿuiɴɴⴡeɼi Ʒeɼaⴡaiɴ, obiiⴡ. ƷillaⱣaⴡɼaic

---

¹ *The third.* The Annals of Connacht add αcuɼ ɴí ɼeⴡamaɼ aɴ
ⴡiaɼ aili, "and we know not the
other two."

² *Comarb of Patrick;* i.e. the suc-
cessor of St. Patrick, or archbishop of
Armagh. His name was Maelpatraic
O'Scannail. The Irish of this entry

is written twice in the MS., viz.:—at
the end of one page and beginning of
the next.

³ *Alii.* αli, MS.

⁴ *Ebhdhonn.* Hakon Hakonson is
meant. According to the *Saga Hakonar
Hakonarsonar* the Irish had sent ambassadors to king Hakon, offering to

to attack Mac Carthaigh, until they reached the Mangartach of Loch-Lein, where Gerald Roche was slain by Mac
Carthaigh; and it was said that he was the third[1] best
baron in Erinn. And this was the "joy with sorrow" to
Des-Mumha, for the son of Domhnall Got Mac Carthaigh,
i.e. Cormac, son of Domhnall, was slain on that same day;
and the Foreigners and Gaeidhel suffered great losses on
that day around the Mangartach. The comarb of Patrick[2]
came to Erinn in hoc anno.

The kalends of January on Monday, and the sixteenth
of the moon; anno Domini M.CC.lxiii.; xx.iii. anno cycli
solaris; x. anno cycli lunaris; vi°. anno cycli Indictionis.
Donn O'Breisléin was killed by Domhnall O'Domhnaill
in the bishop's court at Rath-Bhoth, in treachery. A
hosting by Mac William Burk against Fedhlim O'Conchobhair, and against his son, as far as Ros-Comain; and
the Sil-Muiredhaigh fled before them to the North of
Connacht, and the Foreigners obtained neither preys nor
spoils on this occasion. Donnchadh O'Floinn and his
son Tadhg attacked a division of this army, and one
hundred of them were slain, both good and bad, including
Aitin Russel and his son, and the five sons of Cuconnacht
O'Conchobhair, et alii[3] multi; and the army afterwards
returned to their homes in disgrace. Thomas O'Cellaigh,
bishop of Cluain-ferta-Brenainn, quievit in Christo.
Ebhdhonn,[4] king of Lochlann, died in Innsi-Orc, on the
way whilst coming to Erinn. David O'Finn, abbot of
the monastery of the Buill, quievit. Diarmaid Clerech,[5]
son of Cormac Mac Diarmada, mortuus est. Andiles Mac
Finnbharr, dux of Muinter-Geradhain, obiit. Gilla-Patraic,

---

submit themselves to him if he would
come and expel the English. See *Saga
Hákonar Hákonarsonar*, cap. 322;
(Fornmanna Sögur; Kaupmannahöfn,
1835; vol. 10, p. 131); and Munch's
Norske Folks Historie, Christiania,
1858, vol. i., part iv., p. 407. The

Chron. Mannie at 1263 says, "Venit
Haco rex Norvegiæ ad partes Scotiæ
[i.e. Hiberniæ?], et nihil expediens
reversus est ad Orcades, et ibidem
apud Kirkwall mortuus."

[5] *Diarmaid Clerech*; i.e. "Diarmaid
the Cleric."

mac Zilla na nzuippén, ppióp Doipén, pái einiZ ocur
cpábaŏ, quieuic. Maolpaŏaill .h.heiŏin do mapbaŏ
la Zalloib. Maolciapán .h.Maoileoin, ab Chluana
mic Nóip, quieuic. Cocaŏ mór evip čomapba Pacpaic
ocur erpuc na Miŏe in hoc anno. Caippleu do ŏenum
do Mac Uilliam Úupc az Aŏ in zail ipin Chopann.
Meačaip .h.Ruaŏán do mapbaŏ lá Zalloib abťell, a
nooppur ŏempail Chille Seipcnén, in hoc anno. Ecaoin
inzen hi Fhlannacáin moprua erc. Sampaŏ po ŏe
ipin mbliaŏain rin.

 Kt. Enaip pop maipc, ocur peachc ficheŏ cuippe;
anno Domini M.cc.lx.quapco; xxiii.anno cicli polapir;
xi. anno cicli lunapir; iii.anno cicli inoiccionir.
Cocaŏ mór do ŏenum dApc.h.Mhaoilpečlainn pop
Zhalloib na Miŏe, ocur áp mop do ŏabaipc dó poppa
imón mÚpopnač, ocur an neoč nach ap mapŏaic diŏ
po báiŏic iao. Muipcepcach, mac Domnaill hi Aipc,
do mapbaŏ, ocur a muinncep do lopcuŏ, lá Donn
Mház Uiŏip in hoc anno. Cocaŏ mór do eipže evip
pí Saxan ocur pí Úpeacan, ocur iaplaŏa Saxan do
eipže do Eoŏapo ocur dá mac, ocur caŏ do chup
ecoppa diŏlinaiŏ, ocur Eoŏapo pí Saxan ocur a mac
do żabáil ann, ocur Ioan dé Uepoún, ocur áp diáipmŏe
maille ppiú pin do ŏabaipc ecoppa. Aonžur .h.Clú-
máin, erpuc Luizne, do éz a mainircip na Úuille, iap
cup a erpucóiŏe ŏe pava ŏaimpir peimi rin. Cpeč
mór do ŏenum do Dhealŏnaiŏ ap Shiol nAnmchaoa,
ocur coiz mic hi Mhaoaŏáin do mapbaŏ ann ŏeóp.
Coinne mór ecip Zhalloib Epenn, im ziurŏir na
hepenn, ocur im Iapla Ulaŏ, ocur im Mac Zepailc,

---

¹ *War.* cocaŏ. This was a dispute regarding the right of the archbishop of Armagh to make a visitation of the diocese of Meath, which Ware states was arranged in a provincial synod held at Drogheda in the year 1262. See Ware's *Bishops* (*Armagh*, under Patrick O'Scanlain, and *Meath*, under Hugh de Tachmon).

² *His people.* It would be more correct to say the territory occupied by his people.

³ *Edward.* This is apparently a mistake for Henry III.

son of Gilla-na-nGuissén, prior of Doirén, a man eminent for hospitality and piety, quievit. Maelfabhaill O'hEidhin was slain by Foreigners. Maelchiarain O'Maeleoin, abbot of Cluain-mic-Nois, quievit. A great war[1] between the comarb of Patrick and the bishop of Midhe in hoc anno. A castle was erected by Mac William Burk at Ath-in-gail in the Corann. Meachair O'Ruadhain was killed by Foreigners, in treachery, in the door of the church of Cill-Seiscnen, in hoc anno. Etain, daughter of O'Flannagain, mortua est. A very hot summer in this year.

The kalends of January on Tuesday, and the twenty-seventh of the moon; anno Domini M.cc.lx.quarto; xxiiii.anno cycli solaris; xi.anno cycli lunaris; vii.anno cycli Indictionis. A great war was waged by Art O'Maelsechlainn against the Foreigners of Midhe; and he inflicted a great slaughter on them about the Brosnach; and such of them as were not slain were drowned. Muir-chertach, son of Domhnall O'hAirt, was killed, and his people[2] were burned, by Donn Mac Uidhir in hoc anno. A great war arose between the king of the Saxons and the king of Britain, and the Saxon earls opposed Edward[3] and his son; and a battle[4] was fought between them, in which Edward,[3] king of the Saxons, and his son were taken prisoners, and John de Verdun, and a great slaughter besides was committed between them. Aenghus O'Clumh-ain, bishop of Luighne,[5] died in the monastery of the Buill, after having resigned his bishopric a long time before that. A great depredation was committed by the Dealbhna on Sil-Anmchadha, and five sons of O'Mada-dhain were slain there moreover. A great meeting between the Foreigners of Erinn, (including the Justiciary[6] of Erinn, and including the Earl of Ulster, and Fitz-Gerald,

---

[4] *A battle.* The battle of Lewes is doubtless meant.

[5] *Bishop of Luighne.* That is to say, bishop of Achonry.

[6] *The Justiciary.* Richard de la Rochelle, justiciary of Ireland from A.D. 1261 to 1266.

ocuṛ ım ṁαıṫıḃ Ʒαll Єṗenn oṛın αmαṫ, ṗe Ḟeıḃlım
.h.Conchoḃαıṗ, ocuṛ ṗe hᾼoḃ .h.Conchoḃαıṗ α mαc,
ın ᾼṫ Luαın. Єαʒlα ṁóṗ ocuṛ αnḃάṫαḋ ḋo ʒαḃάıl
nα nʒαll oḋ ṫonncoḋαṗ αnṫ ḟocṛαıḋe ḃίάıṗṁıḃe ṗo
ḃoı .h.Conchoḃαıṗ ocuṛ α mαc, conıḋ hί comαıṗle ḋo
ṗónṗαṫ Ʒαıll αnnṗın ṗίṫ ḋo ḋenum ṗe .h.Conchoḃαıṗ
ocuṛ ṗe nα mαc; ocuṛ ḋo ṗınneḋαṗ αṗṗ α hαıṫle.
Cocαḋ moṗ ḋo eṗṡe eṫıṗ Mαc Uıllıαm Ḃuṗc, .ı. Iαṗlα
Ulαḋ, ocuṛ Mαc Ʒeṗαılṫ ıṗın mḃlıαḋαın ṗın, ʒuṗ
mılleḋ uṗṁoṗ nα hЄṗenn eṫoṗṗα, ʒuṗ ʒαḃ αnṫ Iαṗlα
α ṗαıḃı ḋo ṫαıṗlénαıḃ α Connαchṫα αʒ Mαc Ʒeṗαılṫ,
ocuṛ ʒuṗ loıṗc α ṁαınéṗα uıle, ocuṛ ʒuṗ αıṗʒ α
muınnṫeṗα uıle ḋon ṫocαḋ ṗın. ᾼṗṫ .h.Mαoılṛechlαınn
ḋo loṗcαḋ αṗαıḃe ḋo ṫαıṗlénαıḃ ocuṛ ḋo ṗṗάḋḃαılṫıḃ
α nʼOeαlḃnα ocuṛ α mḂṗeʒṁuıne, ocuṛ α Cαllṗuıḋe,
ocuṛ ṗo ḃίṫuıṗ nα Ʒαıll eıṗḋıḃ uıle, ocuṛ ṗo ʒαḃuṗṫαṗ
ḃṗαıʒḋe ṫαoıṗech αn ṫíṗe uıle ıαṗṗın; ocuṛ Loṫ Luαṫα
ḋo loṗcuḋ ḋó ḃeóṗ. Ʒıúṗḋıṗ nα hЄṗenn, ocuṛ Seoαn
Ʒoʒάn, ocuṛ Ṫeαṗóıḋ Ḃuıṫıléıṗ, ḋo ʒαḃαıl ḋo Mαc
Ʒeṗαılṫ α ṫempαll ṫoıṗṗecṫα. Cαıṗṗlén Loṫα Meṗcα
ocuṛ cαıṗṗlén ᾼṗḋα ṗαṫαın ḋo ʒαḃαıl ḋo Mαc Uıllıαm
ınα lαım ṗṗéın ın hoc αnno. Oomnαll .h.hЄʒṗα, ṗí
Luıʒne, ḋo ṁαṗḃαḋ ḋo Ʒhαlloıḃ. Cúṁuıʒe O Cαṫάn,
ṗı Cίαnαchṫα, cαṗṫuṛ eṗṫ ṗeṗ ᾼoḃ ḃuıḋe. Ḃṗαıṫṗı
Mınúṗα ḋo ṫαḃαıṗṫ ʒo hᾼṗḋ Mαchα Leıṗın αıṗḋeṗṗıc,
.ı. le Moelṗαḋṗαıc O Scαnnαıl, ocuṛ αn ṗeṗ ceḋnα, .ı.
Mαolṗαḋṗαıc, ḋo ḋenum ḋíʒe αṫımṫell ᾼıṗḋ Mαṫα αn
ḃlıαḋαın ṗın.

ᚴꞇ. Єnαıṗ ṗoṗ ḋαṗḋαoın, ochṫmαḋ uαṫhαḋ ṗuıṗṗe;
xxu. αnno cıclı ṗolαṗıṗ; xıı. αnno cıclı lunαṗıṗ; uııı.
αnno ınḋıcṫıonıṗ; M.cc.lx.quınṫo. Ṫomάṛ Mαc Ḟeṗʒαıl

[1] *Street-towns.* For the meaning of street-town (ṗṗαıḋ-ḃαıle), see note [6], p. 258, *supra*.

[2] *The Justiciary.* See note [6], p. 447.

[3] *A consecrated church.* The church of Castle-Dermot in the county of Kildare.

[4] *Aedh Buidhe.* Apparently Aedh Buidhe (yellow Hugh) O'Neill, chieftain of Cenel-Eoghain, sl. 1283. The three concluding entries for this year

and the other nobles of the Foreigners of Erinn), and Fedhlim O'Conchobhair, and Aedh O'Conchobhair, his son, at Ath-Luain. Great fear and consternation seized the Foreigners when they saw the countless multitude that accompanied O'Conchobhair and his son; and the resolution the Foreigners then adopted was to conclude peace with O'Conchobhair and his son, which they did forthwith. A great war arose between Mac William Burk, i.e. the Earl of Ulster, and Fitz-Gerald, in this year, so that the major part of Erinn was destroyed between them; and the Earl seized all the castles Fitz-Gerald had in Connacht, and burned all his manors, and plundered all his people, during this war. Art O'Mael-sechlainn burned all the castles and street-towns[1] in Dealbhna, and in Breghmhuine, and in Calraighe, and expelled the Foreigners out of them all, and afterwards took the hostages of the chieftains of the entire district; and Loch-Luatha was also burned by him. The Justiciary[2] of Erinn, and John Gogan, and Tibbot Butler were taken prisoners by Fitz-Gerald in a consecrated church.[3] The castle of Loch-Mesca, and the castle of Ard-rathain, were seized by Mac William Burk into his own hand in hoc anno. Domhnall O'hEghra, king of Luighne, was slain by Foreigners. Cumhuighe O'Cathain, king of Cianachta, captus est per Aedh Buidhe.[4] Friars Minor were brought to Ard-Macha by the archbishop, i.e. Mael-patraic O'Scannail; and the same man, i.e. Maelpatraic, made a trench[5] round Ard-Macha in this year.

The kalends of January on Thursday, the eighth of the moon; xxv. anno cycli solaris; xii. anno cycli lunaris; viii. anno Indictionis; M.cc.lx.quinto.[6] Thomas, son of

---

are not given in the Dublin copies of the Annals of Connacht.

[5] *A trench.* The sinking of a trench *round the church* of Armagh, by Arch-

bishop O'Scannail, is recorded by the Four Masters under the year 1266.

[6] *Quinto.* quincto, MS.

2 G

mic Οιαρmαοα, εγρυς Οιlεγιnn, quιειτ ιn Cγιγτο.
Τοmάγ .h.Maιcín, εγρυς Lιιξne,, quιειτ. Caιγlén
Slιξιξ οο γξαοιleξ lα hαοξ .h.Conchobαιγ, οcuγ cαιγlén
αn ξhenο γαοα οcuγ cαιγlén Κάξ αιγο cγαιξe οο
lογcαο οcuγ οο γξαοιleο leιγ ξeóγ. Mαιnιγτιγ Τhοξαιγ
Φhατγαιc οο lογcαο ιγιn mblιαοαιn γιn. Ταοξ Mαc
Φhιnnξαιγ οο ṁαγξαξ οο Chonchobαγ Mhάξ Κάξnαιll,
οcuγ οο mαc Οomnαιll hι Φεγξαιl, ιn hoc αnno.
Φειξlιm mαc Cατhαιl cγοιξοεγτ hι Conchobαιγ, γι
Connαchτ, γεγ coγαnτα οcuγ coξαιξτι α cúιξιξ γειn,
οcuγ γεγ coγαnτα α cαγαο γογ ξαch leιξ ; γεγ αιγcτι
οcuγ ιοnnαγξτα α εγcαγαο ξαch ιnαξ αmbίοιγ ; γεγ lάn
οenech οcuγ οenξnum ; γεγ lάn οοιγγοεγcuγ οcuγ οuγ-
γumuγ α nΘγιnn οcuγ α Saxαnαξ, οο éξ ιαγ mbuαιξ
nonξτα οcuγ nαιξγιξe, οcuγ α αξlucαο α mαιnιγοιγ nα
mbγάτhαγ γγεcιuγ α Κογ Chomαιn τuc γειn αmαξ οο
Οhíα οcuγ οοn ογο γοιme γιn. αοξ .h.Conchobαιγ,
.ι. α mαc γειn, οο ξαξαιl γιξe Connαchτ ταγ éιγ α ατhαγ,
οcuγ αξ γεαξ γιξ οο ξenum ξó αγ Uιξ Φαιlξe. Loιγcτι
οcuγ mαγξτα ιomξα οο ξenum ξó αnn ; οcuγ αγ nιmγόξ
ξο hαξ Luαιn οό, Cατhαl mαc Ταοξ hι Conchobαιγ οο
ξαllαο οό, οcuγ α héξ οαγéιγ α ξαllτα. Muιγceγταch,
mαc Cατhαιl, mιc Οιαγmαοα, mιc Ταοξ hι Mhαοιl-
γuαnαξ, γι Mhuιξe Luιγξ, οο éc ιγιn blιαοαιn γιn.
Ξιllα nα nαom .h.Cuιnn, ταοιγεch Muιnτεγι Ξιollξάn,
mογτuuγ εγτ. Cαthαl Mhάξ Κάξnαιll, τάιγγech
Muιnnτιγe hΘolαιγ, mογτuuγ εγτ. Mυιγεξαξ .h.Cεγ-
ξαιll, ταιγγech Cαllγαιοhe, mογτuuγ εγτ. Mαοlbγιξοe
.h.Ξγúcαn, οιγξιnοech Οιlεγιnn, mογτuuγ εγτ. Mυιγιγ
mαc Νειll hι Conchobαιγ οο ξοξα οοξύιm εγγιcοιοε
Οιlεγιnn ιn hoc αnno. Coιγne οο ξenum οό Τhomαl-
ταch .h.Conchobαιγ, οαιγοεγρυς Connαchτ, γε Οαυιο
Φιnοαγξγάγ οcuγ γe mαcαξ Muγchαοα, οcuγ mογάn
οο muιnnτεγ αn αιγοεγγυιc οο ṁαγξαο αn lά γιn οόιξ

Ferghal Mac Diarmada, bishop of Oilfinn, quievit in Christo. Thomas O'Maicin, bishop of Luighne,[1] quievit. The castle of Sligech was demolished by Aedh O'Conchobhair; and the castle of Benn-fhada and the castle of Rath-aird-craibhe were burned and demolished by him also. The monastery of Tobar-Patraic was burned in this year. Tadhg Mac Fhinnbhair was killed by Conchobhar Mac Raghnaill, and by the son of Domhnall O'Ferghail, in hoc anno. Fedhlim, son of Cathal Crobhderg O'Conchobhair, king of Connacht—the protector and supporter of his own province, and the protector of his friends on every side; the plunderer and extirpator of his enemies wherever they might be; a man full of bounty and prowess; a man full of distinction and honor in Erinn and Saxon-land—died after the triumph of unction and penitence, and was interred in the monastery of the Friars Preachers in Ros-Comain, which he had previously granted to God and the Order. Aedh O'Conchobhair, i.e. his own son, assumed the sovereignty of Connacht after his father, and executed his royal depredation on the Ui-Failghe, where he committed many burnings and killings; and, on his return to Ath-Luain, he blinded Cathal, son of Tadhg O'Conchobhair, who died after having been blinded. Muirchertach, son of Cathal, son of Diarmaid, son of Tadhg O'Maelruanaidh, king of Magh-Luirg, died in this year. Gilla-na-naemh O'Cuinn, chieftain of Muinter-Gillgan, mortuus est. Cathal Mac Raghnaill, chieftain of Muinter-Eolais, mortuus est. Muiredhach O'Cerbhaill, chieftain of Calraidhe, mortuus est. Maelbrighde O'Grugan, airchinnech of Oilfinn, mortuus est. Maurice, son of Niall O'Conchobhair, was elected to the bishopric of Oilfinn in hoc anno. A conference was held by Tomaltach O'Conchobhair, archbishop of Connacht, with David Prendergast and the Mac Murchadhas; and a great number of the archbishop's people were slain by them on that day at

2 G 2

α Cill meɓóin. Ꝺeꝛɓoꝛgaill, inɡen hi Ꝺhuɓꝺα, .i. mαthαiꝛ Tomαlтαiᵹ hi Conchoɓaiꝛ, aiꝛꝺeꝛpuic Connαcht, ꝺo éᵹ iαꝛ mbuαiɓ nαiᵺꝛiᵹe. Cocαꝺ moꝛ eꝺiꝛ ꝛí Sαxαn ocuꝛ Siomαnn Muꝛꝛoꝛꝺ. Muꝛchαꝺ mαc Suiɓne ꝺo ᵹαɓáil le Ꝺomnαll mαc Mαᵹnuꝛα, ocuꝛ α ᵺinꝺlucαɓ α láim αn iαꝛlα, ocuꝛ α éᵹ iꝛin pꝛiꝛún.

Kt. Enáiꝛ ꝛoꝛ αine, ocuꝛ ix. ꝺec ꝛuiꝛꝛe; αnno Ꝺomini M.cc.lxui ; xxui. αnno cicli ꝛolαꝛiꝛ; xiii. αnno cicli lunαꝛiꝛ; ix. αnno cicli inꝺicтioniꝛ. Mαᵹᵹαmαin mαc Ceiᵺeꝛnαiᵹ hi Cheꝛín, ꝛí Ciαꝛꝛαiᵹhe, ꝺo ᵐαꝛbαꝺ lα ᵹαlloiɓ Ꝺhúnα móiꝛ in hoc αnno. Mαᵹᵹαmαin .h.Cuilén, ꝛí nα Clαonᵹlαiꝛi, ꝺo ᵐαꝛbαꝺ ꝺá ᵐnαi ꝛein ꝺαon ɓuille ꝺo ꝛcín, тꝛe éꝺ, αn bliαꝺαin ꝛin. Cαiꝛlén Tiᵹe Ꝺháchoinne ꝺo ɓꝛiꝛꝛeɓ ocuꝛ ꝺo ꝼαꝛꝛuᵹαꝺ αn bliαꝺαin ꝛin, ocuꝛ Conmαicne uile ꝺꝼáꝛuᵹαꝺ. Ꝺomnαll .h.hEᵹꝛα, ꝛí Luiᵹne, occiꝛuꝛ eꝛт αᵹ loꝛcαɓ αiꝛꝺ nα ꝛiαꝺ ꝼoꝛ Ꞡhαlloiɓ in hoc αnno. Toiꝛꝛɓeαlbαch, mαc αoɓα, mic Cαᵺαil cꝛoibꝺeꝛc, ꝺo éᵹ α mαiniꝛꝺiꝛ Cnuic Muαɓi iꝛin mbliαꝺαin ꝛin. Ꝺiαꝛmαiꝺ ꝛuαɓ, mαc Conchoɓαiꝛ, mic Coꝛmαic Mic Ꝺiαꝛmαꝺα, ocuꝛ Ꝺonncαᵺα mαc Ꝺuinn óiᵹ Mhéᵹ Oiꝛechтαiᵹ, ꝺo ɓαllαꝺ lá hαoɓ .h.Conchoɓαiꝛ. Sαɓɓ, inᵹen Cαᵺαil cꝛoibꝺeꝛᵹ, moꝛтuα eꝛт. Mαoilíꝛα .h.hαnαinn, pꝛióiꝛ Roꝛα Comán ocuꝛ αᵺα Líαᵹ, quieuiт in Cꝛiꝛтo. Ꝺuiꝛᵹéiꝛ ɓheoil αn тáchαiꝛ ꝺo loꝛcuꝺ ꝺo Ꝼhlαnn ꝛuαɓ .h.Ꝼhloinn, ocuꝛ moꝛán ꝺo Ꞡαlloiɓ αn ɓαile ꝺo ᵐαꝛbαꝺ ɓó. Cαiꝛléin ocuꝛ αꝛɓαnnα imɓα ꝺo loꝛcuꝺ

---

[1] *Simon Mufford.* An attempt at writing the name of Simon de Montfort (the younger). This entry and the succeeding one are not in the Ann. of Connacht (Dublin copies).

[2] *Son of Maghnus;* i.e. of Maghnus O'Conchobhair, or Manus O'Conor.

[3] *The Earl.* Walter de Burgo, earl of Ulster. This event is given by the Four Masters at the year 1267, under which date it is also entered *infra.*

[4] *The 19th.* The MS. has xx. ꝺec, a mistake for ix. ꝺéc, or nαomαꝺ ꝺéc.

[5] *Ciarraighe.* There were many districts in Ireland called Ciarraighe. The one here referred to was Ciarraighe Maighe, or "Ciarraighe of the plain," otherwise called Clann-Ceithernaigh, a district nearly co-extensive with the present parish of Kilkeevin, barony of Castlerea, and county of

Cill-medhoin. Derbhorgaill, daughter of O'Dubhda, i.e. the mother of Tomaltach O'Conchobhair, archbishop of Connacht, died after the victory of penitence. A great war between the king of the Saxons and Simon Mufford.[1] Murchadh Mac Suibhne was apprehended by Domhnall, son of Maghnus,[2] and surrendered into the hands of the Earl ;[3] and he died in the prison.

The kalends of January on Friday, and the nineteenth[4] of the moon; anno Domini M.CC.lxvi; xxvi. anno cycli solaris; xiii. anno cycli lunaris; ix. anno cycli Indictionis. Mathghamhain, son of Ceithernach O'Cerin, king of Ciar-raighe,[5] was slain by the Foreigners of Dún-mór in hoc anno. Mathghamhain O'Cuilén, king of the Claen-ghlais, was killed by his own wife, with one thrust of a knife, through jealousy, this year. The castle of Tech-Dachoinne was broken down and laid waste in this year; and all Conmaicne[6] was laid waste. Domhnall O'hEghra, king of Luighne, occisus est whilst burning Ard-na-riadh against the Foreigners, in hoc anno. Toirdhelbhach, son of Aedh, son of Cathal Crobhderg, died in the monastery of Cnoc-Muaidhe in this year. Diarmaid Ruadh, son of Con-chobhar, son of Cormac Mac Diarmada, and Donncatha, son of Donn Og Mac Oireghtaigh, were blinded by Aedh O'Conchobhair. Sadhbh, daughter of Cathal Crobhderg, mortua est. Maelisa O'hAnainn, prior of Ros-Comáin and Ath-Liag, quievit in Christo. The borough of Bel-an-táchair was burned by Flann Ruadh O'Floinn; and many of the Foreigners of the town were slain by him. Several castles and corn-fields were also burned

Roscommon. Dr. O'Donovan errs (*Four Mast.*, p. 401) in stating that the district in question was in the county of Mayo. See O'Dubhagain's *Topogr. Poem*, ed. O'Donovan, p. 63.

6 *Conmaicne.* There were four districts in Connacht called Conmaicne. The Conmaicne here indicated was probably Conmaicne-Dúna-móir, or Conmaicne of Dún-mór, now the barony of Dunmore, county Galway, adjoining the barony of Tech-Da-choinne, or Tiaquin, in the same county, in which the castle of Tech-Dachoinne was situated.

ocur do millev a tír Phiacrac bó teor. Tomárr .h.
Maolconaire, airctovechain Tuama, quievit in Crirto.
Aob .h.Conchobair, rí Connacht, do tul irin mbreifne
daitriozhao Airt mic Cathail riabaiz hi Ruairc, ocur
ríze do tabairt do Conchobar buive, mac Amlaoib,
mic Airt hi Ruairc, ocur braizve tairrech na breifne
uile do zabáil dó. Errucóive Luizne do zabáil do
Thomár .h. Mhiavacán, ocur zráva in dá erruc rin
do tabairt an aon ló. húza Mac Zoirdelb mortuur
ert. Aob.h.Muireghaizh do marbav in hoc anno.
Sloizev la hUilliam burc docum hi Maoilrechlainn,
ocur morán do báthav díb i nAt Croeva, ocur a nimrúb
zan nert zan braizve do zabáil don dul rin. Toza
erruic do tocht on Roim zo Cluain ferta brénainn,
ocur a zráva erruic do tabairt a nAt na ríz an
Domnach ria Nodluic. Ar mór do tabairt do droinz
do muinnter hi Conchobair, .i. do Loclainn mac
Diarmava mic Mhuircertaiz, ocur do Mac Ceiter-
naiz, ocur do mac Domnaill duib hi Ezra, ar bret-
nachaib ocur ar Laizhnechaib iarthair Connacht, ocur
aoin cend déz ar .xx. da zcendaib do tizlucav do
.h.Conchobair doib. Cormac mac Zillacrirt Mic
Diarmava do lot, ocur a héz don lót rin. Zráva
erruic do tabairt ar bráthair rrericúr, .i. Ua Scóra, in
Ard Mata docum Ráta bot Thire Conaill. Maoileóin
bodar .h.Maolconaire mortuur ert.

Kt. Enáir for Satarn, ocur x. ficheo ruirre; anno
Domini M.cc.lxciii.; xxviii. anno cicli rolarir; x°.quarto

---

and destroyed by him in Tir-Fhiachrach. Thomas O'Maelchonaire, archdeacon of Tuaim, quievit in Christo. Aedh O'Conchobhair, king of Connacht, went into the Breifne to depose Art, son of Cathal Riabhach O'Ruairc; and he gave the sovereignty to Conchobhar Buidhe, son of Amhlaibh, son of Art O'Ruairc, and took the hostages of all the chieftains of the Breifne. The bishopric of Luighne[1] was assumed by Thomas O'Miadhachán, and the degrees of these two bishops[2] were conferred on the same day. Hugo Mac Goisdelbh mortuus est. Aedh O'Muiredhaigh was killed in hoc anno. An army was led by William Burk against O'Maelsechlainn; and a great number of them were drowned in Ath-crochdha, and the rest turned back without obtaining sway or hostages on this occasion. A bishop-elect[3] came from Rome to Cluain-ferta-Brenainn, and his episcopal degree was conferred on him at Ath-na-righ the Sunday before Christmas. A great slaughter was committed by a party of O'Conchobhair's people, viz.:—by Lochlainn, son of Diarmaid, son of Muirchertach, and by Mac Ceithernaigh and the son of Domhnall Dubh O'hEghra, on the Britons[4] and Lagenians[5] of the West of Connacht, thirty-one of whose heads were presented to O'Conchobhair by them. Cormac, son of Gilla-Christ Mac Diarmada, was wounded, and died of the wound. The degree of bishop was conferred in Ard-Macha on a Friar Preacher, i.e. O'Scoba,[6] *appointed bishop* of Rath-Both of Tir-Conaill. Maeleoin Bodhar[7] O'Maelchonaire mortuus est.

The kalends of January on Saturday, and the thirtieth of the moon; anno Domini M.cc.lxvii; xxvii. anno cycli

---

Four Masters call them "Luighne," i.e. inhabitants of the district comprised in the present barony of Leyny, county of Sligo. But Leyny is not in the West of Connacht.

[6] *O'Scoba.* Cairbre (or Carbery)

O'Scoba, whose death is recorded under the year 1275 *infra.*

[7] *Maeleoin Bodhar;* i.e. "Maeleoin (Malone) the deaf." From this Irish word *bodhar* is seemingly deriv. Eng. *bother,* and its cognate *pother.*

anno cicli lunapir; x. anno cicli indictionip. Maoilpechlainn, mac Cončobair, mic Aoda, ocur Conchobar réin
a athair, ocur Aod a derbrathair, do éz a naon raiče.
Murchad Mac Suibne do zabáil do Dhomnall mac
Máznura hI Conchobáir a nUmall, ocur a činnlucad
do Uáter a búrc, .i. Iarla Ulad, ocur a éz a prirrún
an Iarla iarrin. Brian, mac Toirrdhelbaiz, mic
Ruaidri hI Conchobair, do éz a mainirtir Chnuic
Muaide irin mbliadain rin. Druim Cliab do lorcud
uile cona tizib [ocur] templaib. Crec mór do denum
do Ghalloib iarthair Chonnacht ar Chairrri Dhroma
cliab, ocur do airzedair Er dara. Crec mór eli do
denum do Mac Uilliam búrc ar .h.Conchobair, zur
airzertar Tir Mhaine ocur Clann Uadach. Erruc
Cluana rerta, .i. Románach, do dul tairir docum an
rápa. Donnchad, mac Ruaidri, mic Aoda hI Conchobair, do marbad do Ghalloib in hoc anno. zalar
mór do zabáil Aoda hI Chonchobair, condechaid a
čárc rá Erinn uile, ocur a černó arr rlán. Alir,
inzen Mic Carrzamna, mortua ert. Cocad mór a
Saxanaib itir rí Saxan ocur Simann Suronn.

Kt. Enáir ror domnach, ocur .xi. ruirre; anno
Domini M.cc.lxuiii.; xxuiii. anno cicli rolarir; xu.
anno cicli lunarir; xi.anno indictionir. Conchobar
.h.Briain, rí Tuadmuman, do marbad la Diarmaid
mac Muircertaiz hI Briain, ocur a mac, .i. Seonín,
ocur a inzen, ocur mac a inzene, .i. mac Ruaidri hI
zrádda, ocur Dubločluinn .h. Ločluinn, ocur Tomár
.h. Beollán, et alii multi, do marbad maille rriú do
mnaib ocur dreraib nach áirimter runn; ocur ro

[1] *Conchobhar.* He was apparently
of the family of O'Conchobhair, or
O'Conor.

[2] *Apprehended.* This is a repetition.
See the concluding entry for the year
1265.

[3] *Simon Suforn.* This is an attempt
at writing the name of Simon de
Montfort, which is written "Simon
Mufford," under the year 1265. In
Mageoghegan's version of the Annals
of Clonmacnois it assumes the form
"Sufforne."

[4] *Killed.* Mageoghegan (Annals of
Clonmacnois, 1268) says "in Corcomroe (county of Clare), in the campe

solaris; x°. quarto anno cycli lunaris; x. anno cycli Indictionis. Maelsechlainn, son of Conchobhar,[1] son of Aedh, and his father Conchobhar himself, and his brother Aedh, died in one quarter. Murchadh Mac Suibhne was apprehended[2] by Domhnall, son of Maghnus O'Conchobhair, in Umhall, and was surrendered to Walter Burk, i.e. Earl of Ulster; and he died in the Earl's prison afterwards. Brian, son of Toirdhelbhach, son of Ruaidhri O'Conchobhair, died in the monastery of Cnoc-Muaidhe in this year. Druimcliabh was all burned, with its houses [and] churches. A great depredation was committed by the Foreigners of the West of Connacht on *the inhabitants of* Cairpre-Dromacliabh; and they plundered Es-dara. Another great depredation was committed by Mac William Burk on O'Conchobhair, when he plundered Tir-Maine and Clann-Uadach. The bishop of Cluain-ferta, i.e. a Roman, went across to the Pope. Donnchadh, son of Ruaidhri, son of Aedh O'Conchobhair, was killed by Foreigners in hoc anno. A great illness seized Aedh O'Conchobhair, so that the report thereof spread throughout all Erinn; but he recovered safely from it. Alice, daughter of Mac Carghamhna, mortua est. A great war in Saxon-land between the king of the Saxons and Simon Suforn.[3]

The kalends of January on Sunday, and the eleventh of the moon; anno Domini M.cc.lxviii; xxviii. anno cycli solaris; xv. anno cycli lunaris; xi. anno Indictionis. Conchobhar O'Briain, king of Tuadh-Mumha, was killed[4] by Diarmaid, son of Muirchertach O'Briain; and his son, i.e. Seonin,[5] and his daughter, and his daughter's son, i.e. the son of Ruaidhri O'Grada, and Dubhlochlainn O'Lochlainn, and Thomas O'Beollain, and many more[6] women and men, who are not enumerated here, were slain along with them;

called the Siwdayne;" from which he is known in history as "Conor *na Siudaine* O'Brien."

[5] *Seonin*; pron. *Shoneen*; the dimin. of Seon, or John.

[6] *More*. aℓɪ, for aℓɪɪ, MS.

mαrbαꝺ Ꝺιαrmαιꝺ ꝼéιη ιηꝺ ꝛo ceꝺóιr αmαιl ꝛo ꝛℓιᵹ.
Αṁlάιḃ .h. ꝼeꝛᵹαιl ꝺo ṁαrbαꝺ lα ᵹαlloιḃ α meαḃαιl.
Mάᵹηυꝛ Mhάᵹ Oιꝛechταιᵹ, ꝺυx ℓlαιηηe Tomαlταιᵹ,
qυιeυιτ. Rαᵹηαιlτ, ιηᵹeη hι Conchobαιꝛ, beη Chαṫαιl
hι Mαꝺαḃάιη, qυιeυιτ. Mυιꝛιꝛ ꝛυαꝺ Mαc ᵹeꝛαlτ
ꝺo ḃάꝺhαꝺ αꝛ mυιꝛ Eꝛeηη, lυchτ lυιηᵹe, αᵹ τeαchτ ó
ꝛιᵹ Sαxαη ꝺιηηꝛoιᵹeꝺ ηα hEꝛeηη. Cαꝛꝺℓαlυꝛ αητ
ιmꝛιꝛ Róṁαηαch ꝺo ṁαrbαꝺ ꝺoηα Seιꝛꝛιꝛꝺηιḃ αᵹ
coꝛηυm ηα cꝛίꝛꝺαιᵹechτα. Αoꝺ mαc Conchobαιꝛ hι
ꝼhlαιḃḃeꝛταιᵹ, oιꝛꝛιꝛꝺél Eηαιᵹ ꝺúιη, moꝛτυυꝛ eꝛτ.
Toιꝛꝛꝺhelbαch óᵹ, mαc Αoꝺα, mιc ꝼeꝺlιm, mιc Cατhαιl
cꝛoιḃꝺeꝛᵹ, ꝺαlτα .h. mḃꝛιúιη, qυιeυιτ. Coιηηe ꝺo ꝛoᵹꝛα
ꝺo ᵹhαlloιḃ Eꝛeηη α ηΑᵹ lυαιη αꝛ Αoꝺ .h.Conchobαιꝛ.
Ro ℓιηóιl .h.Conchobαιꝛ, ιmoꝛꝛo, ιηα ᵹcoιηηe αηηꝛιη,
ocυꝛ τυc mαιꝺm αꝺḃαιl ꝼoꝛꝛα α bꝼeꝺhαιb Αᵹα lυαιη,
ocυꝛ ꝛo mαrbαꝺ ꝛochαιꝺe ꝺιḃ αηη. Ꝺomηαll mαc
Tαιꝺᵹ hι Mhαηꝺαchάιη ꝺo ṁαrbαꝺ, ocυꝛ τeιcheꝺ ꝺα
mυιηητιꝛ υαꝺ, .ι. ꝺo Thαꝺc .h. ꝼhlαηηαᵹάη ocυꝛ ꝺo
ᵹιllαcꝛιꝛτ .h. bιꝛη, α .υιιι. ƙτ. Eηαιꝛ. ꝼeꝛᵹαl .h.
Mαolṁυαꝺ, ꝛί bꝼeꝛ Ceαll, ꝺo ṁαrbαꝺ lα ᵹαlloιb.
Mαolꝛechlαιηη Mhάᵹ Coℓlαιη ꝺo mαrbαꝺ lα ᵹαlloιb.
Ꝺυḃᵹαll Mαc Rυαιꝺꝛι, ꝛί ιηηꝛι ᵹαll ocυꝛ Oιꝛιꝛ
ᵹhαoιꝺel, qυιeυιτ. Ꝺomηαll .h. ᵹꝛάꝺꝺα, ꝺυx ℓéηel
Ꝺυηᵹαιle, moꝛτυυꝛ eꝛτ. Loℓlαιηη mαc Ꝺιαrmαꝺα hι
Conchobαιꝛ ꝺo ṁαrbαꝺ ꝺo Ꝺαυιꝺ Αυυlb ocυꝛ lα hιḃ
Cιηαoℓα; ocυꝛ τoꝛcꝛαꝺαꝛ ꝼéιη ιηꝺ ꝛo ceꝺóιꝛ. Ꝺιαꝛ-
mαιꝺ, mαc ιη αᵹℓeιꝛιᵹ hι Ꝺhꝛιαιη, ꝺo éc. Mαᵹᵹαmαιη
.h. Ꝺꝛίαιη ꝺo ᵹαbάιl, ocυꝛ α ℓιꝛꝛbαꝺ lα Ꝺꝛιαη ꝛυαꝺ

---

1 *In return.* ιηꝺ, lit. "in it," MS.
2 *Clann - Tomaltaigh.* The word
Tomaltaigh is represented by ꝺoṁ in
the MS.; but the Annals of Connacht
read Tomαlταιᵹ.

3 *Ruadh*; i.e. "the red."

4 *Fedha-Atha-Luain.* The Faes (or
woods) of Ath-Luain; the name of

O'Naghten's country, in the barony of
Athlone, and county of Roscommon.

5 *And his people ran away from him.*
ocυꝛ τeιcheꝺ ꝺα mυιηητιꝛ υαꝺ,
MS. In the text this clause follows
after the words ꝺo mαꝛbαꝺ, "was
slain." The Annals of Connacht read
"ocυꝛ x̅. ꝺα mυιηητιꝛ mαιℓℓꝛ,"

and Diarmaid was himself immediately slain in return[1], as he deserved. Amhlaibh O'Ferghail was killed by Foreigners, in treachery. Maghnus Mac Oirechtaigh, dux of Clann-Tomaltaigh[2], quievit. Raghnailt, daughter of O'Conchobhair, wife of Cathal O'Madadhain, quievit. Maurice Ruadh[3] Fitz-Gerald was drowned in the sea of Erinn, with a ship's crew, whilst coming to Erinn from the king of the Saxons. The Roman Emperor Carolus was slain by the Saracens whilst defending Christendom. Aedh, son of Conchobhar O'Flaithbhertaigh, official of Enach-dúin, mortuus est. Toirdhelbhach Og, son of Aedh, son of Fedhlim, son of Cathal Crobhderg, foster-son of the Ui-Briuin, quievit. Aedh O'Conchobhair was summoned by the Foreigners of Erinn to a conference at Ath-Luain. O'Conchobhair, moreover, mustered *his forces* to meet them there, and inflicted a great defeat on them in Fedha-Atha-Luain,[4] where a great number of them were slain. Domhnall, son of Tadhg O'Mannachain, was slain, viz. by Tadhg O'Flannagain and Gilla-Christ O'Birn, on the 7th of the kalends of January; and his people ran away from him.[5] Ferghal O'Maelmhuaidh, king of Feara-Ceall, was killed by Foreigners. Maelsechlainn Mac Cochlain was killed by Foreigners. Dubhgall Mac Ruaidhri, king of Innsi-Gall and Airer-Gaeidhel, quievit. Domhnall O'Grada, dux of Cenel-Dunghaile, mortuus est. Lochlainn, son of Diarmaid O'Conchobhair, was killed by David Aulb, and by the Ui-Cinaetha; and they were themselves immediately slain in return,[1] Diarmaid, son of the Aithcleirech[6] O'Briain, died. Mathghamhain O'Briain was taken prisoner, and mutilated, by Briain Ruadh O'Briain, in

---

for ocuꞃ ꝺeıchnebaꞃ ꝺɑ mꙋınnꞇıꞃ. maıꞇꞇe ꝼuꞃ, i.e. "and ten of his people along with him," which is more likely to be correct, and with which reading the Four Masters agree.

[6] *Aithcleirech.* By *aithcleirech* is meant an ex-cleric, or rather a cleric who had been suspended, or forced to retire from the clerical profession.

.h. mbrialn, a noíżail a achar. Conchobar .h. Cellaiż, rí Uí Mane, morcuur erc. Ccongur .h. Dálaiż, .i. rói noána ocur tiże aoioheo, quieuic.

Ictt. Enair ror maire, ocur aili riched rurre; anno Domini M. cc. lxix.; primur annur cicli rolarir; xui. annur cicli lúnarir; xii. annur cicli inoictionir. 1mar .h. birn, óżlaoč ocur lán rerżráča occo .h. Conchobair, do rążbáil anc raożuil do lár a člainn ocur a čonáiż iar cinneð a ðecha a Ror Chommáin, a main-iroir na mbrachar rreciur. 1uiróir nua do čoiżechc a nerinn o rí Saxan .i. hoirerð Surrorn, do čercużao ocur do rocrużao na hErenn. Cc čoiżechc a Connachcaib iarrin, ocur Żaill Erenn maille rir, ocur cairlén do čenum a Ror Chomán dóið; ocur irreð roðera rin do čenum, .i. Ccoð .h. Cončobair do ðeich a nżalur ocur a nerláinci an can rin. Taðż mac Neill mic Mhuireżhaiż hI Conchobair do marbao do crerrénach do muinncer a brachar réin an Oilrinn, żo rír čona, in hoc anno; ocur ro marbao an rerrénač rein na érinc ro cedóir. brian mac Domnaill onið hI Eżra do marbao a Slizech la Żalloib, in hoc anno. Denmiðe, inżen Toirrohelbaiż mic Ruaiðri, .i. ben Maolmuire Mhic Shúiðne, quieuic. Serrraio mac Doimnaill člannaiż Mic Żillaþatraic, rí Sléibe blaðma, do éż in hoc anno. Þatriciur .h. Scannail, comarba Þatraic a nCcro Mhača, do éż; in Crirto quieuic. Crirðina, inżen hI Neachtuin, ben Diarmaoa

---

[1] *His father*; i.e. Conchobhar (na Siudaine) O'Briain. See note [4], page 457.

[2] *Robert Sufforn*, Robert D'Ufford. The name is corruptly written Hoirerð Surrorn in the MS. See note [5], p. 228 *supra*.

[3] *Son of Ruaidhri*; i.e. of Ruaidhri O'Conchobhair, the last monarch of Ireland.

[4] *Seffraidh.* Jeffrey.

[5] *Clannach.* A sobriquet signifying "prolific," from clann, children, offspring.

[6] *Sliabh-Bladhma.* Slieve Bloom, a mountain on the confines of the King's and Queen's Counties. It formed the western boundary of the ancient territory of Ossory; and hence the Mac Gillapatricks (now Anglicised

revenge for his father.[1] Conchobhar O'Cellaigh, king of A.D. Ui-Maine, mortuus est. Aenghus O'Dalaigh, i.e. an eminent professor of poetry, and *keeper* of a house of hospitality, quievit.

The kalends of January on Tuesday, and the twenty-second of the moon; anno Domini M.CC.lxix.; primus annus cycli solaris; xvi. annus cycli lunaris; xii. annus cycli Indictionis. Imhar O'Birn, servant and confidential man to Aedh O'Conchobhair, withdrew from the world, from the midst of his children and affluence, after resolving to pass his life in Ros-Comain, in the monastery of the Friars Preachers. A new Justiciary came to Erinn from the king of the Saxons, i.e. Robert Sufforn,[2] to settle and pacify Erinn. He afterwards proceeded into Connacht, accompanied by the Foreigners of Erinn; and a castle was erected in Ros-Comáin by them. And the reason it was erected was that Aedh O'Conchobhair was at that time in sickness and ill-health. Tadhg, son of Niall, son of Muiredhach O'Conchobhair, was most unfortunately slain by a soldier of his own brother's people, at Oilfinn, in hoc anno; and the soldier was himself immediately killed in retaliation for it. Brian, son of Domhnall Dubh O'hEghra, was killed in Sligech, by Foreigners, in hoc anno. Benmhidhe, daughter of Toirdhelbhach, son of Ruaidhri,[3] i.e. the wife of Maelmuire Mac Suibhne, quievit. Seffraidh,[4] son of Domhnall Clannach[5] Mac Gillapatraic, king of Sliabh-Bladhma,[6] died in hoc anno. Patricius O'Scannail, comarb of Patrick in Ard-Macha, died;[7] in Christo quievit. Christina, daughter of O'Neachtain, wife of Diarmaid

[1269.]

Fitzpatricks), lords of Ossory, were sometimes designated by the title of lords of Sliabh-Bladhma. See note [12], page 371, *supra*.

[7] *Died.* Ware (*Bishops*, under

Armagh) states that Archbishop O'Scannail died on the 16th of March, 1270, under which year his death is again recorded in the present chronicle.

Miðiᵹ Mic Ὀιαρμαɒα, .ι. an ᵬen ɒob ḟerr ɒealᵬ ocuſ
ɒenum, enech ocuſ ιonnrαcuſ, cιαll ocuſ cράbαɒ ɒo ᵬόι
an̄ αon αιmſιr rρία, ocuſ ιſ mό cumαoιn αr an orɒ lιαᵬ,
ɒo éᵹ ιαr mbuαιᵬ nonᵹᵵα ocuſ nαιᵵrιᵹe. Αᵭ .ħ. Ϝιnn,
rόι ḟenmα ocuſ oιrſɒιᵹ Ɛrenn, morᵵuuſ erᵵ. Cαιrlén
Slιᵹιᵹh ɒo ᵬenum ɒo Mac Muιrιſ Mιc ᵹerαιlᵵ an
blιαɒαιn rιn. Eᵭṁιlιᵬ Mαc Cαιrᵵén ɒo mαrbαᵬ
ɒħ̄Uα Αnlúαιn. Ὀomnαll .ħ. Ϝerᵹαιl, ocuſ Αᵭ
.ħ.Ϝerᵹαιl α mαc, ɒo ṁαrbαᵬ ɒo Ᵹhιllα n̄α nαom
.ħ. Ϝerᵹαιl ocuſ ɒo Ᵹhαlloιb, ιn̄ hoc αnno.

Kᵵ. Ɛnαιr ɸor Ceɒάιn, ocuſ ᵵreſſ uαᵵhαᵬ ſuιſſe;
αnno Ὀomιnι M.cc.lxx. Secuṅɒur αṅnuſ cιclι rolαrιſ;
xιιι.αṅnuſ cιclι lúnαrιſ; xιιι. αṅnúſ ιnɒιcᵵιonιſ.
Slιᵹech ɒo loſcuɒ lά .ħ.n̄Ὀomnαιll ocuſ lα Cénel
Conαιll, ocuſ mαc Ḃreαllαᵹ an ᵵαιrſ hι Mhαoιl-
ᵬrénαιnn ɒo ṁαrbαɒ ɒon ᵵuſαſ rιn. Coᵹαɒ mόr ocuſ
eſſαonᵵα ɒo eιrᵹe eɒιſ .ħ.Conchobαιſ, .ι. Αᵭ mαc
Ϝélιm, ocuſ Ůάᵵer α Ḃúrc, .ι. ιαrlα Ůlαᵬ; ocuſ nίſ
ḟéɒrαᵵ Ᵹαιll ιn̄αιɒ Ᵹαοιɒel α neᵵᵵrάιn; ᵹuſ ᵵιnόιl anᵵ
ιαrlα Ᵹoιll n̄α hƐrenn mαιlle ſιſιn Ᵹιuιſɒιſ, ᵹo ᵵαn-
ᵹαɒαr ɒιᵬlίnαιᵬ mόr ſluαιᵹheɒ α Connάchᵵαιᵬ, ᵹo
ſαnᵹαɒαr Roſſ Chommάιn an ceɒ αᵹαιᵬ, ocuſ αſſιᵬé
ᵹo hOιlſιnn ιn ɒαrα αᵹαιᵬ, ocuſ αſſιᵬé ᵹo Ϸorᵵ Leιce,
ᵹuſ ᵹαᵬαɒαr ſoſſαɒ ocuſ lonᵹſorᵵ αᵹ Ϸorᵵ Leιce an
oιᵬᵭe rιn; ocuſ ɒo ſόnſαᵵ comαιſle αr α ᵬάſαᵭ, ocuſ
ιſſί comαιſle ɒo ſonſαᵵ, .ι. anᵵ ιαrlα ocuſ mαιᵵe Ᵹαll
Ɛrenn ɒo ᵬul ᵵαr Sιonαιṅṅ ſoιſ ι nΑᵭ cαſαᵬh Conαιll
ιn ᵵαn rιn. Ὀάlα rιᵹ Connαchᵵ ιmorro, .ι. Αᵭα mιc
Ϝélιm hι Conchobαιſ, ɒo ᵬόι rιᵬéιn beᵹάn ɒo ṁαιᵵᵬh

---

[1] *Diarmaid Midhech.* "Diarmaid
the Midhian;" so called, apparently,
from having been fostered in Midhe
(Meath).

[2] *O'Finn.* The Four Masters write the
name O'Finnaghtaigh (O'Finaghty);
but in the Dublin copies of the so-

called Annals of Connacht it is .ħ.Ϝιnn
(O'Finn). In Mageoghegan's version of
the Annals of Clonmacnoise he is called
"Hugh O'Fflynn, a good musitian."

[3] *Were slain.* ɒo mαrbαɒ; written in the marg., with a mark of ref.
to the proper place in the text.

Midhech[1] Mac Diarmada, i.e. the handsomest, best formed, most hospitable, worthy, sensible, and pious woman of her time, and the most bountiful to the Grey Order, died after the victory of unction and penitence. Aedh O'Finn,[2] the most eminent professor of music and minstrelsy in Erinn, mortuus est. The castle of Sligech was erected by Mac Maurice Fitz-Gerald in this year. Echmhilidh Mac Cairtén was slain by O'hAnluain. Domhnall O'Ferghail, and his son, Aedh O'Ferghail, were slain[3] by Gilla-na-naemh O'Ferghail and the Foreigners, in hoc anno.

The kalends of January on Wednesday, and the third of the moon; anno Domini M.CC.lxx.; secundus annus cycli solaris; xvii. annus cycli lunaris; xiii. annus Indictionis. Sligech was burned by O'Domhnaill and the Cenel-Conaill, and the son of Breallach-an-chairn[4] O'Maelbhrenainn was killed on this expedition. A great war and dissension arose between O'Conchobhair, i.e. Aedh, the son of Fedhlim, and Walter Burk, i.e. the Earl of Ulster; and neither the Foreigners nor the Gaeidhel could reconcile them. The Earl assembled the Foreigners of Erinn, together with the Justiciary,[5] when they all went on a great hosting into Connacht, and proceeded to Ros-Comain the first night, and from thence to Oilfinn the second night, and from thence to Port-leice; and they rested and encamped that night at Port-leice. And on the morrow they held a council, and the resolution they adopted was, viz., that the Earl and the chiefs of the Foreigners of Erinn should then go eastwards across the Sionainn at Ath-caradh-Conaill.[6] As regards the king of Connacht, however, i.e. Aedh, son of Fedhlim O'Conchobhair, he was

---

[4] *Breallach-an-chairn;* i.e. "the blubber-lipped man of the cairn."

[5] *Justiciary.* Jacques D'Audeley.

[6] *Ath-caradh-Conaill.* "The ford of Conall's weir." Dr. O'Donovan states that this was the name of a ford on the Shannon, near Carrick-on-Shannon; but the name has long been obsolete. *Four Masters,* A.D. 1270, note [l].

a muinncipe ap cinn na nZall a MaZ Nippi, ocup po
an an Zuipóip ocup beZán ḋonc flúaiZ maille pip alla
ciap ḋonc Shionainn aZ iopnaiḋe an lapla cona muinncip. Ḋála an lapla, ap nḋul ḋó cap Cĕ capaḋ Conaill
poip po eipiZ-uacḣaḋ ḋo muinncip hI Conchobaip ḋóiḃ
a coillciḃ Conmaicne, ocup po mapbaḋ beZán ḋonc
flúaiZ Zhall annpin. Ccḣc chena, níp anpaḋ na
Zaill ḋon peim ocup ḋon puacḣap pin pop a paḃaḋap
no Zo panZaḋap MaZ Nippi, ocup po Zaḃpac poppaḋ
ocup lonZpopc ann an oiḋĕe pin. Ḋála na nZall, imoppo,
ippí cóṁaiple cucpac ap an lapla, píĕ ḋo ḋénum pe
.h.Conchobaip ḋon chup pin, ocup a ḋepḃpacḣaip, .i.
Uilliam óZ mac Ricaipḋ ṁóip mic Uilliam cuncúp, ḋo
ĕaḃaipc a laim ṁuinncepi hI Conchobaip an peḋ ḋo
biaḋ .h.Conchobaip a ciZ an lapla aZ peḋuZaḋ; ocup
ḋo pónaḋ aṁlaiḋ. Ocup ap nḋula ḋo Uilliam óc a
cech hI Conchobaip po Zaḃaḋap muinncep hI Conchobaip é, ocup ḋo mapbaḋ Seon Ḋuilepín ocup a mac
ap an lácḣaip pin. Oḋ ĕuala, imoppo, anc.lapla pell
ḋo ḋenum ap a bpácḣaip, po Zluaip moĕpáĕ ap ná
ĕápaĕ Zo hCĕ an ĕip pop Sinuinn, ocup ip aṁlaiḋ ḋo
ḃoi .h.Conchobaip in ḋá oiḋĕe pin ina cimĕeall mup
ĕiop leoman lonn, laiṅḋ, leḋapcach, a cimĕeall a
ḃiḋḃaḋ aZ á mbáppuZaḋ, conap leiZ caiĕeṁ na coḋlaḋ
na companaḋ ḋóiḃ. Ro épiZ Cɑḋ .h.Conchobaip ipin
ló ceḋna pin. Ḋala Zall, imoppo, ap nḋul ḋóiḃ ḋocum
in áĕa ipin maiḋin ap a ĕápach, ip annpin puZ Coipp-
ḋhelbach.h.Ḃpíain oppa, ocup po immpo anc lapla
pein ppip, ocup po ṁapḃ hé Zan ĕuiḋiuZaḋ ó neoĕ oile.

---

[1] *Ath-caradh-Conaill.* See note [6], p. 463.

[2] *Coillte-Conmaicne.* "The woods of Conmaicne." Apparently the same as the "Fedha Conmaicne" referred to under the year 1247 *supra.*

[3] *William the Conqueror.* William Fitz-Adelm de Burgo, who is some-times called "the Conqueror" by Irish writers, on the ground that he had subjugated the province of Connacht.

[4] *Duilefin.* This name is written "Doilifin" in the Annals of Connacht, "Dolifin" by the Four Masters, and "Dolphin" in Mageoghegan's version

in Magh-Nisse, before the Foreigners, with a few of the chiefs of his people; and the Justiciary, accompanied by a small number of the army, remained on the western side of the Sionainn, awaiting the Earl and his people. With regard to the Earl, after he had gone eastwards past Ath-caradh-Conaill[1] a few of O'Conchobhair's people opposed them at Coillte-Conmaicne,[2] where a small number of the army of Foreigners were slain. Nevertheless, the Foreigners desisted not from the career and expedition in which they were engaged until they reached Magh-Nissi, where they rested and encamped that night. As to the Foreigners, moreover, the advice they gave to the Earl was, to make peace with O'Conchobhair on this occasion, and to deliver his brother, i.e. William Og, son of Richard Mór, son of William the Conqueror,[3] into the hands of O'Conchobhair's people whilst he (*O'Conchobhair*) should be in the Earl's house arranging *the peace*. And this was accordingly done. And after William Og had gone into O'Conchobhair's house, O'Conchobhair's people took him prisoner; and John Duilefin[4] and his son were slain on the spot. When the Earl, moreover, heard that treachery had been practised against his brother, he proceeded early on the morrow to Ath-an-chip on the Sionainn. And O'Conchobhair was *during* these two nights *marching* round them, as a furious, raging, tearing lion goes about his enemies when killing them, so that he permitted them neither to eat, sleep, nor be at rest. O'Conchobhair moved on the same day.[5] As regards the Foreigners, moreover, after going to the ford on the morrow Toirdhelbhach O'Briain overtook them, and the Earl himself turned on him, and slew him without assistance from any other person. With regard to the

---

of the Annals of Clonmacnois. The present form of the name is Dolphin.

[5] *Day.* This sentence seems mis-

placed, and should probably be transferred to the beginning of the preceding sentence.

2 H

Oαla Connacht, imoppo, pucpαo oppα pαoi pin, ocup
oo cuipeb α noepeb αpp α mionαb, ocup po meαbαb oα
copach. Ccho chenα, po meipbizeo α meipnech ipin
maižin pin, ocup po mαpbαb nαonbαp oo maichib α
pioipeoh αp αn láthαip pin, pα Ricapo nα Coille, ocup
pα oSheon buioilép; ocup ní pepp cá lion opin αmaċ
po pázbαo αnn; ocup po pázbαo ceo ech conα luipechαib
ocup conα noilláuib αnn; ocup po mαpbαo Uilliam
óz iαppin ipin mbpαižoenup αmbói α haiċle mic hi
bpiαin oo mαpbαo lαipin iαplα. Imċup Ccoα hi Conchobαip iαppin, po lez cαiplén Ceα Cnžαile, ocup
cαiplen Sleibe Luzα, ocup cαiplen Chille Calmáin,
ocup po loipc Rop Comán ocup Rinn oúin, ocup Uille
Uαnach; ocup po eipiž cocαo móp eoip bhpiαn puαb
.h.mbpíαin ocup Zαll, ocup cpeαchα mópα oo oenum
oo oppα, ocup cαiplen Chláip Ceα oá ċαpαoh oo žαbáil
oó. Cpeċα oo oenum oon iαplα ocup oo Zhαlloib
Connacho α Cíp Oililα αp muinncip Ccoα hi Conchobαip, ocup Oαuio Cúipín oo mαpbαo αp αn cpeiċ
pin. Comáp .h.Rαižilliž oo mαpbαo lα Zαlloib nα
hOippe. Mαc Mupchαoα ċαppαiž hi Pepžαil oo
mαpbαo oo Zαlloib. Comαpbα Pαpαic quieuio. Zopα
ocup oommα móp α nEpinn uile in hoc αnno. Cαhαl
mαc αn Liαċαnαiž hi Conchobαip, αb nα Cpinóioe αp
Loċ Cé, nαuip epo in hoc αnno. Lαbαoip, .i. pí Ppαnc,
oo éc αn bliαoαin pin. Eobαpo, mαc pí Sαxαn, oo oul

[1] *Richard-na-Coille*; i.e. "Richard of the Wood," who is stated in the Annals of Ulster to have been the Earl of Ulster's brother.

[2] *Cill-Calmáin.* The castle of Cill-Calmáin "stood near the old church of Kilcolman, in the parish of the same name, barony of Costello, and county of Mayo." *O'Donovan*, Four Masters, A.D. 1270, note °.

[3] *Clár-Atha-dha-charadh.* "The plain of the ford of two weirs;" probably the old name of the town of Clare, near Ennis, county of Clare.

[4] *The Ober.* Now Nobber, county of Meath. The form of the name in the text, nα hoippe, is the gen.; nom., αn opαip (or αn obαip)=Lat. opus-cris; and by the incorporation of the n of the article with its subst. (obαip) the corrupt form nobαip (Nobair) is produced. See Mr. Joyce's

Connachtmen, however, they came up with them (*the Foreigners*) at this time, when their rear was dislodged, and their van was routed. In short, their courage was confounded in this place, and nine of their principal knights were slain on the spot, including Richard-na-Coille[1] and John Butler; and it is not known how many more were lost there; and one hundred horses, with their mail coverings, and with their saddles, were left there; and William Og was killed in his captivity immediately after the son of O'Briain had been slain by the Earl. As regards Aedh O'Conchobhair's subsequent proceedings, he demolished the castle of Ath-Anghaile, and the castle of Sliabh-Lugha, and the castle of Cill-Calmáin,[2] and burned Ros-Comáin, and Rinn-dúin, and Uille-Uanach. And a great war arose between Brian Ruadh O'Briain and the Foreigners, and great depredations were committed by him on them, and the castle of Clár-Atha-dha-charadh[3] was taken by him. Depredations were committed by the Earl, and by the Foreigners of Connacht, in Tir-Oililla, on the people of Aedh O'Conchobhair; and David Cuisín was slain on this foray. Thomas O'Raighilligh was slain by the Foreigners of the Ober.[4] The son of Murchadh Carrach O'Ferghail was slain by Foreigners. The comarb of Patrick quievit.[5] Great famine and scarcity in all Erinn in hoc anno. Cathal, son of the Liathanach O'Conchobhair, abbot of the Trinity[6] in Loch-Cé, natus est in hoc anno. Lewis, i.e. the king of France, died this year. Edward, son of the king of the Saxons, went to the Holy

---

very valuable paper on *Changes and Corruptions in Irish Topographical Names*; Proceed. R. I. Acad., vol. ix., p. 229, *sq.*

[5] *Quievit*. The death of the comarb of Patrick (Archbishop O'Scannail) has been incorrectly recorded under the year 1269 (p. 460, *supra*).

[6] *Abbot of the Trinity*. And subsequently bishop of Elphin. See Harris's ed. of *Ware's* works, vol. i, p. 631.

2 H 2

ιρη Ταλαm ναοmṫα ϋια ċορnum. Ἰρ αnnρα mbliαϋαιη ρin, ιmορρο, ϋο ċuαιϋ cρἰοċ οcuρ ρορcenϋ αρ ollαṁnαċτ αn ϋuṫρúiliẓ hi Mhαolċοnαιρe οcuρ Ὁunlαιnẓ hi Mhαolċοnαιρe, οcuρ ρο ρuiϋeρϋαιρ Ταnαιϋe mόρ, mαc Ὁuinnίn mic Neiϋe mic Conαιnẓ Ϭuiϋe hi Mhαolċοnαιρe, α cαṫαοιρ ollαmnαċτα ċόιẓeϋ Chonnαċτ, uτ ροeτα ϋιχιτ :—

Ro ċαιṫ Ταnαιϋe τρeοραċ,

Mαc Ὁuinnίn, ollαm eolαċ,

Ὁα ρicḣiτ bliαϋαn bloιϋι

Cΐρ lάρ Leρρα Leiρτοιle.

ḳτ. Enαιρ ρορ ṫαρϋαοιn, οcuρ α ceṫαιρ ϋέẓ ρuιρρe ; αnnο Ὁοmini M.cc.lχχ.ρρimο ; τeρτιuρ αnnuρ cicli ρolαριρ ; χuiii. αnnuρ cicli lunαριρ ; χiiii. αnnuρ ιnϋicτιοnιρ. Uάτeρ α Ϭúρc, ιαρlα Ulαϋ οcuρ τιẓeρnα Ꝣαll Connαċτ, ϋο έẓ α cαιρlén nα Ꝣαιllṁe ϋο ẓαluρ αοn ρeċτṁαιne, ιαρ mbuαιϋ nαṫριẓe. Τοmάρρ Mαc Muιριρ ϋο éc α mbαιle Loċα Mερcα. Ιοṁαρ .h.Ϭιρη, lάn ρeρẓράϋα Coϋα hi Conchobαιρ, ρί Connαċτ, ϋο éẓ ιρη mbliαϋαιη ρin α Roρ Chοmάιn, ιαρ mbuαιϋ nαṫριẓe, οcuρ α αϋlucαϋ ιnτι ιn quαρτο ċαllαιnϋ ℉hebρα. Coϋ mαc Cοmαρϭα Chοmmαιn hi Conchobαιρ ϋο mαρϭαϋ ϋο Τοmαρρ Ϭuiτιlέρ αẓ Muιne ιnẓíne Cρeċάιn. Ὁοṁnαll .h.℉loιnn ϋο mαρϭαϋ ϋο mαc Roιϭín Lαιẓléιρ ιρη lό ceϋnα, α cinn uαċταραċ Ꝅρuṫρα. Mαṫẓαmαιn .h.Conchobαιρ ϋο mαρϭαϋ ϋο Ꝣhαllοιϭ Ὁhúιn mόιρ. Ṅicόl mαc Seοαn Ϭeρϋun, τιẓeρnα Οιρẓιαll, ϋο mαρϭαϋ lα Seρρραιẓ .h.Ϭρeρẓαιl οcuρ lα muιnnτeρ nα hCΐnẓαιle αιρchenα. Conchobαρ mαc Τιẓeρnαιn hi Conchobαιρ ϋο mαρϭαϋ lα Mάιlρechlαιnn

---

1 *Dubh-súilech* ; i.e. "the black-eyed."

2 *Tertius.* τeρcιuρ, MS.

3 *Thomas Mac Maurice*; i.e. Thomas Fitz-Maurice Fitz-Gerald.

4 *Cumarb-Comain.* Ordinarily the words Comarb Comain would signify "successor of (St.) Coman," but here they form a compound which represents a single proper name, as in the compounds of *cele, gilla, mael,* &c., See under the year 1244, *supra*, where

Land, to defend it. In this year it was, moreover, that an end and termination was put to the ollaveship of the Dubh-súilech[1] O'Maelchonaire, and of Dunlang O'Mael-chonaire; and Tanaidhe Mór, son of Donnin, son of Nedhe, son of Conang Buidhe O'Maelchonaire, was established in the ollave's chair of the province of Connacht, ut poeta dixit :—

> The guiding Tanaidhe,
> Son of Donnin, a learned ollamh,
> Spent forty happy years
> In the middle of Lis-Leirthoile.

The kalends of January on Thursday, and the fourteenth of the moon; anno Domini M.cc.lxx.primo; tertius[2] annus cycli solaris; xviii. annus cycli lunaris; xiiii. annus Indictionis. Walter Burk, Earl of Ulster, and lord of the Foreigners of Connacht, died in the castle of the Gaillimh, of a week's illness, after the victory of penitence. Thomas Mac Maurice[3] died in Baile-Locha-Mesca. Imhar O'Birn, a prime confidant of Aedh O'Conchobhair, king of Connacht, died in this year at Ros-Comain, after the victory of penitence; and he was interred therein on the fourth of the kalends of February. Aedh, son of Comarb-Comain[4] O'Conchobhair, was slain by Thomas Butler at Muine-inghine-Crechain.[5] Domhnall O'Floinn was killed by the son of Robin Laighleis on the same day, at the upper end of Sruthair. Mathghamhain O'Conchobhair was killed by the Foreigners of Dún-mór. Nicholas, son of John Verdun, lord of Oirghiall, was slain by Jeffrey O'Ferghail, and by the people of the Anghaile besides. Conchobhar, son of Tighernan O'Conchobhair, was slain by Maelsechlainn, son of Art

---

the election of Comarb-Comain as bishop of Elphin, by a section of the chapter, is recorded. In some pedigrees he is called Maelisa O'Conchobhair.

[5] *Muine - inghine - Crechain.* This name signifies the "shrubbery of Crechan's daughter."

mac Cipt hí Ruaipc, ocuy lá Clann Fepṁoiġe. Caiylén Tiġe Templa, ocuy caiylen Sliġiġ, ocuy caiylen Cta Liaġ, do bpiyyeṫ la hCCoṫ .h.Conchobaip in hoc anno.

Kt. Enaip ṗop CCine ocuy cuiceṫ pichit puippe ; anno Domini M.cc.lxx.yecundo ; bliaḋain deipiṫ naiḋecḋa hí ; quaptuy annuy cicli yolapiy; xu. annuy indictioniy. Enpi buiṫilép, tiġepna Uṁaill, ocuy hoiṫpe Mebpic do mapbaḋ la Cathal mac Conchobaip puaiḋ, ocuy la macaiṫ píġ Connacht, in hoc anno. Caiylen Royya Comán do bpiyyeḋ la hCCoṫ .h.Conchobaip. Taḋġ dall, mac CCoḋa mic Cathail cpoiḃdepġ, .i. ant aḋḃap píġ iy ẏepp do ṫí dá ċuigiḋ ẏein no ġup dallaḋ la muinteþ Raiġilliġ hé, do éġ in hoc anno. Iamuy Dodálaiġ, .i. ġiuiydip na hEpenn, do ṁapbaḋ la .h.mḃpoin ocuy le yochaide do Connachtaiṫ. Muipġep, mac Donnchaḋa mic Thomaltaiġ hí Mhaolpuanaiġ, yói einiġ ocuy enġnuma Epenn, do éġ a Muṗbach. Cn Mhiḋe do loycaḋ ġo ġpanapḋ la hCCoṫ.h.Conċoḃaip. Cth Luain do loycuḋ ocuy [an] dpoiċeḋ do bpiyyeṫ. Donnchaḋ mac ġilla na naoṁ Mhéġ Sháṁpaḋáin do ṁapbaḋ la Tomáy Mháġ [Sh]ampaḋáin, .i. a depḃpathaip yéin. Ricapḋ Diuiḋ, in bapún dob uaiyle i nEpinn, quieuit. Loinġep móp la hCCoṫ.h.Conchobaip ap Loċ Ríḃ, condepna loipce móya ocuy uilc iṁḋa eli.

Ktt. Enáip ṗop Domnach, ocuy yeiyeḋ uaċaḋ puippe ; anno Domini M.cc.lxx.teptio ; ppimuy annuy Decennouenaliy cicli ; quinto anno cicli yolapiy; ppimuy annuy indictioniy cicli. Conchobap buiḋe, mac CCṁlaiḃ mic CCipt hí Ruaipc, pí Ḃpeiẏne, do mapbaḋ la macaiṫ Conchobaip mic Tiġepnáin hí Con-

---

1 *Clann-Fermaighe.* Otherwise written "Clann-Fernmhaighe." See note 3, p. 350 *supra.*

2 *Decennovenalian.* ixᵒᵃ., MS.

3 *James Dodalaigh.* This is an

attempt at writing the name of Jacques D'Audeley, Lord Justice of Ireland.

4 *O'Brain.* Now Aglicised O'Breen, and Breen, without the O'. Mageogh-

O'Ruairc, and by the Clann-Fermaighe.[1] The castle of Tech-
Templa, the castle of Sligech, and the castle of Ath-liag,
were broken down by Aedh O'Conchobhair in hoc anno.

The kalends of January on Friday, and the twenty-
fifth of the moon; anno Domini M.cc.lxx. secundo. It
was the last Decennovenalian[2] year; quartus annus cycli
solaris; xv. annus Indictionis. Henry Butler, lord of
Umhall, and Hoitse Mebhric were slain by Cathal, son of
Conchobhar Ruadh, and by the sons of kings of Connacht, in hoc anno. The castle of Ros-Comáin was broken
down by Aedh O'Conchobhair. Tadhg Dall, son of Aedh,
son of Cathal Crobhderg, i.e. the fittest person in his
own province to be a king, until he was blinded by Muinter-Raighilligh, died in hoc anno. James Dodalaigh,[3] i.e.
the Justiciary of Erinn, was slain by O'Brain,[4] and by a
multitude of Connachtmen. Muirghes, son of Donnchadh,
son of Tomaltach O'Maelruanaigh, the most eminent for
hospitality and prowess in Erinn, died in Murbhach.
Midhe was burned as far as Granard by Aedh O'Conchobhair. Ath-Luain was burned, and [the] bridge broken
down. Donnchadh, son of Gilla-na-naemh Mac Shamhradhain, was killed by Thomas Mac [Sh]amhradhain, i.e.
his own brother. Richard Tuit, the noblest baron in
Erinn, quievit. A large fleet by Aedh O'Conchobhair on
Loch-Ribh; and he committed great burnings, and many
other injuries.

The kalends of January on Sunday, and the sixth of
the moon; anno Domini M.cc.lxx.tertio;[5] primus annus
Decennovenalis cycli; quinto anno cycli solaris; primus
annus cycli Indictionis. Conchobhar Buidhe, son of
Amhlaibh, son of Art O'Ruairc, king of Breifne, was
killed by the sons of Conchobhar, son of Tighernan

---

egan, in his version of the Ann. of
Clonmacnois, says that "James
Dowdall (*recté* Jacques D'Audeley),

deputye of Ireland, was killed by
O'Bryen and some Connaghtmen."
[5] *Tertio.* τεɲcɩo, MS.

chobaiṗ; ocuṗ ṗo ṁaṗḃ ṗom an mac ṗob ḟeṗṗ ꝺiḃṗiuṁ, .i. Tiʒeṗnan mac Conchobaiṗ. Eochaiꝺ Mháʒ Mhaṫʒaṁna, ṗí Oiṗʒiall, ꝺo ṁaṗḃaꝺ la .h.nꝆluain ocuṗ la Cenel Eoʒain, ocuṗ moṗán eli nach aiṗṁiꝺṫeṗ maille ṗṗiṗ, in hoc anno. Cṗeċ ꝺo ꝺenum ꝺo Shiuṗṫán Ꝺexeṫaṗ iṗin Choṗann, ocuṗ beʒán ꝺo macaiḃ ṗiʒ Connachṫ ꝺo ḃṗeiṫ ꝼoṗṗa, ocuṗ aimʒlicuṗ comaiṗle ꝺo ꝺenum ꝺóiḃ ann ṗin ṫṗe ꝼoṗʒoll a nꝺaoineḋ, ʒuṗ maṗḃaꝺ Ꝺomnall mac Ꝺonnchaꝺa mic Mhaʒnuṗa, ocuṗ Maʒnuṗ mac ᴀiṗṫ, ocuṗ Oiṗechṫaċ mac ᴀoꝺaʒain, ocuṗ ᴀoꝺ .h.ꝺiṗn, eṫ alii mulṫi. Moṗṗluaiʒeꝺ la mac Muiṗiṗ Mic ʒeṗailṫ a Tuaꝺhṁumain, ʒuṗ ʒaḃ bṗaiʒꝺe ocuṗ neṗṫ aṗ .h.mḃṗiain. Coṗmac mac Ꝺiaṗmaꝺa mic Ruaiꝺṗi moṗṫuuṗ eṫ. Ioṗṗṗaiꝺ ʒenuille ꝺo ṫeachṫ na ʒiúṗꝺiṗ a nEṗinn o ṗíʒ Saxan in hoc anno. Ꝺoṁnall Ioṗṗuiṗ, mac Maʒnuṗa mic Muiṗceṗṫaiʒ Muimniʒ, ꝺo innaṗḃaꝺ a hꝊmall ocuṗ a hIṗṗuṗ ꝺo ʒhalloiḃ in hoc anno. Ruaiꝺṗi .h.ꝼlaiṫbeṗṫaiʒ ꝺo ionnaṗḃaꝺ a iaṗṫaṗ Connachṫ ꝺo ʒhalloiḃ muṗ an ceꝺna.

Kt. Enáiṗ ꝼoṗ Luan, a rechṫmaꝺ ꝺhéc ṗuiṗṗe; anno Ꝺomini M.cc.lxx.quaṗṫo; ṗecunꝺo anno Ꝺecennouenaliṗ cicli; ui. anno cicli ṗolaṗiṗ; ṗecunꝺuṗ annuṗ inꝺicṫioniṗ. ᴀoꝺ mac ꝼélim mic Caṫhail cṗoibꝺeṗʒ, ṗí Connachṫ ṗria ṗé .ix. mbliaꝺna, ꝺo éʒ a quinṫ noin Mai iṗin mbliaꝺain ṗin; ꝺia Ꝺaṗꝺaoin aṗái laiṫe ꝼeachṫṁaine, iꝺ eṫ inuenṫio ṗancṫe cṗuciṡ; Ri ṗo ꝼalmaiʒ ocuṗ ṗo ꝼáṗṗaiʒ Connachṫa aṗ ʒhalloiḃ ocuṗ ʒhaoiꝺelaiḃ ḃiꝺiṗ na aʒhaiꝺ; Ri ꝺo ṗaꝺ maꝺmanna móṗa mince ꝼoṗ ʒhalloiḃ ocuṗ ʒhaoiꝺelaiḃ; ocuṗ Ri ṗo ṫṗaṗcaiṗ a cúiṗṫenꝺa ocuṗ a ʒcaiṗléna; Ri ṗo ʒaḃ

---

[1] *Maghnus;* i.e. Maghnus O'Conchobhair, or Manus O'Conor.

[2] *Art.* Another member of the family of O'Conor.

[3] *Alii.* aLi, MS.

[4] *Ruaidhri.* Ruaidhri O'Conchobhair.

[5] *Domhnall Irruis;* i.e. Domhnall

O'Conchobhair; and he slew the best of these sons, viz., Tighernan, son of Conchobhar. Eochaidh Mac Mathghamhna, king of Oirghiall, and many more along with him who are not specified, were killed by O'hAnluain and the Cenel-Eoghain in hoc anno. A depredation was committed in the Corann by Jordan de Exeter, when a few of the sons of kings of Connacht overtook them; but they adopted an imprudent resolution at the suggestion of their people, so that Domhnall, son of Donnchadh, son of Maghnus,[1] and Maghnus, son of Art,[2] and Oirechtach Mac Aedhagain, and Aedh O'Birn, et alii[3] multi, were slain. A great hosting by the son of Maurice Fitz-Gerald into Tuadh-Mumha, when he took hostages, and obtained sway over O'Briain. Cormac, son of Diarmaid, son of Ruaidhri,[4] mortuus est. Geoffroi Geneville came to Erinn, as Justiciary from the king of the Saxons, in hoc anno. Domhnall Irruis,[5] son of Maghnus, son of Muirchertach Muimhnech, was expelled by the Foreigners from Umhall, and from Irrus, in hoc anno. Ruaidhri O'Flaithbhertaigh was expelled from the west of Connacht, by the Foreigners, in like manner.

The kalends of January on Monday, the seventeenth of the moon; anno Domini M.cc.lxx.quarto; secundo anno Decennovenalis cycli; vi. anno cycli solaris; secundus annus Indictionis. Aedh, son of Fedhlim, son of Cathal Crobhderg, king of Connacht during the space of nine years, died on the fifth of the nones of May in this year, on a Thursday as regards the day of the week, id[6] est Inventio[7] Sanctæ Crucis: a king who emptied and wasted Connacht against the Foreigners and Gaeidhel who were opposed to him; a king who inflicted frequent great defeats on Foreigners and Gaeidhel, and a king who demolished their courts and castles; a king who took

---

of Irrus, a territory represented in name and extent by the present barony of Erris, county of Mayo.

[6] *Id.* ꙇꞇ, MS.

[7] *Inventio.* ꙇnꙋꙇncꙇo, MS.

bṛaiġḋe ḣ.mḃṛiuin ocuṛ Chenel Conaill ; Ṛí ba ṁó
ġṛáin ocuṛ coṛcṫṛ ḋo ṛiġaiḃ Eṛenn ; ḟeṛ milḻṫi ocuṛ
ḻeṛṛaiġṫi na hEṛenn uiḻe ṛe ṛeḋ a iṅṅe ocuṛ a
uaiṛḻe ocuṛ aimṛiṛe ḟeiṛṛin, uṫ ṗoeṫa ḋiṫiṫ :—

     Nai mḃḻiaḋna ḋon Aoḋ enġaċ
     Aġ coṛṅum ṫeaḻḻaiġ Theṁṛaċ ;
     Níṛ ḃḟann ṛe ṛaġaiḻ an ḟeṛ,
     Aṅaġaiḋ Ġhaḻḻ iṛ Ġhaoiḋeaḻ.

Eoġan, mac Ruaiḋṛí mic Aoḋa mic Caṫhail cṛoiḃḋeṛġ,
ḋo ṛiġhaḋ na ionaḋ ḋo Connachtaiḃ ; ocuṛ ġiḋeoh niṛ
ḃo ḟaḋa an ṛiġe ṛin ḋo ṛaḋaḋ ḋó, óiṛ ní ṛaiḃe achṫ
aon ṛaiṫi a naṛḋ ḟḻaiṫeṛ ċúiġiḋ Chonnachṫ in ṫan ṛo
maṛḃṛaṫ a ḋeiṛḃṛine ṛein hé a ṫempuḻḻ bṛaṫhaṛ
Roṛṛa Comain, .ı. Ruaiḋṛi mac Toiṛṛḋhelḃaiġ mic
Aoḋa hı Conċoḃaiṛ, uṫ ḋiṫiṫ ṗoeṫa :—

     Mac Ruaiḋṛi na ṛí ṛáiṫi,
     Ḋo ġeiġ ḃṛeġ níṛ ḃuan ṛṅáiṫi ;
     Ḋo ṛaḋ ṛḻuaġ Oiḻiġ ġan aṛ
     An oiġiḋ ḋo uaiṛ Eoġan.

Aoḋ, mac Caṫhail ḋaiḻḻ mic Aoḋa, ṁic Caṫhail cṛoiḃḋeṛġ, ḋo ṛiġhaḋ ḋo Chonnachtaiḃ ṫaṛéiṛ Eoġain mic
Ruaiḋṛi, ocuṛ niṛ ḃó ṛaiḋe a ṛiġe ṛiḋé, uaiṛ ni ṛaiḃe
achṫ aon ċaoiciḋiṛ a ṛiġe an ṫan ṛo maṛḃaḋ ḻe Máġ
Oiṛechtaiġ, .ı. Tomaltach, ocuṛ ḻa .ḣ. mḃiṛn, uṫ ḋiṫiṫ
ṗoeṫa :—

     Aoḋ mac Caṫhail, cṛoḋa an ṛmachṫ,
     Ro ċoṛṛain coiġeḋ Chonnachṫ ;
     Caoiciḋiṛ ḋUa Chṛeiḋe maṛ ṛin
     Ina ċeḻe ḋo Cṛuachain.

---

¹ *Poeta.* The stanzas here quoted
are from the poem already referred to
(p. 314, note ¹), by Donn Losc O'Maelchonaire, on the kings of Connacht.

² *The tribe of Temhair.* Teaḻḻaiġ
Theṁṛaċ: ṫeaḻḻaiġ is the gen. of
ṫeaḻḻaċ, which signifies a hearth,
and also a tribe or family. Teaḻḻaċ
Theṁṛaċ, the tribe of Temhair(Tara),
is a bardic name for the Irish people.

³ *One quarter;* i.e. of a year.

⁴ *Cathal Dall;* i.e. "Cathal (or
Charles) the Blind."

⁵ *Tomaltach.* In the Annals of
Connacht, which are but a copy of
the original of the present chronicle,
he is called "Tomaltach an Grainsigh
Sruthra," or "Tomaltach of the grange
of Sruthair" (Shrule, county of Mayo).

the hostages of the Ui-Briuin and Cenel-Conaill; the most formidable and triumphant king of the kings of Erinn; the destroyer and improver of all Erinn during the period of his own renown, dignity and time, ut poeta[1] dixit:—

> Nine years was the valiant Aedh
> Defending the tribe of Temhair;[2]
> Not weak was the man to be found
> Against Foreigners and Gaeidhel.

Eoghan, son of Ruaidhri, son of Aedh, son of Cathal Crobhderg, was made king in his place by the Connacht-men; but this sovereignty which was conferred on him was not of long duration, for he was only one quarter[3] in the supremacy of the province of Connacht when his own kinsman, i.e. Ruaidhri, son of Toirdhelbhach, son of Aedh O'Conchobhair, killed him in the Friar's church of Ros-Comain, ut dixit poeta[1]:—

> The son of Ruaidhri, who was king for a quarter,
> Was not a lasting fibre of a beauteous branch;
> The host of Oilech, without slaughter, inflicted
> The tragic death which Eoghan received.

Aedh, son of Cathal Dall,[4] son of Aedh, son of Cathal Crobhderg, was made king by the Connachtmen, after Eoghan, son of Ruaidhri; but his sovereignty was not of longer duration, for he was only one fortnight in the sovereignty when he was slain by Mac Oirechtaigh, (i.e. Tomaltach),[5] and by O'Birn, ut dixit poeta[1]:—

> Aedh, son of Cathal—valiant the sway—
> Defended the province of Connacht;
> A fortnight was the descendant of Creidhe[6] thus
> As a husband to Cruachan.[7]

---

[6] *Descendant of Creidhe.* Ua Chnerѣe. There is no mention in the O'Conor pedigrees of this Creidhe, whose descendant Aedh is here stated to have been, and the text is probably corrupt.

[7] *Husband to Cruachan.* Cruachan (now Rathcroghan, in the county of Roscommon) was the ancient seat of the kings of Connacht, who were poetically designated its husbands or companions.

Ταὄჳ, mac Τοιρρὄhelbαιჳ mic Ααὄα mic Cαthαιl
croιὄοεrჳ, ὄο ríჳhαὄ ταρéιr Ααὄα mic Cαthαιl ιrιn
mblιαὄαιn ceὄna. Ααcht čena, nír ὄό bec ιn errbuὄ αon
ὄlιαὄna τrι rίჳ ὄο ríჳαιὄ Connαcht ὄο τuιτιm ιnnτe, .ι.
Ααὄ mac Γeὄhlιm, ocur Εoჳhan mac Rυαιὄrι, ocur
Ααὄ mac Cαthαιl ὄαιll, uτ ruprα ὄιχιmur. Τιჳernán
mac Ααὄα hι Rυαιrc, ríჳ ὄreιϝne, morτuur erτ.
Ὄomnall, mac Maჳnυrα mic Μurcerταιჳ Μuιmnιჳ
hι Conchobαιr, rόι eniჳ ocur enჳnumα na hΕrenn uιle,
morτuur erτ. Ταὄჳ mac Cerὄαιll ὄuιὄe hι Όhαluιჳ,
ollαm Ααὄα hι Conchobαιr ϝe ὄán, ὄο éჳ ιn hoc αnno.
Ჳιllα na naom, mac Ααὄα mic Ααṁláιb hι Γerჳαιl,
αon roჳα ταoιrech Ερenn uιle na αιmrιr ϝeιn, ὄο éჳ
ιαr mbuαιὄ naιτrιჳe, ιαr na ὄeιτ τrιčα blιαὄαn α
ჳcenὄur čloιnne Conmaιc mic Γerჳυrrα, αჳ cornum na
hΑnჳαιle ϝe Ჳαlloιb ocur ϝe Ჳαιὄelαιb αιρčena, ocur
Cαthαl mac Ჳιllα na naom ὄο ჳαbáιl ταoιrιჳechtα
ιαrrιn, ocur α ὄeιτ .ιχ. mblιαὄna ιnnτe. Cαthαl Μháჳ
Γhlαnnchαιὄ, ταιrreač Όαrτrαιჳe, morτuur erτ.
Μαoιlrečlαιnn, mac Ααṁláιb mic Ααιρτ hι Rυαιrc, rί
Όαrτrαιჳe ocur Chloιnne Γerṁαιჳe, ὄο marbαὄ lá
Conchobαr mac Όomnαιll mic Νeιll hι Rυαιrc, α Cιll
Γorჳα, ocur α ríჳαὄ ϝeιn ιαrrιn. Όomnall óc, mac
Ααṁláιb mic Ααιρτ hι Rυαιrc, morτuur erτ.

Ϳcτt. Εnáιr ϝor ṁαιρτ; α hochτmαὄ ϝιčeὄ ϝuιrρe;
αnno Όomιnι Μ.cc.lxx.quιnτο; ιιι. αnno ὄecennouenαlιr·
cιclι; ιιι. αnno ιnὄιcτιonιr; uιι. αnno cιclι rolαrιr.
Rυαιὄrι mac Τοιρρὄhelbαιჳ hι Conchobαιr ὄο ჳαbáιl
ὄá bráthαιr ϝeιn, .ι. ὄο Τhαὄჳ mac Τοιρρὄhelbαιჳ, ocur
Ταὄჳ mac Cαthαιl mιc Όιαrmαὄα ὄο αrჳuιn uιle lαιr;
ocur αn Rυαιὄrι ceὄna ὄο élúὄ αr αn lαιṁὄechαr rιn, .ι.
Conchobαr .h.hΑαιnlιὄe ὄá ὄreιτ leιr, ocur τόραιჳechτ

---

[1] *Cathal Dall.* See p. 474, note [4].
[2] *Cerbhall Buidhe.* "Cerbhall (or Carroll) the Yellow."
[3] *Clann-Fermhaighe.* This name is also written "Clann-Fernmhaighe."

See note [3], p. 350 *supra*. It is anglicised "Glanfarne" by Roderick O'Flaherty, in a marginal note.
[4] *By him;* i.e. by Tadhg, son of Toirdhelbhach (O'Conor).

Tadhg, son of Toirdhelbhach, son of Aedh, son of Cathal Crobhderg, was made king after Aedh, son of Cathal, in the same year. No trifling loss was it in one year, indeed, three kings of the kings of Connacht to have fallen in it, viz., Aedh son of Fedhlim, and Eoghan son of Ruaidhri, and Aedh, son of Cathal Dall,[1] ut supra diximus. Tighernan, son of Aedh O'Ruairc, king of Breifne, mortuus est. Domhnall, son of Maghnus, son of Muirchertach Muimhnech O'Conchobhair, the most eminent of all Erinn for hospitality and prowess, mortuus est. Tadhg, son of Cerbhall Buidhe[2] O'Dalaigh, chief poet of Aedh O'Conchobhair, died in hoc anno. Gilla-na-naemh, son of Aedh, son of Amhlaibh O'Ferghail, the choicest of all the chieftains of Erinn in his own time, died after the victory of penitence, after having been thirty years in the chieftainship of the descendants of Conmac, son of Fergus, defending the Anghaile against the Foreigners, and against the Gaeidhel besides: and Cathal, son of Gilla-na-naemh, assumed the chieftainship afterwards, and enjoyed it nine years. Cathal Mac Flannchaidh, chieftain of Dartraighe, mortuus est. Maelsechlainn, son of Amhlaibh, son of Art O'Ruairc, king of Dartraighe and Clann-Fermhaighe,[3] was slain at Cill-Forga by Conchobhar, son of Domhnall, son of Niall O'Ruairc, who was himself made king afterwards. Domhnall Og, son of Amhlaibh, son of Art O'Ruairc, mortuus est.

The kalends of January on Tuesday, the twenty-eighth of the moon; anno Domini M.cc.lxx.quinto; iii. anno Decennovenalis cycli; iii. anno Indictionis; vii. anno cycli solaris. Ruaidhri, son of Toirdhelbhach O'Conchobhair, was taken prisoner by his own brother, i.e. by Tadhg, son of Toirdhelbhach; and Tadhg, son of Cathal Mac Diarmada, was completely plundered by him.[4] And the same Ruaidhri escaped from this confinement, viz., Conchobhar O'hAinlighe took him with him; and they were pursued,

vo ðenum ꝛoꝛꝛα, ocuꝛ Conchobαꝛ .h.hⱭꝉnlⱶe vo mαꝛbαv αnnꝛın. Conchobαꝛ, mαc ꝼeꝛⱶαıl, mıc Vonnchαvα
ṁıc MhuıꝛceꝛⱵαⱶ, vo mαꝛbαv vá ḃꝛαıⱵꝛıḃ ꝛeıꝛꝛın.
Ɑꝛⱦ, mαc Cαⱦαıl ꝛıαbαⱶ hı Ruαıꝛc, ꝛí ḃꝛeıꝛne, vo
mαꝛbαv lα Máⱶ ꝼhınnḃαıꝛ ocuꝛ lα Muınnⱦeꝛ Ȝheꝛα-
ðán, ⱶo nȜαlloıb mαılle ꝛꝛıú, α nȜꝛαnáꝛv, ocuꝛ áꝛ α
muınnⱦıꝛe vo chuꝛ. Cαıꝛbꝛe.h.Scóꝛα, eꝛꝑuc Ráⱦα
boⱦ, ın Cꝛıꝛⱦo quıeuıⱦ. h.lαoıðıⱶ, .ı. eꝛꝑuc Chılle
hⱭlαıð, quıeuıⱦ ın Cꝛıꝛⱦo. Tomáꝛ Mháⱶ Sháṁꝛαðáın
vo mαꝛbαv lα Cénel Vúαchαın. Mαc Conconnαchⱦ hı
Rαıⱶıllıⱶ vo mαꝛbαv lα Cloınn Cαⱦαıl ꝑeꝛ volum.
Mαıðm móꝛ ꝼoꝛ Ȝhαlloıb α nUllⱦoıb, ⱶo ꝛαnıc vα cev
cenn ocuꝛ vá cev ech αn áıꝛeṁ ðıð, cum mulⱦıꝛ αluꝛ.

Jⱦ. ꝺnαıꝛ ꝼoꝛ Ceváın, ocuꝛ .ıx. uαⱦhαv ꝛuıꝛꝑe ; αnno
Vomını M.cc.lxx.ꝛexⱦo ; quαꝛⱦo αnno cıclı lunαꝛıꝛ ;
quαꝛⱦo αnno ınvıcⱦıonıꝛ ; uııı. αnno cıclı ꝛolαꝛıꝛ.
Ɑⱥv Muımnech, mαc ꝼeıðlım mıc Cαⱦαıl cꝛoıbveꝛc,
vo Ⱦochⱦ αꝛ αn Mumαın, ocuꝛ α ðol α nuchⱦ hı
Vóṁnαıll ; ocuꝛ .h.Vomnαıll vo Ⱦınól lαıꝛ, ocuꝛ
ⱦoıⱶechⱦ vóıḃ vıḃlınαıḃ ⱶo hꝺⱦαnαch, ocuꝛ ımꝑóð
vllα Vomnαıll αnnꝛın ; ocuꝛ ⱦochⱦ vo mαc ꝼeıðlım ꝼeın
α meꝛc Chonnαchⱦαıb αꝛꝛıðé, ocuꝛ beıð vo αnn. Clαnn
Toıꝛꝛvhelbαıⱶ, ımoꝛꝛo, vo Ⱦochⱦ αꝛ ⱦíꝛ íαꝛ ꝛın, ocuꝛ
loıꝛⱦí moꝛα vo ðenum ðóıḃ, ocuꝛ nıꝛ ⱶαḃꝛαⱦ vo Ⱦenn
αꝛ ⱦíꝛ αchⱦmαv ꝛın nαmá. Vıαꝛmαıv mαc Ȝıllαmuıꝛe
hı Moꝛnα, ꝛí Ulαv, moꝛⱦuuꝛ eꝛⱦ. Cꝛeⱥ vo ðenum vo

---

[1] *Muirchertach.* Muirchertach (or
Murtough) O'Conor.

[2] *Cathal Riabhach*; i.e. "Cathal the
Tawny."

[3] *Quievit.* Ware (*Bishops*, Harris's
ed., p. 271) states on the authority
of the "Annals of Lough-Kee (Loch-
Cé)," that Bishop O'Scoba died at
Rome; but it is clear that Ware did
not quote from the original of the
present volumes, as there is no mention
of Rome either in this MS., or in the
so-called Annals of Connacht.

[4] *Cenel-Duachain.* More usually
written Cenel-Luachain, as in the
Four Masters, and under the year
1284, *infra*; but Cenel-Luachain is
probably a corruption, arising from
the aspiration of the letter ð in the
form Cenel-Dhuachain (pron. Cenel-
Uachain), and the attraction of the
letter *l* of *Cenel* over to the second
word of the name.

[5] *Aedh Muimhnech.* "Aedh (Hugh)
the Momonian," so called from his
having been fostered in Munster.

and Conchobhar O'hAinlighe was then slain. Conchobhar, son of Ferghal, son of Donnchadh, son of Muirchertach,[1] was killed by his own brethren. Art, son of Cathal Riabhach[2] O'Ruairc, king of Breifne, was slain by Mac Finnbhair and Muinter-Geradhain, accompanied by Foreigners, at Granard; and a slaughter of his people was committed. Cairbre O'Scoba, bishop of Rath-Both, in Christo quievit.[3] O'Laidhigh, i.e. bishop of Cill-Alaidh, quievit in Christo. Thomas Mac Shamhradhain was slain by the Cenel-Duachain.[4] The son of Cuconnacht O'Raighilligh was slain by the Clann-Cathail, per dolum. A great victory was gained over the Foreigners in Uladh, so that two hundred of their heads, and two hundred horses, were counted, cum multis aliis.

The kalends of January on Wednesday, and the ninth of the moon; anno Domini M.cc.lxx.sexto; quarto anno cicli lunaris; quarto anno Indictionis; viii. anno cycli solaris. Aedh Muimhnech,[5] son of Fedhlim, son of Cathal Crobhderg, came out of Mumha, and went to seek O'Domhnaill's protection; and O'Domhnaill mustered his army; and they both came to Echanach, where O'Domhnaill turned back; and the son of Fedhlim went from thence amongst the Connachtmen, where he remained. The sons of Toirdhelbhach, however, came afterwards into the district, and committed great burnings; but they obtained no power in the district except this alone. Diarmaid, son of Gillamuire O'Morna,[6] king of Uladh, mortuus est. A depredation was committed by the sons of Toirdhelbhach on the son of Fedhlim and the sons of

---

Mageoghegan, in his version of the Annals of Cionmacnoise, states that Aedh Muimhnech was "a base sonne" of Fedhlim O'Conor, whose legitimate son Aedh, king of Connacht, was slain in the year 1274, as above recorded.

[6] *O'Morna.* The Four Masters give

the name as Diarmaid O'Gillamuire (Dermot O'Gilmurry), and instead of "king of Uladh," state that he was "lord of Leth-Cathail," a district now represented, both in extent and name, by the barony of Lecale, county of Down.

ćloınn Toıppohelbaıž ap mac Péólım, ocuf ap macaıb
Mıc Oıapmaoa, ocuf Žılla Cpıft .h. Máılbpenaınn
oo mapbab leo an lá fın. Cpeć oo ćenum oo mac
Péólım ap Chloınn Muıpceptaıž, žup ŕhapbfat Clann
Mhuıpceptaıž Žılla na naınžeal .h. Conpóı a tóp-
aıžecht na cpeıće fın, ocuf oaoıne ımóa elı oo muıntep
mıc Péólım. Oo fížne Ruaıópı mac Toıppohelbaıž
cpeć ŕhóp elı ap Muıntep Nechtaın, ocuf Muıntep
Nechtaın oo ćabaıpt ŕhaóma faıp ocuf oo buaın na
cpeıće óe; ocuf Oomnall mac Neıll mıc Conžalaıž hı
Ruaıpc oo ŕhapbab, ocuf ıf fpıf aoeıpćí Žılla an ımme,
ocuf oaoıne ımóa elı maılle fpıf oo muıntep Ruaıópı.
Žılla Cpıft .h.Neachtaın ocuf Uıllıam .h.Neachtaın
oo mapbab la Ruaıópı mac Toıppohelbaıž ıapfın.

Ktt. Enaıp fop Aıne, ocuf fıćtech fuıppe; anno
Oomını M.cc.lxxuıı; quınto anno cıclı lunapıf; ıx.anno
cıclı folapıf; quınto anno ınoıctıonıf. Opían puab
.h.Opıaın, pı Muman, oo žabaıl a meabaıl oo mac
Iapla Claıp, ıap žcup a bpola an aon foıóech, ocuf ıap
noenum ćaıpoeffa Cpıoft oóıb, ocuf ıap otabaıpt
ŕhınn, ocuf ćloz, ocuf bacall Muman oa ćelı oóıb; ocuf
a ćappaınž oo mac an Iapla ıoıp foéoaıb ıapfın. Žılla
Cpıft .h. bıpn, fep žpáóa oAćŏO .h.Conchobaıp, oo
mapbab oon Žılla puab mac Lóchlaınn hı Conchobaıp,
ı nuaćbuf. Opaon .h.Maolmoıćeıpže, ab Cenannuf, ın
Cpıfto quıeuıt. Caıflen Roffa Comáın oo lezab oo·
mac Péólım, ocuf oo Ohomnall .h.Oomnaıll, ocuf oo
Connachtaıb maılle fpıf. Cpeć ŕhóp oo ćenum oo
Theallać Echach ap Chénel Ouacháın a nžlınn oá

Mac Diarmada; and Gilla-Christ O'Maelbhrenainn was slain by them on that day. A depredation was committed by the son of Fedhlim on the Clann-Muirchertaigh; and the Clann-Muirchertaigh killed Gilla-na-naingel O'Conroi, whilst in pursuit of this prey, and several others of the son of Fedhlim's people. Ruaidhri, son of Toirdhelbhach, committed another great depredation on Muinter-Nechtain; but Muinter-Nechtain defeated him and took the prey from him; and Domhnall, son of Niall, son of Conghalach O'Ruairc—who was usually called Gilla-an-imme[1]—was slain, and many other persons of Ruaidhri's people along with him. Gilla-Christ O'Nechtain and William O'Nechtain were afterwards slain by Ruaidhri, son of Toirdhelbhach. •

The kalends of January on Friday, and the twentieth of the moon; anno Domini M.cc.lxxvii.; quinto[2] anno cycli lunaris; ix. anno cycli solaris; quinto[2] anno Indictionis. Brian Ruadh O'Briain, king of Mumha,[3] was apprehended, in treachery, by the son of the Earl of Clare, after they had poured their blood into the same vessel,[4] and after they had formed gossipred, and after they had exchanged mutual vows by the relics, bells, and croziers of Mumha; and he was afterwards drawn[5] between steeds by the Earl's son. Gilla-Christ O'Birn, a favourite of Aedh O'Conchobhair, was most cruelly slain by the Gilla-ruadh, son of Lochlainn O'Conchobhair. Braen O'Maelmocheirghe, abbot of Cenannus, in Christo quievit. The castle of Ros-Comain was thrown down by the son of Fedhlim, and by Domhnall O'Domhnaill, and by the Connachtmen along with him. A great depredation was committed by the Tellach-Echach on the Cenel-Duachain,[6] in

---

the covenant were written. "Yellow Book of Lecan," an Irish MS., class H. 2. 16, Trin. Coll., Dublin, col. 313.

[5] *Drawn*. The Dublin copy of the Annals of Inisfallen represent O'Brien as having been executed by hanging.

[6] *Cenel-Duachain*. This name seems to have been first written "Cenel-Luachain" in the text, and then altered to "Cenel-Duachain" by the original hand. See note [4], p. 478. The Annals of Connacht read "Cenel-Luachain."

ὄυιλe, ὄαη ṁαηὄαὄαη Conchobaη Ṁὰᵹ Ὄhoηchαιὄ eτ αλιι μυλτι.

Ḱττ. Θηαιη ƒoη ƒαταηη, ocυη ρηιμ ƑυιƑƑe; anno Ὄomini M.cc.λxx.octαυo; x. anno cicλι ƑoλαηιƑ; ηexτo anno cicλι λυηαηιƑ; υι. anno ιηὄιcτιonιƑ. Ταὄᵹ, mαc Τoιηηὄheλbαιᵹ, mιc Αoὄα ṁιc Cατhαιλ cηoιbὄeηᵹ, ὄo mαηbαὄ ὄo ĕλαιηη Chατhαιλ Ṁιc Ὄιαηmαὄα, ιαη ηὰ ὄeιτ τeoηα bλιαὄηα α ᵹceηηυƑ Connαchτ, υτ ρoeτα ὄιxιτ, .ι. Ὄonn λoηᵹ .h. Μαoλconαιηe:—

> Uα Conchobaιη Chλυαηαcα,
> Μαc Τoιηηὄheλbαιᵹ, τηι bλιαὄηα;
> Cὰĕ ƒα ηιᵹe ὄo ηeιη Τ   ;
> Ᵹeιλλ an τιηe ὄo τιomαιηᵹ;

ocυη Αoὄ Μυιṁnech mαc Ƒeιὄλιm ὄo ᵹαbὰιλ ηιᵹe Connαchτ. Ruαιὄηι mαc Τoιηηὄheλbαιᵹ, ηιᵹὄαṁnα Connαchτ, ὄo mαηbαὄ ὄo Ᵹhιλλα CηιƑτ Ṁὰᵹ Ƒhλαηη- chαιὄ ocυη ὄo Ὄhαητηαιᵹιὄ ὰιηĕena, αη boηὄ Ὄηoma cλιαὄ, ocυη an ρeηηυη ηιαbαch mαc Τιᵹeηηὰιη hι Con- chobαιη, ocυη ὄαoιne ιmὄα eλe nαch ὰιηιṁτeη ηυηη. Ὄonnchαὄ ocυη Ƒeηᵹhαλ ocυη Ᵹιλλα CηιƑτ, τηι mιc Μυιηᵹeηα mιc Ὄonnchαὄα mιc Τomαλταιᵹ, ὄo ṁαηbαὄ λα Ταὄᵹ mαc Ὄomnαιλλ 1ηηυιη. Ƒλαιτbeηταch .h. Ὄoιṁín, ηí Ƒheη Μαnαĕ, ὄo mαηbαὄ ιηιn mbλιαὄαιn ηιn. Ματṁ Cυιηnĕe ὄo ταbαιητ ὄo Ὄhonnchαὄ mαc Ƀηιαιn ηυαιὄ hι Ƀηíαιn, ocυη ὄo mαcαιὄ eλι hι Ƀηιαιn, αη mαc 1αηλα Cλαιη, ᵹυη λoιηceτ τempuλλ Cuιnnche·α ceηὄ α μυιnτιηe, ocυη ᵹυη λoιηceὄ ocυη ᵹυη mαηbαὄ ὄάιne ὄιάιηṁιὄe αnnηιn, ocυη ᵹonὄechαιὄ mαc an 1αηλα ηó λάιṁ αηη υατhαιb, ƒóηίoη. Τomάηη .h.Cυιnn, eηρuc Cλυαnα mιc Noιη, quιeuιτ. Τomαλταch Ṁὰᵹ Oιηechτ- αιᵹ, ηιᵹ ταoιηηeĕ Shιoλ Μυιηeᵹhαιᵹ, ὄo ṁαηbαὄ λαη nα Τúατhαιb ιn hoc αnno.

---

¹ *Alii.* αλι, MS.

² *Ut.* ιτ, MS.

³ *Donn Losg.* "Donn the Lame." In the so-called Annals of Connacht (under A.D. 1224) he is called "Donn-

chadh Bacach," i.e. "Donnchadh the Lame."

⁴ *Aedh Muimhnech.* See note ⁵, p. 478.

⁵ *Domhnall Irruis;* i.e. Domhnall

Glenn-dá-dhuile, on which occasion they slew Concho-bhar Mac Dorchaidh, et alii[1] multi.

The kalends of January on Saturday, and the first of the moon; anno Domini M.cc.lxx.octavo; x. anno cycli solaris; sexto anno cycli lunaris; vi. anno Indictionis. Tadhg, son of Toirdhelbhach, son of Aedh, son of Cathal Crobhderg, was slain by the sons of Cathal Mac Diarmada, after having been three years in the government of Connacht, ut[2] poeta dixit, i.e. Donn Losg[3] O'Maelchonaire:—

> O'Conchobhair of Cluain-ca,
> The son of Toirdhelbhach, *was king* three years;
> All, during his reign, were obedient to Tadhg:
> The hostages of the country he collected;

and Aedh Muimhnech,[4] son of Fedhlim, assumed the sovereignty of Connacht. Ruaidhri, son of Toirdhelbhach, royal heir of Connacht, was slain by Gilla-Christ Mac Flannchaidh, and by the Dartraighc likewise, on the borders of Druim-cliabh; and the Swarthy Parson, son of Tighernan O'Conchobhair, and many other persons not enumerated here, *were slain*. Donnchadh, and Ferghal, and Gilla-Christ—three sons of Muirghis, son of Donnchadh, son of Tomaltach—were slain by Tadhg, son of Domhnall Irruis.[5] Flaithbhertach O'Doimhín, king of Feara-Manach, was slain in this year. The defeat of Cuinnche was inflicted by Donnchadh, son of Brian Ruadh O'Briain, and by O'Briain's other sons, on the son of the Earl of Clare, when they burned the church of Cuinnche over the heads of his people; and persons innumerable were burned and slain there, but, alas![6] the Earl's son escaped safely from them. Thomas O'Cuinn, bishop of Cluain-mic-Nois, quievit. Tomaltach Mac Oirechtaigh, king-chieftain of Sil-Muiredhaigh, was slain by the Tuatha in hoc anno.

of Irrus, or Erris, in the county of Mayo. His surname was O'Conor.

[6] *Alas*. τόπιοη. Mageoghegan, in his version of the Annals of Clon-macnois, referring to this exclama-tion, which he must have found in his original, observes "for which escape myne author sayeth that him-selfe was sorry."

]ctt. Eṅαιρ ρορ Ḋoṁnach, ocuρ αιle ṫéc ρuιρρe; αnno
Ḋoṁιnι M.cc.lxxιx.; xι. αnno cιclι ρolαριρ; uιι. αnno
cιclι lunαριρ ᴇᴛ ιnṿιcᴛιoṅιρ. Ꞇoṁαlᴛαch, mαc Ꞇoιρρṽhelbαιᵹ, mιc Mhαoιlρechlαιnn hι Conchobαιρ, αιρṽ
eρρuc Ꞇuάmα, ράι Eρenn uιle αρ eᵹnα ocuρ αρ eoluρ,
αρ eιnech ocuρ αρ uαιρle, αρ ᴛροċραιᵹechᴛ ocuρ αρ
ᴛιṽlucαṽ ρéṽ ocuρ mαoιne ṽo ċάċ α ᵹcoιᴛċιnne, ṽo éᵹ
ιαρ mbuαιṽ nαιᴛριᵹe ιn hoc αnno. Mαιlρeċlαιnn
mαc Ꞇoιρρṽhelbαιᵹ ṽo mαρbαṽ ιn hoc αnno. Conchobαρ, mαc Ḋιαρmαṽα mιc Mhαᵹnuρα hι Conchobαιρ,
occιρuρ eρᴛ. Ᵹιllα αn Choιṁṽeṽh .h.Ceρḃαllάιn, eρρuc
Chéneoιl Eoᵹαιn, quιeuιᴛ. Muρchαṽ.h.ℵechᴛαιn ṽo
mαρbαṽ ṽo Ḋomnαll.h.ℵechᴛαιn, ocuρ compαc ṽo
ρóᵹρα ṽo Roιbeρṽ .h.ℵechᴛαιn, .ι. ṽeρbραᴛhαιρ Muρ-
chαṽα, αρ Ḋomnαll ιαρριn; ocuρ Roιρeρṽ ṽo mαρbαṽ
muρ αn ceṽnα ιριn compuc ριn. Ḋomnαll mαc Ᵹιllα
Cριρᴛ hι ℵechᴛαιn ṽo mαρbαṽ lα hάoṽ .h.Conċenαιnn
ιn hoc αnno.

]ctt. Eṅαιρ ρορ Luαn, ocuρ ᴛρeρρ ριcheṽ ρuιρρe;
αnno Ḋoṁιnι M.cc.lxxx.; xιι. αnno cιclι ρolαριρ; uιιι.
αnno [cιclι] ṽecennouenαlιρ eᴛ ιnṽιcᴛιoṅιρ. ᴵmρeραιn
ṽo eιρᵹe eṽιρ αᵒṽ Muιmnech, mαc Ϝélιm mιc Cαᴛhαιl
cρoιbṽeρc, ρι Connαchᴛ, ocuρ Clαnn Mhuιρċeρᴛαιᵹ
Muιmnιᵹ hι Conchobαιρ, ιn hoc αnno; ocuρ αᵒṽ
Muιmneċ ṽo ṁαρbαṽ leo α Coιll αn ṽαιnᵹιn; ocuρ
Mαoιlρeċlαιnn mαc Mάᵹnuρα ṽo ᵹαbάιl ṽóιṽ αn lά
ριn, ocuρ α ṗuαρlucαṽ uαᴛhαιb ṽllα Ḋhomnαιll αρ
ceιᴛρι ceṽ bó ocuρ αρ xx. ech; ocuρ Cαᴛhαl, mαc Conchobαιρ ρuαιṽ, mιc Muιρċeρᴛαιᵹ Muιmnιᵹ, mιc Ꞇhoιρρ-
ṽhelbαιᵹ ṁóιρ hι Conchobαιρ, ṽo ριᵹhαṽ ṽo Con-
nαchᴛαιḃ ιαρᴛαιn. Seoαn.h.Lαoιṽιᵹ, eρρuc Chιlle

---

¹ *Son of Toirdhelbhách;* i.e. of
Toirdhelbhach O'Conchobhair, or Turlough O'Conor.

² *Bishop of Cenel-Eoghain;* otherwise, bishop of Derry.

³ *Coill-an-daingin;* i.e. "the wood of
the *daingen* (or stronghold)" Mageoghegan (Annals of Clonmacnois) understood Coill-an-daingin, or Koyll-an-
daingin, as he writes it, to be a proper

The kalends of January on Sunday, and the twelfth of the moon; anno Domini M.cc.lxxix; xi. anno cycli solaris; vii. anno cycli lunaris et Indictionis. Tomaltach, son of Toirdhelbhach, son of Maelsechlainn O'Conchobhair, archbishop of Tuaim, the most eminent man in all Erinn for wisdom and knowledge, for hospitality and nobility, for munificence, and for distributing jewels and valuables to all in general, died after the triumph of penitence in hoc anno. Maelsechlainn, son of Toirdhelbhach,[1] was slain in hoc anno. Conchobhar, son of Diarmaid, son of Maghnus O'Conchobhair, occisus est. Gilla-an-Choimdedh O'Cerbhalláin, bishop of Cenel-Eoghain,[2] quievit. Murchadh O'Nechtain was killed by Domhnall O'Nechtain; and Domhnall was challenged to fight by Robert O'Nechtain, (i.e. Murchadh's brother), and Robert was also killed in this fight. Domhnall, son of Gilla-Christ O'Nechtain, was killed by Aedh O'Conchennain in hoc anno.

The kalends of January on Monday, and the twenty-third of the moon; anno Domini M.cc.lxxx; xii. anno cycli solaris; viii. anno [cycli] Decennovenalis et Indictionis. A contention arose between Aedh Muimhnech, son of Fedhlim, son of Cathal Crobhderg, king of Connacht, and the descendants of Muirchertach Muimhnech O'Conchobhair, in hoc anno; and Aedh Muimhnech was killed by them in Coill-an-daingin;[3] and Maelsechlainn, son of Maghnus, was taken prisoner by them on the same day, but was ransomed from them by O'Domhnaill for four hundred cows and twenty horses. And Cathal, son of Conchobhar Ruadh, son of Muirchertach Muimhnech, son of Toirdhelbhach Mór O'Conchobhair, was afterwards made king by the Connachtmen. John O'Laidigh, bishop of Cill-Alaidh, in

---

name; but Dr. O'Donovan (Four Mast., ad. an.) translates "the wood of Dangan." The Irish word *daingen* seems cognate with the Fr. *donjon*, and Engl. *dungeon*.

hαClaið, in Cpirτo quieuiτ. Maτa mac Maӡnura hi
Conchobair, ab na búille, quieuiτ.

Ictt. Enair ror čéτaoin, ocur a ceτhair uaτhad
ruirre ; anno Domini M.cc.lxxx. primo; xiii. anno cicli
rolarir; ix. anno cicli lunarir eτ indicτionir. Taðӡ,
mac Caτhail, mic Cončobair, mic Dhiarmada o
nabarτar Mic Diarmada, riӡ Mhoiӡe Luirӡ, rói
neiniӡ ocur nenӡnuma ocur nuairle na hErenn, morτuur erτ. Caτ Dírirτ váčμič edir Conallchaib ocur
Eoӡanchaib, dú aτorčuir Domnall óӡ .h. Domnaill, rí
an τuaircerτ, .i. rer dár ӡialladar Fir Manach ocur
Oirӡialla, ocur urmór Ӡaoidel Connachτ ocur Ulað
achτmaӡ beӡ, ocur rir mbreirrne .bór ; ocur anτ aon
ӡaoidel rob rerr einech ocur oirechur ; reichem coiτ-
čend iarτhair Eorra ocur rnaτad uamma na hairoriӡe,
ocur rarča dluτaiӡτe ӡach deӡ rechτa ; ocur ionnamail[1]
Chonaire mic Eoirrceóil ar óiӡe aӡ ӡabáil riӡe, ocur
cnú mullaiӡ Ӡhaoidel ar ӡairced, ocur medh cormail
Chaτhail croibderӡ ar áӡ ocur innroiӡed ; ocur a
adnacal co honórach a mainirdir na mbráτhar a
n'Doire Choluim čille, iar mbreiτ buada ӡach uile
maiτerrai ; ocur irriad ro ir rerr do marbad maille
rrir irin maiðm rin, .i. Maolruanaid .h. baoiӡill,
τaoirech na Tri Tuaτ, ocur Eoӡan mac Mhaoilτrech-
lainn mic Domnaill móir hi Dhomnaill, ocur Ceallač
.h. báiӡill, .i. mac Ӡilla bhriӡde, anτ én τaoirech rob.
rerr oinech ocur τidnacul, ocur ir mó do rӡaoil il
maoine ar eiӡrið, do bí an aon aimrir rir, ocur dob
rerr lám ocur uairle; ocur Andiler .h. baiӡill, ocur
Dubӡall a mac; ocur Máӡ Fhlannchaið, τáirioč Dar-
τraiӡe; ocur Domnall Mac Ӡillarhinnén, τairrech
Muinnτire Feodačán; ocur Enna .h. ӡairmleӡhaiӡh,
ard τáirrech Cheneoil Móain ; ocur Cormac mac an

---

1 *Parallel.* ionnamail for ionnramail, MS.

Christo quievit. Matthew, son of Maghnus O'Conchobhair, abbot of the Buill, quievit.

The kalends of January on Wednesday, and the fourth
of the moon; anno Domini M.cc.lxxx.primo; xiii. anno
cycli solaris; ix. anno cycli lunaris et Indictionis. Tadhg,
son of Cathal, son of Conchobhar, son of Diarmaid (from
whom the Mac Diarmadas are named), king of Magh-
Luirg, the most eminent man in Erinn for hospitality,
prowess, and nobility, mortuus est. The battle of Disert-
dá-chrich between the Cenel-Conaill and Cenel-Eoghain, in which fell Domhnall Og O'Domhnaill, king of
the North—i.e. a man to whom submitted the Feara-
Manach, and the Oirghialla, and nearly the majority of
the Gaeidhel of Connacht and Uladh, and also the men
of Breifne; the best Gaeidhel for hospitality and dignity;
the general guardian of the west of Europe, and the
knitting needle of the arch-sovereignty, and the
rivetting hammer of every good law; the parallel[1] of
Conaire, son of Edirscel, in purity when assuming sovereignty; the top nut of the Gaeidhel in valour; the equal
of Cathal Crobhderg in battle and attack: and he
was honourably interred in the monastery of the Friars
in Doire-Choluim-Chille, after obtaining the palm of
every goodness. And these were the best who were
slain along with him in that battle, viz. Maelruanaidh
O'Baighill, chieftain of the Three Tuatha; and Eoghan,
son of Maelsechlainn, son of Domhnall Mór O'Domhnaill;
and Ceallach O'Baighill, i.e. the son of Gilla-Brighde—the
chieftain who, of all his contemporaries, was the best
for hospitality and generosity, and who distributed
various gifts in largest measure to learned men, and who
was the best for munificence and nobility; and Andiles
O'Baighill, and his son Dubhgall; and Mac Flannchaidh,
chieftain of Dartraighe; and Domhnall Mac Gilla-fhinnén,
chieftain of Muinter Pheodacháin; and Enna O'Gairmleghaigh, high chieftain of Cenel-Móain; and Cormac,

ḟiṗ leiġinn hi Domnaill, ταiṗṗech Ṗánαd, ocuṗ Ṡillα
an Choimḋeḋ. h. Maolḋúin, ṗi Luiṗʒ, ocuṗ Caṗmac
mac Caṗmaic hi Dhomnaill, ocuṗ Ṡillα na nóʒ mac
Dál ṗe docαiṗ, ocuṗ Mailṗechlainn mac Neill hi
ḃṗaʒill, ocuṗ Andileṗ mac Muiṗċeṗταiʒ hi Dhoṁnaill, ocuṗ Maʒnuṗ Mháʒ Cuinn, ocuṗ Ṡillα na naom
.h.heoċaʒáin, ocuṗ Muiṗċeṗτach.h.Ḟlaiṫḃeṗταiʒ, ocuṗ
Muiṗcheṗτach Mac an Ullταiʒ, ocuṗ Ḟlaiṫḃeṗταċ
Mháʒ ḃhuiḃechán, ocuṗ dáine imḃα ele nach áiṗiṁτeṗ
ṗunn. Caṫ eli in hoc anno iτiṗ na ḃaiṗédαċḃ ocuṗ
an Ciomoṗóʒach, ocuṗ ṗo ṁeabhad ṗoṗ na ḃaiṗéd-
achaiḃ, ocuṗ ṗo maṗbaḋ ann Uilliam ḃaiṗéd ocuṗ
Adám Ṗleimend, ocuṗ daoine imḃα eli ; ocuṗ do ḃí
diaṗ do Ṡhaoidelaiḃ annṗin do leiṫ an Chiṁṗóʒaċ,
ocuṗ do ċinnṗeτ aṗ ḃeoḋachτ ocuṗ aṗ lúṫ, ocuṗ aṗ
lamach, do ċáċ uile annṗin, .i. Taiċlech.h.Duḃḋa ocuṗ
Taiċleċ .h.ḃaiʒill in diaṗṗ híṗin.

Ktt. enaiṗ ṗoṗ ḃaṗdáin, ocuṗ cuiʒed déʒ ṗuiṗṗe ;
anno Domini M.cc.lxxxii ; xiiii. anno ciċli ṗolaṗiṗ ;
x. anno ciċli lunaṗiṗ eτ indicτioniṗ. Muiṗċeṗτach
Mac Muṗchada, ṗí Laiʒen, ocuṗ Aṗτ Mac Muṗchada,
a deṗḃṗaτhaiṗ ṗiḋé, do maṗbaḋ la Ṡalloiḃ in hoc
anno. Taiċleċ mac Mhaolṗuanaiḋ hi Dhuḃḋa, ṗi
.h.ḃḟhiacṗaċ Muaiḋe, .i. an ṗeṗ ṗoḃ ṗeṗṗ oinech ocuṗ
enʒnum, ocuṗ bá mó cendaiṗṗe ocuṗ cointinn ṗe
Ṡalloiḃ ocuṗ ṗe Danaṗaiḃ im a ḃuṫhaid, aʒ á díḋen, ·
do maṗbaḋ la hAdam Ciomṗóʒ aṗ Tṗaiʒ neoċaile.
Laṗṗaiṗṗionna, inʒen Chaτhail cṗoiḃdeṗʒ hi Conchobaiṗ, ben Dómnaill óiʒ hi Domnaill, .i. an ḃen doḃ
uaiṗle ocuṗ doḃ ṗéile ocuṗ doḃ ṗeṗṗ cṗuτh do ḃí an
eṗinn na haimṗiṗ ṗein, quieuiτ in Cṗiṗτo. Maṫa
.h.Raiʒilliʒ, dux Muinnτeṗi Maolṁoṗḋa, do éʒ in hoc

---

[1] The Ferleighinn; i.e. "the Lector."
[2] Mac-an-Ultaigh. "Son of the
Ultonian." The name is now usually
written "M'Nulty."

[3] Danars. This name, originally
applied to the Danish invaders, was
subsequently used to signify robbers,
ruffians, or desperadoes. See Dr.

son of the Ferleighinn[1] O'Domhnaill, chieftain of Fánad;
and Gilla-in-Choimdedh O'Maeldúin, king of Lurg; and
Cormac, son of Cormac O'Domhnaill; and Gilla-na-nóg
Mac Dáil-re-dochair; and Maelsechlainn, son of Niall
O'Baighill; and Andiles, son of Muirchertach O'Domhnaill; and Maghnus Mac Cuinn; and Gilla-na-naemh
O'hEochagáin; and Muirchertach O'Flaithbhertaigh; and
Muirchertach Mac-an-Ultaigh;[2] and Flaithbhertach Mac
Buidhechán; and several other persons who are not
enumerated here. Another battle in hoc anno between
the Barretts and the Cusack; and the Barretts were
defeated, and William Barrett, and Adam Fleming, and
many other persons, were slain; and two of the Gaeidhel
were present on the Cusack's side, who excelled all
there in vigour, agility, and dexterity, viz.:—Taichlech
O'Dubhda and Taichlech O'Baighill were these two.

The kalends of January on Thursday, and the fifteenth
of the moon; anno Domini M.cc.lxxxii.; xiiii. anno
cycli solaris; x. anno cycli lunaris et Indictionis. Muirchertach Mac Murchadha, king of Laighen, and Art Mac
Murchadha, his brother, were slain by Foreigners in hoc
anno. Taichlech, son of Maelruanaidh O'Dubhda, king
of Ui-Fiachrach-Muaidhe, i.e. the best man for hospitality
and prowess, and who had most conflicts and contentions
with Foreigners and Danars[3] regarding his country, whilst
protecting it, was killed by Adam Cusack on Traigh-
Eothaile. Lassairfhiona, daughter of Cathal Crobhderg
O'Conchobhair, wife of Domhnall Og O'Domhnaill,[4] i.e. the
most noble, and hospitable, and beautiful woman that was
in Erinn in her own time, quievit in Christo. Matthew
O'Raighilligh, dux of Muinter-Maelmordha, died in hoc

Todd's ed. of the "*War of the Gaedhil
with the Gaill*," Int., p. cxc., note 4,
and p. 152, note 1.

[4] *Domhnall Og O'Domhnaill.* The
Four Masters state that Lassairfhionna

(lit. "wine-flame") was the wife of
Domhnall Mor O'Domhnaill, who died
in the year 1241, and the mother of
his son, Domhnall Og, or young
Daniel.

αnno. Ʒilla Ιορρα Μας Τιʒερnάιn, ουχ Τheαllαιʒ Dhunchαοα, quieuiτ. Cαṫαl mαc Ʒillα nα nαom hΙ Ϝerʒαil, ταιρρech nα hΑƱnʒαile ϝρι ρe .ix. mbliαοnα, οο éʒ ϝορ Ιniϝ Cuαn ϝορ αƀuinn Cluαin liϝ Ƅeιc mιc Conοlα, .ı. ρí Τeṫƀα; ocuϝ ιϝ αϝϝιn ρο τuιceοh αnτ ιomαιρe ϝαοα, uαιρ αοuƀαιρτ αn ϝeρ ϝάιϝοιne ϝe Cαṫαl ʒuραƄ αρ αn ιomαιρe Ƅϝαοα οο ʒéƄαο ϝé Ƅάϝϝ; ʒuρ αƄ uιme ϝιn no hϝechnαƀ Cαṫαl αnτ ιomαιρe ϝαοα ʒαn α ṫαʒαll οο ʒϝéϝϝ. Seϝϝραιο mαc Ʒillα nα nαom οο ʒαƄάιl ταιριʒechτα ιαϝϝιn. Snechτα ρο ṁορ o Νοοlαιc co ϝeιl Ƅρíʒοe ιϝιn mbliαοαιn ϝιn.

Ϳcτ. Εnαιρ ϝορ Αοιne, ocuϝ ϝeιϝϝeο αxeτ ϝuιϝϝe; αnno Domιnι M.cc.lxxx.τeρτιο; xu. αnno cιclι ϝolαϝιϝ; xι. αnno cιclι lunαϝιϝ eτ ιnοιcτιonιϝ. Αοƀ Ƅuιƀe .h.Νeιll, ρí Chénel Εoʒαιn, ocuϝ ριʒƀαṁnα Ερenn uιle áιρchenα, ocuϝ Ƅαρρ eιnιʒ ocuϝ ʒαιϝcιο Ʒαοιοel, ocuϝ αon ρoʒα αn τuαιρceρτ αρ ṫιοnαcαl ϝéο ocuϝ eαllαιʒ ocuϝ echϝαιο, ocuϝ ϝeρ Ƅuƀ mo ʒϝάιn ocuϝ coρcuρ οο Cénel Εoʒαιn nα αιmϝιρ ϝeιn, οο ṁαρƄαο, lα Ƅριαn Μhάʒ Μhαṫʒαmnα, ρι Οιρʒιαll, ocuϝ lα hΟιρʒιαllαƀ αιρčenα, ocuϝ lα Ʒillα Ιορρα ρuαο mαc Domnαιll hΙ Ραιʒιllιʒ, ιn hoc αnno. Ταƀc mαc Domnαιll Ιoρρuιρ hΙ ConchoƄαιρ οο loτ lα Luιʒnιƀ, ocuϝ α ʒαƄάιl, ocuϝ α ṫιοlucαο οο Chαṫαl .h.ConchoƄαιρ, ocuϝ α éʒ οια loτ ιn hoc αnno. Αƀ clιαƀ ocuϝ Ceαll Chριϝτ οο loϝcαο ιn hoc αnno.

Ϳcτ. Εnαιρ ϝορ ϝαṫαρn, ocuϝ ρechτmαο uαṫαο ϝuιϝϝe; αnno Domιnι M.cc.lxxx.quαρτο; xuι. αnno cιclι ϝolαϝιϝ; xιι. αnno cιclι lunαϝιϝ eτ ιnοιcτιonιϝ. Simαnn Dexeταρ οο mαρƄαο lα Ƅριαn.h.Ƅϝhloιnn

---

[1] *Cluain-lis of Bec Mac Connla;* i.e. "the meadow-fort of Bec, son of Connla," king of Tebhtha, or Teffia, whose death is recorded in the Annals of the Four Masters under A.D. 766. The place has not yet been identified.

[2] *Understood.* ρο τuιceοh. This is an obscure way of saying that the prophecy which follows was manifested or fulfilled. The expression commonly used by the Irish writers in similar cases is ρο ϝιραο, "was verified."

[3] *Festival of Brighid;* i.e. the first of February.

anno.   Gilla-Isa Mac Tighernáin, dux of Teallach-Dunchadha, quievit. Cathal, son of Gilla-na-naemh O'Ferghail, [1282.]
chieftain of the Anghaile during nine years, died on Inis-
Cuan on the river of Cluain-lis of Bec Mac Connla,[1] i.e.
king of Tethbha; and it is from this that the "long ridge"
was understood ;[2] for the prophet told Cathal that he
would die on the "long ridge," wherefore it was that Cathal
used always to avoid visiting the "long ridge." Jeffrey,
son of Gilla-na-naemh, assumed the chieftaincy afterwards.
Very great snow from Christmas to the festival of
Brighid[3] in this year.

The kalends of January on Friday, and the twenty- [1283.]
sixth of the moon; anno Domini M.cc.lxxx.tertio ;[4] xv.
anno cycli solaris ; xi. anno cycli lunaris et Indictionis.
Aedh Buidhe O'Neill, king of Cenel-Eoghain, and also
royal heir of all Erinn; head[5] of the hospitality and valour
of the Gaeidhel, and the most distinguished[6] of the North
for bestowing jewels, and cattle, and horses; and the most
formidable and victorious man of the Cenel-Eoghain in his
own time, was slain by Brian Mac Mathghamhna, king of
Oirghiall, and by the Oirghialla likewise, and by Gilla-Isa
Ruadh, son of Domhnall O'Raighilligh, in hoc anno. Tadhg,
son of Domhnall Irruis[7] O'Conchobhair, was wounded by
the Luighne, and taken prisoner, delivered to Cathal
O'Conchobhair, when he died of his wound, in hoc anno.
Athcliath and Christ's Church were burned in hoc anno.

The kalends of January on Saturday, and the seventh [1284.]
of the moon ; anno Domini M.cc.lxxx.quarto ; xvi. anno
cycli solaris; xii. anno cycli lunaris et Indictionis. Simon
de Exeter was slain[8] by Brian O'Floinn and the two sons

---

[4] *Tertio.* ᴄᴇᴩᴄɪᴏ, MS.

[5] *Head.* ʙᴀᴩᴩ (lit. "summit"),
MS. The Four Mast. have ᴩᴇᴄᴄᴇ
"ridge pole."

[6] *Most distinguished.* ᴀᴏɴ ᴩᴏᵹᴀ,
lit. "one choice," MS.

[7] *Domhnall Irruis;* i.e. Domhnall,

of Irrus, or Erris, a district in the
county of Mayo. See note [5], p. 472,
supra.

[8] *Slain.* In Mageoghegan's version
of the Annals of Clonmacnois the
place where Simon de Exeter was
slain is called Fert-Gedye.

ocur Lá δá mac h1 Fhlannaʒain, .1. Diarmaid ocur
Maoilrechlainn. Cocad mór ocur erαonta δo eirʒe
α Connachtaib treimid ríδé, ocur creča móra δo
δenum δo Ʒhalloib im Choirrfliaδ, ocur airioc iomlán
δo tabairt δona Ʒalloib hírin δo muinter na
Trinóitte, ocur δo manchaib na búille. Dún mor
δo lorcud la Fiachra.h.bfhloinn. Muirir .h.Conco-
δair, erpuc Oilerin, in Crirto quieuit. Donnchad
.h.briain, rí Tuadmuman, δo marbad la Toirrδhel-
bach .h.mbriain. Ʒilla Iorra Mhág Thiʒernáin, arδ
taoirrech Cénel mbrenuinn, quieuit. αmlaδ .h.To-
maltaiʒ, toʒα confirmaitiʒe erpucoiδe Oilerinn, in
Crirto quieuit. Ʒilla Ira mac an Liathanaiʒ h1
Conchobair, ab Oilén na Trinóiδe ar Loč Cé, δorδ
Premonrtra, δo toʒα δocom erpucóiδe Oilerinn iar
rin. Duδʒaill mac Maʒnura h1 bhaiʒill, taoirrech
Cloiche Chinnfaolaδ, δo marbad la muinter h1 Maoil
ʒaoiče. Mac na hoiδče Mhág Dhorchaiδ, taoirrech
Chénel Luacháin, δo éʒ in hoc anno.

|ctt. enáir ror Luan, ocur α hochtmad δéʒ fuirre ;
anno Domini m.cc.Lxxx.quinto ; xuii. anno cicli rolarir ;
xiii. anno cicli lunarir et inδictionir. Simón .h.Ruaire,
erpuc na breirne, in Crirto quieuit. Maiδm mor δo
tabairt δo Mhaʒnur .h.Conchobair ror αδám Ciomróʒ ocur ror Ʒhalloib iarthair Connacht, αʒ Leic
erra δara, δú inar marbad iliomad δaoineδ, ocur
inar ʒabad Coilin Ciomróʒ, .1. α δerbratair, α mbraiʒ-
δenur taréir α muinnteri δo marbad, δo činn na
fliʒed δo leiʒen δó féin. Maiδm δo tabairt δo Pilip
Mac Ʒoirδelδ ror muinter Mhaʒnura h1 Conchobair,
ror Sliab Ʒham, δú inar marbad morán δo ʒlarrláič

¹ *Cenel-Brenainn.* In the Annals of
Clonmacnois, Gilla-Isa (Gelasius)
Mac Tighernáin is said to have been
chieftain of Tellach-Dunchadha ; and
the present entry seems a repetition of
one under the year 1282, recording

the "quievit" of a Gilla-Isa Mac
Tighernáin.
² *Cenel-Luachain.* Written "Cenel-
Duachain" under the year 1275. See
note ⁴, p. 478 *supra.*

of O'Flannagain, i.e. Diarmaid and Maelsechlainn. A
great war and dissension arose in Connacht through
this, and great depredations were committed round Corr-
sliabh by the Foreigners; but full restitution was given
by these Foreigners to the community of the Trinity,
and to the monks of the Buill. Dún-mór was burned
by Fiachra O'Floinn. Maurice O'Conchobhair, bishop of
Oilfinn, in Christo quievit. Donnchadh O'Briain, king
of Tuadh-Mumha, was slain by Toirdhelbhach O'Briain.
Gilla-Isa Mac Tighernáin, high chieftain of Cenel-Brenainn,[1] quievit. Amhlaibh O'Tomaltaigh, the confirmed
elect of the bishopric of Oilfinn, in Christo quievit. Gilla-
Isa, son of the Liathanach O'Conchobhair, abbot of Trinity
Island on Loch-Cé, of the Premonstre order, was afterwards elected to the bishopric of Oilfinn. Dubhgall, son
of Maghnus O'Baighill, chieftain of Cloch-Chinnfhaeladh,
was slain by O'Maelghaithe's people. Mac-na-hoidhche
Mac Dorchaidh, chieftain of Cenel-Luachain,[2] died in hoc
anno.

The kalends of January on Monday, and the eighteenth
of the moon; anno Domini M.cc.lxxx.quinto; xvii. anno
cycli solaris; xiii. anno cycli lunaris et Indictionis.
Simon O'Ruairc, bishop of the Breifne,[3] in Christo quievit.
A great defeat was inflicted by Maghnus O'Conchobhair
on Adam Cusack and the Foreigners of the West of
Connacht, at Lec-Essa-dara, where a great many persons
were slain, and where Colin Cusack, i.e. his (*Adam's*)
brother, was taken into captivity[4] after his people had
been slain, in consideration of being allowed himself to
depart. A defeat was inflicted by Philip Mac Goisdelbh
upon Maghnus O'Conchobhair's people, on Sliabh-Gamh,
where a great many recruits and inferior persons were

---

[3] *Breifne.* The bishopric of the Breifne is now represented by the diocese of Kilmore.

[4] *Into captivity.* Apparently as a pledge to secure the payment of the sum stipulated to be given by Adam Cusack to Maghnus O'Conor, for permitting him to depart unmolested.

ocuſ vſoġ̇vaoiniḃ. Ailíſ inġen Coſmaic moſtua eſt. Ruaivſi .h.ġávſa, ſi Sleiḃe Luġa, vo ṁaſbaṽ la Mac Ḟeoſuiſ ſoſ a loċ ſein. Enſí Mac Ᵹillaſinnéin moſtuuſ eſt.

Ict. Enaiſ ſoſ ṁaiſt, ocuſ ix. mav ſicheʋ ſuiſſe; anno Domini M.cc.lxxx.ui.; xuiii. cicli ſolaſiſ; xiiii. cicli lunaſiſ et invictioniſ. Moſ ſluaiġev la hiaſla Ulaṽ a Connachtaiḃ, ᵹuſ ṁill moſán vo ṁ̇ainiſ-vſechaiḃ ocuſ vo ceallaiḃ Connacht, ocuſ ᵹiṽevh vo ġaṽ neſt ᵹaċa conaiſ ſainic, ocuſ vo ġaṽ bſaiġve Connacht uile; ocuſ ſuᵹ ſluaiġ Connacht laiſ iaſſin, ocuſ vo ġaṽ bſaiġve Conaill ocuſ Eoġain, ocuſ vo aċſiġ Domnall mac Bſiain hi Neill, ocuſ tuc ſiġe vo Niall ċúlánach.h.Neill in vulav ſin. Eaſſach an Ḃóṽiċe in hoc anno. Muiſiſ maol Mac Ᵹeſuilt moſtuuſ eſt in hoc anno. Domnall .h.hAinliġe, vux Chéneoil Doſſa, quieuit uiii. Ict. Aſſiliſ.

Ict. Enáiſ ſoſ Cevaoin, ocuſ veaċmav uathav ſuiſſe; anno Domini M.cc.lxxxuii; xix. anno cicli ſolaſiſ; xu. anno cicli lunaſiſ et invictioniſ. Diaſ-maiv Mivhech, mac Diaſmava, mic Muiſġeſſa, mic Cathail Mic Diaſmava, ſi Muintiſe Mhaolſuanaiv, .i. ant aon vuine ſo ba ſine ocuſ ſob uaiſle vía ċinevh, vo éᵹ in hoc anno. Floiſint.h.Ᵹibeallán, aiſċi-veochain Oileſinn, ſeallſom ſeſſa ocuſ eoluiſ, ocuſ intlechta, ocuſ ċleiſċechta, quieuit in Cſiſto. Ᵹilla na neaċ .h.Mannaċáin, ſi na Tſi Tuaċ, moſtuuſ eſt uii. ivuſ Septembſiſ. Maolſechlainn mac Tomaltaiġ Mhéᵹ Oiſechtaiġ vo ṁaſbav la Toiſſvhelbach mac Eoᵹain hi Conchobaiſ, a nvíᵹailt a athaſ vo ṫſéiᵹen

---

1 *His own lake.* Now Loch Gara (anciently called Loch-Techet), in the barony of Coolavin, county of Sligo.

2 *The spring;* i.e. the Spring season.

3 *Mael;* i.e. " the bald."

4 *Aprilis.* aiſt., MS.

5 *Diarmaid Midhech.* "Diarmaid (or Dermot) the Meathian;" so called, apparently, from having been fostered in Meath.

6 *Quievit.* The death of this ecclesiastic is entered in the Annals

slain. Alice, daughter of Cormac, mortua est. Ruaidhri O'Gadhra, king of Sliabh-Lugha, was killed by Mac Feorais on his own lake.[1] Henry Mac Gillafhinnén mortuus est. A.D. [1285.]

[1286.] The kalends of January on Tuesday, and the twenty-ninth of the moon; anno Domini M.cc.lxxxvi.; xviii. cycli solaris; xiiii. cycli lunaris et Indictionis. A great hosting by the Earl of Ulster into Connacht, when he destroyed many of the monasteries and churches of Connacht; and he obtained sway, nevertheless, in every place through which he passed, and received the hostages of all Connacht; and he afterwards took with him the army of Connacht, and obtained the hostages of *Cenel*-Conaill and *Cenel*-Eoghain; and he deposed Domhnall, son of Brian O'Neill, and gave the sovereignty to Niall Culanach O'Neill, on this occasion. The spring[2] of the cow-mortality in hoc anno. Maurice Macl[3] Fitz-Gerald mortuus est in hoc anno. Domhnall O'hAinlighe, dux of Cenel-Doffa, quievit viii. kalendas Aprilis.[4]

[1287.] The kalends of January on Wednesday, and the tenth of the moon; anno Domini M.cc.lxxxvii.; xix. anno cycli solaris; xv. anno cycli lunaris et Indictionis. Diarmaid Midhech,[5] son of Diarmaid, son of Muirghes, son of Cathal Mac Diarmada, king of Muinter-Maelruanaidh, i.e. the oldest and noblest man of his kindred, died in hoc anno. Florence O'Gibellan, archdeacon of Oilfinn, a philosopher in wisdom, learning, intellect, and clerkship, quievit[6] in Christo. Gilla-na-nech[7] O'Mannachain, king of the Three-Tuatha, mortuus est vii. idus Septembris.[8] Maelsechlainn, son of Tomaltach Mac Oirechtaigh, was killed by Toirdhelbhach, son of Eoghan O'Conchobhair, in revenge for the abandonment of his father

---

of Ulster (Dublin copy) under the year 1283.

[7] *Gilla-na-nech*; i.e. "the servant of the horses." "Gilla-na-nog" ("servant of the young"). *Four M.*

[8] *Septembris.* ꞅepꞇimi, MS.

oo Thomaltach oo macaiḃ Toippohelbaiġ. Ruaiopi
Sinoach quieuit.

Ktt. Enaip pop Dapoaoin, aġuf aonmao xxᵉᵗ puippe;
anno Domini M.cc.lxxxuiii.; xx. anno cicli polapip;
xui. anno cicli lunapip. Cathal, mac Taioc, mic Cathail
Mic Diapmaoa, oo ġaḃáil piġe Mhoiġe Luipġ in hoc
anno. Maġnuf .h.Conchobaip, mapaon pe bpuaip leip
oo Chonnachtaiḃ, ocuf .h.mBpiuin ocuf Conmaicne oo
ṫoiġecht leip oo ġaḃáil piġe Connacht oó péin, acuf
oo aiṫpiġhao a ḃepḃpathap, .i. Cathal mac Conchobaip
puaio, ocuf teacht oóiḃ ġo hAḃ Slipion, áit a paiḃe
Cathal cona pocpaioe, ocuf cumapc oo tabaipt oóiḃ
leth ap leṫ oiapoile, ocuf Cathal oo ġaḃáil annpin,
ocuf maioṁ oo ṫabaipt ap a ṁuinntep; ocuf oo haiṫ-
piġheo é pein, ocuf oo haipġeoh upṁop Connacht oon
ċup pin; ocuf piġe oo ġaḃáil oo Mhaġnuf pein ap
éiġin in tan pin ap bélaiḃ a pinnpep bpathap, iap ná
ḃeiṫ peacht mbliaona co leith i piġe amail ippeipt
ant uġoap :—

    Mac Conchobaip piġoa puaio,
    Ba pí Connacht ṫep ip tuaio,
    Leiṫ ḃliaoain ipp a peacht pin
    Riġe Cathail a Cpuachain.

Donnchao piaḃach, mac Maġnupa mic Muipceptaiġ
Muimniġ, quieuit. Teċ oo ġaḃáil ipin ġeṁpiuo ceona
pin pop Mhaġnuf .h.Conchobaip oo Thoippohelbach
mac Eoġain hi Conċobaip, ipin Rop móp, ocuf oo
Mhaoilpechlainn .h.Phlannaġáin maille ppip; ocuf
oo comaiple Phiachpa hi Phloinn oo pónao an

---

¹ *The sons of Toirdhelbhach.* Probably a mistake for "the sons of
Tomaltach." As the sentence stands
in the text, Toirdhelbbach O'Conchobhair is represented as taking vengeance on the son of Tomaltach Mac

Oirechtaigh for an offence committed
by Toirdhelbhach's own sons against
his own father, through the instru-
mentality of Tomaltach.

² *Ruaidhri Sinnach*; i.e. "Ruaidhri
the Fox" (O'Catharnaigh). See note ²,

by Tomaltach to the sons of Toirdhelbhach.[1]	Ruaidhri
Sinnach[2] quievit.

The kalends of January on Thursday, and the twenty-first of the moon; anno Domini M.cc.lxxxviii.; xx. anno cycli solaris; xvi. anno cycli lunaris. Cathal, son of Tadhg, son of Cathal Mac Diarmada, assumed the sovereignty of Magh-Luirg in[3] hoc anno. Maghnus O'Conchobhair, accompanied by those of the Connachtmen, Ui-Briuin, and Conmaicne, whom he got to join him, came to take the sovereignty of Connacht for himself, and to depose his brother, i.e. Cathal, son of Conchobhar Ruadh; and they proceeded to Ath-Slision, where Cathal was with his army; and they gave battle to one another on both sides, when Cathal was taken prisoner, and his people were routed; and he himself was deposed; and the greater part of Connacht was plundered on this occasion. And Maghnus then forcibly assumed the sovereignty himself, in the face of his elder brother, who had been seven years and a-half in the sovereignty, as the author[4] said :—

> The son of the royal Conchobhar Ruadh
> Was king of Connacht, north and south ;
> Half a year and seven lasted
> The sovereignty of Cathal in Cruachan.[5]

Donnchadh Riabhach, son of Maghnus, son of Muirchertach Muimhnech, quievit. A house was captured in the Ros-mór, in this same winter, against Maghnus O'Conchobhair, by Toirdhelbhach, son of Eoghan O'Conchobhair, and by Maelsechlainn O'Flannagain along with him; and by the advice of Fiachra O'Floinn this attack

p. 404 *supra.* In the so-called Annals of Connacht it is added that Ruaidhri died on the 6th of the ides of March.

[3] *In.* an, MS.

[4] *The author.* Donn Losg O'Maelchonaire, from whose poem called *Duan na Righraidhe*, or the "Poem

of the Kings," some stanzas have been previously quoted. See note [3], p. 482.

[5] *Cruachan.* Rath-Cruachan, or Rathcroghan, in the County of Roscommon, anciently the chief residence of the kings of Connacht.

2 K

innroigeo rin. Acht chena, ro loiteḋ Maġnur rein
annrin, ocur ro marbaḋ Raġnall Mhág Raġnaill,
tóirrech Mhuinnteri hEoluir, ḋaon urchor roiġḋi,
ocur ro loitteḋ Niall ʒealḃuiḋe.h.Conchobair ann.
Ro marbaḋ, imorro, ḋaoine iomḋa eli ann; ocur ro
benaḋh eich ocur éḋáil iomḋa ḋiḃ. Sluaiʒeḋ la
Maġnur .h.Conchobair ḋéir a leiʒir o na lottaib rin
arriol Muireġhaiʒ, ʒurror ʒaḃ a mḃraiġḋe ʒo huiliḋe.
Sluaiʒeḋ laran iarla ruaḋ, .i. Rirḋerḋ, mac Uaitéir,
mic Ricairḋ, mic Uilliam conʒcúr in ġaḃaltair, ḋocom
Chonnacht, ʒo tánic ʒo Ror Chomáin ḋinnroiʒeḋ
Maġnura mic Conchobair ruaiḋ, ri Connacht an tan
rin, ocur ḋinnroiʒeḋ Mic ʒerailt ocur ṁuinntire an
riʒ; ocur ḋo tinoilriot uile ar a činn, ocur ḋo ġren-
ḋaiġret ant iarla ró teacht recha rin; comiḋ hi
comairle ḋo riʒne ant iarla annrin imthecht arrin
tir amaċ, ocur a rlúaiʒ ḋo rʒaoileḋ iarrin. Sḋearrán,
airḋerpuc Tuama ḋá ġualann, ocur ʒiuirḋir na hErenn,
quieuit. Uilliam Mac Pheoruir ḋo toġa ḋočom air-
ḋerpucóiḋe Thuama iarrin.

Ktt. Enair ror raťarn, ocur aile uaťaḋ ruirre;
anno Domini M.cc.lxxxix.; xxi. anno cicli rolarir;
xuii. anno cicli lunarir; recunḋur annur inḋictionir.
Taḋʒ .h.Flannaʒán, tairrech člainni Cathail, quieuit.
Maťa .h.Sʒinʒín, ollam Chenel Conaill, mortuur ert.
Erpuc Conmaicne, .i. an ʒaill erpuc, Milir a ainm,
quieuit. Simón .h.Finnachta, airčiḋeochain Oilerinn,
in Crirto quieuit. Sluaiʒeḋ la Maġnur .h.Conchobair
ocur la Ricarḋ Diuiḋ, ocur lá ʒalloiḃ na Miḋe maille
rrir, ḋocum hi Mhaoilrechlainn, ocur ḋočum rer Miḋe
áirčeena, co tucaḋ maiḋm rorrai anḋ rin inar marbaḋ

---

1 *Occupation*; i.e. the Anglo-Nor-
man occupation of Ireland. See *ante*,
p. 464, note 3.

2 *Ollamh*; i.e. chief professor. The
Four Mast. call O'Sgingin "arḋ
renčaiḋ," "chief antiquary."

3 *Bishop of Conmaicne*; i.e. of Ardagh, which diocese comprises Con-
maicne-Maighe-Rein (the southern
part of the county of Leitrim, called
Mac Raghnaill's country), and the
Anghaile, Annaly, or O'Farrell's

was made. However, Maghnus himself was wounded there, and Raghnall Mac Raghnaill, chieftain of Muinter-Eolais, was killed by the discharge of an arrow; and Niall Gealbhuidhe O'Conchobhair was wounded there. Many other persons also were slain there, and several horses and spoils were taken from them. A hosting by Maghnus O'Conchobhair, after having been cured of these wounds, to Sil-Muiredhaigh, all whose hostages he took. A hosting to Connacht by the Red Earl, i.e. Richard, son of Walter, son of Richard, son of William the Conqueror of the Occupation[1]; and he went to Ros-Comáin, to attack Maghnus, son of Conchobhar Ruadh, at that time king of Connacht, and to attack Fitz-Gerald and the king's people. And they all assembled before him, and challenged the Earl to pass beyond that place, so that the resolution which the Earl then adopted was, to go out of the territory, and subsequently disperse his army. Stephen, archbishop of Tuaim-dá-ghualann, and Justiciary of Erinn, quievit. William Mac Feorais was afterwards elected to the archbishopric of Tuaim.

The kalends of January on Saturday, and the second of the moon; anno Domini M.CC.LXXXIX.; xxi. anno cycli solaris; xvii. anno cycli lunaris; secundus annus Indictionis. Tadhg O'Flannagain, chieftain of Clann-Cathail, quievit. Matthew O'Sgingin, ollamh[2] of Cenel-Conaill, mortuus est. The bishop of Conmaicne,[3] i.e. the foreign bishop, whose name was Miles, quievit. Simon O'Finnachta, archdeacon[4] of Elphin, in Christo quievit. A hosting by Maghnus O'Conchobhair, and by Richard Tuit, with whom were the Foreigners of Midhe, to O'Maelsechlainn and all the Feara-Midhe; and a great defeat was then inflicted on them, in which Richard

country, in the present county of Longford. The "Gall Espuc," or "foreign bishop," named Miles, is called "Milo of Dunstable" by Ware. *Bishops*, Harris's ed., p. 251.

[4] *Archdeacon*. The Four Masters say that Simon O'Finnachta was aıɼċınneaċ, or "Erenagh," of Elphin.

2 K 2

Rιcαρ꜀ Dιυιτ, .ι. ιη bαρύη ιγ υαιγle ꝺo τόι ιη꜀ εριηη
αη ταη γιη, ocυγ α bγαιτρεchα mαιlle γριγ; ocυγ
ρο mαρbαꝺ αη꜀ Sιαcυγ mαc ιη꜀ εγρυιc hí Chellαιξ;
ocυγ ρo mαρbαꝺ [ꝺαιηε ιmꝺα αιle] αηη τεογ. ꝼιαchρα
.h.ꝼloιηη, ꝺυx Shιl Mhαoιlρυαιη, ιη ꝼεγ ρob ꝼεγγ ιocητ
ocυγ ꝼιγιηηε, ocυγ comαιγce, εηεch ocυγ εηξηυm ꝺo
τᴀoιγγεchαιꝑ Coηηαcητ υιle, ꝺo ꝺυl ꝺoꝺεηυm cleαmηυγα
ρε ξαlloιꝑ, ξυγγυγ mαρꝑ mαc Rιcαιγꝺ ꝼιηη mιc Uιllιαm
bύγc, ocυγ Mαc ꝼheoρυιγ, α meαꝑαιl hé. Slυαιξεꝺ
mόρ lα Mαc Mυιγιγ ocυγ lα Mαc ꝼheoρυιγ ꝺoċυm
αη ċαlꝑαιξ ṁoιγ hí Choηċobαιγ ocυγ ηα mαc ριξ
lαιξηεch αιγchεηαι, ocυγ τυcαꝺ mαιꝺm mόρ ꝼoρρα
ιηαγ mαρbαꝺ Mαoιlιγ Dexéταγ ocυγ ξαιll ιmꝺα εle,
mαιlle γρι ειċ ιmꝺα ꝺo ꝑéιη ꝺιꝑ αη꜀ ꝑoγγ.

Ktt. εηαιγ ꝼoγ ꝺomηαch, ocυγ τγεγγ ꝺéc ꝼυιγγι;
αηηo Domιηι M.cc.xc.; xxιι. αηηo cιclι γolαγιγ; xuιιι.
αηηo cιclι lυηαγιγ; τεγτιυγ αηηυγ ιηꝺιcτιoηιγ. Cαιγ-
ρρι .h. Mαoιlγeċlαιηη, γί Mιꝺε, ꝺo mαρbαꝺ ꝺo Mhάξ
Coċlάη ocυγ ꝺo Dhelꝑηα α meαꝑυιl. Çoηξαlαċ Mαξ
Eoċαξάη, ꝺυx Cheηeoιl bꝼhιαchα mιc Neιll .ιx. ξιαllαιξ,
moγτυυγ εγτ. Uιllιαm Mαc ꝼheoρυιγ ꝺo ξαbάιl αιγꝺ-
εγρυcoιꝺe Τυαmα. Iη꜀ εγρυc .h.Seταchαιη, .ι. εγρυc
Cιlle Mιc Dυαċ, qυιευιτ. Slυαιξεꝺ lα Domηαll mαc
bγιαιη hí Neιll α Céηél ηEoξαιη, ξυγ ċυιγ Nιαll O Neιll
αγ ειξιη αιγꝺε, ocυγ ξυγ ξαꝑ ꝼειη αη ριξε αllογγ α
ηειγτ. Αoꝺ .h.Domηαιll ꝺo αιτγιξhαꝺ ꝺια ꝺεγbγα-
τhαιγ bυꝺéιη, .ι. ꝺo Thoιγγꝺelbαch .h.Dhomηαιll, ocυγ
αη ριξε ꝺo ξαbάιl ꝺό ꝼειη τγε cυmαchταιꝑ ċιηιꝺ α
mατhαγ, .ι. Clάιηηε Domηαιll, ocυγ ξαlloclαeċ ηιmꝺα elι.

---

1 *Siacus.* This is the Irish form of
the name "Jacques."

2 *The Bishop O'Ceallaigh.* Apparently Thomas O'Ceallaigh, or
O'Kelly, bishop of Clonfert. See
note 3, p. 434 *supra.*

3 *Persons.* The words within
brackets are supplied from the so-
called Annals of Connacht. In the
Annals of Clonmacnois it is stated
that "Meyler Persey, with many
others, was slain."

4 *Tertius.* τεγτιυγ, MS.

5 *The race of Fiacha.* The territory
of Cenel-Fiacha, Anglicised Kenal-
iagbe and Kinelea, originally comprised the district extending from
Parsonstown, in the King's county,

Tuit, i.e. the noblest baron at that time in Erinn, was slain, and his brothers along with him; and Siacus,[1] son of the Bishop O'Ceallaigh,[2] was slain there, and [several other persons][3] were also slain there. Fiachra O'Floinn, dux of Sil-Maelruain, the most clement, truthful, protecting, hospitable, and valorous man of all the chieftains of Connacht, went to contract a marriage alliance with the Foreigners, when the son of Richard Finn, son of William Burk, and Mac Feorais, slew him in treachery. A great hosting by Mac Maurice and Mac Feorais, against the Calbhach Mór O'Conchobhair and the other Lagenian princes; and a great defeat was inflicted on them, in which Meyler de Exeter and many more Foreigners were slain; and numerous horses were moreover taken from them.

A.D.
[1289.]

The kalends of January on Sunday, and the thirteenth of the moon; anno Domini M.CC.XC.; xxii. anno cycli solaris; xviii. anno cycli lunaris; tertius[4] annus Indictionis. Cairbre O'Maelsechlainn, king of Midhe, was slain by Mac Cochlainn and the Delbhna, in treachery. Conghalach Mac Eochagain, dux of the race of Fiacha,[5] son of Niall of the Nine Hostages, mortuus est. William Mac Feorais assumed the archbishopric of Tuaim. The Bishop O'Setachain,[6] i.e. bishop of Cill-Mic-Duach, quievit. A hosting by Domhnall, son of Brian O'Neill, to Cenel-Eoghain, out of which he forcibly expelled Niall O'Neill; and he assumed the sovereignty himself by means of his power. Aedh O'Domhnaill was deposed by his own brother, i.e. Toirdhelbhach O'Domhnaill, who assumed the sovereignty himself through the power of his mother's kindred, i.e. the Clann-Domhnaill, and several other Gall-oglaechs.[7]

[1290.]

to the hill of Usney, in Westmeath; but in later times was reduced to the limits of the district forming the present barony of Moycashel, county of Westmeath. The territorial and family name of Cenel-Fiacha was derived from Fiacha, son of Niall of the Nine Hostages, monarch of Ireland in the early part of the fifth century. See O'Donovan's ed. of *O'Dubhagain's Topographical Poem*; Appendix, p. viii.

[6] *Bishop O'Setachain.* Ware states that his Christian name was David.

[7] *Gall-oglaechs;* lit. "foreign young heroes," and usually Anglicised "gallowglasses."

Ictt. Θnαιρ ρορ Luαn, οcυρ α cethαρ xxet ρυιρρε;
αnnο Dοmιnι Mο. ccο. xc. ρριmο; bliαδαιn δεριδ
nοιεcδα hι; xxο. τερτιο αnnο cιclι ρολαρυρ; quαρτυρ
αnnυρ ιnδιcτιοnιρ. Τοιρρδhelbαch mαc Θοζαιn hι
Conchοbαιρ, ιn ρερ ιρ mό οcυρ δο bυδ αιlne οcυρ δοb
ρερρ enech οcυρ enznum, οcυρ δοb ρeρρ δαδδυρ ριζ, δο
mαρbαδ le Nιαll nζelδυιδe .h.Conchοbαιρ. Slυαζheδ
mόρ lα hιαρlα Ulαδ α Τιρ Θοζαιn, δαρ αδριζ ρé
Dοmnαll mαc bριαιn hι Neιll, οcυρ δαρ ριζhαδ lαιρ
Nιαll Culánαch.h.Neιll; οcυρ mυρ δο ράζυιδ ιnτ
ιαρlα ιn τιρ ρο mαρbαδ Nιαll Culαnαch.h.Neιll le
Dοmnαll.h.Neιll. Τιζ ιnτ ιαρlα δο ριδιρ οcυρ ρο
ριζhαδ lαιρ mαc Αοδα bυιδe, .ι. Nιαll. Ro hιnnαρbαδ
Dοmnαll .h.Neιll αρ αn τιρ αmαδ, τρe cumαchταιδ ιn
ιαρlα. Slυαιζeδ elι lαραn ιαρlα ceδnα ριn α Τιρ
Chοnαιll, δοcum Τhοιρρδhelbαιζ hι Dhοmnαιll, ζυρ
αιρζ ιn τιρ υιle ιδιρ διll οcυρ τυαιδ, conάρ ραρζαιbρeτ
bρéιδ ρορ αlτόιρ, ιnα leαbυρ αιρρριnn, ιnά coιleδ
αιρρριnn, α cellαιδ Chéneοιl Conαιll; οcυρ τυc ιn
cρeιδ ριn α Connαchταιδ. Ocυρ τάnιc co hOlριnn ιαρριn
οcυρ τυcαδαρ Connαchτα ρel bραιζδe δό ιn ταn ριn,
οcυρ δο ιmδιζ ιαρριn. Conδοbαρ .h.Dυδδα, ρι .h.
bρhιαδραch, δο δάδαδ αρ Sιnυιnn αζ τeαchτ mαιlle ρe
Connαchταιδ ι conne ιn ιαρlα ceδnα ριn. Comδοcbáιl
δοζαιδ δο δenυm δο Chαthαl.h.Conchοbαιρ οcυρ δο
Nιαll ζelδυιδe.h.Conchοbαιρ, οcυρ δά ζαch lυchτ δάρ
éιριζ leo δο Ghαlloιδ οcυρ δο Ghαοιδelαιδ, δο αδριζhαδ
Mhαζnυραι hι Conchοbαιρ, ρι Connαchτ; οcυρ ιmερ-
ραιn δο δαbαιρτ δοιδ δά δelι αζ Cαραιδ Chúlmαοιle,
οcυρ Cαthαl δο lοτ αnnριn; οcυρ Mυρchαδ mαc Ταιδc
mιc Αιnδριαρρα hι Conchοbαιρ δο mαρbαδ αnn lα
Nιαll nζeαlδυιδe.h.Conδοbαιρ, οcυρ δοιne elι, οcυρ

---

¹ *Annus.* αnδυρ, MS.

² *Deceptive hostages.* ρel bραιζδe.
The chronicler apparently meant to
imply that the Connachtmen, al-

though giving hostages to the earl
of Ulster, did not intend to submit
tamely to his rule.

³ *Caraidh-Culmhaile;* i.e. the weir

The kalends of January on Monday, and the twenty-fourth of the moon; anno Domini M°. cc°. xc°. primo. It was the last Decennovenalian year; xx°. tertio anno cycli solaris; quartus annus[1] Indictionis. Toirdhelbhach, son of Eoghan O'Conchobhair, the greatest, handsomest, most hospitable and valorous man, and the best fitted to be a king, was slain by Niall Gelbhuidhe O'Conchobhair. A great hosting by the Earl of Ulster to Tir-Eoghain, when he deposed Domhnall, son of Brian O'Neill, and when Niall Culanach O'Neill was made king by him ; and just as the Earl left the district, Niall Culanach O'Neill was slain by Domhnall O'Neill. The Earl came again, and the son of Aedh Buidhe, i.e. Niall, was made king by him. Domhnall O'Neill was expelled out of the country through the power of the Earl. Another hosting by the same Earl to Tir-Conaill, against Toirdhelbhach O'Domhnaill, when he plundered the entire country, both church and territory, so that they neither left a cloth upon an altar, nor a mass-book, nor a mass-chalice, in the churches of Cenel-Conaill : and he carried this spoil into Connacht. And he went subsequently to Oilfinn ; and the Connachtmen then gave him deceptive hostages,[2] after which he departed. Conchobhar O'Dubhda, king of Ui-Fiachrach, was drowned in the Sinuinn, whilst coming with the Connachtmen to meet the same Earl. A war was conjointly raised by Cathal O'Conchobhair, and by Niall Gelbhuidhe O'Conchobhair, and all the Foreigners and Gaeidhel who adhered to them, to depose Maghnus O'Conchobhair, king of Connacht; and they gave battle to each other at Caraidh-Culmhaile;[3] and Cathal was wounded there ; and Murchadh, son of Tadhg, son of Andrias O'Conchobhair, was slain there by Niall Gelbhuidhe O'Conchobhair ; and other persons *were*

of Culmhaile, or Collooney, in the county of Shgo. In the Dublin copy of the Annals of Ulster, which have the event under the year 1287, the place is called " Caraidh-Culaind, alias [Caraidh]-Culmhaile."

eich imða ðo ðein ðo ṁuinnτep Maᵹnuρα ann; ocuρ
maɩðm ðo ṫαbαɩρτ ραɩρ ρein, ocuρ α ðul αρρ α τοραð α
eɩρɩοṁuɩl ρó lαiṁ; ocuρ cρečα móρα ðo ðenum ðo
ṁuɩnnτeρ Chaτhαɩl ocuρ ðo Nɩαll ᵹelðuɩðe α Cαɩρbρɩ,
οɩρ ní ρaɩðe Cαθαl ρein αρ αn ρɩοðαl ρɩn ταρéɩρ α
luɩτ. Αchτ čenα ρο αɩρcρeτ Cαɩρρρɩ uɩle ó Chnuc
Lαοɩᵹén co heρρ ðαρα. Ðálα Maᵹnuρα hɩ Conchobαɩρ,
ɩmoρρo, ɩαρ τοchτ ðo Sɩol Muɩρeᵹhαɩᵹ ocuρ ðá αορ
ᵹραðα ρeɩρρɩn, ocuρ Ᵹαll Roρρα Comαɩn cuɩᵹe ðαρ éɩρ
ɩn mαðma ρɩn, ðá ρuρταchτ, ταnɩc ροime ɩαρ nα ðαραch
α coɩnne nα ᵹcρeč ρɩn, ocuρ ρuc ρe oρρα αᵹ Sραɩť ɩn
ρéράɩn ocuρ ρón Αonαch, ocuρ ρο benαð α cρechα ðɩð.
Ocuρ ρο ɩmťɩᵹ Nɩαll ρein αρ eɩᵹɩn αραn maɩðm ρɩn;
ocuρ ρο mαρbαð αnn Tomαρ Mαc Ᵹοɩρðelb; ocuρ ρο
ᵹαbαð α ðeρbρατhαɩρ .ɩ. Ðαuɩð Mαc Ᵹοɩρðelb, ocuρ ρο
mαρbαð ɩρin lαɩmðechuρ ρɩn é ɩαρρɩn; ocuρ ρο mαρbαð
móράn ðonτ ρlúαɩᵹ ɩðɩρ Ᵹhαlloɩb ocuρ Ᵹhαɩðelαɩɓ. Ocuρ
τοchτ ðo Nɩαll αρ ρɩť ðon τíρ ɩαρρɩn, ocuρ α ρeρonn ρein
uɩle ðo ṫαbαɩρτ ðó. Αɩṁleρ ocuρ ɩomcαρροeɩτ ðo eρᵹe
eτɩρ Mhαᵹnuρ ocuρ Nɩαll, oɩρ ρο hɩnnɩρρeð ðo Maᵹnuρ
ᵹuρ ρeαll Nɩαll ραɩρ, ocuρ ρóbαɩρτ ɩn τɩρe ðo ράᵹðáɩl
ðo Nɩαll ɩαρρɩn. Αɩρᵹťe moρα ðo ðenum αρ Nɩαll ðo
Maᵹnuρ, ocuρ ðɩmuρ Neɩll ðo τοɩρnem co móρ ðo nα
hαɩρᵹnɩð hɩρɩn. Αoð .h.ραllαmαɩn, τáɩρρech Chlαɩnnɩ
Uαðαch, ðo éᵹ ɩρin mblɩαðαɩn ρɩn. Ðɩαρmαɩð .h.ρloɩnn,
ταɩρρech Sɩl Mhαɩlρuαɩn, moρτuuρ eρτ. Αoð .h. Domnαɩll ðo ᵹαbáɩl α ρɩᵹe ρein ðo ρɩðɩρ, ocuρ Τοɩρρðhel-
bαch .h. Domnαɩll ðo ɩnnαρbαð. Lucαρ Mαc Ᵹɩllα-
ρuαɩð, αɩρčɩðechαɩn Oleρɩnn, quɩeuɩτ. Eoρúť Mháᵹ
Cραɩť, αb Ločα Cé, moρτuuρ eρτ.

Ɉcττ. Enαɩρ ρορ ṁαɩρτ, ocuρ uɩð uαthαð ρuɩρρe; anno

---

¹ Cnoc-Laighén. The Annals of
Connacht say, o čnucc Lαɩᵹén ɩnnɩαρ
"from the west, from Cnoc-Laighén,"
thus indicating that Cnoc-Laighén
was in the western part of Cairbre.
It is the hill now called Knocklane,

in the west of the barony of Carbury,
county of Sligo.
² Ros-Comain. The second word
of this name (Comain) is an interlinea-
tion by a later hand in the MS.
³ Captivity. The MS. has lαɩm,

slain; and several horses were there taken from the people of Maghnus; and he was himself defeated, but escaped safely by means of his bravery. And great depredations were committed in Cairbre by Cathal's people, and by Niall Gelbhuidhe; for Cathal himself was not on this expedition, in consequence of his wound. They plundered all Cairpre, however, from Cnoc-Laighén[1] to Es-dara. As regards Maghnus O'Conchobhair, moreover, when the Sil-Muiredh-aigh, and his own favourites, and the Foreigners of Ros-Comain,[2] had come to his assistance after this defeat, he proceeded on the morrow to meet those depredators, and came up with them at Srath-in-fherain, and about the Aenach; and their preys were taken from them. And Niall himself escaped by force from this defeat; and Thomas Mac Goisdelbh was slain there, and his brother, i.e. David Mac Goisdelbh, was taken prisoner, and was afterwards slain in that captivity.[3] And a great many of the host, both Foreigners and Gaeidhel, were slain. And Niall subsequently came on terms of peace to the district, and all his own land was given to him. Enmity and mutual complaints occurred between Maghnus and Niall, for it was reported to Maghnus that Niall had acted treacherously by him; and Niall afterwards tried to leave the district. Great depredations were committed on Niall by Maghnus, and Niall's pride was very much humbled by these depredations. Aedh O'Fallamhain, chieftain of Clann-Uadach, died in this year. Diarmaid O'Floinn, chieftain of Sil-Maelruain, mortuus est. Aedh O'Domhnaill assumed his own sovereignty again, and Toirdhelbhach O'Domhnaill was expelled. Lucas Mac Gilla-ruaidh, archdeacon of Oilfinn, quievit. Edrúth Mac Craith, abbot of Loch-Cé, mortuus est.

The kalends of January on Tuesday, and the fifth of   [1292.]

---

abl. of *lam*, "hand;" but the Annals of Connacht more correctly read | *laimoechup*, which is a deriv. from *laim*, and signifies " captivity."

Domini M°. cc°. xc°.ii. ; xxiiii. anno cicli rolapir; u. anno indictionir; primur annur cicli Lunapir. Sluaiʒed láran Iapla docum Maʒnura hI Choncobaip, co tanic co Ror Chomáin, ocur do imtiʒ ʒan ʒeill ʒan eicipe do ʒabáil. Ro len Maʒnur .h.Conchobaip co Miliuc hé, dap rapuʒad Connacht, ocur do cuaid ina tech, ocur ruaip ʒach ní ra raibe on Iapla don chup rin. Sluaiʒed ele laran Iapla ceona rin docum Luiʒne, ʒur aipʒ upmop in cipe uile, ocur ʒidedh cena, ní tanic Domnall .h. hEaʒpa ina teach, ocur ni tuc ʒeill ina ecipe don dul rin dó. Niall ʒealbuicche.h.Conchobaip, mac Muipeʒhaiʒ mic Ααoda daill mic Toippdhelbaiʒ móip, .i. pi Connacht, do mapbad do Thadʒ mac Ααindpiarrai mic bpiain Luiʒniʒ hI Conchobaip, ocur do Tuathal mac Muipcepcaiʒ. Máʒ Coċlán, .i. pí Delbna, do mapbad na duthaid rein do hSheppin Mac Pheopuir, cpe rorʒall in Iapla, in hoc anno. Donnchad mac Eoʒain hI Conchobaip do éc in hoc anno. Soṁaiple .h.ʒaipmleʒhaiʒ do mapbad dUa Neill. Ααndiler .h.Doċapcaiʒ, cáirrech Αρda Miδaip, quieuic.

Ictt. Enaip ror dapdaoin, ocur reirred dhéc ruippe; anno Domini M°.cc°. xciii.; xxu°. anno cicli rolapir; recundur annur cicli Lunapir; ui. annur indictionir. Maʒnur, mac Conchobaip ruaid, mic Mhuipcepcaiʒ Muimniʒ, mic Thoippdhelbaiʒ móip, .i. pi Connacht rpi ré u. mbliadan co leit, amail roipʒler in riled :—

> Ua Conchobaip in chnir ʒil,
> Mac mic Muipcepcaiʒ Muimniʒ,
> Cuiʒ bliadna co leith re luad
> bá pí Maʒnur na mapcrluaʒ,

do éʒ in hoc anno iap na δeit raite i nʒalap ; .i. rep ra

---

1 *Lunaris.* Lunappu, MS.

2 *In violation of Connacht*; i.e. in despite of the wishes of all the people of Connacht.

3 *Into his house.* The expression

"went into his house," is equivalent to saying "submitted to him."

4 *Son of Muirchertach*; i.e. of Muirchertach (or Murtough) O'Conor.

5 *Secundus annus.* reʒcdur añor, MS.

the moon ; anno Domini M°.cc°.xc°.ii. ; xxiiii. anno cycli solaris ; v. anno Indictionis ; primus annus cycli lunaris.[1] A hosting by the Earl against Maghnus O'Conchobhair, when he went to Ros-Comain ; and he departed without taking pledges or hostages. Maghnus O'Conchobhair followed him to Milic, in violation of Connacht,[2] and went into his house,[3] and obtained all that he desired from the Earl on this occasion. Another hosting by the same Earl to Luighne, when he plundered the greater part of the district ; but, nevertheless, Domhnall O'hEghra went not into his house,[3] and gave him neither pledges nor hostages on this occasion. Niall Gelbhuidhe O'Conchobhair, son of Muiredhach, son of Aedh Dall, son of Toirdhelbhach Mór (i.e. king of Connacht), was slain by Tadhg, son of Andrias, son of Brian Luighnech O'Conchobhair, and by Tuathal, son of Muirchertach.[4] Mac Cochlain, i.e. the king of Delbhna, was killed in his own country by Sifin Mac Feorais, at the instigation of the Earl, in hoc anno. Donnchadh, son of Eoghan O'Conchobhair, died in hoc anno. Somhairle O'Gairmleghaigh was slain by O'Neill. Andiles O'Dochartaigh, chieftain of Ard-Midhair, quievit.

The kalends of January on Thursday, and the sixteenth of the moon ; anno Domini M°. cc°. xciii. ; xxv°. anno cycli solaris ; secundus annus[5] cycli lunaris ; vi. annus Indictionis. Maghnus, son of Conchobhar Ruadh, son of Muirchertach Muimhnech, son of Toirdhelbhach Mór, i.e. king of Connacht during five years and a half, as the poet[6] explains—

> O'Conchobhair of the fair skin,
> The grandson of Muirchertach Muimhnech :
> Five years and a half, to be mentioned,
> Was Maghnus of the cavalry hosts a king—

died in hoc anno, after being ill during a quarter ; viz. the

---

[6] *The poet.* Donn Losg O'Maelchonaire, in a poem enumerating the kings of Connacht, called *Duan na Righraidhe,* or the "Poem of the Kings," copies of which are preserved in the collection of the Royal Irish Academy. See note [4], p. 497 *supra.*

mó ʒpαin ocuʃ corʃcuʃ α cαɫαιb ocuʃ α compαcαιb; ʃι ʃob ʃeʃʃ enʒnum ocuʃ enech ιnɔ Eʃιnn. Ꙃeɔ mαc Eoʒαιn hι Conchobαιʃ ɔo ʃιʒhαɔ ɔon ʒιuʃóιʃ ocuʃ ɔo muιnnceʃ ʃι Ꙃαχαn ιαʃʃιn; ocuʃ ιn ɔechmαɔ lá ɔαʃéιʃ α ʃιʒɫα α ʒαbαιl ɔo Mαc Ꙃeʃαιlc α meɓαιl, ocuʃ cαocα ɓα muιnnceʃ ɔo mαʃɓαɔ; ocuʃ cʃeαɫα móʃα ɔo ɓenum ʃαιʃ ιαʃʃιn. Cαɫαl ʃuαɓ .h.Conchobαιʃ ɔo ʒαbáιl ʃιʒe Connαchc ιαʃʃιn, ocuʃ α mαʃbαɔ α cιnn ʃαιɫe ɔo Ruαιɔʃι mαc Ꙃonnchαɔα ʃιαɓαιʒ hι Conchobαιʃ, α meɓuιl; ocuʃ Oeɓ mαc Eoʒαιn ɔo lecuɔ ιmmαɫ, ocuʃ ʃιʒe Connαchc ɔo ʒαbαιl ɔó cʃe neʃc ιn Ꙃιuʃóιʃʃ. Muʃchαɔ.h.Mαιlʃechlαιnn, ʃι Mιɓe, ɔo éc ιʃιn mblιαɔuιn ʃιn. Ʃeʃʒαl.h.Rαιʒιllιʒ, cαιʃʃech Muιncιʃe Mhαιlmóʃɓα ʃʃι ʃé ɓα ɓlιαɔαιn ɔéc, ɔo mαʃbαɔ αʃ lαʃ α Lonʒʃuιʃc ʃeιn ɔo Chellαιʒ Ꙃhúnchαɔα, ιn hoc αnno. Cαιʃʃι Rαɔʃαιc ocuʃ Coluιm Cιlle ocuʃ bʃιʒɔe ɔo ʃoιllʃιoʒαɔ ɔo Nιcol Mháʒ Mhαoιlιʃʃα, ɔo comαʃbα Rαɔʃαιc, ɔo ɓeιɫ α Ꙃαbαll Rαɔʃαιc, ocuʃ α cocbáιl ɔó; ocuʃ ɔeιʃ α cocbαlα ɔó ʃeʃcα ocuʃ mιʃɓuιle móʃα ɔo ɓenum ɓoιɓ, ocuʃ eιʃʃιum ɔo ɓenum ʃcʃíne cumɔαιʒɫe co honoʃαch ɔoιɓ ιαʃʃιn. Moʃ, ιnʒen Ʃhelιmm hι Conchobαιʃ, moʃcuα eʃc. Ʃlóιʃιnc.h.Ceʃbαllán, eʃʃuc Chenel Eoʒαιn, quιeuιc ιn Cʃιʃco. Muιʃɫeʃcαch .h.Ʃlαnnαʒαιn, ɔuχ ɫlαιnne Cαɫαιl mιc Mhuιʃeʒhαιʒ, moʃcuuʃ eʃc. Ꙃhá ɫαoιʃech Chellαιʒ Ꙃhúnchαɔα ɔo éʒ ιn hoc αnno. Cuαɫαl mαc Muιʃɫeʃcαιʒ hι Conchobαιʃ occιʃuʃ eʃc. Cαɫαl Mαc Ꙃιαʃmαɔα, ʃι Muιnncιʃe Mαolʃuαnαιɔ,

[1] *Hoc.* oc, MS.

[2] *Bishop of Cenel-Eoghain;* i.e. bishop of Derry.

[3] *Descendants of Cathal.* This Cathal was the son of Muiredhach Muillethan, king of Connacht, whose death is recorded in the Chron. Scotorum under the year 698 = 701. The tribe name of the sept was Clann-Cathail, whose territory comprised the parishes of Kilmacumshy, Kilcorkey, and Shankill, and the greater part of the parishes of Creeve and Elphin, in the county of Roscommon. See O'Donovan's ed. Four Mast., A.D. 1289, note [s].

[4] *Two chieftains.* The chieftains of

most formidable and victorious man in battles and conflicts; the most puissant and bountiful king in Erinn. Aedh, son of Eoghain O'Conchobhair, was afterwards made king by the Justiciary and the king of the Saxons' people; but on the tenth day after his election he was taken prisoner by Fitz-Gerald, in treachery, and fifty of his people were slain; and great depredations were committed on him after that. Cathal Ruadh O'Conchobhair subsequently assumed the sovereignty of Connacht, but was slain before the end of a quarter by Ruaidhri, son of Donnchadh Riabhach O'Conchobhair, in treachery; and Aedh, son of Eoghan, was released, and assumed the sovereignty of Connacht through the power of the Justiciary. Murchadh O'Maelsechlainn, king of Midhe, died in this year. Ferghal O'Raighilligh, chieftain of Muinter-Maelmórdha during the space of twelve years, was killed in the middle of his own residence by the Tellach-Dunchadha, in hoc[1] anno. It was revealed to Nicholas Mac Maelisa, comarb of Patrick, that the relics of Patrick, and Colum-Cille, and Brighid were in Sabhall-Patraic; and they were disinterred by him; and great virtues and miracles were performed by them after they had been disinterred by him; and he subsequently made an honourably covered shrine for them. Mor, daughter of Felim O'Conchobhair, mortua est. Florence O'Cerbhal-láin, bishop of Cenel-Eoghain,[2] quievit in Christo. Muirchertach O'Flannagain, dux of the descendants of Cathal[3] son of Muiredhach, mortuus est. Two chieftains[4] of Tellach-Dunchadha died in hoc[1] anno. Tuathal, son of Muirchertach O'Conchobhair, occisus est. Cathal Mac Diarmada, king of Muinter-Maelruanaidh, was treacher-

---

Tellach-Dunchadha ("household of Dunchadh," now Tullyhunco, county of Cavan) were of the family of Mac Tighernain, or Mac Kernan. The

Christian names of the two above referred to are given in the so-called "Annals of Connac " as Duarcan and Sitrec.

vo ʒabáil lα hCCoõ mαc Eoʒαin hi Conchobαiр, α bρill,
тρe ƒoρʒαll Conchobαiр mic Тαichliʒ, ocuр Mαilρečlαinn
hi Ƒhlαnnαʒαin, ocuр тShil Muiρeʒhαiʒ áiρchenα.
Ocuр vo αiρʒeт Mαʒ Luiрʒ uile iviр čill ocuр тuαiõ;
ocuр тαnic millev Connαchт uile αр nα holcαib рin.
Cαтhαl Mαc Diαρmαvα, рi Muiʒe Luiрʒ, vo õul αр
eiʒin αр α čuiõρiʒiõ, ocuр cρeαč mōρ vo õenum õó
iαρρin αр cloinn Cαтhαil hi Ƒlαnnαcαin.

Ктt. Enαiр ƒoр Oeine, ocuр iρρechтmαv ƒichev ƒuiρρe;
αnno Domini M°.cc°.xc°.quαртo; xxui. αnno cicli
рolαρiр; iii. αnnuр cicli lunαρiр; uii. αnno invicтionir.
Muiρčeρтαch mαc Mαʒnuρα hi Conchobαiр, inт αõõuρ
ρiʒ vob ƒeρρ vo Connαchтαiõ, vo ṁαρbαõ le Тαõʒ mαc
CCinvρiαρρα hi Conchobαiр, ocuр lα Domnαll mαc
Тαiõc, ocuр becán vá muinnтeρ mαille ρiр vo mαρbαõ
αnn. CCoõ mαc Eoʒαin hi Conchobαiр vo õenum cρeč
ƒoр Chlαinn Muiρčeρтαiʒ. Domnαll .h. hEʒρα, рi
Luiʒne, võéc in hoc αnno. Moeilρečlαinn .h. Ƒlαnnαʒαin,
тαiρρech Clαinne Cαтhαil, vo mαρbαõ vo Chαтhαl mαc
Тαiõc mic Diαρmαvα, αр ρáiтт Sliʒiʒ, iρiṅ mbliαvαin
рin. Donnchαv Mαc Conρnαṁα, тαiρρeč Muinnтiρe
Cinαiõ, moρтuuр eрт. Cαρραč in čαiρn Máʒ Тhiʒeρnán,
тαiρeč Тellαiʒ Dhúnchαvα, moρтuuр eрт. Cαтhαl
mαc Тαiõc Mic Diαρmαvα, рi Muiʒe Luiрʒ, in ƒeρ ρob
ƒeρρ enech ocuр enʒnum, moρтuuр eрт. Deρõαil, inʒen
Тαiõʒ mic Cαтhαil Mic Diαρmαvα, moρтuα eрт.
Cαiρρlen Sliʒiʒ vo leʒαõ lα hCCoõ .h. Conchobαiр.
Mαolρuαnαiv mαc ʒillαcρiiт vo ʒαbαil ρiʒe Muiʒe
Luiрʒ. Inт iαρlα vo ʒαbáil [vo] Mαc ʒeραilт, ocuр
buαiõρeõ Eρenn uile vo õoiʒechт тρiv рin. Cρeč
mōρ ṁeαõlα vo õenum vo Mαc ʒeραilт ocuр vo

---

1 *Son of Taichlech*; son of Taichlech Mac Diarmada, who died A.D.
1297.

2 *Quarto.* ᚸᚱᚾᚉᚩ, MS.

3 *Carrach - in - chairn*; lit. "the
rough faced man of the cairn." The
Four Mast. call him Duarcan, without
mentioning the sobriquet.

ously taken prisoner by Aedh, son of Eoghan O'Conchobair, at the instigation of Conchobhar, son of Taichlech,[1] and of Maelsechlainn O'Flannagain, and the Sil-Muiredhaigh likewise. And they plundered all Magh-Luirg, both church and territory; and the destruction of all Connacht proceeded from these injuries. Cathal Mac Diarmada, king of Magh-Luirg, escaped by force from his bonds, and committed a great depredation afterwards on the sons of Cathal O'Flannagain.

The kalends of January on Friday, which was the twenty-seventh of the moon; anno Domini M°.cc°.xc°. quarto;[2] xxvi. anno cycli solaris; iii. annus cycli lunaris; vii. anno Indictionis. Muirchertach, son of Maghnus O'Conchobhair, the best qualified of the Connachtmen to be a king, was killed by Tadhg, son of Andrias O'Conchobhair, and by Domhnall, the son of Tadhg; and a few of his people were slain there along with him. Aedh, son of Eoghan O'Conchobhair, committed depredations on the Clann-Muirchertaigh. Domhnall O'hEghra, king of Luighne, died in hoc anno. Maelsechlainn O'Flannagain, chieftain of Clann-Cathail, was slain by Cathal, son of Tadhg Mac Diarmada, on the street of Sligech, in this year. Donnchadh Mac Consnamha, chieftain of Muinter-Cinaith, mortuus est. Carrach-in-chairn[3] Mac Tighernáin, chieftain of Tellach-Dunchadha, mortuus est. Cathal, son of Tadhg Mac Diarmada, king of Magh-Luirg, the best man for bounty and prowess, mortuus est. Derbhail, daughter of Tadhg, son of Cathal Mac Diarmada, mortua est. The castle of Sligech was thrown down by Aedh O'Conchobhair. Maelruanaidh, son of Gilla-Christ,[4] assumed the sovereignty of Magh-Luirg. The Earl[5] was taken prisoner [by] Fitz-Gerald, in consequence of which all Erinn was thrown into a state of disturbance. A great, treacherous depredation was committed by Fitz-

---

[4] *Gilla-Christ*; i.e. Gilla-Christ Mac Diarmada.

[5] *The Earl.* Richard Burk, or De Burgo, called the Red Earl.

Mac Fheopuip pop Connachtaib, ocur Αοδ mac Eogain h1 Chonchobaip do ramailt daičpighad, ocur an típ uile do milled doib; ocur nip gabrat nept bud mó iná rin don dul rin. Diapmaid mac an Liačánaig h1 Conchobaip occirur ert, et repultur ert i nOilén na Tpinnoide pop Loč Cé. Dauid Mac Gilla Eppáič do mapbad do macaib Domnaill duib h1 Egpa.

Ict. Enaip pop ratopn, ocur ochtmad uathad ruippe; anno Domini M.cc. xc. quinto; xxuii. anno cicli rolapir; quaptur annur cicli lunapir; uiii. anno indictionir. Int iapla ceona do legud arr do Mac Gepailt tpe nept pig Saxan, ocur ap bpaigoib maiči a čineð rein dfagail arr do Mac Gepailt. Bpian, mac Αοδα buiðe mic Dhomnaill óig mic Οεδα meith, pi Chénel Gogain, do mapbad la Domnall mac Bpiain h1 Neill, ocur ap mór do Galloib ocur do Ghoeidelaib maille ppir. Domnall .h.Cellaig, pi .h.Maine, do ég i naibid manaig leith a mainirtip Cnuic Muaiðe, in hoc anno. Conn Mac Bpanán, taippech Coppcačlainn, do mapbad le macuib .h.Cellaig, ocur ré pop lupg a each iap na ngaid. Tomaltach Mac Bpanán do gabáil táipigecht ina inað iappin, ocur a mapbad la macuib Chonallað a níc i naičpech do mapbad la Tomaltach poimepiðé. Caiplen Muige Duma ocur caiprlen in Baile núaið,

---

[1] *The same Earl.* Richard Burk, the "Red Earl," whose capture by Fitz-Gerald is recorded under the preceding year.

[2] *Brian.* Brian O'Neill.

[3] *Aedh Meth;* i.e. "Aedh the Fat."

[4] *Was slain.* The Four Mast. say décc, "died."

[5] *The sons of Cu-alladh.* The Four Masters state that Tomaltach Mac Branan was slain by "Muinter-Conallan," "who were located," Dr. O'Donovan observes (Four Mast., A.D. 1295, note q,) "in the plain of Connaught, to the west of the territory of Corc-achlann." If such a family existed they are not mentioned in any of the Irish chronicles or genealogical books, as far as the editor is aware; but in any case the entry in the text, which represents the sons of Cu-alladh (lit. "wild dog") slaying his murderer, is apparently more correct than the statement of the Four Mast., which would give the Muinter-Conallán (a tribe, or sept) only *one* father.

[6] *Baile-núadh;* i.e. New-town. Dr. O'Donovan (Four Mast., note ad an.)

Gerald and Mac Feorais on the Connachtmen. They attempted to depose Aedh, son of Eoghan O'Conchobhair, and the entire country was destroyed by them; but they obtained no greater sway than this on the occasion. Diarmaid, son of the Liathanach O'Conchobhair, occisus est, et sepultus est in Trinity Island on Loch-Cé. David Mac Gilla-Erraith was slain by the sons of Domhnall Dubh O'hEghra.

The kalends of January on Saturday, and the eighth of the moon; anno Domini M.cc.xc.quinto; xxvii. anno cycli solaris; quartus annus cycli lunaris; viii. anno Indictionis. The same Earl[1] was set at liberty by Fitz-Gerald, through the power of the king of the Saxons, good hostages of his own family having been obtained from him by Fitz-Gerald. Brian,[2] son of Aedh Buidhe, son of Domhnall Og, son of Aedh Meth,[3] king of Cenel-Eoghain, was slain by Domhnall, the son of Brian O'Neill; and a great slaughter of the Foreigners and Gaeidhel along with him. Domhnall O'Cellaigh, king of Ui-Maine, died in the habit of a gray monk, in the monastery of Cnoc-Muaidhe, in hoc anno. Conn Mac Branan, chieftain of Corc-Achlann, was slain[4] by the sons of O'Cellaigh, whilst seeking for his horses after they had been stolen. Tomaltach Mac Branan afterwards assumed the chieftainship in his place, and was slain by the sons of Cu-alladh,[5] in revenge of their father who had been previously killed by Tomaltach. The castle of Magh-dumha, and the castle of Baile-núadh,[6] and

---

says, "according to Grace's Annals . . . . this castle is in the county of Wicklow, and that called Newcastle M'Kynegan." But no such inference can be drawn from Grace's brief statement, "Laginenses Hiberni Lageniam vastarunt, Novum castrum (not Novam villam) cum aliis cremarunt." It is apparent from the context that the castle of Baile-núadh, or New-

town, was in the county of Longford, in which the castle of Magh-dumha (Moydoe) is situated, and which contained O'Ferghail's territory of Anghaile. There are two townlands named Newtown in the parish of Moydoe, in that county; and it appears from an Inquisition taken at Granard in 1604, that there was then a castle of *Newton* in the barony of Granard.

ocur cairrlen Muiże bpercraiðe ðo leżað la Seppraið .h.bpeżżail in hoc anno. Cocað mór ιτιρ ρí Fpanc ocur ρí Saxan. Cożað mop a Típ Conaill in hoc ánno. bpaiżðe bpiain Mhéż Shámpaðain ocur żilla 1pra Mhéż Dhopchaið ðo żabail ðo żilla 1pra .h.Raiżilliż iṅ hoc anno.

ִKtt. Enaip rop Domnach, ocur noeṁað ðhéc puippe; anno Domini M.cc.xcui.; xxuin. anno cicli rolapir; quinto anno cicli lunapir; ix. anno inɔictioṅir. Ccoð mac Eożain hi Conċhobaip ðo aiṫpiżhað ðia oipecht rein, ocur Clann Muipcepταiż ðo ṫabaipt ðon típ na inað, ocur cenður an tíρε, ocur a bpaiżðe, ðo ṫabaipt ðo Conchobap puað mac Cathail puaið hi Conchobaip; ocur an típ uile ðo ṁilleð ιτιρ čill ocur tuath tρeran aṫpiżhað rin ðo ðenum ðoið. Cpič Caippri uile ðo lopcuð ocur ðo milleð ðo Chlainn Muipcepταiż, ocur ðul ró čempluib in τíρε ðóið. Do ðíżuil Día ocur Colum Cille ocur Muipe, ιρa tempaill ðo rápaiżheð anṅrin, na żniṁapta rin roppa iappin. Dala Ccoða hi Conchobaip, imoppo, ðo činoilríðe rluaż mór ðo żhalloið ocur ðo żhoeiðeluið ra Uilliam búpc ocur ra Tepoið a bupcc, żo tanżaðap co mainiττιρ na búille, ocur co pabaðap certpa hoðče innte, ocur po millret imat apbanna ocur iṁṁenna ap reð in tíρε co léip. Ocur tancotap taiριż an tíρε ina ṫeč anṅrin, ocur pucrat leo iað co teč in 1apla ðo ðenum ríða rpi hCcoð .h.Conchobaip; ocur żé ρο żeallrat ni ρο comaillret an ríč, oip ðo aontuiżret ðopiðir ap techt ðá tiżið re Clainn Muipcepταiż. Dala Oeða hi Conchobaip iappin, tanic irna Tuathaib, ocur tuc .h.Feрżai ocur Máż Rażnaill maillere himepcech-aið na Conṁaicnech laip; ocur ðo čuip techta ðocum Mic Dhiapmaða ocur ðocum hi Fhlannażán, ocur

1 *Anno.* αṅnur, MS.
2 *Theobald.* Tepoið; also fami-liarly written "Tibbot."
3 *They.* Aedh O'Conchobhair and his allies, William and Tibbot (or Theobald) Burk.
4 *For.* oi for oip, MS.; and also Annals of Connacht.

the castle of Magh-Brecraidhe, were razed by Jeffrey O'Ferghail in hoc anno. A great war between the king of France and the king of the Saxons. A great war in Tir-Conaill in hoc anno. The hostages of Brian Mac Shamhradhain, and of Gilla-Isa Mac Dorchaidh, were taken by Gilla-Isa O'Raighilligh in hoc anno.

The kalends of January on Sunday, and the nineteenth of the moon; anno Domini M.CC.XCVI.; xxviii. anno cycli solaris; quinto anno[1] cycli lunaris; ix. anno Indictionis. Aedh, son of Eoghan O'Conchobhair, was deposed by his own sept, and the Clann-Muirchertaigh were brought into the district in his place, and the sovereignty of the district, and its hostages, were given to Conchobhar Ruadh, son of Cathal Ruadh O'Conchobhair; and the entire district was destroyed, both church and territory, through this deposition having been effected by them. The territory of Cairpre was all burned and destroyed by Clann-Muirchertaigh; and they attacked the churches of the district; but God, and Colum-Cille, and Mary, whose churches were then profaned, avenged these deeds on them afterwards. As regards Aedh O'Conchobhair, however, he assembled a great army of Foreigners and Gaeidhel, including William Burk and Theobald[2] Burk, who proceeded to the monastery of the Buill, in which they remained four nights; and they destroyed much corn and property throughout the entire district. And the chieftains of the district went then into his house; and they[3] took them with them to the Earl's house, to make peace with Aedh O'Conchobhair. And though they promised, they did not observe this peace; for[4] on going home they again sided with the Clann-Muirchertaigh. As to Aedh O'Conchobhair, he went after this into the Tuatha, and brought with him O'Ferghail and Mac Oirechtaigh, together with the forces of the Conmaicne; and he dispatched messengers to Mac Diarmada and O'Flannagain, who returned into the

ιηητόδ δόιδ ριη ιγ τίρ ναρέιγ ηα τεchταιρεchτεδ ριη
να ροchτμιη; ocuγ γο Len Conchobaρ ρμαδη ίαν μαρ
ρμαιρ αξ ιμρμδ μαιδε ρειη ιαν, ocuγ cρεch νο δέιη
δίδ ιαρριη. 1μρμδ α τοραξεchτ α cρειδε, ocuγ δρειτ
ρμιρρε δόιδ αξ cenn δέιττι Τιρε Τυαthαιl, ocuγ Conchobaρ ρμαδ νο μαρδαδ αηηγιη, ocuγ Loδlaιηη μαc
Conchobaιρ νο ξαδάιl αηη, ocuγ Μαξηυγ μαc Τομαl-
ταιξ νο ξαδάιl αηη δόρ, ocuγ began να ηναοιηιδ νο
μαρδαν αηη μαιlle ρριύ. Ἀcoδ .h.Conchobaιρ ocuγ
Μαc Ὀιαρμανα, ocuγ ηα hοιρεchτα αιρδεηα, νο δεημμ
cρειδε μόιρε νιξlα αρ Chlοιηη Μμιρcερταιξ ιριη lό
cενηα ριη. Loδlaιηη μαc Conchobaιρ νο δαllαδ δόιδ,
ocuγ α έc ι ηυthαρ α δαllτα. Ξιlla 1ρρα μαc αη
lιαδαηαιξ, εγρμc Ὀλεριηη, ιη Cριγτο qμιεμιτ ι Ρογ
Comáιη, xx. οιδδε ρια mbellταιηε, ocuγ α αδlucaν α
μαηιγτιρ ηα δύιlle. Ὀερδορξμιll, ιηξεη hι. Chlοιηη
Ἐρρα, μορτμα ερτ, ετ ρεπμlτα ερτ ιη μοηαγτεριο
canoniconum ρontiρ Ρατριcι. Μόρρlμαιξεν Le ρι
Saxan co μαιthιδ Ξhall Ἐρεηη μαιlle ρριρρ, .ι. Ριρδερν
α δύρc ιαρla Ulαδ, ocuγ Μαc Ξεράιlτ, ocuγ ιοάη Ἐινο-
μμρ; ocuγ α ηνμl μιle co hἈlbμιη, ξμρ ξαδγατ ηερτ
μόρ ιηητι νοη νμl ριη. Ἀcht chena ρο μιllρετ τμαδα
ocuγ τερμμιηη, οιρεchτα ocuγ εξlμρα co hιμδα ιηητε,
ocuγ co háιριδδε μαηιγτιρ δρατhαρ ρρέcιμρ νο ργριορ
δόιδ, conαρ ράξμιδρεττ clοδ αρ δlοιch δι; ocuγ ρο
μαρδρατ ριρ ξραιδ ocuγ μηα ιμδα ιηητε δόρ.

---

[1] *Their prey.* α cρειδε; i.e. the prey taken from Mac Dermot and O'Flannagan by Conchobhar Ruadh.

[2] *Céite-Tire-Tuathail.* "The green hill of Tir-Tuathail." The district of Tir-Tuathail comprised the parish of Kilronan, in the northern part of the county of Roscommon. The name of the *Céite* (pron. *Kéite*) is probably still preserved in that of Keadew, a townland in this parish.

[3] *From the effects thereof.* The MS. has ι ηυthαρ α δαllτα, which is lit. "in the illness of his blinding."

[4] *Mac-an-Liathanaigh.* "Son of the Liathanach." "The Liathanach" was a member of the family of O'Conchobhair, or O'Conor, as appears from an entry under 1295, *supra.*

[5] *Es.* Es-Ui-Fhloinn, "the cataract of O'Flynn," now Assylin, near Boyle, in the county of Roscommon. For some notice of this place, which was also called Es-mic-nEirc, see Reeves's *Adamnan,* p. 281.

district after these messages had reached them. And Conchobhar Ruadh followed them when he found them abandoning himself, and subsequently took a prey from them. They turned back in pursuit of their prey,[1] which they overtook at the head of Céite-Tire-Tuathail,[2] where Conchobhar Ruadh was slain, and Lochlainn, son of Conchobhar, was taken prisoner; and Maghnus, son of Tomaltach, was also taken prisoner there, and a few of their men were slain there besides. Aedh O'Conchobhair and Mac Diarmada, and the other tribes, committed a great retaliatory depredation on the Clann-Muirchertaigh on the same day. Lochlainn, son of Conchobhar, was blinded by them; and he died from the effects thereof.[3] Gilla-Isa Mac-an-Liathanaigh,[4] bishop of Oilfinn, in Christo quievit in Ros-Comain, twenty nights before May-day, and was interred in the monastery of the Buill. Derbhorgaill, daughter of O'Floinn of Es,[5] mortua est, et sepulta est in monasterio canonicorum Fontis Patricii.[6] A great hosting by the king of the Saxons, accompanied by the chiefs of the Foreigners of Erinn, viz. :—Richard Burk, Earl of Ulster, and Fitz-Gerald,[7] and John Fitz-Thomas; and they all went to Alba, and obtained great sway in it on that occasion. However, they destroyed numerous territories and termons,[8] oirechts[9] and churches, in it; and, in particular, razed a monastery of Friars Preachers,[10] so that they left not one stone of it on another; and they also killed many ecclesiastics and women there.

---

[6] *Fontis Patricii.* Tober-Patrick, or Ballintober, in the barony of Carra, and county of Mayo.

[7] *Fitz-Gerald.* The Four Mast. call him Gerald Fitz-Gerald.

[8] *Termons.* Termon lands, or lands within the liberties of a monastery.

[9] *Oirechts.* By *oirecht* is meant the district or patrimony of an airech, oirech, or chieftain of a certain grade; as also the people thereof.

[10] *Monastery of Friars Preachers.* St. Andrew's, probably. See Rishanger's Chronicle, ad an. (Riley's ed., London, 1865, p. 188).

ḱtt. Enaip pop ṁaipt, ocup ɒeċmaɒ piċeɒ puippe;
αɴɴo 'Oomiɴi Ɱ°.xx°.xc°.peptimo; ppimup αɴɴup polapip cicli; ui. αɴɴo cicli luɴapip; x. αɴɴo iɴɒictioɴip.
Coɴċobap, mac Taiċliċ, mic 'Oiapmaɒa, mic Coɴ-
ċobaip, mic 'Ohiapmaɒa, mic Taiɓg, .i. pí Ɱhuiże
Luipg ocup Cciptiż, ocup piɴɴpep bpaċap ocup tiżepɴa
hᵹleċta Ɱhaolpuaɴaɒ, ocup pep pob pepp cop ocup
comaipce, żal ocup żaipceɒ, tpoɒo ocup taċup, iɴɴ-
poiżeɒ ocup aɴṁuiɴ, ɒíɴ ocup ɒeż tepmoɴɴ, pipɴɴe
ocup plaiċeṁɴup ɴa aimpip peiɴ, ɒo éc iɴ ḃliaɒaiɴ piɴ
ap mḃpeiċ ḃuaɒa ó ɓomuɴ ocup ó ɓemuɴ; ocup α
aɓlucaɒ α maɴiptip ɴa ḃúille α leaḃai α pen ocup α
piɴɴpep poime. Eɴpi Ɱhág Oipeċtaiż, eppuc Coɴɒaipe
ocup maɴaċ liaċ ɒopɒ ɒipipti, quieuit. Ɱażɴup
.h.Cciɴliże, taippeċ Cheɴél 'Ooppa, ɒo ṁapbaɒ ɒo
mac α bpaċap, .i. mac ɒepbpaċap α aċap, ocup ɒo
Ɱuiɴɴtep Eoluip, pep ɒolum, ag Eɴaċ ɓuiɓ. Uilliam
.h.'Ouɓċhaiż, eppuc Chluaɴa, ɒo ṁapbaɒ ɒepcap ap
tuitim ɒá eċ. Ɱóppluaiżeɒ le hEoḃapɒ, .i. pí Saxaɴ,
ipiɴ Eppaiɴc, co muipɴ ocup żo moipṁeɴmuiɴ, ocup
żiɓeɒh táɴic aipɒe żaɴ tpeɴ żaɴ tpeipi ɒoɴ ɒula piɴ.
Ɱoeilpeċlaiɴɴ mac Ḃpiaiɴ, .i. ab ɴa ḃúille, ɒo żaḃáil
eppucoiɒe Olepiɴɴ, ocup Ɱapiaɴ .h. 'Ooɴɴaɒaip ɒo
ɓoża pemipɒe, ocup α ɒula ɒo Róiṁ i ɴimċopɴum ɴa
heppucoiɒe, ocup α éż ap αɴ tupup piɴ. Cu Ulaɒ
.h.hCcɴluaiɴ ocup α ɒepbpaċaip, ocup Ccoɴżup Ɱaż
Ɱhaⱦżamɴa, ocup mopáɴ eli ɒo ṁaiⱦiḃ α muiɴtipe
maille ppiú, ɒo mapbaɒ ɒo Żhalloiḃ 'Ohúɴa 'Oelgaɴ
ag impuɓ ɓóiḃ oɴ Iapla ipiɴ mḃliaɒaiɴ ceɒɴa piɴ.

ḱtt. Enaip pop ċetáiɴ ocup αoɴmaɒ ɒhéc puippe;

---

1 *Slicht-Maelruanaidh*; i.e. the offspring of Maelruanaidh, ancestor of
the Mac Dermots of Roscommon,
whose tribe name was Sil-Maelruan-
aidh.

² *Condere.* Connor, in the county
of Antrim. This is a mistake, as Henry
Mac Oirechtaigh, or Mageraghty, was
bishop of Derry. See O'Donovan's
ed. Four Mast., A.D. 1297, note ʸ.

The kalends of January on Tuesday, and the thirtieth of the moon; anno Domini M°.xx°.xc°.septimo; primus annus solaris cycli; vi. anno cycli lunaris; x. anno Indictionis. Conchobhar, son of Taichlech, son of Diarmaid, son of Conchobhar, son of Diarmaid, son of Tadhg, i.e. the king of Magh-Luirg and Airtech, the eldest of his brothers, and lord of Slicht-Maelruanaidh,[1] the best man of his own time for covenant and guarantee, valour and prowess, battle and conflict, attack and restraint, protection and good asylum, veracity and government, died in this year, after triumphing over the world and the devil, and was interred in the monastery of the Buill, in the grave of his ancestors and elders. Henry Mac Oirechtaigh, bishop of Condere,[2] and a gray monk of the order of the Desert,[3] quievit. Maghnus O'hAinlighe, chieftain of Cenel-Doffa, was slain by his kinsman's son, i.e. the son of his father's brother, and by Muinter-Eolais, per dolum, at Enach-dubh. William O'Dubhthaigh, bishop of Cluain,[4] was killed by a concussion, after falling off his horse. A great expedition *was led* into France by Edward, i.e. the king of the Saxons, with cheerfulness and great spirits; but he came out of it, nevertheless, without *obtaining* sway or power on that occasion. Maelsechlainn Mac Briain, i.e. the abbot of the Buill, assumed the bishopric of Oilfinn; and Marian O'Donnabhair was elected previously, and went to Rome to contest the bishopric, and died on that journey. Cu-Uladh O'hAnluain, and his brother, and Aenghus Mac Mathghamhna, and a great many more of the nobles of their people along with them, were killed by the Foreigners of Dun-Delgan, whilst they were returning from the Earl in the same year.

The kalends of January on Wednesday, and the [1298.]

---

[3] *Order of the Desert;* i.e. the Cistercian order.

[4] *Cluain;* i.e. Cluain-ferta-Brenainn, or Clonfert, in the county of Galway.

anno Domini M.cc.xc.octauo; ſecunᴅo anno ciċli
ſolaſiſ; ſeſtimo anno ciċli Lunaſiſ; xi. anno inᴅictioniſ. Tomaſ Fimuiſiſ, baſun moſ uaſal ᴅo clainn
Ʒeſailt, fiſ iſaiti int oiʒſi cam, moſtuuſ eſt in hoc
anno. Tomáſ .h. hOiſeċtaiʒ, ab Eſſa Ruaiᴅ, quieuit
in Cſiſto. Saᴅb inʒen Oeᴅa buiᴅe hi Neill, ben
Taiᴅʒ mic Ɑinᴅſiaſſa hi Conchobaiſ, [ᴅo ecc] i toſach
eſſaiʒ in hoc anno. Dſian bſeʒach Maʒ Shamſaᴅan,
taiſeċ Tellaiʒ Eċaċ, ſeſ ſob ſeſſ enech ocuſ enʒnum
ᴅo ᴅí na aimſiſ ſein, ᴅo ṁaſbaᴅ la hOeᴅ mBſeiſſnech
.h. Conchobaiſ, ocuſ la Clainn Muiſcheſtaiʒ, na tiʒ
ſein a Cúil O nʒuaiſe in tſeſ lá ᴅo ſamſaᴅ. Donn-
chaᴅ mac Domnaill hi Eʒſa, aᴅbuſ ſi Luiʒne, ocuſ
an mac ſiʒ ᴅob ſeſſ enech ocuſ oiſbeſt na ᴅuċaiᴅ
ſein, ᴅo ṁaſbaᴅ a meᴅuil ᴅia bſaṫaiſ ſéin, .i. ᴅo
Dſian ċaſſach .h. Eaʒſa. Domnall ſuaᴅ Mháʒ
Caſſṫaiʒ, ſi Deſſmuman, quieuit. Feſʒal .h. Feſ-
ʒhail, eſſuc ṫiſe Conaill, quieuit in Cſiſto. Eaſſuc-
oiᴅe Cluana ᴅo ʒaᴅail ᴅabaiᴅ Cille Décaiſ, .i. Uilliam
.h. Finnén, iſin mbliaᴅain ſin.

Ktt. Enáiſ ſoſ ᴅaſᴅoein, ocuſ aili ſicheᴅ ſuiſſe;
anno Domini M.cc.xcix.; teſtio anno ciċli ſolaſiſ;
uiii. anno ciċli Lunaſiſ; xi. annuſ inᴅictioniſ. Ɑlax-
anᴅaiſ Mac Domnaill, in ſeſ ſob ſeſſ eneċ ocuſ
uaiſle itiſ Eſinn ocuſ Ɑlbain, ᴅo ṁaſbaᴅ le hɑlax-
anᴅaiſ Mac nDubʒaill, maille ſe háſ ᴅiáiſṁiᴅe
ᴅia muinnteſ maille ſſiſ. Muiſiſ .h. hOcan, eſſuc
Chille Dalua, quieuit. Seoan Ɑlamaſa, int oen
ſuᴅiſe iſ beoᴅa ocuſ iſ laiᴅiſe, ocuſ ᴅob ſeſſ enech
iſin Miᴅe, ᴅo maſbaᴅ le Seſſſaiᴅ .h. bFeſʒail i

---

[1] *Clann-Gerailt*; i.e. the descendants
of Gerald, or family of Fitz-Gerald.

[2] *Died.* ᴅo ecc. Omitted in the
MS., and supplied from the Annals of
Connacht.

[3] *Tir-Conaill.* The Four Mast., who
have the death of Ferghal O'Ferghail
under the year 1299, call him bishop
of Raphoe, which diocese comprises
the territory of Tir-Conaill, or county
of Donegal.

eleventh of the moon; anno Domini M.cc.xc.octavo; secundo anno cycli solaris; septimo anno cycli lunaris; xi. anno Indictionis. Thomas Fitz-Maurice, a great, noble baron of the Clann-Gerailt,[1] who was called the Crooked Heir, mortuus est in hoc anno. Thomas O'hOirechtaigh, abbot of Es-Ruaidh, quievit in Christo. Sadhbh, daughter of Aedh Buidhe O'Neill, wife of Tadhg, son of Andrias O'Conchobhair, [died][2] in the beginning of spring in hoc anno. Brian Bregach Mac Shamhradhain, chieftain of Tellach-Echach, the most bountiful and puissant man that was in his own time, was slain by Aedh Breifnech O'Conchobhair and the Clann-Muirchertaigh, in his own house at Cuil-O'Guaire, on the third day of summer. Donnchadh, son of Domhnall O'hEghra, one fit to be king of Luighne, and the most bountiful and renowned prince in his own country, was slain in treachery by his own brother, i.e. Brian Carrach O'hEghra. Domhnall Ruadh Mac Carthaigh, king of Des-Mumha, quievit. Ferghal O'Ferghail, bishop of Tir-Conaill,[3] quievit in Christo. The bishopric of Cluain[4] was assumed by the abbot of Cill-Bécain, i.e., William O'Finnén, in this year.

The kalends of January on Thursday, and the twenty-second of the moon; anno Domini M.cc.xcix.; tertio anno cycli solaris; viii. anno cycli lunaris; xii. annus Indictionis. Alexander Mac Domhnaill, the best man for hospitality and nobility both in Erinn and Alba, was slain by Alexander Mac Dubhghaill, together with a countless slaughter of his people along with him. Maurice O'hOgain, bishop of Cill-Dalua, quievit. John Alamara,[5] the most active, powerful, and bountiful knight in Midhe, was slain by Jeffrey O'Ferghail, in pursuit of a prey. A

---

[4] *Cluain;* i.e. Cluain-mic-Nois, or Clonmacnois.

[5] *Alamara.* Mageoghegan, in his version of the Annals of Clonmacnois, writes this name "Delamare," which is the correct form.

tóraiġecht creiche. Caṫ aḋbail do ṫabairt do ri
Tairtri ocur do ri bḟerménia, maille re na bḟuaradar
do ṫocbáil eli maille rriú, do hḟoḋḃán, .i. ri na
Baibilóne, ocur do na Seirrirdíniḃ airċena, a mi
meḋóin in ḟóġṁair, .i. im ḟeil Muire mór do rionnrad;
ocur a bṙirreḋ ar na Seirrirdíniḃ, ocur ár díairṁiḋe
do ṫabairt forra, ocur in talam noeṁ do ġabáil dona
riġuiḃ cedna.

Ktt. Enáir ror Aoine, ocur trerr uaṫad ruirre;
A.D. M.ccc.; quarto anno cicli rolarir; ix. anno
cicli lunarir; xiii. anno indictionir. Teróid Buitilér,
barún mor uarral, mortuur ert. Ioan Prendarcarr
do ṁarbad do mac Fiacra hI Ḟloinn in hoc anno.
Cairlen Aẗa cliaṫ in Chorainn do ṫinnrcedal leirin
Iarla ruaḋ irin mbliadain rin. Seoinín óc Mac
Muirir do ṁarbaḋ, ocur doeine imḋa eli maille rrir,
la Conchobar mac Fiacra hI Ḟloinn. Feḋlimiḋ Mag
Carrṫaiġ, aḋbar rí Dermuman, mortuur ert. Con-
ġalaċ.h.Loċlainn, erruc Corcumruaiḋ, in Crirto
quievit. Eochaid mac Domnaill hI Airt, tairreċ ċlainni
Cellaiġ, do ṁarbaḋ do Ḡhallaib in hoc anno. Ġairm
ċoitċend do ṫoiġecht ón Róiṁ innaimrir Bunaraciur
pápa .viii. ar reḋ na Crirtaiḋechta uile, ocur ror ġaċ
cedmad bliadain ticed an ġairm rin, ocur bliadain raċa
aduerḃi rria; ocur do ṫiced rlúaġ díairṁiḋe a huile
ṫíruiḃ na Crirtaiḋechta ron nġairm rin día noilitri co
Roim; ocur loġhad na nuile ḟecctha dḟaġail doiḃ innte
tréran raċ rin. Adam Sdóndún, tiġerna Cera, mortuur
ert. Uilliam Mhág Ḟhlannchaḋa, tairreċ Dartraiġe,
do ṁarbad la hUalġarg .h.Ruairc in hoc anno.

<hr>

1 *Armenia.* The MS. has Fer-
menia, as if the chronicler understood that by Armenia was meant
"men of Menia." The battle in question was the great battle of Damascus,
fought in the year 1300. See Rishanger's Chron. (Riley's ed.), pp. 443
and 466.

2 *Festival of Mary.* The festival of
the Annunciation, or 15th of August.

3 *Ath - cliath - in - Chorainn;* "the
hurdle-ford of the Corann," now Balli-
mote, in the barony of Corran, county
of Sligo.

4 *Bishop of Corcumruaidh.* The
Annals of Connacht say more cor-

great battle was given by the king of the Tartars and
the king of Armenia,[1] together with all whom they got
to join them, to Soldan, i.e., the king of Babylon, and to
the other Saracens, in the middle month of harvest, i.e.,
about the great festival of Mary[2] exactly; and the battle
was gained over the Saracens, and a great slaughter was
inflicted on them; and the Holy Land was occupied by
the said kings.

A.D
[1299.]

The kalends of January on Friday, and the third of
the moon, A.D. M.ccc.; quarto anno cycli solaris; ix. anno
cycli lunaris; xiii. anno Indictionis. Tibbot Butler, a
great, noble baron, mortuus est. John Prendergast was
slain by the son of Fiachra O'Floinn in hoc anno. The
castle of Ath-cliath-in-Chorainn[3] was commenced by the
Red Earl in this year. Seoinin Og Mac Maurice was
slain, and many other persons along with him, by Conchobhar, son of Fiachra O'Floinn. Fedhlimidh Mac
Carthaigh, who was qualified to be king of Des-Mumha,
mortuus est. Conghalach O'Lochlainn, bishop of Corcumruaidh,[4] in Christo quievit. Eochaidh, son of Domhnall O'hAirt, chieftain of Clann-Cellaigh, was slain by
Foreigners in hoc anno. A general invitation came from
Rome in the time of Pope Boniface VIII., throughout all
Christendom; and in each hundredth year this invitation
was wont to be issued, and it was usually called a "year
of grace;" and a countless multitude from all the countries
in Christendom were wont to go in pilgrimage to Rome at
this invitation; and they would obtain forgiveness of all
sins there through this grace. Adam Staunton, lord of
Cera, mortuus est. William Mac Flannchadha, chieftain of
Dartraighe, was slain by Ualgharg O'Ruairc in hoc anno.

[1300.]

---

rectly, erpuc Finnabrac Corcmod-
ruaid, "bishop of Finnabhair of
Corc-Modhruaidh," i.e. bishop of Cill-
Finnabhrach, or Kilfenora, which

diocese is co-extensive with the district or barony of Corca-Modhruaidh,
Corcumruaidh, or Corcomroe, in the
county of Clare.

Ktt. Enaip pop τomnach, ocup a cethap vég puippe;
anno Domini M°.ccc. ppimo; quinto anno cicli polapip; x°. anno cicli lunapip; xiiii. anno invictioniṗ.
Pinnġuala, inṫen Ṗéðlim .h. Conchobaip .i. banab
Chille Cpaoḃnaτ, in Cpiṡτo quieuiτ. Copmac mac
Copmaic hi Mhaoilpechlainn vo ṁapbaẟ la mac Aipτ
hi Mhailpechlainn, .i. mac a veṗbpaτhap aτhap pein.
Ṡilla Ioppa Mac Ṗipḃiṡiṫ, ollam .h. ḃṗiacpach
Muaiẟ, pói penċupa ocup pṡélaiẟechτa, ocup pili-
echτa, ocup compóivechτa, ocup elaẟna imẟa eli,
vhéc in hoc anno. Cpeach ṁóp vo ẟénum voeṗh mac
Caṫail hi Chonchobaip ocup vo Chloinn Mhuipċep-
τaiṫ aipċéna, ap Thaẟc mac Ainvpiappa a Moiṫ
Céivne. Maẟa Mháṫ Cpaiḃ, pacapτ móp Apva
Capna, pói nvéippe ocup nvoennachτa, quieuiτ in
Cpiṡτo. Caṫal .h. Máilevúin vlḃ Ṗhiacpaḃ Muaiẟ,
.i. aipv pechτaipe pi Connachτ, vo éc in hoc anno.
Muipċepτach Mac Conpnama, aḃḃap τaippiṫ Muin-
τipe Cinaiẟe, vo mapbaẟ la Clainn Muipċepτaiṫ in
hoc anno. Sluaiṫev la pí Saxan i nAlbain, ocup
Mac Ṡepailτ, ocup Mac Ṗheopuip, ocup maiṫi Ṡall
Connachτ ocup Epenn uile inéṫmuip Iapla Ulaẟ, ó
ċoeiciẟip pia Luṫnupaẟ co Samain, ocup ṫan lop nepτ
vo ṫabáil voiḃ innτi.

Ktt. Enaip pop Luan; ocup cuiciẟ piched puippi;
anno Domini .M.ccc. pecunvo; pexτo anno cicli polapip; xi. anno cicli lunapip; xu. anno invictioniṗ.
Domnall puaẟ Mháṫ Cappτhaiṫ, pí Depmuman,
.i. an Ṡoeivel po buv pine ocup pob uaiple, ocup
pobuv pepp enech ocup enṫnum, ocup po buv mó
ṫpáin ocup copcup i caṫaib ocup a comlonnaiḃ vo
Ṡhoeivelaiḃ Epenn uile, vo éc iap mbuaiv naiτpiṫe ipin
mbliavain pin. Mílip, eppuc Luimniṫ, mac mic Iapla

---

¹ *Domini.* Dº, MS.
² *Ollamh.* pron. "Ollave;" i.e. a
very learned person.

³ *Andrias.* This Andrias, or Andrew,
was the son of Brian Luighnech
O'Conchobhair (slain in 1181), who

The kalends of January on Sunday, and the fourteenth of the moon; anno Domini[1] M°.ccc. primo; quinto anno cycli solaris; x°. anno cycli lunaris; xiiii. anno Indictionis. Finnghuala, daughter of Fedhlim O'Conchobhair, i.e., the abbess of Cill-Craebhnat, in Christo quievit. Cormac, son of Cormac O'Maelsechlainn, was slain by the son of Art O'Maelsechlainn, i.e., the son of his own father's brother. Gilla-Isa Mac Firbisigh ollamh[2] of Ui-Fiachrach-Muaidhe, a most eminent professor of history, story-telling, poetry and computation, and of many other sciences, died in hoc anno. A great depredation was committed by Aedh, the son of Cathal O'Conchobhair, and by the Clann-Muirchertaigh also, on Tadhg, son of Andrias,[3] in Magh-Ceidne. Matthew Mac Craith, great priest of Ard-Carna, a most charitable and humane man, quievit in Christo. Cathal O'Maelduin, of the Ui-Fiachrach-Muaidhe, i.e., the chief steward of the king of Connacht, died in hoc anno. Muirchertach Mac Conshnamha, one fit to be chieftain of Muinter-Cinaith, was killed by the Clann-Muirchertaigh in hoc anno. A hosting to Alba by the king of the Saxons, accompanied by Fitz-Gerald, and Mac Feorais, and the chiefs of the Foreigners of Connacht, excepting the Earl of Ulster, *which lasted* from a fortnight before Lammas until All-hallowtide; but they obtained not complete sway in it.

The kalends of January on Monday, and the twenty-fifth of the moon; anno Domini M.ccc. secundo; sexto anno cycli solaris; xi. anno cycli lunaris; xv. anno Indictionis. Domhnall Ruadh Mac Carthaigh, king of Des-Mumha, i.e. the oldest and noblest, the most bountiful and valiant, and the most formidable and triumphant Gaeidhel, in battles and conflicts, of all the Gaeidhel of Erinn, died after the victory of penitence in this year. Miles, bishop of Luimnech, who was the grandson

---

was the son of Turlough the Great O'Conor, monarch of Ireland, and the ancestor of the family of O'Conor Sligo.

Laigen eiriðein, in Crirto quieuit. Erpuc Corcaige .i.
mac Donnchaða, ocur hé na manach liað, quieuit in
Crirto. Ruaiðri mac Domnaill hi Egra, aððup rí
Luigne, ðhég in hoc anno. Creaca móra do ðenum
ðOeðh mac Cathail hi Conchobair ar Thaðc mac
Anðriarra hi Conchobair, ocur ar Shitriuc mac an
čairnig Mhég Fhlanncharð, a Mag Ceirne, in bliaðain
ceðna rin. Bóðít mór ocur ár ar četruið uile irin
mbliaðain rin. Maigirtir Soiamna .h. braccán,
airderpuc Cairil, quieuit. Donn Mhág Uiðir, rí
fer Manacħ, rói na hErenn uile i nðérc, i nðoenðacht
ocur i nengnum, quieuit. Uilliam .h. Finnén, ab
Chille ðécán, ocur erpuc Cluana mic Noir iarrin, in
Crirto quieuit. Cathal mac Domnaill Mhég Ragnaill, ðaṁna čoeirrig Muintire hEoluir, do ṁarbað
le Fergal Mhág Rágnuill, .i. mac ðerbrathar a athar
fein.

Ktt. Enair for ṁairt ocur reirreð uathað fuirre ;
anno Domini M.ccc.tertio ; reptimo anno cicli rolarir ; xii. anno cicli lúnarir ; primur annur inðic-
tionir. Nicól Mhág Mhaoilírra, airderpuc Arða
Mača, int oen čleirech ir ðiaða ocur ir ðeigenaig do
ðí i nErinn na aimrir fein, in Crirto quieuit. Moeilrechlainn mac briain, erpuc Olefinn, do ég in hoc
anno. Donnchað .h. Flannagán, ab na búille, do gabáil .
erpucoiðe Olefinn iarrin. Diarmaið .h. Flannagán,
tairréč Thúaith Ráta, ocur a ðá mac maille frir, do
marbað do muinter Dhomnaill mic Anðriarra hi
Conchobair, ocur ðaoine maiče eli ðá muintir fein

1 *The Earl of Laighen;* or Earl of
Leinster; apparently Earl William
Marshall, although the five sons of
William Marshall died without legiti-
mate issue.

2 *Mac Donnchadha.* In Ware's catalogue of the bishops of Cork he is
called "Robert Mac Donogh, a Cister-
tian monk of great learning." See
Harris's *Ware,* vol. i., p. 559.

3 *Hoc.* óc, MS.

4 *Aedh.* A marginal note in the
copy of the Annals of Connacht pre-

of the Earl of Laighen,[1] in Christo quievit. The bishop of
Corcach, i.e. Mac Donnchadha[2], (and he was a gray monk),
quievit in Christo. Ruaidhri, son of Domhnall O'hEghra,
one fit to be king of Luighne, died in hoc[3] anno. Great
depredations were committed by Aedh,[4] son of Cathal
O'Conchobhair, on Tadhg, son of Andrias O'Conchobhair,
and on Sitrec, son of the Cairnech Mac Flannchchaidh, in
Magh-Ceidne, in the same year. A great destruction of
cows, and mortality amongst all cattle, in this year.
Master Stephen O'Bragan, archbishop of Caisel, quievit.
Donn Mac Uidhir, king of Feara-Manach, the most eminent man in all Erinn for charity, and humanity, and
prowess, quievit. William O'Finnén, abbot of Cill-Bécan,
and afterwards bishop of Cluain-mic-Nois, in Christo
quievit. Cathal, son of Domhnall Mac Raghnaill, heir
to the chieftaincy of Muinter-Eolais, was slain by Ferghal Mac Raghnaill, i.e. the son of his own father's
brother.

The kalends of January on Tuesday, and the sixth of
the moon; anno Domini M.ccc. tertio; septimo anno cycli
solaris; xii. anno cycli lunaris; primus annus Indictionis.
Nicholas Mac Maelisa, archbishop of Ard-Macha, the most
godly and generous cleric[5] that was in Erinn in his own
time, in Christo quievit. Maelsechlainn Mac Briain, bishop
of Oilfinn, died in hoc anno. Donnchadh O'Flannagain,
abbot of the Buill, assumed the bishopric of Oilfinn afterwards. Diarmaid O'Flannagain, chieftain of Tuath-
Ratha, and his two[6] sons, and many superior men of his
own people along with them, were slain by the people of
Domhnall, son of Andrias O'Conchobhair, after they had

---

served in the library of Trinity College, Dublin, reads "ᴅoᴍ óoɪᵹ ɪꞃó
Ꝺeᴅʜ Ɓꞃeɪꞃnech," "I think he is
Aedh Breifnech," i.e. Aedh the Breifnian, son of Cathal Ruadh O'Conchobhair.

[5] *The most godly and generous cleric.*
The expression in the text, "ɪnᴄ oen
ċᴌeɪꞃech ɪꞃ ᴅɪaᴅa ⁊ ɪꞃ ᴅeɪᵹenaɪᵹ,"
lit. signifies "the one cleric that was
most godly and generous."

[6] *Two,* aᴅá for óá, MS.

malle ꝼ꞉uꞃ, aꞃ cecꞁc ꝺo ꝺenum cꞃeıce ꞇ Caıꝛꝛ꞉ ꝺoıꞇ. Coıꞃꝛꝺꞁelbacꞁ mac Ꝺomnaıll óꞇꝣ ꞁı Ꝺꞁomnaıll, ꝺa nꞡoıꝛꞇ Coıꞃꝛꝺꞁelbac Cꞁnuıc ꞇn ṁaꝺṁa, .ı. ꞃı Cıꞃe Conaıll ꞃe ꝺá blıaꝺaın ꝺꞁéc ꞇnnce ocuꞃ na ꞁecmuıꞃ; ꝼeꞃ coccacꞁ coꞃnamacꞁ, ocuꞃ Cúcullaınn claınnꞇ Ꝺalaıꞡ aꞃ ꞡaıꞃceꝺ, ꝺo maꞃbaꝺ la ꞁαꝺꞇ mac Ꝺomnaıll óıꞡ .ı. a ꝺeꞃbꞃacꞁaıꞃ ꝼeın, ꞇaꞃ coꞡaꝺ ꝼaꝺa, ocuꞃ ꞇaꞃ mılleꝺ moꞃáın ꞇmón cıꞃ aꞃ ꞡacꞁ coeꝺ, ocuꞃ áꞃ aꝺbaıl elı maılle ꝼꞃ꞉uꞃ ꝺo Cꞁenel Coꞡaın ocuꞃ ꝺo ṁaꞇꝺꞇꝺ Ꞡꞁall ꞇn cuaıꞃceꞃc, ocuꞃ ꝺo Cꞁonnallcꞁaıꝺ ꝼéın áꞃcꞁena, ocuꞃ Muıꞃceꞃcacꞁ Mꞁáꞡ Ꝼꞁlanncꞁaıꝺ, caıꞃꞃecꞁ Ꝺaꞃcꞃaıꞡe. Ro maꞃbaꝺ ann Ꝺonn .ꞁ.Caꞇán, ꞃı bꝼeꞃ ꞡCꞃaıꝺe ocuꞃ Cꞇannacꞁcaı, ocuꞃ Ꝺonncꞁaꝺ Mac Menmaın, ocuꞃ αꝺꝺ Mac Menmaın, ꝺá mac ṁꞇc ꞇn ꝼꞇꞃ leıꞡꞇnn ꞁı Ꝺꞁom-naıll, ocuꞃ Nıall mac Neıll ꞁı Ꝺꞁaıꞡıll, ꝺeꞡ aꝺbaꞃ caıꞃꞡ na Cꞃı Cúacꞁ, Mac Uꞡoꞃꞃa ocuꞃ a mac ocuꞃ a ꝺeꞃbꞃáꞇaıꞃ, ocuꞃ αꝺám Sanꝺaıl, ocuꞃ Ꞡoıll ocuꞃ Ꞡaoıꝺel ꞇmꝺa óꞃın amacꞁ; ocuꞃ αꝺꝺ .ꞁ.Ꝺomnaıll ꝺo ꞡabaıl a ꝼlaıꞇıꞃ ꝼeın ꞇaꞃꞃaın móꞃ coꞃcuꞃ ꞃ꞉n, ꞡuꞃ ꝺó cuan aꞃ cıunacaꞇꝺ, ocuꞃ cuıle aꞃ cꞃáꞡꞁaꝺ ocuꞃ aꞃꝺ ꞡoecꞁ aꞃ nımꞇecꞁc a cꞇꞡeꞃncuꞃ ꞇaꞃ ꝺcꞃeꞇṁꞃꞇ. Sloıꞡeꝺ móꞃ le ꞃꞇꞡ Saxan ꞇ nαlbaın, ocuꞃ caꞇꞃaꝺa ꞇmꝺa ꝺo ꞡaꝺáıl ꝺoıꝺ ꞇnncı; ocuꞃ anc ꞇaꞃla ꞃuaꝺ .ı. Rıcaꞃꝺ a búꞃc, ocuꞃ Ꞡaıll ocuꞃ Ꞡoeıꝺel ꞇmꝺa ꝺo ꝺul a ꞁCꞃꞇnn coꝺꞁlac móꞃ, ocuꞃ neꞃc ꝺo ꞡaꝺáıl a nαlbaın ꝺóıꝺ ꝺon- ꝺulaꝺ ꞃꞇn. Ceꞃóıꝺ a búꞃc .ı. ꝺeꞃbꞃacꞁaıꞃ ꝺon ꞇaꞃla, ꝺo éꞡ á Caꞃꝛaıꞡ Ꝼeꞃꞡuꞃa oıꝺce Noꝺlac ꞇaꞃ ceacꞁc ónc ꝼluaıꞡeꝺ

---

1 *Cnoc-in-mhadhma*; i.e. "the hill of the defeat," seemingly the name of some hill in Tir-Conaill.

2 *The Cuchullainn.* Cuchullainn, the Cuthullin of Mac Pherson, was one of the principal heroes of the ancient Irish, whose valour, prowess, and accomplishments, have been much celebrated by Irish writers from the earliest times. For some interesting notices of his career, see Mrs. Ferguson's *Story of the Irish before the Conquest*, p. 83, *et seq.*

3 *Clann-Dalaigh.* Descendants of Dalach, who died A.D. 868, and from whom his descendants, the O'Donnells of Tir-Conaill, have derived the tribe name of Clann-Dalaigh.

A.D.
[1303.]

gone to commit a depredation in Cairpre. Toirdhelbhach, son of Domhnall Og O'Domhnaill, who was usually called " Toirdhelbhach of Cnoc-in-mhadhma,"[1] i.e. the king of Tir-Conaill during twelve years, both in it and out of it— a warlike, active man, and the Cuchullainn[2] of the Clann-Dalaigh[3] in valour—was slain by Aedh, the son of Domhnall Og, i.e. his own brother, after a long war, and after much destruction had been committed on all sides throughout the country, and a prodigious slaughter along with him of the Cenel-Eoghain, and the chiefs of the Foreigners of the North, and of the Cenel-Conaill themselves likewise, and Muirchertach Mac Fhlannchaidh, chieftain of Dartraighe. Donn O'Cathain, king of Feara-Craibhe and Cianachta, was slain there, and Donnchadh Mac Menmain and Aedh Mac Menmain—the two grandsons of the Ferleighinn[4] O'Domhnaill ; and Niall, son of Niall O'Baighill, the good material of a chieftain of the Three-Tuatha ; Mac Ughossa[5] and his son, and his brother, and Adam Sandal, and numerous Foreigners and Gaeidhel besides. And Aedh O'Domhnaill resumed his own sovereignty after this great triumph, so that after a while his government was like a sea growing calm, a tide ebbing, and a high wind subsiding.[6] A great hosting by the King of the Saxons to Alba, when they took several cities ; and the Red Earl, i.e. Richard Burk, and a great many Foreigners and Gaeidhel, went from Erinn with a large fleet, and obtained sway in Alba on this occasion. Tibbot Burk, i.e. the Earl's brother, died at Carraig-Fergusa on Christmas night, after returning from this

---

[4] *The Ferleighinn*; lit. "the Lector."

[5] *Mac Ughossa.* In the Annals of Connacht (Dublin copies) the name of this individual is written ꟺac .h.ꞡoꞃꞃa, "son of O'Gossa;" but Mageoghegan, in his version of the Annals of Clonmacnois, Anglicises it "O'Heossy," a name now represented by Hosey, or Hussey, and sometimes corruptly written Oswell.

[6] *Subsiding.* These similes, which are not found in the so-called Annals of Connacht, are used to signify the general lull that succeeded the resumption of the sovereignty of Tir-Conaill by Aedh O'Domhnaill.

2 M

ṁn. Domnall óᵹ Mac Carṫaiᵹ, ṙí Dermuman, morṫuur erṫ. Maᵹnur Mháᵹ Samraḋáin, dux Tellaᵹ Eċaċ, occirur erṫ. Niall Mac Ᵹillaṙinnen morṫuur erṫ. Muirir, mac Uilliam ᵹalloa Mhéᵹ Eoċaᵹain, hi quarṫ noin Iuin quieuiṫ.

Ctt. Enair ror Ceooein, ocur rechṫmao ṫéc ruirre; anno Domini M.ccc.quarto; octauur annur cicli rolarir; xiii. annur cicli lunarir; recunoo inoicṫionir. Maċa mac Ᵹilla Irra hi Raiᵹilliᵹ, ri Breirne, oo ṁarbaḋ oo Tellaċ Dhúnchaoa ar Achao na corra, ocur a ᵹallóᵹlaiċ oo ṁarbao maille rrir ann. Maᵹ Samraḋáin ocur Máᵹ Dhorċaiḋ oo ᵹuin ann ṫór rarú. In ċonooeir .i.ben Rioveroo a Búrc .i. Iarla Ulaḋ, morṫua erṫ. Uáṫṫer a Búrc, oiᵹri inn Iarla ceona rin, ṫéc irin mbliaoain rin. Conchobar, mac Oeṫa hi Conchobair, oo marbao la Toirberṫ .h.bḟhlaiṫberṫaiᵹ, ar noenum ṫuirril ocur meṫla ṫórum ar Dhonnchao .h.ḟhlaiṫberṫaiᵹ; ocur in Toirberṫ hírin oo ṫuiṫim ar an laṫair ceona rin. Uilliam óc, mac Uilliam ᵹalloa Mhéᵹ Eochaᵹan, quieuiṫ hi prio io Octimbir in hoc anno.

Ctt. Enair ror Oeine, ocur ochṫmao richeo ruirre; A.D. M.ccc.quinto.; ix. anno cicli rolarir; xiiii. anno cicli lunarir; terṫio anno inoicṫionir. Muircerṫach .h.Conchobair Ḟhailᵹe, ocur Moelmórḋa a braṫair eli, .i. an Calbach .h.Conchobair, ocur nonbar ar richiṫ oia muinṫir maille rriú, oo ṁarbao oo ṙir Piarur Mac Ḟheoruir a meṫail ᵹránna, a cairlen Mic Ḟheoruir. Maiṫm la hAoḋ mac Cathail hi Conchobair, ocur la Clainn Muirċerṫaiᵹ airchena, ar Muinnṫer Raiᵹilliᵹ, co torchair ann Pilip .h. Raiᵹilliᵹ, ocur oiᵹri Chlainne Suiṫne, ocur Mháᵹ

1 *William Galldha;* i.e. "William the Foreign (or the Anglicised);" so called from his relations with the English.

2 *Octavus.* octaḃó, MS.

3 *Toirbert.* This name is written

ħoiberṫ, i.e. "Hubert," by the Four Masters.

4 *His other brother Maelmordha.* The Four Mast. are more correct in making the Calvach "the other bro-

hosting. Domhnall Og Mac Carthaigh, King of Des-
Mumha, mortuus est. Maghnus Mac Shamhradhain, dux
of Tellach-Echach, occisus est. Niall Mac Gillafhinnen
mortuus est. Maurice, son of William Galldha[1] Mac
Eochagain, quievit on the fourth of the nones of June.

The kalends of January on Wednesday, and the seventeenth of the moon; anno Domini M.CCC. quarto; octavus[2]
annus cycli solaris; xiii. annus cycli lunaris; secundo
Indictionis. Matthew, son of Gilla-Isa O'Raighilligh,
king of Breifne, was slain by the Tellach-Dunchadha on
Achadh-na-corra, and his gallowglasses were slain there
along with him. Mac Shamhradhain and Mac Dorchaidh
were wounded there, moreover, along with them. The
Countess, i.e. the wife of Richard Burk, i.e. the Earl of
Ulster, mortua est. Walter Burk, the same Earl's heir,
died in this year. Conchobhar, son of Aedh O'Conchobhair, was killed by Toirbert[3] O'Flaithbhertaigh, after he
had committed wrong and treachery against Donnchadh
O'Flaithbhertaigh; and this Toirbert fell on the very
same spot. William Og, son of William Galldha[1] Mac
Eochagain, quievit the day before the ides of October in
hoc anno.

The kalends of January on Friday, and the twenty-
eighth of the moon; A.D. M.CCC.quinto; ix. anno cycli
solaris; xiiii. anno cycli lunaris; tertio anno Indictionis. Muirchertach O'Conchobhair Failghe, and his
other brother Maelmordha,[4] i.e. the Calbhach O'Conchobhair, and twenty-nine of their people along with
them, were slain by Sir Piers Mac Feorais, in abominable
treachery, in Mac Feorais's castle.[5] A defeat was inflicted by Aedh, son of Cathal O'Conchobhair, and by
the Clann-Muirchertaigh also, on Muinter-Raighilligh, in
which Philip O'Raighilligh, and the heir of Clann-Suibhne,

---

ther," and a different person from
Maelmordha.

  [5] *Mac Feorais's castle.* Mageoghegan calls it "Castle-Feorais." The

ruins of this castle, now known as
Castle-Carbury, in the barony of
Carbury, and county of Kildare, are
still in existence.

2 M 2

Ởhuιρρce .ι. cenὀ ὀο ξαllόξlαοčαιɓ αn τίρe, mαιlle ρe-
ceὀ αρ χl.αιτ ὀο ὀὄειnιɓ elι mαιlle ρριύ. Ởοnnchαὀ
.h.ρlαιɓeρταιξ, eρρυc Cιlle hΌlαιὀ .ι. ιnτ αοιn eρρυc
ιρ ξenmnαιὀe ocυρ ιρ cραιɓὄιξe ὀο ɓί ιn αοn αιmριρ
ρριρ, qυιeυιτ. Ϲοιρρὀhelɓαč mαc Ởριαn ρυαὀ hι
Ởριαιn mορτυυρ eρτ. Μαčα όc .h. Rαξιllιξ ὀο
mαρɓαὀ lα Ϲellαč n'Ởúnchαὀα. Ἀοὄ οξ .h. Ϝeρξαιl ὀο
eξ ιρ-ιn mɓlιαὀαιn ceὀnα ριn. Cαιρρlen nuα Ιnὀρι
hἘοξαιn ὀο ὀenum láραn ιαρlα ρυαὀ ιn ɓlιαὀαιn ριn.

Ιctt. Ἐnαιρ ρορ ρατhαρn ocυρ .ιχ. ριcheὀ ρυιρρe; Ἀ.Ό.
Μ.ccc.ρeχτο; χαnnυρ cιclι ρolαριρ; χυ. αnnυρ cιclι lunαριρ; quαρτο αnno ιnὀιcτιοnιρ. Ϲοιρρὀhelɓαch .h.Ởριαn,
ρι Ϲυαὀṁumαn, ιnτ οen ὀυιne ροɓ οιρeξὄα ocυρ ρο ɓυὀ
mo áξ ocυρ enξnum α comαιmριρ ριρ ρein, mορτυυρ eρτ.
Ởοnnchαὀ .h. Ởριαιn, α mαc ρein, ὀο ριξαὀ nα ιοnαὀ.
Ϝeρξαl Μháξ Rαὀnαιll, ταιρρech Μυιnτιρe hἘοluιρ, ὀο
mαρɓαὀ ὀο Μhαčξαṁαιn Μháξ Rαὀnαιll .ι. α ὀeρ-
ɓρατhαιρ ρein, ocυρ lα ὀροιnξ ὀα οιρechτ ρein, ρeρ
ὀolum. Ϲοξαὀ mόρ ιτιρ Ἀοὄ mαc Ἐοξαιn hι Conchοɓαιρ, ρι Connαchτ, ocυρ mαιče cρίl Μυιρeξhαιξ mαιlle
ρριρ, ocυρ Ἀοὄ mαc Cατhαιl hι Conchοɓαιρ co mοραn
ὀο mαcαιɓ ρίξ ocυρ ταιρeč Connαchτ, ιmαὀοen ρe
τοeιρechαιɓ ocυρ ρe hοιρechταιɓ ρeρ mỞρeιρρne áιρčenα,
ιmόn Sιnυιnn ρρι ρe τρι mίρ no α cethαιρ, conὀeρnαὀαρ
ὀρein ὀο mαcυιɓ ρίξ Ἐeὀα mιc Cατhαιl ρορɓυιρ ιρ nα
Ϲυατhαιɓ mαροen ρe ροchαιὀιρ ιmὄα, ξυρ ξαɓρατ cρechα
mόρα ocυρ αιρξne ὀíαιριṁὄe; ocυρ ρυcρατ τοιρ ṁόρ
ρορρα. Ϝlαnn mαc Ϝιαchρα hι Ϝhlοιnn ὀαṁnα ταιρριξ
cρίl Μhoeιlρυαιn, ocυρ Ởριαn mαc Ởοnnchαὀα ριαɓαιξ

---

[1] *Brian Ruadh* ("Brian the Red").
The Four Masters incorrectly say
"son of Niall Ruadh O'Briain."

[2] *The New Castle*; i.e. Greencastle,
in the parish of Moville, barony of
Inishowen (Inis-Eoghain), and county
of Donegal.

[3] *Twenty-ninth.* ιχ. ριcheὀ; which
should be ιχ., or ninth, in order to
agree with the criteria for the preceding and following years, which
give the age of the Moon on the 1st
of January in each, respectively, as
twenty-eight and twenty.

and Mac Buirche, i.e. the head of the gallowglasses of the
country, together with one hundred and forty other
persons, were slain. Donnchadh O'Flaithbhertaigh, bishop
of Cill-Aluidh, i.e. the most chaste and devout bishop of
his time, quievit. Toirdhelbhach, son of Brian Ruadh[1]
O'Briain, mortuus est. Matthew Og O'Raighilligh was
killed by the Tellach-Dunchadha. Aedh Og O'Ferghail
died in this same year. The New Castle[2] of Inis-Eoghain
was erected by the Red Earl in this year.

The kalends of January on Saturday, and the twenty-
ninth[3] of the moon ; anno Domini M.ccc.sexto ; x. annus
cycli solaris ; xv. annus cycli lunaris ; quarto anno
Indictionis. Toirdhelbhach O'Briain,[4] king of Tuadh-
Mumha, the most illustrious, valiant, and puissant man
of his own time, mortuus est. Donnchadh O'Briain, his
own son, was made king in his place. Ferghal Mac
Raghnaill, chieftain of Muinter-Eolais, was killed by
Mathghamhain Mac Raghnaill, i.e. his own brother, and
by a party of his own tribe, per dolum. A great war
between Aedh, son of Eoghan O'Conchobhair, king of
Connacht, (with whom were the chiefs of the Sil-Muiredhaigh), and Aedh, son of Cathal O'Conchobhair, with
whom were many sons of kings and chieftains of Connacht, together with the chieftains and tribes of the men
of Breifne also ; *and it was waged* on both sides of the
Sinuinn during the space of three or four months, when
a number of the sons of kings attached to Aedh son of
Cathal encamped with large forces in the Tuatha, and
captured great preys, and countless spoils ; but a great
number of pursuers overtook them. Flann, son of Fiachra
O'Floinn, heir to the chieftaincy of Sil-Maelruain, and
Brian, son of Donnchadh Riabhach O'Conchobhair,

---

[4] *Toirdhelbhach O'Briain.* This is
apparently a repetition of the entry
under the preceding year, recording
the death of "Toirdhelbhach, son of
Brian Ruadh O'Briain." The Four
Mast. also repeat the entry.

hI Choncobaip, mápoen pe ooeinib iméa eli, oo rhapbao
ap lunʒ na cpeiče oon tóip, ocup mopan opaʒoóʒ oona
cpeachaib, ocup blaò eli oo ťpeiť app óip. Ippiat tpa
ba pepp oo ťí ap na cpeachaib pin .i· Ruaiòpi mac
Cathail hI Conchobaip, ocup Oonnchao, mac Conchobaip
in čopain, mic Pepʒail, mic Ohonnchaoa, mic Muip-
čeptaiʒ Mic Oiapmaoa, aòbap piʒ Mhuiʒe Luipʒ ocup
Muintipe Mhailpuanaiò ap áʒ, ocup ap oinech, ocup
ap enʒnum conuiʒe in la pin ; ocup ippeo panic poime
pin co Lonʒpopt hI Conchobaip, ocup loipcip pailíp
pi Connacht mapoen pe tiʒiò in Lonʒpuipt. Ɓepip
Oeoh.h.Conchobaip paip in lá pin, ocup benup na
cpecha óe, ocup oičentap hé pein iaptain. Maʒiroip
Tomápp.h.Náan, oipchioechain Raťa ƀoť, ocup toʒa
eppuic na hecailpi ceona hé ƀóp, in Cpipto quieuit.
Roiƀepo Ɓpiuip, mór rhoep Caippʒe, oo ʒabáil [piʒe]
nCClban ap eiʒin inaʒhaio pí Saxan. Oomnall Tuip-
tpeč.h.Neill oo mapbao a tuipiol la lucht tiʒe hI
Neill in hoc anno. Sip Uilliam Ppinoapʒápp, pioipe
ba mó nopp ocup uippoepcup na aimpip pein in Epinn,
moptuup ept. Cpeč rhop oo òenum oo Chlainn Muip-
čeptaiʒ a cpič Caipppi, oú ap mapbao Oauio.h.
Coerháin, ƀpuʒhaio ceoaċ conáiʒ, ocup Oonnchao Mháʒ
Ɓhuiòechain, ocup ooeine iméa eli maille ppiú. Ɓpian
Cappach .h. heʒpa oo rhapbaò la Copmac .h.ƀPhlan-
nacán. Nicól .h.Oonnchaoa, .i. pacapt oo ťí na óiʒ

---

[1] *Whilst protecting*. The text has ap lunʒ na cpeiče, which literally means "in the track of the prey," i.e. following after it and acting as a rere guard.

[2] *Conchobhar - in - chopain*; i.e. "Conchobhar (or Conor) of the cup."

[3] *Palace*. A marginal note in the Dublin copies of the Annals of Connacht observes that pailíp Chluana

Ppaoič, "the palace of Cluain-Fraich" is intended. Cluain-Fraich, or Cloonfree, as the name is now written, is a townland situated a little to the west of Strokestown, in the county of Roscommon, containing an immense square fort within which the "palace" probably stood.

[4] *Domhnall Tuirtrech*; i.e. Domhnall the Tuirtrian, so called from having been fostered in the district of

together with many other persons, were killed whilst protecting[1] this prey by the pursuers, and a great part of the preys was detained, and another part of them was carried off. The most distinguished in committing these depredations were, viz., Ruaidhri, son of Cathal O'Conchobhair, and Donnchadh, son of Conchobhar-in-chopain,[2] son of Ferghal, son of Donnchadh, son of Muirchertach Mac Diarmada, one qualified to be king of Magh-Luirg and Muinter-Maelruanaidh as regards prosperity, bounty, and prowess until this day. And he (*Donnchadh Mac Diarmada*) went before this to O'Conchobhair's fortress, and burned the palace[3] of the king of Connacht, together with the houses of the fortress. Aedh O'Conchobhair overtakes him on the same day, and takes the preys from him ; and he is himself afterwards beheaded. Master Thomas O'Naan, archdeacon of Rath-Bhoth, and also bishop-elect of the same church, in Christo quievit. Robert Bruce, great steward of Carraig, assumed [the sovereignty] of Alba by force, in opposition to the king of the Saxons. Domhnall Tuirtrech[4] O'Neill was slain, by accident,[5] by the household of O'Neill in hoc anno. Sir William Prendergast, the most famous and illustrious knight in his own time in Erinn, mortuus est. A great depredation was committed by the Clann-Muirchertaigh in the territory of Cairbre, when David O'Caemhain, a rich, affluent farmer, and Donnchadh Mac Buidhechain, and many more persons along with them, were slain. Brian Carrach O'hEghra was killed by Cormac O'Flannagain. Nicholas O'Donnchadha, (i.e. who was a priest and

---

Hy-Tuirtre, in the south of the present county of Antrim, for an account of the exact situation and extent of which, see Reeves's *Ecclesiastical Antiquities*, pp. 82, 292-297.

[5] *By accident.* α τυιρϻοl. τυιρεl, abl., τυιρϻοl, is glossed *casus* in a

passage quoted from an ancient Irish MS. by Zeuss (*Gram. Celt.*, vol. i., p. 12). Instead of "α τυιρϻοl," the Four Mast. say "ιn ιομϸαιċne," i.e. through mistake, or unintentionally. But τυιρεl also means "injury," "injustice."

inoraic ı nUruim ēliaē, oo maņbaē oon Ʒheņņan ouē
oona ēaıņéoach, ʒan ćūıņ ʒan ćınaıē acht maņuaē
maņtņa oo ımbeņt ľaıņ; quıeuıt ın Cņıľto; ocuľ ʒać
oen ʒeēuņ ľaıoıņ oo ľaē anma atáıo ņé ľıćıt lá oo
loʒhaō a ľecta aıʒe ʒach mınce uaıņ ʒeēuņ hí.

Ctt. enaıņ ľoņ ōomnach, ocuľ ľıcheō ľuıņņe; anno
Oomını M.ccc.uıı; xı. anno cıclı ľolaľıľ; xuı. anno
cıclı lunaľıľ; quınto anno ınoıctıonıľ. Oonnchaō
Muımnech.h.Cellaıʒ, ľı.h.Maıne, ľóı ćoıtćenō oľeņ-
uıē Eņenn uıle ım bıaō ocuľ ım éoach, ım óņ ocuľ
ım aıņʒeo, ocuľ ım eallać, oo éʒ aņ mbņeıt ēuaōa ó
ōoman ocuľ ó ōemun; ocuľ Taōʒ .h. Cellaıʒ .ı. a
macľōé, oo éʒ ıaľľın. Luıľınt .h.Lachtnán, ab Eľľa
Ruaıo, ocuľ ab na ēuılle athaıo elı, ocuľ ab Chnuıc
Muaıōe ıaľľın, ocuľ eľľuc Cılle Mıc Ouać ľoōeoıʒ, ın
Cņıľto quıeuıt. Conchobaņ mac Ľıachņa hı Ľhloınn,
ouıne óʒ ba ľeņņ coʒao ocuľ ľoʒuıl ľoņ Ʒhalloıē ocuľ
Ʒhoeıoeluıē na aımľıņ ľeın oá ľaıē ı Connachtuıē uıle,
oo héc; ocuľ a aēlucao co huaľľal onoľach a manıľtıņ
na ēuılle maņoen ľı a bņathaıņ. eaćoņuım .h.Maıne
oo loľcao le oņonʒ oo macaıē ľıʒ.h.Maıne ľeın.
Ʒoıll Roľľa Comáın uıle oo ṁaņēao le Oonnchao
Muımnech.h.Cellaıʒ ľé na éʒ ľel beʒ, ı nctt eľcņach
Cúan oo ľunoņao, oú atoņchaıľ Pılıp Muınnteņ ocuľ
Sean Muınnteņ ocuľ Máʒıu Oņıú, máņoen le .lxx. ıoıņ
ṁaņēao ocuľ ʒabáıl; áıt ınaņ ʒabao ľıľľıam Roľľa
Commáın, ocuľ Oıaņmaıo Ʒall mac Oıaņmaoa, ocuľ
Coņmac Mac Ceıćeņnaıʒ; ocuľ ľo leıʒeō a ľoľņaıoe
aľľ ēóņņ, ocuľ ľo léıʒeo ıao ľeın ıaľ tņıoll, ocuľ oo
ľóņľat ľıt aľ ľon an ēaıle oo loľcao la hemann

---

1 *Gerran-dubh.* A sobriquet signifying the "Black Horse."

2 *Domini.* ꝺ⁰, MS.

8 *Quinto.* quıncto, MS.

4 *Donnchadh Muimhnech*; i.e. Donnchadh (or Donough) the Momonian.

5 *Made peace.* "Gave satisfaction"
would be a more correct expression.
The entire entry is rather loosely
worded; but it may be inferred from
it that Ath-easerach-Cuan (Ahas-
cragh, in the east of the barony of

pure virgin in Druim-cliabh), was killed, without cause or
offence, by the Gerran-dubh[1] of the Barretts, who subjected him to a martyr's death ; quievit in Christo ; and
every one who recites a pater for the good of his soul has
six score days' remission of his sins as often as he recites it.

The kalends of January on Sunday, and the twentieth
of the moon; anno Domini[2] M.ccc.vii.; xi. anno cycli solaris;
xvi. anno cycli lunaris; quinto[3] anno Indictionis. Donnchadh Muimhnech[4] O'Cellaigh, king of Ui-Maine, the
most generous of all the men of Erinn respecting food and
clothing, gold and silver, and cattle, died after obtaining
victory over the world and the devil; and Tadhg O'Cellaigh, i.e. his son, died afterwards. Laurence O'Lachtnain, abbot of Es-Ruaidh, and for a time abbot of the
Buill, and afterwards abbot of Cnoc-Muaidhe, and ultimately bishop of Cill-Mic-Duach, in Christo quievit.
Conchobhar, son of Fiachra O'Floinn, the best young man
in all Connacht in his own time for making war and
depredations on Foreigners and Gaeidhel, died ; and he
was nobly *and* honourably interred in the monastery of
the Buill, along with his brother. Echdruim-Ui-Maine was
burned by a number of the princes of Ui-Maine themselves.
The Foreigners of Ros-Comain were all slain by Donnchadh Muimhnech O'Cellaigh, a short time before his
death, in Ath-escrach-Cuan, to wit, where Philip Munter,
and John Munter, and Matthew Drew fell along with
seventy others who were either slain or taken prisoners ;
where the sheriff of Ros-Comain, and Diarmaid Gall Mac
Diarmada, and Cormac Mac Ceithernaigh were taken
prisoners ; but their forces were still allowed to depart ;
and they themselves were let go after a while ; and they
afterwards made peace[5] for the burning of the town by

Kilconnell, and county of Galway),
had been burned by Edmond Butler,
who became viceroy of Ireland in
1312, and that O'Kelly had slain

some of the English of Roscommon,
in retaliation for the proceeding, and
detained the sheriff of Roscommon and
others until they made satisfaction.

buiτιléιη ιαηηιη. Θουβαηο móη, ηι Saxan ocuη bηe-
ταη ocuη Αlban, ocuη οιυιce na Ʒαηcuιne, ocuη τιɡeηna
na hEηenn, quιeuιτ ιn Cηιητο, ιηιn cóιɡeο blιαοaιn
οéc aη ғιcheο a ғlaιτιuηa, ocuη ιηιnτ ηeιηηeο blιαοaιn
ηéηcατ a αòιηη. Coηóιn ηι Saxan ocuη bηeαττan, ocuη
Θηenn ocuη Αlban, οο τabaιητ οΘουbαητ óɡ mac
Θ̇οbaιηο ιαηηιη. Oοnnchαο .h.ғlannaɡan, ab na
buιlle ηηι ηe u. mblιαοan, ocuη eηηuc Oleηιnn ηηι ηe
τηι mblιαοan co leιτh, ηeιchem coιτċenn cηαιὸοech
cηιὸech ιαητhaιη Eoηηa uιle; ηeη naη éη οáṁ na
οeoηaιὸ, ocuη naη ιmοeηɡ nech ηιam ηá ὸιαὸ no ηα
ṁoeιnιὸ; cenο comaιηce ocuη caὸuηa ιn cuιcιο co
coιτcenn; ηeη lán οο ɡoeιη ocuη οο ɡlιcuη, ocuη οο
ċoηnum ɡacha caιnɡne ηó τabηaὸ laιṁ; ηeη οeηɡeċ
οeιɡcηιὸeċ, ηeη ηocηaιὸ ηoċaητanach; ηeη buιlιὸ bιnn
bηιαċηach ηé ṁílla macachτa macánτa, quιeuιτ ιn
Cηιητο ιαη mbuaιὸ onɡτa ocuη aιτηιɡe, ocuη he a
τηeablaιτ ηe heοh .u. míη; ιn x°. Ktt 1ulιι quιeuιτ.
Oomnall, [mac Taιὸɡ], mιc bηιaιn, mιc Αιnοηιαηηa,
mιc bηιaιn Luιɡnιɡ, mιc Choιηηοelbaιɡ móιη hι
Conchobaιη, τanaηοe Connachτ uιle, ocuη ιn οamna
ηιɡ οo bu mo τoιce ocuη τηom ċonáċ, ocuη οo bu mo
enech ocuη enɡnum, ocuη ηo bu mo ғlaιτemnuη ocuη
ηeηon οò bí a Connachτ, oιη οob é ғαο a ғeηaιnn
o Choιηηғlιαὸ na Seɡηa co Coel uηqι, οo ṁaηbαὸ
aη ιmmηuacαο le hΑ̇οὸ mbηeιғηnech, mac Cathaιl
ηuaιο hι Conchobaιη; ocuη ιηηé ηuηɡon, .ι. Oιaηmaιο
mac Sιmóιn na τηáɡa; ocuη ηo ɡab Oía aιɡe uaιη
οo ὸí beo ιn aɡhaιο ηιn no co τaηηαιο ғαcaητ ocuη
coηη Cηιητ ocuη onɡαο é aη na ὸaηach; ocuη aοbαċ
ιαηηιη; ocuη ηucαο annηιn οocum Choιηηηleιb a ċoηη,
ocuη ní ηucαο ιηιn aιmηιη ὸeιɡenaċ le οuιne maηὸ

---

1 *Childlike.* macachτa, MS., apparently for macὸachτa, a deriv.
from mac, son, or child.

2 *In x°.* ιn x p̄ū, MS.

3 *Royal heir.* οamhna ηιɡ; usually written ηιοamhna, i.e. "materies
regis."

Edmond Butler. Edward the Great, king of the Saxons, and of Britain, and of Alba, and duke of Gascony, and lord of Erinn, quievit in Christo in the thirty-fifth year of his reign, and in the sixty-sixth year of his age. The crown of the king of the Saxons, and of Britain, and Erinn, and Alba, was afterwards given to young Edward, the son of Edward. Donnchadh O'Flannagain, abbot of the Buill during the space of five years, and Bishop of Oilfinn during the space of three years and a half—the devout, cordial, general protector of all the west of Europe; a man who never refused guest or stranger, and who never offended any one regarding food or property; head of guarantee and respect of the province in general; a man full of wisdom and skill, and who defended every affair which he took in hand; a charitable, good-hearted man; a quiet, amiable man; a courteous, sweet-worded, mild, childlike,[1] honest man—quievit in Christo, after the triumph of unction and penitence, having been suffering during a period of five months: in x°.[2] kalendas Julii quievit. Domhnall, [son of Tadhg], son of Brian, son of Andrias, son of Brian Luighnech, son of Toirdhelbhach Mor O'Conchobhair, tanist of all Connacht, and the royal heir[3] of greatest property and wealth, of greatest hospitality and prowess, of greatest sovereignty and possessions that was in Connacht, (for the extent of his land was from Corr-sliabh-na-Seghsa to Cael-uisce), was slain in an encounter with Aedh Breifnech, son of Cathal Ruadh O'Conchobhair. And the person who wounded him was Diarmaid, son of Simon-na-tragha.[4] And God was merciful to him, for he lived that night, and until he saw the priest, and received the Body of Christ and unction, on the morrow; after which he died. And his body was then taken to Corrsliabh, and there was not taken with a dead body in

---

[4] *Simon-na-tragha.* "Simon of the Strand." Perhaps the name should be printed "Diarmaid son of Simon of the Strand."

comméꝺ α ꞃucαꝺ αꞃ αn ꞃocꞃαꝺe ꞃin ꝺαlṁuıꝺ
ocuꞅ ꝺéꝺıꝺ ocuꞅ ꝺınnılıꝺ, ꝺo mαꞃcꞃlúαᵹαıꝺ ocuꞅ ꝺo
ċeċeꞃnαċαıꝺ, lαıꞃ ꝺocum α ċılle; ocuꞅ ꞃo hαꝺluıceꝺ
co huαꞃꞃαl onoꞃαċ α ċαıꞃꞃe α mαnıꞅꞇıꞃ nα búılle.
Ꞇαꝺc, mαc Ṁhαılꞅechlαınn, mıc ꝺhonnchαꝺα, mıc
ꝺhomnαıll, mıc Mαᵹnuıꞃ, mıc Ꞇhoıꞃꞃꝺhelbαıᵹ ṁóıꞃ
hı Conchobαıꞃ, ꝺo mαꞃbαꝺ le Cαꞇhαl, mαc n'ꝺomnαıll, mıc Ꞇhαıꝺᵹ hı Conchobαıꞃ. Cαꞃꝼꞇoluꞅ mαc αn
Lıαċαnαıᵹ hı Conchobαıꞃ ꝺo ċoᵹα ꝺoċum eꞃꞅucoıꞇe
Oleꞃınn ꝺon ꝺαꞃα leꞇ, .ı. αb nα Ꞇꞃınnóıꝺe αꞃ Loċ Cé
eıꞃíꝺe; ocuꞅ ꞇucαꝺ α ᵹꞃαꝺα α coꞃαıꝺ αꞃꝺα Mαċα;
ocuꞅ ꝺo ꝺí ꞃé ꞇꞃı blıαꝺnα co leıꞇ αᵹ cαıċeṁ ꞇoꞃαꝺ
nα heꞃꞅucoıꞇe, ocuꞅ ꝺo ꞇoᵹhαꝺ ımoꞃꞃo ꝺon leıꞇ elı
mαᵹıꞅꝺeꞃ Mαlαıꞅꞃı Ṁhαᵹ Coeꝺα, ꞇꞃe neꞃꞇ Uıllıαm
Mıc Ꝼheoꞃuıꞅ, .ı. αıꞃꝺeꞃꞅuc Connαchꞇ ın ꞇαn ꞃın. ꝺo
ċóıꝺ ꝺon Roım, ocuꞅ ꝺo ꝺí ꞃe heꝺh ꞇꞃı mblíαꝺαn ınnꞇı,
ocuꞅ ꞇánıc nα eꞃꞅuc íαꞃꞅın. Uıllıαm Mαc Ꝼheoꞃuıꞅ,
αıꞃꝺeꞃꞅuc Connαchꞇ, ꝺo ꝺul ꝺo Roıṁ ın hoc αnno.
Mαoılꞅechlαınn .h. Ᵹαıꞃmleᵹhαıᵹ, αꞃꝺ ꞇαıꞃꞃech Chenel
Móαın, moꞃꞇuuꞃ eꞅꞇ. Mαᵹnuꞃ Ṁhαᵹ Oıꞃechꞇαıᵹ quıeuıꞇ. ꝺıαꞃmαıꝺ mαc ꝺonnchαꝺα ꞃıαbαıᵹ ꝺo mαꞃbαꝺ
lα Moelꞃuαnαıꝺ Mαc n'ꝺıαꞃmαꝺα. Cαꞇhαl mαc Mαᵹ-
nuꞃα ꝺo mαꞃbαꝺ lα Cαꞇhαl mαc ꝺomnαıll mıc Ꞇhαıꝺc
hı Conchobαıꞃ. Ꞇαꝺc, mαc Bꞃıαın, mıc αnꝺꞃıαꞃꞃα,
mıc Bꞃıαın Luıᵹnıᵹ, mıc Ꞇhoıꞃꞃꝺhelbαıᵹ moıꞃ, ꝺo ꝺul
ceım oılıꞇꞃı ꝺoċum mαnıꞅꞇꞃech nα búılle, ocuꞅ α ꝺul
ınnαıbíꝺ mαnαıᵹ leıꞇ ınnꞇe, ocuꞅ α éᵹ ꝺo ᵹαluꞃ αon

1-3 *Droves—garments—cattle.* The text is so obscurely worded that it is not easy to ascertain the object for which cattle and clothing were introduced into the funeral procession, unless to be distributed as alms to the poor, or as dues to the clergy.

4 *Cartholus.* This is an attempt at representing the name Carolus. Under the year 1270, *supra,* where the birth of this ecclesiastic is recorded, he is called "Cathal," the Irish for Charles.

5 *On the one part.* Ware (*Bishops,* at Elphin; Harris's ed. of *Ware,* vol. i., p. 631) says by "one part of the Canons" of the church of Elphin.

6 *Malachi Mac Caedha.* Called Malachy Mac Aedha (or Mac Hugh)

later times such a quantity of droves,[1] and garments,[2] and cattle,[3] of cavalry, and of kerns, as were taken in this procession with him to his sepulchre ; and his remains were nobly and honourably interred in the monastery of the Buill. Tadhg, son of Maelsechlainn, son of Donnchadh, son of Domhnall, son of Maghnus, son of Toirdhelbhach Mor O'Conchobhair, was killed by Cathal, son of Domhnall, son of Tadhg O'Conchobhair. Cartholus,[4] son of the Liathanach O'Conchobhair, i.e. the abbot of the Trinity in Loch Cé, was elected to the bishopric of Oilfinn on the one part,[5] and his degree was conferred in the choir of Ard-Macha ; and he was three years and a half enjoying the profits of the bishopric, when Master Malachi Mac Caedha[6] was, however, chosen on the other part, through the power of William Mac Feorais, at that time archbishop of Connacht.[7] He[8] went to Rome, and remained there during the space of three years, and came back afterwards as bishop. William Mac Feorais, archbishop of Connacht, went to Rome in hoc anno. Maelsechlainn O'Gairmleghaigh, high-chieftain of Cenel-Moain, mortuus est. Maghnus Mac Oirechtaigh quievit. Diarmaid, son of Donnchadh Riabhach,[9] was killed by Maelruanaidh Mac Diarmada. Cathal, son of Maghnus,[10] was killed by Cathal, son of Domhnall, son of Tadhg O'Conchobhair. Tadhg, son of Brian, son of Andrias, son of Brian Luighnech, son of Toirdhelhach Mor, went on a pilgrimage to the monastery of the Buill, in which he assumed the habit of a gray monk ; and he died of one day's illness,

by Ware, *loc. cit.* Mageoghegan, in his version of the Annals of Clonmacnois, sub anno, writes the name "Molussy Magaoy."

[7] *Archbishop of Connacht;* i.e. archbishop of Tuam.

[8] *He;* i.e. Malaitsi Mac Caedha, or Malachi Mac Aedha.

[9] *Donnchadh Riabhach.* "Donough the Swarthy." Probably a son of Donnchadh Riabhach O'Conchobhair, mentioned at the year 1306.

[10] *Son of Maghnus;* i.e. of Maghnus O'Conchobhair, or Manus O'Conor. The Four Masters state that the person slain was Tadhg, the son of Maelechlainn, son of Donough, son of Donnell, son of Maghnus, son of Turlough O'Conor.

λαοι ιαρ mbreiċ ḃuaḋ ó ḋomun ocur o ḋeamun. Αιλλḃe,
inġhen Ταḋċ hi Conchobair, morτua erτ.   Claiηη
Mhuircerτaiġ vo ċechτ a Maiġ Ceτne, ocur arḃanna
criċe Cairbri, ocur morán varbur ṫíre hOililla vo
lorcuv leo, ocur arḃanna in Choruinn mar an ceona
vo ṁilleḋ ocur vo lorcuv ḋoiḃ ; ocur von τoirrrin
ro marbav Ταḋċ mac Maġnura.   Αṁláiḃ mac Αirτ
mic Cathail hi Ruairc vo ṁarbaḋ vo mac Ferġail
ġairḃ Mhéġ Shamraḋáin in hoc anno.

Ιctt. Enair ror luan ocur rrim ruirre ; anno Oomini M.ccc.uiii. ; xii. anno cicli rolarir ; xiii. anno cicli
lunarir ; rexto anno Invicτionir.   Creċ ṁor vo ḋenum
vo Mhoelruanaiḋ Mac Oiarmava ar macaiḃ Oomnaill hi Conchobair a criċh Chairpri.   Creaċ ṁór eli
vo venum vo Ḃrian.h.Ohuḋva, ocur vo ġalloiḃ luiġne,
ocur vo.h.bḟíacraċ ar na macaiḃ ceona rin Oomnaill hi Conchobair. · Creaċ eile lá cloinn Muirċer-
τaiġ ar na macaiḃ rin Oomnaill hi Conchobair, ocur
riav ar nvenum ríḋa ṙú roime rin, ocur ar τabairτ
ḃraiġvi ḋóibh ; ocur τanȝavor clainn Oomnaill íarrin
co Sliaḃ ḋá én ; ocur ni rucrat leo achτ a neich ocur
a néiviġ ocur a nȝroiḃe ; ocur óv ċualavar ȝaill
luiġne ocur.h.bḟíacraċ an ni rin, ro ċinóilret ocur
vo lenrat co Sliaḃ vá en. Αchτ chena ro imróvar mic
Ohomnaill hi Conchobair friu, ocur Mac Oonn-
chava, ȝur ġaḃavur na ȝoill ḃrirret ċuca, ocur ȝur
ċeċevar rompu, ocur τucaḋ maiḋm rorra, ȝurrur
lenrat mic Oomnaill íav co leic Erra vara ; ocur ro
marbaḋ leó Tommac mac ḃhalvair, conrvarla ḃuna
ḟinne, ocur a verḃrathair maille frir, ocur voeine

---

1 *Ferghal Garbh.* "Farrell the
Fierce (or the Rough)." At the end
of this entry, which concludes folio
62 *b* of the vellum portion of the MS.,
the scribe has added the note, mire

rilir rȝnirrτ "I am Philip [qui]
scripsit." See note 4, p. 58, *supra.*

2 *Lec-Esa-dara*; lit. "the flag (or
flat rock) of Es-dara," or Ballysadare,
county of Sligo.

after obtaining victory over the world and the devil.
Ailbhe, daughter of Tadhg O'Conchobhair, mortua est.
The Clann-Muirchertaigh went into Magh-Ceidne, and
the corn crops of the district of Cairbre, and a great part
of the corn of Tir-Oililla, were burned by them; and
the corn crops of the Corann also were destroyed and
burnt by them; and it was on this expedition that Tadhg,
son of Maghnus, was slain. Amhlaibh, son of Art, son of
Cathal O'Ruairc, was killed by the son of Ferghal Garbh[1]
Mac Shamhradhain in hoc anno.

[1308.]

The kalends of January on Monday, and the first
of the moon; A.D. M.ccc.viii.; xii. anno cycli solaris;
xvii. anno cycli lunaris; sexto anno Indictionis.   A
great depredation was committed by Maelruanaidh
Mac Diarmada on the sons of Domhnall O'Conchobhair, in the territory of Cairbre.   Another great depredation was committed by Brian O'Dubhda, and the
Foreigners of Luighne, and the Ui-Fiachrach, on
the same sons of Domhnall O'Conchobhair.   Another
depredation was committed by the Clann-Muirchertaigh
on these sons of Domhnall O'Conchobhair, after they
had previously made peace with them, and given them
hostages.   And the sons of Domhnall proceeded after
this to Sliabh-dha-en, and took with them only their
horses, accoutrements, and steeds; and when the Foreigners of Luighne and the Ui-Fiachrach heard this, they
mustered and followed to Sliabh-dha-en.   The sons of
Domhnall O'Conchobhair, however, and Mac Donnchadha
turned upon them, and the Foreigners suffered a defeat,
and fled before them, and were routed; and the sons of
Domhnall pursued them to Lec-Esa-dara;[2] and Thomas[3]
Mac Walter, constable of Bun-finne, and his brother
along with him, and many other persons, were slain by

---

[3] *Thomas.* The MS. reads Commac.
The form in the Annals of Connacht
is Comas. The person slain was
probably Thomas, son of Walter Burk.

ιmɓα elι. Cpeč ṁóp oιxαlτα oo ɓenum ɓαͨoɓ ṁαc
Cατhαιl αp Ruαιopι ṁαc Cατhαιl, pop α oepbpατhαιp
peιn, ocur Mαχnuιp mαc Mαχnuιp oo mαpbαo lαιp αnn,
ocur oαoιne elι nαch αιpṁτep punn. Ͷoṁnαll mαc
Comαpbα Commáιn hI Conchobαιp, αιpčιoechαιn Ole-
pιnn, quιeuιτ. Sιmón.h.Pιnoαchτα quιeuιτ ιn Cpιrτo.
Imop Mαc Xéɓenoαιχ mopτuur epτ. Pιαppur Cαpur-
τón, pιoιpe po uαppαl, ocur lαn pep χpαoα pí Sαxαn,
oo τeαchτ ι nepιnn, ocur .h.Ͷιumαppαιχ oo ṁαpbαo
lαιp ιpιn mblιαoαιn ceonα. Soιχnen τeneo oo τuιτιm
oo nem ιnouαpp ι mαnιrτιp Roppα Commáн, χup
bpιr ιn mαnιrτιp oιoče pele Sͨoeppαιn ιαp Noolαιc
móιp. Cαιpc αmmí ṁαpτα ιn hoc αnno, ocur oíͨ pop
ɓαoιnιɓ ocur pop čeτpαιb ιnnτι, ocur oοιneno ṁóp pop
ιnnτe.

|Ctt. Θnáιp pop Ceoáιn ocur αιlι ɓéc puιppe; αnno
Ͷomιnι M.ccc.ιx.; xιιι. αnno cιclι polαpιr; xuιιι. αnno
cιclι lunαpιr; uιι. αnno Inoιcτιonιr. αͨoɓ, mαc Θoχαιn,
mιc Ruαιopι, mιc αͨoɓα, mιc Cατhαιl cpoιɓoepc, pí Connαchτ, ocur αͨɓαp pι Θpenn ocur αpoιle oo cpιochαιb,
αp uαιrle ocur αp enech ocur αp enχnum, αp oeιlɓ ocur
αp ɓeχι ɓenuιm, oo mαpbαo lα hOeͨoɓ mͷpeιppnech mαc
Cατhαιl puαιͷo hI Conchobαιp, ι Coιll ιn člαͨáιn ι cpιͨ
ͷpeιppne, ocur mopán elι oo ṁαιτhιb Connαchτ mαlle
pμιr, .ι. Conchobαp Mαc Ͷιαpmαoα, ocur Ͷιαpmαιo
puαͷo mαc Ταιoc mιc αͨnoριαppα hI Conchobαιp, ocur.
Ͷιαpmαιo mαc Cατhαιl čαppαιχ Mιc Ͷιαpmαoα, ocur
αͨoɓ mαc Muιpčepταιχ mιc Ταιoͨoχ mιc Mhαoιlpuαnαιͷo,

---

them. A great retaliatory depredation was committed by Aedh,[1] son of Cathal, on Ruaidhri son of Cathal,[2] his own brother; and Maghnus,[3] son of Maghnus, was slain there by him, and other persons not enumerated here. Domhnall, son of Comarb-Comain[4] O'Conchobhair, archdeacon of Oilfinn, quievit. Simon O'Finnachta quievit in Christo. Imhar Mac Gebhennaigh mortuus est. Piers Gaveston, a very noble knight, and prime favourite of the king of the Saxons, came to Erinn; and O'Diumasaigh was slain by him in the same year. Lightning fell down from heaven on the monastery of Ros-Comain, which broke down the monastery, on the night of the festival of Stephen after Great Christmas. Easter in the month of March in hoc anno; and there was destruction of people and cattle in it,[5] and also great inclemency of weather in it.[5]

The kalends of January on Wednesday, and the twelfth of the moon; A.D. M.CCC.IX.; xiii.[6] anno cycli solaris; xviii. anno cycli lunaris; vii. anno Indictionis. Aedh, son of Eoghan, son of Ruaidhri, son of Aedh, son of Cathal Crobhderg, king of Connacht—and one fit to be king of Erinn and other lands for nobility, and bounty, and prowess, for figure and comeliness—was slain by Aedh Breifnech, son of Cathal Ruadh O'Conchobhair, in Coill-in-chlachain in the territory of Breifne; and many more of the nobles of Connacht were slain along with him, viz., Conchobhar Mac Diarmada, and Diarmaid Ruadh, son of Tadhg, son of Andrias O'Conchobhair; and Diarmaid, son of Cathal Carrach Mac Diarmada; and Aedh, son of Muirchertach, son of Tadhg, son of Maelruanaidh;

---

mistake of eight years has been committed, the number nineteen being given instead of twenty-seven, which is the correct enumeration. A greater mistake has been committed under the year 1231, which is represented as the 19th instead of the 8th of the solar cycle. But as these errors do not affect the accuracy of the chronology, which is otherwise sufficiently exact, it has not been thought necessary to correct them as they occur.

2 N

ocuſ Διαρmaιο óc .h.hεlιδε, ſlaιτ bρυghaιο cévach
conaιʒ, ſιal, ſοιſοιnεch, ocuſ Mοεlοοṁnaιʒ ʒallóʒlaεč,
ocuſ ʒιlla na noεm Mac Ccovacán, ollam Connachτ
ſε ſεinεchuſ, ocuſ ſóι coιṁδεſſ čοιττεnn ιn ʒach cεſο
αιſčεna, vo τuιτιm von lucht ſοιſ ιſιn lo cεvna, ocuſ
ſaʒaſτach.h.ɒoῦaιlén vo lucht τιʒε Tomalταιʒ Mιc
ɒonnchava, ocuſ voειnε ιmṡa εlε mallε ſſ ́ ſιn;
ocuſ nιſ luʒa ιna cεv ιn εſbuv vιῦlιnaιῦ.   Ccοῦ bſειſſ-
nεch vo čοιʒεchτ ιſ τιſ ιaſſιn, ocuſ na τſι Τuaṫa vo
τεcht ιna ṫεch.

ιmṫuſa Mhοεlſuanaιδ Mιc ɒhιaſmava, ſι Muιʒε
Luιſʒ, τaιnιc ſιδéιn cona ṫóιčιm τεʒlaιʒ ocuſ τſuιm
ṫιnóιl ιna ṫιmčεll aſ laſ ṁεδοιn τſίl Muιſεʒhaιʒ,
vo čοſnum ſιʒε ocuſ ſlaιτιuſa vιa ṡalτa .ι. vſhειδlιm
.h.Conchobaιſ, ocuſ vo čuιſ τεchτa voċum a ṫaſav
ʒall.ocuſ ʒoειvεl aſ ʒach lειth, ocuſ vo ιnnſοιʒεv
Uιllιam búſc cona bſaιṫſιῦ; ocuſ τaιnιcſιδé co τιn-
nεſnach ſιſιn τεchταιſεcht ſιn; ocuſ ſo ſuιδεſvaſ aſ
mín Mhuιʒε hOι, ocuſ aſ ſιaδ Raṫa Cſuachan co
ſειτſεch ſίſčalma, ιmmεſc ιmmιſcιδ ιn τίſε, vá
τáṫuʒhav aſ εʒla ocuſ aſ oṁan na noιſεcht ſιn vo
aonτuʒav lε hCcoῦ mbſειſſnεch mac Caṫaιl hι Con-
chobaιſ, ocuſ vo ʒaῦ ſειn τιʒεſnτuſ na τaoιſεch ocuſ
uſlaṁuſ na nuſſaιʒhεv, ocuſ ſo ṫaῦaιʒ a ċιſſa ocuſ
a čóſanna ocuſ a čánachuſ, ocuſ ſóſ ſo ṫaῦaιʒ ſεοva
ſ ́ινε ocuſ ſlaṫa ſιʒ Connachτ cona uιlε ṡlιʒεva o ῦεʒ
co móſ; ocuſ τucſaτ Sιl Muιſεʒhaιʒ a nvaιnʒεn uιlε

---

[1] *Maeldomhnaigh Galloglaech*; i.e.
Maeldomhnaigh the gallowglass.

[2] *Eastern party.* lucht ſοιſ. This
is apparently corrupt, as ſοιſ is an'
adverb, meaning "eastwards." But
it has been translated "eastern," it
appearing that by lucht ſοιſ the
people of Breifne were intended.

[3] *Went into his house.* This is a
mode of expression equivalent to

saying that the people of the "Three
Tuatha" submitted to Aedh Breifnech
(Hugh the Breifnian) O'Conchobhair.

[4] *For himself.* This portion of thē
text is very confusedly written. In
the preceding sentence it is stated
that Maelruanaidh MacDermot's object in coming into the territory of
Sil-Muiredhaigh was to defend the
sovereignty for his foster son, Fedhlim

and Diarmaid Og O'hElidhe, a wealthy, generous, digni-
fied prince-farmer, and Maeldomhnaigh Galloglaech;[1]
and Gilla-na-naemh Mac Aedhagain, chief professor of
Connacht in law, and a man equally eminent in all other
sciences, fell by the eastern party[2] on the same day,
and Foghartach O'Dobhailen by the household band of
Tomaltach Mac Donnchadha; and many other persons
fell along with these.   And the loss on both sides was not
less than one hundred.   Aedh Breifnech came into the
district afterwards, and the "Three Tuatha" went into
his house.[3]

As regards Maelruanaidh Mac Diarmada, king of
Magh-Luirg, he came, surrounded by his household
troops and heavy muster, into the very middle of Sil-
Muiredhaigh, to defend the sovereignty and supremacy
for his foster-son, i.e., for Fedhlim O'Conchobhair, and
sent messengers to his friends on every side, both
Foreigners and Gaeidhel, and unto William Burk and his
brothers, who came quickly on receiving the message.
And he (*Maelruanaidh*) encamped strongly, ever power-
fully, on the plain of Magh-Ai, before Rath-Cruachan,
amidst the inhabitants of the country, to conciliate them,
for fear and terror lest these tribes should unite with Aedh
Breifnech, son of Cathal O'Conchobhair; and he himself[4] received the government of the chieftains, and the
submission of the sub-chieftains.   And he exacted his
rents, and his stipulations, and his tributes; and he exacted, moreover, the family and princely jewels of the
king of Connacht, with all his dues both small and great.
And the Sil-Muiredhaigh all pledged their engagement

O'Conchobhair; but here he is represented as obtaining the sovereignty himself, and exacting the
rights and privileges attaching thereto.   Some words have probably been
omitted by the transcriber in this

place, unless the expression, "ᴅo
ᵹaḃ ꝼeın ᴄıᵹeꝑnᴄuꝑ," &c., i.e.
"he [Maelruanaidh] himself received
the government," is by mistake
for "ᴅo ᵹaḃ ꝼeᴅlım ᴄıᵹeꝑnᴄuꝑ,"
"Fedhlim assumed the sovereignty."

ocur a luġa na cippnóír in cizepncur do neoċ oile
achc dópum chena. Canic Moelpuanaiḋ ocur Uilliam
búpc maille pe píl Muipeġhaiġ co hOilpinn. Dála
Ccoḋa mic Cathail, imoppo, do ċuaiḋ a conne in 1apla
irin Miḋe, ocur do impóipioc na cuaċa innoinechc
paip dia éir. 1ap cechc dCcoḋ bpeippnech appan
Miḋe po puiḋercap i nUachcap ċípe, ocur do póne
cpeċ ṁop ap Ccoḋ.h.bḟlannaġain iappin, ocur po
ċaiċcpcaip in cpeċ pin ino Uachcap ċípe. Conchobap
mac Donnchada h1 bpiain do ṁapbaḋ do Ʒalloib co
duḃ a mebail. Cathal mac an Liaċanaiġ h1 Conchobaip, 1. app na Cpinnóide, do cóġa docum eppucoide
Oilepinn. Ruaidpi mac Cathail ocur.h.ḟloinn do dul
ap an maċaipe, ocur mac Mic ḟheopuir do mapbaḋ
leo don dulaḋ pin. Coinne dḟoġpa ecip mac Cathail
ocur Uilliam búpc aʒ Cċh Slippen, ocur bpippeḋ
coinde do cochc ecoppa, ocur maiḋm do ċabaipc ap
mac Cathail, ocur dpong ṁop dia muincep do mapbaḋ
and. Uilliam búpc do ḋul co mainipcip na buille
iappin, ocur apḃaip imḋa do ṁilleḋ ocur do lopcuḋ
innce. Mac Uilliam do dul cap pliaḃ píop, ocur mac
Cathail do chup ap a lonʒpuipc dó, ocur Donnchaḋ
.h.ḟionnachca do mapbaḋ do ċoipech pluaiġ Mic
Uilliam, ocur daoine eli nach aipiṁcep punn. Cpeċ
do ḋenum la Mac Uilliam ap Cloinn ḟepmaide,

---

[1] *To him;* i.e. to Maelruanaidh,
unless the text is corrupt, which is
not unlikely. In Mageoghegan's
version of the Annals of Clonmacnois the Sil-Muiredhaigh are made
to pledge themselves "to Felim, the
said Moilroney's foster son." The
Four Masters state that the Sil-
Muiredhaigh conferred the lordship
on Ruaidhri, the son of Cathal O'Conor
[i.e. the brother of Aedh Breifnech];
but this is most probably a mistake.

[2] *Tuatha.* The "Three Tuatha," or

"three Territories"; ancient districts
in the present county of Roscommon.

[3] *In Uachtar-thire.* The Annals of
Connacht say, ina lonʒpopc pein i
nuachcap ċípe, "in his own camp
in Uachtar-thire."

[4] *Wickedly.* co duḃ; lit. "blackly."
This event is repeated under the next
year (the last entry), where O'Briain,
or O'Brien, is stated to have been
slain do na Ʒallaib duḃa, "by
the Black Foreigners," which is also
the expression used by the Four Mas-

and oaths that they would not give the sovereignty to any other person but to him[1] alone. Maelruanaidh and William Burk went to Oilfinn, together with the Sil-Muiredhaigh. As to Aedh, son of Cathal, however, he went to meet the Earl in Midhe, and the Tuatha[2] at once turned against him when he had left. After Aedh Breifnech came out of Midhe, he encamped in Uachtar-thire, and subsequently took a great prey from Aedh O'Flannagain, and consumed this prey in Uachtar-thire.[3] Conchobhar, son of Donnchadh O'Briain, was wickedly[4] slain by Foreigners, in treachery. Cathal, son of the Liathanach O'Conchobhair, i.e., the abbot of the Trinity,[5] was elected to the bishopric of Oilfinn. Ruaidhri, son of Cathal, and O'Floinn went upon the Machaire;[6] and the son of Mac Feorais was slain by them on that occasion. A meeting was proclaimed between the son of Cathal[7] and William Burk, at Ath-Slissen; and a rupture took place between them, and the son of Cathal was defeated, and a great number of his people were slain there. William Burk went subsequently to the monastery of the Buill, and much corn was destroyed and burned in it. Mac William went down beyond the mountain,[8] and the son of Cathal[9] was expelled from his fortress by him; and Donnchadh O'Finnachta was slain by the captain of Mac William's army; and many other persons not enumerated here *were also slain.* A depredation was committed by Mac William on the Clann-Fermaighe;[10] and another predatory expedi-

---

ters, who have the entry under the year 1310.

[5] *Abbot of the Trinity;* i.c. Trinity Island in Loch-Cé.

[6] *The Machaire.* Machaire Chonnacht, or the "plain of Connacht;" the level part of the county of Roscommon, lying between Elphin and Strokestown.

[7] *The son of Cathal;* i.e. Ruaidhri,

the son of Cathàl O'Conchobhair, and brother of Aedh Breifnech.

[8] *The mountain.* Corrsliabh, or the Curlieu hills, on the borders of the counties of Roscommon and Sligo.

[9] *The son of Cathal.* The Four Masters say "Ruaidhri, the son of Cathal."

[10] *Clann-Fermaighe.* See note 3, p. 350, *supra.*

ocur cneč ele λαιr go beinn Ghulbain ocur τairri buð ťuaið.

Ictt. Enair ror ðarðaoin, ocur a trerr richeð ruirre; anno Domini M.ccc.x.; xiiii. anno cicli rolarir; xix. anno cicli lunarir; octauo anno Inoictionir.[1] Tanaiðe mór .h.Moelconare, ollam Shil Muireghaigh[2] Muilleťain re riliðecht ocur re rencur, ðo éc i torrach na bliaðna rin irinð errach cruaið. Cneč mór, rrir i nabarťaoi crech in tóiten,[3] ðo ðenum ðOcoh breirrnech mac Cathail hi Conchobair ar Moelruanaið Mac nDiarmaða, i Clochar hi Muir- gile, ocur Donnchað mac Donnchaða Mic Diarmaða ðo gabáil ann, ocur a ben, .i. ingen hi Fhlannagain, ðo marbað ann ťór; mná ocur lenim, ocur ðaeine imða eli ðo marbað ocur ðo lorcuð ann, ocur long- port ðo gabáil ðóir inð Uachtar ťíre re hucht Mic Diarmaða. O ðo čualaið Uilliam búrc in ní rin ro gaď longport a Cill Lommað ar inchaib[4] Coða mic Cathail. Ir annrin ðo cuir Coð mac Cathail techta co hinčleiťe ðočum a brathar .i. Ruaiðri mac Cathail, ða raða rrir techt maille re reðuin, ocur ðul co cairlén buna rinne taréir Uilliam búrc ðá rágťail. Dála Ruaiðri mic Cathail, imorro, ocur Coða mic Mhaȝnura, ocur muinntire Coða breirrnigh, ro činóil- ret ðiblínuið, ocur ðo airȝret ocur ðo loircret cairlen bhona rinne co nuile maiťer. Dala Oeða mic Cathail, ir amlaið ro ťóiriðe in tan rin ocur buannaða ðo čeiťirn congabála ina ročáir agá iomčoiťéð; ocur

---

tion was made by him as far as Benn-Ghulbain, and
beyond it northwards.

The kalends of January on Thursday, and the twenty-
third of the moon; A.D. M.CCC.X.; xiiii. anno cycli solaris;
xix. anni cycli lunaris; octavo[1] anno Indictionis. Tanaidhe Mór O'Maelchonaire, chief professor of Sil-Muiredh-
aigh-Muillethain[2] in poetry and history, died in the
beginning of this year, in the hard spring. A great
depredation, which was usually called "Crech-in-tóiten,"[3]
was committed by Aedh Breifnech, son of Cathal O'Conchobhair, on Maelruanaidh Mac Diarmada, in Clochar-
Ui-Muirghile; and Donnchadh, son of Donnchadh Mac
Diarmada, was taken prisoner there, and his wife, i.e.
the daughter of O'Flannagain, was killed there; *and
several other women, children, and men were killed and
burned there; and they (*the depredators*) established
themselves in Uachtar-thire, to watch Mac Diarmada.
When William Burk heard this thing he encamped at
Cill-Lommad, in front[4] of Aedh, son of Cathal. Then
it was that Aedh, son of Cathal, secretly sent messengers to his brother, i.e. Ruaidhri son of Cathal, desiring
him to proceed with a band, and go to the castle of
Bun-finne, which William Burk had left. As regards
Ruaidhri son of Cathal, moreover, and Aedh, son of
Maghnus, and Aedh Breifnech's people, they all mustered,
and plundered and burned the Castle of Bun-finne,
with all its contents. As to Aedh, son of Cathal, he
had at that time by him some buannadha[5] belonging
to a defensive band who were protecting him; and

---

transactions (Annals of Clonmacnois)
corresponds with the account above
given, translates ꝛ ınchaıb "in the
sight of;" but the correct meaning is
"in front of," "in presence of," or
"before."

[5] *Buannadha.* Buannadha, or buan-
naghta, were persons employed in

military service, for whose maintenance the chief exacted from his subjects a tribute called *buanaght,* or
bonaght. The Anglo-Irish exaction of
"coigne and livery" was an aggrava-
tion of that of the Irish *buanaght.* See
Davis's *Discoverie of the State of Ireland,* London, 1613.

Seonac Mac Uiᵹilin pá cenꝺ ꝺon ċeꞇipɴ conᵹṁáʟα
pin. Αċꞇ chena óꝺ ċonnαιpcpιum mαc hI Conchobαιp
co huαιᵹnech, ꞇαpéιp α muιɴꞇιpe ꝺá ḟáᵹbáιl nα uαꞇhαꝺ
ιαp nιmꞇechꞇ αp pιꞇal ꝺonα ꝼιnne uαꝺα ꝺοιꞇ, po
éιꝺepꝺαιp hé pein ιn ꞇαn pιn conα muιnꞇep, ocuꞃ po
ιnnpαιᵹ mαc hI Conchobαιp ιαp nα ċoᵹαp peme pιn .ι. αp
nᵹeαllαꝺ α ṁαpꞇα αp pupáιleṁ Uιllιαm ꞇupc ꝺo
ċιnn lóιᵹιꝺechꞇα, ocuꞃ mαpꞇuιp Αoꝺ ꞇpeιꝼpnech mαc
Cαꞇhαιl puαιꝺ hI Conchobαιp ιn ꞇαn pιn, αmαιl po
ᵹeαll ꝺo Uιllιαm ꞇupc peme pιn ; ocuꞃ ꝺob é ιnꞇ Αoꝺ
ꞇpeιꝼpnech pιn.h.Conchobαιp αnꞇ αꝺbuꞃ pιᵹ ꝺob ꝼepp
ꝺo ꞇí ι nƐpιnn ιnα αιmpιp pein, ꝺα nꝺconαιᵹeꝺ Dια hí
ꞇó. O pαnιc, ιmoppo, pᵹéʟα ιn ṁαpꞇα Αeꝺα ꞇpeιꝼpnιᵹh
ꝺocum Uιllιαm ꞇupc, ocuꞃ ꝺocum Mιc Dhιαpmαꝺα ocuꞃ
ꞇṁl Muιpeᵹhαιᵹh co Cιll Lomαꝺ αιpchenα, po ᵹluαιpeꝺαp
α ceꝺóιp ꝼop cpeαchαιb ꝺocum ṁuιnɴꞇιpe Αoꝺhα ꞇpeιꝼp-
nιᵹ, ocuꞃ po leιcpeꞇ α pιpꞇe co ꞇennán ꞇpechṁoιᵹe ꞇó
ċuαιꝺ, ocuꞃ co Mαᵹ Céꞇne nα bꝼhoṁópαċ. Iɴɴꞇαιᵹep
Uιllιαm ꞇupc ιαppιn ιnα pιꞇιnᵹ co lαp ṁeꝺοιn ꞇṁl
Muιpeᵹhαιᵹh, ocuꞃ coιnnιṁeꝺιp ꝺα ceꝺ peppénach ꝼoppα
.ι. Mαc Uιᵹιlín conα puꞇꞇα, ocuꞃ nι pαιꝺe bαιle α Sιol
Muιpeᵹhαιᵹ uιle ᵹαn ᵹnαꞇ ꞇuαnnα, nα ꞇuαꞇ ᵹαn ꞇαbαch,
nα ꝼlαιꞇ ᵹαn ꝼoppαch pe ꝼeꝺh ꝼopláṁuιp Uιllιαm ꞇupc
ꝼoppα ꝺαpéιp Αoꝺα. Oꝺ ċonnαιpc Mαolpuαnαιꝺ Mαc
Dιαpmαꝺα α ꞇαlꞇα αp nα ꞇíʟpιuᵹαꝺ po nα ꞇuꞇhαιꝺ,
ocuꞃ ꞇpomα ꞇαbαċ ᵹαch ꞇuαιꞇι nα ꞇιmċell, αchꞇ ċenα po
ṁoꞇhαιᵹ pιum co móp ᵹαιll ιᵹá cenᵹαl ocuꞃ αᵹ α cuιꞇ-
pιuᵹαꝺ ꝺocum bec neιpꞇ, oιp bα ꝺeιmιn lα ᵹαllοιb ꝺá
mαꝺ αnꞇꝼαnn cιpιom nα oenαp comαꝺ leo pειn cóιᵹeꝺ
Connαchꞇ co comláɴ pó commuꞃ. Ippí comαιple, ιmoppo,
αp αp cιnneꝺ lαpαn cuιnᵹιꝺ .ι. α ꞇαlꞇα ꝺo ꞇeᵹ ċócꞇáιl

[1] *Seonac.* Mageoghegan writes this name "Johnock."

[2] *Bonaght.* See note, [5] p. 551.

[3] *Ignored.* αp nα ꞇíʟpιuᵹαꝺ. In Mageoghegan's version of the Annals of Clonmacnois the corresponding expression is "set nought by."

[4] *He;* i.e. Fedhlim O'Conchobhair, MacDermot's foster-son. The text is here very loosely worded.

Seonac[1] Mac Uighilinn was the commander of this defensive band. Nevertheless, when he observed the son of O'Conchobhair quite alone, after his people had departed from him when they went away from him on the expedition to Bun-finne, he armed himself, together with his people, and attacked the son of O'Concho-bhair, against whom he had previously conspired, (i.e. after he had promised to slay him, at the instigation of William Burk, in consideration of a reward); and he then slew Aedh Breifnech, son of Cathal Ruadh O'Conchobhair, as he had before that promised to William Burk. And this Aedh Breifnech O'Concho-bhair was the best qualified to be king that was in Erinn in his own time, if it had pleased God to allow it. As soon as the news of the murder of Aedh Breifnech, moreover, reached to William Burk, and to Mac Diarmada, and to the Sil-Muiredhaigh also, to Cill-Lomad, they immediately proceeded on preying expedi-tions to Aedh Breifnech's people, and sent their bands to Bennan-Brechmhaighe northwards, and to Magh-Cetne of the Fomorians. William afterwards returns back into the midst of the Sil-Muiredhaigh, and quarters two hundred mercenaries upon them, viz.:— Mac Uighilin with his rout; and there was not a town in all Sil-Muiredhaigh without habitual bonaght,[2] nor a district without exaction, nor a prince without op-pression, during William Burk's rule over them after *the death of* Aedh. When, however, Maelruanaidh Mac Diarmada observed his foster-son ignored[3] regarding his inheritance, and the heavy exactions levied from every district around him, he felt strongly that the Foreigners were limiting and restricting him to little power; for the Foreigners were convinced that if he[4] alone were weak the entire province of Connacht would be under their sway. The resolution adopted by the hero, there-fore, was to elevate his foster-son over all on this occa-

óρ čach τon chuρ ριη, ocuρ α ριξατ αρ ειξιη cen ρα
ḟuiρech ; ocuρ ρucuρταιρ λαιρ hé αρ Cαρη Ḟραοιč ṁic
Ḟιτhαιξ, ocuρ το ριξuρταρ αρ αη cαρη hé το ρειρ ηóιρ
ηα ηοεṁ ocuρ Ταconηα Eρρα το ḟuηηρατ, αmαιλ ιρ
ριξτα, ocuρ ιρ οιρεξτα, ocuρ ιρ λιηmuιρe το ριξhατ οeη
τuιηe τά čιηeτh ρειρριη ο ρé Bριαη mιc Echach Μuιτ-
ṁeτόιη ιηηuαρρ ξuρ αη λαιčē ριη. Ιαρ bḟειρ, ιmoρρο,
τḞheιτλιm mαc Οeτα mιc Eoξαιη ρe coιξeτ Conηαchτ,
το ρóιηe α οιτe α ḟριčáιλeṁ ιη οιτčε ριη το ρειρ cuιmηe
ηα ρeη ταοιηeτ ocuρ ηα ρeη λebαρ, ocuρ ιρρι ριη bαηuιρ
ριξ ιρ ριξτα ocuρ ιρ οιρεξτα το ροηατ το ριξ Conηαchτ
ριem ξuρ αη λαιčē ριη. Coρmαc .h.Ḟλαηηαξαη, τáιρρeč
Τuαč Ráčα, το mαρbατ λα hEηρí Μαc Ξιλλαρίηηéη,
ταιρρeč Μuιηητιρe Peoταcáιη, ιmmeαbαιλ. Cαιρλéη
Sλιξιξ το ξeηum λαραη ιαρλα ιη hoc αηηo. Ḟιche τuηηα
ρίοηα το chuρ ρó čιρ α Μαξ Ceτηe. Ḟιηηξuαλα, ιηξeη
Μαξηuρα hΙ Conchobαιρ, quιeuιτ ιη Cριρτο. Μαcραιξ
Μháξξ Uιτιρ, ρίταmηα Ḟeρ Μαηαch, ocuρ Τοηη Μαc
Ξιλλαṁιchιλ, τux Chλοιηηe Conξαιλe, το mιλλeτ ocuρ το
λορcuτ λα Ροαλτ Μhαξ Μhαčξαṁηα. Ḟeρξαλ Μháξ
Τhορchαιτ το héc ιη hoc αηηo. Uηα, ιηξeη Οeτα mιc
Ḟheτλιm, moρτuα eρτ ιη hoc αηηo. Sιυβáη ιηξeη hΙ
Chonchobαιρ Ḟhαλξe, uxορ Μuιρceρταιξ ṁóιρ Μhéξ
Eočαξáιη, ταιρeč Cheηeoιλ Ḟhιαchαιτ, moρτuα eρτ,
Ḟeρξαλ, mαc Μuιρceρταιξ ṁóιρ Μeξ Eočαξαιη, το
mαρbατ ιριη αηξαιλe, ocuρ ιρρί ριη ceτ ḟαλα ηα hαηξαιλι

---

[1] *Carn-Fraich-mhic-Fidhaigh*; the
Carn of Fraech, son of Fidhach; now
Carnfree, near Tulsk, in the county of
Roscommon, where the O'Conors were
usually inaugurated kings of Connacht. The Fraech, son of Fidhach,
from whom Carn-Fraich has been
named, is the subject of a Gaelic
poem published (Edinburgh, 1862)
from the *Dean of Lismore's Book*, by
the Rev. Thomas M'Lauchlan and

Mr. William F. Skene, who would fain
prove (*Dean of Lismore's Book*, p. 54,
note [3]) that Carn-Fraich was in Scotland! "It is not easy identifying the
topography of this poem," they add;
but it would be surprising if the task
were easy, considering the district
(Perthshire) selected by them as the
field of their investigation.

[2] *Es*; i.e. Es-Dachonna, or the
cataract of (St.) Dachonna; also

sion, and forcibly to make him king, without much delay. And he took him with him upon Carn-Fraich-mhic-Fidhaigh,[1] and inaugurated him on the carn according to the practice of the saints, and of Dachonna of Es[2] in particular, in the most regal, most illustrious, and fullest manner that any man of his own family had been inaugurated from the time of Brian, son of Eochaidh Muidhmhedhoin, down to that day. After Fedhlim, son of Aedh, son of Eoghan, had espoused the province of Connacht, moreover, his guardian ministered to him that night in accordance with the traditions of the old men, and the old books; and this was the most regal, and most illustrious wedding feast of a king that had ever been made for a king of Connacht until that day. Cormac O'Flannagain, chieftain of Tuath-Ratha, was slain by Henry Mac Gillafinnén, chieftain of Muinter-Pheodachain, in treachery. The castle of Sligech was erected by the Earl in hoc anno. Twenty tuns of wine were sent ashore in Magh-Cetne. Finnghuala, daughter of Maghnus O'Conchobhair, quievit in Christo. Macraith Mac Uidhir royal heir of Feara-Manach, and Donn Mac-Gillamichil, dux of Clann-Conghaile, were destroyed and burned by Roalbh[3] Mac Mathghamhna. Ferghal Mac Dorchaidh died in hoc[4] anno. Una, daughter of Aedh, son of Fedhlim, mortua est in hoc anno. Siubhán,[5] daughter of O'Conchobhair Failghe, uxor of Muirchertach Mór Mac Eochagain, chieftain of Cenel-Fiachaidh, mortua est. Ferghal, son of Muirchertach Mór Mac Eochagain, was slain in the Anghaile, and this was the first cause of enmity between the people

called Es-mic-Eirc, and now Eas-Ui-Floinn, or Assylin, near the town of Boyle, in the county of Roscommon. For an account of the formalities attending the inauguration of the kings of Connacht, see Hardiman's ed. of O'Flaherty's *Iar Connaught*, p. 139, and O'Donovan's *Hy-Fiachrach*, p. 426.

[3] *Roalbh*. A Hibernicised form of Ralph or Rodolph.

[4] *Hoc.* oc, MS.

[5] *Siubhán;* i.e. Joanna.

ocur Cheneoil Ƒιαchaιδ. Slοιζεδ lá Seffραιζ .h.bƑeρ-
ζαιλ co Ďún Uαδαιρ, αιτ ιnαρ nαρbαδ Ďomnαll mαc
Oeδhα óιζ hι Ƒeρζαιλ, ocuρ Oeδ nάζ Mhαοιλιρρα, ocuρ
ζοƒƒραιζ mαc Muιρcερταιζ. Conchoβαρ .h.bριαιn, mαc
ριζ δοb Ƒeρρ nα αιmριρ, δo nαρbαδ δo nα ζαλλοιb δυδα
ιmmeαδuιλ.

Ɉcττ. Enαιρ ƒορ Ɑοιne, ocuρ cettρι uαthαδ ƒuιρρe;
αnno Ďomιnι M.ccc.xι.; xu. αnno cιclι ρolαριρ; ρριmuρ
αnnuρ cιclι λunαριρ; ιx. αnnuρ ιnδιcτιοnιρ. Muιρcερταch móρ, mαc Conζαλαιζ Meζ Eochαζάιn, δux čeneoιλ
Ƒιαchαιδ mιc Νeιλλ .ιx. ζιαλλαιζ, occιρuρ eρτ ó ζhαλλοιδ.
Cρeč nóρ δίζλα lα Clαιnn Muιρcερταιζ Muιmnιζ α
Connαchταιδ, δάρ nαρbαδ leo ζιλλα Cριρτ, mαc Muιρ-
ζeρρα, mιc Ďhonnchαδα Mιc Ďιαρmαδα, ocuρ Ɑoδ
mαc Cορnαιc, ocuρ Uιλλιαm Mαc ζιλλα Eρράιδ, ocuρ
Ďonnchαδ mαc Čomαλταιζ, ocuρ δáιne mαιče ιmδα
ele mαλλe ƒριu. Ďá mαc Uιλλιαm leιδ α búρc δo
nαρbαδ δonα mαcuιδ ριζ λαιζnechα. Sιuρτάn Ďexe-
ταρ δo čochτ ƒορ cρeιč α Mαζ λuιρc, ocuρ Ταδc
.h.hɑιnlιδe, ταιρρech Cheneoιλ Ďoƒƒα, δo nαρbαδ α
τóραιζechτ nα cρeιce ριn. Ďomnαλλ .h. bιρn, δux
Τhíρe bριuιn, mορτuuρ eρτ. Máιλίρα .h.Ďáλαιζ, ρóι
nδánα ocuρ nenιζ, δo héc ιn hoc αnno. Ďomnαλλ,
mαc Ɑnlαιb, mιc Ɑιρτ hι Ruαιρc, ρι bρeιƒƒne, δo héc
ιn hoc αnno. Slοιζeδ móρ le hUιλλιαm búρc ιριn
Mumαιn ι nαζhαιδ αn Chlάραιζ, ocuρ cαč δo čαbαιρτ
δá čéλι δοιδ, ocuρ .bριρρeδ αρ αn Clάραč, ocuρ mαιδm
móρ δo čαbαιρτ ƒαιρ αnnριn. Uιλλιαm búρc ƒeιn δo
ζαbáιλ αρ δeρeδ α muιnnτeρι, ocuρ ρe αζ lennhuιn αn

1 *Seffraigh.* Geoffrey.

2 *Goffraigh.* Godfrey.

3 *Black Foreigners.* This seems to be a repetition of an entry under the year 1309. See note 4, p. 548.

4 *Descendants of Fiachadh.* Usually called Cenel-Fhiachaidh, from whom the district extending from Parsons-town, in the King's county, to the hill of Uisnech, in the county of West-meath, was called Cenel-Fhiachaidh, or "Kenaliaghe," as the name is written in Anglo-Irish documents.

5 *Niall-nai-ghiallach.* "Niall of

of the Anghaile and Cenel-Fiachaidh. A hosting by
Seffraigh[1] O'Ferghail to Dun-Uabhair, where Domhnall,
the son of Aedh Og O'Ferghail, and Aedh, son of Mael-
Isa, and Goffraigh,[2] son of Muirchertach, were slain.
Conchobhar O'Briain, the best son of a king in his time,
was slain by the Black Foreigners,[3] in treachery.

A.D.
[1810.]

The kalends of January on Friday, and the fourth of
the moon; anno Domini M.ccc.xi; xv. anno cycli solaris;
primus annus cycli lunaris; ix. annus Indictionis. Muirchertach Mór, son of Conghalach Mac Eochagain, dux of
the descendants of Fiachadh,[4] son of Niall-nai-ghiallach,[5]
occisus est by the Foreigners. A great retaliatory depredation *was committed* in Connacht by the Clann-Muir-
chertaigh-Muimhnigh, when Gilla-Christ, son of Muirghes,
son of Donnchadh Mac Diarmada, and Aedh, son of
Cormac,[6] and William Mac Gilla-Erraith, and Donnchadh, son of Tomaltach,[7] together with many other
good men, were slain by them. Two of William Liath
Burk's sons were slain by the Lagenian princes. Jordan
de Exeter came on a predatory expedition into Magh
Luirg, and Tadhg O'hAinlidhe, chieftain of Cenel-Doffa,
was slain in pursuit of this predatory band. Domhnall
O'Birn, dux of Tir-Briuin, mortuus est. Mael-Isa O'Dalaigh, a most eminent man in poetry and hospitality, died
in hoc anno. Domhnall, son of Amhlaibh, son of Art
O'Ruairc, king of Breifne, died in hoc anno. A great
hosting by William Burk into Mumha, against the Clarach;[8] and they gave battle to each other; and the Clarach[8] was worsted, and a great defeat was inflicted on him
there. William Burk was himself taken prisoner in the
rere of his people, whilst he was following up the rout;

[1311.]

---

the nine hostages," or more correctly
"nine-hostage-taking Niall," monarch
of Ireland, who was slain A.D. 405.

[6] *Son of Cormac*; i.e. son of Cormac
Mac Diarmada, or Mac Dermot.

[7] *Tomaltach*. Also a member of
the family of Mac Diarmada.

[8] *The Clarach*; i.e. Richard de
Clare. Cox states that the Burkes
were defeated.

ṁaṫma, ocuʃ ʒɪŏ hé ʃŏ ʒabaɔ ann ɪʃ aɪʒe ɔo ꝟóɪ buaɪŏ
ċoʃcaɪʃ ɪn ċaṫa ʃɪn. Cocaɔ moʃ ɪ Tuaŏmumuɪn ɪʃɪn
mblɪaɔaɪn ʃɪn, ocuʃ caṫ ɔo ṫabaɪʃṫ ɔo Ɔonnchaɔ Mac
Conmaʃa ocuʃ ɔá oɪʃechṫ ʃeɪn, .ɪ. ɔo ṫʃɪċaɪṫ ceɔ
.h.Caɪʃʃɪn, ɪnnaʒhaɪɔ hɪ bʃɪaɪn ocuʃ ʃeʃ Muman uɪle,
ocuʃ Ɔonnchaɔ Mac Conmaʃa ɔo ṁaʃbaɔ ann, ocuʃ
maɪṫe a oɪʃechṫa uɪle; ocuʃ Ɔomnall .h.Ʒʃáɔɔa,
ṫaɪʃeċ Cheneoɪl Ɔúnʒaɪle, ɔo ṁaʃbaɔ ann, ocuʃ áʃ
ʃɪáɪʃṁŏe ɔo ṫabaɪʃṫ eṫuʃʃa ɔɪꝟlɪnaɪꝟ. Ɔonnchaɔ
.h.Ꝟʃɪaɪn, ʃí Tuaŏṁuman, ocuʃ ɔeʒ aŏbaʃ ʃí Eʃenn,
ɔo maʃbaɔ a meꝟuɪl la Muʃchaɔ mac Maṫʒamna
hɪ Ꝟʃɪaɪn. Loċlaɪnn ʃɪabach .h.Ɔeʒhaɪɔ ɔo ṁaʃbaɔ
la Maċʒamuɪn mac Ɔomnaɪll Connachṫaɪʒ hɪ Ꝟʃɪaɪn.
Seonaċ Mac Uɪŏɪlín ɔo ṁaʃbaŏ ɪn Ʒhʃuélaɪʒ a mbaɪle
ṫoʃaɪʃ Ꝟʃɪʒɔe, ocuʃ a maʃbaɔ ʃeɪn ɪnɔ ʃo ceɔóɪʃ, ocuʃ
ŏon ʒeʃʃʃaṁṫhaɪʒ ɔaʃ ṁaʃꝟ ʃé Oeɔh Ꝟʃeɪʃʃnech mac
Ċaṫaɪl ʃuaɪŏ hɪ Conchobaɪʃ ɔo maʃbaɔ é ʃéɪn; ocuʃ
bennachṫ ɔon ṫé ʃuʃmaʃꝟ. Cʃeċ ṁóʃ ɔo ŏenum la
Ʃeɔhlɪm .h.Conchobaɪʃ, ʃɪ Connachṫ, aʃ Cloɪnn Muɪʃ-
ċeʃṫaɪʒ aʃ boʃɔ Mhuɪʒe Ceṫne, ocuʃ Maoɪleċlaɪnn
ṁac Conchobaɪʃ ʃuaɪŏ, ʃʃɪʃ a ʃáɪṫɪ cenn a[n] meɪŏɪl,
ɔo maʃbaɔ ann, ocuʃ ɔaɪne ɪmŏa elɪ maɪlle ʃʃɪʃ ꝟóʃ.
Ɔɪaʃmaɪɔ cleɪʃech .h. Ꝟʃɪaɪn, ʃɪ Muman, ɔo aɪṫʃɪ-
ʒhaɔ, ocuʃ Muɪʃceʃṫach .h.Ꝟʃɪaɪn ɔo ʃɪʒhaɔ na ɪonaŏ
ɪáʃʃɪn. Ꝟʃɪan Mháʒ Mhaċʒamna, ʃí Oɪʃʒɪall, moʃ-
ṫuuʃ eʃṫ.

Kɫɫ. Enaɪʃ ʃoʃ ʃaṫoʃn, ocuʃ xu. ʃuɪʃʃe; anno
Ɔomɪnɪ M°.ccc.xɪɪ.; ʃecunɔuʃ annuʃ cɪclɪ lunaʃɪʃ;

---

1 *Seonac.* This name is written
Johnock, and also John Oge, or
"young John," by Mageoghegan, in
his translation of the Annals of Clonmacnois.

2 *The Gruélach.* The Four Masters
write the name "Gruidelach," which
appears a more correct form; but the

individual so designated has not been
identified.

3 *A blessing.* This prayer is not
found in any other Irish chronicle
except the Dublin copies of the so-
called Annals of Connacht; but Mageoghegan, in his version of the Annals of Clonmacnois, observes "myne

and although he was there taken prisoner, it was he that had the triumph of that battle. A great war in Tuadh-Mumha in this year, and Donnchadh Mac Conmara and his own tribe, viz., *the people of* the cantred of Ui-Caisín, fought a battle against O'Briain and the men of all Mumha; and Donnchadh Mac Conmara and all the chief men of his tribe were slain there; and Domhnall O'Grada, chieftain of Cenel-Dunghaile, was slain there; and a countless slaughter was committed between them on both sides. Donnchadh O'Briain, king of Tuadh-Mumha, and the good material of a king of Erinn, was slain in treachery by Murchadh, son of Mathghamhain O'Briain. Lochlainn Riabhach O'Deghaidh was slain by Mathghamhain, son of Domhnall Connachtach O'Briain. Seonac[1] Mac Uighilin killed the Gruélach[2] in Baile-tobair-Brighde, and was himself immediately slain in return; and it was with the short-handled axe with which he slew Aedh Breifnech, son of Cathal Ruadh O'Conchobhair, that he himself was slain; and a blessing[3] attend the person who killed him. A great depredation was committed by Feidhlim O'Conchobhair, king of Connacht, on the Clann-Muirchertaigh, on the border of Magh-Cetne, and Maelechlainn,[4] son of Conchobhar Ruadh, who was usually called "Cenn-a[n]-meidhil,"[5] was slain there, and several other persons also along with him. Diarmaid Clerech[6] O'Briain, king of Mumha, was deposed, and Muirchertach O'Briain was afterwards made king in his place. Brian Mac Mathghamhna, king of Oirghiall, mortuus est.

The kalends of January on Saturday, and the fifteenth[7] of the moon; anno Domini[8] M°.ccc.xii.; secundus annus

[1312.]

author prayeth God to reward him that killed him [Mac Uighilin], for murthering Hugh Brenagh, as before is recited."

[4] *Maelechlainn.* ṁαoιℓeℓαιnn, MS.; the m being incorrectly marked with the aspirate sign.

[5] *Cenn-an-meidhil;* lit. "head of the harvest band."

[6] *Diarmaid Clerech;* i.e. "Diarmaid the cleric."

[7] *Fifteenth.* The MS. has xu.ᴅec, which is wrong.

[8] *Domini.* ᴅ°., MS.

ın .x. Inꝺıcꞇıonıꞃ. Uıllıαm Mαc Ꝑheoꝛuıꞃ, αıꝛꝺeꝛꝛuc Ꞇuαmα, quıeuıꞇ. ƀenꞇꝺechꞇ .h.ƀꝛαcáın, eꞃꝛuc Luıᵹne, quıeuıꞇ. Mαlαıꞇı Mαc Oeꝺhα ꝺo ꞇoᵹα ꝺocum αıꝛꝺeꝛ- ꝛucoıꝺe Ꞇuαmα α heꝛꝛucoıꝺe Oleꞃınn. Ꝑeꞇꝛuꞃ Cαꝓuꞃ- ꝺún occıꞃuꞃ eꞃꞇ. Cαıꝛc α mí ṁáꝛꞇα ın hoc αnno. Ꝺeꝛƀαıl, ınᵹen Mhαᵹnuꝛα hı Conchobαıꝛ, moꝛꞇuα eꞃꞇ. Cꝛoċ noem ꝺo ꞇocƀáıl α mαınıꞃꞇıꝛ nα ƀúılle ın hoc αnno.

Ⰾⱅⱅ. Enαıꝛ ꝛoꝛ Luαn, ocuꞃ uı.eꝺ ꝛıcheꝺ ꝛuıꝛꝛe ; αnno Ꝺomını M.ccc.xııı. ; ꞇeꝛꞇıuꞃ αnnuꞃ cıclı lunαꝛıꞃ ; xı. αnnuꞃ ınꝺıcꞇıonıꞃ. Clemenꞇ ꝓαpα ın Cꝛıꞃꞇo quıeuıꞇ. Ꝺıαꝛmαıꝺ clépech .h.ƀꝛıαın, ꝛı Ꞇuαꝺṁumαn, moꝛꞇuuꞃ eꞃꞇ. Ꝛoıbeꝛꝺ ƀꝛuıꞃ, ꝛí Albαn, ꝺo ꞇoıᵹechꞇ αꝛ oıꝛeꝛ nα hEꝛenn. Ꝛí Ꝑꝛαnc ꝺo éc ın hoc αnno. Ᵹıllα ıꝛα Mháᵹ Ꝺhoꝛchαıꝺ, ꞇαıꝛꞃech Cenel Luαċáın, ꝺo mαꝛƀαꝺ lá Conchobαꝛ cαꝛꝛαch mαc Ꝺomnαıll Mıc Ꝺıαꝛmαꝺα. Cαꞇhαl mαc Muꝛchαꝺα ċαꝛꝛαᵹ hı Ꝑeꝛᵹαıl moꝛꞇuuꞃ eꞃꞇ. Ꞇıᵹeꝛnán mαc Neıll hı Ꝛuαıꝛc occıꞃuꞃ eꞃꞇ. Ꞇαꝺc, mαc Aınꝺꝛıαꝛꝛα, mıc ƀꝛıαın Luıᵹnıᵹ, mıc Ꞇhoıꝛꝺhelb- αıᵹ moıꝛ hı Conchobαıꝛ, ꝺo éc ın hoc αnno, ıαꝛ mbeꞇ ꝛel ꝛαꝺα ꝺó ı nαıbıꝺ ṁαnαıᵹ leıꞇ, ıαꝛ mbꝛeıꞇ ƀuαꝺα o ꝺomαn ocuꞃ o ꝺemαn ; ocuꞃ α αꞇlucαꝺ co huαꝛꝛαl onóꝛαch α mαınıꞃꝺıꝛ nα ƀúılle.

Ⰾⱅⱅ. Enαıꝛ ꝛoꝛ ṁαıꝛꞇ, ocuꞃ α .uıı. uαꞇhαꝺ ꝛuıꝛꝛe ; αnno Ꝺomını M.ccc.xııı. ; quαꝛꞇuꞃ αnnuꞃ cıclı lunαꝛıꞃ ; xıı. αnnuꞃ ınꝺıcꞇıonıꞃ. Nıαll mαc ƀꝛıαın hı Neıll, .ı. αnꞇ oen mαc ꝛıᵹ ꝺob uαıꝛle, ocuꞃ ꝺob onóꝛαıᵹe, ocuꞃ ꝺob ꝛeꝛꝛ enech ꝺo Chenel Eoᵹαın nα αımꝛıꝛ ꝛeın, ꝺꝛαᵹαıl ƀαıꝛ ın blıαꝺuın ꝛın. Nıαll .h. Ꝺomnαıll

---

1 *William.* This entry is transposed in the original, in which it follows the date m°.ccc.xıı. It is curious that a similar mistake occurs in the Dublin copies of the so-called Annals of Connacht, and in Mageoghegan's version of the Annals of Clonmacnois, where the entry is mixed up with the criteria for the year, thus, "William Breming- ham [i.e. Mac Feorais], archbishop of Twaim, the 2nd day of the Moon, be- fore the 10th indiction died." This is not the only remarkable coincidence between the original from which Ma- geoghegan compiled his chronicle and that of the present Annals, if indeed

cycli lunaris; x. Indictionis. William[1] Mac Feorais, arch-bishop of Tuaim, quievit. Benedict O'Bracain, bishop of Luighne,[2] quievit. Malachi[3] Mac Aedha was elected to the archbishopric of Tuaim from the bishopric of Oilfinn. Petrus Capusdún[4] occisus est. Easter in the month of March in hoc anno. Derbhail, daughter of Maghnus O'Conchobhair, mortua est. The Holy Cross was raised[5] in the monastery of the Buill in hoc anno.

The kalends of January on Monday, and the twenty-sixth of the moon; anno Domini M.CCC.xiii.; tertius annus cycli lunaris; xi. annus Indictionis. Clemens papa in Christo quievit. Diarmaid Clerech[6] O'Briain, king of Tuadh-Mumha, mortuus est. Robert Bruce, king of Alba, came on the coast of Erinn. The king of France died in hoc anno. Gilla-Isa Mac Dorchaidh, chieftain of Cenel-Luachain, was slain by Conchobhar Carrach, son of Domhnall Mac Diarmada. Cathal, son of Murchadh Carrach O'Ferghail, mortuus est. Tighernan, son of Niall O'Ruairc, occisus est. Tadhg, son of Andrias, son of Brian Luighnech, son of Toirdhelbhach Mor O'Con-chobhair, died in hoc anno, after having been a long time in the habit of a gray monk, after triumphing over the world and the devil, and was nobly *and* honourably interred in the monastery of the Buill.

The kalends of January on Tuesday, and the seventh of the moon; anno Domini M.CCC.xiiii; quartus[7] annus cycli lunaris; xii. annus Indictionis. Niall, son of Brian O'Neill, i.e., the noblest, and most honourable, and most bountiful prince of the Cenel-Eoghain in his own time, died this year. Niall O'Domhnaill occisus est. A

---

his original was not the latter. See note 3, p. 558.

[2] *Bishop of Luighne;* i.e. bishop of Achonry.

[3] *Malachi.* maɫaıtı, MS. The Four Masters write the name Maelechlainn.

[4] *Petrus Capusdún.* This is an attempt at writing the name of Piers Gaveston.

[5] *Raised.* ꝺo tocbáıɫ. It is not clear whether the Chronicler meant "was elevated," or "was dug up."

[6] *Diarmaid Clerech.* See note 6, p. 559.

[7] *Quartus.* ꝗrɼꞇo, MS.

occipup ept. Maiồm το ὲabaipt το Ruaiopi mac
Cathail hI Conchobaip pop Mhuinntip Raiᵹilliᵹ αᵹ
Ὀpuim leὲan. Maᵹnup mac Ὀomnaill hI Eᵹpa το
ṁapbaτ la Maᵹnup mac Uilliam hI Eᵹpa, pep τolum.
Caὲ αᵹ Spiṅ leiὲ i nΑlbain, áit ατορ̇pαταp popᵹlαὃ
Ghall Saxan la Roibepτ bpuṕp, .i. pí Αlpan, ocup pé
αᵹ copnum Αlban ap eiᵹin ; áit ina τopcpaτop iap-
laτα ocup pιτipeὃa po imὃa, ocup ταoine τiáipṁiὃe
eli aipchena, mapoen pe hiapla Glóppeταp, pep ba mó
oiᵹpecht ocup uaiple ocup onóip το ὃí a Saxain uile
in pep pin. Gilla in Choimmτheὃ mac Cinaoith hI
Ghopmṕúiliᵹ, oipὲinτech Olepinn, ocup Gopmlaiὲ inᵹen
Mic bpanáin, .i. a ṕéiτὲiὃ pópτa, moptui punt. Roalὃ
Mhάᵹ Mhaὲᵹamna το ṁapbaτ la a bpaiὲpiὃ ppein.
Maὲa Mhάᵹ Ὀhuiὃne, eppuc na bpeippne, quieuiτ in
Cpiᵹτo. Maὲa Maᵹ Τiᵹepnáin, τux Τellaiᵹ Ὀhunchaτa,
το ṁapbaτ la Cathal mac Ὀomnaill hI Ruaipc, .i. τά
ὃalτa, ap láp a ὲiᵹe pein pep τolum. Mathᵹamuin
mac in ὲaoiὲ, τaippech peτha na Saiτne, moptuup ept.

Κtt. Enaip pop Ceττein, ocup ocht τéᵹ puippe ; anno
Ὀomini M.ccc.xu. ; u. annup cicli Lunapip ; xiii. inτic-
τionip. Eτὃapτ ṁac Iapla Αlban .i. mac Roibepτ
bpuiṕp, ocup Iapla Caippᵹe intí Eτὃapτ pin, το ὲoiᵹ-
echt τoὲum Epenn ap oipep Ulaὃ ὃuὃ ὲuaiὲ ; Lucht ὲpí
ceτ lonᵹ bá peὃ a Lín ; ᵹup combuaiὃip ocup ᵹup coim-
cpiὲnaiᵹ a iὃna áiᵹ ocup ippaile Epe uile co coiὲὲenτ
eτip Ghall ocup Ghaoiτel ; ocup po aipᵹ, imoppo, popᵹla

[1] *Srubh-leith;* lit. "gray point."
In Mageoghegan's version of the so-
called Annals of Clonmacnois the name
is written "Screvelin or Strevling."
Trokelowe writes it "Strivelyne,"
i.e. Stirling. The celebrated battle
of Bannockburn is referred to.

[2] *Airchinnech.* oipᶜc for oip-
ὲiτech, MS. The correct form iˢ
aipὲinτech, or oipὲinτech, as in
the Annals of Connacht. For the

meaning of aipὲinτech, or *Herenach,*
see Reeves's *Adamnan,* p. 364, note[m],
and Todd's *St. Patrick,* p. 160.

[3] *Roalbh;* i.e. Ralph, or Rodolph.

[4] *Mac Dhuibhne.* The Four Masters
write the name macc Uibne (Mac
Uibhne) ; but this is an incorrect
form arising from the omission of the
first letter (τ) of the last member of
the name, which, being aspirated, is
not sounded in the pronunciation.

defeat was inflicted by Ruaidhri, son of Cathal O'Concho-bhair, on Muinter-Raighilligh, at Druim-lethan. Magh-nus, son of Domhnall O'hEghra, was slain by Maghnus son of William O'hEghra, per dolum. A battle at Srubh-leith[1] in Alba, where the chief men of the Saxon Fo-reigners fell by Robert Bruce, i.e., the king of Alba, who was defending Alba by force; where a great many earls and knights fell, and persons innumerable besides, toge-ther with the Earl of Gloucester, who was the man of greatest inheritance, and nobility, and honour in all Saxon-land. Gilla-in-Choimdedh, son of Cinaeth O'Gormshuil-igh, airchinnech[2] of Oilfinn, and Gormlaith, daughter of Mac Branain, (i.e. his wedded wife), mortui sunt. Roalbh[3] Mac Mathghamhna was slain by his own brethren. Matthew Mac Dhuibhne,[4] bishop of the Breifne, quievit in Christo. Matthew Mac Tighernain, dux of Tellach-Dun-chadha, was slain by Cathal, son of Domhnall O'Ruairc, i.e. his foster-son, in the middle of his own house, per dolum. Mathghamhain Mac-in-chaeich,[5] chieftain of Fidh-na-Saithne,[6] mortuus est.

The kalends of January on Wednesday, and the eighteenth of the moon; anno Domini M.CCC.XV.; v. annus cycli lunaris; xiii. Indictionis.. Edward, son of the Earl of Alba, (i.e. this Edward was the son of Robert Bruce, and Earl of Carrick), came to Erinn, on the coast of Uladh in the north, with a fleet of 300 ships, and his valorous and warlike fame confounded and terrified *the people of* all Erinn in general, both Foreigners and Gaeidhel. And he plundered, moreover, the principal part of Uladh,

---

[5] *Mac-in-chaeich*; lit. "son of the blind [man]."

[6] *Fidh-na-Saithne*; i.e. "the wood of Saithne." The territory of Saithne comprised the present barony of Bal-rothery West, county of Dublin, and the name of Fidh-na-Saithne is ap-parently still preserved in that of Holywood (Latinized "Sanctum Ne-mus"), in the same barony. See Dr. Reeves's note on the extent of the territory of Saithne, in the appendix to O'Donovan's ed. of *O'Dubhagain's Topog. Poem* (p. 5). It may be added that there is a townland called "Nevit" (*neimhed*, asylum) in the neighbour-hood.

Ulaꝺ, ocur ro loirc Raiṫ ṁór Mhuiᵹe line ocur Dun
Delᵹan, ocur ꝺo ṁarḃ α nꝺoeine; ocur ꝺo loirc
αṫ Ḟirꝺiaꝺ mic Daṁáin iarrin. αcht chena ro
ᵹaḃurꝺar braiᵹꝺi ocur tiᵹerntur ṫoiᵹeꝺ Ulaꝺ uile
ᵹan frearraḃra, ocur ꝺo ꝺeónaiᵹertar a ᵹairm ꝺo
ṫaḃairt ina ri Erenn, ocur ro aontaiᵹret Ᵹoeiꝺel
Erenn a tiᵹernur ꝺo ṫaḃairt ꝺó; ocur ꝺo ᵹoireꝺar
ri Erenn ꝺe. Oꝺ ṫualaiꝺ Rirꝺerꝺ a ḃúrc, .i. Iarla
Ulaꝺ, Eꝺḃarꝺ aᵹá inꝺoiᵹeꝺ, ro ṫinóilrum rluaᵹa
ṁóra ar ᵹach airꝺ ina comꝺail co Ror Comáin ar
túr, ocur arriꝺe co hαṫ luain, ocur ar reꝺ na Miꝺe
ocur Muiᵹe ḃreaᵹh; ocur Feꝺlim.h.Conchobair, ri
Connacht, ar an rloiᵹeꝺ rin maille frir; ocur
timcell ḟicet cat ba reꝺ comaireṁ a rluaiᵹ. αcht
cena nir choiᵹleꝺar Ᵹaill ꝺon ꝺulaꝺ rin noeṁ iná
neimeꝺ ꝺá nemnaiꝺe, na tuaṫ iná termonn, can
ċnam ocur can coimmilleꝺ ar riarlaoiꝺ Erenn ó
Shinuinn ḃuꝺerr co Cúl Raṫain ḃuꝺ ṫuaiꝺ, ocur co
hInnir Eoᵹain; ocur o rancoꝺar ar oen ċonair inn
imerce aꝺbail oenrlúaiᵹeꝺ rin co ḃreᵹhaiḃ, aꝺ-
ċonncaꝺar ṫuca ina comꝺáil Emunn ḃuitileir .i.
ᵹiurtír na hErenn, tríċa cat coimċenᵹailti ar na
comaireṁ ꝺon chur rin. αcht chena ro ṫoirmirc
int Iarla a tocht rin ina ṫóiċim na ina ṫinól fein,
oir ba ꝺoiᵹ lair hé fein cona ṫrlúaiᵹ ꝺo ꝺichur
Eꝺḃuirꝺ ocur αlbanach a hErinn. Ir ann bói int
Iarla an oiꝺċe rin i nαṫ Ḟirꝺiaꝺ re taoḃ Sleiḃe
ḃreᵹ, ocur Eꝺḃarꝺ ḃriúir maroen fria hUlltoiḃ ocur
fria hαlbanċaḃ aᵹ Inir Coein mic Deᵹhaiꝺ. Do
riacht int Iarla ar a ḃarach inanꝺiaiꝺ, ocur ꝺo ᵹaḃ
roᵹaꝺ ocur lonᵹport aᵹ Luᵹṁaꝺ, ocur ꝺo cuaiꝺ
imorro Uilliam ḃurc ꝺfaᵹail eluimme ar Eꝺḃurꝺ
co nαlbanchaiḃ, ocur ro marbaꝺ uaṫaꝺ eturra a
comurc annrin. Imṫúra Eꝺḃairꝺ co na feꝺuin
imorro, ꝺo ᵹluair feme tre ruráilem hi Neill ocur
Ulaꝺ airċena, ocur téiꝺ ar a ḃárach ar uiꝺeꝺhaiꝺ

and burned Rath-mor of Magh-Line and Dun-Delgan, and killed their people; and he afterwards burned Ath-Fhir-diadh-mic-Damhain In fine, he obtained the hostages and sovereignty of all the province of Uladh without opposition, and consented to be proclaimed as king of Erinn. And the Gaeidhel of Erinn agreed to give him their sovereignty, and proclaimed him king of Erinn. When Richard Burk, i.e. the Earl of Ulster, heard that Edward was advancing towards him, he assembled large armies from every direction to meet him at Ros-Comain, in the first place; and *he proceeded* from thence to Ath-Luain, and along Midhe and Magh-Bregh. And Fedhlim O'Conchobhair, king of Connacht, was along with him on this hosting. And the number of his army was about twenty battalions. However, the Foreigners on this expedition spared neither saint nor asylum, however sacred, nor territory, nor termon, without wasting and completely destroying, throughout the extent of Erinn from the Sinainn in the south to Cul-Rathain in the north, and to Inis-Eoghain. And when this great multitudinous army came together into Bregh, they saw Edmond Butler, i.e. the Justiciary of Erinn, coming to join them, having on the occasion thirty battalions well united and counted. Nevertheless, the Earl prevented him from going in his own procession or assemblage, for he considered that he himself, together with his army, could expel Edward and the men of Alba from Erinn. The Earl was that night at Ath-Fhirdiadh, by the side of Sliabh-Bregh, and Edward Bruce, with his Ulidians and men of Alba, at Inis-Cain-mic-Deghaidh. The Earl went on the morrow in pursuit of them, and occupied a place of rest and encampment at Lugh-mhagh; and William Burk went, moreover, to obtain an advantage over Edward Bruce and the men of Alba, and a few persons were slain between them in an encounter. As regards Edward and his forces, however, he advanced, through the persuasion of O'Neill and the other Ulidians, and proceeded on the morrow, by

imτechτα co Cúl Raτhaιn ρότυαιδ, ocuρ co hoιρeρ
Innρι hEoξaιn, ocuρ ρο leξρeτ δροιčeτ Chúla Raτaιn
ρe haξhaιδ ιn Iaρla. Lenuρ ιnτ Iaρla ιαδ, ocuρ ξαδυρ
Lonξρορτ α Cúl Raτaιn αρ ιnchαιδ Ulaδ ocuρ Eoδαιρδ
ιmmón αδαιnn, co náρ ράξαιδρeτ διδλιnυιδ coιll no
machaιρe, na ξορτ na ξemaρ, na ρορραδ, ná ραδαll, na
cιll, cen δοδ ocuρ cen διαn Loρcaδ, υaιρ nιρ δό
coιmρech cumaιρc nó caτaιξτe na ρlúaξa ριn ρe ροιle,
οιρ δο δί αn δhanna bρuτmaρ δορb τomuιn αξά
neδράιn; achτ αon ní, δο τίδιρ δeδτα δeρṁáρa eτορρα
αδιú ocuρ αnall ιmón αδuιnn ξach Láoι. Oδ čualaιδ
Eoδúρδ bρuιρ ρeδυρ Pheδλιm hI Conchobaιρ, ρí
Connachτ, δο čuιρ ρeρρα ρolaιξτe δá ιnnροιξeδ, δο
τaιρρριn Connachτ cen comροιnn ρό na τomuρ, ocuρ élúδ
δό on ιaρla δο τορnum a čúιξιδ ρeιn. Ro éιρδ Pédλιm na
ρυιξle ριn co ροιξιδnech, ocuρ ρο αonταιξ la hEoδαρδ
δon δulaδ ριn. Imτuρa Ruaιδρι mιc Caτhaιl ρuaιδ hI
Conchobaιρ, óδ čonnaιρc Connachτa αρ na bρolṁuξαδ
δο ξluaιρ υaτhaδ δο αξalluιm Eoδuιρδ coξ Cúl Raτaιn
αρ ριαρλαoιδ Chenéóιl Conaιll ραιρ, ocuρ δο ξell
δEoδúρδ conδιčuιρρeδ ξaιll υaδ ó čennuρ Connachτ,
ocuρ δo δeonaιξ Eoδúρδ δó ιαρριn coξaδ δο δenum αρ
ξhalloιδ, ocuρ ξan ροξuιl ιná διδeρξ δo δenum αρ
Pheδλιm, na ιmτechτ a ρeρuιnn. Ní heδh ριn, ιmορρο,
δο ρóne Ruaιδρι, achτ ρo τιnóιl Connachτuιξ ocuρ
bρeιρρnιξ ocuρ ξallóξlaeč ιmδa maιlle ρριú, ocuρ ρο
ιnnραιξ ξo ceρτ láρ Shíl Muιρeξhaιξ ocuρ Chonnachτa
αιρčena, ocuρ δo loιρc a ceδóιρ ρράδδaιle Slιcιξ ocuρ
αč cliaτ ιn Choρuιnn, ocuρ caιρlén móρ Chιlle Col-
maιn, ocuρ baιle τοραιρ bριξδe, ocuρ Dún Iomδán
conα caιρlenuιδ, ocuρ Roρ Chomáιn, ocuρ Rιnnδúιn,
ocuρ baιle αčα Luaιn, máρoen ριρ na huιle τιξιδ baδαρ
ιn ξach conaιρ δáρ ιmτιξ; ocuρ ρo ριρ ρé τenδ ocuρ

<hr/>

1 *The river;* i.e. the Bann.

regular marches, northwards to Cul-Rathain, and to the
border of Inis-Eoghain; and they broke down the bridge
of Cul-Rathain before the Earl. The Earl follows them, and
encamps at Cul-Rathain in front of the Ulidians and
Edward, about the river,[1] so that both parties left neither
wood nor plain, nor field, nor corn crop, nor residence, nor
barn, nor church, without burning and wholly destroying;
for these armies were not able to encounter or fight with
each other, as the rapid, fierce, deep Bann was separating
them. Nevertheless, severe skirmishes occurred between
them on one side and the other, about the river, each day.
When Edward Bruce heard of the excellence of Fedhlim
O'Conchobhair, king of Connacht, he sent secret messages
to him, offering him undivided power over Connacht,
if he would steal away from the Earl to defend his own
province. Fedhlim listened patiently to these words,
and agreed with Edward on that occasion. With regard
to Ruaidhri, son of Cathal Ruadh O'Conchobhair, when
he perceived that Connacht had been evacuated he proceeded, accompanied by a few, eastwards through the
middle of Cenel-Conaill to Cul-Rathain, to converse with
Edward; and he promised Edward that he would expel
the Foreigners from the government of Connacht; and
Edward subsequently consented that he might make war
on the Foreigners, but that he should not commit spolia-
tion or robbery on Fedhlim, or go into his land. This was
not what Ruaidhri did, however; but he assembled the men
of Connacht and Breifne, and numerous gallowglasses along
with them, and proceeded right into the middle of Sil-
Muiredhaigh, and of Connacht likewise, and immediately
burned the street-town of Sligech, and Ath-cliath-in-
Chorainn, and the great castle of Cill-Colmain, and Baile-
tobair-Brighde, and Dun-Iomdhain with its castles, and
Ros-Comain, and Rinn-duin, and the town of Ath-Luain,
together with all the houses that were in every route
through which he passed. And he afterwards claimed

τιʒeρnur aρ Mac nΌιαρmαɒα ιαρριn, ocur ní bρuαιρ
ʒιαll ιná eɒιρe uαɓ ; ocur ρo ʒαɓ ʒeιll ocur bραιʒɒe
Shíl Muιρeʒhαιʒ áιρčena ; ocur ρóρ ρo ριʒρατ ρoρ
Chαρn Ɣραoιč hé ιαρριn ; ocur ρo ɓóι αʒ ρuιρech eɒιρ
Shíl Muιρeʒhαιʒ αnnρéιn ρe heɒh ocur ρe hαchαιɒ,
αʒ cnαm ocur αʒ comčαιčeіn ʒαch comαρραn ιnα čιm-
čell αn ѓéιɒ nαρ ɓáɒ ριαραč ɒó ɒíɓ, ocur ρóρ αʒ
ρuιρech ρe ράchαɒ Ɣeιɒlιm ocur αnτ ѓlúαʒ ɓóι ι
nUllταιb ιnα ѓochαιρ. 1mčuρα Ɣeιɒlιm hι Conchobαιρ,
ρí Connαchτ, óɒ čuαlαιɓ Ruαιɒρι nα ριčιnʒ ɒocum
Connαchτ ɒo čορnum ριʒe ɒó ѓéιn, ocur ɒo čuιc mαρ
čαρlα ɒá čuρuρ ɒó, ocur ɒo ιnnιρ ɒon 1αρlα ʒo nʒeɓαɒ
Ruαιɒρι cnαιm coʒαιɒ ɓá éιρι . ιnα ѓeρonn, ocur ρo
ιαρρ ιnτ 1αρlα co τιnneρnαch lαιρ ɒočum Connαchτ
ɒá cορnum. Cchτ chenα nι ρocαιρ ρuαιρριum nα
ρlιʒče ρeme, oιρ nι ραιɓe αen lá cen cρeιč no cen cατ
αρ ѓeɒh Ulαɓ ocur Oιρʒιαll, no co ραnιc co Ʒραnαρɒ
ocur co Coιll nα nαmuρ, ocur co ρocραιττe Seoαιn hι
Ɣeρʒαιl, .ι. ɒeρbραchαρ α ѓαchαρ, αιτ ιnαρ ɒíčαιʒheɒ
α ɒαeιne, ιαρ néluɒ ιn éɒálα uαɒαραn co nα ѓeɒuιn
ɒo čeαɒαιʒ ɓá čαeιρechαιɓ ocur ɒá uιρρíʒαιɓ báɒαρ
nα ѓochαιρ αρ αnτ ѓlóιʒeɒ τuαιčɓιl ριn α mιonαɒ ѓeιn
ɒo ιnιρoιʒeɒ, ocur ɒul ɒóιɓ ɒocum ριʒe Ruαιɒρι ριαρú
no ɓeιɒíρ αρ αneol nα ѓochαιρ ριum, óιρ mαɒ τρén
ɒαmρα ɒo ριɒιρρe beιčιρρι αʒαm ; αchτ oen ní, o nαch
ιnѓιočα moιɒιρι ocur Ruαιɒρι ɒon ɒulαɓ ρo ρe ρoιle,
beιmmιτ αρ αon čonαιρ αρ nɒιαρρ ρe heɓ αρ coʒαιɒ.

---

[1] *Carn-Fraich.* See note [1], p. 554
supra.

[2] *Return.* ράčh, apparently for
ράchαɒ. The editor has not met
this word elsewhere, and has followed
Mageoghegan's version of the so-called
Annals of Conmacnois in translating
it "return." The Dublin copies of
the Annals of Connacht have Ḱάčh,
for cαchαιb "battalions."

[3] *Northern.* τuαιčɓιl. The word
τuαιčɓιl (deriv. from τuαιɒ,
"north") signifies also "left-hand-
wise," and "unlucky." See O'Donovan's ed. of the *Book of Rights,*
p. 2, note e.

[4] *Guardian;* i.e. Maelruanaidh Mac
Diarmada, or Mulrony Mac Der-
mot. The MS. has mιρι (I., i.e.
Fedhlim), but the Dublin copies of the

sway and sovereignty over Mac Diarmada, but obtained neither pledge nor hostage from him ; and he took the pledges and hostages of all Sil-Muiredhaigh ; and they also subsequently inaugurated him on Carn-Fraich;[1] and he thus remained amongst the Sil-Muiredhaigh during a space and period, wasting and impoverishing such of the neighbours around him as were not obedient to him, and also awaiting the return[2] of Fedhlim and the army that was in Uladh with him. As to Fedhlim O'Conchobhair, king of Connacht, when he heard that Ruaidhri was on his way back to Connacht, to contest the sovereignty for himself, and understood how it fared with him on his journey, he told the Earl that Ruaidhri would make war in his land in his absence; and he earnestly besought the Earl *to return* with him to Connacht, to defend it. Nevertheless, he did not find the ways before him quiet, for not a day passed without a depredation or battle, in his passage through Uladh and Oirghiall, until he came to Granard, and to Coill-na-namus, to the people of John O'Ferghail, i.e., his mother's brother, where his men were reduced in number. After their spoils had been taken away from them by the army, he permitted his chieftains and princes who were along with him on this northern[3] expedition to go to their own homes, and submit themselves to the sovereignty of Ruaidhri, rather than they should be wanderers with him, "for if I am again powerful," (*said he*), "you shall be with me. Nevertheless, as my guardian[4] and Ruaidhri cannot be reconciled with each other on this occasion, we shall both act together during the period of our war."

Annals of Connacht read moıꝋıřı for mo oıꝋıřı ("my guardian"), which seems more correct, and which has therefore been substituted for the word in the text. Mageoghegan, whose account of these transactions

in his version of the Annals of Clonmacnois agrees very literally with the foregoing narrative, seems also to have understood that M'Dermott, "his [Fedhlim's] own ffoster ffather," was meant.

Imtéapa ino Iapla ocup Uilliam búpc ocup na nʒall
áipcena, o nach bpacatap Peiolim aʒá bpuptacht, ocup
a plúaiʒ pein ap painnpeol, po inntovap ap a naip ó
Chuil Rathain co caiplén Coinvipe. Do čonncovap
Ullta ocup Albanaiʒ an ni pin vo lenpat co tinnep-
nach int Iapla co Convepe, ocup ap coimpiachtuin
voib vočum tpova vo čabaipt vá čele, po ʒabav
Uilliam búpc co na puvepivib annpin, ocup vá mac
mic in mílib, ocup po teich int Iapla pein cen puipech
ap invevhaib imteachta óta pin co panic i Connachta.
Ro innpaiʒpet a čaipve Ʒall vá ʒach leiš int Iapla
ap toiʒecht vó a nvóčup in Iapla vá bpóipivin no va
bpuptocht on éʒen, ocup tancotap imoppo a čapuiv
Ʒhoeivel ino oeinecht ina čech in tanpin mup an ceona;
ocup ippiat bá pepp tanic annpin .i. Peolim .h. Concha-
baip, pí Connacht, ocup Muipceptach .h. Ópiain, pi
Tuavmuman, ocup Maelpuanaiv Mac Diapmava, pí
muinntipe Moelpuanaiv, ocup Ʒillibept .h. Cellaiʒ,
pí .h. Maine, iap ná nvíchup on vuthaiv uile. Ocup
óv čonnaic Maolpuanaiv Mac Diapmava imav na
naičpiʒ ocup na ninnaptach i naein tiʒ vo ʒabh naipe
he, ocup tuc vá bpéitip nach áipémtói hé pein na
aičpiʒ na na ionnaptach i naein tiʒ vopivipi, acht
ʒo pachav pe oipbept búvéin ina čip amuil no čoip-
bépav intoicce vó; ocup tanic ap inchaib Taivʒ hi
Chellaiʒ, ocup vo póne Tavc copmaileʒ pivá vó pe
Ruaivpi vo činn a vuthaivie, ocup bpaiʒve vo čabaipt
vo Ruaivpi mac Cathail vópum. Aov ballač, mac
Maʒnupa, mic Conchobaip puaiv, mic Muipceptaiʒ
Muimniʒ, vo mapbav a bpill la Cathal mac n'Domnaill
hi Conchobaip, ocup Aov mac Aipt, ocup Diapmaiv
mac Simóin na tráʒa vo mapbav vóib čópp, i nvíʒuil

---

¹ *To give.* vo čabaipt; repeated in MS.

² *By them.* From this it is apparent that some other person, or persons,

participated in the slaying of Aedh Ballach O'Conor and the others mentioned, probably the brother (or brothers) of Cathal, whose father

With regard to the Earl and William Burk, and the other Foreigners, when they saw Fedhlim not assisting them, and their own army dispersed, they turned back from Cul-Rathain to the castle of Condere. As soon as the Ultonians and men of Alba observed this, they quickly followed the Earl to Condere; and on their meeting to give[1] battle to one another, William Burk with his knights, and the two sons of Mac-an-mhilidh, were taken prisoners there, and the Earl himself fled without delay, by regular marches, from thence until he arrived in Connacht. His Foreign friends on every side approached the Earl on his arrival, in the hope that the Earl would relieve or help them from oppression; and his Gaeidhelic friends came then together into his house in like manner. And these were the best who came there, viz, Fedhlim O'Conchobhair, king of Connacht, and Muirchertach O'Briain, king of Tuadh-Mumha, and Maelruanaidh Mac Diarmada, king of Muinter-Mael-ruanaidh, and Gilbert O'Cellaigh, king of Ui-Maine—all of whom had been expelled from the entire district. And when Maelruanaidh Mac Diarmada observed the great number of deposed and expelled persons assembled in the same house, he was seized with shame, and he vowed that he would not again be reckoned in any house as one deposed or expelled, but that he would go by his own efforts into his country as opportunity should offer. And he went into the presence of Tadhg O'Cellaigh; and Tadhg con-cluded a semblance of peace on his part with Ruaidhri, for his inheritance, on condition that he should give hostages to Ruaidhri, son of Cathal. Aedh Ballach, son of Maghnus, son of Conchobhar Ruadh, son of Muirchertach Muimhnech, was slain in treachery by Cathal, son of Domhnall O'Conchobhair; and Aedh son of Art, and Diar-maid, son of Simon-na-trágha, were also slain by them[2] in

["their father," as the text has it] had been killed by Diarmaid, son | of Simon - na - trágha ("Simon of the Strand"), in the year 1307.

1 nαϑαη ϑo ṁαηbαϑ ϑo Ϭhιαηмαιϑ. Cηeϭα móηα ϑo
ϑenυm ϑo ϭlοιnn Ϭomnαιll αη ϭlοιnn Mhυιηϭeηϭαιξ
αη α ϭáηαch, ocυη Maξnυη mαc Maξnυηα, ocυη Ϭomn-
αll mαc Maξnυηα ϑo mαηbαϑ lá clοιnn Ϭomnαιll
αη lοηξ nα cηeιϭe ηιn; ocυη Ϭomαlϭαch Mαc Ϭonn-
chαϑα ϑo ξαϑáιl ηóη ϑon lυchϭ ceϑnα ηιn; ocυη
ιmϭechϭ ϑοιb α nυchϭ Ξhαll ϑαηéιηι nα néchϭ ηιn ϑo
commαeιϑem. Oϑ chυαlα Feϑhlιm.h.Conchοbαιη nα
hechϑα móηα ηιn ϑo ξlυαιη υαϑhαϑ ϑá óeηη ξηáϑα
ηeιηηιn mυη αηαϑαϑαη clαnn Ϭomnαιll hι Conchobαιη ocυη Rυαιϑηι ocυη Maξnυη, Cαϑhαl ocυη Mυιη-
ceηϑαch, Ϭonnchαϑ ocυη Seαn .ι. mec Ϭomnαιll mιc
Ϭαιϑc hι Conchοbαιη, mαηοen ηe mbηαιϑηιϑ αιηϭenα.
O ϭáηηαιϑ Feϑhlιm αϭαιηιηιn ιαηηιn ϑo ηóηe cηeιϭ
mοιη αη bηιαn.h.nϭυϑϑα α ceϑóιη, ocυη ϑo ηóηe
cηeαϭ móη ι nαιηϭech αη Ϭhιαηϭech nξαll Mαc
nϭιαηmαϑα, ocυη ϑo mαηϭ móηán ϑα mυιnnϭeη, ocυη
ϑo lοιηc α αηϭαnnα ocυη ϑιξe ιmϑα, ocυη ϑo ηone
cηeϭ ṁοη elι αη ϭlαιnn Chαϑhαιl hι Fhlαnnαξáιn; ocυη
ιηηí conαιη αηυcαϑ ιn cηeϭ ηιn ϑοϭυm ϭοηαϑ Chúlα
Cυιηc, ocυη nιη ηϑϑαϑ α hιmmáιn ηe mαeιϭe nα
mónαϑ, ocυη ηe méϑ nα cηeιϭe, ηe ϭηeιηηι ocυη ηe
ϭηυιm lιnmυιηe nα ϭóηα, óιη ηυcηαϑ ηοηξlα ξlαηηlαιϭ
nα Ϭυαϭ ocυη ηοcηαιϑι ϭlαιnne Cαϑhαιl hι Fhlαnnαξáιn ηυιηηe, ocυη Maξξαmυιn Mhάξ Rαξnαιll, ϭαιηηeϭ
Mυιnϭιηe hϭolυιη, conα bηαιϑηιη ocυη conα ϭοιmϭιnοl.
Oϑ ϭυαlα, ιmοηηο, mαc Ϭιαηmαϑα comαιηc ocυη coṁ-
ξáιη nα cηeιϭe αξ ϑυl ϑοϭυm nα cαηαϑ ηο lenυηϭαη
lοηξ nα cηeιϭe ξο Cυllϭάϭαη, ocυη óϑ ϭonnαιηc αn
cηeαϭ íαη ná cυιϭechαϑ ocυη ιαη ná ηοηϑóϑ, αchϭ

---

1 *Diarmaid.* See under the year
1307 (p. 539 *ante*). At the end of
this entry, which concludes fol. 66 *a*
of the vellum portion of the MS., the
scribe has added the note, ηξυιηιm
ϑo ϭαϭυ ηηυιηne, i.e. "I cease for
want of a dinner."

2 *Viz.* The MS. has the usual
abreviation for ocυη, "and," but the
Annals of Connacht have .ι. for
"viz."

8 *Coraidh-Chúla-Cuirc;* i.e. "the
weir of Cúil-Cuirc."

4 *They.* The persons who had

revenge for their father having been killed by Diarmaid.[1] Great depredations were committed by the sons of Domhnall on Clann-Muirchertaigh on the morrow, and Maghnus son of Maghnus, and Domhnall, son of Maghnus, were slain by the sons of Domhnall whilst pursuing this prey; and Tomaltach Mac Donnchadha was furthermore taken prisoner by the same band, who went under the protection of the Foreigners after having committed these deeds. As soon as Fedhlim O'Conchobhair heard of these great exploits, he went with a few of his own confidants to where the sons of Domhnall O'Conchobhair were, viz.,[2] Ruaidhri and Maghnus, Cathal and Muirchertach, Donnchadh and John, viz., the sons of Domhnall, son of Tadhg O'Conchobhair, together with their other brethren. When Fedhlim succeeded in joining them, subsequently, he immediately committed a great depredation on Brian O'Dubhda; and he committed a great depredation, in Airtech, on Diarmaid Gall Mac Diarmada, and killed a great number of his people, and burned his corn fields and many houses; and he committed another great depredation on the sons of Cathal O'Flannagain. The place whither this prey was conducted was to Coraidh-Chúla-Cuirc;[3] and it could not be driven owing to the softness of the bog, the extent of the prey, and the strength and heavy number of the pursuing band; for the majority of the recruits of the Tuatha, and the forces of the sons of Cathal O'Flannagain, and Mathghamhain Mag Raghnaill, chieftain of Muinter-Eolais, with his kinsmen and muster, overtook it. When Mac Diarmada, however, heard the noise and clamour of the prey going towards the weir, he followed the track of the prey to Culbháthar; and when he observed the prey divided and detained, (for they[4] liked not that it should not be

---

attempted to rescue the prey from Fedhlim O'Conor's adherents. This part of the entry is so loosely constructed that it is not easy to interpret the literal meaning of the original in correct and intelligible English.

chena ní hé ba háil ꝺoiꝗrium acht ꝗan a ꝗáꝡḃáil aꝗá ꝗiaꝺnuiḃ. Iaꝗꝗin ꝗo ꝗéč aꝗ a eꝗcaiꝗꝺiḃ co hamiaꝗꝗꝺa, uꝗḃaꝺach, ocuꝗ tuc táꝗ ocuꝗ taꝗcuꝗſal ꝗoꝗꝗa, acht ꝗéꝗ ḃó huathaꝺ na ꝗaꝗꝗaꝺ ḃuꝺéin in tan ꝗin, óꝺ čoniaiꝗc imoꝗꝗo in loem lethan laꝗꝗamain lán imꝺa ꝗo ḃói aꝗ comaiꝗ a tꝗoꝺa ꝺo čoiꝗnem; acht atá ní chena, ꝗo maꝗḃaꝺ Conchobaꝗ ꝗúaꝺ mac Oeꝺa Ḃꝗeiꝗꝗniꝗ hI Conchobaiꝗ, ocuꝗ Matꝗamain Mháꝗ Ráꝺnaill, taoiꝗꝗeč Muinntiꝗe hƐoluiꝗ, ocuꝗ .h. Maoilṁiaꝺaiꝗ, ꝺux Muinntiꝗe Ceꝗḃalláin, ocuꝗ moꝗán ꝺo maiꝡiḃ Muinntiꝗe hƐoluiꝗ maille ꝗú aꝗ an lathaiꝗ ꝗin, ocuꝗ tuc maiꝡm ꝗoꝗ ꝗach ꝗocꝗaiꝺe ele ꝺá ꝗaiḃ anꝗin aꝗ ꝗaꝗꝺóḃ a éꝺála ó Ꝟheꝺlim; ocuꝗ ꝗucaꝗtaꝗ ꝗein in cꝗeč laiꝗ iaꝗꝗin, ocuꝗ níꝗ aiꝗic ꝺia huiꝗꝗiꝗhib hí; ocuꝗ ꝗanic in oiꝺče ꝗin co ḃúill, ocuꝗ ꝗánic aꝗ a ḃáꝗach ꝺaꝗ Seꝗuiꝗ ꝗiaꝗ tuaiḃ, ocuꝗ aꝗꝗiꝺé tꝗe Chúil O ḃꝟhinn, ocuꝗ aꝗ ꝗuꝺ in Choꝗuinn, ocuꝗ a cꝗič Luiꝗne, ait aꝗaiḃe Ꝟéiꝺlim co na ꝟeꝺuiꝗ iꝗá ḃꝟuꝗnuiꝺe. Imꝡúꝗa Ruaiꝺꝗi mic Cathail hI Conchobaiꝗ, imoꝗꝗo, óꝺ čualaiꝺ na cꝗecha móꝗa ocuꝗ na héchta aiꝺḃle ꝗin ꝺo ꝺenum ꝺo Mac Ꝺiaꝗmaꝺa, ocuꝗ a ꝺul aꝗ oein ꝟeol ꝗe na ꝺalta, ꝺo ꝗóne ꝗein tinol co tinneꝗnach, ocuꝗ ꝺo ꝗóne ꝗoꝗlonꝗꝗoꝗt a mbaile ṁóꝗ hI Ꝟhloinn, ocuꝗ ꝗo ṁill cáꝺuꝗ na cille .i. Ɛꝗꝗa Ꝺáconna ocuꝗ manach na ḃúille aiꝗchena, im eallač ocuꝗ im aꝗḃonnuiḃ; ocuꝗ ꝗóꝗ ꝺo čuaiḃ Tomaltach mac Muiꝗꝗeꝗꝗa, mic Ꝺhonnchaꝺa, mic Tomaltaiꝗ, cona oiꝗecht ocuꝗ cona muinnteꝗ, ꝺočum Ꝟheiꝺlim. Iꝗ annꝗin ꝺo chúaiꝺ Ꝺiaꝗmaiꝺ ꝗall aꝗ Cꝗuačán, ocuꝗ ꝗoiꝗiꝗ ꝗaiꝗm ꝗi ꝺe. Táinic ꝗóꝗ an tan ꝗin Taꝺꝗ.h.Cellaiꝗ cona ꝗocꝗaiꝺe a bꝟuꝗtacht Ruaiꝺꝗi mic Cathail, ocuꝗ ꝺo lenmain a ꝟlánaiꝗechta aꝗ Mac nꝺiaꝗmaꝺa

---

1 *Es-Daconna.* See note ², p. 554 *supra.* The text incorrectly reads Ɛꝗꝗa ocuꝗ Ꝺaconna "of Es and Daconna." Mageoghegan (Annals of Clonmacnois) translates "made little respect of the reverence due to the church of Es-Daconna, and preyed the monks of Boyle;" but the Dublin

left with its owners), he afterwards looked furiously, angrily at his enemies, and heaped reproach and insult on them, though there were then but few in his own company, even though he saw the broad, flaming, immense phalanx which was ready to repulse his attack. In fine, Conchobhar Ruadh, son of Aedh Breifnech O'Conchobhair, and Mathghamhain Mac Raghnaill, chieftain of Muinter-Eolais, and O'Maelmhiadhaigh, dux of Muinter-Cerbhalláin, and a great number of the nobles of Muinter-Eolais along with them, were slain on the spot; and he (*Mac Diarmada*) defeated all the other bands that were there detaining his spoils from Fedhlim, and carried off the prey himself afterwards, and restored it not to its owners. And he came that night to Buill, and proceeded on the morrow across Seghais to the north-west, and from thence through Cul-O'Fhinn, and through the Corann, and into the territory of Luighne, where Fedhlim, with his forces, was awaiting them. As regards Ruaidhri, son of Cathal O'Conchobhair, however, when he heard that these great depredations and prodigious exploits had been committed by Mac Diarmada, who had allied himself with his foster-son, he himself made an expeditious muster, and established a camp in Baile-mór-O'Floinn, and profaned the church, i.e. Es-Daconna,[1] and the monks of the Buill likewise, respecting cattle and corn. And Tomaltach, son of Muirghes, son of Donnchadh, son of Tomaltach, with his tribe and people, went also to Fedhlim. It was then that Diarmaid Gall went upon Cruachan, and was proclaimed king. Tadhg O'Cellaigh came then, moreover, to the assistance of Ruaidhri, son of Cathal, and to enforce[2] his guarantee on Mac Diarmada, who had

---

copies of the Annals of Connacht say that "Cill-Athrachta, Es-Daconna, and the *monastery* of the Buill" were profaned.

[2] *Enforce.* oo tenmain; lit. "to follow," i.e. to compel Mac Diarmada to fulfil the terms of the covenant made on his part with Ruaidhri, by Tadhg O'Cellaigh, a short time previously.

ιαr cαιlleᵭ α ċαιɴʒɴe ρe Rᴜαιɔrι, ocᴜſ ᴅo ċᴜαᴅαr
ᴅιᵬlíɴαιᵭ ı leɴmαιɴ Pɦeιᴅlιm ocᴜſ Mιc Dιαrmαᴅα ocᴜſ
ɴα ɴoιrecɦᴛ ᵬóı ɴα ᵬṗóċαιρ, co Lιᴛιρ Lᴜιʒɴe, ocᴜſ
co ſleᵬe Sleᵬe ʒαṁ, ocᴜſ ʒo ʒlιoɴɴ Pαᴛρoιṁ ᴅo
ſᴜɴᴅραᵭ, áιᴛ ιɴαρ mαρᵬαᴛαρ ιlṁíle ᴅo ᵬᴜαιᵭ ocᴜſ
ᴅo ċαeιριᵭ, ocᴜſ ᴅo ċαιρlιb, ocᴜſ ᴅo ɴocɦᴛαᴅαρ mɴá
ᴜαιρle, ocᴜſ ᴅo ṁιllſeᴛ leɴιm beʒα ocᴜſ mιɴᴅαoιɴe
ᴅoɴ ᴛᴜρᴜſ ſιɴ, ocᴜſ ɴíρ mιlleᴅ ſe cᴜιmɴe ɴα ɴᴅαoιɴeᵭ
ριαm ᴜιρeᴅ ſιɴ ᴅellαċ αρ oeɴ láᴛɦαιρ ʒαɴ ᴛαρᵬα.
Imᴛúρα Mαolρᴜαɴαιᴅ Mιc Dιαρmαᴅα, óᴅ ċᴜαlαιᵭ
ſιᴅéιɴ .Dιαρmαιᴅ ʒαll ᴅo ſᴜιᴅe ı cαᴛαιρ ċαᴅᴜρα α
ċιɴιᵭ .ı. ı Cαιρρις Loċα Cé, ocᴜſ α ᴅᴜl αρ Cρᴜαċáɴ ᴅá
ριʒɦαᴅ, ocᴜſ ιαρ ɴoιρleċ α ᵬó ſeιɴ ᴜιle α ɴʒlιoɴɴ
Pαᴛρoιm, ᴅo ʒlᴜαιρ ſoιme co ɴα lᴜcɦᴛ ᴛιʒe ocᴜſ co
ɴα lᴜcɦᴛ ᴛeʒlαιʒ ᵬᴜᴅéιɴ co cαlαᴅ ɴα Cαιρρʒe, ocᴜſ
ᴛᴜcᴜſᴅαρ ᴅρᴜιm ſρι Sιɴᴜιɴɴ, ocᴜſ ρo αιρʒeſᴛαρ o
Sɦιɴᴜιɴɴ co cαραιᵭ Cúlα Cᴜιρc áιᴛ αραᴅᴛαρ oιρecɦᴛα
ɴα ᴛρí Cιαρραιᴅe .ı. Cιαρραιᴅe ιαρᴛαραcɦ ocᴜſ Cιαρραιᴅe
Mɦoιʒe ocᴜſ Cιαρραιᴅe Αιρᴛιʒ coɴα ɴellαιʒιᵭ ocᴜſ co ɴα
ɴιɴɴιlιᵭ co ɦᴜιlιᴅe ; ocᴜſ ɴι ᴅóιʒ coɴᴅeρɴαᴅ ιſιɴ αιmſιρ
ſιɴ ιɴɴſoιʒeᴅ ᵬᴜᴅ cρóᴅα ocᴜſ ᵬᴜᴅ beoᴅα ocᴜſ bᴜᴅ mo
éᴅáιl ιɴα ιɴ cρeċ ſιɴ, óιρ ρo cριᴛɴαιʒeᴅ ιɴ cúιʒeᴅ co
comláɴ; ocᴜſ ſóρ ρᴜcαᴅ beɴ Dιαρmαᴅα ʒαll α cιmιᴅecɦᴛ
ιſιɴ cρeιċ ſιɴ, co ɴᴜαᴛɦαᴅ ᴅá bαɴᴛραcɦᴛ mαιlle ſριά ;
ocᴜſ ɴíρ ʒαᴅ Dιαρmαιᴅ ſαιme ɴα ſeſſcαιρecɦᴛ ριαm
ᴅαρéιρ ɴα cρeċ ſιɴ. Αcɦᴛ cɦeɴα ρo ɦιɴɴιſeᴅ ᴅᴘɦeιᴅ-
lιm.h.Coɴcɦoᵬαιρ ocᴜſ ᴅá oιᴅe bα ᴅo ᵬeιᴛ α Mαʒ Lᴜιρʒ
ᴅαρéιρ ɴα cρeιċe ſιɴ, ocᴜſ ᴅo ċᴜαᴅαρ ᴅá ɴιαρραᵭ ιɴ
ᴅαρɴα ſecɦᴛ, ocᴜſ ɴíρ ſáʒᵬαᴅαρ ecɦ ιɴá bó α ɴᴅíoɴ
ιɴá ɴᴅíċleιᴛ ιɴɴᴛe; ocᴜſ ᴛᴜcſαᴛ ιαρραᵭ αρ Dɦιαρmαιᴅ

---

1 *Caladh-na-Cairge.* The *caladh,*
callow, or shore, of the Rock [of Loch-
Cé], Mac Dermot's chief residence,
in Loch-Cé, county of Roscommon.

2 *Caraidh-Cúla-Cuirc.* See note ³,
p. 572.

³ *Ciarraidhe-iartharach;* i.e. "Western Ciarraidhe," a branch of the Ciarraidhe settled in the barony of Cos-
telloc, county of Mayo. Mageoghegan
says "Lower Ciarraidhe."

violated his covenant with Ruaidhri; and they both
went in pursuit of Fedhlim and Mac Diarmada, and the
tribes that were with them, to Letir-Luighne and the
slopes of Sliabh-Gamh, and to Glenn-Fathroimh in particular, where they killed many thousand cows, and
sheep, and horses; and they stripped gentlewomen, and
destroyed small children and little ones, on this journey;
and never during the memory of the people was so much
cattle uselessly destroyed in one spot. With regard to
Maelruanaidh Mac Diarmada, when he heard that Diarmaid Gall had sat in the chair of honour of his family,
i.e. in the Rock of Loch-Cé, and had gone upon Cruachan
to be made king, and that all his own cows had been
slaughtered in Glenn-Fathroimh, he advanced with his
own retainers and household band to Caladh-na-Cairge;[1]
and he turned his back to the Sinainn, and plundered
from the Sinainn to Caraidh-Cúla-Cuirc,[2] where the
tribes of the three Ciarraidhe were, viz., Ciarraidhe-
iartharach,[3] and Ciarraidhe-Mhaighe,[4] and Ciarraidhe-
Airtigh,[5] with all their flocks and cattle; and it is not
likely that there was made in that time an incursion more
valorous, and more energetic, and more rich in spoils
than this foray, for the province was entirely con-
vulsed. And the wife of Diarmaid Gall was, moreover,
taken captive in this foray, together with a few of her
female attendants; and Diarmaid never enjoyed quiet
or happiness after these spoliations. It was reported to
Fedhlim O'Conchobhair, and to his guardian, however,
that there were cows in Magh-Luirg after this depredation, and they proceeded to seek for them a second time,
and left neither horse nor cow in a place of security,
or hiding-place, in it. And they sought for Diarmaid

---

[4] *Ciarraidhe-Mhaighe.* See note [5], p. 452.

[5] *Ciarraidhe - Airtigh.* Another branch of the Ciarraidhe, settled in the territory of Airtech, now the parish of Tibohine, county of Roscommon.

nᵹall, oᴄup puaippium pabaᵭ pompuᴅ ᴅon cup pin,
ocup nip ᵭó ᴄapᵭa ᵭó; acᴄ ᵹep ᵭó ᴄpom a ᵭóip ocup
a ᴄinól ap a cinn nip páᵹaiᵭpeᴄ ech iná ᴅuine, ocup
bá poen polaṁ Maᵹ Luipᵹ ᴅapéip na cpeᴄ pin.   ηi
ᵭiᵭ, imoppo, ᴅion no ᴅeᵹcaomna a ᴄuaiᵭ nó a ᴄepmonn
a Maᵹ Luipᵹ ocup a Maᵹ hOi co huiliᵭe, acᴄ a
healᵭa ocup a hinnile, a happap ocup a héᴅach ᴅa
ᵭpaᴅach ᴅona halᴄópaib ocup aᵹá ᴄabaipᴄ ᴅo ᵹallóᵹ-
laeᴄaiᵭ ocup ᴅo ᴄpeppénchaib ina noliᵹᴄenup.   baile
ᴅhúna móp ᴅo lopcuᴅ le Ruaiᴅpi.h.Conchobaip in
hoc anno. Eaᴄᴅpuim .h. Maine ᴅo lopcuᴅ ocup a
caiplén ᴅo leᵹaᴅ. Tpiᴄa ceᴅ Maonṁuiᵹe ᴅapᵹuin
ocup ᴅo lopcuᴅ le Taᴅc .h. Cellaiᵹ. Peiᴅlim.h.Con-
chobaip ocup Mac ᴅiapmaᴅa, ocup Tomalᴄach Mac
ᴅonnchaᴅa, ocup clann ᴅomnaill hí Conchobaip, ᴅo
ᴅul uile a nuchᴄ ᵹhall iapᴄhaip Connachᴄ, ocup
Tip nEnna, ocup Tip ηechᴄain, ocup Muinnᴄep
Cpeaᴄáin, ocup Conmaicne ᴅhúna móip ᴅo milleᴅ
eᴅip ᵭeoin ocup éᴅeoin. Riᴄᴅepᴅ a búpc, .i. iapla
lllaᵭ, ap puᴄ Epenn ᵹan ᴄpén ᵹan ᴄpeipi pe heᴅh na
bliaᴅna pin. Teᴅhmanna inᵹanᴄacha imᵭa ap puᴅ
Epenn uile in bliaᴅain pin .i. ᴅiᵭ ᴅoeineᴅ co hilimᵭa
innᴄi, ocup ᵹopᴄa ocup ᵹallpaᴅa éxamla. Mapᵭᴄa
ᴅaeineᴅ ocup ᴅoineᴅ ᴅopuilinᵹ ᴅiᵹᵭalaᴄ innᴄe ᵭóp.
Aᴅᵭ.h.ᴅomnaill pí ᴄipe Conaill, ᴅo ᴄoiᵹechᴄ a
Caipbpi, ocup cpiᴄ Caipppi uile ᴅo ṁilleᴅ laip ᴄpe
comaiple a ṁná.i. inᵹen Mhaᵹnupa hí Conchobaip; ocup
ᴅul ᴅi péin mapoen pe bpuaip ᴅo ᵹallóᵹlaeᴄuibh ocup
ᴅo Chloinn Mhuipᴄepᴄaiᵹ pó ᴄemplaib ᴅpoma cliaᵭ,
ocup mopán ᴅo ᴄlépᴄiᵭ ocup ᴅo compopbaib ᴅpoma
cliaᵭ ᴅo apᵹuin lé innᴄe in hoc anno. Caipplén Sliᵹ
ᴅo leccaᴅ ᴅUa ᴅhomnaill ᴅon ᴄoipc pin, ocup éᴅála
mópa ᴅpaᵹail ᴅóiᵭ ann. Taᴅc.h.hUiᵹinn, pói ᴄoiᴄᴄenn

---

1 *West of Connacht.* iapᴄhaip | of Clonmacnois) says "Ighter Con-
Connachᴄ. Mageoghegan (Annals | naught," i.e. Lower Connacht.

Gall, but he got notice of their coming on this occasion; and it was of no use to him, for, though great his force and muster before them, they left neither horse nor man; and Magh-Luirg was an empty waste after these depredations. There was, moreover, neither defence nor protection in district or termon in all Magh-Luirg and Magh-Ai; but the flocks, cattle, and corn, and the cloths taken from off the altars, were given as wages to gallowglasses and mercenaries. The town of Dún-mór was burned by Ruaidhri O'Conchobhair in hoc anno. Echdruim-Ui-Maine was burned, and its castle thrown down. The cantred of Maenmagh was plundered and burned by Tadhg O'Cellaigh. Fedhlim O'Conchobhair, and Mac Diarmada, and Tomaltach Mac Donnchadha, and the sons of Domhnall O'Conchobhair joined the Foreigners of the West of Connacht;[1] and Tir-Enna, and Tir-Nechtain, and Muinter-Creacháin, and Conmaicne-Dúna-mór were destroyed, both wilfully and unwilfully. Richard Burk, i.e. the Earl of Ulster, was *a wanderer* throughout Erinn, without sway or power, during this year. Numerous wonderful diseases throughout all Erinn this year, viz., a destruction of people in great number *occurred* in it, and famine, and various distempers. Slayings[2] of people, and intolerable, destructive bad weather also *happened* in it. Aedh O'Domhnaill, king of Tir-Conaill, came into Cairbre, and all the territory of Cairbre was destroyed by him through the counsel of his wife, i.e. the daughter of Maghnus O'Conchobhair; and she herself, together with all she found of the gallowglasses and the Clann-Muirchertaigh, attacked the churches of Druim-cliabh, where several of the clerics and comarbs of Druim-cliabh were plundered by her, in hoc anno. The castle of Sligech was thrown down by O'Domhnaill on this expedition; and great spoils were found there by them. Tadhg O'hUiginn, a man

---

[2] *Slayings*. mαρβτα, plur. of mαρβαὄ, which is the form of both the infin. and participle pres. of the verb mαρβαιm, I kill, or slay.

gacha cerроє, οά mbenann ɼe ɼɪlɪɞechτ, moɼτuuɼ eɼτ. Οomnall Maʒ Τhɪʒeɼnáɪn, οux Τhellaɪʒ Οhúnchaοa, οcuɼ ɪɼ ɼɼuɼ aοeɼɮáɪ ɪɪ ɼaɪɮneɮ, οo ɰaɼbαο οo Chαthal na τoeɼɼech.h.Ruaɪɼc. Cɰlαɪɞ.h.Ɏeɼʒαɪl moɼτuuɼ eɼτ.

ʃctt. Enαɪɼ ɼoɼ ɮαɼοαoɪɼ, οcuɼ .ɪx. ɼɪcheο ɼuɪɼɼe; anno Οomɪɪ M.ccc.xuɪ; ɼeατo anno cɪclɪ lunαɼɪɼ; xɪɪɪɪ. ɪɪοɪcτɪoɪɪɼ; xx. anno cɪclɪ ɼolαɼɪɼ. Cαοɞ .h.Οomnαɪll οcuɼ Cenél Conαɪll uɪle οo ɮɪɪól ɼluαʒhαο ɰóɼ, οcuɼ τoɪʒechτ α Cαɪɼɼɼɪ οoɼɪɞɪɼ οóɪɞ, οcuɼ α ɪοul co cαɪɼlén Conchobαɪɼ οon τoɪɼc ɼɪɪ; οcuɼ Ruαɪοɼɪ mαc Οomnαɪll hí Conchobαɪɼ οo ɼcαɼthαɪn ɼe nα bɼαɪɮɼɪɞ ɼeɪn, οcuɼ ɼɪɞ οo ɮénum ɞó ɼe .h. n'Οomnαɪll, οcuɼ τɪʒeɼnuɼ Cαɪɼɼɼɪ οo ɮαbαɪɼτ οó; οcuɼ Οeɼɞoɼʒαɪll ɪɪʒen Mhαʒnuɪɼ hí Conchobαɪɼ οo ɼαɼοóɞ ɮeɪɮɪɼne ʒαllóʒlαech, οcuɼ luαɮ οo ɮαbαɪɼτ οóɪɞ οo ɮɪnn mαɼɞτhα Ruαɪοɼɪ mɪc Οomnαɪll hí Conchobαɪɼ; οcuɼ α ɰαɼbαο leo ɪαɼum οαɼ ɼáɼuʒαο ɰɪnnαɪɞ Τɪɼe Conαɪll τucαɞ ɞó ɼeme ɼɪɪ; οcuɼ cɼeαɮα móɼα οo ɮénum οo Chenél Conαɪll αɼ οɪɼechτ cɼɪɮe Cαɪɼɼɼɪ. Cɼeɮ lα Ɏeɞlɪm .h.Conchobαɪɼ αɼ ɮlαɪnn ɪn Ɏhαɪlʒɪʒ, áτ ɪnαɼ ʒαbαο Rɪcαɼο ɼeɪn οcuɼ áɼ α ɰuɪnnτeɼɪ mαɪlle ɼɼuɼ. Ro ɮɪɪóɪl Ɏeɞlɪm ɪαɼɼɪn ɼluαʒ móɼ οo ʒhαlloɪb οcuɼ οo ʒhαeɪοelαɪb ɼá Mαc Ɏheoɼuɪɼ οcuɼ ɼα Mhαelɼuαnαɪο Mαc n'Οɪαɼmαοα, οcuɼ ɼα ɮláɪnn Οomnαɪll hí Conchobαɪɼ, οo ɮoɼnum ɼɪʒe ɼe Ruαɪοɼɪ mαc Cαthαɪl, οcuɼ τucαοαɼ ɪ nαɪʒhɮe αnoeɪɼechτ οɪnnɼoɪʒeο τɼɪl Muɪɼeʒhαɪʒ. Ro hɪnnɪɼɼeο ɼɪn οo Ruαɪοɼɪ.h.Conchobαɪɼ, οo ɼɪʒ Connαchτ, οcuɼ ɼe ɼoɼ Mullαɮ ɼíɪʒ α Cloɪnn Chon-

1 "The Saithnech," or "Saithnian." He was so called, probably, from having been fostered in the territory of Saithne. See note 6, p. 563 supra.

2 Cathal-na-taisech; i.e. "Cathal (or Charles) of the chieftains."

3 Domini. Ο°., MS.

4 Caislen-Conchobhair. "Conchobhar's castle," now Castleconor, in the parish of the same name, barony of Tireragh, and county of Sligo.

5 The Failghech. See note 4, p. 434 supra.

6 With. ɼe, written twice in MS.

7 Mullach-Fidhig. "The summit of Fidheg." The MS. has Mullαɮ ɼíɪʒ, which appears to be a mutilated form of the name. The Annals of

generally eminent in all arts pertaining to poetry, mortuus
est. Domhnall Mac Tighernain, dux of Tellach-Dunchadha, who was usually called "the Saithnech,"[1] was
slain by Cathal-na-taisech[2] O'Ruairc. Amhlaibh O'Ferghail mortuus est.

The kalends of January on Thursday, and the twenty-
ninth of the moon; anno Domini[3] M.ccc.xvi.; sexto anno
cycli lunaris; xiiii. Indictionis; xx. anno cycli solaris.
Aedh O'Domhnaill and all the Cenel-Conaill mustered a
large army; and they came again into Cairbre, and went
to Caislen-Conchobhair[4] on this occasion; and Ruaidhri,
son of Domhnall O'Conchobhair, separated from his own
brothers, and made peace with O'Domhnaill, and gave
him the lordship of Cairbre. And Derbhorgaill, daughter
of Maghnus O'Conchobhair, retained a band of gallowglasses, and gave them a reward for the killing of Ruaidhri,
son of Domhnall O'Conchobhair, who was subsequently
slain by them in violation of the relics of Tir-Conaill,
which had previously been pledged to him; and great
depredations were committed by the Cenel-Conaill on
the inhabitants of the district of Cairbre. A depredation
by Fedhlim O'Conchobhair on the sons of the Failghech,[5]
when Richard himself was taken prisoner, and a slaughter
of his people was committed. Fedhlim afterwards assembled a great army of Foreigners and Gaeidhel, including
Mac Feorais, and Maelruanaidh Mac Diarmada, and the
sons of Domhnall O'Conchobhair, to contest the sovereignty with[6] Ruaidhri, son of Cathal; and they advanced
together towards Sil-Muiredhaigh. This was reported to
Ruaidhri O'Conchobhair, king of Connacht, who was
then encamped on Mullach-Fidhig[7] in Clann-Conmhaigh,

Connacht read mullt proicchi (for
Mullach Fidighi). Mageoghegan (Annals of Clonmacnois) writes the name
"Mullach ffie Ikie." Clann-Conmhaigh, now Clanconoo, or Clan-Con-
way, anciently the inheritance of the
family of O'Finaghty, and in later
times of the branch of the Burke
family called Mac David, is a district
to the west of the river Suck, in the
barony of Ballymoe, and county of
Galway.

maiꝺ, aꞃ ꝼeiċhem aꝃ ꝼáꞇꝃepꞇuiꞓ Ꝼeꞃꝺim, ocuꞃ ꞃé a
bꝼoꝃlonꞓpoꝃꞇ annꞃin. Iꞃ annꞃin aꝺconncoꝺaꞃ Ꝼeꞃꝺim
co ꞃoꞃníaꞇꞇa ꞃoꞃꞃanach ı ꞇoꞃach a ꞇeꞓlaiꞓ ꝺá ninn-
ꞃaiꞓeꝺ, ocuꞃ Maelꞃuanaiꝺ Mac Ꝺiaꞃmaꝺa maille ꞃe
na cuiꞃꞃꝼine, ocuꞃ ꞃe na luchꞇ lenmana ꝼeiꞃꞃin na
ꝼochaiꞃ; ocuꞃ ꞃo ꝺaꝺaꞃ ann, ımoꞃꞃo, clann Ꝺomnaill
hI Conchobaiꞃ ocuꞃ clann Ꝺonnchaꝺa mic Ꞇhomal-
ꞇaiꞓ, maꞃoen ꞃe Ꞓalloıb ıaꞃꞇaiꞃ Connachꞇ, na ꞇóiċim
ocuꞃ ına ꞇinól ꝺoċum ꞇóċaiꞃ ṁónaıꝺ Conneꝺha.
Ꝺoꝟáꝺaꞃ Connachꞇa ꝺon ꞇoeıꞓ eli ım Ruaıꝺꞃi mac
Caꞇhaıl hI Conchobaiꞃ, ꞃi Connachꞇ, ocuꞃ ım Ꝺiaꞃmaıꝺ
nꞓall Mac n'Ꝺiaꞃmaꝺa, ım ꞃiꞓ Mhuıꞓe Luiꞃꞓ an ꞇan
ꞃin, ocuꞃ ım Chonnachꞇaıꞓ áiꞃċena; ocuꞃ ꞇucꞃaꞇ ı
naiꞓꞇe uile ꝺá ċéli aꞃ ṁónaꝺ ın ꞇoċaiꞃ, ꝙcuꞃ ꞇucꞃaꞇ
ꞇachuꞃ ꞇulꝟoꞃb ꞇinneꞃnach ꝺaꞃoıle annꞃin. Ccchꞇ
chena ꞃo bꞃiꞃꞃ ımaꝺ na láṁ ocuꞃ na naꞃm, maille
ꞃe héꝺeꝺ na nꞜall, aꞃ Ruaıꝺꞃi, conꝺꞃoċaiꞃ ann ꞃí
Conꝺachꞇ, Ruaıꝺꞃi mac Caꞇhaıl .ı. cenn ꞓoile ocuꞃ
ꞓaiꞃcıꝺ na nꞜaoıꝺel, ocuꞃ ꝼeꞃ ꝺíꞇláiꞇꞃiꞓ Ꝺanaꞃ ocuꞃ
ꝺíꝟeꞃꞓach ocuꞃ ınnaꞃꝟꞇa allmuꞃach ocuꞃ echꞇaꞃ-
ċıneoıl a hEꞃınn; ocuꞃ aꝺꞃoċꞃaꞇaꞃ na ꝼochaiꞃ ann
Ꝺiaꞃmaıꝺ ꞓall Mac Ꝺiaꞃmaꝺa, ꞃı Muıꞓe Luiꞃꞓ, ocuꞃ
Coꞃmac Mac Ceꞇeꞃnaıꞓ, ꞃı Ciaꞃꞃaıꞓe, ocuꞃ Ꞓilla
Cꞃıꞃꞇ Mac Ꝺiaꞃmaꝺa, ocuꞃ Ꝺiaꞃmaıꝺ mac Ꝼeꞃꞓail
Mıc Ꝺhiaꞃmaꝺa, ocuꞃ Conneꞓán Mac Connecán, ocuꞃ
Ꝺomnall Mac Connecán, ocuꞃ Ꝺonnchaꝺ mac Ruaıꝺꞃi,
ocuꞃ ceꝺ ꞓallóꞓlaech maille ꞃiú, eꞇ alıı mulꞇı nobileꞃ
eꞇ ıꞓnobileꞃ. Ꝺo loiꞇꞇeꝺ ꝺon leıꞇ anaıll ann Moel-
ꞃuanaıꝺ Mac Ꝺiaꞃmaꝺa, ocuꞃ Ꝺomnall h.Ꝺaoıꞓill,
ocuꞃ Ropuc Mac Ꝼheoꞃuiꞃ: un. Ꝃcꞇ. Maꞃꞇu ꝺo ꞃónaꝺ
na ꞓníṁa ꞃin. Ro aiꞃꞓ Ꝼeꞃꝺim aeꞃ ꞓꞃáꞇa Ruaıꝺꞃi
hı Conchobaiꞃ ıaꞃꞃin. Ro ꞓaꝟuꞃꞇaꞃ ꝼein ꞃiꞓe Con-

[1] *Tochar-móna-Coinnedha.* "The causeway of Coinnidh's bog." See note [3], p. 284 *supra.*

[2] *The bog of the causeway.* mónaꝺ ın ꞇochaiꞃ; the *mónadh* (bog) which

gave name to the causeway, or *Tochar*, mentioned in last note. This "Monadh-in-tochair" may however be a proper name.

[3] *Ciarraighe*; otherwise Ciarraighe-

observing Fedhlim's proceedings. Then it was that they perceived Fedhlim advancing towards them vigorously, fiercely, at the head of his retainers, accompanied by Maelruanaidh Mac Diarmada with his own kindred and followers. And the sons of Domhnall O'Conchobhair, and the sons of Donnchadh, son of Tomaltach, together with the Foreigners of the West of Connacht, were also there, in his advance and muster towards Tóchar-móna-Coinnedha.[1] The Connachtmen were on the other side, including Ruaidhri, son of Cathal O'Conchobhair, king of Connacht, and Diarmaid Gall Mac Diarmada, king of Magh-Luirg at that time, and the other men of Connacht. And they all faced one another on the bog of the causeway,[2] and then delivered a fierce, sudden battle to each other. The superior number of the hands and weapons, however, together with the mail-armour of the Foreigners, vanquished Ruaidhri, so that the king of Connacht, Ruaidhri, son of Cathal—i.e. the head of the valour and bravery of the Gaeidhel, and the extirpator of pirates and bandits, and the expeller of foreigners and stranger-tribes from Erinn—fell there; and there fell along with him there Diarmaid Gall Mac Diarmada, king of Magh-Luirg, and Cormac Mac Cethernaigh, king of Ciarraighe,[3] and Gilla-Christ Mac Diarmada, and Diarmaid, son of Ferghal Mac Diarmada, and Connegán Mac Connegán, and Domhnall Mac Connegán, and Donnchadh son of Ruaidhri, and one hundred gallowglasses along with them, et alii[4] multi nobiles et ignobiles. Of the other side, Maelruanaidh Mac Diarmada, and Domhnall O'Baighill, and Robuc Mac Feorais, were wounded there. On the 7th of the kalends of March[5] these deeds were done. Fedhlim afterwards plundered the favorites of Ruaidhri O'Conchobhair, and then assumed himself the sovereignty

---

Maighe, or Clann-Cethernaigh. See
note [6], p. 452 *supra*.

[4] *Alii.* αli, MS.
[5] *Of March.* mαρcıı, MS.

nacht αnnpin o Cpp Ruaιo co hechtξe, ocup po
ξαbuptap .h. mbpuin bhpeιppne, ócup po benuptap
poξα bpαιξoe oιb, ocup po pιξaptap Uaιapξ.h.Ruaιpc
poppa, ocup oo ξαb bpaιξoe Chlaιnne Cellaιξ ocup hι
Mhaoaoáιn, ocup .h. nOιapmaoa ocup hι Cξpa ocup
hι Ohuboa; ocup oo chúaιo ιappιn oo oíchup Ξhall
ιapthaιp Connacht, ocup oo loιpceo laιp baιle ατα
Lethaιn, ocup oo mapbao Sоιamna oeχétap ocup
Mιlιo Ξoccan, ocup Uιllιam Penopecáp ocup Ioan
Soónoún ann, .ι. pιoιpeoha uaιpLe ιaopιoéιn; ocup po
mapbao ann Uιllιam Laιξléιp maιlle pe háp oιáιpmιoe

[ιna pochaιp; ocup oo haιpcceo ocup oo loιpceo ιn tιp
uιle laιp o chaιplen ιn Coppan co Rooba etιp cιll ocup
thuaιth, ocup taιnιcc oa tιξ ιappιn co naιthιup ocup to
netalaιo mopa leιp. Acup oo chooap a ceooιp a coιmoáιl
Leξe Moba co Mιlιc na Sιnoa, ocup oo loιpc aξup oo
bpιp caιplen Mιlιcc; ocup taιnιcc Muιpcheaptach
.h.bpιaιn, pιξ Tuaomuman, ιna tech anopιn, ocup pιl
mbpιaιn puaιo ιno αιξιo apoιlι; ocup po ιmpo co Rop
Coman oa lecao. Aξup o po chuala Peιolιm Uιllιam
bupcc oo toιoecht hι Conoachtaιo a hAlpaιn oo poξaιp
tιnol a muιnntιpe co hen ιnao oa hιnoapbao. Aξup
pob e po tιnol taιnιcc ano .ι. o Cp Ruaιo co hechtξι.
Aξup taιnιcc Oonochao.h.bpιaιn, pι Tuaomuman ιna
toιp ocup ιna tιnol, ocup .h.Maelechlaιnn pι Mιoe,
ocup .h. Ruaιpc, pι bpeιpne, ocup .h.Pepξaιl pι Con-
maιcne, acup Taocc.h.Cellaιξ pι .h.Mane, ocup mopan
aιlι oo macaιo pιξ acup taιpech hepenn oo techt ιna

<blank> ¹ *Countless multitude.* áp oιáιp-
mιoe; lit. "countless slaughter."
These words conclude folio 67 *b* in
the MS. H. 1, 19, Trin. Coll., Dublin,
after which occurs a hiatus extending
to A.D. 1413. The deficiency (which
ends with the bracket on p. 144, vol.
II.) has been supplied from a copy of
the so-called Annals of Connacht,

preserved in Trin. Coll., Dublin (class,
H. 1, 1–2, indicated by the letter B
in the notes appended to the following
pages), collated with another copy of
the same Annals in the Library of the
Royal Irish Academy, classed 23, F,
13, distinguished by the letter C in the
following foot notes. See the Introduction.

of Connacht from Es-Ruaidh to Echtghe. And he seized
the territory of the Ui-Briuin-Breifne, and took choice
hostages from them, and made Ualgharg O'Ruairc king
over them; and he took the hostages of Clann-Cellaigh,
and O'Madadhain, and Ui-Diarmada, and O'hEghra, and
O'Dubhda. And he afterwards went to expel the Foreigners
of the West of Connacht; and Baile-Atha-lethain was
burned by him, and Stephen de Exeter, and Miles Cogan,
and William Prendergast, and John Staunton, were slain
there, (viz., these were noble knights); and William Laighleis was slain there, and a countless multitude[1] [along with
them. And the entire country was plundered and burned
by him, from the castle of the Corran to Rodhba, both[2]
church and territory; and he returned home afterwards
with gladness, and with great spoils. And they went[3] forthwith[4] to Milic-na-Sinda, to meet the people of Leth-Modha;
and he burned and demolished the castle of Milic; and
Muirchertach O'Briain, king of Tuadh-Mumha, went into
his house there, the descendants of Brian Ruadh being
opposed to each other.[5] And he turned back to Ros-
Comain, to demolish it.[6] And when Fedhlim heard that
William Burk had arrived in Connacht from Alba, he
commanded a muster of his people to one place, to expel
him. And this was the muster that came there, viz., all
from Es-Ruaidh to Echtghe. And Donnchadh O'Briain,
king of Tuadh-Mumha, came in his following and
muster; and O'Maelechlainn, king[7] of Midhe; and
O'Ruairc, king[7] of Breifne; and O'Ferghail, king[7] of Conmaicne; and Tadhg O'Cellaigh, king[7] of Ui-Maine, and
many more[8] of the sons of kings and chieftains of Erinn,

---

[2] *Both.* eτιη=inter, B. eαρap, C.

[3] *They went.* ρο choραp, B.. ρο
ċuαρap, C.

[4] *Forthwith.* α ceρoιp, B. α
cceρóιp, C.

[5] *Opposed to each other.* ιnρ αιᵹιρ

αpoιλe, C. In this MS. the practice
of aspirating is very loosely observed.

[6] *To demolish it;* i.e. the castle of
Ros-Comain.

[7] *King.* pιᵹ, B. pι, C.

[8] *More.* αιλι, B. eιλe, C.

defective.
supplied
" Annals
nnacht."]

τinol, ocuς α nvol viblinαit co hαcth na ριξ ι conne
Uilliam buρc ocuς Mιc Feoρuiς ocuς ξαll Connαcτ
αρchena, ocuς cατh vo comoραv ετuρρο a nvoρuς ιη
baili, ocuς bριςεv αρ ξαιvelαιt anηςιn, ocuς Feivlιmιv
.h.Conchovαις, ςι Convαcht, ocuς αvvαρ ςιξ Eρenn can
ςςεαςαvρα, vo mαρvαv ann, ocuς Ταvξ .h.Cellαιξ, ςι
.h.Mαιne, ocuς ochταρ αρ χx.ιτ vαρ vual ςιξι .h.Mαιne,
vo τοιτιm mαρoen ςις anv ; ocuς Mαξnuς mαc Vomnαill
.h.Chonchovαις, τanαιςτι Connαcht, ocuς αρτ .h.hεξρα,
ςι Luιξne, ocuς Maelechlαιnn cαρραch .h.Ouvvαι, ocuς
Muιρceαρταch mαc Conchuvαις .h.Ouvvα, ocuς Con-
chuvαρ occ .h.Ouvvα, αξuς Viαρmαιv Mαc Viαρmαvα,
αvvαρ ςιξ Moιξι Luιςξ, ocuς Muιρcheαρταch mαc Ταv-
lιξ mιc Viαρmαvα, ocuς Muιρceαρταch mαc Viαρmαvα
mιc Feςξαιl, ocuς Mαilechlαιnn oc mαc Mαξnuςα,
αcuς Seααn mαc Muρchαv .h.Mαvαvαn, ocuς Vomnαll
mαc αevα .h. Conchenαinv, ςιξ.h.nViαρmαvα, ocuς
Muιρcheαρταch α veρvραταις mαρoen ςις, ocuς Muρchαv .h. Mαvαvαin, ocuς Vomnαll.h.vαιξιll, ocuς
Vonochαv .h. Mαilmuαιv conα muιηnτις mαille ςις,
ocuς mαc Muρchαv Meξ Mαthξαmnα ocuς cέv vα
muιnτις mαille ςις, ocuς Niαll Sιnnαch, ςι ςες Techbα,
conα muιηnτις, ocuς Feςξαl mαc Seoαin ξαllvα.h.Feς-
ξαιl, ocuς Uilliαm mαc αevα oιcc .h. Feςξαιl, ocuς
Tomaς mαc αmlαιv.h.Feςξαιl ; αξuς vo mαρvαv ann
beuς coιceς vo člαιnn Vonnchαιv .ι. Tomαlταch mαc.
ξιllα Cριςτ Mιc Vonnchαv, ocuς Muρchαv Mαc
Vonnchαv, ocuς Conchovαρ mαc Ταιvξ, ocuς Muις-
ceαρταch ocuς Maelςεačlαιnη Mαc Vonnchαv ; ocuς
vo mαρvαv anv beuςς Eoιn Mαc αevαcαn, bςεčεm
.h.Conchuvαις, ocuς ξιllα na nαεm mαc Vαιlςεvocαις

---

1 *Between them.* ετuρρο, B.
eατορρα, C.

2 *King.* ςι, B. ςιξ, C.

3 *Fit to be king.* αvvαρ ςιξ ;
lit. " materies regis."

4 *Og.* " The young." oc, B. οξ, C.

5 *Donnchadh.* Donough. Vonochαv, B. Vonnchαv, C.

6 *Son.* The Four Masters call him
Murchadh (or Murrough), and add
that he was the son of Murchadh Mac
Mathghamhna.

came in his muster. And they all went to Ath-na-righ, against William Burk, Mac Feorais, and the other Foreigners of Connacht; and a battle was fought between them[1] at the door of the town, and the Gaeidhel were defeated there, and Feidhlimidh O'Conchobhair, king of Connacht, and undisputed heir presumptive to the sovereignty of Erinn, was slain there, and Tadhg O'Cellaigh, king[2] of Ui-Maine, and twenty-eight persons entitled to the sovereignty of Ui-Maine, fell there along with him; and Maghnus, son of Domhnall O'Conchobhair, tanist of Connacht; and Art O'hEghra, king of Luighne; and Maelechlainn Carrach O'Dubhda; and Muirchertach, son of Conchobhar O'Dubhda; and Conchobhar Og O'Dubhda; and Diarmaid Mac Diarmada, who was fit to be king[3] of Magh-Luirg; and Muirchertach, son of Taichlech Mac Diarmada; and Muirchertach, son of Diarmaid, son of Ferghal; and Maelechlainn Og[4] Mac Maghnusa; and John, son of Murchadh O'Madadhain; and Domhnall, son of Aedh O'Concennainn, king of Ui-Diarmada, and his brother Muirchertach along with him; and Murchadh O'Madadhain; and Domhnall O'Baighill; and Donnchadh[5] O'Maelmhuaidh, together with his people; and the son[6] of Murchadh Mac Mathghamhna, and one hundred of his people along with him; and Niall Sinnach, king of Feara-Tethbha, with his people; and Ferghal, son of John Gallda O'Ferghail; and William, son of Aedh Og O'Ferghail; and Thomas, son of Amhlaibh O'Ferghail. And five of the Clann-Donnchaidh[7] were also slain there, viz., Tomaltach, son of Gilla-Christ Mac Donnchaidh, and Murchadh Mac Donnchaidh, and Conchobhar son of Tadhg, and Muirchertach and Maelsechlainn Mac Donnchaidh. And John Mac Aedhagan, O'Conchobhair's brehon, and Gilla-na-naemh,[8] son of Dal-redochair O'Dobhailen, the

---

[7] *Of the Clann-Donnchaidh.* ꝺo ꝼlꝺinn ꝺonꝺchꝺiꝺ, B. The Mac Donoughs of Tirerrill.

[8] *Gilla - na - naemh.* ᵹiꝺllꝺ nꝺ nꝺemh, C.

.h.Oobaɩɫen, ɾeɾ ɩmoɾchaɩɾ na honchon, ocuɾ Comaɾ .h.Conaɫɫan, a cɩmċɩoɫɫ a cɩʒeɾna; ocuɾ ní heŏ aṁaɩn, achc nɩ huɾaɾa a ɩnoɩɾɩn aɾ maɾbhaŏ anoɾɩn vo Muɩṁnechaɩŏ ocuɾ vo Mɩŏeachaɩŏ, ocuɾ oɾeɾaɩbh Eɾeno aɾchena, uc vɩxɩc an ɾɩɫɩ :—

Moɾ oɾeɾaɩŏ hEɾeno uɩɫɩ accɩmcheɫɫ ɩn moɾ muɩʒɩ,
Moɾ mac ɾɩʒ nach abɾaɩm aɩnm vo maɾbaŏ ɩɾɩn moɾ maɩŏm;
Oo ɾɫuaʒ Mɩŏe ocuɾ Mumhan, cɾuaʒ ɫem cɾɩŏe an caċuʒaŏ.

La ɾan Laŏɾaɾ maɩɾcɩɾ vo ɾonaɩc na ʒɩɩṁa ɾɩn; aʒuɾ ɾeɾ cɾɩ mbɫɩaŏan .xx. Feoɫɩmɩŏ aʒ a maɾŏaŏ, ocuɾ coɩcc bɫɩaona vo ɩɾɾɩʒɩ ʒuɾ ʒaŏ Ruaɩŏɾɩ macc Cachaɩɫ ɾuaɩŏ ɩna cheno ɩ ɾe heŏ Leŏ bɫɩaona, ocuɾ Leŏ bɫɩaŏaɩn aɩɫɩ voɾam caɾéɩɾ Ruaɩŏɾɩ ɩɾɩn ɾɩʒɩ ʒuɾ maɾbaŏ ɩɾɩn chach ɾɩn Ccha na ɾɩʒ. Ruaɩŏɾɩ na ɾeo, mac Oonochaɩo mɩc Eoʒaɩn mɩc Ruaɩŏɾɩ .h. Conchuŏaɩɾ, vo ɾɩʒaŏ ɩaɾɾɩn. Sɫuaʒaŏ aŏŏaɫ moɾ La hUɩɫɫɩam Ŏuɾc hɩ Sɩɫ Muɩɾeŏaɩʒ ɩaɾɾɩn, ocuɾ .h. Conchoŏaɩɾ ocuɾ Sɩɫ Muɩɾeŏaɩʒ uɫɩ vo venam ɾɩcha ɾɾɩɾ achc Mac Oɩaɾmava nama. Ceachc voɾam a Maʒ Luɩɾʒ ɩaɾɾɩn, ocuɾ cɾeacha moɾa vo chaŏaɩɾc vo Leɩɾ o Cch ɩn chɩp ocuɾ a hUachcaɾ Cɩɾɩ, ocuɾ ɩn cɩɾ uɫɩ vo Loɾcaŏ ocuɾ vo ṁɩɫɫeŏ voɩŏ, acuɾ a nɩmchechc ʒan chach ʒan cumaɩŏ. Ruaɩŏɾɩ mac Oonochaɩŏ vachɾɩʒaŏ vo Mac Oɩaɾmava ɩaɾɾɩn, ɩaɾ na Ŏeɩŏ ɾaɩŏɩ co Leŏ ɩncɩ. Oeɾŏoɾʒaɩɫɫ ɩnʒen Maʒnuɾa .h.Conchoŏaɩɾ, ben Ceŏa.h.Ooṁnaɩɫɫ, moɾcua eɾc. Macha mac Coɾmaɩc moɾcuuɾ eɾc. Ruaɩŏɾɩ na ɾeo, mac Oonochaɩŏ mɩc Eoʒaɩn, ɾɩ Connachc, vo maɾbhaŏ a ɾɩɫɫ La Cachaɫ mac Ceŏo mɩc Eoʒaɩn, ocuɾ a éveo

---

standard bearer, and Thomas O'Conallan, were slain there around[1] their lord. And not alone this; but it is not easy to tell all that were then slain of Momonians and Meathians, and of the men of Erinn likewise, ut dixit the poet.[2]

> Many of the men of Erin all, around the great plain—
> Many sons of kings, whom I name not, were slain in the great defeat:
> Sorrowful to my heart is the conflict of the host of Midhe and Mumha.

On the day of St. Laurence the martyr these deeds were committed;[3] and Fedhlimidh was twenty-three years old when slain; and he had been five years in the sovereignty of Connacht when Ruaidhri, son of Cathal Ruadh, assumed it in opposition to him during the space of half a year; and he was another half year after Ruaidhri in the sovereignty until he was slain in this battle of Ath-na-righ. Ruaidhri-na-fedh,[4] son of Donnchadh, son of Eoghan, son of Ruaidhri O'Conchobhair, was afterwards made king. A prodigious hosting by William Burk afterwards into Sil-Muiredhaigh, and O'Conchobhair and all the Sil-Muiredhaigh made peace with him, except Mac Diarmada alone. He afterwards went into Magh-Luirg, and brought great preys with him from Ath-in-chip and from Uachtar-tire; and the entire country was burned and destroyed by them; and they went away without[5] battle or conditions. Ruaidhri, son of Donnchadh, was subsequently deposed from the sovereignty by Mac Diarmada, after having been[6] a quarter[7] and a half in it. Derbhorgaill, daughter of Maghnus O'Conchobhair, wife of Aedh O'Domhnaill, mortua est. Matthew Mac Cormaic mortuus est. Ruaidhri-na-fedh,[4] son of Donnchadh, son of Eoghan, king of Connacht, was slain in treachery by Cathal, son of Aedh, son

---

of Athlone, county of Roscommon, where Ruaidhri was fostered.

[5] *Without.* cin, B. ᵹαn, C.

[6] *After having been.* ιαρ nα bιʈ B. ιαρ nα bειʈ, C.

[7] *A quarter;* i.e. of a year.

ᴅοn ταεᵬ ιϝτιᵹ ιm Chαthαl ; οcuϝ ιϝ ϝιϝ αᴅuᵬαιϝτ
Ruαᴅϝι ϝαιϝιm ᴅϝoch mαc ϝιᵹ, ιαϝ τhecmαιl ϝcεnε
Ruαᴅϝι ιϝιn εᴅεᴅ.

ᴋᴌ. εnαιϝ ϝoϝ Sατhoϝn, οcuϝ x.uαthαᵬ ϝuιϝϝι ; αnno
ᴅomιnι M.ccc.xuιι. ; ϝεϝτιmo αnno cιcλι λunαϝιϝ ; xιι.
ιnᴅιcτιοnιϝ ; xxᵒ. ϝϝιmo αnno cιcλι ϝoλαϝιϝ. Τoιϝϝ-
ᵬεαλᵬαᵬ mαc Αεᴅα mιc εoᵹαιn ᴅo ϝιᵹαᵬ ᴅo Chonnαch-
ταιᵬ ιn hoc αnno. Roιbεϝᴅ α ᵬϝuιϝ .ι. ϝι Αλϝαn, ᴅo
τεαᵬτ α nεϝιnn mαιλλε ϝε móϝαn ᴅo ᵹαλλocλαεchαιᵬ
α ϝuϝταchτ α bϝαthαϝ .ι. εᴅubαϝᴅ α ᵬϝuιϝ, οcuϝ ᴅo
ᴅιchuϝ ᵹαλλ α hεϝιnᴅ. Mαιλιϝ ᴅεxετϝα, τιᵹεαϝnα
Αthα λεᵬαιn, ᴅo mαϝᵬαᵬ λα Cαthαl mαc ᴅοᵯnαιλλ
.h.Conchuᵬαιϝ, οcuϝ ᴅo ᴅοᵯnαλλ mαc Ταιᵬᵹ mιc ᴅoᵯ-
nαιλλ ιϝϝαιϝ .h. Conchoᵬαιϝ, αϝ boϝᴅ nα Μεthεnαch
ᴅϝomα cλιαᵬ, οcuϝ cεthϝι ϝιϝ .x. αλι mαϝoεn ϝιϝ.
Cαιϝλεn Αthα cλιατh ιn Choϝαιnᴅ ᴅo bϝιϝεᵬ ιn hoc
αnno. ᴅonᴅchαᵬ .h. bϝιαιn ϝι Μuᵯαn οcιϝuϝ εϝτ.
Μαελεαᵬλαιnn cαϝϝαch Μαc ᴅιαϝmαᴅα, αᴅᵬαϝ ϝιᵹ
Μοιᵹι λuιϝᵹ, αᵹuϝ Μαᵹnuϝ .h. ϝλαnnαcαn, ᴅαᵯnα
ταιϝιch Cλοιnnε Cαthαιλ, ᴅo mαϝᵬαᵬ λα ᵹιλλιbεϝᴅ
Μαc ᵹοιϝᴅελb, οcuϝ Conchuᵬαϝ mαc Comαϝϝα Comαn
.h.Conchuᵬαιϝ, ετ αλιι muλτι. Μαιᵬm Chιλλι moϝι ϝoϝ
mαc Ruαᴅϝι οcuϝ ϝoϝ ϝεϝαᵬ bϝειϝnε, οcuϝ ᴅo mαϝbαᴅ
.uιι. xx.ιτ ᵹαλλocλαεch ᴅo muιnτιϝ [ᵯειc] Ruαᴅϝι αnᴅ ;
οcuϝ ᴅα mαc Αεᴅα bϝειϝnιᵹ .h.Conchuᵬαιϝ ᴅo ᵹαᵬαιλ.
αnᴅ, οcuϝ ᴅonnchαᵬ mαc Νειλλ .h.Ruαιϝc, αᵹuϝ Conchuᵬαϝ buιᵬε Μαᵹ Τιᵹεαϝnαn, ταιϝεch Τελλαᵹ ᴅun-
chαᴅhα, ᴅo ᵯαϝbhαᴅh αnᴅ, οcuϝ Μαᵬᵹαᵯαιn Μαᵹ
Τιᵹεαϝnαιn, οcuϝ ιn ᵹιλλα ϝuαᵬ mαc ιnᴅ αιϝchιnᴅιch

---

1 *And.* This clause to the end is
omitted in C.

2 *Touched.* From this it would
appear that Ruaidhri had attempted
to kill his slayer. See note 6, p. 599.

3 *Kalends.* The characters ꞇƀ are
added to the abbrev. " ᴋᴌ.," to indicate that B is the Dominical Letter
for the year.

4 *To Erinn.* α nεϝιnn, B. α
nεϝιnn, C.

5 *From Erinn.* α hεϝιnᴅ, B. α
hεϝιnn, C.

6 *By Domhnall.* The Four Masters
represent this Domhnall as slain
along with De Exeter ; but they are
most probably wrong.

of Eoghan; and Cathal wore his coat of mail on the
inside; and[1] it was to him that Ruaidhri said, "I perceive
a bad son of a king," after Ruaidhri's knife had touched[2]
the coat of mail.

The kalends[3] of January on Saturday, and the tenth
of the moon; anno Domini M.CCC.XVII.; septimo anno
cycli lunaris; xv. Indictionis; xx°. primo anno cycli
solaris. Toirdhelbhach, son of Aedh, son of Eoghan,
was made king by the Connachtmen in hoc anno. Robert
Bruce, i.e. the king of Alba, came to Erinn[4] with a great
number of gallowglasses, in aid of his brother, i.e. Edward Bruce, and to expel the Foreigners from Erinn.[5]
Meiler de Exeter, lord of Ath-lethan, was slain by Cathal,
son of Domhnall O'Conchobhair, and by Domhnall,[6] son
of Tadhg, son of Domhnall Irruis O'Conchobhair, on the
border of the Methenach[7] of Drium-cliabh, and fourteen[8]
other men along with him. The castle of Ath-cliath-in-
Chorainn was broken down in hoc[9] anno. Donnchadh
O'Briain, king of Mumha, occisus est. Maelechlainn
Carrach Mac Diarmada, one qualified to be king of
Magh-Luirg, and Maghnus O'Flannagain, who was
qualified to be chieftain of Clann-Cathail, were slain by
Gilbert Mac Goisdelbh; and Conchobhar, son of Comarb-
Comain O'Conchobair, et alii multi, *were slain.* The vic-
tory of Cill-mor over the son of Ruaidhri and the men of
Breifne; and seven score gallowglasses [of the son[10]] of
Ruaidhri's people were slain there; and Aedh Breif-
nech O'Conchobhair's two sons were taken prisoners
there; and Donnchadh, son of Niall O'Ruairc, and Con-
chobhar Buidhe Mac Tighernain, chieftain of Tellach-
Dunchadha,[11] were slain there, and Mathghamhain Mac
Tighernain, and the Gilla-ruadh, son of the Airchinnech

---

[7] *Methenach.* The name of a river near Drumcliff, in the county of Sligo.

[8] *Fourteen.* ceꞇhꞃi x., B. ceiꞇꞃo x., C.

[9] *Hoc.* hocc, B.

[10] *Of the son.* ṁeic; supplied from the Four Mast.

[11] *Of Tellach-Dunchadha.* Ꞇellach (*recté* Ꞇellaiġ) Ꞇunchaꝛha, B.

5. defective,
t supplied
n "Annals
Connacht."]

Meᵹ Tiᵹeαρnαn, ocuρ Nιcol Mαc ιn mαιᵹιρτιρ, ocuρ mοραn αιlι ᴅα cιneᴅ oριn αmαch. Mαelιρα ρuαᴅ Mαc Ccᴅαᵹαιn, ραι Cρenᴅ α mbρειτemnαchτ ρenα-chαιρ, moρτuuρ eρτ. Rαᵹnαll Mαᵹ Rαᵹnαιll, ταιρech Muιnτeρι hColαιρ, ᴅo ᵹαbαιl ᴅα oιρeαcτ ρeιn α ριll, ocuρ ταιρech ᴅo ᴅenαṁ ᴅo Seρραιᴅ Mαᵹ Rαᵹnαιll ιαρ ριn. Ꞡoρτα ρo móρ ιριn blιαᴅαιn ριn α nⲆριnn uιlι. Ꝺoṁnαll ριαᴅαc Mαc Muρchαᴅα, ριᵹ oιρρᴅeαρτ Lαιᵹen, moρτuuρ eρτ.

Ƈττ. Cnáιρ ρορ Ꝺoṁnαc, ocuρ αenmαᴅ xx.ιτ ρι-ιρρι; αnno Ꝺomιnι M°.ccc°.xuιιι; octαuo αnno cιclι lunαριρ; ρριmo αnno ιnᴅιcτιonιρ; xιι. αnno cιclι ρolαριρ. Mαᴅṁ móρ ᴅo chαbαιρτ α nⲆlιᴅ lα hꞸα Ceρbαιll αρ Ꞡαllαιb, ᴅu αρ mαρbαᴅ Ccᴅαm Mαρeρ ocuρ Ꞡαιll ιmᴅα αιlι mαιlle ριρ. Slúαᵹ móρ ᴅo τιnol ᴅo Mαelρuαnαιᴅ Mαc Ꝺιαρmαᴅα, ᴅo ριᵹh Mοιᵹι Luιρᵹ, ocuρ ιρ ιατ bα ρeρρ ᴅo bαι αρ ιnτ ρlúαᵹ ριn .ι. Toιρρᴅeαlbαc .h. Conchobαιρ, ρι Conᴅαchτ, ocuρ Uαl-ᵹαρᵹ .h. Ruαιρc, ριᵹ bρeιρne, αᵹuρ Conchobαρ.h. Cellαιᵹ, ρι .h. Mαιne, ocuρ Tomαlταch Mαc Ꝺonn-chαιᴅ, τιᵹeαρnα Tιρι hOιlellα. Ccuρ α nᴅol ᴅιblιnαιᴅ ᴅιnnραιᵹιᴅ Cαthαιl mιc Ꝺoṁnαιll .h.Conchobαιρ co ρáρα choιllιᴅ; ocuρ ταρcαιᴅ Cαthαl coṁαᴅα móρα ᴅοιᴅ ᴅo cιnᴅ ᵹαn ᴅol ċuιᵹι, ocuρ nιρ ᵹαbραᴅ uαᴅα; αᵹuρ ᴅo ιnᴅραιᵹeαᴅαρ nα mαιthι ριn co láρ meᴅon α Lonᵹphuιρτ; ocuρ nι αρ τeιcheᴅ nα αρ τιme ᴅo chuαιᴅ ᴅοραm ριn, ocuρ ᴅo ιnᴅραιᵹ Cαthαl αρ nα τιᵹιᴅ αmαch ιαᴅ co ρραechᴅα ρορmιατα, ocuρ coṁραιcιτ ρρια αροιlι αnnριn; αchτ ατα nι chenα, mαρbᴅαρ Conchuᴅαρ .h. Cellαιᵹ, ρι .h. Mαιne, αρ ιn lαthαιρ ριn, ocuρ bριαn

---

1 *His*; i.e. Conchobhar Buidhe (the Yellow) Mac Tighernan's.

2 *Mac Aedhagain.* mαc Ccᴅαcαn, B. mαc Ccᴅαᵹαn, C. The name would now be written Mac Egan, or Egan without the "Mac."

3 *Brehonship of Fenechas.* Fenechas is a term employed to signify the laws of the ancient Irish, commonly called the code of Brehon Laws.

4 *Mortuus est.* This entry is not in C.

5 *Kalends.* The Dominical Letter for the year (A) is added.

Mac Tighernain, and Nicholas Mac-in-Maigistir, and many more of his[1] kindred besides. Maelisa Ruadh Mac Aedhagain,[2] the most eminent man in Erinn in the Brehonship of Fenechas,[3] mortuus est. Raghnall Mac Raghnaill, chieftain of Muinter-Eolais, was taken prisoner by his own tribe, in treachery; and Jeffrey Mac Raghnaill was afterwards made chieftain. Very great famine in this year in all Erinn. Domhnall Riabhach Mac Murchadha, illustrious king of Laighen, mortuus est.[4]

The kalends[5] of January on Sunday, and the twenty-first of the moon; anno Domini M°. ccc°. xviii.; octavo anno cycli lunaris, primo anno Indictionis; xxii. anno cycli solaris. A great defeat was inflicted in Eile, by O'Cerbhaill, on the Foreigners, where Adam Mares was slain, and many other[6] Foreigners along with him. A great army was assembled by Maelruanaidh Mac Diarmada, king of Magh-Luirg, and the noblest who were in this army[7] were Toirdhelbhach O'Conchobhair, king of Connacht, and Ualgharg O'Ruairc, king of Breifne, and[8] Conchobhar O'Cellaigh, king of Ui-Maine, and Tomaltach Mac Donnchaidh, lord of Tir-Oilella. And they all proceeded to attack Cathal, son of Domhnall O'Conchobhair, to Fása-choillidh.[9] And Cathal offered them liberal terms, on condition that they would not go to him; but they did not accept them from him. And these nobles advanced to the very middle of his fortress; but this occurred not through flight or timidity on his part. And Cathal advanced furiously, bravely, against them from out of the houses, and they encountered[10] each other. However, Conchobhar O'Cellaigh, king of Ui-Maine, was slain in

---

[6] *Other.* aili, B. eile, C.

[7] *Army.* ſluaᵹ, B. ſluaᵹaᵭ, C.

[8] *And.* aᵹuſ. Repeated in B.

[9] *Fása-choillidh.* Foſa choillio, B. The Four Masters have Fása-choillidh, as in C. It means "the

waste of the wood," would now be pronounced Fossakilly, and was the name of a woody district in the present barony of Carbury, county of Sligo.

[10] *Encountered.* cuṁſaicit, B. coṁſaicit, C.

[S. defective.
ext supplied
om "Annals
' Connacht."]

mαϲ Ϲoιρρϸhϵlbαιʒ .h.Conϲobαιρ, αϐϐαρ ριʒ Connαϲhϲ,
oϲuρ ϐριαn Ϻαϲ Ϻαʒnuρα, oϲuρ Cαϲhαl mαϲ ʒιllα
Cριϲϲ Ϻιϲ ϸιαρmαϸα, ϵϲ αlιι mulϲι nobιlϵρ ϵϲ ιʒno-
bιlϵρ ϵϲιρ lϵϲhαϸ oϲuρ mαρbhαϸ. 1n Cαϲhαl ϲϵϸnα ριn
ϸιnϸραιʒιϸ Connαϲhϲ ιαρριn, oϲuρ ϸo ρonϵ ϲρϵαϲhα
móρα αρ Ϻαϲ nϸιαρmαϸα, oϲuρ ϸo ʒαϐ ρϵιn ριʒι
Connαϲhϲ; oϲuρ ϸo hαϵριʒαϸ lϵιρ Ϲoιρρϸhϵαlbαϲh
Uα Conϲhuϐαιρ, oϲuρ ϸo ϲhúαιϸ ρo ϸιϲιn Uιllιαm ϐuρϲ
oϲuρ uιlι ʒαll Connαϲhϲ ιαρριn. ʒιllα αn Comϸϵϸ
mαϲ Cιnαιϲh .h. ʒoρmʒαιlι, oϲuρ ʒoρmlαιϲh ιnʒhϵn Ϻιϲ
ϐραnαn α ϐϵn, ϸo ϸol ϸéϲϲ ρon αm ριn .ι. oιρϲhιnnϵϲh
Oιlιριnϸ ϵρϸϵ. Sϵoαn mαϲ .h. Νϵιll .ι. mαϲ ϸoṁnαιll
.h.Νϵιll, ϸo mαρϐαϸ lα hαϵϸ Uα nϸoṁnαιll α nϸoιρϵ
Choluιm Cιllϵ, oϲuρ mαϲ ϸoṁnαιll oϲuρ ϸαιnϵ ιmϸα
αιlι ϸo mαρϐαϸ oϲuρ ϸo ϐáϲαϸ αn lá ϲϵϸnα. Rιϲαρϸ
α Clαρα moρϲuuρ ϵρϲ. ϴϸuϐαρϸ α ϐριuιρ, ρϵρ mιllϲι
nα hϵιρϵnn ulι ϲo ϲoιϲϲϵnϸ ϵιϸιρ ʒαllαιϐ oϲuρ ʒαιϸϵl-
αιϐ, ϸo ṁαρϐαϸ lα ʒαllαιϐ ϵρϵnϸ ϲρια nϵρϲ ϲαϐαιʒϵ
oϲuρ ϲρoϐαϲϲ oϲ ϸún ϸϵlʒαn ; oϲuρ Ϻαϲ Ruαιϸρι ρι
1nnρι ʒαll, oϲuρ Ϻαϲ ϸomnαιll, ρι Oιριρ ʒαιϸϵαl, ϸo
ṁαρϐαϸ mαραϵn ριρ αnϸ, mαιllϵ ρϵ nαlbαnϲhαιϐ
mαιllϵ ρριu. αʒuρ nι ϸϵρnαϸ o ϲhuρ ϸoṁαιn o ϸo
ϸιϲhuιρϵϸ ρινϵ ρoṁρα α hϵιριnϸ ʒnιoṁ bα ρϵρρ
ϸϵϵραιϐ ϵρϵαnϸ uιlι ιnα αn ʒnιoṁ ριn. Uαιρ ϲαινιϲ
ʒoιϲ oϲuρ ʒoρϲα oϲuρ ϸιϲh ϸαινϵ ρϵ lινϸ αρ ρoϸ
ϵρϵnϸ ϵϐ ϲρι mϐlιαϸαn. ϲo lϵϲ, oϲuρ ϸo ιϲhϸαιρ nα
ϸαινϵ ϲαn αṁαραρ α chϵlι αρ ρoϸ ϵρϵnϸ. Sϵoαn Uα

---

[1] *Either.* ϵϲιρ, B. ϵαϸαρ, C.
Although translated "either," the
word ϵϲιρ=Lat. *inter;* and the expression ϵϲιρ lϵϲhαϸ oϲuρ mαρbhαϸ lit. means "between wounding
and killing."

[2] *Committed.* ϸo ρonϵ, B. ϸo
ριnnϵ, C.

[3] *Protection.* ϸιϲιn, B. ϸιϸϵαn, C.

[4] ϸoιρϵ. ϸoρι, B. ϸoιρϵ, C.
ϸoιρϵ Choluιm Cιllϵ (the Irish

name of Derry) signifies " Colum
Cille's oak wood."

[5] *Mac Domhnaill.* In place of
" Mac Domhnaill," Mageoghegan
(Annals of Clonmacnois) says "the
same Aedh," i.e. Aedh (or Hugh)
O'Domhnaill. But the Four Masters
agree with the form in the text,
which, however, should probably be
mαϲ Uι ϸoṁnαιll, "the son of
O'Domhnaill."

A.D. [1318.]

that field, and Brian, son of Toirdhelbhach O'Conchobhair, heir to the sovereignty of Connacht, and Brian Mac Maghnusa, and Cathal, son of Gilla-Christ Mac Diarmada, et alii multi nobiles et ignobiles, were either[1] wounded or killed. The same Cathal attacked Connacht afterwards, and committed[2] great depredations on Mac Diarmada; and he assumed himself the sovereignty of Connacht, and Toirdhelbhach O'Conchobhair was deposed by him. And he (*Toirdhelbhach*) subsequently sought the protection[3] of William Burk and all the Foreigners of Connacht. Gilla-an-Choimdedh, son of Cinaeth O'Gormghaile, i.e. the airchinnech of Oilfinn, and Gormlaith, daughter of Mac Branan, his wife, died about this time. John, the son of O'Neill, i.e. the son of Domhnall O'Neill, was slain by Aedh O'Domhnaill in Doire[4]-Choluim-Cille; and Mac Domhnaill[5] and many other persons[6] were drowned and slain the same day. Richard de Clare mortuus est.[7] Edward Bruce, the destroyer of all[8] Erinn in general, both Foreigners and Gaeidhel, was slain by the Foreigners of Erinn, through the power of battle and bravery, at[9] Dun-Delgan; and Mac Ruaidhri, king of Insi-Gall, and Mac Domhnaill, king of Airer-Gaeidhel, together with the men of Alba, were slain there along with him; and no better deed for the men of all Erinn[10] was performed since the beginning[11] of the world, since the Fomorian race was expelled from Erinn, than this deed; for theft,[12] and famine, and destruction of men occurred throughout Erinn during his time, for the space of three years and a half; and people used to eat one another, without doubt,

---

6 *Many other persons.* ᴅᴀoıne ᴛomᴅα eıle, C.

7 *Mortuus est.* According to Pembridge's Annals, Richard de Clare was slain by O'Brien and Mac Carthy.

8 *All.* uli, B. uile, C.

9 *At.* oc, B. ag, C.

10 *Of all Erinn.* Ereann uili, B. Eireann uile, C.

11 *Since the beginning.* o thus, B. ó tos, C.

12 *Theft.* go, falsehood, B. C has goit, theft, which seems more in harmony with the context.

MS. defective.
Text supplied
from "Annals
of Connacht."]

Ferġail do marḃaḋ doen orchur troiġti da mac féin. Serraiḋ Ua Ferġail .i. mac Ġiolla na naem .h. Ferġail toirech muintire hAnnġaile, do éc iar forba .ui. mbliaḋan .xxx.at a flaiṫeara. Sneaċta do na friṫ raṁail re heḋ cian in hoc anno.[1] Cathal mac Ġiolla Criord daill Meg Raġnaill occirus[2] ert.[3]

Kt.[4] Enair for Lúan, ocur aili uathaḋ fuirri; anno Domini M°. ccc°. xix.; ix.anno cicli lunaris; ii. anno indictionir;[5] xx.iii. anno cicli rolarir. Erpog Ratha boṫ .i. Enri mac an Crorain, in Crirto quieuit. Tomar mac Cormaic .h. Domhnaill, ab Era Ruaiḋ, do thoġa dochom Erpogoidi Ratha boṫ. Errac[6] Doiri, aġur Ua Banan erpuce Clochair, aġur erpoc Cluana ferta Brenaind,[7] in Crirto quieuerunt. Aine ingean Mic Diarmada, ben Mic Conrnaṁa, mortua ert. Echmarcach Mac Branan, dux Corca Achlann,[10] do ṁarḃaḋ Tomultaiġ .h. Mailbrenaind, ocur Echmarcach féin do dol [déc] da ġonaiḃ an trer lá daéiri rin. Domhnall .h. Neill, ri Tiri hEoġain, dinnarbaḋ ar a riġi ocur ar a flaiṫer tre nert Ġall ocur clainne Aeḋa buiḋe, ocur crecha móra do denaṁ la feraiḃ Manach a fell fair. A riġi féin do ġaḃail dó aridiri. Brian mac Domhnaill .h. Neill do marḃaḋ le cloinn Aeḋa buiḋe.

Kt. Enair for Mairt, acur trer.x. fuirri; M.°ccc°. xx.°; iii. anno indictionir; xx.iiii. anno cicli rolarir.

---

[1] Hoc. o., for oc, B. hoc, C.

[2] Dall; i.e. "the Blind."

[3] Occisus. o., B. ocrirurr C.

[4] Kalends. The Dom. Letter (G) is added in the marg. in B.

[5] Indictionis. This clause is repeated in C.

[6] The bishop of Doire. Errace Doiri, B. Earpoce Doiri, C. His name was Odo (or Hugh) O'Neill.

[7] Bishop of Cluain-ferta-Brenainn.

Gregory O'Brogy, who was made bishop of Clonfert in 1308.

[8] Christo. qrirto, B.

[9] Quieverunt. quieuit, B.

[10] Corca-Achlann. The MSS. have Corca Aċhcṫ (for Corca-Ath-chlann). The proper form is Corca Seachlann, i.e. the "tribe of Seach-lann." A marginal note reads, "Aoḋ Brernech mac Cathail ruaiḋ, Ruaidri mac Caṫail ruaiḋ, Feḋlimiḋ mac Aeḋa mic Eoġain,

throughout Erinn. John O'Ferghail was killed with one shot of an arrow by his own son. Jeffrey O'Ferghail, i.e. the son of Gilla-na-naemh O'Ferghail, chieftain of Muinter-Anghaile, died after completing thirty-six years in his government. Snow, the like of which was not observed for a long time, fell in hoc[1] anno. Cathal, son of Gilla-Christ Dall[2] Mac Raghnaill, occisus[3] est.

The kalends[4] of January on Monday, and the second of the moon; anno Domini M°.ccc°.xix.; ix. anno cycli lunaris; ii. anno Indictionis;[5] xxiii. anno cycli solaris. The bishop of Rath-both, i.e. Henry Mac-an-Crosain, in Christo quievit. Thomas, son of Cormac O'Domhnaill, abbot of Es-Ruaidh, was elected to the bishopric of Rath-both. The bishop of Doire,[6] and O'Banan, bishop of Clochar, and the bishop of Cluain-ferta-Brenainn,[7] in Christo[8] quieverunt.[9] Aine, daughter of Mac Diarmada, wife of Mac Consnamha, mortua est. Echmarcach Mac Branan, dux of Corca-Achlann,[10] slew Tomaltach O'Mael-bhrenainn; and Echmarcach himself died of his wounds the third day after that. Domhnall O'Neill, king of Tir-Eoghain, was expelled from his sovereignty and lordship through the power of the Foreigners, and of Clann-Aedha-Buidhe; and great depredations were committed on him, in treachery, by the Feara-Manach. His own sovereignty was again assumed by him. Brian, son of Domhnall O'Neill, was slain by the Clann-Aedha-Buidhe.

The kalends[11] of January on Tuesday, and the thirteenth of the moon; M°.ccc°.xx°.; iii. anno[12] Indictionis; xxiiii.

Toippohelbach mac Aoba mic Eogain, acuf Cathal mac Domhnaill mun am po a nefaonta pe ceile. Hac ttug po a topab? cpuag an pgel pin; i.e. "Aedh Breifnech, son of Cathal Ruadh; Ruaidhri, son of Cathal Ruadh; Fedhlimidh, son of Aedh, son of Eoghan; Toirdhelbhach, son of Aedh, son of Eoghan, and Cathal, son of Domhnall, were about this time at enmity with each other. Did not this produce its fruit? A pitiful story is this!" They were all members of the O'Conor family.

[11] *Kalends.* The Dom. Letters (F E) are added in the margin in B.

[12] *Anno.* The year of the Lunar cycle also has been added in B, and then expunged.

[S. defective.
xt supplied
m "Annals
Connacht."]

Conne mop eivip Chathal .h. Conchuḃaip aṡup Maelpuanaiġ Mac Diapmava, convepnpat píd cunnail
caipveaṁail; ocup Mac Diapmava vo ṫeacht ipin
típ iappin. Ṗell vo venaṁ von Chathal cetna pin
ap Mac n'Diapmava, ap mullaċ Topaṁnach, ocup a
ġaḃail ann, ocup Spáinne inġen Mic Maṡnupa, ben
Mic Diapmava, vo ġaḃail a pupt na Caipṡi, ocup in
típ vo lomapcain iap pin; ocup Maelipa vono Macc
Œvaṡan, ocup a mac, ocup Tomoltach Mac Vonochaiḋ, tiṡepna Tipe Oiliolla, vo ġaḃail anv pop. Œvh
mac Taivcc .h. Chonchoḃaip, veṡ aḃṫap piṡ Connacht
ap veilb ocup ap venaṁ, ocup ap uaipli, ocup ap enech,
vo ṁapḃaḋ vo Mac Maptin, ocup a ṁapḃaḋ péin ina
viġail. Mathṡaṁain mac Voṁnaill Connaċtaiġ .h.
Ḃpiain, tanaipte Muṁan, vo ṁapḃaḋ vo Cloinn Cuilen
in hoc anno. Mop, inġen .h. Ḃaiṡill, ben .h.Ṗepṡail,
moptua ept.

Ḱt. Enaip pop Vapvain, ocup cethpamaḋ piched
puippi; xi. anno cicli lunapip; quapto anno invictionip;
xxii. anno cicli polapip. Spáinne inġen Mic Maṡnupa, ben Maelpuanaiġ Mic Diapmava, moptua
ept. Ruaiḋpi na peo, mac Vonochaiḋ mic Eoṡain
.h.Chonḃoḃaip, vo ṁapḃaḋ vo Chathal mac Œvα
mic Eoṡain, pep volum. Cappaic Locha Ce vo vpipeḋ
la Cathal mac Voṁnaill .h. Chonḃoḃaip, piṡh Connacht. Ḃóvith móp ap put Epeann uile, vo na ppith
paṁail piaṁ. Maṡnup Ua hŒnluain, pi Opṫep, vo
vallaḋ ocup vo ppochaḋ via ḃpathaip péin, .i. vo

---

1 *Friendly.* caipveṁail, B.

2 *Port-na-Cairgi.* "The bank (or
shore) of the Rock;" i.e. the shore of
the lake, opposite to Mac Dermott's
Rock in Loch-Cé, in the county of
Roscommon.

3 *Tomaltach.* Tomoltach, B.
Voṁnall, C.

4 *Lord.* tiṡepna, B.; omitted in C.

5 *Of Connacht.* Coṅṅ aṗ, B.
Coṅṅ, C.

6 *As regards form, and figure.* ap
vē (for veilb) ocup ap venaṁ,
B. C has ap vénaṁ tiṡeapna,
"as regards lordly figure."

anno cycli solaris. A great meeting between Cathal O'Conchobhair and Maelruanaigh Mac Diarmada, when they made a prudent, friendly[1] peace; and Mac Diarmada afterwards came into the country. Treachery was practised by the same Cathal against Mac Diarmada on Mullach-Toramhnach, and he was taken prisoner there; and Grainne, Mac Maghnusa's daughter, Mac Diarmada's wife, was taken prisoner at Port-na-Cairgi;[2] and the country was completely plundered afterwards; and Macl-Isa Donn Mac Aedhagain, and his son, and Tomaltach[3] Mac Donnchaidh, lord[4] of Tir-Oilella, were also taken prisoners there. Aedh, son of Tadhg O'Conchobhair, one well qualified to be king of Connacht[5] as regards form, and figure,[6] and nobility, and generosity, was slain by Mac Martin, who was himself slain in retaliation. Mathghamhain, son of Domhnall Connachtach O'Briain, tanist of Mumha, was killed by the Clann-Cuilen in hoc anno. Mor, daughter of O'Baighill, wife of O'Ferghail, mortua est.

The kalends[7] of January on Thursday, and the twenty-fourth of the moon; xi. anno cycli lunaris; quarto anno Indictionis; xxv. anno cycli solaris. Grainne, daughter of Mac Maghnusa, wife of Maelruanaidh Mac Diarmada, mortua est. Ruaidhri-na-fedh, son of Donnchadh, son of Eoghan O'Conchobhair, was slain[8] by Cathal, son of Aedh, son of Eoghan,[9] per dolum. The Rock of Loch-Cé was demolished by Cathal, son of Domhnall O'Conchobhair, king of Connacht. A great cow-destruction throughout all Erinn, the like of which was not known before. Maghnus O'hAnluain, king of Oirthera, was blinded and emasculated by his own brother, i.e.

---

[7] *Kalends.* The Dom. Letter (D) is added in the margin in B and C.

[8] *Slain.* This is a repetition, the murder of Ruaidhri-na-fedh (or Rory of the Faes) being already recorded under the year 1316. The Four Masters have the event, however, under the present year.

[9] *Son of Eoghan;* i.e., son of Eoghan O'Conchobhair, or Owen O'Conor.

[d fective.
supplied
"Annals
onnacht."]

Nιαll mαc Conuλαδ .h. Ccnluαιn ceδαιn αn bραιċ. Nιαll Uα hCcnluαιn, ρι Οιρċeρ, δο mαρδαδ δο Ζαλλοιδ Dúιnne Delzαn α meδαιl.   Mαιδm mορ δο ċhαδαιρτ δο Ccnδριu Mαc Feοραιρ οcuρ δο Ζαλλαιδ nα Mιδe αιρ mhαcαιbh-ριξ .h. Fαιlzι.

Jct. Enαιρ ρορ Ccιne, οcuρ cuιceδ uαċαδ ρuιρρι; M.ccc.xx.11.; xιι. αnnο cιclι lunαριρ; ιι. αnnο ιn-διcτιοnιρ; xxuι. αnnο cιclι ρολαριρ.   Cocαδ mορ eιδιρ ριξ Sαxαn οcuρ α ιαρlαδα buδeιn.   Mαċhα .h. hΘο-ċhαιξ, eρροg Ccρδαchαιδ, quιeuιτ.   Mορchαδ mαc Ζιllα nα nαeṁ .h. Feρξαιl, ταιρeċ nα hCcnzαιlι ρρια ρe τρι mbliαδαn, δο mαρδαδ ρeρ δολum ι Cluαιn lιρ δecι, δο mαc α δeρρbραċαρ ρeιn, .ι.   Seόιnιn .h. Feρξαιl.   Muιρcheαρταch mαc Ccṁlαιδ .h. Feρξαιl δο mαρδαδ ιριn lo ceαδnα δια bραċαιρ ρeιn .ι. δο Loch-lαιnδ οcuρ δο Rοιbeρδ, ρeρ δολum.   Lochlαιnδ mαc Ccṁlαιδ .h. Feρξαιl δο mαρδαδ lα Seόιnín .h. Feρξαιl ιαρριn.   Donδchαδ mαc Donδchαδα Mιc Dιαρmαδα mορτuuρ eρτ.   Enρι mαc Ζιllιριnneιn, ταιρech Muιn-τιρι Feοταchαn, δο mαρδαδ δο chloιnn Ccmlαιδ Meg Uιδιρ ιn hoc αnnο.   Ζιllιbeρδ .h. Cellαιξ, ρι .h. Mαιne, δο hecc ιn hoc αnnο.   Mαelρuαnαιξ Mαc Dιαρmαδα, ρι Mοιξι Luιρξ, δο ξαδαιl οcuρ δαρcαιn le Conchοδαρ mαc Ταιδcc .h. Chonchuδαιρ, οcuρ δο lucht τιξι Cαċhαιl .h. Conchuδαιρ, ι Cluαιn Cummαιρcc.   Rιcαρδ Mαc Feοραιρ, τιξheαρnα Ccτhα nα ριξ, mορτuuρ eρτ.   Uιl-lιαm lιαċ, mαc Uιllιαm mοιρ, mορτuuρ eρτ.   Mαιδm mορ δο ċhαδαιρτ δο bριαn .h. bριαιn αρ Ζαλλοιδ.   Ccnδριαρ Mαξ Mαιlιn, αρδ mαιξιρτιρ δλιξιδ nuα οcuρ ρen δλιξheδ, hι lex οcuρ α cαnοιn, quιeuιτ.   Ζιllα nα nαeṁ, mαc Seρραιδ, mιc Ζιllα nα nαeṁ, δο ξαδαιl

---

[1] *By Niall.* δο Nιαll, C. B in-correctly reads Doṁnαll. The Four Masters and Mageoghegan agree with the reading of C.

[2] *Kalends.* The Dom. Letter (C) is added in the margin in B.

[3] *Brothers.* B and C have bραċαιρ, "brother;" but the Four Masters more correctly read bραιċριbh, abl. plura of bραċαιρ.

[4] *William Liath;* i.e. William [Burk] the gray (or hoary).

by Niall,[1] son of Cu-Uladh O'hAnluain, on Spy-Wednesday. Niall O'hAnluain, king of Oirthera, was slain by the . Foreigners of Dun-Delgan, in treachery. A great defeat was inflicted by Andriu Mac Feorais, and by the Foreigners of Midhe, on the sons of kings of Ui-Failghe.

The kalends[2] of January on Friday, and the fifth of the moon; M.ccc.xxii.; xii. anno cycli lunaris; v. anno Indictionis; xxvi. anno cycli solaris. A great war between the king of the Saxons and his own Earls. Matthew O'hEothaigh, bishop of Ard-achadh, quievit. Murchadh, son of Gilla-na-naemh O'Ferghail, chieftain of the Anghaile during the space of three years, was slain, per dolum, in Cluain-lis-Bece, by his own brother's son, i.e. Seóinin O'Ferghail. Muirchertach, son of Amhlaibh O'Ferghail, was slain the same day by his own brothers,[3] viz., by Lochlainn and Robert, per dolum. Lochlainn, son of Amhlaibh O'Ferghail, was afterwards slain by Seoinin O'Ferghail. Donnchadh, son of Donnchadh Mac Diarmada, mortuus est. Henry Mac Gillafinnen, chieftain of Muinter-Pheodachain, was slain by the sons of Amhlaibh Mac Uidhir in hoc anno. Gilbert O'Cellaigh, king of Ui-Maine, died in hoc anno. Maelruanaidh Mac Diarmada, king of Magh-Luirg, was taken prisoner and plundered by Conchobhar, son of Tadhg O'Conchobhair, and by the household of Cathal O'Conchobhair, in Cluain-Cummaisc. Richard Mac Feorais, lord of Ath-na-righ, mortuus est. William Liath,[4] son of William Mor, mortuus est. A great defeat was inflicted by Brian O'Briain on Foreigners. Andrias Mac Mailin, high master of new laws and old laws, in Lex and in Canon,[5] quievit. Gilla-na-naemh, son of Jeffrey, son of Gilla-na-naemh,[6] assumed the chieftainship of the

---

[5] *In Lex and in Canon;* otherwise in Civil and Canon Law.

[6] *Gilla-na-Naemh;* i.e. Gilla-na-naemh O'Ferghail, or O'Farrell.

fective.
upplied
Annals
iacht."]

ταιριξεαċτα να hαϲнζαιlι ιη hoc anno. Maelpuαναiξ, mac ζιlla Cpιrτ, mιc Conċuϐαιp, mιc Copmaιc, mιc Τomαlταiξ να Capcι, pι Mυιξι Lυιpcc, mopτυυp eρτ.

ƙτ. Ƈναιp pop Sαταpнн, ocuρ peacht vecc rυιppι; M.ccc.xxιιι.; xιιι. anno cιclι Lυηαpιr; reɣτo anno ιηϑιcτιoнιr; xxιιι. anno cιclι rolαpιr. Cαppι ιη pcpecaн, mac Copmaιc .ḣ. Maιleacħlαιnn, pι Mιϑe, occιpur eρτ la peραιϐ Cell. Maelmopϑα Mac Ɛochacαн qυιeυιτ. Seoιнιн .ḣ. Feρξαιl vo mapϐαϑ vo cloιηн Seoαн .ḣ. Feρξαιl ιη hoc anno. ḣ. Ɛξpα vo mapϐαϑ vo Connmachαн ιη hoc anno.

ƙτ. Ɛναιp pop Ꝺomναċ, ocuρ peachτmαϑ .xx. rυιppι; xιιιι. Lυηαpιr cιclι; uιι. anno ιηϑιcτιoнιr; xx. octauo rolαpιr cιclι. Uιllιαm ƀúpc mac Uιllιαm mopτυυp eρτ. Caτhαl mac Ꝺoṁнαιll, mιc Ταιϑξ, mιc ƀpιαιн, mιc Ꝺηϑpιαr, mιc ƀpιαιн Lυιξнιξ, mιc Τoιppϑelϐαiξ ṁoιp .ḣ.Conchoϐαιp, pι Connacht, occιpur eρτ o Τoιppϑealϐαċ, mac Ꝺϵϑα, mιc Ɛoξαιн .ḣ.Conċoϐαιp .ι. ιντ aen ξαιϑιl ιr beoϑα ocuρ ιr bpιξṁuιpe vo ƀι a naen aιmrιr rυιr, a Τιp ƀpιαιн να Sιnnα ιη hoc anno; ocuρ Maιleaċlαιnn mac Τoιppϑealϐαiξ .ḣ.Ꝺoṁнαιll, ocuρ ζιlla Cpιrτ occ Mac Ꝺonvchαϑα, et alιι mulτι, vo ṁapϐαϑ mαραen rιr, a nochτmαϑ callαιnn Sepτιm-bpιr, ιap να ϐeċ .uι. blιαϑna co leċ ιppιξι Connacht vanveoιн ζαll ocuρ ζαιϑel; ocuρ Τoιppϑealϐach vo pιξαϑ ιαppιn vo Connachταιϐ ule. Ιn bóvιτh cέvna ιnv Ɛpιnn ulι ιη hoc anno, ocuρ ιr rrιrιϑe avbeιpτι ιη maelvoṁнαiξ. ζιlla Cpιrv Uα ƀιpн mopτυυp eρτ.

---

1 *Tomaltach of the Rock*; i.e. Tomal-tach Mac Dermot, called Tomaltach "of the Rock," from the Rock of Loch-Cé, the chief residence of the chieftains of Magh-Luirg, in Roscommon. For Τomαlταiξ, B incorrectly reads Ꝺoṁнαιll.

2 *Kalends.* The Dom. Letter (B) is added in the margin.

3 *Hoc.* hocc, B.

4 *Moon.* The entry M.ccc.xx.quap-το, which should follow according to the usual rule of the Chronicler, is represented by "quapτo" only in both MSS. The Dom. Letters (A G) are added in the margin in B.

5 *Mortuus est.* This is possibly a repetition, as the William Burk Mac

Anghaile in hoc anno. Maelruanaidh, son of Gilla-Christ, son of Conchobhar, son of Cormac, son of Tomaltach of the Rock,[1] king of Magh-Luirg, mortuus est. [1322.]

The kalends[2] of January on Saturday, and the seventeenth of the moon; M.ccc.xxiii.; xiii. anno cycli lunaris; sexto anno Indictionis; xxvii. anno cycli solaris. Cairbre-in-screcain, son of Cormac O'Maelechlainn, king of Midhe, occisus est by the Feara-Cell. Maelmordha Mac Eochagain quievit. Seoinin O'Ferghail was slain by the sons of John O'Ferghail in hoc[3] anno. O'hEghra was slain by O'Connmachan in hoc anno. [1323.]

The kalends of January on Sunday, and the twenty-seventh of the moon;[4] xiiii. lunaris cycli; vii. anno Indictionis; xx. octavo solaris cycli. William Burk Mac William mortuus est.[5] Cathal, the son of Domhnall, son of Tadhg, son of Brian, son of Andrias, son of Brian Luighnech, son of Toirdhelbhach[6] Mor O'Conchobhair, king of Connacht, i.e. the most active and vigorous Gaeidhel of his time, occisus est by Toirdhelbhach, son of Aedh, son of Eoghan O'Conchobhair, in Tir-Briuin-na-Sinna, in hoc anno, (and Maelechlainn, son of Toirdhelbhach O'Domhnaill, and Gilla-Christ Og Mac Donnchadha, et alii[7] multi, were slain along with him), on the eighth of the kalends of September, after having been six years and a half in the sovereignty of Connacht in spite of Foreigners and Gaeidhel; and Toirdhelbhach was afterwards made king by all the Connachtmen. The same cow-destruction[8] in all Erin in hoc anno; and it was it that was usually called the Maeldomhnaigh. Gilla-Christ O'Birn mortuus[9] est. [1324.]

William here referred to may have been the William Liath [Burk], son of William Mor, whose death is entered under the year 1322. The same repetition occurs in the Ann. Four Masters.

[6] *Of Toirdhelbhach.* [7] ⁊ɼɼ., for Toiɼɼohelbaiʒ, B. Ꝺonncħ., for Ꝺonnchaꝺa, C.

[7] *Alii.* aḽ, B.

[8] *Cow destruction;* i.e. the bóoich, or murrain, mentioned under the year 1321.

[9] *Mortuus.* moɼcuɼ, B.

ʒfective.
upplied
Annals
racht."]

Ict. Enαιp pop Mαιpτ, ocup ochτmαδ uατhαδ puιppι;
M.ccc.xxu.; xu. cιclι Lunαpιp; octαuo αnno ιnδιcτιonιp; ppιmo αnno cιclι polαpιp. Domnαll mαc
bpιαιn Uι Neιll, pι Ulαδ, mopτuup epτ. Dιαpmαιτ
Uα Mαιlbpenαιnδ, pιʒ τoιpech Cloιnne Concobαιp,
mopτuup epτ. Cú Ulαδ .h. Neιll mopτuup epτ .ι. mαc
Domnαιll mιc bpιαιn .h. Neιll ιn Cú Ulαδ pιn, αcup
α mαpbαδ δo poιpατ clαnn Neιll mιc bpιαιn .h. Neιll
.ι. clαnn δepbpαταp α αthαp peιn. ʒιllα Cpιpτ
cleιpec Mαc Dιαpmαδα mopτuup epτ. bpιαn Uα
ʒαδpα mopτuup epτ. Iη bóδιτh póp αp puτ Epenδ.

Ict. Enαιp pop Cedαoιn, ocup xιx.mαδ puιppι; αnno
Domιnι M.ccc.xxιιι.; xuι. αnno cιclι Lunαpιp; ιx. αnno
ιnδιcτιonιp; pecunδo αnno cιclι polαpιp. Rιpδαpδ α
bupc .ι. αnτ Iαplα puαδ, τιʒeαpnα Ulαδ ocup Conδαchτ, αcup αen poʒα ʒαll Epenδ uιlι, δo hecc ιpιn
blιαδαιn pιn αnτe pepτum Peτpι αδ uιnculα. Cocαδ
mop eιδιp pιʒ Ppαnc ocup pιʒ Sαxαn ιn hoc αnno.
Lupιnτ .h. Lαchτnαn, epboʒ Olιpιnn, ιn Cpιpτo quιeuιτ.
Meτpα Seoαn O Pιnδαchτα δo τoʒαδ δochum nα
heppocoιδι cednα ιαp pιn. Imhαp Mαʒ Rαʒnαιll,
ταιpech Muιnτιpι hEoluιp, occιpup epτ o [α] bpαιthpιb
buδeιn. Nιcol .h. hEδhιn mopτuup epτ.

Ict. Enαιp pop Dαpδαoιn, ocup .x.mαδ .xx. puιppι;
αnno Domιnι M.ccc.xx.uιι.; xuιι. Lunαpιp cιclι; x. αnno
ιnδιcτιonιp; τepτιo αnno cιclι polαpιp. Cocαδ mop
eιδιp pιʒ Sαxαn ocup α ben buδeιn, .ι. ιnʒen pιʒ Ppαnc,
ocup pι Sαxαn δo αthpιʒαδ δon cocαδ pιn, ocup α mαc
peιn δo pιʒαδ δι α nαʒαιδ α αthαp, ocup copoιn pιʒ
δo τhαbαιpτ δó τpια chomαιple Sαxαn uιlι. ʒopmlαιc
ιnʒen Mιc Dιαpmαδα, ben Mαʒnupα mιc Domnαιll
.h.Conchobαιp. ταnαιpτe Conδαchτ pe heδ, ocup

---

[1] *Kalends.* The Dom. Letter (F) is added in the margin in B.

[2] *Cow-destruction.* The bóδιτh, or murrain, referred to in note [6], p. 603.

[3] *Choicest.* αen poʒα; lit. "one choice," C. αen pαʒα, B.

[4] *Metra.* Meꞑ (probably a mistake for "Maigistir"), B and C.

The kalends[1] of January on Tuesday, and the eighth of the moon; M.CCC.XXV.; xv. cycli lunaris; octavo anno Indictionis; primo anno cycli solaris. Domhnall, son of Brian O'Neill, king of Uladh, mortuus est. Diarmaid O'Maelbhrenainn, king-chieftain of Clann-Conchobhair, mortuus est. Cu-Uladh O'Neill mortuus est; i.e. this Cu-Uladh was the son of Domhnall, son of Brian O'Neill; and the sons of Niall, son of Brian O'Neill, viz., the sons of his own father's brother, killed him. Gilla-Christ Cleirech Mac Diarmada mortuus est. Brian O'Gadhra mortuus est. The cow-destruction[2] still throughout Erinn.

The kalends of January on Wednesday, and the nineteenth of the moon; anno Domini M.CCC.XXVI.; xvi. anno cycli lunaris; ix. anno Indictionis; secundo anno cycli solaris. Richard Burk, i.e. the Red Earl, lord of Uladh and Connacht, and the choicest[3] of all the Foreigners of Erinn, died in this year, ante festum Petri ad Vincula. A great war between the king of France and the king of the Saxons in hoc anno. Laurence O'Lachtnain, bishop of Oilfinn, in Christo quievit. Metra[4] John O'Finnaghta was afterwards elected to the same bishopric. Imhar Mac Raghnaill, chieftain of Muinter-Eolais, occisus est by his own kinsmen. Nicholas O'hEdhin mortuus est.

The kalends[5] of January on Thursday, and the thirtieth of the moon; anno Domini M.CCC.XXVII.; xvii. lunaris cycli; x. anno Indictionis; tertio anno cycli solaris. A great war between the king of the Saxons and his own wife, i.e. the daughter of the king of France; and the king of the Saxons was dethroned through this war; and his own son was made king by her in opposition to his father, and a king's crown was given to him through the counsel of all the Saxons. Gormlaith, Mac Diarmada's daughter, for a while the wife of Maghnus, son of Domhnall O'Conchobhair, tanist of Connacht, and

---

[5] *Kalends*. A marg. note in B. gives D as the Dom. Letter for the year.

banríʒan.h.ꝋaine aʒ Conchuƀap.h. Cellaiʒ ꝺep ꝋaʒ-
nupa, ocuṙ banríʒan ᴌuiʒne aʒ Ꝼepʒal.h. eʒpa, ocuṙ
ben pob ꝼepp nóp ocuṙ enech ocuṙ ꞇinꞇacaꝺ ꝺa cineꝺ
ꝼein hi, a hec iap mbuaiꝺ naiꞇpiʒhe. eꝺuƀapꝺ, pí
ᴤaxan, iap mbuain a piʒi ꝺe quieuiꞇ. Ceꝺm mop ꝺon
ʒalap bpec ap puꞇ epenꝺ uli co popleꞇhan, co ꞇucc
ꝺiꞇh ap ꝺainiƀ beca ocuṙ mopa ipin bliaꝺain pin.
ꝋailechlainn piaƀach, mac ꝺoṁnaill, mic Caiꝉc.h.
Conchuƀaip, ꝺo ꝺol [ꝺéʒ] ꝺon ʒalap pin. Ꝼepʒal mac
Ualʒaipc.h. Ruaipc mopꞇuup epꞇ. Culén Ua ꝺimupaiʒ
mopꞇuup epꞇ. ᴤaꝺƀ inʒen ꝋic ᴀeꝺacan mopꞇua epꞇ.

Ct. enaip pop Cine, aʒup aenmaꝺ .x. puippi;
ꝋ°. ccc°. xx°. uᴠ.; xᴠ. cicli ᴌunapiṙ; xi. anno inꝺic-
ꞇiónip; quapꞇo anno cicli ṡolapiṙ. ꝋailechlainn o
Raiʒilliʒ ꞇiʒeapna ꝋuinnꞇipi ꝋaolmopꝺa, ꝺo ʒaƀail
ocuṙ ꝺo loꞇ ꝺo ʒallaiƀ na ꝋiꝺe; aʒuṙ a puaplucaꝺ
ap bpaiʒꝺiƀ, ocuṙ a ꝺol ꝺecc ꝺa ʒonaiƀ ina ꞇiʒ ꝼein
iappin. Ꞇopnach ocuṙ ꞇenꞇich anbail ipin bliaꝺain
pin, ʒup milleꝺ mopan ꝺo ṁep ocuṙ ꝺo ꞇopaꝺ epenꝺ
uili, ocuṙ cup papaꝺap apbanna pinna papa. Ceꝺm
ʒalaip ʒo coiꞇcheanꝺ ap puꞇ epenꝺ uili, ppiṙ inabap-
ꞇhai ṡlaeꝺan, pe heꝺ ꞇpi lá no ceꞇhaip ap cech nech
ꝺa nʒaƀaꝺ, ʒup bo ꞇanaipꞇe baiṙ ꝺo he. Inꞇ iapla
ꝺonn ꝺo ꞇeachꞇ a nepinꝺ in hoc anno .i. Uilliam ƀupc
mac pip ᴤeoan mic in iapla puaiꝺ. ꝺonꝺchaꝺ puaꝺ
.h.ʒaꝺpa, ocuṙ coiʒep ꝺa cineꝺ ꝼein maille piṙ, occipi
punꞇ. Conċuƀap ꝋac ƀpanain, aꝺƀap ꞇaipiʒh Copca
Cchlann, ꝺo mapƀaꝺ la muinꞇep Cnʒaili. ꝺaibeꞇ
ꝋac Ʒilla Comʒaill ʒalloclaech, ocuṙ ceꞇhpi pip ꝺeaʒ
ꝺa ṁuinnꞇip maille piṙ, ꝺo ṁapƀaꝺ la ꝺonꝺchaꝺ nʒall
mac ꝺoṁnuill.h.Conchuƀaip, ocuṙ ꝺonꝺchaꝺ ꝼein ꝺo
ꞇpomloꞇ anꝺ beuṙṙ. ꝺuƀepa inʒean .h. elipe, ben

---

1 *Galar-brec;* lit. "speckled disease,"
i.e. the small-pox.

2 *Kalends.* The Dom. Letters (C B)
are added in the margin in B.

3 *Slaedan;* i.e. a cough or influenza.

4 *Five.* coiʒep, C. cocep, B.

5 *Corca-Achlann.* Copca Cꞇhcꞇ.
in B and C. See note [10], p. 596.

queen of the Ui-Maine with Conchobhar O'Cellaigh, after
Maghnus, and queen of Luighne with Ferghal O'hEghra,
(and who was the woman of greatest reputation, hospitality, and liberality, of her own kindred), died after
the triumph of penance. Edward, king of the Saxons,
after his sovereignty had been taken from him, quievit.
A great epidemic of the "galar-brec"[1] throughout all
Erinn widely, which brought destruction on people small
and great, in this year. Maelechlainn Riabhach, son of
Domhnall, son of Tadhg O'Conchobhair, died of this
disease. Ferghal, son of Ualgharg O'Ruairc, mortuus est.
Culén O'Dimusaigh mortuus est. Sadhbh, daughter of
Mac Aedhagain, mortua est.

The kalends[2] of January on Friday, and the eleventh of
the moon; M°. ccc°. xx°. viii.; xviii. cycli lunaris; xi. anno
Indictionis; quarto anno cycli solaris. Maelechlainn
O'Raighilligh, lord of Muinter-Maelmordha, was apprehended and wounded by the Foreigners of Midhe; and
he was released on *giving* hostages, but afterwards died
of his wounds in his own house. Terrible thunder and
lightning in this year, so that much of the fruit and
produce of all Erinn was destroyed, and corn grew
whitish and empty. An epidemic disease generally
throughout all Erinn, which was called "slaedan,"[3]
and lasted during the space of three or four days
with every person whom it attacked, so that it was
next to death to him. The Brown Earl, i.e. William
Burk, son of Sir John, son of the Red Earl, came to
Erinn in hoc anno. Donnchadh Ruadh O'Gadhra, and
five[4] of his own kindred along with him, occisi sunt.
Conchobhar Mac Branan, heir to the chieftainship of
Corca-Achlann,[5] was slain by the people of Anghaile.
David Mac Gilla-Comghaill, gallowglass, and fourteen
men of his people along with him, were slain by
Donnchadh Gall, son of Domhnall O'Conchobhair;
and Donnchadh himself was also greatly wounded there.
Dubhesa, daughter of O'hElidhe, wife of Domhnall,

defective.
supplied
"Annals
nnackt."]

Ɗoṁnaill mic Ɑinꝺriar, an inᵹeṅ mic oclaeċ iꞃ ꝼeꞃꞃ ꝺo ḃi a naen aimꞃiꞃ ꞃꞃia, ocuꞃ ꝺoḃ ꝼeꞃꞃ clú ocuꞃ ꝺo ḃo mo conach, ꝺo écc iꞃin ḃliaꝺain ꞃin. Ᵹaeċ móꞃ ꝺoꞃulaċṫa iꞃinṫ ꞃaṁꞃaꝺ, aᵹuꞃ ṫeꞃca biꝺ, ocuꞃ imaꝺ éṫaiᵹ. Cꞃech moꞃ la Uaṫeꞃ a Ḃuꞃc aꞃ Coṅnachṫaiḃ, cuꞃ haꞃceꝺ moꞃan leiꞃ ꝺaeꞃ ᵹꞃaꝺa Ṫoiꞃꞃꝺhealḃaiᵹ .h.Conchoḃaiꞃ, ꞃiᵹ Coṅnachṫ. Siꞃ Seon Mac Ꝼeoꞃaiꞃ, iaꞃla Luᵹmaiᵹ .i. anṫ aen Ḃaꞃun ꝺo ba beoꝺa ocuꞃ ꝺo ba ḃꞃiᵹṁuiꞃe, ocuꞃ ꝺoḃ ꝼeꞃꞃ enech, ocuꞃ ꝺo ꞃo mo ṫinꝺlaicṫi ꝺo ḃi a neꞃinn, ꝺo maꞃḃaꝺ a ꞃill ꝺa ṁuinnṫiꞃ ꝼein .i. ꝺo Ᵹallaiḃ Oiꞃᵹiall, ocuꞃ moꞃan ꝺo Ᵹhalloiḃ ocuꞃ ꝺo Ᵹhaiꝺelaiḃ maiṫi ꝺo ṁaꞃḃaꝺ maꞃaoen ꞃiꞃ; aᵹuꞃ ꞃi na ꞃenma .i. Mael-ꞃuanaiᵹ Mac Ceꞃḃaill .i. in ᵹiolla caech, ocuꞃ ꝺeꞃḃꞃa-ṫaiꞃ aili ꝺó ꝺo maꞃḃaꝺ maꞃoen ꞃiꞃ; ocuꞃ ni ꝼeꞃ co ṫainicc na co ṫiccꞃa choiꝺ̃ċi a choṁmaiḃ ꝺo ṫimpanach. Muiꞃiꞃ .h. Ᵹibillan, aꞃꝺ maiᵹiꞃṫiꞃ Eiꞃeann a nꝺliᵹiꝺ nua ocuꞃ a ꞃenꝺliᵹiꝺ, hi canoin ocuꞃ i lex, ꝼellꞃom ꞃeꞃa aᵹuꞃ ꞃiꞃeolaiꞃ; ꞃai nꝺana aᵹuꞃ nOᵹmoꞃachṫa ocuꞃ elaꝺan nimꝺa eli; cananach coꞃaꝺ hi Ṫuaim ꝺa ᵹua-lann, aᵹuꞃ a nOilꝼinꝺ, aᵹuꞃ a nɑchaꝺ Conaꞃi, aᵹuꞃ i Cill Ɑlaiꝺ aᵹuꞃ a nEnach ꝺuin, aᵹuꞃ i Cluain ꝼeꞃṫa Ḃꞃenainꝺ, oiꞃicel aᵹuꞃ ḃꞃeiṫeamh coiṫchenꝺ na haiꞃꝺ-eꞃpocoiṫi uli, in Cꞃiꞃṫo quieuiṫ. Ṫomaꞃ Ua Mellan, eꞃpuc Enaiᵹ ꝺuin, ꝺo ecc hi cuiꞃṫ an ꝼapa in hoc anno. Ḃꞃian mac Ṫomalṫaiᵹ Mic Ɗonꝺchaiḃ ꝺo maꞃ-ḃaꝺ ꝺo Ḃhꞃian mac Ṫaiꝺcc Mic Ɗonꝺchaiḃ. Uilliam iaꞃla Ulaꝺ ꝺo ṫinol ṫꞃluaiᵹ moiꞃ ꝼa Ṫhoiꞃꝺhealḃaċ .h.Chonchoḃaiꞃ, ꞃi Conꝺachṫ, ocuꞃ ḃa Muiꞃcheaꞃṫach .h.mḂꞃiain, ꞃi Ṫuaꝺmuṁan ocuꞃ Muṁan aꞃchena,

---

[1] *Son of Andrias.* The Four Masters say "son of Tadhg," i.e. Tadhg O'Conor, the son of Brian, the son of Andrias, which is probably correct.

[2] *The Gilla-caech;* i.e. "the one-eyed fellow."

[3] *Canon and Lex;* i.e. Canon and Civil Law.

[4] *Of Ogham writing.* nOᵹmo-ꞃachṫa. Mageoghegan (Annals cf Clonmacnoise) translates it "the speech which in Irish is called Ogham," and adds that it is "composed of the dipthongs, and tripthong·, and consonants of Irish, wherein they are added together, whereof the words are framed."

son of Andrias,[1] the best daughter of a hero of her time, and the woman of best reputation and greatest wealth, died in this year. Great, intolerable wind in the summer, and scarcity of food, and much drought. A great depredation by Walter Burk on the Connacht-men, when a great number of the favourites of Toir-dhelbhach O'Conchobhair, king of Connacht, were plun-dered by him. Sir John Mac Feorais, Earl of Lugh-mhagh, i.e. the most active, vigorous, hospitable and liberal baron that was in Erinn, was killed in treachery by his own people, viz., by the Foreigners of Oirghiall; and a great number of noble Foreigners and Gaeidhel were slain along with him; and the king of minstrelsy, i.e. Maelruanaidh Mac Cerbhaill, i.e. the Gilla-caech,[2] and another brother of his, were slain along with him; and it is not known that there came, or will ever come, so good a harper. Maurice O'Gibillan, high master of Erinn in new laws and old laws, in Canon and Lex;[3] a philosopher in wisdom and true knowledge; an eminent professor of poetry, and of Ogham writing,[4] and many other arts; a canon chorister in Tuaim-da-ghualann, and in Oilfinn, and in Achadh-Conaire, and in Cill-Alaidh, and in Enach-dúin, and in Cluain-ferta-Brenainn, and the official and general judge of all the archbishopric, in Christo quievit. Thomas O'Mellain,[5] bishop of Enach-dúin, died at the Pope's court in hoc anno. Brian, son of Tomaltach[6] Mac Donnchaidh, was slain by Brian, son of Tadhg Mac Donnchaidh. William Earl of Ulster assembled a great army, including Toirdhelbhach O'Con-chobhair, king of Connacht, and Muirchertach O'Briain, king of Tuadh-Mumha, and of Mumha besides, against

---

[5] O'Mellain. The name is written .h. melt. in B, but Ua Meallan in C. The Four Masters write h.Mellaız, "O'Mellaigh," and add

that the bishop died irin Roim, i.e. "in Rome."

[6] Tomaltach. Tom., B. Chas Dom-naill, the genit. of Domhnall, or Daniel, which is wrong.

% defective.
t supplied
n " Annals
Connacht."]

a naᵹaιᵭ bριαιη baιη .h. bριαιη.　　Maιᵭm λe bριαη
mban O mbριαιη αρ Ua mbριαιη, ᴅu αηαρ mαρᵬαᵭ
Conchubaρ .h. bριαιη, ᴅeᵹ αᵭᵬαρ ριᵹ Eριεηᴅ αρ méᴅ
αᵹuρ ᴅeιλᵬ, αᵹuρ αρ eηech, mαιλλe ρe ceᴄhρι ριchιᴄ
eιᴅιρ mαιch αᵹuρ ραιch.　　Coιηηe moρ ρα Cch cιηᴅ
λocha ᴅeιchεᴅ eιᴅιρ Uαᴄeρ mαc Uιλλιαm buρc αᵹuρ
ᵹιλλιbeρᴅ Mαc ᵹοιρᴅeλᵬ ᴅoη ᴅαρα λeᵬ, ocuρ Mαeλ-
ρuαηαιᵹ Mαc ᴅιαρmαᴅα, αᵹuρ Comαλᴄαch α ᵭαc,
αᵹuρ Comαλᴄαch Mαc ᴅoηᴅchαιᵭ, αᵹuρ cλαηη Mαeλ-
ρuαηαιᵹ αρchεηα ᴅoη λeιch αιλe.　　bρeιριmh mαᴅhmα
ᴅo ᴄhαbhαιρᴄ αρ mαc Uιλλιαm, ᴅαρ mαρᵬαᵭ bριαη
mαc Cαιᴅᵹ Mιc ᴅoηᴅchαιᵭ λe α ᵬραᴄhαιρ ρeιη, α
ηᴅιᵹαιλ bριαιη mιc Comuλᴄαιᵹh Mιc ᴅoηchαιᵭ ᴅo
mαρᵬᴅom ρemhe ριη.　　ᴅoηηchαᴅ ᵹαλλ mαc ᴅoᵭηαιλλ
.h.Choηchuᵬαιρ ᴅo mαρᵬαᵭ λα hCcᴅh, mαc Cαιᴅᵹ,
mιc Mαιλechλαιηη, mιc Mαᵹηuρα.

ɪCl. Eηαιρ ρορ ᴅoᵭηαᵬ, αᵹuρ αιλι ριchᴇᴅ ρuιρρι;
m.°ccc.°xx.°ιx.; xιx. cιcλι λuηαριρ; xιι. αηηo ιηᴅιcᴄιoηιρ;
u. αηηo ρoλαριρ cιcλι.　　Cαᴅcc mαc Cοιρρᴅhelbαιᵹ
.h.Coηchuᵬαιρ ᴅo ᵭαρᵬαᵭ ᴅo ᴅιαρmαιᴅ.h.ᵹαᵬρα ι me-
ᵬαιλ.　　Cαᴄhαλ mαc ᴅoᵭηαιλλ.h.Ruαιρc, ᴅeᵹ αᵭᵬαρ ριᵹ
bρeιρηe, ᴅo mαρᵬαᵭ λα cλoιηη Seααιη.h.ρeρᵹαιλ ocuρ
λα ᵹαλλoιᵬ Mιᵬe, ρeρ ᴅoλum, ocuρ ᴅρoηᵹ ᴅα muιηᴄιρ
mαιλλe ριρ.　　Muιρᵬeαρᴄach mαc ᴅoᵭηαιλλ.h.Coηchu-
ᵬαιρ, ᴄιᵹeρηα Cαρρρι, ocuρ ᴅeᵹ αᵭᵬαρ ριᵹ Coηηαchᴄ,
moρᴄuuρ eρᴄ.　　Cαᴄhαλ, mαc Ccᴅα, mιc Eoᵹαιη.h.Choη-
chobαιρ, ᴅo ᴅιchuρ αρ ecιη αρ ηα ρeᴅαιᵭ ocuρ α Cιρ
Mαιηe, ᴄρe ρορᵹαλλ Uαᴄeρ α buρc αρ cλoιηη Cellαιᵹ
ocuρ αρ ιᵬ Mαιηe.　　Cocaᵭ moρ eιᴅιρ Cοιρρᴅhelbαch

---

¹ *Meeting.* coηᴅι, B. coιηηe, C.

² *Tomaltach.* ᴅoᵭηαλλ, C.

³ *On the other part.* ᴅoη ᴅαρα λeιch (instead of ᴅoη λeιch αιλe), B and C.

⁴ *Donnchadh Gall;* i.e. Donough the foreigner. This name is written ᴅoη̄ ᵹαλλ in B, and ᴅoηηᵹαλλ in C.

The Four Masters write it Donnchadh Galldha (Donough the Anglicised); but the preferable form is ᴅoηη-chαᴅ ᵹαλλ, as it is elsewhere written. See page 606.

⁵ *Maghnus;* i.e. Maghnus O'Con-chobhair (or Manus O'Conor).

Brian Bán O'Briain. An overthrow *was given* by Brian
Bán O'Briain to O'Briain, in which Conchobhar O'Briain,
the good material of a king of Erinn as regards stature,
form, and bounty, was slain, together with fourscore
both good and bad. A great meeting[1] near Ath-cind-
Locha-Techet between Walter, son of William Burk, and
Gilbert Mac Goisdelbh, on the one part, and Maelruanaidh
Mac Diarmada, and his son Tomaltach,[2] and Tomaltach[2]
Mac Donnchaidh, and the Clann-Maelruanaidh besides,
on the other part.[3] A defeat was inflicted on Mac William, on which occasion Brian, son of Tadhg Mac Donnchaidh, was slain by his own kinsman, in revenge of
Brian, the son of Tomaltach Mac Donnchaidh, whom he
had previously slain. Donnchadh Gall,[4] son of Domh-
nall O'Conchobhair, was killed by Aedh, the son of
Tadhg, son of Maelechlainn, son of Maghnus.[5]

The kalends[6] of January on Sunday, and the twenty-
second of the moon; M.°ccc.°xx.°ix.; xix. cycli lunaris;[7]
xii. anno Indictionis; v. anno solaris cycli. Tadhg, son
of Toirdhelbhach O'Conchobhair, was slain by Diarmaid
O'Gadhra, in treachery. Cathal, son of Domhnall
O'Ruairc, the good material of a king of Breifne,
was killed by the sons of John O'Ferghail, and by the
Foreigners of Midhe, per dolum, and a number of his
people along with him. Muirchertach, son of Domhnall
O'Conchobhair, lord of Cairbre, and the good material
of a king of Connacht, mortuus est. Cathal, son of
Aedh, son of Eoghan O'Conchobhair, was forcibly expelled from the Fedha,[8] and from Tir-Maine, by the
order of Walter Burk to the Clann-Cellaigh and the
Ui-Maine. A great war between Toirdhelbhach

---

[6] *Kalends.* The Dom. Letter (A)
is added in the margin in B.

[7] *Cycli lunaris.* Repeated in MSS.
B and C.

[8] *The Fedha.* "The Woods," or
"Faes," a district in the barony of
Athlone, and county of Roscommon,
formerly the patrimony of the family
of O'Neachtain, or O'Naghten.

2 R 2

lefective.
supplied
" Annals
rnacht."]

.h.Conchuḃaıp, pı Conꝺachꞇ, ocuр clann Maelpuanaıᵹ, cup mılleꝺ mopan eaꞇoppa ꝺıḃlınaıḃ. Cpeach lα Tomalꞇach Mαc Ꝺıαpmαꝺα αp Ꝺıαpmαıꝺ .h. Ꝑlannα-can, ꞇαıpech Cloınne Cαꞇhαıl. Ꝑıne ınᵹen Ꝑepᵹαıl .h.Ꝛαıᵹıllıᵹ, ben Tomulꞇαıᵹ Mıc Ꝺıαpmαꝺα, mopꞇuα epꞇ ın ꞇpeαр lα pıα noꝺlαıc moıp. Ꝺαboᵹ ꝺonn mαc Uıllıαm Ꝺupc, pıꝺıpı po chonαıᵹ, mopꞇuup epꞇ.

Ꝗꞇ. Ꝺnαıp pop Lυαn, ocuр ııı. uαꞇhαꝺ pυıppı; M.ccc.xxx.; ppımup αnnup Lυnαpıp cıclı; xııı. αnno ınꝺıcꞇıonıp; peaꞇo αnno polαpıp cıclı. Mαᵹnup, mαc Ꝗeꝺα Ꝺpeıppıᵹ .h. Conchoḃαıp, ꝺo mαpḃαꝺ lα Cαꞇhαl, mαc Ꝗeꝺα, mıc Ꝑoᵹαın .h. Conchoḃαıp, hı Ꝑepαnn nα ꝺαpαch, ocuр Sımαnn mαc ınꝺ Ꝑhαılᵹıᵹ ꝺo mαpḃαꝺ mαpαen pıp. Ꝗmmuр Lonᵹḃuıpꞇ le Toıppꝺhelbach .h.Conćoḃαıp αp ḃαıꞇep mαc Uıllıαm Ꝺupc, α Lecmαıᵹ α Moıᵹ Luıpᵹ, ocuр α pυαᵹαꝺ αppıꝺe co Cαıpċı Lıαcc pαꝺα, ocuр Ꞡılleberꝺ Mαc Ꞡoıpꝺelḃ, ꞇıᵹeαpnα Sleḃı Luᵹα, ꝺo ꞇeαċꞇ peꝺαn móp ı pυpꞇαchꞇ Mıc Uıllıαm Ꝺupc, ocuр Tomalꞇαch Mαc Ꝺonꝺchαıꝺ ꝺo ꞇeαchꞇ peꝺαn αılı ı pυpꞇαchꞇ Mıc Uıllıαm. Ꝗᵹur ımpυꝺ ꝺo nα pluαᵹαıḃ pın ꝺıḃlınαıḃ αp .h. Conchuḃαıp co pαncα-ꝺαp Ꝗꞇh Ꝺıpıpꞇ Nυαꝺαn, ocuр becαn ꝺo muınꞇıp .h.Chonćoḃαıp ꝺo mαpḃαꝺ pon αꞇh, .ı. Ꝺonnchαꝺ mαc Ꝺoṁnαıll Mıc Mαꞇhᵹαṁnα ocuр Mαc Ꞡıllα Comᵹαn, ocuр ꝺαıne elı boр nach αpımꞇhep punn; ocuр Uα Con-chuḃαıp ꝺo ımꞇeαchꞇ co beoꝺα nopmαp ıp nα Tυαꞇhαıḃ ıαppın. Ꝗᵹur ᵹαḃuр Mαc Uıllıαm Lonᵹpopꞇ αn αꝺαıᵹ pın α Cıll Lomαꝺ αp ınchαıḃ .h. Conchuḃαıp. Sluαᵹαꝺ Conꝺαchꞇ uılı ꝺo ꞇınol ꝺo Mαc Uıllıαm, eꝺıp Ꞡαll

---

[1] *Mac-ind-Fhailgigh*; i.e. son of the "Failgech," or needy person. The "Failgech," from whom the family name of "Mac-ind-Fhailgigh," or "Mac-in-Fhailghe" (now probably Mac-Nally), and the tribe name of "Clann-in-Fhailghe" were derived,

has not been identified. See note [4], p. 434, *supra*.

[2] *Cairthi-liag-fada*; lit. "the long stone pillar." Dr. O'Donovan suggests that the townland of Cnoc-a-Cartha (hill of the pillar stone), in the parish of Killukin, county of

O'Conchobhair, king of Connacht, and the Clann-Maelruanaidh, and much property was destroyed between both parties. A depredation by Tomaltach Mac Diarmada on Diarmaid O'Flannagain, chieftain of Clann-Cathail. Aine, daughter of Ferghal O'Raighilligh, the wife of Tomaltach Mac Diarmada, mortua est the third day before Great Christmas. Daboc Donn Mac William Burk, a very wealthy knight, mortuus est.

A.D.
[1329.]

The kalends of January on Monday, and the third of the moon; M.CCC.XXX.; primus annus lunaris cycli; xiii. anno Indictionis; sexto anno solaris cycli. Maghnus, son of Aedh Breifnech O'Conchobhair, was killed by Cathal, son of Aedh, son of Eoghan O'Conchobhair, in Ferann-na-darach; and Simon Mac-ind-Fhailgigh[1] was slain along with him. A camp attack was made by Toirdhelbhach O'Conchobhair on Walter Mac William Burk, in Lecmagh in Magh-Luirg, whom he drove from thence to Cairthi-liag-fada.[2] And Gilbert Mac Goisdelbh, lord of Sliabh-Lugha, came with a large force to the assistance of Mac William Burk, and Tomaltach Mac Donnchaidh came with another force to the assistance of Mac William; and both these armies turned against O'Conchobhair until they reached Ath-Disert-Nuadan;[3] and a few of O'Conchobhair's people were slain about the ford, viz. :— Donnchadh, son of Domhnall Mac Mathghamhna, and Mac Gilla-Comghain, and other persons also who are not enumerated here. O'Conchobhair went afterwards actively, proudly, into the Tuatha; and Mac William fixed his camp that night[4] at Cill-Lomad, in presence of O'Conchobhair. The armies of all Connacht, both Foreigners and Gaeidhel, were subsequently mustered by Mac William, with the

[1330.]

Roscommon, where a pillar stone stands, may be the place indicated. See *Four Mast.*, O'Donovan's ed., A.D. 1330, note °.

[3] *Ath-Disert-Nuadan.* The "ford of Disert-Nuadan," absurdly Anglicised

"Estersnow," the name of a parish in the barony of Boyle, and county of Roscommon. Ɔ⅄ⅽℏ, the first member of the name, is written αὑ in B.

[4] *Night.* αὑαⅼ℈, B. αⅰὀċⅰ, C.

[MS. defective.
Text supplied
from "Annals
of Connacht."]

ocuʃ ʒαιδελαιʒ, vo ʒαɓαιλ ʃιʒι Conʋαchτ vo ʃειn ιαʃ ʃιn. Sιτh cunnαιλ cαιʃvεμαιλ vo vεnαʃ̃ vo Mαc Dιαʃμαvα αcuʃ vlla Chonchoɓαιʃ ιαʃ ʃιn. Slυαʒαʒ λα .h. Rυαιʃcc co ʃιɓ̆ αn ατhα, ocuʃ ιn ɓαιλι vo εʃʒι voιɓ ιαʃʃιn, ocuʃ μαιɓ̆μ vo τhαɓαιʃτ αʃ .h. Rυαιʃc, ocuʃ Ɑʃτ. h. Rυαιʃc, αɓ̆ɓαʃ ʃιʒɓʃειʃne, vo μαʃɓαʒ αnn, ocuʃ μoʃαn αιλι ειvιʃ μαιτh αʒuʃ ʃαιτh. Ʒιλλα Iʃα ʃυαʒ .h. Rαιʒιλλιʒ̆, ʃι Mυιnnτιʃε Mαιλμoʃɓα ocuʃ nα ɓʃειʃne υιλι ʃε μoʃαn vαιμʃιʃ ʃεμhε ʃιn, vo εcc ιnα ʃεnoιʃ ʃατhʃ̃αʃ ʃo chonαιʒh ιαʃ μɓʃειτh ɓυαɓ̆α o vεʃ̃αn αcuʃ o vomhαn. ɓεnεvεcτ.h.ʃlαnnαcαn, ʃʃιoʃ Cιλλι μoʃι nα Sιnnα, quιεuιτ ιn Cʃιʃτo. Mαιλεchλαιnv Mαc Cαʃμαιc, ɓʃυʒαιɓ̆ cεvαch conαιch, vo εcc ιn hoc αn̄no.‑ Mαελιʃα vonv Mαc Ɑεvαcαn μoʃτυuʃ εʃτ. Mαιɓ̆μ μoʃ λα Conchoɓαʃ, μαc Ταιvcc, μιc ɓʃιαιn, μιc Ɑιnvʃιαʃ, μιc ɓʃιαιn λυιʒnιʒ̆, μιc Τoιʃʃvεαλɓαιɓ̆ μóιʃ.h.Chonchuɓαιʃ, αʃ Dαʃτʃαιʒιɓ̆, coʃ μαʃɓαɓ̆ μoʃαn vιɓ̆ λειʃ. Τoιʃʃvhελɓαch .h. Conchuɓαιʃ vo μαʃɓαɓ̆ λα μuιnτιʃ Uατεʃ μιc Uιλλιαμ ɓuʃc oc τεαchτ o τιʒ̆ ιnv ιαʃλα.

Ḱττ. Εnαιʃ ʃoʃ Mαιʃτ, ocuʃ cετhʃαʃ̃αɓ̆ .x. ʃuιʃʃι; M.°ccc.°xxx.° ʃʃιμo; ʃεcunvo αnno cιcλι λunαʃιʃ; xιιιι. αnno ιnvιcτιoιn̄ιʃ; ʃεʃτιμo αnno cιcλι ʃoλαʃιʃ. Mαελʃυαnαιʒ̆ Mαc Dιαʃμαvα, ʃι Moιʒι λuιʃʒ, vo ʃαcɓαιλ α ʃιʒε ocuʃ α ʃλαιɓ̆ιuʃα, ocuʃ vo ʒαɓαιλ αιɓιτι μαnαιʒ̆ λειτh ιμε α μαnιʃτιʃ·nα ɓuιλλε ιn hoc αnno, ocuʃ α εcc ιαʃ ʃιn, ocuʃ Τomαλταch α ʃ̃αc ʃειn vo ʒαɓαιλ nα ʃιʒε cεvnα ιn ʃεʃεɓ̆ λα ιαʃ μɓεαλταιnε. ʃεʃʒαλ μαc Mαιλεchλαιnv chαʃʃαιʒ̆ Mιc Dιαʃμαvα vo μαʃɓαɓ̆ λα Ταvcc μαc Cατhαιλ μιc Domnαιλλ .h. Conchoɓαιʃ. Móʃ ʃλuαʒαɓ̆ λα Uατεʃ μαc Uιλλιαμ ɓuʃcc hι Mαιʒ λuιʃʒ, ocuʃ ιn τιʃ υιλι vo λoʃcuɓ̆ vo αchτ α cελλα nαμα; ocuʃ τucc ʃε cαvuʃ ocuʃ comαιʃcι μαιτh voιɓ̆; αʒuʃ cιɓ̆ εɓ̆ nιʃ λειcc Τomuλταɓ̆ conα ʃεvαιn ɓuvειn

---

¹ "*Brughaidh cédach;*" i.e. a rich farmer.

² *Victory.* The letters N.B. (nota bene) are added in the margin in B.

³ *Kalends.* A marginal note in B and C indicates that the Dom. Letter for the year is F.

object of seizing the sovereignty of Connacht for himself. A prudent, amicable peace was afterwards made by Mac Diarmada and O'Conchobhair. A hosting by O'Ruairc to Fidh-an-atha, when *the people of* the town opposed them, and O'Ruairc was defeated, and Art O'Ruairc, who was qualified to be king of Breifne, was killed there, and a great many more, both good and bad. Gilla-Isa Ruadh O'Raighilligh, king of Muinter-Maelmordha and all the Breifne for a long time previously, died a prosperous, wealthy senior, after obtaining victory over the devil and the world. Benedict O'Flannagain, prior of Cill-mor-na-Sinna, quievit in Christo. Maelechlainn Mac Carmaic, a wealthy brughaidh cédach,[1] died iu hoc anno. Mael-Isa Donn Mac Aedhagain mortuus est. A great victory[2] by Conchobhar, son of Tadhg, son of Brian, son of Andrias, son of Brian Luighnech, son of Toirdhelbhach Mór O'Conchobhair, over the Dartraighe, when a great number of them were slain by him. Toirdhelbhach O'Conchobhair was slain by the people of Walter Mac William Burk, whilst coming from the Earl's house.

A.D.
[1330.]

The kalends[3] of January on Tuesday, and the fourteenth of the moon; M.°ccc.°xxx.° primo; secundo anno cycli lunaris; xiiii. anno Indictionis; septimo anno cycli solaris. Maelruanaidh Mac Diarmada, king of Magh-Luirg, resigned his kingdom and sovereignty, and assumed the habit of a gray monk in the monastery of the Buill in hoc anno, and died afterwards; and his own son Tomaltach assumed the same sovereignty the sixth day after May-day. Ferghal, son of Maelechlainn Carrach Mac Diarmada, was killed by Tadhg, son of Cathal, son of Domhnall O'Conchobhair. A great hosting by Walter Mac William Burk into Magh-Luirg, when the entire country was burned by him, except the churches alone, to which he gave good respect and protection. Nevertheless, Tomaltach and his own army did not permit them to remain

[1331.]

coṁnaiᵹ ᴅoiḃ cin α ninᴅṗaiᵹeḃ co hollaṁ ocuṗ co hapel ina coṁṗoᵹuṗ; aᵹuṗ τuccṗaτ ᵹoill ṗuaicc τṗomleτhan ᴅo τomolτach, cuṗ maṗḃaᴅaṗ ṗoṗinᴅ ᴅo luchτ in τiṗe; aᵹuṗ ciᴅeḃ niṗ miaḃ la Mac nᴅiaṗmaᴅa in ṗoiṗenn ṗin ᴅo maṗḃaᴅ ᴅoiḃṗim ᴅia ṁuinnτiṗ aᵹuṗ can α noiᵹail ṗoṗṗo. Mailiṗ Maᵹ Ɵochaᵹan ᵹuieuiτ in τeṗτia jct. 1enaiṗ.

jct. Ɵnaiṗ ṗoṗ Ceτain, ocuṗ cuiᵹeḃ ṗicheaτ ṗuiṗṗi; anno ᴅomini M.°ccc.°xxx.° ṗecunᴅo; τeṗτio anno cicli lunaṗiṗ; xu. anno inᴅicτioniṗ; uiii. anno cicli ṗolaṗiṗ. Uaτeṗ mac ṗiṗ Uilliam ḃuṗc ᴅo ᵹaḃail laṗin iaṗla nᴅonn, ocuṗ α ḃṗeiḃ leiṗ iaṗ ṗin co caiṗlén nua inᴅṗi hƐoᵹain, aᵹuṗ α ᴅul ᴅecc ᴅon ᵹoṗτa hi ṗṗiṗun in chaiṗlein ṗin. Maiτhi Ꮯlpan ᴅo maṗḃaᴅ leiṗin mᴅaillᴅelḃaċ iṗin bliaᴅain céaᴅna. Maiᴅm ḃeṗna in mil ṗoṗ τomulτach Mac nᴅiaṗmaᴅa, ṗi Muiᵹi luiṗᵹ, ocuṗ aṗ mac Uilliam ḃuṗc, la mac inᴅ iaṗla aᵹuṗ la τomalτach Mac ᴅonᴅchaiḃ, inaṗ maṗḃaᴅ moṗan ᴅo muinnτiṗ mic Uilliam ḃuṗc. Uilliam ᵹallᴅa mac Muiṗcheaṗτaiᵹ móiṗ Mecc Ɵochaᵹain, ᴅux Cenel Ṗiachaiḃ, moṗτuuṗ eṣτ immi Nouembeṗ.

jct. Ɵnaiṗ ṗoṗ Ꮯine, aᵹuṗ ṗeiṗiḃ uaτhaḃ ṗuiṗṗi; anno ᴅomini M.ccc.xxx.iii.; quaṗτo anno cicli lunaṗiṗ; ṗṗimo anno inᴅicτioniṗ; ix. anno cicli ṗolaṗiṗ. Uilliam ḃuṗc .i. iaṗla Ulaḃ, ᴅo maṗḃaᴅ la ᵹallaiḃ Ulaḃ, aᵹuṗ na ᵹoull ṗin uili ᴅo τoiτim ann iτiṗ chṗochaᴅ ocuṗ maṗḃaᴅ ocuṗ τaṗṗaing la muinτiṗ ṗi Ꮪaxan. Ꮯeḃ .h.ᴅomnaill, ṗi τiṗi Conaill ocuṗ ṗeṗ Manach, aᵹuṗ ᴅo ᵹaḃ bṗaiᵹτi ᴅa cṗich Caiṗṗṗi ocuṗ na ḃṗeiṗne, ocuṗ aᴅḃaṗ ṗiᵹ cuiᵹiḃ Ulaḃ uile, ocuṗ leτhᴅṗommann Ɵṗenn

---

¹ *Severe.* τṗomleτhan; lit. "heavy-wide."

² *Kalends.* The Dom. Letters for the year (E D) are added in the margin in B.

³ *New Castle.* Green Castle, near the mouth of Lough Foyle, in the barony of Inishowen, and county of Donegal.

⁴ *The Baliol.* This name is written ḃaillᴅelḃach in the MSS., as if compounded of ḃall, a member, and ᴅelḃach, an adj. derived from ᴅelḃ,

A.D.

[1331.]

[1332.]

[1333.]

without quickly and ably advancing against them, into their neighbourhood; and the Foreigners gave a severe[1] repulse to Tomaltach, and killed a number of the people of the district; but Mac Diarmada did not think it creditable that this number of his people should be killed by them, without revenging it on them   Meiler Mac Eochagain quievit in tertia kalendas Januarii.

The kalends[2] of January on Wednesday, and the twenty-fifth of the moon; anno Domini M°ccc°xxx.° secundo; tertio anno cycli lunaris; xv. anno Indictionis; viii. anno cycli solaris.   Walter, son of Sir William Burk, was taken prisoner by the Brown Earl, who afterwards took him with him to the New Castle[3] of Inis-Eoghain; and he died of hunger in the prison of that castle.   The nobles of Alba were slain by the Baliol[4] in the same year.   The victory of Berna-in-mil was gained over Tomaltach Mac Diarmada, king of Magh-Luirg, and over Mac William Burk, by the Earl's son and Tomaltach Mac Donnchaidh, in which a great number of Mac William Burk's people were slain.   William Gallda,[5] the son of Muirchertach Mór Mac Eochagain, dux of Cenel-Fiachaidh, mortuus est in the month of November.

The kalends[6] of January on Friday, and the sixth of the moon; anno Domini M.ccc.xxxiii.; quarto anno cycli lunaris; primo anno Indictionis; ix. anno cycli solaris.   William Burk, i e. the Earl of Ulster, was slain by the Foreigners of Ulster; and all these Foreigners fell in return, having been either hanged, slain, or torn asunder,[7] by the king of the Saxons' people.   Aedh O'Domhnaill, king of Tir-Conaill and Feara-Manach, and who took the hostages of the two districts of Cairbre, and of the Breifne; one qualified to be king of the entire province of Uladh, and the prop of all Erinn as

"figure." The form ḃailiolach is, however, added in the marg. in both MSS

[5] Gallda.   This is a sobriquet signifying the "Anglicised."

[6] Kalends   The Dom. Letter for the year (C) is added in the margin in B and C.

[7] Torn asunder. cappaing; lit. "drawing."

[MS defective. Text supplied from "Annals of Connacht"]

uili ap enech ocur ap engnaṁ, ocur ap rmacht, ocur ap piaḃail; acur rear ir mo ler ṫoic do Ʒallaiḃ ocur Ʒaiḋealaiḃ bioir a naen aimrir frir, moptuur ert iap mbreith buaḋa o deṁan ocur o doṁan, ocur iap mbeith da bliaƷain ap ċaoƷad appiƷi Tire Conaill, ocur iap nƷaḃail aibici manaiƷ leith imbi, iar rairroin ocur aithriƷi, quieuit. Conchuḃar.h.Doṁnaill, a ṁac rein, do Ʒaḃail riƷe Tire Conaill taper a athar, ocur imchornamh do ḃeith etir Conchoḃar aƷur Art .i.h.Doṁnaill, .i. mac a athar rein, imon riƷi, acur Art do Ʒaḃail le Conchuḃar.h.nDoṁnaill, ocur a ṁarḃaḋ leir ro cedoir. Tomaltach Mac Donochaiḋ, tiƷearna Tire Oiliolla, rai neniƷ ocur nenƷaṁa, aƷur rer rob rerr comairci ocur caḋur aƷur ririnne do ḃai a naen aimrir frir, moptuur ert. Feḋlimiḋ.h.Doṁnaill, ant aen mac riƷ dob uarli aƷur dob ailli, aƷur dob appach-ta, aƷur ir mo rir araiḃi ruil na rochaiḋe aƷur rer nErenn uili, do ecc irin ḃliaḋain rin. Ʒilleberd Mac Ʒoirdelḃ do marḃaḋ ap lár a tiƷi rein la Cathal Mac Diarmada Ʒall, rer dolum. Aeḋ Mac Conrnaṁa, tairech Muinntire Cinaith, quieuit. Macc na hoidchi MaƷ Flannchaiḋ do marḃaḋ la Connachtaiḃ. Dono-chaḋ mac Aeḋa.h. CellaiƷ do Ʒaḃail la Toirrḋealḃach Ua Conchubair, ri Connacht. Sith do rocra a Ratreser do cloinn Uilliam Burc a hucht riƷ Saxan. Conchuḃar Mac Branan, toirech Corca Achlann, moptuur ert ui. idur Ienair.

ƘCt. Enair ror Satharn, aƷur rechtmaḋ .x. fuirri; M.ccc.xxx iiii.; quinto anno cicli lunarir; primo anno indictionir; x. anno rolarir cicli. MorrluaƷaḋ la Connachtaiḃ uili eidir Ʒallaiḃ ocur Ʒaiḋelaiḃ irin Muṁain dochom MeƷ Conmara. braiƷdi ocur neart

¹ *Mac-na-hoidchi;* lit. "son of the night."

² *Rath-Secher.* This appears to have been the name of some place, probably in Connacht, which has not been identified.

³ *Corca-Achlann.* Corca Achct., B and C. See note ¹⁰, p. 596.

regards bounty and prowess, repression and rule; and the man by whom Foreigners and Gaeidhel fell most in his own time—mortuus est after obtaining victory over the devil and the world, and after having been fifty-two years in the sovereignty of Tir-Conaill, and after assuming the habit of a gray monk,—after confession and penance, quievit. Conchobhar O'Domhnaill, his own son, assumed the sovereignty of Tir-Conaill after his father; and a contention occurred between Conchobhar and Art O'Domhnaill, i.e. his own father's son, regarding the sovereignty; and Art was taken prisoner by Conchobhar O'Domhnaill, and was immediately slain by him. Tomaltach Mac Donnchaidh, lord of Tir-Oilella, a most eminent man for bounty and prowess, and the best of his contemporaries for guarantee, honour, and truth, mortuus est. Fedhlimidh O'Domhnaill, the king's son who was the most noble, the most comely, and most illustrious, and from whom the multitudes, and the men of all Erinn, expected most, died in this year. Gilbert Mac Goisdelbh was slain in the middle of his own house by Cathal Mac Diarmada Gall, per dolum. Aedh Mac Consnamha, chieftain of Muinter-Cinaith, quievit. Mac-na-hoidchi[1] Mac Flannchaidh was slain by Connachtmen. Donnchadh, son of Aedh O'Cellaigh, was taken prisoner by Toirdhelbhach O'Conchobhair, king of Connacht. Peace was proclaimed at Rath-Secher,[2] to the sons of William Burk, on the part of the king of the Saxons. Conchobhar Mac Branan, chieftain of Corca-Achlann,[3] mortuus est vi. idus Januarii.

The kalends[4] of January on Saturday, and the seventeenth of the moon; M.CCC.XXX.iiii.; quinto anno cycli lunaris; primo[5] anno Indictionis; x. anno solaris cycli. A great hosting by all the Connachtmen, both Foreigners and Gaeidhel, into Mumha, to Mac Conmara, from whom

---

[4] *Kalends.* The Dom. Letter (B) is added in the margin in B and C.

[5] *Primo.* So in B and C. But it is by mistake for "secundo."

defective.
supplied
"Annals
nnacht."]

do dol doib fair. Tempoll do lorcad do dreim dont
fluag fin arrabadar ochtmada ar ced do dainib eitir
maith ocur traith, ocur diar facart maille friu, et
comburti fuerunt. Deicnebar do muinntir Donnchaid
riabaig mic Maielechlainn charraig Mic Diarmada
do badad ar Loch Teched. Tadcc, mac Cathail, mic
Domnaill.h.Conchobair, mortuur ert. Seonacc, mac
Muirceartaig moir Mec Eochacan, dux Cenel Fia-
chaid, mortuur ert in .xiiii. Ct. ienair. Donnchad
Mac Conrnama, tairech Muintire Cinaith, mortuur
ert.

Ct. Enair for Domnac, ocur ochtmad .xx.it fuirri ;
M.ccc.xxx.u. ; ui. anno cicli lunarir ; tertio anno indictionir ; xi. anno cicli rolarir. Finnguala, ingen
.h.briain, ben Toirrdelbaig.h.Chonchobair, mortua ert.
Seoan mac Airt.h.Eghra do gabail le mac in iarla,
ocur forccla a muintiri do arccain do. Crech la
Cloinn Domnaill .h. Conchobair ar cloinn Muirir
trucaig mic Geralt, du ar marbad mac mic Muirir.
Creach noigailti la cloinn Muirir ar cloinn Domnaill
cedna iarrin. Iarthar Connacht uli do milled le
hEmann a Burcc ; daine imdo do marbad, ocur
creacha ocur loircthi acur uile diarmithi do denamh
do for ar mac an iarla acur ar cloinn Ricaird a Burc
irin bliadhain ceadna ; acur rith do denamh doib re
roile iar rin. Snechta mor irin errach cur dithaig
urmor minen Ereand uili.

Ct. Enair for Luan, ocur naemhad uathad fuirri ;
M.°ccc.°xxx.°ui. ; uii. anno cicli lunarir ; quarto anno
indictionir ; xii. anno cicli rolarir. Tomaltach Mac
Diarmada, rig Moigi Luircc, fer ro bo mo grain ocur
corcar ar a ercardoib, ocur fer ror ferr enech ocur

---

[1] *Ten.* deicenbar, C. x.enbar
for deicenbar (or deicnebar), B.

[2] *The Earl's son.* mac nDiarmada (Mac Diarmada) B. The same
name was also written in C., but

afterwards expunged, and mac an
iarla (the Earl's son) substituted.

[3] *Kalends.* The Dom. Letter (G) is
added in the marg. in B, but C has G F.

[4] *xxxvi.* xxvi., C.

hostages were exacted, and over whom sway was obtained, by them. A church was burned by a division of this army, in which were one hundred and eighty persons both good and bad, and two priests along with them; et combusti fuerunt. Ten[1] of the people of Donnchadh Riabhach, son of Maelechlainn Carrach Mac Diarmada, were drowned in Loch-Teched. Tadhg, son of Cathal, son of Domhnall O'Conchobhair, mortuus est. Seonac, son of Muirchertach Mór Mac Eochagain, dux of Cenel-Fiachaidh, mortuus est in xiiii. kalendas Januarii. Donnchadh Mac Consnamha, chieftain of Muinter-Cinaith, mortuus est.

The kalends of January on Sunday, and the twenty-eighth of the moon; M.CCC.XXXV.; vi. anno cycli lunaris; tertio anno Indictionis; xi. anno cycli solaris. Finnghuala, daughter of O'Briain, wife of Toirdhelbhach O'Conchobhair, mortua est. John, son of Art O'hEghra, was taken prisoner by the Earl's son; and the principal part of his people were plundered by him. A depredation *was committed* by the sons of Domhnall O'Conchobhair on the descendants of Maurice Sugach Fitz-Gerald, on which occasion the son of Mac Maurice was killed. A retaliatory depredation was afterwards committed by the Clann-Maurice on the same sons of Domhnall. The West of Connacht was all destroyed by Edmond Burk; a great many persons were slain; and innumerable depredations, and burnings, and injuries were also committed by him on the Earl's son,[2] and on the Clan-Rickard Burk, in the same year; but they afterwards made peace with one another. Great snow in the spring, which destroyed the greater number of the small birds of all Erinn.

The kalends[3] of January on Monday, and the ninth of the moon; M.°ccc.°xxx.° vi.[4]; vii. anno cycli lunaris; quarto anno Indictionis; xii. anno cycli solaris. Tomaltach Mac Diarmada, king of Magh-Luirg, the most formidable and triumphant man against his enemies, and the man of

defective.
supplied
"Annals
nnacht."]

almrana, caðar accur comairce ina aimrir rein, becc
in nono Kalenvar Iunii .i. aðaiᵹ Domnaiᵹ na Trinnoiti,
ina tiᵹ rein i calað na Cairci, et repulcur ert i man-
irter na builli co huaral onorach; ocur Conchoðar
mac Tomaltaiᵹ .i. a mac rein, vo riᵹað ina inav.
Teboiv a burc .i. Mac Uilliam, mortuur ert. Mailer
mac Siurtan vecetar mortuur ert. Maiðm la hEoᵹán
.h.Mavavan ar cloinn Ricarv a burc, inar marbað
reirer aᵹur tri richit ivir maith aᵹur raith. Creach
mor la cloinn Diarmava ᵹall ocur la mac Feivlimið
.h.Conchoðair, ror Cloinn ᵹoirvelᵇ, ocur Maviucc
mac balvrin vo marbað ina toraiᵹecht. Crech mor
le hemanv mac Uilliam burcc ar Cloinn Cathail, var
haircev Conchoðar .h. Flannaᵹan ocur vaine imvo eli
amaille rir, ocur Maileaᶜlainn.h.Flannaᵹan vo marbað a toraiᵹecht na creichi rin; ocur vo ᵹaðavarran
verbratair vo Mac in milið a toraiᵹecht na creichi
rin. Conchuðar Mac Diarmava, ri Moiᵹi Luirᵹ, ocur
Aeð mac Feðlimið, mic Aeða, mic Eoᵹhain.h.Chonchu-
ðair, ocur lucht tiᵹi.h.Conchoðair maraen riu, acur
clann Donvchaið ocur ᵹlarlaith criche Cairrᵹi im
Cormac mac Ruaivhri, vo vol ar creich a Tir Fiachrach currancɕavar mullaᶜ Ratha; ocur ba an tire vo
teiᶜev rompa. Marbévala mora ocur caraill imva,
ocur beccan vechaið ocur vo roᶜroð imva vo thaðairt
leo; aᵹur vaine vo marbað leo; ocur a teacht rein
rlán va tiᵹiᵇ. Diarmaitt .h. Flannaᵹan, vux Cloinne
Cathail, mortuur ert. Toirrvelᵇach Ua Conchoðair, ri
Convacht, vo tinol imircech na Tuatha ocur Cloinne

---

1 *Junii.* luni, B and C.

2 *Night.* aðaiᵹ, B. āv, for anv,
"on," or "in," C.

3 *Caladh-na-Cairgi.* "The shore
of the Rock [of Loch Cé]."

4 *Of Tomaltach.* Tom, for Tomaltaiᵹ, B. Domnaill, C.

5 *Mac Waltrin.* mac balvrin, B.

mac bailtirín, C. The name signifies "son of little Walter," and was
that of a member of the Clann-Goisdelbh, or Clann-Costello.

6 *O'Flannagain.* h. Flanvacan,
B. The form of the name in C, .h.
Flannaᵹan, is the more usual.

7 *They;* i.e. the Clann-Cathail.

greatest bounty and almsgiving, of greatest honour and guarantee in his own time, died in nono kalendas Junii,[1] i.e. on the night[2] of Trinity Sunday, in his own house in Caladh-na-Cairgi,[3] et sepultus est nobly, honourably, in the monastery of the Buill ; and Conchobhar, son of Tomaltach,[4] i.e. his own son, was made king in his stead. Tibbot Burk, i.e. the Mac William, mortuus est. Meiler Mac Jordan de Exeter mortuus est. A victory by Eoghan O'Madadhain over the Clann-Rickard Burk, in which three score and six were slain, both good and bad. A great depredation by the sons of Diarmaid Gall, and by Fedhlimidh O'Conchobhair, on the Clann-Goisdelbh ; and Maidiuc Mac Waltrin[5] was slain in pursuit of the prey. A great depredation by Edmond Mac William Burk upon the Clann-Cathail, on which occasion Conchobhar O'Flannagain[6] was plundered, and many other persons along with him ; and Maelechlainn O'Flannagain was slain whilst in pursuit of this prey ; and they[7] took Mac-in-mhilidh's brother prisoner in pursuit of this prey. Conchobhar Mac Diarmada, king of Magh-Luirg, and Aedh, the son of Fedhlimidh, son of Aedh, son of Eoghan O'Conchobhair, together with O'Conchobhair's household band, and the Clann-Donnchadha, and the young soldiers of the territory of Cairbre, including Cormac the son of Ruaidhri,[8] went on a predatory expedition into Tir-Fiachrach until they reached Mullach-Ratha ; but the cows of the district fled[9] before them. Many inanimate spoils, and several horses, and a few steeds, and a great quantity of small cattle were brought away by them ; and people were slain by them ; and they came home safely. Diarmaid O'Flannagain[6], dux of Clann-Cathail, mortuus est. Toirdhelbhach O'Conchobhair, king of Connacht, mustered the moveable forces of the Tuatha, of Clann-

---

[8] *Ruaidhri*; i.e. Ruaidhri, the son of Domhnall O'Conchobhair.

[9] *Fled.* ꝺo ꞇeiꞇeꝺ ; i.e. were driven off.

'efective.
supplied
'Annals
nacht."]

Cαċαιl, ocup Cloinne Conchoḃαιp, αġup Moıġı Luıpż co hαpτech, ocup cαιplen mop Mıc Żopṽelḃ ṽo żαḃαιl ṽo, ocup α ḃuıpeṽ ιαppın, ocup ceτhıpnn conżḃαlα αn bαιlı ṽo τeαċτ αmαċ αp comαpcı Mıcc Ṽıαpmαṽα. Τpınnoıτ O Nααn, αpṽmαıżıpτıp α nelαṽnαıḃ ımṽα, α lex occup ı cαnoın, quıeuıτ ın Cpıpτo. Ṽoṁnαll mαc Seoαn mıc Ṽomnαıll .h. Chonchoḃαıp mopτuup epτ. Nıαll mαc Conchoḃαıp mıc Ταıṽcc occıpup epτ ṽupchup τpoıżṽı.

Ιcτ. Θnαıp pop Ceταın, αġup pıchıτ puıppı; M.°ccc.°xxx.uııı.; uıııı. αnno cıclı lunαpıp; quınτo αnno ınṽıcτıonıp; xııı. αnno cıclı polαpıp. Sıṽ ṽo ṽenαṁ ṽUıllıαm mαc ıαplα Ulαṽ ocup ṽo Ḃpıαn bán .h. Ḃpıαın, ocup cαch pepαnṽ ṽαp polṁαıż pe po mαc αnṽ ıαplα ṽo lécαn ṽó αp α chıp pein ṽo τhαḃαıpτ áp. Sıṽ ṽo ṽenαṁ ṽo αeṽ pemαp Uα Néıll pe hOpżıαllαıṽ ocup pe pepαıṽ Mαnαch. Poplonżṗupτ ṽo ṽenαṁ lα Τoıpp-ṽheαlbαch .h. Conchoḃαıp, pı Connαchτ, ıc ατh Lıαż α nαżαıṽ Θmαınṽ α Ḃupc. Seoαn .h. pαllαṁαın, ṽux Cloınne hUαṽαċ, mopτuup epτ. Ταṽc Mαż plαnnchαıṽ, ṽux Ṽαpτpαıżı, ṽo mαpḃαṽ lα Copbmαc mαc Ruαıṽpı mıc Ṽoṁnαıll .h. Chonchoḃαıp, mαpαen pe mopαn elı, α nṽıżhαıl τSeoαın mıc Ṽoṁnαıll; ocup cpeαchα mopα ṽo ṽenαṁ αp Ṽαpτpαıżıṽ, ocup mαc Muıpıp Meż plαnnchαıṽ ṽo mαpḃαṽ αn lα céṽnα. Ταṽc ocup Mαılechlαınn, ṽα mαc ıṁαıp Meż Rαżnαıll, ṽo żαḃαıl ṽo Chατhαl Mαż Rαżnαıll, ocup Cατhαl Mαż Rαżnαıll ṽo mαpḃαṽ α τópαıżechṽ lα cloınn ıṁαıp ocup lα hUıllıαm Mαc Mατhżαṁnα, .ı. Conchoḃαp occup Τom-ulταċ meıc ıṁαıp ınṽpın, ocup ocḃαṽ αn τıpe αmαılle ppıu, ocup Mαżnup mαc pepżαıl ṽo mαpḃαṽ ṽoıṽ ın

1 *Great castle.* cαıplen móp. This castle, called Castlemore-Costello, or Castlemore, is situated in the barony of Costello, and co. of Mayo.

2 *Lex and Canon;* i.e. Civil and Canon Law.

3 *Kalends.* The Dom. Letter (E) is added in the margin in B.

4 *His own rent:* i.e. such rent as O'Brien elected to pay. The Four Masters say α ccíop pein, "their own rent," i.e. the rent of the lands.

Cathail, Clann-Conchobhair, and Magh-Luirg, to Airtech; and the great castle[1] of Mac Goisdelbh was taken by him, and afterwards broken down; and the kern who guarded the place came out on the guarantee of Mac Diarmada. Trinnoit O'Naan, high master in many sciences, in Lex and Canon,[2] quievit in Christo. Domhnall, son of John, son of Domhnall O'Conchobhair, mortuus est. Niall, the son of Conchobhar Mac Taidhg, occisus est by a shot of an arrow.

The kalends[3] of January on Wednesday, and the twentieth of the moon; M.°ccc.°xxx.vii.; viii. anno cycli lunaris; quinto anno Indictionis; xiii. anno cycli solaris. Peace was made by William, son of the Red Earl, and Brian Bán O'Briain; and all the lands that he (*O'Briain*) had wasted against the Earl's son were given to him, on condition of his own rent[4] being paid for them. Peace was concluded by Aedh Remhar O'Neill with the Oirghialla and the Feara-Manach. A fortified camp was formed by Toirdhelbach O'Conchobhair, king of Connacht, at Ath-Liag, against Edmond Burk. John O'Fallamhain, dux of Clann-Uadach, mortuus est. Tadhg Mac Flannchaidh, dux of Dartraighe, was slain by Cormac, son of Ruaidhri, son of Domhnall O'Conchobhair, together with many more, in revenge of John, son of Domhnall; and great depredations were committed upon the Dartraighe; and the son of Maurice Mac Flannchaidh was slain the same day. Tadhg and Maelechlainn, two sons of Imhar Mac Raghnaill, were taken prisoners by Cathal Mac Raghnaill, and Cathal Mac Raghnaill was killed in the pursuit by the sons of Imhar— (viz., these sons of Imhar were Conchobhar and Tomaltach)—and by William Mac Mathghamhna, and by the young men of the country along with them; and Maghnus, son of Ferghal,[5] was killed by them on the

---

[5] *Son of Ferghal.* The Four Masters write the name Ua Ꝼeṅġail, or O'Farrell; but the Maghnus in question was probably the son of Ferghal Mac Raghnaill, who was slain in 1306, as above recorded.

defective.
supplied
"Annals
onnacht."]

la ceaona, ocur Taöc Maz Raznaill vo zaöail na
toirizechta iarrna znioṁaiö rin.   Doṁnall ruaö
.h. Mailli ocur Copmacc O Mailli vo ṁaröaö vo
cloinn Mebrice ocur vo zallaiö eli maille rriu, avaiz
reli Stepain. In maizirtir .h. Roclan quieuit in Cripto.
Matha .h. hUicinn, rai voána ocur voennachta,
quieuit. Enri Mac Martin vo maröaö in hoc anno.
Maiöm mor ar Toirrvelöach .h. Conchoöair, ri Connacht, re cloinn Cellaiö, ocur Toirrvhelöach rein
vo lot ano, ocur vo zaöail, ocur a eich ocur a etiö
vo racbail vo ano, maille re hár mór vo ṫainiö.
Luzaiv .h. Oálaiz, erruc Cluana muc Noir, in Cripto
quieuit. Tomar mac Copmaic .h. Doṁnaill, erpoz
Tiri Conaill .i. rai necna ocur cráöaiö, verci ocur
vaennachta, in Cripto quieuit. Donochaö mac Muir-
ceartaiz moir Mec Eochacan, vux Cenel Fiachaiö,
occirur ert o Uiö Failzi.

Kl. Enair ror Darvaoin; ocur aen uachav ruirri;
M.°ccc.°xxx.° octauo; ix. anno cicli lunarir; rexto anno
invictionir; xiiii. anno cicli rolarir. Donochaö mac
Ruaiöri .h. Concubair occirur ert in hoc anno.
Ruaiöri Maz Uivir, ri rer Manach ocur Locha hErne,
in rer ir mó ro tiönaicc varccet ocur vellach ocur
vetach vo vaṁaiö ocur vollaṁnaiö Erenv ina aimrir
rein, mortuur ert. Emanv a burc .i. mac Iarla Ulaö,
vo zaöail la hEmann a burcc, ocur cloch vo chup ra
na öraizit, ocur a chup a Loch Merca iar rin; azur
tanicc milleö zall Connacht ocur a chiniö rein trít
rin; azur vo zaö Toirrvhelbach .h. Conchobair neart
Connacht iar rin, ocur vo hinnaröaö Eṁan mac

---

1 *Assumed.* vo zaöail; repeated in C.
2 *Clothes.* etiö; i.e. his coat of mail.
3 *Son of Cormac.* mac Copmaic,
C. mac Carmaicc, B.
4 *Bishop of Tír Conaill:* otherwise

5 *Kalends.* The Dom. Letter (D)
is added in the margin in B.
6 *O'Conchobhair.* This name has
been omitted in B.
7 *Of money.* varccet; for vo

same day; and Tadhg Mac Raghnaill assumed[1] the chieftaincy after these events. Domhnall Ruadh O'Maille and Cormac O'Maille were slain by the Clann-Mebhric, and by other Foreigners along with them, on the night of Stephen's festival. The Master O'Rothlan quievit in Christo. Matthew O'hUiginn, a man eminent for poetry and humanity, quievit. Henry Hac Martin was killed in hoc anno. A great victory over Toirdhelbhach O'Conchobhair, king of Connacht, by Clann-Cellaigh; and Toirdhelbhach himself was wounded there, and taken prisoner; and his horse and clothes[2] were left there by him, together with a great slaughter of people. Lughaidh O'Dálaigh, bishop of Cluain-mic-Nois, in Christo quievit. Thomas, son of Cormac[3] O'Domhnaill, bishop of Tir-Conaill,[4] i.e. a man eminent for wisdom, piety, charity, and humanity, in Christo quievit. Donnchadh, son of Muirchertach Mór Mac Eochagain, dux of Cenel-Fiachaidh, occisus est by the Ui-Failghe.

The kalends[5] of January on Thursday, and the first of the moon; M.°ccc.°xxx.° octavo; ix. anno cycli lunaris; sexto anno Indictionis; xiiii. anno cycli solaris. Donnchadh, son of Ruaidhri O'Conchobhair,[6] occisus est in hoc anno. Ruaidhri Mac Uidhir, king of Feara-Manach and Loch-Erne, the man who, in his own time, presented most of money,[7] of cattle, and of clothing to the learned men and chief poets of Erinn, mortuus est. Edmond Burk, i.e. the son of the Earl of Ulster, was taken prisoner by Edmond Burk; and a stone was tied round his neck,[8] and he was afterwards thrown into Loch-Mesca; and the destruction of the Foreigners of Connacht, and of his own family, occurred through this. And Toirdhelbhach O'Conchobhair assumed the sway of Connacht after that,

---

[8] *Round his neck.* ꝼꝺ ꝼꝺ ḃꞃꝺíᵹіꞇ, C. ꝼꝺ ḃꞃꝺíᵹіꞇ, B. Roderick O'Flaherty (*Iar Connaught*, Hardiman's ed., p. 48) states that Edmond Burk was "turned into a bag, and cast out of the [Earl's] island into the lake, with stones tyed to the bag." The letters N.B. are added in the margin.

Uilliam buꞃcc a Connachταιꞃ amach; ocuꞃ ꞃo milleꞅ
ꞇuaτha ocuꞃ cella ιαꞃταιꞃ Connachτ uli; ocuꞃ ꞃo
ꞇinol Emanꞅ a buꞃc coꞃlach moꞃ ꞅo lonჳaιꞃ ocuꞃ baꞃ-
caιꞃ, [acuꞃ] ꞃo baι aꞃ olenaιꞃ na ꞃaιꞃꞃci ꞃe heꞅ ciana.
Luჳni ocuꞃ in Copanꞅ ꞅo ꞃolmuჳaꞅ ocuꞃ ꞅo ꞃáꞃꞃuჳaꞅ,
ocuꞃ a τιჳeaꞃnaꞃ ꞅo ჳaꞃaιl ꞅa nჳaιꞅelaιꞃ ꞅuτhcuꞃa
buꞅein, aꞃ nꞅιchuꞃ a nჳall eꞃτιꞃ. Ταꞃc mac Ruaιꞅꞃι
mic Caτhaιl ꞃuaꞅ .h. Concoꞃaιꞃ, ꞃιꞃ ꞃáιτι an bꞃaτach
ꞃιჳin, ꞅo ჳaꞃaιl ꞅo Thomaꞃ Mac Saꞃꞃaꞅaιn, ocuꞃ
moꞃan ꞅa ꞃuinτιꞃ ꞅo maꞃbaꞅ. Maჳ Saꞃꞃaꞅaιn ꞅo
ꞅol co ꞇech .h. Conchuꞃaιꞃ ιaꞃ ꞃin, ocuꞃ oc ꞇeachꞇ ꞅo
o τιჳ .h. Conchuꞃaιꞃ aꞃ aιꞃ, clann Muιꞃceaꞃταιჳ ocuꞃ
Muιnτeꞃ Eolaιꞃ ꞅo coꞃꞇinol aꞃ a chinꞅ, ocuꞃ Maჳ
Saꞃꞃaꞅaιn ꞅo ჳaꞃaιl ꞅoιꞃ, acuꞃ moꞃan ꞅa ꞃuιnnτιꞃ ꞅo
ꞃaꞃꞃaꞅ. Deꞃbaιl ιnჳen Chaτhaιl mιc Muꞃchaꞅa, ben
Donꞅchaιꞃ mιc Αeꞅa oιc, quιeuιꞇ. Caoιꞃιꞅ Eꞃenꞅ ꞅo
écc ιn hoc anno achꞇmaꞅ becc. Cocaꞅ moꞃ eιꞅιꞃ ꞃιჳ
Fꞃanc aჳuꞃ ꞃιჳ Saxan ιn hoc anno.

Кт. Enaιꞃ ꞃoꞃ Αιne ocuꞃ aιlι .x. ꞃuιꞃꞃι; anno Domιnι M.ccc.xxx.ιx.; x. anno cιclι lunaꞃιꞃ; uιι. anno
ιnꞅιcꞇιonιꞃ; xu. cιclι ꞃolaꞃιꞃ. Ruaιꞅꞃι Ua Cellaιჳ,
ꞃι .h. Maιne, ꞅo maꞃꞃaꞅ la Caτhal mac Αeꞅa mιc
Eoჳaιn .h. Conchobaιꞃ, ac ꞅola o τιჳ .h. Conchuꞃaιꞃ ꞅa
τιჳ ꞃeιn ιn hoc anno. Τomaꞃ Maჳ Saꞃꞃaꞅaιn ꞅo bι
alláꞃ aჳ cloιnn Muιꞃcheaꞃταιჳ ꞅo lecuꞅ amach.
Pláιჳ móꞃ o τꞃιcc ocuꞃ o ꞇꞃneaꞇτa aꞃ ellach ocuꞃ aꞃ
ჳoꞃꞇaιꞃ ჳeꞃaιꞃ Eꞃenꞅ o caιcτιჳιꞃ ꞅo ჳemꞃιꞅ co blaιჳ
ꞅon eꞃꞃach. Sluaჳaꞅ moꞃ la hΑeꞅ ꞃeꞃaꞃ .h. Neιll
ꞅochom Τιꞃι Conaιll, ꞅaꞃ maꞃbaꞅ mac Seoaιn .h. Neιll

---

1 *Out of them.* eꞃτιꞃ, C. eꞃιꞃ, B.
2 *The.* an, C.; omitted in B.
3 *Bratach righin;* i.e. "the tough
standard (or flag)."
4 *From.* o. C. oꞃ. B.

6 *Clann - Muirchertaigh;* i.e. the descendants of Muirchertach Muimhnech
(or Murtough the Momonian) O'Conchobhair, who was the son of Turlough
Mór, monarch of Ireland. Instead of

and Edmond Mac William Burk was expelled out of
Connacht; and the territories and churches of all the
West of Connacht were spoiled. And Edmond Burk collected a large fleet of ships and barks, [and] remained on
the islands of the sea for a long time. Luighne and the
Corann were depopulated and wasted, and the sovereignty was assumed by their own hereditary Gaeidhel,
after the expulsion of their Foreigners out of them.[1]
Tadhg, son of Ruaidhri, son of Cathal Ruadh O'Conchobhair, usually called the[2] "Bratach righin,"[3] was taken
prisoner by Thomas Mac Samhradhain; and many of his
people were slain. Mac Samhradhain went afterwards
to O'Conchobhair's house, and on his return from[4] O'Conchobhair's house the Clann-Muirchertaigh and Muinter-
Eolais assembled before him; and Mac Samhradhain was
taken prisoner by them, and several of his people were
slain. Derbhail, daughter of Cathal Mac Murchadha,
wife of Donnchadh, son of Aedh Og, quievit. The sheep
of Erinn died in hoc anno, excepting a few. A great
war between the king of France and the king of the
Saxons in hoc anno.

The kalends of January on Friday, and the twelfth of
the moon; anno Domini M.CCC.XXX.IX.; x. anno cycli
lunaris; vii. anno Indictionis; xv. cycli[5] solaris. Ruaidhri
O'Cellaigh, king of Ui-Maine, was slain by Cathal, son
of Aedh, son of Eoghan O'Conchobhair, whilst going
from O'Conchobhair's house to his own house, in hoc
anno. Thomas Mac Samhradhain, who was detained a
prisoner by the Clann-Muirchertaigh,[6] was set at liberty.[7]
A great plague from frost and snow on the cattle and
green cornfields of Erinn, from a fortnight of winter to a
part of the spring. A great hosting by Aedh Remhar
O'Neill to Tir-Conaill, on which occasion the son of John

---

cĉ. h.; but this is a repetition, as h.
is the abbrev. for huıb, or uıb, the
dat. plur. of ua, or o, "descendant."

[7] *Set at liberty.* do lec amach,
for do lecud amach (lit. "was let
out"), B. do leıʒen amach, C.

defective.
supplied
"Annals
nnacht."]

ocur Zoppaiḋ .h.'Doṁnaill le muintip .h.'Dochaptaiż. Emanḋ mac Uilliam ḃupcc ḋinnapḃaḋ a hUltaiḃ cona lonżur. Ben mic inḋ iapla Ulaḋ .i. inżen Coippḋhealbaiż .h. Ḃpiain, ḋo chaḃaipt ḋo Coippḋealḃaċ .h. Conchoḃaip pi Connachc, ocur 'Depḃail inżen Aeḋa .h. 'Dhoṁnaill ḋo lecaḋ ḋo ipin bliaḋain pin. Cocaḋ mop ap poḋ na Miḋe eiḋip Zallaiḃ ocur Zaiḋelaiḃ. Apḃanna Epenḋ ḋo milleḋ, ażur żopta mop innti. Cempall Cille Ronain ḋo ḋenaṁ la Pepżal Muiṁnech .h. 'Duiḃżennan in hoc anno.

Kt. Enaip pop Satapnn, ocur cper .xx. puippi; M.°ccc.°xl.; xi. anno cicli lunapir; uiii. anno inḋictionir; xui. cicli polapir. Coṁtocḃail cocaiḋ móip eiḋip Mainechaiḃ .i. etip Caḋcc mac Caiḋcc .h. Cellaiż, ḋa tucc Coippḋhealbach .h. Conchoḃaip upplamur .h. Maine, ocur Uilliam mac 'Donḋchaiḋ Muiṁniż .h. Cellaiż, cup cuipeḋ Uilliam mac 'Donḋchaiḋ Muiṁniż apin tip amach, ocur po lenpat uli'e, cup impo Uilliam ppiú, ocur cup ṁapḃaḋ 'Donḋchaḋ mac Aeḋa .h. Cellaiż, ocur cup żaḃaḋ Caḋcc .h. Cellaiż, acur cup loteḋ, ocur a écc ḋa lot iapaṁ. Maelpechlainn .h. Zaipmleaḋaiż, taipech Cenel Moain, moptuur ert. Clann Ualżaipż .h. Ruaipc .i. 'Doṁnall ocur Aoḋ, ocur Zilla Cpiorḋ, ocur Ruaiḋpi ḋo ḋol ap cpeich ḋochum Cathail mic Aeḋa Ḃpeipniż; ocur ḋo ponpat cpeach lán móp, ocur ḋo mapḃaḋ Conchoḃap, mac 'Donḋchaiḋ piaḃaiż, mic Mażnura, mic Muipċeaptaiż Muiṁniż leo in lá pin, ażur mopan aili maille pir; ocur ipí pin ceḋ pola Muinntipi Ruaipc ocur Cloinni Muipcheaptaiż Muiṁniż mic Coippḋhealbaiż móip; ocur ḋo pone Cathal mac Aeḋa Ḃpeipniż in topaiżecht ċpoḋa iap pin, ḋap poptaḋ mopan ḋon chpeich, ocur ḋap mapḃaḋ 'Domnall .h. Ruaipc, aen poża mac piż

---

[1] *In it*; i.e. in the same year.   [2] *Kalends.* The Dom. Letters (B A) are added in the margin in B.

O'Neill, and Godfrey O'Domhnaill, were slain by O'Dochartaigh's people. Edmond Mac William Burk was driven
to Uladh, together with his fleet. The wife of the
Earl of Ulster's son, i.e. the daughter of Toirdhelbhach
O'Briain, was taken to wife by Toirdhelbhach O'Conchobhair, king of Connacht, and Derbhail, daughter of
Aedh O'Domhnaill, was abandoned by him, in this year.
A great war throughout Midhe, between Foreigners and
Gaeidhel. The corn crops of Erinn were destroyed, and great
famine *ensued* in it[1]. The church of Cill-Ronain was built
by Ferghal Muimhnech O'Duibhgennain in hoc anno.

The kalends[2] of January on Saturday, and the twenty-
third of the moon ; M.° ccc.° xl. ; xi. anno cycli lunaris ; viii.
anno Indictionis ; xvi. cycli solaris. A great war arose
amongst the Ui-Maine, i.e. between Tadhg, son of Tadhg
O'Cellaigh, to whom Toirdhelbhach O'Conchobhair had
given the government of Ui-Maine, and William, son of
Donnchadh Muimhnech O'Cellaigh ; and William, son of
Donnchadh Muimhnech, was sent out of the district ; and
they all pursued him, but William turned upon them,
when Donnchadh, son of Aedh O'Cellaigh, was slain, and
Tadhg O'Cellaigh was taken prisoner and wounded ; and
he died afterwards of his wound. Maelsechlainn O'Gairm-
leghaig, chieftain of Cenel-Moain, mortuus est. The sons
of Ualgharg O'Ruairc, viz., Domhnall, and Aedh, and
Gilla-Christ, and Ruaidhri, went on a predatory expedition to Cathal, son of Aedh Breifnech ; and they committed a very great depredation ; and Conchobhar, the
son of Donnchadh Riabhach, son of Maghnus, son of
Muirchertach Muimhnech, was on that day slain by
them, and many more along with him : (and this was
the first rupture between Muinter-Ruairc and the descendants of Muirchertach Muimhnech, son of Toirdhelbhach Mór). And Cathal, son of Aedh Breifnech, made a
valorous pursuit afterwards, when a great part of the
prey was detained, and Domhnall O'Ruairc, the choicest

na Όρειρηε uιle, ocuρ σαρ ξαбασ Ξιlla Cριοσ.h.
Ruαιρc ocuρ Mαc Coηρηαῖα, αcuρ σαρ ταρбασ ηοραη
elι αηη ρορ. Τασc ηαc Ruαιόρι ηιc Cαthαιl.h.Conchub-
αιρ, σο bι αllαιῖ αc .h.Ruαιρc, σο lecoη αηαch αρ
coῖρuαρlαcασ Ξhιlla Cριοσ .h. Ruαιρcc. Άceσ ηαc
Feσlιηισ .h.Concoбαιρ σο ξαбαιl σο Τοιρρσhealbach
.h.Conchoбαιρ, ρι Conναchτ, .ι. σο σερбραthαιρ α αthαρ,
ocuρ α čuρ α cαιρleη Rορα Coηαιη σα čοῖεσ. Cocασ
ηορ ocuρ εξαεηtα αόбαl σο ερξι ειòιρ .h.Conchoбαιρ
ocuρ Mαc Όιαρηασα tριαραη ξαбαιl ριη, ocuρ cuρ
ηιlleσ ηοραη εαtαρρο σιбlιηαιб. Ξuαραchτ ηορ
σραξбαιl σO Chonchoбαιρ ο Mαc Όιαρηασα ιριη Co-
ραησ, cuρ cuιρεασ σα αιῖσεοιη ε αρtech α ηбαlι ιη
ηutα, ocuρ ρισ σο σεηαῖ σοιб αρα hαιthle ριη ρε
chele. Sιuρtαη ρuασ Mαc Ξοιρσelb σο ηαρбασ σο
Chαthαl Mαc Όιαρηασα ξαll ιη hoc anno. Cαthαl
Mαc Όιαρηασα ξαll, αεη ρόξα ηαc ριξ Connαchτ αρ
ξαιl αcuρ αρ ξαιρcισ, αρ tρερι ocuρ αρ tαlchuιρεchτ,
σο ῖαρбασ σο Όοnσchασ ριαбαč ηαc Mαιleαčlαιηη
chαρραξ Mιc Όιαρηασα, ρερ σolum, α Lιρ Selbαιξ
ι Cloιηη Chončuбαιρ. Mαξηuρ ηαc Cαthαιl ηιc Όοῖ-
ηαιll .h. Chonchoбαιρ σο ηαρбασ lα Cαthαl ηαc Άεσα
Όρειρηιξ .h. Conchoбαιρ. Όριαη occ Mαξ Sαῖραсαιη
σο ηαρбασ lα Τεllαč Όunchασα. Θοξαη.h.hεσιη, ρι
.h.Fιαchραch Άισηε, occιρuρ ερτ α ρuιρ. Θοξαη ηαc Sερ-
ραισ Mεξ Rαξηαιll ocuρ Άceб .h. Mαιlηισαιξ σο ηαρбασ αροιlι. Άσσαη Mαξ Τεthεσαη quιευιτ ιη Cριρtο.
Fιlιb .h. Όubξennαη, ollαῖ Conηαιcηε, ηορtuuρ ερτ.
ιηαξ ιηξεη Mιc Ξορσelb, beη Θοξαιη ηιc Fιηξιη, quιευιτ. Uιllιαη Mαc Ξορσelb, ηαc Ξιlleбερσ, σο ηαρбασ
αρ ξρειρ ιριη Όρειρηι lα Τεαllαch Θchòach. Ruαιòρι

---

1 *Unwillingly.* σα αιησεοιη, B.
σα αιῖσεοιη, C.

3 *Aidhne.* Άònι, B. Άιòne,
C.

1 *Vigour.* tαlčheῖ, for tαlchuιρεchτ. B. tαlcῖuιραchτ, C.

4 *Occisus est.* οū cιρз 2, B. οū cιρ
2, C.

of the princes of all the Breifne, was slain, and Gilla-
Christ O'Ruairc and Mac Consnamha were taken prisoners, and many more were slain there besides. Tadhg,
son of Ruaidhri, son of Cathal O'Conchobhair, who was
detained a prisoner by O'Ruairc, was set at liberty in
consideration of the release of Gilla-Christ O'Ruairc.
Aedh, son of Fedhlimidh O'Conchobhair, was taken prisoner by Toirdhelbhach O'Conchobhair, king of Connacht,
i.e. his father's brother, and placed in confinement in the
castle of Ros-Comain. A great war and terrible dissension arose between O'Conchobhair and Mac Diarmada
through this capture, so that much property was destroyed
between them both. O'Conchobhair was put in great
jeopardy by Mac Diarmada in the Corann, when he was
unwillingly[1] driven into Baile-in-mhuta; and they immediately afterwards made peace with each other.
Jordan Ruadh Mac Goisdelbh was killed by Cathal Mac
Diarmada Gall in hoc anno. Cathal Mac Diarmada Gall,
the choicest of the princes of Connacht for prowess,
valour, might and vigour[2], was slain by Donnchadh
Riabhach, son of Maelechlainn Carrach Mac Diarmada,
per dolum, at Lis-Selbhaigh in Clann-Conchobhair.
Maghnus, son of Cathal, son of Domhnall O'Conchobhair,
was slain by Cathal, son of Aedh Breifnech O'Conchobhair. Brian Og Mac Samhradhain was killed by the
Tellach-Dunchadha. Eoghan O'hEdhin, king of Ui-
Fiachrach-Aidhne,[3] occisus est[4] a suis. Eoghan, son of
Jeffrey Mac Raghnaill, and Aedh O'Maelmhiadhaigh
killed one another. Adam Mac Techedhan quievit in
Christo. Philip O'Duibhgennain, ollamh[5] of Conmaicne,
mortuus est. Imag, daughter of Mac Goisdelbh, wife
of Eoghan Mac Finghin, quievit.[6] William Mac Goisdelbh, son of Gilbert, was slain in a conflict in the
Breifne, by the Tellach-Echach. Ruaidhri, son of

---

[5] Ollamh; i.e. chief poet, doctor, or professor.

[6] Quievit. This entry is not in C.

'ective.
pplied
innals
icht.']

mac Mαɜnuɼα .h. eɡɼα moɼτuuɼ eɼτ. Mατhα
mac αnɒαιɒ .h. Rαɨɜιllιɓ ɒo ṁαɼɓαɓ lα hαⁿɒɼιαɼ
mac bɼιαιn.h.Rαɨɜιllιɜ, ocuɼ cɼechα moɼα ɒo ɒenαṁ
ιɼιn bolcαn ιαɼ ɼιn. τempoll Cιlle Ronαιn ɒo loɼcαɓ
ιn hoc αnno. Nιαll .h. hUιcιnn, ɼαι nɒαnα, ɒo bαɓαɓ.
Conchuɓαɼ .h. Ɒoṁnαιll conα τhιnol ɒo τeαchτ α Con-
nαchταιɓ.

ƘL. Enαιɼ ɼoɼ Luαn, ocuɼ ɼeαchτ uατhαɓ ɼuιɼɼι;
αnno Ɒomιnι M.°ccc.°xL.°ɼɼιmo; xιι. αnno cιclι lunαɼιɼ;
ιx. αnno ιnɒιcτιonιɼ; xuιιι. cιclι ɼolαɼιɼ. Mαιɒm moɼ
ɒo τhαɓαιɼτ ɒo mαc Uιllιαm buɼc αɼ cloιnn Muιɼιɼ,
ɒu αɼ mαɼɓαɓ τomαɼ Mαc Muιɼιɼ ocuɼ Muιɼιɼ mαc
Seonαc ɼuαιɓ, ocuɼ ɼechτ .xx. mαɼoen ɼιu. Ɒoṁnαll
Mαɜ Ɒoɼchαɓ, ɒux Cenel Luαchαιn, moɼτuuɼ eɼτ.
Ɒonɒchαɓ mαc meιc nα hoιɒchι Meɜ Ƒlαnnchαιɓ ɒo
mαɼɓαɓ lα hαCeɓ mαc ταιɒcc Meɜ Ƒlαnnchαιɓ ιn hoc
αnno. Uα Ɜαιɼmleαɓαɨ, ɒux cenel Muαn, moɼτuuɼ
eɼτ. bɼιαn .h. Ƒloιnn, ταιɼech τellαιɜh Cuɼnαιn,
moɼτuuɼ eɼτ. Cατhαl Mαc Ceτheɼnαιɜ ɒo mαɼbαɒ
ɒo eɼcuɼ. Cαιɼlen Roɼα Commαιn ɒo ɜαɓαιl ɒo τoιɼɼ-
ɒelɓαch .h. Conchoɓαιɼ, ocuɼ αeɒ mαc Ƒeιɒlιmιɒ
.h.Conchoɓαιɼ ɒo bι ιllαιṁ ιɼιn chαιɼlen ɒɼ τɼeιc ɒo
Choncoɓαιɼ he. Seonαc Mαɜ Mατhɜαṁnαι ɒo choɼ α
hOɼɜιαllαιɓ. Cuconnαchτ .h.Cuιnn, ɒux Muιnτιɼe Ɜιl-
lαɜαιn, moɼτuuɼ eɼτ. Ɒιαɼmαιɒ ɼuαɓ, mαc Coɼmαιc
oιcc Mιc Ɒιαɼmαɒα, moɼτuuɼ eɼτ.

ƘL. Enαιɼ ɼoɼ Mαιɼτ, ocuɼ .uιι.mαɒ x. ɼuιɼɼι; αnno
Ɒomιnι M.° ccc.° xL.° ɼecunɒo; xιιι. αnno cιclι lunαɼιɼ;
x. αnno ιnɒιcτιonιɼ; xuιιι. cιclι ɼolαɼιɼ. ιn ɜιllα
ɒuɓ Mαɜ Uιɒιɼ ɒo bαɓαɓ αɼ loch heιɼne αɼ ɒeιɼeαɓ

---

¹ *Afterwards.* ιαɼ ɼιn, B. αɼ α
hαττle, C.

² *Seventh.* This is an error, as New
Moon occurred on the 23rd of December, 1340. Similar errors are frequently noticeable in this chronicle.

See Introd. The Dominical letter
(G) is added in the margin.

³ *O'Floinn.* h.Ƒι., B. C. incor-
rectly reads h.Ƒlαnnɓαιɓ. The
Four Masters write the name Uα
Ƒloιnn, or O'Flynn.

Maghnus O'hEghra, mortuus est. Matthew, son of Annadh O'Raighilligh, was slain by Andrias, son of Brian O'Raighilligh, who afterwards[1] committed great depredations in the Bolcan. The church of Cill-Ronain was burned in hoc anno. Niall O'hUiginn, an eminent poet, was drowned. Conchobhar O'Domhnaill went into Connacht, with his muster.

The kalends of January on Monday, and the seventh[2] of the moon; anno Domini M.°ccc.°xl.° primo; xii. anno cycli lunaris; ix. anno indictionis; xvii. cycli solaris. A great defeat was inflicted by Mac William Burk on the Clann-Maurice, on which occasion Thomas Mac Maurice, and Maurice, son of Sconac Ruadh, and seven score persons along with them, were slain. Domhnall Mac Dorchaidh, dux of Cenel-Luachain, mortuus est. Donnchadh, son of Mac-na-hoidhchi Mac Flannchaidh, was killed by Aedh, son of Tadhg Mac Flannchaidh, in hoc anno. O'Gairmleghaigh, dux of Cenel-Moan, mortuus est. Brian O'Floinn,[3] chieftain of Tellach-Curnain[4], mortuus est. Cathal Mac Cethernaigh was killed by a fall. The castle of Ros-Comain was captured by Toirdhelbhach O'Conchobhair; and it was Aedh, son of Fedhlimidh O'Conchobhair, who was imprisoned in the castle, that betrayed it to O'Conchobhair.[5] Seonac Mac Mathghamhna was expelled from Oirghiall. Cuchonnacht O'Cuinn, dux of Muinter-Gillagan, mortuus est. Diarmaid Ruadh, son of Cormac Og Mac Diarmada, mortuus est.

The kalends[6] of January on Tuesday, and the 17th of the moon; anno Domini M.° ccc.° xl.° secundo; xiii. anno cycli lunaris; x. anno Indictionis; xviii. cycli solaris. The Gilla-dubh Mac Uidhir was drowned on Loch-Erne, in the rear of a predatory party. A great

[4] Of Tellach-Curnain. Ceallach Cuṙnan, B. Ceallac Cuṙnain, C. But ceallach, which signifies a household, or family, makes ceallaich, or ceallaiġh, in the gen.

[5] Betrayed it to O'Conchobhair. Instead of the expression do treic do Choncobair he, as in B, the words do leiġen amach, "was let out," occur in C.

[6] Kalends. The Dominical Letter (F) is added in the margin.

cɼeıċɲ. Coṁeɲʒı coccaıḃ moıɲ ɒo eɲʒı eıɒıɲ Toıɲɲɒel-
ḃaċ .h.Conċoḃaıɲ, ɲı Conɒaċc, ocuɼ Conċoḃaɲ Mac
Oıaɲmaɒa, ɲı Moıʒı Luıɲʒ; ocuɼ Emaɒ a ḃuɼc ɒeɲʒı
le Mac Oıaɲmaɒa, ocuɼ Œḃ mac Ɣeıṫlımıṫ .h. Conċuḃaıɲ, ocuɼ Oonċaṫ .h. ḃıɲn ɒux Tıɲı ḃɼıuın na
Sınna; ocuɼ .h.ḃıɲn ɒo ċuɼ .h.Conċuḃaıɲ a ċempoll
Olıɼınn, aɲ nɒol ɒoɼum ɒo ʒaḃaıl ʒıll cɼeıċı ɒo
ɼonɼacc muınncıɲ ḃıɲn aɲ hoḃeɲɒ a ḃuɼcc ɼemeɲıɒe,
ocuɼ cuıc ɒo ʒalloclaeċaıḃ .h.Conċuḃaıɲ ɒo maɲḃaṫ
ɒoıḃ ɼan cónɼcaɲla, .ı. ɼa Mac Ruaıṫɲı. Cocaṫ
coıcċenɒ ocuɼ olc aṫḃal ɒo ɼáɼ a Connaċcaıḃ ulı
an can ɼın, ocuɼ Clann Muıɲċeaɲcaıʒ ım Œṫ mac
Œeɒa ḃɼeıɼnıʒ, ocuɼ ım Caċal mac Œeɒa ḃɼeıɼnıʒ,
ocuɼ ım Caɒc mac Ruaıṫɲı ɒo coṁeɲʒı leo ɼın ulı,
ocuɼ moɲan ɒo mılleṫ ɒoıḃ ɒaɲḃannaıḃ an cıɼı aɲ
cuɼ. Ɣell ʒɲanna ɒo ɒenaṁ aɲ cloınn Uıllıam ḃuɼc
cɼıɼ ɼoɲʒall .h. Ċonċoḃaıɲ, ɒaɲ maɲḃaṫ Comaɼ a
ḃuɼc le Cloınn Muıɲıɼ, ocuɼ ɼe na noıɲeċcuɼ ɼeın,
ocuɼ Seonın a ḃuɼc ɒo maɲḃaṫ aɲ ın aɼcı ceaṫna le
cloınn Rıcaıɲɒ. Caċal mac ʒılla Cɼıoɼɒ Mıc Oıaɲmaɒa ɒo maɲḃaṫ ɒƔeɲʒal .h.Caɒc aɲ ın cocaṫ ceɒna
ɼın. Ɣeɲʒal mac ʒılla Cɼıoɼɒ ɼınn mıc Coɲmaıc ɒo
maɲḃaṫ aɲ ın cocaṫ ceɒna ɼın. ḃɼıɼım ḃɼoʒɒa ɒo
ċaḃaıɲc ɒo Mac Oıaɲmaɒa ocuɼ ɒa macaıḃ ɼıʒ aɲ
.h.Conċoḃaıɲ a mḃeol Œċa Slıɼen, ɒaɲ lınʒeṫ anc
aċ ɼaıɼ, ocuɼ ɒaɲ maɲḃaṫ anɒ Oıaɲmaıɒ mac ḃɼıaın
.h.Ɣeɲʒaıl .ı. ɼeɲ a aıɼı ɼeın ıɼ ɼeɼɼ ɒo baı ɒo
Ċonmaıcnıḃ uıle, ocuɼ mac hoḃeɲɒ a ḃuɼc, ocuɼ
Conċoḃaɲ mac Oonɒċaıḃ ɒuıḃ .h.Elıɒe. Seoan Maʒ
Maċʒaṁna, ɼaı nenıʒ ocuɼ nenʒnaṁa, ɲı Oɼʒıall, ɒo
ɒola aɲ cɼeıċ ɒoċum Roaılb Meʒ Maċʒaṁna, ocuɼ

---

[1] *O'Conchobhair*. h.Conċuḃaıɲ,
B. The name Conċuḃaıɲ has been
omitted in C.

[2] *He*, i.e. O'Conchobhair. ɒoɼum

[3] *For a depredation*. cɼeıċı (lit.
"of a depredation"); omitted in C.

[4] *Ruaidhri*; i.e. Ruaidhri O'Conchobhair, or Rory O'Conor.

A.D.
[1342

war broke out between Toirdhelbhach O'Conchobhair, king of Connacht, and Conchobhar Mac Diarmada, king of Magh-Luirg; and Edmond Burk and Aedh, son of Fedhlimidh O'Conchobhair, and Donchadh O'Birn, dux of Tir-Briuin-na-Sinna, sided with Mac Diarmada; and O'Birn drove O'Conchobhair[1] into the church of Oilfinn, after he[2] had gone to obtain pledges for a depredation[3] which the Muinter-Birn committed previously on Hubert Burk; and some of O'Conchobhair's gallowglasses were slain by them, including the constable, i.e. Mac Ruaidhri. A general war, and great enmity, grew in all Connacht at that time, and the Clann-Muirchertaigh, with Aedh son of Aedh Breifnech, and with Cathal son of Aedh Breifnech, and with Tadhg son of Ruaidhri,[4] sided with all those at first; and a great quantity of the corn of the country was destroyed by them. An ugly act of treachery was committed on the Clann-William-Burk, at the instigation of O'Conchobhair, when Thomas Burk was slain by the Clann-Maurice whilst in their own assembly; and Seonin Burk was slain in the same way by the Clann-Rickard. Cathal, son of Gilla-Christ Mac Diarmada, was slain by Ferghal O'Taidhg in the same war.[5] Ferghal, son of Gilla-Christ Finn Mac Cormaic was slain in the same war. A fierce overthrow was given by Mac Diarmada and his princes to O'Conchobhair, at Bel-atha-Slisen, where the ford was passed in spite of him, and where Diarmaid, the son of Brian O'Ferghail—i.e. the best man of all the Conmaicne[6] of his own age—and the son of Hubert Burk, and Conchobhar, son of Donnchadh Dubh O'hElidhe, were slain. John Mac Mathghamhna, a man eminent for bounty and prowess, king of Oirghiall, went on a predatory expedition against Roalbh[7] Mac Mathghamhna, and was

---

[6] *Of all the Conmaicne.* oo Chonṁicniḃ uiḺe, B. oo Chonnṝaiḃ uiḺe, "of all the Connachtmen," C.

[7] *Roalbh.* ṘoaiḺḃ, B. Ṙoaiḃ, C. "Roalbh" is a Hibernicised form of Ralph, or Rodolph.

ctive.
pplied
nnals
cht."]

a ṁapbhaď cona ʒalloʒlaeċaiɓ ap ɔeipeď a chpeiche,
ocuʃ iʃ commoʃ ɔo mapɓaď acuʃ ɔo baiɓeď iaɔ. Copmac
mac Ruaiďpi mic Ɔoṁnaill .h.Chonchobaip ɔo ʒaɓail
la Conċoɓap mac Ταiɔc, ocuʃ le Ruaiďpi mac Cathail
.h.Conchoɓaip, iʃin ɓliaďain ceɔna ʃin, ocuʃ Conchobap
ɔo ʒaɓail le Ɓpian mac Ruaiďpi, ocuʃ a chaɓaipt a laiṁ
Conchoɓaip Mic Ɔiapmaɔa, ocuʃ a chop ɔo iapʃin ap
in chappaic ɔa choṁeɔ.   Ɔoṁnall .h. Ɔochapταiʒ,
ταiʃech Αpɔa Miɔaip, ʃai neniʒ ocuʃ nenʒnama, ɔepci
ocuʃ ɔoennachta, ɔo éʒ ina τiʒ ʃein in hoc anno, ocuʃ
Seoan .h. Ɔochapταiʒ ɔo ʒaɓail a inaiτ ɔa epi.   Sil
Muipeɔaiʒ uili iɔip ɔeoin ocuʃ aimhɔeoin ɔo ɔilʃiu-
ʒuɓ ʃiʒ Connachτ .i. Ɔoippɔhelbach mac Αoɓa mic
Eoʒain .h. Chonċubaip; ocuʃ iʃ iaτ iʃ oipeʒɔa po
epiʒ ɔo an ταn ʃin .i. Emunɔ mac Uilliam Ɓupc, ocuʃ
Conchoɓap Mac Ɔiapmaɔa, ʃi Moiʒi Luipʒ, cona
bpathpaiɓ ocuʃ cona oipeachτ uile, ocuʃ Αeɓ mac
Αeɔu Ɓpeiʃniʒ, mic Cathail puaiɔh hI Chonchuɓaip,
ocuʃ Ταɔc mac Ruaiďpi .h. Conchuɓaip, ocuʃ Cathal
mac Αeɔa Ɓpeiʃniʒ mic Cathail puaiɓ, ocuʃ pochpaiɔe
Ɓpeiʃne ocuʃ Conmaicne, ocuʃ Αoɓ mac Ɣeɔlimiɓ mic
Αeɔa mic Eoʒain; ocuʃ Ɔoippɔhelbach ɔo chup apin
τip amach leo uli map napb inʒnaɓ.   Αcuʃ conaɔ i
coṁaiple τucʃaτ a chapaiɔ ɔo iapʃin ɔol ɔo τiʒ Mic
Ɔiapmaɔa iʃin oiɔche; acuʃ ʃuapaταp Clann Muip-
ċeapταiʒ ʃiʃ na coṁaipli ʃin, ocuʃ ɔo inɔliτep pemhe
ap ʃliʒτiɓ ocuʃ ap bepnaɓaiɓ baeʒail an Lonʒḃupτ,
ocuʃ ταniccʃim ταpʃiɓ ʃin uli iʃan oiɔche ʃe ɔopcha
ɔiʃ no τpiap mapcaċ; ocuʃ ɔo epʒiɔ ɔo ap τochap in
Lonʒḃupτ, ocuʃ ɔo chuaiɓ ταpʃʃa ap ταpaɔ a lama
laiɔipi, ocuʃ ɔo loiτ ʃe Cathal mac Αeɔa Ɓpeiʃniʒ.
Ocuʃ ni paiɓi a ʃipʃ ʃin aʒ Mac Ɔiapmaɔa no co

---

1 *The Rock*; i.e. the Rock of Loch-
Cé, Mac Dermot's castle.

2 *Willing and unwilling*; i.e. those
who were willing to oppose Tur-

lough, and those who were forced by
others to oppose him.

3 *Of the fortress*; i.e. on the way to
the fortress.

slain, with his gallowglasses, in the rear of his band; and as many of them were drowned as slain. Cormac, son of Ruaidhri, son of Domhnall O'Conchobhair, was taken prisoner by Conchobhar, the son of Tadhg, and by Ruaidhri, son of Cathal O'Conchobhair, in the same year; and Conchobhar was taken prisoner by Brian, the son of Ruaidhri, and delivered into the hands of Conchobhar Mac Diarmada, who afterwards placed him in the Rock[1] to be imprisoned. Domhnall O'Dochartaigh, chieftain of Ard-Midhair, a man eminent for bounty, prowess, charity, and humanity, died in his own house in hoc anno, and John O'Dochartaigh assumed his place after him. The Sil-Muiredhaigh all, both willing and unwilling,[2] renounced the king of Connacht, i.e. Toirdhelbhach, son of Aedh, son of Eoghan O'Conchobhair; and the most distinguished who then opposed him were Edmond Mac William Burk, and Conchobhar Mac Diarmada, king of Magh-Luirg, with his brothers and with all his people; and Aedh, son of Aedh Breifnech, son of Cathal Ruadh O'Conchobhair; and Tadhg, son of Ruaidhri O'Conchobhair; and Cathal, son of Aedh Breifnech, son of Cathal Ruadh; and the armies of Breifne and Conmaicne; and Aedh, the son of Fedhlimidh, son of Aedh, son of Eoghan: and Toirdhelbhach was sent out of the country by them all, which was not surprising. And the advice which his friends gave him afterwards was to go at night to Mac Diarmada's house. And the Clann-Muirchertaigh received intelligence of this advice, and assembled before him on the roads, and in the dangerous passes of the fortress;[3] but he went past all these in the dark night,[4] with two or three horsemen; and he was opposed on the causeway of the fortress, but he passed through them by the force of his strong hand, and wounded Cathal, son of Aedh Breifnech. And Mac Diarmada

---

[4] *Night.* aꝺ, for aꝺaiᵹ or aꝺaiꝺ B. oiꝺche, C.

ctive.
plied
inals
kt."]

cuala re an.comairc an malluġu accuṛ in maṛġnech aṛ
ṛoṫ an lonġphuirt chuice, ocuṛ vo eṛiġ co hopand ocuṛ
vo ṛuaiṛ ṛe .h. Conchobaiṛ, ocuṛ vo chuiṛ ṛe vaine
ṫaṛiṛi leiṛ va chuṛ iṛin caṛṛaicc; acuṛ vo baí
ṛoṛġlai ṛeachtṁaine inti, accuṛ vo ṫeiġdiṛ vaine
maiṫe in tiṛi chuce cech lai aṛ cuaiṛt; ocuṛ ni
ḟuaiṛ Mac Diaṛmava ced ṛiṫa ḟṛiṛ, ocuṛ o nach
ṛuaiṛi vo tindlaic he co caiṛlen Ṛoṛa Coman, ocuṛ ṛo
ṛaccaib andṛin he. Conchuḃaṛ ṛúad Maġ Eochacan,
vux Cenel Ḟiachaib, vo maṛḃad vo Ġallaib. Ṫomaṛ
.h. Cinġa moṛtuur eṛt. Muiṛiṛ Mac Eochaġan quieuit.
Simon mac Conchobaiṛ mic Simoin mic Ġilla Appaic,
taiṛeċ vo ṫaiṛeċaib Luiġni, moṛtuur eṛt. Muṛchad
mac Ṫomaltaiġ .h. Ḟlannacan .i. an ṫṛeṛ vuine aṛ
ṛeaṛṛ vo bi vo Chloinn Chaṫail, vo ṁaṛḃad vo
ġalloġlachaib mic Caṫail. Aed mac Aeda Ḃṛeiṛniġ,
mic Caṫail ṛuaid .h. Chonchoḃaiṛ, vo ṛiġad vo Chonnachtaib ocuṛ vo mac Uilliam Ḃuṛcc in cet Luan von
ġeṁṛiud, ocuṛ tanaiṛtecht Connacht vo ṫaḃaiṛt vo
Aed mac Ḟedlimid .h. Conchoḃaiṛ; ocuṛ Tiṛ nOiliolla
vo ṫabhaiṛt d'Ḟeṛġal Mac Diaṛmava, ocuṛ Tadġ
mac Ṫomaltaiġ mic Muiṛġiuṛa Mic Donochada vo
innaṛbad aṛ a duṫaiġ ṛein vo Chonchoḃaṛ Mac
Diaṛmava ocuṛ va bṛaiṫṛichaib; ocuṛ Mac Donnchada vo ḃeiṫ imaṛaen ṛe Toiṛṛdhelbach .h. Con-
chuḃaiṛ.

Conchuḃaṛ .h. Doṁnaill, ṛí Tiṛe Conaill, ocuṛ
ṛoidech vinġbala d'Eṛinn uli va ndeonaiġed Dia vo
hi, aṛ a uaṛli ocuṛ aṛ a uṛdeaṛcuṛ, ocuṛ aṛ ṛebuṛṛ
eniġ ocuṛ enġnamha, vo maṛḃad vo Niall .h. Doṁnaill
.i. mac a aṫaṛ ṛein, ocuṛ tech Ḟindṛoiṛ vo loṛcad
ṛaiṛ, ocuṛ .h. Doṁnaill vo vol aṛin tiġ amach, ocuṛ
a ṫoitim iaṛ ṛin a ndoṛaṛ a tiġi ṛein, iaṛ mbṛeiṫ

---

[1] *The execration.* an malʾu, apparently for an malluġu, B. Omitted in C.

[2] *Found.* ṛoiṛ, B. ṛuaiṛ, C.
[3] *The Rock;* i.e. the Rock of Loch-
Cé, Mac Dermot's residence.

knew not of this until he heard the tumult, the execration,[1] and lamentation throughout the fortress, when he suddenly went, and found[2] O'Conchobhair, with whom he sent trusty persons to conduct him to the Rock.[3] And he remained in it the greater part of a week; and the nobles of the country were wont to visit him each day. And Mac Diarmada did not obtain leave to make peace with him; and as he did not, he escorted him to the castle of Ros-Comain, where he left him. Conchobhar Ruadh Mac Eochagain, dux of Cenel-Fiachaidh, was slain by Foreigners. Thomas O'Cinga mortuus est. Maurice Mac Eochagain quievit. Simon, son of Conchobhar, son of Simon Mac Gilla-Arraith, one of the chieftains of Luighne, mortuus est. Murchadh, son of Tomaltach O'Flannagain, i.e. the third best man that was of the Clann-Cathail, was slain by the gallowglasses of Cathal's son.[4] Aedh, the son of Aedh Breifnech, son of Cathal Ruadh O'Conchobhair, was made king by the Connachtmen and Mac William Burk, the first Monday of the winter; and the tanistship of Connacht was given to Aedh, the son of Fedhlimidh O'Conchobhair; and Tir-Oilella was given to Ferghal Mac Diarmada, and Tadhg, son of Tomaltach, son of Maurice Mac Donnchadha, was expelled from his own country by Conchobhar Mac Diarmada, and by his brethren; and Mac Donnchadha joined[5] Toirdhelbhach O'Conchobhair.

Conchobhar O'Domhnaill, king of Tir-Conaill, and one worthy to rule all Erinn, if God had willed it, by reason of his nobility, eminence, and the excellence of his bounty and prowess, was slain by Niall O'Domhnaill, i.e. his own father's son: (the house of Finn-ros was burned over him, and O'Domhnaill went out of the house, and fell afterwards in the doorway of his own house),

---

[4] *Cathal's son*; i.e. the son of Cathal O'Conor.

[5] *Joined.* ᵈᵒ ᵇᵉᵢᵗʰ ᵢᵐᵃᵃᵉⁿ lit. "was along with."

[MS. defective. Text supplied from "Annals of Connacht."]

buαdhα o deman ocur o dorhan; ocur dronʒ mor do
Lucꞇ ꞇiʒi .h. Domnaill do Lorcαdh ocur do marbαd
αnn beor. Niαll .h. Domnαill do riʒαd Lα droinʒ do
ꞇhαirechαib ꞇiri Conaill.   Flαnn occ .h. Domnαl-
Lαin, ollαṁ dαnα .h. Chonchobαir, quieuiꞇ. Domnαll
.h. Cuindlir, rαi renchαrα, occirur erꞇ o 1d Diαrmαdα.
Tomαr mαc ʒillα Coirclid, rαi neniʒ, in Crirꞇo quieuiꞇ.
Mαꞇhα Mαc Mαʒnurα, brυʒαid Lochα hErne, quieuiꞇ
in Crirꞇo.

Kꞇ. Enαir ror Ceꞇαin, ocur ochꞇmαd .xx. ꞇuirri;
αnno Domini Mº.cccº.xL.iii.; xiiii. cicli Lunαrir; xi.
αnno indicꞇionir; xix. cicli rolαrir. Toirrdhelbαch
.h. Concobαir do ʒαbαil α riʒi rein dorididi, ocur
rich do denαṁ do Mαc Diαrmαdα rirri. Slαine
inʒen .h. briαin, ben Toirrdhelbαiʒ .h. Chonchobαir
beur, ocur ben mic Iαrlα Ulαd hi remiride, morꞇuα
erꞇ. Derbαil inʒen Aedα .h. Domnαill do ꞇeαchꞇ
αr cuαirꞇ co hInir Doiʒri doꞇum Chonchubαir Mic
Diαrmαdα, ocur ʒαlαr α heccα diα ʒαbαil αnd
rin, ocur α hαdnαcαl α mαnirꞇir nα builli iαr rin.
Dubhcαblαid inʒen Conchobαir Mic Diαrmαdα, ben
Ui bhipi, quieuiꞇ. Tomαr Mαc Sαmpαdαin, dux
Tellαich Echαch, quieuiꞇ. Murcheαrꞇαch .h. briαin,
ri Tuαdmuṁαn, morꞇuur erꞇ; ocur Diαrmαid
.h. briαin do riʒαd inα inαꞇ; ocur α innαrbα rin
Le briαn .h. mbriαin, ocur mαiꞇhe Tuαdmuṁαn do
rocrα do iαr rin. Uillec mαc Ricαird mic Uilliαm
Leiꞇh, mαcαṁ ʒαll Erend uili αn enech ocur αn
enʒnαṁ, quieuiꞇ. Cαꞇhαl .h. Mαdαdαn, rαi Erenn,
do mαrbαd do cloinn Ricαird. Donochαd cLerech

---

1 *Tir-Conaill.* Instead of Conαill, as in B, C incorrectly reads Conn̄ for Connαchꞇ.

2 *O'Cuindlis.* The Four Masters write the name O'Coinleisg, but the form O'Cuindlis (from which is derived the name of Candlish?) is correct.

3 *Eminent historian.* rαi renchα,

for rαi renchαrα, B. rαi renchα-dαiʒ, C.

4 *Brughaidh.* A "brughaidh" was a wealthy farmer, of great authority.

5 *Kalends of January.* The word Enαir (January) is omitted in B. The Dominical Letter (E) is added in the margin.

after obtaining victory over the devil and the world ; and a great number of O'Domhnaill's household band were moreover burned and killed there. Niall O'Domhnaill was made king by a number of the chieftains of Tir-Conaill.[1] Flann Og O'Domhnallain, O'Conchobhair's chief poet, quievit. Domhnall O'Cuindlis,[2] an eminent historian,[3] occisus est by the Ui-Diarmada. Thomas Mac Gilla-Coisglidh, a man eminent for bounty, in Christo quievit. Matthew Mac Maghnusa, brughaidh[4] of Loch-Erne, quievit in Christo.

The kalends of January[5] on Wednesday, and the twenty-eighth of the moon ; anno Domini M°.ccc°.xl.iii. ; xiii. cycli lunaris ; xi. anno Indictionis ; xix. cycli solaris. Toirdhelbhach O'Conchobhair assumed his own sovereignty again, and peace was made with him by Mac Diarmada. Slaine, O'Briain's daughter, Toirdhelbhach O'Conchobhair's wife, and previously the wife of the Earl of Ulster's son, mortua est.[6] Derbhail, daughter of Aedh O'Domhnaill, came on a visit to Inis-Doighre, to Conchobhar Mac Diarmada, where her death sickness seized her ; and she was afterwards interred in the monastery of the Buill. Dubhchabhlaigh, daughter of Conchobhar Mac Diarmada, wife of O'Birn, quievit. Thomas Mac Samhradhain, dux of Tellach-Echach, quievit. Muirchertach O'Briain, king of Tuadh-Mumha, mortuus est, and Diarmaid O'Briain was made king in his place ; and he was expelled by Brian O'Briain, to whom the chieftains of Tuadh-Mumha afterwards submitted. Ulick,[7] son of Richard, son of William Liath, the greatest of all the foreign youths of Erinn in bounty and prowess, quievit. Cathal O'Madadhain, the most eminent man in Erinn, was killed by the Clann-Rickard.

---

6 *Mortua est.* So in B. ꝺeᵹ, C. The clause ocuꝛ ben mic Iaꝛla Ulaꝺ hi ꝛemꝛꝺe is omitted in C.

7 *Ulick.* The MSS. B and C have Ulḃ., which may represent William as well as Ulick, but the Four Mast., Ann. Ult., and Mageoghegan, have the name Ulick.

[MS defective. Text supplied from " Annals of Connacht."]

Uα Maılbpenaıno, cananač copao a nOıɼınn, oo mapbao oupchap tpoıgtı la muınntıp hobepo mıc Oauıo ouınn mıc Uıllıam. Cathal mac an Lıathanaıg, ab na Tpınnoıtte ɼop Loch Cé, ocuɼ toga eɼpuıcc Olıɼınn, ın Cpıpto quıeuıt. Maıom mop le Claınn Ɽeopaıɼ ocuɼ le Claınn Rıcaıpo aɼ Manechaıб, ou aɼ mapбao en mac pıg oec oo claınn Cellaıg, ɼa Conchobap ceppbach .h. Cellaıgh. Nıall .h. Ooṁnaıll oo athpıgao la hCCengup .h. n Ooṁnaıll acuɼ la Ooṁnall noub .h. mbaıgıll, ocuɼ le hUa n Oochaptaıg, acuɼ le neapt CCeoa pemaıp .h. Neıll, ocuɼ le Claınn tSuбne apchena, ocuɼ CCengup oo pıgaб oıб oıblınaıб. Nıall oo ool ıɼ tıp apıoıpı ; ocuɼ Clann Muıpcheaptaıg oo oıchup apın Oreıɼne le hUalgapg .h. Ruaıpc, ocuɼ la Toıppoealbach .h. Concoбaıp, ocuɼ le Taocc Mag Ragnaıll, ocuɼ a nool a Tıp CCeoa ; ocuɼ CCengup .h. Ooṁnaıll oo čaбaıpt Tıpı hCCeoa oıб eıoıp ɼep ocuɼ apбap, ocuɼ cona maıthıp apchena ; acuɼ ımpıɼaın oo thaбaıpt oo Oengup .h. Oomnaıll ocuɼ oo Chlaınn Muıpčeaptaıg ıapɼın oo Nıall .h. Ooṁnaıll, ocuɼ maıбm oo thaбaıpt ɼop Nıall oıб, oap mapбao CCnoılıp .h. baıgıll ocuɼ a ṁac .ı. taıpech Tıpı hCCnmıpeč, ocuɼ Eogan mac CCıpt .h. Ooṁnaıll, et alıı multı. Tempoll Cıllı Ronaın oo oenaṁ. Iohannep .h. Ɽlaıčıṁ, eɼpog Cıllı hCClaıб, quıeuıt. Seoan Mag Eoaıб, eɼpacc Conmaıcne, quıeuıt. Conchoбap Mac Oıapmaoa pı Moıgı Luıpg, ocuɼ tuılı opoaın ocuɼ oıpıchaıɼ cloınne Maelpuanaıg moıp, mıc Taıocc, mıc Cathaıl, mıc Conchoбaıp, oo ecc ına tıg ɼeın peachtṁaın pıa pamhaın, oıa pathapnn apaı laıthı peachtṁaıne, ıap mbpeıth buaбa o oeman ocuɼ o ooṁan ; ocuɼ a aбlacaб a manıptıp na buıllı ; ocuɼ Ɽepgal Mac Oıapmaoa, a oepbpačaıp ɼeın, oo pıgao ına ınao.

---

¹ *Loch-Cé.* The last syllable (Cé) is omitted in C.   ² *Both.* eıoıp (lit. " between "), B. eaoaɼ, C.

Donnchadh Clerech O'Maelbhrenainn, a canon chorister at Oilfinn, was killed with a shot of an arrow by the people of Hubert, son of David Donn Mac William. Cathal Mac-an-Liathanaigh, abbot of the Trinity on Loch-Cé,[1] and bishop-elect of Oilfinn, in Christo quievit. A great victory by the Clann-Feorais and Clann-Rickard over the Ui-Maine, in which eleven princes of the Clann-Cellaigh were slain, along with Conchobhar Cerbhach O'Cellaigh. Niall O'Domhnaill was deposed by Aengus O'Domhnaill, and by Domhnall Dubh O'Baighill, and by O'Dochartaigh, and by the power of Aedh Remhar O'Neill, and by the Clann-Suibhne; and Aengus was made king by them all. Niall went again into the country; and the Clann-Muirchertaigh were expelled out of the Breifne by Ualgharg O'Ruairc, Toirdhelbhach O'Conchobhair, and Tadhg Mac Raghnaill; and they went into Tir-Aedha, and Aengus O'Domhnaill gave them Tir-Aedha, both[2] grass and corn, and with all its other benefits. And a battle was afterwards fought by Aengus O'Domhnaill and the Clann-Muirchertaigh against Niall O'Domhnaill, when Niall was defeated by them; on which occasion Andiles O'Baighill, i.e. the chieftain of Tir-Ainmirech, and his son, and Eoghan, the son of Art O'Domhnaill, et alii multi, were slain. The church of Cill-Ronain was built.[3] Johannes O'Flaithimh, bishop of Cill-Alaidh, quievit. John Mac Eoaidh, bishop of Conmaicne,[4] quievit. Conchobhar Mac Diarmada, king of Magh-Luirg, and fountain of the dignity and nobility of the descendants of Maelruanaidh Mór, son of Tadhg, son of Cathal, son of Conchobhar, died in his own house a week before Allhallowtide, on a Saturday as regards the day of the week, after having overcome the devil and the world, and was interred in the monastery of the Buill; and Ferghal Mac Diarmada, his own brother, was made king in his place.

---

[3] *Built*; i.e. rebuilt, it having been burned in 1340.

[4] *Bishop of Conmaicne*; i.e. Bishop of Ardagh.

[MS. defective. Text supplied from "Annals of Connacht."]

ſct. Enaıp ɼoɼ Ɗaɼɔaoın, ocuɼ nomaᵭ uachaɔ ɼuıɼɼı; anno Ɗomını Ɯ°.ccc°.xL quapco; xu. cıclı Lunaɼıɼ; xıı. anno ınɔıccıonıɼ; xx. anno cıclı ɼolaɼıɼ. Ɯomaɼ mac Cachaıl ɼıaᵭaıᵹ .h. Ruaıɼcc ɔo maɼᵭaᵭ La Claınn Ɯuıpcheaɼcaıᵹ ın hoc anno. Ɑeᵭ, mac mıc Roaıᵭ Ɯeᵹ Ɯachᵹamna, moɼcuuɼ eɼc .ı. ɼıᵹ Oıɼᵹıall; acuɼ Ɯuɼchaᵭ oᵹ, mac Ɯuɼchaɔha móıɼ, mıc Ɓpıaın na coılıᵹ aıɼɼınn, ɔo ɼıᵹaᵭ ana ınac, ocuɼ a éᵹ a cınɔ ɼeachcmaıne. Ɯaᵹnuɼ, mac Eochaɔa mıc Roaılb, ɔo ᵹaᵭaıl ɼıᵹe nOıɼᵹıall ıaɼ ɼın. Ɑɼc moɼ mac Coɼbmaıcc .h. Maıleaᵭlaınn, ɼı Ɯıᵭe, ɔo maɼᵭaᵭ ɔo Coɼbmac ballach .h. Maılechlaınn, aᵹuɼ ɼıᵹı Ɯıᵭe ɔo ᵹaᵭaıl ɔo ɼeın ıaɼɼın. Uıllıam, mac Ɯachᵹamna Ɯeᵹ Raᵹnaıll, ɔo maɼᵭaᵭ le macaıᵭ Cachaıl Ɯeᵹ Raᵹnaıll. Ɯacha, mac ᵹılla Cɼıoɼɔ cleɼıᵹ Ɯıc Ɗıaɼmaɔa, ɔo maɼᵭaɔ ɔo muınncıɼ Elıɔı aɼ ın Coɼɼɼlıaᵭ. Eɼɼocc Luᵹnı ın Cɼıɼɔo quıeuıc. Ɯuɼchaᵭ mac Maılmuaɔ .h. eᵹɼa, ab na Ɓuılle ocuɼ ɔamna eɼɼaıcc Luᵹne, quıeuıc.

ſct. Enaıɼ ɼoɼ Sachaɼnn, ocuɼ .xx. ɼuıɼɼı; Ɯ°.ccc°.xL.quınɔo; xuı. cıclı Lunaɼıɼ; xııı. anno ınɔıccıonıɼ; xxı. cıclı ɼolaɼıɼ. Ɯoıɼɼɔelᵭach mac Ɑeᵭa mıc Eoᵹaın .h. Conchoᵭaıɼ, ɼı Connachc ɼɼıa ɼe .xxı. blıaᵭan, ocuɼ ɔeᵹ aᵭᵭaɼ ɼıᵹ Eɼenn ɔa nɔeonaıᵹeᵭ Ɗıa ɔo í, ɔo maɼᵭaᵭ ɔuɼchuɼ cɼoıᵹcı a ɼıɔ Ɗoɼuɔa a Ɯuınncıɼ Eolaıɼ, ıaɼ nɔol ɔo conᵹnaᵯ ɔó Le Ɯaᵹ Raᵹnaıll anaᵹhaıᵭ Cloınne Ɯuıɼ-cheaɼcaıᵹ Ɯuıᵯnıᵹ .h. Conᵭoᵭaıɼ co Loch Ɑıɼınn, ocuɼ Clann Ɯuıɼᵭeaɼcaıᵹ Ɯuıᵯnıᵹ ocuɼ ın chuıɔ elı ɔo Ɯuınncıɼ Eolaıɼ ɔıa leneaᵯaın co ɼıɔ Ɗoɼuᵭa,

---

¹ *Kalends.* The Dom. Letters (D C) are, as usual, added in the margin.

² *Grandson.* mac mıc. The Four Mast. state that Aedh was the *son* of Roalbh (Ralph) Mac Mathghamhna.

³ *Roalbh.* A Hibernicised form of Ralph or Rodolphus.

⁴ *Brian-na-coiligh-aifrinn*; lit., "Brian of the mass-chalice." He was of the family of Mac Mathghamhna, or Mac Mahon.

⁵ *Cormac Ballach;* i.e. Cormac the freckled.

⁶ *Muinter-Elidhe.* "People of Elidhe," or family of O'Hely. The first

The kalends[1] of January on Thursday, and the ninth of the moon; anno Domini ᴍº.ccc.xl.quarto; xv. cycli lunaris; xii. anno Indictionis; xx. anno cycli solaris. Thomas, son of Cathal Riabhach O'Ruairc, was slain by the Clann-Muirchertaigh in hoc anno. Aedh, grandson[2] of Roalbh[3] Mac Mathghamhna, i.e. the king of Oirghiall, mortuus est; and Murchadh Og, son of Murchadh Mór, son of Brian-na-coiligh-aifrinn,[4] was made king in his place, and died in the course of a week. Maghnus, son of Eochaidh, son of Roalbh, assumed the sovereignty of Oirghiall afterwards. Art Mór, son of Cormac O'Mael-echlainn, king of Midhe, was slain by Cormac Ballach[5] O'Maelechlainn, who afterwards assumed the sovereignty of Midhe for himself. William, son of Mathghamhain Mac Raghnaill, was slain by the sons of Cathal Mac Raghnaill. Matthew, son of Gilla-Christ Clerech Mac Diarmada, was slain by Muinter-Elidhe[6] on the Corr-sliabh. The bishop of Luighne[7] in Christo quievit. Murchadh, son of Maelmhuaidh O'hEghra, abbot of the Buill, and intended bishop of Luighne,[7] quievit.

The kalends[8] of January on Saturday, and the twentieth of the moon; ᴍº.cccº.xl. quinto; xvi. cycli lunaris; xiii. anno Indictionis; xxi. cycli solaris. Toirdhelbhach, son of Aedh, son of Eoghan O'Conchobhair, king of Connacht during a period of twenty-one years,[9] and one well fitted to be king of Erinn, if God had vouchsafed it to him, was killed by a shot of an arrow in Fidh-Dorudha in Muinter-Eolais, after he had gone as far as Loch-Airinn to assist Tadhg Mac Raghnaill against the descendants of Muirchertach Muimhnech O'Conchobhair; and the descendants of Muirchertach Muimhnech, and the other section[10] of the Muinter-Eolais,

[1345.]

---

member of the name, muinᴄeᴘ, is written muinᴄiᴘᴄiᴘ in C.

[7] *Of Luighne*; i.e. of Achonry.

[8] *Kalends.* The Dom. Letter (B) is added in the margin.

[9] *Years.* This clause is omitted in C.

[10] *The other section.* The Dublin copy of the Annals of Ulster have bloᴅ, "a part."

[MS. defective. Text supplied from "Annals of Connacht."]

ocur a maptad ap Suiptin na rpideogi a rid Doruda, amail aoubramap romainn; ocur ni minic do ronnad riam le roigid, ó do maptaoh Niall .ix. giallach mac Echach Muidmeodoin le hEochaid mac Enna Cennrilaid, gniom ba mó ina in gnim rin do genam le roigit; acur Aed mac Toippdhelbaig do rigad ina inat iar rin. Brian .h. Fergail, deg addar tairig na hAngaile, moptuur ert.

Kl. Enair for Domnac, ocur prim ruirri; M°.ccc°.xl°.rexto; xuii. cieli lunarir; xiiii. anno indictionir; xxii. cieli rolarir. Cocad addal mor do rár eidir Ualgarg .h. Ruairc ocur Ruaidri mac Cathail .h. Conchobair, ocur troid do thabairt da celi a Calraidhe Locha Gile, ocur maidm do thabairt ar .h. Ruairc and rin, ocur a galloglaeca uli do maptad and .i. Mag Burci ocur mac Neill chaim, agur a muinntir uli drorgla do maptad maroen riu, acur .h. Ruairc rein do lenmain, ocur a maptad la Maelruanaid Macc Donnchaid in lá rin. Ceithre meic Cathail mic in caich Meg Ragnaill do gabail air loch an rcuir do Chonchobar Mag Ragnaill, ocur Tomoltach Mag Ragnaill da mbreith lair co cairt Corcraig, ocur a maptad do annrin iaram. Comarba Paoraic .i. Dauid Mag Oireachtaig, in Crirto quieuit. Cú Ulad Mac Cathmail, dux Cenel Feradaig, do maptad la Domnall Mac Cathmail. Maidm la Brian Mag Mathgamna for Gallaib, co ranicc .ccc. cenn a comaredh leo co haen lathair.

---

[1] *Fidh-Dorudha*; i.e. "the wood of Dorudh"; now Fedaro, a townland in the parish of Annaduff, barony of Mohill, and county of Leitrim.

[2] *Gurtin-na-spideoige*; "the little field of the robin redbreast." There is no place at present bearing this name at or near Fedaro.

[3] *Done with an arrow.* This repetition (do genam le roigit) is not necessary to the grammatical construction of the passage, the sense of which is complete without it, and seems merely written through mistake.

[4] *Kalends.* The Dom. Letter (A) is added in the margin.

[5] *Anno.* Not in B. Supplied from C.

followed him to Fidh-Dorudha,[1] and he was killed in
Gurtin-na-spideoige[2] in Fidh-Dorudha, as we said above;
(and not often before had there been done with an arrow,
since Niall-nai-ghiallach, son of Eochaidh Muidhmedhoin,
was killed by Eochaidh, son of Enna Cennselach, a deed
greater than that deed done with an arrow) ;[3] and Aedh,
son of Toirdhelbhach, was afterwards made king in his
place. Brian O'Ferghail, who was well qualified to be
chieftain of the Anghaile, mortuus est.

The kalends[4] of January on Sunday, and the first of
the moon; m°.ccc°.xl.° sexto; xvii. cycli lunaris; xiiii. anno[5]
Indictionis ; xxii. cycli solaris. A terrible war arose
between[6] Ualgharg O'Ruairc and Ruaidhri, son of Cathal
O'Conchobhair; and they gave battle to each other in
Calraidhe-Locha-Gile ; and O'Ruairc was there defeated,
and all his gallowglasses were slain there, viz., Mac
Burci, and the son of Niall Cam,[7] and mostly all their
people along with them ; and O'Ruairc himself was pursued, and was slain by Maelruanaidh Mac Donnchaidh
on that day. The four sons of Cathal Mac-in-caich[8]
Mac Raghnaill were taken prisoners on Loch-an-Scuir by
Conchobhar Mac Raghnaill, and Tomaltach Mac Raghnaill took them with him to Caisel-Cosgraigh, where
they were afterwards killed by him. The comarb of
Patrick, i.e., David Mac Oirechtaigh, in Christo quievit.
Cu-Uladh Mac Cathmhail, dux of Cenel-Feradhaigh, was
slain by Domhnall Mac Cathmhail. A victory over the
Foreigners by Brian Mac Mathghamhna, so that·three
hundred heads were counted in one place.[9] Niall

---

[6] *Between.* eroip, B. eaoaip, C.

[7] *Son of Niall Cam.* mac Neill
chaim. O'Donovan (Four Mast., ad
an.) understands mac Neill chaim
to be the proper name Mac Neill, with
the epithet "cam," or the "crooked";
but as "chaim" is the gen. form of
"cam," the correct translation is
"son of Niall Cam."

[8] *Cathal Mac-in-Caich*; i.e. Cathal
(or Charles) son of the "Caech" (mo-
noculus).

[9] *Counted in one place.* The expression co puince .ccc. cenn a coih-
apeih leo co haen lachaip, literally translated, would read "so that
300 heads came into calculation by
them to one place."

[*MS. defective.
Text supplied
from "Annals
of Connacht.*"]

Niall .h. Ꝺoṁnaill ocuꞃ Clann Muiꞃcheaꞃtaiᵹ, ocuꞃ
mac Feiꝺlimiꝺ .h. Conchobaiꞃ, ocuꞃ Muiꞃᵹiuꞃ Mac
Ꝺiaꞃmaꝺa, ꝺo lenmain Ruaiꝺꞃi mic Cathail a Cul
Maile, ocuꞃ maiꝺm immiꞃcech ꝺo thaḃaiꞃt ꝺoiḃ ꞃaiꞃ
ocuꞃ aꞃ Cloinn Ꝺonꝺċaiꝺ, ocuꞃ áꞃ aḋḃal ꝺo taḃaiꞃt
ꝼoꞃꞃo ꝺiblinaiḃ eiꝺiꞃ báthaꝺ ocuꞃ loꞃcaꝺ, ocuꞃ leꞇaꝺ,
ocuꞃ ꝼuilliuꝺ, ocuꞃ cꞃeacha moꞃa leiꞃ. Cocaꝺ moꞃ
eiꝺiꞃ mac n'Ꝺiaꞃmaꝺa ocuꞃ Maᵹnuꞃ mac Ꝺiaꞃmaꝺa
ᵹall in hoc anno, ocuꞃ ꝼell ꝺo ꝺenaṁ ꝺo cloinn Bhail-
ꝺꞃin mic Ꝫoꞃꝺelb aꞃ Maᵹnuꞃ mac Ꝺiaꞃmaꝺa ᵹall ina
ꞇiᵹ ꝼein, ocuꞃ a ṁaꞃḃaꝺ anꝺ, acuꞃ Coꞃmac caech mac
Finᵹin anꝺ ḃeuꞃ. O Ceꞃḃuill ꝺo ṁaꞃḃaꝺ la Oꞃꞃaiᵹuiḃ.
Conchoḃaꞃ.h.ḃiꞃn occiꞃuꞃ eꞃꞇ uiii. Ƈꞇ. Maꞃꞇii.

Ƈꞇ. Enaiꞃ ꞃoꞃ luan, acuꞃ aili .x. ꝼuiꞃꞃi; anno
ꝺomini Mº.cccº.xl.uii.; xuiii. cicli lunaꝼiꞃ; xu. inꝺic-
ꞇioniꞃ; xxiii. cicli ꞃolaꞃiꞃ. Ᵹilla na naeṁ, mac Seꝼꞃaiꝺ,
mic Ᵹilla na naeṁ .h.Feꞃᵹail, ꞇaiꞃech na hɑnᵹaili,
ꝺo eᵹ hi Cluain liꞃ ḃeci iaꞃ caiꞇheṁ ꝺo ꞃe mbliaꝺna
.xx. inn aꝺꞇennaꞃ na hɑnᵹaili, iaꞃ mbꞃeiꞇh buaꝺa ó
ꝺemon ocuꞃ o ꝺoṁan, ocuꞃ Cathal mac Muꞃchaꝺa mic
Ᵹilla na naeṁ .h. Feꞃᵹail ꝺo ᵹaḃail ꞇaiꞃechꝺa ꝺa eꞃ.
Muiꞃᵹiuꞃ Mac Ꝺiaꞃmaꝺa ꝺo maꞃḃaꝺ ꝺo Seoan ꞃuaꝺ
mac Ꝺauiꝺ a ḃuꞃc. Ꞇaꝺc Maᵹ Raᵹnaill, ꝺux Muinꞇiꞃe
hėolaiꞃ, ꝺo ᵹaḃail ꝺo Cloinn Muiꞃcheaꞃtaiᵹ in hoc
anno. Ᵹallocclaᵹ .h. Ruaiꞃc ꝺo maꞃḃaꝺ acuꞃ ꝺo ᵹaḃail
la Cloinn Muiꞃcheaꞃtaiᵹ iaꞃ na ꝼaᵹail a Muinꞇiꞃ
ėolaiꞃ. Uilliam mac Ꝺabi miliꞃ ꝺo maꞃḃaꝺ ꝺo
Ꞇhaꝺc ꞃuaꝺ Mac Ꝺiaꞃmaꝺa ᵹall immḃali in ꞇobaiꞃ.
Enꞃi mac Œeꝺa buiꝺe .h.Neill moꞃꞇuuꞃ eꞃꞇ. Ꞇomaꞃ
Mac Œiꞃꞇen, ꞃi .h.nEchach Ulaꝺ, ꝺo cꞃochaꝺ ꝺo

---

¹ *A great defeat.* maiꝺm immiꞃcech. By this expression is meant a
defeat involving the dispersion, or
migration, of the vanquished party.
immiꞃcech is an adj. deriv. from
immiꞃce a migratory expedition.

² *Both.* eiꝺiꞃ (lit. "inter"), B.
eaꝺaꞃ, C.

³ *Hoc.* hocc, B.

⁴ *O'Cerbhaill.* This entry and the
following are not in C.

O'Domhnaill and the Clann-Muirchertaigh, and the son
of Fedhlimidh O'Conchobhair, and Maurice Mac Diarmada, followed Ruaidhri, the son of Cathal, to Cul-maile,
where they inflicted a great defeat[1] on him and on the
Clann-Donnchaidh; and a great slaughter was committed
on them respectively, both[2] by drowning, burning,
hacking, and wounding; and great spoils *were taken*
besides. A great war between Mac Diarmada and
Maghnus Mac Diarmada Gall in hoc[3] anno; and treachery was practised by the sons of Waldrin Mac Goisdelbh on Maghnus Mac Diarmada Gall in his own house,
and he was slain there; and Cormac Caech Mac Finghin
was also *slain* there. O'Cerbhaill[4] was slain by the
Osraighe. Conchobhar O'Birn occisus est viii. kalendas
Martii.

The kalends of January on Monday, and the twelfth
of the moon; anno Domini M°.ccc°.xl.vii.; xviii. cycli lunaris; xv. Indictionis; xxiii. cycli solaris. Gilla-na-naemh,
son of Jeffrey, son of Gilla-na-naemh O'Ferghail, chieftain
of the Anghaile, died in Cluain-Lis-Bece, after having
spent twenty-six years in the chief government of the
Anghaile, after overcoming the devil and the world;
and Cathal, the son of Murchadh, son of Gilla-na-naemh
O'Ferghail, assumed the chieftaincy after him. Maurice
Mac Diarmada was slain by John Ruadh Mac David
Burk. Tadhg Mac Raghnaill, dux of Muinter-Eolais,
was taken prisoner by the Clann-Muirchertaigh in hoc
anno. O'Ruairc's gallowglasses were slain or captured[5] by the Clann-Muirchertaigh, after having been
found in Muinter-Eolais. William Mac David Milis[6]
was slain by Tadhg Ruadh Mac Diarmada Gall, in Baile-
in-tobair. Henry, son of Aedh Buidhe O'Neill, mortuus
est. Thomas Mac Airten, king of Ui-Echach-Uladh,

A.I
[134

[134

---

[5] *Slain or captured.* The expression
in the text, ꝺo mαꝛbαꝺ αcuꝛ ꝺo
ᵹαbαιꝈ, literally means "were slain
and captured."

[6] *Mac David Milis.* mαc ꝺꝺ bι
mιꝈιꝛ. The word mιꝈιꝛ is probably for Lat. *miles.* The usual form
of the name is "Mac David Burk."

'S. defective.
rt supplied
m "Annals
Connacht."]

Gallaib. Eogan Ua Madadan, ri tril nacnmchada, mortuus est; acus Murchad Ua Madadan, a mac fein, do rigad iar sin. Finnguala, ingen Eogain mic Finghin, uxor Feargail Muimnigh .h. Duibgennan, airchindech Chille Ronain, quieuit. In gilla dub Mac Gillimochua quieuit. Fergal mac Cormaic do marbad, ocus ni fer cia dormarb.

Kt. Enair for Mairt, ocus xxiii. fuirri; Mº.cccº.xlº. octauo; xix. cicli lunaris; primus annus indictionis; xx. quarto cicli solaris. Cathal .h. Fergail, dux Muintire hUngaile fria ré leit bliadna, mortuus est. Niall garb .h. Domnaill do marbad la Maghnus meblach .h. nDomnaill, fer dolum. Maelechlaind Mag Orechtaigh, dux Muinntiri Raduib, mortuus est. Donnchad Mac Bradaigh, dux Cuili Brighdin, quieuit in Cristo. Cocad mor do ergi eidir Fergal Mac nDiarmada ocus Ruaidri mac Cathail mic Domnaill, ocus longport Micc Diarmada do lorcad do mac Cathail. Mac Diarmada do tinol a charad do Chonnachtaib, ocus dol doib andiaig mic Cathail co baile in muta, ocus do loirced an baile leo eidir cloich ocus crand, ocus nir lamad cend do tocbail doib no co tancadar da tigib; ocus tuccadar ambai do braighdib isin baili leo fa mac .h. Ruairc, ocus tancadar slan da tigib iar sin.

---

[1] *Airchinnech*. Herenach, or Erenach. B. and C. read airchideochain, "archdeacon"; but this is obviously a mistake. The office of Herenach of Cill-Ronain (Kilronan, county of Roscommon) was hereditary in the family of O'Duibhgennain.

[2] *Ferghal Mac Cormaic*. This name should perhaps be printed " Ferghal, son of Cormac [Mac Diarmada]."

[3] *Kalends*. B has the Dom. Letters (F E) in the margin.

[4] *Maghnus Meabhlach*; i.e. "Maghnus (or Manus) the deceitful."

[5] *Donnchadh*. Repeated in C.

was hanged by Foreigners. Eoghan O'Madadhain, king of Sil-Anmchadha, mortuus est, and Murchadh O'Madadhain, his own son, was subsequently made king. Finnghuala, daughter of Eoghan Mac Finghin, uxor of Ferghal Muimhnech O'Duibhgennain, airchinnech[1] of Cill-Ronain, quievit. The Gilla-dubh Mac Gillamochua quievit. Ferghal Mac Cormaic[2] was slain; and it is not known who slew him.

The kalends[3] of January on Tuesday, and the twenty-third of the moon; M°.ccc°.xl°. octavo; xix. cycli lunaris; primus annus Indictionis; xx. quarto cycli solaris. Cathal O'Ferghail, dux of Muinter-Anghaile during the space of half a year, mortuus est. Niall Garbh O'Domhnaill was slain by Maghnus Meabhlach[4] O'Domhnaill, per dolum. Maelechlainn Mac Oirechtaigh, dux of Muinter-Raduibh, mortuus est. Donnchadh[5] Mac Bradaigh, dux of Cuil-Brighdin, quievit in Christo.[6] A great war arose between[7] Ferghal Mac Diarmada and Ruaidhri, son of Cathal,[8] son of Domhnall;[9] and Mac Diarmada's fortress was burned by the son of Cathal. Mac Diarmada assembled his friends of the Connachtmen, and they pursued the son of Cathal to Baile-in-mhuta, and the town was burned by them, both[10] stone and wood;[11] and no one dared to oppose them until they arrived at their homes; and they brought with them all the captives that were in the town, including O'Ruairc's son, and came home safely afterwards.

---

[6] *In Christo.* Omitted in B.

[7] *Between.* eιτιρ, B. eαυαρ, C.

[8] *Son of Cathal.* B. and C. have "son of Diarmaid," which is incorrect, as appears from the context, as well as from the Ann. Four Mast.

[9] *Domhnall;* i.e. Domhnall O'Conchobhair.

[10] *Both.* eιτιρ (=Lat. inter), B. eαυαρ, C.

[11] *Stone and wood;* i.e. stone and wooden edifices.

Lightning Source UK Ltd.
Milton Keynes UK
UKOW05f1124020216

267589UK00010B/171/P